Handbook of Clinical Social Work

Aaron Rosenblatt

Diana Waldfogel

General Editors

Handbook of Clinical Social Work

Jossey-Bass Publishers
San Francisco • Washington • London • 1983

HANDBOOK OF CLINICAL SOCIAL WORK
by Aaron Rosenblatt, Diana Waldfogel, General Editors

Library of Congress Cataloging in Publication Data
Main entry under title:

Handbook of clinical social work.

Includes bibliographies and index.
1. Social service—Addresses, essays, lectures.
2. Social case work—Addresses, essays, lectures.
I. Rosenblatt, Aaron. II. Waldfogel, Diana. III. Title: Clinical social work. [DNLM: 1. Social work. 2. Social work, Psychiatric. WM 30.5 H236]
HV43.H315 1983 361.3′2 82-49042
ISBN 0-87589-562-X

Manufactured in the United States of America

The paper in this book meets the guidelines for permanence and durability of the Committee on Production Guidelines for Book Longevity of the Council on Library Resources.

JACKET DESIGN BY WILLI BAUM

FIRST EDITION

Code 8310

The Jossey-Bass
Social and Behavioral Science Series

Preface

Handbook of Clinical Social Work is a milestone in the history of social work—the first time that so many eminent practitioners and scholars have united in a common effort to prepare a comprehensive, in-depth review of all components of clinical social work. Until now, no standard reference has existed to serve everyone in the field—including practitioners, teachers, and students. The *Handbook* is intended to fill that gap by presenting the best, most current thinking about all aspects of theory, research, and practice.

To ensure broad and up-to-date coverage, we invited leading experts in social work to serve as section editors for the eight major parts of the volume. Scott Briar, Kay L. Dea, Ann Hartman, Stuart A. Kirk, John Allen Lemmon, Elizabeth C. Lemon, Harry Specht, and Harold H. Weissman are a truly outstanding group of editors who worked diligently to make the *Handbook* an invaluable contribution to the field. In turn, they commissioned the contributors—all authorities on particular subjects—to write chapters in their areas of expertise. Then, editors and chapter authors combined their talents and drew on their experiences in social work and clinical practice, as well as on empirical studies conducted in social work and related professions, to offer detailed information and advice. Every effort has been made to include a variety of viewpoints, specialties, and theoretical orientations; in no way did we, or the contributors, intend the individual chapters to represent a consensus of opinion.

Because of the diversity of views and breadth of coverage, various audiences will benefit from the *Handbook*. The material is addressed to practitioners working in either agency settings or private practice; to administrators and supervisors in a wide range of social service agencies (such as family service agencies, child welfare agencies, public welfare agencies, hospitals, and community health centers); to faculty members charged with preparing students for social work careers; and to students studying social work in graduate programs or professional schools.

Readers can use the *Handbook* to (1) familiarize themselves with major theories for producing beneficial change in clients (including behavioral, psychodynamic, cognitive, communications, and family approaches); (2) expand their knowledge of new assessment techniques and intervention strategies—with children, parents, families, ethnic minorities, and socially disadvantaged or oppressed groups; (3) obtain recommendations for effectively using specific assessment techniques and treatment approaches with particular clients and problems; (4) keep current with research methods, findings, and applications; (5) understand how policy issues—such as social services financing and regulation of practice—affect day-to-day work; and (6) promote continued professional development by increasing their knowledge of particular topics.

The volume is organized into eight sections, each covering a major area of practice. Section One, "Knowledge Base of Clinical Social Work," provides a broad overview of the major content areas of clinical practice and reviews progress in developing a scientific base for clinical social work. The second section, "Theories for Producing Change," then examines theories supporting the use of numerous resources in bringing about beneficial change in clients. These resources include the environment, life experiences, the group, the family, the worker-client relationship, learning, cognition, and insight. The authors suggest ways in which social workers can use each resource.

In Section Three, "Education and Methods for Clinical Practice," practitioners, supervisors, instructors, and students present their views of several casework and treatment approaches. Focusing on how various treatment methods are taught, learned, and utilized, chapters also cover interactions between clients and therapists, treating parents along with children, and making use of cross-cultural perspectives.

By generating new knowledge about the factors influencing human problems, research can help change social work practice. Section Four, "New Applications of Research in Clinical Practice," demonstrates how research methods and findings provide valuable information about ways of responding effectively to problems; also considers measurement issues and significance testing in single-case studies for the benefit of clinical social workers.

Clinical social work practice is affected not only by policy matters but also by values and ethical considerations. Section Five, "Policy Issues in Clinical Practice," discusses some of the major issues confronting social workers—such as resource allocation, funding of services, and certification and licensure—and shows what impact they have on day-to-day practice. Section Six, "Values, Ethics, and Legal Issues," highlights principles of ethical practice and helps social workers resolve common ethical dilemmas by providing information on legal and ethical codes, clients' rights, work with minority clients, and confidentiality.

Section Seven, "Practice Settings," next considers both the traditional fields of practice in social work and the emerging ones; it describes the special delivery systems, methodological approaches, and interprofessional networks unique to each. And the final section, "Current and Future Trends in Clinical Social Work," assesses new clinical methods, such as primary prevention and data-based approaches, currently in various stages of development and refinement.

The practicing profession of social work, like other professions, encourages its members to probe and explore, to learn from experience and cut loose the bonds of tradition. As editors we wanted the same spirit of freedom and experimentation to be felt here, to avoid parochial interests and allow a variety of contending viewpoints. We also wanted the *Handbook* to look both backward and forward—backward to a close examination of the foundations of the profession and forward to the new structures that may rise to prominence. We hope that the diversity of viewpoints and specialties represented by the contributors have enabled us to achieve the desired balance.

January 1983

Aaron Rosenblatt
Albany, New York

Diana Waldfogel
Boston, Massachusetts

Contents

The Editors

Aaron Rosenblatt is professor and director of doctoral studies, School of Social Welfare, State University of New York, Albany. He received his B.A. degree in American history from Wayne State University (1946); his M.A. and M.S. degrees in American history and social work, respectively, from Columbia University (1948 and 1956); and his D.S.W. degree from Columbia (1965).

Rosenblatt has previously served as professor and director of social work, Department of Psychiatry, Langley Porter Psychiatric Institute, University of California, San Francisco; as faculty member, Department of Psychiatry, Einstein College of Medicine, Yeshiva University; and as director of research, Council on Social Work Education. His professional affiliations include the National Association of Social Work; he has been on the editorial boards of *Journal of Social Service Research* and *Social Work,* and for many years he was book review editor for *Social Casework.*

In addition to more than sixty articles on such topics as patients' responses to mental illness, social work education, and women's contributions to the helping professions, Rosenblatt has most recently published *Social Research and the Practicing Professions* (coedited with Thomas Gieryn, 1982).

Diana Waldfogel is professor and dean, School of Social Work, at Simmons College, where she previously served as associate dean (1977–1979) and director of field work (1970–1977). She received her A.B. and M.S.W. degrees from Wayne

State University in 1944 and 1947, respectively, and has taken advanced courses and seminars in clinical work and family treatment.

Waldfogel's clinical background has been primarily in child guidance and work with families and children; her supervision and consultation work has been in the field of mental health—in mental health clinics, mental hospitals, and child guidance clinics. In addition to teaching casework and supervision courses in a variety of settings and colleges, she has worked for many years as a supervisor and caseworker.

Since 1968, Waldfogel has been active in the National Association of Social Workers (NASW), serving as delegate to the national assembly several times; since 1977 she has been on the editorial committee of NASW's *Practice Digest* journal. She has also been involved in the Council on Social Work Education and was a member of the advisory committee on the Utilization of Research from 1977 to 1979. Her continuing interests are in supervision, work with families and children, and ethics in social work.

Contributors

Jo Ann Allen is associate professor, School of Social Work, University of Michigan, Ann Arbor, and family therapist, Ann Arbor Center for the Family.

Sharon Berlin is assistant professor, School of Social Work, University of Wisconsin, Madison.

Martin Bloom is professor, School of Social Work, Virginia Commonwealth University.

Scott Briar is professor and dean, School of Social Work, University of Washington.

Donald Brieland is professor and dean, Jane Addams College of Social Work, University of Illinois, Chicago.

Jerome Cohen is professor, School of Social Welfare, University of California, Los Angeles.

Beulah R. Compton is professor and acting dean, School of Social Work, Indiana University.

Jon R. Conte is assistant professor, School of Social Service Administration, University of Chicago.

Shirley Cooper is director of child clinical services, Department of Psychiatry, Mt. Zion Hospital and Medical Center, San Francisco.

Kay L. Dea is associate dean, Graduate School of Social Work, University of Utah.

Golda M. Edinburg is director of social work, McLean Hospital, Belmont, Massachusetts.

Joel Fischer is professor, School of Social Work, University of Hawaii.

Louise A. Frey is associate dean, Division of Continuing Education, School of Social Work, Boston University.

Charles D. Garvin is professor, School of Social Work, University of Michigan, Ann Arbor.

Carel B. Germain is professor, School of Social Work, University of Connecticut.

Wallace J. Gingerich is associate professor, School of Social Welfare, University of Wisconsin, Milwaukee.

Eda G. Goldstein is associate professor, School of Social Work, New York University.

William E. Gordon is professor emeritus, School of Social Work, Washington University, St. Louis.

Burton Gummer is associate professor, School of Social Welfare, State University of New York, Albany.

Terese M. Halpin is social worker, Special Education District of Lake County, Gurnee, Illinois.

David A. Hardcastle is professor and dean, School of Social Welfare, University of Kansas.

Russell D. Hart is family therapist, Together, Inc., Marlboro, Massachusetts.

Ann Hartman is professor, School of Social Work, University of Michigan, Ann Arbor.

Walter W. Hudson is professor, School of Social Work, Florida State University.

Shirley Jenkins is professor, School of Social Work, Columbia University.

Hessa B. Kadet is clinical social worker, Department of Social Service, Framingham Union Hospital, Framingham, Massachusetts.

Stuart A. Kirk is professor and dean, School of Social Welfare, State University of New York, Albany.

Joan Laird is assistant professor, Department of Social Work, Eastern Michigan University.

John Allen Lemmon is professor, Department of Social Work Education, San Francisco State University.

Elizabeth C. Lemon is professor, School of Social Work, Simmons College.

Charles S. Levy, previously professor, School of Social Work, Yeshiva University, is now freelance consultant in New York.

Rona L. Levy is associate professor, School of Social Work, University of Washington.

Florence Lieberman is professor, School of Social Work, Hunter College, City University of New York.

Gary A. Lloyd is professor, University of Southern Mississippi, and president, Divorce & Family Mediation Associates, Inc., New Orleans.

Sophie Freud Loewenstein is professor, School of Social Work, Simmons College.

Anthony N. Maluccio is professor, School of Social Work, University of Connecticut.

Carol H. Meyer is professor, School of Social Work, Columbia University.

Ruth R. Middleman is professor, Raymond A. Kent School of Social Work, University of Louisville.

Henry Miller is professor, School of Social Welfare, University of California, Berkeley.

Samuel O. Miller is associate professor, School of Social Work, Columbia University.

Edward J. Mullen is professor, School of Social Service Administration, University of Chicago.

Nancy K. Neale is associate professor, Department of Sociology, Appalachian State University.

Connie Philipp is assistant professor, Department of Psychiatry, University of California, San Francisco.

Philip R. Popple is associate professor and director, Social Work Program, Department of Sociology, Anthropology, and Social Work, Auburn University.

William J. Reid is professor, School of Social Welfare, State University of New York, Albany.

Victoria S. Roemele is clinical assistant professor, School of Social Work, Smith College; lecturer on psychiatry, School of Medicine, Harvard University; and staff social worker, Department of Psychiatry, Cambridge Hospital, Cambridge, Massachusetts.

Gerald Schamess is associate professor, School of Social Work, Smith College.

Steven Paul Schinke is associate professor, School of Social Work, University of Washington.

Arthur Schwartz is professor, School of Social Work and Community Planning, University of Maryland.

Jerald Shapiro is assistant professor, Department of Social Work Education, San Francisco State University.

Barbara Bryant Solomon is professor, School of Social Work, University of Southern California.

Harry Specht is professor and dean, School of Social Welfare, University of California, Berkeley.

H. John Staulcup is vice-president, Perfect Software, Inc., Berkeley, California.

Herbert S. Strean is distinguished professor, Graduate School of Social Work, Rutgers University.

Paul Terrell is lecturer and academic administrator, School of Social Welfare, University of California, Berkeley.

Edwin J. Thomas is professor, School of Social Work, University of Michigan, Ann Arbor.

Joseph L. Vigilante is professor and dean, School of Social Work, Adelphi University.

Froma Walsh is associate professor, School of Social Service Administration, University of Chicago, and faculty member, The Family Institute of Chicago.

Mary L. Waring is professor, Graduate School of Social Service at Lincoln Center, Fordham University.

Harry Wasserman is associate professor, School of Social Welfare, University of California, Los Angeles.

Harold H. Weissman is professor, School of Social Work, Hunter College, City University of New York.

Suanna J. Wilson is currently consulting in Arlington, Texas.

Introduction: Clinical Social Work

Diana Waldfogel
Aaron Rosenblatt

There was great hope for social change in the 1960s when the term *clinical social work* came into the language. With considerable optimism, members of the social work profession enlisted as soldiers in the war on poverty and the war against racism. In the course of this crusade, the term *casework* and the discipline it represented came to be viewed as inadequate, as being too concerned with adjusting people to negative social realities at a time when it seemed large-scale efforts were required to bring about structural changes in society. *Clinical social work* thus entered the language—an early appearance was in the California State licensing law of 1968 (Bandler, 1979)—in response to this need for a new nomenclature and for a redefinition of direct practice. In the ensuing years, caseworkers dramatically expanded their activities in client advocacy, outreach, education, and prevention; increased their use of varying modalities in work with groups and families; considered a broader variety of psychosocial theories of treatment; and paid special attention to the pluralistic needs of their clients resulting from ethnic and racial differences.

The diverse aspects of expanded practice also began to be reflected in social work organizations. In 1971, for example, the National Association of Social

Workers (NASW) responded to the urgent need for additional social workers by establishing a new level of membership for social workers with a baccalaureate degree. Many social workers with master's degrees (psychiatric social workers in particular) objected to this broadening of membership criteria as being a regressive measure, dropped their NASW memberships, and began to form local chapters of their own clinical societies. This movement culminated in the formation of the National Federation of Societies for Clinical Social Work (NFSCSW). Other, equally well-trained workers chose not to join these clinical societies but instead in 1976 formed a Clinical Registry, which lists the names of all clinical social workers in NASW who meet the established criteria. Both organizations currently work closely together to achieve professional goals regarding licensing and delivery of services to needy groups, although there are still political differences between the two.

A third influential organization is the Council on Social Work Education (CSWE), which has been responsible for accrediting schools of social work conferring M.S.W. (Master of Social Work) degrees and in 1974 began accrediting programs conferring the B.S.W. (Bachelor of Social Work) degree. (Doctoral programs receive their accreditation as part of the university accreditation practice.) By 1981 there were approximately 300 accredited B.S.W. programs and 88 accredited M.S.W. programs, and educators have argued about the role and function of workers emerging from these two entry-level programs. One issue, for instance, is whether the title "clinical social worker" should be reserved only for those obtaining master or doctoral degrees in social work or whether this restriction creates unnecessary divisiveness within the profession. Another issue is whether or not clinical social work is a specialization within the social work profession and, if so, what kind of education should be required.

The definition of clinical social work is still unresolved, and it will not be resolved in this book. The fact that "clinical" is derived from the Greek word *klinike*, for "medical treatment at sickbed," has given some of the handbook's contributors discomfort, for the word seems to connote a concern with elitist practice, narrowness of perspective, or too-close ties to the earlier specialty of psychiatric social work or else the opposite of all these—too broad or all-inclusive a term, encompassing all of direct practice.

In *Toward a Definition of Clinical Social Work* (Ewalt, 1980), Jerome Cohen reports on a task force he chaired for the NASW-sponsored National Invitational Forum on Clinical Social Work in June 1979, which was charged with formulating a definition of clinical social work. The task force, he says, "perceived the *person-in-situation* perspective as continuing to be the base on which an understanding of clinical practice is to be built" (p. 25). He then proceeds to state the group's proposed definition as follows:

> Clinical social work involves a wide range of psychosocial services to individuals, families, and small groups in relation to a variety of human problems of living. Such practice may be carried out under both private and public auspices. It is concerned with the assessment of interaction between the individual's biological, psychological, and social experience, which provides a guide for clinical intervention. A distinguishing feature is the clinician's concern with the social context within which individual or

> family problems occur and are altered. Clinical social work, therefore, may involve intervention in the social situation as well as the person situation. Three major principles by which clinical social work produces change or maintenance of function are (1) through the interpersonal relationship with the clinician; (2) through alterations in the social situation; (3) through alterations of relationships with significant persons in the life space of the individual [p. 26].

Another definition, quoted by Carol Meyer (see Meyer, Garber, and Williams, 1979, and Meyer's chapter in this handbook), is offered in the NASW's Clinical Registry: "The clinical social worker is, by education and experience, professionally qualified at the autonomous practice level to provide direct, diagnostic, preventive, and treatment services to individuals, families, and groups where function is threatened or affected by social or psychological stress or health impairment." The purpose of clinical practice in social work, Meyer suggests, is "to improve social functioning," which summarizes the theoretical position offered by Harriett Bartlett (1970).

Whatever the actual definition of clinical social work, it is clear that the *need* for the term has been brought about by the following circumstances: (1) a blossoming of new theoretical bases used by social workers; (2) a change in the size of the "client unit" to include not only individuals but also families and groups, thus requiring a variety of modalities to fit new situations; (3) a renewed interest in the social environment, along with an awareness that the casework perspective has not been sufficiently concerned about planned interventions designed to affect social systems; and (4) a renewed desire to establish an empirical research base to undergird practice.

The term *clinical social work*, as used in this handbook, is intended to demonstrate the present nature of a varied and purposeful, productive, and ever-unfolding practice. The varied perspectives offered by the contributors here is striking. Indeed, the conflict between the "diagnostic" and "functional" schools, which seemed so impossible in the 1950s, appears simple compared to the proliferation of theories requiring resolution today (Miller, 1979). In general, however, two main streams of theory are represented: the behavioral, from the pioneer work of Watson and Skinner, and the psychodynamic, from the work of Freud, Hartmann, and Winnicott. Many other theories—such as cognitive, gestalt, communications, and role—are emerging as newly important. Some models, such as task-centered treatment, are attempting to combine elements of the behavioral and psychodynamic approaches. The various forms of systems theory also represent a major contribution to clinical practice. For example, family therapy has forced psychodynamic therapists to take into account the systemic properties of family interaction, and problems once considered to result primarily from individual psychology have come to be viewed as resulting from interaction between family members. This shift in perspective has required social work clinicians to incorporate a different strategy of intervention and a new standard by which to measure change, and today a dozen or more theories of family therapy vie for the attention of clinicians. Some theorists are attempting to reconcile psychological and social systems theories in order to advance the power of family therapy.

The varying theories and modalities cut across the traditional fields of practice and require a new organization of specialization. In order to bring about some order in the face of so much change, the Council on Social Work Education appointed Carol Meyer, Ralph Garber, and Constance Williams to examine specializations. In 1979 they presented a report proposing the organization of specializations around segments of the environment with which people interact (Meyer, Garber, and Williams, 1979). Some of these suggestions identified the sectors of health, justice, education, economics, and family.

Still, much remains to be done. The level of clinical intervention in the social environment is still undetermined. Methods of assessment and intervention strategies for use in changing the social environment have not been put into operation to the same degree as they have in work with individuals. Clinicians are struggling to identify appropriate actions that go beyond advocacy for individual clients, which has always been one aspect of the practitioner's role. Clinicians have no well-developed theory they can use to decide when they should refer problems to other experts. The strategies of prevention offer some reason for hope. The use of educational methods and active support of natural networks, helpers, and self-help endeavors hold promise of developing new ways of addressing the social environment.

The 1980s are an exciting time in social work. We hope that this handbook will make a significant contribution to the developing practice of clinical social work.

References

Bandler, L. S. "The Evolution of Clinical Social Work: Continuity and Change." In *Change and Renewal in Psychodynamic Social Work: British and American Developments in Practice and Education for Services to Families and Children.* Oxford, England: Proceedings of the Oxford Conference, 1979.

Bartlett, H. M. *The Common Base of Social Work Practice.* New York: National Association of Social Work, 1970.

Ewalt, P. (Ed.). *Toward a Definition of Clinical Social Work.* Washington, D.C.: Proceedings of the National Association of Social Work Conference, 1980.

Meyer, C. H., Garber, R., and Williams, C. W. "Specialization in the Social Work Profession." Council on Social Work Education, Commission on Educational Planning, Subcommittee on Specialization, 1979. (Mimeograph.)

Miller, R. R. "Clinical Learning as a Developmental Process." In *Change and Renewal in Psychodynamic Social Work: British and American Developments in Practice and Education for Services to Families and Children.* Oxford, England: Proceedings of the Oxford Conference, 1979.

Handbook of Clinical Social Work

Section I

Knowledge Base of Clinical Social Work

Harold H. Weissman
Section Editor

Freud has been quoted as saying "We shall probably discover that the poor are even less ready to part with their neuroses than the rich, because the life that awaits them when they recover has no attraction" (Coles, 1964). This statement captures the essence of the dilemma facing clinical social workers. Can one really focus on psychological difficulties with a man, woman, or child overwhelmed by material and social problems? Are clinical skills relevant for dealing with situational troubles?

Answers to this dilemma have shifted back and forth over the decades, from all casework is psychotherapy to social action is therapy, from disengagement with the poor to advocacy for the poor. Is there really a definite answer? Probably not, if we take the mission of clinical social work to be helping people. Such a mission allows no room for swearing allegiance to a particular helping method or theory until it can be scientifically proven to be better than any other, in any situation. It might be said that clinical social work has neither eternal clients nor techniques, only an eternal interest, helping people.

Williams (1965) argued a decade and a half ago that caseworkers who had been nurtured on Freud and the ego psychiatrists must employ the bulk of their training in study-diagnosis rather than treatment or action. She was skeptical about "the dictum that study-diagnosis and treatment are parts of the same process," pointing out that "many of us can offer a wealth of information and deep insights about our clients, individually and collectively, but we are befuddled about how this information is fashioned into a treatment program which will (1) not alienate our clients and (2) have some impact on their personality and behavior. Our traditional training leaves us ill equipped to . . . initiate and progressively execute a treatment program when we may be debating what in our storehouse of knowledge is to be used and even how we are to evaluate success."

For her, a partial answer was the thoughtful use of concrete services, or what was called in past decades environmental manipulation.

> Concrete services . . . suggest to me a way in which the social work profession may begin to break into the deprived person's view of us as "magical . . . unfeeling . . . preachy." I would define concrete services simply as any substantive act on the part of the practitioner which is readily discernible to the client, ideally proposed by the client, and having about it the potential for immediate relief from stress. I would see it as employing action in behalf of the client rather than instruction or information given to the client so that he might act in his own behalf. I subscribe to concrete service because I believe it "start(s) where the client is," gives the social worker a means of diagnosing the deprived (who recoil from history taking), counteracts their sense of hopelessness and distrust, relieves stress, and demonstrates good will. . . . Unfortunately, we sometimes place too much stress on concrete service . . . when, in essence, it is only the beginning for a significant proportion of our clients. . . . I believe the concrete service has a temporary, limited, palliative effect, making the person "feel good" but not clearly suggesting to them the need to review the B-H-H (Blameless-Hopeless-Helpless) syndrome, a symptom of defeat and despair which is so blatantly compounded in their daily lives. Let us remember that we are with our clients one or two hours a week, we are not the world to them. . . . Further, encapsulated concrete services are not going to change that world. What we are talking about, after all, is the use of concrete services to change the clients' view of their world so that they might more productively engage it. Are we not then talking about some, however limited, form of behavioral change or educative process? . . . I think so, and for that reason view concrete services as the . . . essential, irreversible step to be used planfully along an ongoing continuum.

Readers will find in the chapters of this section a continuation of Williams' discussion and analysis about the *techniques* and *focus* of clinical social work as they apply to all groups, not simply the poor. Is clinical social work a specialty, a psychotherapeutic approach to practice? Is it an umbrella term, covering a variety of approaches to helping people on a one-to-one basis? Or does it deal with the interface between people and their environment, aiming both at liberating and supporting their adaptive capacities and at increasing the responsiveness of the social environment to their needs?

Eda Goldstein suggests that one of the problems related to developing a scientific base for clinical social work is in the abstractness of many of its concepts. In addition, the historical tendency to separate knowledge of individuals and strategies for helping from understanding the social environment and approaches to changing society has not contributed to systematic theory building.

The general and abstract nature of person-environment concepts and their lack of specificity as a guide to intervention limit the appeal of the ecological perspective to those currently engaged in direct practice. Without operational concepts to describe the active and natural processes of coping and adaptation, without principles for action derived from these concepts, and without systematic research on the effectiveness of practice with specific types of maladaptive transactions, it is tempting to fall back on old, familiar formulations about what is wrong with people and how to correct those problems.

Carel Germain traces the technological advances in clinical social work with individuals, groups, and families. Germain raises serious issues about the development of technology and the ways it is diffused in the profession. She asks an important question with significant ramifications for our understanding of clinical social work: "Are university-based social workers talking only to themselves and to one another in formulating practice approaches?" In other than the family field, why have practice formulations been developed almost solely by university-based social work educators? It may be that a knowledge base that is primarily dependent on professors who do not practice is inevitably a knowledge base that must be broad and abstract.

Joseph Vigilante examines the value base of the social work profession. Quoting Apteker he notes, "The framework of social work, as we know it, is a set of values." Having made this observation, he articulates the dilemmas presented to clinical social workers. The basic one, still unresolved and at the top of the agenda in the '80s, is the frequent conflict between equally good values. What is good for some clients may not be good for others. For example, confidentiality taken to the extreme can breed a preciousness of practice and a breakdown in service. Vigilante also traces the argument over whether values are instruments of professional practice or only guidelines for practice and a moral justification for the profession.

Arguments over the proper focus of clinical social work are not new. Philip Poppel traces the development of the institutional context of social work practice in all of its intricacies. Should it be under private auspices or public? Should it have a case focus or a reform focus? Or is the debate irrelevant for decisions about what social work is, or what clinical social work will be, determined not so much by theoretical discussions as by social conditions? History and experience show that social work has responded to the practical needs of people in real situations. These needs have varied in terms of the perceptions of the people themselves, and of society, as evidenced by social movements and public concerns. Thus the general acceptance by the authors in this section of a broad definition of clinical social work which concerns the person-in-situation is that it allows for specific foci at specific points in time. Any other definition would severely limit the ability of social workers to meet people's needs as they emerge over time.

What is left for the reader to decide? To what extent is the focus on values productive in the '80s? To what extent has the focus on values obscured the need to develop adequate, validated theories of practice? Are the values we espouse the same as the values espoused by our clients? Have we been value-based or have we been value-bound?

In this section, the authors have posed certain issues to which the authors in subsequent sections will return for further analysis and discussion, in some cases with greater specificity. In approaching these issues I should like to recall a former teacher of mine, one who would have been pleased to define herself as a clinical social worker of the person-environment perspective. Hazel Osborn died in 1980. She was one of the great stylists in social work, a term that is not used in this volume, but that signifies a personal projection of one's approach to one's work. Her words to me in defining the role of the clinical social worker are as appropriate now as they were when I was one of her students twenty-five years ago. "Most problems are potentially solvable through psychoanalysis or salve. We usually start with salve." By this she meant that people's needs must define the method we use, and not the other way around.

References

Coles, R. "Journey into the Mind of the Lower Depths." *New Republic,* February 15, 1964, pp. 11–12.

Williams, M. "Detailed Notes of a Professional Social Worker in a Mobilization for Youth Neighborhood Service Center." Mimeographed. New York: Mobilization for Youth, 1965.

1

Issues in Developing Systematic Research and Theory

Eda G. Goldstein

The scientific commitment of the social work profession has been reflected in persistent efforts to develop and systematize its theoretical and technological base. Since its transformation from a charitable undertaking performed by well-meaning volunteers to an activity requiring paid, trained workers, social work practice has passed through many phases in its search for a scientific base. Briar and Miller (1971, pp. 30–31) describe this quest as "often frantic . . . silly and brilliant; courageous and fearful. Dogmas have been generated and stubbornly defended; heresies proclaimed; dissent squelched. But . . . the search for theory and method has been inexorable."

After a general commentary on the definition and scope of clinical social work at the present time, the chapter will review significant issues and developments in the evolution of the knowledge base of social work practice. The following main points will be made: (1) that the development of the knowledge base of social work reflects the borrowing of theoretical systems from the behavioral and social sciences on the one hand and the refinement of interventive technology on the other, (2) that there has been a tendency to rigidify these systems of ideas and their related technology, (3) that the historical tendency to separate knowledge of individuals and strategies of people-helping from knowledge of the social environment and approaches to society-changing has fragmented rather than unified theories of social work, and (4) that the gap between the profession's scientific commitment and the minimal degree to which professionals have engaged in practice-based research has slowed the consolidation of a scientific base. This chapter then will address the importance of clinical social work as a unifying direct practice framework. Clinical social work is built on a broad knowledge of transactions between people and their environments and a deep understanding of human behavior. Current problems in developing a unified direct practice framework will be discussed, along with the significance of a multifaceted research strategy for evolving and consolidating its scientific base.

The Current Scene

In the decade of the 1980s, a significant feature of the social work profession is its reaffirmation of both aspects of its historical commitment: enhancing individual functioning and promoting a social environment more responsive to human needs. Direct practice has returned to the forefront of the concerns of the profession after its partial eclipse in the 1960s and early 1970s. During those times emphases on society-changing rather than people-helping, challenges to traditional conceptions of practice, and attacks on the theoretical systems that informed practice cast a pall on workers involved in and committed to direct practice.

Despite its resurgence, however, the direct practice sector is in disarray; its proponents lack unity and its critics are vigorous (Germain, 1980). A proliferation of highly specialized approaches has fragmented practice, and attempts to unify it have suffered from a lack of operational concepts. The research base of practice is weak. Meanwhile the accretion of knowledge in the behavioral and social sciences along with business and computer technology continue to have staggering effects. Furthermore, social work in the 1980s occurs in an increasingly conservative sociopolitical atmosphere in which its values, services, and practices are questioned and criticized. These factors combine with contracting economic resources to result in the loss of financial support from vital human services. At a time when clients' needs and problems are exceedingly complex, issues of diminished status, governmental regulations, accountability, cost-effectiveness, third-party payments, and program evaluation dominate practitioners' lives.

Various coping responses have emerged. One is for followers of a particular approach to "do their own thing," tool up as much as possible, and acquire the necessary credentials to compete effectively for the consumer's interest and for financial compensation. Behavior therapists, psychotherapists, family therapists, cognitive therapists, and so on, abound. A second coping response is unorganized eclecticism. A third is to evolve a conception of social work practice that allows both for the complexity of the interaction between clients' personalities and their social circumstances and for the diversity of approaches to intervention linked by an overarching "social work" perspective.

Thus debate about the definition of social work practice continues. This debate encompasses differences of opinion about what is or is not social work practice, what constitutes evidence for the effectiveness of specific approaches with specific clients, what theoretical perspectives, if any, should underpin practice, and what is the best way to acquire the necessary research base. Perhaps the key question is whether or not it is crucial to the survival and growth of the profession to evolve (and rigorously evaluate) a distinctive and unifying practice theory out of which meaningful specializations can emerge.

Recent efforts at defining clinical social work reflect all these issues (Minahan, 1980). The term *clinical social work* is laden with complex and even contradictory meanings. To many practitioners it connotes a specialty—a psychotherapeutic approach to practice that aims to improve or modify individual coping capacity and that relies on theories of the inner person, the ego, and the world of object relations (Frank, 1980). To other practitioners clinical social work is an umbrella covering a host of seemingly unrelated approaches to helping people. To still others clinical social work affirms the significance of a broad range of individualized services aimed at "(1) liberating, supporting, and enhancing people's adaptive capacities and (2) increasing the responsiveness of physical and social environments to people's needs" (Germain, 1980, p. 483). Those who share this third view argue that clinical social work deals with the interface between people and environments (Germain, 1979; Germain and Gitterman, 1980).

The task force on clinical social work of the National Association of Social Workers (NASW) presented its view at the First Annual Invitational Forum on Clinical Social Work in Denver in 1979: "The person-in-situation perspective was reaffirmed as the guiding principle for all forms of clinical social work practice. Within this perspective, however, variations in method may legitimately be used, depending on setting and needs to be addressed. Psychotherapeutic activitiy is deemed to be a part of but not the whole of clinical social work practice" (Ewalt, 1980, p. 23). Furthermore it identified clinical social work "as one type of social work practice neither capable of or intending to direct its attention toward all the concerns of the social work profession" (Cohen, 1980, p. 25). Thus clinical social work is differentiated from community organization, social planning, and social change strategies. Nevertheless it encompasses all helping efforts directed at enhancing social functioning, involving a "wide range of psychosocial services to individuals, families, and small groups in relation to a variety of human problems in living" (Cohen, 1980, pp. 25–26).

An important question for the 1980s is whether clinical social work practice will become unified around such a broad definition and will be linked meaningfully to other social work specializations, whether it will remain an umbrella concept sheltering practice models whose theoretical linkages are obscure or contradictory, or whether it will become a psychotherapeutic approach to practice requiring highly specialized knowledge and skills. At the present time clinical social work is still in search of its identity and its constituency. At the heart of this issue is the question whether clinical social work practice will be able to identify, consolidate, and systematize its knowledge base.

Although attempts to provide a scientific basis to philanthropy in the latter part of the nineteenth century reflected the earliest manifestations of social work's scientific commitment, the urgency of developing a distinctive body of theory and skills became apparent when Flexner (1915) argued that social work was not a true profession because it lacked such a common core. Social workers have since recognized that the "hallmark of a profession is its shared body of common knowledge" (Simon, 1977, p. 397). In elaborating on Goode's (1969) suggestion that the possession of a body of abstract knowledge is essential in conferring professional status, Kirk (1979) noted that it is also the possession of such a core that forms the basis for professional authority over education, training, and the terms and the nature of services.

Nevertheless, a successful response to the challenge to social work to define its core of knowledge and skills has been and continues to be elusive. One major reason stems from the profession's dual commitment to people-helping and society-changing. Although potentially complementary, throughout social work's history these goals have repeatedly been polarized, and the enthusiasm of practitioners has swung from one goal to the other. This in turn has fragmented the knowledge base of the profession: theories of individual functioning have formed one pole and knowledge of environments, society, and culture another. Although the integration of theories of person and environment is often espoused, it has not been reflected in practice (Mailick, 1977; Siporin, 1970). Efforts to develop a unified conception of practice using knowledge of transactions between person and environment have been handicapped by deficiencies in making the concepts operational; they therefore have not led to the consolidation of practice or of its scientific base (Goldstein, 1980).

A second major reason that social work has had difficulty defining its scientific base has been its reluctance to study the process and outcome of its practice modalities and technology. Although a research tradition exists within the profession, the research models that were prevalent for many years grew out of the social rather than biophysical sciences and involved large-scale survey and small group research. Moreover, while the measurement of variables (adopted from psychology) has been pursued, the evaluation of practice, the testing of assumptions, and the investigation of therapeutic processes, such as change, have been neglected. Thus, the research foundation of practice is weak (Kirk, 1979; Simpson, 1979).

Over two decades ago Kadushin (1959) commented on the "disturbing characteristics" of the knowledge base of the social work profession. First among these characteristics was that "the borderline between social work hypothesis and fact is often tenuous. A seemingly truthful, self-evident hypothesis achieves the status of fact by sheer repetition. Yet the history of science is strewn with the debris of self-evident propositions" (p. 48). Kadushin further discussed the lack of consistent efforts to conceptualize social work knowledge, the noncumulative nature of that knowledge, and the fact that most of it had been borrowed from the behavioral and social sciences and consequently suffered from the problems associated with borrowed knowledge. He looked to the future for the amelioration of some of the negative consequences of these factors. Almost twenty years later, Simon, in discussing the conceptual frameworks for social work practice, referred to the knowledge base of social work as its Achilles heel. She described the incompleteness of social work theory, pointed out the insufficient identification and organization of basic social work knowledge, and called for the profession to engage in a systematic attempt at "knowledge-building and knowledge-ordering" (Simon, 1977, p. 400).

In this connection, Siporin, has distinguished between two essential components of all social work knowledge: foundation knowledge, which he views as "consisting of personality theory, social theory, and an element of the latter, social welfare theory," and practice theory, which he defines as concerned with planned intervention and change activities in regard to personality and social systems (1975, p. 94). Obviously, neither type of knowledge is the exclusive domain of social work. It is in the area of what Siporin terms "distinctive content," which refers to the knowledge that is shaped by social work's values, mission, and goals, and which is given special emphasis, that the social work profession has encountered special difficulties.

Reviewing the historical development of the theories that have informed social work practice and the complex issues this evolution has highlighted raises important considerations for the definition of clinical social work and for the consolidation of its scientific base.

Evolution of the Knowledge Base of Practice

Morality and Religion as Theory. When the social work profession evolved in the late nineteenth and early twentieth centuries, moral, religious, and socio-political values associated with English and American Protestantism and capitalism were intertwined. Together they constituted the "theory" of human behavior that shaped helping efforts (Woodroofe, 1962; Lubove, 1971; Hollis, 1963; Briar, 1971). The times gave birth to the idea that philanthropy could be "scientific." According to Hamilton (1958, p. 13), however, "the truth was simply that the causes of behavior were little understood. The culture imposed its morals and values on social work, as well as on all the humanistic professions."

One author notes that in the early days of the Community Organization Society (COS) in London, which gave birth to its counterpart and later to social casework in the United States, the main assumption about human behavior was that "with certain rare exceptions, 'self-dependence' was possible for all men, and if they failed to attain it, the fault lay in themselves, and not in any external causes" (Woodroofe, 1962, pp. 33–34). Thus the COS embodied the view that individuals rather than social conditions were the main focus of helping efforts. Moreover, the organization of society was taken as a given, not as the object of change.

When the COS developed in the United States, the focus on the individual was prominent. Nevertheless there were those who differed with the view that individuals were wholly responsible for their fate and who looked to social conditions as the main determinants of individual problems. The settlement and social reform put more emphasis on society's role in fostering or inhibiting individual well-being. Siporin (1970, p. 13) writes of this period that "From 1892 to 1917, and especially at the beginning of the century, the new profession of social work emphasized social legislative action, social institutional reform, and broad preventive programs. . . . As Richmond later recalled, she was one of the caseworkers who were 'often waved aside as having outlived [their] usefulness because legislation and propaganda, between them, would render social work with and for individuals unnecessary.'"

Thus two antagonistic trends existed in the early history of the profession. The individual and society were polarized. There was no broad agreement on what the focus of understanding and intervention ought to be. The immediate legacy, however, was the more individualistic view. Thus the beginning consolidation of social casework in the years after World War I gradually moved the social focus into the background.

Emphasis on Technology. Before 1917 social casework developed into an activity requiring paid, trained workers (Woodroofe, 1962; Lubove, 1971). The new profession's scientific pursuit focused on developing a sound way of evaluating people and their environments so that intelligent decisions about whether and how to give help could be made—that is, the emphasis was on developing a methodology rather than on developing social work's knowledge base.

The "science" of fact-gathering about the client in his social situation was epitomized by Richmond's *Social Diagnosis* (1917), which put forth study, diagnosis, and treatment as the principles underlying social casework. Richmond described what she thought to be the most fundamental aspect of the casework method—the systematic collection of facts about the nature of the problem the client presented. She felt that caseworkers must have knowledge of the individual, the family, and the community. Perhaps paradoxically, her emphasis on understanding and "treating" environmental conditions, and thus her more sociological emphasis, was in the context of her advocacy of a highly individual-centered approach. Although Richmond did not see people as "morally responsible for their plight" (Meyer, 1970, p. 39), she did view the individual as unique in the way he or she dealt with social factors, and thus as the proper focus of casework. Mailick points out (1977, p. 403) that while Richmond repeatedly discussed the social situation of her clients, her focus "was guided principally by an interest in their relevancy to the diagnosis of the individual or family need . . . The conceptual links between the individual and his situation were weak." Mailick further noted that Richmond did not try to develop a conceptual framework about the social environment.

In fact, no major theoretical perspective on human behavior commanded Richmond's attention, though she repeatedly stressed the need for more systematic understanding of human behavior and the importance of growth in personality as a casework goal. Further, Germain (1970) has pointed out that Richmond's adoption of the study, diagnosis, and treatment paradigm linked social work to the medical model in which clients were seen as "diseased" people in need of "healers" and social workers were viewed as "social physicians or general practitioners of charity."

Psychiatry and Psychoanalytic Theory. The shell-shock casualties of World War I, the adjustment needs of soldiers returning to civilian life, and the Child Guidance Movement of the early 1920s brought social workers in hospitals, clinics, and family agencies into greater contact with psychiatric principles and practices. While somewhat socially and community oriented psychiatric treatment approaches already existed, for instance in the work of Adolph Meyer and Richard Cabot, the psychiatric deluge contributed to the "swing away from the socioeconomic determinism of the previous era to the psychological determinism of the 1920s" (Woodroofe, 1962, p. 121).

Out of the host of psychologically oriented theories, Freud's ideas gained momentum in the United States, supplying social caseworkers with a powerful set of ideas to help them understand human behavior and to guide individual helping strategies. Psychoanalytic theory stressed the impact of unconscious, irrational, instinctual forces in early childhood and the significance of subjective and fantasied reality in shaping behavior. It postulated fixation points in childhood that determined later psychosexual stages. It explained the role of defenses (as protections against anxiety) and the individual's tendency to repeat early childhood conflicts and experiences in adult life—even in the helping relationship itself.

Social workers embraced psychoanalytic theory as a way of understanding clients' failure to make changes in their lives or their choosing to refuse help altogether. The problems that clients presented, the "bad" circumstances in which they lived, and their "uncooperativeness" could now be seen as rooted in their early life experiences and could be treated by "uncovering" their unconscious conflicts. Client uncooperativeness could now be understood as "resistance."

All casework practice became infused with psychoanalytic theory and techniques. Among the more important ones were indirect, reflective, and "passive" as well as interpretive techniques for eliciting unconscious conflict. This led to what many have termed "excesses" (Hamilton, 1958) and to what others (Meyer, 1970) have called "wrong turns" in the profession because they sidetracked social workers from their fundamental concern with the development of a helping method that would enhance their clients' social functioning. The theme underlying these criticisms was that psychoanalytically oriented casework narrowly addressed the inner person rather than environmental transactions. "It was one of the aberrant features of the attempt to carry psychoanalytic principles and techniques primarily concerned with the neurotic into casework that treatment became so preoccupied with the inner life as almost to lose touch with outer reality and the social factors with which social workers were most familiar" (Hamilton, 1958, p. 23).

The use of psychoanalytic theory in social casework practice was also criticized for its pessimistic and deterministic view of people and its reliance on a medical or disease model (Yelaja, 1974). It was attacked too for leading to a process that robbed individuals of responsibility for moving their lives forward, created undue dependency, and promoted an unrealistic, never-ending exploration of the past.

A schism developed between social workers of the diagnostic school and those of the functional school that was inaugurated by the publication of *A Changing Psychology in Social Casework* (Robinson, 1930). Functional casework, developed initially by Taft (1937, 1950) and Robinson (1930, 1950), drew on the theories of Otto Rank (1929, 1947), which were thought to be more humanistic than the diagnostic approach. Rank viewed individuals as more active and creative in seeking health, capable of changing themselves and their environment within the limits of their capacities, and able to use relationships to move toward their life goals. Rank saw each person as a unique whole, motivated by a will that pushed toward expression to overcome life fears and death fears.

The widening of this schism between diagnostic and functional caseworkers occurred during the severe economic depression of the 1930s, when greater and greater numbers of "worthy" people of "good character" found themselves in desperate financial circumstances and required economic assistance. For the first time, government-sponsored public agencies employed social workers who had previously worked in mental health and family agencies. These workers struggled with how to give help to their new clients—through psychological means or through supplying necessary services.

Functional casework adopted an approach to clients that could offer them a relationship, irrespective of need, in which the clients could learn to assert their will and fulfill their uniqueness. The use of relationship became linked to the function of the agency. Thus, the client seeking assistance could be helped by means of the casework relationship to accept or reject the agency's service and in the process emerge more fully.

This functional approach was criticized for leading to its own excesses in that its stress on client self-determination, individual responsibility, and the casework relationship as an end in itself led to the deprivation of needed services and to what were experienced as punishing and withholding techniques used to evoke a supposedly necessary struggle.

Yet another current that existed during the period that was dominated by the psychoanalytic view and the controversy between the diagnostic and functional schools emphasized the social determinants of behavior. Numerous theorists tried to develop a conceptual framework that linked individuals to their environment and led to social treatment or to intervention using a situational perspective (Mailick, 1977; Siporin, 1970). Among these were Ada Sheffield, Fern Lowry, Ernest and Harriet Mowrer, Edward Lindermann, Pauline Young, and Bertha Reynolds. Social treatment in its various forms was concerned with clients' social situations in interaction with their needs and was directed at creating a better fit between person and environment. Social intervention was distinguished from psychotherapy, but as Siporin notes (p. 16), this notion was "out of tune with the prevailing Freudian ethic and the preoccupation with personality change through psychological procedures. . . . The term social treatment fell into disuse and was replaced by . . . the limited procedures of 'environmental manipulation.'"

Beginning in the later 1930s, though more significant in the post-World War II period, revisions in psychoanalytic theory that drew attention to the ego became assimilated in the United States. Anna Freud, Hartmann, Kris and Lowenstein, Rapaport, and Erikson emphasized the importance of the ego's innate, conscious, rational, adaptive, problem-solving capacities, the autonomous or conflict-free areas of ego functioning, and the adaptive role of defense. They refocused the importance of both the individual's interaction and relationship with external reality and the interplay of current and past biopsychosocial factors in lifelong development.

In the 1940s and 1950s numerous social workers identified with the diagnostic school, or psychosocial model, became associated with attempts to assimilate psychoanalytic and ego psychological concepts into the knowledge base of social casework and with attempts to differentiate casework from psychotherapy. Prominent among them were Lucille Austin (1948, 1956), Bernard Bandler (1963), Louise Bandler (1963), Grete Bibring (1950a, 1950b); Eleanor Cockerill and others (1953), Annette Garrett (1958), Gordon Hamilton (1940, 1951), Florence Hollis (1949, 1964), Isabel Stamm (1959), and Charlotte Towle (1950, 1954). In summarizing the contributions of ego psychology, Stamm (1959, pp. 87–88) wrote that social workers viewed ego psychology as providing "a connecting link between concepts about instinctual drives and unconscious conflict and concepts about social role and its ties to the structure and functioning of institutions."

During this period ego psychology affected all aspects of casework practice and moved social casework away from its exclusive focus on the inner depths of clients. It provided a theoretical rationale for delineating the client's functioning in the here and now, assessing the nature of the client's adaptive as well as maladaptive ego functioning, identifying the situational factors that might be part of the problem but could become part of the solution, creating more selective developmental histories of past events as they pertained to current functioning, and determining the internal and external resources that might be mobilized on behalf of the client to produce the desired changes.

Ego psychological concepts led to treatment approaches that aimed to improve or sustain adaptive ego functioning by working with the individual and by working with the environment. Working with the ego required the social worker's respect for the client's defenses and for his capacity for autonomous, effective ego functioning. The real nature of the client-worker relationship became important, in contrast to an exclusive focus on its distorted transference aspects. Further, the relationship was seen positively as a tool for bettering the client's functioning. According to ego psychology, change might be produced not only through insight but also through freeing up and enhancing innate ego capacities (without necessarily altering underlying personality conflicts), providing experiences in the worker-client relationship that would "correct" for past developmental failures or deprivations, providing opportunities in the casework relationship and in real life in which new behavior could be exercised and reinforced, and creating environmental supports for effectively exercising specific ego functioning. The phases of casework—that is, the engagement or initial phase, the working-through or middle phase, and the termination or end phase—were reconceptualized so that the importance of engaging clients in a helping relationship in which they could exercise their innate ego capacities and take more responsibility for directing their own treatment and their lives became apparent. Greater selectivity and more circumscribed exploration, intervention, and monitoring of progress in the middle phase was advocated. The termination phase was viewed as "therapeutic" in its own right—as a time for clients to test out their ability to manage their own lives—and the posttermination phase became more critical as it was necessary to ensure continued environmental support after the formal end of treatment.

Ego psychological concepts reclaimed a crucial role for environmental and sociocultural factors in shaping behavior and in providing opportunities to develop, enhance, and sustain ego functioning. Efforts to translate this view of the environment into social casework method gave credence to the assessment of and work with the environment. New terms evolved: environmental manipulation, social treatment, and environmental modification. Under the impact of ego-psychological concepts, Hamilton's formulation of the person-in-situation configuration developed (1940). As she tried to link person and environment, she espoused a multicausal view of human functioning in which psychosocial diagnosis was situational.

Despite this extensive development of theory and refinement of technique, casework remained focused on the individual. Mailick (1977, p. 407) writes that Hamilton's ideas in particular were not fully realized in her time. "The profession was enmeshed in the medical metaphor and found difficulty in relinquishing a linear cause-and-effect world view. Limited to one perspective, practice continued to concentrate on the individual. The study of the situation was viewed as a separate activity, not an integral part of a unitary whole."

Other Contributions. Through the 1940s and into the 1950s, other personality theories affected social work practice, although none equaled the significance of orthodox and ego-psychological Freudian thought. Theorists such as Adler, Horney, Fromm, and Sullivan (the neo-Freudians or social psychologists) were known for their focus on the social and interpersonal context of human behavior and on the significance of these contexts during treatment. Alexander's (1946) writings, which influenced many social workers, shed light on the relationship dimension of the therapeutic process, particularly its realistic and potentially corrective aspects, as well as on ways of shortening, focusing, and managing it. Theorists such as Maslow, Murray, and Lewin emphasized a more holistic and growth-oriented view of personality. They enriched the profession's ways of understanding the person-in-situation complementarity that many social work theorists were struggling to conceptualize. Piaget became important for his work on cognitive development, and Robert White's writings about the individual's inherent drive toward mastery and competence began to generate interest.

Efforts to incorporate social science theory had long been a part of the social work tradition, but the theory itself was underdeveloped. While notable exceptions existed, social workers had less interest in social science theory and the social environment than they did in personality theory. Furthermore, while the sociology of Durkheim, Merton, and Parsons, among others, was known to social workers, these theories were used to illuminate the environmental context of individual behavior rather than the functioning of complex environmental systems in their own right (Kammerman and others, 1973).

It was not until the 1950s that social science knowledge itself underwent rapid development and transformation and began to be assimilated by social work. The study of the structure and processes of small groups, of marriage and the family, of complex organizations, of the impact of social class, bureaucratization, and urbanization, of power and authority, of social roles, and of sociocultural influences offered social work new ways of conceptualizing the social environment (Stein, 1963).

Theoretical concepts from these areas contributed immeasurably to the development of group work and community organization and to the use of more interpersonal types of intervention, such as marital and family casework. Nevertheless, insofar as the impact of these concepts on the casework process is concerned, while caseworkers acquired a sophisticated understanding of the impact of environmental factors, they continued to see the environment as a backdrop for the individual (Kadushin, 1959; Kammerman and others, 1973).

An important development in the 1950s stemmed from efforts to incorporate new concepts from personality and social science theory. Helen Perlman developed a distinctive problem-solving casework model (1957). She tried to bridge the gap between diagnostic and functional caseworkers as well as to offer correctives for practices that she viewed as dysfunctional for the client. Significant among these were long waiting lists, the high dropout rate associated with lengthy diagnostic processes, and the practice of engaging in a relationship with the client that had no purpose with respect to the client's problem.

Drawing heavily on the writings of Hartmann, Erikson, White, and Piaget as well as on social psychology, Perlman evolved a casework approach that was based on the premise that all human living is effective problem solving and that emphasized the rational, flexible, and growth-oriented aspects of individuals. Client difficulties were viewed as stemming from disruptions of normal problem-solving capacities in relation to specific situations and from deficiencies in some combination of client motivation, capacity, and opportunity (Ripple and Alexander, 1964).

In its attention to both the nature of the problem the client presented and the assessment of the client's motivation, capacity, and opportunity, Perlman's model deemphasized many of those aspects of the "inner man" thought to be essential to assessing personality. It was criticized for elevating the conception of the rational and cognitive ego to a loftier place vis-á-vis instinctual and unconscious motives in behavior.

Changing Views of Practice. Beginning in the 1960s and throughout the 1970s, multiple factors within society and within the social work profession converged to radically change the role and nature of direct practice. The 1960s ushered in an emphasis on large-scale programs financed by the federal government. In contrast to the 1940s and 1950s, which emphasized the psychological and interpersonal causes of individual and familial pathology, human problems now were seen as stemming from social conditions. This atmosphere supported a thrust within the social work profession to turn its attention to social planning and social change.

This focus on social rather than psychological factors in client difficulties was accompanied by a challenge to the utility of the medical model and its view of people as afflicted with diseases that could be diagnosed and treated. An antilabeling and antitreatment sentiment gathered support, and many types of client difficulties seen by the social worker were redefined as problems in living, failure to conform to society's norms, or forms of social deprivation.

Casework services, which had dominated social work until this time, came under attack. They were viewed as linked too closely to the medical model, too allied with psychodynamic theories, too narrowly conceived, too expensive, and too lengthy (Wasserman, 1974, p. 48). The accumulating results of research on casework effectiveness with individuals and families (Mullen, Dumpson, and others, 1972) were disheartening to supporters of casework and were used as ammunition by critics. In commenting on the historical evolution of social casework's scientific commitment and the place to which it had arrived, Germain wrote (1973, p. 126):

> During the 1880s a beginning conviction about the usefulness of science in handling the problems of charities and corrections crystallized in the commitment to scientific method known as scientific philanthropy. The charity organization movement saw its inchoate processes of social diagnosis and social treatment culminate in Richmond's 1917 conceptualization. Over succeeding decades social casework strengthened its scientific commitment by absorbing knowledge from the behavioral and social sciences, developing a method based on the logical principles of scientific inquiry and adopting scientific attitudes of objectivity and open-mindedness. In these same years social casework, as an art, developed its system of values and its service of humanistic concern. Despite its long adherence to the values of science and humanism, however, social casework reached the 1970s at a low point of externally based criticism.

The Proliferation of Practice Models. Concurrent with the emphasis on social rather than psychological factors and with the attack on traditional practice methods, there was concern about the increasing numbers of people in need of preventive and rehabilitative services, the limited manpower resources, and the too lengthy and expensive treatment approaches. Cutbacks, changes in priority, and increasing demands for accountability, efficiency, and consumerism in the early seventies, all supported a search for types of intervention that would lead to quicker and more easily documented payoffs for large numbers of people. The rapid accretion of knowledge in the behavioral and social sciences that began in 1950s supported group work and community organization as methods of practice. Summarizing the scope of knowledge for practice at this time, Kammerman and others emphasized the relevance of social science theories for intervention in both macrosystems and microsystems. They pointed out the relevance of sociology, political science, and economics for what they called "macropractice," and of sociology, social psychology, and anthropology for "micropractice." The direct practice arena witnessed the proliferation of different types of microsystems intervention.

In two major texts that addressed the theoretical basis of social casework and social work treatment in the 1970s (Strean, 1971; Turner, 1974), role theory, communication theory, general systems theory, cognitive theory, behavioral modification theory, family systems theory, and crisis theory assumed major significance, diminishing the earlier exclusive emphasis on psychoanalytic theory and ego psychology as foundation theories. Additionally, two summaries of theories of social casework intervention (Roberts and Nee, 1970; Turner, 1974) cited no fewer than nine interventive models: the psychosocial approach, the functional approach, the problem-solving model, behavior modification, family therapy, crisis intervention, the socialization approach, the client-centered system, and existential social work. Siporin regrouped all the models into six major theoretical helping approaches plus an additional theoretical perspective: social provision, interactional, psychoanalytic, existentialist, sociobehavioral, problem-solving, and ecosystems theory. He argued for an integrated but eclectic and pluralistic approach to practice and theory building in which the diverse elements were consistent with social work knowledge and values and were tested and validated through research. He was aware that such an eclectic position is open to diverse orientations, some aspects of which may or may not be capable of synthesis (1975, p. 155).

Professional Diversity and Disunity. These developments of the 1960s were significant in shaping the direction of the profession. They restored the "social" to social work by reaffirming the profession's commitment to social change and by recognizing the impact of the social environment on human development and dysfunction. The direct practice wing of the profession moved away from its exclusive reliance on casework, with its psychodynamic base, toward diverse types of intervention with individuals, families, and groups. These developments reflected the profession's responsiveness to changing times and to growth in other disciplines.

These changes also led to polarization and alienation, as the emphasis on social change seemed to eclipse the profession's commitment to direct practice. Large numbers of practitioners dedicated to individualized work felt that the profession turned its back on their interests and expertise (Frank, 1980). Specialization without solidification of a common core of knowledge and skills led to splintering into special interest groups and fragmentation of the knowledge base. Many social workers appeared to have more in common with members of other fields than with the members of certain specialities within their own ranks. Rather than deriving strength from a strong base, remaining in close touch with it, and strengthening it in turn, specialization weakened the common core so vital to the status and survival of the whole profession.

The Role of Research

Thus far this historical review has dealt mainly with the borrowing of knowledge from the social and behavioral sciences and the development of models for practice, against the backdrop of shifting emphases within society and the profession. The role of research in verifying the theoretical assumptions underlying the practice models, in clarifying the nature of the helping process, and in evaluating the effectiveness of intervention models has not been discussed. One reason is that while there is a long tradition of social work research, the results do not comprise an organized body of data.

Until World War II the main emphasis in social work research was large-scale community surveys. Typically these would describe exhaustively the multiple characteristics of the people and social conditions of large areas or populations (MacDonald, 1960; Stuart, 1971). An assumption underlying these studies was that systematic information about needs would lead to programs geared to address them. But because these surveys were so monumental, they often became diffuse and superficial. One corrective was to ask more focused questions. While there were some attempts to study the outcomes of interventions, social casework relied largely on an intensive case-study method begun by Richmond.

After World War II social work researchers emerged in new garb. Margaret Blenkner's article, "Obstacles to Evaluative Research in Social Casework" (1950), was a classic article calling for more outcome research and discussing the problems of undertaking it. Hunt and Kogan (1950) developed one of the earliest methodologies for assessing client outcome. While research efforts increased in the 1950s, they largely studied the effects of agency services rather than the effects of social work method and theory. Moreover, since these studies lacked the rigor of experimental designs, the important variables in outcome could not be isolated. Even in their efforts at gross evaluation, the designs did not shed light on advancing our understanding of therapeutic processes.

A second postwar trend was to study aspects of the interventive process. One example comes from Hollis's work on a way of analyzing the components of social workers' interventions in an effort to understand their impact on clients. Commonly such process studies have not been tied either to specific hypotheses following from social work theory or to outcome variables.

In the 1960s two important studies ushered in a time of intensified efforts to study social casework: *Girls at Vocational High* (Meyer, Borgatta, and Jones, 1965) and the *Cheming County Evaluation of Casework Service to Multiproblem Families* (Brown, 1968). The significance of these studies was that they did not support the efficacy of social casework over control groups. While the methodology of these studies was criticized in many quarters, the impact of their results was intensified when rigorous reviews of additional evaluation studies performed during this period were published (Mullen, Dumpson, and others, 1972; Fischer, 1973). Mullen and Dumpson (1972, p. 10) concluded in their discussion of thirteen such studies that "the emerging picture of professional intervention is far from clear. The evidence does not definitely indicate that such intervention is effective or ineffective. We are now confronted with a large number of outcome evaluations and have not had the wisdom, skill, or time as professionals to integrate their meaning. Our immediate task is to determine the reasons for our failures and the meaning of our success." What the studies also reflected was the lack of precision in designing interventive models in ways that could be studied.

As Mullen and Dumpson point out (1972, p. 10): "Many projects fail to reach their goals because the following questions [have] been inadequately considered: On what basis and toward what end will who do what to whom, for how long, and what effect, and with what benefits?" Perlman (1972, p. 194) made the following similar and important points regarding the nature of some of the social casework processes studied:

> Although technical faults may be found here and [there] in these studies, nevertheless it is clear that each was individually and carefully designed. . . . But the process being studied—casework—was not designed at all. There is no evidence that the caseworkers sat down and asked themselves exactly what services or provisions people with needs and deficits would want and find useful, nor did they ask what reasonable results might be anticipated. Or what, if any, special emphasis or forms of psychological influence toward change might be called for and utilized. Or, what the clients' perception of service might be and, consequently, what clarifications and agreements would have to be reached. And so on. Instead, one repeatedly receives the impression that caseworkers are turned loose on clients, adjured to do casework or give casework, as if casework were a theory to be bestowed upon a person or an immutable process, or as if casework help bore small relation to the nature of the material with which it [was] involved.

While the collective results of these evaluation studies contributed to the attack on traditional methods of helping and to casework's low ebb, the role of evaluation research in social work asserted itself strongly. Research methodology became increasingly rigorous, utilizing variations on the prototypical designs. Clearly those intervention models whose concepts were most easily operationalized and measurable were the most easily studied. Thus, the new task-centered casework, brief intervention models, and forms of behavioral intervention lent themselves to the measurement and control of variables and to the evaluation of clear-cut inputs and outcomes. More difficult to research in this way are the more dynamically oriented interventions, which have especially complex client, social worker, intervention, and outcome variables. The trend toward this type of research has been buttressed by the demands for cost-effective social work services. A program evaluation component is now usually tied to services offered.

These trends have led to renewed debate, however, as to whether outcome evaluation in itself is sufficient to forward our building of practice theory, particularly when the research involves expensive, large group designs that do not clarify the meaning of the results or permit us to test specific theoretical assumptions. A search exists for more versatile research designs that permit the intensive analysis of the multiple factors that affect client change or that allow discrete questions to be investigated expeditiously. The goal is not to return to studies of process rather than outcome, but to design studies that unite the two so as to advance our understanding of the interventive process with specific types of clients under specific circumstances.

Future Directions

The importance of direct practice is being reaffirmed in the 1970s and 1980s. Two sometimes opposing trends can be identified: a continuing thrust toward specialization and another toward integration. As discussed at the beginning of the chapter, at the present time clinical social work is split with respect to which of these trends it should embrace and thus with respect to what it calls its scientific base.

One segment of the split is represented by those who review social work history and feel that the recent priority the profession has given to macrosystem intervention has crippled direct practice. They hold the view that in-depth understanding of human problems has been forsaken in favor of emphasizing the social determinants of behavior or performing abstract analyses of system functioning. They argue that meaningful services have been replaced by global programs, or by mechanistic and opportunistic though easily researchable practices.

Individuals who share this view agree that psychotherapeutic intervention, whether with individuals, families, or groups, and whether under private or public auspices, is not only a legitimate function of social workers but also a specialization requiring a distinctive knowledge base, skills, and training. Although there is some overlap, it is safe to say that social workers interested in therapeutic work with individuals regard ego psychological object relations theory or psychoanalytic developmental psychology as the main theoretical underpinnings of practice, whereas those interested in treating families and groups regard family systems theories and theories of group processes as foundation theories. The stereotype of practitioners who hold either of these preferences sees them as preferring to call themselves "therapists" rather than social workers for reasons of status, licensing, and third-party payment for private fees.

Any review of social work history must acknowledge the significance of the foundation theories cited above for their contribution, however controversial, to the development of social work practice. An unfortunate by-product of the ways the theories were applied in social work was that they became too wedded to a monolithic and narrow approach to practice. Nevertheless, these "excesses" and the subsequent counterreaction were predictable. The theories continue to be useful but their associated technologies are too restrictive for social work. Even the theories themselves, despite their more recent focus on the interpersonal context of behavior, (a) continue to ignore the role of the environment and of person-environmental transactions in causing problems in coping or adaptation, and (b) lead to practices that stress intervention directed at what is "wrong" with the person. Further, there is little that is distinctive to social work in this exclusive orientation. Moreover, the concepts and their practice implications lack a systematic research base, and the research evidence that does exist is either equivocal or negative.

For all these reasons defining a clinical social work specialization around a psychotherapeutic knowledge and technological base is regressive for social work. While a clinical social worker may need to understand these theories and their technology, and while such knowledge should be part of formal social work education, this theoretical and technological model should not define the scientific basis of clinical social work nor constitute the totality of theory in clinical social work training.

The other segment of the current split within the profession reviews the history of social work and sees negative consequences of the profession's tendency to emphasize one aspect or the other of its dual mission—people-helping and society-changing. Those who share this view argue that this tendency to polarize has inhibited the development of the foundation and practice theories essential to consolidating social work's scientific base. They advocate overcoming the artificial dichotomy in practice between work with people and work with their environments, and they call for using theories that focus on person–environmental transactions (Hearn, 1969; Gordon, 1969; Germain, 1979; Meyer, 1970, 1976). These authors see the goal of social work as restoring, maintaining, and enhancing social functioning by improving individual coping and adaptation and by ameliorating environmental conditions.

An illustration of the richness of this integrating perspective (along with its gaps) is seen in the ecological or life model approach to practice as described by Germain (1979, pp. 7–8).

> Ecology is a form of general systems theory: ecologists have always been system thinkers concerned with the relation among living entities and other aspects of their environments. Ecology . . . rests on an evolutionary, adaptive view of human beings (of all organisms) in continuous transactions with the environment. . . . The perspective is concerned with the growth, development, and potentialities of human beings and with the properties of human environments that support or fail to support human potential. . . . In an ecological view, [social work] practice is directed at improving the transactions between people and environments in order to enhance adaptive capacities and improve environments for all who function within them. To carry out the professional purpose requires a set of environmental interventions and a set of interventions into the transactions between people and environments to complement the sets available for intervening in coping patterns of people.

Underpinning the ecological perspective are the concepts of coping and adaptation, a stress on the rational, cognitive, problem-solving aspects of people, the need and quest for personal and social competence, and the necessity for adaptive fits between an individual's phase-specific needs and environmental resources. It draws on aspects of ego psychology associated with Hartmann, Erikson, and White, on general systems theory and human ecology, on crisis theory, and on conceptions of therapeutic milieus applied to the physical and social environmental systems as they impinge on and are affected by people. It gives a prominent role to intervention in the social environment as well as to work with individuals (Germain and Gitterman, 1980).

Germain and others are aware that many of their unifying concepts are still at too high a level of abstraction to help practitioners, other than by giving them a broad organizing perspective. Practitioners need practical knowledge to guide their actions. For example, "The traditional means for defining problems of individual, family, or systems pathology lead to concepts that are operational and that can guide intervention and that have reality for practitioners. However, concepts that link the individual and environment are difficult to operationalize. The term 'interface' comes to mind. It may be conceptually useful, but efforts to apply it in practice lead one to feel as if one were working in cracks, or in between chairs, or in empty spaces. This is because social workers have not yet made concepts relating to interface phenomena come alive in ways that do justice to the complexity of an individual's transactions with the environment" (Goldstein, 1980, p. 174). Thus, the general and abstract nature of person–environment concepts and their lack of specificity as a guide to intervention place serious limits on the appeal of this perspective to people currently engaged in direct practice. If the psychotherapeutic orientation seems too narrow to some, this broadened perspective seems amorphous and frustrating to others. And so we have yet another polarization within the direct practice arena.

A further weakness of this unifying perspective is that its concepts are not only hard to operationalize, they are even harder to research. This is true particularly if the model of research viewed as optimal in these times calls for clear-cut, easily documented inputs and outcomes and tightly controlled variables. Such a model may be more suited to the pure sciences and to areas of inquiry in which the knowledge base is more refined.

Siporin's distinction between foundation theory and practice theory, discussed at the beginning of the chapter, identifies the former as descriptive and explanatory personality (or behavior) and social theories, and the latter as theories of how social work helps change personality and social systems (Siporin, 1975, p. 118). Clearly, while research is essential in both areas, each requires different research strategies. Further, research addressing the relationship between concepts from both areas is complex. Turner (1974, p. 14) suggests that what a practitioner does may not necessarily follow from the theories he says he follows, and he recommends studying what practitioners actively do. While this represents one useful approach, too great a tendency to look at practice in isolation from the theoretical concepts alleged to guide it does not do justice to the necessary linkages between foundation knowledge, practice theory, and operational interventions. It is clear that a multifaceted approach to both process and outcome research must develop models that give a key role to practitioners. Fortunately, research models are evolving that integrate practice and research and point to promising directions in helping practitioners formulate and study issues of importance to them (Briar, 1979; Scheurman, 1979; and Jayaratne and Levy, 1979).

Another difficulty in the path of integration is the lack of clarity within the profession as to the role of specialized knowledge and skills. Is a practitioner with a sociobehavioral orientation working at the interface between people and environments if he or she attempts to relieve a client of a crippling phobic symptom that impairs social functioning? Is a practitioner sufficiently ecological if he or she uses psychotherapeutic skills to enhance autonomous ego functioning? Is the social work practitioner dealing with interface phenomena if he or she engages in intensive family therapy aimed at modifying family communication roles and structure? Since these practitioners overlap to such a great extent with practitioners in other fields, can their functions be viewed as sufficiently distinctive to social work, and if so, what is the factor that makes them so?

Gordon and Schutz (1977, p. 423) have suggested that the answer to such questions lies in assessing whether new social work specializations are concerned "with some interface between persons and their environments." They imply that the practitioner may work on one side or another of the interface so that, for example, the practitioner may view a person's limited coping capacity as the cause of the difficulty and thus work to improve such coping, "but as long as a dual focus is used to achieve a better match between coping capability and environment . . . a social work specialization may be identified." Presumably the clinical social worker will need a core of knowledge and skills that guides assessment and intervention as well as specialized knowledge and skill in particular types of intervention selected from a large repertoire of available helping approaches.

The challenge to clinical social work is to find ways of resolving the issues discussed here. The heart of the struggle will lie in achieving clarity about the values underlying and the goals directing social work practice, and in narrowing the gap between commitment to a scientific approach and its achievement.

References

Alexander, F., and French, T. M. *Psychoanalytic Therapy*. New York: Ronald Press, 1946.

Austin, D. N. "Identifying Research Priorities in Social Work Education." In A. J. Rubin and A. Rosenblatt (Ed.), *Sourcebook on Research Utilization*. New York: Council on Social Work Education, 1979.

Austin, L. N. "Trends in Differential Treatment in Social Casework." *Social Casework*, 1948, *29*, 203–211.

Austin, L. N. "Qualification of Social Caseworkers for Psychotherapy." *Journal of Orthopsychiatry*, Jan. 1956, pp. 47–57.

Bandler, B. "The Concept of Ego-Supportive Therapy." In H. J. Parad and R. Miller (Eds.), *Ego-Oriented Casework*. New York: Family Service Association of America, 1963.

Bandler, L. "Some Aspects of Ego Growth Through Sublimation." In H. J. Parad and R. R. Miller (Eds.), *Ego-Oriented Casework*. New York: Family Service Association of America, 1963.

Bibring, G. "Psychiatry in Social Work." In C. Kasius (Ed.), *Principles and Techniques in Social Casework: Selected Articles, 1940–1950*. New York: Family Service Association of America, 1950a.

Bibring, G. "Psychiatric Principles in Casework." In C. Kasius (Ed.), *Principles and Techniques in Social Casework: Selected Articles, 1940–1950*. New York: Family Service Association of America, 1950b.

Blenkner, M. "Obstacles to Evaluative Research in Social Casework." *Social Casework*, 1950, *31*, 54–60; 97–105.

Briar, S. "Incorporating Research into Education for Clinical Practice in Social Work." In A. Rubin and A. Rosenblatt (Eds.), *Sourcebook on Research Utilization.* New York: Council on Social Work Education, 1979.

Briar, S., and Miller, H. *Problems and Issues in Social Casework.* New York: Columbia University Press, 1971.

Brown, G. E. (Ed.). *The Multi-Problem Dilemma.* Metuchen, N.J.: Scarecrow Press, 1968.

Cockerill, E. E., and others. *A Conceptual Framework of Social Casework.* Pittsburgh: University of Pittsburgh Press, 1953.

Cohen, J. "Nature of Clinical Social Work." In P. L. Ewalt (Ed.), *Toward a Definition of Clinical Social Work.* Washington, D.C.: National Association of Social Workers, 1980.

Ewalt, P. L. (Ed.). *Toward a Definition of Clinical Social Work.* Washington, D.C.: National Association of Social Workers, 1980.

Fischer, J. "Is Casework Effective?" *Social Work,* 1973, *18,* 5–21.

Flexner, A. "Is Social Work a Profession?" In *Proceedings of the National Conference of Charities and Corrections.* Chicago: The Conference, 1915.

Frank, M. G. "Clinical Social Work: Past, Present, and Future Challenges and Dilemmas." In P. L. Ewalt (Ed.), *Toward a Definition of Clinical Social Work.* Washington, D.C.: National Association of Social Workers, 1980.

Garrett, A. "Modern Casework: The Contribution of Ego Psychology." In H. J. Parad (Ed.), *Ego Psychology and Dynamic Casework.* New York: Family Service Association of America, 1958.

Germain, C. B. "Casework and Science: An Historical Encounter." In R. W. Roberts and R. H. Nee (Eds.), *Theories of Social Casework.* Chicago: University of Chicago Press, 1970.

Germain, C. B. "Social Casework." In H. B. Trecker (Ed.), *Goals for Social Welfare 1973–1993: An Overview of the Next Two Decades.* New York: Association Press, 1973.

Germain, C. B. *Social Work Practice: People and Environments.* New York: Columbia University Press, 1979.

Germain, C. B. "The Social Context of Clinical Social Work." *Social Work,* 1980, *25,* 483–488.

Germain, C. B., and Gitterman, A. *The Life Model of Social Work Practice.* New York: Columbia University Press, 1980.

Goldstein, E. G. "Knowledge Base of Clinical Social Work." *Social Work,* 1980, *25,* 173–178.

Goode, W. "The Theoretical Limits of Professionalization." In A. Etzioni (Ed.), *The Semi-Professions and Their Organization.* New York: Free Press, 1969.

Gordon, W. E. "Basic Constructs for an Integrative and Generative Conception of Social Work." In G. Hearn (Ed.), *The General Systems Approach: Contributions Toward an Holistic Conception of Social Work Practice.* New York: Council on Social Work Education, 1969.

Gordon, W. E., and Schutz, M. L. "A Natural Basis for Social Work Specialization." *Social Work,* 1977, *22,* 422–427.

Hamilton, G. *Theory and Practice of Social Casework.* New York: Columbia University Press, 1940.

Hamilton, G. *Theory and Practice of Social Casework.* (2nd ed.) New York: Columbia University Press, 1951.

Hamilton, G. "A Theory of Personality: Freud's Contribution to Social Work." In H. J. Parad (Ed.), *Ego Psychology and Dynamic Casework.* New York: Family Service Association of America, 1958.

Hearn, G. (Ed.). *The General Systems Approach: Contributions Toward an Holistic Conception of Social Work Practice.* New York: Council on Social Work Education, 1969.

Hollis, F. "Techniques of Casework." *Social Casework,* 1949, *30,* 235–244.

Hollis, F. "Contemporary Issues for Caseworkers." In H. J. Parad and H. Miller (Eds.), *Ego-Oriented Casework.* New York: Family Service Association of America, 1963.

Hollis, F. *Casework: A Psychosocial Therapy.* New York: Random House, 1964.

Hunt, J. McV., and Kogan, L. S. *Measuring Results in Social Casework: A Manual for Judging Movement.* New York: Family Service Society of America, 1950.

Jayaratne, S., and Levy, R. L. *Empirical Clinical Practice.* New York: Columbia University Press, 1979.

Kadushin, A. "The Knowledge Base of Social Work." In A. J. Kahn (Ed.), *Issues in American Social Work.* New York: Columbia University Press, 1959.

Kammerman, S., and others. "Knowledge for Practice: Social Science in Social Work." In A. J. Kahn (Ed.), *Shaping the New Social Work.* New York: Columbia University Press, 1973.

Kirk, S. "Understanding Research Utilization in Social Work." In A. Rubin and A. Rosenblatt (Eds.), *Sourcebook on Research Utilization.* New York: Council on Social Work Education, 1979.

Lubove, R. *The Professional Altruist.* New York: Atheneum, 1971.

MacDonald, M. E. "Social Work Research: A Perspective." In N. A. Polansky (Ed.), *Social Work Research.* Chicago: University of Chicago Press, 1960.

Mailick, M. "The Situational Perspective in Social Work." *Social Casework,* 1977, *58,* 400–412.

Meyer, C. H. *Social Work Practice: A Response to the Urban Crisis.* New York: Free Press, 1970.

Meyer, C. H. *Social Work Practice: The Changing Landscape.* New York: Free Press, 1976.

Meyer, H. J., Borgatta, E. F., and Jones, W. C. *Girls at Vocational High: An Experiment in Social Work Intervention.* New York: Russell Sage Foundation, 1965.

Minahan, A. "What Is Clinical Social Work?" *Social Work,* 1980, *25,* 171.

Mullen, E. J., Dumpson, J. R., and others. *Evaluation of Social Intervention.* San Francisco: Jossey-Bass, 1972.

Perlman, H. H. "Once More with Feeling." In E. J. Mullen, R. Dumpson, and others, *Evaluation of Social Intervention.* San Francisco: Jossey-Bass, 1972.

Perlman, H. H. *Social Casework: A Problem-Solving Process.* Chicago: University of Chicago Press, 1957.

Rank, O. *The Trauma of Birth.* London: Paul, Trench, Truber and Co., 1929.

Rank, O. *Will Therapy and Truth and Reality.* New York: Knopf, 1947.

Reynolds, B. "Between Client and Community." *Smith College Studies in Social Work,* 1934, *5* (1), whole issue.

Richmond, M. L. *Social Diagnosis.* New York: Russell Sage Foundation, 1917.
Ripple, L., and Alexander, E. *Motivation, Capacity, and Opportunity.* Chicago: University of Chicago Press, 1964.
Roberts, R. W., and Nee, R. H. *Theories of Social Casework.* Chicago: University of Chicago Press, 1970.
Robinson, V. P. *A Changing Psychology in Social Work.* Chapel Hill: University of North Carolina Press, 1930.
Robinson, V. P. *The Dynamics of Supervision Under Functional Controls.* Philadelphia: University of Pennsylvania Press, 1950.
Scheurman, J. R. "On Research and Practice-Teaching in Social Work." In A. Rubin and A. Rosenblatt (Eds.), *Sourcebook on Research Utilization.* New York: Council of Social Work Education, 1979.
Simon, B. K. "Diversity and Unity in the Social Work Profession." *Social Work,* 1977, *22,* 394–400.
Simpson, R. L. "Understanding the Utilization of Research in Social Work and Other Applied Professions." In A. Rubin and A. Rosenblatt (Eds.), *Sourcebook on Research Utilization.* New York: Council on Social Work Education, 1979.
Siporin, M. "Social Treatment: A New-Old Method." *Social Work,* 1970, *15,* 13–25.
Siporin, M. *Introduction to Social Work Practice.* New York: Macmillan, 1975.
Stamm, I. "Ego Psychology in the Emerging Theoretical Base of Social Work." In A. J. Kahn (Ed.), *Issues in American Social Work.* New York: Columbia University Press, 1959.
Stein, H. "The Concept of the Social Environment in Social Work Practice." In H. J. Parad and R. Miller (Eds.), *Ego-Oriented Casework.* New York: Family Service Association of America, 1963.
Strean, H. F. *Social Casework: Theories in Action.* Metuchen, N.J.: Scarecrow Press, 1971.
Stuart, R. "Research in Social Work." In R. Morris, and others (Eds.), *Encyclopedia of Social Work,* 1971, *2,* 1098–1122.
Taft, J. "The Relation of Function to Process in Social Casework." *Journal of Social Work Process,* 1937, *1* (1), 1–18.
Taft, J. "A Conception of Growth Process Underlying Social Casework." *Social Casework,* 1950, *31,* 311–318.
Towle, C. "The Contribution of Education for Social Casework to Practice." *Social Casework,* 1950, *31,* 318–326.
Towle, C. *The Learner in Education for the Professions.* Chicago: University of Chicago Press, 1954.
Turner, F. J. *Social Work Treatment.* New York: Free Press, 1974.
Wasserman, S. L. "Ego Psychology." In F. J. Turner (Ed.), *Social Work Treatment.* New York: Free Press, 1974.
Woodroofe, K. *From Charity to Social Work in England and the United States.* Toronto: University of Toronto Press, 1962.
Yelaja, S. A. *Authority and Social Work: Concept and Use.* Toronto: University of Toronto Press, 1971.
Yelaja, S. A. *Functional Theory for Social Work Practice.* New York: Free Press, 1974.

2

Technological Advances

Carel B. Germain

Before the 1960s, when its kinship system of technologies began to expand, clinical social work's genogram would have been simple to construct, as shown in Figure 1. In the 1980s, however, clinical social work has a richness of technology previously unimaginable. Thus, a genogram of the casework side of clinical social work in 1980 is more complex, as shown in Figure 2. Until 1957 there were only two major approaches in social casework: the diagnostic (now called psychosocial) and the functional. The third, appearing in 1957 and called the problem-solving approach, sought to blend the other two. In the face of criticisms related to the rediscovery of poverty in the sixties and in response to continuing theoretical developments, the three approaches were elaborated and refined, incorporating ideas from new bodies of theory. While all three remain prominent today, each has also generated new but related approaches.

Also in the sixties and seventies some theorists undertook to effect more drastic change in approaches to casework by moving away from the Freudian or Rankian systems of psychoanalytic thought on which the original three were based. Such efforts took two directions. One followed the path of general systems theory and the other took the path of learning theory and behaviorism.

Because the newer approaches push toward, or at least lend themselves to, an integrated clinical practice, Figure 2 should be regarded as a genogram that begins with casework but moves toward a broader conception of practice. Methods of working with families and groups are now integral parts of clinical social work even though their technologies do not have as long a history or as full a development in the profession as those of casework.

The origins of group work lay in the settlement movement, the recreation movement (including organized camping), and the Deweyan progressive education movement, as shown in Figure 1. Early practitioners who came from the settlements bequeathed to group work a legacy of interest in social justice and

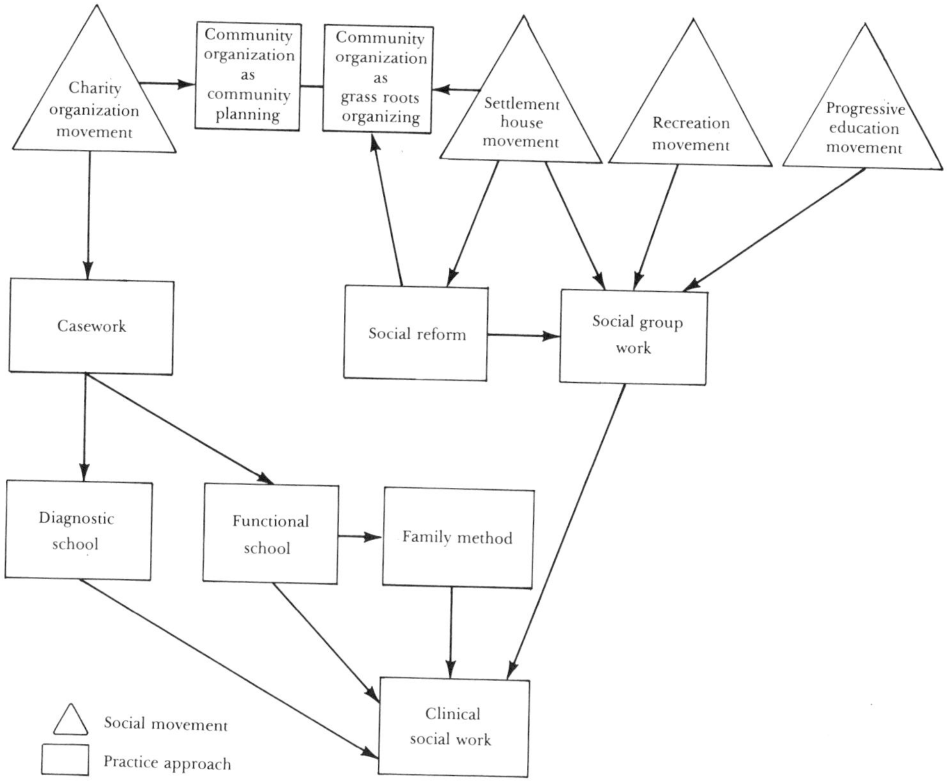

Figure 1. Clinical Social Work Before the 1960s

social reform. Those from the recreation and camping movements brought their interest in programs and activities that produce growth and enjoyment. Those from progressive education brought the conviction that the small group is a means of learning the skills needed for effective participation in a democratic society. Thus group work did not originate as a problem-focused method of service but as a method of social goals: growing, learning, and experiencing the pleasures and benefits of shared activities (Middleman, 1968, p. 26). In the late 1950s two new group work approaches joined the original social goals one. These were the reciprocal (or interactionist) approach and the remedial approach, which moved close to the medical/disease metaphor of the diagnostic school (Papell and Rothman, 1966), and which is now known as the preventive and rehabilitative approach. By 1980 a genogram of clinical social work from the group work side (Figure 3) was quite as complex as that from the casework side (Figure 2).

Work with the family unit is as old as social work itself, since charity workers and settlement workers were always concerned with the family as the unit of their attention. But in the 1920s a marked shift of emphasis from the family to the individual occurred in social casework (American Association of Social Workers, 1929). The emphasis moved back to the family in the later 1930s, but only as a backdrop for understanding the individual or as people to be manipulated on behalf of the individual. During the 1950s developments in the social

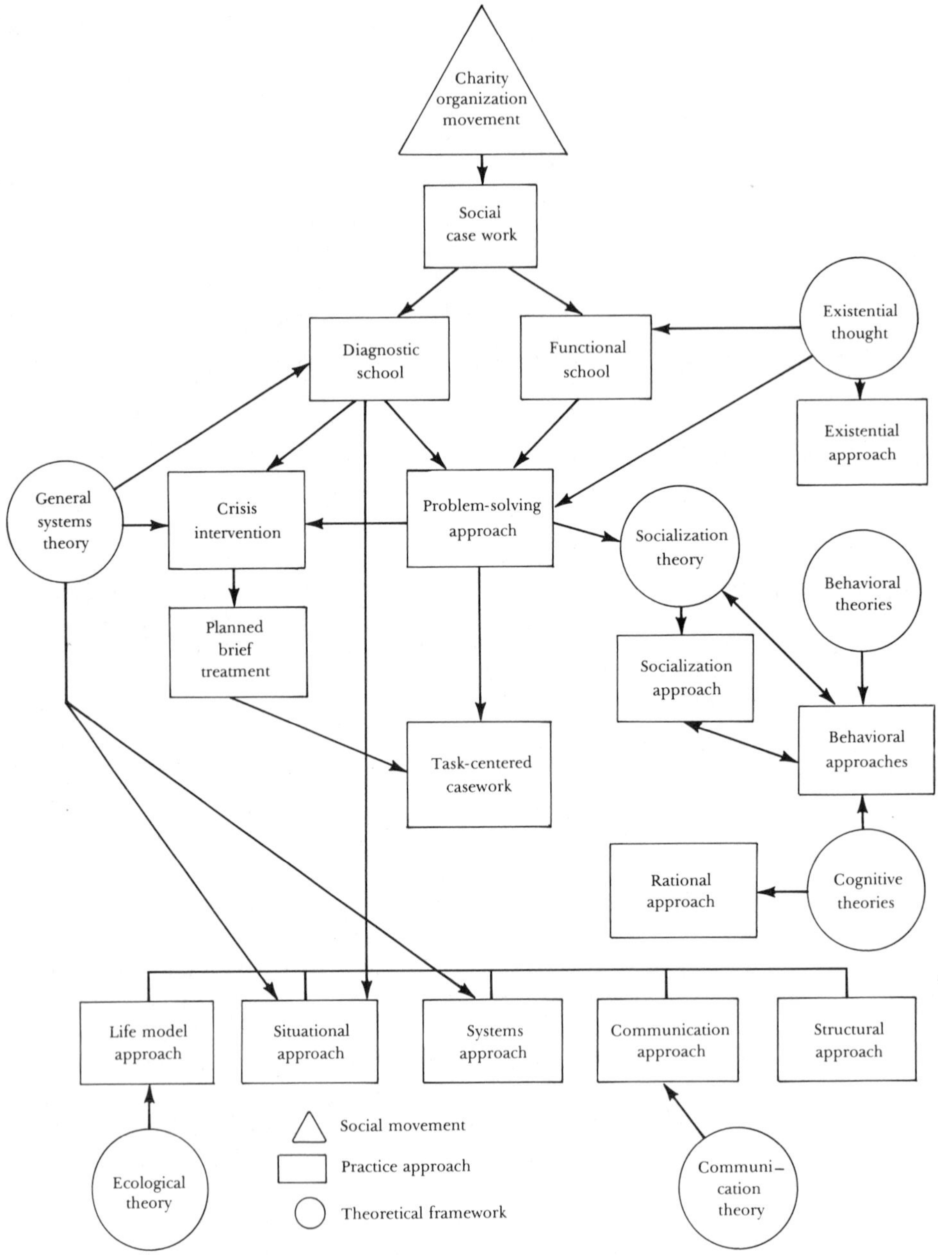

Figure 2. Casework Approaches, 1980. (Not all are examined in this chapter.)

sciences, psychiatry, and social casework itself reawakened the interest of the diagnostic school in the family as the unit of help. The functional school had already moved into the arena of family-focused service ten years before. In 1980 there is a large and growing number of approaches to family therapy, mostly developed by psychiatrists and a few psychologists. Figure 4 shows several that

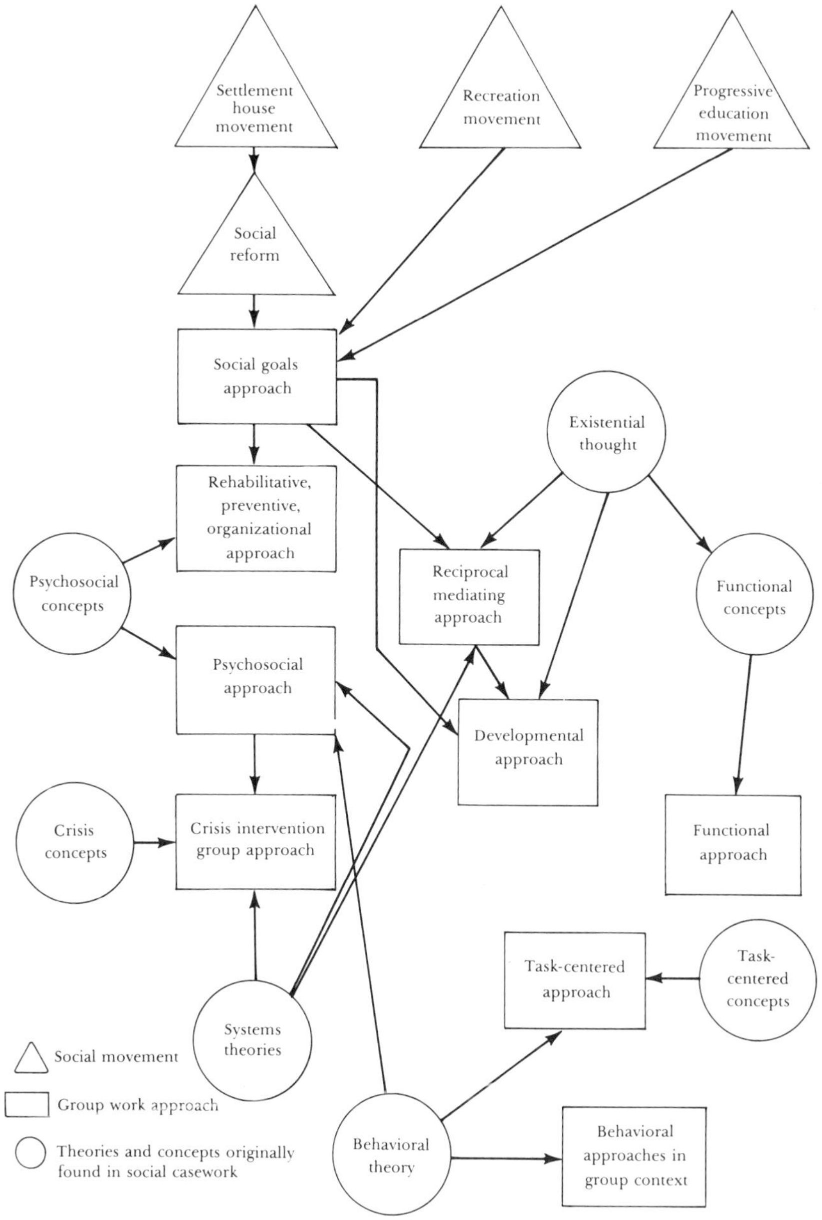

Figure 3. Group Work Approaches, 1980. (Not all are examined in this chapter.)

have been developed further by social workers and that exemplify social work purpose.

Many other technologies developed outside social work are being adopted in whole or in part by some clinical social workers. These include but are not limited to Gestalt therapy, primal therapy, transactional analysis, rational-emotive

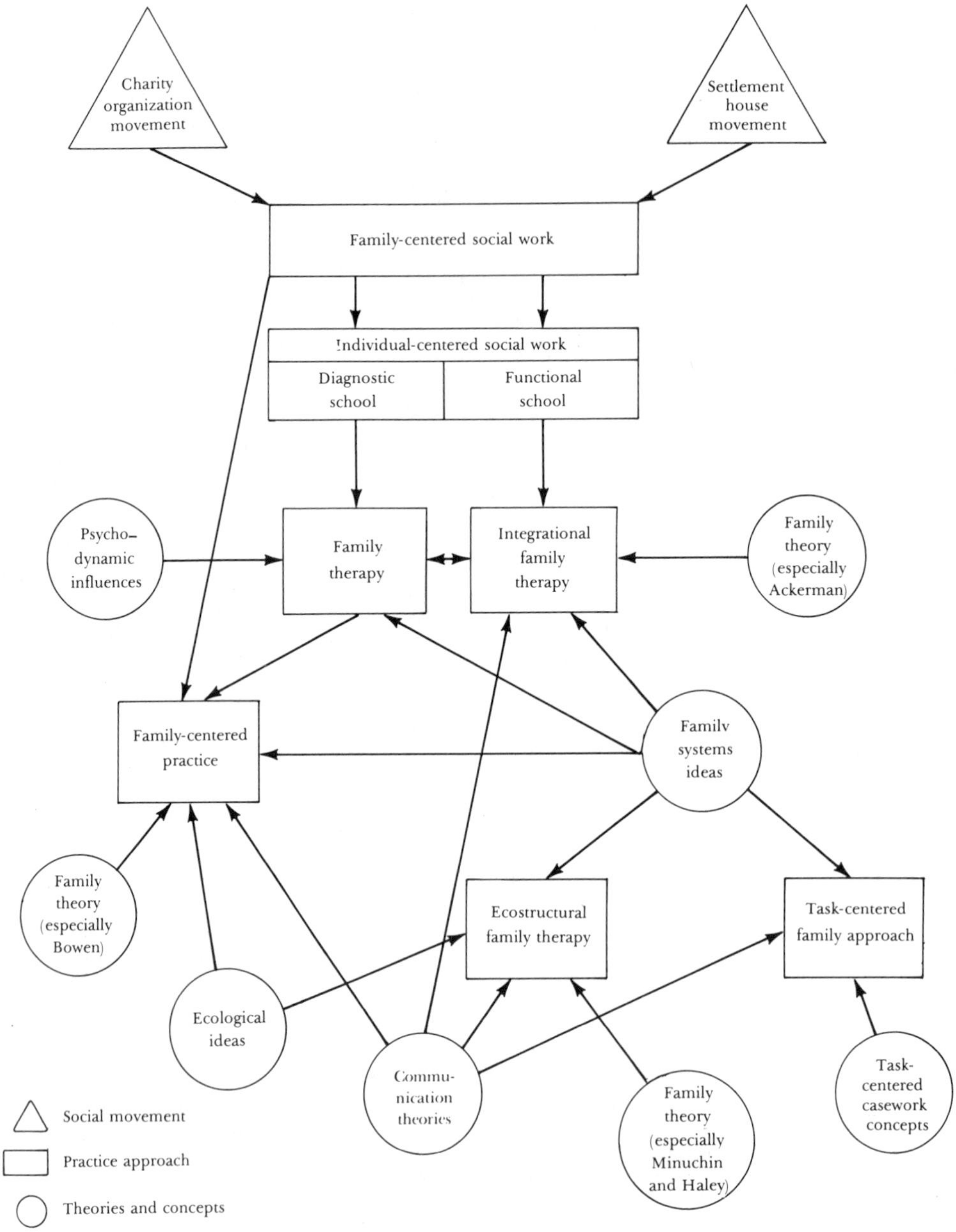

Figure 4. Family Approaches, 1980.

therapy, bioenergetic analysis, biofeedback, and transcendental meditation (Beck, 1978). They are not included in this chapter even though, depending on one's point of view, they either enrich or becloud the practice of clinical social work.

The chapter proposes first to trace the historical development of technology in clinical social work in the light of three thematic threads—a scientific orientation, a medical/disease metaphor, and the commitment to person-in-situation—and second to assess the state of the art in clinical practice by a gross comparative analysis of present-day technologies.

Before proceeding with these tasks, however, we must take account of the troublesome lack of agreement in the literature concerning the meaning of such terms as *approach, model, method, skill,* and *technique.* For the purposes of this chapter, *approach* refers to recognizable or recognized prescriptive entities often called practice models. The term approach is preferred over the more common *model,* because of the confusion between a theoretical model in science, useful for its predictive value, and a practice model—so-called—that merely sets forth the several dimensions of a coherent, consistent approach to social work practice but has no predictive value.

Method is used to designate practice activities with a particular size unit. Traditionally casework, group work, and community organization have been called methods, although this may change as more and more schools of social work move away from method specializations. In this chapter method will continue to refer to an orderly, systematic way of working with an individual, a family, or a natural or formed group. (In some instances, method was used earlier also to indicate subdivisions in types of treatment with individuals, and this will be noted when necessary.) *Skill* is used to refer to a particular area of practitioner action, such as observation, engagement, data collection, assessment, contracting, setting goals and planning, and achieving goals. *Technique* is used to designate a more specific procedure within such an area of skill.

In this usage, then, an approach may embrace more than one method. Any one method is made up of a number of skills, each of which in turn is made up of a number of techniques. All of these—approach, methods, skills, and techniques—are considered to make up technology. *Technology* is the application of theory and knowledge to practice, and it is guided by professional values. Finally, and perhaps most troublesome of all, is the definition of clinical social work. This chapter relies on the tentative definition included in the report of the National Association of Social Workers Task Force on Clinical Social Work Practice (Cohen, 1980) as being congruent with social work purpose, values, and historic commitment:

> In the report [of the Task Force], the "person-in-situation" perspective is reaffirmed as the guiding principle for all forms of clinical social work practice. Within this perspective, however, variations in method may legitimately be used, depending on setting and needs to be addressed. Psychotherapeutic activity is deemed to be a part but not the whole of clinical social work practice. The boundary of such practice, the particular role of clinical social work within the mission of the social work profession, is thought to be represented by the ability to conduct a bio-psychosocial assessment of persons-in-situations and to conduct or facilitate interventions based on these assessments [Ewalt, 1980].

With all of this now specified, it should be evident that one author cannot present the full richness of technological developments in clinical social work. The selection that follows inevitably reflects my interests and the limitations of space.

Historical Developments: Casework Technology

Social casework had its origins in the charity organization movement borrowed in the late nineteenth century from Victorian England. The movement in both countries was identified with church-related and other voluntary almsgiving and reflected a concern with making charity more efficient by eliminating fraud and duplication. It was characterized by a deep suspicion of public tax-supported aid that stemmed from Elizabethan Poor Law notions about the causes of poverty and the fear of pauperism. The causes of indigency were assumed to lie with the indigent themselves, except in the cases of widows and orphans, where the fault lay in circumstance. Pauperism was a disease caused by too generous aid. So the charity organization movement emphasized moral uplift, which became the responsibility of the friendly visitor, a middle-class exemplar. In the United States the movement was also pervaded by attitudes derived from the Puritan ethos, Calvinism, the Protestant ethic, and, later, social Darwinism.

The interest in scientific philanthropy, although pertaining narrowly to the management and control of giving, restored an earlier but ambivalent interest in the scientific study of social problems and the use of scientific methods in caring for dependent classes (Germain, 1971). These interests in scientific methods were buttressed by the need to justify professionalization, as friendly visitors were replaced by paid agents (Lubov, 1965). The agents, or caseworkers as they came to be called, were expected to be more effective than volunteers because their work could be based on scientific methods. This aspiration required training, and, together with the striving for professional status, led in 1898 to the first educational program for those embarking on charity work, the New York School for Philanthropy.

The search for a scientific method (technology) was set in motion by the remarks of Abraham Flexner at the 1915 National Conference of Charities and Corrections (NCCC) the prestigious social work forum of the day. Flexner, a prominent social scientist who had reformed medical education in the United States, said that social work could not become a profession because it lacked a distinctive professional method (Flexner, 1915). In response, Mary Richmond, the respected charity organization leader and teacher of casework, rallied caseworkers to the task of method development (Richmond, 1917a). Over the years, that task remained a preoccupation of the casework segment of the profession.

There is nothing wrong, of course, in such a quest for a more and more effective technology. The criticism over the decades, beginning with the differentiation of cause and function (Lee, 1929) and reaching its strident peak in the 1960s and 1970s, was that casework directed its preoccupation with technology (function) solely to problems of personal change, ignoring problems of institutional change (cause). Tension was also generated, in part, by the adoption of a medical/disease metaphor for casework. As early as the 1880s and 1890s, the charity organization group had adopted a medical idiom, describing its practitioners as social doctors engaging in social therapeutics (Germain, 1971). The idiom fit the conception of pauperism as a disease, and it was congruent with the social Darwinian views of the times. When hospital-based caseworkers joined their charity colleagues in the early 1900s, the disease metaphor of diagnosis and treatment was strongly reinforced. As a platform for helping, however, the metaphor was somewhat ameliorated by an altruistic concern for the relief of misery (however ambivalent), the democratic value placed on individuality and autonomy, and the humane traditions of Judaic and Christian thought. Nevertheless, it tended to view problems as lodged within the person and to obscure social causation and external processes.

By 1917, when Richmond published her influential *Social Diagnosis,* it appeared that she had relinquished some of the paternalistic and social Darwinian attitudes of her early and middle years in the charity organization movement (Pumphrey, 1956; Germain, 1971; Germain and Hartman, 1980). By the publication of *What Is Social Casework?* in 1922, it was clear that her years of analyzing, generalizing, and systematizing the experiences of charity workers had mellowed her own professional development. There was also evidence of her sympathetic use of ideas she had earlier disparaged, particularly the ideas of settlement workers, social reformers, and members of labor groups. By then, her ideas may also have reflected the widening views of caseworkers as they moved into hospitals, courts, psychiatric settings, schools, and child placement.

Even though Richmond remained aloof from the psychoanalytic ideas that greatly interested her younger contemporaries—Jarrett, Reynolds, Robinson, and Taft—she was, perhaps, influenced by new ideas emerging from the mental hygiene movement that had begun in 1909. Clearly she was respectful of the ideas of the psychiatrist Adolph Meyer, whom she trusted and admired. Where *Social Diagnosis* was a treatise on social evidence and was situational in emphasis, *What Is Social Casework?* is psychosocially oriented (Meyer, 1973). It is concerned with the interaction between person and environment.

Richmond asserted that the *combination* (italics in the original) of two diagnostic and two treatment processes is the hallmark of the trained caseworker (1922, p. 102). The two diagnostic processes are those through which insight is gained into "personality as it now is, together with the ways in which it came to be what it now is," and "into the resources, dangers, and influences of the social environment" (1922, p. 103). The two treatment processes are the direct action of mind upon mind, and indirect action through the social environment. The distinction between direct and indirect action persisted with significant consequences.

It is tempting to see an evolving and continuous link between [Richmond's analysis] and contemporary ideas regarding work with individuals, families, and groups; consultation and collaboration; reaching out; and ego-oriented treatment. It would be specious to do so, however, for these contemporary ideas arose from very different theoretical sources. What seems quite clear in Richmond's views, however, is (1) a dual concern with person and environment in both diagnosis and treatment, (2) the status of indirect treatment accorded to environmental work, and (3) the continuing use of the medical/disease metaphor.

The early postwar years saw the development of professional associations, journals, and forums that provided opportunities for professional interchange and solidarity. They supported the development of technology and the elaboration of idea systems, including the scientific orientation, its concretizing through a medical/disease metaphor, and the commitment to person-in-situation.

With the rapid spread of the method of casework to fields beyond charity, however, concern grew for identifying the generic features of the method in the light of differences appearing in different fields. A group of individuals "aware of the current practices of social caseworkers" (American Association of Social Workers, 1929, p. 23) met annually to try to define casework. Their conclusion that generic casework was the same for all fields was published in 1929. It specified some twenty-five elements of the technology, including data analysis, diagnosis, interviewing, prognosis, and client participation. Reference was also made to providing such services and tangible resources to those in need as money, job referrals, child placement, housing referrals, medical care, and so on, using community resources. In all, the report explicitly reinforced a scientific orientation and the medical metaphor. Although the notion of personal defect was replaced by the idea of maladjustment, the focus remained on personal change, with social provision an aspect of treatment.

In a searching review of the literature, Alexander (1972) demonstrated that in the 1920s psychoanalytic ideas had not yet taken hold among social workers except for a few in a few northeastern cities. In an earlier review of the curricula of schools of social work, Hellenbrand (1965) reached a similar conclusion. While not affecting the main body of casework practice, psychoanalytic theory nevertheless influenced the ideas of some leaders who, then and later, contributed to technological developments. The Smith College School for Psychiatric Social Work was established in 1918. Its Associate Director was Mary Jarrett, whose 1919 paper before the National Conference of Social Work had electrified the audience (Jarrett, 1919). Taft reported with excitement about the NCSW meeting in 1919: "The conference was swept off its feet. In every section, psychiatrists appeared on the program. The psychiatric social worker was present in person for the first time and violent indeed was the discussion which raged about her devoted head—what should be her training, what her personality, and what the limitations of her province? Should she remain forever different from every other caseworker or should every other caseworker be reborn in her likeness? That was the meeting which burst its bounds and had to be transferred to a church a block away. Dignified psychiatrists and social workers climbed out of windows in order to make sure of a good seat" (quoted in Robinson, 1962, p. 125).

Various streams of experience—dynamic psychiatry, psychotherapy, mental hygiene, psychoanalysis, and wartime experiences with shell-shocked soldiers—came together in the appearance of a new entity called psychiatric casework. In a paper a year earlier, Jarrett had prophesied a change in direction for casework, from social and economic to psychiatric. She had suggested that this would provide the scientific base needed to attract college graduates actuated by the scientific spirit (Jarrett, 1918, p. 283).

The growing excitement among at least some leaders of the profession culminated in the 1930 publication of Virginia Robinson's dissertation, *A Changing Psychology in Social Casework*. In an earlier paper (1921) Robinson had complained of the overemphasis on environmental work in casework practice and its literature. She now declared that all through the twenties caseworkers had seized upon particular Freudian concepts such as psychic determinism, unconscious needs, and the influence of family relationships on individual development. "From this point of view, later environmental pressures and obstacles became less and less significant and important" (p. 37). The findings of Hellenbrand and of Alexander suggest that Robinson may have mistaken the part for the whole. Such a degree of absorption was probably true only of the Boston–New York–Philadelphia network of caseworkers in family and child guidance agencies. Bertha Reynolds recalls the heady discussions of the new ideas in those years when she met with Robinson, Libbey, and Dawley in Philadelphia and with others in New York and Boston (Reynolds, 1963, p. 101).

In any case the book had the effect of an earthquake, according to the review written by Reynolds in *The Family* (1931). Her own reaction was one of wonder and delight. The book was based largely on the psychoanalytic theory of Otto Rank, Freud's dissident disciple, and, to some extent, on Gestalt psychology. The fundamental human problem was considered to be the relationship of self to others from birth to death; the solving of other problems thus hinged on patterns of relating to others. So, for Robinson, the casework relationship assumed primacy over matters of technology. In place of technology, a relationship was to be created in which the client's growth process could be "released." Robinson rejected technique because it suggested that the worker knew what was best for clients and could motivate or manipulate them in that direction. Hence she repudiated history taking and diagnosis as manipulative.

Robinson acknowledged that social reform was necessary, but she concluded that it was not the province of the caseworker. Casework was to be individual therapy rather than social welfare: "only in this field of the individual's reaction patterns and in the possibilities of therapeutic change in these patterns through responsible self-conscious relationships can there be any possibility of a legitimate professional casework field" (1930, p. 185).

Reynolds later reported that after her review had been published she received a warning from Florence Sytz: "'The time has not yet come when social workers can confine their interest and activity to the realm of emotional adjustment, either for themselves or their clients.' She found attempts to do so as amusing as when 'an application of mental hygiene to our fears is offered as a solution for the industrial depression'" (Reynolds, 1963, p. 121).

Indeed, the country was rapidly being engulfed by the Great Depression. With the need for financial help so widespread, charity became relief, administered by new public relief bureaucracies. Many historians have pointed to the change in function this imposed on the family service agencies, which until then had continued to discharge their original charitable function (Hartman, 1972). While many staff members were recruited by the public agencies, those who remained in family agencies were freed to continue developing psychodynamic ideas in achieving personality change. Their efforts were augmented by those of their colleagues in child guidance clinics and other psychiatric settings where caseworkers labored side by side with psychiatrists. Robinson's book had cleared the way, and, ironically, the depression permitted a renewed interest in issues of psychologically oriented technology in the midst of environmental intransigence.

Client need became a central theme in diagnosis and treatment within the diagnostic school of casework thought. An emphasis on the client's situation as the interaction between person and environment had been introduced by Sheffield. She refined it as need-situation (1931), and while most of her systemslike ideas apparently had little influence, the notion of need-situation was picked up by Lowry (1936). It referred to the interaction among the elements of a person, situation, and the particular need, and underscored the fact that situational needs were influenced by personality factors. Thus it led to more sophisticated notions of differential diagnosis and treatment.

Lowry's formulation reflects this new direction. It permitted her to dispense with the distinction made earlier, and to be made again later, between direct and indirect treatment (with its subtle suggestion that work in the environment is of a lesser nature). She also connected the nature of the client's need to the treatment activities selected, almost an articulation of diagnostic categories with treatment categories, which she termed *criteria for selection.*

Lowry mentions few techniques and skills. She was disenchanted with the preoccupation with technique because of two dangers that lay in it: (1) a tendency to search for a need to fit the technique instead of searching for a technique to fit the need and (2) a tendency for client selection to depend more on the client's ability to use the agency's technique than on the agency's ability to meet the client's need. These were challenging thoughts, but they were destined to be submerged by an increased reliance on the medical disease metaphor, a continued striving for professionalism whose lodestar was sought in psychiatric casework, and the lack of dynamic concepts of the environment. Lowry's fear that greater prestige was being accorded psychological needs and greater dignity was being attached to the techniques associated with them remained a reality.

In 1937 Taft published her now well-known paper on the functional approach. A member of the Pennsylvania School's full-time faculty since 1934, following sixteen years' practice at the Philadelphia Children's Aid, Taft was a psychologist by training. She was nevertheless identified with the social work profession as practitioner, writer, and teacher. She had been analyzed by Rank in New York in 1926 and was greatly influenced by his ideas. She was not aware of the estrangement between Rank and Freud until the break became an open one in 1930 (Robinson, 1962, p. 120).

It seems doubtful that the difference in Rankian and Freudian ideas alone could have caused the violent clash that occurred between two schools of casework thought. But in searching for a way to distinguish casework from therapy, Taft and Robinson hit upon agency function. They conceptualized the agency as a relatively stable force against which clients could experience their own will as they decide to accept or not accept the agency's service. Thus Taft concluded that "the approach to social work via the needs of the individual applicant is an approach that leads to inevitable failure and confusion, since it focuses attention and effort on something that can never be known exactly or worked on directly. Even the client, himself, can only discover what his need *really* is by finding out what he does in the helping situation" (1937, p. 8; Taft's italics).

Taft also rejected social study and diagnosis, the essence of the scientific method advanced by the diagnostic school, as resting on deterministic causality. The centrality of agency function and the rejection of scientific method were gauntlets flung down.

The challenge was picked up by the doyenne of the diagnostic school, Gordon Hamilton (1941), and the conflict raged through the forties and well into the fifties. It is hard for today's clinical social worker to understand what the conflict was about, yet even now terms such as *helping process, beginnings, endings,* social work *function,* and *service* can reawaken indignation in some who participated in that struggle. For others, these are but useful descriptive terms independently arrived at and devoid of ideological intent. By now, however, most would agree that the functional school provided generally accepted and valued concepts such as relationship, self-determination, and the use of time and fees as dynamics in help.

A scientific orientation, the medical metaphor's emphasis on pathology instead of growth, and the focus on technique had been the objects of the functionalists' attack. One consequence of the conflict seems to have been a renewed commitment to all three by the much larger diagnostic school. On the assumption that scientific understanding depends in part on the classification of phenomena, attention was given all through the war and postwar years to classifying treatments and problems and to trying to match one to the other.

Grete Bibring (1947), a Boston psychoanalyst who had worked many years with social workers as a teacher and consultant, formulated a typology of skills that caseworkers drew on in formulating their own. The delineation of these skills and techniques seemingly led to the conceptualization of treatment types based on increasing "depth," that is, it led to different levels of treatment, ultimately to unconscious and repressed content. An example is one presented by Hollis (1949) at a landmark event in 1948, the Symposium on Psychotherapy and Casework sponsored by the Boston Psychoanalytic Society and Institute. Its purpose was to examine the overlap that was already observable "in the work of the psychiatrist doing psychotherapy and the caseworker doing treatment in which there is some danger of each discipline either losing its identity or stressing it too much" (1949, p. 219). The Hollis paper divided treatment into four types: environmental modification, psychological support, clarification, and insight development. Environmental modification was designed to reduce pressure in the physical or human environment and included providing social services and modifying the attitudes of others. Techniques were described for the three types of psychological treatment, with transference aspects handled differently in each. Each type was deemed suitable for particular personality structures. Clarification was limited to conscious material and insight development represented greater "depth" (suppressed and unconscious but not deeply repressed material).

In the previous year Austin (1948) had presented a classification that would preserve the two main methods in casework: social therapy and psychotherapy. In her awareness of the ego's adaptive capacities, Austin went farthest among the authors of classifications to preserve the significance of the environment. She recognized that positive experiences in the transference and in real life situations, which can be fostered by the worker, can bring about better adaptations. In addition to considering environmental work as a separate type of therapy, Austin placed appropriate activity in the environment among the techniques in psychotherapy. The upshot was that the insidious distinction between direct and indirect treatment was erased.

By the middle 1950s it was generally recognized that for the caseworker treatment content was limited to conscious and preconscious material. Although there were references to the ego in the range of schemes (Hamilton, 1951; Family Service Association of America, 1953; Community Service Society of New York, 1958; Cockerill and others, 1952), for the most part they referred to its defensive functions. The typologies developed by the Family Service Association and the Community Service Society were based solely on whether or not defenses should be modified, surely a narrow conception of casework function even for that era. Although Freud's newer conceptions of the ego had appeared in 1933, the interest of diagnostic caseworkers in psychoanalytic ideas as a base for technological development seems to have been largely engaged by libidinal aspects and the unconscious until the work of the later ego psychologists began to appear in the middle fifties.

The problem-solving approach was introduced by Perlman in 1957. She described it as an eclectic approach built upon her education and experience in the diagnostic framework but supplemented by functional concepts of relationship, engagement, agency function, partialization, and the will. In the effort to combine what was most useful in both schools, Perlman favored a humanistic orientation over a scientific one, so there is also a thread of existential thought in her approach and a distrust of scientific method because of the deterministic features of study-diagnosis-treatment. Her more recent formulation (1970) retains many functional ideas and strengthens the existential thread, but it also makes a stronger rapprochement with ego psychology. The later work also underscores the use of social role concepts as a bridge to the interpersonal environment. The focus is on role as the frame for personality in social functioning, with little attention given to the influence exerted by the social and cultural structures in which roles are embedded.

While the problem-solving approach does not rely explicitly on the medical/disease metaphor, nonetheless the burden for change still seems to be on the client: "Poor thinking, poor learning, blurred perception, inappropriate or inept coping are symptoms of some functional failures or inadequacies or blocking" (Perlman, 1970, p. 132), "some breakdown or impairment in one or more of his emotionally invested roles" (p. 143). Perlman describes the controlled problem-solving efforts of the helping process as "the responsible and skilled means by which frail or dwarfed or distorted ego capacities might be empowered or reformed or restored to effectiveness" (p. 133).

In the early formulation technology was minimal beyond eliciting the client's participation and providing knowledge or guidance. Work in the environment was described as using community resources as aids in problem solving. In the later work the psychological techniques of sustainment, ventilation, exploration, clarification, confrontation, and reinforcement, among others, are deemed useful. Greater attention is given to the environment; reference is made to influencing the behavior of others in the environment or changing life conditions bearing upon the problem by using material supports or organized services and by strengthening linkages with the client's social network. The person-in-situation commitment is clear.

Many contemporary approaches with individuals, families, and groups incorporate elements of problem solving that reflect the continuing influence of Perlman's approach. Hallowitz, for example, has developed a family therapy approach with a problem-solving component (1970, 1979). Perlman's work appears to have helped stimulate the initial development of the task-centered approach (Reid and Epstein, 1972). Perlman's problem-solving approach is likely to sustain its influential position, particularly if cognitive theory and cognitive-behavioral therapy come to the fore, as now seems likely. While not formally linked to these developments, the approach lends itself to such connections. Also of critical significance to clinical social work is Perlman's development of Dewey's ideas about the problem-solving process for practice and her connecting these to ego psychological ideas of adaptation, coping, and mastery. Somers has traced the independent development of problem-solving in group work (1976).

In 1965 Smalley published the definitive reformulation of the functional approach. She refined and elaborated the work of Robinson, Taft, and other leaders in functional thought by systematizing generic principles. These principles come close to a technology in an approach that considers technique to be manipulative. Still, Smalley cautions that techniques (which she consistently places within quotation marks) are not to be regarded as discrete entities or as interventive acts, as in the diagnostic school. Rather, they are integral parts of a process directed to the purpose inhering in agency function and the casework method. While continuing to reject a scientific method based on a medical/disease metaphor, Smalley restored a scientific orientation by accepting a behavioral science base rooted not in nineteenth-century ideas of causality but in twentieth-century ideas of patterns, processes, relationships, emergence, potentiality, and purpose in human life.

Smalley specifies no "techniques" for the environment. Her fourth principle refers to the worker's helping the agency clarify, modify, or even give up its purpose, but she does not encourage the worker as an employee to seek changes in policies, procedures, and structures. A later theorist attempted to bring the approach more in line with interests and concerns of the 1980s by suggesting a more change-oriented stance toward the agency: "Caseworkers are no longer satisfied that they cannot effect a policy change without its being counterproductive to their casework effort" (Yelaja, 1979, p. 137). The person-situation commitment, however, is not really present in the practice formulation, despite Yelaja's assertion that Smalley saw method and social purpose as inseparable, because through them client interests and broad social interests are served. What seems to linger is Robinson's notion that casework is not social welfare and its province does not include environmental change.

The very early influence of functional social work on the development of family therapy in social work will be examined at a later point. Functional social work also moved to embrace the group method relatively early in its own history (Phillips, 1950, 1957). The contemporary functional conception of a group approach (Ryder, 1976) is congruent with Smalley's generic principles. These early moves to embrace family and group approaches are not surprising, since an interest in generic practice has been a hallmark of the functional school.

In 1964 Hollis, following the Richmond-Hamilton tradition, introduced a major reformulation of the diagnostic approach, including its technology. Calling casework a psychosocial therapy, Hollis maintained both the commitment to person–situation and the commitment to a scientific method rooted in a medical/disease metaphor. The distinction between direct and indirect action is maintained, thereby making environmental work secondary as a tool for client change. In the 1964 schema, the first four categories of direct treatment of the client were considered to be also useful for dealing with the client's environment of other people; a fifth category of indirect treatment (social provision) was added in 1972. The revised schema shows efforts to conceptualize indirect treatment more dynamically, taking into account the influence of systems theory on casework thought.

A strength of this formulation is its research base: a microscopic analysis of client-worker interactions in interviews from six highly specialized agencies, testing and replication in other settings, and further development by others (for example, Turner, 1978). Historically, the psychosocial approach has been a dominant one. It was developed, and continues to be developed, largely in terms of a one-to-one method. Nevertheless, the family therapy method developed by Scherz (1970) is rooted in the diagnostic tradition while incorporating systems and communication theories. Northen's formulation of the group method is directly related to the psychosocial approach (1969, 1976).

Historical Developments: Group Work Technology

Figure 3 showed that group work's origins were very different from those of casework. Its early development was associated with a long line of distinguished pioneer group workers (Wilson, 1976; Middleman, 1968). The original social group work approach (termed *social goals* by Papell and Rothman, 1966) has been continually enriched and elaborated upon (for example, Hartford, 1972, 1976). Its commitment to person-in-situation, its growing orientation to science in the sense of a knowledge-based method that retains a humanistic component, and its shunning a medical/disease metaphor are all very clear.

The preventive and rehabilitative approach, building perhaps on earlier work done in psychiatric settings (Redl and Wineman, 1958; Konopka, 1949) has been identified with the work of Vinter and his colleagues (Vinter, 1959; Glasser and others, 1974). Where the social goals approach viewed the group as an entity with a life of its own in which the relationships among members were valued, the preventive and rehabilitative approach regarded the group as a vehicle for individual treatment. Thus it came close to diagnostic casework and to the concept of group therapy. The medical/disease metaphor was discernible in the social worker's responsibility for making individual diagnoses and treatment plans for the group members. Less interest was shown in member participation or in the development of group autonomy, and environmental issues were not addressed (Papell and Rothman, 1966). In its most recent reformulation, however, significant refinements and developments are evident (Glasser and Garvin, 1976). The medical metaphor has given way to an adaptive point of view, and the approach clearly reflects a strong person-in-situation commitment. Goals refer to client social functioning or client environment. The group is still the context for achieving individual goals, but it is also a means whereby members help each other attain goals. The social worker's tasks include assessing individual-social situations, deciding whether to use the group method for individual and environmental change, establishing the group's composition, and intervening to make or promote change (for example, choosing targets, strategies, and techniques for personal or environmental change).

The approach also makes a creative contribution to the theory of practice in specifying four ideal types of organizations in which groups are served. These organizations function to reduce anomie (for example, a rap center), provide socialization (a school), provide social control (a mental hospital), or provide resocialization (a sheltered workshop). This conception brings a salient aspect of the social environment into clear and telling focus; and the approach incorporates the differential effects of each organizational type on clients, workers' tasks, and group process.

Like other approaches, the preventive-rehabilitative one rests on phases of the contact, termed *stages in the treatment sequence* (Glasser and Garvin, pp. 104–107). These are (1) arranging intake, composition, and location, (2) selecting targets and forming groups, (3) planning individual and system change, (4) executing and evaluating the change plan, (5) renegotiating or terminating contracts. Glasser and Garvin believe their formulation has the potential for a generic approach to individual, group, family, and environmental change.

Over the past twenty years William Schwartz has been developing and refining the reciprocal or mediating approach. It rests on a mediating function through which the social worker seeks to bring about a better relation between people and social institutions. It also assumes a symbiotic or reciprocal need between the individual and society and between the group and the agency. The group is defined as "a collection of people who need each other to work on certain common tasks, in an agency that is hospitable to those tasks" (Schwartz, 1971, p. 7). Thus the group must have a purpose, defined in terms of tasks that are embedded in a relevant agency function. The approach views the worker as having two clients: the group as a whole and the individual member. Diagnosis and treatment goals have no place in the approach, but personal and social factors are not ignored. The ultimate "valued outcome" is the group's achievement of a mutual aid system.

Schwartz identified a number of skills or worker behaviors which were augmented by the work of Shulman (1979). They are conceptualized in terms of the temporal phases of the helping process and are associated with valued outcomes for each phase. They represent contributions to the technology of clinical social work practice with groups.

The reciprocal approach is existential and humanistic. It also echoes functional emphases on beginnings, middles, and endings, on process, and on engagement, agency function, and the rejection of diagnosis and treatment goals. Clearly, it reflects the commitment to person-in-situation, renounces the medical/disease metaphor, and embraces a scientific orientation. That orientation is toward theory that underpins the worker's function and skills of helping, bolstered by a philosophy of helping and a theory of action. The reciprocal approach is also a generic one, being applicable to individuals as well as to groups. Moreover, in Schwartz's judgment, it is not limited by whether the group is "natural or formed, therapeutic or task-oriented, open or closed, voluntary or captive, time-limited or extended, age-or-sex homogeneous or heterogeneous, or [by] other quite legitimate small-group distinctions" (1976, pp. 185–186).

Closely related to the reciprocal and social goals approaches, yet with distinctive attributes of its own, is the developmental approach (Tropp, 1971, 1976). The distinctiveness arises, in part, from the very strong threads of existentialism and humanism running through it and from its emphasis on natural transitions and changes in life tasks as these lead to self-realization (within a context of interdependence). Of particular interest is the careful spelling out of the "how" in technology, that is, the professional presentation of self that underpins the "whats" of worker activity. These components are compassion, mutuality, humility, respect, openness, empathy, involvement, support, expectation, limitation, confrontation, planning, enabling, spontaneity and control, role and person, science and art. They are enriched by the specification of the implicit message each conveys to the group.

Historical Developments: Family Practice Technology

An analysis of the development of family approaches is less straightforward than one of individual and group approaches because of multiple streams of thought influencing them. The simplest way to begin is to recall that the family was the unit of social work attention for a long time. It came to be ignored in the 1920s in favor of a focus on the individual, but was reinstated in the functional school in the early 1940s and to some degree in the diagnostic school in the 1950s.

The functional school sought to specify a unique function performed by a family service agency that could then be used to define the agency's varied services. The function was found in the seemingly obvious but apparently overlooked intent to deal with problems affecting the family as a whole (Gomberg, 1944). To deal with the family required a knowledge base in family structure and development. Family agencies, particularly in Philadelphia and New York, were influenced by this point of view. Under Gomberg's leadership, for example, the Jewish Family Service of New York made—and continues to make—fundamental contributions to family therapy (Ackerman and others, 1961), now infused with psychoanalytic and social science concepts.

Writing out of this long tradition and about contemporary practice, Sherman (1979) calls the approach integrational family therapy, because there is a dual focus on the family system and process and on family members as individuals. Interventions are geared to both intrapsychic and interpersonal processes. They are derived from basic concepts of homeostasis, positive and negative complementarity, and symmetrical relationships and communication. But techniques are not spelled out, although there are faint echoes of functional ideas about beginnings. Nevertheless there is a strong infusion of the psychodynamic influence of Ackerman and others. The scientific orientation is clear in the span of knowledge and theory deemed relevant, and a medical/disease metaphor is implicit. Diagnosis is geared to understanding the dynamic place of the individual's symptom in the matrix of family relationships; it is inescapably geared to person-in-situation, but within the micro-environment of the family. The approach refers to work with persons in the family's social network and to social provision and recognizes the societal and cultural contexts of family life, but intervention at those levels is considered beyond the scope of the family therapist.

Within the diagnostic tradition, movement toward the family as the object of help and not merely the backdrop to the individual began with the work of Pollak at the Jewish Board of Guardians in New York (1952, 1956). The Family Service Association of America and the McCormick Fund jointly sponsored conferences on family diagnosis in 1957 and in 1959. At the latter, Pollak presented a model for healthy family functioning, structured along the marital axis and overburdened by middle-class values (Pollak, 1960). As an outgrowth of the 1959 conference, the McCormick Fund established a three-year Midwest Seminar on

Family Diagnosis and Treatment under Pollak's leadership (Pollak and Brieland, 1961), which generated practitioner interest in family work.

During these years, Scherz of the Chicago Jewish Family Service was developing a social work approach to family therapy based on (1) the adaptive point of view in ego psychology, (2) crisis theory and its concern with life tasks, (3) systems theory, and (4) communication theory (Scherz, 1967, 1970). The family was the unit of investigation and treatment, although heavy weight was put on the marriage. And the family was viewed as a system with developmental stages and tasks of its own. Treatment was conceptualized as modifying elements of relationships and communication that interfere with the successful resolution of individual and familial life tasks. Techniques used in individual approaches were deemed useful in family treatment, but were to be directed to interactional processes or to an individual in the interest of the total group. The approach recognized transference phenomena and considered different "levels" of treatment, from symptom relief or crisis resolution to interpretation of motives and intrapsychic conflict affecting behavior toward others. The commitment to person-in-situation and to a scientific orientation are clearly present. The attempt to move away from the medical/disease metaphor is not completely successful.

Contemporary Developments in Technology

In the early 1960s social casework suffered severe criticism for allegedly having forsaken the poor in favor of verbal, introspective, middle-class clients having no severe environmental problems. At the same time, many caseworkers were drawn into the new community-based poverty programs. In their efforts to meet both the criticism and the demands posed by the life circumstances of their new clients, caseworkers sought out new knowledge. Information from the social sciences, particularly about differences in values, norms, and behaviors across subcultures of social class, race, and ethnicity, and about the impact of poverty and discrimination on development and functioning, was added to the knowledge base of most practitioners. The new information led some to the view that psychoanalytic theory was less useful than it had been held to be. Other practitioners, perhaps the majority, pursued the growing interest in the adaptive point of view within psychoanalytic theory—that is, ego psychology. While the new knowledge enriched diagnostic understanding, new techniques for intervention based on such understanding did not appear until the 1970s and 1980s. An exception was the new approach of crisis intervention, although related more directly to the developments in ego psychology and role theory than to concerns about the poor per se.

The new approach of crisis intervention and a new form of service, planned brief treatment, emerged in the 1960s. Where adopted, they changed the temporal structure of service and the pattern of practice. Crisis intervention arose from new ideas about the ego's response to critical life events. It assumed that brief treatment provided during the height of the crisis was more effective than longer treatment provided later after the crisis had been poorly resolved. Planned short term service in problems of psychosocial functioning was supported by the findings of Reid and Shyne (1969). Their experiments contrasting brief and extended forms of casework began in 1964 at the Community Service Society in New York (in earlier times, this family service agency had been known as the Charity Organization Society). This work led, in part, to the later development by Reid and Epstein (1972) of the new task-centered approach.

The approach of crisis intervention was developed by several social workers within the diagnostic tradition who had been influenced by their work with the Harvard psychiatrist Gerald Caplan (Kaplan and Mason, 1960; Parad, 1965; Rapoport, 1962a, 1962b, 1970). Psychoanalytic insights were combined with social science concepts of role, family structure, life style, values, and social network in order to explain and handle the problems created by a stressful precipitating event. Emphasis was placed on immediate professional response to the personal, interpersonal, and environmental dynamics released by the crisis state. Successful resolution was viewed as completing the coping tasks in an orderly sequence. History taking focused on current rather than historical data, although in many instances, the crisis state led to a reawakening of unresolved old conflicts that might now be worked through. Goals were limited, for example, to relieving symptoms or restoring the optimal level of functioning before the crisis. In general, established techniques were to be used for (1) cognitively restructuring the situation and integrating the crisis event, (2) accepting distorted affect, attitudes, or responses and placing them in a rational context, (3) mobilizing and using interpersonal and institutional resources (Rapoport, 1970). In general a more directive and active style by the practitioner was advocated in crisis intervention than in other forms of treatment.

Crisis theorists drew not only on the psychosocial approach but also on the problem-solving approach. The scientific orientation of crisis intervention and its commitment to person-in-situation are firm. It avoids the medical/disease metaphor and is the first approach examined that directs itself explicitly to prevention. Intervening in the crisis state precipitated by a critical life even can forestall maladaptive outcomes. Moreover, the approach is applicable to families and groups (Parad and others, 1976; Scherz, 1970; Golan, 1979) as well as individuals.

The task-centered approach has achieved a remarkable level of development since its initial appearance. Related to Perlman's problem-solving approach and to Reid's earlier work with Shyne on planned brief treatment, the task-centered approach focuses on the tasks required to solve specific problems identified by the client. As much as possible is done by the client, but where "more is needed, more is supplied, to the extent necessary to help the client resolve his difficulties" (Reid, 1979, p. 482). Hence while client participation is involved in every step of the process, the social worker also has tasks, and the whole is formalized in a contract that explicitly specifies the nature and duration of the service. Problems represent temporary breakdowns in coping, and treatment rests on the human capacity for autonomous problem solving; hence the medical/disease metaphor is rejected. The person-in-situation commitment is firm, since the approach recognizes psychological and environmental obstacles to problem solving. Both obstacles and the resolution of problems arise from the same elements: the individual's dysfunctional patterns of belief and/or action or uncooperative social systems (Reid, 1979, p. 481).

Significantly, no differential weights are applied to personal and environmental factors, although only the micro-environment is considered. Thus obstacles are dealt with whether they are generated internally or externally. One of the strengths of the approach is that is can be used with a range of problems faced by people receiving social work services in a wide range of settings (Reid and Epstein, 1977). But more than that, because it is eclectic and nonideological, it can also be used as a set of activities within some other practice approach (Reid, 1978). It fits into assumptions made by other models as long as the focus is on resolving problems through cognitive and behavioral action.

Another strength of the approach lies in its usefulness with families and formed groups. Conjoint forms involving marital or parent-child dyads make use of the technology developed for individual work, but strategies and techniques are geared to resolving interpersonal problems through reciprocal, shared, and individual tasks (Reid, 1978). Work with formed groups is subject to different principles, since individual problems are now being treated within a group context. The client system is viewed as the individual, but the group members, under the guidance of the leader, help each other carry out their problem-solving tasks. The leader uses three types of intervention: direct influence to secure change in the individual; indirect influence to change group conditions; activities on behalf of members outside the group (Garvin and others, 1976).

Still another strength is that "research monitoring is an integral part of the service design and serves as a basis for progressive modifications of the model" (Garvin and others, 1976, p. 238). Hence a scientific orientation is present, and its behavioral science base is now more developed than it was initially. Practitioners can now draw upon psychoanalytic, cognitive, social learning, communication, and family systems theories as needed to help clients complete their tasks and resolve their problems.

Contemporary approaches to clinical social work practice depart, to varying degrees, from former theoretical or ideological assumptions. In general, they have emerged either out of behavioral and learning theories or out of general systems and ecological theories. Some of the approaches already examined draw on one or both of these idea systems to some degree, but this section will identify several approaches that are significantly different from their predecessors. They will not be examined in the detail accorded the older approaches because of the complexity of their technologies and the availability of their extensive literature.

The pioneer work of Thomas (1967, 1970) introduced sociobehavioral techniques to social work and his continuing work has helped generate widespread interest and use. (Most recently the work of Fischer, 1978, and Fischer and Gochros, 1975, reflects and contributes to the growing interest. Many others have contributed to the development including Stuart, 1979, and Briar and Miller, 1971.) McBroom (1970, 1976) has advanced a related approach, socialization, in which the emphasis is on teaching competence in social functioning. Initially, behavioral approaches seemed to many social workers to be too narrow since they focused on specific units of behavior and environmental contingencies, as though all human activity were determined by the environment. But increasingly the approaches are incorporating mediating processes, both internal factors of cognition (Werner, 1965, 1979) and feelings and external factors of a social and cultural nature. The more this trend develops, the closer the behavioral approaches will draw to systems-oriented approaches. Conversely, because the systems approaches, or at least the ecological ones, are concerned with cognition, action, and feeling components of adaptation and effective coping with stress, they may draw closer to the sociobehavioral approaches that incorporate behavioral-cognitive therapy.

Stuart describes the changes to be made in behavior as having to occur in one of four areas: ". . . the antecedents and consequences of desirable behavior must be strengthened, and the antecedents and consequences of problematic behaviors must be weakened. In some instances, antecedents which fail to control certain behaviors must be 'conditioned' to produce these reactions, while in other instances antecedents which give rise to problematic behaviors must be 'deconditioned'" (1979, p. 444). A criticism of using behavioral approaches in social work has been that, beyond the specific conditioning and reinforcing aspects of the micro-environment, the approaches do not address the larger social purpose implied by the person-in-situation commitment (a criticism which can be made of some other approaches that profess the commitment but do not implement it). Stuart recognizes the use of community resources where material need exists as a necessary condition for trying to change behavior. In addition he refers to the potential for introducing behavioral change at the macro-environmental level of the community or society. Thus there are three levels of manipulating behavior: modification of the individual's behavior directly; modification of the micro-environment, that is, the behaviors of other people involved as conditioners or reinforcers of the problematic behavior (for example, a parent or spouse); and modification of the macro-environment, that is, the attitudes, values, and expectations of the larger community that are deemed responsible for maladaptive behaviors of clients. Recognizing the value issues and the dangers in them, Stuart urges open discussion to ensure that this powerful technology will be constructively applied. Other social workers may be less sanguine, and some may continue to believe that the person-situation commitment is still at issue. For example, while Fischer (1978) advances an eclectic approach involving change efforts at the individual and systems levels, his technology focuses on individual change.

A significant strength of behavioral approaches lies in their research component. More than other approaches, they are enriched by extensive findings on methods and techniques from outside social work, and they are increasingly characterized by a steady flow of validating studies within social work. The use of single organism designs (Bloom and Block, 1977) is being generalized to single system designs and can be expected to lead to a more research-oriented stance on the part of social workers of all persuasions.

The scope of the behavioral technology is extended by its use in the context of families and groups (for example, token economies), by its selective incorporation in certain other approaches, as noted earlier in the chapter, and by the selective use of its techniques by practitioners within all approaches.

Because of its research stance, the scientific orientation and method is clearest of all in these approaches. While the medical/disease metaphor is not in evidence, the onus for behavioral change is on the individual. The person-in-situation commitment is still not clear, but is likely to become clearer as more internal elements enrich the conception of the person and more societal and cultural elements are taken into account.

The systems and ecological approaches have been developed by theorists who were educated for and practiced in older approaches and traditions, so that residual theoretical threads may inhere in each formulation. No attempt will be made to tease them out. Easily discernible, however, are the serious and purposeful efforts to repair the severance of person from situation. The introduction of social systems ideas to social work is credited to Lutz (1956), and the introduction of general systems ideas to Hearn (1958). In 1974 Stein produced a sophisticated comparative analysis of general systems theories.

For practice, Meyer presented a framework in 1970 and revised it in 1976. Goldstein (1973), Pincus and Minahan (1973), and Siporin (1975) all presented full conceptualizations, including well-developed technologies. Middleman and Goldberg presented a structural conception in 1974 that in some ways is unique but still appears to fall within systems approaches. Tentatively included under the systems conception is an approach based on communication theory (Nelsen, 1980); as it is released and distributed, it will undergo study and application.

From the standpoint of technology, Siporin's is an interesting formulation because of its use of situational theory (which echoes the earlier interests of Sheffield and Lowry) (Siporin, 1972). Innovative as it is, it provides a thread of continuity to social work's origins. It returns the situation to both diagnosis and treatment. Diagnosis consists of three components: a situational assessment, a statement of the problem, and an assessment of the personality or character of the client as an individual and/or social system. The situational assessment is an external element (which is often internalized). How the individual defines the situation is influenced by both personal and sociocultural factors, so the definition itself is an element in the situation. The three components must be brought together in an integrative evaluation that can be used in planning or designing a course of action to resolve a problem or to meet a need (Siporin, 1975).

Especially valuable in Siporin's formulation is its avoidance of the indirect-direct distinction and its inclusion of a category of influencing and improving the social welfare resource system. Among the skills pertinent to that category are planning for and creating new social programs and helping formulate or reformulate social welfare policy. This category is presented as the responsibility of the practitioner and is of neither lesser nor greater value than the responsibility for helping with internal and external resources. In their own ways the other systems approaches also emphasize, via their technologies, the social worker's simultaneous responsibility toward both person and situation.

The ecological perspective is roughly parallel to general systems ideas, but it is derived more from the biological sciences than from the physical sciences, which gave rise to general systems ideas. Examples of ecological approaches are the family-centered approach (Hartman, 1978, 1979a, 1979b), approaches related to ecostructural family therapy (Aponte, 1976, 1979; Hoffman, 1971, 1976), the life model approach (Germain and Gitterman, 1980), and the competence approach (Maluccio, 1981). Perhaps the critical practical difference in the ecological perspective is its striving toward (1) identifying and conceptualizing transactions between people and environments, that is, the reciprocal processes or exchanges between person and environment and (2) finding pathways into transactional processes and developing interventions for changing them from maladaptive to adaptive ones.

The life model approach builds on the creative ideas of Bandler (1963), was first enunciated in 1968 and 1973 (Germain), was identified as a model of change in 1971 (Oxley), and continues to be inspired and enriched by the work of René Dubos and other biologists and by that of stress theorists. It is in the process of evolving, and many social workers are presently contributing to its development and applying it to practice. The approach conceptualizes people's problems in living as arising out of maladaptive transactions between them and their environments. So far, adaptation, stress, and coping have been identified as such transactional processes. There is reason to assume that achieving competence, autonomy, identity, self-esteem, and relatedness to others and to the natural world is also transactional in nature, requiring simultaneous attention to person and situation. In practice such adaptive achievements are often the foci of concern and sometimes are among the goals of intervention. Hence the technology must include practice principles and skills directed to those transactional processes across levels of human organization.

Both the family-centered and ecostructural approaches view the family as an environment in which individual members live, grow, and develop while the family itself is embedded in a social and cultural environment with which it must maintain an adaptive exchange. Both are richly eclectic in their use of systems, communication, and other frameworks. In Hartman's approach, which draws on Bowen's conceptions, members are helped to move across emotional cutoffs and to reconnect to extended kin, open up channels of communication that have been closed, uncover secrets, and so on, so that the extended family becomes itself a resource for change. Hartman believes that the approach is not limited to family therapy, but can be used with individuals and groups. It is usable in all fields of practice, and Laird and Hartman have both applied it to child welfare (Hartman, 1979a, 1979b; Laird, 1979).

Aponte, drawing on Minuchin's conceptions, seeks to modify the family-structural underpinning of a problem by shaping and influencing the behavioral and transactional patterns within the family. He has also used the approach in helping a family and environmental system to reach a better fit within an ecological context (1976). Similarly, Hoffman, making use of the ideas of Minuchin, Haley, and Bateson, has developed ways of understanding and then intervening in the transactional, cyclical positive and negative feedback processes that result in maladaptive family relationships and communications. The applicability of some of her ideas to environmental systems was demonstrated in the early stage of their development by Hoffman and Long in the widely read "A Systems Dilemma" (1969).

Systems and ecological approaches are distinguished from the others previously examined by the following attributes: (1) since problems are defined in transactional terms, the onus for change does not rest on the client alone, (2) the unit of client-worker attention is expanded to include the life space or the field of relevant systems, (3) human beings are viewed as active, purposeful, goal-seeking organisms whose development and functioning are outcomes of transactions between their genetic potential and their environment plus degrees of freedom from the determining influence of either, (4) a reorienting of interventive procedures toward releasing growth, adaptive transactions, and improved environments. Not every approach necessarily exhibits every characteristic. In general, however, all make an effort to implement the person-in-situation commitment, not only theoretically or philosophically, but in their technologies. The medical/disease metaphor is firmly repudiated, and the scientific orientation is present in the sense of a systematic approach to practice and a theory base. Areas currently needing development are research on effectiveness, on the match between interventions and outcome, and on the use of these approaches for particular needs, particular people, or particular situations.

The State of the Art

Thomas Kuhn's ideas about crisis and revolution in science were used to understand the nature of the crisis that faced casework theory and practice throughout the 1960s (Germain, 1970). Briefly, Kuhn's thesis (1962) is that normal science is characterized by relatively stable periods of research guided by a generally accepted paradigm. The paradigm is a structure of law, theory, applications, and instrumentation from which coherent research traditions spring. Such peaceful periods are interrupted by crises induced when the accepted paradigm becomes increasingly unable to account for newly discovered phenomena. Unease grows among the researchers, some defensively denying or suppressing the problems, some trying even harder to fit new problems to the old paradigm, and others—especially younger scientists or those new to the discipline—directing their efforts to developing a new paradigm that will solve new problems better than the old paradigm can. The crisis erupts when the new problems can no longer be ignored. Out of the battle that rages between the supporters of the old and the new, resolution occurs when the new supplants the old for most members of the discipline. Kuhn's additional point is that such decisions are made not on rational grounds alone but on irrational ones, such as matters of taste. He concluded that science does not grow by peaceful accretions to its base of knowledge, but by these intellectual revolutions in paradigms.

As fascinating as this thesis is, I now believe that it was wrong to use it in 1970 as an analogue for the development of new approaches to clinical social work practice. In the first place, Kuhn himself declares that the behavioral sciences have not yet developed paradigms, so a professional practice based on these sciences must also be in a preparadigmatic state. In the second place, this review suggests that there is nothing like a revolution taking place in the development of a practice paradigm. If anything, it suggests that the approaches, some of which were running on parallel tracks anyway, are moving closer together—enriching each other, partaking of the same bodies of new theory, and tolerating the presence of one another. This is not to deny the presence of argument and debate, often as acrimonious now as they were during the height of the diagnostic-functional conflict. But that is often enriching and very different from what Kuhn had in mind in explaining the rise of Copernican astronomy and its revolutionary triumph over the Ptolemaic paradigm.

So, rather than our discovering a revolution in practice paradigms, this review confirms the notion that "the historian of science always finds that the number of germinal ideas is limited and that they tend to reappear, spiral-wise, at increasingly higher levels of sophistication" (Bertalanffy, 1967, p. 60). With respect to social work, ideas about person and situation, as well as scientific orientation, methods, and metaphors, appear and reappear and are shaped both by the social forces of each era and by the changing aspirations of the profession itself.

In this era, the 1980s, it does seem that practice is reaching toward a deepened commitment to people and environments, many approaches are struggling to be free of the distortions of the medical/disease metaphor, and most approaches are seeking to incorporate and integrate scientific and humanistic orientations. On the scientific side, most approaches are lagging behind the research achievements of the behavioral and task-centered approaches, but that can be remedied. On the humanistic side, an emphasis on or interest in developing strategies and techniques for primary prevention is missing from most approaches except, perhaps, for some types of crisis intervention. But that, too, can be remedied.

It also appears that there is a common movement toward an integrative practice, stronger among the group approaches than among the individual approaches so far, and strongest of all among the systems approaches. Once the unit of attention is expanded, problems are defined transactionally, and causality is located in reciprocal rather than in linear processes, it is inevitable that practitioners and educators will reach the conclusion—as Lowry did so many years ago, and Studt (1968) more recently—that people's needs must define the method, and not the other way around.

What remains critical for the future—of clinical social work in particular and of all social work in general—is the development of what we might call a social work science. Basic research into the exchanges between people and environments that are pertinent to social work, the transactional aspects of the particular stresses that propel people into social work services, and the nature of successful coping strategies used by various populations, together with studies of social work technologies vis-á-vis particular stresses and particular populations are a few examples of needed content for a social work science. The approach that so far comes closest to providing a framework for a social work science is the structural approach of Middleman and Goldberg (1974). Although now underdeveloped, the framework provides loci for knowledge-building activities and the means for sorting out social work objectives, processes, and technologies. And it does not borrow from any other discipline or theory. In any case, we seem to be reaching a point where we will, like professional practices more advanced than our own, begin building on the work of one another, "spiral-wise, at increasingly higher levels of sophistication," instead of rediscovering the obvious, quite separately, in each era.

With one exception, all fomulations examined, as well as others not examined, have been proposed and developed by university-based social work educators. Some of these educators are also directly involved in practice, and all, from Richmond on, have had years of practice experience. But their salient identity is that of professional school faculty. The exception is found in the family method: Gomberg, Scherz, Sherman, Aponte, and Hoffman are identified with the world of practice even though they may be engaged in formal teaching activities. Why the exception is confined to the family method will be an interesting question to pursue. But, for now, it seems evident that practitioners lack the time and flexible financial arrangements to participate in formulating technological frameworks. And this is a serious constraint on the profession's ongoing development. It leads us to ask how much university-based social workers talk only to one another in formulating practice approaches. Do their formulations reflect the actualities of practice? We can be relatively confident that they do when the approaches are tied to a research base of field testing. Even so, however, an accurate answer can only be provided by a study of practice that samples geographic regions, fields of practice, and agency settings in a sufficiently representative way.

A fundamental problem exists when a few exert considerable influence on the practices of the many. It rubs up against our generally anti-elite stance. And the problem becomes a knotty one, considering the large numbers of social workers who have practiced without the benefit of professional education and, presumably, without the benefit of the technological frameworks so confidently put forth by social work educators.

A related issue, the resolution of which must also await research, concerns the social processes by which the ideas of a few intellectual leaders and innovators are disseminated through the profession. What personal and social characteristics influence the acceptance of their ideas? To what degree is the acceptance achieved on rational grounds (including the pressures and opportunities of social and cultural forces at play in the external environment)? Instruments for dissemination are at hand in a growing number of books and journals and in conferences, postgraduate study, continuing education, and staff development activities. How wide a circle is reached is not known, but the observation has frequently been made in other fields as well as our own that the average practitioner or theorist tends to read or otherwise attend to content that is congruent with what she or he already believes. These and other questions concerning the introduction, refinement, and dissemination of technologies in clinical social work beckon us on to further study.

References

Ackerman, N., and others (Eds.). *Exploring the Base for Family Therapy.* New York: Family Association of America, 1961.

Alexander, L. "Social Work's Freudian Deluge: Myth or Reality?" *Social Service Review,* 1972, *46,* 517-538.

American Association of Social Workers. *Social Casework Generic and Specific,* A Report of the Milford Conference. New York: American Association of Social Workers, 1929.

Aponte, H. J. "The Family-School Interview: An Eco-Structural Approach." *Family Process,* 1976, *15,* 303-312.

Aponte, H. J. "Diagnosis in Family Therapy." In C. Germain (Ed.), *Social Work Practice: People and Environments.* New York: Columbia University Press, 1979.

Austin, L. "Trends in Differential Treatment in Social Casework." *Journal of Social Casework,* 1948, *29,* 203-211.

Bandler, B. "The Concept of Ego-Supportive Psychotherapy." In H. J. Parad and R. R. Miller (Eds.), *Ego-Oriented Casework: Problems and Perspectives.* New York: Family Service Association of America, 1963.

Beck, D. F. *New Treatment Modalities: An Outline of Some Options and Source Materials.* New York: Family Service Association of America, 1978.

Bertalanffy, L. von. *Robots, Men, and Minds.* New York: Braziller, 1967.

Bibring, G. "Psychiatry and Social Work." *Journal of Social Casework,* 1947, *28,* 203-210.

Bloom, M., and Block, S. "Evaluating One's Own Effectiveness and Efficiency." *Social Work,* 1977, *22,* 130–136.

Briar, S., and Miller, H. *Problems and Issues in Social Casework.* New York: Columbia University Press, 1971.

Cockerill, E., and others. "A Conceptual Framework for Social Casework." Unpublished manuscript, University of Pittsburgh, 1952.

Cohen, J. "Nature of Clinical Social Work." In P. L. Ewalt (Ed.), *Toward a Definition of Clinical Social Work.* Washington, D.C.: National Association of Social Workers, 1980.

Community Service Society of New York. *Method and Process in Social Casework.* New York: Family Service Association of America, 1958.

Ewalt, P. L. (Ed.). *Toward a Definition of Clinical Social Work.* Washington, D.C.: National Association of Social Workers, 1980.

Family Service Association of America. *Scope and Method of the Family Service Agency. Report of the Committee on Methods.* New York: Family Service Association of America, 1953.

Fischer, J. *Effective Casework Practice: An Eclectic Approach.* New York: McGraw-Hill, 1978.

Fischer, J., and Gochros, H. *Planned Behavior Change: Behavior Modification in Social Work.* New York: Free Press, 1975.

Flexner, A. "Is Social Work a Profession?" In *Proceedings of the National Conference of Charities and Corrections.* Chicago: The Conference, 1915.

Freud, S. *New Introductory Lectures on Psychoanalysis.* New York: Norton, 1933.

Garvin, C., and others. "A Task-Centered Approach." In R. Roberts and H. Northen (Eds.), *Theories of Social Work with Groups.* New York: Columbia University Press, 1976.

Germain, C. "Social Study: Past and Future." *Social Casework,* 1968, *49,* 403–409.

Germain, C. "Casework and Science: A Historical Encounter." In R. Roberts and R. Nee (Eds.), *Theories of Social Casework.* Chicago: University of Chicago Press, 1970.

Germain, C. "Casework and Science: A Study in the Sociology of Knowledge." Unpublished doctoral dissertation, Columbia University School of Social Work, 1971.

Germain, C. "An Ecological Perspective in Social Casework." *Social Casework,* 1973, *54,* 323–330.

Germain, C., and Gitterman, A. *The Life Model of Social Work Practice.* New York: Columbia University Press, 1980.

Germain, C., and Hartman, A. "People and Ideas in the History of Social Work Practice." *Social Casework,* 1980, *61,* 323–331.

Glasser, P., and Garvin, C. D. "An Organizational Model." In R. Roberts and H. Northen (Eds.), *Theories of Social Work with Groups.* New York: Columbia University Press, 1976.

Glasser, P., and others (Eds.). *Individual Change Through Small Groups.* New York: Free Press, 1974.

Golan, N. "Crisis Theory." In F. Turner (Ed.), *Social Work Treatment.* (2nd ed.) New York: Free Press, 1979.

Goldstein, H. *Social Work Practice: A Unitary Approach.* Columbia: University of South Carolina Press, 1973.

Gomberg, R. "The Specific Nature of Family Casework." In J. Taft (Ed.), *A Functional Approach to Family Casework.* Philadelphia: University of Pennsylvania Press, 1944.

Hallowitz, D. "The Problem-Solving Component in Family Therapy." *Social Casework,* 1970, *51,* 67–75.

Hallowitz, D. "Problem-Solving Theory." In F. Turner (Ed.), *Social Work Treatment.* (2nd ed.) New York: Free Press, 1979.

Hamilton, G. "The Underlying Philosophy of Casework Today." In *Proceedings of the National Conference of Social Work,* 1941.

Hamilton, G. *Theory and Practice of Social Casework.* (Rev. ed.) New York: Columbia University Press, 1951.

Hartford, M. *Groups in Social Work.* New York: Columbia University Press, 1972.

Hartford, M. "Group Methods and Generic Practice." In R. Roberts and H. Northen (Eds.), *Theories of Social Work with Groups.* New York: Columbia University Press, 1976.

Hartman, A. "Casework in Crisis 1932–1941." Unpublished doctoral dissertation, Columbia University School of Social Work, 1972.

Hartman, A. "Diagrammatic Assessment of Family Relationships." *Social Casework,* 1978, *59,* 464–476.

Hartman, A. "The Extended Family as a Resource for Change: An Ecological Approach to Family-Centered Practice." In C. Germain (Ed.), *Social Work Practice: People and Environments.* New York: Columbia University Press, 1979a.

Hartman, A. *Finding Families: An Ecological Approach to Family Assessment in Adoption.* Beverly Hills, Calif.: Sage, 1979b.

Hearn, G. *Theory Building in Social Work.* Toronto: University of Toronto Press, 1958.

Hellenbrand, S. "Main Currents in Social Casework 1918–1936." Unpublished doctoral dissertation, Columbia University School of Social Work, 1965.

Hoffman, L. "Deviation-Amplifying Processes in Natural Groups." In J. Haley (Ed.), *Changing Families.* New York: Grune & Stratton, 1971.

Hoffman, L. "Breaking the Homeostatic Cycle." In P. Guerin (Ed.), *Family Therapy: Theory and Practice.* New York: Gardner Press, 1976.

Hoffman, L., and Long, L. "A Systems Dilemma." *Family Process,* 1969, *8,* 211–234.

Hollis, F. "The Techniques of Casework." *Journal of Social Casework,* 1949, *30,* 235–244.

Hollis, F. *Casework: A Psychosocial Therapy.* (2nd ed.) Random House, 1972.

Jarrett, J. "The Training School of Psychiatric Social Work at Smith College." *Mental Hygiene,* 1918, *2,* 582–594.

Jarrett, J. "The Psychiatric Thread Running Through All Casework." In *Proceedings of the National Conference of Social Work,* 1919.

Kaplan, D., and Mason, E. "Maternal Reactions to Premature Birth Viewed as an Acute Emotional Disorder." *American Journal of Orthopsychiatry,* 1960, *30,* 539–552.

Konopka, G. *Therapeutic Group Work with Children.* Minneapolis: University of Minnesota Press, 1949.

Kuhn, T. S. *The Structure of Scientific Revolutions.* Chicago: University of Chicago Press, 1962.

Laird, J. "An Ecological Approach to Child Welfare: Issues of Family Identity and Continuity." In C. Germain (Ed.), *Social Work Practice: People and Environments.* New York: Columbia University Press, 1979.

Lee, P. "Social Work: Cause and Function." In *Proceedings of the National Conference of Social Work,* 1929.

Lowry, F. "The Client's Needs as the Basis for Differential Approach in Casework Treatment." *The Differential Approach in Casework Treatment.* New York: Family Welfare Association of America, 1936.

Lubov, R. *The Professional Altruist.* Cambridge: Harvard University Press, 1965.

Lutz, W. *Concepts and Principles Underlying Social Casework Practice.* New York: National Association of Social Workers, 1956.

McBroom, E. "Socialization and Social Casework." In R. Roberts and R. Nee (Eds.), *Theories of Social Casework.* Chicago: University of Chicago Press, 1970.

McBroom, E. "Socialization Through Small Groups." In R. Roberts and H. Northen (Eds.), *Theories of Social Work with Groups.* New York: Columbia University Press, 1976.

Maluccio, A. N. (Ed.). *Promoting Competence in Clients: A New/Old Approach to Social Work Practice.* New York: Free Press, 1981.

Marcus, L. "Communication Concepts and Principles." In F. Turner (Ed.), *Social Work Treatment.* (2nd ed.) New York: Free Press, 1979.

Meyer, C. H. "Purposes and Boundaries—Casework Fifty Years Later." *Social Casework,* 1973, p. 54.

Meyer, C. H. *Social Work Practice: A Response to the Urban Crisis.* (2nd ed.) New York: Free Press, 1976.

Middleman, R. *The Non-Verbal Method in Working with Groups.* New York: Association Press, 1968.

Middleman, R., and Goldberg, G. *Social Service Delivery: A Structural Approach to Social Work Practice.* New York: Columbia University Press, 1974.

Nelsen, J. *Communication Theory and Social Work Practice.* Chicago: University of Chicago Press, 1980.

Northen, H. *Social Work with Groups.* New York: Columbia University Press, 1969.

Northen, H. "Psychosocial Practice in Small Groups." In R. Roberts and H. Northen (Eds.), *Theories of Social Work with Groups.* New York: Columbia University Press, 1976.

Oxley, G. "A Life-Model Approach to Change." *Social Casework,* 1971, *52,* 627–633.

Papell, C., and Rothman, B. "Social Group Work Models: Possession and Heritage." *Journal of Education for Social Work,* 1966, *2,* 66–78.

Parad, H. (Ed.). *Crisis Intervention.* New York: Family Service Association of America, 1965.

Parad, H., and others. "Crisis Intervention with Families and Groups." In R. Roberts and H. Northen (Eds.), *Theories of Social Work with Groups.* New York: Columbia University Press, 1976.

Perlman, H. H. *Casework, A Problem-Solving Process.* Chicago: University of Chicago Press, 1957.

Perlman, H. H. "The Problem-Solving Model in Social Casework." In R. Roberts and R. Nee (Eds.), *Theories of Social Casework.* Chicago: University of Chicago Press, 1970.

Phillips, H. (Ed.). *Achievement of Responsible Behavior Through Group Work.* Philadelphia: University of Pennsylvania School of Social Work, 1950.

Phillips, H. *Essentials of Group Work Skill.* New York: Association Press, 1957.

Pincus, A., and Minahan, A. *Social Work Practice: Model and Method.* Itaska, Ill.: Peacock, 1973.

Pollak, O. *Social Science and Psychotherapy for Children.* New York: Russell Sage Foundation, 1952.

Pollak, O. *Integrating Social Science and Psychoanalytic Concepts.* New York: Russell Sage Foundation, 1956.

Pollak, O. "A Family Diagnosis Model." *Social Service Review,* 1960, *34,* 19–28.

Pollak, O., and Brieland, D. "The Midwest Seminar on Family Diagnosis and Treatment." *Social Casework,* 1961, *42,* 319–324.

Pumphrey, M. "Mary Richmond and the Rise of Professional Social Work in Baltimore." Unpublished doctoral dissertation, Columbia University School of Social Work, 1956.

Rapoport, L. "The State of Crisis: Some Theoretical Considerations." *Social Service Review,* 1962a, *36,* 211–217.

Rapoport, L. "Working with Families in Crisis: An Exploration in Preventive Intervention." *Social Work,* 1962b, *7,* 48-56.

Rapoport, L. "Crisis Intervention as a Mode of Brief Treatment." In R. Roberts and R. Nee (Eds.), *Theories of Social Casework.* Chicago: University of Chicago Press, 1970.

Redl, F., and Wineman, D. *The Aggressive Child.* New York: Free Press, 1958.

Reid, W. *The Task Centered System.* New York: Columbia University Press, 1978.

Reid, W. "Task-Centered Treatment." In F. Turner (Ed.), *Social Work Treatment.* (2nd ed.) New York: Free Press, 1979.

Reid, W., and Epstein, L. *Task Centered Casework.* New York: Columbia University Press, 1972.

Reid, W., and Epstein, L. (Eds.). *Task Centered Practice.* New York: Columbia University Press, 1977.

Reid, W., and Shyne, A. *Brief and Extended Casework.* New York: Columbia University Press, 1969.

Reynolds, B. "A Changing Psychology in Social Casework, A Review." *The Family,* 1931, *12,* 111–114.

Reynolds, B. *An Uncharted Journey.* New York: Citadel Press, 1963.

Richmond, M. "The Social Case Worker's Task." In *Proceedings of the National Conference of Social Work,* 1917a.

Richmond, M. *Social Diagnosis.* New York: Russell Sage Foundation, 1917b.

Richmond, M. *What Is Social Casework?* New York: Russell Sage Foundation, 1922.

Robinson, V. "Analysis of Processes in the Records of Family Case Working Agencies." In *Proceedings of the National Conference of Social Work,* 1921.

Robinson, V. *A Changing Psychology in Social Case Work.* Chapel Hill: University of North Carolina Press, 1930.

Robinson, V. *Jessie Taft, Therapist and Social Casework Educator.* Philadelphia: University of Pennsylvania Press, 1962.

Ryder, E. "A Functional Approach." In R. Roberts and H. Northen (Eds.), *Theories of Social Work with Groups.* New York: Columbia University Press, 1976.

Scherz, F. "The Crisis of Adolescence in Family Life." *Social Casework,* 1967, *48,* 209–216.

Scherz, F. "Theory and Practice of Family Therapy." In R. Roberts and R. Nee (Eds.), *Theories of Social Casework.* Chicago: University of Chicago Press, 1970.

Schwartz, W. "On the Use of Groups in Social Work Practice." In W. Schwartz and S. Zalba (Eds.), *The Practice of Group Work.* New York: Columbia University Press, 1971.

Schwartz, W. "Between Client and System: The Mediating Function." In R. Roberts and H. Northen (Eds.), *Theories of Social Work with Groups.* New York: Columbia University Press, 1976.

Sheffield, A. "Three Interviews and the Social Situation." *Journal of Social Forces,* 1924, *2,* 692–697.

Sheffield, A. "The Situation as the Unit of Family Case Study." *Journal of Social Forces,* 1931, *9,* 465–474.

Sherman, S. "Family Therapy." In F. Turner (Ed.), *Social Work Treatment.* (2nd ed.) New York: Free Press, 1979.

Shulman, L. *The Skills of Helping Individuals and Groups.* Itaska, Ill.: Peacock, 1979.

Siporin, M. "Situational Assessment and Intervention." *Social Casework,* 1972, *53,* 91–109.

Siporin, M. *Introduction to Social Work Practice.* New York: Macmillan, 1975.

Smalley, R. *Theory for Social Work.* New York: Columbia University Press, 1965.

Somers, M. L. "Problem-Solving in Small Groups." In R. Roberts and H. Northen (Eds.), *Theories of Social Work with Groups.* New York: Columbia University Press, 1976.

Stein, I. *Systems Theory, Science, and Social Work.* Metuchen, N.J.: Scarecrow Press, 1974.

Stuart, R. B. "Behavior Modification: A Technology of Social Change." In F. Turner (Ed.), *Social Work Treatment.* (2nd ed.) New York: Free Press, 1979.

Studt, E. "Social Work Theory and Implications for the Practice of Methods." *Social Work Education Reporter,* 1968, *16,* 22–24, 42–46.

Taft, J. "The Relation of Function to Process in Social Case Work." *Journal of Social Work Process,* 1937, *1,* 1–18.

Thomas, E. J. (Ed.). *The Socio-Behavioral Approach and Applications to Social Work.* New York: Council on Social Work Education, 1967.

Thomas, E. J. "Behavioral Modification and Casework." In R. Roberts and R. Nee (Eds.), *Theories of Social Casework.* Chicago: University of Chicago Press, 1970.

Tropp, E. *A Humanistic Foundation for Group Work Practice.* (2nd ed.) New York: Selected Academic Readings, 1971.

Tropp, E. "A Developmental Theory." In R. Roberts and H. Northen (Eds.), *Theories of Social Work with Groups.* New York: Columbia University Press, 1976.

Turner, F. *Psychosocial Therapy.* New York: Free Press, 1978.

Vinter, R. "Group Work's Perspectives and Prospects." In *Social Work with Groups.* New York: National Association of Social Workers, 1959.

Werner, H. *A Rational Approach to Social Casework.* New York: Association Press, 1965.

Werner, H. "Cognitive Theory." In F. Turner (Ed.), *Social Work Treatment.* (2nd ed.) New York: Free Press, 1979.

Wilson, G. "From Practice to Theory: A Personalized History." In R. Roberts and H. Northen (Eds.), *Theories of Social Work with Groups.* New York: Columbia University Press, 1976.

Yelaja, S. "Functional Theory for Social Work Practice." In F. Turner (Ed.), *Social Work Treatment.* (2nd ed.) New York: Free Press, 1979.

3

Professional Values

Joseph L. Vigilante

In 1967 Herbert Aptekar wrote, "The framework of social work, as we know it, is a set of values" (p. 19). Nathan Cohen expressed the centrality of values to social work practice and education in his terse description of the development of the profession: "Humanitarianism in Search of a Method" (Cohen, 1958, p. 3). Before Cohen, many leading thinkers in social work had traced social work and social services from the earliest recorded history through the medieval tradition in the church to the development of the great democratic political systems. Most believed that the Judeo-Christian ethic had had a profound influence on the development of the social work profession (Bisno, 1952; Lindeman, 1955; Tierney, 1959; McCormick, 1948; Maimonides, 1951). William Gordon believes that "the values which flow from social work's purposes and methods" constitute "the major substance of social work" (Gordon, 1965a, p. 20). In his zeal for illuminating the importance of the value base of social work, Gordon has advocated shifting the research emphasis of the profession from one concerned with functions and activities to one that addresses the "value-knowledge realm" (Gordon, 1965). Other well-known writers before and after him (Gordon Hamilton, 1951; Helen Harris Perlman, 1976; and Charles Levy, 1973) have made similar arguments. Perlman, for example, pleads that professional values be transmuted from "idea" into "form, quality, or direction of behavior" (1976, p. 382). While echoing Cohen's affirmation of the relationship between humanitarianism and the social work profession, her plea poses a fundamental epistemological dilemma for all helping professions: Can

Note: The writer acknowledges with appreciation the editorial assistance of Daniel Sieg, Graduate Assistant to the Dean, Adelphi University School of Social Work.

values be transmuted into instruments of professional practice, or do they serve only to guide practice and morally justify the profession? This article will attempt to show how values are currently used as instruments of practice.

Values, like theories, are not immutable. They are subject to changes in customs, mores, and norms of behavior in social systems. Consequently, they must be understood as fully as possible by a profession that is interlaced with social forces. Changes, for example, regarding societal conceptions of life and death, sexual behavior, privacy, alienation, coercion, and self-actualization challenge the helping professions at the very roots of their philosophical commitments. L. G. Swack (1978) calls attention to the stress caused by population growth and mobility, burgeoning knowledge, proliferating information, technological growth, and demands for more governmental control of social institutions. She states that implicit in the belief that professionals will be effective problem solvers and decision makers are assumptions that sound professional ethical codes underlie their practice.

One of the most profound and vital changes our society experienced during the decades of the fifties, sixties, and seventies was the drastic rejection or revision of traditional values. These values had helped to define for hundreds of years the roles and relationships between parents and children, between peers, between the sexes, between men and women in the work place, between people and the social institutions purported to serve them, and between people and their governments. The roles of professionals vis-à-vis their clients have also changed greatly. We continue to be in a state of flux during which these relationships are tested, redefined, and revamped to meet the complexities of the problems that people bring to professionals for help. We face new dilemmas in protecting the professional's freedom to exercise his or her skill while recognizing clients' rights to be protected from inappropriate invasions and exposure and assaults upon their autonomy. Privacy accompanied with sense of self is important for social workers too, whose practice is so closely related to the social experiences and social pressures of the client community. Problems in using values in practice have multiplied at least as rapidly as the problems of the society. This condition is exacerbated because our knowledge of the genesis and use of values in social work practice does not measure up to what is required for a profession that is steeped in ministering to psychosocial conditions so greatly influenced by social values.

Recent rapid changes in sexual mores, for example, have prompted a proliferation of articles in many professions considering the relationship between heretofore accepted professional values and sexual conduct. Hare-Mustin (1974) reports on recently developed treatment of sexual dysfunction using genital intercourse as a psychotherapeutic technique. She discusses it in the light of changing sexual mores and with respect to three of the American Psychological Association's ethical standards. These standards deal with competency, community expectations, and client relationships. (The article soberly concludes that the use of such techniques is unethical.)

Other issues have prompted discussions of the relationship between values and clinical practice. The increase in third-party payments for clinical services is an example. The growing appearance of third-party payers, peer review structures, and governmental surveillance tends to erode the traditionally understood principles of confidentiality between professionals and clients. Traditional interpretations of confidentiality appear to be no longer functional. Consequently many professionals are calling for a clearer understanding of the values bearing upon confidentiality and privileged communication and a more precise set of principles for assessing these hallmarks of the professional relationship (Plaut, 1974). As the delivery of human services is entrusted to an ever-widening array of human services specialists, some of whom have no, or only limited formal education, the concern for values in the delivery of human services is increasingly pertinent.

In social work literature the examination of values has for the most part been directed at justifying the goals and methods of the profession as an institution. Such value justification has been manifested in terms of concern for the rights of individuals, increased opportunities for self-determination, and the evidence that many individuals require professional help in coping with the complexities of post-industrial societies. The long-range goals of the profession tend to be couched in value terms: enhancing, functioning, preserving the dignity and worth of individuals, and serving a humanizing function in society (Perlman, 1976; Gordon, 1965a and 1965b; Lodge, 1980).

What Are Social Work Values?

Among writers who have identified some of the problems connected to the value orientation of social work are Herbert Aptekar (1967), Felix Biestek (1953), Herbert Bisno (1952), Charles Levy (1973), Muriel Pumphrey (1959), Barbara Varley (1968), and Harold Lewis (1972). The Code of Ethics of the National Association of Social Workers (NASW) also provides useful insights into the values of the profession (National Association of Social Workers, 1980).

Eduard C. Lindeman (1955), a philosopher who occupied a faculty position at the New York School of Social Work, Columbia University, during the 1940s and 1950s, was an early explorer and teacher of the value base of social work. Lindeman had a profound impact upon Herbert Bisno, one of the first social work educators to organize and clarify professional values, and both men acknowledged the direct influence of Philip Klein (1940). Bisno's book *The Philosophy of Social Work* was among the first to collect and group professional values in a manner that had implications for practice (1952, pp. 6–65):

> Each individual by the very fact of his existence is of worth.
>
> Human suffering is undesirable and should be prevented, or at least alleviated, whenever possible.

All human behavior is the result of interaction between the biological organism and its environment.

Man does not "naturally" act in a rational manner.

Man is amoral and asocial at birth.

There are both individual and common human needs.

There are important differences between individuals and they must be recognized and allowed for.

Human motivation is complex and frequently obscure.

Family relationships are of primary importance in the early development of the individual.

"Experiencing" is an essential aspect of the learning process.

The rich and/or powerful are not necessarily "fit."

"Socialized individualism" is preferable to "rugged individualism."

A major responsibility for the welfare of its members rests with the community.

All classes of persons in the community have an equal right to the social services; there is a community responsibility to relieve adequately and without discrimination all members of the community.

The federal government is thought to have an important responsibility in providing for health, housing, full employment, education, and various types of public assistance and social insurance.

Public assistance should be based on the concept of need.

Organized labor makes a positive contribution to community life and should be accepted as a constructive, rather than destructive force.

There needs to be complete social cooperation of all race and ethnic groups, on the basis of complete equality and mutual respect.

Freedom and security are not mutually exclusive.

Bisno's values are not organized into levels of abstraction, nor are they classified in a mutually exclusive manner; yet they represent long-felt social work beliefs, recorded together perhaps for the first time.

Bisno's work explicitly identified what social workers, as professionals, "believed in." It remained for Muriel Pumphrey seven years later to report on the prevalence of these values in the curricula of graduate schools of social work. Pumphrey also classified professional values as *ultimate* and *proximate,* and she attacked the problem of internal value conflicts, probably the most difficult problem encountered by scholars attempting to translate values into professional behavior. She identified eight ultimate professional values most frequently taught in schools of social work. In abbreviated form, these are as follows (Pumphrey, 1959, pp. 43–44):

1. Each human being should be regarded by all others as an object of infinite worth. . . .
2. Human beings have large and as yet unknown capacities for developing both inner harmony and satisfaction and ability to make outward contributions to the development of others.
3. In order to realize his potentialities every human being must interact in

giving and taking relationships with others, and has an equal right to opportunities to do so.
4. Human betterment is possible . . . human beings have the capacity to change. Change per se is not sought, but change toward personal and social ideals is something "better."
5. Change in a positive direction for individuals, groups or organized societies may be speeded up by active and purposeful assistance or encouragement from others. . . .
6. The most effective changes cannot be imposed. Man's potentialities include his capacity to discover and direct his own destiny. . . .
7. Human effort should be directed to constant search for enlarged understanding of man's needs and potentialities. . . .
8. The profession of social work is . . . committed to the preservation and implementation of these values.

Lest the reader be led to underestimate the complexity of Pumphrey's work by this simplified accounting, it is important to note that she recognized these highly abstract values as subject to great confusion in practice. She offers an extensive discussion of the importance of "paired values" (for example, the value of freedom of speech is paired with the value of the rights of all individuals to protection through social control in the adage, "You can't shout 'fire' in a crowded theatre") and of middle-range (proximate) values for purposes of operationalizing values in practice, a concern also expressed by Perlman in another context, discussed below. Pumphrey did not investigate the ordering and utilization of proximate values to the extent that she did ultimate values. She suggested that much more remains to be done in researching this aspect of values in social work education and practice. Most important, she affirmed a distinction between a professional's personal values and the values of the profession. In a related study in the area of personal and professional values, Douglas Posey (1978) found a correlation between social role or rank in the profession and adherence to certain values.

Value as Instruments of Practice

An important manifestation of professional values in social work is their use in the direct helping process—that is, as instruments of direct practice (J. L. Vigilante, 1974; Lewis, 1972; F. W. Vigilante, 1980). This chapter will primarily be concerned, henceforth, with values as tools of practice. My approach assumes the time-honored philosophical base of the profession—the Judeo-Christian, humanitarian, humanistic ethic. It will not distinguish between "direct practice" and "indirect practice" (micropractice or macropractice), since it is further assumed that professional values have equal application to both forms.

Values are precisely identified as instruments of practice by Charles Levy's quotation from Parsons: "A value-*pattern* . . . defines a *direction of choice, and consequent commitment to action*" (Levy, 1973, p. 36). He adds, quoting from Gouldner's (1968, p. 136) discussion of Talcott Parsons, "In principle, a value pattern may be relevant to the orientation of a class of actors to the whole of the 'human condition,' and, specifically to a conception of the desirable type of society." Levy introduces yet another challenge of transmuting values into practice (1973, p. 36): "It is the job of the social worker in society that determines, and perhaps even dictates his preferences regarding persons, practices, and conditions which relate to the job. The job, and those to whom it is directly or indirectly addressed, shapes the rules by which his values, and his actions, will be measured or evaluated." In other words, Levy suggests that professional values are shaped not only by time and custom but by the social roles of individual professionals. This view suggests the most profound professional conflicts. It has long been recognized that values are not forever fixed and that they are influenced by custom, practice, and social change. But the suggestion that *professional* values, as contrasted to professionals' personal values, differ as a function of hierarchical status within the profession appears to challenge the validity of the assumption that a set of generally accepted professional values dominates practice. These observations, made by a leading scholar in this area of practice, demonstrate the need for much more research into what values are used in practice and how.

The value patterns referred to by Levy suggest their instrumentality in the practice of social work in a variety of ways. Of primary importance is the fact that those values which Pumphrey and Bisno specified tend to operate in the way schools of social work select their students. Individuals who apply to schools of social work tend to profess the values identified by Bisno, Pumphrey, and others, and the selection process of the schools uses evidence of adherence to these values as criteria for admission (Berengarten, 1949, 1951, 1964; Bishop, 1948; Council on Social Work Education, 1957; Steinman, 1968; J. L. Vigilante, 1980). For this reason these values might be expected to have a direct effect on the nature of practice.

Levy (1973) recommends three major categories of values in social work: (1) values as preferred conceptions of people, (2) values as preferred outcomes for people, and (3) values as preferred instrumentalities for dealing with people. His observations regarding the relationship between the interpretation of values and the role one occupies in the professional hierarchy suggests a closer relationship between the values expressed by agency executives and the board of directors than between the values of direct service workers and executives. For the purpose of understanding values specifically as practice tools, I subdivide Levy's third category into four categories: (1) who social work clients shall be, (2) where and how clients are seen, (3) priorities with respect to the relationships among client, agency, and worker, and (4) the effect of values on professional judgments. I believe, with Levy, that identified professional values are the preferred instruments for decision making in the helping process.

Who Are Social Work Clients?

Traditionally, social work has served the so-called underclasses of the society. These groups tend to include, among many others, individuals who are the victims of poverty, of physical or mental handicaps, of alienation following immigration, or of discrimination because of minority status, and individuals who are deviants. As social work became more professionalized, its services appealed to a larger part of the mainstream of the social system. But, for all intents and purposes, most of the clients of social work still come from the underclasses.

One might easily speculate that it is the value orientation of the profession that leads it to place high priority on providing opportunity to those with the fewest opportunities. Many social workers have been impressed by John Rawls's book (1971) *A Theory of Justice.* Rawls expounds "the difference principle," which states that good must be distributed in a way that benefits the least advantaged—providing a safeguard against antisocial application of classic utilitarianism, which would subordinate the rights of a few to the greater good of the many. This work is used increasingly in social work theory courses. Rawls's general theory of distributive justice has particular relevance to social work practice.

It would appear that most social workers, with the exception of a few who primarily engage in private practice, continue to serve this underserved population by choice. (Although there are no hard data on this subject, it seems apparent that most social workers in private practice are not servicing underclass populations. Private practice specialization is a phenomenon that has increased rapidly since about 1960.) Most social work clients continue to be mainly dependent populations. The number of social workers in child care, child protective services, child abuse, and children's service organizations, combined with workers who serve the aged, the emotionally and physically handicapped, and legal deviants, far surpasses the number who work with persons not suffering from these conditions of dependency or handicap.

Where and How Are Clients Seen?

It is well known that social agencies tend to be located in marginal areas where underclass populations live. The values of the profession, cited earlier, demand as a part of providing opportunities for self-fulfillment that services be established where they are accessible to clients. These values, of course, are not always realized, but they seem to be borne out for the most part.

Many social work clients are seen in groups. In fact, group work has been identified by the NASW as a professional specialization. Social workers' leadership in developing services for groups during the 1930s was a departure from the methods of the other helping professions. The group work and community organization methods serve large numbers of people. These methods meet the needs of populations en masse (in response to values of the profession) while serving them in a manner in which the values of socialization and engagement are enhanced. Social workers believe that healthy socialization patterns are direct and necessary derivatives of healthy group experiences.

The values of the profession also suggest that clients or their representatives should participate in developing social agencies' professional practice policies. It is not unusual for clients to be represented on boards of directors and advisory boards, although one would hope for it to be a more common practice. Professional values also strongly imply offering service at times convenient to clients (after work, during lunch periods, late evenings, weekends, and so on). This value, too, is not always realized in practice. Perhaps the greatest breach of it can be seen on those occasions when youth-serving agencies are closed on school holidays.

Professional values are often in conflict with the policies of the social agency as defined by the board of directors, even if the board includes clients or their representatives. Increasingly, this conflict between the professionalism of workers and the policies of the agency is becoming more open, and there is some evidence that social agency policies are beginning to provide greater autonomy for professional decision making. It is expected that professional values will be viewed as a central focus of agency service. The professional association of social workers holds as fundamental values the assumptions that the agency's policies should exist foremost for the benefit of clients, not workers, and that client needs should be given the highest priorities in program planning. Although these values are not always manifested in social agency practice, a serious breach of the values might subject an agency to censure by the professional association.

Using Values Directly with Clients

The application of the professional values of social work is manifested in a helping relationship in which the inevitable authority of the profession is not abused, but is exercised through a sharing of the professional's resources with the client. From the beginning the worker and the client (or clients) together define, plan, and agree on what the helping relationship will be. This process applies to all specializations of practice. Before any helping relationship is established, the worker and the client should agree on their respective roles and, usually, on a specific point in time at which they will reevaluate these roles and consider a new contract. Throughout the process it is expected that the professional will try to avoid intimidating the client, to enable the client to freely make choices about using the service, and to enable the client to express his or her feelings about the professional, the agency, and the nature of the process. Professional decisions regarding the use of collateral contacts (persons or institutions with interest in or knowledge about the client), community contacts, or contacts with a school or a physician should be made only with the agreement and active participation of the client, who should have the full knowledge of not only the reasons for the contact but how it is expected to help. The social worker is expected to encourage clients to evaluate the risks in involving other persons. For example, decisions such as whether or not a spouse will be seen or whether a family will be seen together are influenced not only by the client's desires and interests but also by the mutual examination of the meeting's impact upon a variety of the client's systemic relationships. The professional is expected to consider with the client how the worker's involvement will help the relationship between client and teacher, for example, or between client and family. Deciding whether seeing the entire family might help or hinder the family relationships should be mutually explored. At times such an involvement may not be seen as immediately helpful, though it may be desirable in the long run. If clients participate in arriving at these decisions, they may hold a conviction about the decision that can help them stay with their choice.

The worker's decision to intervene more actively (for example, whether he or she should give advice) should be influenced by an assessment of several professional values in combination, such as the client's entitlement to self-growth and self-determination, the importance of familial and social relationships, and accepted social imperatives.

The professional social worker's judgments about how he or she will use particular psychosocial helping skills, when to use them, and with whom are subject to the influence of professional values. For example, within the context of the psychosocial condition—the professional domain of social work practice—a decision to emphasize the importance of resources in the social environment, rather than those within the individual, is often determined in part by the worker's commitment to professional values. Balancing "individual" good and "group" good, for example, probably has a direct influence upon which part of the psychosocial complex will demand most of the worker's efforts from time to time. This orchestration of individual and social forces (within a value frame of reference) is perhaps the most challenging test of professional skill.

Another example of the worker's use of professional values may occur in a situation where a family's well-being is threatened by the presence of an alcoholic parent. The value of maintaining an integrated family in spite of the alcoholism of the parent is balanced by the rights of the other individuals in the family for a life unencumbered by the parent's disabling dependence. The social worker's process will be based upon a combination of professional judgments about the strengths of individual family members, as well as the family's potential ability to bear the burden. Penetrating these analyses will be a balancing of the rights of the group vis-à-vis the rights of the individual.

In a recent study Phillips (1980) found that the practice of social work graduate students was influenced by their adherence to the value which holds that society has a responsibility for the welfare of its members. Social workers were more ready than other professional students to take a clinical situation devoted to individual change and move it toward an effort at achieving social change.

Values and the Code of Ethics

By reading a social worker's process recording of sessions with individuals, groups, or communities, one can see where values have influenced professional behaviors and where they have not. Professional values set forth professional expectations that cannot be totally and completely fulfilled. It is the chase that characterizes their use in practice. The professional Code of Ethics is the instrument for monitoring the chase.

At present the profession's use of the Code of Ethics requires much improvement. We have not yet developed a smooth system for successfully defining whether a professional has breached the code in many situations. Nor are we clear about the legal expectations of professional behavior. As human problems and professional solutions increase in complexity, whether and how the code has been transgressed becomes increasingly difficult to determine. The development of a sophisticated system of "case law," based upon breaches of the code and reporting both the alleged transgressions and the remedial action taken (along with the reasoning process of the professional judges), has not yet been accumulated, analyzed, or categorized. In the four years before the 1979 meeting of the Delegate Assembly of the National Association of Social Workers, the association directed its attention to the content of the Code of Ethics as well as methods of enforcing it. Two task forces worked throughout this period to rewrite the code. For many social workers the revised code still falls short of explicating desired professional behaviors. Applying the code in a more sophisticated manner is a primary challenge to a profession that acknowledges itself to be highly influenced by philosophical values in its practice. The development of a system of case law that can help monitor the Code of Ethics would appear to be a fundamental prerequisite to further understanding the use of values in practice.

Professional Values and Social Policy

Social values obviously have a close relationship to social policy. The stated goals in official constitutions and documents that define democratic governments provide ample evidence. These democratic-humanitarian values are applied to the development and maintenance of human service institutions. How they are used can significantly affect social policy in the future.

When to suggest various options for decision making in a client's or group's life may have the most far-reaching impact not only upon the individual and his primary group or family but also upon the wider social system. Indeed, the crucible in which social policy for social welfare is put to the test is very often the relationship between a social worker and a client. The effect of social policies upon client groups will often depend upon value judgments made by workers in the line of practice. For example, whether certain social policies designed to enhance parent-child relationships, marital relationships, youth-peer relationships, or parent-child-school relationships will have the desired results often depends upon how these policies are interpreted and used by professionals.

The future of certain service programs in public assistance, the goals of government policies regarding adoption, work with welfare clients, or juvenile court probation policies may well be related to the subtlety and skill with which professionals apply their professional value system. The close relationship between social policy practice and direct service may be clearly seen in the application of professional values. It seems possible that it is the use of professional values in social policy practice, as in direct service practice, that distinguishes the social work method from other professional disciplines concerned with social policy.

References

Aptekar, H. H. "American Societal Values and Their Influence on Social Welfare Programs and Professional Social Work." *Journal of Social Work Process,* 1967, *16,* 17–36.

Berengarten, S. "A Pilot Study to Establish Criteria for Selection of Students in Social Work." In *Social Work as Human Relations: Anniversary Paper of the New York School of Social Work and the Community Service Society of New York.* New York: Columbia University Press, 1949.

Berengarten, S. "A Pioneer Workshop in Student Selection." *Bulletin of the New York School of Social Work,* 1951, *44,* 3–12.

Berengarten, S. *Admission Predictions in Student Performance in Social Work Education: An Unduplicated Count Study of Applicants for Admission and Enrolled Students Entering Schools of Social Work, Fall Term 1961–62.* New York: Council on Social Work Education, 1964.

Biestek, F. P., "The Non-Judgmental Attitude." *Social Casework,* 1953, *34,* 235–239.

Bishop, M. E. *The Selection and Admission of Students in the School of Social Work.* Philadelphia: University of Pennsylvania Press, 1948.

Bisno, H. *The Philosophy of Social Work.* Washington, D.C.: Public Affairs Press, 1952.

Cohen, N. *Social Work in the American Tradition.* New York: Dryden Press, 1958.

Council on Social Work Education. *Selection of Students for Schools of Social Work: A Report by the 1953 Committee on Admissions.* New York: Council on Social Work Education, 1957.

Gordon, W. E. "Toward a Social Work Frame of Reference." *Journal of Education for Social Work,* 1965a, *1* (20), 19–26.

Gordon, W. E. "Knowledge and Value: Their Distinction and Relationship in Clarifying Social Work Practice." *Social Work,* 1965b, *10,* 32–39.

Gouldner, A. W. On Talcott Parsons. "On the Concept of Value-Commitments." *Sociological Inquiry,* 1968, *38,* 136.

Hamilton, G. *Theory and Practice of Social Casework.* (2nd ed.) New York: Columbia University Press, 1951.

Hare-Mustin, R. T. "Ethical Considerations in the Use of Sexual Contact in Psychotherapy." *Psychotherapy: Theory, Research and Practice,* 1974, *11,* 308–310.

Klein, P. "The Social Theory of Professional Social Work." In H. E. Becker, H. Becker, and F. B. Becker (Eds.), *Contemporary Social Theory.* New York: Appleton-Century-Crofts, 1940.

Levy, C. S. "The Value Base of Social Work." *Journal of Education for Social Work,* 1973, *9* (36), 34–42.

Lewis, H. "Morality and the Politics of Practice." *Social Casework,* 1972, *17,* 404–405.

Lindeman, E. C. "The Roots of Democratic Culture." In H. B. Trecker (Ed.), *Group Work Foundations and Frontiers.* New York: Whiteside, 1955.

Lodge, R. *Combatting Alienation: The Social Worker as Humanizing Agent.* Davis, Calif.: International Dialogue Press, 1980.

McCormick, M. *Thomistic Philosophy in Social Casework.* New York: Columbia University Press, 1948.

Maimonides, M. *The Guide for the Perplexed.* London: Routledge & Kegan Paul, 1951.

National Association of Social Workers. "Code of Ethics of the National Association of Social Workers as Adopted by the 1979 NASW Delegate Assembly, Effective July 1, 1980." NASW Policy Statements 1. Washington, D.C.: National Association of Social Workers, 1980.

Perlman, H. H. "Believing and Doing: Values in Social Work Education." *Social Casework,* 1976, *57,* 381–390.

Phillips, D. "An Exploration of Comparative Professional Values." Unpublished doctoral dissertation, Adelphi University, 1980.

Plaut, E. A. "A Perspective on Confidentiality." *American Journal of Psychiatry,* 1974, *131,* 1021–1024.

Posey, D. "Personal and Professional Values Among Colorado Social Workers." Unpublished doctoral dissertation, Graduate School of Social Work, University of Denver, 1978.

Pumphrey, M. W. *The Teaching of Values and Ethics in Social Work Education.* A Project Report of the Curriculum Study, Vol. 13. New York: Council on Social Work Education, 1959.

Rawls, J. *A Theory of Justice.* Cambridge, Mass.: Harvard University Press, 1971.

Steinman, R. "Values in Occupational Choice and Occupational Selection: A Comparative Study of Admissions Decisions in Social Work Education." Unpublished doctoral dissertation, Brandeis University, 1968.

Swack, L. G. (Ed.), *Dilemma of Our Time: The Individual Versus the System.* Cleveland: Case Western Reserve University, 1978.

Tierney, B. *The Medieval Poor Law: A Sketch of Canonical Theory and Its Application in England.* Berkeley: University of California Press, 1959.

Varley, B. "Social Work Values: Changes in Value Commitments of Students from Admission to MSW Graduation." *Journal of Education for Social Work,* 1968, *4,* 67–85.

Vigilante, F. W. "Self-Preoccupation as a Predictor of Performance in Graduate Social Work Education." Unpublished doctoral dissertation, Yeshiva University, 1980.

Vigilante, J. L. "Between Values and Science: Education for the Profession During a Moral Crisis, or Is Proof Truth?" *Journal of Education for Social Work,* 1974, *10,* 107–115.

4

Contexts of Practice

Philip R. Popple

The social work profession is currently in a state of flux, as it has been over the entire course of its history. As usual we are debating whether services should have an individual or a social change focus. We are debating what our core skill is or whether we even have a core skill that is uniquely our own. We debate who should be and who should not be considered a social worker. On top of all this we wonder why we cannot settle down, become organized, and develop as a profession in a manner similar to medicine or law. The answer to these questions is that social work is imbedded in an institutional context, and interacts with this context as part of its mission. As the institutional context changes over time, so must the profession. Medicine deals with the human body, which remains stable; the legal profession deals with a body of law that changes over time, but also with legal principles that remain stable. Social work, on the other hand, deals with public and voluntary programs concerned with immediate problems and priorities and reflecting values and beliefs that are constantly shifting. If a major health program is enacted, it will influence medical services but not the basic nature of medicine. A major Supreme Court decision will influence the material a lawyer works with, but the function and practice of law will not change. A major public welfare bill (such as the 1962 Amendments to the Social Security Act), however, can change the basic structure of social work and the focus of practice. Because the mission of the social work profession is a moving target, so to speak, it is imperative that social workers understand their institutional context, for only then will they be able to understand the nature of their practice.

The purpose of this chapter is to discuss the historical development of the institutional context in which clinical social work is embedded. The institutional context is conceptualized here as being made up of three primary interwoven threads. The first thread is the development of the social work profession and issues such as what is social work, who can legitimately be called a social worker, and what are appropriate settings for social work practice. The second thread is public social welfare policy and issues such as what services should government pay for, who should provide them, and what results are expected. The third thread is private social welfare policy and deals with questions of what services should be provided by the voluntary sector, how money can be raised to fund these services, and what the relationship between private social welfare, government, and the business community should be.

Although the topic of this handbook is clinical social work, it is not possible to separate out the institutional context of clinical social work from that of social work in general. Therefore, this chapter will look at the development of the institutional context of social work in general with those events of particular relevance to clinical social work highlighted.

Because this subject is broad and complex, many important events are given short shrift and many details are left out. Those wishing a more extensive treatment are referred to Leiby (1978) and Lubove (1965).

Historical Development of Clinical Social Work

Before the Civil War very little existed in the United States that could, by any stretch of the imagination, be considered social work as we think of it today. What social welfare programs there were, were based on the 1601 English Poor Law, which firmly established family responsibility for dependent persons and assigned responsibility for those with no family to the smallest unit of government. Generally, dependent children were apprenticed, if possible, or were boarded at the cheapest place; able-bodied persons were put to work; and the old or incapacitated who did not have families were either given a small grant (outdoor relief) or were placed in an institution (indoor relief). Institutions were very popular for dealing with a variety of social problems, with specialized institutions being established for the old, blind, deaf, and mentally defective, and for dependent children. A few private charitable agencies, such as the Association for Improving the Condition of the Poor and the St. Vincent De Paul Society, existed in large cities and dealt with needy persons on a case-by-case basis. However, except for a small number of administrators, members of regulatory bodies such as state welfare boards, and matrons who provided menial help, very few people were engaged in anything that even vaguely resembled what we now think of as social work.

Before the middle of the nineteenth century, there was really very little need for a profession such as social work. The United States was what Leiby (1978) refers to as "the rural democracy." The country was large and undeveloped; the population was small, prosperous, and homogeneous (except for blacks and Indians, whose social welfare concerned few other people); and the economy was relatively simple. The traditional institutions of the family, the marketplace, and the church were well able to handle any social welfare problems that arose.

In the second half of the century, American society changed drastically, and a number of interacting forces created a situation in which social work developed. Trattner (1979, p. 71) cites the following figures to illustrate the immensity of the "economic revolution" that occurred. In 1860 about $1 billion was invested in manufacturing, yielding an annual value of manufactured products of nearly $1.9

billion and providing work for approximately one million three hundred thousand workers in American factories. By 1900 capital investment had risen to more than $12 billion, the yearly value of products was over $11 billion, and the number of factory workers had risen to five and a half million. Accompanying this economic growth was an increase in population, much of it due to immigration (in 1901, one in seven Americans had been born abroad), massive and chaotic growth of cities, stratification of society (a small group of wealthy businessmen at the top and a large group of poorly paid laborers on the bottom), and a business cycle characterized by periods of depression and unemployment alternating with periods of growth. Added to all this was the development of a faith in the seemingly unlimited potential of science, technology, and rationality for solving the problems of modern life and a belief that problems should be dealt with by specialized professions.

Society in the late nineteenth century became so complex that the traditional institutions could no longer deal with the problems occurring between people and their social environment. Two newly emerging organizations, the settlement houses and the charity organization societies, attempted to resolve these problems. The settlements were devoted to solving problems between persons and their social environment by changing the environment. The charity organizations sought to resolve them by changing the individual. Together these two types of organizations formed the roots of the social work profession in the United States. Their differing perspectives on the solution to social problems have continued to be one of the unresolved (and perhaps unresolvable) debates in social work.

The Settlement House Movement. The settlement movement was a transplant from Victorian England, where it had begun as a part of a broad attempt to preserve human and spiritual values in an age of urbanization and industrialization. Many settlement workers, particularly in England, were motivated by religious conviction. They were closely allied with the Protestant social gospel movement, which sought to establish a kingdom of God on earth through social reform.

The earliest settlement house in England was Toynbee Hall, founded in 1884 by Samuel Barnett. Barnett believed that it would be socially beneficial for university men to live in the worst area of London. He felt they were cut off from the real work of the world, they were restless, and they needed to do something useful. Barnett also felt that the workingmen were cut off from culture and civilization and that association with the university atmosphere of the settlement would benefit them. Toynbee Hall was strongly Protestant. Barnett hoped that it would lead to a spiritual reawakening of both the laborers and the university men. He believed "that the things which make men alike are finer and better than the things that keep them apart, and that these basic likenesses . . . easily transcend the less essential differences of race, language, creed, and tradition" (Addams, 1938, p. 112).

Stanton Coit, a young American who had earned a doctorate at the University of Berlin, spent three months at Toynbee Hall. After his return to New York, he founded the Neighborhood Guild in 1886, the first settlement in the United States. The settlement idea grew rapidly here. In 1897 there were seventy-four; by 1900, over a hundred; by 1905, more than two hundred; and by 1910, over four hundred.

The settlements stressed the social and economic causes of poverty rather than the individual causes. Whereas the philosophy of the charity organizations led to private charity and spiritual uplift, the philosophy of the settlements led to social and economic change. The settlements stressed the neighborhood ideal and rejected the idea of enlightened self-interest, emphasizing instead the interdependence of social groups in an organically structured society. One settlement advocate suggested that the settlement was a "great modern protest against the heresy that wealth makes character, that education can establish an aristocracy, that one can rise to a social pinnacle without obligation to those who have contributed to that rise" (Davis, 1967, p. 17).

Settlement workers were less interested in changing individuals than they were in changing social conditions. Their reform activities generally began in the immediate neighborhood of the settlement and addressed mundane issues such as the number of bathhouses, trash collections, housing conditions, recreation facilities, and the like. The settlement workers and the neighborhood residents engaged in political action directed at these issues (Jane Addams got herself appointed trash inspector for the Hull House neighborhood) and set up programs to meet neighborhood needs. Fairly typical settlement programs consisted of daycare services, literacy classes, social clubs, and the like (Trolander, 1975; Davis, 1967).

In addition to neighborhood programs, settlement workers engaged in broader social reform activities. Hull House residents spearheaded the fight against child labor during the early years of the twentieth century and were successful in getting legislation passed and the Children's Bureau established (Trolander, 1975). Settlement workers were key participants in the labor movement and in the push to enact public welfare statutes and civil rights statutes for blacks and immigrants. One important contribution the settlements made to the cause of civil rights for blacks was their aid in founding several important self-help organizations. In 1909 settlement workers helped create the National Association for the Advancement of Colored People. Its first meeting was held at Henry Street Settlement in New York. Of the thirty-five members on the executive committee, eight were settlement workers. In addition, settlement workers aided in forming the National Urban League in 1910 and participated as delegates to the 1921 Pan-African Congress held in London, Brussels, and Paris under the leadership of W.E.B. DuBois (Trattner, 1979).

At the same time another group of social workers was working with social problems on the other side of the person-in-situation equation. They sought to solve social problems by changing the individual. By the end of the Progressive Era, this type of social work was known as social casework. Although the social work techniques of administration, community organization, and group work can be traced to the settlements, workers there did not intentionally foster the development of technique. The settlement workers prided themselves on being pragmatists. They were skeptical of those seeking to develop methods and techniques. It was the caseworkers who began to chase the elusive status of "profession" and who consciously sought to meet its criteria, mainly that a profession have an expert technique that is uniquely its own.

Charity Organization Societies and the Beginning of Social Casework. After the Civil War private charities in America multiplied at a rapid rate. Many persons began to view the relief situation as excessive and chaotic. Relief workers began to argue for the elimination of outdoor relief and for the improvement of relief operations, particularly in regard to paying more attention to the individual needs of those helped and to coordinating the work of relief agencies. Experiments in systematizing and coordinating relief activities began in several areas of the country (Pumphrey and Pumphrey, 1961).

The destitution in Buffalo, New York, during the winter of 1876, and the inadequate relief situation, became a concern to Stephen Humphreys Gurteen, Assistant Minister of St. Paul's Church, and T. Guilford Smith, an active parishioner and rising businessman. The two decided to take steps to rectify the situation. As part of their plan, Gurteen spent the summer of 1877 in London observing the work of the Society for Organizing Relief and Repressing Mendicancy. When Gurteen returned to Buffalo, he and Smith established America's first Charity Organization Society (COS), forerunner of today's Family Service Associations. The COS movement spread rapidly. Seven additional societies were in operation by the end of 1879, and the movement had grown to ninety-two societies by 1892. "Phases of Charity," Gurteen's printed lectures, which sketched a consistent ideology for the movement, gained wide circulation. His *Handbook of Charity Organization* published in 1882, became its text (Lewis, 1977).

The COS movement addressed itself to urban destitution, the increase in poverty, and the potential for explosive conflict between social classes. It held that destitution could be reduced, hardship ameliorated, and mendicancy prevented by instituting a system of scientific charity, abolishing public relief, and replacing the existing chaos in almsgiving by systematically coordinated private philanthropy. The primary technique was "friendly visiting." This consisted of a wealthy volunteer befriending a needy family and through his or her example and guidance showing the family the way out of poverty. The COS motto was "not alms but a friend." Social harmony was supposed to result from the mutual respect that would develop as the well-to-do initiated reciprocal friendly relations with poor families. In addition to individual aid the COS's had other goals, such as promoting interagency cooperation and community education. Interagency cooperation was operationalized by registering cases. Every COS operated a community-wide registration bureau, the object of which was to ensure that each case got to the proper agency and to prevent the duplication of services and/or aid. In regard to community education the societies sought to educate "the poor and the rich in their respective duties to each other." The poor were to learn diligence, abstinence, and thrift, as basic to self-support; the rich were to give modestly of their money and generously of their time by participating in COS work (Lewis, 1977, p. 97).

Pumphrey (1959) has described the dual functions of social welfare programs as compassion and protection. Certainly there was a good deal of compassion involved in the work of the COS, but originally its function appears to have been mainly the protection of society against massive social upheaval. The middle and upper classes in America were becoming alarmed at the widespread social unrest they were witnessing. One writer near the turn of the century reported: "At the present time the social instinct, tending toward congestion in the urban centers, the influx of foreign elements, the non-assimilation or resistance of Americanizing influences, new industrial conditions, the failure or indifference of the church to its social mission, make the modern city a storm center" (Tolman, 1898,

p. 20). Scientific charity was felt to be the urban community's surest safeguard against revolution. Charity organizations represented an instrument of urban social control. Robert Treat Paine said that friendly visiting was the "only hope of civilization against the gathering curse of pauperism in the great cities" (Gettleman, 1975, p. 51).

In a manner similar to the settlements, the early charity organizations were staffed with a few paid employees and a larger number of volunteers. The employees, called *agents,* were low-paid, low-status technicians. The volunteers, called *friendly visitors,* were the decision making and "treatment" staff. The societies felt that paid employees lacked the spontaneity of volunteers. The paid worker could offer skill, but only the volunteer offered herself. It was this friendship between classes that was supposed to uplift the poor and avert the worst consequences of urban-industrial society.

There was a definite division of labor between the volunteer and the paid agent. Each district had a volunteer committee that kept records and formulated plans for each case. The agents made investigations, reported the results to the volunteer committee, and then carried out the committee's decisions. The volunteer friendly visitor assigned by the committee did not deal with the mundane business of relief, but rather offered the family friendship whereby she was supposed to uplift the family.

This early emphasis on the moral influence of the volunteer rather than on the skill of a paid specialist was a natural outgrowth of the societies' social philosophy. The COS people rejected the influence of the environment or the subconscious on the lives of people. It was felt that people were free agents who could control their destinies commensurate with their abilities and moral fiber. Any lapse into dependency was a result of intemperance, improvidence, indolence, ignorance, or some other personal defect. Thus, what was needed for the solution of social problems was not social but individual change, and the way to bring this about was friendly visiting. Also, what was needed for effective friendly visiting was not technical training or scientific understanding of human behavior, but moral insight.

In the years between 1877 and 1900, the role of the volunteer friendly visitor gradually diminished, and the role of the paid agent was upgraded, until at the turn of the century Mary Richmond was pushing for education for "the profession of applied philanthropy" (1897, p. 186). There were several reasons for the decline in the volunteer's importance and the increase in the importance of the paid agent. One reason was simply numbers. Since the number of cases requesting aid far outstripped the number of volunteers, only a small proportion of cases could be assigned to visitors.

Probably the main reason for the decline in friendly visiting was simply the contact of theory with reality. Because of extensive contacts with poor people, the COS movement was quickly forced to drop its cherished belief that poverty was the result of personal moral shortcomings. By the turn of the century, COS representatives realized that the causes of poverty were social, economic, and psychological rather than the result of personal moral failure. If moral failure was not the cause of poverty, then friendly visiting was not the solution. While volunteers continued to play an important role in charity organizations after the 1890s, they were gradually replaced in client contact positions by staff trained in methods of investigation and in the social sciences.

The Expansion of Social Casework. A special skill applied to a special function is a basic criterion of any profession. After 1900, in keeping with the general social trend toward professionalization, caseworkers made a concerted effort to limit, define, and clarify their particular knowledge and technique and to delineate a special function, beginning in charity organizations.

At the turn of the century, COS workers began to feel that they had a skill. This feeling was crucial to the development of professional education and identification. Also the feeling was prevalent that facts and more facts were needed and that case records should therefore be kept as a guide to the worker and an aid to seeking out the causes of poverty. Since adequate investigation and recording were tasks that required skill and training, it seemed clear that they should be done by professional staff. In keeping with this feeling COS agencies had been groping toward investigation techniques and methods of diagnosis and treatment that would result in an understanding of the unique problems of each client.

Prior to the early 1900s what is now known as social casework had been limited to children's aid and charity organization societies. However, along with reforms that recognized the important effects of the environment on different aspects of people's well-being, social work began to spread into new areas. "Employment in several institutions whose effectiveness had been limited by a failure to consider the social environment of clients or patients was a decisive episode in the development of social work as a profession. . . . The knotty problems of adjustment which social workers confronted in these institutions sparked a search for the expertise which differentiated them from other members of the staff and justified claims to professional status" (Lubove, 1965, p. 22).

In 1905 Dr. Richard C. Cabot introduced medical social work at Massachusetts General Hospital. He had wondered how much illness could be traced to social conditions such as "vice, ignorance, overcrowding, sweatshops, and poverty" (1909, p. 33). Cabot felt that the hospital did not really treat the sick, but only isolated physical symptoms. Often it failed to cure patients who returned to the environment that had produced the illness in the first place. He felt that social services would overcome the hospital's separation from the social roots of disease and contribute to the development of preventive medicine.

Medical social workers had to decide early if they were to identify with nursing or social work. Identifying with nursing would have been an obvious step, as many early medical social workers were trained nurses, and nurses already had an established place in the hospital. However, social workers set out to sever any ties they had with nursing for two reasons: (1) they felt that medical social work required different and special skills and (2) the nursing profession was clearly subordinate to the physician, and the medical social worker wanted to be the physician's equal.

The enlistment of medical social workers marked an important stage in the development of professional social work. Charity organizations and child welfare societies provided too narrow a base for a profession, and the settlements had few paid staff, most of them not particularly interested in professionalization. Medical social work added an entirely new institutional setting in which to explore the implications of casework theory and practice.

Shortly after Cabot introduced the first medical social work program, a second casework specialty emerged—school social work. Like the hospitals, schools felt they had lost contact with the child's environment, and reformers began to stress establishing such contact. Although school social work was a casework specialty, it received its initial impetus from settlements and civic organizations rather than from charity organizations. In New York in 1905 four settlements cooperated in sponsoring two visiting teachers for three school districts. By 1913 boards of education began to confer official status on visiting teachers. In 1921 school social work received an additional boost when the Commonwealth Fund decided to sponsor it in connection with its five-year program for preventing delinquency.

The progressive educator and the school social worker viewed the child as the key to the problem of urban social control. The ethnic and class divisions of urban society troubled the progressive generation no less than the nineteenth-century COS spokesman. In fact, the search for solutions to these problems was to a great extent the essence of progressivism. For the progressive generation the public school assumed special significance as an instrument of acculturation and social control. The visiting teacher's contact with the child in his own environment was the "logical place to detect symptoms of future inefficiency, whether they be departures from the mental, social, or physical standards" (Hodge, 1917, p. 225). Like medical social work, visiting teaching helped shape the social caseworker's image as being a skilled professional representing a social institution.

Just as Cabot, a physician, had taken the initiative in promoting medical social work, psychiatrists in rebellion against the prevailing institutional methods of care for the mentally ill worked to integrate therapy with environment. In conjunction with the mental hygiene movement, they substituted a clinical, empirical approach to mental illness for the institutionalization and custodianship of the nineteenth century. Prominent in this movement was Dr. Adolph Meyer, who envisioned the development of community mental health programs. The mental hospital would be the nucleus of the system, but it had to be "socialized" like Cabot's general hospital. Meyer felt that the cornerstone of success in the socialized mental hospital was the "organization of social work and home visitation" (Lubove, 1965, p. 60).

The development of specialists in medical, school, and psychiatric aspects of social work left no one responsible for the most important social institution—the family. It gradually dawned on charity workers that specialization had made them experts on family adjustment, and, as faulty adjustment to one's environment superseded moral defects as an explanation of dependency, they perceived their task to be the discovery of internal and external pressures that interfered with normal family life. Poverty came to be viewed as a symptom of a breakdown in family cohesion or of an unsatisfactory relation to other social institutions. Family casework stemmed from the friendly visiting of the charity organization societies. As it was not suddenly thrust into a host institution (hospital or school), it did not have the same stimulus to define its professional functions and knowledge base as did the other specialties.

Thus, by the end of the Progressive Era, four social work specializations had emerged related to what is now referred to as clinical social work. Medical, school, psychiatric, and family social work all shared a common core: they all were based on casework, they all emphasized changing the individual as the solution to social problems, and they all held the opinion that this could be done by developing an expert technique.

The Quest for Professionalization, 1915–1930. Although social workers in the settlements never developed a great interest in achieving professional status, persons working in the casework field became interested in it at a very early date. As early as 1897 Mary Richmond, a Charity Organization Society leader, said of persons entering charity work: "Surely, they have a right to demand from the profession of applied philanthropy (we really have not even a name for it) that which they have a right to demand from any other profession—further opportunities for education and development, and incidentally the opportunity to earn a living" (1897, p. 182). From the time of Richmond's paper until 1915, the move to professionalize social work slowly built momentum. Social casework began to be practiced in a variety of settings, and schools of social work began to emerge. The Russell Sage Foundation began to actively support the development of a profession of social work, financing the National Association of Societies for Organizing Charity, formed in 1911, and providing seed money for four schools of social work between 1907 and 1915. However, the professionalization movement did not achieve critical mass until 1915, when Abraham Flexner, famed critic of the medical profession, was asked by the National Conference of Charities and Corrections to study social work and analyze it as a profession.

Flexner began his report by clearly defining the concept "profession," something that had not previously been done in a satisfactory manner. He listed six criteria: "Professions involve essentially intellectual operations with large individual responsibility and learning; this material they work up to a practical and definite end; they possess an educationally communicable technique; they tend to self-organization; they are becoming increasingly altruistic in motivation" (1915, p. 581).

In several important criteria Flexner found social work lacking. The main source of its deficiency, he felt, was the broadness of its boundaries. Professions had to have definite and specific ends. However, "the high degree of specialized competency required for action and conditioned on limitation of area cannot possibly go with the width and scope characteristic of social work." Flexner felt that this lack of specificity seriously affected the possibility of professional training: "The occupations of social workers are so numerous and diverse that no compact, purposefully organized educational discipline is feasible" (1915, pp. 585–588).

Flexner's conclusion was that at the stage of development social work had reached in 1915 it could not legitimately be considered a profession. However, he voiced an optimistic, although cautionary, note at the end of his paper: "At the moment, therefore, . . . it may be that social work will gain if it becomes uncomfortably conscious that it is not a profession in the sense in which medicine and engineering are professions; that if medicine and engineering have cause to proceed with critical care, social work has even more" (1915, p. 590).

On the same program with Flexner, several leading social workers presented papers outlining their ideas as to how social work could correct the deficiencies outlined by Flexner and thereby achieve full professional status. Jeffrey Brackett of the Boston School for Social Workers, Edward T. Devine of the New

York School of Philanthropy, and George Mangold of the Missouri School of Social Economy all presented papers. Porter R. Lee, of the New York School, presented the report of the Committee on the Professional Basis of Social Work. The interesting fact is that all of these reports emphasized the individual treatment aspect of social work, and, while recognizing social work's involvement with social problems, relegated it to a position of secondary importance. The reports also stressed the necessity of developing an educationally communicable technique. These two areas of emphasis directly reflected the deficiencies identified by Flexner.

In the fifteen years between the Flexner Report and the onset of the Great Depression, social work rapidly professionalized and narrowed to a casework focus. A number of factors contributed to this, a major one being the swing to the right of American society following the First World War. Hofstadter has explained the reason for this shift as follows: "The war purged the pent up guilts, shattered the ethos of responsibility that had permeated the rhetoric of more than a decade. It convinced the people that they had paid the price for such comforts of modern life as they could claim, that they had finally answered to the full progressive demand for sacrifice and self-control and altruism. . . . The pressure for civic participation was followed by widespread apathy, the sense of responsibility by neglect, the call for sacrifice by hedonism" (1955, p. 273). In this atmosphere an approach to social problems aimed at changing the individual was more acceptable than one aimed at changing society; casework accordingly was emphasized by social workers.

Another reason for social work's movement toward an individual treatment approach following the Flexner Report was simply that caseworkers were interested in improving their professional status, and social reformers and settlement workers were not. Schools of social work offered few courses of interest to settlements, and those that did generally offered psychiatrically oriented group work. Only a few settlement workers had formal professional training or qualified for membership in the American Association of Social Workers (AASW). Furthermore, settlement leaders publicly belittled the importance of social work education, casework, and psychiatry. In their own national professional organization and in local federations in New York and Chicago, settlements continued to place more emphasis on social issues than on professionalization (Trolander, 1975, p. 47).

It was the caseworkers who concentrated on satisfying Flexner's criteria of professionalization. In 1917 the name of the National Conference of Charities and Corrections was changed to the National Conference of Social Work, to reflect what was felt to be its professional orientation. Also in 1917 Mary Richmond's book *Social Diagnosis* was published and was heralded as providing the theoretical base necessary to support casework's claim of professional expertise. Having seen the benefits professional organization had yielded for the medical profession, social workers formed the American Association of Hospital Social Workers in 1918, the American Association of Social Workers in 1920, the American Association of Visiting Teachers in 1922, and the American Association of Psychiatric Social Workers in 1924. These professional organizations, particularly the AASW, became the institutionalized vehicle for furthering the fulfillment of Flexner's professional criteria. In the 1920s the AASW concerned itself with defining the various specialized areas of social work through a series of job function studies. It actively began recruiting able young men and women into social work careers and became concerned with improving salaries and status, drawing up a code of ethics, and inaugurating special institutes and courses to upgrade the skills of workers already in the field. The AASW maintained an exchange for job placement, tried to define both the rights and the responsibilities of agency workers, and sought to establish objective standards for accrediting professional schools and certifying trained personnel (Chambers, 1967, p. 92).

Two important events accelerating social work's shift toward individual treatment were the concurrent discoveries of the opportunity to provide services to people above the poverty level and the application of psychoanalytic theory to social work practice. Shortly after America's entry into World War I, the American Red Cross set up a Home Service Division to provide casework services to uprooted soldiers and their families. Social workers in this setting quickly found themselves dealing with problems, such as war-induced neurosis, for which their experience gave no help. In a search for solutions they quickly joined up with psychologists and psychiatrists and discovered Freud. In 1918 Smith College established its School of Psychiatric Social Work to provide training for this specialty. While Richmond's *Social Diagnosis* and the casework practice based on it had emphasized external forces acting on the individual, the psychoanalytic approach emphasized internal forces. In 1918 Mary Jarrett predicted that casework was "about to pass into a psychological phase." In support of her argument that this was desirable she argued that 50 percent of the cases cited by Richmond in *Social Diagnosis* presented "clearly psychiatric problems" and another 15 percent suggested the possibility of a "psychopathic condition" (Lubove, 1965, p. 79). The conceptual attractiveness of psychoanalytic theory, plus the opportunity to work with physicians in a clinical setting, plus the fact that psychoanalysis provided the theoretical base Flexner had criticized social work for lacking, all furthered the dominance of the individual treatment approach in social work during the 1920s.

During the years that social work was professionalizing, another movement was occuring that was to have a profound effect on the institutional context of clinical social work. This was the movement toward financial federation—better known as the community chest. Federated funding began in America in 1887 with the creation of the Associated Charities of Denver. The idea did not catch on immediately, and it was not until World War I that a sizable number of "war chests" appeared to meet the emergency need for social services. Thousands of people never before considered able to participate in philanthropy gave small quantities of money, and the aggregate of these small gifts (along with some large gifts, of course) produced a level of support never before available to social services. After the war the same social climate characterized by belief in efficiency, rationality, and expertise that had supported social work professionalization was receptive to the idea of financial federation. Despite some resistance by social workers, the movement grew so rapidly that by the middle 1920s over two hundred cities had adopted the community chest idea.

The main effect of financial federation was that it centralized control of social services. Private funding of social agencies was placed under one central agency, and this agency tended to be controlled by the businessmen who were large givers. The result was that agencies became more conservative, because to advocate causes unpopular with the business community was to risk loss of funding from the local community chest, and with nearly all givers belonging to the chest, alternate sources of funds were very rare. In a study of the response of the social settlements to the Great Depression, Trolander found that manufacturers' associations advised their members to make contributions to community funds "contingent on the promise that no part of the contribution should be used to promote the passage of, or to carry on propaganda for, any 'social-service labor program'" (1975, p. 21). The net result of federated funding was to further push organized social work away from social reform and toward the individual treatment–casework model.

By the end of the 1920s social work was beginning to think of itself as a full-fledged profession based on a body of theory and skills related to individual treatment; only lip service was given to social reform. However, one problem remained: Was social casework one profession practiced in a variety of settings, or was it a series of loosely related professions? The Milford Conference, consisting of executives and board members who had been meeting periodically since 1923, released its report in 1929. This report reflected the determination of social work leaders to establish a group identity based on a generic skill. In summarizing its conclusion in 1929 it reported the "emergence of a strong conviction unanimously held by the members . . . that a functional conception which has come to be spoken of as 'generic social case work' was much more substantial in content and much more significant in its implications for all forms of social case work than were any of the specific emphases of the different casework fields" (American Association of Social Workers, 1929, p. 3). According to this conception, caseworkers differed not in purpose or in methodology but in administrative setting. Each setting required a measure of specialized knowledge and technique, but the "distinguishing concern" of all caseworkers was the "capacity of the individual to organize his own normal social activities in a given environment" (p. 16).

Thus by 1930 social work had become "professionalized," and this largely meant that it had come to define itself as being expert in individual treatment and not responsible for social reform. In less than a third of a century the evolution had been dramatic. In 1906 Edward T. Devine, in his presidential address to the National Conference of Charities and Corrections, had painted a broad responsibility for social work: "It is embodied in a determination to seek out and to strike effectively at those organized forces of evil, at those particular causes of dependence and intolerable living conditions which are beyond the control of the individuals whom they injure and whom they too often destroy. Other tasks for other ages. This be the glory of ours, that the social causes of dependence shall be destroyed" (1906, p. 15). By 1930 this view had been greatly altered, as can be seen from Miriam Van Waters's presidential address to the National Conference of Social Work: "Social work has realized that a program cannot make men moral, religious or happy. . . . The true springs of action are in the internal nature of man. Hence, the uselessness of programs, particularly those dependent upon State action or force" (1930, p. 19).

The Great Depression and the Development of Social Work in the Public Sector. The 1920s in the United States was a time of unprecedented prosperity: factories sought to turn out goods fast enough to meet demand; every month avid investors snapped up hundreds of millions of dollars in new securities; colleges and movie theaters were jammed. In this atmosphere President Hoover was able to say "we in America are nearer to the final triumph over poverty than ever before in the history of any land." But this triumph was not to come, for abruptly in October of 1929 the stock market crashed. By the end of 1929 the value of securities had shrunk by $40 billion. Hundreds of thousands of families lost their homes, millions of unemployed walked the street, and tax collections fell to such a low that school teachers could not be paid in many areas. The United States had faced depressions before, in 1837, 1873, and 1893, but these had each lasted only a few years. The Great Depression of 1929 was to last a full decade (Nevins and Commager, 1966, pp. 470–471).

President Hoover reacted to the depression with faith that natural forces in the economy would correct the situation if the government did not interfere. He did not entirely repudiate the responsibility of the national government to act, but he did hold firm to the English Poor Law principle that relief was exclusively the concern of private charity and local governments. Hoover's philosophy regarding the desirability of the federal government's engaging in welfare activities was summed up in his statement that "You cannot extend the mastery of government over the private lives of people without at the same time making it the master of their souls and thoughts." He therefore limited national government response to pumping money into businesses in the form of contracts for roads, public buildings, loans, and so forth, thinking this would stimulate the economy and aid the natural forces of recovery. His tactic for dealing with the crisis was graphically illustrated in December of 1930 when he approved an appropriation of $45 million to feed the livestock of Arkansas farmers but opposed an additional $25 million to feed the farmers. The natural forces that Hoover placed so much faith in did not work. By 1932 the number of unemployed was over twelve million, five thousand banks had closed, thirty-two thousand businesses had failed, and national income had declined from $80 billion to $40 billion.

By the time Franklin Roosevelt entered office in 1933, the economic situation was so bad that people were questioning whether the American system was viable any longer. Disorder was spreading and threats of revolution were heard. It is beyond the scope of this chapter to give even a superficial analysis of Roosevelt's New Deal programs. Suffice it to say that he quickly repudiated Hoover's doctrine of government nonintervention in the area of welfare. In the place of Hoover's doctrine Roosevelt substituted the philosophy he had developed as governor of New York and had implemented in that state under the Wicks Act. This philosophy was that people in need have a right to governmental aid because this aid is financed out of tax dollars paid when they were employed. Thus, receiving welfare payments was no different from sending children to public school or asking for police protection. Under this philosophy, with social worker Harry Hopkins as his assistant, Roosevelt implemented a wide range of public welfare programs, beginning with the 1933 Federal Emergency Relief Act (FERA) and culminating in the 1935 Social Security Act, a beginning, if incomplete, attempt of the federal government to assume responsibility for cradle-to-grave security for the citizens of the nation.

The direction in which social work had been heading for many years before the depression put the profession in a poor position for responding to the crisis.

For years most social workers had opposed the establishment of a public welfare system. Two factors went into this opposition. First, social workers generally believed that government agencies were corrupt, inefficient, and political and therefore were not settings conducive to providing high quality social services. Second, they felt that the existing network of private agencies was capable of meeting the dependency needs of American society. There were notable exceptions, such as Grace and Edith Abbott, Jane Addams, and Gertrude Vaile, but the majority of social workers, particularly in casework agencies, subscribed to these beliefs.

When the depression hit, the majority of poor relief came from private donations and was administered through private family service agencies. Aid was distributed on a highly individualized basis according to the old notion that economic dependency was a symptom of some basic individual deficiency requiring treatment. The coming of the depression had two rapid and profound effects on family service agencies. The first was that when private money ran low, as it quickly did, local governments began distributing aid through the family agencies. In less than a year after the crash, well over half of the aid distributed by private agencies came from public funds. The second was that the depression shocked social workers into realizing that social and economic forces were at the root of many of the problems they were dealing with. As Paul Kellogg, editor of *The Survey,* said, "You cannot deal effectively with an inferiority complex on an empty stomach" (Trattner, 1979, p. 238). His message was clearly that social workers needed to concentrate on social, political, and economic issues, as well as on understanding the psychology of the individual.

When the Federal Emergency Relief Act was passed in 1933 it changed the structure of social services in the United States. Immediately upon assuming office, Harry Hopkins, administrator of the act, formulated Regulation Number 1, which stated that all public money was to be administered by public agencies. This regulation effectively ended the relief-giving function of private social work agencies. Another provision of the FERA was that each local administrator was to employ at least one experienced social worker and at least one qualified supervisor for every twenty employees. The net effect of these regulations was to move a major social work function and a large number of social workers out of private and into public agencies.

This rapid change in the institutional context of social work created several problems for the profession. The first was that family agencies, historically the backbone of the profession, were stripped of one of their main functions, that of providing a range of services to families facing financial difficulty. The family agencies dealt with this problem by firmly embracing the growing interest in psychoanalysis and developing highly skilled "casework treatment to assist individuals in removing their own handicaps" (Axinn and Levin, 1975, p. 194). Another problem was that social workers had not been entirely incorrect when they had stated that large public agencies were not settings conducive to quality social services. The entry of social workers into the public sector brought them a whole new range of problems and created the need to study organizations and administration as well as traditional subjects in order to be effective professionals in the new arena.

The number of people employed in social work jobs doubled from forty thousand in 1930 to eighty thousand in 1940 (Trattner, 1979, p. 238). Most of the new positions were in the public sector and were filled by people with little, if any, social work training and experience. What should have emerged from the depression was a new social work, encompassing both public and private agencies and both professional and lower-level workers. Unfortunately, what happened is that two separate, but overlapping, professions emerged. Graduate social workers, while accepting public welfare as a legitimate field of practice, were unwilling to accept anyone without graduate training as a professional social worker. Welfare departments, however, did not have the funds to hire people with professional training and so were staffed mainly by B.A. graduates. These workers without professional training were not allowed into the professional association, and schools offering training on the undergraduate level were not accredited by the association of professional schools. As a result, public welfare workers generally joined unions, if they joined anything, and land grant colleges joined together and formed their own body for accrediting undergraduate programs. An even greater problem was that many professionally trained social workers felt that because welfare was now the responsibility of public agencies, the social work profession no longer needed to be concerned with it and could get back to what they perceived as the core of social work—the psychological adjustment of the individual.

The Return to Prosperity, 1940–1960. The Second World War brought an end to the depression that Roosevelt's New Deal programs had succeeded in ameliorating but not ending. In 1940 the gross national product (GNP) had increased to a level equal to the boom year of 1929. Between 1940 and 1960 the GNP increased fivefold. Population growth, which was minimal during the depression, also boomed. In the 1940s population grew by twenty-one million and in the 1950s by an additional thirty million, most of the increase due to the birthrate. Generally the era was characterized by optimism and prosperity, unfortunately accompanied by complacency and conservatism.

Social work during this era was characterized by a pulling back from large social issues such as public welfare and a return to a preoccupation with the problems of the individual and with developing techniques for dealing with these problems. There were many reasons for this trend. Many social workers felt that after the passage of the Social Security Act environmental problems were being dealt with by the political system and so they could return to concern with individual adjustment problems. Also, they shared the widespread belief in mass prosperity. Experts who should have known better, such as social workers and economists, believed that poverty was fast becoming a minor problem. In his best seller *The Affluent Society,* published in 1958, the economist John Kenneth Galbraith stated that America had essentially solved the problems of scarcity and poverty. This belief tended to make the poor invisible and concern with them seem remote and almost antiquarian.

In addition to the conditions that caused many social workers to abandon large social issues, there were also conditions that reinforced their interest in the individual psyche. The massive testing of military recruits during the war uncovered a startling number of psychological and educational problems. Wartime programs to deal with these problems illustrated the usefulness of psychological and social science knowledge. After the war the National Mental Health Act was passed (1946) and funded (1948), and in 1949 the National Institute of Mental Health was established. The institute encouraged research and training dealing with the individual causes and solutions to social problems. In the private sector social workers were also encouraged to look at the psychological roots of problems. The psychotherapeutic orientation that had begun in the 1920s found wide acceptance in the 1940s and 1950s, partly because this approach made sense not only to social workers but also to the people who supported social agencies. The general feeling could be summed up as a belief that "the social system works, therefore problems are due to some defect of the individual, therefore the appropriate approach is to find and cure the defect." In evidence, 85 percent of students in schools of social work during the 1950s chose casework as their major. This interest in individual counseling was reinforced by the fact that more and more persons above the poverty line were turning to social workers for help. A 1960 study of family service agencies revealed that 9 percent of clients were upper class and 48 percent were middle class (Leiby, 1978, p. 282).

Along with the return to a primary concern with individual treatment, graduate schools and graduate-trained social workers moved to consolidate and reaffirm their dominance of the social work profession. In the early 1940s, the social work unions died out, leaving the untrained or undergraduate-trained social workers without any association to represent their interests. In 1955, after a long period of negotiation and several years of a temporary association, seven associations of specialists merged to form the National Association of Social Workers (NASW). The majority of employees in the public sector, not having the M.S.W., were not welcome. In a similar fashion the National Association of Schools of Social Administration (NASSA), the accrediting body for undergraduate programs, and the American Association of Schools of Social Work, the graduate accrediting body, merged to form the temporary National Council of Social Work Education. The council sponsored a major study of social work education, the Hollis-Taylor report (1951), which recommended that social work training be confined to the graduate level. As a result the temporary association was replaced in 1952 by the Council on Social Work Education (CSWE), which accredited only graduate programs. The effect of the demise of the unions and NASSA and the rise of NASW and CSWE was to define less-than-graduate-trained social workers out of the profession.

While the main trend in the 1940s and 1950s was to move away from public welfare and toward a focus on individual treatment, there were events that prepared the way for social work to return to a concern with larger issues. In 1952 *Community Planning for Human Services* by Bradley Buell was published. This book was based on a comprehensive study of social work in St. Paul, Minnesota. The main finding was that 6 percent of the families served absorbed over half the services. But the services were not coordinated, each agency saw only a part of the problem, and no one tried to put it all together. Buell argued that the medical model, focusing on individuals, case by case, was inappropriate. A public health model was indicated—that is, an approach characterized by community-wide intervention directed toward a large number of cases (Buell and others, 1952, p. 9). Another event that moved the social work profession back toward public welfare was the passage of the 1956 Social Security Act amendments. These amendments stated that public assistance should provide services as well as money payments. Large federal expenditures were authorized to help states provide social services. Although no money was actually appropriated, it was clear that Congress felt that social workers should be involved in public welfare.

The 1960s—Social Work Broadens Its Scope. By the end of the 1950s the country was feeling restless and ready for a change. John F. Kennedy was campaigning for the presidency on the assertion that the country was stagnating and promised that he would get it "moving again" toward "new frontiers." Shortly after his election the 1960 census was completed and revealed that the country clearly had a need to get moving again. The census data revealed that the New Deal and the Second World War had not eliminated poverty as had been generally believed. Further, the data indicated that poverty was not restricted to people living in certain deprived areas or to members of certain groups, as Galbraith had asserted, but that it was ubiquitous. A number of books based on the new data made clear the extent of poverty, the most influential being Michael Harrington's *The Other America: Poverty in the United States* (1962).

In light of this "rediscovery of poverty," the federal government attempted to attack the problem from three different approaches under three different presidents during the sixties. Each approach had different specific effects on social work, but each contributed in its own way to widening the scope of the profession.

The approach of the Kennedy administration was embodied in Public Law 87-543, known as the Social Service Amendments, signed into law on July 25, 1962. This law grew out of the recommendations of the Ad Hoc Committee on Public Welfare, appointed by Health, Education, and Welfare Secretary Ribicoff in May 1961, and a report prepared by George Wyman at about the same time. Wyman was an administrator with experience in a wide variety of social welfare agencies including local, state, and federal as well as voluntary agencies. The Committee's and Wyman's recommendations were heavily influenced by advice from social workers and other experts who contended that providing intensive social services would rehabilitate and bring financial independence to the poor. The act provided increased federal support (75 percent) to the states to enable them to provide social services to recipients of public assistance. In reality the act represented a very old approach—providing individual services to help people lift themselves out of poverty, with little attention directed toward altering the social conditions that caused the poverty (Trattner, 1979, p. 255).

The Social Service Amendments rapidly increased the number of social workers in public welfare settings. Recommendation number 12 of the Ad Hoc Committee stated, "To make possible the rehabilitative services so strongly advocated [by the committee], the goal should be established—that one third of all persons engaged in social work capacities in public welfare should hold master's degrees in social work." Money was allocated for welfare departments to send employees to graduate school, and schools across the country began to incorporate additional public welfare content into their curricula.

When social workers advocated providing professional services to welfare recipients, they did so in the belief that these services would improve recipients' lives and would be judged on this basis. Unfortunately, Congress supported the services in the belief that they would help people become self-supporting, thereby reducing the welfare rolls, and judged them on this basis. After the passage of the amendments the welfare rolls rose at a faster rate than ever, making social workers suspect in policy makers' eyes and causing them to look for a new approach.

The new approach came in 1964 when, in his State of the Union Message, President Johnson called upon Congress to enact a thirteen-point program that would declare "unconditional war on poverty." In July of 1964 the Economic Opportunity Act established the Office of Economic Opportunity. The Act also created VISTA, the Job Corps, Upward Bound, the Neighborhood Youth Corps, Operation Heat Start, and the Community Action Program.

There were a number of reasons behind President Johnson's War on Poverty. One was pressure from the civil rights movement for an attack on hunger and poverty. An example of the intensity of this pressure was a march for "jobs and freedom" that brought two hundred thousand people to Washington, D.C., and culminated in a historic speech by Martin Luther King. The major reason, however, was probably the growing awareness of the extent of poverty in the United States and the continued growth of the welfare rolls, despite the Social Service Amendments. It is significant that the War on Poverty programs made no provision for social work services, placing faith instead in self-help activities encouraged by the Economic Opportunity Act's provision for "maximum feasible participation" of the poor.

Although social workers were originally ignored by policy makers involved in the war on poverty, they were soon brought in because program administrators and community residents felt a need for their competencies in community organization, administration, and direct work with clients. The demand for social workers skilled in approaches other than traditional casework quickly resulted in schools broadening their curricula to include more emphasis on macro interventions. As Axinn and Levin have said, "The thrust of the War on Poverty and particularly of community action programs moved many social workers, and the profession itself, from a therapeutic to a reform approach, from a psychoanalytic to a social science base" (1975, p. 247).

If anything, however, the War on Poverty programs were even less successful than the Social Service Amendments. Congress and taxpayers stuck to reducing welfare rolls as the primary criterion for success, and far from shrinking, the rolls increased at a record rate, more than one million persons being added between 1963 and 1966. In addition, the War on Poverty drew severe criticism for other reasons: mayors were upset because the federal government was funding programs over which they had no control; members of Congress were upset by lawsuits brought against government agencies by government-funded legal services; citizens were upset by the aggressiveness and hostility of the poor, who had found voice through the "maximum feasible participation" concept. As a result of these criticisms the Economic Opportunity Act of 1966 sharply curtailed community action.

Toward the end of President Johnson's term in office, the mood of the country began to drift to the right. In 1966, on the same day the new Economic Opportunity Act was signed into law, the Republicans gained fifty-one seats in Congress, mostly from liberal Democrats. In 1968 the Republicans added the White House to their list of victories. With the conservative mood of the country, sentiment grew for limiting "soft" services, such as casework and community action, and emphasizing "hard" services, such as daycare and work training programs. The Social Security Amendments of 1967 reflected this mood, setting up the Work Incentive Program and instituting a formula whereby a welfare recipient's grant was reduced by only a percentage of earned income when that person became employed. Also funded was daycare for welfare recipients who were employed or in training.

Along with the emphasis on so-called hard services came an emphasis on management and accountability. The high cost and low results of services provided during the 1960s challenged skeptics and critics. Not only was accountability to taxpayers demanded by public officials, but accountability to users of services was demanded from within the social work profession. The result was that the scope of social work continued to widen during the conservative years of the late sixties as schools broadened their curricula to include more work in administration, planning, and research.

Current Trends and Issues Effecting Clinical Social Work

At the beginning of this chapter the institutional context of social work was conceptualized as made up of three primary threads—public social welfare policy, private social welfare policy, and the profession of social work. As the historical survey has unfolded it has been shown that each of them has been affected by recurrent issues. Primary among these issues has been whether the focus of social work and social welfare should be on individual treatment or on social change; which services should be provided by the public sector and which by the private; and who can legitimately be considered a social worker in terms of practice setting and level of training. As we have moved through the seventies and into the eighties, these issues appear no closer to resolution than they were in our past.

Public Social Welfare Policy. The 1970s provided no massive breakthroughs in the area of social welfare policy. Most of the events were a continuation of trends already apparent in the 1960s. In 1969 President Nixon unveiled his Family Assistance Plan, which was intended to replace existing cash assistance programs with one unified, if stingy, minimum guaranteed annual income. The plan placed a premium on work and little emphasis on social services. It immediately ran into controversy and was eventually defeated except for one small part: the Supplemental Security Income program (SSI) that was enacted in October 1972 and went into effect on January 1, 1974. Under this program financial assistance to the elderly, the blind, and the disabled became 100 percent federal. The program is administered by the Social Security Administration and deals only with financial assistance; since the state still provides social services to these groups, the act has had little effect on social workers.

The enactment of Title XX of the Social Security Act in December of 1974 has had a much greater effect on social work. Under this act money is allocated to the states for the purchase of social services. The intent of Title XX was to unify separate social service programs, to transfer decision making to the states and communities, and to put a lid on the open-ended funding that has been the rule under other purchase-of-service programs. The ceiling was originally $2.5 billion, but was raised to $2.7 billion for 1980 and is scheduled to be increased by $100 million each year for the next five years. Under Title XX the federal government pays 75 percent of the cost of service and the state pays the other 25 percent.

Under Title XX the states must each submit an annual plan that shows how the money is to be used to meet federal program goals. These goals, arranged in a hierarchy, are (1) achieving economic self-support, (2) achieving self-sufficiency, (3) preventing or remedying neglect, abuse, and exploitation, (4) preventing inappropriate institutional care, and (5) securing institutional care when other forms of care are not appropriate. In addition the states must demonstrate that at least 50 percent of the services go to Aid to Families with Dependent Children (AFDC), SSI, or Medicaid eligible persons. Under Title XX a wide range of social services has been funded, and a great deal of money has been directed toward social work education and training.

Public social welfare policy continues to emphasize program management and accountability, although not to as great an extent as during the Nixon and Ford years. Chauncey Alexander makes the interesting assertion that federal emphasis on management has really been a ploy for attacking service objectives. He says the emphasis on management technology "has included such techniques as the reduction or elimination of ideologically undesirable services such as community action agencies and neighborhood health centers; the accusation of inefficiency of cost-productiveness; the substitution of administrative personnel for career professionals; the alteration of service objectives behind the facade of changes in management techniques . . . ; and disregard for consumers and professionals" (1977, pp. 844–845). Whatever the reason, social welfare organizations are being required to meet increasingly strict management guidelines in order to receive federal funds. This emphasis on management and accountability has an obvious effect on service: workers are being required to spend an ever increasing amount of time documenting their services, leaving less time to actually provide the services.

President Carter attempted a major public welfare reform when he unveiled the Jobs and Income Security Program on August 6, 1976, proposing that it become effective in October 1980. The plan proposed the sweeping abolition of the existing welfare system with its patchwork of benefits, including AFDC, food stamps, and SSI. These would be replaced with a two-tier system—a job program for those who were able to work, and an income maintenance program for those who were not. The proposal called for creating one million four hundred thousand job slots for persons able to work but unable to find jobs. The schedule of benefits was designed so that those finding work in the private sector would always be better off than those in public service jobs. Those unable to work would receive benefits from a single program. Unfortunately, President Carter became so quickly mired in political problems that his Jobs and Income Security Program was placed on the back burner, where it remained until he left office.

A significant trend over the past decade has been the separation of social services from eligibility determination in public welfare. In 1972 Health, Education, and Welfare regulations mandated that these functions be separate. Before the mandate both functions were generally performed by a social worker. Since the mandate the social worker only performs services, while eligibility is determined by nonprofessional technicians. This separation, along with SSI and Title XX, which have furthered the separation of services, has led some to speculate on the development of a completely free-standing social service system in this country, that is, one that has no connection to income maintenance. However, as Weaver

(1977, p. 1132) has pointed out, Title XX requires that 50 percent of services be given to welfare eligible persons, and the Title XX goals emphasize self-support. Thus, the historic link between services and cash assistance remains, and the criterion for success of public social service programs continues to be how many people get off the welfare rolls.

Private Social Welfare Policy. The history of social welfare in the last fifty years has been one of a steady decline in the proportion of social services provided by the private sector. In 1930 the voluntary sector provided almost all social service; by the 1970s the proportion provided by voluntary agencies had shrunk to less than 10 percent. The current situation can be illustrated by looking at children's services. A 1973 survey conducted by the National Center for Social Statistics revealed that 94 percent of children receiving services were receiving them from public agencies. Of the services provided to the remaining 6 percent by private agencies, one third were being purchased by public agencies. With government dominating social services, voluntary organizations are faced with two questions: What activities do they finance and how? (Murphy, 1977, p. 478).

An activity that is having a great effect on voluntary social welfare and partially forcing an answer to these questions is contracting for services by public agencies. This practice got a boost from the Nixon administration's "new federalism," which returned tax money to localities—to meet locally determined needs—through revenue sharing. Very little revenue sharing money was devoted to social services, but when Title XX was implemented in 1975 it established a form of special revenue sharing for the specific purpose of encouraging the states to furnish social services for low-income individuals and families. Although receiving government funds through contracting has been a great help to many agencies, it has also caused a number of problems. Levin indicates that the main ones are that agencies have found themselves in dire straits when government funds were withdrawn; contracts are subject to time limits and uncertain renewal; the government approach requires sophisticated management techniques and the ability to account for outcomes as well as for finances; and government funds are "provided to accomplish the purposes of government" (1977, p. 1578). Generally, government funding for voluntary agencies creates problems of program planning, management, integrity, and autonomy.

One of the traditional roles of voluntary agencies has been to encourage and sometimes goad government to perform its civic duties better and to pay closer attention to social needs. The government now pays so much attention to social needs that the voluntary sector is in something of a quandary over what its function should be. Coughlin (1966) has maintained that direct service is the primary role of voluntary agencies. The Volunteerism Project of the United Way concluded in its 1970 report that it is impossible for the voluntary sector to compete with the public sector in providing direct services. Instead the project committee felt that the responsibility of voluntary agencies is to provide leadership, develop new service methods, and enable millions of people to play a role in helping their neighbors. Even further away from direct services is Schorr's notion that social reform is the primary purpose of voluntary social welfare (1968, p. 253).

One of the clear trends of the 1970s and the foreseeable future is that voluntary agencies, like their public counterpart, will continue to be under much pressure to improve management and planning practices and to develop accountability mechanisms. Toward this end the United Way of America Service Identification System was introduced in the mid 1790s and updated a few years later. Local United Ways use this system to identify local needs, rank them, and direct funding toward agencies whose services fall under the high priority rankings. The purpose of this system is to direct funding toward community needs rather than toward agency needs. Another tool that has been developed is the book *Accounting and Financial Reporting—A Guide for United Ways and Not-for-Profit Human Service Organizations,* published by the United Way of America in 1974. The purpose of this guide is to persuade agencies to keep records in a way that makes it possible to prepare an annual report in accordance with uniform standards. Local United Ways have put pressure on agencies to adopt the standards.

Even more serious than the debate over the appropriate direction for voluntary service is the fear that the voluntary sector is perceived by many as an anachronism. In a report on private institutions, Alan Pifer president of the Carnegie Corporation of New York, expressed concern that a majority of citizens may "be quite content to see private institutions generally handed over to public control" (1970, p. 11). This concern is given substance by the slow growth in United Way campaigns, averaging less than 6 percent per year since 1965. When population growth and inflation are taken into account, the success of campaigns has actually declined. As voluntary agencies have historically been the settings most amenable to the practice of clinical social work, this lack of clarity of focus and apparent decline in support should be of great concern.

The Profession of Social Work. For most of its history the profession of social work has appeared to be heading in one direction. Although there have been minor shifts in emphasis, social work has moved steadily toward becoming an all graduate-trained profession whose main focus is providing skilled treatment to individuals. However, with the expansion of public programs, the expansion of the number of positions defined as social work but requiring only a bachelor's degree, and the pressure for an emphasis on community organization, social action, policy, and administration, social work has lost this focus. In the preface to the most recent *Encyclopedia of Social Work,* the editor states that "it may well be that the 1970s will be perceived as having been nondirectional" (Turner, 1977, p. vii). Kahn and Kammerman, in a paper read before an NASW Professional Symposium, refer to social work as a "profession in disarray" (1979, p. 3). And Minahan, in her first statement as editor of *Social Work,* reports that "searching for unity" is the profession's big issue (1978, p. 362). Prominent among the issues being debated in this search for unity are the issues that have been debated since social work emerged out of the settlements and the Charity Organization Societies: What is the level of preparation and qualification for a person to be considered a social worker? What types of practice constitute professional social work? And what legal regulation is appropriate and desirable for the practice of social work?

The issue of level of preparation and qualification of professional social workers has largely been resolved, although not to everyone's liking. In the early 1950s when NASW and CSWE were formed, it was with the clear idea that only persons with the M.S.W. degree were qualified to be professional social workers. The prevailing belief was that it was only a matter of time before there would be enough of them to fill all social work jobs. However, programs continued to expand at a rate faster than schools could turn out graduates, and by the mid 1960s it was obvious that there would never be enough M.S.W.'s to staff all direct services. The number of M.S.W.'s in practice doubled during the 1960s, from twenty-six thousand to fifty-two thousand, but they remained less than one fifth of the total direct service staff in social agencies. In 1970, after a long struggle, NASW began admitting persons with bachelor's degrees as members, and in 1974 CSWE began to accredit undergraduate social work programs. Persons opposed to these changes have pointed out that social work is the only profession ever to lower its entrance requirements and that by doing so the status and effectiveness of the profession has been damaged.

What the appropriate focus of the social work profession should be is another subject of current debate. After two decades of almost exclusive focus on individual treatment, social work swung sharply in the direction of reform in the 1960s. Social workers began taking jobs with social action groups; community organization specializations in schools of social work boomed; NASW altered its bylaws to state that the profession has a dual obligation to use "both social work methods and . . . social action" to prevent and alleviate "deprivation, distress, and strain." The association also hired a lobbyist and appointed a committee to devise methods of translating data from practice into social policy. The movement toward social action hit its zenith in 1970 when Chauncey Alexander, Executive Director of NASW, stated that "as a profession we have recognized that we must change our basic societal institutions" (1971, p. 2), and the Community Service Society of New York, one of the nation's oldest social agencies, announced that it was discontinuing casework services. The Executive Secretary of COS, Dr. James G. Emerson, stated, "If you don't deal with the pathology of the ghetto, all the individual counseling you do with a person is not going to help" (Trattner, 1979, p. 266). Although the interest in reform has subsided a great deal in the conservative years of the 1970s, the focus of social work on so-called macro methods has been sustained through an increasing interest in management and planning techniques. A survey by Kazmerski and Macarov found that in 1966 only 16 percent of graduate schools of social work offered concentrations in administration and management, that by 1970 this had increased to 30 percent, and that by 1975 it had increased to 50 percent (1976, p. 2). Also, federal policy has changed to allow the use of federal training funds to develop management training programs for upper and middle managers in the public social services.

The macro focus of social work, particularly the reform focus, has created a good deal of controversy. Many persons have argued that social reform is the responsibility of every citizen and cannot be claimed as the responsibility of any one profession. Others, such as Specht, have argued that social work's rather naive efforts at reform have alienated many supporters and may eventually result in the "deprofessionalization of social work" (1972, p. 4). The focus on management, because of its obvious necessity and conservative nature, has created less controversy. Nevertheless, many within the profession feel that management and planning cannot be justified as unique social work methods and probably should be left to schools of business and public administration.

An issue related to both level of preparation and focus of the profession is licensing. Beginning in the 1930s there has been some interest in regulating social work legally. There are two sets of reasons for this interest. The first set has to do with protecting the public and consists of arguments that social work is a technical specializaton that can result in great harm if practiced by people without proper qualifications. Because of this, the argument goes, the government under its mandate to ensure public safety should assume the responsibility of regulating social work services. The second set of reasons has to do with enhancing the status of the profession. Licensing would increase the status of the profession, protect its domain against competition, and make social workers and agencies eligible for third-party vendor payments. This latter point becomes increasingly important as health insurance programs expand and proposals for a national health insurance program proliferate. Most health benefits programs—Medicaid is a good example—will directly pay for services only if they are provided by a licensed practitioner. In 1973 NASW developed a model licensing bill and recommended that state chapters use it in developing their own proposed statutes. The model statute recommends three levels of licensure based on educational qualifications: certified social worker (with M.S.W. or higher degree), social worker (B.S.W. degree), and social work associate (junior college degree). An examination in addition to educational criteria is recommended (NASW, 1973). Currently, social work is regulated by law in twenty-five states. Licensing has come under attack from persons who feel that it is elitist and is being advocated to exclude people from the profession inappropriately. On the other hand, it has come under attack from those who feel it is not exclusive enough, that there is no reason to include B.S.W.'s and junior college graduates. The feeling is that these people provide only routine services under close supervision (that is to say, nonprofessional services) and that licensing should only cover those with the M.S.W. degree who provide individual treatment.

The issues discussed above have led to one of the most serious schisms to hit social work since the depression, when bachelor-level workers joined unions and graduate social workers joined one of the professional associations. During the 1960s people interested in traditional psychodynamic casework became more and more alienated from the profession as it moved to lower entrance requirements, broaden the definition of social work, and even recommend licensing people who were previously not considered eligible to join the professional association. In 1969 this dissatisfaction led to the formation, in California, of the first Society of Clinical Social Work. The next year a society was formed in New York, and by 1977 there were societies in twenty states. These are all independent organizations affiliated with the National Federation of Societies of Clinical Social Work. Generally these groups feel that social action is a personal, not a professional duty, that "to confuse professional practice with social action is to prejudice by identification rather than afford the perspective necessary for clinical interaction" (J. Alexander, 1977, p. 365). They feel that the development of the generic curriculum and B.S.W. programs has watered down the quality of social work education. Alexander goes so far as to argue that clinical social work should split off from the rest of the profession, because different interests and practice methods "have differentiated us from those who were our peers. We are related to them, but no longer the same as them. The direct service advocates and the indirect service adherents, traveling in different directions, relating to diverse goals, and trained in separate methods, have evolved into two different professional entities bearing as many differences as similarities. If this is so, I would like to conceive of our parting not as a schism, but as an unfolding of differentiated professionals and professions each having its own validity" (p. 366).

The social work profession has been quick to recognize and respond to the threat posed by the secession of clinical social workers. Richan stated that "this issue of professional cohesion is paramount, if social work is to deal with its other problems" (1973, p. 161). In 1971 the Executive Director wrote to the membership of NASW about the need for professional unity: "Probably the most persistent obstacle to social work unity that we note from the national office vantage point is the dichotomy of clinical practice versus social action. NASW has made much headway in the last year in combating this destructive polarization, but old experiences and attitudes die hard" (C. Alexander, 1971, p. 10). This statement has been followed up by concrete action such as the establishment of a Registry of Clinical Social Workers by NASW. At the present time it appears that the rift between clinical social work and other specializations is closing and that we will face the problems of the 1980s as a unified profession.

References

Addams, J. *Twenty Years at Hull House.* New York: Macmillan, 1938.

Alexander, C. A. "From the Director: Enigma of Unity," *NASW News,* 1971, *16* (10), col. 1.

Alexander, C. A. "Management of Human Service Organizations." In J. B. Turner (Ed.), *Encyclopedia of Social Work.* (17th ed.) New York: National Association of Social Workers, 1977.

Alexander, J. "Organizing for Excellence." *Clinical Social Work Journal,* 1977, *5,* 363–366.

American Association of Social Workers. *Social Casework Generic and Specific. A Report of the Milford Conference.* New York: American Association of Social Workers, 1929.

Axinn, J., and Levin, H. *Social Welfare—A History of the American Response to Need.* New York: Dodd, Mead, 1975.

Buell, B., and others. *Community Planning for Human Services.* New York: Columbia University Press, 1952.

Cabot, R. C. *Social Service and the Art of Healing.* New York: Moffat, Yard and Company, 1909.

Chambers, C. *Seedtime of Reform—American Social Service and Social Action, 1918–1933.* Ann Arbor: University of Michigan Press, 1967.

Coughlin, B. J. "Interrelationships of Governmental and Voluntary Welfare Services." In K. Close (Ed.), *Social Welfare Forum.* New York: Columbia University Press, 1966.

Davis, A. F. *Spearheads for Reform: The Social Settlement and the Progressive Movement, 1890–1914.* New York: Oxford University Press, 1967.

Devine, E. T. "Presidential Address." In *Proceedings of the National Conference of Charities and Corrections.* Chicago: The Conference, 1906.

Flexner, A. "Is Social Work a Profession?" In *Proceedings of the National Conference of Charities and Corrections.* Chicago: The Conference, 1915.

Galbraith, J. K. *The Affluent Society.* Boston: Houghton Mifflin, 1958.

Gettleman, M. E. "Philanthropy as Social Control in Late Nineteenth Century

America: Some Hypotheses and Data on the Rise of Social Work." *Societas,* 1975, *5,* 49–59.
Harrington, M. *The Other America: Poverty in the United States.* New York: Macmillan, 1962.
Hodge, L. H. "Why a Visiting Teacher?" In *Addresses and Proceedings of the National Education Association,* 1917.
Hofstadter, R. *The Age of Reform: From Bryan to F.D.R.* New York: Knopf, 1955.
Hollis, E., and Taylor, A. *Social Work Education in the United States.* New York: Columbia University Press, 1951.
Institute of Community Studies. *Citizen Action on Urban Problems—Report of the Voluntarism and Urban Life Project.* New York: United Way of America, 1970.
Kahn, A. V., and Kammerman, S. B. "The Personal Social Services and the Future of Social Work." Paper presented at the NASW Professional Symposium, San Antonio, November 1979.
Kazmerski, K. J., and Macarov, D. "Administration in the Social Work Curriculum." New York: Council on Social Work Education, 1976.
Leiby, J. *A History of Social Welfare and Social Work in the United States.* New York: Columbia University Press, 1978.
Levin, H. "Voluntary Organizations in Social Welfare." In John B. Turner (Ed.), *Encyclopedia of Social Work.* (17th ed.) New York: National Association of Social Workers, 1977.
Lewis, V. "Charity Organization Society." In J. B. Turner (Ed.), *Encyclopedia of Social Work.* (17th ed.) New York: National Association of Social Workers, 1977.
Lubove, R. *The Professional Altruist—The Emergence of Social Work as a Career.* Cambridge, Mass.: Harvard University Press, 1965.
Minahan, A. "Social Work Unity: Yesterday and Today." *Social Work,* 1978, *24,* 362–363.
Murphy, M. J. "Financing Social Welfare: Voluntary Organizations." In J. B. Turner (Ed.), *Encyclopedia of Social Work,* 1977, *17,* 478–484.
National Association of Social Workers. *Legal Regulation of Social Work Practice.* Washington, D.C.: National Association of Social Workers, 1973.
Nevins, A., and Commager, H. S. *A Short History of the United States.* New York: Knopf, 1966.
Pifer, A. "The Jeopardy of Private Institutions." *Annual Report.* New York: Carnegie Corporation, 1970.
Pumphrey, R. E. "Compassion and Protection: Dual Motivations in Social Welfare." *Social Service Review,* 1959, *33,* 21–29.
Pumphrey, R., and Pumphrey, M. (Eds.). *The Heritage of American Social Work.* New York: Columbia University Press, 1961.
Richan, W. C. "The Social Work Profession and Organized Social Welfare." In A. J. Kahn (Ed.), *Shaping the New Social Work.* New York: Columbia University Press, 1973.
Richmond, M. E. *Social Diagnosis.* New York: Russell Sage Foundation, 1917.
Richmond, M. E. "The Need of a Training School in Applied Philanthropy." In *Proceedings of the National Conference of Charities and Corrections.* Chicago: The Conference, 1897.

Schorr, A. L. *Explorations in Social Policy.* New York: Basic Books, 1968.

Specht, H. "The Deprofessionalization of Social Work." *Social Work,* 1972, *17,* 3–15.

Tolman, W. "Association for the Improvement of the Conditions of the Poor Notes." Vol. 1. February 1898.

Trattner, W. I. *From Poor Law to Welfare State—A History of Social Welfare in America.* (2nd ed.) New York: Free Press, 1979.

Trolander, J. A. *Settlement Houses and the Great Depression.* Detroit: Wayne State University Press, 1975.

Turner, J. B. (Ed.). *Encyclopedia of Social Work.* (17th ed.) New York: National Association of Social Workers, 1977.

Van Waters, M. "Presidential Address." In *Proceedings of the National Conference of Social Work,* 1930.

Weaver, E. T. "Public Assistance and SSI." In J. B. Turner (Ed.), *Encyclopedia of Social Work.* (17th ed.) New York: National Association of Social Workers, 1977.

United Way of America. *Accounting and Financial Reporting—A Guide for United Ways and Not-for-Profit Human Service Organizations.* Alexandria, Va.: United Way of America, 1974.

Section II

Theories for Producing Change

Ann Hartman
Section Editor

To attempt an overall conceptualization or framework for the organization of theory for clinical social work practice, one must be brave, foolhardy, or very naive. In fact, a little of each would probably help to meet the challenge posed in this section. Siporin (1979, p. 76) has commented that "the theoretical paradigm for clinical social work is in a state of disarray." Certainly, as one considers the range, number, and variety of theoretical perspectives that support clinical social work practice, this disarray would seem inevitable. Social workers draw on theory from the social sciences, particularly from sociology, social psychology, anthropology, and psychology. They draw from theories about the environment, about mankind's biological nature, and about the transactions between the biological and psychological person and the environment. And, as theoretical perspectives and knowledge in the relevant physical and social sciences become more diverse, so does the theory that may inform our practice.

Yet another source of knowledge and theory has added to our riches but also to our disarray. Practice theories developing in different schools of therapy are also finding their way into clinical social work. Such therapies include transactional analysis, Gestalt, rational emotive, reality, behavior modification, bioenergetic, existential, and Zen, to name but a few.

There are many divergent perspectives within clinical social work practice itself. In 1969, the Charlotte Towle Symposium explored some of these perspectives. These explorations were published in Roberts and Nee (1970), *Theories of Social Casework,* and seven different approaches, models, or bodies of practice theory were identified and described in some detail. They were the psychosocial approach, the functional approach, the problem-solving model, behavior modification, family therapy, crisis intervention, and the socialization model. Presenting their positions were major proponents for each practice perspective, namely, Florence Hollis, Ruth Smalley, Helen Harris Perlman, Edwin Thomas, Frances Scherz, Lydia Rapoport, and Elizabeth McBroom. This meeting was a milestone in the history of clinical practice theory development and in the sociology of knowledge of the profession. In her summary, Bernice Simon remarked about the great diversity in casework theory. She reported that "a goal of unitary theory is probably not appropriate or healthy for the development of practice that must address itself to a myriad of difficult baffling, and little understood human problems" (Roberts and Nee, 1970, p. 393).

Four years later, in his first edition of *Social Work Treatment: Interlocking Theoretical Approaches* (1974), Francis Turner identified fourteen thought systems in social work treatment. In his second edition, published in 1979, ten years after the Charlotte Towle Symposium, the number had grown to nineteen. With the exception of socialization theory, all the perspectives presented in the Symposium were also included in Turner's book.

In a recent essay review of six books on practice theory, Siporin (1979) writes, "We need a model, a coherent potent theoretical framework and set of helping procedures addressed specifically to the specialized practice of clinical social work" (p. 77). Whether such a goal is indeed desirable can be argued. However, a review of clinical social work practice literature tells us that we are very far from that point. In fact, the trend seems to be toward increasing diversity rather than integration and unity.

In the context of such a rich and disorderly picture, this section on theory for clinical social work practice was developed. A somewhat different route has been taken in the organization and conceptualization of this material and thus, for it to be understandable, some explanations and definitions are necessary. First, in developing a framework for presenting theories for clinical practice, it seemed important to have in mind some conception, tentative definition, or description of clinical social work practice itself. This definitional issue has generated a great deal of lively discussion over the years and was recently the focus of a 1978 national symposium in Denver, sponsored by the National Association of Social Workers (Cohen, 1980). A wide range of views were presented and discussed, and, although certainly no agreement was reached or single perspective developed, Cohen's account of the work of the NASW Task Force on Clinical Social Work represented a useful synthesis for many. As reported by Cohen, the task force proposed that "the practice of clinical social work involves a wide range of psychosocial services to individuals, families, and small groups in relation to a variety of human problems in living. . . . At least three major principles by which clinical social work produces change or maintenance of function can be identified. Such goals can be reached through the interpersonal relationship with the clinician; they can be brought about through alterations in the social situation; they can be brought about through alterations of relationships with significant persons in the life space of the individual" (p. 26). This familiar description can help guide our thinking about theory for practice.

Perhaps the initial key task in conceptualizing theory for social work practice is that of establishing boundaries around the unit of attention. Following Cohen's definition, the clinical social worker's unit of attention includes, as has historically been the case, the person in the situation, the human being in his or her life space. Establishing this definition of the unit of attention also indicates the parameters of the knowledge and theory that are considered to be relevant to practice.

The second concept in need of clarification is that of theory. Hearn (1958) has defined theory as "an internally consistent body of verified hypotheses" (p. 8). He warns, however, that such verification should always be considered provisional. In fact, Hearn supports a "searching attitude which would regard theory as tentative and would hold, therefore, that present theory should be used only as policy . . . as the present best basis for action and decision" (p. 9). Joel Fischer (1978) emphasizes that theory is explanatory and relates to the relationships between variables. Webster's original definition of *theory* is "a mental viewing." *Theory* in this sense is defined as "a mental plan of the way to do something." This action statement holds particular appeal in thinking about theory for practice, for doing.

To summarize, the objective of this section of the handbook is to present the principles and the relationships between those principles that comprise and support mental plans for the practice of clinical social work.

Clinical Practice Theory as Change Theory

Clinical practice is devoted to bringing about planned change. As Fischer (1978) has pointed out, "The fact that caseworkers . . . increasingly are adopting the use of the term *intervention* . . . suggests increasing acceptance of the notion that caseworkers do, in fact, take an active role in planning and carrying out action to influence the behavior, activities, and/or situations of others" (p. 59).

By *change* is meant "an alteration in an existing field of forces" (Bennis, Benne, and Chin, 1961, p. 315), or, less cryptically, change is considered to have occurred when some aspect or aspects of a situation are in some way different at one point in time than they were at a previous point in time. The concept of difference is repeatedly used in outcome research and in efforts to establish accountability systems in clinical social work practice. The final enquiry is usually some form of the question "Did it make any difference?"

Of course, there are different kinds and rates of change. Therapeutic change can be seen as taking place slowly or incrementally through, for example, long-term supportive treatment models or in "open growth" family treatment approaches. Or, change may be rapid and dramatic, as sometimes occurs in crisis intervention or in strategic approaches to family therapy. In fact, one of the ways clinicians differ is in their views of the parameters, durability, and foci of change efforts.

Furthermore, for some, maintenance, which is frequently the goal of clinical practice, is not considered change. However, maintenance is not usually aimed at the continuation of the status quo but at the support and stabilization of a situation that has been under threat of dissolution or collapse. Enhancing the stability of a situation and ameliorating the stressors that are undermining it can certainly be considered a change process.

Change, however, to be an outcome of a professional intervention, must be a planned process. The professional planning of change must be informed by principles and procedures systematically derived from an identified body of knowledge (Fischer, 1978) and must be guided by clearly enunciated values. Planned change should include a fact-gathering and assessment process, specified goals and objectives, and interventive strategies that are related to the assessment, the knowledge base, and the desired outcome. Theories for clinical practice, then, can be thought of as those propositions and prescriptions that give direction to assessment and guide the selection of particular interventive strategies to achieve desired outcomes. In the last analysis, theory for clinical practice is at least to some extent theory about change. Thinking about clinical theory as change theory leads one to examine clinical practice by asking the following questions:

1. What are the instruments or resources for change that clinical social workers use in their change efforts?
2. What aspect of the person–situation complex is mobilized in the change effort?
3. What sources of power are tapped?

The following vignette serves to illustrate.

David, age 10, is having difficulty learning in school. Let us assume that the goal or objective of intervention is the enhancement of his learning. Different clinical social workers, although agreeing on the identification of the problem and the desired outcome, may use very different resources for change and varying interventive strategies to achieve the desired objective. Such change strategies may include individual play therapy with the child, referral to a big brother program, coaching the teacher in the use of behavioral techniques in the learning situation, family therapy, group therapy with several boys having the same difficulties, work with school administration, teachers, and parents toward the amelioration of stressful tensions in the school environment, or arranging for a volunteer teenage tutor for David.

In each of these interventive strategies, different resources for change are mobilized and brought to bear on "the system of David in his life space." These resources include the environmental context, new life experiences, the family, a group, a therapeutic relationship and opportunities for enhanced insight into his situation, new learning opportunities, and planned reinforcements.

This example leads to the notion that different approaches in clinical practice might be characterized or identified by the alternate resources for change that are used.

Using the resource for change as the major criterion for the development of a typology of practice approaches has a precedent in social work practice theory building. Mary Richmond's famous typology divided casework practice into the use of the environment and "action of mind upon mind" (1921, p. 102). In 1948, Lucille Austin, in her landmark article "Trends in Differential Treatment in Social Casework," added a third category based on the resource for change, which she called "experiential therapy." Describing this kind of intervention, she writes (1948, p. 331) that "change is brought about through the use of the transference as the dynamic for providing a corrective emotional experience and through stimulating growth experiences in the social reality."

The chapters that follow explore theories that support the use of eight different resources for change within the person–situation complex. The discussion is not meant to be comprehensive. There is also considerable overlapping of topics, which may at times be considered duplication or may contribute to integration of different perspectives.

The underlying view that leads to the development of these resources is that the person-in-situation is an immensely complicated transactional system. An analysis of that person–situation complex reveals a series of subsystems and subsystems of subsystems, any one of which may become the focal point and resource for bringing about change. A systems view tells us that change in one subsystem will reverberate and bring about change throughout the system and that different kinds of interventions may bring about similar outcomes. Thus, to return to our case example of David, it is possible, or even likely, that any of the interventions described could result in the improvement of David's learning.

The following resources for change will be considered: the environment, life experience, the group, the family, the worker–client relationship, learning, cognition, and insight. Figure 1 is a visual representation of the person–situation system, with the resources for change specified. Clearly, these resources are not mutually exclusive categories or specific models of change. They are, rather, resources that can be used singly or in combination to make a difference in the person–situation system.

The linkages among the various resources that can be used to bring about change are multiple. For example, the worker–client relationship, as a necessary if not sufficient part of the change effort, will usually occur in conjunction with the use of other resources. Cognitive change may be a major resource in work with groups and with families, as in the case of reframing. Furthermore, there are important linkages between cognition and learning. Behavior assignments (learning strategies) are frequently used in family or in group treatment, and the fulfillment of these assignments becomes an important part of life experience. There are strong linkages between learning and the environment, as most meaningful learning experiences take place through alterations of some aspect of the environment. There are also important linkages between insight development and the worker–client relationship, in that frequently insight develops through a growing understanding of the client's unconsciously motivated responses to the worker.

In asking the authors of the following chapters to present theory supporting the use of different resources for change, the following questions were suggested. Although there was no effort to impose an outline to limit the explorations of the writers, the questions do define issues that arise when clinical practice theory is conceptualized as change theory. The questions were:

1. What is the nature of the resource or instrument of change?
2. What is the relationship between that resource or instrument and the client or the client's psychosocial functioning?
3. How and why is it that the resource for change has such power to alter or enhance the client's psychosocial functioning?
4. What does the preferential use of this resource for change say about the nature of human beings?
5. How and why is it that the clinical social worker may have access to this source of power for change?

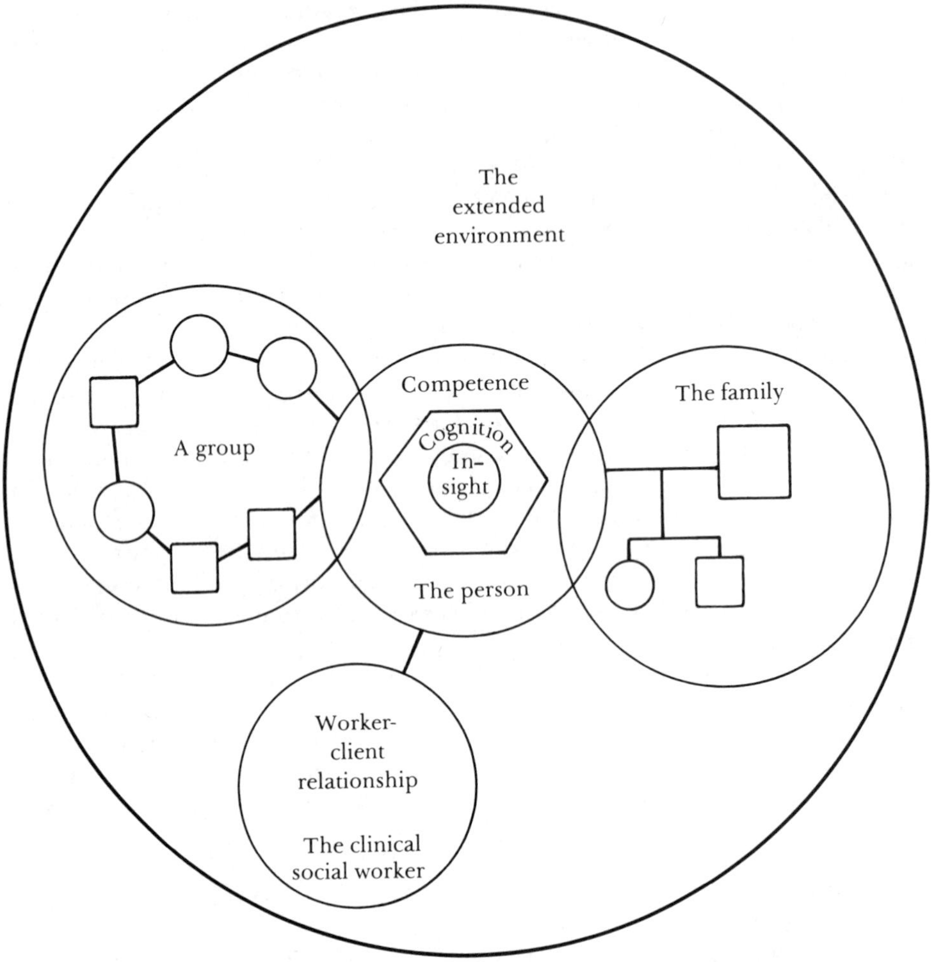

Figure 1. The Unit of Attention in Clinical Social Work—Potential Resources for Change.

6. What practice theory propositions guide the use of this resource for change? This question includes propositions about when, how, why, and with whom this resource for change should be used.
7. What is the current state of research on the theory supporting use of this resource or instrument for change? To what extent has it been tested or demonstrated? What areas are fully developed? What areas are in need of development?
8. What are the strengths and particular contributions of this theoretical base?

Most of these questions have been dealt with, at least to some extent, by the authors. Considering these questions may help the reader to compare and integrate the extensive and rich excursions into the theory base for clinical practice that follow.

Theory for Clinical Practice

In Chapter Five, Carel Germain summarizes current theory about the environment. Social workers have always used the environment as a resource for change, usually through environmental manipulation or the delivery of services. Historically, the environment has been seen as affecting the individual but relatively separate from the individual. Although social workers have always been concerned with the relationship between the person and the environment, until the development of systems theory, we have not had the conceptual tools to describe that complex transactional relationship.

Germain, in her application of an ecological perspective to social work, has focused on the person–environment transaction. Drawing from ecology, biology, ethology, and other life sciences as well as from organizational theory, she characterizes major aspects of the physical environment, both natural and built, and the social environment. She also describes the importance of culture in shaping the social and built environments and in the perception and meaning of the natural environment. Using the concepts of adaptedness, stress, and coping, she examines the reciprocal, transactional relationships between people and environments and the importance of "goodness-of-fit" between people and environments. In describing both nutritive and noxious elements in the physical and social environments, she suggests that the restoration of goodness-of-fit between person and environment is an appropriate and important change strategy for clinical social workers. She also points to the organizational environment and its power in defining and altering the way clinical services are delivered. In changing the nature of those services, she emphasizes the clinical social worker's role in understanding how his or her practice is affected by the organizational context. At times, the most effective and far-reaching effort for change on the part of a clinical social worker may be directed at that very organizational structure.

The restoration of "goodness-of-fit" between clients and their environments, including the organizations in which they are served, can only grow out of an understanding of the dynamic reciprocal transactions that occur between people and their world.

By including the built and natural physical environment within the areas of concern to the clinical social worker, Germain has expanded the boundaries around the unit of attention. Although the NASW Task Force's definition of *clinical social work* includes the social environment, no mention was made of either the built or the natural physical environment. These concepts are important aspects of an ecological perspective, and they provide additional interventive opportunities and resources for change through, to mention only two examples, the use of resources in nature and manipulation of spatial arrangements in the delivery of service.

In Chapter Six, Anthony Maluccio presents theory supporting the use of life experience as a resource for change. Underlying his position is the assumption that human beings are striving, active organisms who are fundamentally motivated to seek stimulation, to cope with challenge, to accomplish, to master, to feel competent and self-determining. In the tradition of Austin's third or "experiential" category of intervention, Maluccio, focusing with Germain on the relationship between person and environment, describes the theory that can give direction to the planned and conscious use of life experiences to afford clients opportunities for the enhancement of a sense of competence and a strengthened sense of self.

While Germain focuses primarily on the environment when examining the potential for change in person–environment transactions, Maluccio focuses on the person in transaction with that environment. Calling on the work of ego theorists Hartmann, White, Rapaport, Erikson, and Gladwin, among others, Maluccio explores adaptation, autonomy, and competence as concepts with biological, psychological, social, and cultural significance. He points to the interdependence of these three concepts and to the fact that adaptation, autonomy, and competence are strongly influenced by learning through life experience.

At the heart of Maluccio's position is the view that change may take place through the planned provision of life experience or the conscious exploitation of life events for learning. Mastery growing out of such experience leads to an enhanced sense of identity and self-esteem, which in turn strengthens motivation and confidence in facing new and increasingly complex life tasks.

Much of human life is lived in groups, and Charles Garvin, in Chapter Seven, explores theory supporting the use of natural and formed groups as resources for change. Closely related to Maluccio's discussion of life experience, Garvin's discussion indicates that group membership can provide clients with new, corrective, or enriching experiences through which they can grow and change. Garvin believes that group practice should be firmly integrated into clinical practice, both for enhanced socialization of clients who wish to search out new ways of attaining goals and of assuming new roles and for resocialization of clients who have been defined as deviant and need the opportunity to acquire new behaviors, coping strategies, and alternative roles.

Turning to social science theory and to practice theory, Garvin explores the sources of power for change that can be found in a group. Such sources include the power of group cohesiveness (which motivates group members to give up certain behaviors and attitudes to retain membership in the group), the importance of association with others in the development of self-worth and identity, and the effectiveness of the group in developing problem-solving and goal-attainment strategies, which in turn enhance the individuals' capacities to achieve their goals. Furthermore, the group offers experience in social interaction, which can enhance the awareness of patterns of relationship and can provide an opportunity to develop and practice new ways of relating.

The use of the group as a resource for change may, as Garvin points out, be combined with other change resources. Not only may the group offer life experience, it may also direct its efforts toward the environment to enhance the goodness-of-fit between group members and the environment, particularly in the reciprocal model of group work. The relationship with the group leader may well be a resource for change, as can be the development of insight and of new cognitive structuring of problems and solutions in the group process. The group is also frequently used to enhance behavior modification approaches, as the group can be an important source of reinforcements.

A particularly significant characteristic of the group that has vital meaning in the use of groups in clinical practice is that group forces exemplify the fundamental human conflict between belonging and separateness. In the group, the person has a opportunity to experience, to objectify, and to come to terms with these two dimensions of human experience and human identity.

The belonging and separateness theme is also central to Joan Laird and Jo Ann Allen's exploration of the rapidly expanding theory and knowledge of family therapy in Chapter Eight. After briefly reviewing the knowledge from the social and behavioral sciences that contributes to an understanding of the family, the authors focus on family theory and practice theory developed from clinical research and practice with families.

There have been several efforts to categorize the divergent approaches of family therapists. Laird and Allen offer the reader a new and very useful framework for these theoretical approaches. These authors differentiate among approaches to the use of the family as a resource for change by identifying various targets for change. Family theories and family therapists may be differentiated in terms of their focus on communication processes, rule-governing processes, family organization and structure, differentiation and growth processes, family-environment transactional processes, and learning processes.

In examining the theory developed around the focus on each of these processes, Laird and Allen explore the different views of family function and dysfunction. They also examine the major hypotheses about the resources for and the nature and targets of change. The chapter ends with a discussion of the common themes that offer some unity to this rapidly growing and rapidly differentiating practice, and the authors provide suggestions for areas for possible integration and research.

There are some commonalities between this presentation and some of the other discussions. For example, the view of the family-environment transaction as the focus of change is congruent with Germain's ecological perspective, and the experiential aspects of several of the family treatment perspectives are in harmony with Maluccio's discussion of the use of life experience. Behavioral approaches with families are, of course, similar to the overall behavioral perspectives presented by Schwartz, and there are fascinating but as yet insufficiently explored linkages between altering family communication and family rules and Middleman's discussion of cognitive and perceptual processes as resources for change.

Some of the differences between family and other perspectives are also striking. When the family system is central, there is usually much less attention given to the inner life of the individual than we find in most other approaches. Also, considering that both family therapists and group therapists use groups as a resource for change, it is interesting how little exchange seems to have taken place between group theory and family theory, at least in terms of acknowledgment or conceptualization. The major commonality appears to be a concern with belonging and individuation. In the practice theory supporting most other approaches to change, the role of the worker is conceptualized quite differently. In family work, the worker may "join" the family, may "stay out" of the family, or may act as teacher of communication or coach. However, for the most part, the role of the transference in the change process is excluded, and the transference itself is discounted or consciously kept to a minimum. Although family therapists differ in their use of insight, insight development is not generally considered an instrument for change and, in fact, may even be viewed as an obstacle in this context.

The basic tenet of the theoretical position presented by Arthur Schwartz in Chapter Nine is that most human behavior is learned. The major resource for change, therefore, lies in the capacity of human beings to learn new behaviors and to unlearn old behaviors. Behavior modification practice is based on learning theory and on the empirical research that has demonstrated, with animals and humans, in the laboratory and in life, how learning takes place.

Schwartz traces the development and expansion of behavioral theory over the past fifty years and discusses the relevance for practice of new approaches. He describes the classical conditioning theory and radical environmentalism of Watson and Wolpe, the operant conditioning theories of Skinner, and the work on motivation and cognition of Bandura and Beck. He demonstrates that learning theory has been additive; each time a major new breakthrough is made in the understanding of how people learn, another dimension is contributed to the theory and to the practice. Schwartz suggests that these developments in learning theory have shown that human beings learn in a variety of ways, that the contingencies that influence learning and behavior are many, and thus that many practice approaches may focus on problems of learning. It is Schwartz's view that much of the strong critical reaction to behavior modification practice is based on the faulty assumption that current practice is still primarily based on simple stimulus–response theory and procedures.

On the contrary, contemporary learning theory and attendant behavior modification approaches exhibit breadth and variety and have much in common with and may well have something to offer other approaches to practice. For example, the strong emphasis on the role of the environment in shaping and changing behavior is congruent with much of social work practice. The behaviorist's effort has been to operationalize and measure specific person–environment interactions and to manipulate some aspect of these interactions. The ecological systems view may well concur in the focus on person–environment interactions but would object to the behavior modifier's effort to isolate variables and to reduce what a systems thinker would conceptualize as highly complex transactional systems to linear cause-and-effect relationships.

The planned use of life experience to practice and learn behavior is highly complementary to the work presented by Maluccio, as is Bandura's interest in Robert White's concept of self-efficacy and the importance of efficacy expectation as an element of motivation. The growing interest on the part of some behaviorists in internal mediating factors in behavior, such as belief systems, perceptual distortions, and cognitive structures, links these theoreticians and practitioners with others studying the relevance of such factors in adaptation and change.

Learning and knowing are also central concepts of the next two chapters. In Chapter Ten, Ruth Middleman explores a body of theory that is somewhat less familiar to most clinical social workers but holds considerable promise as a basis for the development and implementation of new practice approaches. Middleman's explorations of the complex area of perception and cognition may provide a basis for future applications to clinical practice.

She begins her discussion of perception and cognition by focusing on how practitioners' biases determine where they look, how they look, what they look for, and what they see. She describes some examples that clinicians may study to gain more conscious awareness of and control over their own cognitive views of clients in their situations. After reviewing some recent theoretical developments in the study of perception and cognition, she discusses perception in behavioral, problem-solving, and ecological approaches. Of particular interest is the conviction that emerges as the chapter unfolds that clinicians may well be working with perception and cognition far more than they know and that the conscious awareness and use of these processes may lead to more precision and effectiveness.

Middleman also explores some of the newest developments in the study of thinking. She describes the current interest in brain hemisphere specialization, in holistic thinking, and in creativity, and discusses the implications for practice. She also describes emerging theory concerning the variety of cognitive styles and suggests that a differential assessment of cognitive style can be important in understanding and working with both students and clients.

In conclusion, Middleman comments on the importance of the clinician's attention in giving direction and shape to practice. It may well be that the profession has not paid sufficient attention to cognition and perception as an area for self-awareness.

Jerome Cohen also explores the world of knowing and places insight and understanding in the center of his view of clinical practice by taking the position that "the goal of intervention should always remain the same, to enhance understanding."

Cohen begins his discussion by specifying the several meanings of the term *insight* and indicating how each of the meanings is expressed in clinical theory and practice. His definitions include seeing into a situation or into the self, understanding the inner nature of things, understanding the unconscious processes contributing to a mental problem or emotional conflict, and immediate learning without recourse to trial and error. These different kinds of insight are found in the clinical literature and form the basis of Cohen's explorations into the relationship between insight and clinical practice.

In establishing the context for his presentation, Cohen describes the psychoanalytic view of insight and the central position occupied by insight development in psychoanalytic treatment. He contrasts this with the perspective of those working in a behavior modification framework, who tend to take an opposite view of the efficacy of insight development in bringing about change. Cohen points out that divergent views of change and the relation of insight to change grow from very different conceptions of human motivation and of the sources of human behavior.

Having established the parameters of his discussion, Cohen turns to a historical discussion of the role of insight in the practice of clinical social work. He describes the differential integration into clinical social work practice of the psychoanalytic view of insight and change, from Gordon Hamilton's tentative consideration of this new body of theory and knowledge in the 1940s to the highly developed psychoanalytic perspectives found in the late 1950s in the work of Austin, Hollis, Garrett, and the British social worker Irvine. In the 1960s, attention turned away from psychodynamic factors to a consideration of social variables and insight into social situations. In the 1970s, there was a rekindling of interest in psychodynamically oriented clinical practice.

Throughout this history, Cohen raises several questions concerning change: How important is the development of insight in the change process? To what extent does the clinical social worker use interpretation to bring about change? How does the clinical social worker deal with the client's transference? Is interpretation of the transference used to enhance the client's self-understanding and to bring about change?

Although these issues are resolved differently by different generations of clinical social workers, Cohen holds to the view that insight and the client's enhanced understanding of the why and the how of intrapersonal and interpersonal events are an essential aspect of clinical change. Without such understanding, Cohen believes that change is relegated to habit or automatic functioning.

In the Chapter Twelve, Herbert Strean examines the worker–client relationship as the context of change and as a resource for change. Strean summarizes a range of theoretical contributions to the understanding of the worker–client relationship and examines the relevance of each of these views of the relationship to change processes. He begins with psychoanalytic theory and an examination of the transference that he believes is present in all therapeutic relationships. The power of the transference as an instrument for change is seen not only through the development of insight but also in the alleviation of the demands of the superego. Turning to the contributions of ego psychology and role theory, Strean reviews these bodies of theory and points out how an enhanced understanding of the ego and of role can make more precise the experiential use of the worker–client relationship in helping clients in the resolution of developmental crises, the mastery of life tasks, and the successful enactment of new roles.

The work of Carl Rogers is also discussed, since Rogers placed special emphasis on the healing power implicit in the therapeutic relationship, particularly the restorative effect of the experience of unconditional positive regard. This approach is in sharp contrast to the use of relationship as an instrument for change in behavior modification, where, as Strean points out, the worker's response to clients may indeed be conditional and may serve as positive or negative reinforcement in the change process. Strean concludes his review by briefly describing the contributions to relationship theory made by Adler, Sullivan, and Lewin. Strean urges that continued research be done on the evaluation of the worker–client relationship in treatment.

In the chapters on theory for clinical practice that follow, we have the opportunity to understand the client in his life space through the perspectives of eight different authors. Each perspective adds to our understanding of that complex system and opens new possibilities for helping.

References

Austin, L. N. "Trends in Differential Treatment in Social Casework." In C. Kasius (Ed.), *Principles and Techniques in Social Casework.* New York: Family Service Association of America, 1950.

Bennis, W. G., Benne, K., and Chin, R. *The Planning of Change.* New York: Holt, Rinehart and Winston, 1961.

Cohen, J. "Nature of Clinical Social Work." In P. Ewalt (Ed.), *Toward a Definition of Clinical Social Work.* Washington, D.C.: National Association of Social Workers, 1980.

Ewalt, P. L. *Toward a Definition of Clinical Social Work.* Washington, D.C.: National Association of Social Workers, 1980.

Fischer, J. *Effective Casework Practice.* New York: McGraw-Hill, 1978.

Gordon, W. E. "Notes on the Nature of Knowledge." In *Building Social Work Knowledge.* New York: National Association of Social Workers, 1964.

Hartman, A. "To Think About the Unthinkable." *Social Casework,* 1970, *51,* 467–474.

Hearn, G. *Theory Building in Social Work.* Toronto: University of Toronto Press, 1958.

Pincus, A., and Minahan, A. *Social Work Practice: Model and Method.* Itasca, Ill.: Peacock, 1973.

Pinkus, H., and others. "Education for the Practice of Clinical Social Work at the Master's Level: A Position Paper." *Clinical Social Work Journal,* 1977, *5* (4), 253–268.

Richmond, M. *What Is Social Casework?* New York: Russell Sage Foundation, 1922.

Roberts, R., and Nee, R. *Theories of Social Casework.* Chicago: University of Chicago Press, 1970.

Siporin, M. "Practice Theory for Clinical Social Work." *Clinical Social Work Journal,* 1979, *7* (1), 75–89.

Turner, F. J. *Social Work Treatment: Interlocking Theoretical Approaches.* New York: Free Press, 1974. (2nd ed. 1979.)

5

Using Social and Physical Environments

Carel B. Germain

From its beginnings, social work has been interested in the environment, although the degree of interest has varied with methods, areas of interest, and geographic regions. The reasons for this uneven attention are historical, sociological, and epistemological. Interest in the environment as a resource for change has been increasing during the past decade, however, probably because of new environmental issues. Public concern is growing about the presence of hazardous wastes in our communities, about asbestos and lead in our schools and dwellings, about other toxic substances in work places, and about the pervasiveness of polluted air, water, and food in urban and rural areas. All are serious threats to the nation's present and future health. An even more immediate danger is the energy crisis and consequent worldwide recession and inflation. The assumption of politicians and economists that a certain rate of unemployment is necessary to control inflation is not acceptable to those who must bear the burden, nor is it acceptable to those who care about the well-being of their fellows. Unemployment contributes to disabling depressive states, physical illness, suicide, disrupted families, alcohol and drug abuse, and emotional disturbance. Moreover, extensive shifts in values, norms, and life-styles since the 1960s have affected all the professions, including that of social work, and have forced them to take greater account of the environment. The shifts include changes in family structures and functions, in the status of women (and hence of men), and in sexual practices. The shifts are associated with demographic changes in the marriage, birth, and divorce rates, in the age ratios of the population, and in the numbers of women in the work force.

It would be a poor practice indeed that took little account of the impact of these and other environmental phenomena on the lives of those whom we serve, on agency and worker practices, and on the profession. I believe that clinical social workers are acutely aware of the impact of environmental forces on their clients and themselves. Everywhere, services are being redesigned to fit the needs of oppressed groups; interest is growing in group and community methods of mobilizing people to influence environmental processes. Graduate students are learning how to change organizational processes and how to influence the legislative processes at local, state, and federal levels. The professional association is lobbying in matters of health and mental health, international peace, income maintenance, human rights, and human services. Individual practitioners are joining these efforts and forming coalitions across disciplines and professions to influence issues of nuclear energy, defense spending, the ERA, the rights of children, and the treatment of experimental animals and endangered species. The outlook for increasing activity on the part of the profession toward these and other environmental issues is promising—even within a dismal political and economic context.

The forces so far described are macroenvironmental, whereas this chapter is concerned with the *microenvironment,* or the immediate *life space,* of individuals, families, and groups. Nevertheless, the macroenvironmental phenomena have been purposely mentioned at the beginning of this chapter because of their fundamental significance in continually shaping the microenvironment—the social and physical settings in which people live. The clinical relevance of the microenvironment arises from the ways people experience and take action in their environment—that is, from the association between the environment and people's cognitions, perceptions, motivations, feelings and emotions, values, attitudes, and sense of identity and effectiveness. In turn, the ways people experience and take action in their environment are influenced by individual factors of age, sex, culture, physical and emotional states, genetic endowment, and previous experience as well as by macroenvironmental factors. The clinical relevance of the interaction between people and their environments may involve (1) changing aspects of the social or physical environment; (2) protecting, supporting, or mobilizing aspects of the environment that support growth; and (3) designing and using environmental instruments of help; adding or subtracting someone or something to or from the life space; or otherwise restructuring life situations.

For purposes of analysis, this chapter distinguishes between physical and social environments and between them and the culture. Nevertheless, their complex interaction must be kept in mind. The physical setting—whether natural or built—shapes the nature of the social interaction that takes place there. For example, the arrangement of objects within space will influence distance/intimacy behaviors as people seek to fulfill their needs for privacy and for interaction. Conversely, the social structure of a setting will influence how its physical aspects are used and the responses it evokes. In an organization such as a hospital, for example, physical arrangements reflect social stratification through the use of uniforms, badges, signs, glass partitions, the location and design of separate dining and lounge facilities, allocation of office and parking space, and other territorial behaviors. These are all designed to regulate role behaviors by creating social separateness and emotional distance between staff and patients and among the various levels of staff.

Cultural values and norms influence both social and physical settings. People's perceptions of the relationships between human beings and the natural world are determined by culture. Some groups view nature as an entity to be subjugated and exploited, others view it as an entity to be respected and revered in harmonious coexistence, and still others view nature as a mysterious and ominous force to which humans must submit. Culture influences the uses of land and the location and design of buildings. Reciprocally, social and physical environments can contribute to cultural change. A simple example can be found in the influence exerted by transportation systems (especially automobiles and airplanes) and communication systems (especially films and television) on values, norms, and life styles. Different social structures, such as nomadic, agrarian, and urban societies, create different kinship systems and norms of interaction and different knowledge and belief systems. In contemporary society, rural and urban social and physical conditions contribute differentially to the development of new value systems and modification of traditional value systems.

In these and other respects, environments are dynamic and complex, which may be a reason for the relative underdevelopment of the concept of environment in social work theory. Early contributors to conceptual development included Pollak (1952, 1956), Lutz (1956), Hearn (1958), Coyle (1958), Stein and Cloward (1958), Stein (1960), Polsky (1962), and the anthropologist Kluckhohn (1958). Knowledge of environments is now being codified, and new theory about environments and people-environment transactions is being developed in environmental psychology, geography, planning and architecture, anthropology, behavioral medicine and social psychiatry, biology, genetics, and ecology. Not all of it can be mentioned in this chapter; it is hoped that the small sampling provided will suggest the breadth of what is available. The next section reviews the work of several biologists, ecologists, and behavioral scientists that provides a base for connecting environmental theory and ideas about people-environment transactions to the social worker's concern with social functioning. Elements of environments will be examined in the following section, and the final section will summarize uses of the environment as a resource for change.

People-Environment Transactions: Emerging Theory

Adaptation. A well-known geneticist, the late T. Dobzhansky, taught through his research and writing that genetic endowment does not determine the traits of a person, but it does govern the responses of the body and mind to environmental forces (Dobzhansky, 1956, 1970, 1973). The microbiologist René Dubos (1968a) has declared that the physical and mental personality is built out of these responses. For both scientists, heredity and environment are complementary, but this interplay is supplemented by a degree of freedom from both determinants in development and functioning. This principle holds true for all organisms, but it is most clearly seen in the case of humans because of the operations of intelligence and culture in transcending biological, psychological, and environmental limits.

Ecologists have developed a systemic view of the relations between organisms, and among species within a given biome, which provides a useful metaphor for viewing the relations between human beings and all aspects of their social and physical environments within a given culture. The metaphor assumes that neither people nor environments can be fully understood except in the context of their reciprocal relations. The exchanges between them represent adaptive processes that permit survival of the organism and enlarge the capacity of the environment to support more diversity of life forms. Such adaptations over evolutionary time lead to the development of genetically based characteristics through processes of genetic variability and environmental selection. The characteristics persist because they assure survival in the evolutionary environment in which the characteristics appeared. Hartmann (1958), the ego theorist, used these biological and evolutionary ideas in his thesis that the human infant arrives in the world equipped for survival through primary autonomous ego functions of motility (including repostural tendencies, the reflexes of sucking and rooting, and crying), cognition and perception, and other functions that connect the infant to the expectable environment. The infant is preadapted by evolutionary processes. Hartmann postulated a sphere of secondary ego autonomy in which other personal characteristics develop through interaction of drives and the environment; in this process, drive energy becomes neutralized through identification with parents and others. In the light of today's knowledge, it may be more accurate to assume, with Dobzhansky, that all personal characteristics have a genetic base of potentiality, but whether they will actually appear in the individual will depend on the nature of environmental experiences. Some characteristics (like those of Hartmann's primary sphere) are less dependent on the environment for expression than others (like those of Hartmann's secondary sphere). But all represent a mixture of genetic endowment and environment experience supplemented by some freedom to select environments by which to be influenced.

Dubos (1968b) argues that the mass, urbanized, technological environments created by human beings exert excessive adaptive demands on human beings. The demands exceed the biological and psychological limits that evolved over the millennia when humans lived in small bands of hunters and gatherers. Elements of poor fit between human nature and the environments created by humans are responsible for certain physical illnesses, emotional disturbances, and social disruptions of our times. Because of the evolved plasticity of human beings, we can tolerate nonsalutary environments more readily than is good for the quality of life. Physiological and behavioral responses may maintain an immediate adaptive balance but may result in degenerative and chronic physical disease or emotional disorders later. For example, an infant's or young child's adaptation to undernutrition by restricting activity makes survival possible, but the insuffient diet interferes with normal brain development and cognition and may also result in life-long physical and mental apathy.

Some environments have nutritive elements that release genetic potential, support optimal development, and promote adaptive functioning (however defined in a given culture); and other environments have nonnutritive elements that stifle genetic potential, inhibit full development, and interfere with adaptive functioning. Our knowledge about nutritive and nonnutritive elements is rudimentary. In some instances, we must operate on assumptions that may turn out to be reflections of our own cultural values rather than verities of universal human nature. A simple example is our assumption that babies and young children are able to form only one primary attachment, which not only flies in the face of evidence from other kinds of societies in which very young children form attachments to several caretakers but is also contradicted by recent ecological research about the role of fathers in early development (Lamb, 1976). This example may not be so simple, however, as we confront the research that suggests there is not only a critical period of attachment for the infant (Bowlby, 1973) but also a reciprocal critical period right after birth for particular maternal responses to be elicited if mother–infant interaction is to proceed easily (Klaus and Kennell, 1976). That all of this is complex and so far insufficiently understood is underscored by the debate initiated (Gross, 1979) by Rossi's (1977) article on these biosocial aspects of parenting.

Another "simple" example is the assumption that slum neighborhoods are disorganized. Research has demonstrated that slums are far from being disorganized social systems. They possess rich structures of mutual aid systems and social networks (Stack, 1974; Valentine, 1978). Certain of their physical aspects are valued and become part of the sense of connectedness to place and to others (Fried, 1969). And, there are highly developed adaptive institutions, such as religion, music, language, and humor, that mediate the harsh environment (Draper, 1979; Valentine and Valentine, 1970). This example also is not so simple, insofar as it does not take account of the dangers of dilapidated housing, poor schools, and poor medical care and the absence of safe and attractive parks, libraries, museums, and other amenities withheld by the larger society.

Our knowledge of the physiological effects of nonnutritive environmental elements may be a little more advanced than our knowledge of behavioral effects. We now know, for example, that maternal smoking, drug and alcohol use, and undernutrition all have negative consequences for the developing fetus. We know more about the relation between environmental hazards and the emergence of physical illness. But the doctrine of specific etiology, which advanced medical knowledge in the late nineteenth and the early twentieth century, is no longer helpful. The single germ theory of disease does not fit what is, in fact, a complex relationship among host, environment, and invader. The old mind–body dichotomy is yielding to a holistic view of body, mind, and environment, even for illnesses that are genetically based.

Within the emerging holistic framework, it is sometimes difficult to determine which environmental elements are nutritive and nonnutritive. Other difficulties arise from the great genetic diversity of human beings, which requires environmental diversity for the expression of different characteristics. However, we know very little about environmental properties that support the development of individuals with differing potentialities (Dobzhansky, 1976, p. 167). What we do know is that there is greater diversity in the human gene pool than is being released by present environments.

Recent innovative research carried out by social workers may help to specify aspects of person–environment fit in particular environments. Coulton (1979, 1980) is studying empirical manifestations of person–environment fit among hospitalized adults. Wetzel (1978a, 1978b) is studying depression in working women from the standpoint of person–environment fit, or *congruence*. Maluccio's (1979) research touched on the fit between client and agency arrangements. Continued efforts in these directions should increase our knowledge about nonnutritive and nutritive elements in particular environments.

Transactions. Reciprocal relations between person and environment are best described by the concept of *transaction.* Most social workers are familiar with the systems notion that living entities must exchange information, energy, and matter with their environments if both are to survive and grow. But the nature of the exchange is sometimes difficult to understand and specify. The idea of transaction captures the reciprocal quality more effectively than the more familiar idea of interaction. Interaction is a linear, unidirectional process between two or more entities in which one entity is the antecedent or independent variable that causes the response of the other as dependent variable, or effect. Transaction, by contrast, conceptualizes what goes on over time between two or more entities where each is reciprocally influencing the other (Dewey and Bentley, 1949). In this sense, then, *transactions* are the processes by which people continually shape their environments and are shaped by them, over time. *Interaction* refers to a stimulus-response relationship regarded as a single complete behavioral unit.

The distinction is important because it affects notions of causality. The interactional view rests on the concept of linear chains of cause and effect. Although these chains do exist in some behavioral phenomena, the transactional view explains more complex phenomena in terms of ongoing processes of reciprocal influence. Here, the theorist and clinician focus on the consequences of the action of one part of the unitary system on the operations of another part rather than on a linear chain of cause and effect. In such a closed feedback loop, an effect becomes a cause and a cause can be an effect (Powers, 1973). Living systems depend on both positive and negative feedback loops for survival and growth. Negative feedback is good because it keeps behavior within system limits by correcting errors and deviations and by maintaining stable functioning. The danger in negative feedback is its potential for creating rigidity in the system's response to internal or external changes. An example is the inability of a father and mother to grant appropriate autonomy to an adolescent daughter or son. Positive feedback is good because it allows innovative behavior beyond usual system limits. The danger in positive feedback is its potential for amplifying errors and thus for encouraging destructive processes that disrupt the person-environment behavioral system. An example is the serious disruptions caused in rural boom towns by the nation's search for more sources of energy: "Craig, Colorado may serve as an example. Coal development caused Craig to grow from 7,000 people in 1973 to 10,300 in 1976. The Denver Research Institute found that this 47% increase in population was accompanied by a 22% increase in crimes against property, a 130% increase in child abuse and neglect, a 352% increase in family disturbance, a 623% increase in substance abuse, a 900% increase in crimes against persons, and a 1,000% increase in child behavior problems" (Davenport and Davenport, 1980).

In trying to change such feedback loops at the individual, family, or group level, the social worker may seek to interrupt negative feedback processes that prevent needed change in behavioral systems or positive feedback processes that escalate change beyond the system's limits (Maruyama, 1963). Since the operations of one part of the system have consequences for other parts, interventions may proceed in different directions and take different forms. In the case of depression, for example, interventions might include work on feedback processes that sustain and intensify the problem, including exchanges between the person and the spouse, children, parents, network, work place, school, or even treatment facility. Hoffman has demonstrated such interventions in work with families and groups (1971, 1976) and with client-organization relations (Hoffman and Long, 1969).

The transactional view can be pushed to an extreme position, such that the relationship between or among entities defines the phenomenon, eliminating the conception of two independently defined entities engaged in interdependent action (Pervin and Lewis, 1978, pp. 16–17). This would mean, for example, that there is no organism and no environment but only an organism-environment relationship. In this theory, the entities in a relationship owe their existence and definition to each other. In practice, however, it is possible for the social worker to view person and environment in transactional terms while also considering them interactionally as having separable attributes of their own. While regarding person and environment as a unitary system of reciprocally influencing parts, the social worker is also concerned with the nature of the person and the nature of the environment. The specification of the environment's separable properties will be taken up later in the chapter, but the specification of those of person is beyond the chapter's scope.

Related to transactionalism is the biological view of adaptedness as a relationship between organism and environment. "No entity in itself is adapted, it is adapted to something else, that is, the environment" (Weiss, 1949). Behavior is then conceived of as the efforts of the organism to achieve goodness-of-fit between itself and the environment. Adaptedness, or fit, is a transactional relationship that, over time, manifests both stability and variability through the operation of positive and negative feedback.

Stress and Coping. When the transactions go well, the fit is good—that is, people's growth, health, and social functioning bring personal and social satisfaction within the given cultural group, and the environment's capacity to support growth, health, and social functioning is protected and promoted. When transactions do not go well, people's biological, cognitive-perceptual, emotional, and social development and functioning may be impaired, and environments may become polluted, which further impairs adaptive capacities. These upsets in the fit or congruence between the needs, values, or goals of the individual and the properties of the environment are conceptualized as stress. In human beings, goodness-of-fit is never fully achieved because of continual internal and external changes, so the degree of fit is the critical feature. Poor fit causes stress; unmitigated stress sharply reduces the fit. Coping responses to stress represent efforts to restore the previous level of fit or to improve upon it. Like adaptedness or fit, stress also is not a property of the individual or the environment alone; it is the expression of a relation between them.

Several investigators have advanced a transactional model of stress (Cox, 1978; Van Harrison, 1978; Lazarus and Launier, 1978). These models also distinguish between actual and perceived elements of demand and capability to meet the demand. This distinction is important because it allows for individual variations in what is experienced as stress (Hinkle, 1961). By contrast, the well-known life-change scales for predicting stress and illness assume that certain life-changes are experienced similarly by all persons (Holmes and Rahe, 1967), without taking into account individual perception and other mediating factors (Mechanic, 1974a; Rabkin and Struening, 1976). The Lazarus model, which is used in this chapter, is also a cognitive as well as a perceptual model, in that stress is considered to arise only after there has been a cognitive appraisal of discrepancy (lack of fit) between perceived demand and perceived capability for meeting it. At that point, the person experiences a subjective, emotional state of stress. Demands may be generated internally by needs, wants, values, attitudes, and so on, or externally by environmental events and processes. Capability includes both personal and environmental resources for meeting the perceived demand. The model postulates three stress-relevant relationships between person and environment—harm/loss, threat, and challenge. Harm/loss refers to damage already done, and threat refers to anticipated harm/loss. Harm and threat of harm may both be present, as when the loss of a loved one is accompanied by anticipated long-term changes in status. Challenge differs from the other two in its preponderance of positive feelings associated with an expectation of mastery and gain.

The experience of stress evokes coping responses, which may be physiological (for example, release of adrenalin), cognitive (for example, avoidance, considering alternative solutions), or behavioral (for example, overeating, seeking information). Effective coping reduces or eliminates the stress. Ineffective coping results in unrelieved or even intensified stress. If marked stress continues unabated there is danger of physical illness, emotional disturbance, or social disruption, which may in turn cause new or additional stress. In the case of physical illness, unrelieved stress is not disease-specific; rather, it increases the susceptibility of the individual to a variety of disease agents, probably by altering the body's endocrine balance (Cassel, 1974).

Coping responses serve as feedback processes revealing how the organism is doing. They include information from internal reactions and from the environment (Lazarus and Launier, 1978, p. 308). As feedback, they can affect the actual or perceived demand or capability, the appraisal of discrepancy, the stress experience, or the coping strategies themselves (Cox, 1978, pp. 18–21). For example, securing information might alter the demand by reducing it; the defense of denial might alter it in the short run but increase it in the long run. Asking for network support might increase capability; resorting to alcohol might decrease capability. The actual experience of stress may be heightened by physiological responses, such as gastric distress, palpitations, or increased thirst. Environmental approval or disapproval of coping manuevers might alter them in one direction or another, for the better or for the worse. Like adaptedness and stress, coping also expresses a particular relation between person and environment. It is more fully understood as transactional rather than as a personality attribute alone.

The transactional aspect of coping is illumined by Mechanic (1974b). Coping requires personal resources, but such resources depend on environmental provisions and supports. An individual's coping skills depend on the quality of preparation afforded by past and present environments; their success depends on which behaviors are valued and which are condemned in a given social system. The capacity to maintain a favorable degree of internal comfort and self-esteem in order to begin problem solving requires not only internal resources but social supports. The environment must also provide information, time to develop coping strategies, and space for autonomous action (White, 1974). And, finally, coping ability depends on the effectiveness of the solutions provided by the culture. In a period of rapid social change, institutionalized solutions to problems tend to lag behind new demands, so that many persons will experience coping failures and added stress. Single-parent families and working mothers are increasing in numbers, for example, yet adequate childcare arrangements have not yet been provided in industry, universities, and neighborhoods. The major stresses in modern society are less amenable to individual solutions because of their complexity; they seem to require group solutions. The move toward self-help and mutual aid groups reflects the salience of group solutions in matters of health and mental health, changes in social status, and other areas of life. They can help protect individuals from stress and enhance their coping abilities.

These conceptions of adaptation, stress, and coping have implications for clinical practice. Social workers have the skills to intervene at transactional levels of demand, capability appraisal, emotional experience of stress, and coping responses—although practice has not been conceptualized in quite that way. For example,

> We may consider with the individual, family, or group the feasibility of acting on an external demand in order to change its nature or reduce its threatening quality, or we may direct our mutual attention to mobilizing or strengthening actual capability. At the next level we may seek to influence the perceived demand or perceived capability in order to bring them closer to the actual, especially where either demand or capability is over- or underestimated. We often initiate a process of reappraisal in which the misappraisal of discrepancy between perceived demand and perceived skills and resources may be corrected. And interventions are also directed to mobilizing and supporting more effective coping responses [Germain, 1979].

But the social work practitioner has the added responsibility for monitoring and seeking to correct organizational factors that create stress instead of alleviating it or that undermine coping efforts instead of supporting them. Good practice has always relied on advocacy in behalf of individual clients. What is suggested here is that organizational interventions to change stressful procedures to enhance coping are the responsibility of all social workers and not just those designated as community organizers or as nonclinical practitioners. Such interventions to introduce innovative programs may also be significant preventive strategies as well as therapeutic strategies.

Environmental Elements

A focus on person–environment fit, that is, on their transactions, does not eliminate the necessity to understand the separate characteristics of each. This section will review some of the attributes of social and physical environments and their spatial and temporal dimensions.

Social workers may be more aware of the dynamic nature of the social environment than they are of the physical environment. The social work theorists of the 1950s described the influence on human behavior of such social variables as family structure, social role, social class status, ethnic membership, and bureaucratic structure and functioning. During the 1960s, research studies of the influence of these variables on childrearing patterns, social interaction, verbal and nonverbal communication, and helping relationships were introduced into the curricula of schools of social work. Practitioner interest in the social environment was bolstered by rapid developments in milieu therapy and family therapy and advances in the study of small group dynamics, intergroup relations, and community development. In this chapter, the family, formed group, and neighborhood are regarded, like the individual, as entities being served. Hence the review of developing knowledge of the social environment is limited to social networks and bureaucratic structures.

Social Networks. Human beings become socialized through relationships with others that tend to expand in widening circles over the life span until old age, when they tend to contract. It is through involvement with others that people develop the sense of self and individuality. Humankind evolved in the structure of small bands (Bowlby, 1973; Dubos, 1968), so that isolation and unwanted distance from others violate deep needs for relatedness. Without relatedness, the human being may die or may be in danger of profound mental disturbance. From the symbiosis of infancy to the reciprocity of caring in adulthood, relatedness to others is a biological as well as a social imperative. Even the pain of loss and loneliness can be endured if the sense of relatedness to the human world holds out against the death-threatening sense of unrelatedness (Will, 1959). The same may be said about the sense of relatedness to the world of nature, which we will discuss later.

Weiss (1973) has made a useful distinction between two kinds of loneliness, that of emotional isolation, which results from the loss or lack of an intimate attachment (usually with a spouse, lover, parent, or child) and that of social isolation, which is the consequence of lacking a network of involvements with peers of some sort. The loneliness of emotional isolation can only be assuaged by reintegration of the lost relationship or the formation of a new one following the successful resolution of grief. The loneliness of social isolation can only be assuaged by engagement with a social network. Neither attachment nor engagement can be substituted for the other; both are required for human well being. For example, a child who is lonely because all his peers are away for the summer is not likely to find his mother an adequate substitute playmate. Another child, who has lost a parent, will not alleviate the pain of the lost attachment through the company of peers. Adults also need both the security of a reciprocal attachment and the social integration of engagement with a network of others. Neither can substitute for the other (Weiss, 1973, p. 148). From this perspective, the helpfulness of widow-to-widow programs, for example, may lie in their integrative and instrumental functions as one moves into a new status and faces new coping tasks (Silverman, 1976). Peers who have faced a similar situation and its tasks can provide significant support and guidance to the newly bereaved. They cannot, however, be expected to substitute for the lost attachment or to relieve the pain of grief.

These aspects of human development (over evolutionary time in the case of the species and over the life span in the case of the individual) support the growing professional interest in social networks. The concept refers to a web of interpersonal relations in which the linkages between and among members serve as pathways of communication and channels for the exchange of resources, information, judgments, and opinions. The network is not merely an aggregate of social relationships, now covered by the concept of significant others. Rather, it is a system in which the linkages themselves influence the behavior of individual members (Mitchell, 1969). Different kinds of networks appear to serve differing functions (Litwak and Szelenyi, 1969). Ties of kinship are characterized by permanence; thus, kin networks are able to provide support and resources over the long term and across great geographical distances. Ties among neighbors are based on face-to-face contact and immediate proximity, and they tend to lack permanence in this era of increased geographic mobility. Thus, neighbors are more apt to exchange resources and services that do not require a long-term commitment, such as help with child care, transportation, and equipment. Ties among friends lack, to some degree, the permanence of kinship ties and often the proximity of neighbors' ties. But, because friendship rests on a base of mutual regard and affection, friends tend to exchange guidance, advice, and emotional support.

Social networks, mutual-aid systems, self-help groups, and natural helpers are important environmental instruments in both primary prevention and restorative intervention (Caplan, 1974; Caplan and Killilea, 1976). Cassel (1974), for example, has taken the position that social supports mediate the effects of stress as a causal factor in physical illness. He recommends that efforts to prevent physical disease should be directed to improving and strengthening social supports instead of reducing exposure to stressful life events, which may be less feasible. In cases of mental illness, Hollister (1977) suggests the use of social supports for primary prevention in building resistance to stress and managing reactions to stress. In social work, Collins and Pancoast (1976) studied the functions of the natural helper in primary prevention, and they have extended their work into the area of protecting children from abuse and neglect (Collins, 1980; Pancoast, 1980). Patterson (1977) and her colleagues identified the distinctive qualities and techniques of natural helpers in a rural area of Kansas. Shapiro (1971) studied the activities of natural helpers among the tenants of single room occupancy hotels that made it possible for the residents to cope more effectively with multiple stresses. In their linkages to formal support systems, natural helpers can be effective sources of referral to agencies (Lee and Swenson, 1978). The influence of social networks on whether a potential client applies to an agency for help or, on applying, remains in the contact was demonstrated by Mayer and Rosenblatt (1964). These studies provide information on how to locate rural or urban natural helpers as resources for prevention of disordered functioning, and they also underscore the need for caution and skill in working with natural helpers. Social work consultation can help extend the scope and effectiveness of natural helpers, but it must not undermine the confidence and intuitive capacities that make natural helpers so helpful. Social networks are also significant means of support in restorative intervention. Speck and his colleagues, for example, devised a treatment approach with families having a schizophrenic member, in which a family's entire social network up to 100 members is convened for problem solving (Speck, 1967; Speck and Attneave, 1973; Speck and Ruveni, 1969).

Experience with systems of natural helping suggests that two human motives are frequently involved, altruism and the need for reciprocity in giving and receiving. As a concept, altruism has recently taken on the character of an ideological controversy in the new discipline of sociobiology. Sociobiologists assert that the altruistic sacrifice of an individual's life in behalf of a related individual, which is genetically programmed behavior in certain insects and possibly in some birds, is similarly programmed in higher animals, including human beings (Wilson, 1975). Human altruism, from this perspective, is derived from an evolutionary survival device favoring the preservation of genes of a kinship group rather than of an individual, although Wilson does concede that "the form and intensity of altruistic acts are to a large extent culturally determined" (Wilson, 1978, p. 153). Other biologists disagree with the thesis of genetic determinism and declare that altruism of humans is different from that of insects and birds, does not originate in genetic programming, and is learned in the individual's social environment. Thomas (1977, pp. 1462, 1463) observes that, because of this acrimonious debate, the idea of altruism "has lost much of its amiable aspect, and instead of being a newly recognized, rather delightful fact of life to be reflected on in puzzlement, it has become the topic of an intermittently ill tempered doctrinal dispute among professionals. . . . The term *altruism* as used in these discussions . . . is a narrow definition indeed. I would prefer to broaden it to include all behavior that can be interpreted as indicating goodwill or helpfulness or friendliness, or what we would all accept as good nature. There is much more of this in the world than we used to believe. . . ."

This broadened conception of altruism describes what seems to take place in social networks and related groups. Such qualities have been found to make possible coping with harsh environments in inner-city neighborhoods (Stack, 1974; Valentine, 1978). When slum neighborhoods are subjected to urban renewal, the loss of network affiliations causes many displaced residents to experience grief and prolonged depression (Fried, 1969). The lack of physical facilities that would foster the development of social networks in high-rise public housing projects is thought to contribute to the vandalism and feelings of alienation experienced by many residents (Newman, 1973; Yancey, 1971).

Implied in Thomas's description is the notion of reciprocity. Human beings have a need to give as well as to receive, and in helping others they help themselves. Very often this is the explanation given by natural helpers for their interest in helping. Reciprocity is the basis of success of self-help groups, and even of formed groups led by professionals (Lee and Park, 1978). Members exchange ideas, instruct one another in new ways of coping, and offer emotional support to one another. In poor communities, the principle of reciprocity makes the whole system of mutual aid possible among kin, friends, and neighbors. Most important of all, perhaps, is that these forms of informal help—networks, self-help groups, and natural helpers—represent natural life processes, not clinical processes. They emerge from people's caring for one another, and, being noninstitutionalized, they carry no stigma of dependency, deviancy, or other labels. Indeed, in the case of self-help and mutual aid systems serving oppressed groups, the environment is improved for everyone in a kind of recycling process, in which the members work to eliminate the very problems that had victimized them.

Bureaucratic Organizations. Human beings must adapt to the changes they make in physical and social environments. The changes may make adaptation easier or harder, or they may have mixed effects, depending on intervening personal and social-cultural variables. Complex organizations are among the environmental forms created by human beings to solve certain complex problems and to achieve particular goals in various areas of life. With the rise of the Industrial Revolution, bureaucracy evolved as a way of organizing to achieve greater productivity, efficiency, and profits through rational methods of management in business and industry. The form spread to other areas of endeavor, even to charity. Scientific philanthropy in the late 1800s and early 1900s was so called because it bureaucratized alms-giving by the use of management methods to control duplication and fraud. In contemporary society, public and private bureaucracies provide products and services that families and individuals once provided for themselves. Systems of work, health care, education, religion, child care, transportation, and care of the elderly and infirm structure their services, production, or other activities in bureaucratic forms. Etzioni (1964, p. 1) writes: "We are born in organizations, educated by organizations, and most of us spend much of our lives working for organizations. We spend much of our leisure time paying, playing, and praying in organizations. Most of us will die in an organization, and when the time comes for burial, the largest organization of all—the state—must grant official permission."

In many instances, complex organizations serve their purposes well, but over time they sometimes tend to create problems for those who are served by them, work in them, or are otherwise engaged in exchanges with them. In the 1980s, more and more professions are conducting their practices in bureaucratic organizations, with attendant strains and tensions between organizational requirements or needs and professional interests. Social workers have long practiced in such settings and now have an enlightened concern about the impact of the organization on clients, themselves, and their practice. The concern has led to interest in understanding how organizations work and how to make them work better. The aim is to help one's agency to be more responsive to client needs and aspirations and to the imperatives of professional practice.

Most theoretical work on organizational innovation analyzes organizational change introduced at the top. But in recent years social workers have developed concepts and principles for lower-level staff to use in initiating change (Brager and Holloway, 1978; Germain and Gitterman, 1980; Patti, 1974; Patti and Resnick, 1972; Wax, 1968, 1971; Weissman, 1973). In general, these concepts demonstrate that a systematic problem-solving approach to organizational change—which roughly parallels the systematic approach to other change efforts in social work practice—can achieve improvements in service. However, when the organization is the object of change, the practitioner needs another body of knowledge (organizational theory) and a set of politically oriented skills to be used in addition to the accustomed interpersonal skills of helping. The body of organizational theory is large and growing. Organizational properties that are especially pertinent to change efforts by social workers are *centralization, formalization,* and *stratification* as these manifest themselves in the organization's formal and informal systems (Hage, 1980; Hage and Aiken, 1970). The change-oriented practitioner needs to understand how the interplay of these properties affects services and shapes practice.

Centralization refers to the distribution of power in an organization; it is manifested by authority in the formal system and by influence in the informal one. Practitioners, because of their location in the organization's formal system, may have little authority but often have more informal influence than they realize. Initiating and implementing a successful change will require garnering or increasing one's influence and mustering that of others who are likely to be supportive of the goal.

Formalization refers to the presence of rules that help to maintain efficiency, impartiality, and fairness. Rules are found in the regulations generated by the formal system to support the achievement of the organization's goals. Over time, however, the rules may take on a life of their own and may begin to subvert goals by their rigidity or their latent functions in serving organizational needs rather than client needs and practitioner needs. Rules may also be found in the customs, norms, and traditions that develop in the informal system. These, too, are forceful regulators and may operate to help make services more effective by circumventing formal rules; or they may operate to interfere with effective service by giving primacy to staff interests. It is essential that the practitioner monitor the impact of formal policies and informal customs on the quality of service and on the practitioner's opportunity to exercise professional judgment.

Stratification refers to the distribution of rewards within the organization, manifested by status in the formal system and prestige in the informal system. High status is rewarded by higher income and other perquisites. Similarly, persons, groups, or departments having greater prestige are likely to enjoy more space and other amenities. In settings where another profession is in charge, matters of stratification may bear heavily on social work services. Even in such settings, however, social workers can gain prestige in the same way they gain influence—through professional competence, attractive personal and interpersonal qualities, and exchange relationships with other staff members. Matters of status and prestige often account for competitiveness between disciplines or departments, and they can affect the allocation of scarce resources. Thus, issues of status and prestige can affect change efforts, especially where the goal of change may threaten the self-interests of the staff.

Implicit in this description of organizational properties is the need for an organizational analysis or assessment in order to ascertain the feasibility of the goal of change and to plan strategies for achieving it. The phases of analysis and planning rest on an understanding of the internal structural dynamics of the organization *and* its relations with its political, economic, and sociocultural environment. Particularly important is the identification of internal and external forces that can be expected to support the change effort and those that are likely to oppose it. Strategies will be needed to mobilize and support the one set of forces and to neutralize or by-pass the other set. Once the plan is settled on, the phases of entry and engagement follow, during which effort is directed to securing adoption of the change goal. A range of skills is available for this task, including program demonstration, joint problem solving, persuasion, negotiation, and bargaining; which skill is called upon will depend on the degree of consensus. Following agreement of the relevant decision makers on the goal, the phases of implementing and institutionalizing the change can begin. Experience has shown that modest, perhaps incremental, and sometimes more far-reaching change can be achieved in complex organizations when the practitioner possesses the requisite knowledge and skill, a clear sense of professional ethics and accountability to clients, and a commitment to individualized quality services.

The Physical Environment. In contrast to the social environment, the physical environment is sometimes viewed as a static background for human action. But the physical environment is, in fact, a dynamic, transacting feature in people's life space. It can evoke human behavior and it can be shaped by human behavior. It has its own imperatives to which people must adapt, yet people also use it for their adaptive needs and purposes. The physical environment comprises cosmic influences, the earth's seasons and its climates, the world of plants and animals, and the landscape of earth, water, sky, and air—the web of life into which human beings, like all organisms, must fit. The physical environment also comprises the endless variety of architectural structures, utilitarian and aesthetic objects, and means of transportation and communication that are constructed by human beings. Actually, what human beings build and fashion are as "natural" as what other species construct, but it is convenient to distinguish between the natural world and the built world for purposes of description and analysis. We will examine the natural world first.

Biologists question whether human beings can retain physical and mental health without remaining in intimate touch with the world of nature that shaped human nature (Dubos, 1968b, p. 150). From a similar evolutionary perspective, a psychiatrist has written of the human being's kinship with the natural world in what he terms *normal development* and *schizophrenic development* (Searles, 1960). Using ideas from ego psychology, Searles suggests that there is a difference between mature and disturbed relatedness to the natural world, which parallels the difference in mature and disturbed relatedness to other human beings. In states of ego disorganization, where personal boundaries are diffuse, it may be as difficult to distinguish the self from the physical environment as from another human being. In both cases, the yearning for unity may be equally compelling and the possibility of engulfment equally terrifying. Immature at-one-ness with the natural world, accompanied by a loss of one's distinctiveness as a human being, is not reversible at will. By contrast, mature relatedness to the natural world leads to a sense of kinship with it but without the loss of one's sense of individuality and humanity. Mature relatedness also includes the ability to experience the physical environment in its realness (Searles, 1960, p. 135) as menacing, benevolent, or innocuous, as the case may be, and the ability to change one's response as the environment changes. For Searles, the years of childhood and youth are spent in differentiating one's self from the social environment of significant others and the physical environment of nature and cherished physical objects. The balance of life is spent in achieving a reintegration with both worlds while maintaining separateness and individuality. Searles (pp. 120ff) caps his analysis with a delineation of four categories of fruitful effects of mature relatedness to nature: (1) the assuagement of various painful and anxiety-laden states of feelings; (2) the fostering of self-realization; (3) the deepening of one's feeling of reality; and (4) the fostering of one's appreciation, and acceptance, of one's fellow men.

If justification were needed for including the physical environment in the social worker's unit of attention, it is found in this analysis. Settlement workers of long ago were aware of the needs of inner-city residents for renewal and refreshment in the natural world, and so they developed fresh-air camps for children and their mothers. Today's programmatic developments are in this tradition, including camping for inner-city families (Vassil, 1978), overnight trips for chronic psychiatric patients (Shearer, 1978), and wilderness therapy for delinquent and disturbed youths (Cataldo, 1979). The use of gardening projects and horticultural therapy is expanding (Lewis, 1976). The significance of pets has been recognized for isolated persons living alone (Bikales, 1975) and for those in residential treatment settings. And researchers studying patients at the University of Maryland Hospital reported that pet owners were found statistically to be more likely to survive a heart attack than were those who had no animal companions (Friedmann and others, 1980).

A growing literature analyzes the transactions between people and the built world and the consequences of these transactions for behavior, health, and mental health (for example, Hinkle and Loring, 1977; Moos, 1976; Proshansky and others, 1970, 1976; Tuan, 1977). Some investigations of the impact of architecture and design on institutional and community life underscore the importance of social workers' seeking opportunities to participate as consultants in building plans in settings where they practice so that a better fit may be achieved between clients' needs and design elements. The impact of urban layouts, housing, transportation, parks, and spatial structures on women in their homes, at work, and in their neighborhoods suggests a need for new kinds of assessments and interventions in the problems women clients bring to social workers (*Signs,* 1980). Spivack (1973) offers a framework for analyzing setting needs and setting deprivations at critical points in the lives of individuals and families, and he analyzes their impact on the performance of individual and family life tasks. This framework can aid the social worker and client in deciding what changes are needed to improve the environment, increase person-environment fit, and support adaptive functioning.

One dimension of both the social and physical environments is space—its arrangement, its influence on behavior, and its use in the service of adaptation (Germain, 1978). Space has been shown to affect social relations in hospitals, schools, and other congregate settings (Sommer, 1969) and in family life (Henry, 1973; Kantor and Lehr, 1975; Lennard and Lennard, 1977). Concepts of spatial behavior—using the physical environment to create a social one—include territoriality and home range, borrowed from ethology (Esser, 1971; Stea, 1970; Scheflen and Ashcraft, 1976); personal distance (Hall, 1966); and body buffer zones (Kinzel, 1970).

A second dimension of both physical and social environments is time. Concepts of biological, social, cultural, and psychological time have been discussed by Germain (1976). Environmental rhythms and cycles have been entrained into the biological structures of all organisms. Biological time refers to such bodily tempos as sleep cycles, regular fluctuations in body temperature, menstruation, and the rhythmic operations of heart and lungs. Upsets in these and other biological rhythms account for the unpleasantness of jet lag and the stress created by night shift and swing shift work. Social time refers to rhythmic cycles generated by such social institutions as work places, businesses, schools, hospitals, and social agencies, which may not fit with people's biological rhythms or their cultural orientations to time. Such cycles include the temporal structure of the work day, work week, pay period, and provisions for leave. Cultural time includes orientations toward punctuality, the value ascribed to past, present, or future time, and the perceptions of and responses to issues of duration, frequency, and pacing of social processes and events. Psychological time refers to one's perception of time as full or empty of significant experience and of its flow as an opportunity for constraint against such experience. Time's passage may be felt as fast or slow. People who lose their sense of time (or their orientation to space) because of illness, psychiatric disturbance, or loss of sensory acuity as in aging may experience panic and disorganization or may withdraw from interaction with the environment. These dimensions of time influence people's behavior by contributing to smooth social interaction when there is congruence or to conflicted expectations and perceptions when there is not. Temporal arrangements at the work place may interfere with temporal requirements of family life. The cultural orientations to time held by client populations may be different from those held by staffs of health settings and social agencies. This incongruence can lead to problems in service provision. Members of social systems develop temporal behaviors that, like their spatial behaviors, help to define social positions and roles and to regulate intimacy and distance among the participants (Kantor and Lehr, 1975).

Drawing together many streams of thought about social and physical environments, Altman (1975) has constructed a transactional, perceptual paradigm of people's regulation of social relations. He suggests that people use personal and spatial behaviors (we can add temporal behaviors) to maintain a desired degree of openness or closedness of their self/other boundaries. When more social interaction occurs than is desired, the person, family, or group will experience an unpleasant state of social crowding (not to be confused with density of numbers) or individual intrusiveness. When there is less social interaction than desired, the person, family, or group will experience an unpleasant state of social isolation. Either outcome may give rise to emotional or physiological stress as an appraisal is made of imbalance between the perceived demand for a certain degree of social interaction or solitude and the capability to meet the demand. The behaviors to control the interchange across the self/other boundary include territorial and personal distance behaviors; nonverbal, paraverbal, and verbal behaviors (Draper, 1979); and such environmental aids as doors, locks, partitions, hedges, fences, and signs. The definition of what constitutes a desirable degree of interaction, the behaviors used to achieve it, and the state actually achieved are influenced within any given culture by mediating factors of personal characteristics, interpersonal characteristics, and environmental properties. Interventions directed to personal characteristics are not within the scope of this chapter. Nevertheless, interventions directed to interpersonal and environmental characteristics would have to take into account communication styles and cognitive, perceptual, affective, and motivational states as these influence receptiveness or resistance to social engagement. Such interventions might be directed to the interpersonal processes in family or group life, including spatial and temporal behaviors used to keep people apart or keep them together. Environmental interventions might include changing spatial or temporal arrangements in the physical environment so that privacy and sociableness are both available options.

Summary: Use of the Environment as a Resource for Change

In this chapter, adaptedness, stress, and coping have been analyzed as expressions of reciprocal, transactional relationships between people and environments. The fit between people's needs and goals and environmental properties is the critical factor in social functioning. Hence, it is of central interest to clinical social workers. Most people seek social work help because they are experiencing unpleasant stress or, in the case of those referred for service, someone or some institution in the environment is stressed by their behavior. In either event, the person–environment fit is awry. Fit may be restored in certain instances by change in the person, in many instances by change in the environment, and perhaps in most instances by change in the transactions between them, including those pertaining to adaptations, stress, and coping. The significance to clinical social work of the Maruyama–Powers model of closed loops of positive and negative feedback, the Lazarus model of stress and coping, and the Altman model of boundary maintenance in social relations lies in their holistic view of person and environment. Interventions can be addressed to any element within each model, as the situation requires, to bring about a better fit; the models are equally applicable to work with individuals, families, and groups.

Transactional interventions must take into account the qualities of both individual and environment. Pertinent personal qualities include age, sex, physical and emotional states, cognition–perception, personality, and values. Pertinent environmental qualities include physical hazards; overstimulation or understimulation; opportunities for growth, learning, and pleasure; arrangements for sociability and privacy; messages conveyed bearing on self-worth and identity; and provisions for successful achievement of life tasks (Saegert, 1976; Steele, 1973). Errors in transactional interventions may be committed unless the qualities of both individual and environment are considered. For example, it is easy to assume that network relations are desirable because human beings are social beings. But people differ in their needs for solitude and sociability; some prefer to be, and function adaptively as, loners. Or, a network may represent a poor person–environment fit. People may wish to free themselves from a network because of problems it raises in terms of independence, or in terms of values, or because it lacks reciprocity.

Elements of physical and social environments may be analyzed in terms of their potential usefulness for social workers. Social networks, natural helpers, mutual aid systems, the natural and built worlds, and relevant concepts of space and time all offer potential as environmental instruments of prevention and help. Nutritive environmental elements can be used to evoke and support adaptive functioning by enriching the sense of identity and self-esteem, increasing competence, and enhancing relatedness. Decision making and action in the environment contribute to self-directedness. Nonnutritive elements of physical and social environments, or of space and time, can be changed through the efforts of natural helpers and self-help groups. Changing the environment requires knowledge, skill, and commitment by the social worker and the active participation of the persons being served. The elderly, the ill, and children are very dependent on the environment and therefore the least able to effect change. In such instances, the social worker may carry greater responsibility in the change effort but must always seek the client's participation, however modest. Finally, it is important to recognize that physical and social environments are arenas for new cognitive and behavioral experiences, which can bring pleasure, mastery, and a new sense of self.

References

Altman, I. *The Environment and Social Behavior.* Monterey, Calif.: Brooks/Cole, 1975.

Attneave, C. "Social Networks as the Unit of Intervention." In P. Guerin, Jr. (Ed.), *Family Therapy: Theory and Practice.* New York: Gardner Press, 1976.

Bikales, G. "The Dog as 'Significant Other.'" *Social Work,* 1975, *20*(2), 150–152.

Bowlby, J. "Affectional Bonds: Their Nature and Origin." In R. S. Weiss (Ed.), *Loneliness, The Experience of Emotional and Social Isolation.* Cambridge: M.I.T. Press, 1973.

Brager, G., and Holloway, S. *Changing Human Service Organizations: Politics and Practice.* New York: Free Press, 1978.

Caplan, G. *Support Systems and Mental Health.* New York: Behavioral Publications, 1974.

Caplan, G., and Killilea, M. *Support Systems and Mutual Help: Multidisciplinary Exploration.* New York: Grune & Stratton, 1976.

Cassel, J. "Psychosocial Processes and 'Stress': Theoretical Formulation." In R. Kane (Ed.), *The Behavioral Sciences and Preventive Medicine.* DHEW Publication No. (NIH) 76-878. Washington, D.C.: U.S. Department of Health, Education, and Welfare, 1976.

Cataldo, C. "Wilderness Therapy: Modern Day Shamanism." In C. Germain (Ed.), *Social Work Practice: People and Environments.* New York: Columbia University Press, 1979.

Collins, A. "Helping Neighbors Intervene in Cases of Maltreatment." In J. Garbarino and S. H. Stocking (Eds.), *Protecting Children from Abuse and Neglect.* San Francisco: Jossey-Bass, 1980.

Collins, A., and Pancoast, D. *Natural Helping Networks: A Strategy for Prevention.* Washington, D.C.: National Association of Social Workers, 1976.

Coulton, C. "A Study of Person-Environment Fit Among the Chronically Ill." *Social Work in Health Care,* 1979, *5* (1), 5–17.

Coulton, C. "Developing an Instrument to Measure Person-Environment Fit." *Journal of Social Service Research,* 1980, *3,* 159–173.

Cox, T. *Stress.* Baltimore: University Park Press, 1978.

Coyle, G. *Social Science Knowledge in the Education of Social Workers.* New York: Council on Social Work Education, 1958.

Davenport, J., and Davenport, J. "Boom Towns Bring Social Malaise to Energy-Rich West." *NASW News,* 1980, *25* (6), 3.

Dewey, J., and Bentley, A. *Knowing and the Known.* Boston: Beacon Press, 1949.

Dobzhansky, T. *The Biological Base of Human Freedom.* New York: Columbia University Press, 1956.

Dobzhansky, T. *Genetics of the Evolutionary Process.* New York: Columbia University Press, 1970.

Dobzhansky, T. "The Myths of Genetic Predestination and Tabula Rasa." *Biology and Medicine,* 1976, *19* (2), 156–170.

Draper, B. J. "Black Language as an Adaptive Response to a Hostile Environment." In C. Germaine (Ed.), *Social Work Practice: People and Environments.* New York: Columbia University Press, 1979.

Dubos, R. "Environmental Determinants of Human Life." In D. Glass (Ed.),

Environmental Influences. New York: Rockefeller University Press and Russell Sage Foundation, 1968a.

Dubos, R. *So Human an Animal.* New York: Scribner's, 1968b.

Esser, A. *Behavior and Environment.* New York: Plenum Press,1971.

Etzioni, A. *Modern Organizations.* Englewood Cliffs, N.J.: Prentice-Hall, 1964.

Fried, Marc. "Grieving for a Lost Home." In L. Duhl (Ed.), *The Urban Condition.* New York: Simon & Schuster, 1969.

Friedmann, E., and others. "Animal Companions and One-Year Survival of Patients After Discharge from a Coronary Care Unit." *Public Health Reports,* July-August 1980, *95* (4), 307-312.

Germain, C. "Time, an Ecological Variable in Social Work Practice." *Social Casework,* 1976, *57* (7), 419-426.

Germain, C. "Space, an Ecological Variable in Social Work Practice." *Social Casework,* 1978, *59* (9), 515-522.

Germain, C. "The Ecological Approach in Social Work: Some Notes on People-Environment Transactions." Paper presented at Sixth NASW Professional Symposium, San Antonio, Texas, Nov. 1979.

Germain, C., and Gitterman, A. *The Life Model of Social Work Practice.* New York: Columbia University Press, 1980.

Gross, H. E., and others. "Considering 'A Biosocial Perspective on Parenting.'" *Signs, Journal of Women in Culture and Society,* 1979, *4* (4), 695-717.

Hage, J. *Theories of Organization: Form, Process, and Transformation.* New York: Wiley, 1980.

Hage, J., and Aiken, M. *Social Change in Complex Organizations.* New York: Random House, 1970.

Hall, E. *The Hidden Dimension.* New York: Doubleday, 1966.

Hartman, A. In E. Tolson and W. Reid (Eds.), *Models of Family Treatment.* New York: Columbia University Press, 1981.

Hartmann, H. *Ego Psychology and the Problem of Adaptation.* New York: International Universities Press, 1958.

Hearn, G. *Theory Building in Social Work.* Toronto: University of Toronto Press, 1958.

Henry, J. *Pathways to Madness.* New York: Vintage Books, 1973.

Hinkle, L. "Ecological Observations of the Relation of Physical Illness, Mental Illness, and the Social Environment." *Psychosomatic Medicine,* 1961, *23,* 289-296.

Hinkle, L., and Loring, W. (Eds.). *The Effect of the Man-Made Environment on Health and Behavior.* DHEW Publication No. (CDC) 77-8318. Washington, D.C.: U.S. Department of Health, Education, and Welfare, 1977.

Hoffman, L. "Deviation-Amplifying Processes in Natural Groups." In J. Haley (Ed.), *Changing Families.* New York: Grune & Stratton, 1971.

Hoffman, L. "Breaking the Homeostatic Cycle." In P. Guerin (Ed.), *Family Therapy: Theory and Practice.* New York: Gardner Press, 1976.

Hoffman, L., and Long, L. "A Systems Dilemma." *Family Process,* 1969, *8,* 211-234.

Hollister, W. "Basic Strategies in Designing Primary Prevention Programs." In D. Klein and S. Goldston (Eds.), *Primary Prevention: An Idea Whose Time Has Come.* DHEW Publication No. (ADM) 77-447. Washington, D.C.: U.S. Department of Health, Education, and Welfare, 1977.

Holmes, T., and Rahe, R. "The Social Readjustment Rating Scale." *Journal of Psychosomatic Research,* 1967, *14,* 121-218.

Kantor, D., and Lehr, W. *Inside the Family.* San Francisco: Jossey-Bass, 1975.

Kinzel, A. "Body-Buffer Zone in Violent Prisoners." *American Journal of Psychiatry,* 1970, *127* (1), 59-64.

Klaus, M., and Kennell, J. *Maternal-Infant Bonding.* St. Louis: Mosby, 1976.

Kluckhohn, F. "Variations in the Basic Values of Family Systems." *Social Casework,* 1958, *39* (2), 63-72.

Kolata, G. "Behavioral Development: Effects of Environments." *Science,* 1975, *189,* 207-209.

Lamb, M. *The Social Role of the Father in Child Development.* New York: Wiley, 1976.

Lazarus, R., and Launier, R. "Stress-Related Transactions Between Person and Environment." In L. Pervin and M. Lewis (Eds.), *Perspectives in Interactional Psychology.* New York: Plenum Press, 1978.

Lee, J., and Park, D. "A Group Approach to the Depressed Adolescent Girl in Foster Care." *American Journal of Orthopsychiatry,* 1978, *48* (3), 516-527.

Lee, J., and Swenson, C. "A Community Social Service Agency: Theory in Action." *Social Casework,* 1978, *59* (6), 359-369.

Lennard, S., and Lennard, H. "Architecture: Effect of Territory, Boundary, and Orientation on Family Functioning." *Family Process,* 1977, *16* (1), 49-66.

Lewis, C. "People/Plant Interaction: Human Perspectives in Horti-Culture." *Hortiscience,* 1976, *11* (1), 4-5.

Lewis, T. "Notes of a Biology Watcher: Facts of Life." *New England Journal of Medicine,* 1977, *295* (25), 1462-1464.

Litwak, E., and Szelenyi, I. "Primary Group Structure and Their Functions: Kin, Neighbors, and Friends." *American Sociological Review,* 1969, *34* (4), 465-481.

Lutz, W. *Concepts and Principles Underlying Social Work Practice. [Social Work Practice in Medical Care and Rehabilitation Settings.* Monograph no. 3.] New York: National Association of Social Workers, 1956.

Maluccio, A. *Learning from Clients.* New York: Free Press, 1979.

Maruyama, M. "The Second Cybernetics: Deviation-Amplifying Mutual Causal Processes." *American Scientist,* 1963, *51,* 164-179. Reprinted in W. Buckley (Ed.), *Modern Systems Research for the Behavioral Scientist.* Chicago: Aldine, 1968.

Mayer, J., and Rosenblatt, A. "The Client's Social Context." *Social Casework,* 1964, *45* (9), 511-518.

Mechanic, D. "Discussion of Research Programs on Relations Between Stressful Life Events and Episodes of Physical Illness." In B. S. Dohrenwend and B. P. Dohrenwend (Eds.), *Stressful Life Events: Their Nature and Effects.* New York: Wiley, 1974a.

Mechanic, D. "Social Structure and Personal Adaptation: Some Neglected Dimensions." In G. Coelho and others (Eds.), *Coping and Adaptation.* New York: Basic Books, 1974b.

Mitchell, J. (Ed.). *Social Networks in Urban Situations.* Manchester: Manchester University Press, 1969.

Moos, R. *The Human Context: Environmental Determinants of Behavior.* New York: Wiley, 1976.

Newman, O. *Defensible Space.* New York: Collier Books, 1973.

Pancoast, D. "Finding and Enlisting Neighbors to Support Families." In J. Garbarino and S. H. Stocking (Eds.), *Protecting Children from Abuse and Neglect.* San Francisco: Jossey-Bass, 1980.

Patterson, S. "Toward a Conceptualization of Natural Helping." *Arete,* 1977, *4* (3), 161-173.

Patti, R. "Organizational Resistance and Change: The View from Below." *Social Service Review,* 1974, *45,* 367-383.

Patti, R., and Resnick, H. "Changing the Agency from Within." *Social Work,* 1972, *17* (4), 48-57.

Pervin, L., and Lewis, M. "Overview of the Internal-External Issue." In L. Pervin and M. Lewis (Eds.), *Perspectives in Interactional Psychology.* New York: Plenum, 1978.

Pollak, O. *Social Science and Psychotherapy for Children.* New York: Russell Sage, 1952.

Pollak, O. *Integrating Social Science and Psychoanalytic Concepts.* New York: Russell Sage, 1956.

Polsky, H. *Cottage Six.* New York: Russell Sage, 1962.

Powers, W. "Feedback: Beyond Behaviorism." *Science,* 1973, *179,* 351-356.

Proshansky, H., and others (Eds.). *Environmental Psychology.* New York: Holt, Rinehart and Winston, 1970. (2nd rev. ed. 1976.)

Rabkin, J., and Struening, E. "Life Events, Stress, and Illness." *Science,* 1976, *194,* 1013-1020.

Rossi, A. "A Biosocial Perspective on Parenting." *Daedalus,* 1977, *6* (2), 1-32.

Saegert, S. "Stress-Inducing and Reducing Qualities of Environments." In H. Proshansky and others (Eds.), *Environmental Psychology.* (2nd ed.) New York: Holt, Rinehart and Winston, 1976.

Scheflen, A., and Ashcraft, N. *Human Territories: How We Behave in Space and Time.* Englewood Cliffs, N.J.: Prentice-Hall, 1976.

Searles, H. *The Non-Human Environment.* New York: International Universities Press, 1960.

Shapiro, J. *Communities of the Alone.* New York: Association Press, 1971.

Shearer, R. "Overnight Trips for Chronic Psychiatric Patients." *Social Work,* 1978, *23* (4), 324-325.

Signs, Journal of Women in Culture in Society, 1980, Supp. *5* (3). Special Issue, "Women and the American City."

Silverman, P. "The Widow as Caregiver in a Program of Preventive Intervention with Other Widows." In G. Caplan and M. Killilea (Eds.), *Support Systems and Mutual Help: Multidisciplinary Explorations.* New York: Grune & Stratton, 1976.

Sommer, R. *Personal Space: The Behavioral Basis of Design.* Englewood Cliffs, N.J.: Prentice-Hall, 1969.

Speck, R. "Psychotherapy of the Network of a Schizophrenic Family." *Family Process,* 1967, *6,* 208-214.

Speck, R., and Attneave, C. *Family Networks: Retribalization and Healing.* New York: Pantheon, 1973.

Speck, R., and Ruveni, U. "Network Therapy—A Developing Concept." *Family Process,* 1969, *8* (2), 182–190.

Spivack, M. "Archetypal Place." In W. Preiser (Ed.), *Environmental Design Research. Vol. 1.* Stroudsburg, Pa.: Dowden, Hutchinson and Ross, 1973.

Stack, C. *All Our Kin: Strategies for Survival in a Black Community.* New York: Harper Colophon Books, 1974.

Stea, D. "Home Range and the Use of Space." In L. Pastalan and D. Carson (Eds.), *Spatial Behavior of Older People.* Ann Arbor: University of Michigan–Wayne State University, 1970.

Steele, F. *Physical Settings and Organizational Development.* Reading, Mass.: Addison-Wesley, 1973.

Stein, H. "The Concept of the Social Environment in Social work Practice." *Smith College Studies in Social Work,* 1960, *30,* 187–210. Reprinted in J. Parad and R. Miller (Eds.), *Ego-Oriented Casework.* New York: Family Service Association of America, 1963.

Stein, H., and Cloward, R. *Social Perspectives on Behavior.* New York: Free Press, 1958.

Tuan, Y. *Space and Place.* Minneapolis: University of Minnesota Press, 1977.

Valentine, B. *Hustling and Other Hard Work.* New York: Free Press, 1978.

Valentine, C., and Valentine, B. "Making the Scene, Digging the Action, and Telling It Like It Is: Anthropologists at Work in a Dark Ghetto." In N. Whitten and J. Szwed (Eds.), *Afro-American Anthropology.* New York: Free Press, 1970.

Van Harrison, R. "Person–Environment Fit and Job Stress." In C. Cooper and R. Payne (Eds.), *Stress at Work.* New York: Wiley, 1978.

Vassil, T. "Residential Family Camping: Altering Family Patterns." *Social Casework,* 1978, *59* (10), 605–613.

Wax, J. "Developing Social Work Power in a Medical Setting." *Social Work,* 1968, *10,* 62–71.

Wax, J. "Power Theory and Institutional Change." *Social Service Review,* 1971, *45* (3), 274–288.

Weiss, P. "The Biological Bases of Adaptation." In J. Romano (Ed.), *Adaptation.* Ithaca, N.Y.: Cornell University Press, 1949.

Weiss, R. S. *Loneliness: The Experience of Emotional and Social Isolation.* Cambridge: M.I.T. Press, 1973.

Weissman, H. H. *Overcoming Mismanagement in the Human Service Professions.* San Francisco: Jossey-Bass, 1973.

Wetzel, J. "Depression and Dependence Upon Unsustaining Environments." *Clinical Social Work Journal,* 1978a, *6* (2), 75–89.

Wetzel, J. "The Work Environment and Depression: Implications for Intervention." In J. Hanks (Ed.), *Toward Human Dignity.* Washington, D.C.: National Association of Social Workers, 1978b.

White, R. W. "Strategies of Adaptation: An Attempt at Systematic Description." In G. Coelho and others (Eds.), *Coping and Adaptation.* New York: Basic Books, 1974.

Will, O. "Human Relatedness and the Schizophrenic Reaction." *Psychiatry,* 1959, *22* (3), 205–223.

Wilson, E. *Sociobiology.* Cambridge, Mass.: Harvard University Press, 1975.

Wilson, E. *On Human Nature.* Cambridge, Mass.: Harvard University Press, 1978.

Yancey, W. "Architecture, Interaction, and Social Control: The Case of a Large-Scale Public Housing Project." *Environment and Behavior,* 1971, *3* (1), 3–18. Reprinted in H. Proshansky and others (Eds.), *Environmental Psychology.* (2nd ed.) New York: Holt, Rinehart and Winston, 1976.

6

Planned Use of Life Experiences

Anthony N. Maluccio

As with the weather, it seems that nearly everyone in social work talks about the importance of life experiences in the growth and functioning of human beings. Indeed, social workers often informally use life experiences, such as life crises, events, and activities, in their efforts to help clients.

Unlike the weather, there has been little effort to analyze, synthesize, and further develop our knowledge in this area. Perhaps life experiences are so obvious that they are taken for granted and their role is undervalued. As a result, in social work practice, their potential is not fully exploited and their use is oversimplified. It is as if life experiences simply *happen* in the course of social work intervention rather than being consciously used on the basis of careful assessment of client needs and formulation of client goals.

Yet, as early as the 1940s, social work theorists pointed to the significance and complexity of life experiences. In particular, in her classic formulation of casework methods, Austin (1948) added "experiential treatment" to the earlier bimodal typology of "environmental manipulation" and "insight therapy." By experiential treatment, she meant the active use of life experiences, as well as the caseworker-client relationship, to bring about change in the client's situation. Even before 1948, early social group workers in such settings as settlement houses and community centers emphasized the provision of recreational and cultural experiences to promote individual growth and personality development.

Note: For their thoughtful criticisms and suggestions, I wish to thank Ann Hartman, the University of Michigan School of Social Work, and Mary Frances Libassi, the University of Connecticut School of Social Work.

More recently, Oxley (1971) highlighted the role of life experiences in the life-model approach to casework treatment. The life model has since emerged as a useful framework for social work practice in general (Germain and Gitterman, 1980). Its major emphasis is on improving the adaptive fit so that reciprocal processes between people and their environments will be more conducive to the development of human potential and the improvement of environments. The planned use of life experiences is a major feature of this perspective on practice.

With the advent of the life model and the emergence of new bodies of knowledge, especially in the sociobehavioral sciences, the professional use of life experiences in social work practice may be said to be coming of age. This chapter examines the significance of life experiences for clinical social work, the theoretical perspectives supporting their use as resources for (and instruments of) change, and the central practice principles guiding workers in using them professionally in a conscious and purposeful fashion.

Life Experiences and Clinical Social Work

Before going further, we should define *life experiences*. This term refers to processes and events or experiences that unfold in the natural course of people's lives. Life processes include such human functions as motivation, cognition, emotion, and perception. Life experiences include simple occurrences, such as meeting a new friend, as well as complex life tasks and developmental crises or challenges, such as the birth of a child or the death of a parent. Other examples are such events as beginning a new job or getting a promotion, activities in areas such as work and recreation, and relationships with significant persons in one's social networks.

The therapeutic potential of life experiences and activities has been emphasized by a number of theorists and researchers. The contributions of such social work pioneers as Austin (1948) have already been mentioned. Others have shown that engaging in goal-directed action can stimulate people's coping efforts, strengthen their adaptive capacities, and facilitate growth (Maluccio, 1974). In her naturalistic studies on child development, Murphy (1962) points out that the feelings of satisfaction and mastery resulting from a child's successful completion of an activity are closely linked with his or her sense of self-worth and capacity to gain respect from others. On the basis of research showing how the meeting of new challenges enhances the child's sense of adequacy, pride, and pleasure, Murphy (1962, p. 374) observes: "Through the successive experiences of spontaneous mastery of new demands and utilizing new opportunities for gratification, the child extends and verifies his identity as one who can manage certain aspects of the environment. Through his coping experiences the child discovers and measures himself and develops his own perception of who and what he is and in time may become." Although Murphy's formulations are derived from research with children, her observations have essential meaning regardless of age.

The value of life experiences is also emphasized in psychoanalysis by Alexander (1946, p. 40), who indicates that "there is no more powerful therapeutic factor than the performance of activities which were formerly neurotically impaired or inhibited." Stressing that the experience of success in significant activities encourages new trials and enhances the person's well-being, Alexander

(1946, p. 40) concludes that "successful attempts at productive work, love, self-assertion, or competition will change the vicious cycle to a benign one; as they are repeated, they become habitual and thus eventually bring about a complete change in the personality."

Similarly, Menninger (1967) asserts that, in the course of mental illness, life events and processes can have a beneficial impact on the person. He observes (p. 297) that "hundreds of impersonal things contribute to recovery—everything, in short, which belongs to a healthy way of living. This means the opportunity and the encouragement to work, to play, to create, to communicate, to enjoy beauty."

As research findings demonstrate, "people experience positive change as a result of life experience without therapy" (Oxley, 1971, p. 627). Moreover, as many argue, insight is neither sufficient nor necessary to achieve change; with or without self-understanding, human beings change through natural life processes such as maturation, interaction, action, learning, and crisis resolution (Oxley, 1971).

In short, life events and experiences are the heart and soul of psychosocial functioning and can serve as powerful resources for change. To achieve the central purpose of helping clients to enhance their functioning, clinical social workers should therefore make conscious use of these resources by (1) building on the client's natural life processes and events and (2) planning and prescribing new experiences that are geared to the client's unique needs and qualities.

Opportunities to do so can be found in typical case situations. Thus, a crisis, such as the father's death in a young family, is approached as a challenge to the mother; the social worker can suggest various strategies for helping her to mobilize her own resources and strengthen her parenting skills. A child having trouble making or keeping friends is encouraged and supported in playground activities; the worker becomes a coach who provides information and teaches skills. A deinstitutionalized psychiatric patient who is overwhelmed by the complexity of city living is helped to negotiate the bus system, shop for food and clothing, and apply for a job; success in these basic life experiences enhances psychosocial functioning and builds a sense of competence and self-worth.

Philosophical Base

Our philosophical assumptions about human nature guide our thinking and action as social workers and influence our choice of theoretical perspectives. Optimum use of life experiences in clinical practice requires, above all, commitment to the view of human beings as striving, active organisms who are capable of organizing their lives and developing their potentialities as long as they have appropriate environmental supports.

Especially noteworthy in this regard are the ideas of various humanistic thinkers, such as Angyal (1941), with his concepts of autonomy, self-determination, and human striving toward active mastery of the environment; Maslow (1954), with his emphasis on positive personality growth and human motivation toward self-actualization; and Allport (1960), with his view of personality as an open system in contrast to the psychoanalytic notion of personality as semiclosed.

Although the terms and their underlying assumptions vary, the formulations of these and other thinkers basically refer to the human being's motivation to seek stimulation, to cope with challenges, to accomplish, to master, to feel competent and self-determining.

By virtue of its positive emphasis on growth and adaptation, the humanistic perspective leads to deemphasis of pathology and conviction about the human being's capacity for change throughout the life cycle. Implementing this perspective in practice may necessitate changes in our views of human beings, and especially a shift in our attitudes toward clients; many workers have been trained only too well to emphasize pathology and overlook or deemphasize human strengths and latent potentialities for change. It is no accident that a study of perceptions of treatment in a family service agency showed that there were striking differences in the perspectives of clients and social workers: "In general, clients presented themselves as *proactive,* autonomous human beings who were able to enhance their functioning and their competence through the use of the service and of resources in themselves and their social networks. Workers, on the other hand, tended to view clients as *reactive* organisms with continuing problems, underyling weaknesses, and limited potentialities" (Maluccio, 1979a, p. 102). As an example, in the case of a woman who had received a job promotion, the client talked about her increased sense of competence and enhanced self-image, while the worker expressed much concern about her ability to cope with the additional pressures and responsibilities.

Theoretical Perspectives

Theoretical support for the professional use of life experiences as resources for change comes from various theorists with a humanistic orientation and from a range of disciplines as diverse as ego psychology and learning theory. A number of integrative themes come particularly from ecology, general systems theory, ego psychology, and crisis theory.

Human Organisms as Open Systems. From general systems theory comes the notion of the human organism as constituting one part in an interconnected, interdependent, and complementary set of parts. As with any other living organism, each person is constantly influenced by—and in turn exerts influence upon—other systems of varying levels, such as family, school, community, work, or culture. In other words, human beings are defined as open systems engaged in a continuous process of growth and adaptation.

In the science of ecology, human beings are also seen as involved in dynamic transactions with their environment, specifically in a continuing struggle to maintain a "moving equilibrium" while faced with a complex and changing array of environmental challenges. Similarly, in biology there is emphasis on the interplay between the person and the environment, a process of mutual adaptation in which each human being responds in a personal and creative manner.

Crisis theory elaborates the notion of the human organism as an open system even further. It holds that persons are especially amenable to change when they are facing a crisis (such as the loss of a family member) or a life transition (such as retirement). Golan (1978) explains this phenomenon: "During the resolution of the crisis, the individual tends to be particularly amenable to help. Customary defense mechanisms have become weakened, usual coping patterns have proved inadequate, and the ego has become more open to outside influence and change. A minimal effort at this time can produce a maximal effect; a small amount of help, appropriately focused, can prove more effective than more extensive help at a period of less emotional accessibility" (p. 9).

Crises and life transitions are an integral part of living. For instance, according to Erikson (1959), people grow and achieve their identity through the successive resolution of developmental crises characterizing each stage of the life cycle.

In clinical social work, a client's crisis or life transition presents opportunities for enhancing his or her psychosocial functioning: "All life transitions require changes in the self-image, ways of looking at the world, the processing of information derived from cognition, perception, and feeling, patterns of relating to others, uses of environmental resources, and goals. All require the restructuring of one's life space" (Germain and Gitterman, 1980, p. 7).

Goodness-of-Fit. A related idea is that of the "goodness-of-fit" between people and their environments, an idea that is characteristic of the ecological perspective and life model of practice (Germain and Gitterman, 1980). This concept, which has been used extensively in stress theory, refers to the complex transactional relationship between human beings and their environments. The complementarity or "goodness-of-fit" between people's needs and qualities and environmental demands and characteristics strongly influences human competence and adaptation. For this reason, some researchers conceptualize human adaptation in terms of the fit between the characteristics of people and the properties of the impinging environment (French, Rodgers, and Cobb, 1974).

In clinical practice with individuals, families, or groups, the notion of goodness-of-fit suggests that, in each client situation, crucial questions should be considered in relation to the environment and its properties. For example, how nutritive or supportive is it? What is the quality of life events impinging on the person at any given point? What needs to be added to—or subtracted from—the environment in order to render it more nutritive and thus conducive to the successful negotiation of life challenges? Which life experiences are constructive for the person and should be supported or mobilized? Which life experiences interfere with the person's struggle to achieve a dynamic equilibrium and should therefore be modified?

As these questions suggest, in each client situation, life experiences represent a crucial variable in the person–environment transaction. They influence, positively or negatively, the person's struggle to achieve a dynamic equilibrium and thus influence his or her psychosocial functioning. Consequently, they can affect any change efforts that clients and social workers undertake.

Competence Development. Knowledge from various disciplines, particularly ego psychology, is essential in understanding how human beings achieve competence and effective functioning. Adaptation, autonomy, and competence are among the central concepts that are especially pertinent to the professional use of life experiences as resources for change and as instruments of competence development (Maluccio, 1981).

Adaptation. In the past several decades, through the contributions of such theorists as Erikson (1959), Hartmann (1958), and White (1959, 1963), ego psychology has moved from emphasis on the dynamics of defense mechanisms to explication of the independent, adaptive, and maturational aspects of the ego. In the classical Freudian view, the ego was seen as arising out of conflict among the id, superego, and reality; its key function was that of mediator or synthesizer. Departing from this view, Hartmann (1958) postulates the existence of a "conflict-free sphere" of the ego from which emerge "executive" functions, such as thought, perception, and motility.

Hartmann (1958, pp. 22–37) indicates that adaptation involves a reciprocal relationship between organism and environment. He distinguishes between a *state of adaptedness* between the organism and the environment and the *process of adaptation* through which that state is achieved. In his formulation, adaptation is a creative endeavor that is influenced by the environment, the person's constitution, and his or her developmental phase. The individual's biologically endowed potentialities emerge and develop in response to the reality situation encountered in the environment. In Hartmann's view, human organisms not only adapt to the environment but also are capable of changing it in order to meet their needs. Hartmann defines three forms of adaptation: (1) *autoplastic,* that is, a change of self or a change in the individual's psychosocial system; (2) *alloplastic,* that is, effecting changes in the environment itself; and (3) *seeking a new environment* that is advantageous for the individual's functioning.

In his psychosocial, epigenetic formulation of ego development, Erikson (1959) places further stress on the role of the environment in personality growth. Elaborating on Hartmann's earlier formulation concerning the individual's adaptation to "an average expectable environment," Erikson highlights the individual's constant and active interaction with the environment as particularly crucial to his or her development. Similarly, from the perspective of biology, Dubos (1965) focuses on the dynamic interplay between people and their environment, a process that leads to each human being's unique way of developing himself or herself.

Contrary to the simplistic view sometimes reflected in social work writings, adaptation does not imply passive submission or mere adjustment by the human organism to the environment. On the contrary, the formulations of ego psychologists, ecologists, and others serve to make alive the notion of the person as an active rather than merely a reactive participant in interaction with the environment. Thus, Dubos (1965) stresses: "Experience shows that human beings are not passive components in adaptive systems. Their responses commonly manifest themselves as acts of personal creation. Each individual person tries to achieve some self-selected end even while he is responding to stimuli and adapting to them" (p. xviii).

In short, adaptation is a dynamic, creative process that demands continual effort and a variety of strategies on the part of the organism. White (1974, pp. 46–49) views defense, mastery, and coping as the chief strategies of adaptation. In his formulation, *defense* refers to the organism's efforts to deal with danger or anxiety, such as the fear of rejection from another person. *Mastery* denotes successful performance in meeting task requirements under ordinary circumstances, such as in learning how to swim. *Coping* refers to efforts to meet new or difficult demands, such as when a child goes to school for the first time.

As the preceding formulations suggest, the process of adaptation is a complex one requiring a variety of personal resources, constructive life experiences, and broad social and environmental supports.

Autonomy. The concept of adaptation is closely related to that of autonomy, which may be defined as the person's capacity for self-government with relative freedom from instinctual and environmental forces. Autonomy may be viewed as the inner sense of safety and well-being. The higher the number of opportunities for adaptive responses available to the person, the higher is the degree of his or her autonomy.

In a class paper, Rapaport (1958) synthesizes and further develops scattered ideas on ego autonomy from the psychoanalytic school of thought. He defines *ego autonomy* as the individual's relative independence from the id or internal drive forces as well as from external reality or the environment. Drawing from Piaget's (1952) theory of cognitive development, Rapaport suggests that the development, maintenance, and effectiveness of ego autonomy require stimulus-nutriments from within as well as from outside the organism. External stimulus-nutriments include all that is perceived in the environment, such as positive feedback from another person and rewarding life experiences. Internal stimulus-nutriments include personal values, ideologies, and drives.

Miller (1962) examines the concept of autonomy in the light of experimental, biographical, and clinical evidence from situations of sensory deprivation, isolation, and stress. He proposes various revisions in Rapaport's theory of ego autonomy, underscoring the importance of ego activity in adaptive measures. Examples of ego activities successfully employed by prisoners, explorers, and other human beings in situations of extreme stress or deprivation include the following: mental exercises, reading, log-keeping, work, turning to religion, humor, reliance on ideology, and devotion to nonhuman companions. Engagement in these activities promotes maintenance of ego autonomy. In contrast, ego passivity or lack of involvement in activities results in impairment of autonomy (p. 16).

In his reevaluation of the theory of ego autonomy, Holt (1967, pp. 492–500) clarifies that a key function of stimulus-nutriments or inputs from the external world is to provide *opportunities* to use and develop ego skills in addition to offering support and information. In other words, if a person is to develop necessary skills, such as relating to one's peers, dealing with anxiety-provoking situations, or making decisions, he or she must have adequate opportunities to practice these skills in real-life situations. Environmental inputs should support and nourish the individual's efforts to develop ego skills.

In his penetrating analysis of autonomy in a mass age, Bettelheim (1960, pp. 73–79) focuses on the threats to ego development and autonomy arising in a complex, industrialized, mass society. These threats include infringement on human freedom, excessive external management of human affairs with little personal decision making, and other dehumanizing processes. In clinical social work, interventive activities and life experiences can often be mobilized to counteract these threats and promote the client's autonomy.

Competence. Competence is generally defined as the network of skills, knowledge, and talents that enable the person to interact effectively with the environment (White, 1963). Since it is a central concept in the theoretical base supporting the planned use of life experiences as resources for change (Maluccio, 1981), it will be considered at some length.

From the perspective of ego psychology, White (1959, 1963) has made the most notable contribution to the study of human competence. First, he has modified the orthodox drive theory of human motivation by postulating the existence in the organism of inborn "independent ego energies," or a special category of biologically given motivation toward dealing with the environment that he terms "effectance" or "competence motivation." White departs from classical psychoanalytic formulations by hypothesizing that the drive toward effectance is powered by its own psychic energy rather than being dependent on the neutralization of sexual and aggressive energies.

In explicating the concept of effectance, White (1963, pp. 24–43) cites extensive evidence from research on animal behavior and early childhood development demonstrating that a human organism's efforts to reach out to the environment through such processes as manipulation and exploration cannot be adequately explained on the basis of traditional motivational theories rooted in instinctual drives and tension reduction. Noting that much activity and learning occur even when the basic drives of the organism are satisfied, White postulates that an autonomous drive toward competence motivates the human being to keep trying out the effectiveness of his or her ripening capacities for action. The person is compelled to seek competence in dealing with instinctual as well as environmental demands through the force of his or her independent ego energies. The ego is strengthened through the individual's "action upon the environment, feelings of efficacy, and cumulative growth of a sense of competence" (p. 150).

White's formulation is essentially a biopsychological one. In contrast, in their conceptualization of social competence, Inkeles (1966) and Gladwin (1967) stress societal rather than psychological referents. Inkeles is concerned primarily with role performance and societal requirements; consequently, he defines *competence* as "the ability effectively to attain and perform in three sets of statuses: those which one's society will normally assign one, those . . . which one may reasonably aspire to, and those which one may reasonably invent or elaborate for one's self" (p. 265).

Gladwin (1967) also emphasizes the importance of social processes and interactions. He believes that competence develops along three major interrelated axes: (1) "the ability to learn or to use a variety of alternative pathways or behavioral responses in order to reach a given goal"; (2) the ability to comprehend a variety of social systems within society and in particular to utilize the resources that they offer; and (3) effective reality testing involving not only "lack of psychopathological impairment but also a positive, broad, and sophisticated understanding of the world" (p. 32).

Smith (1968), a social psychologist, proposes an integrative conception of competence that also rests on the interaction between behavior and environment. In his formulation, competence involves intrinsic as well as extrinsic motivation, social skills as well as personal abilities, and effective performance for *self* as well as *society* in one's social roles. Smith asserts that both intrinsic motivation of the organism and social reinforcement are necessary in socialization and personality development. He therefore states that competent functioning is affected by key factors in the personal system of the organism as well as by strategic components in the social structure. The key factors in the personal system are: the sense of *efficacy* or *potency* in controlling one's destiny; the attitude of *hope;* and a favorable level of *self-respect* or *self-acceptance.* Corresponding key features in the social system are: *opportunity* (for example, supports or resources), which stimulates and reinforces the sense of hope; *respect by others,* which provides the social ground for respect of self; and power, which guarantees access to opportunity (pp. 312–313).

These varying formulations contribute to a comprehensive conception of competence in its multiple biological, psychological, social, and cultural aspects. There is uniform emphasis on the notion of the human organism's drive toward dealing effectively with the environment. There is also agreement that personality growth takes place in the context of the dynamic interplay between the qualities of the organism and the characteristics of the impinging environment. Such a transactional view helps to sensitize practitioners to the impact that environmental demands and properties have on the personal, interpersonal, or social competence of human beings.

Significance for Competence Development. Theoretical perspectives relating to competence, autonomy, and adaptation show that, to develop their competence and achieve effective functioning, human beings need a variety of opportunities and supports that are matched to their changing needs and qualities. These perspectives therefore help social workers to appreciate more deeply the significance of the context of human behavior and to guide them in identifying, understanding, and manipulating life experiences and environmental obstacles and resources affecting a client's psychosocial functioning.

Autonomy, adaptation, and competence are closely related and interdependent concepts. There is a reciprocal relationship between a person's adaptation at any given point and his or her competence. Adaptive behavior may be viewed as the outer manifestation of competence. Similarly, self-esteem may be regarded as the individual's perceived competence. And, key components of self-esteem are a sense of mastery over the environment, feeling positively valued by others, and being autonomous.

Learning and Human Behavior. The crucial role of learning in human behavior is an underlying theme in the theoretical perspectives discussed thus far regarding competence development, the view of human organisms as open systems, and the notion of the goodness-of-fit between people and their environments. Indeed, most theories of human behavior and personality development implicitly or explicitly postulate that behavioral change is the result of learning. Ego psychology, for example, stresses that people grow and change as they learn new ways of coping and adapting.

The learning process is an even more prominent component of other theories. For instance, socialization theory emphasizes that, through social interaction with others, human beings learn about themselves and each other. As defined by Merton and others (1957, p. 287), *socialization* is "the process by which people selectively acquire the values and attitudes, the interests, skills, and knowledge—in short, the culture—current in groups of which they are, or seek to become, members."

In addition, learning is a cornerstone of behaviorism. The latter embodies an extensive formal learning theory in which the learning process is systematically examined. Although there are diverse views within behaviorism, a key theme is that learning through conditioning shapes human behavior.

Despite their widely different philosophical and theoretical assumptions, ego psychology, behaviorism, and socialization theory share the view that learning through life experiences is an important influence on human behavior and personality development.

Principles of Practice

The theoretical orientations presented in this chapter lead to a particular practice approach requiring a redefinition of the helping process in clinical social work. The process is one in which client and worker are actively involved in making conscious and planful use of life experiences—natural or otherwise—to (1) meet the client's needs, (2) support his or her adaptive strivings, and (3) promote his or her growth and psychosocial functioning. Selected practice principles and strategies flowing from such a redefinition are discussed and illustrated in this section.

Client-Worker Relationship and Roles. As part of the focus on life experiences, the client-worker relationship is "redefined as one in which two people are working on a shared project. Each brings a special expertise to the task" (Hartman, 1979, p. 264). The worker encourages client autonomy and reduces worker authority and the mystique of treatment. The worker seeks to decrease social distance from the client and nurture "a relationship that manifests openness, authenticity, honesty, and human caring" (Germain, 1979, p. 18).

At the same time, the worker should be sufficiently aware of the client's life situation to be able to identify opportunities for the client to use and build on relevant life processes and events. In typical life situations, it is often possible to identify opportunities to help clients exercise their decision-making function, become engaged in action on their own behalf, and use their cognitive powers. In this process, "Every effort is made to mobilize and employ natural systems for change rather than to develop new or artificial systems. For example, the client is encouraged to work through troublesome relationships with major figures in life with the people involved rather than with the therapist through the medium of transference" (Hartman, 1979, p. 263).

To take full advantage of life experiences, workers should regard clients as partners in the change process; they should also define clients as *resources,* that is, as having assets and potentialities that can be mobilized on their behalf. This means, among other aspects, that clients should play active roles and participate meaningfully in such areas as assessment, goal formulation, and selection of interventive strategies. If workers consciously seek such opportunities, frequently they can find many ways to help clients to meet their needs and at the same time enhance their competence and autonomy (Maluccio, 1981, p. 15). In some residential treatment centers, for example, parents of placed children are actively involved in the treatment program through such means as serving as resources to the childcare staff and participating in team meetings. Through these experiences, they are helped to improve their self-esteem and ultimately their coping capacities as parents.

As clients are thus empowered to take action on their behalf, the roles of social workers are also defined in complementary terms. In particular, as suggested by Studt (1968), workers are viewed primarily as catalysts, as enabling agents who help the client to identify and use appropriate experiences or create new experiences and resources. The worker plays diverse roles and uses a variety of approaches to help provide the conditions necessary for clients to achieve their purposes, engage in their natural developmental processes, and carry out their tasks. In addition to the role of therapist, a worker may need to serve as guide, strategist, teacher, broker, or advocate.

The focus on life experiences and a redefined client-worker relationship can lead to benefits that at times go beyond the client's immediate need. For example:

> A social worker in a day care center became acquainted with a young mother, Mrs. Jenkins, when she dropped off and picked up her child each day. Mrs. Jenkins began to linger for short conversations with the worker. Eventually, she asked the worker to visit her at home so that they could talk further about some of her concerns.
>
> Mrs. Jenkins then expressed much dissatisfaction with her life; she felt lonely, unfulfilled, and unhappy over the lack of contact with other adults. People in her neighborhood tended to keep to themselves. Although she was yearning for opportunities to develop her interests and to form close relationships with others, her environment provided little challenge.
>
> As the worker became aware of Mrs. Jenkins' needs and qualities, she encouraged her to try to create an informal support system in the neighborhood, thus making the environment more nurturing. Mrs. Jenkins brought considerable knowledge and skills to this task. She had a good understanding of the needs and characteristics of the community. She also had skills in arts and crafts. The worker had information about—and access to—formal agencies and was able to involve the appropriate ones in the project.
>
> Mrs. Jenkins and the worker began to hold informal arts and crafts events at the day care center for parents and children in the neighborhood. This not only provided an opportunity for families to have fun together but also began to produce the kind of informal support that Mrs. Jenkins had wanted.
>
> While playing the role of enabler and community organizer, the worker respected and supported Mrs. Jenkins and helped her to create opportunities that were responsive to her needs and talents. In turn, Mrs. Jenkins, as an effective leader, attained satisfaction through her participation in meaningful activities and enhanced her sense of competence. At the same time, with the worker's encouragement, she created an environment that was more supportive and challenging for herself as well as other mothers in the area.

Assessment. A fundamental feature of clinical social work is the individual assessment of each client. A major purpose of assessment should be to identify potential opportunities to employ life experiences in each case situation. To be able to do so effectively, the worker needs to complement clinically based assessment procedures with other methods, such as participant observation. As much as is feasible and appropriate, the worker should become involved in the client's life situation and seek to understand through direct experience what is going on with the client in relevant contexts, such as the family, neighborhood, or school.

Competence Clarification. To make professional use of life experiences as resources for change, workers should understand, as clearly as possible, each client's competence and the multiple factors affecting it (Maluccio, 1981, pp. 13–14). Consequently, principles such as the following should guide the worker in the course of assessment:

- *Clarifying the competence of the client system.* The worker addresses the questions such as these: What are the unique capacities, skills, attitudes, motivations, and potentialities of the client? What are the particular areas of coping strengths? Which areas of competence need to be reinforced or supported? Which life experiences may be mobilized to stimulate or support the process of change?
- *Clarifying the characteristics of the impinging environment that influence the client's coping and adaptive patterns.* This involves exploring areas such as the following: the critical environmental demands and challenges confronting the client; the actual or potential supports available in the environment; and the blocks, obstacles, and deficits that interfere with the person's life processes and adaptive strivings.
- *Clarifying the goodness-of-fit between the clint system and its impinging environment.* Some relevant questions are: How nutritive is the environment in relation to the client's needs? Does it contain the ingredients necessary to support, nourish, and challenge the person? What needs to be changed to make the transaction more mutually rewarding, to achieve a better adaptive fit, and to help the person to use and build on his or her life experiences? What new experiences or activities should be specifically planned?

The following vignette suggests how the use of these principles as a part of the assessment can lead to the conscious use of life experiences as instruments of change.

> A worker in a halfway house located on the grounds of a large psychiatric hospital began to work with a resocialization group of five middle-aged women who had been diagnosed as schizophrenic. Every one of them had been in the hospital at least four years. They had recently been transferred to the halfway house to test their readiness to return to the community.
>
> In examining the functioning of group members from a competence perspective, the worker was impressed by the variety of existing skills and strengths. For instance, three of the women had been successfully holding part-time jobs in the hospital. One was an excellent cook. Another one wrote poetry that delighted the other patients. All of them had been regularly attending group activities.
>
> The worker thus identified the clients' varied skills and potentialities for competent functioning. At the same time, she recognized various environmental blocks. Above all, as a result of having been labeled as sick, the women were not receiving positive feedback from their family or from staff members. The worker, therefore, set out to improve the goodness-of-fit between these persons and their environment by changing other people's perception of them and their qualities, by offering encouragement and support, and by providing further opportunities for development of their skills and talents. For instance, she planned a structured "life skills" workshop for group members and then helped them to practice their new skills through a variety of specific and repeated activities, such as shopping in local supermarkets, going to the movies in town, and taking the bus to a nearby city. These activities were developed on the basis of the worker's assessment of each person's needs and qualities and purposively related to specific goals formulated with each client.

Problem Definition. The planned use of life experiences as resources for change also requires that human difficulties be viewed as "problems in living" or as manifestations of the poor fit or lack of mutuality between people and their environments. These problems include developmental crises, such as adolescence; life transitions, such as marriage or divorce; and discrepancies between a person's needs and environmental resources, such as the situation of a single mother who is finding it hard to care for her children due to the lack of day care services in her neighborhood.

Problems or needs thus are not seen as specific weaknesses or properties of the person. "Behavior is not viewed as sick or well but is defined as transactional—an outcome of reciprocal interactions between specific social situations and the individual" (Kelly, 1973, p. 538).

As a result of this orientation, human problems, needs, and conflicts are redefined in transactional terms so as to suggest ways of intervening in the person–environment transaction. For instance, problems are translated into adaptive tasks or meaningful life experiences, which provide the client with opportunities for competence development. Change efforts can then be directed toward supporting the client's coping strategies and learning of necessary skills. For example, a parent referred for child neglect is defined as needing to learn skills in child care and is provided with a homemaker and a parent aide, who offer concrete help while also serving as role models. A couple experiencing marital discord is encouraged to clarify and define factors that lead to their persistent arguments. A young unmarried mother is defined as having a problem in role transition rather than an underlying personality conflict and is provided with activities that help her to gain competence as a new parent.

Intervention

The major thrust of the theoretical and practice orientation presented in this chapter is that life itself can serve as the arena of social work intervention when the therapeutic potential of life experiences is consciously exploited on behalf of clients. Various principles help guide interventive activities in this approach to practice.

Relevance. To begin, the particular experiences or activities should flow from the assessment and be relevant to the client's life situation; they should be meaningfully related to the person's needs or goals and consonant with his or her natural life processes. The issue of relevance is especially important in crisis situations, such as the following:

> Mrs. Fort is a middle-aged woman who seems incapable of functioning following her husband's recent death. She has become extremely dependent on her adolescent children, who are frightened and frustrated by her behavior. The children have been avoiding her, thus contributing to her loneliness and depression. Their physician refers the Forts to a family service agency.
>
> After helping Mrs. Fort to work through some of her grief reaction, the social worker involves her and the children in formulation of multiple tasks designed to promote her independent functioning as well as to change the family's interactional patterns. For example, instead of constantly

avoiding their mother, the children agree to go with her to visit relatives at least once weekly. Mrs. Fort agrees to let them go out on their own several evenings weekly rather than feeling that all of them should always keep her company. The worker instructs the children to sit down individually with their mother and share with her their hopes for the future—something that they had routinely done with their father. The worker encourages Mrs. Fort to make decisions in such areas as necessary housing repairs. He also helps her to pursue a variety of activities, including shopping for some badly needed clothes for herself and beginning to look for a job.

As they perform these varied tasks, Mrs. Fort and her children develop a new interactional equilibrium in their family system, which had been severely threatened by the loss of the husband and father. New role behaviors and communication patterns emerge, enabling them to offer each other some gratification as a changed family unit. In addition, as she gradually performs her individual tasks with the worker's and children's support, Mrs. Fort enhances her sense of autonomy, gains some desperately needed feelings of competence, and improves her skills in dealing with the environment. All family members thus profit from engagement in a variety of individual as well as joint activities and experiences.

In response to the disruption and dysfunctioning provoked by a family crisis, the worker in the above case selected a variety of relevant experiences intended to strengthen each person's coping patterns and restore the family's interaction and functioning as a system. As shown by Minuchin (1974) in his structural approach to family therapy, appropriately chosen experiences within as well as outside treatment sessions can be used to restructure the family environment so that it is more satisfying and growth producing for family members. The following example illustrates ways of accomplishing this purpose.

The Turner family was rapidly drawing apart following the parents' divorce. Mrs. Turner had custody of her three teenagers. She was preoccupied not only with her own feelings and needs but also with the children's increasing behavioral and learning problems. When her oldest son dropped out of high school, Mrs. Turner talked with a school social worker and shared her desperation about herself as well as the children. With her permission, the worker arranged a joint session with Mrs. Turner and the son and daughter who were still in school. In this session, the worker recognized this family's struggle to cope with the impact of the divorce by avoiding each other. At the same time, he sensed their tender feelings for one another and wish for closer relationships.

The family responded positively to the worker's suggestion that, for the next two weeks, they arrange to participate in a variety of activities together, including dinner at least every other night, visiting the maternal grandmother in a convalescent home, and attending a basketball game. All family members agreed to participate in each of these activities and to discuss their experiences with the worker in a follow-up session.

In the subsequent session, the children reported that, as they and their mother came together, they were able to share with her their confusion over the divorce, anger toward both parents, and fears of further losses. Mrs. Turner, on the other hand, indicated that she was able to let her children know about her growing dissatisfaction and disappointment in the mar-

> riage and her self-doubts since the divorce. The son who had dropped out of school still refused to return but appreciated his mother's concern for him and his future. All family members expressed their satisfaction in being able to come together. The children also began to talk about maintaining their relationship with their father by including him in selected family activities.

Competence Building. Workers should always be on the lookout for specific opportunities to help clients to build their competence. As the preceding examples indicate, workers often can help clients to make use of a life event to promote growth and change through mastery. In addition, at times workers need to plan and design new experiences that provide further opportunities for clients. For instance, it has been shown that helping parents of children in foster care to become involved in a parents organization can have multiple benefits for clients who typically feel powerless: it can lead to new roles for the parents (as resources for each other), a new sense of mastery as human beings, and improved competence as parents (Carbino, 1981). As another example, a worker arranges a school conference for a father who is upset by his teenage son's learning difficulties and frustrated by what he perceives as the school's lack of interest:

> In the conference, Mr. Mosley speaks assertively about his son's rights and expresses his concern for him. He responds to a teacher's obvious hostility toward the son by pointing out that she has been rejecting Bob and that Bob, therefore, reacts negatively. He hears the interest and concern of the other teachers regarding the boy. He offers suggestions as to how Bob might be handled in school and emphasizes ways in which he could discipline him at home and expect more from him in relation to his school work.
>
> In short, with support from the worker before and during the conference, Mr. Mosley succeeds in expressing his feelings, confronting school personnel, and gaining their acceptance. School personnel respond more positively to him as they see him in a different light as a result of his performance during the conference. In his subsequent efforts to deal with his son's continuing school difficulties, Mr. Mosley then begins to move from his previous pattern of angry outbursts against the school system toward making realistic expectations clear to his son.

Timing and Location of Help. As underlined especially by crisis theorists, the timing of helping efforts is crucial. While a person is struggling to resolve a crisis, "new ego sets may emerge and new adaptive styles learned which will enable the person to cope more effectively with other situations in the future. However, if help is not available during this critical period, inadequate or maladaptive patterns may be adopted which can result in weakened ability to function adequately in the period ahead" (Golan, 1978, p. 9).

In addition to timing, the location of helping efforts should be considered carefully. Interventive activities should take place as much as possible within the client's natural life context. While the office setting is often appropriate for certain purposes, it should not be routinely viewed as the ideal context for help. On the contrary, in many situations its remoteness from the client's life space can undermine change efforts or reduce their impact. Good opportunities to use life events effectively are often missed because of excessive reliance on artificial or formal procedures, such as the office interview.

One way to take into account the factors of timing and location is to use the *life space interview,* a technique that Fritz Redl (1959) defined as clinical exploitation of life events or on-the-spot provision of emotional first aid. In clinical social work, there are frequent opportunities to use life space interviewing and thus help clients to take advantage of the therapeutic potential of natural life experiences. For example, in residential treatment centers, handling a child's explosion within the cottage *as it happens* is much more effective than waiting until the child is due to see his therapist several days later. In a hospital setting, social workers attached to the emergency room have opportunities to intervene in the midst of shock and grief in ways that are powerful. At times, they may also be able to foster informal sharing and mutual aid in the waiting room itself.

Another way to maximize the impact of experiences is to station social workers at the "crossroads of life" (Meyer, 1976; Reynolds, 1934). Practice could become more meaningful and rewarding if workers functioned more regularly in the natural surroundings of clients; they would be better able to discover and encourage the clients' dormant potentialities and mobilize resources in their environment.

Client Participation. Social workers should use the experience or activity in such a way that client involvement is maximized. As supported by various theoretical perspectives reviewed earlier, the worker consciously seeks to provide opportunities for clients to exercise their decision-making function, become engaged in action on their own behalf, and use their cognitive powers. As seen in the following example, a paramount question is: How can the experience or activity be used to mobilize the person's own life processes and strivings toward growth?

> Mrs. Brewer is a middle-aged widow who has been referred to a mental health clinic by her physician because of her hypertension, obesity, and prevasive unhappiness and depression. She is desperate for help as a result of the physician's warning that her hypertension has been increasing steadily. For years she has been unsuccessfully trying to lose weight.
>
> In a family session involving Mrs. Brewer's two teenage daughters, it becomes apparent that the family as a whole has considerable difficulty in expressing anger or dealing with anxiety. Whenever Mrs. Brewer gets angry, upset, or discouraged, she withdraws to her room. The daughters are quite concerned about her behavior but avoid discussing it with her; instead, they usually bring extensive plates of rich food to their mother, who quickly devours everything.
>
> Choosing to deal directly with family dynamics, the worker points out how the daughters are interfering with their mother's efforts to lose weight and how each family member finds it difficult to express her feelings, particularly negative ones. Focusing on their mutual concerns, the worker helps the family to formulate these goals: communicating their feelings more openly with each other; becoming engaged in more gratifying joint activities within as well as outside the home; and helping Mrs. Brewer to lose weight.
>
> When it is evident that all family members concur in these goals, the worker helps them to define several pertinent tasks. First, they are to plan at least one pleasurable joint activity every other day, such as watching a

favorite movie on television. Second, Mrs. Brewer and her daughters are to express their feelings of anger openly during several family sessions at the clinic. Third, the daughters are not to bring any food to their mother whenever she retreats into her room; instead, they should reach out to her by making themselves available to talk. At the same time, Mrs. Brewer agrees to talk or do something constructive while one of the daughters is in her room.

As each of these tasks is defined, the worker systematically elicits each family member's understanding of it as well as her feelings about it. In addition, she explains the rationale for each task. For example, she indicates that, by expressing their negative feelings within the therapeutic sessions, they will release natural, pent-up feelings that are preventing them from achieving the kinds of relationships that they desire with each other.

As Mrs. Brewer and her daughters carry out these tasks, a number of significant changes begin to take place within the family system. For instance, its members learn to convey their feelings and concerns directly rather than through food. At the same time, as Mrs. Brewer receives from her daughters some of the attention that she has been craving, she has less need to overeat.

As each family member has the experience of expressing her feelings within the therapeutic environment, the worker faces them with another, more complex task, namely, expressing their angry feelings toward each other at home. During each session, she reviews with them how each task is proceeding and provides encouragement and positive feedback whenever appropriate. Slowly and with much difficulty, Mrs. Brewer and her daughters are able to begin to change their mutually destructive patterns of communication and interaction.

As this example illustrates, client participation in the helping process can be enhanced through the use of tasks, homework assignments, and other procedures that are common in such treatment approaches as behavior modification and family treatment. Through these means, new behaviors are coached and rehearsed with the worker and then practiced out in the world. The client's life experiences are thus altered, and change follows in his or her coping and functioning. As the case of the Brewer family demonstrates, even a small improvement in communication can enhance the feeling tone within a family and facilitate further gains.

Restructuring the Environment. The use of life experiences as resources for change also requires a supportive and nutritive environment. In many instances, this means that the environment needs to be modified or restructured to facilitate or support the client's coping efforts and adaptive strivings (Germain and Gitterman, 1980).

Various approaches may be used toward this end. At times, it is necessary to remove obstacles in the person's transactions with key systems, as when the practitioner provides information or advocacy to parents who are trying to deal with a school or welfare system. In other situations, potential resources in the person's social networks are identified and mobilized in support of the client, as when a neighbor is encouraged to visit an isolated older person. Or new resources are introduced into the client's life, as when a parent aide is enlisted to work with a parent who has been referred for child neglect. In other instances, it is necessary to create a new environment, such as placement of a teenager in a group home.

There are many other ways the environment can be enriched to support the client's efforts to cope with life challenges. These include a variety of structured experiences, such as camping programs for families involved in child abuse, wilderness programs for aged psychiatric patients, and visual arts projects with aged persons living in single-room occupancy hotels. The experience of "creating and participating in a novel and supportive environment releases growth and adaptive functioning in individuals, families, and groups" (Germain, 1981, p. 329).

To use life experiences effectively, human beings also need to learn or improve skills in negotiating their environments and choosing the right environment; this is a critical task throughout the life cycle (Moos, 1976, p. 419). To make choices, the person should have sufficient and accurate environmental information. Prior information about environments, or "anticipatory guidelines," can be very useful in the coping efforts of those facing life transitions, or such challenges as marriage, divorce, relocation, or retirement. Supplying information about institutional aids (such as preretirement counseling) as well as informal resources (such as self-help groups) is a crucial function of the social worker.

Client Feedback. Finally, to make professional use of life experiences, it is essential that workers obtain, on a regular basis, the views of clients concerning interventive activities. Feedback from the client can help the social worker to assess the effectiveness and relevance of the particular intervention by ensuring that the worker is attuned to the client's feelings, needs, and qualities. Also, the process of giving feedback can be a valuable experience for clients; it can help to promote their competence by providing them with opportunities for decision making and increasing their sense of control over their lives (Maluccio, 1979a, pp. 200–207).

Research Issues

The planned use of life experiences as resources for change is strongly supported by practice as well as by different theoretical perspectives. Further research is needed, however, to test these theories and to demonstrate the validity of the practice propositions and principles delineated in this chapter.

Perhaps the greatest need is for more extensive research on how human beings cope naturally with life challenges or problems in living. With few exceptions, the theories social workers draw from have been generated and tested largely through research on pathology. For instance, personality theories, such as psychoanalysis or behaviorism, are based primarily on practice or research with people who are experiencing difficulty in their transactions with their environment and therefore come to the attention of professional helpers. Similarly, most family treatment modalities, as well as research and theories on the family, are characterized by a pathological orientation and "an overly solemn and grim emphasis" (Leichter, 1974, p. 216).

Yet, we know that most people manage successfully with natural life tasks and everyday problems without professional help. Indeed, there is research evidence suggesting that even applicants placed on the waiting list of social agencies improve their functioning without professional intervention (Sloane and others, 1975). These persons apparently find and use informal resources in their social networks.

More naturalistic research on how human beings manage to cope, change, and grow would lead to further understanding of life experiences and their role as resources for change. Examples of pioneering work in this area are the expanding body of research on crisis intervention and the series of studies on coping carried out with children and adolescents by Murphy and her associates (Murphy, 1962; Murphy and Moriarty, 1976).

A shift in the focus of research away from pathology and toward competence could lead to substantial changes in social work theory and practice. More systematic and proven guidelines could emerge for helping people to enhance their functioning through natural change processes and through resources in their life context.

Conclusion

A person's autonomy and competence evolve in response to the dynamic transaction between the person and the environment. Human beings change and grow through the enduring sequence of transactions with the environment and through their involvement in meaningful life experiences.

Clinical social workers can help their clients to enhance their psychosocial functioning through systematic attention to, and encouragement of, people's active engagement with their impinging environment and through helping to provide a milieu that is nurturing as well as challenging. Social work intervention can play an essential *triggering function* by carefully mobilizing the client's coping capacities, life processes, and strivings toward growth.

A study of client perception of the helping process at a family service agency supported such an approach. Most clients reported that the worker's intervention helped them in a variety of ways—to make better use of resources in their environment, to reach out to others more freely, to act more positively on their needs, to interact with significant others in ways that elicited more positive feedback, or to enhance their hope and motivation for change. As clients in this study spoke, there was "the suggestion of an almost regenerative quality to their functioning: as they had the experience of coping more effectively and gaining some mastery over their environment, they went on to rekindle dormant capabilities and develop new coping patterns" (Maluccio, 1979a, p. 189).

Through further systematic and purposive emphasis on life experiences as resources for, and instruments of, change, social workers can help to enhance their clients' natural coping processes.

References

Alexander, F. "Extratherapeutic Experiences." In F. Alexander and T. M. French, *Psychoanalytic Therapy*. New York: Ronald Press, 1946.

Allport, G. W. "The Open System in Personality Theory." *Journal of Abnormal and Social Psychology*, 1960, *61*, 301–310.

Angyal, A. *Foundations for a Science of Personality*. New York: Commonwealth Fund, 1941.

Austin, L. N. "Trends in Differential Treatment in Social Casework." *Social Casework*, 1948, *29*, 203–211.

Bettelheim, B. *The Informed Heart*. New York: Free Press, 1960.

Carbino, R. "Developing a Parent Organization: New Roles for Parents of Children in Foster Care." In A. N. Maluccio and P. A. Sinanoglu (Eds.), *The Challenge of Partnership: Working with Parents of Children in Foster Care.* New York: Child Welfare League of America, 1981.

Dubos, R. *Man Adapting.* New Haven, Conn.: Yale University Press, 1965.

Erikson, E. H. "Identity and the Life Cycle." *Psychological Issues,* 1959, *1,* (entire issue).

French, J. R. P., Jr., Rodgers, W., and Cobb, S. "Adjustment as Person-Environment Fit." In G. V. Coelho, D. A. Hamburg, and J. E. Adams (Eds.), *Coping and Adaptation.* New York: Basic Books, 1974.

Germain, C. B. "Ecology and Social Work." In C. B. Germain (Ed.), *Social Work Practice: People and Environments.* New York: Columbia University Press, 1979.

Germain, C. B. "The Ecological Approach to People-Environmental Transactions." *Social Casework,* 1981, *62,* 323-331.

Germain, C. B., and Gitterman, A. *The Life Model of Social Work Practice.* New York: Columbia University Press, 1980.

Gladwin, T. "Social Competence and Clinical Practice." *Psychiatry,* 1967, *30,* 30-43.

Golan, N. *Treatment in Crisis Situations.* New York: Free Press, 1978.

Hartman, A. L. "The Extended Family as a Resource for Change: An Ecological Approach to Family-Centered Practice." In C. B. Germain (Ed.), *Social Work Practice: People and Environments.* New York: Columbia University Press, 1979.

Hartmann, H. *Ego Psychology and the Problem of Adaptation.* New York: International Universities Press, 1958.

Holt, R. R. "Ego Autonomy Re-evaluated." *International Journal of Psychiatry,* 1967, *3,* 481-512.

Inkeles, A. "Social Structure and the Socialization of Competence." *Harvard Educational Review,* 1966, *36,* 30-43.

Kelly, J. G. "Ecological Constraints on Mental Health Services." *American Psychologist,* 1973, *28,* 535-539.

Leichter, H. J. "Some Perspectives on the Family as Educator." *Teachers College Record,* 1974, *76,* 175-217.

Maluccio, A. N. "Action as a Tool in Casework Practice." *Social Casework,* 1974, *55,* 28-36.

Maluccio, A. N. *Learning from Clients—Interpersonal Helping as Viewed by Clients and Social Workers.* New York: Free Press, 1979a.

Maluccio, A. N. "Promoting Competence Through Life Experiences." In C. B. Germain (Ed.), *Social Work Practice: People and Environments.* New York: Columbia University Press, 1979b.

Maluccio, A. N. "Competence-Oriented Social Work Practice—An Ecological Approach." In A. N. Maluccio (Ed.), *Promoting Competence in Clients—A New/Old Approach to Social Work Practice.* New York: Free Press, 1981.

Maslow, A. H. *Motivation and Personality.* (2nd ed.) New York: Harper & Row, 1954.

Menninger, K. *The Vital Balance.* New York: Viking Press, 1967.

Merton, R. K., and others. *The Student Physician.* Cambridge, Mass.: Harvard University Press, 1957.

Meyer, C. H. *Social Work Practice.* (2nd ed.) New York: Free Press, 1976.

Miller, S. C. "Ego Autonomy in Sensory Deprivation, Isolation and Stress." *The International Journal of Psychoanalysis,* 1962, *43,* 1–20.

Minuchin, S. *Families and Family Therapy.* Cambridge, Mass.: Harvard University Press, 1974.

Moos, R. H. *The Human Context: Environmental Determinants of Behavior.* New York: Wiley, 1976.

Murphy, L. B., and Moriarty, A. E. *Vulnerability, Coping and Growth.* New Haven, Conn.: Yale University Press, 1976.

Murphy, L. B., and others. *The Widening World of Childhood.* New York: Basic Books, 1962.

Oxley, G. B. "A Life Model Approach to Change." *Social Casework,* 1971, *52* (10), 627–633.

Piaget, J. *The Origins of Intelligence.* New York: International Universities Press, 1952.

Rapaport, D. "The Theory of Ego Autonomy: A Generalization." *Bulletin of the Menninger Clinic,* 1958, *22,* 13–35.

Redl, F. "Strategy and Technique of the Life Space Interview." *American Journal of Orthopsychiatry,* 1959, *29,* 1–18.

Reynolds, B. C. "Between Client and Community: A Study of Responsibility in Social Casework." *Smith College Studies in Social Work,* 1934, *5,* 5–128.

Sloane, R. B., and others. *Psychotherapy Versus Behavior Therapy.* Cambridge, Mass.: Harvard University Press, 1975.

Smith, M. B. "Competence and Socialization." In J. A. Clausen (Ed.), *Socialization and Society.* Boston: Little, Brown, 1968.

Studt, E. "Social Work Theory and Implications for the Practice of Methods." *Social Work Education Reporter,* 1968, *16,* 22–24, 42–46.

White, R. W. "Motivation Reconsidered: The Concept of Competence." *Psychological Review,* 1959, *66,* 297–333.

White, R. W. "Ego and Reality in Psychoanalytic Theory." *Psychological Issues,* 1963, *3* (entire issue).

White, R. W. "Strategies of Adaptation: An Attempt at Systematic Description." In G. V. Coelho, D. A. Hamburg, and J. E. Adams (Eds.), *Coping and Adaptation.* New York: Basic Books, 1974.

7

Theory of Group Approaches

Charles D. Garvin

The idea that social workers can use groups to help individuals has existed from the inception of the profession of social work. The first professionals to work with groups worked in such agencies as settlement houses, YMCAs and YWCAs, and youth organizations. Their intent was to use group experience to socialize individuals to urban environments, to preserve their cultural identities, and to facilitate their participation in the democratic process.

Those who worked with groups in these agencies in the late nineteenth and early twentieth centuries came from a variety of professions and disciplines, including education, recreation, sociology, psychology, and social work. Because of the interest of social workers and educators in group work, schools of social work began offering related courses in the 1920s. The first such training was begun in 1923 at Western Reserve University. Early organizations of group workers admitted members from the fields of education and recreation.

Social workers have often sought to distinguish their approach to groups from that of other professions by calling it *social group work*. We refer simply to *group work* in this chapter because we believe such semantic distinctions fail to resolve the current debates on the boundaries of clinical social work with groups.

Mary Richmond, who contributed so much to the development of casework, also encouraged the interest of social workers in group processes. For example, she referred to "the new tendency to view our clients from the angle of what might be termed *small group psychology*" (1920, p. 256). The pioneers in the use of groups in social work, however, drew very broadly for their theoretical foundations. They perceived a strong kinship with political ideas that linked small-group processes to the growth of democracy, such as in the writings of

Follett (1926) and Lindeman (1921). They also sought to apply the progressive educational ideas of John Dewey (1933), in which group processes dealing with the problems of living were seen as educational tools.

Although the late 1920s saw the creation of group-work training in some schools of social work, there was controversy among group workers and the larger population of social workers as to whether group work was a social work method. This issue was largely settled in 1935 when the National Conference of Social Work instituted a section on group work and Grace Coyle (1935) and Wilbur Newstetter (1935) presented papers clarifying the philosophy and methods that linked group work to social work.

Group workers continued to develop the theoretical base for this method throughout the following decades in ways that sometimes paralleled and sometimes diverged from analogous developments in other social work methods, such as casework and community organization. Theoretical and practice changes took place in the 1960s, however, that had significant effects on the development of group work. These changes consisted of the effort to integrate practice theory about work with individuals, families, and groups into a body of knowledge applicable to all. Thus, workers increasingly were viewed as offering a full range of services in ways dictated by the needs of clients rather than by the specialization of the worker. This emphasis, however, has diminished to a degree the attention paid to group theory. In this chapter, we view group theory as linked to theory for all clinical practice and as possessing unique elements. This view of group work as integrated with the other modalities within the field of clinical social work is controversial; some theoreticians still emphasize the unique aspects of group work (Tropp, 1976). The validity of seeing group work as an integrated part of clinical social work is not fully established, despite the fact that (1) almost all clinical social workers are now provided with training in group approaches, (2) groups are used as a means of helping clients in all types of clinical settings, and (3) we no longer divide clinical social workers into caseworkers and group workers.

Practice Settings

Various types of groups are relevant to clinical social work. For example, groups are used in psychiatric settings to help clients acquire social skills, cope with interpersonal conflicts, and enhance their ability to perceive social realities. In child welfare settings, groups are used to help individuals work on problems regarding loss and separation. In school settings, groups help children to support each other and to cope with psychological and social impediments to learning. In correctional settings, groups can help people to respond to social and psychological forces that promote deviance. In family settings, groups help individuals as well as families to fulfill or modify their family roles.

Certain agencies that historically served to nurture group work, such as community centers and settlement houses, continue to sponsor groups. Some groups in these agencies have the traditional function of helping people learn appropriate social roles. Recently, other groups have been established in these agencies as a way of helping retarded persons, individuals released from mental institutions, and similar clients to function in their own community environments.

In early group theory, group work was viewed as a separate method from other social work approaches, and the group theory applicable in one setting was applicable in others, at least in a general way. Most group work occurred in community institutions where clients functioned relatively adequately and did not require rehabilitative services. Some theorists (Lang, 1980) still hold to this posture, but we believe that the proliferation of settings and the diversity of group purposes require a range of group theories rather than a single approach. This idea does not preclude the idea that group tasks and dynamics may be similar in all settings, but the ways workers accomplish these tasks will vary by group purpose and setting—a variance that we will reflect throughout this chapter.

In seeking to organize ideas about the way clinical practice with groups varies, we developed a typology of purposes (Garvin, 1981). This typology draws from the work of Vinter (1963), who described the two major functions of agencies as the socialization and resocialization of the client. *Socialization* refers to helping persons viewed as "normal" whose tasks relate to role transitions. *Resocialization* refers to helping those who are considered deviant and who are often labeled with either psychiatric or criminal justice terms (or both) and who require rehabilitation.

In using these categories to analyze group services, we subdivided them one step further. Socialization was viewed as comprising two purposes, *anomie reduction* and *role attainment*. Our use of the term *anomie* is similar to that of Hartman (1969) in her discussion of its application in casework—"a state of societal demoralization, of normlessness, created by the dysfunction of goals and norms for reaching these goals" (p. 132). An example of a group used for this purpose is one of women in a family agency meeting to decide how they wish to relate to the changing roles of women in our society.

Role-attainment purposes are those that help members to fulfill roles they have chosen but for which they require the help of others to perform. A group of high school students supporting each other, with the help of a social worker, in meeting school requirements is an example of this purpose.

Resocialization was viewed, in turn, as including the purposes of *social control* and *alternative role attainment*. *Social control,* as a purpose, refers to groups formed to affect behavior (which includes, in our definition, all actions, affects, cognitions, and attitudes) of members who have not yet acknowledged the need for such services. The social control purpose raises many complex issues whose consideration lies beyond the purpose of this chapter. An example of such a group is one conducted in an institution for delinquents to orient new inmates to the institution.

Alternative role attainment refers to the purpose of helping voluntary clients, through groups, to change their behavior to fulfill socially acceptable roles. These individuals often are suffering from dysfunctional personality patterns that promote severe interpersonal conflicts and other dysfunctional relationship patterns. A group of people who attend an outpatient psychiatric clinic because of their poor social relationships is an example of a group with this purpose.

This typology is not meant to present a set of mutually exclusive purposes but rather purposes that may occur singly or in combination in any group. The value of this conceptualization is to clarify group purposes for the worker and the group members and to suggest practice theories that are useful at times that a specified purpose prevails. Practice problems emerge when purposes are unclear or when purposes of agencies, members, workers, or others in the community conflict. An example of such problems occurred in an inpatient facility in which group members were told that the purpose was alternative role attainment—namely, to help them prepare for life in the community. In reality, the purpose was a form of social control—to secure the members' conformity to institutional rules that in fact were not related to their ability to function in the community.

Now that we have presented the historical context and contemporary agency settings and purposes for group work, we move to our presentation of relevant theory for practice. In this discussion, we distinguish between *behavior theory* and *practice theory*. The former consists of statements about human behavior and its causes; the latter consists of principles regarding the way practitioners should act to facilitate changes in behavior. Since practice theory draws from behavior theory, we begin our discussion with the latter.

Behavior Theory

Since a group is composed of individuals and often is established to help individuals attain their goals, practice with groups must draw from such theories of individual behavior as psychoanalytic theory, role theory, and behavioral theory. Little is unique, however, about the social worker's use of these approaches when working with groups. We will therefore focus on theories about groups as such and about individual behavior in group situations.

So far, we have used the term *group* as if its definition were self-evident. Actually, social psychologists and others who study groups have struggled to define and clarify the term. First, a distinction must be made between small groups and large ones, as the properties of these entities differ. (For clinical work, we are primarily interested in the small group.) Second, a distinction must be made between the variables that characterize any group from those that emerge as the group develops. We believe that both of these issues are resolved in a definition proposed by Shaw (1976, p. 11): "A group is defined as two or more persons who are interacting with one another in such a manner that each person influences and is influenced by each other person. A small group is a group having twenty or fewer members." (In group work, the number is more likely to be eight to ten.)

The size of the group is limited by the requirement in the definition that each person influences and is influenced by each other person. This requirement implies face-to-face interaction that is not possible in large, formal organizations. The minimum number of two is given, although groups of two have characteristics that differ from larger groups (Berelson and Steiner, 1964, p. 360). For this reason, we will primarily describe processes for groups that consist of more than two members.

When a group comes into existence and begins to evolve, other properties emerge. These properties include a definition of the boundaries of the group (who is and is not included in membership), goals the group seeks to attain, norms that control the behavior of group members, and patterns of interaction among members (group structure). Some writers include these properties in their definition of a group, whereas we see these properties as consequences of group development rather than as intrinsic to all groups.

Groups play a major role in the social functioning of all individuals; everyone's behavior, at all stages of the life cycle, is influenced, learned, and nurtured in the context of groups. The child's first learning takes place in the family, which remains throughout life one of the most powerful group forces to which we are exposed. In young childhood, the individual begins the process of peer-group association that continues throughout life. Problematic group conditions present in either the family or the first peer groups are major causes of maladaptive behavior. When individuals reach school age, they must function in the classroom, which is another form of group environment. After education is completed, people must function in work environments, most of which require interaction with employees, clients, and managers in groups. Finally, people seek to meet still other needs through such community groups as those in churches, political organizations, and recreational facilities.

The implications of these facts about human association to group theory are manifold. First, in whatever way the social worker interacts with clients, clients' problems will affect their group associations. The worker must understand the meaning of interactions in groups in order to understand the client's problems and help the client to plan effective ways of coping with them. Second, social work practice is increasingly devoted to working directly with the groups in which problems occur. Community mental health facilities and other community-oriented services now seek to work with families, groups of neighbors, naturally formed peer groups, and groups drawn from the social networks of clients. Finally, social workers will form groups of unrelated persons. Such groups can become replications of other groups in the client's life. The rationale for forming such groups is that the client can transfer what he or she has learned in the social-work group to other associations.

Small-Group Concepts. To analyze group events, social scientists have generated a series of concepts to refer to the full range of group phenomena. We will present these concepts with reference to the phases of group development to which they are most relevant. Group development itself is one of the most important concepts from small-group theory (Bennis and Shepherd, 1956; Garland, Jones, and Kolodny, 1965; Hartford, 1972; Sarrie and Galinsky, 1974; Tuckman, 1965). The idea of group development stems from the finding that all groups are likely to progress through a series of phases. The identification of these phases can help the practitioner to predict events and identify barriers to the group's progress.

Hartford (1972, p. 67) examined many studies that dealt with group development and developed a scheme that integrated them, as follows:

I. Pregroup Phases
    A. Private Pregroup Phase
    B. Public Pregroup Phase
    C. Convening Phase
II. Group Formation Phase
III. Integration, Disintegration and Conflict, Reintegration or Reorganization Synthesis Phase
IV. Group Functioning and Maintenance Phase

V. Termination Phases
   A. Pretermination Phase
   B. Termination
   C. Posttermination Phase

This view of phases does represent an idealization of group life, inasmuch as, at any moment, group members might experience events typical of several phases. In addition, all groups do not advance through every phase; many groups, for example, terminate without ever progressing beyond the group formation phase, and yet they accomplish the purposes for which they were formed. Groups also may experience a regression to earlier phases as well as a forward movement.

Hartford's scheme recognizes that a conception of group development must include events that occur prior to the group's first formal meeting. These events are the thoughts and experiences that propel individuals toward the group as well as the discussions that members have with each other before the meeting. Unless the existence of these events is recognized, subsequent situations will be difficult to comprehend. Similarly, after the last formal meeting of the group, group forces continue to be manifested in the reaction of the members to the ending of the group experience and the use they make of that experience in later situations.

A number of additional concepts are relevant to these phases. An important concept for the pregroup phase is that of *group composition.* This term is used as a noun to describe the actual array of individuals and their attributes in the group; it is also used as a verb to refer to the act of creating a group that consists of members with selected attributes. A great deal of research and theory exists that describes both the effects of different group composition arrangements (Shaw, 1976, pp. 194–236) as well as how the worker should compose a group (Bertcher and Maple, 1974).

In the group formation phase, several processes begin. One is the determination of *group purpose,* or the function to be fulfilled by the group. We described earlier in this chapter one approach to categorizing group purposes in terms of socialization and resocialization. A related concept is *group goal,* which refers to the desired outcome of the work in which the group members engage. Thus, a group goal in a group whose purpose is anomie reduction might be that all the members will clarify their values regarding their sexual identity.

Another concept that applies to group formation as well as to all other phases of the group is *group cohesiveness.* The concept of cohesiveness on a group level is analogous to the concept of relationship on a one-to-one level and refers to "the degree to which members are motivated to remain in the group" (Shaw, 1976, p. 197). Cohesiveness is a product of all the forces that act to retain members in the group (Festinger, 1950), such as the attraction that exists among the members as well as the value members place on the goals, the activities, the purposes, and the prestige of group membership. Members also remain in a group if the outcomes of membership in that group are deemed to be better than the outcomes of alternative affiliations.

The group moves into the next phases when it has reached consensus on its purpose and goals, has achieved some cohesiveness, and has begun to choose and implement activities to attain its goals (often referred to by social psychologists as *group tasks* and by social workers as *group program*). Phase III refers to integration, conflict, and reintegration because all descriptions of development note that, after goals and purposes are identified, conflicts develop among potential leaders, especially among emerging leaders and those who fulfilled leadership roles during the formation phase. This conflict results in a diminution of cohesiveness, and groups will require internal or external supports to survive these conflicts.

As groups continue to function, the *group structure* becomes more elaborate, and group processes are devoted to attaining the goals of the group and to maintaining the cohesion of the group. *Group structure* is defined by Shaw (1976, p. 446) as "the pattern of relationships among the differentiated parts of the group." This differentiation occurs along the following dimensions:

1. *Sociometric or affectional:* This refers to the pattern of attraction and rejection among group members and is manifested in the existence of *subgroups* (two or more individuals in the group who are attracted to each other and interact more with each other than with persons not in the subgroup) and *isolates* (persons who have few interactions with other group members).
2. *Communications:* This refers to the pattern of who communicates, verbally and nonverbally, with whom and about what in the group.
3. *Roles:* This refers to the statuses that are created in the group and how persons fulfill them. These statuses include both formal roles (chairperson, secretary) as well as roles that grow out of group interactions (mediator, clown, scapegoat). Leadership roles are an important component of the role structure.
4. *Division of Labor:* This refers to how tasks are allocated among group members.
5. *Power:* This refers to the patterns of influence that exist within the group.

Group process refers to changes in group conditions over time. Elsewhere, we have analyzed two types of group processes: task processes, which relate to determining and attaining the goals of the group, and social-emotional processes, which relate to the maintenance of the group (Garvin, 1974). In that analysis, we identified task processes as consisting of the processes of goal determination and goal pursuit. Social-emotional processes, as suggested by Mills (1967, p. 58), occur on three levels: behavior, emotion, and norms.

Social-emotional processes at the *behavioral level* are directed at reducing behaviors that can lead to the destruction of the group. These processes occur when members seek to control the behavior of others in the group, particularly those who are defined as deviant. Social-emotional processes at the *emotional level* are expressions of liking and disliking among members. Social-emotional processes at the *normative level* occur as members define norms of acceptable and unacceptable group behavior and translate many of these norms into group rules.

We also identified two processes that can fulfill either task or social-emotional functions, depending on the content of the interaction. One of these processes is that of *role differentiation.* It occurs as the group determines the roles that are required of members and as members interact around role requirements. Some of these roles relate to task functions of the group; others, to social-emotional functions. Another process that fulfills either function is that of *communication-interaction.* This process occurs as members communicate in order to coordinate their various roles to carry out the overall purposes of the group.

The final phase is that of *termination.* Prior to the actual termination, groups undergo a period of preparation for and reactions to the ending. Hartford calls this period pretermination. It can include a constructive effort to deal with feelings about endings, to plan what members will do after termination, and to evaluate the group experience. In any case, group members will experience many of the same feelings and reactions that people have at any termination. These include depression, anger, and denial as well as elation and anticipation. The unique aspect of termination of a group experience is the multiple number of separation reactions a member may have because of the number of individuals in the group. In addition, separation reactions can be experienced in relation to the group as an entity.

The actual group ending is often observed with a ceremony or celebration to symbolize the finality of that ending. Members will look for ways of saying farewell to others and for symbolizing what the group has meant to them. It is also possible for some members to deny the meaning of the event by failure to attend the last session or to participate in its events.

The posttermination phase occurs as the individuals who had been in the group recall group events in association with later situations. On these occasions, they may seek to contact other group members or even to reinstitute the group.

Contrasting Theories. All small-group theories must account for the group conditions to which the above concepts refer, but there are a variety of such theories, and each has a different way of organizing concepts to account for group phenomena. Following is a listing of the major small-group theories that have relevance for clinical social work with groups.

1. *Field Theory:* This approach, first associated with the work of Kurt Lewin (1947), has been elaborated upon by many other writers (Cartwright and Zander, 1968; Festinger, Schachter, and Back, 1950; Lippitt, 1939). It organizes group processes in terms of their relationship to attaining group goals. These processes occur in the "life space" of the group and are conceptualized as being the results of forces that move the group and its members toward or away from "regions." This movement is referred to as *locomotion;* related concepts are *power fields* and *group forces.*
2. *Social-Exchange Theory:* This approach relates the behavioral notions of Skinner (1953) to the complex interactions in group situations. The ideas of Skinner regarding the effects of reinforcement and punishment on behavior are seen as the basis of social exchanges among group members. These exchanges are influenced by economic and political factors, such as costs of the exchange and the justice or injustice of exchanges (Homans, 1961). Thibaut and Kelley (1959) have examined interpersonal transactions in terms of the possible outcomes for each participant, the control each has on the outcomes of others, and how participants create benefits.
3. *Social Systems Theory:* In a broad sense, all small-group theories are systemic because they must account for individual and group behavior in terms of the interaction of systems at various levels of social organization. The writings of Parsons (1951) have been particularly influential on small-group investigators because of his delineation of the functioning of systems and the way systems interact. According to Nixon (1979), a central aspect of this approach is its view of the functional problems of social systems as focusing on problems concerning (1) *integration,* or how the parts of a system fit together as a

whole; (2) *pattern maintenance,* or how the major patterns of culture and interaction in a system are maintained; (3) *goal attainment,* or how a system organizes and controls the pursuit of its tasks and goals; and (4) *adaptation,* or how a system relates to its environment. Bales has made a major contribution to small-group theory through his presentation of how small groups fulfill these functions (1950, p. 73) and how groups function to maintain equilibrium (1950, p. 157).

4. *Psychoanalytic Theory:* A number of writers have used psychoanalytic concepts to understand events occurring in groups (Bion, 1959; Foulkes, 1964). These writers view many group processes as outgrowths of distortions related to transference phenomena. They also view many group transactions as familial reenactments. Bion investigated emotional responses to leadership, particularly to the therapist. He found that such responses often prevent the group's work as members engage in "fight" or "flight" or "pair" with each other in response to their feelings toward the leader.

The Influence of Groups on Members. Groups influence the behavior of members in "active" ways when some individuals in the group seek to modify the behavior of other members in the group. This effort to change member behavior can be viewed as the product of forces designed to accomplish group purposes and to maintain the group over time. Some of these "active" forces that function to train members to fulfill group functions are socialization efforts. For example, some members train others to perform leadership activities in the group and reinforce them for performing these. Another socialization effort for which some members modify the behavior of other members is to reduce deviant behavior in the group—behavior that violates group norms or in other ways interferes with group functioning.

Groups also influence behavior in "passive" ways when they create group *conditions* that lead to the modification of member behavior. The group in these circumstances has not singled out individual members as the targets of such forces. When group members make rules, agree on the opinions they hold, or behave in similar ways, these conditions are often viewed by all or most members as expected of all group members.

The active and passive influences groups exert on members may be either highly compatible or incompatible with the purposes of clinical social work practice. These forces may help members to engage in socially acceptable behavior, accurately perceive reality, or fully make use of the group experience. They can also have the opposite effects on members. The task of the clinical social worker is to assess such forces accurately and to work toward their constructive rather than destructive consequences. To aid in this assessment, we will now indicate the ways groups control the behavior of members.

Groups control the behavior of members by affecting their perceptions, cognitions, emotions, behavior, self-concept, and ways of problem solving. A further delineation of these effects follows:

1. *Perceptions of Reality* A considerable amount of research demonstrates that group members tend to perceive reality in ways that conform to the perceptions of others in the group, even when this contradicts their own judgments (Asch, 1955; Deutsch and Gerard, 1955; Sherif, 1936; Sherif and Sherif, 1969). This often occurs when there is some ambiguity regarding "reality."

2. *Understanding of Situations* In addition to members' perceptions, what members think about the meanings of their perceptions is similarly affected. One way this effect has been studied is in terms of *attributions*, that is, the explanations people hold of the causes of events (Shaw, 1976, pp. 327–328; Strong, 1978). One important kind of attribution affected by group processes is whether members believe their problems are a result of shortcomings in themselves or their environment. The importance of this attribution in clinical groups is that it can determine the kinds of goals members work toward. According to Strong (1978) when others indicate to individuals that they have previously acted in certain ways, they will be likely to attribute the cause of the event to themselves. When others define the behavior as unique, the causes of the behavior more likely will be attributed to the environment.
3. *Affective Responses* Group conditions can affect the emotions of group members; that is, certain group events tend to elicit or reduce particular emotions. Conformity to group norms, for example, is likely to reduce anxiety in members (Shaw, 1976, p. 185). In any group, some members are likely to function as social-emotional leaders. They, more frequently than others, will seek to reduce tensions in the group by providing emotional support and release through such techniques as humor (Bales, 1958). Such emotions as anger, elation, or anxiety can spread to others in the group through a process of contagion (Redl, 1966). This is most likely to occur when the emotion is first expressed by high-status members and when the group is cohesive (Polansky, Lippitt, and Redl, 1950).
4. *Behavior* Groups affect the actions of members in a number of ways. Perhaps most directly, groups can selectively reinforce behaviors of members by determining how rewards are to be distributed. These rewards can take the form of assigning the member to desired group positions, or they can be an allocation of its available resources. Negatively, the group can punish undesired behavior by criticizing it, by withdrawing resources from members, and ultimately by excluding the member from the group (Nixon, 1979, pp. 122–154). Schachter (1951), in a much-cited piece of research, demonstrated that, when a member acts in a deviant manner in a group, there will be a steady increase in communications to that person in an effort to secure conformity. Such persons may ultimately be dropped from group membership.

   A number of other processes operate in groups to control the behavior of members. One referred to earlier is that members tend to imitate each other's behavior; the behavior of high-status members is most likely to create this effect. The group also can control the behavior of members through the information it supplies members about the behavior itself, about the situation that is the occasion for the behavior, and about the consequences of behavior.
5. *Identity and Self-Concept* According to Hartford (1972), "not only do one's values, beliefs, and behaviors seem to stem from his interaction with others, but one's very impression of himself or herself—one's identity, one's assessment of his own worth, also develop from associations with others" (p. 34). This is accomplished partially through the process of seeing one's self through others. This idea of the "looking glass self," as discussed by Mead (1934), was one of the earliest and most important ideas in social psychology.

   Research has demonstrated that, when people's ideas of themselves differ from those held by the group, it is the former that is likely to change (Manis, 1955). Another approach to this issue has been to examine how groups affect the difference between how one sees one's self (actual self) and how one would like to see one's self (ideal self). In research conducted in human relations training groups, the discrepancy between the member's actual self-concept and ideal self-concept was reduced more in the experimental group than in the control group (Gassner, Gold, and Snadowsky, 1964). This shows the powerful effects groups can have on such phenomena.

6. *Problem Solving* Finally, groups are likely to affect both the processes individuals use to solve problems and the quality of the solutions they reach. Research has consistently shown "that groups produce more and better solutions to problems than do individuals" (Shaw, 1976, p. 64). However, the amount of time required for a group to solve a problem is usually greater than for an individual. One can train group members in a logical approach to problem solving, such as moving consecutively through phases of information gathering, assessment of information, and choosing alternatives based on this assessment. If group norms favor such an approach, members will be more systematic in their problem-solving efforts (Coche and Douglas, in press; Coche and Flick, 1975; Sarason and Ganzer, 1973).

Practice Theory

Models of Practice. All current approaches to social work practice with groups draw from the above concepts from small-group theory as well as from psychology, sociology, social psychology, and other social sciences. In addition, clinical practitioners with groups borrow techniques and concepts from such professional disciplines as clinical psychology, psychiatry, public health, and nursing. Despite a similarity in their knowledge and theory base, writers about social work in groups have developed a diversity of practice theories. In one effort to identify the similarities and differences among these theories, Schwartz (1971) wrote: "There was a kind of 'medical' model in which 'the steps of the helping process are described by assuming a sequence of movements through which the worker investigates, diagnoses, and treats the problem under consideration.' There was a 'scientific' model in which the steps in the helping process resemble closely the problem-solving sequence by which the scientific worker moves from the unknown to the known.' And there was a 'model of the organic system in which the total helping situation is viewed as a network of reciprocal activity, and in which it is impossible to describe accurately any part of the system without describing its active relationship to the other moving parts'" (p. 1255).

Another paper that has had a great influence on the delineation of group-work models is that by Papell and Rothman (1966). They also identified three group-work models: the *social goals model,* the *remedial model,* and the *reciprocal model.* The *social goals model* is closely related to the ideas of the early group-work theorists who emphasized the value of social groups in the enhancement of democratic participation. This model is still influential among clinical social workers because of its recognition of the struggle for human rights and the assumption of a responsible role in society. Both of these dimensions relate to the potency of groups for changing social conditions.

The *remedial model* emerged during the movement to establish groups in rehabilitation settings. It is closely related to Schwartz's reference to a medical model. The worker, in this approach, helps members identify and solve individual problems in functioning; the worker does this through an assessment of the members as individuals as well as of group conditions (Vinter, 1974a). Because of the emphasis in this model on individual treatment planning, it has been used extensively in clinical social work settings, and it has facilitated the establishment of group services in those settings.

The *reciprocal model* focuses on the processes through which individuals and groups transact for their mutual benefit. The worker facilitates such transactions in the role of mediator (Schwartz, 1976).

In addition to differences in technique between the remedial and reciprocal models, there are also philosophical differences. The remedial model is strongly positivist, and the reciprocal model is strongly existential. In the former, a scientific and positivist bias is manifested in an emphasis on individual goals, the encouragement of group goals that will support these, and the use of social science as well as social work research to inform and test goal-oriented practice procedures. In the reciprocal approach, according to Schwartz (1976, p. 175), existential ideas "are expressed through a curiosity about processes, the nature of experience, the influence of feelings on human behavior, and the conduct of people in interaction."

In a departure of Papell and Rothman's conceptualization of group-work models, two consecutive editions of the *Encyclopedia of Social Work* (1971 and 1977) commissioned theoretical papers on group practice by representatives of the reciprocal model (Schwartz) and the remedial model (Garvin and Glasser, 1974; Glasser and Garvin, 1977) but commissioned Tropp to describe a third model, which he calls a *developmental* approach. Tropp (1977) describes his practice theory as "starting with a strong emphasis on the common group goal and the democratic process of group involvement" (p. 1321).

The most recent effort to identify models of group work was that of Roberts and Northen (1976), *Theories of Social Work with Groups.* Their volume includes the same authors as the *Encyclopedia of Social Work* as well as several persons who had written group-work or small-group-theory texts (Northen, Hartford). Ryder, who has been identified with the *functional approach,* described that model. Several persons who have associated casework models with group work were also included in this collection: McBroom on socialization through groups, Parad and his colleagues on crisis reduction in groups, and Garvin, Reid, and Epstein on the application to groups of the latter two authors' task-centered approach. A chapter by Wilson on history and one by Somers on approaches to problem solving in group work are also part of this collection.

Roberts and Northen summarized and compared the work of the authors and concluded that these authors did not represent totally distinct approaches to group work. This comparison included the writer's views of behavioral science foundations, target populations, criteria for group-member selection, and worker interventions. Those who had similar positions on one of these dimensions often had different positions on others. The authors sought an internal consistency for their models and achieved this by combining elements of practice in different ways. In the next section, we will describe some of these elements and comment on some similarities and differences that exist among theorists of group practice.

Practice Principles. Clinical social workers in group situations share basic values, even when they employ different practice theories. These values can have special implications in the group situation. For example, the general emphasis in social work on respect for individuals and self-determination implies that *neither* the worker nor the group should deny these rights to individual group members. The self-determination of the group should also be respected. A further implication for group work is that the worker and the group may act at times to benefit some members as long as harm is not done to other members. These values remind the worker to be watchful for the inevitable pressures for conformity in groups that are not therapeutic for the members.

One way of discussing practice theory and principles is in reference to the phases of group development described earlier in this chapter. During the *pregroup phase,* the worker, in ways consistent with agency goals, determines the general purpose for which the group is to be formed (or, in the case of a preexisting group, the purpose for which service is to be offered). In formed groups, the worker selects potential members for the group and prepares the members for the group experience.

Group purposes are usually expressed in terms of goals the group will help the members achieve. Workers should consider group purposes carefully as these will influence decisions on group composition, group program, and choice of intervention. The worker offering group services can identify purposes for a group by assessing the needs of the client through questionnaires or interviews. In fact, any problem that can be considered in a one-to-one treatment situation may also be dealt with in a group if the client wishes to be helped that way. A major exception may be when a family approach should be the choice because the problem is clearly rooted in family functioning. Even then, groups composed of several families have been successfully formed (Bowen, 1971).

Although a full range of problems have been worked on in groups, not all individuals can or should be served that way. The problem, however, with research findings on this topic is that they relate to particular kinds of groups, and one type of group experience may be appropriate for a client whereas another may not. For example, Yalom (1975, p. 225) studied dropouts from group psychotherapy and discovered that some gave reasons, such as distance to meetings and scheduling problems, that may represent resistance to the group. Some drop-outs had become deviants in the group, others reacted negatively to the intimacy that evolved, and still others were concerned about contagion to themselves of emotions and behaviors of others.

Variables workers consider when they choose members for groups include age, sex, ethnicity, group-participation characteristics, and interpersonal behaviors. Workers choose members who are enough alike to identify with and to attract one another yet different enough to learn from one another (Bertcher and Maple, 1974). Yalom (1975, p. 271) argues, however, that service-group cohesiveness is essential for group effectiveness and that cohesion is based on interpersonal attraction.

Research findings have shown that members who were prepared for group treatment were more likely to have desired outcomes than those who were not (Yalom, 1975, pp. 290–298). Orientation to groups can include a description of group processes, norms, and expectations. The idea that the members will be expected to share thoughts and feelings with each other and help each other can be instilled. The worker can acknowledge that sharing in groups may be difficult and that first meetings, when members get to know each other, can be frustrating.

If additional procedures or experiences are anticipated by the worker, they should also be presented.

During the group formation phase, the worker helps the members determine their purposes and their group norms. The worker also helps the members to discover commonalities among themselves as one basis for developing trust in each other and creating a cohesive group. Members are likely to experience ambivalence toward the group if they simultaneously anticipate desirable outcomes and fear undesirable ones. The worker helps the members to reduce this ambivalence through discovering and reinforcing their caring for one another; at the same time, fears about the group are acknowledged and reduced.

One way that members can determine their purpose for the group and relate this to the worker and agency purpose is to identify individual goals. A group purpose can then be created that will further these individual goals. The models of group work we have identified approach the determination of individual goals differently. Those who use the remedial model elicit concrete, often long-term, individual goals; those who use the reciprocal model give greater emphasis to the immediate demands the group and the members place on each other. This latter approach is more oriented to the shifting nature of individual aspirations as a result of interactional processes.

Almost all models of group work refer to a "contract" as an outcome of the formation phase. Here, again, different models have contrasting ideas about the nature of the contract. In the reciprocal approach, the worker seeks complementarity between what the members need and what the agency offers. In the remedial approach, the worker seeks an agreement on the specific goals the members will seek to attain, the procedures that will be used in the group, and the roles of the worker and the members. Since there can be many types of agreements sought within the group, we enumerate these: (1) between the members and the worker; (2) between the group-as-a-whole and each member; (3) among several members; (4) between a single member and the worker.

Another issue that divides theorists is whether or not to generate a psychosocial assessment of each member, as is required in the remedial model. Tropp (1976), in contrast, seeks data on "what concern the members have *in common*, based on how they describe, evaluate, and respond to their own and others' experiences in coping." He also suggests that workers should assess the group-as-a-whole as a basis of preparing for group meetings (p. 218).

During the middle phases of the group's existence, the worker will employ interventions directed at individuals, subgroups within the group, the group-as-a-whole, and the environment of the group. Interactions with individuals enhance problem-solving abilities or participation in the group. The techniques the worker uses are the same ones used in a one-to-one helping situation. These include confrontation, interpretation, and assignment of tasks. The worker in a group situation must be aware, however, that one-to-one interactions will have effects on other members because of their observability. In fact, this is often the intent of the worker. Of course, the worker should refrain from such interactions when they will have detrimental effects on others.

An important worker decision is when to engage in one-to-one interactions in the group as opposed to facilitating the way members help one another. (Inexperienced workers will often overuse the former type of intervention.) The worker should interact with individuals when it is not possible to use group processes at the moment and a delay will seriously hinder the member's goal attainment. Workers should also use this approach when group processes become destructive and when the worker seeks to model helping behaviors for group members.

Workers may also interact with a subgroup when they seek to mediate interactions taking place among these members. The worker may also work with a subgroup created as a committee or task force. The worker will help these subgroups to clarify their charge, to secure resources, and to learn the skills required to fulfill their mandate.

The unique element of the group-worker's role is to facilitate changes in the structures and processes of the entire group. Schwartz (1976), in reference to the reciprocal model, describes workers as facilitating group processes by helping the members "search for common ground between the needs of clients and those of systems they have to negotiate" and by "detecting and challenging the obstacles that come between the members and their systems" (p. 190). The worker also contributes information, shares his or her own vision and feelings, and helps "define the limits and requirements of the situation in which the work takes place" (p. 190).

In working with the entire group, the worker will make use of *program,* which is defined as the activities and tasks the worker introduces or supports in furtherance of group or individual goals. Almost all group-work publications since the earliest ones have described the use of program (Vinter, 1974b; Wilson and Ryland, 1949). The types of programs that have been used by group workers include discussion, arts and crafts, games, role plays, music, cooking, and group trips. Vinter (1974b) has identified the variables a worker must consider in selecting a group activity, such as the way the activity promotes interactiveness, distributes rewards, controls behavior, promotes physical movement, and requires competence.

Workers also seek to help the entire group engage in effective problem solving. Strategies they use include (1) teaching the group the principles of problem solving, (2) resolving communication problems that hinder this process, (3) helping the group obtain information, and (4) working with emotions that hinder rational consideration of issues. The worker must also provide support and encouragement to the group when problem-solving activities are lengthy and frustrating.

Still another way of affecting group structures and processes is *mass group process commentary* (Yalom, 1975, pp. 169–190). This involves making comments, and inviting the members to do likewise, regarding the nature and meaning of interactions among members and between members and the worker. This exploration of group process has two effects: (1) it helps members become aware of and plan changes in structures and processes that interfere with attaining the purposes of the group, and (2) members can become aware of and seek to modify the ways they cope with interpersonal relationships both within and outside the group. Several writers have conceptualized group processes in ways that facilitate this kind of commentary, including Bion (1959) through his idea of "basic assumption cultures" and Whitaker and Lieberman (1964) through their concept of focal group conflicts.

Workers with groups, like all social workers, may also interact with systems outside the group on behalf of individual members as well with as the group-as-a-whole. In doing this, they use techniques associated with such roles as advocate, broker, and mediator (Compton and Galaway, 1979, pp. 337–345). The group worker must also be sensitive to how the service agency affects group structures and processes. Some of the ways agencies have such effects on groups is through creating their purposes, establishing their referral patterns, allocating their resources, approving their change targets, creating their physical environments, interacting with their indigenous leaders, favoring specific change theories, and modeling interactional patterns through the agency's own structures and processes.

The worker also draws from practice principles when the group enters its termination phases. These phases may occur after only four or five sessions in some groups, such as those created to help clients with specific transitions, or after a year or more in groups that were formed either to support persons with chronic problems or to provide intensive group therapy. In all cases, the worker's termination goals are to help members deal with feelings about termination, to reduce attraction to and dependence on the group, and to generalize learning from the group to other settings.

To accomplish these goals, the worker may:

1. Encourage the members to practice behaviors learned in the group in such situations as their family, school, and workplace.
2. Help the members to seek out support from persons outside the group for these behaviors.
3. Prepare members for the fact that the environment will not always be supportive and help members to plan coping strategies for nonsupportive environments.
4. Identify the feelings members may have about termination and help them to cope with these. Of particular importance is challenging a denial of termination feelings.
5. Facilitate the ways members relinquish ties to other members and the worker by supporting relationships outside the group and the members' new skills of independent functioning.
6. Evaluate with the members the effects of the group experience in both its beneficial and nonbeneficial respects. Evaluation should be done continually throughout the group experience so that the termination evaluation constitutes a summation of previous feedback processes. This final evaluation helps the members to make plans for subsequent experiences and helps the worker to identify strengths and weaknesses in his or her ways of working with the group. A way of leading into a final evaluation is a summary of the group's experiences.

Research on Practice with Groups. A number of useful summaries of social work research findings relevant to group work have been compiled (Maas, 1966, 1971, 1979). In addition, there are comprehensive compilations of research on group psychotherapy, and much of this research can be extrapolated to social work practice with groups (Bednar and Kaul, 1978; Grunebaum, 1975; Lewis and McCants, 1973; Parloff and Dies, 1977). A few examples of group work research are Navarre, Glasser, and Costabile (1974) on group work with public assistance clients; Garvin, Reid, and Epstein (1976) on task-centered group work; Sarri and Vinter (1974) on group work in schools; Rose (1977) on behavioral approaches; Lawrence and Walter (1974) on adult behavioral groups; Wittes and Radin (1969) on group approaches with preschool parents; and Kaplow and Terzieff (1971) on group work with unmarried mothers.

The research and summaries of research to which we have referred support many of the practice principles we have identified. It is well established that groups can provide benefit to a wide variety of clients, although little is known about those situations in which individual or group modalities clearly excel. In addition, research findings support the value of preparing members for groups and the value of increasing group cohesion through identifying similarities among members. A clear goal orientation increases the likelihood of attaining goals, and a contract between members and workers secures commitment to performing their respective tasks.

Training in problem solving does enhance the quality of solutions. More research needs to be done on the use of different types of groups and interventions with different client populations and situations. Such investigative efforts may help workers to choose among various practice theories. Research should also be done on issues posed by existential writers, such as how worker actions can enhance the authentic quality of group processes and how each member benefits from them. Research also should be done, from a positivist perspective, on how persons develop their goals in groups and the effects of different ways of choosing goals. Clients vary in their commitments to their goals, and this phenomena also needs to be better understood.

Conclusion

Group practice has the advantage of reflecting the idea that much of life is lived in groups and that an enhancement of life is dependent on enriching the way people function in group situations. Social theorists have contributed to clinical practice by enriching the understanding of group processes and the knowledge of how to intervene in group situations for the benefit of individuals. This type of understanding is rapidly becoming integrated into social work practice. However, *all* of life is *not* lived in groups. All workers must be aware of the need to help individuals develop their identities and achieve their goals, often in opposition to group forces. In this respect, the following statement of Yalom (1975) about group members who were positive about their group experiences is clearly relevant: "They realized that there were limits to the guidance and support they could receive from others and that the ultimate responsibility for the conduct of their lives was theirs alone. They learned also that though they could be close to others, there was nonetheless a point beyond which none could accompany them: there is a basic aloneness to existence which must be faced and cannot be avoided" (p. 87).

References

Asch, S. E. "Opinions and Social Pressure." *Scientific American,* 1955, *193* (5), 31–35.

Bales, R. F. *Interaction Process Analysis: A Method for the Study of Small Groups.* Cambridge, Mass.: Addison-Wesley, 1950.

Bales, R. F. "Task Roles and Social Roles in Problem Solving Groups." In E. E. Maccoby, T. M. Newcomb, and E. L. Hartley (Eds.), *Readings in Social Psychology.* (3rd ed.) New York: Holt, Rinehart and Winston, 1958.

Bednar, R. L., and Kaul, T. O. "Experiential Group Research: Current Perspectives." In S. L. Garfield and A. E. Bergin (Eds.), *Handbook of Psychotherapy and Behavior Change: An Empirical Analysis.* (2nd ed.) New York: Wiley, 1978.

Bennis, W. G., and Shepherd, H. A. "A Theory of Group Development." *Human Relations,* 1956, *9,* 415–437.

Berelson, B., and Steiner, G. A. *Human Behavior.* New York: Harcourt Brace Jovanovich, 1964.

Bertcher, H. J., and Maple, F. "Elements and Issues in Group Composition." In P. Glasser, R. Sarri, and R. Vinter (Eds.), *Individual Change Through Small Groups.* New York: Free Press, 1974.

Bion, W. R. *Experiences in Groups.* New York: Basic Books, 1959.

Bowen, M. "Family Therapy and Family Group Therapy." In H. I. Kaplan and B. J. Sadock (Eds.), *Comprehensive Group Psychotherapy.* Baltimore: Williams and Wilkins, 1971.

Cartwright, D., and Zander, A. (Eds.). *Group Dynamics: Research and Theory.* (3rd ed.) New York: Harper & Row, 1968.

Coche, E., and Douglas, A. A. "Therapeutic Effects of Problem-Solving Training and Play-Reading Groups." *Journal of Clinical Psychology,* in press.

Coche, E., and Flick, A. "Problem-Solving Training Groups for Hospitalized Psychiatric Patients." *Journal of Psychology,* 1975, *91,* 19–29.

Compton, B. R., and Galaway, B. (Eds.). *Social Work Processes.* (Rev. ed.) Homewood, Ill.: Dorsey Press, 1979.

Coyle, G. "Group Work and Social Change." In *Proceedings of the National Conference of Social Work.* Chicago: University of Chicago Press, 1935.

Deutsch, M., and Gerard, H. B. "A Study of Normative and Informational Social Influences upon Individual Judgment." *Journal of Abnormal and Social Psychology,* 1955, *51,* 629–636.

Dewey, J. *How We Think.* Boston: Heath, 1933.

Festinger, L., Schachter, S., and Back, K. *Social Pressures in Informal Groups.* New York: Harper & Row, 1950.

Follett, M. P. *The New State.* New York: Longman, 1926.

Foulkes, S. H. *Therapeutic Group Analysis.* London: Allen & Unwin, 1964.

Garland, J., Jones, H., and Kolodny, R. "A Model for Stages in the Development of Social Work Groups." In S. Bernstein (Ed.), *Explorations in Group Work.* Boston: Boston University School of Social Work, 1965.

Garvin, C. "Group Process: Usage and Uses in Social Work Practice." In P. Glasser, R. Sarri, and R. Vinter (Eds.), *Individual Change Through Small Groups.* New York: Free Press, 1974.

Garvin, C. D. *Contemporary Group Work.* Englewood Cliffs, N.J.: Prentice-Hall, 1981.

Garvin, C. D., and Glasser, P. H. "Social Group Work: The Preventive and Rehabilitative Approach." In P. Glasser, R. Sarri, and R. Vinter (Eds.), *Individual Change Through Small Groups.* New York: Free Press, 1974.

Garvin, C., Reid, W., and Epstein, L. "A Task-Centered Approach." In R. W. Roberts and H. Northen (Eds.), *Theories of Social Work with Groups.* New York: Columbia University Press, 1976.

Gassner, S. M., Gold, J., and Snadowsky, A. M. "Changes in the Phenomenal Field as a Result of Human Relations Training." *Journal of Psychology,* 1964, *58,* 33–41.

Glasser, P. H., and Garvin, C. D. "Social Group Work: The Organizational and Environmental Approach." In *Encyclopedia of Social Work.* Vol. 2. Washington, D.C.: National Association of Social Workers, 1977.

Grunebaum, H. "A Soft Hearted Review of Hard-Nosed Research on Groups." *International Journal of Group Psychotherapy,* 1975, *25,* 185–197.

Hartford, M. *Groups in Social Work.* New York: Columbia University Press, 1972.

Hartman, A. "Anomie and Social Casework." *Social Casework,* 1969, *50,* 131–137.

Homans, G. C. *Social Behavior: Its Elementary Forms.* New York: Harcourt Brace and World, 1961.

Kaplow, E., and Terzieff, N. F. "An Experiment in Group Services to Unmarried Parents." Toronto: Children's Aid Society of Metropolitan Toronto, 1971.

Lang, N. C. "Some Defining Characteristics of the Social Work Group: Unique Social Form." Unpublished manuscript, Faculty of Social Work, University of Toronto, 1980.

Lawrence, H., and Walter, C. "The Effectiveness of Behavior Modification with Adult Groups." Paper presented at the Association for the Advancement of Behavior Therapy Conference, Chicago, Nov. 1974.

Lewin, K. "Frontiers in Group Dynamics." *Human Relations,* 1947, *1,* 5–41.

Lewis, P., and McCants, J. "Some Current Issues in Group Psychotherapy Research." *International Journal of Group Psychotherapy,* 1973, *23,* 268–273.

Lindeman, E. C. *The Community.* New York: Association Press, 1921.

Lippitt, R. "Field Theory and Experiment in Social Psychology: Autocratic and Democratic Group Atmospheres." *American Journal of Sociology,* 1939, *45,* 26–49.

Maas, H. S. (Ed.). *Five Fields of Social Service: Reviews of Research.* New York: National Association of Social Workers, 1966.

Maas, H. S. (Ed.). *Research for the Social Services: A Five Year Review.* New York: National Association of Social Workers, 1971.

Maas, H. S. (Ed.). *Social Service Research: Reviews of Studies.* Washington,, D.C.: National Association of Social Workers, 1979.

Manis, M. "Social Interaction and the Self Concept." *Journal of Abnormal and Social Psychology,* 1955, *51,* 362–370.

Mead, G. H. *Mind, Self, and Society.* Chicago: University of Chicago Press, 1934.

Mills, T. M. *The Sociology of Small Groups.* Englewood Cliffs, N.J.: Prentice-Hall, 1967.

Navarre, E., Glasser, P. H., and Costabile, J. "An Evaluation of Group Work Practice with A.F.D.C. Mothers." In P. Glasser, R. Sarri, and R. Vinter (Eds.), *Individual Change Through Small Groups.* New York: Free Press, 1974.

Newstetter, W. I. "What Is Social Group Work?" In *Proceedings of the National Conference of Social Work.* Chicago: University of Chicago Press, 1935.

Nixon, H. L. II. *The Small Group.* Englewood Cliffs, N.J.: Prentice-Hall, 1979.

Papell, C. P., and Rothman, B. "Social Group Work Models: Possession and Heritage." *Journal of Education for Social Work,* 1966, *2* (2), 66–77.

Parloff, M., and Dies, R. R. "Group Therapy Outcome Research: 1966–1975." *International Journal of Group Psychotherapy,* 1977, *27,* 281–319.

Parsons, T. *The Social System.* New York: Free Press, 1951.

Polansky, N., Lippitt, R., and Redl, F. "An Investigation of Behavioral Contagion in Groups." *Human Relations,* 1950, *3,* 319–348.

Redl, F. "The Phenomenon of Contagion and Shock Effect." In F. Redl (Ed.), *When We Deal with Children.* New York: Free Press, 1966.

Richmond, M. "Some Next Steps in Social Treatment." In *Proceedings of the National Conference of Social Work, 1920.* New York: Columbia University Press, 1939.

Roberts, R. W., and Northen, H. (Eds.). *Theories of Social Work with Groups.* New York: Columbia University Press, 1976.

Rose, S. *Group Therapy: A Behavioral Approach.* Englewood Cliffs, N.J.: Prentice-Hall, 1977.

Sarason, I. G., and Ganzer, V. J. "Modeling and Group Discussion in the Rehabilitation of Juvenile Delinquents." *Journal of Counseling Psychology,* 1973, *20,* 442–449.

Sarri, R., and Galinsky, M. "A Conceptual Framework for Group Development." In P. Glasser, R. Sarri, and R. Vinter (Eds.), *Individual Change Through Small Groups.* New York: Free Press, 1974.

Sarri, R., and Vinter, R. D. "Beyond Group Work: Organizational Determinants of Malperformance in Secondary Schools." In P. Glasser, R. Sarri, and R. Vinter (Eds.), *Individual Change Through Small Groups.* New York: Free Press, 1974.

Schachter, S. "Deviation, Rejection and Communication." *Journal of Abnormal and Social Psychology,* 1951, *46,* 190–207.

Schwartz, W. "Social Work: The Interactionist Approach." In *Social Work Encyclopedia.* Vol. 2. New York: National Association of Social Workers, 1971.

Schwartz, W. "Between Client and System: The Mediating Function." In R. W. Roberts and H. Northen (Eds.), *Theories of Social Work with Groups.* New York: Columbia University Press, 1976.

Shaw, M. E. *Group Dynamics: The Psychology of Small Group Behavior.* New York: McGraw-Hill, 1976.

Sherif, M. *The Psychology of Social Norms.* New York: Harper & Row, 1936.

Sherif, M., and Sherif, C. W. *Social Psychology.* New York: Harper & Row, 1969.

Skinner, B. F. *Science and Human Behavior.* New York: Macmillan, 1953.

Strong, S. R. "Social Psychology Approach to Psychotherapy Research." In S. L. Garfield and A. E. Bergin (Eds.), *Handbook of Psychotherapy and Behavior Change: An Empirical Analysis.* New York: Wiley, 1978.

Thibaut, J. W., and Kelly, H. H. *The Social Psychology of Groups.* New York: Wiley, 1959.

Tropp, E. "A Developmental Theory." In R. W. Roberts and H. Northen (Eds.), *Theories of Social Work with Groups.* New York: Columbia University Press, 1976.

Tropp, E. "Social Group Work: The Developmental Approach." In *Encyclopedia of Social Work.* Vol. 2. Washington, D.C.: National Association of Social Workers, 1977.

Tuckman, B. W. "Developmental Sequence in Small Groups." *Psychological Bulletin,* 1965, *43,* 384–399.

Vinter, R. D. "Analyses of Treatment Organizations." *Social Work,* 1963, *8,* 3–15.

Vinter, R. D. "The Essential Components of Group Work Practice." In P. Glasser, R. Sarri, and R. Vinter (Eds.), *Individual Change Through Small Groups.* New York: Free Press, 1974a.

Vinter, R. D. "Program Activities: An Analysis of Their Effects on Participant Behavior." In P. Glasser, R. Sarri, and R. Vinter (Eds.), *Individual Change Through Small Groups.* New York: Free Press, 1974b.

Whitaker, D. S., and Lieberman, M. A. *Psychotherapy Through the Group Process.* New York: Atherton Press, 1964.

Wilson, G., and Ryland, G. *Social Group Work Practice.* Boston: Houghton Mifflin, 1949.

Wittes, G., and Radin, N. "Two Approaches to Parent Work in a Compensatory School Program." Paper presented at the National Conference on Family Relations, Washington, D.C., Oct. 1969.

Yalom, I. D. *The Theory and Practice of Group Psychotherapy.* (2nd ed.) New York: Basic Books, 1975.

8

Family Theory and Practice

Joan Laird
Jo Ann Allen

Social work practice originated in efforts to strengthen and rehabilitate troubled and destitute families. The early social worker's role in the child guidance movement, in the mental hygiene movement, and in the delivery of health care was to ameliorate noxious elements and mobilize supports in the client's environment. As the family was often the most salient part of that environment, social work practice soon included work with families.

In view of this historical concern with the family, it is not surprising that social workers have found the recent interdisciplinary family therapy movement to be a way of thinking and a way of helping that is highly congruent with their professional goals and attitudes. In this chapter, we will present an overview of the theories that have developed within the family therapy movement—theories that give shape and direction to clinical social work practice with families.

Before embarking on this overview, we will sketch the context within which this body of practice theory will be presented. We will first briefly describe our view of the relationship between social work and the family therapy movement. Following this description of the context, we will discuss what we consider to be the major theories currently informing family therapy. Finally, we will summarize what we perceive to be some of the main commonalities and differences among the theories, and we will point out some of the major unresolved theoretical issues currently under debate.

For the purposes of our discussion, we will define *clinical social work* as that part of social work practice focused on offering direct service in the enhancement of social functioning. *Family therapy* is defined as treatment of psychosocial dysfunction through the use of the family as the context for understanding such dysfunction and as a resource for change.

The family therapy movement is interdisciplinary and includes many social workers who occupy positions of leadership, such as Virginia Satir, Lynn Hoffman, Peggy Papp, Olga Silverstein, Betty Carter, Harry Aponte, Sanford Sherman, and Marianne Walters. Social workers flock to family therapy conferences and account for a large percentage of those enrolled in intensive training programs. Social workers have advocated, often in the face of considerable opposition, for the training and equipment needed to incorporate family perspectives in a range of fields of practice and service delivery settings. Graduate schools of social work have increased family content in both generic and specialized sequences, and some undergraduate programs have developed family-centered curricula in such areas as preparation for child welfare practice.

The present situation is reminiscent of and offers intellectual ferment and excitement similar to that seen in the influence of psychoanalytic thinking on social work in the 1930s. Our task today is to integrate this exciting and useful body of knowledge, theory, and skills into our own practice without losing our professional identity and direction. The emphasis on the social context and the interdisciplinary character of the family therapy movement will aid us in this task. We hope that our discussion of theory drawn from the family therapy movement as a base for family-centered clinical social work practice may make some small contribution to this integrative effort.

Theories for Family Therapy

During the past decade or so there have appeared a number of approaches to summarizing, categorizing, and classifying family theories and leaders. An early, well-known effort was that of Beels and Ferber (1969), who thought that style was probably the most important element in distinguishing among leading family therapists. Theories, which these authors concluded were not fully developed, were often rationalizations for evolving therapeutic practices—a case of thinking following the doing. Major family therapists were divided into "conductors" and "reactors." The conductors are generally more charismatic, action oriented, and controlling in family sessions; the reactors tend to observe and respond to what the family presents. Satir, Ackerman, and Minuchin are examples of charismatic conductors who actively and consciously use the force of their own vigorous personalities to influence change. Beels and Ferber cite Whitaker, Boszormenyi-Nagy, and Haley, among others, as examples of reactors. The reactors do not use their own personalities but rather a variety of assumed roles, depending on their purpose. For them, the theme of power is often central, and the goal of therapy is to devise artful and sometimes paradoxical strategies that can shift power alignments and forces in families.

Guerin (1976) questions this view, stating that "a valid theory should not confine the therapist's repertoire of behavior; otherwise, only those people with a particular style of behavior would be able to use a particular theory, and that theory is then doomed to become a rationalization for a way of doing things" (p. 18). Guerin himself, after giving a fascinating account of the people and ideas that shaped the family therapy tradition, divides family therapists into two basic categories—those who prefer psychoanalytic theory and those who prefer systems theory. These two categories are further divided into subgroups. Psychoanalytic therapists are classified as individual, group, experiential, and Ackerman approach, and systems therapists are classified as general systems, structural, strategic, and Bowen family systems.

Another common way of categorizing approaches to family theory is by "school." Thus we hear the psychodynamic, communication, structural and behavioral "schools" of family therapy. There are weaknesses in this approach. The field of family therapy is still so young and so fluid that it seems premature to suggest that theoretical positions have at this point crystallized into schools. There is considerable debate about what is similar and what is decidedly different among theoretical positions and styles. For example, as Guerin points out, Minuchin was influenced by, among others, both Ackerman, a conductor, and Haley, a reactor, the former influenced by psychoanalytic thinking, the latter by communication theory. The theories and interviewing techniques of strategic therapists such as Haley and systemic therapists such as Palazzoli or Hoffman are highly behavioral. Yet, these theorists are not generally classified, nor would they probably classify themselves, as behavioral therapists. Bowen (1978), who calls his own theory "family systems" and who long ago eschewed psychoanalytic language and ways of thinking to develop new cognitive maps and therapeutic concepts, has often been categorized as psychoanalytically based. Boszormenyi-Nagy also is often placed in this category, yet he describes himself as having been particularly inspired by the dialectic philosophers and the existential thinking of Martin Buber (Boszormenyi-Nagy and Spark, 1973).

An interesting but controversial recent effort by Ritterman (1977) classifies theories of family therapy in terms of the ideal categories or philosophical assumptions on which they are based. She believes most theories can best be described in terms of two ideal paradigms, the mechanistic model and the organismic model. The mechanistic model is said to be characterized as a closed-system, nonholistic model based on linear or deterministic views of causality and is seen, according to Ritterman, in the work of Jackson, Watzlawick, and Weakland as well as in behavioral theories. The organismic model, by contrast, is characterized as an open-system, holistic model based on a dialectical causality and is best represented in the work of structural family therapists, such as Minuchin.

Other efforts to categorize and classify family theory include using the unit of focus of treatment as the organizing variable (Olson, 1975), or the goal of treatment (GAP Report, 1970).

A Framework for Examining Family Therapies

It is clear that, at present, there is neither an integrated body of knowledge nor a single theory of the family that informs the practice of family therapy. Further, as Gurman (1975) points out, family therapists "have generally failed to deal with common themes running through each other's work" (p. 36). As a result, concepts that address the same family phenomena or processes may be called by many different names. We agree with this criticism and hence have chosen to examine major family theories in yet another way. In our view, there *are* important common themes that inform family theory and therapy. What differs is that perspective, view, or aspect of the total family system in its ecological space and over time upon which the theorist chooses to focus, that which is considered most salient and is placed in the center of the lens. These foci identify the theorist's conception of the most appropriate target for change. The choice of focus implies some philosophy about the nature of change and the resources for change that can most profitably be used. These foci can be classified as follows:

1. Communication processes
2. Rule-governing processes
3. Family organization and structure
4. Differentiation and growth processes
   a. Intergenerational level
   b. Current family experiential level
5. Transactional processes with extended environment
6. Behavioral and social learning processes

Clearly, these categories do not define schools of family therapy or particular family therapists. For example, a therapist who focuses on structural difficulties might also focus on communication issues, while a therapist with an intergenerational emphasis might examine issues of structure and communication.

Each of the above foci will be examined in terms of the following categories:

1. Major concepts about the family
2. Ideas about dysfunction in families
3. Major hypotheses about the change process
   a. Nature of change
   b. Resources for change
   c. Targets of change

Communication Processes. As Watzlawick, Beavin, and Jackson (1967) point out, "no matter how one may try, one cannot not communicate" (p. 49). Certainly the observation and alteration of communication patterns is essential to any helping therapy and thus cuts across all of the foci in our scheme. A family is organized, its regulatory system is established, and behavioral patterns and sequences are developed through communication.

Concepts of communication that currently inform much of family therapy practice were developed by such pioneers as Bateson and others (1956), Haley (1956, 1963), Jackson (1968), Satir (1967), Weakland (1956), and Watzlawick (1967), all of whom placed communication at the center of their theories. More recently, Bandler and Grinder (1975) and Grinder and Bandler (1976) have made important contributions to this perspective. Although many family therapists share some common views about communication processes in families, they have different ideas about how to bring about change. We include in this section, then, those therapists who center their attention on communication processes, formulate their ideas of family function and dysfunction in terms of faulty communication, and direct change efforts toward altering and improving family communication. We do not include those therapists who, while using the same or similar communication concepts, direct their focus to changing rules or family structure.

FAMILY CONCEPTS. Therapies directed toward changing family communication are predicated on the idea that the most crucial variable in determining how the family carries out its functions, both in relation to its members and to the extended environment, is its communication system. Members define their ways of being together—their rules, roles, relationships, and values—through the medium of communication. Members must learn how to understand each other on verbal, nonverbal and metacommunication levels. They must also learn how to give adequate and accurate information if they are to have their needs and wants recognized and satisfied. *Clarity* of communication is thought to be a major factor in determining how functional or dysfunctional a family system is in its growth and development and that of its individual members. Satir (1967) emphasizes the importance of *openness:* "An open system permits honest self-expression for the participating members. In such a group or family, differences are viewed as natural, and open negotiation occurs to resolve such differences by 'compromise,' 'agreement to disagree,' 'taking turns,' etc. In open systems, the individual can say what he feels and thinks and can negotiate for reality and personal growth without destroying himself or others in the system" (p. 185).

If communication is open and clear, the family can carry out its functions adequately, individual needs are met, and growth can occur without undue conflict and stress. Each family develops its own style of verbal and nonverbal communication over the years. That style can be affected by a variety of factors, including cultural traditions, life events, and intergenerational themes. Style does not determine quality or adequacy since many styles can result in clear, open communication. How do these therapists define functional, adequate communication? One measure of functional communication is the degree of congruence that exists among the various levels of communication. Satir (1967) states that "a congruent communication is one where two or more messages are sent via different levels but none of these messages seriously contradicts any other" (p. 82).

To understand this idea more fully, it is helpful to turn to Watzlawick, Beavin, and Jackson (1967) once more. These authors point out that a communication both conveys information and at the same time imposes behavior (p. 51). A message contains both a "report" aspect and a "command" aspect (pp. 51–52): "The report aspect of a message conveys information and is, therefore, synonymous in human communication with the *content* of the message. It may be about anything that is communicable, regardless of whether the particular information is true or false, valid, invalid, or undecidable. The command as put, on the other hand, refers to what sort of a message it is to be taken as, and, therefore, ultimately to the *relationship* between the communicants" (p. 51–52). The relationship or "meta" aspect qualifies the content aspect, so that "whenever a person communicates he is not only making a statement, he is also asking something of the receiver and trying to influence the receiver to give him what he wants" (Satir, 1967, p. 78).

If the messages from the different levels "fit" with each other, the result is clear, open communication. The receiver of such communication is not confused by having the nonverbal message, as conveyed by body posture, voice tone, facial expression, and so on, conflict with the verbal message. The receiver can "trust" the message. The nonverbal aspects—behavior and feeling—are congruent with the verbal aspects of the communication.

Of course, the degree of congruence may vary; however, if congruence characterizes most of the communication most of the time in a family, it is likely that messages and consequently roles, rules, and relationships will be clear. It is also likely that members will be free to reveal their needs and wants and will experience a high degree of positive response.

Another idea of importance here is that of symmetry versus complementarity in communication and relationships. This means that relationships are based either on equality or difference. "Symmetrical interaction, then, is characterized by equality and the minimization of difference, while complementary interaction is based on the maximization of difference" (Watzlawick, Beavin, and Jackson, 1967, pp. 68–69). In the extreme, either of these two forms can be dysfunctional. The relationship based on equality can lead to disabling kinds of competitiveness, and the relationship based on difference can lead to a situation in which one person is always in an inferior position. Jackson (1968a) suggests that the "parallel" relationship and style of communication is "the most desirable one for our egalitarian culture" (p. 161). In a parallel relationship, the participants alternate between symmetrical and complementary relationships in response to changing situations. "There may be episodes of conflict concerning particular areas, but since the spouses feel equal to each other, they can be both supportive and competitive without fear, knowing that neither will win all issues at the expense of the other" (Jackson, 1968a, p. 161).

Satir's criteria for terminating treatment illustrate functionality on a communication level. To paraphrase Satir (1967, p. 176), functional communication in relationships exists:

- when family members can complete transactions, check, ask.
- when they can interpret hostility.
- when they can see how others see them.
- when they can see how they see themselves.
- when one member can tell another how he manifests himself.
- when one member can tell another wht he hopes, fears, and expects from him.
- when they can disagree.
- when they can make choices.
- when they can learn through practice.
- when they can free themselves from harmful effects of past models.
- when they can give a clear message, that is, be congruent in their behavior, with a minimum of difference between feelings and communication, and with a minimum of hidden messages.

FAMILY DYSFUNCTION. It should be clear from the foregoing that family dysfunction is understood in terms of faulty communication. In large part, dysfunction is the result of incongruent and contradictory messages. If there is a high level of discrepancy among the various levels of communication, confusion and conflict are created. At the extreme, a high degree of incongruence and contradiction in communication can result in a double bind. Haley (1980) explains double-bind theory as "the idea of describing communication in terms of levels, with the possibility that those levels could conflict and generate a paradox, or bind, when no acceptable response was possible" (p. 16). If no response is acceptable, then dysfunctional behavior is quite likely to arise, especially since the participants in the family are often unable to escape from the situation.

A high degree of incongruent communication tends to lead to a family system in which open self-expression is almost impossible because the individuals cannot trust what they see and hear; they must respond to hidden meanings and distortions. Given this kind of situation, family members cannot openly reveal feelings, needs and wants, and the family cannot carry out its functions effectively. As Satir (1967) points out in her description of a closed communication system, differences are dangerous in such families, and individual growth and development are limited.

Another view of communication dysfunction in families comes from the work of Bandler and Grinder. They suggest that humans portray their experiences by different representational systems and base their communication on those systems. Humans have a number of "output channels," such as language, posture, movement, and voice qualities. These theorists believe that most people organize their worlds according to their most highly valued representational system, which might be auditory, visual, or kinesthetic. That is, individuals understand and interpret their experience primarily through a sense of hearing, seeing, or feeling. To oversimplify, when representational systems of the individuals in the family conflict, accurate and clear communication becomes difficult. "What all this implies for family therapy is that, in the same way that conflicting paramessages produce incongruity, stifling inability to cope, and painful hopelessness in one human being, so, too, conflicting models of the world in the family organism can produce chaos, paralyzing rules, and, thus, prevent family members from being connected with each other in a way that is nourishing to all members of the family" (Bandler and Grinder, 1975, p. 126). Watzlawick, Beavin, and Jackson (1967, p. 56), in discussing discrepancy in the perception of the reality, state that "disagreement about how to punctuate the sequence of events is at the root of countless relationship struggles." Individuals may share experience but interpret it in very different ways. This difference in punctuation can lead to misunderstanding and serious conflict.

The communication view of dysfunction is tied to the idea that "all behavior is the outcome or function of communicative interaction within a social system" (Weakland, 1976, p. 121). In this view, normal behavior as well as dysfunctional behavior is structured and maintained by communication within the family.

THE PROCESS OF CHANGE. Family therapists who focus primarily on communication will obviously direct change efforts toward altering faulty communication processes. These therapists think of change in terms of growth, understanding, and self-awareness. The change process, according to this focus, is partly educative in nature. Family members are helped to understand the contradictions and the confusion in their communication patterns. In describing Satir's work, for example, Beels and Ferber (1972) state: "Satir is determined to teach the family a new language, with which they can resolve the communication problems that she sees as the root of their trouble. To do this, she makes herself the embodiment of clarity and perception in communication, keeping up a running explanatory gloss on what she is doing, and arranges encounters between family members according to her rules" (p. 177).

For these therapists, ideas about the change process are formulated in terms of growth of individual members and the total family system rather than through specific problem solving. Growth may come through improving communication skills, learning new ways of communicating, and reframing past and present experience. "Transforming the system will entail change at the coping level, not at the content level. A change in the *system* of how the people in a family give and receive messages from each other is the goal of family therapy, not the solution of problems—the problems are too many" (Bandler and others, 1976, p. 138).

Since communication processes are intertwined with all other family processes, a change in communication can affect other areas of family functioning. Bandler and Grinder (1975) "begin with the premise that the system (family organism as a whole) has some portion of its shared model of the world impoverished in a way that prevents the processes going on in that system from being nourishing" (p. 126). A change in the deletions, distortions, and generalizations that hinder communication will result in increased capacity of the family members to achieve the experiences they want. Change then essentially must entail decreasing incongruence and increasing congruence among the levels of communication.

Rule-Governing Processes. Another way therapists organize their work is in terms of family rule-governing processes. The Milan Therapy Group led by Mara Selvini Palazzoli, and Lynn Hoffman and Peggy Papp, both associated with the Brief Therapy Project at the Ackerman Institute, are among those who have developed this focus. They are usually identified as systemic or strategic family therapists, as is Jay Haley. The theoretical concepts that underlie the focus on the family as a rule-governing system come from general systems theory, cybernetics, and communication theory. Of the many theorists who have contributed to this perspective, Bateson, Milton Erickson, and Watzlawick are of particular importance.

FAMILY CONCEPTS. When we move the rule-governing process to the center of focus, the family is defined as a "self-regulating system which controls itself according to rules formed over a period of time through a process of trial and error" (Palazzoli and others, 1978, p. 3). The central notion is that every family, just as any natural group, works out its own way of being together through interaction and feedback. Families develop rules about everything. Some rules are overt and some are covert. There are even rules about rules. Each family becomes a systemic unit held together by rules peculiar to it alone. The rules are the basis for the regulatory system, and each family member has a part in maintaining that system.

Systems are not necessarily organized according to hierarchy and power levels, and thus one part of the system is not more important than another in maintaining dysfunction. "With this new orientation, the therapist should be able to see the members of the family as elements in a circuit of interaction. None of the members have unidirectional power over the whole, although the behavior of any one of the members of the family inevitably influences the behavior of the others (Palazzoli and others, 1978, p. 5). Family transactions are seen as a series of behavior responses that in turn influence other behavior responses. Over a period of time, these responses evolve into a series of patterns and rules organized into what Palazzoli calls "the family game." The power lies in the rules of the game, which cannot be changed, or usually even recognized, by family members. Therapy then becomes a process of understanding the family game and its rules and trying to direct interventions toward a change in those rules. Identifying and changing a single central family rule will lead to significant change throughout the system.

A second important principle derived from systems theory is that every living system is characterized by apparently contradictory functions, the homeostatic tendency and the capacity for transformation. Wertheim (1973) has referred to these as morphostatic and morphogenic tendencies. The interplay between morphostasis and morphogenesis in a well-functioning system ensures stability while permitting creativity and growth.

Communication theory is another part of the basis for this focus. The rule-governing behavior of the family system operates through its communication processes, and every family develops rules about communication itself. Theories about double-binding or paradoxical communication, axioms of communication, and analogic and digital modes of communication help therapists to understand family processes and plot strategies for change. Watzlawick (1978) explains the analogic and digital modes: "The one (digital) in which, for example, this sentence itself is expressed is objective, definitional, cerebral, logical, analytic; it is the language of reason, of science, explanation, and interpretation, and therefore the language of most schools of psychotherapy. The other (analogic) is much more difficult to define—precisely because it is not the language of definition. We might call it the language of imagery, of metaphor, of pars pro toto, perhaps of symbols, but certainly of synthesis and totality, and not of analytical dissection" (pp. 14–15). It is the latter that he calls the "language of change." This idea is further developed in his discussions concerning the right and left hemispheres of the brain (the right hemisphere controls the analogic mode and the left controls the digital mode of language).

FAMILY DYSFUNCTION. If one accepts the idea that the family is held together and governed by its own singluar set of rules, it follows that "families in which one or more members present behaviors traditionally diagnosed as 'pathological' are held together by transactions and rules peculiar to the pathology" (Palazzoli and others, 1978, p. 4). The symptomatic behavior is then only a part of, or a "move" in, the pathological transaction, or family game. For example, in the case of a family in which a member has been diagnosed as schizophrenic, in Palazzoli's view, the primary rule is that no one shall define relationships. An open declaration of the relationship is perceived as extremely dangerous since the symmetry is threatened and one member may gain the upper hand. In other words, everyone is involved in a struggle to gain control of the definition of the relationship, but no one can risk the possibility of failure. The game becomes one of disqualifying any definition of relationship by the other, and the participants become locked in a game characterized by the skilled use of paradoxical communication. A symptom then can be seen as a maneuver in the family game and thus as part of the regulatory and morphostatic tendencies of the family. Problematic or symptomatic behaviors can be viewed as serving positive functions in the maintenance of the "pathological" stasis, and any attempts to change these behaviors will be met with corrective feedback from the family. Thus, it becomes a major part of assessment to discover the positive function of the problem for each member of the family and for the system as a whole.

The more rigid the system, the more difficulty it has in dealing with ordinary and necessary change over time. Change, after all, often involves reorganization of the family and changing the rules. In rigid systems, there is no way to change rules, and often it is even forbidden to acknowledge that there are any rules, as in the disconfirmation patterns seen in schizophrenic families. These family systems become "stuck," as Palazzoli has said, and the natural growth and development of individuals and families is thwarted as they progress through the life cycle.

PROCESS OF CHANGE. If there is a natural and powerful tendency to maintain the status quo, and if dysfunctional systems are those that exhibit this tendency to the point of being "stuck," how can change come about? How is it possible to activate the family's capacity for transformation? Palazzoli and others (1978) maintain that "when we change one fundamental rule, the pathological behavior quickly disappears" (p. 4). Insight is not necessary for change and will hinder change if it comes too early since it may be used to combat and disqualify the therapist's intervention. The therapeutic effort is to bring about a transformation or a "leap" to a new rule, which will enable the family system to become "unstuck."

The selection of the rule or rules to be changed grows out of a progressive hypothesizing process, which is an attempt to explain the morphostatic function of the problematic behaviors for every member of the family and the family as a system. As therapy proceeds, the therapist focuses on the feedback responses of the family system. "One has the sensation of proceeding by layers, almost in a circular manner towards the central nodal point, action upon which can trigger the greatest transformation" (Palazzoli and others, 1978, p. 49). This process is based on the general systems notion of a nodal point, Ps, which is that point where the greatest number of functions essential to the maintenance of a system converge. Palazzoli and others (1978) maintain that, "if one directs an intervention toward the nodal point (Ps), one will get maximum change of the system with a minimum expense of energy" (p. 49).

Another important aspect of this approach concerns the dimension of time and how it is used therapeutically. Family system processes occur sequentially; thus, any introduced change must also have time to ripple sequentially throughout the system. The Milan group, for example, sees families at four-week intervals to allow the change, like yeast in bread dough, time to work. The family is discouraged from contact with the therapist during the interval and thus is left with the intervention and is diverted from attempts to disqualify it.

Therapists often find it necessary to deal with resistance to change by the family system. System therapists think of resistance in terms of a natural tendency toward balance and stability or constancy. Hoffman (1979) describes resistance as the system's natural affection for its own coherence. In her view, change is promoted only by therapeutic efforts that respect this tendency. Techniques to positively connote the symptom or problem as being in the interests of preservation of the system are employed to "join the resistance," thus defusing the family's mobilization of its defenses against the intruder who, it is expected, will insist upon change. Papp, (1980) whose concept of the Greek chorus is used similarly, believes "the central issue is no longer how to eliminate the symptoms but what will happen if it is eliminated; the therapeutic argument is shifted from the problem to how the family will survive without it" (p. 46).

For the strategic or system therapist, the *problem* is understood as the family's *solution* to what is another even more threatening or grievous problem. Change is begun by posing a paradox, which can trigger a transformation process that frees the family from its pathological game and its paralyzing rules.

Family Organization and Structure. A third and widely used perspective places family organization and structure at the center of attention. The organizational focus analyzes the family as a whole and the ways in which its parts are demarcated from and related to each other. Salvador Minuchin and his colleagues at the Philadelphia Child Guidance Clinic, including Harry Aponte, Ronald Liebman, Braulio Montalvo, and Marianne Walters, are generally credited with having developed and refined structural family therapy. Jay Haley, who was associated with Minuchin for several years, contributed a great deal to this perspective and has continued to develop his view of the family as a hierarchical organization.

FAMILY THEORY AND CONCEPTS. In describing their work with asthmatic children and their families, Liebman and others (1976, p. 316) list the following general characteristics of structural family therapy:

1. *Structural* refers to the concept of the family as a system consisting of various subsystems.
2. Its basic assumption is that the patient will not be able to give up his symptoms or change his role in the family unless the structure and functioning of the family system are changed.
3. Its therapeutic interventions are directed at correcting dysfunctional behavior patterns in the family.
4. Therapeutically, it is concerned with the present and immediate future, not the past.
5. It is based on observable, transactional, interpersonal processes between and among family members; it is not based on psychoanalytic concepts of the development of psychopathology.

The concept of the family as an organization with a hierarchy of authority is of primary importance. Haley remarks, "Something valuable has been developed from systems and communication theories, while at the same time a new view of organizational power has been developing." He describes an organization as a system of repeating sequences of communication in which "that communication becomes the organization" (1980, p. 25). Being organized necessitates following patterned ways of behaving and existing in a hierarchical arrangement (1976, p. 101). "Not only do all animals form hierarchical organizations, but it is important to note also that the hierarchy is maintained by all the participants. Those of higher status enforce their status by their actions, but those of lower status will act to enforce hierarchy if a higher-status creature does not enforce his status. When animals or humans step out of order, the reestablishment of hierarchy is a group effort with those below as active as those above" (p. 102).

Minuchin, too, speaks of the power hierarchy as essential to family organization and acknowledges it as one of the ways that a system regulates itself. In Minuchin's view, "the family system differentiates and carries out its functions through subsystems" (1974, p. 52). Subsystems can be formed by generation, by sex, by interest, or by function. Clearly, an individual in a family can belong to more than one subsystem and can have different levels of power and skill in each. A child, for example, may have less power when interacting with parents and more when interacting with younger siblings.

Of equal importance is the concept of boundaries among subsystems and between various subsystems and the whole. Subsystem boundaries are expressed in rules defining who participates and what the nature of that participation will be. In addition, boundaries help protect the differentiation of the system. In well-functioning families, the parental subsystem establishes itself in a position of power in relation to the sibling subsystem. "For proper family functioning, the boundaries of subsystems must be clear. They must be defined well enough to allow subsystem members to carry out their functions without undue interference, but they must allow contact between the members of the subsystem and others" (Minuchin, 1974, p. 54).

The idea that the family passes through a series of life stages is crucial to this focus, for it assumes that the family is faced with the task of reorganizing during transitions. Members of the family may leave and others may be added through a variety of circumstances. New subsystems and new alliances may be formed when, for example, a new child, a grandparent, or a step-parent is introduced into the organization. At these times, power and hierarchical arrangements may be altered, with ramifications for each individual member and the system as a whole. Individuals may have to assume new roles or give up others as the organization progresses through successive life stages and faces new developmental tasks.

FAMILY DYSFUNCTION. To organizational theorists, proper family functioning depends on the clarity of boundaries and the capacity of the system to adapt as circumstances change. "Since the family must respond to internal and external changes, it must be able to transform itself in ways that meet new circumstances without losing the continuity that provides a frame of reference for its members" (Minuchin, 1974, p. 52). Given enough flexibility and resources, a family will be able to make the necessary accommodations, even though it experiences stress in the process. No family, however, totally escapes "the pains of accommodation" since every family system, in the course of time, faces stress from extrafamilial forces, transitions in its own evolution, and idiosyncratic problems (p. 60).

Even a family that has been functioning effectively can experience difficulties in achieving the restructuring that is a necessary response to changing circumstances. If the problems and the conflict generated by the stress are resolved through appropriate restructuring and realignment, the family is free to proceed with its own development and the growth of its members. If, however, the family responds to stress by intensifying the rigidity of its organizational boundaries and transactions and by refusing to consider alternatives, dysfunctional patterns will develop. In these situations, an individual family member may be "activated as a symptom-bearer" to maintain the pattern. For example, a spouse subsystem, unable to resolve a stressful issue or relationship, may detour the conflict by attacking a child. Problems also appear in families when status positions are unclear or when there are coalitions across levels of hierarchy (generations), especially when these are secret (Haley, 1976, p. 104). It can be dysfunctional, for instance, for a parent to behave simultaneously as if he or she is in charge of a child and a peer of the child.

Minuchin believes that families can be located along a continuum according to the nature of their predominant boundary arrangements. Families with inappropriately rigid boundaries are located at one end of the continuum, and families with excessively diffuse boundaries are at the other. Most families would fall within the normal range, where boundaries are clear and firm but also responsive to needed change. Dysfunction occurs at the extremes, as seen in the disengaged family, with overly rigid boundaries, and the enmeshed family, with diffuse boundaries.

The disengaged family has such rigid boundaries that "communications across subsystems become difficult, and the protective functions of the family are handicapped" (Minuchin, 1974, p. 54). Individuals from different subsystems become almost inaccessible to each other and "only a high level of individual stress can reverberate strongly enough to activate the family's supportive systems" (p. 55). The disengaged family tends not to respond when response is clearly necessary. A child in such a family, for example, might experience a great deal of difficulty before the parents become actively concerned. The individual who grows up in a disengaged family may function pseudoindependently and lack a sense of belonging and the capacity for interdependence.

At the other end of the continuum is the enmeshed family, in which boundaries are so blurred as to be almost nonexistent. In these systems, there is a heightened sense of belonging, and the lack of subsystem differentiation discourages the development of autonomy. A parent in this family is likely to become inappropriately upset at the slightest variation in a child's behavior. Neither differences nor leaving are easily tolerated.

Minuchin is careful to point out that every family contains enmeshed and disengaged subsystems at certain times. A parent–child subsystem may be enmeshed when children are small and then tend toward disengagement as the children grow. Only in extreme situations will the transactional style result in a faulty organization that may evoke symptomatic behavior and undermine the growth of individual family members.

THE PROCESS OF CHANGE. For Haley (1980), the most effective therapeutic intervention is one aimed at the basic organizational structure. If that structure can be changed, every member of the family will be affected. Minuchin (1974) envisions the therapist as a "boundary-maker, clarifying diffuse boundaries and opening inappropriately rigid boundaries" (p. 56). To change boundaries, structure, and organization is to change the relationship between a person and the family context in which he functions. For Minuchin, this also means change in that person's subjective experience. Therapy is thus directed toward repairing or modifying the family structure so that it can more effectively carry out its functions of "support, regulation, nurturance, and socialization of its members" (p. 14).

During therapy, the therapist becomes an active part of the family organization. Minuchin (1974) calls this "joining" the family and states that "change is seen as occurring through the process of the therapist's affiliation with the family and his restructuring of the family in a carefully planned way, so as to transform dysfunctional transactional patterns" (p. 91). Change occurs through a structural transformation, not through insight or through the exploration and interpretation of past experience.

Differentiation ansd Growth Processes (Intergenerational). Several theorists focus on the relationships between current individual and family dysfunction and powerful intergenerational, extended family, and family of origin themes. Leaders in the use of this perspective include Murray Bowen, Ivan Boszormenyi-Nagy, Geraldine Spark, James Framo, Philip Guerin, Elizabeth Carter, Thomas Fogarty, and Norman Paul.

FAMILY THEORY AND CONCEPTS. While theorists such as Bateson and Haley had discovered and were being influenced by cybernetics and general systems theory in the early 1950s, Bowen, in his pioneering work with schizophrenics and their families, was turning to the natural sciences, such as biology, ethology, and phylogenesis, for both language and concepts to aid his efforts to develop a new way of thinking about emotional disturbance. Eschewing the medically based psychoanalytic model of human behavior, Bowen hoped that the study of emotional problems could share both the language and the greater scientific credibility of the natural sciences.

The central concept in Bowen systems theory is differentiation, a concept that is difficult to define. In a summary (Tolson and Reid, 1981) of Bowen's contribution to family theory, Hartman (1981) concludes that the concept is used interchangeably to refer to intrapersonal, interpersonal, and family system intergenerational processes. Bowen moves back and forth with ease in discussing intrapersonal and intrafamilial differentiation and fusion. This may create confusion, but it is the key both to the theory and to the practice. The concept of differentiation not only conceptualizes parallel intrapersonal, interpersonal, and intrafamilial processes, it also provides the linkages between the levels. In intrapersonal terms, differentiation of self (and its opposite, fusion) refers to the relationship between the intellect (and goal-directed activity) and the emotions (and feeling-directed activity). The well-differentiated person makes plans, is flexible and thoughtful, and can maintain autonomy in the face of considerable stress. The less-differentiated, more fused person is often trapped in a feeling world, is buffeted about by emotionality, makes fewer plans, is often more rigid, and is more susceptible to dysfunction when confronted with conflict or stress.

Differentiation on the interpersonal level means that a person can maintain a solid, nonnegotiable self in interpersonal relationships within and outside the family, taking comfortable "I" positions, not forsaking intellectual and emotional integrity to obtain approval, love, peace, or togetherness. The differentiated person can risk genuine emotional closeness without undue anxiety and is capable of sustained intimate relationships. For the more fused individual, intimacy and closeness may threaten what little sense of self may exist and may lead to extreme stress and a variety of maneuvers to create distance. Geographical or physical distance is not to be equated with differentiation. The differentiated person can leave the family to build his own life without feeling disloyal and still remain emotionally close, or he can stay geographically close without being trapped emotionally in an intense, enmeshed family relationship system. He can choose to be like and to be different at different times, without in either case fearing loss of self.

The differentiated family can accept change and differences among its members. It can allow its members to become autonomous. The fused family, seen in an extreme form in families of schizophrenics, resists new ideas and views change as a threat.

The concepts of differentiation and fusion are also inextricably linked to the family's past through a process of multigenerational transmission. Patterns of adaptation, or ways of preserving family equilibrium, are handed down intergenerationally through powerful myths, themes, prescriptions, and rituals. Current levels of differentiation are determined by a complex combination of factors, such as the differentiation level of parents, sex, sibling position, quality of relationships, and environmental contingencies at developmental transition points. A person's level of differentiation is largely determined by the time he leaves the parental family.

A final concept central to the theory and crucial to understanding the process of dysfunction is that of the *triangle,* or three-person system, which Bowen considers the basic building block of all emotional systems. Bowen (1976) believes "a two-person system may be stable as long as it is calm, but when anxiety increases, it immediately involves the most vulnerable other person to become a triangle" (p. 76). In families, this third person is often a child. During calm periods, the triangle consists of a comfortably close twosome and a less comfortable outsider; during stress periods, the outside position becomes more desirable. Two members of a family form a triangle with another person or a social agency to resolve high levels of tension. It may be that alcohol, excessive work, or other nonhuman resources are often used for the same purpose.

Boszormenyi-Nagy and Spark (1973) view their approach as "the extension of and meeting point between dynamic psychology, existential phenomenology, and systems theory" (p. xiv). They emphasize the subjective growth processes of individual family members, and they believe that mental health is determined by a reciprocal interaction of individual psychological characteristics and the bonds and laws of genetic relatedness. Families develop a hierarchy of obligations or a multigenerational balance sheet of merit and indebtedness, which has tremendous impact on individual members since any move toward differentiation may imply disloyalty. The task of the family therapist is to integrate individual dynamic concepts with current relationships and multigenerational accounts of justice. For Boszormenyi-Nagy and Spark, the study of power games, communication patterns, or rule processes is only marginally relevant and is monothetical since these concepts fail to explain the complexities of human interactions or to encompass the "real essence of human relationships" (1973, p. 17). In the dialectical, paradoxical struggle of each person between individuation and family loyalty, the individual may be sacrificed to pay back multigenerational debts and unresolved obligations from the past in an effort to balance what might be called a "ledger of life."

Paul (1967) and Paul and Grosser (1965) also emphasize the effects of unresolved past events on present dysfunction in families, particularly the inadequate earlier resolution of significant losses. For Paul, a "fixed family equilibrium," or a too rigid homeostasis, combined with a pattern of inability to cope with loss, is common in families with symptomatic members (1965, p. 341). If such losses have occurred in the past, before the birth of the identified patient, a prevailing family sadness appears unexplainable and difficult to treat for a therapist who looks only at the current context.

FAMILY DYSFUNCTION. It is important to emphasize that differentiation, fusion, triangles, multigenerational transmission, invisible loyalties, and unresolved losses are basic human interaction processes. They occur in *all* families and are not in and of themselves maladaptive.

In the Bowen framework, problems occur in marriages and families where the level of emotional fusion between the spouses is intense. People tend to marry others who are about as differentiated as they are, but one spouse often becomes overfunctioning at the expense of the underfunctioning of the other. One gains a little basic self, the other loses self. Undifferentiation (or fusion) in a marriage comes to be manifested in symptoms in three major ways: (1) conflict between the spouses, (2) physical, emotional, or social illness in one spouse, or (3) impairment of one or more children. In the latter instance, the undifferentiation is transmitted to one or more children through a process Bowen terms *family projection*.

For Boszormenyi-Nagy and Spark, family dysfunction occurs when married partners have unpaid, invisible commitments to their respective families of origin and when family members, again out of loyalty, must make personal sacrifices or other adjustments to maintain the illusion of marital harmony. Examples of this are jealous siblings who fight bitterly and the rebellious juvenile delinquent who successfully manages to distract attention from parental discord. This process of "parentification" of children assumes many forms, and the "parentified" child may assume many different roles. In extreme cases, as with the schizophrenic child, the child is caught in an ambivalent, guilty loyalty bind and is often violently hostile to the parents. Parents, however, need not fear loss of loyalty since the child's violence "documents his unchanging involvement and interminable devotion" (1973, p. 161).

THE NATURE OF CHANGE. For those theorists who stress intergenerational issues, change and growth occur in an alteration of intergenerational relationships and in the resolution of troublesome emotional heritages. In Bowen therapy, the goal of therapeutic change is to achieve a higher level of differentiation. "The overall goal is to help individual family members to rise up out of the emotional togetherness that binds us all. The instinctual force toward differentiation is built into the organism, just as are the emotional forces that oppose it" (Bowen, 1978, p. 371).

Although we cannot describe here the range of techniques the client may use in defining a self in the extended family, we note that the goal of therapy is not merely to gain *insight* into one's family experiences. The individual needs to identify those areas where change in *his own* behavior is needed; he needs to plan, implement, and monitor those changes. Significant behavioral change takes place when the client, coached by the therapist, negotiates new ways of relating to and communicating with key members of his extended family. Bowen theory assumes that, as people become more differentiated from their families of origin, they will also become more differentiated in their current work, family, and social roles.

Boszormenyi-Nagy and Spark point out that most people repay at least part of their family emotional indebtedness to parents by becoming parents themselves and making commitments to their own children. Where destructive, undischarged commitments still exist, the change effort centers on exposing these manifestations of loyalty and achieving a better balance between old and new family relationships through repaying the indebtedness. These therapists, as well as Framo

(1976), use sessions with family members to encourage recognizing and reexperiencing unresolved loyalty feelings and unmet obligations.

Paul believes that change takes place through a corrective mourning experience that not only encourages belated grief work but also clarifies the displacement of hostility from the original lost object to current family members (usually the symptomatic member). Paul and Grosser (1965) have developed several creative therapeutic techniques to facilitate what they call "operational mourning," including extended family and family of origin sessions and the use of videotapes of work with *other* families to trigger or release the expression of grief by the family in treatment.

Differentiation Processes (Current Family Experiential Level). Another group of family therapists attempts to direct the work of differentiation of the individual within the interactional context of the family. Examples of therapists who might describe their objectives and therapeutic processes in family treatment as the "open growth" of family members include Donald Bloch, Frederick and Bunny Duhl, Kitty LaPerriere, Ivan Boszormenyi-Nagy, Augustus Napier, and Carl Whitaker. Norman Paul might also be included, although his primary focus is on the issue of loss and mourning.

Those who choose this focus do not differ greatly from Bowen and others discussed previously in their conceptualization of the family as a system or in their formulations of family functioning and family dysfunction. The major difference is in their notions of the change process in therapy. For this group, change takes place in the context of the current family by a working-through process involving the family members and the therapist. The therapy might include members from several generations, but the focus is on the experience of the current family and how to change that experience. The change process depends on an exploration of current family interaction and relationships and the influence of unresolved issues from the past, particularly in the family of origin. In the course of therapy, the family is permitted, and may be even encouraged, to regress. An important requirement for therapeutic change, it is thought, is that families develop the "freedom for a spontaneous enactment of 'pathology'" (Boszormenyi-Nagy and Framo, 1965, p. 107).

If change is to occur, the family must tackle "the binds, conflicts, misperceptions, inequalities, and hungers in this most intimate of groups" (Napier and Whitaker, 1978, p. 271). Change comes as the family members grapple with these issues and experience each other in new ways. As this occurs, individuals are freed of their crippling entanglements with one another, and the family system becomes one in which growth is possible.

It is important to recognize the experiential nature of this change process. Insight is helpful but not sufficient. There must be an emotionally meaningful experience in therapy, "one that touches the deepest level of his person" (Napier and Whitaker, 1978, p. 283). The therapist takes different roles in helping to bring about this growth process, sometimes by engaging an individual family member in an encounter and at other times by directing an encounter between family members. Napier and Whitaker (1978, p. 274) describe this process as follows: "There should come a time when the group has given up on their attempts to force one another to change and when they are ready to use the therapists to generate self-change. This period is somewhat like parallel, or rotating, individual therapy, in that family members intuitively take turns 'being the patient.' These 'public' encounters between the therapist and patient also deepen and intensify the encounters that take place between family members." As this happens, the family develops a more workable model for closeness and for separateness and individuals begin to "be individuals in the psychological sense."

Transactional Processes with Extended Environment. All the theoretical perspectives presented here in some way address the relationship of the family with its extended environment. However, family therapists tend to focus exclusively on the *intimate* environmental context, which usually includes the symptomatic person, the family, and the therapist. The therapist deals with the extended environment only as its influences are mediated through family communication processes. Theorists often stress the importance of the larger social context in *understanding* individual and family behavior, even though interventions are centered within the family system. For example, Minuchin, in the first chapter of *Families and Family Therapy* (1974), presents a number of brilliantly drawn metaphors to emphasize the importance of context in understanding human adaptation, and in fact he describes structural family therapy as a way of approaching man in his social context. Minuchin recognizes that environmental forces continually shape family processes and structure as well as individual thought and behavior, but the family also mediates the transactions between individual and larger social contexts—"its organization and structure screen and qualify family members' experience" (1974, p. 7). Interventions, then, are designed to alter or transform those family structural aspects that contribute to the current dysfunction. Minuchin (p. 14) mentions that "the target of intervention could as well be any other segment of the individual's ecosystem that seems amenable to change-producing strategies," but a model for such interventions has yet to be presented.

Aponte (1976, 1979) describes an approach to structural family therapy that locates problems in the interfaces between individual and family or between family and environment. Stressing the use of the ecological context for diagnosis, he warns that "the technical problem for the therapist is how to approach the complex ecosystem of an individual, a couple, or a family in a way which will not overwhelm the therapist with data, but which will provide the information most relevant to understanding the problem or problems the clients present" (Aponte, 1979, p. 110).

FAMILY THEORY AND CONCEPTS. In some ways, the influence of ecological perspectives and theories on family theory and practice are perhaps the most difficult to delineate. One reason is that definitions of *ecology* and what is meant by an ecological perspective vary. Another reason is that therapeutic principles and techniques based on this perspective are as yet inadequately developed. Further, the methodology for sound ecological research is yet to be discovered, and at present ecologically oriented research receives scant attention in psychology or sociology. Bronfenbrenner (1979), a pioneer in the use of this perspective, points out that "rigorous research on human development using ecologically valid measures on both the independent and dependent side of the developmental equation and at the same time paying attention to the influence of larger social contexts is still the exception rather than the rule. At best, one or two important criteria are met, but other features remain at odds with ecological requirements of equal importance" (p. 13). Bronfenbrenner has argued, however, that much of contemporary research in human development, while perhaps rigorous and elegantly designed, is artificial and lacks relevance to real-life situations (1977, p. 513).

His own conception views the ecological environment as "a set of nested structures, each inside the next, like a set of Russian dolls" (1979, p. 3). The innermost level or ring includes the developing person in his immediate surroundings (the microsystem), and the outermost level includes those overarching patterns of ideology and social institutions common to a particular culture (the macrosystem). In between are the mesosystem and exosystem levels. The former comprises the interrelations among major settings, for example, among family, school, and peer group; the exosystem embraces other specific social structures that do not themselves contain the individual but influence him. Bronfenbrenner interweaves this conception of enlarging rings with both an emphasis on triadic relationships among person, other persons, and larger interpersonal structures and a developmental view of "ecological transitions," or shifts in role or setting that occur throughout the life span.

Other ecological psychologists, also originally inspired by Lewin and, later, Lewin's associates Barker and Wright (1949), have advocated the scientific description of person–environment transactions, naturalistic records of behavior, and the mapping of psychological habitats. Currently there is an interest in studying behavior settings, "the most immediate and the most behaviorally significant human environments" (Wicker, 1979, p. 5).

In social work, Gordon (1969) and Hearn (1969) pioneered the introduction of ecological and general systems concepts to social work theory. More recently, Germain, inspired by, microbiologist René Dubos among others, has taken ecology as a metaphor in her effort to conceptualize an ecologically oriented model of practice (Germain, 1979; Germain and Gitterman, 1980). Attneave (1975) in family theory and Hartman (1978) in social work have made efforts to develop and use new cognitive mapping conceptualizations to aid in thinking ecologically. Germain (1979, pp. 7–8) indicates that the ecological perspective is concerned with "the growth, development, and potentialities of human beings and with the properties of their environments that support or fail to support the expression of human potential." The family is seen as a system that is engaged in constant interchanges with the extended environment in order to obtain the support, nurturance, and stimulation necessary for the survival and growth of its members. The well-being of the family depends on how successful the family is in participating in these transactions. A central concept here is that of adaptation, and thus the focus is on the adaptive balance that exists between the family and its environment.

FAMILY DYSFUNCTION. Edgar Auerswald, perhaps the best-known proponent of an ecological perspective in family therapy, argues that knowledge from the traditional disciplines as they now exist is relatively useless in resolving human and social problems. What is needed is "a realignment of current knowledge and a reexamination of human behavior within a unifying holistic model, that of ecological phenomenology" (1968, p. 111). In his view, neither individual nor family function and dysfunction can be understood separately from the larger environmental field in which it is immersed. Hoffman and Long (1969), in a fascinating case study analyzed by Auerswald, demonstrate how the breakdown of one person can only be understood when the contributions and interrelationships of the family and a variety of larger, impinging social systems are examined. For Auerswald, a systems approach focuses on interfaces and communication processes. The process "begins with an analysis of the *structure* of the field, using the common structural and operational properties of systems as criteria for identifying the systems and subsystems within it. And by tracing the communications within and between systems, it insists that the structure, sources, pathways, repository sites, and integrative functions of messages become clear in addition to their content. In my opinion, this, plus the holistic nonexclusive nature of the approach, minimizes the dangers of excessive selectivity in the collection of data and allows for much more clarity in the contextual contributions to its analysis" (1968, p. 112).

The worker or therapist must become an "explorer," following client need or problem wherever it may lead, using a variety of interventive methods and change strategies, and mobilizing all necessary resources, not just those that rely on verbal communication between the family and the therapist (Hartman, 1974, p. 203).

In a recent analysis, Keeney (1979) defines *ecosystemic epistemology* as "a way of knowing problematic situations through the epistemological framework or paradigm representing cybernetics, ecology, and systems theory" (p. 119). In this paradigm, what differentiates the ecosystemic from the linear theorist is not what system levels are addressed but whether human behavior is understood in terms of linear sequences of cause and effect or in terms of systems. *System* is defined as a cybernetic network that processes information. Ecosystemic epistemology is "concerned with patterns of relationship that are described by metaphors of thought and pattern" (p. 120). The therapeutic situation of family-individual-therapist is one example of an ecological cybernetic information-processing system. The larger social context becomes important primarily as it influences the communication functions of symptoms as indicators for the ecology of relationships. Keeney (1979, p. 120) describes the process as follows: "What becomes critical in diagnosis is knowing how the cybernetic network is interlinked or structured. This idea follows the basic rule of systems theory described by Bateson (1971, p. 244): 'If you want to understand some phenomenon or appearance, you must consider that phenomenon within the context of all *completed* circuits which are relevant to it.' The 'relevant completed circuits' for the therapist refer to the network of complexly intertwined human relationships in which the symptomatic communication has a function."

In an ecological perspective, then, the family is seen within a larger context, which may play a significant role in the family dysfunction. Family and individual symptoms may reflect a poor fit between the family's ability to transact successfully with its larger environment and the qualities of that environment.

THE PROCESS OF CHANGE. The change process, in the view of many ecologically oriented therapists, focuses on strengthening or enhancing the adaptive fit between individuals, families, and environments. Change may take place at the boundaries or interfaces between individuals and families and between individuals, families, and those social institutions on which they depend for meeting their psychological, social, and physical needs.

Theorists of social work have made considerable progress in developing ecological approaches to practice, and we can conclude that this perspective is particularly congruent with the profession's historical commitment to enhance the psychological and social quality of life for those it serves. In family therapy, network therapists have produced the most highly developed model for ecological change. According to Attneave (1976), the term *network* was first defined by English anthropologist J. A. Barnes in 1954 and later redefined as follows: "Every individual in society is seen as linked to several others by social bonds that partly reinforce and partly conflict with one another; the orderliness and disorderliness of social life results from the constraints these bonds impose on the actions of individuals" (1972, p. 1).

Intrigued by the seeing power, excitement, and therapeutic value of such diverse events as tribal healing ceremonies, revival meetings, and such family rituals as weddings and bar mitzvahs, Speck and Attneave have adapted these ideas to family therapy. They assume that "the repair of network relationships will restore orderliness and balance to disordered lives and unbalanced individuals" (Attneave, 1976, p. 223). As Keeney (1979) points out, "when the Navaho medicine man encounters an individual expressing a symptom, his choice of action is to treat the whole tribe in order to bring it back into harmony. In this way, individuals are relieved of symptomatic discomfort through treatment of the whole ecosystem" (p. 122).

The network therapists are not concerned as much with diagnosis or assessment of individual families as with defining the salient social network and its potential for change, with mapping the impact of family on network and network on family, and with understanding the current social matrix through its human representatives. Once that matrix is identified, the goal becomes one of stimulating, releasing, and harnessing its therapeutic potential. Speck and Attneave (1973) describe the process: "By strengthening bonds, loosening binds, opening new channels, facilitating new perceptions, activating latent strengths, and helping to damp out, ventilate, or exorcise pathology, the social network is enabled to become the life-sustaining community within the social matrix of each individual" (p. 641). As Germain points out, whereas family therapists have developed ecological action principles applicable to the intimate environment, family therapy action principles themselves are somewhat limited in application and influence. The task for the future is to translate abstract ecological and systems concepts into principles for practice, and apply them.

Conclusion

Although there is no single theory of the family that underlies the practice of family therapy, there are important common concepts. Most family therapists, in describing the theory base for their practice, include a conceptualization of the family as a system. In so doing, they draw most heavily from general systems theory, cybernetics, communication theory, and ecological theory. Such concepts as feedback and homeostasis are commonly used by family therapists to describe the self-regulating and stabilizing tendencies of family systems. The family is usually considered a stable, rule-governed, but open system that changes over time through interactions with the extended environment. The family is seen as a whole composed of interrelated and interdependent parts, so that a change in one part will produce changes in other parts of the system and in the system as a whole. Like all living systems, the family is said to have an emergent quality; it is more than the sum of its parts, more than the sum of its individual personalities.

Viewing the family as a system has led most family therapists to conceptualize causality as circular rather than linear in nature. This may be the single most important issue differentiating family therapy from individual and most group therapies. A major consequence of accepting a circular view of causality has been a shift in the way pathology has been conceptualized. Family therapists locate dysfunction not in the individual but in the family system or in the individual-family-environment relationships. From a systems perspective, individual symptoms serve a positive function in maintaining the system as a whole. Widespread acceptance of this notion has led to a common view of goals and outcomes that further differentiates family-oriented therapy from individual-oriented therapy. Family therapists may differ as to the precise focus of their interventions, but they do agree that the outcome of the change process should be a basic change in the operation of the family system.

Another common theme uniting many therapists and theorists is communication theory. Olson (1975, p. 33) has pointed out that "communication, verbal and nonverbal, is the means by which one can learn about the family system. As a result, the principles and concepts of system and communication theory are very interrelated" (p. 33). All family therapists must attend to communication in some way in their conceptualizations of family dynamics and in their ideas about practice.

Although most theorists conceptualize the family as a system, there are important variations in meaning. One of the major differences concerns issues of power and hierarchy. Some family therapists reject notions of power and control as nonsystemic and give the various system elements equal importance. Bateson, for example, has said that there is no such thing as unilateral power inasmuch as the person presumably in power is dependent on information from the outside and must respond "to that information just as much as he 'causes' things to happen" (1972, p. 486). Palazzoli and others (1978, p. 5) comment that "none of the members have unidirectional power over the whole." Therapists who take this view of the family believe that "if one looks at a system in a linear, hierarchical way, one cannot see the whole system" (Keeney, 1979, p. 123).

The opposition to this view is most clearly represented by Haley, who emphasizes power and control in his explanation of the family as an organization. From this perspective, all elements of the system are not equally powerful, and the family is structured and organized around hierarchical statuses and powers. This debate over the issues of power and control has implications not only for family theory and change theory but also for describing the therapeutic system itself. As Keeney (1979, p. 122) points out, many therapists see themselves "as a kind of 'power broker' who controls the ways in which power is used and distributed in the family." A strict systems perspective, however, views the therapist "as part and parcel of the system he diagnoses and treats" (1979, p. 123).

Another difference that has clearly emerged among family therapists concerns how the change process is conceptualized. The current dichotomy contrasts "open growth" and "transformation." Probably all family therapists hope that growth in the family system and growth of individual members will occur as part of the change process. Growth takes place as the family is taught new communication skills and ways of relating and thereby gains understanding and insight about itself, its processes, and its effects on individual members. The work of Napier and Whitaker exemplifies the growth model of change. These creative therapists become intensely involved in the family, provide encounters in which the family members experience each other in different ways, and engage the members in a "family-wide growth process" (1978, p. 275).

Other family therapists see change as a kind of "leap" or transformation. Those therapists discussed in the sections on rule-governing processes and structure and organization tend to exemplify this idea of change. They do not consider insight and understanding as being necessary to change; some believe that insight can actually mitigate against change. Transformation therapists tend to be symptom-focused and problem-solving therapists. Recognizing that the symptom serves a positive systemic function, they see change coming through, as Papp (1980) has written, "a series of drastic redefinitions that connect the symptoms with the system in such a way that one cannot be changed without changing the other." In essence, "a perceptual crisis is created, following which the family finds it increasingly difficult to regulate itself through a symptom and begins to regulate itself differently" (p. 46).

This issue of growth versus transformation as the heart of family change is one that will likely persist for a long time. Perhaps what is most needed now is more attention to what kinds of problems yield most easily to what kinds of change efforts.

We have neglected, in this presentation, to survey the current status of research on family therapy. Most analysts stress the urgent need for more critical, research-based evaluation of the continual proliferating approaches to promoting family change, and we add our voices to this appeal. At the same time, we agree with Olson (1975), who reminds us that family therapy is a relatively young approach "which is challenging many of the traditional concepts of psychopathology and approaches to psychotherapy. Exciting projects are also underway which are models for bridging the gap between research, theory, and practice" (p. 51). The next few years should produce some progress in testing whether current theory and practice can meet the rigorous demands of carefully conceptualized evaluative research.

References

Aponte, H. J. "The Family–School Interview: An Eco-Structural Approach." *Family Process,* 1976, *15,* 303–312.

Aponte, H. J. "Diagnosis in Family Therapy." In C. Germain (Ed.), *Social Work Practice: People and Environments.* New York: Columbia University Press, 1979.

Attneave, C. *Family Network Map.* Available from 5206 Ivanhoe N.E., Seattle, Washington, 1975.

Attneave, C. "Y'all Come: Social Networks as a Unit of Intervention." In P. Guerin (Ed.), *Family Therapy: Theory and Practice.* New York: Gardner Press, 1976.

Attneave, C., and Speck, R. "Network Therapy." In A. Ferber and others (Eds.), *The Book of Family Therapy*. Boston: Houghton Mifflin, 1973.

Auerswald, E. H. "Interdisciplinary Versus Ecological Approach." *Family Process,* 1968, *7,* 202–215.

Auerswald, E. H. "Families, Change, and the Ecological Perspective." In A. Ferber and others (Eds.), *The Book of Family Therapy*. Boston: Houghton Mifflin, 1973.

Bandler, R., and Grinder, J. *The Structure of Magic I*. Palo Alto, Calif.: Science and Behavior Books, 1975.

Bandler, R., and others. *Changing with Families*. Palo Alto, Calif.: Science and Behavior Books, 1976.

Barker, R. G., and Wright, H. G., "Psychological Ecology and the Problem of Psychosocial Development." *Child Development,* 1949, *20,* 131–143.

Barnes, J. A. "Class and Committees in a Norwegian Island Parish." *Human Relations,* 1954, *7,* 39–58.

Barnes, J. A. *Social Networks*. Anthropology Module #26. Reading, Mass.: Addison-Wesley, 1972.

Bateson, G. "A Systems Approach." *International Journal of Psychiatry,* 1971, *9,* 242–244.

Bateson, G. *Steps to an Ecology of Mind*. New York: Ballantine, 1972.

Bateson, G., and others. "Toward a Theory of Schizophrenia." *Behavioral Science,* 1956, *1* (4), 251–264.

Beels, C. C., and Ferber, A. "Family Therapy: A View." *Family Process,* 1969, *8,* 280–318.

Beels, C. C., and Ferber, A. "What Family Therapists Do." In A. Ferber, M. Mendelsohn, and A. Napier (Eds.), *The Book of Family Therapy*. New York: Jason Aronson, 1972.

Boszormenyi-Nagy, I., and Framo, J. *Intensive Family Therapy*. New York: Harper & Row, 1965.

Boszormenyi-Nagy, I., and Spark, G. *Invisible Loyalties*. New York: Harper & Row, 1973.

Bowen, M. "Theory in the Practice of Psychotherapy." In P. J. Guerin (Ed.), *Family Therapy: Theory and Practice*. New York: Gardner Press, 1976.

Bowen, M. *Family Therapy in Clinical Practice*. New York: Jason Aronson, 1978.

Bronfenbrenner, U. "Toward a Developmental View of Psychology." *American Psychologist,* 1977, *32,* 513–531.

Bronfenbrenner, U. *The Ecology of Human Development*. Cambridge, Mass.: Harvard University Press, 1979.

Framo, J. "Family of Origin as a Therapeutic Resource for Adults in Marital and Family Therapy: You Can and Should Go Home Again." *Family Process,* 1976, *15,* 193–210.

Germain, C. B. "Introduction: Ecology and Social Work." In C. Germain (Ed.), *Social Work Practice: People and Environments*. New York: Columbia University Press, 1979.

Germain, C. B., and Gitterman, A. *The Life Model of Social Work Practice*. New York: Columbia University Press, 1980.

Gordon, W. E. "Basic Constructs for an Integrative and Generative Conception of Social Work." In G. Hearn (Ed.), *The General Systems Approach: Contribu-*

tions Toward an Holistic Conception of Social Work. New York: Council on Social Work Education, 1969.

Grinder, J., and Bandler, R. *The Structure of Magic, II.* Palo Alto, Calif.: Science and Behavior Books, 1976.

Group for the Advancement of Psychiatry. *The Field of Family Therapy.* Report No. 78. New York: Group for the Advancement of Psychiatry, 1970.

Guerin, P. J. "Family Therapy: The First Twenty-Five Years." In P. J. Guerin (Ed.), *Family Therapy: Theory and Practice.* New York: Gardner Press, 1976.

Gurman, A. S. "Emerging Trends in Research and Practice." In A. S. Gurman and D. C. Rice (Eds.), *Couples in Conflict.* New York: Jason Aronson, 1975.

Haley, J. *Strategies of Psychotherapy.* New York: Grune & Stratton, 1963.

Haley, J. *Problem-Solving Therapy: New Strategies for Effective Family Therapy.* San Francisco: Jossey-Bass, 1976.

Haley, J. *Leaving Home.* New York: McGraw-Hill, 1980.

Hartman, A. "The Generic Stance and the Family Agency." *Social Casework,* 1974, *55,* 199–208.

Hartman, A. "Diagrammatic Assessment of Family Relationships." *Social Casework,* 1978, *59,* 465–476.

Hartman, A. "Bowen Family Systems: Theory and Practice." In E. Tolson and W. Reid (Eds.), *Models of Family Treatment.* New York: Columbia University Press, 1981.

Hearn, G. "Progress Toward an Holistic Conception of Social Work." In G. Hearn (Ed.), *The General Systems Approach: Contributions Toward an Holistic Conception of Social Work.* New York: Council on Social Work Education, 1969.

Hoffman, L. Unpublished paper presented at the 57th Annual Meeting of the American Orthopsychiatric Association, Toronto, 1980.

Hoffman, L., and Long, L. "A Systems Dilemma." *Family Process,* 1969, *8,* 211–234.

Jackson, D. (Ed.). *Communication, Family, and Marriage.* Palo Alto, Calif.: Science and Behavior Books, 1968a.

Jackson, D. (Ed.) *Therapy, Communication, and Change.* Palo Alto, Calif.: Science and Behavior Books, 1968b.

Keeney, B. P. "Ecosystemic Epistemology: An Alternate Paradigm for Diagnosis." *Family Process,* 1979, *18,* 117–130.

Kerr, M. E. "Emotional Factors in Physical Illness . . . A Multigenerational Perspective." *The Family,* 1980, *7,* 59–66.

Lederer, W., and Jackson, D. *The Mirages of Marriage.* New York: Norton, 1968.

Liebman, R., and others. "The Role of the Family in the Treatment of Chronic Asthma." In P. Guerin (Ed.), *Family Therapy: Theory and Practice.* New York: Gardner Press, 1976.

Minuchin, S. *Families and Family Therapy.* Cambridge, Mass.: Harvard University Press, 1974.

Napier, Y., and Whitaker, C. A. *The Family Crucible.* New York: Harper & Row, 1978.

Olson, D. H. "Marital and Family Therapy: A Critical Overview." In A. S. Gurman and D. C. Rice (Eds.), *Couples in Conflict.* New York: Jason Aronson, 1975.

Palazzoli, M., and others. *Paradox and Counterparadox.* New York: Jason Aronson, 1978.

Palozzoli, M., and others. "Hypothesizing—Circularity—Neutrality: Guidelines for the Conductor of the Session." *Family Process,* 1980, *19,* 3-12.

Papp, P. "The Greek Chorus and Other Techniques of Family Therapy." *Family Process,* 1980, *19,* 45-58.

Paul, N. L. "The Role of Mourning and Empathy in Conjoint Marital Therapy." In G. Zuk and I. Roszarmenui-Nagy (Eds.), *Family Therapy and Disturbed Families.* Palo Alto, Calif.: Science and Behavior Books, 1967.

Paul, N. L., and Grosser, G. "Operational Mourning and Its Role in Conjoint Family Therapy." *Community Mental Health Journal,* 1965, *1,* 339-345.

Reuveni, U. *Networking Families in Crisis.* New York: Human Sciences Press, 1979.

Ritterman, M. K. "Paradigmatic Classification of Family Therapy Theories." *Family Process,* 1977, *16,* 29-46.

Satir, V. *Conjoint Family Therapy.* (Rev. ed.) Palo Alto, Calif.: Science and Behavior Books, 1967.

Speck, R. V., and Attneave, C. *Family Networks.* New York: Vintage Books, 1973.

Watzlawick, P. *The Language of Change.* New York: Basic Books, 1978.

Watzlawick, P., Beavin, J., and Jackson, D. *Pragmatics of Human Communication.* New York: Norton, 1967.

Weakland, J. "Communication Theory and Clinical Change." In P. Guerin (Ed.), *Family Therapy: Theory and Practice.* New York: Gardner Press, 1976.

Wertheim, E. S. "Family Unit Therapy and the Science and Typology of Family Systems." *Family Process,* 1973, *12,* 361-376.

Wicker, A. W. *An Introduction to Ecological Psychology.* Monterey, Calif.: Brooks/Cole, 1979.

9

Behavioral Principles and Approaches

Arthur Schwartz

The behavioral orientations to treatment may be the approaches toward which most social workers display the most emotion but perhaps show the least understanding. The behavioral approaches are either vehemently rejected or enthusiastically embraced, usually on the basis of belief and prejudice rather than on a careful consideration of the realities of their qualities, both positive and negative. Some critics have denounced them as being inhumane and thus ultimately ineffective because of the alleged mechanistic orientation to human beings.

The truth is, of course, that the behavior therapies and the behavior therapy techniques tend to be comparatively value free. They are deterministic therapies, as are psychoanalysis and most contemporary helping theories, with perhaps the exception of the Rogerian and the Existential. If behavior therapy, as *any* therapeutic approach, is practiced by a warm, compassionate therapist within a framework of humanistic social work values, then the process of the therapy will tend to be warm and compassionate.

It is unfortunate, but most people tend to respond to the behavior therapies in terms of preconceptions and misperceptions. These preconceptions often paint the behavioral therapies as either all good or all evil when obviously they are neither extreme. These prejudgments, unfortunately, often hinder many practitioners from using a behavioral approach where it may be the most effective or the most economical treatment method.

One reality, not appreciated by most professionals, is that the behavioral orientation represents not one approach but a number of approaches. Furthermore, there are differences among the various behavioral therapies, although the differences may be more of degree than absolute.

Most clinical social workers have been trained in a basically psychodynamic orientation. The behavioral influence on social work has been fairly recent, although behaviorism has a long history in psychology. In general, the behavioral approach to therapy is an outgrowth of the laboratory work of the experimental psychologist. This is exemplified, and perhaps even exaggerated, by the early behavior therapies that were based on stimulus–response psychology. The picture that many have of the behaviorist therapies is that of the behaviorist reconditioning his patient much in the same sense that Pavlov conditioned his dog.

The stereotype of the inhumane behavior therapist is that of the person interested primarily in research first and therapy with a client second. The therapist is in control of the patient, who is merely a passive recipient of treatment. (Needless to say, this is not only unethical and immoral, but this kind of therapist tends not to do good therapy.) Although there has been some truth to the stereotype in the past, and possibly even in the present with a small number of therapists, this view is no longer correct. Because of their backgrounds in the experimental psychology laboratory, early behavior therapists displayed an extreme empiricism. They stressed research and evaluation and focused on specific procedures rather than on the "client in the situation." These procedures were seen to be observable and accountable.

The behavioral approach has been called a procedural approach. The behaviorist, together with the client, plans a program of specific procedures to reach goals that are agreed upon ahead of time. These procedures usually focus on "environmental," or external, factors as contrasted with the "personality" or "traits" or internal factors that are (to oversimplify) the focus of psychodynamic treatment approaches. Most behavioral theory tends to emphasize the environment not only as a *resource* for change but as the *focus* of change.

Recent developments in the behavioral approaches blurred this dichotomy between "inner" and "outer." More and more behavior therapists are going, once more, "inside" the organism—that is, they take into account mental states in addition to the external conditions under which behavior occurs.

This evolution, or return to inner factors, is no accident. Proponents of the behavioral approaches, in demanding substantiation of claims of therapeutic efficacy, have learned that the behavior therapies have proven effective in some areas but have not proven effective in others. Thus, the empirical, experimental orientation of behaviorists has led them to look, once again, "inside" the organism.

A brief overview of the behavioral approaches in psychotherapy in general, and in social work in particular, may help to clarify this evolution.

Pavlov and the Early Behaviorists

Modern behaviorism is generally seen as beginning with Pavlov. Pavlov discovered that, when he put meat powder (an unconditioned stimulus) in front of a hungry dog, the dog would salivate (an unconditioned response). When he paired the presentation of the meat powder with a light, a tone, a bell, or another neutral stimulus, and when he later presented this neutral stimulus without the food powder, the dog would also salivate (a conditioned response). One could then say the dog was conditioned, or trained, or had learned to respond to the bell (or tone or light) in the same way that he responded to the meat powder.

Behavioral theory has continued to evolve from this beginning, but the stimulus-response sequence, as pictured in the above experiments, continues to be the popular view of what behaviorism is today. This is simply incorrect, as we shall see.

Following Pavlov, the American psychologist John Watson introduced behaviorism into America in the 1920s. Watson's behaviorism focused almost completely on the environment, which was a counterposition to the introspectionism then prevalent in American psychology and was in marked contrast to the growing influence of Freudian psychology. Watson, for example, stated that environment was so important that, if you gave him a dozen healthy infants, he would arrange the conditions to produce whatever you wanted, be it doctors, lawyers, or criminals (Watson, 1924). Watson did not advocate the study of emotions because he could not see them and therefore felt he could not measure them. The naive environmentalism of Watson matched the optimistic spirit and the naive belief in "science" that characterized the United States in the 1920s. Watson advocated a "scientific" rearing of children. He used procedures as rigid schedules for feeding rather than demand feeding, treating children as small adults, and treating nurseries almost as sterile laboratories. In addition, Watson and Rayner (1920) attempted to condition very young children to fear furry objects—work that now is considered unethical. Mary Cover Jones (1924) used similar processes to decondition children, reducing the fear by pairing feared objects such as rabbits with the eating of candy.

The behaviorism of the 1920s was a rigid application of principles that, while seemingly scientific, were actually not sufficiently tested. Needless to say, these practices went out of style—in the opinion of this author, justifiably so. However, it is my opinion that much of the rejection of behaviorism today is based on the belief it is the Pavlov-Watsonian extreme environmentalism.

There were early efforts to reconcile stimulus-response concepts with psychoanalytic theory, such as the book *Personality and Psychotherapy* by Dollard and Miller (1950). In fact, interest in behavioral methods was facilitated by the growing questioning of analytically oriented methods, such as the attack by Hans Eysenck (1952), who claimed that untreated neurotics fare just as well as those who receive long treatment through psychotherapy. (This attack has been successfully answered; see Bergin, 1971.)

The primary application of behavioral approaches to clinical situations is found in the work of Joseph Wolpe, a psychiatrist trained in South Africa but currently living in the United States. He adopted the classical conditioning model of Pavlov and Watson, combined it with the drive-reduction work of Clark Hull, and applied these first to the treatment of the phobias and then to other situations. An important early book was *Psychotherapy by Reciprocal Inhibition* (1958).

Wolpe (1969) views the neuroses as habits, which he states are "consistent ways of responding to defined stimulus situations." He states that these habits are acquired through conditioning; that is, we learn them. Furthermore, a fear or anxiety triggered in one situation may generalize to another situation. For example, fear of one animal, perhaps after a frightening encounter, may extend to other animals; a fear of heights may generalize to a fear of flying. These situations are characterized by people responding to cues, and to their environment, with anxiety. These anxieties then form the basis of phobias and other psychological problems.

Wolpe believed that, since most of our neurotic problems (habits) tend to be learned, they can be unlearned and can be replaced by learning more adaptive, prosocial patterns. He drew these conclusions from his doctoral work on neurotic cats, in which he first trained cats to be neurotic and then deconditioned them. This work has led to the unjustifiable assumption that Wolpe considers humans to be the same as cats and rabbits. This is not true. He states that there are certain elements in common among species and that animal neuroses are a model for the treatment of human neuroses. Wolpe, a gentle man, does not depersonalize humans. He actually holds a view that is quite optimistic, that neuroses are *learned* and may be *unlearned.*

Wolpe's best-known procedure is called reciprocal inhibition through systematic desensitization. This technique, commonly referred to as *systematic desensitization,* is probably the most widely practiced behavioral technique used today. It is also the most widely researched and investigated psychotherapeutic technique of any theoretical orientation.

Wolpe's systematic desensitization procedure is based on this view that an anxiety-inhibiting response cannot occur simultaneously with an anxious response (hence the title *reciprocal inhibition*). Thus, he teaches patients to produce a response that is incompatible with anxiety—in particular, the response of *relaxation.* Obviously, one cannot be tense and relaxed simultaneously.

Wolpe believes that if one can learn to feel relaxed in the presence of a noxious stimulus—something that brings on anxiety—that the noxious stimulus will lose the ability to produce anxiety, and the anxiety will not develop into a neurosis, such as a phobia.

Basically, the systematic desensitization is a four-step procedure where (1) the client is trained in deep relaxation, (2) a scale of subjective anxiety is developed, (3) the anxiety hierarchy (the scenes) are presented, and (4) the deconditioning or relearning takes place.

Wolpe has adapted a series of relaxation procedures that he teaches to the client. After the client learns these relaxation procedures, the therapist and client develop a hierarchy, a system of imaginary scenes involving objects of the client's anxieties, which the client will go over in his mind. These scenes are usually based either on such factors as distance from a feared object (for example, distance from a snake) or time from a feared event (for example, time until a feared examination occurs). If the feared object is a snake, the client may be asked to envision a scene where one is first ten feet from the snake, then nine feet, eight feet, seven feet, gradually nearing and (perhaps) even touching the snake (all of this is in the client's imagination).

As we stated above, systematic desensitization is one of the most thoroughly investigated therapeutic interventions. The claims of success and the counterclaims have been extremely controversial. Furthermore, it has been suggested that success is due to variables other than deconditioning, such as extinction, social modeling by the therapist, and even operant conditioning (explained in the next section). In any event, systematic desensitization does seem to be an effective treatment method with the phobias.

A variation of systematic desensitization, where the individual is brought into contact with the feared object in reality, is called *in vivo* desensitization. An example might be an elevator phobic who is asked to enter an elevator and go up one, two, three, or more flights, as long as the anxiety is bearable. When the anxiety is unbearable, he may leave the elevator. He repeats the procedure, floor by floor, first with and then without relaxation techniques, until gradually he is no longer phobic.

Systematic desensitization has led to two additional therapies, implosion and flooding. Implosion is done in imagination while flooding is done *in vivo*. The theory is that, if gradual exposure will cause a stimulus to lose its ability to produce anxiety (the person is slowly desensitized), then massive exposure will result in a rapid reduction in anxiety. A client might imagine being surrounded or inundated with snakes or dirt or whatever is the feared object. In flooding, he might actually handle snakes. In essence, the client stays and "faces" the anxiety. Needless to say, this is a rather controversial and, according to some theorists, an aversive (unpleasant) procedure. Some clients will absolutely refuse to expose themselves to feared objects; others will leave the room in panic.

A very careful assessment of clients is necessary before using either of these procedures. (Of course, a careful assessment is due before using *any* procedure.) One advantage is that, when these procedures do work, they achieve results very quickly. One does not need to use hierarchies or muscle relaxation.

A similar procedure called paradoxical intention was devised not by a behaviorist but by an existentialist psychiatrist, Viktor Frankl (1959). In this method, a patient is encouraged to deliberately try to bring on or exaggerate a symptom. If he fears having a heart attack or fears he will faint, he will try very hard to faint. If he has a fear of vomiting, he will try very hard to vomit, and so forth. This can be an extremely effective procedure with those clients who agree to use it. Some clients, of course, refuse to use it because of their fear of the object. We have found paradoxical intention a useful back-up technique.

Wolpe's deconditioning and counterconditioning theories have had great impact on psychotherapy. Another application of Wolpe's concept of producing other responses that are incompatible with symptoms is called reciprocal inhibition through positive counterconditioning. If a person is tremulous or is passive in the face of somebody who is overbearing, then a response incompatible with this is an emphatic or an assertive response. If, for example, one is pushed out of a line by another person or is dominated by an arrogant salesperson, the approach—in lay language—is to speak up for oneself. The reader will realize that reciprocal inhibition through positive counterconditioning is the basis of the currently popular therapy called *assertiveness training*. An assertive response is incompatible with anxiety and passivity. Contemporary assertiveness training, which goes beyond respondent techniques and uses many complex procedures, is a direct offshoot of the work of Joseph Wolpe.

Another by-product of Wolpe's work is the approach to the treatment of sexual dysfunctions initiated by Masters and Johnson (1966, 1970, 1979). Such exercises as the sensate focus are really forms of systematic desensitization; in their early works, Masters and Johnson credit Wolpe with the origin of these procedures. In the sensate focus, a couple is asked to abstain from sexual intercourse and is directed to caress and to touch each other with no attempt at sexual stimulation.

They then proceed through a hierarchy of exercises in which sexual stimulation is gradually heightened. Various other procedures may be used, depending on the diagnosed dysfunction. The procedure is expected to culminate in mutually satisfying coitus. In behavioral terms, this therapy is a gradual exposure to a noxious or fear-producing stimulus (sexual contact, closeness, intimacy). In many couples, sexual closeness and emotional intimacy are capable of producing anxiety. The gradual approach of Masters and Johnson—the sensate focus—is a gradual systematic desensitization.

Most of Wolpe's therapies focus on changing a response to a noxious stimulus, an approach based on classical or Pavlovian or respondent conditioning. Wolpe's approach is basically an optimistic system. Anxiety is viewed as a learned maladaptive response that can be unlearned and more adaptive responses learned. Of course, these procedures often are not on a conscious level. It is not necessary, according to Wolpe, that there be awareness of the phenomenon that is occurring.

The Aversion Therapies

Some of the earliest therapies that used respondent conditioning (and perhaps are responsible for some of the bad reputation of the behavioral approaches) are the so-called aversion therapies. The aversion therapies were used to change behavior labeled as deviant, such as overdrinking (alcoholism), homosexuality, and fetishism. In the aversion therapies, an unconditioned stimulus that produces an unpleasant consequence—such as electric shock, a chemical, or a drug—is paired with the undesired behavior, such as drinking. In the conditioned reflex therapy of alcoholism (Thimann, 1949), the patient was injected with a drug that produced nausea. Just before the drug took effect, he would drink some of his favorite whiskey. After drinking the whiskey, the drug caused him to vomit. The patient would gradually associate vomiting with drinking whiskey.

The results of aversion therapy are quite controversial, but there is no doubt that it is an unpleasant and aversive procedure. It is also an automatic, reflex-training procedure requiring little, if any, cooperation on the part of the person receiving the therapy. This aspect may be an advantage when a client says that such behavior as drinking "is beyond my control," but there is also the potential for misuse, especially when these therapies are applied without informed consent of the patient. However, the chief problem with the aversion therapies is they merely *remove* a behavior, such as overdrinking; they leave a behavioral void, which the client must then learn to fill with an adaptive behavior (Skinner, 1953).

The aversion therapies were used, as we said, to treat sexual behavior problems, such as homosexuality. The homosexual client received an electric shock while viewing slides of men, but the shock was stopped when pictures of attractive women were shown (Rachman and Teasdale, 1969). Not only is this therapy aversive, but the results seem to be short lived.

A respondent therapy that still is popular—to this author's amazement—is the "bell and pad" technique for the treatment of eneuresis. This therapy goes back to Mowrer (1938). The first drops of urine from a sleeping child complete an electric circuit, which sets off a bell, or a loud stimulus, to awaken the child. He then is supposed to complete urination in the toilet. Recent technology has expanded this apparatus to include not only a bell but a tape recorder telling the child to get up and go to the toilet. This is a punishment procedure that is extremely aversive to the child. Not only is he awakened quickly, but he is deprived of his sleep. There are other effective procedures based on operant approaches of B. F. Skinner, which we discuss below, that are not aversive. They promote and reinforce dryness rather than punish bedwetting, and they have achieved a high degree of success.

Many of the criticisms of contemporary behavior therapies are mistakenly based on the idea that these behavior therapies are essentially the aversion therapies in one form or another. Actually, the aversion therapies are currently used with very few clients—for example, with those suffering from rather serious problems, such as self-destructive behavior, that are not responsive to other interventions (Lovaas and Newsome, 1976). The aversion therapies should only be used as a therapy of final resort. They should also be used only in institutions with proper medical and, above all, proper legal safeguards of patients' rights. They should not be used by social workers unless it is in a team situation with medical and legal protection. These therapies are certainly not benign and may have dangerous side effects. Aversive procedures should not be used when nonaversive procedures, based on positive reinforcement principles, are available.

Other Respondent Procedures

Other stimulus-response procedures include those developed by Cautela (1967, 1970, 1971). They are based on classical conditioning but deal with covert imagery. The first is called covert sensitization. The procedures generally involve a nausea-producing stimulus, disgust on the part of the patient, and an "escape or relief" scene. For example, the client imagines himself engaging in undesirable behavior, such as sitting in a bar and reaching for a drink. He then imagines experiencing an aversive response, such as nausea, which will be relieved only when he leaves the bar and goes out into the open fresh air.

So far we have briefly covered the so-called respondent or classical behavior therapy procedures generally associated with the name of Joseph Wolpe. These approaches are based on a classical conditioning approach, the so-called stimulus-response approach. This approach, while still prominent in some contemporary therapies, is experiencing a resurgence in the application of some of the relaxation procedures to certain problems, such as hypertension (Benson, 1975). However, the respondent approaches in behavior therapy have been to a large degree supplanted and enriched by the operant or instrumental conditioning approach primarily associated with B. F. Skinner.

The Operant Conditioning Approach of B. F. Skinner

The approach of B. F. Skinner is sometimes called operant conditioning because of his view that behavior has an effect on, or "operates," its environment. In the model we have just discussed, the Pavlovian or classical or respondent model, behavior is viewed as a learned, but conditioned, response to stimuli in the environment. Behavior is seen as automatic and reflexive. Because behavior is seen as automatic and reflexive, therapy is aimed at changing the behavior itself, at changing a patient's learned conditioned response to controlling stimuli. This is the basis of the various counterconditioning and aversion therapies.

Skinner's view of conditioning might better be called a contingency approach. Behavior is *not* viewed as an automatic response to stimuli in the environment, but behavior is conceptualized as taking place within an A-B-C framework. There are *antecedent* (A) events, that precede *behavior* (B). Behavior is followed by *consequences* (C). Some consequences cause the rate of behavior to be maintained or to increase, in which case the behavior is said to be *reinforced.* Some consequences will cause the rate of behavior to drop, in which case we say the behavior is *punished.* The antecedent events (A) set the condition and are in a sense the "rules" determining which behaviors (B) will receive which consequences (C). Both the antedecent condition and the behavior are linked to the consequences.

A simple example is that, when we come to a green light, we continue going. The green light (an antecedent condition) tells us which behavior is appropriate, which behavior will be reinforced. We are reinforced by continuing uninterrupted. If we come to a red light, this antecedent condition states that the "rule" is to stop. We stop for a number of reasons, such as not getting a ticket, not being hit by an automobile, and avoiding other potentially aversive consequences. After a while, of course, stopping for the red and green light becomes more automatic, becomes almost a "conditioned" response, but in the beginning it is learned thorugh an A-B-C sequence that determines behavior at a traffic light.

Behavior, in Skinner's operant conditioning view, does not follow automatically and reflexively. In the operant model, we talk about the *probabilities* of behavior. The probabilities of a behavior are governed partially by the antecedent conditions but mostly by the consequences. For example, we described a red light (A) resulting in stopping (B) to avoid negative consequences (C). This sequence of behavior occurs frequently, seemingly automatically. However, when the red light appears at 3 A.M. on a deserted street with no negative consequences in sight, the probability of stopping may decrease considerably. Thus, examining various consequences leads us to more explicit definitions and understandings of behavior. Our behavior is a function of both the rules that are set and the consequences of behavior. Both antecedents and consequences may influence our behavior on a conscious and unconscious level. The interrelations of the antecedent, the behavior, the consequences, and the individual himself are called contingency relationships. The analysis of behavior within the Skinnerian or operant approach is an analysis of the individual within the whole set of his contingency relationships. The concept of contingency relationship is equivalent to the social work principle of the "individual in the situation." It is a dynamic model in the true sense.

The Skinnerian, operant aproach emphasizes examination of the interaction of the individual with his environments, that is, the individual within his contingency relationships. It is a fine-grain analysis of the total contingencies of the individual rather than just one part of one segment. One contingency that is common to both the behavioral approach and the psychodynamic approach is the "history" of the individual. The "history of conditioning" has been compared to "developmental history."

The individual himself—contrary to early behavioral views—is not viewed as a passive respondent but as an active participant in interaction with his contingency relationships. The therapeutic task is to change the environment, to change the contingencies that govern the behavior rather than to change just the behavior itself. The assumption here is that the individual's behavior would then change in response to a changed environment. A simplified example would be the child who receives a great deal of attention from his parents and his teacher when he is late and none when he is prompt. If he were to be praised when he is on time and his late behavior ignored, then being on time might very well increase in frequency. Operant procedures are based primarily on positive reinforcements, that is, on encouraging and rewarding desired behavior rather than on eliminating undesired behaviors through aversive or punishment procedures.

Signals must be *clear,* both as to the behavior required and to the consequences of that (or other) behaviors. If we were driving down the street and the traffic light showed both red and green, we would become confused; our behavior would deteriorate.

The treatment approach in the operant behavioral orientation is fairly explicit and straightforward. First, there is extensive interviewing with a client to determine what he or she would like the final goals of therapy to be. The therapist helps the client to articulate what the client would like to work on and does not want to work on in specific terms. For example, a goal (a terminal repertoire) would not be stated as "to have a healthier ego." It might very well be "to be independent from my parents," independence being defined as living in one's own apartment and working at a job and supporting oneself financially. A terminal goal for a couple would not be a "happier marriage," although that statement might result in a first goal of clarifying what the couple thinks a happy marriage would be. "Having a happier marriage" might consist of the couple going out socially a certain number of times, going on vacation, agreeing more on specific child care issues, and so on. It must be emphasized that the goals and the approach are individualized. They are the client's goals, not the therapist's version of what happiness for the client would be.

A second phase would be to clarify what is now going *well* with the client, what he would not like to change. This leads into a discussion of strengths. What are the strengths, that is, the assets, the resources, the coping skills that can be used in the therapy process? What are the contingencies that maintain both the adaptive behavior—the behavior that is desired—as well as the behaviors that are problematic?

After formulating the goals, the therapist then helps the client to develop a program to use his strengths to achieve the terminal goals. The program is spelled out step by step, often proceeding slowly. It will usually be necessary to formulate intermittant goals.

The goals of the therapy and the program procedures are usually formalized in a contract. The contract may be renegotiated at any time, but never unilaterally by the therapist or the client. Most behavioral therapists would probably agree that a written contract is best, but verbal agreements are fairly common. Some therapists, such as this author, will tape record these transactions or will keep specific notes listing the details.

The use of the contract has long been a feature of behavioral work (Sulzer, 1962) and has been suggested by consumer groups for anybody contemplating therapy (Adams and Orgel, 1975). Specifying the terminal goals, and the subgoals to be achieved on the way to the terminal goals, in a contract increases the understanding of both client and therapist as to what is desired and what will occur. The contract also facilitates evaluation of the effectiveness of the therapy.

Therapy includes procedures for gradually phasing out the therapist, terminating therapy, and making plans for follow-up. In phasing out, the patient gradually assumes more responsibility for planning and monitoring his program steps, but the therapist continues surveillance. Termination may occur when the patient has reached his goals or after a set number of sessions. When appropriate, termination is aided by increasing the intervals between therapeutic sessions.

Throughout the entire course of behaviorally oriented therapy, the emphasis is on contingency analysis and the use of programming procedures to help the client change his contingency relations. The therapeutic interventions usually focus on the following general and sometimes overlapping areas:

1. Behaviors that are not in the individual's repertoire and need to be learned.
2. Behaviors that are in the repertoire but need to be increased in frequency.
3. Behaviors that occur in the wrong situations and need to be put into the right situations.
4. Behaviors that are in the repertoire but must be reduced in frequency or eliminated altogether.
5. Maintaining the treatment effects.

Let us discuss each of these in turn.

1. *Behaviors that are not in an individual's repertoire and need to be learned.* Among the techniques used to teach behavior is *shaping*. In shaping, component parts of the desired final behavior are identified, and those behaviors that increasingly resemble the final desired behavior are reinforced. For example, a patient's terminal goal might be "independence," which he defines as living away from home. An intermediate goal might be to obtain a driver's license. To obtain a driver's license, the steps might be to obtain a driving manual, study it, get a driving permit, take lessons, and then take the driving test (Schwartz and Goldiamond, 1975, pp. 42–43). The therapist selectively reinforces behaviors that facilitate the program and does not reinforce others. Reinforcement includes talking as well as examination of the client's feelings and cognitions. This is an oversimplified example, of course, of a complicated clinical procedure, but it illustrates how the shaping of small steps can help the client to attain large goals and deal with obstacles. The step by step shaping is sometimes called the method of successive approximation.

Another behavioral procedure is *chaining*. Close examination of behaviors shows that they take place in sequences called *chains*. Completing one step is the cue for the next step. For example, lacing a shoe consists of a number of small steps—beginning with picking up the shoelace, touching the lace to the hole, pulling the lace through the hole, and so forth. The examination of behavioral chains is useful in such situations as marital conflict, where the therapy may focus not so much on a specific behavioral interaction but on the whole pattern (chain) of behavior. An argument between partners is really not *one* behavior but a *chain* of behaviors. The therapist helps the couple to examine each step in the chain. This process provides leads for therapeutic intervention for the therapist, indicators for self-change efforts for the couple, and greater understanding of how conflicts occur and escalate for both parties.

Other useful techniques are *prompting* and *fading,* where behaviors are put under more appropriate stimulus control, some classical conditioning procedures, behavioral rehearsal (role playing), modeling, and some of the positive reinforcement procedures listed in the next section.

2. *Behaviors that are in the repertoire but need to be increased in frequency.* There are times when clients already know the appropriate behaviors but need to engage in them more frequently. In this situation, the most frequently used therapeutic procedures are principles of positive reinforcement that either maintain or raise the level of desired behavior. These reinforcements may be material, but more often they are verbal and interpersonal. For example, listening and responding verbally to someone else's talking will usually keep that rate of talking high. Among the more powerful positive reinforcers are the attention and the reactions of the therapist. If we look away, or look bored, we most certainly will not be reinforcing. In therapy, one powerful reinforcer of client speech is simple responses, such as "hm" and "uh-huh!"

We must interject here that, contrary to popular belief, not only does behavioral therapy occur within a meaningful interpersonal relationship, but this relationship is necessary for behavioral therapy to take place. It is a widespread misconception that behavioral therapists do not believe in relationships. Behavioral therapists believe that relationship is a necessary but not a sufficient condition for changing client situations (Schwartz, 1977).

A token economy is a system of positive reinforcement based on the principle that, if certain behaviors are done, the doer will be rewarded with a token. A token is a "generalized reinforcer" that may be exchanged for something the individual wants, much like money may be exchanged for goods or services (Schwartz, in press). In fact, money itself is a token (White, 1971, p. 184).

Token economies are the best known of the behavior therapy applications of positive reinforcement and the most widely used; unfortunately, they are also the most widely misused (see critiques in Kazdin, 1977; Kazdin and Bootzin, 1973; and Schwartz, in press). The token economies, like all behavioral procedures, are conceptually simple but complicated to put into effect. The literature on token economies is extensive; for a good review, see Gambrill, 1977.

A related positive reinforcement procedure is contingency contracting, where two or more parties make a contract to fulfill certain behavioral requirements for certain consequences. Behavioral contracts have been used with some success in work with parents and children (Reese, 1978), with delinquents (Stuart, 1971; Stuart and Lott, 1972), in prisons (Rest, 1973), and with married couples (Jacobson and Margolin, 1979).

The techniques listed in (1) may also be used to increase the frequency of desired behaviors as well as to teach new behaviors.

3. *Behaviors that occur in the wrong situations and need to be put into the right situations.* Sometimes, behaviors occur, but under the wrong stimulus con-

trol. One example might be the student who socializes in the library and tries to study in a noisy student lounge. Helping the client to put the correct behavior under the appropriate antecedent control is a basic therapeutic intervention.

Stimulus control is a useful procedure for helping clients who have "blocks" that hinder their ability to work or study or accomplish other tasks. Procedures involve separating what is appropriate or inappropriate behavior in a particular setting and specifying how the appropriate behaviors should occur. For example, a typical sequence involves setting aside a desk for working on a particular job or project and for nothing else. If the clients feels restless or nonproductive or has another task to do, he must leave and do this elsewhere. The amount of time he spends at the desk working is programmed to increase slowly, and the client is reinforced for accomplishing each step.

Placing behavior under the proper stimulus control is one of the primary interventions in behavioral treatment of obesity. Many overweight people not only eat too rapidly, they do not eat in appropriate places and tend to overeat while engaging in distracting behaviors. Besides reducing the amount that overweight clients eat, the therapist attempts to bring eating behavior under stimulus control in the dining room and to eliminate distractions, such as TV (Mahoney and Mahoney, 1978; Stuart and Davis, 1972).

Stimulus control may also be useful to curtail smoking behavior by allowing smoking only under certain conditions, such as when wearing special smoking jackets or only in special places. One technique is to remove ashtrays in some rooms and to specify that smoking can only occur in the rooms where there are ashtrays (Novar, 1976).

4. *Behaviors that are in the repertoire but must be reduced in frequency or eliminated altogether.* Early behavior therapies focused on reducing or eliminating behaviors that were excessive—for example, children talking out in the classroom, taking of drugs, and alcohol addiction. Most of these earlier techniques tended to be aversive procedures that focused on eliminating the behavior. A more positive approach is to reinforce incompatible behavior. For example, rather than punish children for watching TV when they are supposed to be doing their homework, it is more effective to praise them when they are studying. It would be even better to ignore certain undesired behaviors, such as dirty hands, and reinforce the desired behavior that is incompatible (clean hands). This procedure of ignoring undesired behavior is called *extinction*. Since behavior is maintained by its consequences, attention given to undesired behavior (yelling at a child) may unwittingly reinforce the behavior. Ignoring the behavior, or extinction, is sometimes effective, but it is most effective to combine extinction with reinforcement of the behavior that is desired.

Another technique to reduce behavior is *punishment*. Punishment is an aversive response that follows a behavior and lowers the rate of behavior. Punishment may be either "positive punishment" (presenting an aversive such as spanking) or "negative punishment" (taking something desirable away). It is our feeling that punishment procedures should be avoided whenever possible, although their use might be considered as a treatment of last resort in extreme cases. These procedures should be done only with informed consent and as part of a team with appropriate medical and legal participation. Lovaas (1973), in working with extremely disturbed young children, found that punishment combined with positive reinforcement procedures was effective in extreme cases.

Other ways for reducing behavior are *response costs,* where a reinforcer is removed when a person engages in undesirable behavior. An example is paying a traffic ticket or a fine for an overdue book (Reese, 1978).

Another procedure is *time out,* more technically called time out from positive reinforcement. This technique is most often used with children who are misbehaving. The children are asked to stay in a corner or to go to a "quiet room." A quiet room, unfortunately, may be used for isolation, and the child may sometimes be removed for the convenience of the caretaker rather than for his own benefit. However, when properly used for very short periods of time, and when the rules are completely known to the child, time out may be a way for the child to collect himself.

Other procedures that are used, but that may be complicated, include *satiation* (presenting a very large amount of the reinforcer, which ultimately causes the behavior to drop) and *differential reinforcement* of other behavior (simply reinforcing all behaviors *except* the one you are trying to lessen or eliminate). Differential reinforcement is sometimes called omission training (Schwartz, in press).

5. *Maintaining the treatment effects.* This intervention is also called *generalization* or transfer of learning. There has to be stimulus generalization for a behavior learned under one set of conditions to be carried out in another situation. Behaviors learned in some situations, such as correctional schools, often do not persist once the individual is in his own environment. Gains made in the therapist's office must be maintained outside the therapist's office. It is true that *all* therapies seem to have problems with generalizing and maintaining treatment effects, but the problem may seem exaggerated with the behavioral interventions because they are more specific responses to a more general problem. For example, in such problems as weight control, the long-term follow-up on behavior methods has been rather discouraging (Stunkard and Penick, 1979).

Response generalization occurs when a change in one behavior carries over to other behaviors. For example, improvement in communication between a marital pair may carry over into other areas, such as child care or sexual relations.

The achievement of generalization is one of the active areas of investigation in behavior therapy. There are many ways to achieve continuity of therapeutic effects. If more therapy can be done in the natural environment, and if more "significant others" can be involved in the treatment, then the interventions have a better chance of generalizing (Schwartz, 1965). Another way to maintain therapeutic gains is the conscious use of self-control procedures.

One tenet of the operant behavioral approach is that, the more we can work with the client to analyze his or her own contingencies and have him arrange his *own* behavior, the more he will assume responsibility for change, and the better able he will be to handle future problem situations (Goldiamond, 1965). This is called *self-control.* This emphasis on self-control has intensifed controversy among behaviorists. In the radical behaviorist's view, self-control occurs when there are two or more behavioral alternatives whose effects are conflicting and the individual chooses the alternative that is not met by immediate reinforcement. For example, if an overweight person sees a piece of cake, one response may be to eat the cake. He is immediately reinforced by the taste of the cake. However, if the person does *not* eat the cake but engages in an alternate behavior (such as chewing a piece of celery), then he is showing self-control because the reinforcer is not immediately available. (Celery, or not eating anything, can hardly compare in the reinforcing power of a piece of cake for most individuals.) The trait psychologists would state that the person is "inner motivated"—that his "superego" (or some other metaphor) might be responsible for his not eating the cake. The radical behaviorists would say that the control is still external because the long-term reinforcer (the benefits of avoiding obesity and attaining better health) is maintaining the alternate behavior; that is, the alternate behavior is also under environmental control.

However, viewing self-control as behavior controlled by external factors and conditions is an inadequate explanation. For example, very few people stop smoking because they are risking lung cancer many years in the future. Usually, other factors must be present for people to stop smoking. Recent work in behavior therapy has shown that the idea of self-control presents a dilemma to behavior therapists that can only be resolved by paying increased attention to what is happening "inside the organism." A prominent behaviorist states that there are three classes of behavioral control: *alpha* controls are located in the external environment, *beta* controls are self-generated, and *gamma* controls are biological variables (Kanfer, 1977). Kanfer proposes a dynamic model whose paths interplay. The "internal" variables, particularly the beta self-generated variables, involve such elements as self-esteem.

There are a number of complicated procedures for enhancing self-control by the client. These procedures are discussed in various publications, including Schwartz (in press) and Thoreson and Mahoney (1974). Primarily, the procedures may be divided into two categories. The first is environmental planning, the individual's arrangement of the *antecedent* conditions. For example, as we described earlier, an ashtray may be placed out of the way to deter smoking. The second is behavioral programming, or the individual's management of the *consequences* of his behavior. One example might be the individual rewarding himself with something he enjoys for not smoking, such as watching TV or buying something he wants. If he does smoke, then he cannot reward himself. Of course, there are similarities and overlappings between these two categories of self-control, just as there are similarities between behavioral self-control and the psychodynamic psychotherapies. We believe that the chief application of the operant approach to clinical casework is in the application of the principles and techniques of self-control.

There are times when neither the operant nor the respondent model fully accounts for behavior—for example, in learning new behavior, in learning new uses of language, and in learning behavior for which there are no immediate consequences (for which individuals are neither reinforced nor punished). One approach that addresses the incompleteness of the operant and respondent theories is found in the innovative work of Bandura in what he calls a social learning approach.

The Social Learning Approach of Albert Bandura

Bandura hypothesized that people could learn not only through reinforcement contingencies and through stimulus–response arrangements but also through observation and imitation of others. People learn by copying what others do; they learn vicariously. Others are *models* for our behavior. This is especially true when people learn behavior for which they are not immediately reinforced.

Through moderling, a person observes new patterns of behavior and can deliberately imitate them. A therapist can also use modeling by setting himself as an example, as a means of instruction to teach new behavior. When a person observes a model, he grasps an *entire pattern* of responding as well as the component parts that are emphasized in an operant model. A model can strengthen or weaken behavior, can show the learning person new behavior, and can facilitate new responses by providing a cue. Modeling does not involve the learning of specific, observable contingency relationships, but it involves "imaginal and verbal representations of the modeling stimuli" (Bandura, 1969). In other words, when the client internalizes an image, he has a mental representation of a behavior. He can recall these internal visualizations of behavior and apply (imitate) them in many situations. Bandura's approach *does* focus more on internal variables and is not in keeping with the observable, positivistic orientation of the radical behaviorists. We shall discuss this point further in the next section. Modeling is a complicated process. For further explication, see Bandura (1969, 1971), Rosenthal and Bandura (1978), and Schwartz (in press).

Modeling is certainly part of the psychotherapeutic procedure, and most therapists model behavior, even if it is only verbal behavior. This is sometimes done on a conscious, deliberate basis (Ullman, 1969). Modeling is not similar to countertransference, nor does it mean the therapist is deliberately pushing his values onto the client. There is a great deal of confusion between modeling and the concept of identification. In behavioral modeling, the therapist generally takes a very highly structured approach, deliberately portraying the behavior to be imitated. In other words, the therapist acts as a role model. He will use deliberate, often complex cues to shape behavior. He can model functional behavior, demonstrating to the client how those behaviors may either be combined with old behaviors or replace old behavior. The therapeutic task is then to integrate these new ways of coping and of responding into the client's repertoire.

Modeling may be used in a number of situations with clients. One prevalent usage is the teaching of social skills to mentally handicapped youngsters or to individuals with gaps in skills, such as dating behavior and job applying behavior. Certainly, verbal behavior, assertion training, and social skills training can be taught through demonstration, modeling, and behavioral rehearsal (role playing). These procedures may be combined with assignments to be done during and after the therapy session.

Modeling may also be used effectively in groups. Not only does the therapist offer a model, but each group member is also a potential model and can provide feedback. Symbolic models, such as audiovideo tape and films, may be used; some therapists have even used actors to illustrate behaviors in group situations. For a very good discussion of the use of modeling and the social learning approach in groups, see the works of Sheldon Rose (1972, 1977, 1980).

The work of Bandura and others on modeling, which has added a focus on the internal variables, does not necessarily negate the behaviorists' concentration on the external environment. However, some behaviorists have criticized Bandura's work as a return to "blackbox" or mentalistic psychology. This "internal-external" debate is a current issue among behavior therapists. However, there has been increasing evidence to substantiate the usefulness of a combination of the external (behavioral) and the internal ("mentalistic") approaches. One such synthesis is found in the recent burgeoning work in the cognitive behavioral orientation.

The Cognitive Behavioral Approaches

Bandura's social learning approach uses modeling and is theoretically based on so-called internal mediating factors. Some behaviorists have been reluctant to abandon the data-based, research-oriented approach that focuses on the external. They consider these newer developments as a return to introspectionism (the "black box"), with its accompanying "soft" data and mentalistic concepts that are not based on research or data. It is the experience of this author that behavioral change can often be achieved quite rapidly using operant conditioning approaches and sometimes respondent reconditioning approaches. However, unless the client changes the way he perceives or interprets the experience, unless he changes his way of thinking, these gains will not last. Therefore, it is necessary to intervene in the area of cognition.

This increasing reconsideration of the "interion," or the inner processes of the client, is not entirely new to behavior therapists but represents an increasing emphasis on "private events," a concept found throughout the writings of B. F. Skinner but comparatively ignored by some of his followers.

The increasing emphasis on the internal *does* deemphasize the observable, objective, and measurable phenomenon in favor of the more complex and difficult phenomenon of "thinking." This is an inevitable cost of "getting back inside the organism."

There are a number of different cognitive therapies and a number of different cognitive approaches in the behavioral sciences. In summarizing them, we shall follow the scheme described by Mahoney and Arnkoff (1978), who have divided these therapies into three general classes, cognitive restructuring, the coping skills, and the problem-solving therapies. We shall take each of these in turn.

Cognitive Restructuring. Cognitive restructuring essentially builds upon the work of Albert Ellis (1977), a psychologist, and Aaron T. Beck (1976), a psychiatrist, whose works overlap but complement each other.

Albert Ellis has long rejected psychodynamic approaches in favor of what he calls a "rational-emotive" approach or, more recently, a "cognitive-behavioral" or "rational-behavioral" approach. Ellis believes that many of the problems of individuals are due not so much to what actually happens to them (although these events are important) but what they *think* about the events. He believes that the belief systems of people, particularly their many "false beliefs," affect their responses to situations. One such false belief, reported several times by Ellis, is the belief that one individual must *always* succeed at *everything* he does or else he is worthless. This unrealistic standard of perfection can, and often does, prevent an individual from doing *anything*.

Ellis' work parallels the work of Aaron Beck's recent book on depression (1979) and a previous book on cognitive therapy (1976). Beck concentrates on unravelling the distorted thinking of his patients. He has them examine some of their misperceptions and how these misperceptions affect their actions. Ellis and Beck both agree that there is often a discrepancy between what people perceive something to be and what that something actually is. Problems arise when clients act as if these distorted perceptions are true. Both Ellis and Beck, in various ways, ask clients to examine and dispute their experiences, to engage in "cause and effect" reasoning to detect irrationalities, and to stop overgeneralizing. Both Beck and Ellis help clients to identify their thinking patterns, revise their false beliefs, and learn more adaptive ways of dealing with the realities of their life situations.

Reformulating thinking patterns fits in well with behavioral programming. In the example given above of the person with unrealistically high performance standards, the cognitive restructuring could be done simultaneously with a program of attempting smaller steps in behavior, with criteria lower than perfection as a standard of success.

A pioneer in cognitive restructuring is the psychologist Meichenbaum (1977). He found, in teaching schizophrenics to engage in "healthy talk," that these schizophrenics maintained this healthy talk past the end of therapy. He also found that individuals could be helped to give themselves instructions that would enable them to change their behavior, to substitute adaptive and "healthy" self-talk and behaviors for previously pathological ones. He instructs clients to ask themselves what to do and at the same time give themselves positive messages stating that they are capable of changing the problematic condition. In other words, Meichenbaum combines modeling and operant procedures with self-instruction and cognitive restructuring (Meichenbaum, 1977). Meichenbaum, like many of the newer cognitive behaviorists, promotes "therapeutic packages," a combination of a number of skills that can help the individual to cope better.

Coping Skills. Coping skills are strategies that help the individual deal with problematic situations. They may include cognitive restructuring, muscle relaxation, modeling, or any number of behavioral procedures, such as social skill training. They also include covert modeling (Cautela, 1970), where the client first imagines someone else doing an act and then himself doing the act.

Suinn and Richardson (1971) developed anxiety management training, in which clients respond to anxiety-provoking scenes without the use of any hierarchy. Clients are encouraged to experience the anxiety, to learn to recognize anxiety as a discriminative stimulus for anxiety, and then to cope with the anxiety by using specific procedures. For example, students who had anxiety about mathematics were taught to respond *just* to the anxiety as anxiety, apart from mathematics. They were taught deep muscle relaxation by tape recorder and then were trained to visualize a scene that evoked anxiety. The students then were asked to visualize the anxiety-provoking scene and to terminate it either through visualization of a competent action or through relaxation. This procedure requires no painstaking hierarchies, as does systematic desensitization. After training students to respond to anxiety in general, they generalized the training to anxiety about mathematics classes (Suinn and Richardson, 1971).

Similar to coping skills therapy is *stress inoculation.* Meichenbaum (1974, 1977) teaches relaxation as a coping skill. Stress inoculation, in his view, is the "behavioral equivalent of medical immunization." It has three phases: (1) *educational,* where the client is taught the rationale of these procedures; (2) *rehearsal,* where he acquires specific coping procedures, some of direct action, some of escape routes, and some of cognitive coping; and (3) *application training,* where the client tests these procedures in situations other than target situations and then tries the techniques in the specific situation that causes anxiety. For example, in the *educational phase,* the client is made aware of his patterns of responding, in specific terms that he can understand. When he understands his patterns of behavioral and cognitive responses, he then *rehearses* both *direct coping actions,* such as relaxation exercises and planning escape routes in the event of overwhelming anxieties, and he practices *cognitive coping,* a set of self-statements that he is to make to himself, such as "preparing for a stressor" ("What is it I have to do?" "Develop a plan to deal with it." "When fear comes, just pause." "It's getting better every time I use the procedures.") and a number of others (Meichenbaum, 1977, p. 155).

The client then engages in the third phase, *application training,* where he puts these procedures into practice, first in a clinic or laboratory where he is subjected to artificial and controllable stress, and then, when he feels ready, in a real-life situation, such as standing in line in a bank, approaching a domineering fellow employee, taking an airplane ride, or arguing with his wife.

The reader may note that there are some similarities between the self-statements of Meichenbaum and the "positive thinking" approaches of Norman Vincent Peale and W. Clement Stone. It is true that both Peale and Stone have recognized that "self-talk" has a therapeutic effectiveness. Meichenbaum, however, specifically rejects the kind of stereotyped, formulalike self-talk advocated by Peale and Stone as being too general. Specific self-statements must be tailored to fit the particular problem situation of the individual.

Problem-solving Therapies. Problem solving, as originally advocated by John Dewey, has long been adapted by social workers as a basis of the problem-solving approach to casework (Perlman, 1957). The concept has been extended to behavior therapy by D'Zurilla and Goldfried (1971, 1973) and Goldfried and Davison (1976). The problem-solving approaches within the behavioral orientations facilitate the ability of the client to cope with problems by first helping him to break down the problems into specifics and then equipping him with specific techniques with which to work.

There are five general stages within behavioral problem solving. The first is general orientation, where the client learns that problems are not necessarily pathological but occur throughout everybody's life and must be dealt with. The purpose of therapy is to help him cope better with real-life problems.

The next step is problem definition and formulation, where the client learns to analyze the problem in specific behavioral terms. He learns to avoid using vague terms and to translate the problem, as well as the goals and remedial action, into specific terms.

The next step is generalization of alternatives, where he considers a number of possible solutions, leading to the next phase, decision making, where he selects one to try. The solution should be specific and observable and lend itself to evaluation. The next stage is evaluation, feedback, and (if needed) changing the procedures.

The problem-solving approach represents a synthesis of respondent, operant, and cognitive procedures.

Recent Developments in Behavior Therapy

There have been a number of recent developments with which the reader should become familiar. One is the multimodal therapy of Arnold A. Lazarus. Lazarus, an early collaborator of Wolpe, split with Wolpe over differences of opinion regarding the effectiveness of systematic desensitization. Lazarus has gone through several phases, from technical eclecticism (1967) to a broad-spectrum behavioral approach, then to personalistic psychotherapy (1971). His latest approach, multimodal behavior therapy, is also called treatment of the BASIC ID (Lazarus, 1973). BASIC is an acronym for Behavior, Affect, Sensation, Imagery, and Cognition; ID stands for Interpersonal and the use of Drugs. Each problem area under each of these headings suggests a number of specific techniques that can be applied. The seven areas are, of course, often overlapping. For example, a therapist may suggest assertiveness training to change one aspect of behavior and behavioral rehearsal to change another aspect of behavior. If the client also has problems with affects, the suggested procedure might be desensitization. The therapist may teach the client some forms of relaxation to relieve tension (Sensation), the Gestalt technique of the "empty chair" to relieve problems of Imagery, and so forth. The therapist may use one technique, or two, or up to a dozen or more problem areas (Lazarus, 1976). The multimodal approach uses behavioral cognitive procedures, elements of Gestalt and other techniques, and drugs. The reader may perceive Lazarus' approach to be fragmented, but he claims that these numerous procedures flow into a comprehensive, total approach to the client. Lazarus believes that the *more* therapeutic procedures one can use—procedures that are specific and rooted in empirical research rather than wedded to theory—the more effective will be the intervention.

Bandura's Theory of Self-Efficacy

Bandura's latest theory has great promise for social work. Several behavioral theorists have called this theory "the most complete, clinically useful, and theoretically sophisticated formulation of behavior therapy" (Franks and Wilson, 1978, p. 15).

Bandura states that behavior and human adjustment are governed by respondent conditioning, operant conditioning, and symbolic processes, such as cognition. Any changes, be they behavioral, cognitive, or affective, must be "accompanied by a feeling of mastery." A person must have some *feelings* that he can cope with a problematic situation. There are factors that determine whether or not people believe they can cope. If they believe they can cope, then they may *act* upon the feeling. If they do *not* feel they can cope, then they may not even try. This is what Bandura calls a "motivation to change," a feeling that one can engage in a behavior to try to make a change. Bandura calls the individual's estimate of his ability to engage in the behavior "efficacy expectations."

A second component of the "motivation to change" is whether or not the individual feels there will be *consequences* for him once the behavior is attempted. In other words, what are the expectations of the individual? If the individual should engage in a behavior, or change some aspect of his behavior, does he feel it will actually make any difference to him? This second part, whether or not the changed behavior will make a difference, Bandura calls "outcome expectations." These are often mistakenly collapsed into a misleading unitary concept of motivation. Bandura's position is that these two phases represent different problems and require different types of intervention, some requiring behavioral methods, some nonbehavioral methods. He believes that it is absolutely necessary to make specific differentiation and differential diagnosis between the two. He states that expectations can differ in a number of ways, such as in magnitude (from simple to complex tasks), generality (one instance or many instances), and strength (strong or weak expectations). The individual draws from different sources of information, such as performance, vicarious experience, verbal persuasion, and emotional arousal.

In his writings, Bandura (1977a, 1977b) breaks the theory down into its component parts and suggests not only therapy but fruitful lines of research. We cannot elaborate on each of these phases here. However, each seems to be a unique theoretical position that falls between the frequent vagueness of psychodynamics and the often overly concrete positivism of behaviorism.

Task-Centered Approaches

Sometimes classified as behavioristic are the task-centered approaches connected with Reid (1978) and Reid and Epstein (1972, 1977). The task-centered approaches—applied to casework, group work, and other methods—consist of a time-limited approach to solving problems, including identification of specific problems, exact goals of interventions, and procedures for intervention.

Both Reid and Epstein were trained psychodynamically but in the course of the development of their model have become more focused and more oriented toward the specification of goals, procedures, and evaluation. In that sense, the approach incorporates the behavioral emphasis on operationalism and specification, the use of procedures, and accountability. However, both authors have stated that the task-centered approaches, in essence, may form a treatment framework rather than being a theory itself. Within the task-centered approach, practitioners of different theoretical orientations may practice. The approach is suited for "observable" or "reality-based" problems, of limited scope, for treatment of limited duration, with an emphasis on time-limited treatment. Many behavioral approaches tend to be short term, but the emphasis on time limitation is not an essential part of the behavioral approach. Reid and Epstein's views on time limitation match some of the theories of the functionalists (Smalley, 1970). Their specific procedural approach is similar to the specified step-by-step procedural approaches of some behaviorists.

Summary and Conclusions

We have emphasized that the behavioral approach is not one single approach but, like the psychodynamic therapies, is really a number of approaches. The behavioral approaches are also not a static group of therapies, although there are some behaviorists, as there are some analytically oriented practitioners, who have remained with the same model that they learned early in their professional careers. The behavior therapies are obviously changing and developing. It is still an orientation that may be said to be in process, in transition. In this chapter, we have traced the transition from early stimulus–response psychology, to the operant conditioning of Skinner, to the social-learning approach of Bandura, to the cognitive behaviorists and the various offshoots such as multimodal approaches, to Bandura's theory of self-efficacy, and to task-centered treatment.

In short, the behavioral views as they are developing do not present as fragmented a view of man as some of their vociferous critics have portrayed them. There *are* some differences between behavioral and nonbehavioral therapies, but these differences increasingly become blurred, especially when we talk about the way therapy is actually done as contrasted with how people *say* it is done. One difference is that the behavioral approaches always have focused more on the environment than many other approaches. This is similar to the early emphasis of the early social workers and the social reformers in sociology, who were ardent environmentalists. The importance of the environment is an emphasis that is being revived in social work (see Germain, 1973; Grinnell, 1973; Grinnell and Kyte, 1974, 1975).

In addition to the primacy of the environment, the behavioral practitioner advocates a data-based, research approach to treatment, emphasizing the observable, the recordable, the researchable—in short, the external. Another way of stating this is that most problems will be approached by the behaviorally oriented clinical social worker as problems relating chiefly to the client's environment. They will be seen as problems in social functioning—interpersonal rather than intrapersonal. The behavioral orientations maintain that, while behavior may be altered by changing affects first, it is often easier and more efficient to work on behavior first, which will result in alterations in affects. However, it is the opinion of this author that these behavior changes, which often may occur quite quickly and be quite deep in their ramifications, may not persist unless they are accompanied by a change in the way the client thinks, in his cognitions, in the way the client views his world, and in the way the client thinks about himself. Thus, it is not unusual for readers of contemporary behavioral works to read about changes in a client's "self" (Stuart, 1977).

Partially responsible for this broadening of the methods and of the theoretical base of the behavioral approaches has been the expansion of behaviorists into a number of new areas, some of which have not responded to other psychotherapeutic methods. Social workers using behavioral methods work with one-to-one relationships, dyads, parent training (Miller, 1975; Miller and Miller, 1977), couples (Jacobson and Margolin, 1979; Stuart, 1976), families (Gambrill, 1977), small groups (Rose, 1972, 1977, 1980), in schools (Reese, 1978; O'Leary and O'Leary, 1976), hospitals (Schwartz, in press), and with other client groups. There have been increasing applications of behavioral methods with new classes of clients, such as the aged (Schwartz and Blackman, 1977), the obese (Stuart and Davis, 1972; Loro, 1978), and the anorectic (Stunkard and Mahoney, 1976). There have also been interventions into medical conditions, efforts that will increasingly involve social workers (Knapp and Peterson, 1976). These conditions include cardiac problems (Benson, 1975), hypertension (a problem rife in the ghettos of our cities) (Ragland, 1977), asthma (Knapp and Wells, 1978), burns (Shorkey and Taylor, 1973), and such conditions as seizures, colitis, cerebral palsy, speech difficulties, migraine and tension headaches, and sleep disorders (see Schwartz, in press, chapter six). A general phenomenon, and a critical clinical problem increasingly being presented to social workers both in hospital and out of hospital, is the general area of pain (Fordyce, 1976a, 1976b). It is increasingly seen as a problem coming under environmental (nondrug) control and requiring a team approach.

Through this process of development have come changes in the view of the client's role from that of a passive recipient of some of the early conditioning and reconditioning and aversive treatments to that of a full partner in joint planning and cooperative programming, as in some of the self-control programs (Schwartz and Goldiamond, 1975; Schwartz, 1982). This new role is increasingly appropriate for the broadening of the focus of behavioral workers to include cognitions. This specification of goals, methods, and contracts heightens accountability and client control over the therapeutic process. In short, the behavioral approaches, more than any other helping approach, may embody the social work concept of self-determination.

In the behavioral treatment approaches, the focus and the instrument of change are usually cooperative work between the therapist and the client, with primary focus on the external environment but with increasing emphasis on the cognitions and the internal processes of the client. Behavioral practitioners tend to be more committed to a systematic, data-based research approach to both external and internal processes. They reject some explanations, such as structural explanations and metapsychological explanations, as "mentalistic," as not being amenable to systematic testing; therefore, they can neither be proved nor disproved.

However, in their emphasis on history and learning, behavior therapists are close to some of the more recent "self" theories in psychoanalysis. In essence, behaviorists would go along with some of the "self" theorists in holding that problems are learned behaviors, and thus pathology is also learned behavior that can be unlearned and in its place more adaptive, more productive, and healthier behaviors may be learned. Thus, the behavioral views still remain optimistic in their belief of the eventual possibilities of people to learn, in their propensity for self-development, or, in Rogerian terms, in actualizing their potential.

Since the behavioral procedures tend to be well specified and since behavioral journals are often refreshingly frank and direct in their presentations of procedures and techniques that do not work as well as those that do work, social workers whose primary orientation is not behavioral can learn enough from the literature to start to think about the possible ways of applying some of these procedures to their practice. It must be emphasized that, even though some of the behavioral procedures are direct and may seem simple, they are not simplistic. Some training in the approach should precede application of the procedures. The burden of this kind of training will, for a long time to come, probably be through university extension training and through agency in-service training.

A growing body of research has shown that behavioral procedures are effective in many situations. The irony is that they have not been so effective with the "behavioral problems," such as obesity, smoking, and enuresis, as they have been when combined with other therapeutic methods (Schwartz, in press). Increasingly, they are proving to be effective in situations where they had not previously been considered applicable, such as in the affective disorders, particularly the many forms of depression. There is a growing literature on the use of the behavioral methods with depression. In the view of this author, behavioral methods are excellent in the first part of treatment; they will stop the downward spiral of depression. (For a comprehensive overview of the behavioral methods of treating depression, see Schwartz, in press, chapter five).

In conclusion, the behavioral approaches represent a number of approaches rather than a single, monolithic approach. Social workers need additional tools and therapeutic models to fulfill the growing demands for their services in an increasing number of situations. Knowledge of the behavioral approaches—their applicabilities, their shortcomings, and their potential—will enable current and future social workers to keep pace with the constantly changing demands of the clinical situation.

References

Adams, S., and Orgel, M. *Through the Mental Health Maze: A Consumer's Guide to Finding a Pychotherapist, Including a Sample Consumer/Therapist Contract.* Washington, D.C.: Health Research Group, 1975.

Bandura, A. *Principles of Behavior Modification.* New York: Holt, Rinehart and Winston, 1969.

Bandura, A. (Ed.). *Psychological Modeling: Conflicting Theories.* Chicago: Aldine-Atherton, 1971.

Bandura, A. "Self-Efficacy: Toward a Unifying Theory of Behavioral Change." *Psychological Review,* 1977a, *84,* 191–215.

Bandura, A. *Social Learning Theory.* Englewood Cliffs, N.J.: Prentice-Hall, 1977b.

Beck, A. *Cognitive Therapy and the Emotional Disorders.* New York: International Universities Press, 1976.

Beck, A., and others. *Cognitive Therapy of Depression.* New York: Guilford Press, 1979.

Benson, H. *The Relaxation Response.* New York: Morrow, 1975.

Bergin, A. E. "The Evaluation of Therapeutic Outcomes." In A. E. Bergin and S. L. Garfield (Eds.), *Handbook of Psychotherapy and Behavior Change: An Empirical Analysis.* New York: Wiley, 1971.

Cautela, J. R. "Covert Sensitization." *Psychological Reports,* 1967, *20,* 459–468.

Cautela, J. R. "Covert Reinforcement." *Behavior Therapy,* 1970, *1,* 273–278.

Cautela, J. R. "Covert Extinction." *Behavior Therapy,* 1971, *2,* 192–200.

Cautela, J. R., Flannery, R. B., and Hanley, E. "Covert Modeling: An Experimental Test." *Behavior Therapy,* 1974, *5,* 494–502.

Dollard, J., and Miller, N. C. *Personality and Psychotherapy: An Analysis in Terms of Learning, Thinking, and Culture.* New York: McGraw-Hill, 1950.

D'Zurilla, T. J., and Goldfried, M. "Problem Solving and Behavior Modification." *Journal of Abnormal Psychology,* 1971, *78,* 107–126.

D'Zurilla, T. J., and Goldfried, M. "Cognitive Processes, Problem-Solving, and Effective Behavior." In M. R. Goldfried and M. Merbaum (Eds.), *Behavior Change Through Self-Control.* New York: Holt, Rinehart and Winston, 1973.

Ellis, A. "The Basic Clinical Theory of Rational-Emotive Therapy." In A. Ellis and R. Grieger (Eds.), *Handbook of Rational-Emotive Therapy.* New York: Springer, 1977.

Epstein, L. *Helping People: The Task-Centered Approach.* St. Louis: Mosby, 1980.

Eysenck, H. J. "The Effects of Psychotherapy: An Evaluation." *Journal of Consulting and Clinical Psychology,* 1952, *16,* 319–324.

Fordyce, W. E. *Behavioral Methods for Chronic Pain and Illness.* St. Louis: Mosby, 1976a.

Fordyce, W. E. "Behavioral Concepts in Chronic Pain and Illness." In P. O. Davidson (Ed.), *The Behavioral Management of Anxiety, Depression and Pain.* New York: Brunner/Mazell, 1976b.

Frankl, V. E. *Man's Search for Meaning: An Introduction to Logotherapy.* New York: Washington Square Press, 1959.

Franks, C. M., and Wilson, G. T. *Annual Review of Behavioral Therapy: Theory and Practice, 1978.* New York: Brunner/Mazel, 1978.

Gambrill, E. D. *Behavior Modification: Handbook of Assessment, Intervention, and Evaluation.* San Francisco: Jossey-Bass, 1977.

Germain, C. B. "An Ecological Perspective in Casework Practice." *Social Casework,* 1973, *54,* 323–330.

Goldfried, M. R., and Davison, G. C. *Clinical Behavior Therapy.* New York: Holt, Rinehart and Winston, 1976.

Goldiamond, I. "Self-Control Procedures in Personal Behavior Problems." *Psychological Reports,* 1965, *17,* 851–868. Monograph Supplement 3-V17.

Grinnell, R. M. "Environmental Modification: Casework's Concern or Casework's Neglect?" *The Social Service Review,* 1973, *47,* 208–220.

Grinnell, R. M., and Kyte, N. S. "Modifying the Environment." *Social Work,* 1974, *19,* 477–483.

Grinnell, R. M., and Kyte, N. S. "Environmental Modification: A Study." *Social Work,* 1975, *20,* 313–318.

Jacobson, N. S., and Margolin, G. *Marital Therapy: Strategies Based on Social Learning and Behavior Exchange Principles.* New York: Brunner/Mazel, 1979.

Jones, M. C. "The Elimination of Children's Fears." *Journal of Experimental Psychology,* 1924, *7,* 382–390.

Kanfer, F. H. "The Many Faces of Self-Control, or Behavior Modification Changes in Focus." In R. B. Stuart (Ed.), *Behavioral Self-Management: Strategies, Techniques and Outcomes.* New York: Brunner/Mazel, 1977.

Kazdin, A. E. *The Token Economy: A Review and Evaluation.* New York: Plenum, 1977.

Kazdin, A. E., and Bootzin, R. R. "The Token Economy: An Examination of Issues." In R. R. Rubin and others (Eds.), *Advances in Behavior Therapy.* Vol. 4. New York: Academic Press, 1973.

Knapp, T. J., and Peterson, L. W. "Behavior Management in Medical and Nursing Practice." In W. E. Craighead, A. E. Kazdin, and M. J. Mahoney (Eds.), *Behavior Modification: Principles, Issues and Applications.* Boston: Houghton Mifflin, 1976.

Knapp, T. J., and Wells, A. "Behavior Therapy for Asthma: A Review." *Behavior Research and Therapy,* 1978, *16,* 103–115.

Lazarus, A. A. "In Support of Technical Eclecticism." *Psychological Reports,* 1967, *21,* 415–416.

Lazarus, A. A. *Behavior Therapy and Beyond.* New York: McGraw-Hill, 1971.

Lazarus, A. A. "Multimodal Behavior Therapy: Treating the 'BASIC ID'." *Journal of Nervous and Mental Disease,* 1973, *156,* 404–411.

Lazarus, A. A. (Ed.). *Multimodal Behavior Therapy.* New York: Springer, 1976.

Loro, B. "Bibliography of Behavioral Approaches to Weight Reduction and Obesity from 1962 Through 1976." *Professional Psychology,* 1978, *9,* 278–289.

Lovaas, O. I., and Newsome, C. D. "Behavior Modification with Psychotic Children." In H. Leitenberg (Ed.), *Handbook of Behavior Modification and Behavior Therapy.* Englewood Cliffs, N.J.: Prentice-Hall, 1976.

Lovaas, O. I., and others. "Some Generalization and Follow-Up Measures on Autistic Children in Behavior Therapy." *Journal of Applied Behavior Analysis,* 1973, *6,* 131–165.

McBroom, E. "Socialization and Social Casework." In R. W. Roberts and R. H. Nee (Eds.), *Theories of Social Casework.* Chicago: University of Chicago Press, 1970.

Mahoney, M. J., and Arnkoff, D. "Cognitive and Self-Control Therapies." In S. L. Garfield and A. E. Bergin (Eds.), *Handbook of Psychotherapy and Behavior Change: An Empirical Analysis.* (2nd ed.) New York: Wiley, 1978.

Mahoney, M. J., and Mahoney, K. *Permanent Weight Control.* New York: Norton, 1976.

Masters, W. H., and Johnson, V. E. *Human Sexual Response.* Boston: Little, Brown, 1966.

Masters, W. H., and Johnson, V. E. *Human Sexual Inadequacy.* Boston: Little, Brown, 1970.

Masters, W. H., and Johnson, V. E. *Homosexuality in Perspective.* Boston: Little, Brown, 1979.

Meichenbaum, D. *Cognitive Behavior Modification.* Morristown, N.J.: General Learning Press, 1974.

Meichenbaum, D. *Cognitive Behavior Modification: An Integrative Approach.* New York: Plenum, 1977.

Miller, W. H. *Systematic Parent Training: Procedures, Cases and Issues.* Champaign, Ill.: Research Press, 1975.

Miller, W. H., and Miller, B. *Therapist's Guidebook to Systematic Parent Training.* Champaign, Ill.: Research Press,1977.

Mowrer, O. H. "Apparatus for the Study and Treatment of Eneuresis." *American Journal of Psychology,* 1938, *51,* 163–166.

Novar, L. G. "Self-Control of Smoking Behavior: A Comparative Study of Constructional and Eliminative Approaches." Unpublished doctoral dissertation, University of Chicago, 1976.

O'Leary, S. G., and O'Leary, K. D. "Behavior Modification in the School." In H. Leitenberg (Ed.), *Handbook of Behavior Modification and Behavior Therapy.* Englewood Cliffs, N.J.: Prentice-Hall, 1976.

Perlman, H. H. *Social Casework: A Problem-Solving Approach.* Chicago: University of Chicago Press, 1957.

Rachman, S., and Teasdale, J. *Aversion Therapy and Behavior Disorders: An Analysis.* Coral Gables, Florida: University of Miami Press, 1969.

Ragland, D. R. *Behavioral Approaches to the Treatment of Hypertension: A Bibliography.* (DHEW Publication No. [NIH] 77-1219.) Washington, D.C.: U.S. Government Printing Office, 1977.

Reese, E. P. *Human Behavior: Analysis and Application.* (2nd ed.) Dubuque, Iowa: Brown, 1978.

Reid, W. J. *The Task-Centered System.* New York: Columbia University Press, 1978.

Reid, W. J., and Epstein, L. *Task-Centered Casework.* New York: Columbia University Press, 1972.

Reid, W. J., and Epstein, L. (Eds.). *Task-Centered Practice.* New York: Columbia University Press, 1977.

Rest, E. R. "Rehabilitating Offenders Through Behavioral Change." In B. Ross and C. Shireman (Eds.), *Social Work and Social Justice.* Washington, D.C.: National Association of Social Workers, 1973.

Rose, S. D. *Treating Children in Groups: A Behavioral Approach.* San Francisco: Jossey-Bass, 1972.

Rose, S. D. *Group Therapy: A Behavioral Approach.* Englewood Cliffs, N.J.: Prentice-Hall, 1977.

Rose, S. D. (Ed.). *A Casebook in Group Therapy: A Behavioral-Cognitive Approach.* Englewood Cliffs, N.J.: Prentice-Hall, 1980.

Rosenthal, T., and Bandura, A. "Psychological Modeling: Theory and Practice." In S. L. Garfield and A. E. Bergin (Eds.), *Handbook of Psychotherapy and Behavior Change: An Empirical Analysis.* (2nd ed.) New York: Wiley, 1978.

Schwartz, A. "The Reference Groups of Dieting Obese Women." Unpublished doctoral dissertation, Columbia University, 1965.

Schwartz, A. "Behaviorism and Psychodynamics." *Child Welfare,* 1977, *56,* 368–379.

Schwartz, A. *The Behavior Therapies: Theories and Applications.* New York: Free Press, 1982.

Schwartz, A., and Blackman, D. *Developing Behavioral Therapies for the Institutionalized Elderly: Final Report.* Chicago: School of Social Service Administration, University of Chicago, 1977.

Schwartz, A., and Goldiamond, I. *Social Casework: A Behavioral Approach.* New York: Columbia University Press, 1975.

Shorkey, C., and Taylor, J. "Management of Maladaptive Behavior of a Severely Burned Child." *Child Welfare,* 1973, *52,* 543–547.

Skinner, B. F. *Science and Human Behavior.* New York: Free Press, 1953.

Smalley, R. E. "The Functional Approach to Casework Practice." In R. W. Roberts and R. H. Nee (Eds.), *Theories of Social Casework.* Chicago: University of Chicago Press, 1970.

Stuart, R. B. "Behavioral Contracting with the Families of Delinquents." *Journal of Behavioral Therapy and Experimental Psychiatry,* 1971, *2,* 1–11.

Stuart, R. B. "An Operant Interpersonal Program for Couples." In D.H.L. Olson (Ed.), *Treating Relationships.* Lake Mills, Iowa: Graphic, 1976.

Stuart, R. B. (Ed.). *Behavioral Self-Management: Strategies, Techniques, and Outcomes.* New York: Brunner/Mazel, 1977.

Stuart, R. B., and Davis, B. *Slim Chance in a Fat World: Behavioral Control of Obesity.* Champaign, Ill.: Research Press, 1972.

Stuart, R. B., and Lott, A. "Behavioral Contracting with Delinquents: A Cautionary Note." *Journal of Behavior Therapy and Experimental Psychiatry,* 1972, *3,* 161–169.

Stunkard, A. J., and Mahoney, M. J. "Behavioral Treatment of the Eating Disorders." In H. Leitenberg (Ed.), *Handbook of Behavior Modification and Behavior Therapy.* Englewood Cliffs, N.J.: Prentice-Hall, 1976.

Stunkard, A. J., and Penick, S. B. "Behavior Modification in the Treatment of Obesity: The Problem of Maintaining Weight Loss." *Archives of General Psychiatry,* 1979, *36,* 801–806.

Suinn, R. M., and Richardson, F. "Anxiety Management Training: A Nonspecific Behavior Therapy Program for Anxiety Control." *Behavior Therapy,* 1971, *2,* 498–510.

Sulzer, E. "Reinforcement and the Therapeutic Contract." *Journal of Counseling Psychology,* 1962, *9,* 271–276.

Thimann, J. "Conditioned-Reflex Treatment of Alcoholism, I." *New England Journal of Medicine,* 1949, *241,* 368–370.

Thoreson, C. E., and Mahoney, M. J. *Behavioral Self-Control.* New York: Holt, Rinehart and Winston, 1974.

Ullman, L. P. "Making Use of Modeling in the Therapeutic Interview." In D. R. Rich and C. M. Franks (Eds.), *Advances in Behavior Therapy, 1968.* New York: Academic Press, 1969.

Watson, J. B. *Behaviorism.* New York: Norton, 1924.

Watson, J. B., and Raynor, R. "Conditioned Emotional Reactions." *Journal of Experimental Psychology,* 1920, *3,* 1–14.

White, O. R. *A Glossary of Behavioral Terminology.* Champaign, Ill.: Research Press, 1971.

Wolpe, J. *Psychotherapy by Reciprocal Inhibition.* Stanford, Calif.: Stanford University Press, 1958.

Wolpe, J. *The Practice of Behavior Therapy.* New York: Pergamon Press, 1969.

10

Role of Perception and Cognition in Change

Ruth R. Middleman

Any excursion through the literature that deals with "knowing" is mind-boggling! To understand how we understand, let alone why we understand, remains perhaps our greatest enigma and challenge. This is so despite a long history of interest in and study of the mind, the brain, awareness, and self-knowledge by philosophers, theologians, scientists, mystics, educators, and clinicians. It would seem that the quintessential paradox is, can a brain understand a brain (Cooper, 1980)? This issue has been called our last frontier (Pribram, 1980) and has been summarized as knowing more about outer than inner space—that space inside our heads.

My discussion will deal with certain issues that interest me. Hopefully, these concerns are shared by others who also face the vexing problems of dealing with self and client in clinical practice. I find the consideration of questions of perception and cognition as resources for change to be an experience that elicits more humility than confidence. For, as we shall see, we are into the tangles of metaphysics and epistemology as much as theory and empiricism.

I shall deal with the following areas: disciplined looking and how this is taught; perspective as a limit on "seeing"; consciousness as an information processing system in which perception and cognition are components; perception and clinical practice; cognition and clinical practice; and beyond cognition.

In science, it is often believed that understanding something leads to control of it. This notion, which has both attracted and repelled us over the years, seems frightening when applied to our minds. Mind control is anathema to most social workers because it contradicts the fundamental value of self-determination. It suggests manipulation, which many practitioners eschew as unconscionable, even as they may "unconsciously" influence or change another. And yet, today's clinician has more approaches for effecting client change through mind control methods than ever before.

Miller (Hall, 1980) offers us a useful analogy from astronomy. By understanding the laws of planetary motion, astronomers can predict exactly where the moon is going to be. They can control where to aim the telescopes and where to send the rockets, but they cannot control the moon.

To apply this analogy to the mind, greater understanding of the mind, or consciousness, or knowing should have, as a main effect, an increase in awareness of oneself and perhaps more control over oneself, *not* another. If this analogy is valid, then any increase in precision in understanding and controlling one's self would be of value in clinical practice, where a major method for helping others has always been the conscious use of self. Like the telescope, conscious use of self enables one to know where to look, how to look, what to look for, and thus what to see.

This special use of self-awareness as a precondition for other-awareness has a long history in social work practice theory. For Richmond (1922, pp. 101–102), a central component of social work was insight into the individuality of the other. Behavior could be modified through a process of direct action of mind upon mind. Robinson (1936, pp. 25–50) introduced the concept of professional self as distinct from the personal self, a concept annexed by Reynolds (1942, pp. 261–266) as a distinguishing element of professional practice. By professional self, they meant conscious awareness of what one is doing or the ability to regard self in action and to study one's activities objectively without distracting from a focus on the situation of the client or group. Typically, this seasoned use of one's self was developed after many years of practice. It involved scrutiny and analysis by oneself and one's supervisor until the helping actions become habit, in the sense that attention and energy could be moved from the self to regard the other.

Disciplined Looking: Teaching Approaches

Whether one's purpose is to study or to influence a situation, a first obligation is to get beyond the surface of the observed to its essence, to "see" the other. It is now generally accepted (in science, art, and clinical practice) that it is impossible to separate the observer from the observed. The very choice of what to look at (see Gregg and others, 1979, for a comprehensive review of bias in social science research), as well as the act of looking (Rosenthal and Jacobson, 1968), will distort what is seen. Nevertheless, some approach must be made to help novices achieve a measure of deliberate control so as to distinguish disciplined from intuitive observation. Observation must be relearned. I shall illustrate this by comparing two teaching approaches, one from science and one from social work education.

A learner's diary captures how Louis Agassiz taught zoology students to "see things which other people miss" (Highet, 1950):

> Agassiz brought me a small fish, placing it before me with the rather stern requirement that I should study it, but should on no account talk to anyone concerning it, nor read anything relating to fishes, until I had his permission so to do. To my inquiry "What shall I do?" he said in effect: "Find out what you can without damaging the specimen; when I think that you have done the work I will question you." In the course of an hour I thought I had compassed the fish; it was rather an unsavory object, giving forth the stench of old alcohol. . . . Many of the scales were loosened so that they fell off. It appeared to me to be a case of a summary report, which I was anxious to make and get on to the next stage of the business. But Agassiz, though always within call, concerned himself no further with me that day, nor the next, nor for a week.
>
> At first, this neglect was distressing; but I saw that it was a game, for he was . . . covertly watching me. So I set my wits to work upon the thing, and in the course of a hundred hours or so thought I had done much—a hundred times as much as seemed possible at the start. I got interested in finding out how the scales went in series, their shape, the form and placement of the teeth, etc. Finally, I felt full of the subject and probably expressed it in my bearing; as for words about it then, there were none from my master except his cheery "Good morning." At length, on the seventh day, came the question "Well?" and my disgorge of learning to him as he sat on the edge of my table puffing his cigar. At the end of an hour's telling he swung off and away, saying "That is not right."
>
> It was clear that he was playing a game with me to find if I were capable of doing hard, continuous work without the support of a teacher, and this stimulated me to labor. I went at the task anew, discarded my first notes and in another week of ten hours a day labor I had results which astonished myself and satisfied him [pp. 214–215].

The next steps of Agassiz's laboratory method involved reconstructing fish skeletons from a gallon tank full of assorted bones (a two-month enterprise) followed by increasingly complex tasks of observation and comparison, not praise. We can see that the task was not merely one of learning content but of developing the requisite habits and methods of thinking—a process Bruner (1970) differentiated as *knowing how to* as opposed to *knowing about.* The task was to "think zoology."

Goldberg and I described our methods of teaching social work students how to take account of self and other in the midst of involvement with them by means of direct interactional experience, visualization and imagery experiences, and scrutinized self/other observation (Goldberg and Middleman, 1973, 1975; Middleman and Goldberg, 1972). Our description used videotaped illustrative material, direct interactional experience with the audience, pictures, and expository discussion to convey something about the teaching-learning process. Our objective was much the same as Agassiz's: "Vision-stretching involves the cultivation of deliberate naivete in viewing phenomena. . . , knowledge of one's frame of reference, and the ability to get outside of it" (1973, p. 13).

We helped students to engage their thought biases (biases created by individual differences and by cultural influences) by giving them word lists of different stimuli (for example, circle, cherry, yellow, cube, rose) and asking them to make lists of those belonging together. Afterward, comparisons of the lists and the resulting discussion revealed how each student had individually arranged the information according to the unique categories he had invented. In another teaching situation, students were shown pictures of an interview situation and asked who the people were and what was going on. When the picture showed two women, the older one was always seen as the professional helper, and when the picture was of a man and woman, the man was identified as the helper, irrespective of their relative ages. The man was never seen as the client. It is perhaps most shocking to the more "radical" students, who take pride in expressing egalitarian perspectives, to learn that they have not wholly escaped the influence of their culture.

We also practiced presenting ourselves to another (a "client") and interpreting why we were there. In this role play, students did not know what reaction they would receive but were to concentrate on being responsive to the other and on not abandoning their role. We were not so much concerned at this time with skill in interviewing. Rather, our teaching centered around responsiveness to the client—listening, using ordinary language, and communicating warmth and receptivity through nonverbal as well as verbal channels (1972).

Despite apparent differences, these two approaches to teaching observation share a common aim—to understand certain rules of looking so as to go beyond them in response to the situation at hand, to get beyond technique and become able to respond unselfconsciously with head, hand, and heart. Each approach contains comparable elements—teacher, learner, and content to be learned in a way that is purposeful and congenial to the field of enquiry. Both approaches entail diligent practice of particulars and, in fact, share a learning approach with the Zen master's instructional mode: "In the course of the years the forms which (the learner) perfectly masters no longer oppress but liberate. He grows daily more capable of following any inspiration without technical effort, and also of letting inspiration come to him through meticulous observation" (Herrigel, 1953, p. 63).

Perspective: Believing Is Seeing

Perspective, or world view, forms the background of perception and cognition. Perspective pertains to ideas, knowledge, values, feelings, and attitudes about the world—in other words, one's frame of reference. This has been described as "seeing what one expects to see," the first constraint upon looking. It is required for survival in the environment, for negotiating the complexities of living, and for separating the essential from the trivial (Goldberg and Middleman, 1973).

Having a point of view about self, others, and the environment provides as general orientation of prearranged ideas that keeps one's world in order. This system of ideas, feelings, and predispositions brings comfort and order, linkage to one's own and others' culture and environment, and continuity of tradition and learned notions about "reality." In other words, one's frame of reference determines what has meaning and value, how much openness and difference one can entertain, and what must be ignored or transformed because it doesn't fit with one's expectations and system of beliefs. The clinician's perspective is derived from life experience, from formal and informal education, and from her or his own particular preferences, trials, errors, and successes in dealing with others.

Most clinicians in higher education have had to come to terms with a general cultural perspective that values science more than art. The struggle of Western versus Eastern modes of thinking, of the Apollonian versus Dionysian world views (Holton, 1974), and of the rational and analytical versus the personal and intuitive modes of thinking are well known. The pervasive perspective concerning knowledge, truth, and reality derives from the classical traditions and favors natural science over liberal arts academic disciplines. This general perspective influences the permissable research and practice methods in the social and behavioral sciences, in medicine and psychiatry, and in social work.

Recently, questions have been raised about such a singleness of emphasis perhaps being useful for material technology but limiting and dysfunctional for human and environmental situations. There is increased valuation of seeking the continuities as well as the differences, for the creative and imaginative as well as the analytical. Some have argued for substituting other, more ancient and fundamental ways of knowing for science's way of knowing (for example, Roszak, 1973) or for transdisciplinary views of styles of enquiry as more suitable to the social sciences (Mitroff and Kilmann, 1978). Some have seen the ways of science (formal logic, objectivity, impersonality, skepticism, and so forth) as being more congenial to testing and evaluating ideas and to *discovering* what is or is not rather than the intellectual skills required for *invention* of what could be.

The ways of pure science are being augmented by other orientations and values, by greater acceptance in practice of ad hoc (useful, if not comprehensive) theories, and by disruptive ideas within the disciplines themselves. The new physics, for example, appears to share common ideas with Zen Buddhism (Zukav, 1979). The implications of quantum mechanics—the study of forces in the subatomic or invisible realm—suggest, unlike classical Newtonian physics, that we are not separate from the physical world. We cannot observe something without changing it. The very idea of observer and observed is an illusion. The only access to "reality" is a subjective or personal interpretation of what exists. Each individual's experience of the world depends on one's personal interaction with it. This physics is a far cry from the Universe as Great Machine, with man a mere bystander in a world of unfathomable forces or a cog in a wheel of predetermined events.

More tolerance exists today for diverse and eclectic orientations toward the person-environment transaction. Views about mental health and illness are examples of perspectives that are related to professions' vested interests, to the context of service delivery, and to what clinicians have learned to value and to do. At least three intellectual traditions have been influential: (1) Kraepelin's "scientific" ideology classified and described mental states as entities comparable to physical diseases, thereby moving mental problems from demonology and madness to medicine. (2) Freudian theory included psychological as well as physical origins for mental states. (3) Social work, the human potential movement, and humanistic psychologies have extended the concept of mental illness to include mental health and wellness.

Albee (1969) saw a conceptual dilemma in terms of whether behavior is viewed as *continuous* or *discontinuous*. A continuous perspective would consider all behavior as learned, with problematic behavior as more distorted or exaggerated versions of ordinary behavior. A discontinuous perspective would view problematic behavior as an expression of a mental illness, a mental state different from normal states. Various discrete mental illnesses have particular causes, prognoses, and treatments. The implications of these perspectives for the clinician are obvious.

Perspectives, being limited by values, knowledge, training, and economic, social, and political forces, exert tremendous influence on what the clinician sees and does. Despite such influence, however, many in the helping professions have shifted away from dogmatism to embrace the values of flexibility, adaptability, and versatility. Maslow's view (1966, pp. 31–32) typifies such a perspective and has been influential: "We shall have to include . . . both the techniques of caution and boldness. Mere caution and soberness, mere compulsiveness can produce only good technicians who are much less likely to discover or invent new truths or new theories. The caution, patience, and conservatism which are *sine qua non* for the scientist had better be supplemented by boldness and daring if creativeness is also the hope." Perspectives that value openness and eclecticism in thought and action have contributed to a clinical landscape of unprecedented diversity.

I have discussed disciplined looking and perspective before discussing the conscious awareness of the practitioner as he or she considers the perceptions and cognitions of the client as potential for change. This is more a matter of emphasis than conceptual accuracy since, as we shall see, these global considerations may also be thought of as the clinician's self-awareness. This is not meant to imply any duality of perspective or separation of a clinician-client unit of attention but reflects the inevitable limitations of linear analysis. It seemed necessary to look at the clinician looking before considering awareness more generally.

Consciousness: An Information-Processing System

Consciousness is an appealing concept to organize thinking about perception and cognition. It is used in several senses in the literature: (1) as a theoretical construct referring to the system by which an individual becomes aware, (2) as reflective awareness (the awareness of being aware), and (3) as all forms of awareness. Some recent reviews and rekindled interest in consciousness offer clarity and leads for theory, research, and practice (Goleman and Davidson, 1979; Lee and others, 1976; Ornstein, 1972; Pope and Singer, 1978).

The study of consciousness has enjoyed popularity and disfavor over the years according to prevalent intellectual influences of the times. While appealing and intriguing at the common-sense level, it remained refractory to systematic analysis and study. The metaphor "stream of consciousness," although suggested by James (1890) "stream of thought," persisted more through the attention of the novelist than that of the psychologist or clinician. Always of practical interest to the psychologist, consciousness suffered assaults from several sources. First, the Western preference of dualistic thinking and dichotomies made consciousness elusive. There was mind *and* body, with consciousness linked with mind (soul). There was person *and* environment, with different "specialists" concerned about each. Then, Freudian theory did much to elevate the importance of the unconscious to the detriment of the conscious. Also, the behaviorists, at least until recently, tended to avoid the problem by excluding consciousness from consideration within theories that made no assumptions about substances or a reality that could not be seen.

As of the 1960s, consciousness has reemerged from the background. It is now a central concept within psychology and clinical practice—especially within the cognitive, ego, humanistic, social, transpersonal, and developmental schools of thought. In large part, interest and study have been revived as a consequence of breakthroughs offered by theories and technological advances in communications, information processing, cybernetics, biology, neurophysiology, chemistry, surgery, and, more generally, by a loosening of the boundaries that have separated study of human and mechanical behavior. In short, the energies and resources that produced the Electronic Age have also revealed models and analogues, hardware and technologies with applications to human behavior—for example, the telephone and human communication systems, the computer and the brain, and the hologram and visualization processes.

Although these analogues are hardly exact counterparts of human functioning, they have offered conceptual leads. General systems and open systems concepts have provided intellectual underpinnings for such concepts as transactions, interactions, feedback, and other concepts that can deal with the person-environment entity. New research orientations derived from anthropology and ethology are being developed to study interactional contexts (see, for example, Raush, 1979; Scheflen, 1977), patterning, and description of person-environment systems rather than searching for causal or correlational relationships.

Battista's theory of consciousness (1978, pp. 55–87) offers one useful approach to explore perception and cognition. This conceptual schema, rooted in general system and information theory, is holistic in that it treats mind and body as different levels of a unified hierarchical system. Consciousness is seen as information, with different forms of consciousness as different interlinked levels in the hierarchy. The levels of information, as in the stream of consciousness metaphor, are viewed as a gestalt or field of forces. At each level of information, the amount of consciousness would be a function of the amount of novel information conveyed. For example, old or redundant information at any level would be processed with less consciousness. The person is differentially alert (conscious) or habituated (unconscious), depending on familiarity, expectancy, and so forth. Additionally, any information may be subjective *and* objective since information relates to two hierarchical levels of reality and their interaction. That is, one uses the higher level, experienced subjectively, to impart meaning to the lower level (the source of data), which appears objective (p. 84).

In this formulation, the individual is inherently motivated to reduce uncertainty, which is the equivalent of information transmission. In other words, the person continually, actively seeks information and processes existing information so as to reduce environmental uncertainty. One does not merely respond to stimuli; one is involved in a relational process. Information, viewed as relational, results from the interaction of a receiver with a source, and information can be measured by the amount of uncertainty reduction that a given stimulus provides the receiver.

The hierarchical levels of information in Battista's theory are ordered such that each ascending level plays an evaluative role with respect to the prior level(s).

These levels distinguish among several concepts often used interchangeably in common language: sensation, perception, awareness, self-awareness, and self-realization. I shall summarize distinguishing aspects of the levels:

1. *Sensation:* all physical, sensory information about the environment.
2. *Perception:* information about the sensory level; the meaning of sensation evaluated in terms of some innate or learned frame of reference.
3. *Emotions:* information about perception; the meaning of a perception evaluated in light of innate and/or learned needs and by the context, which imparts meaning to arousal or affect.
4. *Awareness:* information about sensation, perception, and emotions; the meaning of these evaluated through *cognition* (a logical, sequential process using learned categories or constructs) *and/or* through *intuition* (a noncausal, holistic, nonrational process that complements and supplements cognitive thought).
5. *Self-awareness:* understanding the particular ways one processes subjective experience (cognitively and intuitively); the meaning of subjective experience evaluated by reflection on cognition and intuition.
6. *Unition* (synchrony): information about self-awareness; the awareness of being aware; self-realization.

We can consider now that information about the awareness of awareness (unition) includes understanding and evaluating one's subjective experience (self-awareness), which is comprised of cognitions and intuitions (awareness) that hinge upon the meaning of perceptions in light of needs and context (emotions), which emerge from imparting meaning, according to one's frame of reference (perception), to sensory information. Further, it is apparent that what I discussed earlier as *perspective* could be considered here as *perception* (second level). But probably, in terms of the self-control and "sensitivity" to one's own and others' perceptions that is demanded of the practitioner, it is best seen as a fifth-level process: *self-awareness.* We can see also that perception and cognition are related to levels two and four, respectively, and that cognitive processes are only one of two primary ways that information is processed at the level of awareness.

This schema is not posed as new dogma; it is merely one among many ways of thinking about the person in the person–environment situation. Its utility resides in orderliness and compatibility with other theories that deal with explanation of behavior and with intervention. For example, the lack of a sharp distinction between physical and conscious reality pictures the person as an integral part of the environment rather than separate from it. Such a view connects easily with other practice orientations that use systems perspectives (for example, Hartman, 1970; Hearn, 1969; Meyer, 1976), ecological perspectives (Germain, 1979; Germain and Gitterman, 1980), and with transactional (Spiegel, 1971) or interactional emphases (Goffman, 1961; 1963; Heider, 1958; Magnusson and Endler, 1977).

Moreover, the orientation to cognition is compatible with theories of cognitive growth (Bruner, 1964; Piaget, 1954), with affective and intellective experience (Zajonc, 1980), and with the hierarchical taxonomies of cognitive and affective learning domains (Bloom, 1956; Krawthwol and others, 1964). The coordinate relationship of intuitive and cognitive thinking is extensively detailed elsewhere (see Bakan, 1978; Ornstein, 1972; Watzlawick, 1978). Consciousness as a field of forces owes much to Lewinian field theory and to formulations of the early Gestalt psychologists (Wertheimer, Kohler, and Koffka). It also connects with the more recent formulations of communications and family systems theory derived from the Palo Alto Group, with social learning theory (Bandura, 1976), and with other cognitive theorists (for example, Beck, 1976; Ellis, 1962; Kelly, 1955; Lazarus, 1971; Meichenbaum, 1977). Finally, consciousness as information processing seems extremely congenial to many of the current descriptions of diverse approaches to clinical practice (for example, Foreyt and Rathjen, 1978; Lankton, 1980; Lantz, 1978; Nelsen, 1980; Maluccio, 1980; Watzlawick, 1978).

I have tried to identify some of the difficulties involved in examining awareness processes, and I have proposed Battista's information-processing scheme of consciousness as encompassing perception, a level of experience that precedes cognition. Cognition is considered as one means (along with intuition) of imparting meaning to sensation, perception, and emotion. And I have suggested linkages between such a view of consciousness (the reduction of uncertainty by means of information transmission and processing) and various other explanatory systems that clinicians use. I shall now briefly identify certain lines of theory and research that have enriched understanding of perception and cognition.

Issues in Perception

A voluminous literature exists about perception that is impossible to encompass here. Ittleson (1960, pp. 1–39) claims "the entire history of human thought is interwoven with the history of thinking about perception" and offers examples from philosophy, psychology, aesthetics, and science. He defines perception as "that part of the process of living by which each one of us from his own particular point of view creates for himself the world in which he has his life's experiences and through which he strives to gain his satisfactions" (p. 19). It seems important to distinguish perception from mere sensory experience. The classical belief in five sensory receptors is more accurately described as five basic perceptual systems that encompass ten or more sense mechanisms—for example, vestibular, visual, auditory, kinesthetic, tactual, pressure, pain, thermal, smell, and taste senses.

The perceptual systems actively extract and combine information in order to give meaning to sensations (Bartley, 1979). Several sensory receptors combine to form perceptions: smell, taste, tactual, thermal, and pain senses make up the savor perceptual system. Seeing is the combined result of using ears, body muscles, and skin as well as the eyes. The basic orienting system in the inner ear works along with the haptic system (of skin, muscles, and joints), the auditory, the savor, and the visual systems. Thus, perception is a complexity, a mix and match of various sensitive tissues. Far from passively receiving environmental stimuli, one's perception is an active process whereby the individual deals with tasks imposed by the nature of the environment.

Early Gestalt theories of perception, especially visual perception, were concerned with the processes of diffusion, differentiation, and integration—perceiving, organizing or integrating, and interpreting. Key principles of organization—proximity, similarity, common movement, good continuity, and closure—remain important ways of providing order and symmetry to experience.

The concepts of figure/ground and illusions have enduring importance. Cognitive theorists have claimed perception as a cognitive process (Bruner, 1957; Kelly, 1955; Neisser, 1967). That is, we do not perceive things as they are, but we use our brains to interpret them.

Perhaps the most astonishing current ideas about perception and information processing are reported by Pribram (1978, 1980), whose study of the brain, visualization, and information storage suggests that the hologram, a 3-D picture made with laser beams, rather than the camera, is the analogue appropriate for mental imaging. That is, holograms of patterns of waves are the kinds of images stored in the brain that are isomorphic with the world of forces described by quantum physics. According to Pribram, we see objects, not wave forms, only because our sense receptors are all lenslike systems. We create an object world because of the physiological construction of our sensory systems! Furthermore, Pribram (1980, p. 34) questions a favored Gestalt truism, that wholes have properties in addition to the sum of their parts. In the hologram, the whole is contained or enfolded in its parts. The parts have no boundaries; each part is representative of the whole. Thus, tiny total representations of images are stored as patterns throughout the brain. Ideas about perception approach startling proportions!

Perception and Clinical Practice

Since World War II, clinicians have benefited from the intense interest of practitioners, behavioral scientists, and diverse disciplines in the minutiae of interaction at the intrapersonal and interpersonal levels. This interest has been extensively described and translated into practice prescriptions by the communication theorists. The rich literature is too vast to summarize here (see, for example, Watzlawick, Beavin, and Jackson, 1967; Watzlawick, Weakland, and Fisch, 1974). In general, the theorists dealt more with verbal than nonverbal communication (at least until recently) and with communication more than perception.

Reusch and Kees (1956) and Reusch and Bateson (1968) described the function of the many nonverbal information systems as *analogic* in contrast to digital (verbal), as metacommunication that indicated how one should "take" the verbal message. As my summary (1980a, pp. AM5-28) of subsequent nonverbal communication research indicates, nonverbal communication may convey information, express emotions, regulate social interaction, and convey dominant–submissive relationships. Since the major research interests was in expression of information and emotion, it followed that the separate nonverbal channels were studied as partitioned by the known sensory systems (visual, auditory, and so forth), and an enormous array of studies of kinesics, proxemics, facial expressions, and so forth appeared.

Harrison (1974) has attempted a synthesis and reordering of all the nonverbal material into a useful schema, returning to the digital–analogic view as main language codes. The four nonverbal (analogic) language codes are grouped according to how the observable events are produced. The two basic codes are *performance* (including all actions of the person's body) and *artifactual* (including objects, clothing, food, and all things that can be known through the senses). Two "derived" codes are identified as *spatiotemporal* (the context) and *media-*

tory (where persons invent, arrange, or otherwise construct within a medium, such as films or graphs). The derived codes use and interact with the basic codes.

Clinicians currently are knowledgeable and skilled in using all four codes and are attuned especially to decoding information from the client in the performance, artifactual, and spatiotemporal realms. Within the past decade, due especially to the impact of the human potential movement and experiential, or whole-person, teaching–learning approaches, practitioners also encode their communications and structure experiences via the various "nonverbals," which can be seen as using the mediatory code or as *constructed learning experiences* (Middleman, 1980b).

I have linked nonverbal communication to perception since understanding at this level has been typically the major way the clinician decoded the full meaning of others' messages. Naturally, accuracy depended largely on judgment and inference mediated by the clinician's implicit personality theory-in-use. The attention in helping was primarily on the ways the client expressed herself, with the nonverbal seen as ancillary to the main (verbal) message. I have consisently argued for a coordinate, equal valuation of each language code (1968), as in the following comments where I discuss group activities: "There is little value in quibbling over the relative importance of talking and doing as there is merit to the chicken/egg argument. As McLuhan suggests, one need not think that chickens created eggs but can view chickens as the eggs' ingenious way of producing more eggs. In a similar vein, one can view card games or surgical operation teams or dinner parties as social arrangements with known rules, roles, and processes where what is organized is not the activities but turns at talking. . . . It is just as valid to view group experience as activities which form the natural home of speech and offer opportunities for talking every now and then" (Middleman, 1980c, p. 7).

Within the past few years, diverse clinical approaches have emphasized nonverbal interaction with individuals, families, and groups where the clinician actively engages in the situation, not merely decodes the others' nonverbal cues. Use of exercises, guided fantasy, and other experiential techniques, usually launched by the clinician, plunge the helping person directly into diverse expressive modalities that aim to expand sensory awareness, perception, and communication skills. Neuro Linguistic Programming (Bandler and Grinder, 1975; 1976; Lankton, 1980) and Gestalt therapy are noteworthy examples of such emphases.

The NLP practitioner is specially trained to "read" minute nonverbal changes (especially eye movements), to respond within the other's preferred mode of expressiveness, and to harmonize with the other's nonverbal language. The therapist aspires to total sensory self-knowledge and openness by understanding of his own "primary representational systems"—the sensory modes in which one is most sensitive—so as to help the other gain comparable understanding and expansion of representational systems. According to Polster and Polster (1976, p. 269), the Gestalt therapist considers sensory processes "contact functions," the means for making and maintaining contact with others and self and for improving one's clarity, flexibility, directness, and so forth. In both cases, we find a new emphasis on sensation and perception. At a more general level, accurate interpersonal perceptual skills would seem to include such things as identifying emotions, identifying hidden meaning, listening with understanding, and becoming aware of one's own biases and inferences determined by one's beliefs, attitudes, values, motives, errors of inadequate information, distortions, and implicit theoretical preference.

Issues in Cognition

Although information processing is a commonly accepted way of thinking about brain functioning, thinking, and learning, just how the brain processes information remains almost a complete mystery (see, for example, Cooper, 1980). Many attempts have been made to classify types of cognition. For example, Bloom (1956) identified a "cognitive domain" comprised of knowledge, comprehension, application, analysis, synthesis, and evaluation. Gagné (1965) described intellectual or symbol-using skills that involve such processes as distinguishing, combining, tabulating, classifying, analyzing, and quantifying. Furthermore, in any process, one would need concepts, discriminations among concepts, rules to deal with them, and what Bruner termed "cognitive strategies," or the processes needed to find and solve novel problems (remembering, setting priorities, and so forth).

Beyond the complexities involved in cognition itself, the relationship of cognitive with affective processes and with actions is in dispute. Cognitive theorists generally believe cognition precedes emotions: first know, then evaluate. Many therapies have aimed to approach the emotions through cognitions. Zajonc's research (1980) separates this order and further suggests that preferences need no inferences, a position comparable to Lewin's seventh principle of reeducation: changes in sentiments do not necessarily follow changes in cognitive structures (Lewin and Grabbe, 1945).

In the realm of action, Lewin's *life space* concept (1936) introduced a notion of enduring value. The life space is more than the actual physical environment. It is the environment the individual *thinks* is there and the forces that influence his or her goal-seeking actions. Another early theorist concerned with the relationship of cognition to action was Tolman (1932), whose *cognitive map* concept still offers theoretical and practical utility. Tolman placed the individual between the associations of stimuli and responses. The cognitive map, an *internal* representation of routes to goals, brought purposefulness, meanings, and expectations into the learning picture. Yet, the exact relationship between persons' judgments and behavior still remains unclear. Judgments affect behavior, but how this happens is not known. At the physical level, understanding and experience knowledge can be separated in that understanding is a brain function while experiencing involves nerve endings also; beyond this, the interaction remains obscure.

Piaget's study of cognitive development (1954; Piaget and Inhelder, 1969) offers guidance for considering the complexities of cognitive thought. According to Piaget, children's mental structures differ from adults'. Children interact with their environment and construct their understanding of the world out of a quest for order, a desire to make sense of the world and eliminate contradictions. The person continually takes in information (assimilation) that is slightly different from what one knows (ignoring what is too incongruent) and restructures the new knowledge so as to integrate the old with the new (accommodation). The quest for new, slightly more complex information is inherent and impels individuals to progress through four mental stages in a fixed sequence, which may take more or less time according to the individual's choices and decisions about what is appropriate for his or her development.

Intellectual development, according to Piaget, occurs by means of two basic functional imperatives needed for survival—adaptation (the need to survive in the environment) and organization (the need to have well-organized, orderly mental systems). It is influenced further by four interrelated factors—maturation, experience with handling and thinking about objects, social interaction with others, and equilibration, a balancing process whereby the other three factors are integrated. Piaget's four stages—sensorimotor (0–2 years), intuitive thought (4–7 years), concrete operations (7–11 years), and formal operations (11-adult)—are based on how the child represents the world and how the child can act upon the representation.

Piaget's cognitive theory grew from his observations and problem-solving experiments with children. His interest was in their differing explanations of events, which systematically change with age. Earliest preoccupation is with sensorimotor coordinations, followed by abilities to represent objects rather than only actions and sensations, and finally the development of symbolic problem solving and hypothetical and abstract thinking. Piaget was interested especially in processes whereby children grow to see the world not as a set of static perceptual images but as an entity they could transform through mental or concrete activity.

Bruner (1964) built on Piaget's work but developed different categories of representations—the enactive (through actions), the iconic (through images), and the symbolic (through language). He saw these ways of representing the world as technical advances in the use of the mind. Intellectual growth was framed in terms of two forms of competence: (1) *representation,* acquiring ways of representing recurrent regularities in the environment (through action, imagery, and language) and (2) integration, *transcending* the momentary by developing ways to link past to present to future. Bruner saw the key leap in cognitive processing as being able to go beyond the present moment, "beyond the information given." This occurs at about age five to seven, partly through language development.

I have introduced a few of the many theorists who are concerned with the structure and processes of cognition merely as suggestive of a huge realm of inquiry that is possibly less familiar to the clinician than some of the personality theorists. Perhaps the most important contribution of cognitive theories to clinical practice is the linkage, stimulation, and congeniality with other influential lines of thinking. Linkages of special importance would include (1) the stage and phase theories that deal with other realms of development (for example, ego, moral judgment) and with extending developmental thinking through the total life cycle (for example, Erikson, Kohlberg, Loevenger, Levinson); (2) the learning theories and progressive educational approaches, assessment, and evaluation; and (3) the behaviorists, many of whom have revised behavioral theories to include a central mediating role for the individual's cognitions (for example, Bandura, 1969; Lazarus, 1971).

Cognition and Clinical Practice

Cognitive orientations share much with social work's traditional value and knowledge orientations. Examples include self-determination (a view of the client as centrally responsible for his own actions), choice and problem solving with consideration of alternatives, the adaptive quality of cognitive processes, the importance of self-concept and effectiveness in social and occupational realms, and learning through social interaction. The cognitive emphasis on the client as learner is of special importance. It is a concept that also links the client with the clinician as colearners in pursuit of new learning and extension of one's powers.

Cognitively oriented practitioners have assumed three distinguishable roles—facilitator, diagnostician–educator, and ecologist. The facilitator designation emerged mainly from the human potential movement and humanistic psychologies; the diagnostician–educator is linked to the behaviorist tradition; and the ecologist orientation describes a role primarily evolved by social work theorists who focused on both persons and environments. All three are teaching orientations. However, the facilitator usually occupies a less central and controlling place within the helping process than the diagnostician–educator, whose procedures and interventions are more exact and prescriptive, or than the ecologist, whose analytic and planning activities shape and focus the ensuing interventions. All three roles share a long-cherished educational tradition of teacher as arranger of the environment for learning and as specialist in devising the means through which individuals may develop inherent interests and capacities.

Within the facilitator orientation, learning focuses on self–other awareness, coping skills, problem-solving skills, assertiveness, dealing with stress, and, in general, various life transitions and common developmental problems (for example, retirement, divorce, loneliness). Generally, these learning groups are time-limited "structured groups" (see Middleman, 1981) in which the major dynamics for change include the view of the participant as normal (regardless of psychological label) and the use of various teaching–learning approaches derived from educational and cognitive-behavioral perspectives.

Cognitive therapies (the diagnostician–educator orientation) generally emphasize person–environment reciprocal interaction, self-directed modes of behavior change, and notions of self-efficacy (see Wilson, 1978). A common focus is on cognitive processes that may cause adaptive and maladaptive behavior (such as selective attention or symbolic coding). To change problem behavior, the therapist assesses maladaptive cognitive processes and arranges learning experiences (precise procedures) that will alter cognitions and the behavioral–affective patterns they are believed to be correlated with. Thus, the selection of the appropriate procedures is a technical matter of considerable importance. Many discrete procedures have been devised. The procedure, as distinct from a helping "process," is performance based and preferably measurable.

Meichenbaum (1977) developed an approach based on self-instruction that has been influential. Emphasized here are self-monitoring, self-instruction, and identification of thoughts, wishes, and feelings as well as practice and rehearsal, graded performances, and problem solving. Often the procedures are conceptualized as tasks, first enacted with the therapist as monitor and then as homework with self-monitored practice between sessions. Other procedures in current use are cognitive rehearsal (self-talk), distancing (regarding a given thought objectively), decentering (separating self from event or its impact), redefining (recasting of thoughts, self-assessment, wishes, and so forth), and imagining different alternatives or situations.

Many different approaches that use cognitions to approach emotions and behavior enjoy popularity today. Essentially, they emphasize reappraisal and change of maladaptive coping strategies into adaptive ones. Clients are taught the role of cognition in producing the problem, how to monitor maladaptive self-talk, how to recognize signs of difficulty, and how to handle situations differently. The therapist effects changes through the use of modeling and rehearsal, focusing attention on certain particulars, practice, and feedback about performance (knowledge of results). Throughout, the therapist actively teaches, tells, shows, assesses, and offers new ideas and rules for behaving.

Perhaps the first influential cognitive therapist was Ellis (1962), whose emphasis is on verbal persuasion, rational argumentation, and logical reasoning. According to Ellis, irrational interpretations of reality are the fundamental cause of emotional disorders. The therapy consists of helping clients to recognize self-defeating irrational ideas and to replace these with more constructive thoughts. A related approach developed by Beck (1976) also focuses on the acquisition of rational, adaptive thought patterns and on the stylistic qualities of cognitions and distortions (for example, arbitrary inferences, exaggeration of the meaning of an event, overgeneralization).

Various other therapies outside the behaviorist tradition focus on the mental powers, imaging, and reconstructing thoughts to affect physical and emotional processes (for example, Assagioli, 1971; Maltz, 1966) and even to alter the course of physical disease (Scarf, 1980).

The assumption that cognition controls emotions and actions (which psychoanalytic and ego psychology share) is not clearly supported by empirical research. Nor has Bandler and Grinder's typology of eye movements, which is the core of Neuro Linguistic Programming enthusiastically embraced by many clinicians, any support in the extensive CLEM (conjugate lateral eye movements) research that engages scores of neurophysiologists and psychologists today (see Bakan, 1978, pp. 159–184). This is not meant to cast doubt on clinical evidence that the approaches work but merely to acknowledge the gap that often separates clinical and research findings. Clearly, the complex interrelationship among the various levels of consciousness remains obscure; yet, the clinician must practice using the best knowledge and clinical experience one has.

Clinial social workers use cognitive theories of various psychologies, but they also draw from the profession's own rich, unique tradition of focus on the person–environment situation, not just the person. My designation of the role "ecologist" owes much to the clarity and accessibility of an ecological perspective highlighted for social work by Germain (1979).

Despite common usage that relates ecology to environment, the concept of ecology refers equally to individuals, society, and environments. It has to do with achieving balance among the interplay of diverse elements. As used by Aristotle, ecology referred to the stability of the household in relation to the larger society. It deals with the rate, scale, and structure of change, with complementarities and oppositional forces that govern error, excess, and distortion.

The social worker as ecologist aims to correct imbalances, to find out what is not happening, and to identify and fill gaps in the person–environment situation. A characteristic of social work clinical practice identified by Hartman (1980, pp. 36–38) is the "extensive unit of attention" that demands assessment of an extensive universe of data. The clinician-ecologist is thus concerned with selection and distribution of roles, power, resources, tasks, and problem-solving activities. The complex tasks of assessment, planning, setting priorities, and negotiating with clients and others about the matters deserving attention draw heavily from cognitions of self and other. A central, general focus of much social work practice is problem solving, which is primarily cognitive.

Other examples of cognitively oriented practice possibly subsumed within a clinician-ecologist orientation may be identified. Here I would include Reid and Epstein's (1972) emphasis on tasks, analysis of obstacles, modeling, rehearsal, guided practice, and conceptualization of accomplishments; the use of ecomaps and genograms to help clients develop cognitive maps of their position in space and time (Hartman, 1978); and the interest of many in matters of competence and mastery.

Beyond Cognition

During the past decade, two lines of research activity that seem to have enormous potential for increased understanding of the workings of the brain have come to the attention of clinicians—brain hemisphere specialization and cognitive styles. I shall briefly suggest how these lines of enquiry move us "beyond cognition." The research findings on the specialized separate workings of left and right hemispheres of the brain lend credibility to what has always been known to philosophy, the arts, and people helpers: there are two important ways of knowing, not one! The intuitive now has gained equal value to the rational and logical eyes of the scientist. At the same time, research findings from extensive studies of cognitive styles begin to suggest huge variability in the ways different individuals have learned to prefer to process information—different and yet all equally valid. Both of these areas of new knowledge will probably have profound effects on what I have described herein as *perspective* and, within the consciousness typology, as *awareness.*

The Right and Left Hemispheres. Behavioral scientists never totally ignored the subjective, intuitive, holistic realm of experience and knowing. Passing acknowledgment of Polyani's (1967) *tacit knowledge*—of knowing more than one can tell—and of Bruner's "Essays for the Left Hand" (1965) are examples of recognition that rational, cognitive mental processes did not represent the only way the mind works. But, impressive scientific evidence of the specialized dual brain functions—the verbal, linear, analytical thinking of the left hemisphere and the holistic, nonlogical, acoustic or qualitative thinking of the right hemisphere—awaited the recent findings of neurosurgeons with split-brain operations and with stroke victims.

The duality of consciousness, the two types of awareness, is now amply reported with considerable research support (see Bakan, 1978; Ornstein, 1972; Watzlawick, 1978). In fact, Watzlawick (1978) details a therapeutic approach exclusively aimed to tap right brain thinking by means of (1) using right hemisphere language patterns (such as the language of dreams, fairy tales, myths, hypnosis, or puns), (2) blocking the left hemisphere so as to permit the right to dominate (through confusion techniques, paradoxes), and (3) certain specific behavior prescriptions (for example, reframing or offering the illusion of alternatives). Many clinicians following the leads offered in hypnosis and suggestion by Milton Erickson (1976) are responding to the new knowledge offered by understanding the right hemisphere's role in processing information.

The right hemisphere is good at perceiving and expressing novel and complex visual, spatial, and musical patterns—tasks requiring one to keep in mind an overall pattern of relationships, not just the separate parts. It grasps the relations between parts directly, not by any sequence of deductions. It sees patterns, bridges gaps, and can detect patterns even if pieces are missing, as with instances of incomplete information—the form of most problems to be solved. In short, the left hemisphere specializes in analysis, and the right hemisphere effects synthesis. Both hemispheres need to be smoothly integrated—must cooperate rather than interfere with each other—for full awareness.

For example, in problem-solving and decision-making processes, it would appear that part of the thinking processes involved are left brain functions (such as defining, identifying, screening, listing alternatives, evaluating). But, matters of assessment and design of action (and, for the clinician, design of intervention) are judgments or compositions of the right brain, much as are the leaps and insights that are "felt" but not easily described in words.

Various techniques have been described (often in the creativity, management, or training literature) to tap right hemisphere thinking (see, for example, Adams, 1974; de Bono, 1972). I have attempted to conceptualize the expression of right hemisphere thinking within social agencies as dependent on a person–environment transaction. That is, the major elements are creative individuals and organizations that encourage creativity (Middleman and Ifill, 1980). At the person level, such qualities as conceptual fluency, originality, visualizing things as they could be rather than as they are, and comfort in holding one's idea even in the face of opposition would seem important. Organizations that enhance creativity would have such features as valuing creative persons, providing a secure and stable work setting rather than a crisis orientation, and decentralized decision making. An increased appreciation of right hemisphere functions may help to increase the number of ways clinicians understand and approach clients and to a more general grasp of the "art" aspect of clinical practice itself.

Cognitive Style. Cognitive style refers to stable attitudes, preferences, or habitual strategies that determine a person's typical modes of perceiving, remembering, thinking, and problem solving. They are process dimensions that reveal differences in the very form of cognitions as distinct from the content of cognitions or the skill level displayed in cognitive performances. In other words, styles reflect *how* one processes information, not *what* is processed nor *how well.* Aptitudes refer to what the person is able to do; abilities or skills refer to levels of actual accomplishment; and style refers to the way one likes to do something. Whereas abilities may vary from zero to a great deal of any particular content, styles are not measured quantitatively. Any stylistic dimension has adaptive value under certain circumstances, depending on the nature of the situation and the requirements of the task at hand.

Cognitive styles are pervasive dimensions of behavior. Beyond perceptual and cognitive distinctions, they affect the realm of social interactions as well. Messick and others (1976) provide an excellent summary of current study in the area: nineteen different dimensions have been discovered and studied with varying degrees of thoroughness. As examples, we can consider field independent versus field dependent (analytical, impersonal versus global, social orientations), convergent versus divergent thinking, risk taking versus cautiousness, and constricted versus flexible. Jung's personality types may also be considered cognitive stylistic dimensions. His interest was in differences in characteristic ways of seeking information (via the senses or via the imagination) and of reaching decisions (via logical, analytical reasoning or via personalistic value judgments). Another approach to individual variability of information processing styles was devised by Hill, whose elaborate category system demands computer-assisted analysis. Hill (1976) proposed that persons seek meaning from the environment via combinations within four major variables—structural (that is, symbols and their meanings), plus cultural determinants, plus different modalities of inference, plus memory concerns.

The major promises of the cognitive style orientations are the understanding of the infinite variability of individuals and the nonjudgmental evaluation of such differences. One style is not better than another but is only more suitable for certain circumstances. I have developed a Functioning Style Task, which I have used with various adult populations for several years. My category system draws from Sigel's (1967) work on conceptualizing styles and explores three patterns of perception—descriptive, relational, and inferential-categorical. From my experience with students and social workers in various settings, I noticed stylistic conflict and miscommunication among persons with ostensibly similar backgrounds and educations. For example, some consistently attended to detail and routine easily; others could not seem to sort out clutter. Some extracted essences and key components of situations and related these to other comparable situations; others responded to each given event as a discrete and separate happening.

The three dimensions differentiate individuals along the following lines—connections made according to closeness in time, space, or use (relational), according to specific common qualities (descriptive), and according to larger categorical systems (inferential). I shall illustrate these dimensions with a simple example of arranging spices in one's kitchen. Person A arranges them alphabetically (allspice to whole pepper); this approach is *descriptive*. Person B prefers those used most frequently in front (salt, pepper) and those least used behind (tarragon, cayenne); this approach is *relational*. Person C makes arrangements related to different cooking requirements (Italian seasonings, Indian seasonings); this approach is *inferential-categorical*. Although I cannot offer statistical evidence, I have found all three stylistic differences in every task administration. These results regularly come as a remarkable surprise when discussed with the groups, even groups who know each other well. These categories provide an experience-based opportunity to reflect on the variability of individuals.

Conclusion

Like the zoology student who studied the fish, I have become involved with more lines of enquiry than I imagined at the outset. My review may seem more discursive than synthesizing. I have touched the tip of the iceberg or, better, the top of the volcano, and find a ferment of exciting investigation and intervention approaches, with the unsettling realization that much more will erupt momentarily!

Moreover, my awareness is heightened, perhaps disappointingly, by the nagging realization of the limits of my own particular perspective—how inevitably I shall have slanted this review and ignored certain valued thinking of the reader. I have been more descriptive than I should like; no convincing summarizing practice principles have emerged that I can offer with conviction. Nor will this conclusion synthesize the rich realms that so many have explored, that remain still nebulous, and that are taken for granted so often in everyday affairs. My conclusions are more matters of personal emphasis than synthesis. They represent ideas I wish to think about further.

The appeal of consciousness and information processing, despite limited knowledge of their workings at the human level, is considerable. The openness of psychophysically oriented notions about the individual in the environment seems fruitful as compared to various personality (even personality systems) theories, for example. I find the boundaries of person–environment more amorphous, and I find the focus on the present transactional moment as the focus for attention (with past events and history less immediately central) a useful way to think about individuals constructing their particular conscious awarenesses.

Consciousness seems to be a constructive process, with perception depending on the match of one's model of the world with sensory experience. We notice only a tiny fraction of all that goes on around us. We habitually respond to the expected and register mainly the mismatches between what we "know" and what we experience. And, we are programmed (for survival) to jump to conclusions. What is most limited is our attention. Attention governs awareness—awareness of what matters in the living moment as well as how much one is able to remember and bring to bear in the moment. What we manage to attend to remains a matter of individual choice and largely determines the quality of our experience. Therefore, my experience is mine and can never be yours exactly. Moreover, in addition to this individuality in the manner of perception, there are differences in how we deal with or process information. These complexities of perception and cognition deserve much further exploration.

For the clinician, I would emphasize the concept of attention as a most powerful instrument at one's disposal for change (in self and in other). Too bad that this seems like such an obvious thing! Its workings and variability are far from simple minded. I would extend attention in terms of clinical practice to include "attentions," which in common terms connotes ways of showing care and concern for another. There can never be too many attentions of consequence.

I find it curious that empathy is such a well-known concept to clinicians—a concept that connotes intuitive perception of the emotional state of one person by another—and yet, we seem to have no comparable concept that concerns connecting with the thinking processes of the other. Perhaps rapport? But that is less commonly used by social workers and still suggests more feeling than thinking. Our language reveals the valued emphasis of tradition, an emphasis on the emotional life of the individual rather than on the full range of awarenesses with which we must connect.

References

Adams, J. L. *Conceptual Blockbusting.* San Francisco: Freeman, 1974.

Albee, G. W. "The Relation of Conceptual Models of Disturbed Behavior to Institutional and Manpower Requirements." In F. N. Arnoff, E. A. Rubenstein, and J. C. Speisman (Eds.), *Manpower in Mental Health.* Chicago: Aldine, 1969.

Assagioli, R. *Psychosynthesis.* New York: Viking Press, 1971.

Bakan, P. "Two Streams of Consciousness: A Typological Approach." In K. S. Pope and J. L. Singer (Eds.), *The Stream of Consciousness.* New York: Plenum, 1978.

Bandler, R., and Grinder, J. *The Structure of Magic I.* Palo Alto: Science and Behavior Books, 1975.

Bandler, R., and Grinder, J. *The Structure of Magic II.* Palo Alto: Science and Behavior Books, 1976.

Bandura, A. *Principles of Behavior Modification.* New York: Holt, Rinehart and Winston, 1969.

Bandura, A. "Social Learning Perspective on Behavior Change." In A. Burton (Ed.), *What Makes Behavior Change Possible?* New York: Brunner/Mazel, 1976.

Bartley, D. H. "What Is Perception?" In D. Goleman and R. J. Davidson (Eds.), *Consciousness: The Brain, States of Awareness, and Alternate Realities.* New York: Irvington, 1979.

Battista, J. R. "The Science of Consciousness." In K. S. Pope and J. L. Singer (Eds.), *The Stream of Consciousness.* New York: Plenum, 1978.

Beck, A. T. *Cognitive Therapy and Emotional Disorders.* New York: International Universities Press, 1976.

Bloom, B. S. (Ed.). *Taxonomy of Educational Objectives.* Vol. 1: *Cognitive Domain.* New York: McKay, 1956.

Bruner, J. S. "On Perceptual Readiness." *Psychological Review,* 1957, *64,* 123–152.

Bruner, J. S. "The Course of Cognitive Growth." *American Psychologist,* 1964, *19,* 1–15.

Bruner, J. S. *On Knowing: Essays for the Left Hand.* New York: Atheneum, 1965.

Bruner, J. S. "The Skill of Relevance, or the Relevance of Skills." *Saturday Review,* 1970, *53,* 66–68, 78, 79.

Bruner, J. S., Goodnow, J. J., and Austin, G. A. *A Study of Thinking.* New York: Wiley, 1956.

Cooper, L. N. "Source and Limits of Human Intellect." *Daedalus,* 1980, *109* (2), 1–17.

de Bono, E. *Po: A Device for Successful Thinking.* New York: Simon & Schuster, 1972.

Ellis, A. *Reason and Emotion in Psychotherapy.* New York: Lyle Stuart, 1962.

Erickson, M. H., Rossi, E. L., and Rossi, S. I. *Hypnotic Realities. The Induction of Clinical Hypnosis and Forms of Indirect Suggestion.* New York: Irvington, 1976.

Foreyt, J. P., and Rathjen, D. P. *Cognitive Behavior Therapy.* New York: Plenum, 1978.

Gagné, R. M. *The Conditions of Learning.* New York: Holt, Rinehart and Winston, 1965.

Germain, C. B. (Ed.). *Social Work Practice: People and Environments.* New York: Columbia University Press, 1979.

Germain, C. B., and Gitterman, A. *The Life Model of Social Work Practice.* New York: Columbia University Press, 1980.

Goffman, E. *Encounters.* Indianapolis: Bobbs-Merrill, 1961.

Goffman, E. *Behavior in Public Places.* New York: Free Press, 1963.

Goldberg, G., and Middleman, R. R. "Visual Teaching: Translating Abstract Concepts into Visual Teaching Models." Paper presented at annual program meeting of the Council on Social Work Education, 1975.

Goldberg, G., and Middleman, R. R. "It Might Be a Boa Constrictor Digesting an Elephant: Vision Stretching in Social Work Education." Paper presented at annual program meeting of the Council on Social Work Education, 1973. *Contemporary Social Work Education,* 1980, *3* (3), 213–225.

Goleman, D., and Davidson, R. J. (Eds.). *Consciousness: The Brain, States of Awareness, and Alternate Realities.* New York: Irvington, 1979.

Gregg, G., and others. "The Caravan Rolls On: Forty Years of Social Problem Research." *Knowledge Creation, Diffusion, Utilization,* 1979, *1* (4), 31–61.

Hall, E. "Giving Away Psychology in the '80s." *Psychology Today,* 1980, *13* (8), 38–50, 97–98.

Harrison, R. P. *Beyond Words.* Englewood Cliffs, N.J.: Prentice-Hall, 1974.

Hartman, A. "To Think About the Unthinkable." *Social Casework,* 1970, *51* (8), 467–476.

Hartman, A. "Diagrammatic Assessment of Family Relationships." *Social Casework,* 1978, *59* (8), 465–476.

Hartman, A. "Competencies in Clinical Social Work." In P. L. Ewalt (Ed.), *Toward a Definition of Clinical Social Work.* Washington, D.C.: National Association of Social Workers, 1980.

Hearn, G. (Ed.). *The General Systems Approach: Contributions Toward an Holistic Conception of Social Work.* New York: Council on Social Work Education, 1969.

Heider, F. *The Psychology of Interpersonal Relations.* New York: Wiley, 1958.

Herrigel, E. *Zen in the Art of Archery.* London: Routledge & Kegan Paul, 1953.

Highet, G. *The Art of Teaching.* New York: Vintage, 1950.

Hill, J. E. *The Educational Sciences.* Bloomfield, Mich.: Oakland Community College, 1976.

Holton, G. "On Being Caught Between Dionysians and Apollonians." *Daedalus,* 1974, *103* (3), 65–81.

Ittelson, W. H. *Visual Space Perception.* New York: Springer, 1960.

James, W. *The Principles of Psychology.* New York: Dover, 1950. (Originally published 1890.)

Kelly, G. *The Psychology of Personal Constructs.* New York: Norton, 1955.

Krathwohl, D. R., and others (Eds.). *Taxonomy of Educational Objectives: Affective Domain.* New York: McKay, 1964.

Lankton, S. *Practical Magic.* Cupertino, Calif.: Meta, 1980.

Lantz, J. E. "Cognitive Theory and Social Casework." *Social Work,* 1978, *23* (5), 361–366.

Lazarus, A. A. *Behavior Therapy and Beyond.* New York: McGraw-Hill, 1971.

Lee, P., and others. *Symposium on Consciousness.* New York: Penguin Books, 1976.

Lewin, D., and Grabbe, P. "Conduct, Knowledge and Acceptance of New Values." *The Journal of Social Issues,* 1945, *1* (3), 56–64.

Lewin, K. *Principles of Topological Psychology.* (F. and G. Heider, Trans.) New York: McGraw-Hill, 1936.

Loevinger, J., Wessler, R., and Redmore, C. *Measuring Ego Development.* San Francisco: Jossey-Bass, 1970.

Magnusson, D., and Endler, N. A. (Eds.). *Personality at the Crossroads: Current Issues in Interactional Psychology.* Hillsdale, N.J.: Erlbaum, 1977.

Maltz, M. *Psycho-Cybernetics.* New York: Pocket Books, 1966.

Maluccio, A. (Ed.). *Building Competence in Clients.* New York: Free Press, 1980.

Maslow, A. H. *The Psychology of Science.* New York: Harper & Row, 1966.

Meichenbaum, D. *Cognitive Behavior Modification.* New York: Plenum, 1977.

Messick, S. A., and others. *Individuality in Learning: Implications of Cognitive Styles and Creativity for Human Development.* San Francisco: Jossey-Bass, 1976.

Meyer, C. *Social Work Practice: The Changing Landscape.* (2nd ed.) New York: Free Press, 1976.

Middleman, R. R. *The Non-verbal Method in Working with Groups.* (Rev. ed.) Hebron, Conn.: Practitioners Press, 1980a.

Middleman, R. R. "The Use of Program: Review and Update." *Social Work with Groups,* 1980b, *3* (3), 5–23.

Middleman, R. R. "The Pursuit of Competence Through Involvement in Structured Groups." In A. Maluccio (Ed.), *Building Competence in Clients.* New York: Free Press, 1981.

Middleman, R. R., and Goldberg, G. "The Interactional Way of Presenting Generic Social Work Concepts." *Journal of Education for Social Work,* 1972, *8* (2), 48–57.

Middleman, R. R., and Ifill, D. *Creativity and Creategenic Organizations.* Louisville: University of Louisville, Kent School of Social Work, 1980.

Mitroff, I. I., and Kilmann, R. H. *Methodological Approaches to Social Science.* San Francisco: Jossey-Bass, 1978.

Neisser, U. *Cognitive Psychology.* New York: Appleton-Century-Crofts, 1967.

Nelsen, J. C. *Communication Theory and Social Work Practice.* Chicago: University of Chicago Press, 1980.

Ornstein, R. E. *The Psychology of Consciousness.* San Francisco: Freeman, 1972.

Phillips, J. L. *The Origins of Intellect: Piaget's Theory.* San Francisco: Freeman, 1969.

Piaget, J. *The Construction of Reality in the Child.* New York: Basic Books, 1954.

Piaget, J., and Inhelder, B. *The Psychology of the Child.* New York: Basic Books, 1969.

Polster, E., and Polster, M. "Therapy Without Resistance: Gestalt Therapy." In A. Burton (Ed.), *What Makes Behavior Change Possible?* New York: Brunner/Mazel, 1976.

Polyani, M. *The Tacit Dimension.* Garden City, N.Y.: Anchor Books, 1967.

Pope, K. S., and Singer, B. L. (Eds.). *The Stream of Consciousness: Scientific Investigations into the Flow of Human Experience.* New York: Plenum, 1978.

Pribram, K. H. "Consciousness and Neurophysiology." American Physiological Society Symposium on Physiological Basis of Mental Functions, July 1978. *Federation Proceedings,* 1978, *37* (9), 2271-2274.

Pribram, K. H. "The Role of Analogy in Transcending Limits in the Brain Sciences." *Daedalus,* 1980, *109* (2), 19-38.

Raush, H. L. "Epistemology, Metaphysics, and Person-Situation Methodology." In *New Directions for Methodology of Behavioral Science.* No. 2. San Francisco: Jossey-Bass, 1979.

Reid, W. J., and Epstein, L. *Task-Centered Casework.* New York: Columbia University Press, 1972.

Reynolds, B. C. *Learning and Teaching in the Practice of Social Work.* New York: Russell and Russell, 1970. (Originally published 1942.)

Richmond, M. E. *What Is Social Case Work? An Introductory Description.* New York: Russell Sage Foundation, 1922.

Robinson, V. P. *Supervision in Social Case Work.* Chapel Hill, N.C.: University of North Carolina, 1936.

Rosenthal, R., and Jacobson, L. *Pygmalion in the Classroom.* New York: Holt, Rinehart and Winston, 1968.

Roszak, T. *Where the Wasteland Ends: Politics and Transcendance in Postindustrial Society.* New York: Doubleday, 1973.

Ruesch, J., and Bateson, G. *Communication: The Social Matrix of Psychiatry.* (2nd ed.) New York: Norton, 1968.

Ruesch, J., and Kees, W. *Nonverbal Communication.* Berkeley: University of California Press, 1956.

Scarf, M. "Images That Heal." *Psychology Today,* 1980, *14* (4), 33-46.

Scheflen, A. E. "Classical Biases and the Structural Approach to Research." *ETC,* 1977, 290-300.

Sigel, I. E. *Sigel Conceptualizing Styles Test.* (Rev. ed.) Princeton: Educational Testing Service, 1967.

Spiegel, J. In J. Papajohn (Ed.), *Transactions.* New York: Science House, 1971.

Tolman, E. C. *Purposive Behavior in Animals and Men.* New York: Appleton-Century-Crofts, 1932.

Watzlawick, P. *The Language of Change.* New York: Basic Books, 1978.

Watzlawick, P., Beavin, J., and Jackson, D. *Pragmatics of Human Communication.* New York: Norton, 1967.

Watzlawick, P., Weakland, J. H., and Fisch, R. *Change.* New York: Norton, 1974.

Wilson, G. T. "Cognitive Behavior Therapy: Paradigm Shift or Passing Phase?" In J. P. Foreyt and D. P. Rathjen (Eds.), *Cognitive Behavior Therapy.* New York: Plenum, 1978.

Zajonc, R. B. "Feeling and Thinking." *American Psychologist,* 1980, *35* (2), 151-175.

Zukav, G. *The Dancing Wu Li Masters.* New York: Morrow, 1979.

11

Insight Development

Jerome Cohen

The use of insight as an instrument of change in clinical social work has been affected by different meanings of the concept itself and by ideological positions regarding treatment. A historical and developmental perspective of social casework reveals how the concepts of relationship and transference were illuminated first by psychoanalytic theory and later by social and behavioral science perspectives. These, in turn, affected the manner in which social casework practice, the direct antecedent of clinical social work practice, was formulated by the leading social work educators and practitioners of each decade since Mary Richmond's identification of the casework process in *Social Diagnosis* (1917). In different situations, varying amounts of attention may be paid to developing insight. In each set of circumstances, the clinician must not only evaluate the client's potential to know and understand himself or herself but must also assess the situation fully to determine how much and what type of insight is appropriate in the context of the services being offered. In addition, the particular cognitive and emotional areas to which the insight is directed and determined to be of value may vary in different approaches to treatment. But the goal of intervention always should remain the same—to enhance understanding. The alternative would foster dependency upon professionals for the solution of each problem that emerges. In that case, the magical or technical wizardry of the treatment person or situation, rather than the developing capacity of the client, becomes the acknowledged source of change.

Because the term *insight* is used so disparately by theoreticians and by practitioners of various persuasions, its nature, the process by which it is achieved, the steps involved in bringing about change, and the nature of the change following the acquisition of insight often are misunderstood or confused. Experience in the fine art of defining made the task no easier for Webster's lexicographers. They too identified a variety of meanings, including (1) the power or act of seeing into a situation or into one's self; (2) understanding the inner nature of things; (3) acknowledgment of a mental problem and awareness and understanding of the nature of that problem and of the unconscious forces contributing to it; and (4) immediate and clear learning that takes place without recourse to trial-and-error behavior (Webster, 1967).

In one way or another, these different definitions identify the main themes on insight that are found in the literature of the various therapeutic professions. The definitions are not necessarily mutually exclusive. Rather, they attend to different kinds of insight that, if used in connection with one another, expand the scope of our understanding and the power of our practice. For example, clinical social work interventions depend on insights about how situations affect clients' responses as well as on insights about clients' intrapsychic states.

Interpersonal, community, and societal conflict may also be understood through insight. For example, recent events in American history have profoundly affected the self-esteem of those who experienced racist or sexist conditions. Self-blame and low self-esteem often arise out of a conviction that one bears sole responsibility for the misery experienced. Clinical efforts over a period of years have helped such individuals to achieve insight into the community and societal forces involved in their circumstances and has frequently released them from the bondage of the defensive adaptations they used to cope with the humiliation they experienced. Thus, insights into social structure can be as important as insights into intrapsychic structure.

The second definition of *insight* is concerned with the understanding of the inner nature of things. Perceptiveness and empathy in regard to self and others are necessary to the clinical use of insight for personal change. Without such understanding, clinical practice is more concerned with compliance than with insight. This is not to suggest that compliance is inappropriate in all circumstances, but social work values dictate that compliance be used only to the extent that it is a specific requirement for client relief or further development.

The specific use of the term *insight* in psychodynamic or psychoanalytic perspectives concerns Webster's third definition: the acknowledgment and the recognition of one's difficulties and the awareness of the unconscious forces contributing to them. This aspect of the definition may be further differentiated into general self-knowledge regarding unconscious processes and highly specific technical meanings given to the term *insight* by some leading psychoanalysts. Menninger, for example, defines *insight* as recognition that (1) specific feelings and attitudes, techniques of behavior, or roles in which people are repeatedly cast form a pattern; (2) that this pattern, which originated long ago, is present in contemporary reality as well as in the analytic relationships; and (3) that this pattern originated for a reason that was valid at the time but persists despite changes in the circumstances that originally determined it. He addresses the integrative aspects by pointing out that "insight is not just seeing that something in the analytic situation is similar to something in childhood, or seeing that something in childhood is reflected in the activities of his contemporary situation, or seeing that something in his contemporary situation is a reflection of something in the analytic situation. In the proper sense of the word and in the useful sense for psychoanalytic technique, insight is the simultaneous identification of the characteristic behavior pattern in all three of these situations, together with understanding of why they were and are used as they were and are" (Menninger, 1958, p. 148).

Webster's final definition concerns the learning process. It specifically addresses the immediate learning that takes place without recourse to trial-and-error behavior. This perspective is most clearly addressed by Köhler (1940) and the subsequent line of psychologists who further developed the Gestalt concept. This form of insight involves the reorganization of elements in such a way that they take on new meanings and provide the necessary conditions to reach new solutions. Once achieved, such insight is thought to be generalizable to new situations of a similar nature.

The Role of Insight in Psychoanalysis

A great deal of attention to the issues of insight in social work derives from the psychoanalytic movement and the early attraction these ideas held for those concerned with the developing theory and practice of social casework, which has recently been redefined as the clinical aspects of social work. Although Freud and the early psychoanalysts paid rather scanty attention to developing the conceptual notion of insight, there is little doubt that they were very much concerned with the nature of self-understanding and the manner in which that produced change in people's lives (Zilboorg, 1951). Even when psychoanalytic theorists differ on the specific meaning of *insight,* one characteristic is always present and central to their thinking—the affective component must be present to develop the kind of understanding that leads to insight and produces change. Intellectual understanding alone is not enough to bring about productive change. Such insight means freely experiencing one's inner world—knowing who we are and have been, who we are with and have been with, and where we are and have been. It is the psychoanalysts' view that such understanding leads to freedom of choice and is a key to insight. But freedom of choice, like all freedoms, does not come without a price. Knowing one's self includes facing the painful aspects of one's self as well as the more pleasurable ones (Shengold, 1980).

Some theorists suggest that the wish to know may be a basic drive. If this were true, then removing barriers or resistances to expressing the drive should be a major goal of any clinician desirous of freeing energies to promote healthy development. Insight is characterized by a process in which emotions are evoked, ideas are clarified, attentiveness and self-observation are in process, organizing functions are operating well, and similarities and contrasts are available. It is a journey toward harmonious integration, surprise, conviction, and the separation and reassemblage of facts, feelings, and issues (Abrams, 1980).

In psychoanalytic perspective, insight involves a quantitative as well as a qualitative way of knowing. There are shifts in the intensity with which individuals hold on to previously powerful ideas about themselves and the significant persons in their past and present. Thus, the transformation presumed to be associated with insight is frequently seen in the form of specific changes in strongly held beliefs, thoughts, and fantasies about such people and events, and it involves a new capacity to deal with them. It is possible, of course, that insight can be based upon "invented truths." The development of a new autobiography depicting events that have been central to identified problems may also involve shifts of affect and beliefs about what one was, is, and can be. In a sense, insight may bear some similarity to behaviorist beliefs associated with the identification of contingency factors thought to promote particular behaviors.

Insight is thought to be enhanced by removing barriers to its development. Defenses, while serving adaptive functions, also serve to inhibit the development of insight, and therefore adaptive functions may require interpretation at appropriate times to identify the defense and the basis for it. The development of transference neurosis and its eventual elimination through interpretation is the fundamental condition in psychoanalytic theory that permits true insight and internal structural change to take place. This is quite different, however, from transference reactions that may occur in all types of helping relationships. From time to time, psychoanalysts have differed in their opinions as to the necessity of the transference neurosis in producing change (Alexander and French, 1946). More recently, there also have been some differences as to the specific nature of the transference neurosis (Kohut, 1977). Nevertheless, the critical nature of the development of a transference neurosis and its resolution remains the essence of the psychoanalytic method. And, it is important to point out that transference, according to the psychoanalyst, not only involves repetition of old experience but also involves the new environment, the new response, and the new holding capacity of the partner in therapeutic work.

It is well to remember that insights are not unblemished blessings for all people. Much like crisis, insight can signify both opportunity and danger. For those who cannot tolerate the regression necessary to gain analytic insight, such efforts can be hazardous and counterproductive. Insight may lead to knowledge of one's own vulnerability as well as strength and therefore requires reasonably secure internal resources to deal with one's self and one's relationship to others. Nevertheless, there is at present a good deal of vigorous reexamination of the conditions under which individuals with various self-structures may be helped by insight-oriented methods. For some analysts, a diagnosis of borderline personality or psychosis no longer automatically eliminates an individual from being an appropriate candidate for developing insight associated with the psychoanalytic method of producing change (Kernberg, 1975). Nor do all psychoanalysts share a similar perspective on the power of insight. Blum, editor of the *Journal of American Psychoanalytic Association,* takes a firm position that interpretation leading to insight is the most powerful agent of the psychoanalytic curative process (Blum, 1980, p. 41); but lack of change despite insight, he admits, is an issue for further research. Other psychoanalysts reject this position and suggest that the understanding of the interaction between analyst and patient, rather than interpretation, is more critical in effecting change. They contend that the reparative process may be accomplished through means other than insight. These analysts emphasize the power of the relationship, in which insight plays a relatively minor role. They advocate facilitating "a corrective emotional experience," in which the patient can reexamine earlier unsatisfactory developmental phases with a more responsive and empathic parenting figure who can help the patient correct maladaptive emotional patterns (Alexander and French, 1946; Scharfman, 1980). In any event, to all these analysts, it is not a single flash of understanding but rather the slow accretion of knowledge through the process of "working through" that is the therapeutically effective mechanism of change. New self-understanding comes from, and is assimilated through, a gradual reconstructive process (Fromm-Reichmann, 1950; Greenson, 1967).

The Role of Insight in Behavior Modification

In the past decade, behavior modification has become one of the most rapidly developing modalities of treatment in clinical social work. Thomas, a leading social work educator long engaged in applying the theory and practice of behavior modification to social work practice, predicted that this method would soon be the prevailing one (Thomas, 1971). Behavior modification promotes change through insight by extinguishing unwanted or troublesome behaviors through reeducation. Unwanted symptoms, whether intrapsychic or interpersonal, are thought to be learned behaviors. They can be replaced with new behaviors by instructing the patient in experimentally derived principles that promote and extinguish maladaptive behaviors. There are a variety of theoretical approaches to bringing about such change. Some are concerned with processes of reciprocal inhibition or systematic desensitization; others eliminate behavior through implosive or flooding techniques (Wolpe, 1969; Stampfl and Levis, 1967). Behaviorists are as concerned as psychoanalysts are with the disabling aspects of anxiety, but they do not perceive the origins of anxiety in terms of repression or unconscious conflict, nor do they believe these matters are of great significance in changing the situation. Although some behavioral theorists, such as Stampfl, have attempted to integrate psychodynamic understanding and behavior modification, their approach is an exception to the general behaviorist perspective, and their ideas have been criticized by learning-theory colleagues.

Bandura (1969), in contrast, gives little credence to psychodynamic issues and believes that the limited success of dynamic psychotherapy derives from persuasion rather than insight. To a great extent, psychiatrist Jerome Frank (1961) shares this position. In Bandura's view, "insight into the presumed psychic determinants of interpersonal responses is of questionable validity and has little effect on behavior" (p. 94). Here he is referring to interpersonal responses, which are more likely than intrapsychic responses to be affected by situational factors. However, there is little doubt that Bandura believes insight is also of little use in changing behaviors that involve only the individual, such as obsessions or compulsive rituals. London (1964), in his comparison of insight and behaviorist or action approaches to understanding and intervention, stresses the issue of compelling motives as the unifying theme in all insight-oriented psychotherapy. "What motivates a man, what drives him, what his reasons are, or goals, or objectives—all these terms mean essentially the same thing, and all may be employed equally aptly in the basic formula of motivation therapy, that motives determine and dictate acts" (p. 54). In contrast, he believes that actionists are more concerned with behavior than motives—with eliciting action rather than producing insight. "But far from trying to bring some secret motives into consciousness, the action therapies' attack on symptoms cavalierly disregards their source, and, aimed at changes in fact, it likewise disavows the crucial need for consciousness. This attacks the very core of Insight Therapy, for it implies that symptoms may not be meaningful expressions of their motive states but may be nonsense learned by chance associations with some unhappy event, and that consciousness may be no help at all in gaining freedom from it" (p. 76). Yelloly (1972) offered a similar analysis in Great Britain, which was addressed more directly to issues of social casework practice.

The Role of Insight in Clinical Social Work

The practice of social work with individuals, families, and small groups has always involved efforts to help clients become more self-sufficient. The goal of personal change, as well as situational change, has been a primary concern of social workers since the beginning of the charity organization movement. This goal has been more clearly articulated since the beginning of professionalization of social casework as defined in Mary Richmond's *Social Diagnosis* (1917). The concept of insight in Richmond's work involves a thorough analysis of the client's social situation, character, and interpersonal relationships. Past relationships, particularly family history, are seen as being indicative of how the client responds to social services as well as to current relationships. Richmond identifies the goal of social diagnosis as (1) full interview with the client, (2) early contact with the family, (3) the search for further insight and for sources of needed cooperation outside the immediate family, and (4) comparison and interpretation of the total picture by the worker to determine the intervention. Fundamental to Richmond's identification of the goals of casework is the worker's "understanding." The gathering of information and the introduction of concepts from history, law, medical diagnosis, and logic lead to a social diagnosis. This social diagnosis serves as the basis for insights regarding what, why, and how the client's problems developed and might be remedied. Richmond was primarily concerned with the caseworker's insights rather than the client's insights. As the theory and practice of social casework developed during the next two decades, the client's insights received more attention.

Prior to the 1940s, insight was primarily a caseworker attribute. The caseworker developed insight and used this understanding indirectly to bring about changes in the client's circumstances. Clients did not themselves need to be concerned with such insights; rather, they were affected by the consequences of the worker's understanding and consequent intervention. The model was in fact much more of a medical model than it was to become, although the analogy has been used more in recent years. The model was similar to medical intervention in that caseworkers gathered information about all facets of the situation, much as physicians use examination and laboratory tests, and then prescribed action to ameliorate or eliminate problems.

The decades of the 1940s and 1950s saw the increasing establishment among caseworkers of psychoanalytic theory as the foundation upon which human behavior and change were to be understood. Analysis offered caseworkers hope that a systematic understanding of the client's irrational behavior might lead the way to changing it and thus solve the dilemma in which the client found himself. In addition, psychoanalytic methods were thought to help clients develop greater self-awareness and lead to an increased capacity to control their lives. Although the psychosocial perspective predominated, there was a clear thrust to work more intensively with the inner world of the client rather than with the external environment, as had been the tendency previous to the 1940s. Yet, social workers were careful not to separate the two. For example, Gordon Hamilton, in the second (revised) edition of her influential volume *Theory and Practice of Social Casework,* counseled that "it is not possible to restrict the casework function to modification of 'outer' conditions, since the problem is usually interpersonal, as well as social. Not only can one not successfully separate environmental and emotional factors, but the client's psychological insights are put to use in meeting 'real' situations" (Hamilton, 1951, p. 4). To counteract the previous concentration on the environment, efforts were made to establish psychological subject matter as an important and concrete factor in helping clients to clarify their problems and to do something to solve them.

With this new emphasis on psychology, caseworkers themselves needed to pay more attention to their own psychological functioning. Insight into their own emotional drives and the manner in which they coped with them was seen as necessary to the understanding and treatment of the client's psychological states. Unconscious motivation and countertransferences became prominent concepts, and insight and self-awareness became prerequisites for ethical helping relationships. To know and accept one's self was viewed as critical to knowing and accepting others (Hamilton, 1951, p. 40).

In spite of this increased attention to insights about the self and the client, a clear boundary for social casework intervention was set at this time. The interpretation of unconscious material was considered to be "dangerous." The goal of casework was to produce insights and understandings of conflicts that were already available or easily made available to awareness; unconscious material remained firmly in the province of psychiatry. To this end, Hamilton suggested that "intrapsychic conflict, as such, is not the preoccupation of casework treatment, but rather the balance between person and environment where, by attention to the less conflicted parts of the personality, the client can be helped to better social functioning and adaptation. The essential nature of basic conflict must, however, be understood in any truly therapeutic endeavor, even though such conflict is not touched directly in limited forms of therapy" (1951, p. 84).

Social group work was not left behind in the excitement that was generated by understanding behavior within the psychoanalytic perspective. Wilson and Ryland (1949) contributed to the application of psychoanalytic theory to social group work practice. In their chapters on supervision and administration, they spoke directly of psychological insights and suggested that the goal of supervision was to assist the worker in developing and using insights into his own feelings, attitudes, reactions, and processes as they are manifested in work with clients as well as with the supervisor. Wilson and Ryland take the position that an awareness of past relationships and their effect on present ones is essential to the development of the group worker and the tasks of group-work intervention. Their discussion of the supervisor–worker relationship, and particularly the development and use of insight by both parties, is similar to that of others who wrote about the process of insight and awareness in worker–client relationship:

> The supervisor must understand the worker as a learner and be able to recognize in him the psychological reactions characteristic of learners. The learning process is a zig-zag of forward and backward movement. It is a dynamic process in which there is considerable struggle; hence, when the forward movement become painful, the individual starts to regress to a more comfortable state of knowledge and experience. The learner is helped by having new learning broken up into portions related to his capacity to accept new knowledge and skill. The learner both wants and fears change.

> In the process of acquiring the professional skill of the social group worker, most individuals face the necessity of making certain fundamental changes in attitudes, values, and norms. These changes the learner resists; he is fearful of what he may become. Moreover, he is in the process of developing the capacity to use insight. To have achieved insight yet be unable to use it is a very painful situation, and therefore the learner must have time to let the insight, like yeast, work within him [p. 539].

The similarity to psychodynamic clinical work is inescapable. Indeed, many social work students and group-work practitioners of that period complained of the similarity and resisted being treated as "patients" by supervisors.

In the 1950s, the place of psychotherapy in casework became an even greater issue. Casework literature urged clinicians to use greater understanding of the self and patient and the clinical relationship to bring about changes in the psychology of clients. The subject of transference became an issue of concern. By the end of the 1940s, a number of leading educators were identifying the increased role that social work was playing in the delivery of psychotherapeutic services. Gordon Hamilton faced the issue boldly for that time in her book *Psychotherapy in Child Guidance* (1947), in which she identified the clinically oriented social caseworker as a practitioner of psychotherapy. The nature of psychotherapy in social casework was identified as an attempt (1) to understand the person in order to assist him in self-understanding, (2) to support the client so that the strengthened ego would be better able to bear up under strain, and (3) to interpret the client's feelings and thoughts so that new insights could be synthesized and new cognitive and emotional habits could emerge. Transference was clearly recognized as an important element in the process, although clinicians were strongly advised to modulate and control the type and depth of transference reactions so that the forces of the unconscious, of which transference was one manifestation, would not be unleashed to overwhelm both client and caseworker. Hamilton and the other leading social casework theorists of the time clearly recognized the psychosocial nature of the psychotherapy they described, and they cautioned against the full development and interpretation of the transference.

Austin (1950) attempted to identify the emerging trends in casework treatment. She separated social treatment approaches from psychotherapeutic approaches and analyzed the various aspects of psychotherapeutic work. She identified insight therapy as a category, although the principles of abreaction, clarification, and manipulation were thought to be used more in casework than was interpretation leading to insight. Austin (1957) further specified the countertransference and transference phenomena that emerge in the treatment relationship and discussed "selected interpretations" that may lead to insight. This article, in which the psychoanalytic perspective is highly developed, ends with the usual concern about recognizing differences between casework therapy and psychoanalysis.

Annette Garrett (1958) further explored the meaning and use of transference in casework. She clearly analyzed other aspects of the therapeutic casework relationship as well as the difference between transference neurosis and transference reactions. It is the transference *neurosis* that Garrett cautions the caseworker to guard against. This very important distinction is frequently missing from the social work literature on transference manifestations in treatment. Transference reactions can no more be avoided in a helping relationship than can the reality manifestations inherent in that process. The regulation of transference phenomena, then, is handled consciously by the clinician according to the nature of the treatment contract. The use of transference in both diagnosis and treatment is clearly identified in Garrett's article, and, while she too approaches interpretation with caution, it is clearly seen as appropriate to clinical social work practice.

Florence Hollis (1949) found herself in accord with Austin about the development of insight as a goal of casework. She later altered her position as a result of her research into the actual practice of intensive social casework in family agencies (Hollis, 1962). At that time, she did not abandon the belief that social workers were involved in psychotherapy, but she distinguished psychotherapy in which free association, frequent contact, and interpretation of unconscious material were used from psychotherapy concerned with the clarification of preconscious content for the purpose of modifying behavior. Hollis directed attention to a variety of ways of modifying behavior short of interpretation of the unconscious elements manifest in transference. She used clarification as an important technique for creating understanding in social casework treatment.

In a series of articles in the 1950s, Elizabeth Irvine presented a particularly lucid account of the British social work perspective on clinical treatment. In her writing, transference and countertransference reactions were clearly matters of considerable importance in the development of insight for worker and client alike. However, transference was not to be the main focus of treatment in clinical social work; rather, it was one way of solving the problems that clients bring to the social work clinician. She saw the aim of much clinical social work as removing the obstacles to healthy growth and development and freeing the spontaneous creative and recuperative power of human beings (Irvine, 1979). She was aware that every relationship combined elements of transference and reality. These included, in varying proportions, (1) the response to the reality of the other person, including the ability to perceive his qualities and to feel and react appropriately to them, and (2) the transference, with its perceptual distortion, inappropriate emotion, and manipulative action. The essential characteristic of transference was the patient's tendency to transform the present person and situation into the image and likeness of an earlier person and situation. She recognized that transference was always present and that it could reach considerable intensity in a casework relationship, even when client and/or worker failed to recognize its existence.

Interpretation of transference and insight gained from it is only one way of dealing with transferred fantasies. Clincial social workers also may deal with transference by remaining steadily concerned and undamaged helpers in their relationship with their clients. In this instance, it is thought that insight may come as proper attention is paid to factors in the clinical relationship that permit the individual to relax his or her defenses and express feelings of anger against those figures and circumstances in his or her background that have been painful and often disabling. Release from such feelings is frequently accompanied by a kind of understanding not previously available, and it may rightfully be called insight. Here, the clinical social worker's attitudes and behavior, as much as his or her interpretations, become the foundation of insight. Irvine points to countertransference as a key factor in understanding and relating to a client's underlying states. Control of the transference manifestations by recognizing the client's current feelings is counseled. Interpreting transference reactions may help clients to understand thoughts and feelings projected in the transference or to remove the veil of distortion and enable the client to experience the reality of the relationship. However, it is not always necessary or appropriate to use this method. Rather, resolving old conflicts through the corrective emotional experiences inherent in the clinical relationship is more frequently espoused as a method of change (Irvine, p. 35).

Irvine, then, adopts the position that the goal in treatment for all clients would not be to achieve increased insight into their past relationships. Rather, the clinical social worker should use the relationship with the client to provide a unique experience in which positive and negative feelings for the clinician are met with understanding and acceptance. Her aim is to arrive at the degree of insight available through reflection and modified interpretation in order to manage the client's experience of their joint effort as positively as possible. Even when possible, caseworkers should not produce and work through a transference neurosis; rather, they should use transference reactions as needed when the present relationship is unduly affected by the residues of past relationships that are inevitably repeated. Clients are seen as having a varied need for more or less interpretive, insight-directed work.

Timms (1964), although viewing the casework relationship as different from psychotherapy, addresses the importance of interpretation to achieve insight in correcting the client's distortion of the social worker. To this end, he identifies three kinds of insight: introspective insight (when a person becomes aware of a previously repressed wish or fear), problem-solving insight (referring to what a person needs to know in order to solve a problem or reach a goal), and practical understanding (referring to what a person actually knows, though he may not be consciously aware of knowing it until it is brought to his attention). This way of defining *insight* would appear to be directly related to clinical social work practice.

During the 1950s, Charlotte Towle (1954) introduced the issues of conscious and unconscious processes in learning as a part of professional education for social work. She identified the manner in which conscious and unconscious processes enriched one another when unhampered by anxiety. She saw the development of insight as critical to reducing anxiety and unlearning old patterns, thereby permitting learning to go on relatively unhampered. Towle was aware that "often insight will be painful, so that seeing one's self realistically in order to regulate emotional responses which distort one's thinking and doing will not always be possible. Sometimes the threat implied may interfere with habitual tendencies to self-inquiry or make the process useless, even though one goes through its motions. The responsible professional worker cannot permit himself the comfort of becoming deeply unconscious of self. He must always be consciously attentive to the import of his activity" (p. 37). She also suggested that learning needed to be a conscious process for the student to manage, comprehend, and integrate learning in a somewhat orderly manner—to help the learner be creative with his effort and intelligence and discourage reliance on "intuitive hunches" or "stereotyped behavior." She refers to insight as a mechanism for making learning conscious. "Guiding insight increases the integrative capacity of the learner. Insight into the processes of invention can increase the efficiency of almost any developed and active intelligence" (p. 160). Towle viewed the process of insight in learning as teaching not only the "*what* and the *how* but also the *why* of professional thinking and doing" (p. 161).

Toward the end of the 1950s, Helen Harris Perlman (1957) drew the profession's attention to social casework as a problem-solving process. She clearly discusses transference and countertransference phenomena, which inevitably occur in establishing a good relationship in casework, but she also begins a powerful movement, extending into the 1960s, in which the reality relationship once again takes center stage. She notes that "in casework practice, our effort is to maintain relationship on the basis of reality; that is, to keep both client and caseworker aware of their joint purpose, their separate and realistic identities and their focus upon working out some better adaptation between the client and his current situation. Transference manifestations need to be recognized, identified, and dealt with as they occur, but the effort is to so manage the relationship and the problem-solving work as to give minimum excitation to transference" (Perlman, 1957, p. 78). This is accomplished by using materials that are readily available to consciousness and are relevant to current life situations. The caseworker may develop understanding and insight into his own functioning, into the client's unconscious processes, and into the relationship between them, but the worker does not necessarily share these with the client. Perlman is aware of the intrusiveness of transference and suggests that "there are instances, however, when the caseworker has managed well enough but when the client's needfulness still distorts the relationship. Occasionally, then, the caseworker will need to place his recognition of this fact directly and openly between him and the client; to point out, gently and understandingly, the realistic difference between himself and the image in which the client casts him; and to suggest that . . . they attempt to keep this difference clear" (p. 80). The transference is to be controlled rather than used in the search for patterns of behavior and for insight into their origins and meanings.

About the same time, Howard Parad (1958) edited a group of papers from the Smith College School for Social Work that addressed the issues of ego psychology and dynamic casework. The bulk of these papers, representing many of the leading theorists associated with dynamic casework, reaffirmed the directions of the previous two decades. However, a paper by Herman Stein foreshadowed a major movement of the 1960s. It was concerned with social science in social work practice and education. Stein (1955, p. 147) noted that "a trained social worker can read with understanding a highly technical psychoanalytic paper but would probably encounter difficulty in comprehending the average article in a journal of sociology; the issues, the concepts, or even the very language itself may not be understood by him." The 1960s and 1970s so radically changed circumstances that today that statement might well be written about psychoanalytic theory. The 1960s and the war on poverty turned the attention of social workers to social science concepts and theory with the same sense of hope that turned the profession to psychoanalytic theory in earlier decades. The hope was for new understanding that would permit more successful intervention, particularly in relation to social work with disadvantaged populations. Elements of theory and empirical data in relation to social class, culture and subculture, value orientations, social role, and labeling and deviant behavior, to name a few parameters, began to enter the discussions in professional meetings, social agencies, and schools of social work (Stein and Cloward, 1958). Awareness of social processes and their influence on behavior reduced the emphasis on insight into the dynamics of unconsciously determined behavior, and there was a corresponding change in the language of the casework literature.

Although changes in social structure were increasingly emphasized as the critical target of change, the individual was not totally ignored. Rather, the concern shifted from psychodynamics to social dynamics. Some theorists thought that casework was ineffective, but others doubted the methods of evaluation that drew such conclusions. From the mid-1960s into the early 1970s, insight-oriented psychodynamic intervention was somewhat out of favor in clinical social work. Clinical social work was concerned with crisis intervention, task-oriented casework, and brief therapy interventions.

New developments in social science during the 1960s influenced social work as well. For example, the concern with ecology led to analysis of ecosystems, which pointed to the interrelationship of environmental factors and led to a systems approach to social work problems (Germain, 1980). Such models provided new insights to social workers, but whether such understanding will lead to interventive power comparable to the assessment power it generates remains an important question.

During the 1970s, interest was renewed in clinical social work and its psychotherapeutic aspects. Clinical social workers felt they had been disregarded, rejected, and made to feel irrelevant. Some workers formed the Federation of Societies for Clinical Social Work to once again promote clinical social work. Others worked within the existing National Association of Social Workers to demand renewed attention to the important tasks of clinical social workers. Psychotherapy has now been officially included in clinical social work practice, and, in various parts of the country, this official recognition has been encoded in licensing laws.

At present, a variety of theoretical positions exist within the practice of clinical social work. No one theoretical perspective has taken over completely. Advocates of each theory are attempting to develop further understanding of their treatment approach. Among the psychoanalytically oriented clinical social workers, issues of insight pertaining to transference and countertransference are being examined with increasing vigor; there is greater concern with developing insights in terms of ego psychology rather than id psychology; and social workers seem to respect rather than fear dealing with the psychic structure.

Conclusion

Insight is a way of knowing and learning. Without it, change is relegated to habit or automatic function. For some purposes in psychosocial functioning, redirection of specific behaviors is appropriate; for others, it is not. Humans are symbolic animals, and, in most intrapersonal and interpersonal events, why behavior occurs is as central as the concern with how behavior occurs. Inasmuch as insight is a cognitive process as well as an affective one, it always involves laws of learning. The function of insight or new knowledge is to prepare the client to maximize his integrative functioning and enable him to change patterns of behavior. When approached in this way, insight has the power to alter or enhance the client's psychosocial functioning. No one can give insight to anyone else; one can only facilitate its occurrence.

References

Abrams, S. "Insight: The Teiresian Gift." Paper delivered at meeting of the American Psychoanalytic Association, San Francisco, May 1980.

Alexander, F., and French, T. M. *Psychoanalytic Therapy*. New York: Ronald Press, 1946.

Austin, L. "Trends in Differential Treatment in Social Casework." In C. Kaius (Ed.), *Principles and Techniques in Social Casework*. New York: Family Service Association of America, 1950.

Austin, L. "Dynamics and Treatment of the Client Anxiety Hysteria." *Smith College Studies in Social Work*, 1957, *27* (3), 167–187.

Bandura, A. *Principles of Behavior Modification*. New York: Holt, Rinehart and Winston, 1969.

Blum, H. P. "The Curative and Creative Aspects of Insight." In H. P. Blum (Ed.), *Psychoanalytic Explorations of Technique*. New York: International Universities Press, 1980.

Frank, J. *Persuasion and Healing: A Comparative Study of Psychotherapy*. Baltimore: Johns Hopkins University Press, 1961.

Fromm-Reichmann, F. *Principles of Intensive Psychotherapy*. Chicago: University of Chicago Press, 1950.

Garrett, Annette. "The Worker–Client Relationship." In H. Parad (Ed.), *Ego Psychology and Dynamic Casework*. New York: Family Service Association of America, 1958.

Germain, C. B. *The Ecological Perspective in Social Work Practice*. New York: Columbia University Press, 1980.

Greenson, R. *The Technique and Practice of Psychoanalysis*. New York: International University Press, 1967.

Hamilton, G. *Psychotherapy in Child Guidance*. New York: Columbia University Press, 1947.

Hamilton, G. *Theory and Practice in Social Casework*. (2nd ed., rev.) New York: Columbia University Press, 1951.

Hollis, F. *Women in Marital Conflict*. New York: Family Service Association of America, 1949.

Hollis, F. "Analyses of Casework Treatment Methods and Their Relationship to Personality Change." *Smith College Studies in Social Work*, 1962, *32* (2), 97–117.

Hollis, F. *Casework: A Psychosocial Therapy*. New York: Random House, 1964.

Irvine, E. *Social Work and Human Problems*. New York: Pergamon Press, 1979.

Kernberg, O. *Borderline Conditions and Pathological Narcissism*. New York: Jason Aronson, 1975.

Köhler, W. *Dynamics in Psychology*. New York: Liveright, 1940.

Kohut, O. *The Restoration of the Self*. New York: International University Press, 1977.

London, P. *The Modes and Morals of Psychotherapy*. New York: Holt, Rinehart and Winston, 1964.

Mattinson, J., and Sinclair, I. *Mate and Stalemate*. Oxford: Blackwells, 1979.

Menninger, K. *Theory of Psychoanalytic Technique*. New York: Basic Books, 1958.

Parad, H. J. *Ego Psychology and Dynamic Casework*. New York: Family Service Association of America, 1958.

Perlman, H. H. *Social Casework, A Problem-Solving Process*. Chicago: University of Chicago Press, 1957.

Richmond, M. *Social Diagnosis*. New York: Russell Sage Foundation, 1917.

Scharfman, M. A. "Insight: Introductory Comments." Paper delivered at meeting of the American Psychoanalytic Association, San Francisco, May 1980.

Shengold, L. "Insight as Metaphor." Paper delivered at meeting of the American Psychoanalytic Association, San Francisco, May 1980.

Stampfl, T. G., and Levis, D. J. "Essentials of Implosive Therapy: A Learning Theory-Based Psychodynamic Behavioral Therapy." *Journal of Abnormal Psychology*, 1967, *72* (6), 496–503.

Stein, H. "Social Science in Social Work Practice and Education." *Social Casework*, 1955, *36* (4), 147–155.

Stein, H., and Cloward, R. *Social Perspectives on Behavior*. Glencoe, Ill.: Free Press, 1958.

Thomas, E. "Social Casework and Social Group Work: The Behavioral Approach." In *Encyclopedia of Social Work*. Vol. 2. Washington, D.C.: National Association of Social Workers, 1971.

Timms, N. *Social Casework Principles and Practice*. London: Routledge & Kegan Paul, 1964.

Towle, C. *The Learner in Education for the Professions as Seen in Education for Social Work*. Chicago: University of Chicago Press, 1954.

Webster's Third New International Dictionary, Springfield, Ill.: Merriam, 1967.

Wilson, G., and Ryland, G. *Social Group Work Practice*. Boston: Houghton Mifflin Co., 1949.

Wolpe, J. *The Practice of Behavior Therapy*. Oxford, England: Pergamon Press, 1969.

Yelloly, M. "Insight," In H. Jehu and others (Eds.), *Behavior Modification in Social Work*. New York: Wiley, 1972.

Zilboorg, G. "The Emotional Problem and the Therapeutic Role of Insight." *Psychoanalytic Quarterly*, 1952, *21*, 1–24.

12

Worker-Client Relationships

Herbert S. Strean

Ever since the formal inauguration of social work practice, when Mary Richmond (1922) averred that a crucial dimension of intervention was "the direct action of mind upon mind," most social work practitioners and theoreticians have considered the worker-client relationship to be a salient feature of treatment. Although those who subscribe to a psychoanalytic orientation contend that the worker-client relationship is indispensable for effective treatment, some behaviorists generally believe that it is not particularly crucial. Be that as it may, the worker-client relationship in social work has not been sufficiently studied theoretically. The purpose of this chapter is to review those theoretical perspectives that can contribute a clearer and richer understanding of the worker-client relationship in social work.

Although many, if not most, social science and personality theories contain concepts that are pertinent to the social worker-client relationship, we have selected those perspectives whose concepts and constructs can contribute in a major way to a further appreciation of the psychological and social dynamics of the worker-client relationship. At the end of this chapter, we will briefly review some of the important theoretical concepts of those theories whose contributions to the worker-client relationship are helpful but not of major significance.

Psychoanalytic Theory

Psychoanalysis has been considered a theory of personality, a form of psychotherapy, a methodological procedure in research, and a value system (Fine, 1975). We shall examine two of its psychotherapeutic concepts, transference and countertransference.

Transference. Anyone who has been engaged in helping others to make changes in their lives recognizes that, in the face of all logic and reason, the client may often behave in a most obstinate manner. According to psychoanalytic theory, the therapeutic relationship and the course of therapy are greatly affected by the patient's *transference*—the feelings, wishes, fears, and defenses that influence his perceptions of the therapist. Transference reactions are *unconscious* attempts by the client to recapitulate with the therapist types of interpersonal interaction that are similar to those he experienced with significant persons in the past. Every client, according to psychoanalytic theory, experiences the therapist not only in terms of how he objectively is but in terms of how the client wishes the worker to be or fears he might be.

The psychoanalytic theorist alleges that, if the therapist does not understand how he is being experienced by the client, he cannot be very helpful. Each client responds to interpretations, clarifications, or environmental manipulation in terms of his or her transference to the therapist. If the client loves the therapist, interventions will probably be accepted, and if the client hates the therapist, the most brilliant and creative interpretation or act will be rejected.

One of the major tasks of the therapist in psychoanalytic therapy is to help the patient see how and why he experiences the therapist the way he does. Why does the patient act like a compliant child and docilely accept everything the therapist says? Or why does he argue with the therapist every time the therapist says something? Why is the therapist's silence experienced by one patient as rejection and by another as love?

Freud (1912) singled out the notion of transference for much discussion. He pointed out that it is a universal phenomenon of the human mind and dominates the person's relations to his environment. He further stressed that transference exists in all relationships—in marriage, in the classroom, in business relations, and in friendships. Because of our unique histories, ego functioning, superego mandates, values, and social circumstances, each of us brings to every new relationship wishes, fears, hopes, defenses, and many other subjective factors that have evolved from previous relationships and that may or may not be appropriate in the new situation. Because these universal phenomena are largely unconscious, they cannot be willed away or consciously modified. They influence our perceptions of the individuals we meet, and very often the reasons we give for responding to people with love, hatred, or ambivalence are rationalizations.

The intimate relationship of client and worker is one in which the client *depends* on the worker. This relationship invariably reactivates feelings and ideas that the client experienced with others he depended on in the past. These feelings and ideas cannot be obliterated, avoided, or neglected. They are normal in any interaction and become intensified in helping situations. If the client has experienced those who nurtured, advised, and educated as essentially positive and well meaning, the client will in all likelihood experience the therapist in the same way. However, there are usually mixtures of love and hate toward parents and other important figures in all individuals, and every therapist will be the recipient of all these feelings.

Although transference reactions are always traceable to childhood, there is not always a simple one-to-one correspondence between the past and present. Sometimes there is a direct repetition, such as when the client is quite convinced that the therapist is almost identical to his father, mother, or siblings. On other occasions, there can be a compensatory fantasy to make up for what was lacking in childhood—in other words, the client fantasizes that the therapist is somebody his mother or father should have been.

When the social worker recognizes that transference always exists in all the relationships that clients have with him, he can look at his therapeutic results more objectively. If the client wants the therapist to be an omnipotent parent to whom he can cling, then he will fight interventions aimed to help him become more autonomous. If the client wants the worker to be a sibling rival, then he will use the worker's interventions to continue his sibling fight. Because the client views all the worker's interventions through the lens of his transference, the worker must explore with the client why he wants to perceive the worker the way he does.

A very common use of transference is the client's projection of unacceptable parts of his psychic structure onto the therapist—sexual and aggressive id wishes, ego defenses, and superego mandates. More often than not, the client projects his own superego onto the therapist and expects punishment or criticism from him. Such projection is related to the way the superego is formed in a child. The process of socialization is one in which the child gives up various modes of instinctual gratification at the request of significant figures. This process is crystallized in the superego, which induces guilt. Guilt is superego punishment. Because the superego is formed in interaction with significant individuals, it can be changed only by such interaction. As the client projects his superego onto the therapist, a consistent comparison of this projection with reality serves to break down the superego in the course of time (Fine, 1971).

Whatever the dynamics of transference are—projection of superego mandates, id wishes, or other unconscious elements—a therapeutic relationship is distinguished from all others *not* by these dynamics but by their place in the relationship, that is, the therapist's attitude toward the transference and the use he makes of it. When a person asks for encouragement, advice, or punishment, the analytically oriented therapist wants to know why these responses are requested. As psychoanalyst Charles Brenner (1976) has said, "The addition of a dash of encouragement, or a measure of scolding or admonition, however tactful and well intended, may seem to hasten the progress. It can, at times, produce symptomatic improvement. But it is no substitute for the analysis of why the patient wants encouragement, admonition, or any other nonanalytic behavior. . . . In the long run, it cannot fail to interfere to a greater or lesser degree with progress" (p. 109).

In summary, according to psychoanalytic theory, transference exists in all relationships. There is no such thing as a client who has "no transference" or in whom transference fails to develop. As clinician and client accept transference as a fact of therapeutic life and constantly study the client's transference responses, they gain an appreciation of the nature of his conflicts and those aspects of his history that are aiding and abetting his current dysfunctional behavior (Menninger, 1958; Sandler, 1973). In classical analysis, the stimulation and working through of the transference is the major instrument of change.

Countertransference. Countertransference is the same dynamic phenomenon as transference, except that it refers to those unconscious wishes and defenses of the therapist that interfere with his objective perception and mature treatment of the client. Frequently, the client represents for the therapist a person of his childhood onto whom past feelings and wishes are projected.

Countertransference as a term was first used by Freud in his paper "The Future Prospects of Psychoanalysis" (1910): "We have become aware of the 'countertransference' which arises in him (the analyst) as a result of the patient's influence on his unconscious feelings, and we are inclined to insist that he shall recognize this countertransference in himself and overcome it. . . . No analyst goes further than his own complexes and internal resistances permit" (p. 141).

The worker–client relationship ceases to be in the service of the client's growth when the therapist becomes unable to deal maturely with aspects of the client's communications that impinge on problems of his own. For example, if the therapist has unresolved problems connected with his own aggression, he may need to placate or be ingratiating with the client. Similarly, if a therapist is threatened by his own unconscious homosexual feelings, he may be unable to detect homosexual implications in a client's material (Sandler, 1973) or may perceive them where they do not exist.

Whenever a worker consistently harbors animosity toward a client, he will inevitably learn that the character trait of the client's that he detests or the behavior that he abhors is similar to a character trait or behavior of his own that he does not wish consciously to acknowledge.

Treatment usually proceeds well when the worker likes the client. If the worker does not really care for the person he treats, this will be reflected in his interventions and the client will sense it. Although a positive countertransference is a desirable attitude, like a positive transference, it must be studied carefully (Fine, 1971).

A temptation for many therapists is to love the client too much. When this occurs, the client is not perceived accurately or treated objectively. In his overidentification, the worker often supports the client against his real or fantasized opponents rather than helping him understand his own role in his interpersonal conflicts. Overidentification frequently takes place in working on marital conflicts when the worker does not want to acknowledge that the client's chronic marital complaint is also the client's own unconscious wish. For example, instead of helping the client see how he unconsciously needs a cold, rejecting, or abusive spouse to protect himself from his fears of intimacy, the worker oversympathizes with the client's plight and voices indignation about how the client is being mistreated.

A therapist is a human being and is more like his client than unlike him (Sullivan, 1953). Because the therapist has wishes, defenses, and anxieties, it is inevitable that his vulnerabilities will be activated in the treatment situation and that he will feel hostility toward some of those whom he wants to help. It is often difficult for social workers to acknowledge their hostility toward their clients because, in our profession, angry feelings are considered a liability. Frequently, hostile feelings in a worker are denied and repressed, and they manifest themselves in disguised and subtle forms. Two of the most common expressions of disguised hostility are the use of the clinical diagnosis as a countertransference expression and alterations of therapeutic plans and techniques. When the worker constantly refers to his client as "that borderline patient whose prognosis is guarded" and fails to individualize and empathize with the client's anxiety and pain, the worker is probably harboring some unconscious hatred toward the client. Similarly, when the client is ready and willing to explore his problems intensively and is not in a hurry to terminate treatment, the worker's wish to alter the therapeutic plan and arrange for a "short-term contract" can be a manifestation of the therapist's unconscious rejection of the client (Fine, 1971; Strean, 1978; Strean, 1979).

Ego Psychology

As psychoanalysis (as a theory of personality, a treatment approach, and a form of research) matured, it began to place more emphasis on the client's ego functions—defenses, locomotion, cognition, memory, perception, rational thought, rational action, and interpersonal relationships—and focused less exclusively on the individual's instinctual development. As part of the shift in diagnostic and therapeutic attention, such ego psychologists as Hartmann (1958) and Erikson (1950) began to emphasize the client's social and cultural matrix when assessing and treating him. Inasmuch as ego psychology acknowledges the importance of "the average expectable environment" (Hartmann, 1958) and the client's "radius of significant others" (Erikson, 1950), it can provide a further enrichment to the ongoing conceptualization of the social worker's interventions with his clients.

It has been postulated that most individuals who visit social workers have difficulty with one or more life tasks. They either have regressed to or are fixated at a certain developmental stage—for example, trust versus mistrust, autonomy versus self-doubt, initiative versus guilt, industry versus inferiority, identity versus identity diffusion—or are having difficulty coping with a current conflict—for example, intimacy versus isolation, generativity versus stagnation, ego integrity versus despair. Erikson (1950) claims that, in order to mature, all people must resolve these eight developmental conflicts. Social workers have used developmental conflicts as a frame of reference in making interventive plans and planning a helpful worker-client relationship (Strean, 1978).

The social worker can conceive of his role in the worker-client relationship as that of "key significant other," who, through his attitudes in the relationship with the client (and activities in the client's milieu), helps the client and resolves universal conflicts. For example, using the theory of ego psychology, the client with a trust-mistrust conflict may be viewed as a child who has been abandoned and needs the protection of a parent figure who will listen to his angry outbursts (some of which may be directed at the social worker) without rejecting him. The worker with this client offers a relationship in loco parentis, which includes help in verbalizing anger and distrust, and later provides the necessary tangible goods and services, such as food, housing, safety, an "on-call" relationship, and other physical and emotional nutrients that will fill voids in the client's life-situation. When this occurs, the client can accept the social worker, to some extent, as a trustworthy person. As a by-product of the social worker-client relationship, the client learns to trust himself a little more.

With clients whose conflicts center around other life tasks, such as autonomy versus shame and doubt, the worker will try to foster and reinforce autonomous attitudes and behaviors of the client.

Ego psychology, with its emphasis on the person as he interacts with others, provides a direction for the worker as he plans his own role in the worker–client relationship. The worker is not only a key significant other who through his attitudes helps the client move up the psychosocial ladder but is also the catalyst who helps those in the client's "radius of significant others" to enact their roles with more maturity so that the client's functioning will be enhanced (Strean, 1975).

Role Theory

With the advent of ego psychology, social workers began to focus more on communication, interaction, and transactions among family members. They found a useful way of describing these phenomena in the concept of social role—behavior that is prescribed by the social situation and governed by the individual's motivations and society's values. The stability of a transactional field, such as a marriage, family, small group, or community, depends on a certain complementarity of roles. Hence, role theory has provided social work with a means of more precisely defining, assessing, and planning intervention for marital, family, group, and community interaction (Biddle and Thomas, 1966).

One means of helping worker and client get off to a good start in their work is by taking a look at their respective *role expectations* (Deutsch and Krauss, 1965). If worker and client share mutual role expectations, the treatment relationship will probably be sustained. However, when the client's expectations of the worker and agency are not clear, the client will probably leave the relationship prematurely (Perlman, 1962; Rosenblatt, 1962; Shyne, 1957; Stark, 1959). For example, if the client views his role as one of receiving financial help as soon as possible, while the worker perceives the situation as one in which he will slowly help the client understand the etiology of his joblessness, there will be a failure in *role complementarity* (Biddle and Thomas, 1966), and the client may withdraw from the agency and the worker.

Very often, the worker expects the client to provide data (tell the story of his life, relate the specifics of problems, and so on), while the client frequently also expects to receive information rather than to provide it. This *role incongruency* has often been cited as one of the reasons for failure to help certain clients, particularly those from lower socioeconomic groups. Many individuals in lower socioeconomic groups do not view verbalizing feelings, thoughts, and memories as a legitimate or prescribed part of any role-set. Overall and Aronson (1961) empirically demonstrated that, when these clients did in fact hold expectations at variance with the actual behavior of the therapist, a higher dropout rate occurred than for clients holding more accurate expectations.

The role theorist would advise the social worker that one of his fundamental tasks, particularly during the early phases of the worker–client relationship, is to clarify the respective role expectations of client and worker so that both may attain some consensus regarding their respective positions and tasks.

Role Equilibrium and Role Disequilibrium. Role theory postulates that the interventive decisions the social worker has to make always involve the choice of promoting either role equilibrium or role disequilibrium in the interaction between worker and client. During the initial phase of the encounter, when the worker is attempting to induce the client to move from the applicant role to the client role, some role equilibrium is necessary; otherwise, there is the danger that the client may leave the situation prematurely. Consequently, for the action-oriented client, some form of social worker action would probably be indicated; for the verbal client, some form of verbal interaction would appear to be the procedure of choice (Perlman, 1962).

Certain role prescriptions that the client presents to the worker must be frustrated; otherwise, the client will not learn new and more adaptive roles. For example, to gratify the wishes and obey the role prescriptions of a demanding, self-destructive client would be, in effect, to join him in his self-destructiveness. Although this client may enact an *explicit role* (Linton, 1938) that at first seems logical to the social worker, such as one of the consistently asking for advice and guidance, if the social worker assumes this *induced role* (Sarbin, 1954), he may further weaken the client's sense of self and autonomy. When a client needs limits, if the role of the social worker is that of frequent giver, the frustration tolerance of the client will not develop. Instead, he will find it difficult to express disagreement or deal effectively with external reality because his *role status* (Biddle and Thomas, 1966) as a dependent, helpless child is consistently reinforced.

There are certain situations in which the social worker can comply with the client's *role prescription* to the benefit of the client. Perhaps the client's prescribed roles have never been acknowledged by previous social workers or other people in authority, and no amount of persuasion or appeals to the client's logic seem to have distracted the client from his requests. Such clients are usually individuals who have suffered a great deal of deprivation—psychological, social, or economic. If they are to sustain the worker-client relationship, their prescriptions (pleas for advice or concrete services) must occasionally be gratified.

In *The Anatomy of Psychotherapy,* Lennard and Bernstein (1960) studied role expectations in the therapeutic situation. They viewed therapy as a social system involving two subsystems, those of role expectations and communication. Their research documented the hypothesis that asymmetry in the system of role expectations is reflected in asymmetry in the system of communication. If therapist and client differ in the expectations each holds for the other, strains will appear, and the participants will attempt to resolve the strains or terminate their interaction.

Role Induction. Psychoanalysts Meerloo and Nelson (1965) in *Transference and Trial Adaptation* contend that, if psychoanalysts wish to take into fuller account the concepts of transference and countertransference, certain problems of role induction that permeate the therapeutic relationship must be considered. One example given by them is that the patient's resistances overtly manifest themselves as a sequence of presented roles, which he mobilizes to influence or compel the analyst to modify his role. By implication, the fundamental tenet of analytic neutrality is questioned by the authors' assertion that the patient's efforts to *induce the analyst to abandon his therapeutic role* and actualize a different role (such as parent, sibling, or lover) are matched by the analyst's efforts to induce the patient to enact a prescribed role (such as explorer of his internal life) despite the latter's resistances.

Role theory helps us to appreciate that, in every treatment relationship, worker and client alike engage in efforts to induce one another to enact the role or roles that each deems necessary to maintain the interpersonal situation. If one of the role partners fails to show appreciation for the other's prescriptions, strain is created, and the role interaction is in danger of being dissolved.

One of the social worker's major tools in treatment is his own role repertoire as a professional. He gives to those who need giving; he frustrates those who need frustration; he is broker, advocate, leader, follower, expert, or neophyte, depending on the dynamic unfolding of the case situation. The social worker attempts to offer a corrective experience by being a new and different role partner who did not or does not exist in the client's socialization experiences. The worker enacts those roles that will help his client assume and strengthen those social roles of his own that promote his individual growth and development.

System Theory

Perhaps the most popular theory used in contemporary social work is system theory. As the role concept became part of social work theory and practice, social workers began to assimilate facets of system theory, which embraces the role concept. Role interactions and transactions are considered to be part of a larger system of group behavior that strives for equilibrium. System theorists view the human personality as an open system in constant interplay with its surroundings, receiving stimuli from the environment and modifying its internal mechanisms to maintain equilibrium.

A few of the principles of systems theory are pertinent to the worker–client relationship. According to the principle of *stability,* systems theory emphasizes input and output and the equilibrating processes that keep the system in a state of stability, or *homeostasis.* Stability means that a change in one part of the system is followed by a change in other parts (Bertalanffy, 1968). Consequently, if a worker has an impact on his client, family members or other key people in the client's environment may resent the client's changes. This in turn may upset the client, who might want to terminate treatment. This principle of stability helps anyone engaged in doing therapy to recognize that a therapeutic relationship can upset an internal or interpersonal homeostatic balance. The worker should always be aware that these disruptions must be faced directly with the client in the treatment encounter.

Another important feature of a social system is the *communication of information.* Communication is an essential feature of the transaction between two or more people. What information is communicated, what is withheld, and the manner in which it is delivered influence the reciprocity or lack of reciprocity between members. If feelings and thoughts are directly communicated without fear of reprisal, the system is stable; if communication is indirect or squelched, resentment arises between members and the system can deteriorate (Ruesch, 1961).

The implications of communication theory for the worker–client relationship are several. For a client to explore his psychological and social problems with the worker, he must experience the worker as one who will not judge, condemn, or reject. If the client anticipates these negative responses, the worker will need to help the client investigate why he anticipates them. Second, if the worker–client relationship is going to strengthen the client's coping capacities, the worker must feel free to discuss issues about which the client is uncomfortable. For example, it can be very reassuring to a client when the worker can discuss homosexuality, dependency, physical handicaps, or death in a direct and frank way. Finally, whenever the worker senses that the client is uncomfortable about something in the client-worker encounter (as can be expressed through the client's silence, absence, or lateness), it can be helpful to the client for the worker to ask what it is about the encounter that makes the client uncomfortable.

A final dimension of system theory that is applicable to the worker–client relationship is the *hierarchical factor.* The hierarchical factor has implications and consequences for communication patterns and relationships among system members. If the worker, through his speech, dress, office furniture, or use of titles, maintains major status differences between himself and the client, he will create barriers in communication and undue formality in the relationship (Stanton and Schwartz, 1954).

Rogerian Theory

Although there are several personality theories that embrace concepts that are applicable to the worker–client relationship (some of which will be reviewed in the concluding section of this chapter), the work of Carl Rogers is very pertinent. Rogers' "relationship therapy," later called client-centered therapy, emphasizes the curative power of the emotional relationship between therapist and client rather than any insight gained by the individual through interpretation (Rogers, 1951).

Unconditional Positive Regard. Although Rogers contends that each person uniquely perceives himself and his environment, there are ways in which the therapist or someone else can "tune in" to the person's perceptions. If the listener holds the client in *unconditional positive regard* (Rogers, 1951) and seeks to enter his frame of reference empathically, the client will be more able to communicate his true feelings and thoughts. If the client is not under *threat*—an experience that is not consistent with the self-picture the client is trying to maintain (Rogers, 1951)—and feels a limited need to be defensive, he will be able to communicate what he is feeling and feel valued for it (Rogers, 1959).

When a client feels that there are no *conditions of worth*—that is, the positive regard of an important person is not made conditional—as he communicates whatever he thinks, his self-esteem rises and he has more energy for functioning (Rogers, 1959). Unconditional positive regard implies "nonpossessive warmth," "genuineness," and "empathy," and these therapeutic attitudes have been demonstrated to exist in successful treatment (Truax, 1973).

In a study conducted by the writer (Strean, 1976), it was demonstrated that the most successful therapists with hospitalized schizophrenic patients are first-year social work students:

> Unperturbed by previous therapeutic failures, unimpressed by the cautionary admonitions of his mentors, unencumbered by a bevy of therapeutic procedures swimming in his head, the social work student *unconditionally regards his or her patient positively* and truly accepts him or her where the patient is. In contrast to experienced professionals, who often unconsciously communicate their therapeutic pessimism to the patient . . .

> the social work student optimistically and very humanely wants to help a real person in a real situation. . . . As we have examined the social work students' demeanor and therapeutic posture in their interviews with schizophrenic patients . . . nonpossessive warmth, genuineness, and empathy were consistently present in the students' therapeutic orientation [pp. 287–288].

Incongruence. When the individual notes behavior that is inconsistent with his self-concept, Rogers postulates a concept of *incongruence,* and it is this state that makes the individual vulnerable to anxiety. According to Rogers (1959), psychological maladjustment exists when the organism denies to awareness significant sensory and visceral experiences. Each client in therapy, according to Rogers, is in a state of incongruence. To help him, the therapist must be in a state of congruence, that is, the therapist's behavior and his concept of self are consistent with one another (1960).

According to Rogerian principles, the therapist must believe in what he is trying to effect for the client. If the worker is not convinced that the family is a worthwhile institution, that sex is an enjoyable interpersonal experience, or that the expression of nondestructive aggression is self-enhancing, these attitudes will be subtly conveyed to the client, and the client will not feel free to mature and function better.

According to Rogers, the personality of the client will change only to the degree that he can sense, however dimly, the empathic understanding and unconditional positive regard the therapist has for him. If the client does not know or feel this, then "no therapeutic relationship will result and no constructive change will take place in the client" (Rogers, 1959).

Learning Theory

Although learning theory makes very few references to the dynamics of the worker–client relationship, some of its concepts are applicable.

All therapy involves learning. Usually, people learn best when they feel *rewarded* and *reinforced.* Consequently, when the therapist affirms or reinforces the client's self-enhancing and self-actualizing statements, there is a good chance that the client will begin to do this for himself.

To learn, one must want something (*drive*), notice something (*cue*), do something (*response*), and get something (*reward*) (Dollard and Miller, 1950). When the worker can help the client get in touch with what he really wants (food, clothing, shelter, love, an opportunity to express certain feelings) and assist him to take action, the client will in all likelihood feel better and function better. As the client feels prized, challenged, and understood, according to learning theorists, he tends to *generalize* (Thorndike, 1932), that is, he begins to approach new situations as he experienced old ones. If, for example, he learned that a social worker is a humane, warm, helpful person, he can be less suspicious in other relationships and find himself to be more cooperative in them.

Learning theory has alerted social workers to the fact that supportive treatment and remarks are essentially rewards that reinforce behavior. Furthermore, withholding supportive remarks or placing limits on the client's self-destructive behavior is essentially *negative reinforcement* that can eventually help to extinguish maladaptive functioning.

Social workers of any persuasion should consider that work with certain, if not most, clients must be bereft of punishment. The nonpunitive atmosphere in the social worker–client relationship can *desensitize* the client when the worker does not provide rewards or reinforcements for immature cravings. The social worker should acknowledge that, regardless of his perspective, he is usually offering the client cues that influence what the worker values, devalues, wishes to work on, and wishes to avoid. Certainly, these cues of the worker will influence the client and affect the treatment outcome.

As Florence Hollis (1968) has suggested, all treatment is replete with approbation or rejecting maneuvers, and all treatment involves some learning and relearning. Therefore, the concepts of positive and negative reinforcement, conditioning, reward, and punishment are applicable in the worker–client relationship.

Other Theories

Adlerian Theory. Alfred Adler, the discoverer of the inferiority complex, postulated that each individual has a unique way of striving for his goals and reaching what is a superior position for him. Based on the individual's constitutionality, his early life experiences, and his inferiorities, the individual finds unique means to arrange his life. If intellectual superiority, for example, is his goal, the individual will organize much of his life in the pursuit of knowledge (Adler, 1927).

To be truly of service to a rich diversity of clients, the social worker must be able to "tune in and be conversant with the client's unique *life style*" (Ansbacher and Ansbacher, 1956). This means that, for the more action-oriented client, the social worker must be able to take action (be an advocate or social broker, make a home visit, see a teacher, go with the client to a legal aid office) rather than just "verbalize." It means being able to converse in the language of the client—slang, at times, concrete words at other times, and perhaps few words at still other times. The idea of life style implies that certain values, norms, and roles of the client cannot easily be altered and perhaps in some cases should not be modified but supported.

According to Adler, each individual feels incomplete and inferior in one way or another; because of the discomfort activated by his feeling of incompleteness, he arranges fantasies that will eventually place him in a position of superiority. *Fictional finalism* implies that much of the individual's behavior can be explained by understanding his final goals. Man, Adler contended, is motivated more by his expectations of the future than by his experiences in the past. Although the final goal may be a fiction, it is an ideal toward which men strive. The individual's goals tend to be more unrealistic the more he is dominated by inferiority feelings; the healthy individual sets realistic goals and faces reality when he is required to do so (Adler, 1927).

The concept of fictional finalism seems to be pertinent to the social worker–client relationship. Every client has fantasies of what he or she would like to have. Whether these fantasies are realistic or not, unless the worker offers some respect for them, he can lose the client. How often have social workers expected clients to adapt to a preconceived therapeutic model without *asking them* what they would like from the social worker and how the social worker should provide it? All clients have fantasies of what they would like to become. Some of these fantasies may be unattainable, but they need airing and exploration before the client can even think of giving them up. Perhaps more clients would become more cooperative if the social worker would offer them the opportunity to first voice and later examine how they would like to be stars, heroes, and Hollywood celebrities.

Sullivanian Theory. All of Harry Stack Sullivan's theory emanates from his view that every behavior has interpersonal significance. The individual cannot be understood without taking into consideration the social and cultural forces that are constantly impinging on him. According to Sullivan, the client cannot be understood or appreciated unless the observer understands the context in which the person is being studied and assessed (1947). For example, if the social worker sees a client in his home, in a store, and in the agency, he may observe three different types of behavior in the same person.

Sullivan's interpersonal orientation helps the social worker recognize the tremendous impact that the staff of nurses, attendants, wardens, and others have on the mental patient, the jailed, and the physically ill. Furthermore, Sullivan's interpersonal orientation defines the client not just as an object of treatment; according to Sullivan, both client and worker are subjects and objects in the interpersonal encounter, with both constantly influencing the other's behavior, for better or worse! Sullivan, like other theorists such as Rogers and Freud, contends that, for the client to modify distortions of himself and others, the best locus for altering attitudes is in a new learning experience in a unique relationship with the therapist (Sullivan, 1947).

Lewinian Theory. Kurt Lewin postulated the notion of the *life space.* It consists of the totality of facts that are capable of determining the behavior of an individual. It includes *everything* that has to be known to understand the concrete behavior of an individual human being in a given psychological environment at a given time (Lewin, 1951).

The Lewinian notion that a fact must exist in the individual's life space before it can influence the person can have far-reaching significance for social workers. One implication of this notion for the social worker is that he must give much credence to the client's subjective diagnosis of his problem. Lewinian theory implies that a client's experience and definition of a problem are what really counts. For example, if he believes his spouse is causing his unemployment, this belief is what is crucial; the worker's definition of the situation, however psychologically astute, is part of the client's "foreign hull"—that is, outside the person's awareness (Lewin, 1951). Implied in this prescription is a proposition for intervention: the most helpful and meaningful interview the social worker can offer the client is one in which he experiences the worker as part of his life space and one in which the worker talks to him in his own psychological language.

Conclusion

The focus of social work, the person–situation constellation, embraces a lot of territory. Consequently, social workers are constant borrowers of knowledge. There are many hazards in borrowing knowledge, but as long as the social work domain remains such an extensive one, borrowing will continue. In this chapter, I have borrowed and tried to elucidate pertinent concepts from selected theories that can be meaningfully applicable to the social worker–client relationship. I am hopeful that this modest project will be continued by others. Perhaps other practitioners and theoreticians will see links to the worker–client relationship that I have not observed, not only from the work of the theorists discussed here, but from other theories and theorists. As social workers continue to attempt to help individuals, families, and groups, no one theory will undergird all our work, and therefore more attempts similar to this one must be pursued.

References

Adler, A. *The Practice and Theory of Individual Psychology.* New York: Harcourt, 1927.

Ansbacher, H., and Ansbacher, R. *The Individual Psychology of Alfred Adler.* New York: Basic Books, 1956.

Bertalanffy, L. *General Systems Theory: Foundations, Development, Application.* New York: Braziller, 1968.

Biddle, B., and Thomas, E. *Role Theory.* New York: Wiley, 1966.

Brenner, C. *Psychoanalytic Technique and Psychic Conflict.* New York: International Universities Press, 1976.

Deutsch, M., and Krauss, R. *Theories in Social Psychology.* New York: Basic Books, 1965.

Dollard, J., and Miller, N. *Personality and Psychotherapy.* New York: McGraw-Hill, 1950.

Erikson, E. *Childhood and Society.* New York: Norton, 1950.

Fine, R. *The Healing of the Mind.* New York: McKay, 1971.

Fine, R. *Psychoanalytic Psychology.* New York: Jason Aronson, 1975.

Freud, S. *The Future Prospects of Psychoanalytic Therapy.* Vol. 11. (Standard ed.) London: Hogarth Press, 1910. (Publication date 1957.)

Freud, S. *The Dynamics of Transference.* Vol. 12. (Standard ed.) London: Hogarth Press, 1912. (Publication date 1957.)

Grinker, R. *Toward a Unified Theory of Behavior.* (2nd ed.) New York: Basic Books, 1967.

Hartmann, H. *Ego Psychology and the Problem of Adaptation.* New York: International Universities Press, 1958.

Hollis, F. "And What Shall We Teach?" *Social Service Review,* 1968, *42* (2), 184–196.

Lennard, H., and Bernstein, A. *The Anatomy of Psychotherapy.* New York: Columbia University Press, 1960.

Lewin, K. *Field Theory in Social Science: Selected Theoretical Papers.* Dorwin Cartwright (Ed.) Westport, Conn.: Greenwood Press, 1975.

Linton, R. "Culture, Society and the Individual." *Journal of Abnormal and Social Psychology,* 1938, *33,* 425–436.

Meerloo, J., and Nelson, M. *Transference and Trial Adaptation.* Springfield, Ill.: Charles Thomas, 1965.

Menninger, K. *Theory of Psychoanalytic Technique.* New York: Basic Books, 1958.

Overall, B., and Aronson, H. "Expectations of Psychotherapy in Patients of Lower Socioeconomic Class." *American Journal of Orthopsychiatry,* 1961, *31,* 421–430.

Perlman, H. "Intake and Some Role Considerations." In C. Kasius (Ed.), *Social Casework in the Fifties.* New York: Family Service Association of America, 1962.

Richmond, M. *What Is Social Casework?* New York: Russell Sage Foundation, 1922.

Rogers, C. *Client-Centered Therapy.* Boston: Houghton Mifflin, 1951.

Rogers, C. "A Theory of Therapy, Personality and Interpersonal Relationships as Developed in the Client-Centered Framework." In S. Koch (Ed.), *Psychology: A Study of a Science.* Vol. 3. New York: McGraw-Hill, 1959.

Rogers, C. *A Therapist's View of Personal Goals.* Wallingford, Pa.: Pnedle Hill, 1960.

Rosenblatt, A. "Application of Role Concepts to the Intake Process." *Social Casework,* 1962, *43,* 8–14.

Ruesch, J. *Therapeutic Communication.* New York: Norton, 1961.

Sandler, J. *The Patient and the Analyst.* New York: International Universities Press, 1973.

Sarbin, T. "Role Theory." In G. Lindzey (Ed.), *Handbook of Social Psychology.* Vol. 1. Cambridge, Mass.: Addison-Wesley, 1954.

Shyne, A. "What Research Tells Us About Short-Term Cases in Family Agencies." *Social Casework,* 1957, *38* (5), 223–231.

Stark, F. "Barriers to Client–Worker Communication at Intake." *Social Casework,* 1959, *40* (4), 177–183.

Stanton, A., and Schwartz, M. *The Mental Hospital.* New York: Basic Books, 1954.

Strean, H. *New Approaches in Child Guidance.* Metuchen, N.J.: Scarecrow Press, 1970.

Strean, H. *Personality Theory and Social Work Practice.* Metuchen, N.J.: Scarecrow Press, 1975.

Strean, H. *Crucial Issues in Psychotherapy.* Metuchen, N.J.: Scarecrow Press, 1976.

Strean, H. *Clinical Social Work.* New York: Free Press, 1978.

Strean, H. *Psychoanalytic Theory and Social Work Practice.* New York: Free Press, 1979.

Sullivan, H. S. Conceptions of Modern Psychiatry. Washington, D.C.: William Alanson White, 1947.

Sullivan, H. S. *The Interpersonal Theory of Psychiatry.* New York: Norton, 1953.

Thorndike, E. *The Fundamentals of Learning.* New York: Columbia University Teachers College, 1932.

Truax, C. "Effective Ingredients in Psychotherapy." In A. Mahrer and L. Pearson (Eds.), *Creative Developments in Psychotherapy.* Vol. 1. New York: Jason Aronson, 1973.

Section III

Education and Methods for Clinical Practice

Elizabeth C. Lemon
Section Editor

"If you would do good you must begin with minute particulars."
Samuel Butler

The following chapters deal with casework and psychotherapeutic approaches currently being practiced by social work clinicians. The focus is on how the approaches are taught, learned, and utilized, and how aspects of this work give rise to problems within the profession as a whole.

The term *clinical social worker* is used to refer to practitioners whose graduate social work education includes the study of, and supervised practice in, various treatment methods and is followed by a continuing and substantial work experience.

Although by no means representative of the whole of clinical work, the treatment of individuals and families constitutes a large and important part of a steadily developing field. Clinicians now provide a considerable portion of the nation's psychotherapeutic services in agency and hospital settings, traditional bases from which much of our knowledge of practice has evolved. The principles of clinical treatment, derived as they are from social casework, are constantly being refined and expanded through the development of new areas of practice and the incorporation of divergent points of view. Yet, despite this activity, actual changes in the way therapeutic procedures are implemented seem to occur with less speed than the recent literature might suggest.

From the 1920s to the early 1960s, psychoanalysis strongly influenced the theoretical base of social casework; it remains a major force in much clinical practice. Derivatives of psychoanalytic theory, like ego psychology or developmental and object-relations theories, while continuing to enlarge and enrich our understanding of personal dynamics and their historical roots, have tended to minimize the part played by everyday realities in promoting and maintaining dysfunctional behavior. Thus, our Freudian heritage can sometimes interfere with our ability to evaluate critically other conceptual models for viewing and working with troubled individuals and families that have been introduced in the more recent past.

Individual casework—open-ended and psychoanalytically oriented, based on a positive relationship—is probably the most well developed of all the approaches used by clinical workers, but its shortcomings are now generally recognized.

Schamess, in his chapter on the treatment relationship reminds us that this one-to-one approach has been of little avail in helping people cope with hostile and unsupportive environments. And Miller, speaking to the problems of cross-cultural treatment, shows that the unique coping strategies of people of color are frequently ignored or viewed as psychopathological by workers in mental health settings.

In general, it would seem that the current trend toward a multimethod practice holds greater promise for meeting widely differing client needs. It is interesting to note that recent writings give more weight to the individual client's cognitive functioning and behavior and less to the client's affect. This change coincides with a closer and more sophisticated look at ethnic and cultural factors, with a new emphasis on more structured, time-limited forms of treatment and the multiperson interview that is concerned primarily with the present. Not all authors imply that the emotions are not important, merely that behavior and cognitive functioning require more attention.

The introduction to casework of a systems and ecological perspective, which directs attention to the complex interdependence of people and social institutions (see Germain's chapter on this subject in the preceding section), encourages the profession to use a more comprehensive framework that will enable us to address multiple factors affecting the personal strivings and adaptive patterns of an individual or family.

These are stimulating ideas, but how much they are being implemented in current practice is uncertain. A recent study in California suggests that old ways die hard. While this may surprise some people more than others, it points to the possibility that the work of Germain and others, although it makes us more aware of the wider social scene, is no substitute for an object-relations theory which aids our understanding of the intricacies of worker/client interaction.

Besides the growth of new ideas, other recent developments in the social work profession include an increase in the number of people entering private practice, the licensing of social workers, and the granting of third-party payments (in many states).

The California study is of special note because it explored similarities and differences between licensed workers in agencies and private practitioners. The study revealed that the gap between these two groups may not be as wide or as significant as we might think (Borenzweig, 1981). The sample consisted of three groups: (1) those whose work was confined to private practice, (2) those employed only in an agency, and (3) those engaged in private as well as agency practice. Some of the findings show the three groups to be similar in many respects. Most remarkable was the discovery that all respondents to the questionnaire stated that their practice was greatly influenced by Freudian theory.

The groups were not at all similar in the populations they served. Here marked differences came to light. Private clients tended to be middle- or upper-class, while those seen in agencies were mostly black, Chicano, and Asian people of lower socioeconomic status. One-to-one interviewing was the most common treatment format among respondents in both groups while "innovative modalities" were used more frequently by agency workers. Private conjoint interviews with married couples were more prominent in the private practice group whereas agency workers used family meetings with greater frequency.

A comparison of respondents who graduated from social work school before 1967 with those who graduated later showed that post-1967 graduates felt more secure in their social work identity; they showed more readiness to ally themselves with the profession and to think of themselves as social workers rather than psychotherapists. A secure identity is dependent upon many factors, and the time of graduation may well be an important variable. It may, for instance, represent a modification of public attitudes in recent years leading to the increased recognition of social workers as independent practitioners. If this is so, it has probably played a part in enhancing our professional self-image; still, whether a secure identity can in any way be related to the year 1967 is hard to tell. Clearly the findings of this particular study cannot be used to make generalizations about clinical work and more research into variations in practice is needed.

The growth of new knowledge and of new ideas about how to apply it therapeutically has made the matter of assessment more complex. The number of factors to be considered when we attempt to arrive at the intervention of choice for a family or individual have increased. Addressing this subject, a National Association of Social Workers Task Force (Cohen, 1980) outlined the areas of theoretical knowledge presently considered necesssary to arrive at a "reasonably adequate" bio/psycho/social assessment of a particular situation. This tripartite classification of knowledge, an effort to consider the whole person and situation, is now generally included in the curriculum of social work at the master's level. While the three parts are obviously intertwined, one is apt to be given greater priority, depending on the field of practice, the worker's orientation, and the client's perception of the situation. For instance, parents seeking treatment for their child from the psychiatric clinic of a large medical establishment will be inclined to view the difficulties as psychological, while parents who petition a juvenile court because they cannot control their child are more likely to be concerned about social behavior.

Ideally, the treatment agreement arising from any assessment is not limited either by professional preference for a particular approach or by the special abilities of the worker doing the evaluation. In practice, the plan will depend upon what services are available. In an era of steadily diminishing funds for social services, cost containment must limit what we can offer. Meanwhile increased awareness of racial discrimination, social injustices, cultural differences, alternative life-styles, and so on, call for greater differentiation in assessment and treatment. The lines of this dilemma are clearly drawn and a rising tide of professional frustration can be expected. Interesting consequences are likely to result from the threats and challenges ahead.

Case study, diagnosis, and treatment have always been more fluid and never quite as discrete and clearcut as the literature would suggest. This is especially so if the time available for study is brief, for instance in an emergency situation. Systematic history-taking that explores different aspects of development is important to a sound assessment, but is appropriate only if the person is not in need of immediate intervention, has voluntarily requested help, or has agreed to explore the service possibilities. When these conditions are not met, it is hoped that the client will receive protection from the supervisory process so that a true appreciation of needs and circumstances may be reached. Collecting information merely because we are aware of its general existence may have no bearing on the wishes and needs of the client. Conversely, failure to explore that which would assist our understanding of why the person needs help limits our ability to engage in any preventive measures.

A skilled worker soon recognizes that some personal facts are not relevant to the presenting problem. The same worker also sees when clients' need to describe their difficulties in their own way and at their own pace takes precedent over fact-gathering. Evaluation is a complex task involving individual judgment and imagination as well as skill. It is an undertaking in which intuition—the rapid making of connections—plays a vital role. The knowledge, training, and skill required for successful diagnosis and treatment are often difficult to classify; experience in one frequently refines and expands our understanding of the other.

One way of coping with the vast amount of knowledge now available is to specialize. Some clinicians tend to focus on one area of practice (such as a hospital setting with surgical patients and their families or working with the aged in a family agency). Another method of meeting this dilemma is to enter private practice. This route is taken by many experienced workers who wish to continue working with clients instead of moving into a supervisory or administrative role. Private practice offers more opportunity for autonomy but may cut off the worker from the mainstream of the profession.

The topics covered in the chapters that follow, while far from comprehensive, are intended to introduce the reader to a range of treatment activities currently subsumed under the term *clinical social work*. The chapters were written to guide students entering the field and to inform workers who may wish to diversify after some initial work experience. To what degree skills required for the various forms of treatment can be acquired during training at the master's level, and whether depth should take precedence over breadth, are the subject of continued discussion (Goldstein, 1980). The increase in number of doctoral programs concentrating on clinical work suggests that the amount of education and experience now needed for independent practice far exceeds that which can be provided in a master's program. Continuing education, as Frey and Edinburg point out in their chapter on this subject, is now essential to professional growth. In some states it is a requirement for license renewal. Whatever the field of practice, keeping abreast of changing conditions and the problems they give rise to provides necessary knowledge for preventive intervention. This may mean reaching out to populations at risk, the introduction of new intake procedures, and the raising of consciousness of clinicians responsible for carrying out treatment.

Wasserman, writing about the teaching of treatment methods, describes ways of helping students synthesize knowledge with their own experiences in order to ease anxieties that are endemic to the education of clinical social workers. Often before they feel prepared to do so, students are required to help people cope with tragedy or stress. This demands a high tolerance for negativism, misery, and neediness, and an ability to manage such feelings without loss of concern and empathy for the client. Speaking from a student point of view, Hart and Kadet underscore this aspect of their learning, making clear the critical part played by fieldwork supervisors and other agency personnel. During the last decade, schools have recognized the educational role of supervisors by granting them academic titles; even so, the extent of their contribution is not always fully recognized or appreciated. Waldfogel discusses various aspects of supervision and consultation, the different form each takes, and the need to particularize in the case of each student according to his or her learning needs.

When faced with a wealth of knowledge and many practice opinions, students are usually stimulated and challenged by the opportunities for learning. They are at the same time bewildered and made anxious by the practical and philosophical diversity of practice; the students believe they must master everything in order to compete in the job market. Supervisors serve an important function here in helping students develop realistic learning goals consistent with their individual talents and prior experiences. The gap between field and classroom tends to fluctuate from time to time, sometimes leaving the burden of integration with supervisor and student.

In their chapters on working with parents (Cooper) and with children (Lieberman), the authors use case vignettes describing the worker/client interaction to illustrate the subtleties inherent in this type of clinical practice in ways that theory, no matter how compelling, cannot convey. Cooper's work shows the value of being flexible enough to change course in treatment in keeping with change in the client's emotional stance, something the more structured forms of time-limited treatment discourage (see Lemon, on planned brief treatment).

Walsh surveys the rapidly developing field of family therapy, in which there has been much collaboration between social work clinicians and professionals from allied disciplines. The multiplicity of approaches reflects differing therapeutic styles as much as differences in theoretical orientation and draws on our understanding of individual dynamics more than was previously acknowledged. Current efforts to link object-relations theory (Friedman, 1980; Kantor, 1980) and ethnic factors (McGoldrick and Pearce, 1982) to an understanding of family systems promise to provide us with a more solid foundation on which to build effective work with more than one family member.

With the skill of a clinician who practices what she teaches, Roemele brings together theory and practice of group treatment. In her chapter she makes very clear the limitations of this modality as well as its therapeutic potential.

Loewenstein's cogent and informative chapter on issues related to women in treatment gives rise to many questions. Not the least of which is how does one choose a therapist—especially if one is poor?

Finally, despite all our efforts to inject new knowledge into practice, much remains to be done. The spirit of inquiry evidenced in the following chapters suggests, however, that so long as clinicians continue to examine the minute particulars of their own practice, they will make a valuable contribution to this profession.

References

Borenzweig, H. "Agency vs. Private Practice: Similarities and Differences." *Social Work,* 1981, *26* (3), 239–244.

Cohen, J. "The Nature of Clinical Social Work." In P. L. Ewalt (Ed.), *Toward a Definition of Clinical Social Work.* Washington, D.C.: National Association of Social Workers, 1980.

Friedman, L. J. "Integrating Psychoanalytic Object-Relations Understanding with Family Systems Interventions in Couples Therapy." In J. K. Pearce and L. J. Friedman (Eds.), *Combining Psychodynamic and Family Systems Approaches.* New York: Grune & Stratton, 1980.

Goldstein, E. "The Knowledge Base of Clinical Social Work." In P. L. Ewalt (Ed.), *Toward a Definition of Clinical Social Work.* Washington, D.C.: National Association of Social Workers, 1980.

Kantor, D. "Critical Identity Image: A Concept Linking Individual, Couple and Family Development." In J. K. Pearce and L. J. Friedman (Eds.), *Combining Psychodynamic and Family Systems Approaches.* New York: Grune & Stratton, 1980.

McGoldrick, M., and Pearce, J. K. *Ethnicity and Family Therapy.* New York: Guilford Press, 1982.

13

Students' Perspective on Graduate Training

Russell D. Hart
Hessa B. Kadet

The first half of this chapter was written by Russell Hart while a first-year graduate student studying for an M.S.W. degree.

Preparation for clinical social work, like training for many other professions, is a multifaceted and rigorous endeavor. Not only does it require learning vast amounts of information on theories of human behavior and development, but it also demands a knowledge of self and a quality of being and relating. One must have not only a head but a heart as well. The practitioner must learn to be critical and analytical in his or her thinking, along with learning how to sustain emotional contact throughout purposeful working relationships that are directed toward therapeutic change.

The demands of learning for action as well as mastery of this knowledge base present special difficulties. How one experiences and responds to the challenges and stresses of clinical social work education is dependent on such factors as previous experience, level of maturity, and the age at which one enters the educational process. That process can at times be a difficult and arduous task, yet it is not without its rewards.

This portion of the chapter will discuss several areas of particular concern arising from my experiences as a social work student. My comments are not only subjective but stem also from many conversations with other first-year students.

Social work students enter graduate school with some sense of competency, since all have been successful at the undergraduate level. All have been wage earners, even if only on a part-time basis. Many have had social work experience. On becoming a graduate student, however, one enters unfamiliar waters. Previous feelings of mastery, competency, and familiarity are replaced by those of uncertainty and anxiety. Questions emerge, such as: What will be expected of me in this new environment? How shall I value my previous work experience? Will it be of any help here? How much can I realistically expect from an academic program when the task to be learned also involves the development of my emotional resources in the service of the helping encounter? Will the knowledge I bring be validated or will I be required to give up my previous frame of reference in order to incorporate new learnings? Will I be able to sift through all of the competing influences and choose for myself that which I think useful? Or will I be so inundated by ideas that I will lose my ability to discriminate? Will the skills I have be useful in this new endeavor, or will I have to give up hard-won gains, with little idea of what will take their place?

Additionally, the educational process requires heavy commitments of time and energy. Relationships and interests outside of school often must be put on hold—sometimes for long periods. Old routines are forsaken. One's personal life must be altered to meet the new requirements.

Most students enter social work education in their twenties, when issues of competency and independence still loom large. Any situation that might be experienced as a backward slide into a previous state of dependency is therefore threatening. Feelings of being overwhelmed can indeed result in regression and dependency. The demands of graduate education, in terms of time and energy, may well be viewed and experienced as a loss of control over one's life. When this occurs, much energy may become directed toward maintaining one's identity by a constant warding off of external influences in order to maintain a feeling of internal cohesiveness. The ways in which each individual mediates and negotiates this process differ. Judging from my own experiences, as well as from my observations of other students, there is often an initial sense of loss and a period of mourning. The mourning may first be expressed in the form of anger or resentment, or hostile acceptance. The trainee frequently looks to the instructor or the supervisor for the "right answers" in order to reduce anxiety. Students may even compete to have the best interpretation or the best paper as a way to reaffirm their sense of competency. Others respond to the transition with excitement and exuberance at the opportunity to increase their knowledge, while still others fluctuate from one state to the other.

The process of learning about other people necessarily entails the risk and challenge of learning about one's self. Reviewing client cases and examining theories of human behavior cannot help but bring into awareness questions about one's own functioning. It is almost impossible for the student to avoid examining his or her own life and relationships in light of new knowledge. In fact, this is clearly a necessity if learning is to go beyond mere intellectualization. Student trainees are likely to see their own families and significant relationships in a new light, and to begin to identify and question their own behaviors and motivations. Unresolved personal issues may emerge and require attention, while issues partially worked through at a previous stage of development may surprisingly reappear, much to one's chagrin. Such reactions involve an element of loss, for integration of this new material requires a giving up of previously held beliefs about one's self. New insights replace gaps in self-knowledge. As Miller (1979) points out: "Clinical learning entails a loss of innocence as one of its hazards."

I recall, for example, a time when I had to set some strong limits on a ten-year-old boy who had difficulty separating at the end of our sessions. The memory of how pathetic and sad he looked as I coaxed him out the door is still vivid, along with the feelings of guilt and anger he evoked. In relating this incident to my supervisor, feelings of sadness suddenly emerged, much to my surprise. The situation afforded me an opportunity to examine my strong reactions and to better understand myself, as well as this particular worker/client relationship.

There is a danger that one may become overly vigilant and critical as a result of this type of self-exploration. Like the medical student who seems to contract whatever disease is being studied that week, so too the social work student may wonder—half in jest, half seriously—if he or she is not borderline manic-depressive. How does the individual learner explain this tumultuous state of affairs to oneself and to others? Reactions are not always so extreme; however, there may be times when one feels that there is either something wrong with one's self or with the educational process, without being clear about exactly what it is.

Clinical work requires that our clients' behavior be carefully observed and analyzed for the purpose of determining how best to help them achieve their goals. Differential diagnosis involves the use of labels and the planning of treatment procedures. At such times the sense of the client as a whole person, as another human being, can be temporarily suspended. When this happens the trainees may feel that they too will be examined in this way. If a clinician can observe what clients cannot see in themselves, then the same may be true for the student/teacher/supervisor relationship. This can be anxiety provoking, particularly when the student is feeling confused, overwhelmed, and struggling to maintain a cohesive sense of self. The student's fear of being in some way like the client can be either exacerbated or decreased by the way in which the instructor or supervisor listens to and responds to questions. The development and use of psychological terminology provides one way of warding off feelings of powerlessness and lack of control. When this happens, classifications are apt to be used pejoratively.

Students differ widely in the ways in which each negotiates, mediates, and copes with the process of change involved in applying what is learned about human behavior. It is difficult for those actively involved to assess how much stress is inherent in the very nature of clinical social work education. Thus, while important but beyond the scope of this chapter, questions about the role of the school and the agency in containing or exacerbating students' anxieties must be considered.

The first year, challenging and tumultuous as it is sure to be, provides the opportunity for growth and increased self-awareness. Adaptation over several months to a highly demanding and challenging situation adds to the learner's sense of achievement and self-esteem, especially when one looks back from the vantage point of examinations successfully completed.

Mastery and adaptation gradually but ultimately take place in the field, in the actual meeting with the client, where theory and application come together over time. Depending on the depth of experience of each individual trainee, there is initially some feeling of helplessness, born of lack of knowledge and skill. As one student stated: "When I first started, I needed my supervisor to tell me what to do from session to session. I felt really lost." From other conversations I heard a common theme: Students assumed that they were expected to present their supervisors with the process recordings of perfect interviews and to have each case expertly assessed and mapped out. It was also evident that there was great fear of making mistakes, alienating the client, or doing harm.

When one of my clients did not show for his appointment three weeks in a row, I was sure that I had somehow increased the client's ambivalence about treatment, despite my supervisor's assurance that I had not. It can be difficult initially to judge how much power and influence one has in the therapeutic situation, when feelings swing quickly from omnipotence to incompetence. Was I accepting enough? Did I push too hard or too little? Did I miss the "real" issue? Should I share my feelings or maintain a sense of detachment? If I knew more and were more skillful, would I be able to turn this case around or move it along faster? If the client had an experienced therapist would he show more improvement? Neither classroom readings nor supervisor seem to offer information and direction fast enough during this frustrating initial period.

Practice inevitably begins before knowledge and performance have solidified. Guilt may result from the feeling that one is practicing on the client and the belief that someone more skillful could have done better and speedier work.

Client demands which overburden the trainee's existing knowledge can be experienced as an assault on self-esteem. One student, conducting her first home visit, was greeted at the door with: "Oh no! Not another young worker. I wish they'd send me someone with experience."

I remember one session early in the year when one of my recently assigned clients poured out an overwhelming amount of material. Later, talking with my supervisor, I said: "He just kept pouring out information and material and I didn't quite know what to do with it all. I tried to make sense of it, tried to slow it down. I ended up making process comments, but he kept on talking." Despite the fact that I had some previous experiernce and some general ideas about how to handle such situations, I never felt sure that I would not get totally confused and disoriented by the quantity of material, or be unable to control its flow.

One of the most difficult elements to contend with in the beginning is this onslaught of intense human emotion—both clients' and one's own. Multiproblem families and individuals suffering from serious traumas and deprivations can overwhelm the student with intense sadness, depression, and anger. In fact, during a first-year class discussion of current issues such as poverty, welfare reform, racism, unwed mothers, battered children, alcoholism, and divorce, silent thoughts roar through the room: How will I deal with all of this? And with what means? How much can I expect from myself in dealing with this? How much will be expected of me? Will I learn enough while I'm here to even make a difference?

Some clients, seeking instant relief, endow the trainee with omnipotent powers, and it is difficult not to accept the role of all-knowing and powerful worker. The propensity to take on too much responsibility for the client's problem is an early pitfall: The client who wants the worker to magically bring about desired changes and the trainee who wants to prove himself form a partnership that is doomed to failure. It is often equally difficult to allow clients to make their own mistakes, or to see them backslide, without feeling responsible. The situation can raise feelings of anger and doubt that alternately can be turned inward and diverted toward the client for his or her refusal to get better.

There is also the experience and awareness of knowing that, no matter how much investment is made by both therapist and client, the amount of change is likely to be partial and provisional. The goal in this case becomes not "well" but "better."

An emotionally deprived eleven-year-old boy became quite dependent during the course of our individual sessions. He wanted more time with me, wanted gifts from me, arrived at the clinic a half hour early, and even came during school vacations when he knew I wouldn't be there. Sometimes this became rather upsetting. Never having worked with children of this age before, I did not know what to expect. His verbal skills and level of awareness were below age appropriateness and my inability to engage him in any more than a three-sentence conversation outside of play activity became painful. Not to know directly what he was feeling or what he wanted rendered useless my usual way of relating and being helpful. It was hard for me to see that our meetings served any useful purpose. In addition, I found this child's growing attachment to me both gratifying and frightening. It gradually became apparent that I could never undo his earlier deprivations—a rather sad awareness. Yet it was evident from his changed behavior in school and at home that our relationship was therapeutic. However, given his poor family situation, even with the aid of community supports, there were definite limitations to what treatment could provide.

It is the gap between expectations and experience, with its resulting discomfort, that forces the student to question, to pore over process recordings, to read and reread clinical literature, and to look to the supervisor for support, encouragement, and direction.

The paradox is that this discomfort resulting from a felt lack of knowledge needs to give way to a feeling of being comfortable with the ambiguity, complexity, and limitations inherent in the therapeutic encounter. Or, one might say, there is a need to become comfortable with the uncomfortable, the vague, the uncertain. Theories and constructs can point the trainee in the right direction by providing frameworks from which to understand behavior, but the frameworks are only guides—they are not the most important element in the therapeutic process. The relationship between the client and therapist would appear to be the key element in which treatment is grounded. The more the trainee is able to give up having "right answers," the more able will the trainee be to see, hear, and feel in the client's presence, and the more will the trainee be likely to get in touch with the unique qualities of the interaction and to learn that "right answers" emerge from the interaction of treatment.

Students can then begin to rely more on their own personal resources in conjunction with classroom learning and supervision; this leads to more autonomous functioning and less dependence on the approval of the supervisor. A search for easy rules and technical guidelines is replaced by the exhilaration of searching for and discovering the client's perspective and understanding significant interpersonal data that facilitates treatment objectives. As energy is redirected from preoccupation with one's own uncomfortable feelings, it may be used in a more creative fashion. One begins to hear the content of the client's messages as well as the underlying feelings, while processing one's own emotional and mental responses. The ability to hear, to feel, and share the client's pain as it occurs without being devastated by it, becomes an essential part of this task.

After the first few months of training students begin to speak in less uncertain terms and with greater excitement. There is an interest in genuine sharing of one's work with other students. The themes in informal meetings and classroom discussion begin to change. "What am I supposed to do?" and "What's the right way to approach this?" become "This is how I handled it" or "This approach did not work. What do you think went wrong?" The questioning occurs at a deeper level—from a desire to know rather than a fear of failure. Theoretical constructs are not as likely to be offhandedly dismissed as irrelevant nor as likely to be swallowed as absolute truths. Rather, each new learning is more apt to be weighed for its relative merits and application to the individual case. The limitations of treatment as well as one's own limitations can be more easily accepted, as one becomes freer to examine the existential stance of each client and able to consider one's interventions without being defensive. The phrase, "It may be my issue . . ." becomes a common statement as trainees consider their own countertransference responses rather than fearing them.

I do not mean to imply that uncertainty vanished within the first year, but rather that, with the accumulation of experience and success, one began to respond with greater enthusiasm, independence, and autonomy.

With better understanding of theory and practice, more penetrating questions emerged. When therapeutic understanding was no longer something to be feared, but rather to be used in a judicious fashion, the question of its differential use arose. Questions were ultimately linked to the development of one's own ideas about how people change and were more frequently involved with examining one's own values.

Because social work trainees are taught to consider the individual, along with his or her environment and adaptation to it, difficulties inevitably arise in defining the roles and boundaries of the social worker as psychotherapist and as social activist. Where, for example, could one's energies best be used? How much time should one spend on changing the conditions and institutions from which clients' problems stem, and how much attention placed on helping the person to make a more effective adaptation? It is hard to refute the belief that individual treatment frequently offers only Band-Aids to those whose problems result from societal inequities of opportunity and resources. During the first year the student usually settles for helping clients gain more power and control over their lives by removing psychosocial obstacles.

Too often questions such as by which route such obstacles might best be overcome are put aside in order to master the more immediate tasks at hand. Ideally, social work affords an opportunity for three methods of prevention—community organization, social reform, and psychotherapy. Yet, for the first-year clinical student the reality is simply that we are only making small improvements. How best to make those improvements lies at the core of the questioning, and is carried over into the second year. Sorting through one's beliefs as to how best to impact on the client population is a process which hopefully does not end after graduation, for the requirements of clinical social work are broad and vast enough to incorporate numerous ways of thinking and modes of responding. I entered my second year of training convinced that there is no one "right way" and that the pitfalls inherent in the present state of social work knowledge and skills are well charted.

References

Miller, Roger. "Clinical Learning as a Developmental Process." Delivered at St. Edmund Hall, Oxford, August 22–26, 1979.

* * * * *

The second half of this chapter was written by Hessa Kadet while a second-year graduate student studying for an M.S.W. degree.

On entering the field the student is quickly faced with questions about the boundaries of clinical social work. One soon learns that members of the profession struggle for a shared definition and a shared identity. The trainee who enters the profession, having chosen a clinical focus and requested a particular type of field work placement, may find that his or her identity is initially defined more by the type of practice than by the social work profession as a whole. This struggle for professional identity seems to parallel the profession's evolution and subspecialization into the broad-based profession that it is today.

The development of a positive professional identity is a particular challenge for the clinical social work trainee who is lerning skills in a setting such as a hospital where a traditional medical model or mental health hierarchy exists. In such a setting medical staff may be providing primary care, and interdisciplinary lines are likely to be sharply drawn which classify psychiatrists as the clinical experts. Clinical social workers with expertise in psychosocial assessment and treatment, innovative program development, teaching, research, and publishing are essential role models cherished by students in such settings.

One enters graduate training having already made some choices about those aspects of social work of greatest interest, but one soon learns that the boundaries between clinical social work, program planning, and policy are really quite fluid. The need to deal with immediate needs of clients, as well as to change the institutional structures that have contributed to them, soon becomes apparent. It is within the context of a relationship through contact of one human being with another that needs for treatment and prevention are identified. In thinking about any case one inevitably moves to considering the need for advocacy and social action.

For the student clinician the relationship between client and worker seems paradoxically both professional and personal. Feelings, thoughts, and actions that occur before, during, and after meeting with clients may be subject to intense scrutiny. Understanding one's reactions based on one's own life experience, attitudes, vulnerabilities, and subjective distortions often requires great investment of

Three years after writing this article I find myself in substantial conflict with it. While I realize its intrapsychic orientation reflects the new clinical knowledge I was acquainted with and immersed in as a student, I feel it fails to pay equal attention to the influence of race, class, and sex on clients' lives.—*Hessa Kadet* emotional energy. Open and safe classroom discussion of experiences and ideas and supportive supervision in the field are a help. In retrospect, it seems that a great deal of anxiety is endemic to clinical training since working with people experiencing significant pain, deprivation, loss, illness, and stress evokes feelings which are often difficult to understand. Thus many students who have not already been in therapy find the need for it.

Prior experience related to social work is an asset as it gives the trainee a sense of confidence and competence which helps especially during the early part of training, but the unlearning or reexamination of existing knowledge and skills is common, whatever experience one brings to training.

My first year of classroom work emphasized the social aspects of human development. This shifted in the second year of training with the introduction to theories of psychopathology and the impact on the treatment process of severe psychological disturbance.

The concern of the first year with a lost sense of competence gives way in the second to questions about one's potential. Feedback from supervisors and teachers remains crucial to the development of confidence about one's performance. At the same time responsibility for one's own learning increases. It becomes easier to identify particular areas of difficulty, rather than waiting for the supervisor to do so. Supervision, essential to clinical learning, creates an atmosphere in which the experience, expertise, and support of the supervisor helps the trainee develop perspective as well as understanding of the treatment process. I found learning easier when the supervisor was able to generalize rather than personalize the clinical learning process. This created an atmosphere in which I felt safe to disclose doubts and openly acknowledge feelings of confusion. Respect for individual learning style and value differences convey the sense of a mutual endeavor, especially when reviewing clinical material and the questions it raises. Supervisors are extremely important, providing the type of acceptance and expectations which make it easier, in turn, to accept clients and help them struggle with difficult, anxiety-provoking events.

The following three vignettes illustrate the way in which clinical learning raises issues, questions, and anxieties which promote learning.

Insight Isn't Everything. A thirty-seven-year-old single black woman employed as a teacher, struggling with depression and long-standing dissatisfaction with many areas of her life, was referred to a trainee at the beginning of the school year. The client was intensely involved with her mother, against whose moralistic, perfectionist, friendly but distant manner the client judged herself inadequate.

During the initial interview the trainee felt a sense of rapport and excitedly looked forward to working with the client. After this initial meeting the client called the clinic director to request a more experienced therapist, noting that while the trainee was "very nice" she felt the high fee she was required to pay was not commensurate with the trainee's level of professional experience. The trainee was disappointed by the client's request which dovetailed with and confirmed her own concerns about her level of competence and ability to help. She personalized the client's concerns and quickly undervalued and overlooked the rapport felt in their meeting. With the benefit of supervision the trainee, recalling her feelings for the client, was able to telephone her. In supporting the client's wish to find a more experienced therapist, the student recommended that rapport be an equally important element in her choice. In the course of this telephone conversation the client decided to return to work with the trainee, and they did so until the end of the academic year. Initially a ten-week contract was made, based on available insurance coverage, but when this was exhausted the client chose to continue seeing the student, even though she had to pay for sessions until insurance coverage was reinstated.

In the early stages the relationship felt very tentative because of the client's difficulty in expressing feelings, particularly about painful issues. The student overfunctioned and bombarded with client with "insights" and "interpretations" in an effort to demonstrate her knowledge. Over time, and with the benefit of supervision, the trust and confidence of both student and client grew. The client was able to express more feelings and a growing acceptance of herself enabled her to separate from her mother.

During the course of their work the client said that it was her expectation that the trainee, a white woman, would be judgmental, particularly around sexual issues; it was such fear, rather than lack of experience, which led her initially to request another therapist. The interest expressed by the trainee's phone call meant a great deal to her and led to her decision to return. Thus she taught the trainee how intrinsic concern for one's clients' best interests sets the stage for change.

The Nature of the Relationship. A twenty-seven-year-old single white fireman came to the clinic after the breakup of a relationship with a woman whom he continued to idealize. He had become deeply involved with this woman in a three-month period and hoped that they would marry. He described a great dependence on others in order to maintain positive feelings about himself. At work and with women he related with a bravado style, which masked his fear of abandonment. In a similar way he idealized the trainee, noting how good she was at what she did, and experienced her as quite powerful, describing meetings as "having gone ten rounds with Ali." After three months, work was interrupted by the trainee's vacation. During the meeting prior to this break, the client commented in a bravado manner that it was too bad he didn't have a few days off as well so that he could go away with her. Shocked, flustered, and concerned that somehow she had unwittingly invited this kind of remark, the trainee quickly proceeded to recite the boundaries and limitations of the therapeutic relationship. She reminded the client that they had an agreement to meet at a prescribed time and place to discuss what he chose to discuss and to focus on him.

It was only after the session, with some distance and thought in supervision, that the trainee could see that what she had quickly interpreted as a seductive invitation could be understood as an expression of the client's sensitivity to loss, felt more intensely when anticipating the trainee's absence. Undervaluing the meaning of the relationship, the trainee recited the rules of the relationship without exploring the feelings behind his comments. The client was intellectually aware of the limitations of the relationship. What he responded to were feelings evoked by being left by someone with whom he had shared many doubts about himself.

But *why* must the boundaries of the professional relationship be maintained? Over a period of the next several weeks, with reading and classroom discussion on the role of trauma and the repetition compulsion and talks with supervisors and other trainees about the treatment process, a deeper understanding emerged. A great deal of clinical learning occurs retrospectively. Process recordings reveal themes and issues missed during the session, leading the student to wonder impatiently when listening, hearing, understanding, and responding usefully will all occur *during* the session.

The compulsion to repeat trauma, although at first seen as a deterministic concept, became extremely useful when viewed as an attempt at mastery, making clear the way in which clients may unwittingly invite responses that reactivate old wounds. Once such patterns become apparent, the therapeutic relationship can be used to talk about, understand, and experience new and more effective ways of dealing with such painful experiences. Ultimately one realizes that it is the special nature of the relationship which allows the client to feel and to reflect rather than act.

Getting Close to One's Self. A chronically troubled adolescent began attending an out-of-town college. Separation from home and academic and social demands precipitated what she described as urgent inner feelings of fragmentation, suicidal impulses, and anger directed at other students who seemed to be adjusting well while she was "falling apart." Fear that she would throw a pair of scissors at her sleeping roommate led her to the college infirmary and eventually into treatment with me. Her history was marked by chronic depression, significant tragedy and loss (including her adoptive mother's death two years earlier), frequent suicidal ideation, and a suicide gesture at age fifteen.

It was difficult to tolerate this young woman's pain, feelings of worthlessness and hopelessness, and her long silences during meetings. I felt an urgency to do or say something to remove or at least reduce her sense of disconnectedness from life. Frightened by her suicidal thoughts, it was difficult not to feel responsible for this young woman's life and to fear that one wrong comment or action during a session or telephone call would prove to be a fatal error. After every session the client would leave the office with a pained grimace and hurried gait. Although at fleeting moments a beginning connection with this young woman was felt, she subtly conveyed her anger that treatment provided very little relief. The meetings, increased in frequency to three times a week, just didn't seem to be helping. I felt that either I wasn't doing enough or was doing something wrong, and I was certain that a more experienced clinician would not be in this predicament. The client was not getting better and I found it difficult to deal with my own feelings of anxiety, helplessness, and responsibility. The client's comment that after meeting with previous therapists or college advisors who had provided "no solutions" she had considered killing herself to show them how insensitive they had been was repeatedly recalled, so that I began anticipating sessions with a feeling of nervousness and dread. Perhaps most difficult to tolerate were negative feelings toward the client, which brought to mind doubts about my potential capacity as a clinician and my very choice of the field.

Supportive supervision, personal reflection, and a framework for understanding the client's developmental needs provided the perspective and distance required to conceptualize and tolerate this difficult clinical learning experience. Several essential issues and ongoing learning tasks emerged. First, I recognized the way that my urgent need to change the client's perception of herself was being communicated, and I gained an understanding of the meaning of this to the client; that is, her intense feelings were as intolerable and unspeakable to me as they were to herself, and this increased the client's fears that her feelings were indeed destructive and could therefore not be expressed. This miscommunication was also impeding the development of my empathic understanding. When I began to recognize intellectually the part played by empathic listening in *containing* acting out, I began to hear my client's expressions of helplessness and despair. This freed me to explore the meaning of her suicidal thoughts. With the help of the classroom work and readings it became easier to accept the emotions evoked by this suicidal, angry young woman as transference phenomena rather than evidence of failure. In addition, it became easier to appreciate the way in which this client's difficulty expressing disappointment and anger stemmed from significant earlier losses. Thus it became clearer how a client's manner of relating may result in the worker accepting responsibility for the client's life and reinforce the expectation that all needs will be gratified in a therapeutic relationship.

Even when the trainee is endowed by the client with special skills and qualities, one's fears about not knowing enough may be easily touched off because much self-esteem is invested in being able to be helpful to everyone. This tendency is closely related to over-responsibility and dovetails with the trainee's personal struggle to determine what she or he can and cannot do.

A great deal of self-scrutiny is required to develop clinical skills. One confronts painful, demanding, confusing, and sometimes frightening situations in which one attempts to "use" one's self in helping another. The relationship as the medium of change may be understood only intellectually in the first year of clinical training. By the second year, with deepening understanding and appreciation for the complexity of the client/worker relationship, its value and use take on greater meaning. Supervision, class discussions, and reading can help to contain and bind the anxiety produced by clinical learning. This provides the framework in which the trainee can view the individual in his or her social situation, against the gradual development of the client/worker relationship. Clinical experience and self-scrutiny, needed to sort out who one is from how one is experienced by clients, make social work training an affective, self-involving learning experience and not a purely academic one. Tolerating feelings and anxiety in oneself and in others is an essential task, a process of change that can be exhausting and excruciating, but also exhilarating. This is particularly true when the student is involved in a program that has grown out of a real need, identified in direct clinical work with individuals and families, and that illuminates ideas about preventive intervention.

Moving from Case to Cause. Rape Crisis Intervention, through which I worked with a woman experiencing the trauma of rape, was founded at a Boston hospital and directed by a social worker to provide immediate and followup medical and counseling services to rape victims and their families. The program involves collaboration, coordination, and consultation with police and attorneys and the sharing of knowledge about medical, legal, and psychological issues faced by rape victims and their families. Twelve followup crisis-oriented counseling sessions were offered to help mobilize coping abilities and social supports.

CASE EXAMPLE. A twenty-three-year-old single white nurse, Ms. A, was seen in the hospital emergency room two hours after she was raped in the basement laundry room of her apartment building in the early afternoon. Immediately following the rape she returned to her apartment where her roommate reported the attack to the police before accompanying her to the hospital. Ms. A, an articulate woman with many interests, strengths, and a wide circle of friends, had moved to Boston two months earlier.

In the emergency room Ms. A was composed and able to focus on those issues of greatest concern to her. These included her fear that the rapist would return to her apartment and fear of walking alone at night. She was anxious, fearful, and preoccupied with whether or not to tell her mother she had been raped. Since she was afraid to do so, she requested that her mother receive counseling in the event of an anticipated visit.

In the initial counseling sessions Ms. A reported no difficulty sleeping or eating. Increasing her involvement with schoolwork seemed to help her regain the sense of control that had been threatened by the assault. Ms. A was committed to taking legal action but was anxious about the court process. She was relieved to learn of the availability of a witness advocate to help her prepare for this. However, when the man concerned was arrested two weeks later while raping a seventh woman, he pleaded guilty to all seven charges, thus precluding the need for Ms. A to appear in court.

In later counseling sessions Ms. A became tearful and anxious around discussion of her mother and chose as the focus of the counseling contract to work on deciding whether or not to tell her mother about the assault. She viewed her mother as fragile and in need of protection, particularly since the death of a close family friend one month earlier. Ms. A had already told her mother by telephone that she had been robbed in the laundry room but had not mentioned the rape. When this omission was explored Ms. A described her uneasiness with the prospect of discussing prior sexual relationships, which she felt would inevitably be revealed in the telling.

Ms. A's own feelings of vulnerability and helplessness resulting from this assault seemed to be transferred to her mother. The theme of the client's difficulty centered around her problem in acknowledging and expressing her own dependent longings to friends and family. She feared that expression of such feelings would result in loss of affection from others. At the third counseling session Ms. A said she had called her landlord to report the need for additional locks on the building, adding that she hoped she would not be labeled as a "troublemaker." I suggested that perhaps she found it hard to accept her angry feelings about the rape and supported the steps she was taking to protect herself.

Ms. A related childhood experiences which seemed to play a part in her response to the rape. After her father's long illness, requiring multiple hospitalizations, and death when she was seven, Ms. A had assumed "adult" responsibilities at home, relied on herself a great deal, and described a "give and take" between herself and her mother, who worked long hours and was unavailable much of the time. She recalled wishing for a sibling, perhaps to share the burden of responsibility. Into adulthood Ms. A idealized her deceased father and had an intensely ambivalent relationship with her mother. The helplessness experienced during the rape reactivated memories of former crises, such as her father's death, and conflicts about dependency and sexuality. Ms. A seemed to feel both the wish for and fear of overprotectiveness by her mother at a time in her life when she was struggling to separate and assert herself as an independent sexual adult, able to take care of herself. During the course of counseling Ms. A's sense of autonomy began to be restored. She decided to discuss the rape with her mother and accepted her right to her own sexual life. She also dealt effectively with her landlord, who was reluctant to accept responsibility for providing adequate protection for his tenants. For me, this case helped make clear the work which clinicians need to do with the community and professionals (other than those directly involved in delivery of mental health services) in order to institute preventive services.

The "Right Way." Students quickly become aware that warmth and concern, while essential elements of clinical work, are not enough. The challenge lies not only in understanding clinical material but learning how to use it.

There is an urgency and impatience inherent in this type of learning, especially when progress or solutions are elusive. Faced with complex, confusing interactions, one hungers for techniques that would structure the treatment situation and contain anxiety. Theoretical frameworks are eagerly sought but, though helpful for this purpose, they tend to interfere with listening and hearing what the client is trying to convey. Developing tolerance for ambiguity, uncertainty, and complexity is one of the hardest tasks for the beginning clinician.

Students frequently enter clinicial training with the unacknowledged but powerful assumption that there is a "right way" to talk with clients and that this is what they will be taught. This can lead to fears that one's comment may be an irremediable mistake and anxieties about exposing one's work to others. The lack of detailed case material in social work literature forces the student to sift through highly theoretical material, which is often difficult to operationalize. What becomes clear in the process of clinical learning is that how we talk with clients depends on our willingness and on our capacity to hear by engaging in a mutual effort to understand.

The trainee's struggle to develop his or her own style becomes easier as experience increases and training progresses. Exposure to the live or videotaped work of a variety of experienced practitioners helps the student relinquish the notion of a "right way," even though one continues to try out, at first self-consciously and later with greater comfort, the styles of supervisors, teachers, and peers, by "borrowing" the wording of a question or response. Slowly the three-minute response becomes more concise.

The realization that the same clinical situation may be handled in different ways by different clinicians, each with an individual style, theoretical orientation, previous experience, and intuitive response, can result in the trainee's feeling alternately liberated and overwhelmed by possibilities.

A Piece of Work. The choice of the social work profession implies some concern for the lives of others, a commitment to human potential and growth, and an investment in helping the client. On a less altruistic note, it is also intensely personally gratifying work. Both conscious and unconscious factors operate in choosing the profession of social work.

During social work training there is a tendency to assume too much responsibility for clients' lives, particularly at the outset when the trainee's wish to help, with the tremendous amount of self-esteem invested in being able to do so, clouds the mutual nature of the professional endeavor.

The ending is an inevitable part of any therapeutic relationship. It is a time when the work that has been done is reviewed along with considering the work that may remain. It is a bittersweet time when the outcome, the meaning, and importance of the relationship gratifies and saddens. It is a time when whatever result has been accomplished may be obscured by unrealistic expectations. And even with a positive, significant outcome, one confronts the limitations of this kind of work.

The ending of the relationship will be experienced differently with each client, depending on the degree and nature of the involvement and the individual's previous experience of loss and separation. But termination that is based not on the resolution of the client's problems but rather on the trainee's completion of time at the clinic or agency presents special issues for both. The client may feel angry that this occurs before his or her problem is resolved and may even wonder whether she or he contributed to the trainee's decision to leave. Students feel guilt and sadness on leaving clients before the work is completed and frequently respond by overfunctioning during the last several weeks of placement in an effort to achieve quicker results. The student must respond to the client's feelings about termination while confronting his or her own reactions to the impending change or loss of relationships with clients, peers, supervisors, and teachers.

Trainees become increasingly aware of their expectations of the ending process. The urgency and need to hear the client express a full range of feelings, particularly anger, may be thought to ensure that the client's experience has been therapeutic. It is at termination that the trainee appreciates most the client as a teacher. Learning to identify that a piece of work has been done, even if it does not provide total relief from distress, and to be at peace with it, is a major task for any student. The limitations of two years of clinical social work training also become clearer. Thus one leaves school with an appreciation for the part that ongoing education and experience play in developing clinical knowledge and skills.

14

Teaching Treatment Methods

Harry Wasserman

This chapter on teaching clinical social work is addressed to those interested in the learning possibilities of neophytes—first-year students in a master's degree program in a school of social work. Specifically, the context of learning with respect to the influences of the macrocosmic and microcosmic environments, the content and process of the classroom situation, and a "theory" of how students learn will be discussed.

Influences of the Macrocosm

It is elementary that all learning and barriers to learning take place both in the immediate world of teacher-student interaction, fieldwork experiences, and university resources, and in the more remote, impersonal, invisible world of economic, political, and social events over which we seem to have increasingly less control. Today, some of these latter forces look ominously dangerous not only to the social services and our ability to serve people decently, but to the very existence of humanity itself. It is as if a pall had been cast over us. Yet we must live and teach and learn with a sense of hope that we shall save ourselves and each other from the abyss. In class we seldom talk about the general, macrocosmic plight, but it is there. Like Plato's people in the cave, we choose the darkness of silence to the light of discussing these horrendous matters—but we are all affected by the darkening shadow.

Less remote, but affecting us more pointedly in our work, is the generalized animus toward the social services. Historically, there is a formidable ignorance in our country about social services and the purposes they serve. This ignorance, combined with a kind of spreading social meanness, perpetrates the crushing of young lives, and the lives of those not so young, and all of those who need some assistance in coping with a seemingly infinite variety of more or less devastating human circumstances.

Social workers are a cognitive minority in this country with respect to the high value we place on social service and the helping process for those who need our knowledge and skills. There are other groups who share our values, but they are not in powerful decision-making positions. Peter Berger (1967) first used this concept of a cognitive minority to describe and explain the situation of those groups in our society which have retained a religious orientation in an increasingly secular Western world. Thus, our minority position, like theirs, is to some extent an embattled one, and necessitates, as Berger points out, the creation of a possible reality which counters the monumental reality of the majority culture.

There are, of course, many healthy trends in our society: the development of mutual help groups, the slow but steady spread of community organization and intermediate technology groups, the help professionals give their clients and patients, and the search of many people for a vision other than the purely materialistic. All of these represent elements of hope and a more decent human existence.

Influences of the Microcosm

The more immediate, more potentially manageable environment is that of the university and the school—their philosophy, leadership, and material and human resources. School situations are affected by short-term and long-term, internal and external forces at play: the rapid academization of social work since the end of World War II; the diverse perspectives of the faculty about the nature, purposes, and functions of social work; the downgrading of the importance of fieldwork; and the recent inflow of students from various racial and ethnic communities.

Becoming academic has not been an entirely salutary process. There are gains and costs. Gains have been made in the creation of a small but significant group of people who have very good theoretical minds and who have contributed important critical thinking to the field; still others are excellent researchers, and some few are very good at both endeavors. There has been, in general, an uplifting of the intellectual core of social work, and the university setting has been the source of this notable advance. But the costs exist, too. Students are not cared for as they once were and our faculty careers are not built around students becoming learned, skilled, sensitive social workers, but around our own productivity in research and publications. Our advancements and the esteem (or lack of it) we have for one another depend more on the authority of our reputations than on our concern about our students' learning experience, growth, and development.

One of the casualties of academization has been fieldwork. There are many signs of this, but the one most noteworthy is the lack of authority and power of the fieldwork faculty. Their low status is a reflection of what we think is important in the education of our students. (I wonder how many D.S.W.s devote a good part of their academic effort researching issues in the field.)

The diversity of philosophies and views held by most social work faculties is at once a source of enrichment and bewilderment for beginning clinical social work students. We seem to be further away from a consensus about the nature, purposes, and functions of social work in our society than we have ever been. How individual and social betterment and change come about, where and to which populations social work should extend its endeavors, confusions about generic social work and specializations within the discipline, and so on—all of these different and often contradictory voices provide students the opportunity to think and to sift through their own presuppositions and biases about their chosen profession, and guide them to confront new ideas and perspectives. On the other hand, in their desire to learn specific ways of working with people on their problematic situations, this unabashed pluralism is a source of confusion. To the neophyte (and to his or her teachers), this Tower of Babel seems more like an errant pluralism, connoting an intellectual disarray rather than an orderly thinking process about the nature of our work.

The relatively recent inflow of students from minority communities has begun to resensitize our faculties to problems arising out of immigration, racism, and poverty, and to how national, regional, cultural, and religious factors influence peoples' ways of living together and doing things. Historical and sociological understanding of ethnic and racial groupings are now as important as the microcosmic interpersonal, intrapsychic variables.

Another circumstance which bears heavily upon our students' learning is the rapid increase in the cost of living. For many of our students, inflation means working at part-time jobs and diminished psychic and physical energies to fulfill their multiple roles as parent, spouse, partial wage earner, and student. Looking at just one item—the cost of gasoline—one wonders how they manage to maintain financial liquidity while having to drive to class, jobs, or fieldwork locations. Many don't. Many are heavily indebted for years to come.

I have briefly sketched out some of the impersonal and more directly impacting trends and forces at work in our educational environments—trends and forces which in more or less invisible ways shape the content and direction of our teaching as well as the resources and perspectives which undergird the students' learning endeavors. Teaching clinical social work does not take place in a vacuum, and the world around us, for both teachers and students, does not hold still.

The Quest for Skill

There are many voices expressing divergent definitions and conceptions of clinical social work. Cutting across these perspectives is a simple, practical point of view which attempts to confront and respond to one of the students' highest goals, namely, to become skilled professionals in their work with clients. Among the primary skills is one which clinical social workers engage in most, namely, interviewing. It is a learned competence that we have taken for granted. We have simply assumed that students would learn how to interview in the field, and that we could well overlook this skill in class except for those instances in which we might analyze social workers' interviewing techniques in "canned" cases or on film or videotape. We have also assumed that somehow we could send beginning students directly into fieldwork situations with little or no preparation from the classroom. Like first-year residents in psychiatry who characteristically are confronted with a caseload of hospitalized schizophrenic patients, our beginning students have to grapple with a wide variety of difficult, problematic, and sometimes catastrophic human situations. For many years we relied on the assumption that in the field the students would begin with simple cases and slowly be introduced to the more complex. Yet, through the years we have come to recognize that this logical progression of learning does not often obtain. Simple cases turn out to be complex, and in some agencies there are seemingly no simple cases. Students are thrown into the human melee to swim or sink. We assumed that fieldwork instructors and other agency staff would somehow see them through. In brief, this approach to teaching and learning became a habitual way of doing things, unexamined and, hence, unanalyzed and unchallenged.

A New Approach. At the University of California, Los Angeles, the clinical social work faculty instituted in 1979 two new learning arrangements for the first quarter of the first-year master's program. As part of the course in social casework, the casework faculty designed a skills laboratory which was convened two hours per week for a period of ten weeks. The principal skill to be learned was interviewing. This skills laboratory was designed to be primarily experiential in nature, but closely linked to the traditional social casework class which also met for two hours per week.

The members of each of four skills laboratories, approximately fifteen students and one teacher, also convened in the casework class. This was designed to build a connection between theory and practice through the respective emphasis of didactic and experiential learning. In brief, the students spent four hours per week learning clinical social work in the first quarter of the first year, and two hours per week in the subsequent two quarters.

Also, in the first quarter, students attended a "professional seminar" designed by the school's field liaison faculty. Here students learned about the scope of social work, the various fields of practice, and the kinds of agencies serving those fields. Discussions took place on the school's field agencies and the nature of the students' experience in the field. Students and teachers met in three groups of approximately twenty students and one instructor. Taken together, these two new "courses" were introduced to facilitate the students' entry into both professional and fieldwork situations. While we did not build an evaluative instrument into the skills laboratory as a learning device, we do have some impressions, including some of the unanticipated outcomes of this experience.

Philosophy and Materials of the Skills Laboratory. It is our sense of things that the art of helping—at least in its initial stages—overarches the various theories of personality and the treatment prescriptions which issue from them. The work of Carl Rogers (1957) and those researchers whom he has influenced, notably Truax and Carkhoff (1967), do not represent philosophical or practical barriers to clinical social workers. Thanks to Rogers, the concepts of warmth, empathy, and positive regard, which are congruent with the values of social work, can be taught in a skills laboratory. Much has been done by clinical and counseling psychologists to operationalize the various dimensions of helping skills. Evans and others (1979, p. 5) indicate that "certain key dimensions of interviewing underlie all counseling and therapeutic approaches." Other informative texts from the fields of clinical and counseling psychology used in the skills laboratory are Bernstein and others (1974) and Egan (1975).

Believing strongly in a skills laboratory fortified by research, faculty members wanted very much to maintain a focus on social work content within that setting. They were fully aware that they were involved in the education of clinical social workers and not simply people learning to do counseling or psychotherapy. Hence, they were prepared to use social casework situations from various fields of practice to illustrate the application of skills.

The skills laboratory is structured along the following lines. The first two sessions are used for the students and the teacher to introduce themselves to each other. Students are encouraged to talk about their interests, concerns, hopes, wishes, and fears about being in school, going into the field, and so forth. Students begin to know each other as their common concerns and anxieties are reflected back to them; they can easily perceive that they are all living through a similar experience even though they come from widely different backgrounds.

Subsequent sessions are devoted to listening to a series of six SASHA audiotapes (Self-Led Automated Series on Helping Alternatives), produced by Goodman (1978). The tapes are interspersed with mini-lectures and role-played interview situations focusing on six interviewing skills. These tapes are entitled: (1) "To Ask or Not to Ask—That's the Question"; (2) "The Ancient Art of Advisement"; (3) "From Silence to Crowding"; (4) "Reflecting the Message"; (5) "The Joys and Sorrows of Interpretation"; and (6) "The Helper Discloses." Two students at a time "role play" a series of social work interviewing situations, while the rest of the students observe and comment upon the completion of the exercise. Students are free to utilize the tapes outside the class. In this way they can practice and sharpen their skills with another learner. Individual use is simply a reinforcement of learnings from the group situation.

Such laboratory groups are a vehicle for many different kinds of learning. Many of the role-playing situations reflect current fieldwork circumstances with which students are faced (for example, clients asking students for advice, or students' discomfort about asking many questions in an interrogatory manner when clients are not talking voluntarily). These commonplace, everyday interactions between student-worker and client are played out within the context of a group of learners confronted with similar situations. Thus, the group is a support system for those suffering from varying degrees of anxiety and feelings of inadequacy and incompetence. This type of group interaction is the polar opposite of the kind of encounter group or T-group where the person's weaknesses are pointed out and subjected to attack. Quite the contrary, these groups provide a milieu where constructive criticism can be easily given and accepted.

Some students can also play out more generalized anxieties about their respective field work and personal situations, thus providing a medium for discussion of the advantages and disadvantages of their fieldwork placements, the similarities and differences among fieldwork instructors, and the commonalities of the problems of living with which clients struggle.

On a more personal level, students may use role-playing sessions to discuss such problems as transportation, lack of money, and difficulties in obtaining good child care. Appropriately, discussion of concerns related to more intimate matters are avoided. Had such matters been raised they would have been discouraged by their teachers.

The laboratory skill groups, initially designed as an experiential learning device, have the added advantage of alleviating stress. For many, if not most, students, entry into a school of social work is a crisis situation. Some students give up decently paid social work positions, others must make new daycare and school arrangements for their children, family and work roles may require rearrangement, and those with little or no experience of social work practice step into an unknown world. For all, social work as a career is seen as a great opportunity, and they undertake this educational effort with an overriding feeling that they must succeed. Failure to demonstrate effectiveness and competence means disaster. They see themselves as being under a great deal of pressure with their self-esteem at stake.

These two "courses"—the skills laboratory and the professional seminar—have been instrumental in alleviating a great deal of the stress. In accordance with some of the principles in treating crisis reactions, students are able to play out their anxieties in a way that allows them to get a firmer cognitive grasp on the nature of their present experience. Teachers give accurate information about the school's expectations, the provision of peer-group support lessens anxieties and fears, and the progress made in interviewing skills through the use of the audiotapes increases the sense of competence.

One of the major learnings of these sessions is a beginning understanding that clinical social work operates under a variety of organizational conditions, and that these conditions either facilitate or constrain social workers in the effective application of knowledge and skills. In some settings, clients and patients come in open acknowledgment that they are seeking help. In other agencies, the reverse is the case: people do not openly request assistance; rather, social workers have to reach out and offer assistance which might be accepted, partially accepted, or refused. From role-playing sessions, students learn that early contacts with clients demonstrate that the latter generally know little about social work or have some misconceptions about it. Some clients have had prior beneficial contacts with social workers; some have not. All of these initial questions can be discussed in these sessions so that students achieve a sense of realism about clinical social work, with its possibilities and encumbrances.

In a skills laboratory, the teacher acts as a facilitator and tries to get everyone to participate in the role-playing and discussion sessions. The teacher leads the discussions but tries not to dominate them; he or she frequently urges speakers to elaborate on their remarks, encourages students to read about subjects discussed, comments on the action taking place in the role playing, and attempts a synthesis of the key points. In brief, the teacher is at times active and at times passive. When students are embroiled in a discussion where they can arrive at certain understandings by themselves, the teacher sits back, observes, and thinks about the content and the process. Where students seem to be floundering, he or she will try to make comments which may open up a different or new pathway into the troublesome area.

In this type of laboratory, two sessions are devoted to the viewing of tapes*

*One tape was produced by Dr. Charles Wahl of the UCLA Department of Psychiatry and a female patient who had recently learned that she was suffering from lung cancer. In the other, made under the supervision of Professor Lawrence Shulman of the School of Social Work, University of British Columbia, a beginning social work student interviews a late adolescent male seeking a group home placement.

which demonstrate the interviewing process in both its skilled and unskilled performances. In this way students can view the common errors beginners make as well as the kind of interviewing which combines knowledge and sensitivity gained through years of experience. In these instances, too, class discussions lead to enlightenment about the interviewing process.

There is no firm research data to indicate that these laboratory sessions have improved students' interviewing skills. Students do, however, report that what they have learned in the sessions has carried over to their work in the field, and that, on the whole, they consider them to be a highly valuable experience. Many students would like the laboratory to be continued into the second quarter of the first year, indicating that they consider this to be an important learning experience. The teachers involved consider these sessions an important innovation in the learning experience of beginning students, which at the same time serve as alleviators of stress.

In addition to readings in counseling and clinical psychology, students are introduced to readings about the art of interviewing from the field of social work. Social work materials are utilized for both their content about interviewing and as sources of social casework illustrations (Garrett, 1942; Kadushin, 1972; Sokol 1971; Shulman, 1979). Again faculty agreed that it was important for students to know that interviewing as a basic skill in clinical social work is important and that an emphasis on value and psychodynamic concepts is congruent with the laboratory experience based on the aforementioned research of Rogers and his "disciples."

The Didactic Element

The didactic element in teaching clinical social work or, for that matter, any course is a reflection of what the teacher believes is important for students to learn. This belief also includes developing the kind of classroom environment that is conducive to learning and presenting the systems of thought which will guide students in their formation as knowledgeable and sensitive social workers.

As an organizing theoretical framework, it seems to me that psychoanalytic ego psychology provides the most perceptive and sensitive lens which orders and makes meaningful the students' observations and thinking about client behaviors. In contrast is the view taken by Rubin and Gertrude Blanck: "We think that there can be only one science of human behavior—either psychoanalytic theory (and therefore, techniques derived from it) is correct or another theory is correct" (quoted in Pinkus and others, 1977, p. 263). In a general way, it is more fruitful to assume that the mysteries and complexities of human behavior cannot be explained by a single system of thought. For this purpose, Strean (1978) has provided a comprehensive and current basic textbook.

There are many social work situations, too numerous to discuss here, for which psychoanalytic thinking and ego psychology do not clarify the social and cultural dynamics at play. From a philosophical point of view, while it may be useful and fruitful in promoting the educational growth of our students to believe that "sharp distinctions do not exist between intrapsychic, interpersonal, and social behaviors" (Cooper, 1977), there are bodies of knowledge other than psychoanalysis which offer illumination. Students are intrigued by the inner workings of the human mind and soul. But they must also understand as profoundly as they can that the ethnic and racial group one is born in, one's parents' social class membership, and religious belief and application have enormous shaping powers as to one's view of the world and one's place in it. Students must understand that economic solvency and work are components of self-esteem, and that people's behavior is shaped by all of these forces as well as those of an immediate situational nature (Siporin, 1972).

Thus, a "soft" position on psychoanalytic theory and ego psychology is taken in the sense that any notion that these theories totally explain the human condition is rejected. However, they do best illuminate (albeit not completely) the connections between the individual's personal developmental history and current behavior, one's ability or disability to live more or less harmoniously with oneself and others in this world, the subtle details of repetitive patterns of behavior, and the blocked psychological (but not social) paths toward the fulfillment of the needs of self-esteem and competence.

This assumes that clinical social work, regardless of the plethora of definitions, incorporates firmly the connotation that its adherents are capable of doing psychotherapy as well as carrying out other social work roles such as resource locator, negotiator, mediator, and acting as broker and liaison on behalf of the clients' well-being. Shirley Cooper (1977) has pointed out that clinical social workers form the unique professional group which has the most experience in combining counseling with the delivery of concrete services. Working from an institutional base affords us the realistic possibility of performing the traditional functions of the social worker as well as that of the clinical psychotherapist.

Strategies of Teaching

Strategies of teaching clinical social work to beginners are contingent upon the answers to five questions: (1) What are the prior educational and work backgrounds of the students? (2) Have they done social work or engaged in any organized helping process, and under whose auspices? (3) What should they know at the end of sixty hours of being together in a didactic class and twenty hours in a skills laboratory? (4) What kinds of field experiences will they have in their respective placements which typically provide a variety of learning experiences? And, finally, (5) What do each of them as individuals bring into their budding professional careers that will ensure their being skilled clinical social workers? In brief, teachers have to get to know the students rather well, and they do this through observations in class and individual conferences.

A good teacher, like a good social worker, begins where the students are, and they are at varied stages of development. A strategy has to be devised which captures the interest of all of the students—one that challenges their capacities to think about the nature of their work.

The analysis and discussion of cases that students are currently carrying in the field is a far preferable teaching strategy to "canned" cases and lectures. Concepts are abstractions of reality, and they are best taught as resonances of concrete, extant life situations and problems. This is the kind of relevance which makes sense to the learners, for they can clearly see the relationship of conceptual thinking to their current experiential learning in the field.

In this context, technical language as metaphor is a theme to which students need to be sensitized. We have many conceptual languages today which describe and explain the principles of diagnosis and treatment. There are the various languages of treatment strategies, human development and its vicissitudes, psychopathology, and so forth. The theoretical concepts are metaphors which indicate a way of thinking about aspects of human thinking, feeling, and behavior. The languages of psychoanalysis, behavior modification, situational behavior, communication, interaction, and system theories all must be translated into an understandable vernacular—into a language which is human—for many of these languages are antihuman. In fact, they are anti-human because they are often taken from fields and disciplines which are not thought of as part of the humanities. They come from engineering (feedback, input, output), from experimental psychology (conditioning, reinforcement, cues), from biology (homeostasis, steady-state, instincts, drives), and so on. And yet we cannot avoid creating new concepts, and would not want to do so if we could. But we must acknowledge a hard truth so that our students will understand and not be mystified by the poverty and awkwardness of our languages. The abstractions we use are, of course, approximations of human happenings, events, experiences, and reactions. In order to avoid mystification and misunderstanding, the concepts have to be translated, demonstrated, and filled with the breath of life, which is pain and suffering, understanding, and contentment—the whole range of human responses to what goes on in people's worlds. For instance, a concept such as "libidinal object constancy" could be translated into the following: the young child begins to feel that the presence of his mother is securely fixed in his mind, and, having it fixed, feels a warmth and security which is both a protection and a foundation for moving ahead to another stage of development. Students find useful the writings of authors like Robert Cole, Studs Terkel, Thomas Cottle, James Agee, Robert Blythe—writers who use a human language to describe and explain what happens to people and what they make happen.

The goal of sensitizing students to clients' languages and their own leads to a normal development—namely, the presentation of case materials without the immediate use of a technical language. Students need to be encouraged to present cases, as this gives them the opportunity to risk themselves as learners. This need not conflict with what a fieldwork instructor might teach in any given case if students are informed that decisions made about cases are those arrived at in the agency between them and their field instructors. Presenting their own cases gives them practice with an audience of their colleagues. (The carry-over from the skills laboratory to the class is evident in the relative ease with which students volunteer.) Using a chalkboard to sketch out the bio/psycho/social factors which the student gives during presentation of the case helps to organize data. After other students have elicited other information from the presentation, the saliency of the historical and current information, the presenting problem(s), the psychosocial dynamics, current functioning, and behavior of the client and the student during the interview can be discussed. In summary, an assessment is made on the evidence available to date. It is the purpose in this kind of exercise to provide the students with a model of analysis which does not simply list items of data under their proper headings, but pinpoints those events, experiences, and reactions which carry the highest significance. From this kind of analysis the student can begin early to develop a sense of reality about the possibilities of treatment, employing Perlman's concept of partialization of problems and our general social work emphasis on seeking out clients' strengths and coping capacities.

After analyzing several cases along these lines, the students can begin to understand the relevance of an organized, systematic approach in the helping process. Many important diagnostic and treatment questions and principles begin to emerge and can be identified. One, for instance—who the client is—is not always evident at the outset of a case (Briar and Miller, 1971). The client may be only one individual, but may also be, and often includes, the significant others in the nuclear or extended families or in the worlds of work or school or friends. From the question of who the client is emerges a second one—who does the client connect with on an ongoing basis? On whom can he or she depend? Who are the reliable, caring people in the client's social world? Who are the people who sustain the client outside the treatment situation? In brief, are there support systems of which the client is a part? If there are, do they need strengthening? And how might this be achieved? If there are none, how has this come about, and what can be done to create one? Reiterated throughout the course is the theme that people live their lives outside our offices; while their contacts with us can be highly significant in overcoming current and sometimes long-standing difficulties, it is in their own social worlds that they have to find and maintain the connections which sustain and enhance their humanity. As a general rule (Reid and Epstein, 1972), it is important that the social worker and the client come to some agreement about what the nature of the problem is and determine what the two of them together are going to work on before the end of the second interview. There are, however, many clinical social work situations that are so complex that two interviews are insufficient to reach agreement about salient problems and goals. The achievement of a contract signifies a true beginning. The notion is emphasized that what clients say are their difficulties may or may not be their most important problems. There are overt problems and underlying ones. It is most fruitful to begin with how the client defines his or her situation, and to see what can be developed from that vantage point. The client may or may not wish to explore and work on deeper problems.

We ought not to impose our own values about the importance of people understanding themselves through therapy. Client self-determination in this matter demands our respect. The question of goals in treatment is difficult when goals cannot be specified. Reaching agreement about objectives is not easy, particularly in those cases where the client is grappling with value issues or deep-seated problems whose psychological and social antecedents are not immediately clear. Increasingly, people are using clinical social workers and other psychotherapists to clarify their values in the sense that they are seeking answers to what is important for them. These revolve around problems of identity, purpose, and meaning in their lives. In our early discussion of case presentations, we begin to see together that diagnosis and treatment are intertwined—that when we are talking about one we are also implicitly including the other. The so-called linear model of treatment, that is, of diagnosis first and then treatment, does not obtain in our work. This is due in part, I believe, to the inevitable subjective elements in the diagnostic-treatment process, and the circular nature of cause and effect. This radical subjectivity is tempered slowly by the realities not only of the client's worlds but by the mutual recognition of the two parties as real persons. The subjective elements of transference and countertransference, of attraction and repulsion, like and dislike—all of the ambivalences implied in the relationship of two people—are pervasive from beginning to ending. In every case I ask the students to look for repeated patterns of behavior and pervasive themes of thinking and feeling. That which is repeated indicates a problematic area of which the client may or may not be aware. At first, the observation is noted, then is subjected to analysis, and kept in abeyance until the proper time for use in treatment—or it may never be brought to the client's awareness. Everything depends on the nature of agreement (contract) in respect to treatment goals; perhaps more importantly, it depends on whether or not such a discussion would be helpful in the therapist's judgment. The timing of introducing sensitive subjects, of making interpretations, or of bringing a formerly beclouded area to a client's awareness is essentially a skill which combines worker sensitivity, intuition, and experience. It is difficult—perhaps impossible—to teach this skill.

Common Themes of Case Presentations

In the first cases presented in class by students from their fieldwork, several common themes emerge. The teacher is thus permitted to teach not only about the individual case but about the events and experiences of people's lives which sometimes crush them, always cause pain and confusion, and most of the time tear them away from the secure moorings of a loving, caring person or family.

Most social work clients have suffered significant losses by death of parents or siblings, or abandonment in the forms of the desertion or divorce of parents. These are losses sustained in the clients' early years. Many of these people show moderate to severe depression, psychosomatic difficulties, or self-destructive tendencies. In others, it is usually possible to identify the theme of a life-long search for the "good parent(s)." Excessive dependency is seen in the manifestations of pursuing love partners who could not provide the parental love sought for; an inability to form satisfying relationships with people and a tendency to hang on to fantasized parental figures who were either infantilizing or coldly detached are commonly found. While it may well be true that for some people early losses do not have irreversible effects (Kagan, 1976), for many people they do. Students can be introduced to a literature (Kohut, 1971; Mahler, 1968; Guntrip, 1971) which addresses itself to the injuries of the self in early development and to the consequences of such injuries. With beginning students it is enough to introduce them to this literature, to have them get a sense of the conceptual metaphors employed by these theorists, and to suggest that if they develop an interest in working with clients suffering from narcissistic, borderline, and schizoid disorders they will have to do some intensive special study in institutes, workshops, and other agencies. It is not practical to go deeply into treatment prospects with clients suffering from early developmental injuries since the students' fieldwork contacts, given current exigencies of the structure and process of many agencies, do not generally permit anything but short-term treatment. And these are typically the kinds of clients who, if they are to make progress even under the condition of voluntarily seeking treatment, have to be engaged in long-term therapy. Even under all favorable conditions they are very difficult to treat successfully. Students in their first year try to assist clients suffering from early damage by working with them on some concrete problems and by giving them some emotional support. In their involvement with borderline and narcissistic clients, students need support from their colleagues, teachers, and fieldwork supervisors. They have to deal with a complicated set of countertransference and realistic reactions to clients who lack trust and who have related to others with at times aggressively hostile and manipulative behaviors as well as the more "acceptable" passive, dependent kinds of behavior. We are aware that what can be done with those suffering from loss, unresolved grief reactions, and other painful trauma is quite limited under present learning conditions and within the constraints of the field. Students are caught in a double-bind situation vis-à-vis these troublesome clients: they are limited by the fact that they are beginners and by the generalized agency pressures toward short-term treatment.

Clients suffering from early trauma (loss, abuse, neglect, successive abandonments, and so forth) often do not trust workers sufficiently to engage themselves in a relationship which might be helpful. These are the clients who struggle all their lives with the issues of symbiosis and separation. Very often they look upon the putative helper as just another person in a long series of people who have little to offer them. Thus the student is in a situation where he or she has to create a case. The student does this by being respectful toward the client and by accomplishing something for the client, either by fulfilling some material need or connecting the client with a potentially helpful resource. This concrete assistance sometimes gives the student the opening needed to engage the client in the initial steps of working together.

While clients suffering from the vicissitudes of the symbiosis-separation process come from all social classes, many social work clients come from those families and groups of all races and ethnic backgrounds where economic and social injustice has been the experience of generations. The majority of the victims of this cruel process are, miraculously, neither demoralized nor defeated. But for those who have paid heavily in social and psychological costs, the clinical social worker must help them move from an attitude of passivity and defeat to that of activity and the will to survive and take control of their lives. We know that in our work with individuals and families, we are not solving any mass problems. Yet we do know that in the long run—when there are high rates of social and individual pathology, where there are highly vulnerable populations (so-called populations "at risk")—a combination of macrocosmic and microcosmic interventions is the only possibility for mass and individual transformations.

One of the themes which commonly emerges is the indissoluble bonds among individual, family, and community. It is an indissoluble triad, for if one of the components weakens, so do the others; where one is strengthened, the others are too. As clinical social workers, we think of the mature individual as one who has achieved the kind of personal autonomy in which attachments and bonds to others are neither restricting nor engulfing, but where respect, love, and mutuality are the basis of human connection. The healthy individual in a disintegrating society eventually becomes submerged in that chaos, just as if he or she might be living in an environment of physically noxious agents.

Another important theme that emerges is the often terrible toll that physical illness takes on those afflicted and on the members of the family. The social and psychological effects of illness and disability are well understood in the abstract. There is an enormous literature, including research findings. Yet, judging by students' fieldwork experience in hospitals and other medical settings, clinical social workers still have difficulty making entry into these situations. When they do, they are often effective and helpful. A family is distressed—in a state of panic about a recently discovered epilepsy in a fourteen-year-old boy; a couple is heartbroken and guilt-ridden about an infant born with many physical anomalies; a woman is hospitalized and is worried about her relationship with her husband and about childcare for her youngsters. Clinical social work can be of enormous help in its special way of combining concrete assistance and counseling to assuage the pain, to give correct information about the nature of the illness, and to provide the kind of human support often missing in our massive organizations. Early in their placements, students become aware of the status of clinical social workers in relation to the other disciplines within the hospital. In some instances, chiefs of services and other staff members respect clinical social work as a humane and effective intervention, while social workers are still interpreting "what we do" to members of the other professions. It is the unevenness of acceptance and effectiveness which students have difficulty understanding at first, but can begin to comprehend after much anguish and frustration when they have gained some sense of their own competence and when they can distance themselves sufficiently to think about the way organizations and professions work.

Defense Mechanisms, Transference, and Countertransference

We see from the start of our classroom deliberations that clients and patients use defense mechanisms as protective devices, that transference reactions are the very stuff of our everyday professional and personal lives, and that resistance to working on whatever has to be worked on permeates the treatment process. On the other hand, clinical social workers experience countertransference reactions and are beset with anxieties, fears, worries, frustrations, depression, and feelings of anger and hostility—all of which are part of working with troubled people. If clinical social work is to retain a human face, the transference and countertransference reactions of clients and workers are to be understood as normal human responses heightened by the anxiety and uncertainty of the encounter, and the threat and danger students and clients feel from such intimate contact. It is this context which magnifies these reactions. Transference and countertransference are also present in less stressful situations.

To understand transference in clients, it is useful to ask students to think of their own transference reactions to various people in their current and past life contexts—teachers, fieldwork instructors, and peers. Ask them to think of possible distorted reactions they have had to people in authority—whether the authority be that of age, status, or role. (Giving students many different examples of distorted interactions between two people permits them to confront their own conflicts in their present school and field situations.) Countertransference issues also arise during case discussions. For instance, a student complains that a particular client accuses him of not being interested in him and the student views the client's reaction as unjustified. Other expressions of hostility directed toward the student by clients may be upsetting for the beginning therapist. Students have to be helped first to express their anger and hurt, and then to understand the nature of the interaction. Concepts such as projection and identification can be explained and their applicability demonstrated in the case under discussion. These bits of knowledge can produce a shift in students' emotional sets. It is very important that students not be blocked from expressing their true feelings under the guise of an impossible standard of universal love and acceptance. If teachers hope that students will learn to embrace an even larger range of human behavior, then they must be willing to permit them to express their own feelings of pain and rejection as these arise in their work with clients. Thus, teachers behave as models for students to emulate.

Involuntary Clients' Resistance

Occasionally in long-term treatment cases, students have the opportunity to make interpretations with respect to a client's transference reactions. For instance, in a case presented to a class a student observed that a client fell silent whenever the question of what went wrong in the client's first marriage was brought up. Finally, the client admitted that the student reminded her of the "other woman" whom she blamed for breaking up her marriage. In reality, student workers have either little opportunity to make transference interpretations or do not feel sufficiently sure of themselves to do so. They think it is the kind of interpretation which, if bungled, will not be helpful to the client. They are content to have treatment proceed within the ambience of a generally positive relationship. This means that clients are able to express themselves, often deeply, without getting hurt.

Given the fact that a sizeable portion of student workers' cases are made up of clients who have not voluntarily requested help, students have to be active in exploring with these clients their questions, doubts, lack of knowledge, and misinformation about social work. These putative clients are resistant at the outset. In class, when situations in which clients initially display reluctance to become engaged in the whole process are discussed, students report that they feel relatively comfortable in talking to clients about early resistance. Resistance to treatment, as it is normally thought of in a psychoanalytic framework—a resistance on the part of the client to deal with some specific content—arises most often in long-term treatment. Beginning students have little opportunity to engage in working through this kind of blockage.

A New Paradigm for Clinical Social Work?

Bloom (1979) contends that a "new paradigm" in mental health work has arisen, one that emphasizes the concept of multifinality in disorder outcome. He writes:

> On the basis of this paradigm, preventive intervention programs can be organized around facilitating the mastery or reducing the incidence of particular stressful life events without undue regard for the prior specification of which forms of disability might thereby be prevented; that is, this

> new paradigm begins by abandoning at the outset the search for a unique cause for each disorder. . . .
>
> If we then keep in mind these two developments—a growing interest in precipitating crisis events rather than in predisposing developmental variables, and the growing acceptance of general as opposed to disorder-specific preventive interventions—we can better appreciate much of the recent research literature. . . .
>
> Of all the explanatory concepts that have been introduced to link individual difficulties with characteristics of the social system, the most compelling have been the concepts of competence and competence building. Much human misery appears to be the result of a lack of competence, that is, a lack of control over one's life of effective coping strategies, and the lowered self-esteem that accompanies these deficiencies [pp. 183–184].

We may come to the tentative conclusion that, while Bloom's formulations and the crisis literature are impressive and insightful, they do not seem to apply—with some few exceptions already cited—to the client populations students currently see in general hospitals, medical clinics, and mental health, family, and developmental disability agencies. It seems as if the bulk of social work clients and patients suffer from chronic medical and psychiatric disorders and social stigmata which have left many of them with shattered self-confidence. They often feel isolated and abandoned, more or less alienated from family and supportive peers, and fail to accomplish the normal tasks of everyday existence. Many are hardly able to deal with either internal or external conflict. What are considered ego strengths—the capacity to cope with small and large problems—are tenuous at best. These are traditional social work clients, not to be seen much in the private practice of any of the mental health professions. For these troubled and troublesome clients, treatment can only become a source of hope and growing self-confidence and competence if they are willing to work at new ways of thinking, feeling, and behaving. The work is slow and plodding for it is done, so to speak, in small bits so that mastery of the smallest activity or task becomes the precursor of future completed activities and tasks. It is not a question of identifying a precipitating event which occurred within a two-week period prior to the first interview, but a series of many, many crises forming a major life-long stress syndrome.

Yet the Bloom formulation is intellectually compelling, for there is an incontestable logic and sense which pervades it. Perhaps it is a problem of how clinicians organize themselves, and where services are offered, and to which populations these are addressed. It is necessary to emphasize that one of the distinguishing characteristics of clinical social work with respect to the other mental health disciplines is the profession of a traditional social work value, namely, that we have a responsibility to offer services to the most vulnerable people in our society whose lives are prevaded by crises. Once we turn our back on the most troubled and shattered, then we shall have lost our raison d'être as a distinctive profession.

Perlman's "In Quest of Coping" (1975) is considered by students to be the finest description and explanation of how clinical social work treatment proceeds with a clear delineation of both worker and client tasks and activities. Perlman's analysis of the cognitive, affective, and behavioral aspects of coping provides students with an abstract mapping of the helping process which can be applied to a wide range of clients.

Learning and Teaching

In student learning it is self-evident that a teacher always engages students with some explicit and, more often, implicit notions about how people learn. Most clinical social workers have come through the kind of educational experience in which we were viewed by our teachers as vessels to be filled, as recipients of transmitted knowledge. In this view, the teacher perceives the student as a passive receptor of knowledge, while being one's self the repository and transmitter of knowledge. If a clinical social work teacher takes a "hard" position on what is to be taught (for instance, a psychoanalytic or a behavioral modification framework), it becomes difficult to avoid assuming the transmitter posture. For in the teacher's mind there is a distinct body of knowledge to be taught, and it is the "right" or "correct" set of formulations. The transmission theory was promulgated by the "founder" of modern education, Comenius (1592–1670), who believed that the minds of children had to be filled and imprinted with the symbols of knowledge. Locke's (1632–1704) idea of the tabula rasa was a restatement of this historically dominant educational view.

A totally different view of how people learn has been advanced by Piaget. He saw the student not only as an active learning person but also as a creator of knowledge. People are active and creative learners because they seek order and need to make sense of things.

In doing diagnostic work, students habitually ask themselves a series of questions. Why does this client behave in a certain way? What are the problems we can work on together? With whom does this client connect in everyday life? What in the client's past history accounts for the situation today? The students begin to collect facts, along with making observations, inferences, and conjectures, and ask themselves some more questions. Beginning with little knowledge, the students rely on a capacity to think and a compelling need to make order and sense of things. Presumably, the students do not yet possess a disciplined sense of self, and yet often enough are able to be very helpful to a client who may be faced with many difficulties and who may be seriously emotionally disturbed. Occasionally we see beginning students do brilliant work with these difficult cases.

How can we account for this paradox, namely, the untutored, undisciplined student who deals brilliantly with the very difficult case? We do not know the complete answer to this question. Some of the important assets the student brings to such a situation are the capacity to think, motivation to learn, the readiness for the challenge to do a good piece of work, a spontaneity unhindered by the explicit and implicit injunctions of a particular framework, and a natural desire to be helpful. This is the kind of student who has a hunger to learn—a hunger which can be further stimulated by class discussions, teachers' references to the apposite literature, informal discussions with colleagues, and the turning over and over in one's own mind of the bio/psycho/social dynamics of the case.

The "soft" position advocated here for teaching allows at once for the learning of a specific theoretical framework and the provision of freedom for the student to look beyond that framework to other ideas, concepts, and formulations. This position further acknowledges that the student is the creator of knowledge when he or she begins to see, for instance, how seemingly unrelated phenomena are connected to each other, and how our internal mental work is a subtle process of combining objective and subjective feelings, thoughts, and actions.

The teacher who believes that students are capable of being actively engaged in learning and creating knowledge for themselves and eventually for others does not give up totally the role of a transmitter of knowledge. There is knowledge to be imparted, but the teacher has to have some sense of limits—a sensitivity to what students can absorb by being talked at. In teaching clinical social work, working on students' current cases provides the kind of classroom process which engages students as active learners. The classroom can be transformed into a case conference structure where student rivalry and competition are inhibited, and cooperation and mutual support are promoted. Thus classroom structure and process reflect a "theory" of education, namely, that of the student as active learner and creator of knowledge.

It is hardly possible to teach clinical social work without doing some direct treatment with clients. Whether in an agency or in private practice, the teacher as practitioner has to test out his or her own knowledge and skills in order for these not to atrophy, and to avoid the pitfall of rote teaching. Just as medical school clinical teachers who never see patients (an unthinkable condition) would be suspect, clinical social work teachers should engage themselves in work with clients. To restrict themselves to the classroom is to be closed off from the kind of learning which teachers need as much as students.

Conclusions

Teaching clinical social work to beginning students is reflective both of one's philosophy about how students learn, and of the nature of our discipline. There is knowledge to be transmitted, but the context and process of transmission create a form which encourages students to think about what they are doing. The expression of their thinking in classroom discussions is at once accepted and subject to challenge, not only by the teacher but by members of the group. In this way students develop a critical posture of their own and others' clinical social work. Above all, it is important for a teacher to convey to students the human importance of their learning endeavors. Tragedy and suffering have been omnipresent in human history. It is our quest, along with other humane professions, to reduce unnecessary suffering. This is a daunting mission given the destructive forces we have to overcome in this world. Yet amidst the moral chaos we find ourselves in, it is imperative that teachers impart to students the conviction that every good piece of work we do with people contributes to the positive, health-inducing forces of the human community. That conviction is the source of enthusiasm for our efforts and hope for the future.

References

Berger, P. L. *The Sacred Canopy.* New York: Doubleday, 1967.

Bernstein, L., and others. *Interviewing: A Guide for Health Professionals.* (2nd ed.) New York: Appleton-Century-Crofts, 1974.

Bloom, B. L. "Prevention of Mental Disorders: Recent Advances in Theory and Practice." *Community Mental Health Journal,* 1979, *15* (3), 179–191.

Briar, S., and Miller, H. *Problems and Issues in Social Casework.* New York: Columbia University Press, 1971.

Cooper, S. "Reflections on Clinical Social Work." *Clinical Social Work Journal,* 1977, *5* (4), 303–315.

Egan, G. *The Skilled Helper: A Model for Systematic Helping and Interpersonal Relating.* Monterey, Calif.: Brooks/Cole, 1975.

Evans, D. R., and others. *Essential Interviewing: A Programmed Approach to Effective Communication.* Monterey, Calif.: Brooks/Cole, 1979.

Garrett, A. *Interviewing: Its Principles and Methods.* New York: Family Welfare Association of America, 1942.

Goodman, G. *SASHA Tape Users' Manual (Self-Led Automated Series on Helping Alternatives).* Los Angeles: Gerald Goodman, 1978.

Guntrip, H. *Psychoanalytic Theory, Therapy, and the Self.* New York: Basic Books, 1971.

Kadushin, A. *The Social Work Interview.* New York: Columbia University Press, 1972.

Kagan, J. "Resilience and Continuity in Psychological Development." In A. M. Clarke and A.D.B. Clarke (Eds.), *Early Experience: Myth and Evidence.* New York: Free Press, 1976.

Mahler, M. S. *On Human Symbiosis and the Viscissitudes of Individualism.* New York: International Universities Press, 1968.

Perlman, H. H. "In Quest of Coping." *Social Casework,* 1975, *56* (4), 213–225.

Pinkus, H., and others. "Symposium Paper." *Clinical Social Work Journal,* 1977, *5* (4), 253–296.

Reid, W. J., and Epstein, L. *Task-Centered Casework.* New York: Columbia University Press, 1972.

Rogers, C. R. "Training Individuals in the Therapeutic Process." In C. Strother (Ed.), *Psychology and Mental Health.* Washington, D.C.: American Psychological Association, 1957.

Shulman, L. *The Skills of Helping: Individuals and Groups.* Itasca, Ill.: Peacock, 1979.

Siporin, M. "Situational Assessment and Introduction." *Social Casework,* 1972, *53* (2), 91–109.

Sokol, B. "Skills of Interviewing." Unpublished manuscript, 1971.

Strean, H. S. *Clinical Social Work: Theory and Practice.* New York: Free Press, 1978.

Truax, C. B., and Carkhoff, R. R. *Toward Effective Counseling and Psychology: Training and Practice.* Chicago: Aldine, 1967.

15

Supervision of Students and Practitioners

Diana Waldfogel

Supervision is almost as old as social work itself. Its central importance in the profession continues despite changes in form and focus that have occurred over the decades. In fact, if there is any one area of practice in the human services that is particularly recognized as having been developed and refined by social work, it is the practice of supervision (Robinson, 1949; Ekstein and Wallerstein, 1972; Cooper, 1979). Literature on the subject emerged from the field in the early 1900s when volunteer workers were supervised by agency boards (Brackett, 1974, originally 1903). As practice and service needs changed, the supervisory process evolved into the combination of administrative, educational, and relationship components that we know today.

Supervision serves important functions for the agency administration, for the individual practitioner, and most importantly for the client. Supervisory personnel are a key source of information, and in meeting administrative requirements for accountability, and provide an overview of service needs. Supervisors are in a position to see similar needs emerging across several supervisees' caseloads. Ideally, they thus can be conduits from lineworker to administration for identifying new or unmet service needs, program imperatives, and training requisites.

Practitioners do not alone carry complete responsibility for their work. The responsibility is shared and they have the purposes and power of the agency behind them, often in the person of the supervisor. For example, in child abuse

Note: Many ideas in this chapter have been developed in discussions with colleagues Louise Frey (Professor, Boston University School of Social Work) and Golda Edinburg (Director of Social Service, McLean Hospital, Belmont, Massachusetts).

cases when legal issues have been raised, supervisors as well as caseworkers have often been held responsible for the practice. Although supervisees, as well as the profession in general, question and challenge the limits of autonomy implicit in such arrangements, many of the issues and situations faced by workers in clinical practice require more than one individual's knowledge, experience, or ingenuity.

Supervision was originally the chief method of training for practice in social work, through an apprenticeship period in agencies. As educators in the profession began developing theory, research, and formal curricula in academic settings and agencies, the teaching content in supervision became more generic and systematic. At present the process ideally combines the teaching of transferable, objective knowlege and the transmission of skills based on theory and research with an individualized method of teaching. It can address the affective needs of the learner as well as the cognitive ones. Through the process, practice wisdom based on experience in the field is transmitted as well.

The ultimate goal of supervision is the best possible service to the client. Supervision is one way of assuring clients of competent help, fair and complete access to the services and resources available, and protection against idiosyncratic practice or decision making (Pettes, 1967). With increased focus on consumer rights, many agencies today have policies of informing clients when their workers are students and interns. In such situations clients are informed that the work is being done under supervision and they may chose to meet the supervisor. Thus supervision is presented openly as a protective part of the structure of help for clients.

Functions and History of Supervision

Administration and education have long been identified as the two primary functions of supervision (Miller, 1971). Over the years other functions have been added. Evaluation was suggested early as an important component, although it is generally viewed as an integral part of administration and education. Charlotte Towle (1963) added the function of helping. "Enabling" is the term used by many to identify a similar need. Kadushin (1976) in his comprehensive book *Supervision in Social Work* suggested "supportive supervision." These additional components of helping, enabling, or supporting are a response to the nature of the work and they are affective as well as cognitive. They address the process and the relationship factors which influence that process and are crucial to its success or failure. The relationship between the supervisor and supervisee affects the objectives and thus its scrutiny is important. Interesting and vital as the relationship may be, however, it is not itself the purpose of supervision, but the vehicle by which supervisory goals are achieved.

The profession of social work grew from practice in social agencies—the Charity Organization Societies in the East and the settlement houses in the Midwest. The needs of the agencies were for accountability and training and these needs formed the basis of the two components of supervision—administration and education. The model of supervision in the two kinds of organizations that developed in the East and Midwest differed, growing out of agency philosophy and activity. The eastern Charity Organization Societies, whose friendly visitors helped families, and from which family agencies and casework methodology developed, used an individual teaching model of supervision which was hierarchical and stressed accountability. Control of the functions of the "visitor," who was the early direct practitioner, was by the agency board. The settlement houses in the Midwest, which focused on social action and systems changes, and from which group work developed, used a more collegial and unstructured model of supervision. Kadushin (1976) suggests that the openness of practice in group work and community organization permitted more autonomy for the practitioners, while the privacy of the casework model suggested the close supervisory model that grew from it.

Family agencies with individually oriented casework blossomed in New York and New England in the 1920s and 1930s, and the individual model of one-to-one supervision focusing on specific cases prevailed. Later, Williamson (1961, first edition, 1950), a groupworker, recommended that all groupworkers as well as caseworkers were entitled to individual time in supervision, indicating a shift from administrative to educational goals and a value preference for the one-to-one model. Public welfare agencies established to meet the crisis of the Depression of the 1930s emulated the private family agencies in their methodology of casework and supervision and also in the individually based model of supervision.

It has been argued that supervision was necessary because the early agency visitors were untrained. Kutzik (1972, 1977) points out, however, that supervision undoubtedly was not utilized at that period, for the original untrained visitors, who were from upper-class society, were in fact the employers, and would not have been supervised by middle- or working-class secretary-agents paid by them. Later the visitors were drawn from the middle and working classes and were paid. Supervision became an arm of the administration and used as a way of achieving agency goals. In other professions such as medicine, nursing, and psychology, supervision has also often assumed both administrative and teaching functions. In some agencies, particularly in large ones, professions have split the administrative and educational functions between two or more people. This may be done for expediency or on the grounds that, as students and workers learn different modalities, they may need supervisors with different kinds of expertise. In some instances, it was felt this would solve some of the problems of supervision—namely, the overly close monitoring, the role conflict, and the overload that can result when one person is doing both administration and education (Austin, 1956; Leader, 1957). Gitterman (1972) and Scherz (1958) presented a convincing position for the alternative, single-supervisor model, on the grounds that the administrative and educational functions are interdependent. Elements of both are always present in supervision, though emphasis may vary. This seems to be the most common practice experience. However, it may be that supervision has been burdened with more administrative responsibility than is necessary and that other channels in agencies could be used or developed to carry some of this.

In discussing the status of social work as a semi-profession, in spite of its aspirations to full professional recognition, sociologists cast supervision as one, among several, of the culprits that deter the profession's progress (Toren, 1969; Perlmutter, 1972). The lack of autonomy implicit in ongoing supervision beyond the training period is cited. Autonomous practice is viewed as a hallmark of the fully professional practitioner. The struggle between autonomy and professionalism goes beyond individual practitioners, whether they work in agencies or in private practice, however, to the issue of autonomy of the profession as a whole. A full profession is viewed as controlling its practice by its own professional norms and as not controlled by a bureaucracy (Wilensky and Lebeaux, 1958). Certainly social workers may find themselves in conflict between the bureaucratic demands of an agency and the demands of their profession, on procedures, standards, and goals. So, however, do other professionals who work in hospitals, clinics, courts, and social institutions. The effort to separate the administrative and educational functions in supervision may be viewed in part as an effort to address this issue of autonomy as well as a way of clarifying the supervisory role. Studies of social workers indicate that workers, by and large, accept administrative supervision. They do not see it as a threat to their autonomy and, in fact, ascribe more authority to their supervisors in administrative matters than those supervisors take for themselves (Kadushin, 1974). Workers recognize the need for accountability. They describe their difficulties, feelings of constraint, and lack of independence as existing more in the educational component of their supervision than in the administrative (Toren, 1969). Some social workers experience considerable unease about the lack of autonomy in decision making in practice situations with clients. Since in clinical practice the desire for individual autonomy must be balanced with the worker's competency, it may be advisable to address autonomy in the context of competency. In addition to supervision, the development of objective criteria of competency at various stages after training might be one way.

A recently articulated point of view is that of applying Robert Merton's role-set theory to the issue of autonomy and control in supervision (Munson, 1976). Such application demonstrates that social work practice is not completely autonomous but functions within organizational necessities.

An enlightening view of the issue of professionalism and autonomy is presented by Howe (1980, p. 179). She suggests that some professions, including social work, are public or mixed rather than private in that they "provide collective services and involve economic externalities that affect the public at large." They will probably continue to be controlled by the public and are unlikely to achieve autonomy. Thus, autonomy as a criterion for professionalism in such professions may be inappropriate. On the other hand, partial autonomy might be achieved by changes within the bureaucratic structure (Epstein, 1973). Success in obtaining licensing for social workers and third-party payments for their services, and the increasing numbers of social workers obtaining advanced degrees, may in the future affect the autonomy issue and supervision in unforeseen ways, both in and outside of agencies.

The creation, or at least fostering, of dependency in supervision is criticized concomitantly with the concerns about autonomy. Misuse of the supervisory relationship may lead to prolonged dependency, inappropriate gratification of the emotional needs of either or both of the supervisory partners, and reduction of autonomy and creativity, but misuse is not inherent in the process. More critical to the dependency issue is the length of time educational supervision is required after training. The two-year training time required for the master's degree in social work is relatively short and supervision is necessary after the degree is received. However, a specific time limitation in combination with standards for objectives attained might improve upon the present open-ended period of continued supervision. States with licensing laws may specify the number of years of supervision—often two after the M.S.W.—required to obtain independent licensed status. Agencies, however, may vary from providing no educational supervision to requiring it indefinitely. The nature of clinical work is emotionally involving and difficult and requires the use of self as the major tool, so the views and support of another professional person may be welcome and desirable throughout a career, but a shift to consultation might be more appropriate after a specified period.

Theories and Principles of Supervisory Practice

Theories of supervision have been drawn from education, social work practice, psychology, psychiatry, and sociology, among others. While drawing on a multiplicity of theories and concepts has enriched and deepened the understanding of practitioners, the failure to distinguish between personality theories, practice theories, and educational theories has at certain times led the process of supervision away from some of its objectives.

Supervision was shaped by practice and gradually patterned itself after the casework method, creating some confusion between goals and process. The inexperienced supervisee was to imitate the experienced worker-supervisor, as it was hoped the clients would imitate the "superior" moral character and success of the early visitor. Supervision was recognized as being educational in intent as well as "overseeing." As a scientific base was introduced into social work practice (Richmond, 1917), and as training became affiliated with academic settings, interest in educational theory developed. Those educational theories which emphasized the individuality of the learner and focused on the learner rather than exclusively on the content to be taught were most compatible to the developing individual casework approach (Towle, 1954).

Without one coherent body of educational theory to apply to the supervision process, social work has made use of various educational principles. Reynolds (1965) contributed greatly to the application of an educational approach by identifying stages of learning which she considered usual and expectable in students. Garrett (1954) further identified expectable progression and regression in student learning in a two-year master of social work program. This helped supervisors understand the progression of learning and regard the anxiety and regression seen in learners as situational rather than pathological. Teaching and learning principles have been enunciated by many other social workers and educators (Pettes, 1967; Knowles, 1972; Kadushin, 1976; Gitterman and Miller, 1977). They generally emphasize the value of building on the learner's past experience, of repetition and focus, of reducing defenses, and of actively involving the learner. They further recommend individualizing the learner, operationalizing what is being taught and generalizing. Morton and Kurtz (1980) add the need for specifying performance outcomes and matching teaching methods to outcomes sought.

Psychoanalytic theory began to infuse the entire field in the 1920s. Many social workers adapted the psychodynamic developmental view to the learning process in the 1950s (Austin, 1952; Towle, 1954). Towle particularly deepened the understanding of learners and learning by showing the relevance of the individual's life experiences, stages, and personal history to the learning process. Psychoanalytical theory introduced the knowledge of unconscious motivation, defenses, and transference which affect learning and the supervisory process as surely as they do all aspects of life. However, the limitation in basing supervision on this theory alone, as was done by some supervisors, was that it located the problems of learning in the personality of the learner. This often diverted the process of teaching, with its attendant growth and change potential, to one of attempted therapy. Psychoanalytical theory illuminated the understanding of human behavior dramatically, but difficulties arose in failing to translate and modify psychodynamic knowledge to meet educational rather than therapeutic endeavors. No one would argue that supervision should be therapy. Techniques were suggested (Hamilton, 1954) for the avoidance of a therapeutic stance: not responding therapeutically to material; referring a supervisee to a therapist, if it seems necessary, rather than dealing with personal material in supervision; keeping discussions focused on the case and the work; and addressing personal issues derivatively or through universalization in relation to the work only. Despite all this, the fact that "being caseworked" is still a common complaint of students indicates that the issues are still not generally resolved (Rosenblatt and Mayer, 1975). "Being caseworked" is not a complaint of workers, however, judging from a survey by Kadushin (1974). Workers are more concerned about autonomy. This gives rise to speculations as to whether workers are more accepting or understanding of the introspection or self-awareness expected in the profession than are students, or whether supervisors treat worker-supervisees, whom they may perceive as colleagues, differently from student-supervisees. Many clinicians feel the increased vulnerability of students is a factor.

Sociological theories, chiefly role theories, have been applied to supervision (Berkowitz, 1952; Munson, 1976). Munson pointed out that, rather than use of a personality system for analysis of supervisory problems, there are advantages to using a role-set frame of reference. It aids in locating problems outside of the personalities of the participants and provides a clearer base for testing practice.

Systems thinking has not been applied in any orderly fashion to supervision although many ideas about supervision are congruent with a systems approach. The work of Hartman (1970) in introducing the application of systems thinking to social work issues and that of Germain (1973, also in this volume) in presenting an ecological perspective seem highly promising as ways of expanding our views of supervision and practice. We have only begun to understand some of the complex interplay of inner and outer forces that influence the supervisory process.

A combination of the psychological and educational approaches led to the important development of the educational diagnosis (Austin, 1952). This has been modified somewhat since that time to reduce the importance of psychological components and emphasize educational assessments. Though the educational diagnosis is important in student supervision, it has equal relevance for supervising workers. Kadushin (1976) described the educational diagnosis as including what supervisees already know, what they need to learn, what they want to learn, and how they want to learn it. The supervisor then tries to ascertain how a particular supervisee can learn it best.

All of these theories and principles enlarge perspectives and deepen knowledge. The task of supervision continues to be that of adapting knowledge—whether from psychodynamic, behavioral, cognitive, social role, systems, or other theories—for educational and administrative use.

Student Supervision

There are distinctions between supervising students in field instruction and supervising workers, although there is also considerable overlap in the two processes.

In the education of students for social work practice, the supervision received in fieldwork placements is seen as a crucial link between academic work and practice experience. Field instructors who supervise the work are usually agency employees but are considered to be a teaching arm of the academic institution as well. Their affiliation requires knowledge of the school's program and objectives, some channels for input into the program, and participation in courses on supervision given by the school. The school's liaison advisor is the official link to the agency supervisor. The basic distinction between worker and student supervision is that the contract in student supervision is between the supervisor and the school and students are assigned to their placement by the school. In worker supervision the contract is between the agency (in the person of the supervisor) and the worker.

There are at least three distinctive requirements of student supervision. They are the need for sharing the supervisory process with an outside institution and person, the increased responsibility for containing anxiety, and the central role of socializing the student into the profession. These requirements occur on both organizational and relationship levels.

Sharing. In supervising students it is necessary to relate the teaching aspects of supervision to the curriculum of the academic program. The priorities of the educational institution must be integrated with the goals of supervision in the practice setting. As the supervisor works collaboratively with the academic institution in the teaching function, and assesses how what is being taught can be integrated into the agency setting, it becomes apparent that the process affects the administrative aspect of the agency as well as the educational one.

On an administrative level, making field instruction effective requires the administrative sanction of both institutions and clear agreement on the compromises that will be made by each of them. Each may have to modify their usual practice or teaching in order to accommodate to student and client needs and to the other institution's goals and policies. Thus, each institution grants some of its authority to the other. For optimally good working relationships, the limits of the authority granted must be clear.

On the educational and relationship levels of supervising students, field instruction requires the supervisor to share the teaching with another person, namely, the school advisor, who also oversees the student's work, develops goals for learning, and knows different aspects of the student's performance (Kent, 1969). The triadic relationship between student, supervisor, and advisor, sometimes seen as troublesome or problematical, can be utilized for learning. At the Tavistock Clinic in London, for example, it is thought that the student can develop increased professional self-awareness from having a triadic experience in addition to the one-to-one relationship in traditional supervision (The Tavistock Clinic, unpublished).

In student supervision, the degree of congruence between the agency's and school's theoretical base, goals for student learning, and practice standards is an important factor. While differences in theoretical perspectives always exist, and may actually help in promoting knowledge and growth for the profession as well as for individuals, too wide a divergence makes the integration of theory and practice impossible for the student. Wide differences, or total disagreement, may lead to fragmentation, choosing sides, or manipulation of one or both systems for survival. When the theoretical bases of workers and supervisors differ, the educational aspect of supervision may be forgone and only the administrative one performed. This is not a solution for student training.

Developing a Professional Identity. A second difference in student and worker supervision is the responsibility of the supervisor of students to aid, with others, the student in the process of socialization into the profession. The development of a professional identity occurs through administrative, educational, and relationship experiences. The socialization process is furthered by the impact and material of classroom teaching, the intense interaction with peers that occurs in school and agency, and contacts with advisors and others during the period of professional education. However, the unique relationship developed with the supervisor often is most important, due to its intimacy, duration, individualization, and focus on ongoing practice. It can become one of the most significant vehicles for identification with the profession and its values, as well as for acquiring knowledge and skills. This identification process is often referred to as role modeling and is certainly not restricted to social work. However, its effectiveness is heightened in supervision because of the intensity of the supervisory relationship. Modeling is encouraged and used in supervision because of the evidence of the power and effectiveness of an important relationship as one way of producing change in human beings. Its use is also based on the notion, commonly held about all human relationships, that "actions speak louder than words." The way people are treated has a more powerful effect on them than do talks, discussions, and lectures. The supervisory relationship thus demonstrates experientially how clients are to be treated, how behavior is viewed, and what the basic values of the profession are. These basic values include understanding and starting where the other person is, treating clients and supervisees and their material with respect and confidentiality, listening, individualizing, assessing situations with care, exploring feelings with sensitivity, respecting defenses, establishing mutuality of goals, putting the client or supervisee's needs before one's own, and advocating for the client's or supervisee's rights or enabling them to do so.

The changes expected and desired in a supervisee are restricted to professional identity and competence, and do not include widespread personality changes (Ekstein and Wallerstein, 1972). Such changes may nonetheless be of considerable depth; they may necessitate giving up previously cherished, deeply ingrained views, prejudices, attitudes, and modes of response. The changes, thus, may be of profound proportions, as discussions with students constantly show.

Containing Anxiety. The containment of anxiety is a third task of student supervision, and is one which is different in degree, only, from the same task in supervising workers. A high level of anxiety is to be expected in highly motivated people entering a new profession in which so many of their own personal values, ideals, and goals are invested. In addition, they are expected to act on behalf of others before they have learned how to do so. The supervisor of students can expect a much higher degree of anxiety than would be expected in trained workers who are already prepared and have demonstrated success to themselves and others.

It is probably also higher than that seen in an untrained worker who will have more limited tasks assigned. Professionals deal in various ways with the anxiety of new members. Educators have pointed out, for example, that medical training has traditionally dealt with anxiety by partializing the person to be dealt with—teaching about a procedure to be performed, a disease entity, or an organ to be treated rather than the whole person. Nursing has handled anxiety by utilizing an authority structure which limits responsibility and decision making. Education utilizes an apprenticeship model where the master teacher is with the practice teacher in much of the early training in the classroom.

Social work, and other mental health professions, expect the worker and the student to be concerned about the whole person, to assume responsibility for making the best decisions possible in an interview, and then to discuss the decisions and modify them if necessary. The burden for supporting the neophyte in this holistic view and with this degree of responsibility is placed on the supervisory process. It is a heavy charge. Obviously, supervisors are not equally supportive; some are overly controlling, and some do not offer sufficient guidance. The supervisory relationship is sometimes felt to be as much of a strain by students as the client one (Rosenblatt and Mayer, 1975). Even with excellent supervision, supervisees can experience the relationship differently, based on their own personalities, stage of professional development, and other factors. A perceptive student, in an unpublished paper (Whaley, 1978), described the conflicting feelings of omnipotence and helplessness which she experienced as she began her work. In retrospect, a year later, she recognized that many of these feelings had been displaced onto her supervisor. There is a need to blame someone for the lack of hoped-for progress early in the treatment process or for the impossibility of knowing everything and helping everyone.

Teaching methods also differ among professions. For example, in medicine, nursing, and education, students do much of their learning in the open. Students are observed in their beginning tasks and they observe their teachers. By contrast, students in the mental health professions traditionally have carried out their interviews and interventions in private from the beginning of their training. They have rarely had natural ways of observing their supervisors at work. Some of this is changing with the new technology of audio-visual aids and one-way screens. Modalities of conjoint interviewing and family therapy also produce new situations where supervisors and trainees may work together in interview situations. But presently there is some legitimacy to the novice's complaint about performing work that he or she has never seen demonstrated, and to the supervisor's anxiety about not actually knowing what the student is doing in interviews. We do not really know which teaching methods create or contain anxiety.

Teaching aspects of supervision exist whether the supervisee is a student or worker. Gaps in knowledge and practice are expected with all workers. New techniques are developed, specialized practice may become required as agency functions change, and research may point in new directions. Workers then may have to learn family treatment, direct treatment of children, time-limited work, and much more, which the relatively short educational years have not covered. Although with workers it is not necessary to integrate a curriculum from an outside institution with the agency practice, there is still the need for supervisors to teach new theory and technique, support supervisees in new and therefore potentially anxiety-provoking situations, and help professionals expand their functions, obligations, and thus ultimately their professional identities. The major difference lies in the fact that the teaching component for workers is based on agency-related requirements and tasks, and not on outside demands. The support and the socialization required are partial, and are built upon already established professional identities. In all instances they are job-related and less broad than the obligations of a supervisor training a student for the profession.

Planning for Supervision

When an agency administration selects one of its employees to become a supervisor, or hires someone new for the task, it has many organizational and competency factors to consider. The person selected must also face educational, organizational, and personal issues in order to be successful in the new role.

Selection of Supervisors. In selecting a supervisor, the first and major consideration of the administration should be whether the person is a well-functioning, respected practitioner. A second is whether the person can conceptualize and clearly articulate practice knowledge. These requirements can usually be ascertained by the administration on the basis of past performance, written evaluations, previously assigned teaching of a limited nature, and references and recommendations of colleagues and supervisors. One cannot teach what one does not know, even with the best will and technique. However, agency realities are sometimes such that workers are catapulted into supervising before they feel ready. Just as students and beginning workers feel they should know everything before they can conduct their first interview, so supervisors feel about beginning supervision. They are often painfully aware of the inevitable gaps in their own education and knowledge, but not everything has to be known at once. The knowledge needed to supervise depends on "the case," the needs of a particular client, the requirements of the agency, and the needs of the supervisee. Beginning supervisors have to be reminded that new knowledge can be acquired. If supervisors can assume a stance of learning as well as teaching, it will not only be beneficial to their relationships with supervisees, but it will relieve them of a great deal of unnecessary pressure.

Teaching Tasks and Methods. The knowledge and skills that can be taught by the supervisor will fall into the general areas covered in the academic curriculum. Theory relevant to the case is discussed and investigated. Research or empirical data relevant to the situation should be considered. The teaching should include the implications of the broader context: agency policies and boundaries, community characteristics, systems relevant to the clinical situation, and social factors that impinge on the clients. Then a tentative selection of methodology, or interventions, is made based on the needs of the clients and the situation, and work is begun by the supervisee. Meanwhile, in supervision there is an ongoing assessment of the learning needs of the supervisee and the most suitable way to address them. The supervisor aids in furthering the development of self-awareness and the use of self in the treatment relationship, and is responsible for assisting in sorting out and identifying transference and countertransference issues as they arise. Throughout, the supervisor is structuring a learning atmosphere and professional relationship which makes intellectual and emotional learning possible.

The supervisor offers support, which helps to contain anxiety; offers realistic encouragement that learning goals can be attained—granting as much autonomy as is compatible with mastery; and offers stimulation for continued motivation to learn.

In order to take on these tasks, the beginning supervisor must consider several emotional and cognitive issues. These include one's own past learning and one's experience in being supervised. It is common to wish to teach as we were taught if we felt it went well, or differently if our experiences were negative, without always considering carefully the need to modify these methods to fit the supervisee now confronting us. It is also advisable to examine one's source of gratification in work, recognizing that supervision requires a shift from treatment to education. The rewards of teaching and supervising are great, but they are different from those of direct service. It is advisable, moreover, to reflect upon one's attitudes and reactions to authority in general and toward the agency or institution in which supervision is to occur. New supervisors, perhaps because of discomfort with their role, sometimes fail to see themselves as an arm of administration or may skirt the authority inherent in the supervisory role. This presents a confusing and inaccurate picture to the supervisee. If the supervisor is either too much in awe of the administration, or too angry with it, he or she cannot fulfill the role of advocate for the supervisee, or appropriately interpret and represent the agency's policies to the worker or student.

It is highly desirable for new supervisors to have a regularly planned opportunity for supervision or consultation on their supervisory practice. A collegial group or a seminar where principles, common problems, and supervisory practice can be discussed is also helpful. When these are not provided or possible, the best that practitioners can do is to consider the intellectual and emotional aspects as honestly as they can and to seek the consultation of a respected third party if serious problems arise. The third party may be an advisor at an academic institution if the supervisee is a student, an administrator in the agency, or an outside consultant.

Personal Characteristics. The personal attributes necessary for supervision are essentially those required of a good clinician: professional self-discipline, self-awareness, and the desire and ability to maintain nonexploitative relationships. Flexibility and maturity are also desirable characteristics. The essential relationship skill needed is the elusive and basic ability to judge the closeness and distance comfortable and appropriate for a particular supervisee in any special instance. These are the characteristics supervisors hope to help supervisees develop in their work with clients. Supervisees attain them in large measure through experiencing them in the supervisory relationship, as well as learning them derivatively from supervisors' assessment and evaluation of clients. The personal attributes, along with knowledge and skill, should form the basis for the selection of supervisors.

The power of the supervisory relationship cannot be overemphasized. In talking with students and new workers, one recognizes its importance and far-reaching effect. Misuse of the relationship can be inhibiting and damaging to professional development. Students entering a school of social work were asked what they knew or had heard about supervision, and one brave group member responded (to nods of agreement from others), "I've heard that it can make you or break you." The perceived power and possible danger of the relationship was thus clearly articulated. The longed-for benefits and comforts are also verbalized when workers and students discuss their hopes for knowledgeability and expertise in their supervisors, and when they request a supervisor who is supportive, understanding, and fair.

Modalities

Supervision can be conducted in a number of different modalities. Each format has certain advantages and disadvantages and each is appropriate or desirable depending on the circumstances, the people involved, and the goals to be attained. There are, however, certain procedures which are considered basic and necessary in all supervisory situations. Providing uninterrupted, regularly scheduled time and a place for conducting supervision within the organization's schedule and space carries the same message it does in a clinical or educational situation. Those statements are administrative sanction, serious professional purpose, and acknowledgment of the supervisee's learning and training needs. A new supervisory assignment begins with establishing a working "contract," which may take several weeks to negotiate and will be a part of the initial ongoing supervisory sessions. Such an agreement includes the agency requirements of the worker, the school requirements if the supervisee is a student, areas the worker wants to focus on or learn, and those that the supervisor believes to be necessary to focus on as well as what he or she feels qualified to teach. Methods for arriving at the goals may be agreed upon and mutual feedback and evaluation procedures discussed. This is the point at which agency job descriptions, evaluation forms, and the former professional experiences of supervisees and supervisors are discussed. Subsequently these issues are brought up in a continuing dialogue to prevent misunderstanding, unrealistic expectations, and the chance of unfair or surprise evaluations on both sides. The focus of supervisory sessions is the supervisee's work. A balance is usually maintained between related administrative issues and policies, professional issues, and the worker's cases or assignments. In clinical supervision it is expected that the major part of the time is spent on the teaching and discussion of clinical practice, but agency, community, and societal issues provide the context in which the clinical work takes place, and are a part of it. Teaching in supervision is from the specific to the general. This provides a helpful complement to formal academic work based on general principles that must be applied to a myriad of situations.

Individual Supervision. The most common format of supervision is that of a weekly conference between supervisor and supervisee. The structure can vary from having a tightly planned agenda, with written or other material prepared by the supervisee and given to the supervisor prior to the conference, to an informal verbal discussion with a flexible agenda. The structured conference with prepared material is generally required for student supervision; in worker supervision, it is more likely to be used with a new employee or when a worker is embarking on a new form of practice. While the informality and private nature of individual supervision can foster a free exchange and a comfortable learning milieu, it can also lend itself to tangential discussions, a personal rather than professional emphasis, or a lack of focused teaching. Therefore certain routines are employed to support more orderly teaching and to ensure a professional relationship. The beginning contract or agreement and requirements are part of that process. The appropriate focus of a teaching conference is the supervisee's specific case or task assignment, not the personal issues or the problems of either partner. Both parties contribute to a decision regarding what cases, work, and issues are to be discussed. A systematic review is made at regularly planned intervals of all the worker's assignments, responsibilities, and cases. Regular times for evaluation are established and carried out. The boundaries of a regularly set time are maintained, as repeated interruptions, changes, or extensions of time generally have the same negative effects that they do in treatment situations. In addition, ongoing feedback about the supervisee's progress in relation to specific work is expected. Regular provision for hearing comments from the supervisee as to the helpfulness of conferences or changes needed in them is also available. These procedures do not preclude friendliness, humane concern, support, understanding, and natural interchange, in the name of professionalism.

One-to-one supervision has long been the preferred method in social work and is assumed to be modeled on the casework method, the most fully developed of the methodologies in social work. But it is also based on a tutorial method of teaching and has many educational advantages. Chief among these is the individualization of the supervisee, as attention can be paid to the particular learning needs of the supervisee related to the specific tasks that must be performed. The level of the supervisee's skills and his or her learning rates and patterns can be observed most accurately, and the immediate needs made known, understood, and met. Time does not have to be shared with others. The supervisee can experience being given to and taken care of to the greatest degree, and thus feel emotionally supported in the demanding learning and work tasks of the profession. The use of the relationship for learning and doing can be maximized. Identification with the supervisor, role modeling, demonstration of professional attitudes, and a positive use of transference can all be more readily used. The profession has been slow to recognize the disadvantages or limitations of this modality, however. Such disadvantages include the restriction inherent in confining learning to one source, the dependency which can develop, the personalization of the relationship which can more easily occur, and the danger of overcontrol which may result from the close scrutiny of work in this modality. Many of these negative effects are the result of the power disparity that exists between the two individuals involved. The presence of other people can modify this disparity or present a differing perspective.

Group Supervision. Group supervision usually consists of three to six supervisees with one supervisor. The supervisor has responsibility for exercising leadership in the group and for the evaluation of each group member. The group usually meets once a week, but individual, or "spot," conferences may also occur as needed with the supervisor and a group member. The use of group supervision seems to be increasing in social work though not at the rate one might expect considering the many advantages that it offers. The format and its advantages, both instrumental and expressive, have been discussed in depth by Kaslow (1972). She postulates that the reluctance to change from individual to group supervision may be due to supervisors' lack of experience with group methods, lack of belief in the efficacy of the group method, and unwillingness to risk oneself. She demonstrates what she considers to be the clear economic advantage of group supervision to agencies. While it is true that less hours are required for actual supervisory conferences, it should be noted that group supervision also requires time for preparation, reading of records, spot conferences, and report and evaluation writing for each group member, as is true in individual supervision.

Judging by the anxiety expressed by supervisors when embarking on group supervision, it seems that their concern about maintaining control and authority in the group is a strong deterrent to change. Some of this concern stems from lack of comfort in dealing with groups, as discussed, but much of it is based in reality. The very advantages of the group stem from reducing the effects of the power disparity and require a new assessment of the role of the supervisor and new responses and actions. The group situation, by reducing the power disparity, can prevent a supervisor from taking an overly authoritative, personal, or therapeutic stance. It also provides the advantage of learning from many members as well as from the supervisor. The participants can offer support which lessens the feelings of loneliness and low self-esteem which can be a part of learning. Raising questions and challenges with peer support is less threatening than in a one-to-one situation. The group situation can dilute dependency on the supervisor. It allows more autonomy, as close monitoring of all the supervisees' work is not possible. There is more freedom for discussing organizational issues as group concern may lend strength and ability to raise criticisms and suggestions for change. Some people can learn better and accept criticism to a greater degree from peers than from authority figures; for them the group situation may increase progress in learning.

There are concomitant disadvantages to group supervision as well. Organizing against the leader may not always be constructive or growth producing. It can be a displacement from other dissatisfactions with the agency, the members' performance, lack of individual attention, or even the insolubility of some of the social problems facing the workers. There are other nonproductive group phenomena such as scapegoating of a member, the tendency of an aggressive or exhibitionistic member to take over, an unfortunate bonding of two or more members, or competitiveness which can develop despite the leader's best efforts. Nonparticipation can be a problem, for shy or uninvested supervisees can hide more easily in a group.

A most useful empirical study comparing individual and group supervision in field instruction was conducted by Sales and Navarre (1970) at the University of Michigan. A sample of 43 students placed with 18 field instructors in group supervision was compared with 104 students placed with 52 field instructors in individual supervision. No significant difference in scores on the Michigan Practice Skill Assessment Instrument was found between the two groups of students. There were some differences on specific items, though they were not statistically significant. The practice skills of diagnostic assessment and of responding appropriately to client communication were somewhat higher for individually supervised students. The group-supervised students were somewhat higher on items of showing interest in agency practice, considering innovation, complying with recording, and identifying their own areas of competence. Students in individual supervision were more satisfied with their mode in the first semester; after that, the difference decreased. The conclusion can be drawn that a mixture of modalities would be beneficial for meeting a variety of learning needs at different stages and for different material.

Peer Group Meetings. Peer group meetings are used for varying purposes, which may include learning, mutual support, or monitoring of practice. Fizdale (1958) first described an effort which grew out of practice in a counseling agency. She later stated that it should probably not have been described as peer group supervision but rather as consultation because there was no evaluative function built into the group. It was formed by a group of "equals" who all had to feel a sense of confidence in each other's work. Since then such groups have proliferated, some within social agencies do not have administrative or evaluative authority, while others do. Occasionally in small agencies and in some private practice group situations, evaluative procedures are used in which the entire group evaluates each member's work. Although members do not necessarily have to be at the same level of experience or expertise, if its members encompass an entire staff and are accountable for the service given by an agency or group practice, the group must be comfortable with the practice of each member and all are responsible for that practice. Frequently in such situations natural leadership and responsibility patterns emerge.

Multiple Supervision. Providing workers and students with more than one supervisor is becoming common, particularly in large organizations. Frequently this is instituted so that personnel may benefit from the expertise of specialists, and sometimes multiple supervision is necessary because administrative responsibility within an institution is divided into geographic areas or various departments, wards, or services. The advantages of multiple supervision are an expanded knowledge and perspective for the supervisee, dilution of personality difficulties between supervisees and supervisors, and a reduction of power disparity. It can be seen that some of the same advantages accrue that do in group supervision, although not in the same manner. One disadvantage is that only an incomplete picture of the supervisee's work may be available. Another is that it affords opportunity for manipulation, conscious or unconscious, or "playing one supervisor against another." Both problems are usually handled by having a primary supervisor who communicates with the others and minimizes the opportunity for incomplete assessment and distortion. For the process to be successful, open communication and mutual respect among the supervisors is necessary and the supervisee must also know that such communication exists and may participate in it.

Group and Team Meetings. Group and team conferences are an effective way to share responsibility among professionals of varying expertise in the process of managing practice and planning for service delivery. As such, they are a valuable addition to supervision but are not a substitute for it. Their primary purpose is to facilitate service and not to address individual learning needs or evaluate worker performance.

Live Supervision. Although the use of live supervision can be considered a technique, made possible by one-way screens, telephones, and microphones in the ear, it is sufficiently different in method and impact to consider it also as a new modality. It has developed chiefly with the growth of family therapy and is most commonly used when there is more than one client interacting with a therapist. Members of the client group must give consent to being observed. At times only a supervisor observes the interview; at other times a supervisor and a peer group observe. All may discuss the interview afterward or, if agreed upon, a supervisor may actually interrupt the interview and affect the course of events immediately.

Advantages of viewing are that the supervisor can observe nonverbal communication and cues and that interaction between family members which may go unnoticed by the therapist can be more easily seen by an outside observer. The use of interruption is more dramatic and controversial.

One technique using the one-way screen is for the supervisee to control interruptions of the treatment situation. The supervisee may stop an interview and tell the clients that he or she wishes to leave the room to confer with colleagues who are observing. The supervisee then returns and reports on the advice, thus integrating the consultation directly into the treatment but controlling its content and use. Another technique, used in some family treatment methods, is to have the supervisor directly intervene during the interview, either by the use of a telephone in the interviewing room, communicating through an earphone worn by the worker, or coming into the interviewing room and making an intervention directly with the clients.

The advantages of being able to change the course of treatment immediately, if it seems so indicated, or give benefit of additional insights in the immediate situation, seem quite evident in live supervision. However, questions arise as to the effect of such personal, direct interventions on the relationship between the clients and their worker and in regard to transference issues in treatment. Some family therapists feel that family therapy as a modality does not elicit and sustain the same amount, depth, or kind of transference that one-to-one treatment does, so that judicious use of interruptions does not unduly interfere with the relationship. Another urgent question raised regards the effect on the supervisee's learning, autonomy, and comfort. Students who were trained with the use of live supervision in a family service agency (Rickert and Turner, 1978) did not report feeling more inhibited, or controlled, than with other methods. Loewenstein (1982) reported on receiving live supervision. She valued enormously the immediate and honest feedback, but cautioned that trainees would confront issues of narcissism, regression, and control. Undoubtedly the emotional impact and usefulness of any supervisory method may vary with the individual trainee, the stage of training, and the supervisor.

Tools

Various tools such as verbal reporting, process records, tapes, role play, and participatory observation are used to facilitate the teaching aspect of supervision. They are all aids in communicating to the supervisor what is happening between the supervisee and clients and are used as the basis for discussion of the cases. The administrative function of supervision is usually better served by formal agency records, statistics, and charts, where an overview of the supervisee's entire workload is more evident.

Verbal Reporting. A considerable amount of spontaneous verbal exchange goes on in all supervision. Some supervisors base their teaching on verbal reporting only, because it has the advantages of spontaneity, immediacy, and a richness not possible in written records. The method is time-saving for both parties but probably advisable chiefly for experienced practitioners. The chief disadvantages are that advance reflection is less likely, it is more difficult to keep to an agenda, and there is no opportunity for the supervisor to prepare in advance, or to bring in knowledge from additional sources.

Process Recording. A major and time-honored tool of educational supervision is the process record, kept separately from the organization's official record. The process record is a chronological selected description of the dynamic interaction that occurred between the supervisee and the client and is written by the supervisee. A method for focusing process recording has been suggested by Dwyer and Urbanowski (1965). The willingness of supervisees to expose their work in the record often increases gradually as trust and confidence in the supervisor develops. The supervisor reads the record in advance of the conference and advisedly selects only two or three important issues to raise with those of the supervisor in order to avoid overwhelming a trainee.

Process recording can permit distortion, forgetfulness, omission, concealment, and self-correction, but it is sufficiently revealing and accurate to allow considerable teaching and understanding. It is valuable despite being time-consuming for it provides both supervisee and supervisor with time for reflection and gives the supervisee maximum control. The method requires self-reflection before the supervisory conference, and even if the supervisee self-corrects while recording, he or she has learned in doing so.

Process recording is most commonly used during the student training period; as training proceeds, its use decreases. It may be used for trained workers in early interviews of newly assigned cases or when new practice methods are being taught. Summary records are used as a further step and they help to move a worker or student toward independence.

Tapes. The use of audio and visual tapes is becoming more frequent and requires the client's consent. Tapes are generally used in carefully selected portions and are useful in allowing the practitioner, the supervisor, or the peer group to hear tone of voice or see visual cues and nonverbal communication. Sharing tapes requires a good deal of trust in the supervisor or group. Selecting the portions for supervision gives the supervisee more control over the situation and material. Even listening or seeing one's own tapes without sharing them can be a powerful learning experience.

Participatory Observation. Mutual observation of supervisor and supervisee can occur in a relatively natural way if they jointly handle a practice situation. For example, intakes can occasionally be done jointly, particularly if a family or couple is involved. Supervisor and supervisee can interview together in marital cases, or they can be co-leaders in a family treatment case or with a group. When they work together the focus is on the work at hand and some of the self-consciousness and anxiety of direct observation is removed. The actual supervision or discussion about the practice which occurs after the interview provides almost immediate feedback.

The problems implicit in such a modality are evident. The chief difficulty lies in the unequal positions of the two participants. Having a supervisor present for a substantial amount of work can severely limit confidence and creative independence. While it can produce constraint on both sides, it is more stifling to the learner. It can create unnecessary competitiveness on both sides, or discouragement on the part of the supervisee, who may feel inadequate with overuse of the technique.

Role Play. Role play can be used during the supervisory conference in both individual and group situations. It is a spontaneous simulation of an interview or practice situation and is usually of limited duration—five or ten minutes. When the supervisee acts the part of the worker, it is generally in order to prepare for a coming interview or event or to practice a technique. When the supervisee acts the part of a client or someone in the client's life situation, it is in order to experience what it feels like to be that person or to be in a particular situation, and thus is a tool for expanding the supervisee's awareness, empathy, and understanding. Because powerful, unexpected, or self-revealing feelings can be aroused or demonstrated by the use of role play, it is advisable to use it briefly and sparingly in supervision.

Formal Evaluations

Formal, written evaluations of employees' and trainees' work written by supervisors are essential to the organization's delivery of quality service. They offer protection to the clients by providing a review of the workload and inform workers and students of how their work is viewed and what they must learn. Evaluations of workers assist in decisions regarding assignments, promotion, tenure, salary, and areas needing improvement. They are official records and are kept for future reference. This practice protects both the agency and the worker, for if agency personnel changes, there is a record of the employee's performance and its content is known to the worker. For students, the evaluation constitutes the written record sent to their academic settings and aids in determining grades in field work. Student evaluations are considered to be primarily an educational tool, though their general content or conclusions may be used as part of the school's composite record.

Evaluations performed at stated times and from objective standards reduce ambiguity about expectations. The evaluation outlines or rating forms used for this purpose vary from agency to agency and school to school. Examples are offered by many writers (Pettes, 1967; Kadushin, 1976; Westheimer, 1977). They are based on requirements for work performance and on learning goals, not on the personality of the worker or student. Evaluations enable supervisees to review the totality of their work, and this view in itself often has the feeling of newness or of a different importance, even when material and information is not new.

Necessary and important as evaluations are, they are often avoided and postponed because of the anxiety they create in both supervisee and supervisor. Kadushin (1976, p. 273) states that "the only thing more anxiety provoking than evaluation is no evaluation." Despite the anxiety engendered, however, honest feedback is desired by most supervisees, and is identified by Levy (1973) as the single most important obligation of a supervisor to a supervisee. The evaluation is the most concrete instrument of such feedback. Evaluations are difficult for supervisees who, like most people, fear and resent being judged. Evaluations are also difficult for supervisors because they can disrupt a comfortable relationship, make manifest the authority of the supervisor, and force the confrontation of difficult issues. Evaluations reveal the knowledge, expertise, lacks, or oversights of the supervisor, just as surely as they delineate the supervisee's strengths and weaknesses. One's supervisory practice is thus exposed to the view of administrators in the agency, to school advisors (if the supervisee is a student), to the supervisee, and to oneself.

Evaluations are an opportunity also for the supervisor to identify learning needs and learning styles. This use is more relevant to student evaluations, since trained workers are usually cognizant of their learning styles. It is wise also to identify strengths in evaluations, not only as a way of supporting supervisees and enabling them to face problems, but also because students and workers frequently do not recognize and value their own strengths and thus fail to build on them.

Basic to good evaluations are: objective criteria shared with the supervisee in advance; ensuring input from the supervisee in the discussion; providing concrete data and examples from practice to support negative and positive points; structuring a way for the supervisee to evaluate the supervision; ensuring that all aspects evaluated have been previously covered, though possibly briefly; and identifying future goals of supervision. The supervisor takes responsibility for the final written document and shares it with the supervisee, who may add a written addendum if disagreements cannot be resolved.

In some agencies experienced practitioners or senior workers are asked to write self-evaluations in which they may identify their own learning and practice goals. This acknowledges their past satisfactory performances, encourages self-direction, and may be more appropriate if they have moved to using consultation rather than supervision. It should be kept in mind that even these documents should be reviewed with an administrator or senior, as it is difficult for anyone to judge their own performance.

The Relationship

The relationship between supervisor and supervisee is often the key to how effectively administrative and educational goals are achieved. Like all human relationships, the supervisory one is complex and operates on several levels simultaneously. The quality and scope of it is determined by: the personalities, abilities, and needs of the participants; the needs, requests, and characteristics of the clients served; the goals and purposes of the agency; the structure and definition of the role of supervision within a particular setting; the standards and requirements of the profession; and social environmental factors outside of the setting, both in the community it serves and in the wider society. The interaction of all these factors influences any supervisory process as well as the overall professional relationship.

The supervisory relationship itself has been discussed by many, chiefly from a psychoanalytical and ego-psychology perspective. Towle (1954) used a psychoanalytical developmental model. Cohen (1979, unpublished paper) has traced the stages of the supervisory relationship using an Eriksonian model. Garland, Jones, and Kolodny (1965) have used an Eriksonian paradigm to describe group stages in treatment, which can also be a way of looking at the process of group supervision. Viewing a relationship as a developmental process is helpful to a supervisor in understanding some of the stages and behaviors observed, and in selecting appropriate techniques or actions for use in supervision. However, a sequential recapitulation of parent-child relationships is not expected in supervision where the two adult parties have had many intervening experiences and opportunities to settle childhood problems. Derivatives of basic human needs and issues are likely to surface in this relationship as they do in all others, however, but when and how they do so will vary with the individual. The understanding of unconscious motivation, defenses, transference, and ambivalence will enlighten supervision as it does therapy, although the knowledge is used and responded to differently. Mattinson (1975, p. 11) has used Searles's thesis of "the reflection process" and applied it to supervision to view one aspect of the relationship in depth: the proposition is that "the processes at work currently in the relationship between client and worker are often reflected in the relationship between worker and supervisor."

Basic human issues present in supervision include trust, autonomy, and competitiveness (or ambivalence about surpassing one's mentor). Trust issues may often be muted in supervision. Most adults who have reached professional status have learned to assess the potential for satisfaction or harm in a new relationship and have developed appropriate self-protectiveness. However, differing desires for closeness and distance, or for revealing and concealing, are evident in all interactions. The supervisor who understands that this is always a relationship dynamic will deal with it by demonstrating a tangible willingness and ability to establish a friendly, but professional relationship which is both safe and helpful and to ally herself with supervisees' feasible hopes and goals for themselves.

The issue of autonomy is commonly the one of most concern to supervisees. This is not surprising, since being accountable as an adult to someone else can be experienced as a threat to independence and competence, and can be viewed as infantilizing. Autonomy is also a central issue in the social work profession, and there is considerable disagreement about who should have the final decision-making authority in practice situations. Struggles with authority are seldom dormant in adult relationships and can be expected to be heightened when there is an inherent power disparity.

A supervisor can minimize the concern for autonomy by carefully establishing the limits and scope of the relationship. It is helpful to depersonalize rules and policies by locating them correctly in the organization and by explaining the reasons for the policies. Setting limits on time, content, and responsibilities and engaging the supervisee in setting mutual goals aids the process. The major objective is to give the supervisee as much control as possible over the work and in the relationship. A supervisor can encourage independence of thought, even when there is disagreement. The responsible action that follows would have to be negotiated.

Supervisees' moves from dependence to independence will be uneven; this may annoy or secretly please a supervisor who either resents or enjoys the dependence of others. It is necessary to allow for expected regression while strongly encouraging forward movement and setting expectations for adequate performance.

The human need for love, and its derivatives of approval and respect, is basic, and supervisees may become anxious when they become competitive with supervisors or when they feel undeserving of approval. The supervisor must try to avoid the competitive arena. It is encouraging and supportive to a supervisee to see that the supervisor is not threatened or jealous of the supervisee's success, and at the same time cannot be coerced into bending rules or distorting the professional relationship.

Recognizing that ambivalence is inherent in all relationships and also that growth and learning take place best in the context of a positive relationship, it becomes the task of the supervisor to foster the positive side of the ambivalence. This is a particularly demanding task when supervision includes an evaluative function. The evaluative function is essential, is valued by and owed to supervisees, but can feel like betrayal. The supervisor is in the same position as parents, teachers, and other authority figures—that of both giving and limiting. It is a difficult role, with a built-in structural conflict which cannot be completely resolved. However, mature people with good will and the self-awareness necessary for functioning as social workers can be expected to negotiate it successfully most of the time.

Social Factors and Roles

Social factors that are consciously known and recognized but go unnoticed or unexamined must be accounted for in the supervisory relationship. We make assumptions about others based on our own experiences and roles and often fail to see how limited, distorted, or idiosyncratic our attitudes and perceptions may be. The roles of workers and supervisors within the organization have been discussed by sociologists and social workers (Munson, 1976). The difficult middle, or conduit, position of supervisors in relation to the workers under them and the administration over them has been explored (Berkowitz, 1952). Just as important are roles outside of the profession. Such factors as race, ethnicity, religion, socioeconomic level, life-styles, gender, sexual orientation, marital status, and age affect the supervisory relationship as they do all others. They are as necessary to scrutinize in relation to supervision as are the unconscious issues that have so long fascinated us. These social factors also require the same sensitivity to dangers of intrusiveness and personalization when explored in supervision that all personal issues do. It is not possible or necessary to examine each of these issues in depth here. Some of them have been discussed elsewhere, and others need further exploration. Royster (1972, pp. 83) has discussed the role conflicts of the black supervisor as "a result of his role as a black, his role as a professional, and his role as a functionary of the agency, as well as the role conflict in the traditional white-black relationship." Current increased consciousness regarding the stereotyped thinking in our society about sex roles, and recognition of the power issues in the male-therapist/female-patient relationship, can illuminate our thinking about similar situations, and their reverse, in supervision. Race and gender are more obvious than some of the other factors raised, however, and it is often the unseen or subtle differences that go unaddressed within ourselves and in others. To make assumptions about other people's attitudes and perceptions based on our own life experiences is never helpful and may be more likely to occur in supervision than in treatment because both partners may assume similarities which they might not with clients. Inner and outer forces and their interplay all affect clinical supervision. We must partialize and select our focus, but if we ignore the existence of either, we do so to the detriment of the supervisory process and the clinical work we supervise.

Ethics

In a broad consideration of ethics in social work practice, the supervisor must take into account obligations to the client being served, the supervisee, the organization or agency, and the profession, and attempt to balance all these competing claims. For this discussion, however, the ethical obligation of the supervisor to the supervisee in the professional relationship is being emphasized.

Both external and internal regulations to govern the use of power are desirable when one person has control over another in some important aspect of life or circumstance. Supervisors may have considerable control over salary, promotion, or grades of supervisees. Also, the supervisory relationship is a "privileged" relationship, since the supervisor is in a position of having knowledge of the supervisee's work, as well as his or her feelings and attitudes which emerge through the work. Thus it is a relationship of uneven power. Levy (1973) has pointed out that an ethical act means one that is "right," not merely best or practical. Among many issues he suggests that the supervisor must consider the worker's suitability and aspirations. Levy believes that the supervisor must give the worker a good start and also feel personally accountable if he or she has contributed in any way to a supervisee's failure. According to Levy, the supervisor's greatest obligation is to give accurate feedback to a supervisee. The supervisor's obligation for confidentiality and consideration of the supervisee's rights also extends beyond the employment period, in writing references or making comments about the supervisee in the future.

Consultation

In considering supervision one is soon led to thinking about consultation and the differences between these two similar processes.

Social work consultation was defined by Rapoport as "a professional method of problem solving involving a time-limited, purposeful, contractual relationship between a knowledgeable expert, the consultant, and a less knowledgeable professional worker as the consultee" (Rapoport, 1971, Vol. I, p. 156).

Kadushin (1977) adds several other components: the help is purely advisory; the consultant is a social worker with experience derived from specialized social work education and practice; the consultee can be an individual, group, organization, or community faced with a job-related problem; and the problem has a social work component. Consultation, unlike supervision, is usually periodic, and, even if it is continuous, it deals with a specific and different case or problem each time. The consultant can be from within or outside of an agency. Consultation involves a more collegial relationship than supervision despite the fact that it is based on a specialist or expertise expectation. The looser relationship stems from two basic assumptions: first, that the process is limited in time or scope; and second, that control, or autonomy, remains with the consultee.

The function of consultation is educational and not administrative, so the consultant usually has no formal input into policy or change within the agency, outside of his or her persuasive or expertise power. Official sanction for the consultant's endeavor must come from the agency, which has administrative responsibility for the practice. Consultants can make a serious professional, ethical, or even legal error in contracting with a practitioner or practice group only, without a formal contract or arrangement with the agency administration. Caplan (1970) has also pointed out that consultation given at the request of one person or group within an agency is limited and partial, for the consultant lacks full knowledge of the context, needs, and goals of the organization. In addition, the consultant's work may never be implemented if consultation is not accepted by those in power to effect change.

Consultation as an educational tool can more readily meet the needs of the adult striving for autonomy and control because the process does not have an evaluative function. Consultees frequently select their own consultants, rather than having them assigned, as with supervisors. In presenting a specific problem they have to identify what it is they wish to learn. Consultees also use only what they wish of what is offered, and such a process may force closer scrutiny of what is useful and what is not. Consultation thus offers, in action, an evaluation of the consultant rather than the consultee.

There are strengths and limitations in both supervision and consultation, and appropriate and inappropriate use of both methods occurs. The profession has been slow in coming to a clear assessment of when each method is most appropriate and has done so by default rather than by plan. Many agencies use both supervision and consultation without clearly identifying them.

The reluctance to move from supervision to consultation may be due to many factors; chief among them is clarity in understanding that mixed models are possible and that an either/or choice may not be desirable within agencies and institutions. For example, administrative supervision may always be necessary for overseeing caseloads, making equitable assignments, doing formal evaluations, implementing policy changes, and developing new policies. However, it is also appropriate that experienced clinicians be expected to make clinical decisions, with consultation on practice as needed. It can be assumed that experienced clinicians should be able to recognize when they are "stuck" or are responding out of character in a situation.

Mental health professions which use a modified consultation approach in teaching during their initial educational training (using many experts for different clinical experiences and no primary supervisor) may lose the benefits of the model developed by social work of overseeing a total learning experience. As we know, the learning patterns of a trainee emerge more clearly in that model, an educational assessment and plan can be established, and the power of the supervisory relationship for modeling and developing self-awareness can be maximized. However, social work, even in its training period, has been modifying its practice of using only one supervisor. The use of supplementary supervisors for teaching specialized skills is now common, and the use of additional modalities such as groups, triadic supervision, and direct observation in family treatment is increasing. Fragmentation is minimized by assigning a primary supervisor.

The reluctance to establish a complete change to consultation is due in part to the relatively short training period for clinicians in social work and the recognition that more education and experience is needed for the demanding nature of and responsibility required in the work. The requirements of some state licensing laws and the certification requirements of the National Association of Social

Work (which requires actual supervision for a specified period, usually two years, after completion of training) seem reasonable and necessary. It seems equally appropriate that a formal, explicit change be made, after a specified period, to mixed models of supervision and consultation, or to consultation only, depending on administrative requirements. Administrative supervision in social agencies and institutions may always be required although its format may change. A public as well as a private need for accountability exists. Educational supervision could be conducted initially as a safeguard when workers change settings or fields of practice, then they could again move to consultation. Such an explicit standard would undoubtedly benefit the functioning of the practitioner and produce a more autonomous image for the profession. Partial rather than complete resolution of some of the problems in supervision may have to suffice, inasmuch as human beings and their social institutions are, alas, imperfect.

References

Austin, L. N. "Basic Principles of Supervision." *Social Casework,* December 1952, pp. 163–217.

Austin, L. N. "An Evaluation of Supervision." *Social Casework,* 1956, *37* (8), pp. 375–382.

Berkowitz, S. J. "The Administrative Process in Casework Supervision." *Social Casework,* December 1952, pp. 419–423.

Brackett, J. R. *Supervision and Education in Charity.* Kennebunkport, Me.: Milford House Publishers, 1974. (Originally published 1903.)

Caplan, G. *The Theory and Practice of Mental Health Consultation.* New York: Basic Books, 1970.

Cohen, M. "A Developmental Approach to Field Work Supervision." Paper presented at the annual conference of Smith College School for Social Work, July 1979.

Cooper, S. "Field Teaching: Acculturation and Education for Clinical Social Work Practice." Lecture in memory of Professor Dorothy Robinson, presented at University of Michigan School of Social Work, Ann Arbor, October 3, 1979.

Dwyer, M., and Urbanowski, M. "Student Process Recording: A Plea for Structure." *Social Casework,* May 1965, pp. 283–286.

Ekstein, R., and Wallerstein, R. S. *The Teaching and Learning of Psychotherapy.* New York: Basic Books, 1972.

Epstein, L. "Is Autonomous Practice Possible?" *Social Work,* March 1973, pp. 5–13.

Etzioni, A. *The Semi-Professions and Their Organizations.* New York: Free Press, 1969.

Fizdale, R. "Peer Group Supervision." *Social Casework,* October 1958, pp. 443–449.

Garland, J. A., Jones, H. E., and Kolodny, R. L. "A Model for Stages of Development in Social Work Groups." In S. Bernstein (Ed.), *Explorations in Group Work: Essays in Theory and Practice.* Boston: Boston University School of Social Work, 1965.

Garrett, A. "Learning Through Supervision." *Smith College Studies in Social Work,* February 1954, pp. 3–109.

Germain, C. B. "An Ecological Perspective in Casework Practice." *Social Casework,* June 1973, pp. 323–330. (Also a chapter in this volume.)

Gitterman, A. "Comparison of Educational Models and Their Influences on Supervision." In F. W. Kaslow (Ed.), *Issues in Human Services.* San Francisco: Jossey-Bass, 1972.

Gitterman, A., and Miller, I. "Supervisors as Educators." In F. W. Kaslow (Ed.), *Supervision, Consultation and Staff Training in the Helping Professions.* San Francisco: Jossey-Bass, 1977.

Hamilton, G. "Self-Awareness in Professional Education." *Social Casework,* November 1954, pp. 371–379.

Hartman, A. "To Think About the Unthinkable." *Social Casework,* October 1970, pp. 467–474.

Howe, E. "Public Professions and the Private Model of Professionalism." *Social Work,* May 1980, pp. 179–191.

Kadushin, A. "Supervisor-Supervisee: A Survey." *Social Work,* May 1974, pp. 288–297.

Kadushin, A. *Supervision in Social Work.* New York: Columbia University Press, 1976.

Kadushin, A. *Consultation in Social Work.* New York: Columbia University Press, 1977.

Kaslow, F. W. "Group Supervision." In F. W. Kaslow (Ed.), *Issues in Human Services.* San Francisco: Jossey-Bass, 1972.

Kaslow, F. W. (Ed.). *Supervision, Consultation and Staff Training in the Helping Professions.* San Francisco: Jossey-Bass, 1977.

Kent, B. *Social Work: Supervision in Practice.* Oxford: Pergamon Press, 1969.

Knowles, M. S. "Innovations in Teaching Styles and Approaches Based upon Adult Learning." *Journal of Education for Social Work,* Spring 1972, pp. 32–39.

Kutzik, A. J. "Class and Ethnic Factors." In F. W. Kaslow (Ed.), *Issues in Human Services.* San Francisco: Jossey-Bass, 1972.

Kutzik, A. J. "The Social Work Field." In F. W. Kaslow (Ed.), *Supervision, Consultation and Staff Training in the Helping Professions.* San Francisco: Jossey-Bass, 1977.

Leader, A. "New Directions in Supervision." *Social Casework,* November 1957, pp. 462–468.

Levy, C. S. "The Ethics of Supervision." *Social Work,* March 1973, pp. 14–21.

Loewenstein, S. F. "Trainees' Initial Reaction to Live Family Therapy Training." In J. Byng-Hall and R. Whiffen (Eds.), *Family Therapy Supervision: Recent Developments in Practice.* London: The Tavistock Clinic, 1982.

Mattinson, J. *The Reflection Process in Casework Supervision.* London: Institute of Marital Studies, The Tavistock Institute of Human Relations, 1975.

Miller, I. "Supervision in Social Work," *Encyclopedia of Social Work,* Sixteenth Issue, Vol. II. New York: National Association of Social Workers, 1971.

Morton, T. D., and Kurtz, P. D. "Educational Supervision: A Learning Theory Approach." *Social Casework,* April 1980, pp. 240–246.

Munson, C. E. "Professional Autonomy and Social Work Supervision." In C. E. Munson (Ed.), *Social Work Supervision: Classic Statements and Critical Issues.* New York: Free Press, 1979.

Perlmutter, F. "Barometer of Professional Change." In F. W. Kaslow (Ed.), *Issues in Human Services.* San Francisco: Jossey-Bass, 1972.

Pettes, D. E. *Supervision in Social Work.* London: Allen & Unwin, 1967.

Rapport, L. "Consultation in Social Work." *Encyclopedia of Social Work,* Sixteenth Issue, Vol. I., p. 156. New York: National Association of Social Workers, 1971.

Reynolds, B. *Learning and Teaching in the Practice of Social Work.* New York: Rinehart, 1965.

Richmond, M. E. *Social Diagnosis.* New York: Russell Sage Foundation, 1917.

Rickert, V. C., and Turner, J. E. "Through the Looking Glass: Supervision in Family Therapy." *Social Casework,* March 1978, pp. 131–137.

Robinson, V. P. *Dynamics of Supervision Under Functional Controls.* Philadelphia: University of Pennsylvania Press, 1949.

Rosenblatt, A., and Mayer, J. "Objectionable Supervisory Styles: Students' Views." *Social Work,* May 1975, pp. 184–189.

Royster, E. C. "Black Supervisors: Problems of Race and Role." In F. W. Kaslow (Ed.), *Issues in Human Services.* San Francisco: Jossey-Bass, 1972.

Sales, E., and Navarre, E. *Individual and Group Supervision in Field Instruction.* Ann Arbor: University of Michigan School of Social Work, 1970.

Scherz, F. M. "A Conception of Supervision Based on Definitions of Job Responsibility." *Social Casework,* October 1958, pp. 435–443.

The Tavistock Clinic. "One-Year Advanced Programme for Social Workers." Unpublished syllabus for training, #2A 1481, The Tavistock Clinic, London (not dated).

Towle, C. *The Learner in Education for the Professions.* Chicago: University of Chicago Press, 1954.

Towle, C. "The Place of Help in Supervision." *Social Service Review,* December 1963, pp. 403–415.

Toren, N. "Semi-Professionalism and Social Work: A Theoretical Perspective." In A. Etzioni (Ed.), *The Semi-Professions and Their Organizations.* New York: Free Press, 1969.

Westheimer, I. J. *Practice of Supervision in Social Work: A Guide for Staff Supervisors.* London: Ward Lock Educational, 1977.

Whaley, K. "Helplessness and Omnipotence: The Two-Headed Monster." Unpublished manuscript, School of Social Work, Simmons College, Boston, 1978.

Whitehead, A. H. *The Aims of Education and Other Essays.* New York: Macmillan, 1929.

Wilensky, H. L., and Lebeaux, C. N. *Industrial Society and Social Welfare.* New York: Russell Sage Foundation, 1958.

Williamson, M. *Supervision—New Patterns and Processes.* New York: Association Press, 1961. (Originally published 1950.)

16

Professional Growth Through Continuing Education

Louise A. Frey
Golda M. Edinburg

Continuous, continued, and continuing education are variations on the theme of learning. *Continuing education* is the name usually given to the formal educational structure which provides opportunities for further learning following completion of basic education. *Continued education* has a more finite quality and implies an identifiable ending to a process. Self-directed *continuous education* is the most applicable to professional social work learning. Because learning should be ongoing throughout a professional career, self-directed continuous education is the subject of this chapter.

Autonomy and Continuous Learning

A key professional attribute is engagement in continuous learning in order to ensure a high quality of work with clients. The current rate of expansion of knowledge tends to shrink proportionately the original educational foundation upon which professional practice is based. The rapid obsolescence of knowledge is a concern in all professions. The external constraints of licensing and certification, the wish for promotions and pay raises, and the reality of job shortages all require updating of knowledge and skills. The decision is not whether to engage in continuous learning, but rather how and with what focus.

For some clinicians there are boundless opportunities; for others the choices may be very limited. Abundant opportunities require development of a plan to achieve a balanced educational program. Where there is a lack of opportunities, the clinician is confronted with creating self-directed learning and mobilizing others to develop formal programs in which all can participate. Whether there are abundant or limited options, the clinician must make a self-directed learning plan which says, "I have taken responsibility for an orderly process in my continuous growth and development as a member of a profession."

Such a statement expresses an attitude about practitioner autonomy, which has implications for the development and general acceptance of social work as a profession. The degree to which social work is regarded as a profession has been discussed extensively in the literature. Recently a number of writers have questioned the negative effect upon professional autonomy of the reliance on certain styles of supervision that act as a means of professional and organizational control (Munson, 1976). Similar questions can be raised about educational methods and their effect upon the development of the profession. The need for different models of supervision and education is apparent.

Amitai Etzioni (1964), a leading theorist on the sociology of organizations, describes social work and social work agencies as semi-professional. The professional organization employs professionals whose training is longer than five years; its goals include the creation and application of knowledge. The professional members are protected by privileged communication and are often concerned with matters of life and death. These conditions do not exist in the semi-professions where control is usually accomplished through organizational regulation and superiors. One aspect of a semi-profession, as compared to a full profession, is the relation between two authority principles: that of knowledge and that of administration. Etzioni writes, "The basis of professional authority is knowledge and the relationship between administrative and professional authority is largely affected by the amount and kind of knowledge the professional has" (1964, pp. 87–88).

Etzioni sees application of knowledge and creativity as basically individual. Ultimate responsibility is to one's conscience for professional decisions. The ultimate responsibility of an administrative act is that it is in line with the organization's rules and regulations and has been approved directly or by implication by a superior.

Whether one agrees or disagrees with Etzioni's formulations about social work as a semi-profession, autonomy in practice appears to be one of the characteristics of a profession. Moving toward greater capacity for autonomous, responsible practice requires building and accumulating knowledge, increased research into the human problems with which practice deals, and research into the methods of practice itself. A self-motivated, self-directed approach to continuous education should be congruent with achieving the goals of autonomous professional practice.

Education and Training

Although the terms *education* and *training* are often used interchangeably, they represent different aspects of learning.

Education is a thinking, inquiring, and problem-solving process which is an expansive experience. It is concerned with building knowledge—providing information, explanation, principles, and concepts which underlie techniques and skills.

Training is a much more limited concept than education. It is a process of preparing for performance in prescribed ways. Training is essential for achieving competence in discrete tasks such as case recording, making statistical and financial reports, and meeting administrative requirements. A person can be taught interviewing techniques for limited practice in social work methods. In-service programs conducted by agencies are generally for training in how to do something rather than for broader educational purposes, but both training and education are attained through a learning process.

Learning is a process which continuously combines the intellect, the emotions, and the motor functions differently in each human being. Reynolds (1970) traced the development of conscious learning as a necessity for the survival of the human species and Freire (1981) points out that the capacity for action based upon conscious thought (reflection and praxis) is unique to the human animal.

Each adult has developed characteristic patterns of learning which include induction/deduction, reflection and observation, abstraction, experience, and experimentation. The mind is an active organ constantly storing, organizing, coding and retrieving information (McKeachie, 1976). The learner is constantly constructing a story or theory about what is perceived. Norman's (1980) analogy is to the mind as an iceberg, most of which is underwater and out of sight of the learner and teacher.

Learning never stops, even though the adult may not be aware of the continual problem solving which goes on each day and in sleep at night. Learning is a problem-solving process of collecting data, sorting it out, analyzing it, and synthesizing it. This process can be done creatively and expansively. Recent research and speculation about the different functions of the two sides of the brain point to ways of using both sides more fully. New investigation into mind-body interrelationships promises much in maximizing our unused capacities for learning. Fortunately we already know enough about learning to encourage our taking control of our own education. In summarizing the state of knowledge about the psychology of learning, McKeachie (1980) gives fifteen major ideas to teachers and learners; most of these are based upon the *active* involvement of learners in the problem-solving process which constitutes learning.

Knowles (1972) has formulated some principles of adult education which stem from the problem-solving aspect of the psychology of learning. He points out that adults generally are and expect to be autonomous and self-directing, that they have a life experience in problem-solving, and that they learn what they need and want to know to carry out their functions, roles, and responsibilities as adults. These social characteristics should provide a readiness for positive continuous education related to the professional role.

Unfortunately, however, there are attitudinal blocks to formal education which are the result of childhood experiences in classrooms. There are also emotional blocks to learning which are the result of developmental experiences in both family and school. These emotional blocks are particularly powerful in learning about clinical relationships. Before discussing these obstacles, some other thoughts about education must be presented.

If education is an opening-out process, the educated person should have developed an attitude about learning which is inquisitive, skeptical, and creative. However exciting this may be, exploring what is new or different may be unsettling and painful. Thinking the unthinkable takes a good deal of courage and basic security. Questioning assumptions or even listening to new ideas may cast doubt upon one's personal value system, current convictions, or knowledge framework. Since learning is an affective and cognitive process, acquiring new knowledge may disrupt one's basic sense of security in knowing what one knows. Frey (1977) points out that patterns of emotional, cognitive, and motor learning are established in early childhood. Throughout life the thrust for independence and autonomy confronts the wish for dependence upon and nurturing by a loving parent figure or acceptance by siblings and peers. The conflict between the regressive wish to be told what to do and the unrealistic wish to do everything on one's own is omnipresent from nursery school to graduate school.

The wish to be loved and nurtured by the teacher (parent) and the wish to exterminate this judging, controlling person are symptomatic of the power disparity attributed by society to the teacher and learner roles (parent/child). Such disparity breeds anxiety and resentment in the learner, who must also struggle for acceptance by peers (siblings). Being the "best" in the classroom means risking friendships and approval by peers. Eventually most students learn that no one loves the teacher's pet—except maybe the teacher. However, the teacher's "love" may last only so long as the pupil does what the teacher wants and continues to appear to be the product of the teacher's skill.

The form these emotional struggles take and how they are handled by the teacher are determined in part by societal prescriptions about education and by the educational philosophy and methods which the teacher has been taught. In the traditional school system it is common practice that teachers "teach," and pupils demonstrate what they have learned by repeating the teacher's words, verbally and in examinations. This mode of education has been referred to as as regurgitative method. It is paradoxical that, although the pupil is doing the regurgitating, it is the teacher who has the illness. Sartre named this the digestive or nutritive concept of education. Along with the narration sickness, Freire (1981) makes an analogy to the banking business. The teacher banks gold in the student depository. When the teacher wants it back, he or she pushes some buttons and collects it with interest, but it is never converted by the learner into some other currency.

The American system of education is a competitive one, suggests Henry, the anthropologist. He calls it "the American Nightmare" (1963, p. 24). Staying on top at any grade level requires a student to demonstrate that he or she is better than someone else. Because cooperative modes are not functional in such a system, it is predictable that learning will be competitive and manipulative. This can be especially difficult for a learner who does not come from the dominant cultural system. The Native American child, for example, who will not raise a hand to answer a question which another child has answered incorrectly, may fail in a typical American school. Such a child is reluctant to violate the values of cooperation which are traditional and were necessary to a tribe's survival. This child will not humiliate a peer even though he or she wishes to have the teacher's approval.

These intrapsychic, social, and cultural influences from childhood have relevance to learning in graduate school. Some students may expect and prefer a rigid and competitive educational structure, while others hope for or are more comfortable with an open, self-directed style of learning and teaching. Achieving a balance between emotional and intellectual learning, between dependence and independence, is not easy for the person learning to be a clinician or for the clinician in the role of teacher. The beginning student is at a stage of learning where intellectual direction and emotional support are essential. A new graduate should have attained a state of competence which permits a greater degree of responsible independence in functioning. If the student has been prepared for this stage of practice by the encouragement of appropriate levels of autonomy during basic education, he or she should be able to articulate areas for further learning in the immediate years ahead. The graduate is most likely to be at the third stage of learning described by Reynolds (1970, pp. 75–91). Having survived the stage of acute self-consciousness and having swum instead of sunk, the new graduate is in the stage of knowing what he or she should do, and being able to do it much of the time—though not consistently and usually not with ease and depth.

It is the stage where motivation to continue learning is high; when there has been enough success in practice, there is willingness and eagerness at this stage to examine one's personal feelings and behaviors and their effect upon practice. It is at this time that clinical supervision becomes an attractive way of learning. (The two-year requirement of postgraduate supervision for admission to membership in the Academy of Certified Social Worker supports its importance.)

Educational supervision is an effective method for learning more about therapeutic relationships and the effects of intrapsychic and unconscious dynamics upon feelings and behavior. Social workers deal with people with serious problems, in which external circumstances and internal responses are uniquely entwined. Facilitating clients' resolution of these complex problems is an emotionally demanding task. Sometimes the behavior and feelings displayed by the client are shocking and repugnant to the clinician. The emotional drain may stimulate unexpected feelings, attitudes, and behaviors which are consciously and unconsciously caused. The clinician may wish to understand his or her reactions in order to keep them from interfering in a client's progress. In addition, differences in race, ethnicity, age, and social and economic status influence the clinician's capacity to work with some clients. Identifying the worker's knowledge gaps, difficulties, and countertransferences, while maintaining his or her autonomy in dealing with clients' problems, is a function of educational supervision. The boundaries of the supervisory relationship preclude it becoming a therapeutic process for working through psychological problems. The clinician has a variety of other educational means in courses, workshops, and consultation to gain increased self-awareness, new perspectives, and support. These structured situations may be less threatening and decrease the possibility of defensiveness which may occur in the one-to-one supervisory relationship.

Reynolds's fourth stage of learning is that of mastery which comes with informed practice. The figure skater who performs precisely (technically) and beautifully (artistically) has achieved mastery of the craft. So too with the clinician who combines the art and science of casework. Achievement of this level of skill may be personally satisfying, but it also holds the danger of lulling the clinician into complacency and a sense of rectitude, thus forestalling new learning. External demands such as licensing may be the prime motivation for continuous learning at this stage. However, the belief in and valuing of continued growth is the internalized professional stimulus. Entering upon Reynolds's fifth stage of learning, which is the teaching of others, is the most humbling means of finding out that one needs to continue to learn.

Opportunities for Learning

Clearly the opportunities for continuous education go beyond enrollment in courses. The integration of the affective, cognitive, and skill needs of clinicians requires experiences which encompass theory, practice, and increased self-awareness. Among the opportunities for learning are supervision, consultation, in-service training, reading and study groups, teaching, publication, professional memberships, research, community activities, and enrollment in formal continuing education courses, workshops, and seminars. Pursuing continuous education requires practical, creative, and imaginative planning by the clinician.

Supervision. The classic method of learning and teaching within an agency is individual supervision. Such learning becomes part of the worker's store of knowledge for use in the present and the future. The clinician who wishes to increase theoretical knowledge, develop and refine skills, and examine attitudes and feelings may have opportunities for individual, group, and peer supervision and consultation.

Supervision is a means of exploring what is known and unknown about specific cases and transferring that knowledge to other cases. It is also useful for questioning assumptions underlying the interventions and for reexamining the basis for emotional aspects of the client/worker relationship. Whether these explorations and inquiries are undertaken depends in part upon the service needs of the clients and the learning needs of the supervisee. A learning plan for supervision can be developed, based on the learner's own assessment of need. However, in supervision such a plan is tempered by the supervisor's perception of learning required for qualitative job functioning. For example, a worker may want to improve clinical diagnostic skills. The supervisor's perception is that the worker's diagnostic ability is at an acceptable level, but that there is a serious problem in the worker's resistance to the use of short-term treatment with clients. Thus, exploration of the worker's resistance is required. However, the more the worker has taken advantage of the opportunity offered in supervision for gleaning new knowledge and increasing self-awareness, the less resistance there will be to understanding the method.

A sound supervisory program is based on agency descriptions of the work to be done by employee. In some instances these descriptions will be broken into tasks and levels of competence. Such a structure could assist the clinician in defining what learning is relevant to job performance. The worker can assess those areas in which he or she wishes to improve and then work out an appropriate educational plan. For example, the worker who decides to learn more about diagnosing and treating the elderly will discover a richness of learning opportunities in exploring biological, psychosocial, and cultural areas; in uncovering new methods of intervention; and in probing personal attitudes toward aging. The clinician may choose a variety of ways to learn, such as preparing full process records on a case or two, discussing several articles, reporting on a workshop, making a home visit, or videotaping an interview in order to analyze how new learnings have been applied. The subsequent supervisory conferences could be devoted to an in-depth discussion of the questions raised or ideas generated. If the agency does not provide clinical supervision, the worker may feel impelled to "buy" supervision outside of the agency. This, however, poses administrative complications related to accountability, confidentiality, and legal liability. Such use of an outside "expert" cannot be supervision which is an agency responsibility. The outside person acts as an educator free of any administrative authority for the worker's performance or the outcome of the case. It is necessary to have the sanction of the agency for engagement of an outside expert, even if the worker plans to pay for this service.

Group supervision is a particularly good way to continue learning. The intepersonal interaction and the variations in ideas, knowledge, points of view, and attitudes can provide the stimulus to free one's thinking and enhance one's creativity. In group supervision there are two learning plans—one for the individual and one for the total group. The group members and the supervisor have the task of blending individual interests into an agenda for the whole group. This is a process of examining all needs, identifying common concerns and unique needs, and working out a way to incorporate all or to eliminate some. The plan for meeting the selected learning needs can include use of publications, observation, tapes, field visits, and theoretical presentations. The group will join with the supervisor in evaluating how well each member's and the group's learning goals were achieved. Other forms of group learning are sometimes called group supervision. However, they are distinguishable from supervision in that there is no group evaluation of the performance of the members.

Peer supervision may be used when a professional has reached a level of competence where regular monitoring by someone in an administrative role is rarely necessary. For the agency clinician, peer supervision requires good morale and an atmosphere which supports interpersonal cooperation rather than competition. The peer group (or pair) would function without the presence of an agency-designated supervisor. The members would meet with the supervisor mainly for administrative purposes. The peers would agree upon learning needs to be addressed and how this would be done. Peer supervision is especially applicable to clinicians in private practice. It has been suggested that group and peer supervision may be more appropriate for encouraging greater autonomy in the profession (Munson, 1976).

Consultation. Giving and receiving expert advice—consultation—enables the practitioner to obtain an opinion from another clinical social worker or other professional with special knowledge in an area of practice. Whether employed by an agency or by a private practitioner, the consultant usually has no administrative responsibility for the worker's performance or the use of the advice. As in supervision this requires the sanction of the agency. The consultation may be on technical issues of practice or it may be geared to reviewing the client's condition and the goals of treatment.

Clinicians can make consultation a more effective learning experience by preparing in advance specific questions on which to focus. For example, a clinician requests consultation regarding a patient who is making no progress in treatment. The patient is acting in a self-destructive manner, cutting herself and taking minor drug overdoses, while demanding more therapy sessions. The frustrated clinician asks that her own intervention techniques be reviewed. As she presents the case material, the worker's negative countertransference becomes very apparent to both herself and the consultant. Rather than focus on this countertransference, the consultant reviews the clinical diagnosis which seemed incorrect. Rethinking the diagnosis enables the worker to modify her approach to the client, resulting in a more appropriate response.

Supervision and consultation are not eligible for formal continuing education credits. However, they offer what may well be the most meaningful learning experiences for the clinician. These learnings can be increased by avoiding a tendency to spend supervisory or consultation time in elaborating on the details of a case, leaving little time for exploration of broader or deeper questions. The determined learner may want to push the consultant for more focused teaching and in-depth review.

In-Service Training. Many agencies have established in-service training programs. They are usually seen as a means of implementing a staff development plan. (Staff development is the organized activity of the agency to increase the capacity of employees to carry out their functions and to move ahead in the agency hierarchy as appropriate.) When the in-service program of an agency is treated as a process aimed at an organized sequence of learning experiences, it is more likely to have relevance and a lasting effect upon the learners.

Staff members can have a role in developing the *educational* aspect of the in-service *training* program. An educational focus would include the statement of overall goals and specific objectives for each course and would attempt to have consistency and sequence among the different courses. An education committee of staff and administration can approach the planning task by assessing learning needs. This assessment can be done by questionnaire, departmental or staff meetings, and individual interviews. The purpose of the questionnaire is not to elicit course titles, but rather to stimulate thought about responsibilities, client needs, and practice problems encountered in meeting these needs. Such a committee can classify the learning needs according to Tyler's (1964) framework of knowledge, skills, and attitudes. Such classification could result in a skills workshop on intake, a knowledge course on diagnosis, and an experiential group to develop greater self-awareness about negative feelings in working with groups. However, if a number of staff members wanted a course on intensive, long-term treatment in an agency whose function was crisis intervention, it would be appropriate for the committee to suggest that these people find a course outside of the agency which will meet their personal educational interests.

Hari's (1977) description of an agency's efforts to change caseworkers' attitudes toward a short-term treatment approach which they wanted to institute demonstrates the resistances and complexities of effecting a change in attitudes. To overcome the negative attitudes of the staff, a study of caseworkers' reactions to participation in time-limited therapy was initiated. At the completion of the project the workers reported that open-ended practice is easier than short-term practice because the latter made greater demands on them. Subsequently, the workers resumed the open-ended approach. Three years later, confronted with long waiting lists and problems with termination of cases, the staff began to study the literature on the dynamics of resistance to terminating. Next they instituted a one-year short-term service project. When 91 percent of the clients reported that the service had been helpful, the staff then became more intersted in methods of short-term treatment and gradually extended the short-term approach to a wide range of clients. It was only when staff members experienced the problem of waiting lists and saw its connection to termination that they became more interested in learning methods of short-term treatment. They then recognized their learning needs. This led to involvement in the service project and a change in attitudes.

Reading and Study Groups. All workers, whether employed in an agency or in private practice, can learn through reading professional publications. Broad or selective reading can be done alone or with the support of a reading club or study group. These self-directed groups generally need the structure of a regular meeting time and an appointed leader. The leader for a session may be the person who is making a presentation or may be another group member who will focus the discussion. In most groups each member has unique experiences, interests, or reactions to the article or book, which can bring depth to the discussion.

The purpose of a reading group may be expanded to provide an opportunity to practice some teaching skills. Teaching about an article requires the leader/teacher to grasp the larger ideas (concepts and principles), relate these to the finer points, and think through the implications of the author's point of view. A peer learning and teaching group can set up learning objectives and measures for evaluation, such as pre- and posttests. All these devices will support the group's motivation, maintain the educational level, and keep the refreshments and socialization in their places.

Teaching. Reynolds suggests that the fifth stage of social work learning is teaching what one has thoroughly learned from practice. Practitioners who begin to teach in an agency, a school of social work, or in continuing education must conceptualize knowledge and make a disciplined, systematic review of the subject matter. They must learn how to tailor knowledge to specific learners' needs. The practitioner experiences a good deal of learning in this process. Because this learning does not have a formal base in a course on teaching, it cannot be awarded continuing education units.

For full-time faculty, the most appropriate learning may not be more courses, but rather more involvement in clinical practice with supervision or consultation from a specialist. Being steeped in practice can avoid the risk of overreliance upon abstract thinking and conceptualization. Just as the practitioners may avoid courses as a defense against anxiety, however, the academician may avoid learning through practice.

Publication. Submitting a paper for publication is an excellent means of learning, although it is usually not recognized as continuing education. Hours and hours of lonely work, often without recognition by others, is the scholar's lot.

Community Activities. Participating on a board, advisory committee, a task force, or a social action project provides opportunity for learning. Working with people who have different perspectives and value systems or who are not in the social work profession can be most enlightening and sobering.

Professional Memberships. Attending meetings of professional organizations is a means of keeping informed and abreast of developments in the field. Participating in committees of these organizations also affords opportunities for learning from members and from activities of the committees.

Research. The means by which a profession meets it responsibility to develop knowledge is research. Participation in a group research project or conducting a small evaluative study alone can be one of the most challenging ways of learning. Even if it is not possible to participate in a research endeavor, it is important to keep an open mind and a spirit of inquiry about the applicability of research findings to one's own work. A research-minded person will raise questions about basic assumptions and current practice methods and will try to apply new knowledge.

Guide to Continuing Education

Courses, workshops, seminars, and institutes are usually regarded as *continuing education* (Gibelman and Humphreys, 1979). In some communities the professional may be besieged by competing brochures, catalogs, and posters designed by universities, professional schools, private entrepreneurs, hospitals, and agencies to entice participants. In communities with limited educational systems the person who wishes to take a course may envy those who are bewildered by a richness of choice. Both are faced with difficult decisions. Cost, location, and time may also be crucial factors.

Enrollment which requires considerable travel, accommodation expense, and time away from home and work may increase the pressure to make the best choice. No matter what the practical reality, it is imperative that the potential consumer have some criteria for judging the quality of the product he or she is considering buying.

Sponsorship. The best guarantees of a quality program are the stability and educational reputation of the sponsor, its capacity to enlist consistently the services of highly skilled teachers, its method of evaluation, and its accreditation to offer Continuing Education Units (CEUs) or academic credits. The kinds and availability of records the sponsoring organization will keep may be very important for participants who are accumulating credits for licensing or licensing renewal.

It is useful to know how the sponsor has ascertained the needs which its program is designed to meet. Does the sponsor have a representative advisory or planning committee which sets policies and standards? If the sponsorship does not include social work planning for the program, the values and philosophy of the profession may be overlooked. When there is no social work input, the applicability of the course offerings should be considered with a discerning eye. Does the sponsor work with agencies to encourage educational leave or to pay all or part of the tuition? Will it offer special courses on site in the agency? How responsive is it to real needs of clinicians?

The educational materials a sponsor offers or makes available are indexes of the quality of the program. Reprints, bibliographies mailed out with registration, and materials on reserve in the library all indicate the degree of educational responsibility assumed by the organization.

Credits. The growing criticism of continuing education in all professions is that it promises too much and results in too little and may lull the participants into thinking that they are up to date. The conscientious social worker will not want to engage in a superficial or titillating program just to obtain credits. CEUs (one for each ten hours of class attendance) are the usual form of credit for continuing education. There are national standards for determining whether CEUs may be awarded (National University Extension Association, 1974). These guidelines include assessing the educational qualifications of the sponsors, faculty, planning process, evaluative process and system for record-keeping, and educational methodology (that is, whether there will be a clear, coherent learning experience with methodology appropriate to the goal).

Continuous learning may include enrollment in a academic program offering credits for a degree. The practitioner may enroll in a master's program in another area such as business management, health planning, or education. There are also Certificates of Advanced Graduated Studies (CAGS) at some universities and doctoral programs in social work and related knowledge fields. Usually these advanced basic courses do not meet the national criteria for continuing education because degree-oriented programs are not considered continuing education. The development of advanced degree programs is crucial to the movement of social work to full professional status. While there are fewer clinical doctoral programs available, the clinician's interest in such can be a catalyst to the universities to begin or reinstate them.

At this time the National Association of Social Workers (NASW) and the Council on Social Work Education are developing social work standards and guidelines for CEU accreditation. Some local social work chapters or organizations have also developed their own criteria. States with licensing or certification laws usually require continuing education credits for relicensing or recertification, but such regulations vary from state to state. Agency practices also differ regarding interest in and requirements for CEU participation. The greatest stimulus for developing CEU credits seems to be coming from the pressures related to licensing and certification.

Educational Formats. Terms describing continuing education offerings are varied and often used quite loosely. There is no guarantee that something which is advertised as a workshop will be a workshop. For the sake of clarity, the following definintions are presented. A *seminar* is a learning process in which each participant is expected to have or acquire considerable knowledge about the subject and to take responsibility for presenting that knowledge for others' consideration. The seminar leader is an expert in this area who facilitates the process and deepens the learning. In planning for seminars, it is assumed that each participant shares responsibility for specifying course content. Seminars are appropriate when the learners have a high level of knowledge and they are interested in deepening their base of understanding.

Many things which are advertised as seminars are not that at all. Instead, they are *classes* in which the teacher has the major responsibility for presenting the material and guiding discussion.

A *conference* consists of a series of deliberations and presentations about the subject of the conference. Usually there are opportunities for group discussions about topics on the conference agenda. A conference group discussion leader is usually a facilitator rather than an educator. Conference attendance is usually not awarded CEUs because there is no organized, coherent educational plan. However, workshops within a conference which meet CEU criteria content may be eligible for award of the CEUs, provided that the conference planners have submitted the plans for approval by an accredited educational sponsor.

Experiential learning may take several forms, such as one-day or weekend intensive events, although other models such as two-hour weekly sessions are also common. The participant may be expected to discuss personal feelings aroused by the experience itself or the topic under discussion. Because there is little formal or organized teaching, learning may be expected to come from within, and what learning does occur may not be what the participant expected. For example, people may enroll in an experiential group in the hope of learning about a method of clinical intervention. This is unlikely if the goal of the experience is examination of the feelings which develop while being in that group. The consumer has to examine the intent, limits, and boundaries of any experiential learning. Many people attend such programs looking for a therapeutic encounter, while others attend so that they might learn a methodology; the leader may have another goal in mind. This makes for interesting group dynamics, but it may not result in the achieving of the educational objectives as originally stated. Clinical practitioners who are hoping to learn new skills and knowledge are again warned to read course descriptions very carefully.

Judging an Educational Offering. Knowing about educational methodology can be useful for judging the suitability of a particular format for meeting one's educational needs. The format should evolve from the course objectives and the content to be learned. The potential student is usually attracted to a program by the description provided in an announcement or public statement of the intent of the sponsor. The more global or vague the description, the less likely it is that the course will be as advertised. The buyer must beware of descriptions containing global promises to "teach" complex subjects in a one-day workshop or a short course. Such descriptions may appear to promise something for everyone—an impossible goal. Parsimony is an important concept in teaching. The more clearly a brochure or course description describes what the *learners will do,* the more certain a consumer can be that the educational planner understands good educational practice. The statement "Compare and contrast three theories of family therapy" contains a demonstrable educational objective which makes clear what the learner will do, but it says nothing about whether the theories will be "learned" or "understood"—two very vague terms (Mager, 1962). Clear statements of objectives should be followed by descriptions of the course content. The more remote the content is from the objective, the more wary the learner should be. The consumer should examine the content to see if it explicates the areas identified by Tyler (1964): the knowledge base which is to be presented, the skills which are to be taught, and the attitudes which are to be explored.

Once the consumer is satisfied that the objectives are reasonable and that the content flows from the objectives, then the next step is to ascertain if all these elements have been put together in a methodological design which will facilitate the learning. For example, in reviewing a brochure for a half-day workshop with the objective of teaching participants to make a social diagnosis, develop short-term treatment goals, and carry out effective treatment with a multiproblem family, it would be obvious that three hours would not allow sufficient time to learn to make a social diagnosis and assessment, let alone identify proper intervention techniques with such difficult cases. Another typical example is the one-day program which features a panel of eight to ten speakers, each of whom has been allotted fifteen to twenty minutes to present a particular perspective on the subject. It is unlikely that there would be sufficient discussion time for those attending to absorb and integrate such a variety of ideas. Nonetheless, some people enjoy such programs and feel that they have learned a good deal in a short time. While it may not be easy to gather full information about a program, informed questioning can give the clinician a better perspective of what is being offered and whether it meets his or her specific needs.

Practical Matters

Costs and Getting Your Money's Worth. The fees charged for a program give very little clue to quality. The price to the consumer is raised by "superstars," traveling "road shows," expensive advertising, extensive mailings, hotel training sites, high status and income level of the intended audience, profit or nonprofit status of the sponsor, and the profit margin expected by private trainers. Current popularity of a topic may also influence the price. The consumer should be aware that those who organize continuing education may have taken courses in the science and technique of marketing for profit. The matter of quality often appears to be an incidential consideration in some of the marketing literature.

Costs may be lowest where an organization, such as a consultation and education service in a community mental health center, offers programs as a community service. A chapter of the NASW, using volunteer labor to develop and teach a program, may also charge low fees (provided that the NASW is not using continuing education as a fundraising device). Because of the ongoing costs of educational programs with paid staff, university-based programs may charge higher fees than those using free labor. Schools of social work are most likely to have a responsibility to meet the needs of all kinds of social workers: clinicians, managers, planners, organizers, and researchers. They must, therefore, offer an array of programs, some of interest to a small number of people while others are guaranteed a large audience and give the appearance of being "money-makers."

Another cost matter which may concern the consumer is that of cancellation, refunds, and extra fees. Good practice would include a clear statement of the conditions for refunds, transfers, and recording fees.

Sometimes sponsoring organizations or particular teachers have a reputation for their classes starting late and finishing early, or having long breaks, whereas other organizations are very careful about fulfilling their total obligations and monitoring the educational experiences by visiting classes and meeting with faculty. The more detailed the schedule of the program, the more likely it will be that the program will be performed as advertised. If the program is clearly organized to provide the opportunity for coherent, organized learning, the more likelihood there is of an enriching educational experience.

Who Pays. The question can be raised about whether the learner, the agency, or the client pay for the education. Even if a learner is agency based, he or she may have to pay tuition, use vacation time, take leave without pay, or attend programs on nonwork time. Private practitioners have to take their own initiative to arrange for learning through supervision, consultation, or attendance at open clinical or academic conferences, meetings, courses, or workshops. They may face the dilemma of losing income to further their education to meet licensing and accreditation requirements.

Even in large agencies committed to student training and staff development, there are limitations on the funds available for in-service education or tuition for courses. To what extent should the agency budget include the educational costs of upgrading practitioners' skills?

In nonprofit agencies, even if there are large endowments, inflationary expenses have led to tight monetary constraints. In hospital and clinic settings, where third-party payers and various rate-setting bodies are asserting tight control over rising costs, the budgeting process is even more restrictive. Cost-base reimbursers such as Blue Cross, Medicare, and Medicaid will pay only for direct patient care; this does not include staff education. While charge-base reimbursers, such as the voluntary insurers, will pay the full daily rate, there must be reasonable limits to the indirect charges they can be expected to carry. With increasing financial constraints, it can be expected that agencies will be limited to teaching the material which has a cost benefit to the particular setting.

The Personal Plan

The professional who wishes to embark on self-directed learning should make a learning plan which maximizes all opportunities to be found in the agency, profession, community, and university. Self-development consists of self-study (the collection of data), self-assessment (diagnosis), a plan of action (setting goals and a means of achieving them), action, and evaluation.

Following are a few examples of learning plans of social workers having different kinds of responsibilities and different levels of competence.

Mrs. Byrnes is a thirty-year-old clinician who has worked for five years in a mental health center with a variety of cases. Her basic skill is in casework with individuals. She has started to work with couples and families and has found this to be an effective modality and comfortable to her. This has increased her interest in becoming more proficient in family therapy. She also enjoys supervising students and hopes someday to do some teaching. Through her self-assessment she has recognized that she has little conceptual knowledge about the family as a social system. She has had no formal skill training and no regular supervision in family therapy techniques.

She also recognizes that if she hopes to do some teaching, she needs knowledge about educational theory and method. Her learning needs and plan, therefore, include formal courses in the theory and method of family work and supervision of her family practice. Through supervision she hopes to deal with her attitudes about various family problems and manifestations of transference and countertransference in her practice. In relation to teaching, she decides that she will put off learning in this area until she achieves competence as a family therapist. She decides that concentration in learning is better for her than diversity.

A senior clinician and administrator, Mr. Williams, has identified a major need to learn more about legal issues related to practice. He also has a secondary interest in becoming more knowledgeable about public service needs. Mr. Williams decides that he will develop a plan to start a study group of social workers and lawyers, and he will let it be known that he is available to serve on a community board.

Another clinician, who wishes to move into an academic role, recognizes that a doctorate is necessary and applies to a school of social work. Still another person knows that clinical research is her immediate interest. Therefore, she takes an advanced course in research methods in a psychology program because there is no local school of social work. She studies statistical methods and plans a series of courses taken with a variety of sponsors which will equip her to carry out research projects.

The following is a plan for charting a self-directed educational program. It is presented as an example of the process involved in educational assessment and planning done by a clinician with two years of professional experience.

The first step in the plan is to identify *long and short range professional goals;* second is to list *current practice responsibilities and priorities;* third is to estimate the *level of competence* related to these responsibilities. The fourth step is to list *learning needs* related to increasing competence, and the fifth is the *plan of action* for achieving the goals. Ms. M. decided that she had two goals: to become a supervisor and a qualified family therapist. She currently did casework with individuals and expected to have six families gradually added to her caseload within the next six months. Her supervisor judged her ready to supervise students. Ms. M. knew that although she had never worked with a family, the agency regarded her as competent enough to begin to do family work: she decided that she needed knowledge on the theory of supervision, skills in techniques, and awareness of her own attitudes and feelings about supervision and authority. She decided to enroll in a basic course in supervision and to receive supervision of her supervisory practice. In terms of her family treatment goals, she ascertained that she needed knowledge of theory and models of family treatment, skill in practice techniques, and awareness of the personal impact of family work upon her own attitudes about families. She planned then to enroll in a local Family Therapy Institute for a systematic series of courses, and begin to work with two families under agency supervision. She planned to discuss the attitudinal and emotional factors with her peers, who were also doing family therapy. Ms. M. planned to evaluate her total plan within six months.

The central theme of this approach to continuous education is that it is the responsibility of professionals to take charge of their continued professional growth. This will contribute to the well-being of clients, the quality of agency services, and the advancement of the profession. For the clinician it can be a means of enrichment, excitement, and satisfaction in being a social worker.

As identified by Erikson (1950), one of the life stages is concerned with choices between generativity or stagnation. In a sense, this choice is continuous throughout a person's development. The tasks of giving birth to new ideas, reaching deeper understandings, and refining skills are accomplished by young, middle-aged, and older people at any stage of their professional life.

Rapoport (1969) wrote of the continued growth and contributions of the social work profession. She recognized the criticisms of the profession but pointed out that the special and unique social work contributions far outweigh any of its limitations. These contributions are made by individuals whose continued engagement in learning has been critical in furthering their own as well as the profession's development.

References

Erikson, E. *Childhood and Society.* New York: Norton, 1950.

Etzioni, A. *Modern Organizations.* Englewood Cliffs, N.J.: Prentice-Hall, 1964.

Freire, P. *Pedagogy of the Oppressed.* New York: Continuum, 1981.

Frey, L. A. "Learning and Teaching with Adults." *Journal of Geriatric Psychiatry,* 1977, *10* (2), 137–149.

Gibelman, M., and Humphreys, N. "Consumer's Guide to Continuing Education." *Social Work,* 1979, *24* (15), 401–405.

Hari, V. "Instituting Short-Term Casework in a Long-Term Agency." In W. Reid and L. Epstein (Eds.), *Task Centered Practice.* New York: Columbia University Press, 1977.

Henry, J. "American Schoolrooms: Learning the American Nightmare." *Columbia University Forum,* 1963, *6,* 24–30.

Knowles, M. "Innovations in Teaching Styles and Approaches Based Upon Adult Learning." *Journal for Social Work Education,* 1972, *8* (2), 32–39.

Mager, R. F. *Preparing Instructional Objectives.* Belmont, Calif.: Fearon, 1962.

McKeachie, W. J. (Ed.). *New Directions for Teaching and Learning: Implications of Cognitive Psychology for College Teachings,* no. 2. San Francisco: Jossey-Bass, 1980.

McKeachie, W. J. "Psychology in America's Bicentennial Year." *The American Psychologist,* 1976, *31* (12), 819–833.

Munson, C. "Professional Autonomy and Social Work Supervision." *Journal of Education for Social Work,* Fall 1976, *12* (3), 95–102.

National Task Force on the Continuing Education Unit. *The Continuing Education Unit, Criteria and Guidelines.* Washington, D.C.: National University Extension Association, 1974.

Norman, D. A. (Ed.). *New Direction for Teaching and Learning: What Goes On in the Mind of the Learners,* no. 2. San Francisco: Jossey-Bass, 1980.

Rapoport, L. "Social Casework: An Appraisal and an Affirmation," Smith College Studies in Social Work, 1969, *34* (3), 213–235.

Reynolds, B. C. *Learning and Teaching in the Practice of Social Work.* (3rd ed.) New York: Russell & Russell, 1970.

Tyler, R. *Basic Principles of Curriculum and Instruction.* Chicago: University of Chicago Press, 1964.

17

Client/Therapist Interactions

Gerald Schamess

When I originally agreed to write about the treatment relationship, I thought it was a subject I understood rather well. As I collected data and reviewed my experiences as a therapist and supervisor, I realized that the concepts I had learned and used for many years did not adequately explain the clinical data. Three questions seemed increasingly important as I thought about the issue. First, what constitutes external reality within the context of the therapeutic situation? Second, is it necessary for the therapist to maintain a positive relationship with the patient throughout the treatment process? Third, can the patient deal effectively with intrapsychic conflicts and negative object experiences without reexperiencing them within the therapeutic interaction? These issues emerge, both implicitly and explicitly, through this chapter.

The chapter contains three sections which I am calling "parts." Part I examines some of the underlying reasons for our gradual disillusionment with psychoanalytic drive theory and for our current interest in ego psychology and object-relations theory. In addition, it contains a rather contentious discourse on the relationship between clinical practice and the real world. Part II summarizes the work of several prominent social work theorists, with emphasis on how they view the treatment relationship. Part III suggests that the treatment relationship is structured by an unacknowledged set of rules and expectations that are inherently frustrating and confusing for the patient. These structural aspects of the relationship exist in stark contrast to the therapist's conscious attitude of concern, empathy, acceptance, and support, thus creating a paradoxical situation that the patient is called upon to resolve. This view of the therapeutic relationship is explored in terms of its implications for both theory and practice.

Part I: The Analytic Model

For more than fifty years, psychoanalytic theory has provided an intellectually compelling and clinically useful theoretical framework for casework practice. Within the last generation a number of casework theorists have played an active role in reformulating analytic concepts to meet the therapeutic needs of social agency clients and programs. Although each of these theorists emphasizes a different aspect of analytic theory, all of them share certain basic assumptions about personality structure and about how human behavior is determined. These assumptions are outlined below.

1. A set of psychodynamic formulations that explain mental phenomena in terms of interacting and opposing motivational forces, operating on an unconscious level within the mind. This conflict model of intrapsychic functioning assumes a basic antagonism between the individual's uninhibited and unmodified search for libidinal or aggressive gratification, and the moral expectations of society.

2. A theory of intrapsychic causality that explains the etiology of emotional disturbance in terms of the individual's failure to successfully master the developmental tasks of early childhood. In this formulation, fixations at, or regressions to, the phase-specific conflicts and levels of ego organization that characterize the oral, anal, phallic, and genital stages of development interfere with normal maturation and are symbolically reproduced as compromise formations in adult symptomatology. In its most traditional form, psychoanalytic theory insists that all adult psychopathology should be evaluated in terms of how the individual has dealt with the oedipus complex.

3. A structural hypothesis that explains mental processes by reference to a tripartite division of the mind into functional groups called id, ego, and superego. These collections of functions evolve in relation to one another during the first six years of life and then interact dialectically throughout the rest of the life cycle. Their interaction is thought to determine the nature of intrapsychic conflict and of personality structure.

4. An adaptive point of view that emphasizes the ego's capacity to modify both intrapsychic functioning and the object world through its ongoing effort to create a (more) harmonious relationship between "instinctual drive forces, internalized restraints and the requirements of the external world" (Moore and Fine, 1968, p. 61).

In a highly condensed way these formulations outline the basic framework of psychoanalytic drive theory. Although drive theory effectively illuminates unconscious meanings and motivations, its applicability to clinical social work practice is limited by at least three important factors. Two of these will be discussed below while the third will be considered somewhat later. First, theoretical formulations that describe psychopathology primarily in terms of intrapsychic conflict, do not, in and of themselves, provide an adequate explanation of the ego-syntonic symptomatology or the inadequacies in ego functioning that we observe in patients with severe character pathology. Second, etiological assessments based on how oedipal issues have been dealt with, do not account for either the unneutralized aggression or the problems in object relatedness that are routinely found in patients whose problems reflect a pervasive sense of emotional impoverishment and/or a perpetual battle with the social environment. Since a very sizeable proportion of social agency clients are characterologically disturbed, emotionally impoverished, and at war with themselves or with the significant people in their lives, these limitations have compelled us to examine other models of mental functioning within the analytic field.

Revised Treatment Models. In our search for models with greater explanatory power, we have explored the applicability of crisis theory (Parad, 1963; Rapoport, 1962), ego psychology (Allan, 1974; Grossbard, 1962; Strean, 1979; Wasserman, 1974; Wood, 1971), and object-relations theory (Blanck and Blanck, 1979; Edward, 1976; Frank, 1980). As we have learned more about ego functioning and character pathology, new treatment approaches have gradually been developed. The traditional analytic model, in which the therapist was viewed as a surgeon who cut away defenses for the purpose of uncovering and interpreting forbidden impulses, was initially modified in its use with neurotic patients and then abandoned entirely in the treatment of more seriously disturbed individuals. In its place, approaches have been designed that enhance ego functioning and promote adaptation without encouraging pathological amounts of regression. These approaches make use of techniques that support defenses (Love and Mayer, 1959), promote cognitive functioning (Blanck and Blanck, 1979), or provide corrective object experiences (Alexander, 1956; French, 1970). Paradigmatic (Spotnitz, 1976; Sternbach and Nagelberg, 1957) and paradoxical interventions (Frankl, 1978; Haley, 1978) have also been developed with the aim of reducing resistance or creating opportunities for rapid symptomatic change.

These technical innovations make it possible to treat patients whose precarious sense of stability and self-esteem is maintained through the use of primitive defense mechanisms such as denial, projection, projective identification, splitting, and idealization (Kernberg, 1975). Since all of these defenses work by providing opportunities for the patient to externalize intolerable feelings of unpleasure, particularly frustration and aggression, they contribute to a pattern of interpersonal interaction in which negative affects, perceptions, and memories are acted out in real relationships with individuals and institutions. The conflicts, frustrations, and disappointments that result from these interactions serve to mask the patient's inner sense of isolation, inadequacy, and self-hatred. Through this process, the patient protects precariously organized ego functions and internalized self and object representations from the disorganizing impact of unmodified instinctual drives and punitive superego precursors. The developmental needs of such patients and their extreme vulnerability to anxiety and depression make it imperative for the therapist to limit regression so that dangerous impulses are not uncovered until the patient can experience them without decompensating. Successful treatment thus depends on an approach that supports and protects defenses until the patient is ready to give them up.

Our ability to study such aspects of ego functioning as perception, defensive organization, and the development of object relations, makes it possible to address some of the issues that have never been adequately explained within the framework of psychoanalytic drive theory. Studies of early childhood development have shifted our attention away from models of oedipal etiology and have made us aware of the connections between maladaptive behavior in adulthood and the developmental arrests and deviations that are first seen in children under the age of three years. Observations about how infants may externalize intense feelings of discomfort, in order to protect themselves and their mothers from the frustration aggression that might endanger positive mental representation of one's mother, provide an interesting and useful explanation of why adult patients experience interpersonal rather than intrapsychic conflict. These new formulations constitute at least a partial response to the issues raised earlier in this chapter, and perhaps more important, establish both a direction and a methodology for future study.

Can Treatment Succeed Without Reference to Social Context? Unexpectedly, and for reasons I do not understand, the development of ego psychology and object-relations theory seems to have exacerbated a long-standing controversy between psychoanalytically and environmentally oriented approaches to treatment. As we have become better able to recognize the importance of the object world as it affects patients in their dyadic and familial interactions, we seem to have become less aware of and less interested in studying the larger social and cultural context in which our patients live. Except for Erikson (1963), most psychoanalytic theorists have never considered the issue of culture to be important enough to examine closely. For clinical social workers, however, it is of central importance. A very high percentage of the patients we work with are economically or socially disadvantaged and, in addition, come from ethnic minorities or immigrant communities that have strong cultural heritages. If we ignore issues of culture and social structure in our practice, we inadvertently blind ourselves to many of the most important influences in our patients' lives.

Nonetheless, when we, as developmentally oriented clinicians, emphasize that patients are able to evoke responses from the object world that replicate the pathogenic responses they experienced in their early childhood relationships (Blanck and Blanck, 1979; Real, 1980; Schamess, 1982), we focus attention on the individual's capacity to control people and events in his or her social environment. To the extent that this point of view influences us, we are inclined to insist that there really are no victims and that every individual, no matter how disadvantaged, plays a role in creating his or her own misery. In taking this position, we implicitly ignore the well-documented body of knowledge that illustrates how the social environment influences such individual characteristics as: self-image, perception of reality, the experience and expression of strong affects, the form and content of interpersonal relationships, and internally experienced moral expectations and value orientations. Although we have known for decades that environmental, intrapsychic, and interpersonal variables are all intertwined, and that the "person-in-situation" configuration (Hollis, 1972) is our most rewarding field of study, we continue to have difficulty in preserving a balance between psychological and sociological explanations of human behavior.

In a society where no less than 25 percent of the population lives at or below the poverty level, where the rate of unemployment for men who are black is almost twice what it is for men who are white, and where any decrease in governmentally subsidized programs first reduces services for AFDC families, general relief recipients, children in public schools, and the aged, it hardly seems necessary to document the existence of a well-established pattern of social inequality that victimizes precisely those people who are least able to protect themselves. By ignoring these realities, we not only stigmatize our patients, but also limit our own effectiveness as therapists. When we treat socially disadvantaged people as if they were totally in control of their own destiny, our clients' self-esteem is undermined not only by the knowledge that they may be a failure in terms of the predominant social norms, but also by a (justified) suspicion that we view them as inadequate and immature. If we attempt to treat environmental problems with techniques that have been developed to influence intrapsychic processes, we repeatedly experience the frustration of not being able to engage certain patients in treatment or of not achieving our treatment goals. In the final analysis (pun intended), the patient's sense of personal inadequacy is then mirrored by our own sense of professional failure.

Our clinical experience indicates that treatment with socially disadvantaged and characterologically disturbed patients is likely to be more effective when the therapist is able to use the relationship to help clients improve the quality of their physical/social environment, while simultaneously encouraging them to explore their inner world (Fantl, 1964; Mayer and Schamess, 1969; Pavenstedt, 1967). In the course of such treatment, the therapist may act as an advocate, an advisor, or a provider of direct help and services, depending on the client's willingness and ability to initiate action on his or her own behalf. When direct help with employment, financial benefits, medical care, or education is offered in ways that are compatible with the patient's cultural background and willingness to use such assistance, the patient experiences both relief from external stress and an increased sense of personal worth. As a result, the patient's capacity to trust the therapist and to speak freely is markedly increased. This process facilitates the development of a corrective relationship because the therapist is gradually perceived as a reliable, empathetic, and potentially gratifying object, both realistically and transferentially.

For all of these reasons, it does not seem useful to make a formal distinction between environmental and psychological forms of casework treatment. In my experience, the two are almost always intertwined. The patient's ability to achieve greater mastery over the social environment typically results in a higher level of self-esteem and an increase in the ego's adaptive capacity. Positive changes in self-esteem invariably lead to an increased ability to deal effectively with the social environment. Successful treatment demands that we recognize the reciprocal nature of these two interacting sets of variables and plan our treatment efforts accordingly.

Part II: Areas of Consensus: A Rich Tradition

In the last twenty years, a number of analytically oriented casework theorists have written about the treatment relationship (Allan, 1974; Bandler, 1963; Feldman, 1960, 1980; Frank, 1976, 1980; Hollis, 1972; Strean, 1979; Wasserman, 1974; Wood, 1971). In their efforts to develop a coherent theoretical rationale for clinical practice, they have made use of concepts drawn from drive theory, ego psychology, object-relations theory, and developmental theory. While some of these concepts are complementary, others represent quite divergent points of view. Given the implicit disagreements between these competing theoretical models, it is interesting to note the substantial areas of consensus regarding important practice issues. The areas of agreement are summarized below.

Characteristics of the Patient Population. Casework agencies assume therapeutic responsibility for significant numbers of people who suffer from very serious emotional disturbances. While clinical social workers treat some individuals with neurotic problems (Frank, 1976; Hollis, 1972; Strean, 1979), a very large proportion of the patients who are seen in social agencies fall into the lower levels of the borderline diagnostic category (Kernberg, 1975), or into the more venerable categories of schizoid character, impulse disorder, or impulse-ridden character disorder. In recent years, clinical social workers have begun to treat increasing numbers of chronically psychotic and partially recompensated patients who are connected to hospital or aftercare settings. In accord with the developmental needs and vulnerabilities of such patients, all of the treatment methodologies that have grown directly out of social work practice emphasize the importance of establishing a nonthreatening, ego-supportive relationship in which the patient is encouraged to develop a positive attachment to the therapist. Techniques that enable the patient to openly express feelings of suspicion, anger, and disappointment serve to reduce anxiety and strengthen the bond between patient and therapist. The therapist's acceptance of negative attitudes and experiences tends to strengthen the patient's sense of self-esteem while providing the opportunity to identify with a more positive (parental) object (Allan, 1974; Strean, 1979; Wasserman, 1974; Wood, 1971).

Unconscious Material. Clinical social workers regularly deal with unconscious material in derivative forms. Exploration of such material is usually done on a symbolic level and metaphorical communication (Feldman, 1960) frequently becomes a major component of the patient/therapist relationship. The therapist is expected to understand the unconscious aspects of the patient's communication and to recognize its symbolic content. Patients, however, are not encouraged to develop insight into their unconscious processes unless they demonstrate both an interest in understanding their motivations and a capacity to do so without decompensating. In general, clinical social workers tend to convey acceptance of the underlying impulse, while exploring, confronting, or limiting the patient's symptomatic or maladaptive behavior (Strean, 1979). When treating patients who openly present primary process material, clinical technique usually involves limiting direct expression of the impulse, while simultaneously trying to strengthen the patient's defensive organization. By helping the patient examine the details of interpersonal interactions, the therapist is able to promote self-observation at a conscious or preconscious level, thereby encouraging the patient to examine behavior, perceptions, and feelings that previously had been ego-syntonic. Hollis (1972) describes this technique as "person-in-situation reflection."

While specific techniques vary considerably, there is general agreement that clinical social work treatment is primarily concerned with the task of promoting adaptation through a process of ego building. Depending on the nature of the individual's phase-specific ego deficiencies, interventions may be designed to strengthen specific ego functions, encourage the ego's integrative capacity, or advance the level of object relatedness. For those who are interested in studying different methodologies for achieving these common goals, it is instructive to compare the technical suggestions made by Allan (1974), Feldman (1980), Frank (1980), Strean (1979), and Wasserman (1974). They provide a rich perspective on the range of diversity within a closely related group of clinical theorists.

Transference. In marked contrast to the opinions of twenty years ago, transference is now recognized as a ubiquitous phenomenon in casework practice. Many of the issues that previously had been discussed in relation to the treatment relationship (dependence, for example) are currently viewed as unconscious repetitions of early object relationships. It is generally accepted that the transference phenomena we encounter are significantly different from the transference neuroses that develop during the course of psychoanalysis. The transferential reactions that emerge during casework treatment usually reflect the patient's need to repeat certain pathogenic object experiences in the hope of gratifying specific wishes and impulses stemming from the oral and anal stages of psychosexual development. From an object-relations point of view, these repetitions typically reflect the wish to establish a symbiotic connection with an undifferentiated object, or, at a somewhat higher level of development, the wish to be taken care of by a need-fulfilling object who will both gratify every impulse and be available whenever needed. Blanck and Blanck (1979) suggest the term "object replication" to distinguish these intense repetitions of very early object relations from the developmentally more mature repetitions that take place in the treatment of people who have achieved object constancy and are capable of viewing the therapist as a differentiated other.

At this point in time, we expect experienced clinicians to recognize transferential reactions and to identify the level of psychosexual development and object relatedness that they reflect. Ordinarily in the course of treatment, transferential feelings are revealed and discussed in the context of examining the patient's interactions with the "other" significant people who inhabit daily life. When the patient talks about relationships with teachers, doctors, lawyers, or police officers, the therapist recognizes that the patient is referring to all of the important people who have played the role of "helper," "nurturer," or "prohibiter" during the course of his or her lifetime. That includes the therapist, of course. When inquiring about what a particular person did to evoke a specific feeling in the patient, or what that person might have done to evoke a different response, the therapist is symbolically asking the patient to help design a corrective emotional experience that will advance the patient's development. On a manifest level, the patient and therapist are discussing some matter of current concern, but on a symbolic level, that discussion will reverberate back to the very earliest object experiences that were problematic to the patient. So, for example, when a therapist carefully and respectfully discusses the patient's wish to become a clinical social worker, acceptance of the patient's need to identify with the therapist is being conveyed, and an atmosphere is being created in which the patient can begin to consider what he or she must do in order to gain pleasure and shape his or her own identity (Wasserman, 1974).

Transferential reactions are discussed more directly when the patient's intensely positive or negative feelings threaten the treatment relationship (Rosenthal, 1980). In such situations the therapist is likely to inquire about whether the patient is having feelings toward him or her that are similar to those described in regard to another object. Interventions of this kind are designed to facilitate an open discussion of the problematic feelings. The therapist accepts the patient's wish, whatever it might be, while simultaneously reinforcing the prohibition against destructive behavior. While such interventions may or may not promote insight, they clearly reduce the patient's anxiety about whether one's impulses will destroy the therapist or provoke the therapist to abandon the relationship. In so doing these interventions touch the core of the characterologically disturbed patient's dilemma: one's feeling of being unloved and unwanted because one is an inherently defective and hateful person (Feldman, 1980; Lieberman and Gottesfeld, 1973). This methodology for dealing with primitive transference phenomena constitutes a major contribution that clinical social work has made to the treatment of seriously disturbed patients.

Part III: A Reformulation of the Treatment Relationship

"All My Clients Love Me." Having summarized a number of the significant areas of agreement within the field of clinical social work, I would now like to turn to one of the major areas of controversy. Several authors have framed the issue in similar ways. "It is appropriate to question whether all of treatment consists in advancing positive identifications or whether there is a point at which more direct exploration of conflictual material is indicated. It would appear that these two elements are not mutually exclusive. . . . When the client has shared his mastery of tasks that have preceded or antedated the current problem it is productive to address directly the more conflictual issues, for in that context positive forces are most prominent in the relationship" (Allan, 1974, p. 34). "The basic premise which has dominated social work theory is that the social worker, by giving warmth, understanding, and even love to the patient through words or in concrete services, can become a 'new object' which is internalized and therefore is capable of curing the past ills. . . . The past cannot be laid to rest by the introduction of a new object without first understanding the forms of the infantile wishes and conflicts as they continue to reoccur in the present and as they emerge in a range of subtleties in the transference" (Schwartz, 1980, p. 2). "We social workers usually deal with immature, deprived people. It is therefore necessary for us to first bring into the relationship with us the rage of the infant at the terrors of helplessness and unmet need, feelings from the period of life before even words could be used to express them. Therefore if a social worker really wishes to help such an individual she must slowly bring out (in the transference) the full rage of the infant, in words" (Feldman, 1980, p. 115).

The following text constitutes my own attempt to understand how feelings of infantile rage, deprivation, helplessness, and self-hatred may be revived and resolved in the context of a treatment relationship that is manifestly soothing and supportive. The focus is still on the relationship—not its content, however, but its structure.

Because the therapeutic relationship is so central to clinical social work practice, we tend to accept its overall form and structure without examining how and why that structure was originally created, what effect it may have on the treatment process, and how it influences the patient's feelings toward the therapist. The idea that the relationship may have a structure beyond its temporal, physical, and financial boundaries has not been seriously considered by most analytically oriented theorists. The subject has been discussed by communication and systems theorists, most of whom agree that the therapist is quite purposeful in establishing and maintaining a position of power in interactions with the patient. While I do not entirely agree with Haley's (1958, p. 200) conclusion that the analytic relationship involves a "patient who by definition is someone compelled to struggle to be one-up and disturbed if he is put one-down," I think he makes a valid point in arguing that the therapist is extremely adept at remaining "one-up" in most, if not all, dealings with the patient.

In spite of the questions raised by this analysis of the treatment relationship, analytic theorists have shown little interest in discussing issues of power, except as projections or displacements of the patient's unresolved intrapsychic conflicts or problematic character traits. When they do talk about the therapist's attitudes in regard to the patient, they emphasize acceptance, empathy, and neutrality. Greenson (1967, p. 216) describes the therapist's posture as one of "compassionate neutrality," while Hollis (1972, p. 266) remarks that the worker's "attitude must be a positive one, with concern for the patient's well-being, liking, respect, acceptance of him as an individual, and a wish for him to be happier or at least more comfortable." While psychotherapists probably should be nonjudgmental, respectful, and compassionate, the idea that these qualities, in and of themselves, are sufficient to explain the patient's involvement with, and attachment to, the therapist seems somewhat ingenuous. Clinical experience indicates that a strictly neutral presentation of self does not provide the patient with any reason to hope for a magical solution to his or her problems. Without such hope, the patient is not likely to invest strong feelings of any kind in the relationship, nor be inclined to remain in treatment. In addition, while the idea of the therapist as a neutral body onto whom transferential feelings are projected is almost an article of faith within the analytic movement, it does not adequately describe either the therapist's activities in regard to the patient, or how the structure of the therapeutic relationship affects the patient's feelings about the therapist. I will return to both of these issues later.

When Freud (1906) first decided that most memories of sexual trauma reflect the patient's libidinal wishes and fantasies rather than the reality of one's familial relationships, he established a far-reaching model for psychoanalytic inquiry. Analytic practice has concerned itself almost exclusively with the study of internal reality and internalized object relations. Object representations are viewed as introjected images of real objects which have been transformed and distorted by the patient's libidinal or aggressive impulses, and by his defenses. When viewed from this perspective, real relationships seem to be less significant, while the patient's instinctual wishes, level of ego organization, nature of superego, and internalized object relations become primary subjects for therapeutic investigation. Given the enormity of Freud's contribution, it seems graceless to fault him for not having achieved a more balanced viewpoint. However, we have had enough clinical experience now to take a view that is somewhat different from his original one. To put the issue metaphorically, it is important to remember not only that Oedipus murdered his father and married his mother, but also that his father had first attempted to murder him. Clinical observations, many of which are derived from object-relations theory or family therapy practice, reinforce this viewpoint and make it necessary for us to view psychopathology not only as a reflection of intrapsychic conflicts or structural deficits, but also as a reciprocal interchange in which two or more people interact in ways that are mutually problematic. These interactions occur as the parties attempt to deal with their own and each other's instinctual wishes, while simultaneously maintaining their intrapsychic and interpersonal equilibrium.

According to traditional theory, transferential reactions arise solely from the patient's prior history of object relations, unless the therapist is having countertransference problems. Presumably there is a clear distinction between the transference relationship and the "real" relationship (Greenson, 1967). From this perspective it is assumed that the patient's transferential feelings are unrelated to anything that is "realistically" happening within the therapeutic interaction. This orientation is consistent with Freud's emphasis on internal processes and is extremely useful in conducting therapeutic sessions. It focuses both the patient's and the therapist's attention on the patient's intrapsychic experiences, thereby making any other focus of attention seem like a distraction or resistance. Unfortunately, as Haley and others point out, this formulation does not conform with what appears to be happening in the ongoing treatment relationship. Since there is considerable evidence to support the view that the therapist works rather hard at keeping the patient in a "one-down" position, one has to wonder why. As most of us know, from personal if not professional experience, being in a "one-down" position tends to evoke a host of intensely unpleasant reactions including anxiety, frustration, helplessness, rebelliousness, and dependence. As these feelings emerge, they revive similar feelings that previously had been conducted with other significant objects in the patient's life, thus precipitating what we usually call transferential reactions.

In the remaining section of this chapter, I will further advance the idea that the structure of the treatment relationship is purposefully, even if not consciously, designed in an ambiguous and paradoxical fashion that evokes anxiety in the patient and thereby precipitates transferential responses. I will also propose that the structure of the relationship provides a social and interactive context within which the problematic aspects of a patient's interpersonal relations are experienced as they occur presently and as they have occurred throughout life. Because I view transferential and structural issues as complementary, I will spend some time discussing current psychoanalytic formulations about the transference relationship, as they bear on clinical social work practice.

An Odd Way to Begin a Relationship. The individual first meeting with a therapist is usually seeking wise counsel, concrete advice, affirmation of one's perception of having been misunderstood and mistreated by the significant people in one's life, and quick relief from conflictual feelings and interpersonal problems. As analytically oriented therapists we view the patient's social and emotional difficulties from an interpersonally oriented, developmental perspective, and do not usually define those difficulties in a way that makes it possible for us to offer immediate relief. Consequently, we try to involve the patient in a treatment process that is rather different from the one anticipated. We offer the patient an empathic ear, an opportunity to talk about feelings and life experiences, and the prospect of a relationship through which that person will gradually arrive at a better self-understanding and thereby learn how to deal more effectively with difficulties.

In order to participate in this relationship the patient undergoes a process of socialization in which he or she gradually learns how to be a reasonably cooperative psychotherapy patient. Even though we would like patients to learn this role quickly and thoroughly, we do not provide many instructions to help them do so. In the initial interview(s), there is discussion about how the patient views his or her problems, a recommendation about a suitable treatment modality, perhaps an effort to "reframe" the problems in terms of the underlying dynamics, and a presentation of some simple rules regarding the time and frequency of sessions, confidentiality, and the fee. If the patient asks how to conduct himself or herself, we suggest talking about the problem, or saying whatever comes to mind, or telling us his or her life story, or discussing something else that is similarly vast and vague. From our viewpoint, this discussion culminates in a "therapeutic contract" that reflects a mutual agreement about how the treatment relationship will develop. From the patient's viewpoint, the discussion leaves him or her with a rather mystifying set of instructions that provide some orientation in time and space, but little guidance about how to conduct oneself or what behavior we expect. As the patient attempts to negotiate these ambiguities, we begin a careful study of how he or she does so. Whether or not we are aware of it, we have placed the patient in a paradoxical situation that he or she must try to resolve—hopefully with some help from us along the way.

It should be apparent that even during these brief initial negotiations we have frustrated the patient's expectations in at least four significant ways. We have not provided immediate relief or concrete advice. Our instructions about the "work" the patient is expected to do are likely to confuse rather than enlighten. We have distracted the patient from the assumption that we will directly influence his or her life in some positive way, and we have reframed the problem so that the patient is now responsible for finding solutions. While in most instances, our attention and understanding is gratifying during the initial stages of treatment, the patient gradually begins to have feelings toward us that are unpleasant, problematic, and reminiscent of the frustrations and disappointments experienced in other significant relationships, past and present. This shifting pattern of historically determined positive and negative feelings toward the therapist constitutes the transferential aspect of the relationship. Since these feelings were first evoked in the patient's interactions with members of the primary family, they are considered "new editions" of early object relations, as they were originally seen through the patient's eyes as a young child (Greenson, 1967, p. 152).

At this point, it is worth noting Freud's (1916, 1966) original observation that there are two distinct types of transferential reactions: those that are object-oriented and grounded in reality, and those that are narcissistic and grounded in the patient's unremitting wish for gratification from the object. Recently, the term "object replication" (Blanck and Blanck, 1979) has been used to describe certain narcissistic transference phenomena. This concept emphasizes the patient's search for replication of primary object experiences, lack of self-object differentiation, wish for immediate narcissistic gratification, and the absence of a reliable "observing ego." Since, as clinical social workers, we treat large numbers of patients who relate to us in either undifferentiated or prematurely differentiated ways, this concept is rather useful. Accordingly, I will use the term "object replication" to describe the transference-like phenomena that arise in the treatment of such patients.

In theory, both object-oriented transferences and object replications arise solely as a result of the patient's unmet developmental needs and intrapsychic conflicts. Presumably the therapist plays no role in evoking these reactions and there is a clear differentiation between the transference relationship and the "real" relationship. Greenson (1967, p. 157) states this view clearly: "The usual restrained, nonintrusive, consistent behaviors and attitudes of the analyst do not *realistically* (italics mine) call for intense reactions" on the patient's part.

Structure of the Treatment Relationship. While these definitions are rather tidy in terms of what they include and exclude, they are phrased in a way that makes it difficult to examine the structure of the therapeutic relationship as it affects the patient's feelings toward the therapist. By structure, I am referring to the interplay between the therapist's self-image as a helping person, expectations about how the patient should respond to him or her, definition of what constitutes therapeutic "work" on the patient's part, and the norms that ordinarily describe and regulate healing relationships in this society. These aspects of the treatment relationship should be viewed separately from the therapist's specific interventions with the patient. They constitute the "external reality" of the therapeutic situation and, therefore, have an effect on the treatment process that is at least partially independent of what the therapist may actually be saying or doing at any given time. Because they constitute a framework within which the therapeutic process takes place and by which it is shaped, the patient is expected to adapt to them in much the same way that it is expected he or she will adapt to the requirements of the social and physical world.

A careful examination of this framework reveals that it is ambiguous and paradoxical in ways that seriously challenge the patient's adaptive capacity. If the patient chooses to remain in treatment, he or she must deal with a set of expectations that are alternately or sequentially confusing, contradictory, gratifying, and frustrating. Efforts to do so give rise to the transferential reactions discussed earlier. This perspective suggests that the patient's feelings toward the therapist reflect both realistic reactions to an intrinsically problematic relationship and transferential reactions that reveal the patient's prior history of difficulties in dealing with significant objects.

The paradoxical structure of the therapeutic situation becomes a highly significant treatment variable because it not only revives the patient's early positive and negative object experiences, but also reproduces them in ways that clearly illuminate the current pattern of adaptive functioning in stressful situations. The inherently problematic nature of the relationship symbolically reproduces the social context within which the patient's maladaptive responses are evoked. As this process unfolds, the patient is compelled to renegotiate early object experiences as well as current ones, regardless of whether they are openly discussed during therapeutic sessions. Feelings of frustration and unpleasure are evoked by the paradoxical structure of the treatment relationship, even if the therapist is acting in ways that are meant to be gratifying and encouraging to the patient.

Ambiguities, Contradictory Expectations, Dilemmas, and Paradoxes. In the material that follows I will provide four examples of ambiguous, contradictory, and paradoxical structures within the treatment relationship. I will attempt to look at each of these from the perspective of several interrelated variables: the therapist's self-image; the therapist's expectations about how the patient should respond to him or her; the therapist's expectations about the "work" the patient should do; some concrete "facts" about what is happening in the relationship; the prevailing social norms; the dilemma that these contradictory expectations create for the patient; and some of the options that are available to the patient as he or she attempts to deal with the contradictions and ambiguities.

1. The therapist generally views himself or herself as a thoughtful, trustworthy professional, and assumes that the patient will perceive these qualities and respond by establishing a "working alliance." Once the alliance is formed, the therapist expects the patient to actively and spontaneously explore thoughts, feelings, and memories while remaining receptive to the therapist's observations and interpretations. As the alliance develops, the therapist has the job of assessing the patient's functioning in terms of ego deficits, internal conflicts, character problems, and other forms of psychopathology. Since the therapist is probing the feelings and experiences that the patient has spent a lifetime defending against, the patient encounters a serious dilemma. If the patient trusts the therapist and talks spontaneously about feelings as expected, he or she risks saying things that might be unacceptable for both of them. If the patient mistrusts the therapist and suppresses or conceals that inner life, the treatment agreement has been broken and the patient is defying the therapist's expectations. In either instance the patient is likely to feel increasingly vulnerable, an emotional state that makes it even more difficult to be trusting and cooperative.

2. The therapist generally views himself or herself as a reliable person who is sincerely concerned about the patient's welfare, encouraging the patient to depend on him or her and implicitly promising to be emotionally available at times of stress and anxiety. In fact, the therapist's empathetic support is only forthcoming for carefully scheduled and measured time periods, at a specified physical location. Particularly during the middle stages of treatment the patient is expected to tolerate a considerable amount of anxiety, depression, and confusion with only limited help from the therapist. This presents the patient with a dilemma of a somewhat different nature. If a patient allows himself to rely on the therapist and accepts the therapist's control over the temporal and physical aspects of the relationship, that patient gives up a significant amount of autonomy and implicitly agrees to regress to a more childlike state within the therapeutic situation. In this state the patient has no way of being certain that the therapist's emotional availability will be adequate to meet his or her needs, or that the therapist has not promised more than can be delivered. If, on the other hand, a patient struggles against the therapist's control by being late, missing appointments, or demanding extra time, he or she may endanger the relationship by undermining the therapist's interest. Patients who are particularly vulnerable to rejection or who are counterdependent find this dilemma especially problematic.

3. The therapist is frequently inclined to view himself or herself as a mentor or "symbolic parent" who can help the patient rework the pathological aspects of internalized representations of parental objects. The therapist prefers to be viewed as a "good" and helpful "parent figure" whose activities are well intended even if they are puzzling or cause distress. In fact, the therapist is an employee whom the patient has hired to provide a specific service. The dilemma here arises from a contradiction between the expectations of the therapeutic situation and the norms of the larger society. In this culture we do not ordinarily view parenting as a paid occupation except in the case of orphans, foster children, or, ironically, servants who take care of their masters. Upon accepting the therapist's definition

of their mutual roles, on a symbolic level, the patient must allow himself or herself to become an orphaned child, in need of substitute parenting. Even so, the financial aspects of the relationship serve to remind, on a regular basis, that the therapist is not really a parent and that intense feelings toward the therapist are, to some degree, artifacts of the treatment situation. This realization adds another level of contradiction and complexity to the relationship, since both patient and therapist maintain some awareness that the therapist is, after all, still an employee who may be fired at any given moment with little or no notice.

4. As a final example, the therapist often believes that treatment offers the patient an opportunity to establish a close and intimate relationship that will increase the capacity to develop rewarding relationships with the other significant people in the patient's life. The therapist views himself or herself as an expert on the subject of relationships and feels quite competent to evaluate the quality of the patient's object relations. The patient is expected to confide in the therapist in ways that transcend what is normative for even the most intimate relationships in this society, and to develop a range of strong feelings toward the therapist, about which the patient will talk openly and honestly. In spite of what he or she expects from the patient, the therapist chooses to remain somewhat of a stranger in the relationship, by masking emotional responses, making sure the patient knows as little as possible about his or her life outside the treatment hour, and frequently deciding not to respond either to the patient's confidences or questions. Normatively, we expect that intimate relationships among adults in this society will be explicitly reciprocal.

The patient is thus faced with the dilemma of whether to confide in someone who is both calculating and distant. By doing so, the patient becomes submissive in a way that both members of the therapeutic relationship would consider pathological if it occurred in any other relationship. If the patient actively opposes the therapist's expectations, a more equal relationship can be maintained but only at the risk of undermining treatment. If this does not pose enough of a dilemma, the patient frequently discovers that, whether or not they are welcome, the relationship has evoked intensely transferential feelings which the patient must then either discuss or attempt to conceal from the therapist.

The paradoxes in the therapeutic relationship can be summarized as follows. To alleviate one's emotional pain, a patient must provide the therapist with information that can produce the deepest wounds. To become free from parental introjects, a patient must allow himself or herself to be controlled and to reexperience the most problematic aspects of what it was like to be a misunderstood and mistreated child. To become independent, a patient must permit himself or herself to be dependent and to feel helpless. Finally, to develop one's capacity for intimacy, a patient must submit to an unequal relationship with a person who is emotionally constrained and physically aloof.

Structure and Transference Intertwined. The idea that paradoxical situations create unusual opportunities for intrapsychic and interpersonal change should come as no surprise to contemporary clinicians. For the last twenty years we have been hearing about the effectiveness of paradoxical structures and interventions from many theorists (Frankl, 1978; Feldman, Nagelberg, and Spotnitz, 1953; Haley, 1978; Palozzoli, 1978; Spotnitz, 1969, 1976; Watts, 1958). In clinical social work practice, the paradoxical elements of the relationship account for much of its effectiveness as an experiential form of treatment.

Each of the realistic dilemmas that the patient must deal with in the treatment relationship evokes some specific aspect of his or her defensive structure and underlying emotional needs. If the relationship did not call forth these mechanisms, it would be nothing more than a prosaic exercise in seeking and giving advice. The patient replays his or her history of real and internalized object relations, precisely because we relate to that person in a confusing and paradoxical way. It is the juxtaposition of an unrealistic and magical wish, with a frustrating and confusing reality, that keeps the patient in treatment. The tension between wish and reality motivates the patient to confront the ghostly object representations from one's past, and examine their haunting effects on significant relationships in the present. The treatment mechanism works in the following way.

By defying the social conventions that require reciprocity in intimate relationships, the therapist creates a pattern of interaction that is hierarchical, asymmetrical, and confusing to the patient. Because the therapist does not ordinarily acknowledge that the expectations are inconsistent or paradoxical, the relationship that develops has much in common with what Bateson (1956) described some years ago as a double bind. As in any such relationship, the therapist's paradoxical expectations precipitate powerful feelings of anxiety that the patient must deal with in order to regain some sense of psychic equilibrium. Given how the relationship is structured, the patient has three major options: fleeing from the therapist; attempting to induce the therapist to interact in a safe and familiar way that replicates some pathogenic relationship from the patient's past; or negotiating a new and different relationship with the therapist, hopefully, but not necessarily, at a higher level of psychosocial development.

During the middle stages of treatment, the patient is most frequently drawn to the second of these options. Throughout that stage of the process, transference and countertransference phenomena are prominant and play an important role in helping the patient express and work through core problems. Transferential reactions are revived in response to the paradoxical and frustrating expectations that the therapist creates within the treatment relationship. These expectations accentuate a level of interchange between patient and therapist in which the patient typically wants something from the therapist that he or she believes the therapist has the power to grant or withhold. This level of relatedness replicates the interactional configuration of childhood in which the parent had "real" power to gratify or frustrate the child. Since the therapist is more likely to explore the patient's wishes than to either gratify or frustrate them, the patient is forced to adapt to the therapist's expectations and delay the need for gratification. This process is ego building and continues for as long a time as the patient wants, needs, or hopes to get something from the therapist. When the patient discovers that the needs and wants have changed and that he or she can either gratify oneself or tolerate a higher level of frustration without becoming symptomatic, the patient begins to lose interest in the therapist and gradually becomes ready to end treatment.

The process by which the patient adapts to the structure of the treatment relationship is analogous to the process by which the child adapts to parental expectations within a family context. Once an attachment to the therapist has been established, the patient is compelled by specific needs and anxieties to deal with the issue of acceptance by the therapist. Depending on one's character structure, the patient may test the therapist's response by making an effort to comply with conduct he or she thinks is expected, by acting in a rebellious and resistant way, or by alternating between compliance and rebellion. Since the expectations themselves are ambiguous and there is usually some discrepancy between what the therapist has requested and what the structure of the relationship seems to call for, the patient experiences a good deal of cognitive and emotional dissonance, and frequently does not know how to comply even when wishing to do so. This dilemma is very similar to the one faced by the young child who tries to understand the spoken and unspoken rules by which one's family is governed and the expectations that one's parents have on a conscious and unconscious level. In this context, the treatment relationship serves metaphorically as an external reality with both social and familial connotations. Within it, the patient's adaptive mechanisms are tested and revealed, both as they originally developed during childhood and as they operate in the patient's current relationships.

As in a family, the process of adaptation is more reciprocal than we sometimes realize. Not only is the patient influenced by the therapist's expectations, but also the therapist is influenced by what the patient wants and expects. All patients tend to induce certain affective and behavioral responses in their therapists, regardless of whether the therapist is aware of it. Characterologically disturbed patients induce stronger reactions because of their need to replicate early object experiences and because their affective life is more primitive and closer to consciousness. Such patients are particularly adept at inducing the therapist to assume a complementary role in relation to them that replicates a pathogenic object experience from childhood (Lieberman and Gottesfeld, 1973; Schamess, 1982; Winnicott, 1975). This process has been noted by a number of different theorists who have described it as induced countertransference (Flescher, 1953; Litner, 1969), projective identification (Kernberg, 1975; Schapiro, 1978), and projective-introjective cycles (Real, 1980). While the therapist may not discover that he or she has adapted to the patient's expectations until after experiencing some very uncomfortable feelings or engaging in some uncharacteristic behaviors, it is important to anticipate that such reactions are likely to occur as the therapist attempts to help the patient renegotiate problematic object relations. In this regard the therapist should be prepared to investigate the following questions with considerable care: What response is the patient seeking from the therapist when presenting particular material? If the therapist responds as the patient wishes, how would that response replicate the patient's interactions with members of his or her primary family? In what ways does the patient attempt to induce particular feelings and behavioral responses in the therapist? What specific anxiety would the patient experience if the therapist were to frustrate, explore, or interpret the patient's need to evoke a particular response?

As the therapist studies what the patient consciously and unconsciously wants from the relationship and how he or she goes about trying to get it, the nature of the patient's problem with significant others becomes apparent in a very real and precise way. When reflecting upon his or her own feelings, the therapist is frequently surprised to discover reactions that are quite similar to the reactions of frustration and unpleasure that other people seem to have in their relations with the patient. This experience allows the therapist to make a rather accurate assessment of just how the patient contributes to interpersonal difficulties. If the therapist places these difficulties in a developmental context, they typically reflect a fixation point, a stage-specific level of anxiety, a set of maladaptive defenses, some inadequacies or malformations in subphase development (Mahler, Pine, and Bergman, 1975), and some specific deficiencies in ego functioning. All of these problems, reflecting either intrapsychic conflict or problematic character formation, are condensed and symbolized in the patient's effort to persuade the therapist to gratify him or her, or at least to alleviate the feelings of anxiety and depression. The treatment relationship can thus be viewed as a microcosm in which the patient's problematic social, familial, interpersonal, and intrapsychic object relations are played out experientially in regard to the therapist.

Clinical Implications. 1. Almost all of the clinical social work literature emphasizes the importance of developing and maintaining a positive therapeutic relationship in order to engage the patient in treatment, provide emotional support, enlarge the patient's capacity for basic trust, offer opportunities for corrective identifications, reduce the pressure of superego prohibitions, promote self-esteem, and enlist active cooperation in efforts at structure building and self-examination. Certainly there is substantial clinical evidence to support the view that a measured amount of support and gratification is therapeutically useful, particularly during the beginning stages of treatment. This is especially true for patients who have been significantly deprived and are mistrustful of a "helping" relationship, and for patients whose cultural background has not prepared them for an ongoing, growth-inducing relationship with a person outside of their immediate family or extended social network.

If my observations about the ambiguous, contradictory, and paradoxical structures within the treatment relationship are accurate, it is important to recognize that the patient cannot experience interactions with the therapist in a totally or even predominantly positive way, regardless of how careful the therapist is to be supportive, encouraging, or gratifying. At best, the patient finds himself or herself in a therapeutic field that is partially gratifying and partially frustrating. While characterologically disturbed patients need positive object experiences and often respond to them by idealizing and identifying with the therapist (Allan, 1974; Wasserman, 1974), it is equally true that the patient's negative feelings are present in the relationship, although usually in a disguised way. If the therapist is not aware of these feelings and does not investigate the symbolic ways in which they are expressed, the patient gradually comes to the conclusion that those hostile feelings make the therapist anxious also. Since the patient consciously wishes to maintain a positive relationship with the therapist, this conclusion strengthens pathological defenses, and treatment founders because there is no opportunity to work through the negative aspects of the repetition compulsion.

2. Although the casework literature speaks extensively about the importance of "process," there is little encouragement for therapists to actively explore the feelings that their patients develop toward them during the course of treatment. Such discussions are almost never found in student case records and are only rarely reported by experienced clinicians. In recent years Feldman (1980) and Strean (1979) have suggested that patients should be encouraged to openly express their negative and critical feelings about the therapist, particularly if those feelings are exaggerated and transferential. Lemon and Goldstein (1978) recommend

the use of a short-term treatment model to promote individuation in certain carefully selected patients with "passive-submissive" character traits. In this approach, patients are encouraged to talk freely about their need for the therapist, and their fear of not being able to cope without the therapist's help. Frank (1980) discusses the importance of "sounding" regularly with patients by asking how the treatment sessions have affected them and what feelings they are having toward the therapist. All of these recommendations contribute to a revised practice framework in which we are encouraged to deal more openly with the patient's "real" and transferential reactions to us.

If the therapeutic relationship is viewed as being inherently problematic for the patient in ways that revive both transferential feelings and the problematic aspects of his or her current relationships, it is particularly important for the therapist to address relationship issues directly, as a major focus of treatment. Developmental theory is necessary in that it provides a background against which the patient's problems can be highlighted and understood in terms of psychodynamics, ego functioning, and, most particularly, the workings of the repetition compulsion. The essence of the treatment process is an ongoing series of affectively influenced negotiations that take place between the patient and the therapist and that provide the impetus for intrapsychic and interpersonal change. While it may or may not be useful to interpret these negotiations, if the therapist has used a developmental perspective to understand their transferential aspects, he or she is in a position either to respond symbolically, or to help the patient verbalize feelings that have been problematic throughout the course of relationships with significant others.

A simple example of this principle can be seen in the treatment of patients who invite the therapist to explain the "reasons" for their problems, as part of their apparent search for self-understanding. When this invitation involves a replication of an early pathogenic relationship with a critical and demeaning parent, it effectively interrupts the treatment process. If the therapist interprets this early relationship, the patient simply perceives the interpretation as another form of criticism. As a result, the more the therapist interprets, the more depressed or rebellious the patient becomes. If, on the other hand, the therapist suggests that the patient is not ready to understand the particular issues, or that it will be better for the patient to try to figure out the issues alone, the therapist both interrupts the transferential replication and brings the patient's anger and frustration at having been criticized by a parent into the immediacy of the ongoing interaction. It should be apparent that both of the latter interventions are paradoxical within the context of a relationship that is designed to promote self-understanding.

3. Finally, if we are serious about the idea that the structure of the treatment relationship is paradoxical in ways that create a double-bind situation for the patient, it seems reasonable to assume that these structures can be altered and controlled on the basis of the patient's developmental and maturational needs. Which structures should be altered, and how that should be accomplished with patients in particular diagnostic groupings, is an issue that is still being explored. For the moment, there are a few suggestive initiatives that are summarized below.

We know that it is possible to change the structure of the relationship so as to create a relatively nurturing and supportive external environment which allows very seriously disturbed patients to remain in treatment without being overwhelmed by anxiety or other intolerable affects. We accomplish this either by eliminating most of the usual therapeutic expectations and allowing the patient to control the relationship until he or she is ready to relate to the therapist (Schwartz, 1978), or by creating a number of very simple and clearly defined expectations that the patient is expected to follow as part of the treatment regime (Ganter, Polansky, and Yeakel, 1967; Jones, 1953).

A second variant approach is described by Love and Mayer (1959). They suggest that in treating patients who make extensive use of projection and denial, it is helpful to actively support those defenses instead of confronting or interpreting them. In so doing, the therapist alters the structural expectation that requires the patient to openly reveal feelings of inadequacy and vulnerability. This approach protects the patient's fragile sense of self-esteem and self-control, until he or she feels ready to look more realistically at problematic feelings and interactions. Other suggested alterations in the therapeutic structure include techniques in which the therapist (1) prescribes the symptom (Frankl, 1978); (2) uses the fee to promote either dependency or greater autonomy and initiative; (3) encourages the patient to talk indirectly about anxiety or guilt through displacements onto other objects; or (4) encourages the patient to be mistrustful and critical of the therapist and to anticipate that therapy may be disappointing or possibly even harmful.

While these interventions are usually classified as paradoxical or paradigmatic (Spotnitz, 1976), they share another common attribute in that they shift the therapeutic structure and force the patient to respond to the therapist in ways that are different from typical interpersonal responses. They also make it impossible for the patient to predict or control the therapist's response as he or she is accustomed to do in other interactions with significant objects. The original structure of the analytic relationship created a similar alteration in "normal" social interaction by seating the therapist behind the couch where he or she would listen silently to most of what the patient says. It appears that such dislocations of social interaction create a level of intrapsychic disequilibrium that not only evokes intensely affective responses, but also creates unusual opportunities for intrapsychic and interpersonal change.

References

Allan, E. "Psychoanalytic Theory." In F. Turner (Ed.), *Social Work Treatment: Interlocking Theoretical Approaches*. New York: Free Press, 1974.

Alexander, F. *Psychoanalysis and Psychotherapy*.New York: Norton, 1956.

Bandler, L. "Some Casework Aspects of Ego Growth Through Sublimation." In H. Parad and R. Miller (Eds.), *Ego-Oriented Casework*. New York: Family Service Association of America, 1963.

Bateson, C., and others. "Toward a Theory of Schizophrenia." In M. Berger (Ed.), *Beyond the Double Bind*. New York: Brunner/Mazel, 1978.

Blanck, G., and Blanck, R. *Ego Psychology II*. New York: Columbia University Press, 1979.

Edward, J. "The Therapist as a Catalyst in Promoting Separation-Individuation." *Clinical Social Work Journal*, 1976, *4*, 172–186.

Erikson, E. *Childhood and Society*. New York: Norton, 1963.

Fantl, B. In J. Cohen (Ed.), "The Work of Berta Fantl." *Smith College Studies in Social Work,* 1964, *34,* 164–251.

Feldman, Y. "Integration of Psychoanalytic Concepts into Casework Practice." *Smith College Studies in Social Work,* 1960, *30,* 144–156.

Feldman, Y. "The Problem of the Giver and Receiver." *Smith College Studies in Social Work,* 1980, *50,* 114–119.

Flescher, J. "On Different Types of Countertransference." *International Journal of Group Psychotherapy,* 1953, *3,* 357–372.

Frank, M. "Psychoanalytic Developmental Theory: A Study of Descriptive Developmental Diagnosis." Unpublished manuscript, School for Social Work, Smith College, 1980.

Frank, M. "A Philosophy of Treatment: Considerations of the Use of Insight and the Corrective Emotional Experience." Address delivered at 7th annual institute of New Jersey Chapter of the National Association of Social Workers, 1976.

Frankl, V. "Paradoxical Intention and Dereflection." In *The Unheard Cry for Meaning.* New York: Simon & Schuster, 1978.

French, T. "Review of Our Studies of the Therapeutic Process." In *Psychoanalytic Interpretations: The Selected Papers of Thomas M. French.* Chicago: Quadrangle Books, 1970.

Freud, S. "My Views on the Part Played by Sexuality in the Aetiology of the Neuroses." *Standard Edition of the Complete Psychological Works of Sigmund Freud.* Vol. 7. London: Hogarth Press, 1906.

Freud, S. "Transference." In J. Strachey (Ed.), *Introductory Lectures on Psychoanalysis.* New York: Norton, 1966. (Originally published 1916.)

Ganter, G., Polansky, H., and Yeakel, M. *Retrieval from Limbo.* New York: Child Welfare League of America, 1967.

Greenson, R. *The Technique and Practice of Psychoanalysis.* New York: International Universities Press, 1967.

Grossbard, H. "Ego Deficiency in Delinquents." *Social Casework,* 1962, *43,* 171–178.

Haley, J. "Obiter Dicta: The Art of Psychoanalysis." *A Review of General Semantics,* 1958, *15,* 190.

Haley, J. *Problem Solving Therapy.* New York: Harper Colophon Books, 1978.

Hollis, F. *Casework: A Psychosocial Therapy.* (2nd ed.) New York: Random House, 1972.

Jones, M. *The Therapeutic Community.* New York: Basic Books, 1953.

Kernberg, O. *Borderline Conditions and Pathological Narcissism.* New York: Jason Aronson, 1975.

Lemon, E. C., and Goldstein, S. "The Use of Time Limits in Planned Brief Casework." *Social Casework,* 1978, *59,* 588–596.

Lieberman, F., and Gottesfeld, M. "The Repulsive Client." *Clinical Social Work Journal,* 1973, *1,* 21–31.

Littner, N. "The Caseworker's Self Observation and the Child's Interpersonal Defenses." *Smith College Studies in Social Work,* 1969, *34,* 95–117.

Love, S., and Mayer, H. "Going Along with the Defenses in Resistive Families." *Social Casework,* 1959, *40,* 69–74.

Mahler, M., Pine, F., and Bergman, A. *The Psychological Birth of the Human Infant.* New York: Basic Books, 1975.

Mayer, H., and Schamess, G. "Long Term Treatment for the Disadvantaged." *Social Casework,* 1969, *50,* 138–145.
Moore, B., and Fine, B. *A Glossary of Psychoanalytic Terms and Concepts.* New York: American Psychoanalytic Association, 1968.
Nagelberg, L., Spotnitz, H., and Feldman, Y. "The Attempt at Healthy Insulation in the Withdrawn Child." *American Journal of Orthopsychiatry,* 1953, *23,* 238–252.
Palozzoli, M. *Paradox and Counterparadox.* New York: Jason Aronson, 1978.
Parad, H. "Brief Ego-Oriented Casework with Families in Crisis." In H. Parad and R. Miller, (Eds.), *Ego-Oriented Casework.* New York: Family Service Association of America, 1963.
Pavenstedt, E. *The Drifters.* Boston: Little, Brown, 1967.
Rapoport, L. "The State of Crisis: Some Theoretical Considerations." *Social Service Review,* 1962, *26,* 213–222.
Real, T. "Projective-Introjective Modalities in Marital Interactions." Unpublished M.S.W. thesis, School for Social Work, Smith College, 1980.
Rosenthal, L. "Resistance in Group Therapy: The Interrelationship of Individual and Group Resistance." In L. Wolberg and M. Aronson (Eds.), *Group and Family Therapy.* New York: Brunner/Mazel, 1980.
Schamess, G. "Boundary Issues in Countertransference." *Clinical Social Work Journal,* 1981, *9,* 244–257.
Schwartz, C. "Failure in the Treatment of a Psychotic Mother and Child: Aspects of Transference and Resistance." Unpublished manuscript, 1980.
Schwartz, D. "Psychotherapy." In J. Shershow (Ed.), *Schizophrenia: Science and Practice.* Cambridge, Mass.: Harvard University Press, 1978.
Shapiro, E. R. "The Psychodynamics and Developmental Psychology of the Borderline Patient: A Review of the Literature." *The American Journal of Psychiatry,* 1978, *135,* 1305–1314.
Spotnitz, H. *Modern Psychoanalysis of the Schizophrenic Patient.* New York: Grune & Stratton, 1969.
Spotnitz, H. *Psychotherapy of Preoedipal Conditions.* New York: Jason Aronson, 1976.
Sternbach, O., and Nagelberg, L. "On the Patient-Therapist Relationship in Some 'Untreatable Cases.'" *Psychoanalysis,* 1957, *5,* 63–70.
Strean, H. *Psychoanalytic Theory and Social Work Practice.* New York: Free Press, 1979.
Wasserman, S. "Ego Psychology." In F. Turner (Ed.), *Social Work Treatment: Interlocking Theoretical Approaches.* New York: Free Press, 1974.
Watts, A. *The Spirit of Zen.* New York: Grove Press, 1958.
Winnicott, D. "Hate in the Countertransference." In *Through Paediatrics to Psycho-Analysis.* New York: Basic Books, 1975.
Wood, K. "The Contribution of Psychoanalysis and Ego Psychology to Social Casework." In H. Strean (Ed.), *Social Casework: Theories in Action.* Metuchen, N.J.: Scarecrow Press, 1971.

18

Treatment of Parents

Shirley Cooper

Nowhere are societal changes more evident than in the structure of the American family. Bronfenbrenner (1973) comments: "The American family is significantly different from what it was only a quarter of a century ago." These changes crucially affect parents and the ways in which they rear children and the problems they encounter.

It is no longer uncommon for children to be raised by a single parent. In 1978 eight million families were supported by women—44 percent more than in 1970. Since 1950, the proportion of first births to unmarried women has more than doubled, accounting for 15 percent of all first births. Ninety percent of unmarried teenage mothers now choose to keep their babies, compared to a decade ago when 90 percent surrendered them for adoption. One baby in five is now born to a mother under nineteen (Huntington, 1975, p. 7). This has serious implications for the future health and psychosocial well-being of such babies and their teenage mothers. Babies born to women under fifteen years of age have three times the number of brain and nervous system disorders of children born to older mothers (U.S. Department of Health, Education and Welfare, reported *San Francisco Chronicle,* December 1979).

Approximately 50 percent of all women now work outside the home—largely in full-time jobs (Keniston, 1977, p. 4). More than half of all married women with school-age children hold a job, and the number of children under three years of age whose mothers work has tripled since 1950 (Huntington, 1975, p. 7). Only one-third of all families have a father as the sole breadwinner (Keniston, p. 4). Four of every ten children born in 1970 will spend a part of their childhood in a single-parent family, usually with the mother (Keniston, p. 4; Huntington, p. 7). The level of divorce in 1974 is 109 percent greater than 1962 and, at its present rate, will result in one child in six losing a parent through divorce (Huntington, p. 7).

More and more parents rear their children in relative isolation without the aid of family resources and traditions to guide their judgments, and "without relief from care-giving duties and without rewards for the difficult task of parenting" (Braun, 1975).

Keniston (1977) comments: "What is new and very American is the intensity of the malaise, the sense of having no guidelines or supports for raising children, the feeling of not being in control as parents, and the widespread sense of personal guilt for what seems to be going awry. For when the right way to be a parent is not clear, almost any action can seem capricious or wrong, and every little trouble or minor storm in one's children's lives can become the cause for added self-blame" (p. 4). As work life becomes increasingly impersonal, ties with neighbors and extended families more attenuated, "and truly intimate outer family relationships rare," husbands and wives tend to put all their emotional hopes for fulfillment into their family life (p. 17).

In spite of this, our social welfare policies are based on the old ideal of the self-sufficient family. Daycare and other forms of assistance remain difficult to obtain, while economic pressures and existing work patterns make the need for such services essential for safe childrearing. Rutter (1981) comments: "Much childcare today falls far short of . . . relatively low-level ideals, and strenuous efforts are needed to improve both the quality of what is already provided and to increase the availability of suitable services for those families who so far lack them." He adds that changes must also be made in "the patterns of employment for parents, which are equally necessary if the needs of young children are to be met" (p. 25).

In short, the "norm" is no longer the rule. Guidelines for parents, once available through one's heritage, family, community, neighborhood, and friends, no longer fit today's rapidly changing conditions. As Bernstein (1978) points out: "Such uncertainty about parenting has led to an unprecedented search for experts to tell us how: how to love, how to fight, how to like ourselves, and especially because it is part of the way we ourselves can change the world, how to raise our children . . . and so a word about experts and how to use the advice they have to offer. As you cut the suit to fit your body and not your body to fit the suit, so take expert advice only if it fits. . . . You will be a better parent for it" (pp. 15–16). In part, this is so because the problems are complex, and the present level of knowledge is such that it can rarely point to a clear course of action. Thus there are broad disagreements among child researchers. Some argue that longitudinal studies demonstrate the impossibility of predicting adult psychopathology from early childhood disorders (Kagan, 1976; Kagan and Klein, 1973), while others argue that even minor failures in early mother-child bonding can be significantly damaging (Klaus and Kennell, 1970). Thus there is no agreement about how to best prevent, on a national level, childhood and adult pathology. Some professionals argue that supplemental programs such as nursery schools support modern family life and are useful and enriching for small children (Tizard, Moss and Perry, 1976), while others insist that for optimal child development consistent care by one adult is the preferred mode (Fraiberg, 1977).

Despite a failure of consensus, evidence mounts from growing numbers of researchers about the reliability of three findings: there is no *one* right way to raise children; the infant enters the world equipped to respond to it in important selective ways and can have powerful effects on parenting; and programs with active parental involvement have the greatest chance of enduring success.

There are marked variations in how readily a child is soothed, the ways in which infants take comfort, and the length of time they remain comforted. Documenting the wide variations among infants from birth, Korner (1971) notes: "We are . . . forever looking for *the* method to raise children, to educate, to cure. One aspect of this trend is to see the mother and the care and stimulation she provides as almost solely responsible for the normality and deviation of her child's development. While this stance feeds into the illusion that with 'the correct methods' and the 'right attitudes' we are in control of our children's destiny, it also produces a lot of guilt. This, in turn, undercuts parental effectiveness in dealing flexibly with a child's strengths and vulnerabilities. The practical implications of our findings are quite clear: In working with parents, it is important that we stress not only their crucial influence on their children's development but also that we free them to see, to hear, to tune in, and to trust their own intuition in dealing differentially with what their children present as separate individuals" (p. 618).

In accord with Korner's findings, Bernstein (1978) observes: "A blanket is not a blanket. To one child, a blanket is something to suck, to another a blanket is something to hide under while playing peek-a-boo, to a third, it provides warmth during sleep, and to yet another, it is a source of security and good feeling to cling to when alone" (p. 21).

Despite the fact that preponderant evidence over the last decade consistently indicates that newborn babies are not passive, receptive vessels to be filled and molded exclusively by their environment (Goldberg, 1977), those who attempt to help parents too often continue to offer advice as if all children are alike. While recognition grows that the infant plays a critical role in shaping the mother-child relationship, affecting the parent-child interaction and thus influencing parental feelings of competence, all too often the child's own propensities, assets, and vulnerabilities remain in shadow while parental behaviors are subjected to the light of sharp scrutiny and criticism. While professionals deny that they search for a culprit upon whom to cast blame for what has gone awry in a child's development, the focus on correcting parental "misdeeds" continues.

There is, however, convincing evidence that as parents are helped to achieve a sense of competence, profound changes can occur in the child and the parent, liberating each to develop independently (Fraiberg and Fraiberg, 1980). As with the child, the parents' capacities differ at different stages of the life cycle. Each life stage can stimulate new growth for the parent, even when it evokes old, unresolved conflicts. Rigid insistence that parents recognize their behavior as deviant can create additional burdens for the total family and serves as a deterrent to their search for help.

Evaluative studies of programs and interventions designed to assist children highlight the importance of involving parents in the helping process. Bronfenbrenner (1976) comments: "The evidence indicates . . . that the involvement of the child's family as an active participant is critical to the success of any intervention program. Without such family involvement, any effects of intervention . . . appear to erode fairly rapidly once the program ends. In contrast, the involvement of the parents as partners in the enterprise provides an ongoing system which can reinforce the effects of the program while it is in operation, and help to sustain them after the program ends" (p. 252).

Group programs which aim to reduce parental isolation have considerable value when they help parents validate their own experiences, review their alternatives, and provide support and advice to other group members. In this way parents become more effective in rearing their children, and many incipient problems are prevented. The work of Reid and her associates (Reid and others, 1973) in establishing a preventive-intervention telephone line and drop-in center and programs such as that of Holman (1979) suggest that effective help can be provided by brief interchanges, ranging from telephone contacts to face-to-face encounters, and time-limited parent groups. Such community programs can provide crucial supports at critical points in the lives of parents and children and are often a major factor in enabling the parents to recognize and accept the need for clinical treatment.

Parent education, while all that is needed by some parents, has become something of a vogue. Almost every social agency has recently entered this field and this work—like all work—ranges from poor to excellent. Programs that provide general education, without regard to the specific needs of the particular person or group, have little utility. They tend to preach rather than to teach. They rarely do harm; however, on occasion they can unwittingly arouse guilt by espousing general standards of excellence while ignoring the parents' particular circumstances.

There is great promise in the tremendous growth in knowledge of children's psychosocial development and those experiences that may facilitate or impede emotional and social development (Rutter, 1981). More is being learned about how affiliations are developed, disrupted, and restored (Ainsworth, 1973; Bowlby, 1973; Maccoby, 1980; Rutter, 1980). Provided with skillful help early enough, some ruptured parent-child relationships posing great risks to the health and development of children have been recaptured (Fraiberg and Fraiberg, 1980). We are beginning to learn more about children's temperamental differences (Chess and Thomas, 1977), about the proximal conditions in the physical and emotional environments which promote development (Wachs, 1979), and even about how one might go about preventing some disorders (Cowen, 1980; Egeland and Brunnquell, 1979).

While much remains unknown or partially understood, we have come a long way! "It was not so long ago—even as recently as fifteen or twenty years ago—that the dominant professional ideology laid the causation of all psychopathology, from simple behavior problems to juvenile delinquency, to schizophrenia, at the doorstep of the mother. . . . Research studies of the past fifteen to twenty years . . . have completely altered these simplistic views" (Chess and Thomas, 1978, p. 245). While professional perspective has changed, those who work with parents in behalf of children still need the constant reminder of Chess and Thomas that "old ideas die hard."

Direct Treatment of Parents

Seeking Helping for a Troubled Child. To make the decision to seek help for one's child is an event which no parent undertakes lightly. The pain of acknowledging that a child is not simply passing through a phase, that one has gone beyond one's own capacity to change the course of events, and that one must now consider exposing private experiences is fraught with difficulty and intense emotion. Sometimes the child's problems have been denied or externalized. By the time the parent seeks help he or she is often under considerable pressure, feeling guilty, ashamed, helpless, angry, and bewildered. Many have already been confronted by some external authority noting that the child's performance is troublesome. The parent often perceives (or endows) the referring person with great authority, confronting the parent's own capacities to judge events and experiences autonomously.

Whether parents have made a personal choice based on their own observations and judgment or are painfully confronted by another, the feelings associated with the beginning efforts to seek help for a child will be fraught with struggle and pain. Resistant or not, portrayed vividly or not, such parental suffering must be met by the clinician with respect, tact, and understanding. Clinicians must recognize that "we can neither rescue children nor hope to accomplish for them the tasks that rightfully belong to the family. Our aim is to help children and parents utilize their own resources more effectively, so that they can live with one another in greater harmony" (Cooper and Wanerman, 1977, p. 182).

At the critical moment of application, clinicians must seek to establish an active alliance and partnership with the parent in order to support the work of treating and helping the child. Since children are rarely able to offer a full picture of the important events in their lives, information must be obtained from the child's caretakers about his or her past and present life. And together, parent and therapist must consider ways to alter those aspects of the child's world which may contribute to the child's difficulty or affect the child's growth.

All parents approach the request for help with presumptions about the helping process—some from prior life experiences, some from ignorance, some extending to or displacing on the therapist the referring person's approach to them. Others seek magical responses and answers, some covertly wish to yield parenting entirely, while others expect punishment and judgment. Covert messages may be implied in the request for help. Understanding these can help the therapist mobilize the most useful and productive alliance in behalf of the child and the parent's best interest.

The parent's help is essential whether the clinical work will be frequent and regular or intermittent and occasional. The unfolding and altering needs of the child and parent will, of course, dictate the frequency and the nature of the work with the parent.

Aims in Treating Parents. Some parents will be required to do no more than pay the bill, support the child's regular attendance at treatment sessions, and exchange important information. Therapist and parent will want to share the conviction that the child's work is proceeding well. Occasional interactions may suffice. However, even within such seemingly limited goals, the parent must experience some mutuality with the therapist and feel assured that the child is in competent and reliable hands.

On the other end of the continuum, parents may be asked to significantly modify their own behaviors, if the child is to profit. Treatment for parents in their own right may be recommended—a decision the parent may or may not be willing to undertake at one time, but be prepared to make at another.

Between these two vastly different objectives, clinical work with parents may aim to:

1. Advise parents about specific parent-child interactions that impair development and relationships or keep the child bound to his or her conflicts and problematic behaviors. Such advice may concern interactions around discipline; management of the child's symptoms; alterations in patterns of ensuring the child's privacy; modulating and regulating stimulation; and management of important life tasks, such as sleeping, eating, and bathing. Less prominent now than a decade ago, but still an issue and a source of struggle, such seemingly less important child activities as haircuts or choice of clothes may also be subject to advice from the clinician.

2. Provide information and advice about the optimal environmental conditions to stimulate growth or repair disruptions in the child's development. Changes in schools, after-school activity, vacation planning, and assistance with a tutor are all within the purview of important parent-therapist interactions, as each takes responsibility for mutually considering and resolving problematic environmental contributions to a child's difficulties.

3. Loosen pathological attachments between the parent and child by focal interventions around specific parent-child interactions which hold problem behaviors in place for both. Such clinical work may not address the parent as a patient but deal with focal aspects of parental behaviors which impinge directly on the child. Some parents will need the support of a sensitive, respectful clinician who is willing to share with the parent the struggle to acknowledge and recognize that the child may be ready to move forward in new ways that may threaten the parent. The parent who has come to trust the child's therapist may, at such times, need increased help in testing out new parenting behavior; this help should persist long enough to ensure that no danger will accrue from these new efforts. Such "moments" in the work with the parent require clinical delicacy and ingenuity. There are times when parents may experience uncertainty, ambivalence, and confusion—perhaps for the first time coming face to face with their own role in contributing to the child's difficulty. It is at such times that the parent may develop sharp resistances to the work, requiring the forging of a new alliance. The work may even be sabotaged by the parent, who may feel pressured to yield parental judgment he or she is yet unprepared to yield.

Work with parents requires a careful assessment of the child, the parents, the child's current environment and past experiences, and the parent's capacity to engage in a serious partnership with the therapist to assist the troubled child. The clinician will need to develop a beginning formulation of the case, arrive at some judgment about who to include in the case of characters to be worked with, and define preliminary treatment goals. Agreement must also be reached about the frequency of encounters for both parent and child, what the work is expected to accomplish, and by what modes these can best be achieved. Some parents may need individual, collaborative work with the child's therapist; others may require a different therapist. While some parents may more profitably be seen as a couple, others make greater gains in groups, while still others may work on interpersonal difficulties most effectively in family therapy. One mode does not contravene the use of others at periodic intervals or as combinations of interventions.

Developing an Alliance. Whatever the aim or the style, effective work cannot be undertaken without a parental alliance, the primary goal in early contacts. The nature of the alliance will shift over time as more information and understanding lead to alterations in the focus of treatment. When such changes occur, frequency in parental contacts or changes in interventions may be required. Trite but true, it is important to acknowledge that no initial assessment of a child and his or her family can yield more than beginning perspectives to be tested over time. As the clinician deepens the understanding of assets, deficits, and needs presented by child and parent, alterations will be made in treating both.

For example: Mrs. Strickler is the mother of two children, eight-year-old Tom and six-year-old Sara. Tom is the product of a brief affair which occurred during Mrs. Strickler's first marriage. Mrs. Strickler's husband and her parents were outraged by the affair and by Tom's birth. Unsupported by her family and divorced by her husband, Mrs. Strickler soon moved with Tom to a new area. She moved restlessly and frequently until she met Sara's father, who for a time provided her with some stability and support. In spite of the intervening pregnancy with her second child, Mrs. Strickler learned a trade and began to work steadily. Tom, however, clearly represented for her her own devalued self-concept as well as a daily reminder of her "transgressions." Deeply but ambivalently attached, Tom and Mrs. Strickler lived together in a state of constant warfare. Paradoxically, as Mrs. Strickler began to rebuild her shifting life, during her association with Sara's father, she discovered that though he offered a refuge and some support he was in many ways as childlike and demanding as her two children. Mrs. Strickler decided to leave Sara's father when Tom was five.

Tom, a restless, angry child, entered school shortly after this separation. Bright, volatile, quick to find and experience insult, Tom soon began to battle peers with open fierceness. The school, having often reprimanded mother as well as son, referred Tom for help when he was eight years old.

Mrs. Strickler approached the agency with ambivalence and profound guilt. Aware that Tom needed help, she nonetheless expected that others would see her as she herself did—responsible for all of Tom's difficulties.

Despite the worker's careful efforts to engage Mrs. Strickler in a nonjudgmental partnership and her empathic recognition of Mrs. Strickler's pain, the client remained aloof and clearly conveyed that any empathy directed toward her was suspect and unreliable. A mild suggestion that Mrs. Strickler might herself benefit from some help was sharply rebuffed. Nevertheless, she brought Tom to his sessions regularly, in spite of her shame about the noisy, raucous sounds emanating from the treatment room. Frequently Tom would burst from the room, accusing the worker of hurting him as she made valiant efforts to limit his destructive play which sometimes escalated out of control. At one such outburst, Tom's mother overheard the worker's comment that "no one deserved such terrible punishments" as Tom had inflicted on a self-representational character in his noisy play. In her next parent session Mrs. Strickler seemed unable to begin. Atypically she spoke haltingly and unsurely about recent events at home with Tom and Sara. For a few moments she sat silently. Sensing the client's inner struggle, the worker observed that Mrs. Strickler seemed to have something on her mind but seemed unsure of whether she wanted to discuss it. Mrs. Strickler faced the worker and asked, "Did you really mean what I heard you tell Tom—that no one deserved so much punishment? I overheard you." The worker assured her that she had, indeed, very much meant what she'd said, adding that Tom's view of himself as such a bad person made it hard for him to hear, but that she did not see him in the same way.

Mrs. Strickler began to weep, acknowledging her similarity to and pain for Tom. She, too, found it hard to believe that the worker did not think that she, too, should be punished for all the bad things she had herself caused to happen. She was sure that everyone, like her parents and herself, blamed her for her indiscretions. The worker gently pointed out that Mrs. Strickler's harsh view of herself sought validation in others, though she surely could not join Mrs. Strickler in painful self-blame.The remaining time was spent on discussing Mrs. Strickler herself as both worker and mother entered a new arena of discourse—Mrs. Strickler's right to get help for herself.

Initially Mrs. Strickler was prepared to establish an alliance with Tom's worker around limited goals. She could support Tom's treatment and met regularly to offer information about events in Tom's world. Not until Mrs. Strickler had tested the worker's empathy and respect for her and Tom, however, could she consider any other alliance. Locked in her own shame and guilt, transferring to others her own demeaned and undeserving view of herself, she painfully struggled with a wish for help and the fear that she deserved nothing good for herself. She felt entitled only to punishment. While workers typically prefer to keep private interchanges between themselves and the child, this inadvertent breach of confidentiality served to trigger the release of new hope for Mrs. Strickler as well as for her young son. The alliance had deepened and taken a new direction.

Eliciting and Exchanging Information. No child can be treated effectively without knowledge about the child's environment and prior experiences. The parents are usually the best source for such data, although information from other caretakers in other settings may contribute importantly to the clinician's understanding. For example, a clinician may receive vital information from physicians who have cared for a child with repeated medical problems. Often such outside sources can help us understand the parent's attitudes and behaviors in response to critical events, though one must take care to hold such information loosely in the mind, since stressful events and institutional contacts may not portray parents at their best. Naturally no information should be sought from anyone outside the family without parental consent.

Just as such information may be distorted, the clinician gathering data from parents must be alert to parental distortion. No history is an objective account of exact experiences; all experiences are filtered through the eyes of the beholder. Memories fade and some material is repressed, while defenses and resistances shade events.

Choices about how to proceed to gather necessary information requires careful consideration and flexibility. Therapists differ in their styles; some prefer a first conjoint meeting with both parents, while others prefer to meet each parent singly. Each has its own advantages and limitations. A joint interview may reveal more information about parental interactions, while separate interviews may disclose more information about a parent's private concerns. A family meeting can reveal how the unit functions together, suggesting how alliances in the family operate and the ways roles are assigned to each of its members. Whatever the approach, such initial encounters can be productive in helping the clinician decide how best to proceed in establishing ongoing contacts with the parents and the child.

The gathering of current and past information is a process requiring skill. Parents need to understand why questions are being put and answers sought. This can serve to educate the parents about the need to keep the therapist abreast of the child's current life experiences. Parents who have been invited to provide the clinician with important information about current changes in the household, visitors to the home, experiences at school, vacations being planned, and so on, will often help the child's clinician understand new and puzzling behaviors which may appear in the course of the child's treatment.

Aaron, age eleven, had been in treatment for over a year. A deeply disturbed boy, his primary alliance was with an older brother whom he strove to emulate. He had been a ready and active participant in his treatment, bounding into the room as soon as he observed the therapist come for him. Suddenly Aaron seemed reluctant to start the interviews; more and more time was spent in the bathroom at the beginning of each session. A meeting with his parent revealed that Aaron's older brother had begun to be truant from school, causing great turmoil and distress within the home. Now Aaron's puzzling behavior could better be understood. Aaron not only mimicked his brother's behavior by being truant from the playroom but soon disclosed that if he continued to work in his treatment, he would be led to reveal his brother's recent behavior and imagined that such disclosures would add to the trouble his beloved brother was already finding himself in. Aaron's compromise to avoid being a "rat fink" was to absent himself as much as possible from his treatment and his therapist.

In gathering information to understand a case, it is useful to order and organize the developmental and historical data into what might be thought of as an "existential flow sheet" (Cooper and Wanerman, 1977, p. 86). This involves clustering the information in the following way:

Date	Age	Event	Context

"Even where historical and developmental data are obtained in the most orderly way, this information emerges in fragments at different moments in an interview or over a series of interviews. For example, one may hear the story of a child's first attendance at school at one time and the story of a grandparent's death much later in a parent's account. It is all too easy to miss the link between such events. The 'existential flow sheet' helps the therapist make appropriate links and, for instance, discover that the two experiences mentioned by the parent have occurred in the same month" (p. 86).

This organization of data provides a cross-sectional view of a family's experiences, thus permitting the discovery of links between experiences, raising speculative questions, and suggesting where omissions may exist to guide further inquiry and enrich perspectives.

Eliciting information from parents is important in its own right. However, as suggested, it serves as well to educate the parents in their partnership roles and to promote an alliance. Responding to questions put by the parents is equally important, once again reaffirming for the parent that he or she has a right to know what lies ahead. However, all parental questions cannot, or in some instances should not, be answered. It is in these encounters that parents can be helped to tolerate some of the ambiguity inherent in any treatment.

Parents often need help in preparing their children for the first encounter with a therapist. While clinicians will certainly want to elicit what ideas the parent may have, since they often provide another view of the parent's attitude about the child and the treatment, they can often use such discussions to further educate the parent. The therapist may then serve as model who offers the important sense that the parents are not alone in this process. Simple, direct suggestions are most useful. The parent will often experience considerable relief when the clinician recommends a straightforward, short statement to prepare the child for the first encounter, learning that evasions and guises often bewilder the child, encouraging secrecy and frightening fantasy. To illustrate, the therapist may recommend the following statement by a parent: "Johnny, I'm taking you to see Mrs. Cooper. She knows about and helps children who have accidents and soil their pants. I hope you'll tell her about this, since we all want to help you with it." No clinician will be naive enough to expect that Johnny will thereafter inevitably reveal his problem readily, but parents can be assured that the therapist will take it from there, helping the child (and his parents) with the attendant anxiety and shame.

The assessment process must be a demonstration of the treatment to come. It is not a process apart from the treatment itself but a sample of what that experience will offer. An early alliance is forged, from the outset in the evolving relationship, in the gathering and giving of information, in helping to find appropriate levels of motivation by reducing anxiety or realistically portraying the seriousness of the situation, fueling neither guilt nor blame, and in respectfully and empathically engaging the parent. It is in these beginning hours that motivation can be enlisted and enhanced, resistances decreased, and an attitude of partnership in problem solving established.

No evaluation is complete without reporting back to the parents the therapist's judgments, understanding, and proposed treatment plan. Once again, these post-diagnostic sessions are not a one-sided affair. Parents will need to understand that an evaluation can yield only beginning and tentative impressions and that some things are yet unknowable. In these sessions, parents have additional opportunities to ask further questions, clarify confusions, and to learn that what concerns them is vitally important. When the post-diagnostic session is well done, it further cements the alliance, reduces parental hopes for magical resolution, and lays the basis for further productive parental work.

Ms. Beadler is the bright, articulate single parent of twelve-year-old Jim. Having left an embattled family in her adolescence, she fought her way through a brief affair with Jim's father while working and attending school. She moved to various parts of the country to ensure promotions in her field, sometimes engaging in brief affairs with men whom she later sharply denigrated. Ms. Beadler had sought help earlier in another city, reporting in staccato tones that the therapist there was "incompetent and silly."

She presents Jim as defiant, constantly battling, resisting her every suggestion or command, and doing poorly in school "in spite of the fact that intellectually he is surely very superior." She cannot understand Jim's refusal to work at school. The therapist is barraged with questions about his own training and experience. Ms. Beadler insists that she wants family treatment to get to the bottom of "this thing," and inquires whether the therapist has "experience with that treatment." The hour can barely be brought to a close. Several times during the evaluation with Jim, Ms. Beadler alters times and makes lengthy telephone calls to the therapist asking for his views as the assessment proceeds.

In the post-diagnostic session, the worker firmly informs Ms. Beadler that he will not see her and Jim in family treatment. His style is totally clear, firm, and unequivocal. He reports that his decision rests on the fact that he intends to treat Jim, that he will not referee battles between them, and that he believes that Ms. Beadler is under considerable stress herself. The problem is not all Jim's.

Ms. Beadler calms down considerably. For the first time, a real interchange occurs, with fewer interruptions and less shrillness from Ms. Beadler. The therapist has passed an important test. Embattled and battling, Ms. Beadler's request for help for her son covertly carried an implicit plea that someone be strong enough to meet her on her own level, to intuit that although she screamed her anger and pain, she was underneath a vulnerable but courageous woman. For Ms. Beadler the best defense was offense. Her request for help for her son implicitly carried the hope that someone see her pain and be strong and alert enough to observe it and stand firmly and autonomously in their own corner, recommending what was necessary for the good of both.

Ms. Beadler is not a typical parent. One does not usually engage in such stormy interchanges throughout an assessment. Some storms simply go underground as the parent decides against further treatment.

Yet the work with Ms. Beadler illustrates the importance of portraying clearly what the clinician believes are necessary foundations for effective work, as well as the ability to pass whatever tests are presented by parents. These tests are not malicious efforts consciously designed to beleaguer clinicians. Most parents need to rightfully test out—through their actual experiences with the clinician—whether they are understood and can entrust their child to a therapist who is competent and reliable.

Ms. Beadler's style of testing also represents an instance in which the parent may implicitly be asking the therapist to help them begin to control behaviors which the parent preconsciously recognizes are counterproductive.

When post-diagnostic information is given perfunctorily or grudgingly, parents often come away with the impression that vast secrets are being withheld. This may arouse suspicion and rivalry. The child's confidentiality must, of course, be respected and safeguarded. As children come to learn that they can more safely report their concerns and pain without fear that their secrets (often vastly magnified by fantasy) will be divulged, the treatment moves forward with greater success. Parents need not know the exact detail of playroom or interview interactions, but they are entitled to know what issues are being addressed, what progress or difficulty is being made or encountered, and what worries and concerns they can help with at home.

We have too often made a dogma out of the important concept of confidentiality, hiding behind it when we feel inept or unclear about its proper use. When parents continue to question their children about what is going on in their sessions, it is often because they feel mystified about the process of child therapy, or they worry about what the child may be disclosing which may lead to the therapist's harsh judgment of their parenting, or they experience correctly that something is being withheld. The therapist must learn to discern which of these are at work and move to deal with them.

When reasonable interventions have been attempted and parental "inquisitions" continue, it may well then reveal that a parent's internal conflicts are fueling such inquiries. It is in this sense that good work provides us with further diagnostic precision about the nature of the problems at hand and leads to more effective interventions.

Ongoing Work. Work with parents includes the entire panoply of therapeutic interventions available to all clinical work. It can include "simply information giving or education on the one end, through clarification, permission, advice, persuasion, facilitation, and channeling or manipulation of feelings, to psychotherapeutic techniques" (Arnold, 1978, p. 4). These interventions in various combinations and emphases are used in dealing with any clinical problem. What distinguishes many parents from the self-referred client is that parents rarely seek treatment for themselves. Thus careful attention to and management of resistances is even more critical than in work with the "motivated client." In working with parents, the nature, level, and shifts in motivation and resistance must be carefully understood. Arnold recommends that when parents present various obstacles and it is yet unclear what predominantly impedes their effective parenting, "it often makes sense to assume at first the simplest and easiest problem" (p. 5). It will soon become clear, he suggests, when it is necessary to alter interventions in keeping with a clearer sense of parental difficulty. To do the most with the least is a time-honored clinical concept, often more honored in the breach than in the doing.

However, it is often possible to quickly recognize factors that could be impeding parental effectiveness. When this occurs a more conscious and rational plan and treatment strategy can be developed—always to be tested and validated by the client. For example, giving straightforward impressions of the child and the possible meaning of his or her behavior can often help a parent gain some perspective on and distance from the child's problem if the parent's own needs do not require that the child's behavior be seen as intentionally designed to thwart the parent. The presentation of information and advice must rest on the therapist's conviction that the parent can make productive use of what is offered. Advice given must be reviewed to determine what has come of it.

Referred by his nursery school teacher, who was aware that Fred and his mother had recently settled in the area following the mother's decision to separate from her husband, Fred was described as a bright, active three-year-old child who had been fighting with peers. He was a sturdy youngster, obviously reacting to the loss of his father and the new, unsettled circumstances in which he and his mother were living. She was trying to establish a new home for herself and her young son but was finding it considerably harder than she had expected. At times she felt burdened by Fred and his needs, and recognized her growing ambivalence about her son. He was hard to control and frequently asked for his Daddy, thereby confronting his mother with her guilt about her actions.

While she acted promptly upon the referral and met regularly with her son's therapist, she was guarded and apprehensive about how the therapist would view her. In the eighth session Fred, who had made a quick attachment to his therapist, was reluctant to leave. He wanted to stay longer, to leave the toys out so that they would be exactly where he put them, and to extend the time so that he could make his therapist a valentine.

As Fred and his therapist returned to the waiting room, Fred greeted his mother, then returned to his therapist and flung himself into his arms, saying, "You are my Daddy now."

Fred's mother was embarrassed and visibly upset. The therapist addressed Fred, commenting: "That is a wish, Fred. Your Mommy and I know that you miss your real Daddy. A little boy would."

In the following meeting with Fred's mother, the therapist was careful to bring up the parting scene. He acknowledged that she must have been pained to hear Fred verbalize his wish and gently explored her right to decide about her marriage, based upon her own needs. Fred's mother was then able to discuss her guilt and ambivalence about Fred and the separation, and was able to avow her concern that Fred's therapist might have judged her harshly for putting her interests before those of her son.

All treatment interventions in work with parents must aim at helping the adult function more effectively as a parent. "Whenever a parent is seen in behalf of his child, there is the danger that the child will enter as ghost into the interview room. The therapist may be tempted to become the advocate for the ghost child. The effort to reach one human being through the needs of another almost invariably ensures that the person in the room will see himself as less valued and less important to the therapist than the ghost hovering between them" (Cooper, 1974, p. 174). This does not imply that we should not advocate for the child; it does suggest that we must have some independent version of what the parent is like—what the parent can tolerate, hear, and use—and that we address the parent in terms of his or her own person and personality.

Tony is five, the oldest of three children in an intact family. After an illness and the birth of his infant brother, Tony began to soil his pants at school, to the shame and chagrin of Mr. and Mrs. Mission. Tony's father, the more patient of the two parents, tried hard to persuade and cajole Tony to use the toilet. Tony's mother, a precise and organized woman, found the messing more upsetting and difficult to manage. Persuaded by a trusted physician that Tony was a healthy child who would probably require only brief help to master recent traumas and his own body, the parents sought professional help. At the conclusion of one session, Tony very much wanted to show his mother a painting he had made and pasted. The therapist agreed and Tony brought his mother in to see his production. Mother entered the room pleasantly, but her affect shifted to one of horror and recoil when she saw that the once pristine room where she had been seen had now turned into a huge mess. She ordered Tony to clean it up. In the next session with Tony's mother, the therapist attempted to explain that the "rules" in the treatment room were not the same as elsewhere and Tony could make a mess if he chose to do so. The mother berated the therapist. It was precisely because Tony could not control his messing that he was brought to treatment. The therapist observed that Tony's symptoms were now in control, that it had been many weeks since he had soiled his pants. Mother seemed taken aback, but her anger and suspicion did not abate.

The therapist acknowledged that Tony's messing had indeed disturbed Mrs. Mission greatly, and that this had probably been even more difficult to tolerate because the new baby demanded so much of her. Slowly relaxing, Tony's mother told of how very much more she enjoyed her children when they were able to move about independently and do more for themselves. One infant with diapers was more than enough. She remembered her responsibilities as a child, to assist her mother in her many younger siblings' care. Her mother had expected obedience, order, and cleanliness. It was not until her younger siblings were well on their own that Mrs. Mission was permitted to leave home to enter college and pursue her own interests. The therapist acknowledged how all the younger ones had gotten in the way and made the pursuit of her own independent interests difficult. She imagined that Tony's soiling brought back images of those hard times.

Mrs. Mission smiled; she had come expecting to tell the therapist that treatment was over. She had been angry—so angry that it probably did remind her of those earlier resentments. She hadn't enjoyed her mother's exaggerated expectations; she assumed Tony didn't always like her commands. Tony was indeed beyond his soiling symptom; nevertheless, his mother reported she still found his clinging to her bothersome. Mrs. Mission reported that her husband had not agreed with her that Tony should stop. The therapist indicated that she thought the treatment was helping Tony and would continue to be of use to him. The mother relaxed visibly and with animation began to discuss her pride in Tony. She smiled as she reported that Tony had just announced that he would no longer take baths with his younger sister; he had told her disdainfully, "You're a baby!" In the last week or so his fantasy baby, Jack, had "grown up." Jack was now big, could open bottles, tie his shoes, and other "big stuff." Tony had also announced to his father that he intended to marry his mother when he grew up. The therapist and mother then spent some time enjoying these new, more grown-up behaviors. The therapist assured the mother that Tony worked hard in his play to let her in on his worries. Mrs. Mission was quite ready to revise her decision to terminate Tony's treatment; she said, "I was just angry for a bit."

The therapist, here, first addressed the mother by conjuring up Tony and allying herself with him. Skillfully and quickly she observed the problem this created and soon turned to the mother's concerns, banishing the ghost and addressing the real person.

Work with the Parents of Adolescents. We have come to recognize that many adolescents do not pass through the "Sturm und Drang" that was customarily viewed as an essential phase before adult maturity could be achieved. While adolescents must loosen ties to their family of origin and begin to consolidate an independent and more cohesive identity of their own, many adolescents manage these tasks far more quietly than we once believed likely.

Nevertheless, those adolescents typically seen for clinical help are frequently those who are locked in struggle with their parents. Adolescent suicide is on the rise and, for each successful suicide, there are many more attempts, testifying to the depression and loss of controls that many adolescents experience as parental ties loosen. Such events as attempted suicide, depressive episodes, impulsive acting out, and rebellious defiance are frightening experiences for parents—more so when these behaviors seemingly erupt from nowhere.

Every stage of parenting requires modulated caretaking and differential responses to the child's developmental behavior. Colley comments: "A mutual respect balance involves neither overcontrol nor undercontrol, neither overpermissiveness nor rigidity, neither intrusiveness nor neglect. It is the middle ground. It recognizes the rights of individuals, whether parents or children, to grow in an atmosphere where neither parents nor children are expected to cater to the whim of the other. Rules, limits, rights, and responsibilities are explicit and parental responses are consistent rather than random. Parents need to provide enough structure for the child so that he may have guidelines while developing, yet possess enough flexibility and awareness of phase-specific characteristics and needs that the child will not be stifled" (1978, p. 47).

Such a balance is often more difficult for parents to maintain when they are dealing with a troubled adolescent. Younger children can be more readily disciplined because they are far less mobile and peers, while important, are not as powerful an influence in countering parental guidance. While the same principles operate in the treatment of parents of adolescents as those guiding the work with younger children, the therapist will often need to establish clearer and firmer ground rules about confidentiality, advise where and in what ways the parents may need to set firm and clear limits, and suggest where overprotectiveness or intrusion must be restricted.

Some adolescents can manage the treatment by themselves. In such instances, parents may be seen infrequently and even not at all. However, care must be taken in assessing the needs of the adolescent and his or her family.

Patricia, age fifteen, worked well with her therapist for over a year. Her parents were seen once a month as a couple and progress had been made in helping them sort out where to take a stand firmly and where Patricia could be permitted to make her own mistakes.

Since things were proceeding well, the parents asked to discontinue meeting with the therapist, agreeing to contact her by phone whenever they felt the need to do so.

Patricia's treatment took a downhill spiral. Only weeks later could she bring herself to inform the therapist that the discontinued parental contacts meant to her that she was solely responsible for the difficulties between herself and her family.

Work with Fathers. The revolution in family relationships has many important influences on parenting. Roles are shifting, as fathers no longer function as sole providers and protectors. Many fathers now actively participate in childrearing and parenting, although this is still more true of middle-class families. They are more available to their children, share in household chores, and often support mothers in their double roles as caretaker and breadwinner. It is no longer a rarity that divorced couples share custody. The recent movie "Kramer vs. Kramer" documents the shifting relationships between parents, and our empathy for both parents is evoked, though we are never told what provoked this seemingly excellent mother to abandon her child.

All too often fathers are seen with less frequency than mothers—if at all. They are not yet viewed as full partners in the treatment enterprise. As we become ever more clear that humans need one another for support, so must we enlist both parents, wherever possible, to support one another in becoming more effective parents. The child invariably profits from several objects with whom to identify—twosomes often engender overcloseness and reduce opportunities for learning and modeling.

Moreover, fathers often feel left out and undermined when their advice and perspective is neither sought nor considered. Therapists and children are not only left without paternal supports; instead, the father may become an active opponent of the treatment, while adversarial collusions and rifts are created within the family.

Work with Disorganized Families. As indicated, the stresses on family life have led to increasing disruptions in many families. Adequate environmental supports are often lacking and those services designed to assist the most disorganized families are often staffed by the least skilled and most burdened of workers. Placement of children away from home is fiscally supported in some measure, albeit insufficiently. Prevention is not yet a real service; it remains a lip service. Far too few efforts are made to implement fully what we already know or to learn more about how to enter potentially problematic situations in families early enough and with the appropriate supplies. Parents cannot provide their children what they themselves do not possess. Parents who have themselves been impoverished often cannot make themselves available to their children. They may, instead, lean on their children for support, bind them in symbiotic fusions to fill their own emptiness, and yet capriciously and unexpectedly detach when faced with overwhelming pressures.

Bandler (1967) delineates five basic pathogenic characteristics in her study of a small group of multiproblem families: a sense of psychological, educational, social, and cultural deprivation; the constant and intense sense of danger from inner impulses and violent and unexpected behaviors from the outer world; the excesses derived from extremes of disorganized stimuli; the absence of patterned, predictable behavior which contributes to a sense of uncertainty and inconsistency; and the lethargy and hopelessness which becomes organized into pervasive passivity.

Yet the work of Bandler, Fraiberg, Anthony, and others suggests that with time and endless patience some disorganized families can provide more effective parenting. Anthony and McGinnis (1978, p. 339) write: "Counseling the very disturbed (borderline or psychotic) parent requires experience and resilience from the counselor and the capacity for endless patience that can put up with interminable recitals of petty resentments, trivial preoccupations, obsessive questioning, repeated recriminations, the breaking of appointments without warning, prolonged telephone calls, unexpected disappearances from the therapeutic scene, and clamorous demands for help at all times of day and night."

These are taxing requirements for any therapist; not many can manage to meet them—certainly not when there are more than a few in any caseload, since such families profoundly threaten therapeutic equilibrium.

However, when we practice what we profess—that children are our most precious resource—we have been able to demonstrate that if help is offered soon enough, long enough, and with differentiated skill and knowledge, progress can be made.

Conclusion

Parenthood is a demanding occupation in a rapidly changing world. While our knowledge about reciprocal relationships between parent and child grows and we increasingly understand the importance of th family as a major shaping influence upon all of its members, this knowledge often lags behind our services and our skills. For the latter, therapists must take responsibility; the former is an indictment of what our society values most and least.

The treatment of parents—like all treatment—requires careful assessment, finely honed listening and responding, differentiated work to ensure that varied parenting styles can be respected and freed for use, and a recognition of when we have gone beyond our capacities to help. However, if we are to assist the many children who need our help, we cannot do so without engaging parents to help their own children.

It is important to add that parenting is a profoundly humanizing experience, giving rise to great pleasure and pride. Those who work to facilitate these experiences can themselves share in the pride and pleasure of helping children and families grow.

References

Ainsworth, M. "The Development of Infant-Mother Attachment." In B. Caldwell and H. Ricciuti (Eds.), *Review of Child Development Research.* Vol. 3. Chicago: University of Chicago Press, 1973.

Anthony, E. J., and McGinnis, M. "Counseling Very Disturbed Parents." In L. E. Arnold (Ed.), *Helping Parents Help Their Children.* New York: Brunner/Mazel, 1978.

Arnold, L. E. "Strategies and Tactics of Parent Guidance." In L. E. Arnold (Ed.), *Helping Parents Help Their Children.* New York: Brunner/Mazel, 1978.

Bandler, L. S. "Family Functioning: A Psychosocial Perspective." In E. Pavenstedt (Ed.), *The Drifters: Children of Disorganized Lower Class Families.* Boston: Little, Brown, 1967.

Bernstein, A. *The Flight of the Stork.* New York: Dell, 1978.

Bowlby, J. *Attachment and Loss II: Separation, Anxiety and Anger.* London: Hogarth Press, 1973.

Braun, S. J. "What's Special About Educational Programs for Young Children." Paper presented at the Conference on Children Under Stress, University of California, San Francisco, 1975.

Bronfenbrenner, U. "American Families: Trends and Pressures." Statement before the Subcommittee on Children and Youth of the Committee on Labor and Public Welfare, United States Senate, September 24–26, 1973.

Bronfenbrenner, U. "Is Early Intervention Effective? Facts and Principles of Early Intervention: A Summary." In A. M. Clarke and A.D.B. Clarke (Eds.), *Early Experience: Myth and Evidence.* New York: Free Press, 1976.

Chess, S., and Thomas, A. "Temperamental Individuality from Childhood to Adolescence." *Journal of the American Academy of Child Psychiatry,* 1977, *16,* 218–226.

Chess, S., and Thomas, A. (Eds.). *Annual Progress in Child Psychiatry and Child Development.* New York: Brunner/Mazel, 1978.

Colley, K. D. "Growing Up Together: The Mutual Respect Balance." In L. E. Arnold (Ed.), *Helping Parents Help Their Children.* New York: Brunner/Mazel, 1978.

Cooper, S. "Treatment of Parents." In S. Arieti and Caplan, G. (Eds.), *American Handbook of Psychiatry.* Vol. 2. (2nd ed.) New York: Basic Books, 1974.

Cooper, S., and Wanerman, L. *Children in Treatment: A Primer for Beginning Psychotherapists.* New York: Brunner/Mazel, 1977.

Cowen, E. "The Wooing of Primary Prevention." *American Journal of Community Psychology,* 1980, *8* (3), 258–284.

Egeland, B., and Brunnquell, D. "An At-Risk Approach to the Study of Child Abuse: Some Preliminary Findings." *Journal of the American Academy of Child Psychiatry,* 1979, *18* (2), 219–235.

Fraiberg, S. *Every Child's Birthright: In Defense of Mothering.* New York: Basic Books, 1977.

Fraiberg, S., Adelson, E., and Shapiro, V. "Ghosts in the Nursery." *Journal of the American Academy of Child Psychiatry,* 1975, *14* (3), 387–421.

Fraiberg, S., and Fraiberg, L. (Eds.). *Clinical Studies in Infant Mental Health: The First Year of Life.* New York: Basic Books, 1980.

Goldberg, S. "Social Competence in Infancy: A Model of Parent-Infant Interaction." *Merrill-Palmer Quarterly,* 1977, *23* (3), pp. 163–177.

Holman, S. "An Early Intervention Program for Developmentally At-Risk Toddlers and Their Mothers." *Clinical Social Work Journal,* 1979, *7* (3), 167–181.

Huntington, D. "Learning from Infants and Families." *Journal of the Association for the Care of Children in Hospitals,* 1975, *4* (1), 5–20.

Kagen, J. "Resilience and Continuity in Psychological Development." In A. M. Clarke and A.D.B. Clarke (Eds.), *Early Experience: Myth and Evidence.* New York: Free Press, 1976.

Kagen, J., and Klein, R. E. "Cross Cultural Perspectives on Human Development." *American Psychologist,* 1973, *28,* 947–961.

Keniston, K., and the Carnegie Council on Children. *All Our Children: The American Family Under Pressure.* New York: Harcourt Brace Jovanovich, 1977.

Klaus, M., and Kennell, J. H. "Mothers Separated from Their Infants." *Pediatric Clinics of North America,* 1970, *17,* 1015–1037.

Korner, A. "Individual Differences at Birth: Implications for Early Experience and Later Development." *American Journal of Orthopsychiatry,* 1971, *41* (4), 617–618.

Maccoby, E. *Social Development: Psychological Growth and the Parent-Infant Relationship.* New York: Harcourt Brace Jovanovich, 1980.

Reid, H., and others. "Preventive Intervention for the Young." Paper presented at the American Orthopsychiatric Association Meeting, New York, 1973.

Rutter, M. "Separation Experiences: A New Look at an Old Topic." *Journal of Pediatrics,* 1980, *95,* 147–154.

Rutter, M. "Social-Emotional Consequences of Day Care for Preschool Children." *American Journal of Orthopsychiatry,* 1981, *51* (1), 4-28.

Thomas, A. "Current Trends in Developmental Theory." *American Journal of Orthopsychiatry,* 1981, *51* (4), 580-609.

Tizard, J., Moss, P., and Perry, J. *All Our Children: Preschool Services in a Changing Society.* London: Temple Smith, 1976.

U.S. Department of Health, Education and Welfare Report as cited by the *San Francisco Chronicle,* 4 December 1979.

Wachs, T. D. "Proximal Experience and Early Cognitive-Intellectual Development: The Physical Environment." *Merrill Palmer Quarterly,* 1979, *25* (1), 3–41.

19

Planned Brief Treatment

Elizabeth C. Lemon

The frequently heard statement that "practice reflects the times in which we live" is nowhere more evident than in the increased use by clinical social workers of planned brief treatment. The term *treatment* in this chapter is used generically and covers all forms of clinical social work interventions and nonphysical treatment, including psychodynamically oriented psychotherapy. In the face of reduced funding for agency-based clinical services, a serious effort to provide therapeutic help which best suits the needs and desires of clients and makes optimal use of their motivation for change is being attempted, and a variety of models or designs for brief treatment are being used and tested. Some that prescribe or limit the duration of therapy from the outset are the work of professionals in allied fields, but the rationale underlying all includes many familiar ideas as well as much clinical knowledge derived from more traditional forms of long-term casework and psychotherapy.

Short-term clinical social work, which has its roots in social casework, is not new (Parad, 1971). What is new is the emergence, during the past decade, of a bewildering array of treatment approaches and the introduction of time-limited contracts that are nonnegotiable. Restricting the duration of treatment is an integral part of some psychoanalytically oriented psychotherapies. It is also a significant feature in certain treatment methods designed by social workers, whereby interventions derived from learning theory and behavior modification are used to promote completion of a well-defined task. The allocation of a specific number of treatment sessions—ranging from four to twenty-four, over periods as long as six months—at the beginning of a therapeutic relationship serves many purposes. While this may be anathema to some there is no doubt that it can provide others, practitioners and clients alike, with an unique opportunity to work on a single aspect of problematic functioning. In addition, some time-limited approaches serve to facilitate the work of the researcher and have been designed with this in mind.

The primary aim in much brief casework is to quickly engage clients in problem-solving activity through a transactional approach, a process designed to enhance autonomous functioning and maximize the client's responsibility for treatment outcome. In an effort to identify the implications of these trends for practice and to provide guidelines for the differential use of short-term approaches, the development of the theoretical bases for brief casework and of psychodynamically oriented short-term therapy will be addressed. Although many of the ideas covered will relate to both families and individuals, this chapter will focus on work with the latter.

History of Brief Casework Treatment

Parad (1971), in her comprehensive overview of historical trends in short-term casework, points out that, from its inception, the varying degrees of emphasis given to the length of casework are closely connected to changes in the larger social matrix as well as to the evolution of therapeutic technique. The duration of much casework has always been brief, for example, medical social work is often confined to the period of the client's hospital stay which, in the majority of instances, is limited to a few days or weeks.

In the 1930s and 1940s, with the development of the diagnostic approach based on modifications of psychoanalytic theory and practice, the assumption was that in-depth long-term casework was the only route to lasting personality change. The worker was required to take full responsibility for making a diagnostic assessment and for planning treatment, the rationale being that unless treatment was diagnostically based, the outcome could be destructive to the client. Opposition to this view came from Jessie Taft, founder of what became known as the Functional School of Social Work at the University of Pennsylvania. Influenced by the ideas of Otto Rank, George Mead, and John Dewey, Taft (1949) considered time, with all the separations and new beginnings the passage of time entails, to be a vital casework tool, one that highlights more than anything else the need for both client and worker to accept the limitations of treatment. Taft's writings, together with those of the early functional theorists (Robinson, 1978; Smalley, 1970) on psychological growth and development, have a remarkable contemporary ring, particularly in their view of casework as a "helping process." In this process the relationship is the central factor, a two-way association entered into with an avowed lack of knowledge about how it will turn out "since the answer has not yet been written" (Smalley, 1977, p. 1281). Taft applied this perspective to the single interview, thereby stimulating interest in the potential for psychosocial growth inherent in the short-term contact (Parad, 1971).

A study by the Family Service Association of America (Casius, 1950), designed to promote understanding of the differing philosophies and concepts underlying casework practice, compared the two schools and in so doing helped make clear the areas of divergence. A major point of cleavage between these two systems was the functionalists' adherence to Rank's concept of will. Both groups saw personality development as the interplay of instinctual needs and outer, or environmental, experience. According to functional theory this interaction operates under the direction of an in-born will to individuation and autonomy, out of which the ego (more frequently called the self) emerges. From the beginning of life the function of the will toward individuation allows the person to act purposefully in dealing with inner and outer forces. Working within a specific time frame becomes, therefore, a strategy for mobilizing the will. By contrast, in Freudian theory, the ego, while holding a central position in the psychic structure, contains no such entity as the Rankian concept of will. Instead it is an organizing force whose chief function is to maintain a balance between inner drives, the superego, and the demands of reality. Ego strength is thought by Freudians to vary according to the vicissitudes of personal development.

When Perlman (1957) first wrote about casework as a problem-solving process, she helped to bring closer the knowledge and practice skills developed by the two schools. She did this by borrowing and incorporating "into a psychodynamic base, certain perspectives and actions from the functional school of casework" (Perlman, 1977, p. 1290). The results of Perlman's ideas are now evident in some of the briefer forms of casework and psychotherapy. Crisis-oriented brief treatment, the best-known form, is an amalgam of theoretical concepts drawn from diverse sources, and can be seen to embody some of Perlman's formulations (Rapoport, 1970).

Probably the most widely practiced of the short-term approaches, crisis intervention is still the subject of many misconceptions (Baldwin, 1977). When Lindemann (1944) published his classic study of the survivors of the Coconut Grove fire, he advanced the premise that sequelae to traumatic events could be prevented by immediate psychotherapeutic intervention. His clinical observations on the responses of the survivors experiencing difficulty in grieving the loss of friends and relatives who died in the fire, and the psychological measures he took to prevent pathological reactions, owed much to Freud's (1966) work on mourning and melancholia. Lindemann's later work and the community mental health center he started in 1948 aroused further interest in this phenomenon and more studies followed (Parad, 1977).

The Community Mental Health Service Act of 1963 made the use of preventive intervention and shorter forms of treatment a major priority. Long waiting lists (Shyne, 1957; Perlman, 1963), shortages of professional staff, and the deinstitutionalization of psychiatric in-patients all contributed to a wider acceptance of the crisis-oriented mode, seen then as now as a strategy for enabling individuals and families to cope more effectively during periods of acute stress. The reasoning here was that at such points of high anxiety, treatment could bring about lasting changes in social and psychological functioning (Bloom, 1965). This argument proved particularly persuasive because the notion of "unanticipated stress" offered workers an opportunity to move away from the diagnostic schema—thought by many to concentrate too much on individual pathology—to closer considerations of socially and environmentally induced stress.

Casework writers have defined a state of crisis as "an upset in a steady state," identified by the presence of two additional factors, one external and the other internal: (1) a hazardous event, and (2) a fluid ego (Rapoport, 1962). Emotional crises of this type were considered to be self-limiting, lasting approximately four to six weeks (Rapoport, 1970). It was assumed that when someone's repertoire of coping mechanisms proves inadequate to deal with sudden and unanticipated changes in the environment, that person's anxiety mounts until the tension can no longer be tolerated. This is the turning point, at which the person makes some type of adaptation in order to bring about a measure of relief. The danger of a maladaptive reaction occurring is high when ego functions are restricted or impaired—particularly if family and other support systems are not available—yet at such times people are readier to seek help and more likely to use it effectively. It follows, therefore, that less therapeutic time would be needed to facilitate optimal adaptation provided the goal was confined to restoring emotional equilibrium through enabling the client to deal more effectively with the changes that have occurred. Once this goal is achieved, treatment could be terminated since there may be no further motivation for change on the client's part.

This philosophy of short-term treatment gained added currency through recognition of the fact that former unresolved or partially resolved traumas were usually reactivated during a state of crisis, thereby affording an opportunity for their reworking in parallel with the client's efforts to gain increased mastery of present circumstances. The emphasis here is on coping with current reality through the use of cognitive and conflict-free functions of the ego, and enlisting the ego's capacity for adapting to the "average expectable environment" (Hartmann, 1939; Rapoport, 1971). Stated differently, crisis-oriented treatment offered a possibility for restoring or improving psychosocial functioning in ways that were compatible with the secondary and tertiary levels of prevention as practiced in the field of public health.

Problems of Definition

Following the educational impact of community mental health services, the public is now more aware of the emotional hazards inherent in both anticipated and unanticipated stressful events and the challenges these provide. The term *psychosocial transition* is now commonly used to describe the changes such events demand in "one's assumptive world" and the emotional disequilibrium this can produce (Parkes, 1971, pp. 101, 103). Examples would be bereavement (Parkes, 1972; Pincus, 1975), surgery (Brown, 1971), divorce (Loewenstein, 1979), and rape (McCombie, 1980). In fact, the range of inner and outer stresses subsumed under the concept of psychosocial transition now covers "any major change which creates the need for the individual to restructure his ways of looking at the world and his plans for living in it" (Parkes, 1971), thereby broadening its scope and making it a synonym for crisis. However, because of its dramatic quality it is likely that the word *crisis* will continue to be a popular metaphor for any type of emotional upset touched off by identifiable changes, regardless of their source and nature. When faced with disruption in their lives more and more people are turning to clinical social workers and other psychotherapists for answers to certain critical questions: "What can I know?" "How can I act?" and "From whom shall I take my values?" (Stierlin, 1980). These questions, which frequently stem from concerns about personal identity and the meaning and purpose of life, arise when individuals are faced with the need to accommodate to changes in the environment, those due to loss of physical functioning, and changes due to maturational development.

As public awareness mounts, the number of identifiable stressors continues to increase and it becomes more difficult to differentiate crisis treatment from casework which is problem-oriented. A model with multiple roots and many heads creates ambiguity for practitioners and researchers because of the all-purpose nature of the definition. Golan (1978), in a comprehensive work on the treatment of situational crises, attempts to bring some order to the subject when she lists the various categories of crises according to the nature of the problem situation and the precipitating factor which leads the client to come for help. Golan renders additional service by first defining and then making useful distinctions between various kinds of stress such as that touched off by accidental, maturational, and other more predictable events.

Marmor (1979) distinguishes between an emergency and a crisis. He considers an emergency to exist when a person cannot cope at all and there is total breakdown in functioning that requires immediate relief. This may include psychiatric hospitalization or tangible support services such as financial aid or child-care. The person in a crisis, on the other hand, according to Marmor, is coping, but poorly, and the situation or condition is likely to get worse unless stress is reduced or the person is helped to manage it better. The value of this distinction is not immediately apparent and the two terms tend to be used interchangeably. In practice, numerous services operate under the rubric of crisis intervention—"hot lines," self-help, and other support groups, as well as emergency services and agencies offering the more traditional types of counseling, psychotherapy, and social casework—making an accurate definition harder to come by. Emergencies are never static; their duration at the time is unknown and appropriate action may quickly proceed from the immediate provision of tangible relief and other anxiety-relieving measures to crisis-oriented psychotherapy. Thus, attempting to classify according to the service initially provided does not help. Also, it seems that in most emergency situations involving an acute emotional crisis, important aspects of the personality may be obscured and people appear less capable than they are, or more so, depending on whether they experience their situation as a threat, a loss, or a challenge (Rapoport, 1970). In any case, a more open approach without a definite treatment plan may be in order, with flexible scheduling of appointments until the worker and client are clearer about the need for additional help.

Planned short-term psychodynamic psychotherapy, on the other hand, is more likely to deal with individuals in conflict but not necessarily in crisis, although a crisis may have been instrumental in bringing them into therapy. The primary goal of this type of treatment is that of "modifying" the patient's coping patterns (Marmor, 1979; Sifneos, 1972). Thus the patient's anxiety tolerance and the extent and availability of family and other supports are decisive factors in assessing whether ameliorative measures need to be taken. The boundaries between short-term psychotherapy and crisis-oriented work are not well drawn and there is much overlapping so that differences are largely a matter of emphasis. Theoretically, crisis-oriented casework is of briefer duration, sharply concentrated on the immediate situation, and ending when emotional equilibrium is regained. But, in fact, extensions occur and treatment continues for various reasons—for example, if the repercussions from a hazardous event persist, as with the birth of a severely handicapped infant whose life may be threatened through repeated surgery (Greenburg, 1979). Work can sometimes proceed beyond the point at which mastery of the presenting problem is established, because of the desire to consolidate gains or to work on other less pressing and more longstanding difficulties. When this happens progress is usually slower and less dramatic.

This prolonging of treatment has given rise to doubts about the usefulness of the crisis model as a base for short-term work, and the practitioner is prompted to ask what distinguishes crisis-oriented treatment from the more traditional forms of casework (Lukton, 1974). Strict time-limited models have developed out of attempts to avoid this kind of confusion. The task-centered system (Reid, 1978), incorporating some of Parad's and Rapoport's ideas about crisis, is perhaps the most widely deployed. Designed to capitalize on the client's "short-lived" motivation for change, the contract for task-centered work is limited to from six to twelve interviews over a period of two to four months.

Task-Centered Casework

Since its inception eight years ago, this empirically developed system has been tested and refined several times (Reid and Epstein, 1972, 1974; Reid, 1978; Epstein, 1980). The task-centered model, which consists of a tight set of guidelines and directives, was a consequence of Reid's earlier research (Reid and Shyne, 1969) on brief and extended casework, and was originally designed for use by B.S.W.s. It has since been tested by first-year M.S.W. students and by experienced social work clinicians. A new approach to old problems, it owes much to casework's central tradition, namely, to Perlman's (1957) notion of a problem-solving process and to Hollis's (1972) classification of casework procedures. It also borrows from Smalley's (1970) work on the use of time limits. What is new about task-centered casework is its design—a pragmatic blueprint calling for partialization of the problem into clearly delineated tasks to be addressed consecutively. This treatment is now accepted as appropriate for the client who is able to acknowledge a precise psychosocial problem the solution to which can be confined to a specific change in behavior or a change of circumstances. The client is further required to be willing to work on the designated problem or to agree to the worker doing so on his or her behalf. For research purposes, Reid has listed the problems as follows: "(1) interpersonal conflicts; (2) dissatisfaction with social relations; (3) relations with formal organizations; (4) difficulties with role performance; (5) decision problems; (6) reactive emotional distress; (7) inadequate social resources; (8) psychological and behavior problems not elsewhere classified; and (9) other and unclassifiable" (Reid, 1978, p. 309).

During intake or assessment the focus is on helping the client identify the problem that is of primary concern. The sequence of events leading to, and succeeding, the problem are explored and clarified. Specific tasks are expected to evolve from this process, and consideration is given to how, in ideal circumstances, the client would like to see the difficulties resolved. Reid would prefer the assessment to be completed in the first interview, at which point a contract should be made. In actuality, this phase usually consists of one to four interviews, including contacts with collaterals, and lasts one to two weeks. Reid (1978) cautions: "To the extent that he follows the model, the practitioner does not offer advice, provide explanations of the client's behavior, or indulge in other forms of change-oriented efforts before a contract is reached" (p. 114). If, after systematic review, a target problem meeting Reid's criteria cannot be agreed upon, then task-centered casework is deemed inappropriate.

In the earliest version, treatment concentrated almost entirely on enabling the client to follow the agreed agenda (Reid and Epstein, 1972), with the worker free to use whatever means were considered most effective in helping to achieve this. A recent protocol with more detailed instructions (Reid, 1978; Epstein, 1980) emphasizes practitioner-client communication and behavioral modes. Task-centered casework now requires that activity be systemized in such a way that the worker responds only to the behavior expected to facilitate completion of the agreed course of action. Reid's (1978) revisions reflect his attempts to establish a practice framework that is midway between psychoanalytically oriented treatment and behaviorism, one which views man as "less a prisoner of his unconscious drives than he is in the theories of psychoanalysis, and less a prisoner of environmental contingencies than he is in the view of the behaviorist" (p. 19). More weight is now given to the collaborative nature of treatment than to technique. The relationship between worker and client is expected to be "of the kind considered fundamental in most forms of interpersonal practice." The evidence suggests, however, that task-centered work differs from other forms of casework in that it involves more direct advice giving on the part of the worker (p. 87).

Guidelines for the final treatment session are planned so as to leave the client in a positive state of mind, but no provision is included for relating to any disappointment or ambivalence he or she might feel about the outcome of treatment. The penultimate session is used to formulate the last set of tasks to be worked on. Ideally, these should be repetitions or modest extensions of former successfully completed tasks. In the final interview those achievements that have accrued since the last session are reviewed and overall progress is assessed in relation to the designated problem. At this time, if necessary, plans are made and directions are given for the client to continue working on "the problem," through applying knowledge acquired during treatment. Particular attention is given to what has been attained to date, and this achievement is used to reinforce the client's sense of mastery. Extensions of up to four sessions can be offered in order to complete work agreed on, or a further contract may be negotiated if additional problems have arisen. In some instances new contracts may, at the client's request, be open-ended, that is, *not* time-limited, but according to Reid the research evidence does not favor frequent dispositions of this kind.

While agreeing that traditional casework can achieve the same goals as task-centered treatment, Reid argues in favor of the latter. He cites the work of Goldstein (1973), who states that there is a good deal of support for the idea that most "lower-class" clients, who form the bulk of many caseloads, prefer structure and direction and a treatment approach that emphasizes action. Goldstein attributes this to educational limitations, cognitive style, and the harsh realities of "lower-class living." The greatest concern of this group is a lack of tangible resources, a problem particularly suited to direct action by the client or the helping agency.

Commenting on Ewalt's (1977) work, Reid remarks that, while mental tasks can be used for purposes of reflection, this is not encouraged. Reflective techniques may be employed to aid clients in examining their beliefs about themselves and their situations, but this is not an integral part of the framework. When these techniques are adopted, they are "always part of a larger focused action strategy" (Reid, 1978, p. 87). By contrast, Mann's (1973) model of time-limited psychotherapy, which is also highly structured but in a different way as will be seen below, utilizes the therapeutic relationship to promote reflection and introspection.

Time-Limited Psychotherapy

This psychodynamically oriented approach was devised by a psychoanalyst to meet the needs of people attending an out-patient psychiatric clinic. Founded on the temporal considerations of the functionalists and certain theories of Mahler (1963), specifically her work on separation/individuation, Mann's therapy addresses the patient's emotional reactions to a strictly time-limited process that makes optimal use of the role of the doctor-patient relationship. Contracts are restricted to twelve hours of direct treatment. Confining the length of therapy to a fixed number of hours, rather than a number of sessions, allows for flexibility in the spacing and length of interviews. For instance, a patient might be offered hourly sessions twice weekly for six weeks, or weekly half-hour sessions for a period of twenty-four weeks. In practice, twelve one-hour weekly appointments is the most common format. The times and dates of each session are scheduled before therapy begins, so the patient is aware in advance of the termination date. An agreement is also reached at the outset on the management of cancellations and missed appointments.

Mann's time-limited therapy focuses on derivatives of what he considers to be a universal problem originating in childhood. It is his belief that the presenting difficulty, whatever it may be, can be traced to conflicts around such issues as self-esteem, dependency, passitivity, or unresolved grief arising from complications in the separation/individuation phase of normal development. To quote Mann: "The recurring life crisis of separation/individuation is the substantive base on which treatment rests" (1973, p. 24).

A decision on the patient's suitability for this type of treatment is usually made at the end of the first interview. If there is any doubt, Mann advises that the evaluation be extended. The therapist shares his or her findings and recommendations in a way that conveys an empathic understanding of the person's distress, a procedure which "brings the patient closer to the therapist" (Mann, 1973, p. 18). This is reassuring to most patients, but it reactivates the timeless wishes and fantasies of childhood, together with the expectations that these will, at last, be met. Mann stays with the patient's affect throughout the treatment and, at the same time, he refuses to digress from the central dynamic of separation/individuation which is the cornerstone of his therapy. If subsequent data and insight lead to doubts about the suitability of this form of treatment for a particular patient, the therapist must be prepared to change course or amend the contract. Resistance is not prominent during the early stages of the relationship since the security of having a set number of sessions to look forward to, plus the therapist's acceptance of the patient's difficulties, fosters the impression that if the instructions are followed like a prescription, a "cure" will follow. During this period the patient's hope for relief is reinforced and anxiety-related symptoms and problems tend to diminish. Interestingly, when the passage of time is commented upon by the therapist, both at the beginning and end of each interview, patients generally do not pay much attention. It is in the second phase of therapy, between the fifth and eighth interview, when expectations of a magical "cure" are not fulfilled, that some disillusionment occurs. The patient's characteristic attempts to cope with such feelings are explored and interpreted. Disappointment with the therapist is made conscious and becomes the center of attention.

With the beginning of the final phase, the reality of impending termination can no longer be avoided. Old patterns of reacting to separation and loss appear, and are dealt with directly by the therapist. As the patient is helped to confront these responses in the interview, basic conflicts are reexperienced in a conscious way: "The genetic source of these affects is relived in the disappointing termination and separation from the therapist to whom the patient has become attached" (Mann, 1973, p. 35). It is essential here to provide an opportunity for examination of feelings and fantasies around termination and to assist the patient in linking them to the presenting problem.

Mann's aim is to provide for the patient a "corrective emotional experience"—a term devised some years ago by Alexander (1946) and since incorporated into social casework theory by Austin (1948), Allan (1963, 1974), Garrett (1958), and Hollis (1972). The main difference between these writers and Mann lies in the latter's concentration on planned time limits and the stress he puts on helping the patient, through interpretation and clarification, to accept the pain associated with termination and to relate this pain to past experiences and present difficulties.

The nonnegotiable nature of Mann's time-limited contract, is certain to precipitate an emotional crisis as termination approaches because the patient is unable to avoid or deal effectively with the emotions evoked by the ending of a valued association at a point when difficulties remain. Working through conflicts in the context of an empathic liason facilitates the substitution of the "good" therapist for earlier and ambivalently held inner-object representations. This is achieved by interpreting the anger and guilt transferred to the therapist from significant others in the patient's past. Termination thus becomes a maturational event which improves self-esteem and raises the capacity for independent functioning.

As distinct from other models of brief psychotherapy which accentuate cognitive functioning as well as the ability to benefit from therapeutic experience (Sifneos, 1972; Malan, 1976), Mann's selection criteria stipulate neither intellectual prowess nor motivation for change. Only people too disorganized to keep regular appointments or those who are actively psychotic, severely depressed, or diagnosed as having borderline personality disorders are screened out. Some borderline personalities are, however, thought to be appropriate, but Mann does not specify how they are chosen. It would seem that those people most likely to act out negative emotions under the stress of termination are considered unsuitable. Since a certain amount of dependence and regression is fostered by the positive transference, brief time-limited treatment is well suited for people with marked passive-dependent traits (Lemon and Goldstein, 1978; Burke, White, and Havens, 1979). Finally, turning from patient to therapist, Mann cautions that this treatment mode is not for the untrained or inexperienced, since the crisis of termination can be distressing for both patient and clinician.

Matching Patient and Therapy

The guides for practice that are put forward by proponents of brief treatment frequently overlap, leaving the individual practitioner with many questions, the most obvious being: Which approach for which client? In a paper on the subject, Burke, White, and Havens (1979) propose a set of indexes based on developmental phases of the adult life cycle, to assist psychodynamically oriented therapists in matching patient and strategy. Three principal classes of therapy are selected in keeping with treatment emphasis and technical considerations: interpretive, correctional, and existential. Mann's model, according to this classification, is seen as primarily existential, and therefore wide-ranging: "Much like Alexander's corrective therapy, Mann's time-limited method seeks to correct the residual effects of unsatisfactory childhood relationships. In Mann's model, however, the conflict is seen as more basic and more universal and a wider group of patients can be treated. Mann also chooses a different therapeutic style because he assumes that an empathic encounter that mirrors the patient's life situation will be sufficient to provide the corrective experience" (Burke, White, and Havens, 1979, p. 180). This schema considers Mann's existential approach to be most effective with passive-dependent patients who have not mastered the classic adolescent conflict, "identity vs. role confusion" (Erikson, 1963, p. 261), a developmental milestone seen as analogous to the separation/individuation phase of childhood and called "early adult transition" by Levinson (1977, pp. 102–103).

"Interpretive" forms of short-term therapy, specifically those of Malan (1976) and Sifneos (1972), are thought the most beneficial for hysterical patients whose normative life task is defined as "intimacy vs. isolation," a stage Erikson locates in early adulthood. While some differences exist between the approaches of Malan and Sifneos, their similarities are more apparent. Both take the same care to select people who are articulate, highly motivated, and quick learners with a history of at least one "meaningful relationship" in their lives. These patients are expected to identify a focal problem and be able to tolerate an anxiety-provoking relationship. Treatment is focused on unconscious conflict, however manifested. A measure of psychological sophistication is a prerequisite for Sifneos's short-term, anxiety-provoking psychotherapy (termed STAPP) because the therapist assumes the role of a detached and unemotional instructor in psychodynamics, confronting and interpreting the patient's defensive maneuvers to avoid self-knowledge. Malan's style is less directive, but is similarly based on an interpretive teaching stance, and he uses the same criteria as Sifneos for choosing patients.

People who are encountering the typical problems of mid-life or mid-adulthood, portrayed by Erikson as the crisis of "generativity vs. stagnation," are thought to be best served by a "corrective therapeutic experience" formulated by Alexander (1946), provided they are relatively well adjusted and functioning on a not less than neurotic level. At this point in the life cycle the concerns of such patients bear upon such matters as personal achievement, the reassessment of life goals, and intellectual and emotional needs and capacities. Such preoccupations tend to reactivate old doubts and conflicts, which in turn interfere with decisions regarding future plans. To call attention to thoughts and feelings about the past is unlikely to prove helpful at a time when the person is looking for guidance in deciding the future direction of his or her life. For this group the optimal therapeutic effect of short-term therapy is expected to come via transference manipulations and a managerial attitude on the part of the therapist.

Burke, White, and Havens, in their formulations, require the clinician to make a careful developmental assessment of the patient prior to treatment. Elements of each life crisis can be found in everyone so it is important to distinguish those features causing distress in the current context. Many clinicians, faced with an array of short-term approaches, find attractive the notion of choosing a particular mode of brief treatment in accord with the individual's (Erikson, 1963) or the family's (Zilbach, 1968) life stage. To date, however, Burke, White, and Havens have considered only three life stages in this regard: early adulthood, adulthood, and mid-life. Of greater significance to clinical social work is the fact that, Mann's model apart, this developmentally based system relates only to people with well-contained neurotic conflicts, who presumably possess adequate economic and social resources. Agency-based clinicians, with cases from different socioeconomic, ethnic, and age groups, are unlikely to adhere to one particular model. With primary regard for the worker-client relationship, social work practitioners are more apt to select from a flexible range of techniques and interventions for meeting the desires and needs of a diverse clientele, always bearing in mind the context of the client's life circumstances.

Mann's time-limited psychotherapy, crisis-oriented casework, and Reid's task-centered system, taken together, offer the worker a useful framework for this purpose. The crisis-oriented model illuminates the way in which anxiety interferes with cognitive functioning and problem solving. The task-centered system provides a practical format for outlining feasible treatment goals and for defining the units of work to be completed in order to achieve these goals. Regardless of the approach, it is the relationship that buttresses, stimulates, and facilitates the client's effort to surmount impediments that stand in the way of meeting his or her objectives. The over-riding value in Mann's contribution lies in his sense of the therapist-client relationship as a continuously changing bond, one that is repeatedly influenced by the limits of time and by the goals being pursued.

Relationship, Communication, and Brief Treatment

In her writing, Perlman (1979) terms relationship "the heart of helping people." She goes on to deplore the fact that the term is currently suffering from neglect at the hands of people who ought to know better: "At a time—now—when 'meaningful relationship' and 'good communication' appear to be highly valued in our society, wanted and eagerly sought in everyday life by most of us, there has been short-shrift given to the recognition of the uses of relationship in the human services. Even in social work, a field in which for many years both theory and practice placed strong and consistent emphasis on the need for a sense of bonding between helper and help-seeker—even there—the literature of the past decade has given the subject scant notice" (p. 2).

The capacity for forming relationships is contingent upon the development of emotional attachments; Perlman illustrates this by pointing to caretakers and other attachment figures as models that influence a person's evolving capacities for future relationships. She stresses that it is the quality of past and present relationships that influence the individual's interpersonal and person-to-task competencies and gratifications. She also makes clear the way in which a professional relationship can become a catalyst, or an enabling factor, when it is used to free the client's energies and foster his or her motivation toward problem solving.

In extending this theme, which supports Mann's position that relationship is a vital component in any emotionally corrective experience, Perlman says that specific aspects of relationship, such as empathy and communication, are now stressed to the neglect of the "how, when, and what." How, for example, does a professional relationship influence a person's desire to work toward changing one's self or one's situation? What are the factors in a client's initial encounter with a worker that quickly promote and sustain a working alliance? These questions are as vital to brief or task-centered work as to any other form of treatment—perhaps more so in view of the time restrictions.

It is instructive to note that such questions have, in the main, proved to be beyond the scope of research, but there seems to be a growing appreciation among behaviorists and others, Reid included, that the role played by relationship in any helping process cannot be ignored (Perlman, 1979; Margolin and Golden, 1974; Schwartz and Goldiamond, 1975).

On the subject of communications, Anderson (1979) views psychodynamics and communication theories as complementary. While there is no general agreement about the meaning of the term "communication," she points to the fact that most schools of psychotherapy claim to help people communicate better. Communication takes place on many levels, and the complexities of this phenomenon are evidenced by the number of theories that seek to explain it. Anderson cites some (1978): "There are theories of general systems, information, balance, symbolic interaction, and many others (Dance and Lance, 1976; Littlejohn, 1978; Meerloo, 1967; Swanson and Delia, 1976; Sereno and Mortenson, 1970). Some of these theories focus entirely on external processes, assuming a black-box concept of input and output (Watzlawick, Beaver, and Jackson, 1967), while others are concerned with meaning and motivation (Hewitt, 1976)" (p. 91).

All the above theories focus on the interactional and circular nature of communication, a phenomenon that cannot be analyzed apart from the idiosyncratic meanings attributed to messages by both sender and receiver. In looking at the potential value of these complex ideas for clinical social work, Anderson continues (1978): "Each communication, verbal and nonverbal, will occur on at least two levels simultaneously: the report or content level, and the command or relationship level. The report level conveys information while the command level tells how the message is to be taken and therefore defines the relationship. . . . While information is important, the relationship level is equally important, if not more so" (p. 95).

Psychodynamic theory has illuminated the way in which emotions affect psychosocial and biological functioning. Communication theories have given us a new slant on how messages can be influenced by the rules and values of the social systems in which they occur. Empathic understanding of the client's anxiety, fears, and concerns, provide the emotional glue that bonds client and worker, supporting the former through the vicissitudes of the problem-solving process. Monitoring the content and patterns of communication makes clearer the points at which the client or family is "stuck," and throws light on the "critical identity images" which messages are designed to maintain (Kantor, 1980).

Whatever their theoretical position, all writers and practitioners agree that in short-term work it is essential to avoid the client's regressing. It is well known that any relationship which is experienced as benign and understanding inevitably evokes some dependent yearnings on the part of the client. In short-term contacts these are contained in a variety of ways—for instance, by reinforcing the client's cognitive understanding of the working nature of the relationship. This does not necessarily exclude acknowledgment of the client's feelings but requires that they be addressed in relation to the core problem or the task at hand. In this way resistance is not ignored and the client is given the opportunity to make connections between his or her feelings and the problem being worked on.

Treatment Contracts

Social work literature, over the past decade, shows the effort being made to bring greater specificity to the goals and focus of social work practice in general through the use of contracts (Maluccio, 1974; Seabury, 1974; Rothery, 1980). This development has had a salutory effect on the profession by indirectly encouraging more frequent reviews of objectives and progress in longer-term and open-ended casework and by making clinicians more aware of time as a factor in accountability. It has also helped to establish brief treatment as an important form of psychosocial therapy, one which is preferred by many clients.

Most writers agree that while it is not a substitute for the long-term work necessary for the alleviation of many chronic difficulties, planned brief treatment is effective for circumscribed conditions and problems. Unfortunately, it is a feature of our age that decisions as to whether treatment is to be short or time-limited, or long-term and open-ended, are often made on the basis of time and money rather than an evaluation of the client's needs and wishes.

An initial understanding of the client's request, the presenting problem, and the client's bio/psycho/social functioning, should be preliminary to any clinical social work intervention (Cohen, 1980). In much short-term work, the initial assessment underlying a treatment contract tends to be confined to a grasp of the client's current problem/situation, some knowledge of why he or she cannot deal unaided with this situation, and a judgment on the client's potential for resolving it more effectively with the worker's help.

The evaluation process is influenced by three things: the clinician's theoretical orientation, the social institutions that impinge on the clinician's particular field of practice, and the client's ability to relate. There are many agencies, medical settings in particular, where people are often referred to social services without any clear idea of how a social worker might help them. In such instances a good deal of reaching out may be necessary before any working alliance or mutually agreed-upon definition of the problem can be arrived at. Brief treatment, whatever the approach, is based on the rapid development of a positive working alliance. This is promoted by enabling the client to tell his or her story, at a comfortable pace, in the way the client feels and understands it. All diagnostic formulations undergo refinement and modification throughout the process of treatment, whatever the conditions of the contract, and the practitioner should be prepared to revise these conditions whenever new understandings of the client's problem or changes in that person's life circumstances emerge.

When introduced, the briefer forms of casework, particularly those which are task-oriented, appeared antithetical to longer-term, open-ended work. Subsequent developments in the task-centered system and an increased use of renegotiable contracts by social workers in general have reduced some of the disparities between long- and short-term treatment. To ensure informed choice and optimal client autonomy, careful attention is now being given to making clear such crucial factors as the expected roles and responsibilities of the parties involved and the objectives and limits of treatment. This clarification process is geared to the client's cognitive style and is a recurring feature of the treatment sessions.

To predict accurately the length of time needed for a client to complete a specific piece of work is still not possible, and hard data on treatment outcome is difficult to find. Mann acknowledges that his twelve hours of treatment time were chosen to meet the training needs of psychiatric residents during a period of long waiting lists. Sifneos's time frame evolved from similar considerations. In practice, after these seemingly arbitrary arrangements had been in operation for some time, it was found that they could, when combined with a carefully spelled out contract, be an aid to the treatment of clients with weak ego boundaries (Oberman, 1967; Briggs, 1979). Conversely, and less surprisingly, the procedure also proved efficacious for others less vulnerable to both social and psychological stress (Sifneos, 1972). There is mounting agreement about the value of time-limited contracts, but because this type of planned brief treatment is relatively new and because there are unknown factors in every situation, the worker must decide at the outset of each case whether the agreement is to be renegotiable. In other words, a most important evaluative decision needs to be reached on whether or not to plan for the possible emergence, during treatment, of unanticipated developments.

There are two sides to the problem. A contact that is non-negotiable restricts both client and worker in their modus operandi, and it intensifies reactions to termination, especially when expectations of either party have not been met. The client's sense of the worker's ability to help in the time allotted is influenced by the client's knowing, at the outset, that an extension may be necessary. Some therapists, such as Oberman in working with borderline personalities, inform the client that sessions may continue beyond the time allotted if so indicated, otherwise regular appointments will cease. Mann does not allow for such provision. In his judgment, those to whom he offers his form of time-limited therapy need to experience the manner in which their difficulties with separation/individuation contribute to their presenting problem.

The clinician's avoidance of termination, with all the feelings this evokes on both sides, is thought by Mann to be a major reason for prolonging unproductive therapy. Precise time-limited arrangements do not rule out, for worker or client, the wish to extend the contact, nor do they preclude either from having strong feelings about ending the relationship. When the termination date is predetermined, the impending end may be experienced as a threat, a challenge, or a loss, rather than as a joint decision by worker and client that treatment goals have been reached. As Shafer (1973) has indicated, the potential for almost every significant human emotion resides in the termination situation. Feelings of gratitude, triumph, deprivation, guilt, unworthiness, anger, disappointment, and defeat are common during the final sessions of any treatment.

Since few of the client's feelings are likely to be consciously available in the short time remaining, it is important that the worker be alert to those that are accessible. When the original agreement is perceived as binding and non-negotiable, emotions accompanying termination are easier to rationalize, and this makes it more difficult for the client to voice negative reactions, such as disappointment in treatment outcome (Miller, 1977). The practitioner's skill in recognizing, eliciting, and responding therapeutically to such reactions is, to a large degree, dependent upon acceptance of one's own limitations as a therapist, the limitations of brief treatment as a helping process, and the therapist's willingness to settle for what has been achieved. The latter point, necessary in bringing the client to a fuller appreciation of the gains that have been made, is best addressed after negative or sad feelings relative to termination have been acknowledged and discussed. If negative responses are not dealt with at this time it is possible that the client may feel invalidated or rejected.

Due to factors beyond the control of either worker or client, a good deal of treatment now being offered is of brief duration. Experience shows that there are numerous practitioners and clients who prefer this type of help. For them the goals of short-term work are more feasible and beneficial than those of lengthier work that aims to change well-entrenched patterns of behavior. The therapeutic relationship apart, there are obvious and important differences between the two modes of treatment. The first is more likely to be used to cope more effectively with a single event or its consequences, in a way which is economical, practical, and almost technical in its pragmatism. The second is looser and more costly, a long-term investment concerned mainly with working toward the goal of personality change. At first sight these two points of view seem to have little in common. On closer examination, a third approach which combines elements of both seems to be emerging. This is due in some measure to the restrictions of third-party payers, such as insurance companies, that limit the amount of reimbursement allowed each year for certain services—a factor which strongly influences the length of treatment at any one time for many clients.

Whether the first experience of professional help is long or short, if successful, the client is more likely to seek further treatment during periods of severe or unusual stress. And, if free to do so, that client will be inclined to return to the same worker, already identified as helpful and trustworthy. This sequence changes the concept of treatment as a relationship that has a precise beginning and end. Agreeing to the client's coming back at a later date, should the need arise, may cushion the impact of the termination process, but it does not exclude or deny it. As Taft (1949) reminds us, life is replete with new beginnings and endings, and these may occur equally with the same professional helper, and in fact often do.

Such a compromise model would appear to move toward the old style practice of the family physician—now greatly missed—who could be counted on to provide service when it was needed. Implicit in this philosophy of treatment is a greater acceptance of the arbitrary and unpredictable nature of many of life's psychosocial, as well as biological, ills. It does not assume there is any permanent immunity from them, but it does suggest that one imperfect answer is a readiness to give help when needed even though this may be of limited duration. The paradox here is that intermittent treatment could lead to the formation of much longer relationships, based, it is hoped, on a healthy dependency. With appropriate assistance clients will return for treatment only after they have exhausted their own resources, including those of the family.

There are signs that this third model has already entered the realm of practice in some quarters (Sobel, 1980), pointing to the fact that there are times when usage precedes and sometimes shapes theory.

References

Alexander, and others. *Psychoanalytic Therapy.* New York: Ronald Press, 1946.

Allan, E. F. "The Super-Ego in Ego Supportive Casework Treatment." *Smith College Studies in Social Work,* June 1963, *33* (3), 117–191.

Allan, E. F. "Psychoanalytic Theory." In F. J. Turner (Ed.), *Social Work Treatment—Interlocking Theoretical Approaches.* New York: Free Press, 1974.

Anderson, C. M. "Family Communication: Words, Messages and Meanings." *Smith College Studies in Social Work,* 1979, *49* (2), 91–110.

Austin, L. N. "Trends in Differential Treatment in Social Casework." *Social Casework,* June 1948, *29,* 203–211.

Baldwin, B. A. "Crisis Intervention in Professional Practice: Implications for Clinical Training." *American Journal of Orthopsychiatry,* 1977, *47* (4), 659–670.

Bloom, B. L. "Definitional Aspects of the Crisis Concept." In H. J. Parad (Ed.), *Crisis Intervention: Selected Readings.* New York: Family Service Association of America, 1965.

Briggs, D. "The Trainee and the Borderline Client: Countertransference Pitfalls." *Clinical Social Work Journal,* 1979, *7,* 133–146.

Brown, E. C., Jr. "Casework with Patients Undergoing Cardiac Surgery." *Social Casework,* 1971, *52,* 611–616.

Burke, J. D., White, H. S., and Havens, L. L. "Which Short-Term Therapy?" *Archives of General Psychiatry,* February 1979, *36* (2), 177–186.

Casius, C. *A Comparison of Diagnostic and Functional Casework Concepts.* New York: Family Service Association of America, 1950.

Cohen, J. "The Nature of Clinical Social Work." In P. L. Ewalt (Ed.), *Toward a Definition of Clinical Social Work.* Washington, D.C.: National Association of Social Workers, 1980.

Dance, F.E.X. and Lance, C. E. *The Function of Human Communication: A Theoretical Approach.* New York: Holt, Rinehart and Winston, 1976.

Epstein, L. *Helping People: The Task-Centered Approach.* St. Louis, Mo.: Mosby, 1980.

Erikson, E. H. *Childhood and Society.* New York: Norton, 1963.

Ewalt, P. L. "A Psychoanalytically Oriented Child Guidance Setting." In W. J. Reid and L. Epstein (Eds.), *Task-Centered Practice.* New York: Columbia University Press, 1977.

Field, M. H. "Social Casework Practice During the 'Psychiatric Deluge.'" *Social Service Review,* 1980, *54* (4), 482–507.

Freud, S. "Mourning and Melancholia." In J. Strachey (Ed.), *The Complete Psychological Works of Sigmund Freud.* Vol. 14. London: Hogarth Press. (Originally published 1925.)

Garrett, A. "The Worker/Client Relationship." In H. J. Parad (Ed.), *Ego Psychology and Dynamic Casework.* New York: Family Service Association of America, 1958.

Golan, N. *Treatment in Crisis Situations.* New York: Free Press, 1978.

Goldstein, A. P. *Structural Learning Therapy.* New York: Academic Press, 1973.

Greenberg, D. H. "Parental Reactions to an Infant with a Birth Defect." Unpublished doctoral dissertation, School of Social Work, Smith College, Northampton, Mass., 1979.

Hartmann, H. "Psychoanalysis and the Concept of Health." In *Essays on Ego Psychology.* New York: International Universities Press, 1964.

Hewitt, J. P. *Self and Society: A Symbolic Interactionist View.* Boston: Allyn & Bacon, 1976.

Hollis, F. *Casework: A Psychosocial Therapy.* (2nd ed.) New York: Random House, 1972.

Kantor, D. "Critical Identity Image: A Concept Linking Individual, Couple, and Family Development." In J. K. Pearce and L. J. Freedman (Eds.), *Family Therapy Combining Psychodynamic and Family Systems Approaches.* New York: Grune & Stratton, 1980.

Lemon, E. C., and Goldstein, S. "The Use of Time Limits in Planned Brief Casework." *Social Casework,* 1978, *59* (10), 588–596.

Levinson, D. J. "The Mid-Life Transition: A Period of Adult Psychosocial Development." *Psychiatry,* 1977, *40,* 99–112.

Lindemann, E. "Symptomatology and Management of Acute Grief." In H. J. Parad (Ed.), *Crisis Intervention: Selected Readings.* New York: Family Service Association of America, 1976, pp.7–21. (Originally published in *American Journal of Psychiatry,* 1944, *101.*)

Littlejohn, S. W. *Theories of Human Communication.* Columbus, Ohio: Merrill, 1978.

Loewenstein, S. F. "Helping Family Members Cope with Divorce." In S. Eisenberg and L. E. Patterson (Eds.), *Helping Clients with Special Concerns.* Chicago: Rand McNally, 1979.

Lukton, R. "Crisis Theory: Review and Critique." *Social Service Review,* 1974, *48* (3), 384–402.

Mahler, M. "Thoughts About Development and Individuals." *Psychoanalytic Study of the Child,* New York: International Universities Press, 1963.

Malan, D. H. *The Frontier of Brief Psychotherapy: An Example of the Convergence of Research and Clinical Practice.* New York: Premium Medicine, 1976.

Maluccio, A. N., and Marlow, W. D. "The Case for the Contract." *Social Work,* 1974, *19* (1), 28–36.

Mann, J. *Time-Limited Psychotherapy.* Cambridge, Mass.: Harvard University Press, 1973.

Margolin, M. H. and Goldman, S. "Beyond Reinforcement: Integrating Relationship and Behavior Therapy." *Clinical Social Work Journal,* 1974, *2* (2), 96–104.

Marmor, J. "Short-Term Dynamic Psychotherapy." *American Journal of Psychiatry,* 1979, *136* (2), 149–155.

McCombie, S. (Ed.). *The Rape Crisis Intervention Handbook—A Guide for Victim Care.* New York: Plenum Press, 1980.

Meerloo, J.A.M. "Contributions of Psychiatry to the Study of Human Communication." In F.E.X. Dance (Ed.), *Human Communication Theory.* New York: Holt, Rinehart and Winston, 1970.

Miller, R. R. "Disappointment in Therapy: A Paradox." *Clinical Social Work Journal,* 1977, *5,* 17-28.

Oberman, E. "The Use of Time-Limited Relationship Therapy with Borderline Patients." *Smith College Studies in Social Work,* 1967, *37* (2), 125-141.

Parad, H. J. (Ed.). *Crisis Intervention: Selected Readings.* New York: Family Service Association of America, 1965.

Parad, H. J. "Crisis Intervention." *Encyclopedia of Social Work.* (2nd ed.) Washington, D.C.: National Association of Social Workers, 1977.

Parad, L. G. "Short-Term Treatment: An Overview of Historical Trends, Issues and Potentials." *Smith College Studies in Social Work,* 1971, *41,* 119-146.

Parkes, C. M. "Psycho-Social Transitions: A Field for Study." *Social Science and Medicine,* 1971, *5,* 101-115.

Parkes, C. M. *Studies of Grief in Adult Life.* New York: International Universities Press, 1972.

Perlman, H. H. *Social Casework: A Problem Solving Approach.* Chicago: University of Chicago Press, 1957.

Perlman, H. H. "Some Notes on the Waiting List." *Social Casework,* 1963, *44,* 200-205.

Perlman, H. H. "Social Casework: The Problem Solving Approach," *Encyclopedia of Social Work.* (2nd ed.) Washington, D.C.: National Association of Social Workers, 1977.

Perlman, H. H. *Relationship—The Heart of the Helping Process.* Chicago: University of Chicago Press, 1979.

Pincus, L. *Death and the Family: The Importance of Mourning.* New York: Pantheon Books, 1975.

Rapoport, L. "A State of Crisis: Some Theoretical Considerations." *Social Service Review,* 1962, *36* (2), 211-217.

Rapoport, L. "Crisis Intervention as a Mode of Brief Treatment." In R. E. Roberts and R. E. Nee (Eds.), *Theories of Social Casework.* Chicago: University of Chicago Press, 1971.

Reid, W. J. *The Task-Centered System.* New York: Columbia University Press, 1978.

Reid, W. J., and Epstein, L. *Task-Centered Casework.* New York: Columbia University Press, 1972.

Reid, W. J., and Epstein, L. (Eds.). *Task-Centered Practice.* New York: Columbia University Press, 1977.

Reid, W. J., and Shyne, A. W. *Brief and Extended Casework.* New York: Columbia University Press, 1969.

Robinson, V. *The Development of the Professional Self: Selected Writings, 1930–1968.* New York: AMS Press, 1978.

Rothery, M. "Contracts and Contracting." *Clinical Social Work Journal,* 1980, *8* (3), 179-187.

Schafer, R. "Termination of Brief Psychoanalytic Therapy." *International Journal of Psychoanalytic Psychotherapy,* 1973, *2* (2), 135-148.

Schwartz, A., and Goldiamond, S. *Social Casework: A Behavioral Approach.* New York: Columbia University Press, 1975.

Seabury, B. A. "The Contract: Uses and Abuses, and Limitations." *Social Work,* 1974, *21* (1), 16-21.

Sereno, K. K., and Mortensen, C. D. (Eds.). *Foundations of Communication Theory.* New York: Harper & Row, 1970.

Shyne, A. W. "What Research Tells Us About Short-Term Cases in Family Agencies." *Social Casework,* 1957, *38* (5), 223-230.

Sifneos, P. E. *Short-Term Psychotherapy and Emotional Crisis.* Cambridge, Mass.: Harvard University Press, 1972.

Smalley, R. E. "The Functional Approach to Casework Process." In R. E. Roberts and R. E. Nee (Eds.), *Theories of Social Casework.* Chicago: University of Chicago Press, 1970.

Smalley, R., and Bloom, T. "Social Casework: The Functional Approach." *Encyclopedia of Social Work.* Washington, D.C.: National Association of Social Workers, 1977.

Sobel, D. "Freud's Fragmented Legacy." *New York Times* Magazine Section. October 26, 1980, pp. 28-31, 102-108.

Stierlin, H. "The Parents' Nazi Past and the Dialogue Between the Generations." Lecture given at School of Social Work, Simmons College, Boston, September 1980.

Swanson, D. L., and Delia, J. G. "The Nature of Human Communication." *Modcom: Modules in Speech Communication.* Palo Alto, Calif.: Science Research Associates, 1976.

Taft, J. "Time as the Medium of the Helping Process." *Jewish Social Service Quarterly,* December 1949, pp. 189-198. (Now called *Journal of Jewish Communal Service.*)

Watzlawick, P., Beaver, J., and Jackson, D. *Pragmatics of Human Communication.* New York: Norton, 1967.

Zilbach, J. J. "Family Development." In J. Marmor (Ed.), *Modern Psychoanalysis.* New York: Basic Books, 1968.

20

Group Treatment

Victoria S. Roemele

Group treatment is a modality used in many clinical settings for diverse therapeutic purposes. In this chapter we will consider a broad range of therapeutic groups in which group process becomes the context for accomplishing individual characterologic and intrapsychic change, improved social and work functioning, adaptive response to personal psychological crisis, reversal of regression in the acute phase of serious emotional disorders, and mastery of developmental challenges. Therapeutic groups have as their goal psychological help for the individual, rather than the furthering of some social, political, or economic change. Groups for these purposes may or may not be therapeutic for their members. This distinction is critical for both leaders and members, as well as for institutions and agencies sponsoring group treatment.

The therapeutic power of groups to treat the psychological problems of individuals has been widely demonstrated in clinical practice. Clinicians who know the usefulness of group treatment and acquire the specialized skills and knowledge necessary to lead therapeutic groups have often proceeded from skepticism to conviction about this modality after having first learned to do individual casework or psychotherapy. In the European and American tradition, one-to-one, or dyadic, treatment for emotional disorders historically preceded group treatment, and has enjoyed an undeniable preference among a majority of mental health professionals. Both theory and practice received a boost from developments attendant to the crisis of World War II, and the decades following the war, 1950–1980, have marked the significant development of group work and group therapy as respected and respectable modalities based upon a body of clinical literature and expertise.

Resistance to the clinical use of groups is intrinsic to the process, it would seem, and figures in much of the theoretical and practical material about group treatment. Traditional social work agencies have probably been the most hospitable to and facilitating of group approaches, partly by virtue of associating group phenomena with health and social adaptation. Social work practitioners have been and continue to be the most likely in the mental health field to develop and support proficiency in working with groups. This is most probably related to the assignment of social workers to poor, resistant, or more disturbed clients who may be in turn assigned to group treatment on the assumption that it is more economical and lends itself to maintaining the psychological stability of persons incapable of the psychodynamic changes thought possible in individual treatment. The subtler pairing of social workers and a less well understood "second-choice" form of treatment has in fact encouraged many social work practitioners to become proficient, even outstanding, group leaders and therapists in many clinical situations. Although relatively few professionals have experienced the therapeutic efficiency of group treatment for themselves, many have acquired significant leadership skills and, by virtue of their participating in groups, have come to appreciate the groups' specific and quite significant therapeutic power.

In conceptualizing group treatment, it is well to look first at the major approaches developed in clinical literature and practice during the past three decades in this country and in England. Each of the approaches is based upon psychodynamic principles which address the central question: "What forces specific to group process further therapeutic goals?" This definition then leads to therapeutic techniques and leadership behaviors that will focus this process upon the individual psychological issues of the members, and a view of how members and leaders affect one another in various stages of group development. This section will also address the question of what settings and what population groups serve especially well, or ill, for group therapy. The second section deals with technical matters of forming groups—composition, contract, kinds of leadership, and training—that critically affect the therapeutic outcome of psychological treatment in groups.

Theories of Group Therapy

Yalom: Interpersonal. In 1964 Irving D. Yalom, a psychiatrist affiliated with Stanford University, published a textbook entitled *The Theory and Practice of Group Psychotherapy,* now in its second edition (1975). The enormous usefulness and currency of this work relates to its validation of group treatment as a modality with great curative potential and its presentation of rational guidelines for clinical leadership of groups with an interpersonal emphasis. For the beginning group therapist, the book is a must; for the experienced clinician, there is much substance to his thorough exploration of those processes he labels "group cohesiveness" and "interpersonal learning" which bring about significant psychological changes in group therapy patients. He presents well the relevant research findings in such critical areas as selection/composition, outcome, leadership behaviors, and differences, if any, between "schools."

Central to Yalom's position is the idea that group process, stripped of its specialized front or trappings, has intrinsic core mechanisms of change which he identifies as "curative factors," some or all of which can combine to produce a therapeutic effect on group members. His conceptualization allows for a broad spectrum of goals ranging from support and inspiration to ambitious change in characterologic structure. The curative factors in group therapy are instillation of hope, universality, imparting of information, altruism, the corrective recapitulation of the primary family group, development of socializing techniques, imitative behavior, interpersonal learning, group cohesiveness, catharsis, and existential factors—most of which are less available, or unavailable, in traditional individual treatment. Thus Yalom directly and convincingly addresses the question of a group's unique power to work upon its members in a positive way. He presents a polemic for groups without giving equal attention to the resistant, destructive, antitherapeutic, and even harmful elements that often thwart the leader's efforts, particularly if they go unnoticed and unattended.

For the group leader, Yalom's position is particularly reassuring, in that he sees the proper functions as other than becoming the focus of powerful transference phenomena to be interpreted in such a way as to produce insight for the group members in an individualized way. This activity requires considerable skill, experience, and tolerance for anxiety, compounded by being confronted by several patients simultaneously. Yalom describes the leader as a careful technological expert who selects, composes, sets the boundaries and conditions, and conducts. Second, the leader becomes a model for interpersonal integrity, sets norms for affective honesty and sensitivity, helps patients understand transference phenomena, and maintains the empathic medium in which interpersonal learning can take place between members. Yalom's view of the essential therapeutic agent in group therapy derives from the interpersonal theories of Harry Stack Sullivan, and the concept of cure brought about through cognitive insight and corrective emotional experience. The inclusiveness and humanistic quality of Yalom's theory and practice makes this book generalizable to any group designed for the treatment of individual psychological ills.

Although Yalom's purpose is to democratize and demystify therapeutic group process, the net effect of the text is to produce a somewhat idealized therapy group. His optimism about groups and generous, carefully developed guidelines for leading a successful group undoubtedly advanced the clinical viability and respectability of group therapy in the permissive climate of the 1960s. While inspiring to beginners, Yalom's presentation falls short of dealing adequately with ongoing frustrations of group leaders whose members are not well-chosen adults capable of interpersonal relatedness sufficient to sustain the vivacious affective movement and full sequential development of a long-term therapeutic group. He did anticipate problems. He cautions against including a member whose ego strength significantly less than that of the other members of a given group. He devotes one chapter to problem patients familiar in the literature, and their management. To prevent dropouts, he advocates thorough preparation of members, exploration of resistance, explanation to increase cognitive understanding for members of how groups work, and interviews to solidify an initial attachment to the leader. He discusses how to avoid dangers of the vulnerable formative phase. In an article on group therapy of alcoholics (1974), Yalom discloses his flexible and imaginative attempt to adapt his own practice to persons whose severe character problems preclude the necessary degree of interpersonal relatedness.

Despite its limitations, Yalom's text has earned for group treatment a legitimacy and scope that has encouraged many clinicians to learn the art and science of group treatment.

Bion-Tavistock and Object Relations. The Bion-Tavistock approach to group leadership has been perhaps as unpopular as Yalom's has been popular. However, during the 1970s in this country, the theoretical assumptions of this view of group process have been increasingly integrated into clinical practice and put to therapeutic use. When Wilfred Bion conducted "study groups" under the auspices of the Tavistock Clinic of London, drawing upon his learning as an army psychiatrist on World War II military hospital wards, he developed a theory of group process and a manner of leadership for which he denied any therapeutic intent. What he observed was the potentiating effect of becoming a group upon the primitive anxieties of all its members, and the defensive behaviors demonstrated in the group's efforts to deal with such anxieties, especially when the presumed leader frustrated the group's wishes for reassurance and direction. Thus, in order to study group process, the leader abstained from responding to the members except interpretively, which often produced confusion, frustration, and anger. The resulting preoccupation with the leader revealed a basic group struggle to find solutions to disquieting states of dependency, feelings of powerlessness, and wishes for magical kinds of relief. In his book, *Experiences in Groups* (1960), Bion describes his experience and the theory of psychodynamic group process he derived from it.

Bion's group theory has as its frame of reference the ideas of Melanie Klein about early psychological development and its relation to psychotic phenomena. This psychoanalytic point of view assumes that the psychic structure of all individuals, regardless of personality development or diagnosis, contains psychotic elements. Bion also believed that every individual had a "group psychology," that is, intrinsic characteristics manifested only in the group context. The psychotic mental state coexists with the nonpsychotic with differing degrees of dominance, organization, and stability depending upon the individual's psychological health and varying with internal and external stress. The psychotic state is characterized by an intolerance for frustration, a predominance of destructive impulses turning love into sadism, attacks against the self with disintegrating effects, and an attempt to deal with these destructive consequences by the mechanism of projective identification. In Bion's clinical practice, he saw participation in an unstructured group as aggravating these tendencies in all individuals. What he called "basic assumption phenomena" were group reactions to psychotic anxieties secondary to the individual's regressive dilemma in the group.

In every group Bion discerned two dynamic groups, or conflicting states: the work group and the basic assumption group. In the work group, the members addressed the task as rationally defined and agreed upon. The concurrent basic assumption demonstrated the defensive resistance to the frustration, difficulty, and pain necessary to accomplishing the task. Bion outlined three basic assumption states: (1) The *dependent group* seeks a leader to fulfill its needs, behaves passively with regard to the wishful fantasy that the leader alone can protect, teach, nurture, and guide, and avoids the work by making of the leader a sort of deity. (2) The group state called *flight-fight* involves the assumption that an enemy exists inside or outside the group from whom the group must escape or defend itself; in this state the preferred leadership is paranoid. (3) In the *pairing* group the group acts as though a couple within the group will, by bringing forth a child or an idea, save the group from having to confront hatred, destructiveness, frustration, and other depressive issues, along with the hard work of individual effort.

What followed from Bion's theories of group process were interpretive interventions by the leader addressed to various aspects of these basic assumptions called "whole group interpretations" in the clinical literature. These called into question assumptions shared by the members with some of the depriving effect traditionally associated with interpretations of individual dynamics, made more powerful by the shared affect. The leader restricted himself to interpretations to the whole group about their shared defensive beliefs, a position often making the leader the object of the group's hostility. The Bion-Tavistock approach clinically has become associated with frustrating, parsimonious, and sometimes obscure and confusing behaviors on the part of a leader that are believed to be inconsistent with therapeutic practice.

When combined with object-relations theory extended to conceptualize the group as a kind of container for all psychological phenomena, wanted or unwanted by the members, the leader's focus on the mechanism of projection in group process has significant therapeutic usefulness, especially in groups whose members' capacities for interpersonal relatedness are seriously impaired by their projective defenses. Often group cohesiveness, as conceived by Yalom, cannot be achieved without active interpretations by the leader to the group as a whole about shared beliefs that constitute a collusive resistance to the hard work of psychotherapy. A generalized interpretation to the entire group includes every member in its sweep and allows each member to take it or leave it, but none to escape it by the device that a given problem or conflict belongs only to the members under scrutiny. While frustrating wishes for personal attention by the leader to individual dynamics, whole-group interpretations addressed to resistant, negative, or destructive elements in the beginning group have the effect of increasing group consciousness and cohesiveness while tersely demonstrating the leader's view of how group dynamics work.

A recent article in the group psychotherapy literature gives both an excellent review of traditional objections to the Bion-Tavistock approach and a model for integrating what is clinically useful about it, without unduly restricting the leader's interventions to the declarative pronouncements of the Tavistock school or losing the richness of personal dynamic material in the group process. The integration of Bion techniques involves allowing individual material and the group associative process to lead inductively toward whole-group interpretations that may then make more sense to other members and allow for better cognitive and reflective use of the leader's interpretations (Horwitz, 1977a). Professionals participating in Bion-Tavistock groups have found that learning from the extremely powerful affective experience produced in part by the leader's frustrating behavior depends to some extent upon previous treatment and knowledge of psychodynamics. Clinicians who use Bion theory and techniques often soften and modify the frustrating and restricting stance of the leader in line with a clinical judgment about the capacities and motivations of a given group's members to use the potential insights.

What Bion offers theoretically is an intrapsychic conceptualization of group process that in practice extends the therapeutic scope of group therapy into areas of pregenital psychodynamics for members whose needs do not conform to the traditional use of groups to address issues of intimacy and individuation. Learning to apply the sparse and frustrating whole-group interventions is a valuable discipline for any group therapist; interpretation of resistance and primitive defensive positions in the group is essential to using group process effectively in any approach.

Ganzarin, in a recent article (1978), demonstrates the clinical effectiveness and therapeutic value of Kleinian object-relations theory in the interpretive work of groups, differentiating a gentler, more individualized approach from the practices associated with Tavistock-type study groups, found in follow-up studies to be negative in their overall effect on patients.

Social Group Work. In the early 1960s investigators at Boston University School of Social Work, drawing from a significant study of empirical data from social work agency groups, produced a sequential schema for stages of development in social work groups. This work was responsive to an articulated need for theory building in the field to guide social work trainees in the therapeutic design of groups whose duration was often determined by academic or programmed years. The model, devised by James A. Garland, Hubert E. Jones, and Ralph L. Kolodny, and published as a collection of papers (Bernstein, 1965, 1970), has proved to be rich in clinical and heuristic properties as well as applicable to a wide range of groups in clinical settings. The model is descriptive of the course of small groups, and normative at the level of the group leader's goal of providing opportunities for improved ego functioning of individual members. It is in the latter sense that this schema has been generalizable to clinical therapeutic goals for the improved functioning of individuals, as distinguished from groups with social tasks and goals other than producing individual change through small group process. This emphasis has been compatible with general social work aims regarding the maintenance and strengthening of those defenses and transactional skills which promote creative social adjustment. Thus, the theoretical structure in its conception was shaped by the therapeutic aims of ego-supportive casework.

The central theme of the group experience is closeness. The five stages through which the group and its members pass are pre-affiliation, power and control, intimacy, differentiation, and separation. The authors describe interpersonal and group phenomena characteristic of each phase and suggest proper behaviors of the group leader to facilitate progress through the stages of development. For the beginning leader this dynamic "map" of the predictable course of the group presumes the corrective recapitulation of individual developmental issues in a neutral or permissive group culture determined by the leader's attitude toward the members' verbal expression and other behaviors as they struggle with the enforced experience of closeness.

Reviewing the stages briefly will reveal their respective diagnostic and therapeutic possibilities. In the pre-affiliation stage the members show their ambivalence toward involvement, a need for distance and protection from the promised closeness, approach and avoidance behaviors, and a process of exploration. The leader provides structure and allows for defensive caution and control to manage anxiety about the new social situation. Members' perception of the group is formed by analogy to social experiences outside the family; their frame of reference is societal rather than familial in this formative period of involvement.

After members establish some emotional investment and the group acquires some internal structure, the phase characterized by power and control struggles occurs. These struggles appear to be mainly an issue between the group and the leader involving the need of the members for both autonomy and the protection of each other. It is during this period that the way in which the leader exercises authority differentiates the treatment group from conventional social groups, especially in response to members' rebellious or challenging words and actions. A nonpunitive, permissive though limiting stance allows for members expression of unacceptable feelings, with the leader assuring a reasonable degree of safety and support for individual controls. This is a period of high tension and risk of dropouts. The frame of reference is traditional and transitional from non-intimate to intimate relationships.

Stage three in this developmental sequence involves the emotional challenge of intimacy; it is a period of intense personal involvement among members and leader where strong familial feelings and the striving for satisfaction of dependency needs dominate the process of the group. This can be a conflictual and transferential experience in the here-and-now of the group where the leader clarifies affective and regressive responses and deals with the general meaning to members of the group.

Once issues of intimacy and recognition of individual needs are dealt with, the group reaches the stage of differentiation, in which the separateness, individuality, and interdependence of members is established, functional roles and shared leadership emerge, and a cohesiveness is attained, all as the result of working through the prior developmental problems in the group context. Group and individual identities are heightened and less colored by displaced associations from earlier experiences. The group at this stage has the internal frame of reference and autonomy to run itself and do its work with diminished dependency on the leader, who becomes a resource person maintaining the group's focus on the process and its meaning.

The fifth stage, separation, involves the process of termination, with regression, recapitulation, and defensive attempts to deal with the anxiety over loss and the breaking of group bonds. The authors discuss typical reactions to separation, both adaptive and maladaptive, and consider the most delicate part of the leader's work the help given in coming to terms, both verbally and through activity, with the ambivalence involved in termination. The authors view their model as useful to clinicians in three principal areas: diagnosis of individual behavior in groups, understanding group behavior in relation to developmental tasks, and interventions by the leader in relation to developmental tasks.

This model, derived from the study of small long-term children's groups, can be extended to illuminate the process of groups composed of emotionally disturbed adults in psychiatric settings and community mental health centers. James Garland and Louise Frey used the model to examine group development at in-patient settings where the group development could be altered by the milieu, member turnover, the intensity of close contact, dependency, and ward cycles of loss and reconstitution (Bernstein, 1970). Of particular interest in their study was the understanding of how problems with object relations in the two major categories of hospitalized patients, schizophrenics and those with character disorders, were reflected in a predictable and definable distortion of stage development reflecting dynamic fixations in the members.

The social group work theory outlined here provides a useful guide for the progress of a group through sequential stages; this approach is based upon the assumption that a developmental recapitulation is corrective emotionally for the individual member of a well-led group. The conceptual framework helps the leader to define and explain a connected series of events, or incidents, in a predictable fashion and with a purpose. Though the framework itself can be supplemented by refined social and dynamic understanding and leaders can themselves define strategies and techniques to foster the progression of the group through its stages, this school lends itself to the use of therapeutic interventions and techniques known as ego-supportive casework.

Child group therapy can be considered a therapeutic subspecialty, perhaps more because of matters of technique than of essential conceptual differences in group process. The social group work theory described above is used as a framework for understanding the developmental process in groups and individuals, with techniques, interventions, and activities adapted to meet differing needs as determined by specific age, sex, or setting. Another widely used and clinically sophisticated approach is known as activity group therapy. This was originated by a pioneer and authority in the field, S. R. Slavson (1943, 1947), in his work with latency-age children with problems around aggression. Slavson developed an age-specific group methodology that was essentially experiential rather than based on verbalization; it utilized as its main therapeutic force the regression in the group and the therapist's capacity to promote change by a dynamic reintegration through activity and attitude.

The Psychoanalytic Tradition. Psychodynamic group psychotherapy developed in this country as a clinical subspecialty of the psychoanalytic movement during the post–World War II period when a number of psychoanalysts, many in the New York City community, put their analytic patients in groups for treatment in turns, sometimes for clinical and sometimes for frankly economic reasons. Group process as such was not employed in the service of the therapy, which was essentially the usual transference analysis with genetic reconstruction with the patient-leader transference axis the active therapeutic dimension.

Psychoanalytic theories of group treatment have mainly derived from concepts about the therapeutic process in individual work. Displacement onto other members and dilution of the intensity of transference feelings toward the leader were viewed as a means of expanding the therapeutic matrix. Such group phenomena were useful to consider those patients dynamically unsuited for intensive individual analytic work. The burden of being a second-choice treatment for less workable patients has slanted clinical thought and practice in most settings influenced by the psychoanalytic hierarchies of diagnosis and treatability. However, the majority of effective group therapists from most disciplines have been trained first in the classical mold and developed an expertise in group work as a subspecialty. This continues to have a major effect on practice, referrals, and professional preference.

The psychoanalytic school of group psychotherapy did develop theories of group process which were analogous to those of individual treatment. In one of the clinically most useful, Whitaker and Lieberman (1964) applied Thomas

French's focal conflict theory to groups. They postulated that group process develops associatively by members expressing a shared concern about some issue. The content of group meetings demonstrates a wish and a reactive fear; this is the group focal conflict. Members deal defensively with this covert conflict and attempt compromise solutions which may be restrictive or enabling. The leader's role is to interpret by flexible means, such as the unconscious, elements in the conflict and to move the group toward more adaptive solutions by flexible means, such as questioning, modeling, and exploring members' idiosyncratic behaviors and beliefs.

This model lends itself to the task of integrating individual dynamics with the thematic group process, allowing the leader to address interpretively, with the individual and the group, the expression of a basic shared dynamic. Group treatment, thus conceptualized, can become a flexible and versatile instrument for experiencing, understanding, and working through problems in a context where the social impact of one's emotional difficulties cannot be denied. Rutan and Alonso (1979) emphasize the power of a long-term dynamic group to work through problems of intimacy and individuation in a social context counteracting the isolation consequent to the breakdown of more traditional social groupings. They contend that the group context offers the specific advantages of allowing the patients' usual presentation of strengths and weaknesses in a true-to-life social situation and of promoting a usable regression by virtue of increased anxiety and emotional contagion.

Clinicians from the psychoanalytic tradition, once immersed in the therapeutically potentiating effect of group, have identified the specific attributes of this modality in treating core personality problems. A skilled group therapist can accomplish basic structural change as defined in the psychoanalytic framework in the process of long-term psychodynamic group therapy. Guttmacher (1973) writes of the particular strength of group therapy in the confrontation and working through of ego-syntonic character pathology. He argues that the therapeutic group culture reproduces a "second chance" analogous to adolescent development in allowing the reflection and modification of one's characteristics through interaction with peers who confront syntonic character traits in a protected situation where the consequent anxiety and conflict can be tolerated, supported, and carried through to a better resolution.

One of the consequences of referring to groups those individuals with difficult, resistant character problems and primitive defensive constellations has been the creation of groups that are homogeneous for particular diagnostic categories. The resulting efforts to use group treatment have produced an impressive understanding of both the process of these disorders and the parameters of possible therapeutic change. In an article describing the holistic treatment of schizophrenic patients, Steiner (1979) relates his psychodynamic formulation of the illness as involving object avoidance, object clinging, and object distortion to a developmental sequence of group treatment. He takes into account the need to modulate anxiety, allow for patients' inability to achieve full maturation into adult roles, and recognize their continued dependency upon a leader perceived as powerful, as the group brings about a significant difference in self-esteem and tolerance for interpersonal relatedness. My own supervisory experience has shown how a group homogeneous for patients with manic-depressive illness and good compliance to lithium therapy can come to contain the disruptive defensive efforts of its members to avoid painful feelings, successfully limit the sadistic abuses and denial interfering with personal relationships, and develop an affective climate and cohesiveness where members can gradually assume some control of their illness by insight and work through powerful depressive anxieties. Thus group treatment for populations once considered candidates for exclusion from psychodynamic therapies has brought hope for patients as well as increased skill to therapists willing to engage in the vigorous interpersonal work required in this area. The literature abounds with clinical accounts of apparently effective group treatment of highly resistant, even unmotivated, individuals. Both in theory and in practice, group treatment in the psychodynamic tradition has extended and amplified the therapeutic process to reach more and more people whose character structure and motivation do not fit the classical patient mold.

Technical Considerations

Before starting a group the leader can profitably focus the expectable anxiety about such a venture upon exploration of all the salient clinical issues. It is important for the prospective leader who is a beginner to seek consultation in order to clarify issues at the conceptual level before embarking upon the search for group members. A good therapeutic group is indeed hard to form in most clinical settings; the task may be simplified where captive populations exist, but this by no means assures success. As Yalom states, the leader's role as an expert technician of the nuts and bolts of group phenomena is a critical factor in the success of the therapeutic group.

In leading workshops for group therapists from many quite varied clinical settings, I have developed an outline to examine specific aspects the leader must attend to in forming a group. Participants think through these issues about a group they wish to start, and present their plans in written form to the group of colleagues in the workshop, whose contributions taken together can constitute an illuminating consultation as well as a demonstration of group process at work. The outline used for the consultation request appears below; a substantive discussion follows on some critical considerations that can make or break a group.

Outline for Consultation

1. Describe dynamically a group you are contemplating in two forms:
   a. A paragraph designed for professional colleagues.
   b. A paragraph explaining the group to prospective members.
2. State time and place of meeting, duration (short-term or open-ended), and fee.
3. Describe patients or clients you wish to have as members. Discuss criteria for selection, composition, exclusions, and referral process.
4. Write a contract for members to agree to and formulate your approach to pregroup preparation of members.
5. State which theoretical approach to group therapy you will follow in the leadership of your group—Yalom, Bion, social group work, or psychoanalytic.

6. Describe your background and experience clinically and what supervision and other support you will need to run this group. Characterize your leadership style and indicate your own resistance to joining or leading groups.
7. Analyze the predictable impact of the setting—agency, institution, or private practice—on the life of your group.
8. Formulate a specific question for consultation. You may want to focus on an issue about which you feel anxious in anticipating the first meeting.
9. Describe how you will conduct the first meeting of your group in some detail, indicating the worst and best fantasies, complications, and challenges, along with your own actions and reactions.
10. Describe interventions and strategies you will employ during the formative phase in your attempt to make a working therapeutic group out of a collection of individuals.

Forming a Therapeutic Group: Critical Considerations. While the best form for a therapist is to approach each group meeting with no agenda and an open mind so as to listen for dynamic themes as they develop within the group, thinking carefully in advance about the formation of any given group provides insight into the therapist's assumptions, wishes, rational goals, theoretical bent, and special interests. The countertransference motivation is particularly important to clarify, as the following examples illustrate. A clinical social worker in an out-patient mental health center contemplated starting a group for step-parents. In consultation she came to understand that in her own family her mother and stepfather had formed a collusive alliance which scapegoated her; when the hope for referrals did not develop, she could tie the motivational question to her own experience. A psychiatric resident who was required to run groups, in forming a group of severe character disorders, came to understand her wish to tackle the goal of changing her own alcoholic mother. A psychology intern began a group for people of mixed character problems (in the twenty-five to forty-year-old range and from working-class backgrounds) who presented failure to separate from home and parents or establish job stability; the patients resembled the intern's own siblings among whom he was the only child to separate successfully and establish a professional identity.

The task of describing a group dynamically for colleagues and prospective members clarifies both personal investments and institutional reasons for preferring to work in groups with certain kinds of patients. In the adoption unit of a family service agency, a worker running intensive short-term groups for parents with adopted infants learned much at both cognitive and affective levels of the client couples' powerful ambivalent feelings toward the baby, their own parents, and the agency. This increased the agency's awareness of its own role.

Through discussing issues of time, place, fee, and duration, a prospective leader again confronts assumptions about his or her role, but here the assumptions are played out at the level of practical reality. Groups that run weekly for three months or less of necessity require a specific task or dynamic focus and behaviors on the part of the leader which focus the members' attention upon the work, their own resistances as soon as they develop, and the predictable wish of members to prolong the group. Closed membership and strategies to limit dropouts are essential to the life of such groups. Successful, short-term group experiences may produce motivation for further group treatment, as is often the experience following group parent education in child guidance practice. Fees for groups are typically lower in private practice than those for individual treatment; in clinics with sliding scales, the same fee for group as for individual treatment may reflect a conviction about the therapeutic potency of group work. The hour a group meets conveys assumptions about the patient's availability, work situation, and the agency or leader's hopes or fears about clients' motivation. Groups for adults typically meet in the late afternoon or evening to accommodate the patients' work schedule; groups for more severely disturbed patients that meet during the working day may convey a pessimistic, even punitive, attitude with regard to the functional rehabilitation of patients. In the course of making these decisions, part of the basic structure of the group is determined.

Determination of membership in therapeutic groups is the prerogative of the leader, though in in-patient settings, for example, eligibility may be automatic for all patients except those specifically excluded while acutely psychotic or otherwise too regressed to participate. Although the leader may take members' opinions into consideration, adding new members or asking a member to leave a group is a decision to be made by the leader, both for administrative and therapeutic reasons—the latter to focus group feelings about such events clearly upon the therapist. Yalom's chapters on selection and composition of therapy groups cover the general considerations for long-term psychotherapy groups. He concedes that there is more art than science in these areas. The available population in any referral situation is of course critical, and referral usually hinges on the issues of trust within clinical communities of colleagues; how well this group leader will treat "my patient" is often an underlying question. The handling of therapist-to-therapist contact about a given patient in concurrent individual and group treatment is often critical in promoting understanding about the usefulness of group treatment.

Yalom is an adequate source for a review of what is known about selection and composition. Pointing out that selection is critical to the fate of a group, he admits that criteria vary widely depending upon the structure, procedure, and goals of the treatment. He concludes that the literature yields a lack of consensus and offers few firm guidelines with many contradictions. The question is most often approached as whom to exclude; diagnostically schizoid, sociopathic, alcoholic, psychosomatic, paranoid, narcissistic, and acutely psychotic individuals are generally viewed as poor therapy group members. However, some groups homogeneous for such disorders can do important therapeutic work on underlying character issues. Patients who do not fit, having some important deviant characteristic, may be extruded by group pressure. Yalom reports findings that indicate certain characteristics that may be used to predict unworkability among group members: lack of psychological sophistication, lack of interpersonal sensitivity, lack of personal psychological insight manifested by use of denial, and severe problems with intimacy. He cautions against including in a group one member whose ego strength is greatly different from that of other members. On the positive side, motivation for group treatment strongly predisposes successful participation. Standard psychiatric classifications seem to be less informative about questions of selection than data about previous interpersonal behaviors, peer relations, and positions taken in other social groups, particularly the family.

Group composition involves choosing for a given group those particular members whose personalities and problems will "jell" into a working mixture. This factor focuses on homogeneity and heterogeneity as critical dimensions; do groups function better when members are more alike than different, and for what characteristics? The general rule is to compose therapy groups that are heterogeneous for psychological conflict areas and homogeneous for ego strength. The dissonance theory, which presumes that differences produce workable tensions in groups, underlies the argument for heterogeneity. Some authors suggest as a technique "group balance" where the therapist attempts to achieve a distribution among various members of the expression of such factors as transference affect, insight, introspective ability, ego strength, aggressiveness, heterosexuality-homosexuality, and the like. Yalom believes a certain type of homogeneity stimulates group cohesiveness and that patients who are vastly different tend to leave groups prematurely. However, the cohesiveness based on likenesses can also block exploration of certain conflicts and become a collusive form of resistance to change.

The use of contracts for members of therapy groups is a particularly important strategy for assembling members committed to working together in therapy, and for addressing the interpersonal behavior of members, that is, how members and leader treat each other over the long term. Rutan and Alonso (1979) provide a most cogent argument for the use of a contract to explore resistance as well as motivation, and to protect the group. Dealing with the prospective members' affective response to the items in a contract required for all members opens for discussion dynamics that affect substantive participation in the therapeutic work of the group; these authors see the process of negotiation as a diagnostic tool and a powerful selector of members, which puts the therapeutic enterprise in terms of mutual responsibility and commitment. As an example, Alonso and Rutan state the specifics of their contract: required attendance at all meetings, agreement to work actively on all issues that brought a member to the group, respect for confidentiality, contact with other members limited to the group, continuation in group until what brought the member is accomplished, announcement of termination to allow enough time for members to respond meaningfully, and payment of bills on time. While contracts may vary, leader and members can use the specific expectations to confront behavior which works against the therapeutic purpose of that group.

Leaders may vary also in the amount and kind of pregroup preparation given to members. Theoretical points of view in part dictate the manner in which ambiguity and level of anxiety are enlisted in the service of the therapy. Rabin and Rosenbaum (1976) classify and describe several elements of pregroup preparation: (1) factual information about time, place, and fee; (2) recorded or printed material introducing patients in an educational way to the process of group treatment; (3) lectures or explanatory interviews orienting patients to the here-and-now process as well as patient and therapist roles; (4) a preparatory, preliminary group experience as a diagnostic aid and reducer of anxiety about participation; and (5) an individual approach yielding data about the patient's patterns of transference and resistance as well as educating the member for entry into group treatment. The authors conclude that individualized preparation best counteracts the destructive effect of members who drop out in the early stages of the group. Individualized contact with the group therapist may produce an initial bond with the leader that encourages continued attendance and effects a kind of early cohesiveness.

Beginning leaders who are untrained in group work face choices about "schools" or theoretical approaches that are often bewildering and biased by personal idiosyncracies rather than clinical fit. The issues of choice of approach, assessment of one's own clinical background, and the need for supervision are often not rigorously considered when a clinician undertakes to "do a group." Indeed, many group leaders are self-taught by the school of trial and error. It is important to seek consultation at the outset and to remember that groups have also especially destructive potential and that some standard group process phenomena are actively antitherapeutic as well as potentially curative. Some excellent individual therapists make poor group leaders, and co-therapy is especially problematic. In short, the complications of group treatment require additional training and educated sensitivities. As Kernberg (1976) notes, the characteristics of leadership and the impingement of institutional structures so powerfully shape group process that psychodynamic knowledge should be supplemented by a subtle awareness of systems factors at work. His map for understanding these phenomena combines systems and object-relations theory in a way that illuminates the effect of mutual psychological projections on the life of therapeutic groups in complex treatment institutions. Group leaders in agencies would be wise to invent comprehensible ways of analyzing factors (such as agency philosophy and events in the larger social order providing the context for a given group) that affect the way referrals are made, leaders are influenced, and process determined.

Finally, a leader's initial behaviors and decisions made in the early meetings of the group can powerfully influence the norms and the transference development. Facing the issue of what kind of leader one intends to be—how one intends to manage anxiety, frustrations, negative matters; how one intends to express interpretive, supportive, and empathic stances; and how one's own self and emotional reactions will be used—conveys important attitudes toward the therapeutic instrument the group affords. Eclectic amalgams are often confusing and at cross purposes. Co-leaders must share a conceptual framework and common strategy in addition to dynamic compatibility. The leader should adopt a consistent approach, though a leader's therapeutic activity may change in some respects with group development. A clinician's convictions about what constitutes true therapy will determine choice of approach, though appropriateness to the members' needs is the prime consideration.

Programmatic Considerations. In most out-patient mental health or social service agencies viable group treatment programs depend upon the energy and interest of one, or a few, clinicians who begin groups and inspire others to do so. Referrals come to group leaders mainly by virtue of their persistent advocacy and the education of their colleagues to the particular value of known groups for certain patients. Seasonal variations and the vicissitudes of student training tend to determine the clinical life and membership of many a group. While a case can be made for economic considerations, Freud rather than Marx seems to prevail in arguments about treatment of choice. Administrative policy favoring and forcing assignments of clinical or agency clients to out-patient therapy groups or to concurrent individual and group treatment is the exception rather than the rule. Grunebaum and Kates (1977) describe patients most suitable for groups in an out-patient setting. The mechanism for creating and maintaining a group therapy program in a given setting is more complex than the issue of selection or the respect awarded various in-house group therapists. Where the agency structure is individualistic and oriented toward the solo practitioner and his or her clientele working in a somewhat isolated context, group modalities seem to compete less successfully with the more manageable dyadic preference. Where there are "teams" on which staff members share knowledge of and responsibility for each other's clients, the staff culture seems readier to expand to multiple-patient groupings for therapy. Group treatment in out-patient settings is seen less as a method for structuring the environment, and more as a specialized and exceptional treatment for a few chosen patients who must be weaned from or shared with the primary individual therapist. Boris (1971) when ministering to the mental health of a small Vermont town, met with groups around a kitchen table rather than purvey therapy through the medium of a mental health clinic. Although some agencies have used natural groups and created groups quite imaginatively for therapeutic purposes, in most out-patient settings group programs seem to grow more from enterpreneurial efforts, responses to special client populations, or training needs, and less from generalized programmatic considerations based on theory or policy.

Specific administrative supports favoring group programs center around attitudes and behavior of senior staff, presence of prestigious or intellectually stimulating teachers of group work, training requirements specifying group therapy as a core modality, and service to clinical populations who present characterologic and interpersonal problems requiring the special leverage of group process to contain, confront, and convert difficulties into more inwardly experienced conflict. Long-term groups can be transferred during their work from one leader to another, but the process requires careful thought on possible contradictory norms and attention to the depressive residue left in the group's life by past therapists. The clinical demonstration of the effectiveness of group therapy comes through conferences, presentation of group process, focus on review of characterologic and other structural change in a given patient, and collaboration of group and individual therapists during concurrent treatment. When the clinical climate is favorable, out-patient centers can begin more effectively to program group treatment as a choice fitting certain clients, with a clarified and effective referral process, ongoing clinical review, and close supervision.

In-patient, or milieu, settings are a different story, and an even more complex and fascinating one. Out-patient settings do not use patient groups to structure the therapeutic "holding" environment in the same way as in-patient, day treatment, and other caretaking agencies, where the patient population spends the greater part of every day, or stays for periods of time, night and day. Group programs in these clinical situations are necessary to provide structure, socialization, and multiple therapeutic impingements on regressed and resistant patients. Groups literally shape and fill the day for people whose current functional disturbance requires this kind of external form as an aid to maintaining or regaining inner organization and social contact. One day treatment center for recently hospitalized psychiatric patients had basically three kinds of groups. The first were meetings for selected patients who could use, within limits, a psychologically focused process dealing with their primitive defenses, fear and need of closeness, and alternating states of hopelessness and denial. Another category of groups dealt selectively with functional deficits consequent to patients' emotional disorders and lack of everyday practical and social skills for survival. Taking the total milieu as the third ongoing group process, workers provided opportunities for patients alone and in solitary activity to shore up schizoid defenses. Staff, by observing the overall pattern of patient behavior on the milieu, can relate this behavior to hopes, fears, and experiences in the patient's family life. Here staff had an opportunity to use interventions based on their understanding.

Another example, in between traditional out-patient and in-patient settings, and a useful example to demonstrate dynamic thinking about group programming, is an adolescent day center, set up with state funding to provide educational and mental health services to a group of about twenty-five adolescents determined to be in need of special services. The students in the day treatment program fall mainly into the diagnostic range of character disorders with a sprinkling of borderline and schizoid individuals. The program, located in a spacious YMCA facility in a large industrial town, was geared to a student population of boys and girls, ages sixteen to eighteen, who came to the treatment center for a seven-hour school day. The staff consisted of teachers and social workers. The clinical staff offered individual counseling to the students and work with patients. The center sought consultation to set up a group program in the third year, after staff had concluded that more structure was indicated clinically for the students to counter unproductive use of the milieu.

In consultation the staff group focused on poor interpersonal relations as a common problem, with basic characterological issues involving poor tolerance for anxiety, depression, closeness, and low self-esteem. Family pathology included alcoholism, parental loss, and lack of protection and nurturance during conflicted adolescent years. The center had become a critical alternative to family support. The first group run by male and female co-leaders was a termination group meeting for five sessions to focus on good-byes. It was predictably a tense, difficult process for all, since good-byes on an interpersonal level could barely be tolerated; the group's struggle to contain the feelings was disrupted by anger and avoidance activity, and leaders experienced frustration.

In planning a more comprehensive group treatment structure for the following year's program, both abstract clinical considerations and the special interests of staff members were taken into account. The use of co-leaders raised the issue of the differences in theoretical orientation and training between teachers and mental health workers, as well as differences in role definition. The shape of a treatment group structure for the center began to emerge from staff ideas. The basic subgroups were to be advising groups consisting of four or five students, with co-managers, a teacher and a counselor. The goals of these groups were case management and promotion of more constructive involvement in the school program through small-group process with a task focus. These subgroups, designed to meet for a half hour every morning and afternoon to discuss school activities and personal concerns about the school setting, would become the vehicle for encouraging a sense of belonging and loyalty among students who shared the same advisors. The treatment or therapy group was planned to meet in three ten-week segments, with short-term therapeutic goals defined in interpersonal terms—a "hello" group, a "how are you doing" group, and a "good-bye" group. The group was conceived as a place where basic characterological issues of individual students could be better understood diagnostically from behavior in small group and dealt with more interpretively. Other specialized activity groups—an environmental group, a current events group, a lunch-cooking group, a driver's license group, a carpentry group—would capture the opportunity to work on specific dynamic issues around deprivation, conflict with authority, and resistance to using opportunities for learning and growth offered by the school. An alumni and parents' group met during nonschool hours. The staff agreed to use the social group work sequential model because it fit the setting and time constraints, and would provide a dynamic approach most compatible with the teachers' background. Group supervision was arranged to continue the process of defining and conceptualizing the specific therapeutic task of each group and to discuss potentially destructive and disruptive effects of small-group dynamics in the treatment center. As clinically predictable, the groups reflected the severe family pathology of members, and were tense experiences for staff, requiring much energy and effort to render them a corrective or therapeutic environment for the reworking of serious character and family problems.

Course of Group Treatment. The questions most often asked by clinicians and clients are: Does group therapy work? Does group therapy produce character change or structural intrapsychic change? Essentially the answer lies in the group leader's skill in producing a working therapeutic group out of a collection of strangers, and in promoting the necessary processes of the "middle game," the usually prolonged period during which forces in the group are brought to bear on the patient's hardened, resistant, and probably syntonic character problems. During this period, both the affective, or experiential, and the cognitive dimensions of the therapy must come together in an interpersonally meaningful way for each member.

The beginning phase of the group has to do with establishing cohesiveness, constancy, and a therapeutic matrix of several persons in which every member and the group as a whole understand the powerful resistances and defensive operations that interfere with the task of the therapy. This task involves mourning lost illusions, understanding the "here-and-now" of personal defenses, and gaining the psychological strength to bear conflict, depression, and frustration in the resolution of problems in the intrapsychic and interpersonal realms. The goals of treatment may not be so different in individual and group psychotherapy, though the path traveled in the course of treatment may not appear or feel the same as in a dyadic relationship.

Each experienced group therapist may develop an essential strategy to conduct the "middle game." Yalom's text gives excellent examples of the powerful effects of what he calls "interpersonal learning," where a shared and corrective emotional experience is combined with cognitive insight to complete the therapeutic loop. I have found that the integration of a psychodynamic, individualized approach with a persistent use of Bion-Tavistock whole-group interpretations provides the most effective approach to the challenge of the repetitious working through and confrontation of the critical middle period. Whole-group interpretations address in a declarative interpretive structure the continuing human propensity to substitute wishful thinking and avoidance for frustration and resolution. For example, in a group of intelligent young adults with depressive and schizoid character defenses, repeated group interpretations may be as follows: (1) the group seems to wish that the leader would give them back their feelings; (2) the group is making one member into the patient; (3) the group acts as though only another member brought love and liveliness into the room; (4) the passivity of which the group complains feels like a demand for love without having to work for it; (5) it would seem that the group assigns to the leader the job of feeling concern for the member in trouble. As powerfully affective issues are worked on in the group, the leader must reinforce the group's capacities to contain the difficult and disavowed feelings in a nonjudgmental climate. The other most important aspect of the work involves highly personal and specific attention to individual members' problematic character traits, defenses, and projections. Since these structures often cover strong anxieties and feelings, interpersonal tensions can be high and members' needs increase for group and therapist support. This period gives the lie to opinions that group treatment is less intense or less adapted to intrapsychic work than individual treatment. However, group leader's resistance to allowing and furthering such basic work in group should not be underestimated. It is hard work requiring considerable skill and emotional stamina.

The task of the leader is more than that of "listening with the third ear" to the thematic presentation of dynamic material in the content of the group, or becoming the focus for elaboration and exploration of transference material. The leader must allow powerful affective "messages" from the group about its wishes, fears, hopes, and disavowed states to permeate her or his own inner life for the duration of group sessions. The leader must also develop the courage to use his or her own reactions to formulate interpretations that further the group members' understanding of how these phenomena shape their inner psychic reality and their outer social reality.

Long-term group treatment allows for the repetition and reinforcement that drives the point home for individual members. In short-term group the leader's capacity to discern and select the basic "assumption" or defensive state and to focus precisely on the central dynamic is crucial to make the most of a time-limited opportunity. For example, in a ten-session group for adoptive parents the worker learned that ambivalence toward the infant, the agency, and the parents' parents was the theme addressed in an atmosphere charged with defensive efforts to deal with the authority attributed to the group leader. Other goals of the leader to educate, support, exhort, or reassure properly gave way to an active interpretive approach to what was "there" in the group process, begging to be dealt with, though the subject was uncomfortable at times to the leader. Group therapists must also trust in the reverberating effects of "letting the chips fall where they may," since the opportunity to explore personal material of each member in great depth and detail is necessarily limited.

Termination. Termination in groups takes three main forms: termination of a member; termination of a leader; or termination of the whole group. In each situation the full range of dynamic possibilities can and do apply with regard to individuals. One interesting phenomenon in groups, of which members and leaders are advised to be aware, is the persistence of a depressive residue after termination which continues to effect the "group life." Basically, the residue seems to consist of unworked-through material about the loss encapsulated in such a way as to block or inhibit further work on the subject. For example, a member leaves a group with complaints about the group and its members and some unfinished interpersonal business. Long after the loss of the member has been given its due, the group may continue at some level to defend against the reproach inflicted by the departing member; the leader should persist in confronting the group with the residue, lest its presence in some subtle fashion forestall work on related issues. In groups used for training which have had a number of leaders, the depressive residue is most clearly problematic; its repeated exploration reveals often considerable resentment, distortions, and resistances which, though understandable, often yield a valuable dynamic formulation for that group. For example, a group homogeneous for patients with borderline character disorders developed a persistent splitting phenomenon in their perception of a past and present leader which constituted a formidable defense against both grieving the old leader and accepting the new. Members of groups that have terminated often internalize "the group" in a way that remains dynamically active, for good or ill, and also reflects the powerful tendency of the group to go on and on even after it has stopped actively meeting. At best, the group affords individuals the experience of separating from something "larger" than themselves, differentiating themselves from a strong base, integrating ambivalence, and mourning the necessary illusions about group cohesion while maintaining the importance of human ties.

Conclusion

In contemplating the use of groups as a therapeutic modality, agencies and individuals are well advised to acknowledge the power of group process, the skill and knowledge it requires to harness this power to therapeutic ends, and the possible abuses and destructive effects of ill-conceived or misled treatment groups. Regular clinical review is required for "quality control" as well as for the continuous growth of the leader, who can easily become involved in the group's dynamics and lose the perspective necessary to maintain an interpretive focus. For the group leader, the role invariably challenges his or her standard therapeutic repertoire and develops an awareness of his or her own "group psychology" and reactions specific to a group situation and the exciting demands of leadership.

References

Bailis, S., Lambert, S., and Bernstein, S. "The Legacy of the Group: A Study of Group Therapy with a Transient Membership." *Social Work in Health Care,* 1978, *3,* 405–418.

Bennis, W. G., and Shepard, H. H. "A Theory of Group Development." *Human Relations,* 1956, *9,* 415–437.

Bernstein, S. (Ed.). *Explorations in Group Work: Essays in Theory and Practice.* Boston: Charles River Books, 1976a.

Bernstein, S. (Ed.). *Further Explorations in Group Work.* Boston: Charles River Books, 1976b.

Bion, W. F. *Experiences in Groups.* New York: Basic Books, 1960.

Boris, H. "The Seelsorger in Rural Vermont." *International Journal of Group Psychotherapy,* 1971, *21,* 159–173.

Boris, H., Zinberg, N., and Boris, M. "Fantasies in Group Situations." *Contemporary Psychoanalysis,* 1975, *2,* 15–45.

Borriello, J. F. "Leadership in the Therapist-Centered Group as a Whole Psychotherapy Approach." *International Journal of Group Psychotherapy,* 1976, *26,* 149–162.

Douglas, T. *Groupwork Practice.* New York: International Universities Press, 1976.

Durkin, H. E. *The Group in Depth.* New York: International Universities Press, 1964.

Ezriel, H. "Psychoanalytic Group Therapy." In L. R. Wolberg and E. K. Schwartz (Eds.), *Group Therapy, 1973: An Overview.* New York: Intercontinental Medical Book Corporation, 1973.

Foulkes, S. H., and Anthony, E. J. *Group Psychotherapy.* New York: Penguin Books, 1965.

Freud, S. "Group Psychology and the Analysis of the Ego." *Standard Edition.* Vol. 18. London: Hogarth Press, 1955. (Originally published 1921.)

Ganzarin, R. "General Systems and Object-Relations Theories: Their Usefulness in Group Psychotherapy." *International Journal of Group Psychotherapy,* 1978, *27,* 441–456.

Grobman, J. "Achieving Cohesiveness in Therapy Groups of Chronically Disturbed People." Unpublished paper, Tufts-New England Medical Center, 1976.

Grobman, J. "The Borderline Patient in Group Psychotherapy: A Case Report." *International Journal of Group Psychotherapy,* 1980, *30,* 299–318.

Grunebaum, H., and Kates, W. "Whom to Refer for Group Psychotherapy." *American Journal of Psychiatry,* 1977, *134,* 130–133.

Grunebaum, H., and Solomon, L. "Toward a Peer Theory of Group Psychotherapy, I: On the Developmental Significance of Peers and Play." *International Journal of Group Psychotherapy,* 1980, *30,* 23–49.

Guttmacher, J. "The Concept of Character, Character Problems, and Group Therapy." *Comprehensive Psychiatry,* 1973, *14,* 513–522.

Horwitz, L. "A Group-Centered Approach to Group Psychotherapy." *International Journal of Group Psychotherapy,* 1977a, *27,* 423–439.

Horwitz, L. "Group Psychotherapy of the Borderline Patient." In P. Hartcollis (Ed.), *Borderline Personality Disorders.* New York: International Universities Press, 1977b.

Kernberg, O. F. "A Systems Approach to Priority Setting of Interventions in Groups." *International Journal of Group Psychotherapy,* 1975, *25,* 251–275.

Kernberg, O. F. "Toward an Integrative Theory of Hospital Treatment." In *Object Relations Theory and Clinical Psychoanalysis.* New York: Jason Aronson, 1976.

Kernberg, O. F. "Leadership and Organizational Functioning: Organizational Regression." *International Journal of Group Psychotherapy,* 1978, *28,* 3–25.

Khantzian, E. J., and Kates, W. W. "Group Treatment of Unwilling Addicted Patients: Programmatic and Clinical Aspects." *International Journal of Group Psychotherapy,* 1978, *28,* 81–94.

Klein, M. *The Psycho-Analysis of Children.* London: Hogarth Press, 1932.

Klein, M. *Contributions to Psycho-Analysis, 1921–45.* London: Hogarth Press, 1948.

Klein, M. *Envy and Gratitude.* New York: Basic Books, 1957.

Malan, D. H., and others. "Group Psychotherapy: A Long Term Follow-up Study." *Archives of General Psychiatry,* 1976, *33,* 1303–1315.

Rabin, H. M., and Rosenbaum, M. *How to Begin a Psychotherapy Group—Six Approaches.* New York: Gordon Press, 1976.

Rioch, M. J. "The Work of Wilfred Bion on Groups." *Psychiatry,* 1970, *33,* 56–66.

Rutan, J. S., and Alonso, A. "Group Psychotherapy." In A. Lazare (Ed.), *Out-Patient Psychotherapy.* Baltimore: Williams & Wilkins, 1979.

Schain, J. "The Application of Kleinian Theory to Group Psychotherapy." *International Journal of Group Psychotherapy,* 1980, *30,* 319–330.

Segal, H. *Introduction to the Work of Melanie Klein.* London: Hogarth Press, 1973.

Slavson, S. R. *An Introduction to Group Therapy.* New York: International Universities Press, 1943.

Slavson, S. R. *The Practice of Group Therapy.* New York: International Universities Press, 1947.

Stanton, A. A., and Schwartz, M. S. *The Mental Hospital.* New York: Basic Books, 1954.

Steiner, J. "Holistic Group Therapy with Schizophrenics." *International Journal of Group Psychotherapy,* 1979, *29,* 195–210.

Sullivan, H. S. *The Interpersonal Theory of Psychiatry.* New York: Norton, 1953.

Whitaker, D. S., and Lieberman, M. D. *Psychotherapy Through the Group Process.* New York: Atherton Press, 1964.

Wolf, A., and Schwartz, E. K. *Psychoanalysis in Groups.* New York: Grune & Stratton, 1962.

Yalom, I. D. "Group Therapy and Alcoholism." *Annals, New York Academy of Sciences,* 1974, *233,* 85–103.

Yalom, I. D. *The Theory and Practice of Group Psychotherapy.* (2nd ed.) New York: Basic Books, 1975.

21

Work with Children

Florence Lieberman

The social work profession has a historical and consistent involvement with children and their families. The profession developed in close relation to the formation of child welfare and family agencies, societies for the prevention of cruelty to children, and child guidance clinics. The latter, originating early in the twentieth century because of concern with delinquent youth, quickly expanded their scope to include the study of child development and the establishment of standards and guidelines for intensive therapeutic work with children. Accompanying these direct-service and clinical activities were significant efforts for social reform and legislation to assist families and their dependent children. The leaders in these movements were prominent social workers from the settlement house movement (Cohen, 1958). Some of their accomplishments included the establishment of the White House Conference and formation of the Children's Bureau.

Throughout the years social workers have been the major therapists for children (Littner and Schour, 1971). Social workers have always seen more children than all other mental health professionals combined and within a variety of settings and fields. Some of the children have been abandoned, abused, or neglected; some are those reacting to inadequate parenting or problems and stresses within the home; others are seriously disturbed children who function within a range of behaviors that are unacceptable to others and nonproductive for the child. Social work clinicians involved with these children have made major contributions to practice theory in relation to the treatment of children. Some have influenced work with children across disciplines and as a result their origins and professional association with social work are often forgotten. Foremost among them are Selma Fraiberg, Leontine Young, Rudolph Ekstein, and Samuel Slavson.

Clinical work with children is a specialty within social work, as it is within all professions. It is different from clinical work with adults because children are not miniature adults. Children act and think differently from adults, have different needs, and therefore need different interventions. In addition, children are realistically dependent upon parents or caretakers for care and protection; they are molded by them and react to them directly in the present rather than in retrospect as adults usually do in treatment (Littner and Schour, 1971). Childhood itself is not a discrete entity. Spanning almost eighteen years, it encompasses different periods, ranging from infancy through adolescence. At each stage—preschool, school age or latency, and adolescence—the child will have particular attributes, abilities, and needs. As a result clinical practice differs for children at different stages; each stage requires special knowledge and methods for effective treatment.

The middle stage, childhood proper or latency, is the focus of attention in this chapter. The child's dependency at this time propels the clinician into multiple relationships with parents or foster parents and as often includes interventions upon a variety of systems that exacerbate or create inner stress by creating external stress for the child. The clinician's first concern will be with the environment; whenever that is diagnosed as pathological for the child, the first focus will be upon changing it because children cannot be expected to adapt to nonsupportive or detrimental conditions. Thus any situation that produces problems is the first target for change. Concomitant with that—or after that, as is diagnostically indicated—the focus is upon progressive developmental changes in the child.

The social work emphasis upon child-in-situation and person-in-situation is the unique contribution of the profession to therapeutic intervention. Though in work with children other professionals generally attend to the child's situation because the child's natural dependency mandates this, no other profession has made as strong a commitment to a clinical assessment of the social environment in relation to the lives and needs of people (Briar, 1976). Thus the starting point in clinical social work with children will be with the parents or other caretakers and the realities which all are experiencing (see Shirley Cooper, "The Treatment of Parents," in this volume, Chapter Eighteen). The ending point with children may occur when there is sufficient improvement in the situation and sufficient progress in the child's development to enable normal growth processes to take precedence. There are circumstances which will demand that work continue with and for individuals within the child's life space even though the child will no longer be seen. In some circumstances, where it is not possible to effect sufficient change in the environment, the clinician may need to continue long-term contact as a support to the child. At times this may mean assisting the child into adulthood. From beginning to end, clinical social work with children will aim to set in motion progressive life processes and suitable environment provisions to facilitate internal maturational processes (Winnicott, 1965).

The methods employed include more than individual casework. In addition to the modalities of family, group, or individual therapy, concrete services, home and school visiting, and advocacy are often indicated. The choice of activity will evolve from a diagnosis of the child and the situation in which the child lives; the treatment plan emerging from this assessment will determine which actions are in the best interest of the child.

The Setting

Children are seen wherever families are seen. They are seen in a variety of social agencies—child guidance clinics, family agencies, children's institutions and special schools, normal school settings, settlement and community settings, the child's own home, or clinicians' private offices. Agencies will vary in function, focus, and resources.

The Agency. The largest number of social workers are salaried employees in agencies and institutions; a much smaller number work autonomously in private practice. The agency can offer security, peer support, supervision, and a wide range of resources. In addition to some concrete services or access to other agencies, there are opportunities to develop a variety of interventions, groups, and family therapy in conjunction with individual work with the child and the family.

Yet there may be conflicts between the goals of the professional and those of the agency. McGowan (1978) suggests that organizations are goal-oriented as contrasted to professionals who emphasize process and the proper use of knowledge and technique. At times, workers have to weigh the children's interests against organizational interests. Explicit goals are often expected in some settings, such as schools or court settings, where there is an effort to obtain measurable results which often may have a strong control component. This is the antithesis of the professional emphasis upon process and client self-determination, even where children are concerned. Clinical social work with children is most successful when the professional has a free choice of differential treatment plans to meet the individual client's needs. Yet organizational structures often have prescribed and limited treatment techniques. Thus the clinical social worker may at times find it necessary to respond to client need beyond the perspective and resources of the immediate agency. In addition, clinical work with children necessitates the ability to engage in multiple relationships, skill in working with a team or with other colleagues, and appropriate knowledge of other resources and referral processes.

The Treatment Room. Children cannot be expected to sit quietly during an interview, thus a formal interviewing room is contraindicated. But few agencies have the space or money for special play rooms that are used exclusively by children. If the usual office is not too decorated, and if the worker will not have to worry about keeping the furniture, walls, and floors in good, clean condition, these rooms can be used for working with children. The addition of a work table and some cupboards or shelves to keep play equipment would suffice for working with most children. Telephones, dictating machines, and typewriters can offer the opportunity for creative work with children. The number of toys that are needed for play therapy with children is very small. Equipment that enables imaginative play and a few appropriate games are usually all that is necessary. In any case, the determination of needed equipment, space, and the method all evolve from a diagnosis of the child and his or her situation.

Diagnosis

The Child's Situation. Because no child can exist without one's own or surrogate family, the assessment process will begin with a study of the people and the circumstances in which the child is living. The majority of children live with their own families, which may include other relatives and the extended family as well as mother, father, and siblings. In addition, there are many children who do not live with their natural parents; they may be the children in foster care because of neglect and abuse, a mother's physical or mental illness, desertion, death, a parent's unwillingness to care for the children, family dysfunction, or the child's unmanageable behavior (Fanshel and Shinn, 1978). When the child's behavior and needs cannot be addressed or managed within an ordinary family situation or a foster care arrangement, residential treatment may be necessitated. Even these "model" families or "therapeutic" settings need to be evaluated to determine if they are meeting the child's changing needs or if they are contributing to the child's difficulties.

The child's day-by-day realities, which include interactions with others, have to be studied. Sometimes a child's sudden deviation from a normal behavior pattern is precipitated by problems within the living situation. The problem may be a critical event in the total family life to which the child is reacting and with which the family is suffering. In other cases, neglect of the child, or a generally unhappy, troubled family system or unreasonable demands imposed upon the child may explain many dysfunctional and chronic behaviors and difficulties.

The Child. Though essential, an emphasis upon environmental circumstances is not sufficient. Even where much of a child's behavior may seem reactive to a pathological situation, the child's development may be skewed because of internalized, pathological adaptations. For example, where the child has experienced abuse or neglect, a focus of therapeutic effort on parents alone has not been successful in resolving the effects on the child's emotional development and relationships (Burch, 1980). Even when the unhealthy environmental situation is improved, children tend to continue to react with old defenses that were learned and internalized when the situation was disturbing to them. Fraiberg, Adelson, and Shapiro (1975) talk of the "ghosts in the nursery," those infantile reactions that continue to be repeated by adults. Studying abusive parents, they found they had been abused or neglected as children. The parents remembered the traumatic facts of their own abuse, but did not remember the accompanying affects and had not worked through the trauma. Instead they reenacted their experiences over and over again with their own children.

Anna Freud (1965) notes that pathogenic factors tend to be operative in external circumstances and internal personal structures: "Once they are intertwined, pathology becomes ingrained in the structure of the personality and is removed only by therapeutic measures which affect this structure" (p. 51). Some developmental interferences and unfavorable circumstances or events have the potential to influence future development and to create fertile conditions for later disturbances. Through the process of internalization, there can be symptom formation, development of certain character traits, or fixation points which can act as an impetus for regression. Children will suffer developmental arrest when they have been deprived of essential and basic requirements such as human contact, caring, and stimulation, as in the institutionalized infants studied by Spitz (1945) or as in cases of extreme child neglect or abuse. These events distort and retard the growth of the personality.

Developmental conflicts occur at all stages. Children have different needs and different developmental tasks during each stage, and every stage requires certain ideal conditions for optimal development of the child's capacities. Similarly during each stage, external events will have different significance depending upon the child's maturity, interest, and understanding. Transitory, phase-specific conflicts will occur and cause anxiety, temporary symptom formation, behavior disorders, and fears. Unresolved developmental conflict can become permanent conflict through internalized restrictions which create anxiety and affect functioning. In these situations, action upon the environment is not enough to help the child.

The Dilemma of Diagnosis. It is not simple to assess the state of a child's health because children vary in their emotional, social, physical, and mental growth. Symptoms and behaviors need to be understood but any one symptom can be the result of multiple causes; a child's symptom is no more than a symbol indicating that some mental turmoil is taking place (Freud, 1970). In addition, it is difficult to learn from children about the problems in their lives. Though children are very sensitive to external conditions, they rarely can complain appropriately and they seldom have the power to change things for themselves. Instead, it is common for them to behave and react, expressing problems within themselves and with others through behaviors, fears, and withdrawal, and through physical, social, and educational difficulties.

The behaviors that prompt parents, foster parents, teachers, and others to think a child needs help tend to be those that disturb the adults in contact with him or her. Many complaints thus reflect adult needs and the beliefs and values of the reporters as well as their reactions to the effect of the behavior on themselves, rather than the child's needs. As a result, the child's viewpoint or need may be neglected (Lieberman, 1979). Yet children who need therapeutic or remedial help are dependent upon adults for recognition of their problems.

Diagnosis, a process of inquiry, understanding, and predictions based on contingencies, consists of a series of hypotheses which are confirmed or negated during the course of treatment. A diagnosis is reached through various means such as observation, facts of past and present, and a variety of tests and statements by the child and caretakers. But many of these processes are fallible.

Retrospective information has been considered a poor source for factual matters (Sears, Raus, and Alpert, 1965). School reports consist of both facts and opinions. The facts are grades and the results of standardized tests, but teachers' grades include subjective opinions about a child's performance. Psychological and intelligence tests tend to be treated as objective rather than conditional (Bachrach, 1974). Yet when psychological tests are summarized and include the psychologist's interpretations, they are diagnostic statements, not facts. Intelligence tests have been under scrutiny for many years. They are generally considered imperfect instruments which permit general predictions about future academic performance and some estimate of what has been learned, but cannot predict performance in all areas of life (Deutsch, 1969; Hobbs, 1975). They have been criticized as not assessing reasoning and creativity (DeVries, 1974).

The psychiatric examination is sometimes used routinely during an intake process. Then children are asked to talk with another adult stranger. Though some children may joke, there is concern about needing a "mental" examination, as the following example illustrates.

Dave, an eleven-year-old boy, had been referred because he didn't get along with peers and seemed isolated and fearful. He appeared to be frightened when first seen, but glanced around the room and seemed to be noting the toys. When the worker indicated she knew that he had seen the psychiatrist, Dr. Smith, Dave just shrugged. Then he said abruptly, "Can I use the toys?" When the worker nodded, he took some paper and drew a picture of a big man and a young boy. In cartoon fashion the following words were written as coming out of the man's lips, each statement enclosed in a balloon:

"Hi, Dave, I'm Dr. Smith. Can I talk to you a little bit?"

"Why not?"

"How do you feel about coming to see me? What makes you not want to talk to me?"

The following issued from the mouth of the boy: "No." Then, "I am not." Finally, in another balloon: "Drop dead!"

It is difficult for children to understand the psychiatric examination or projective tests. Both can evoke frightening, unconscious feelings. Too often these are not clarified for children who, as a result, feel that someone has done something to them rather than helped them.

Professionals often use referral symptoms and other descriptions of behavior to categorize and diagnose children's difficulties. But these tell little about a particular child and cause of the difficulty. Categories and labels do not clarify the etiology of the problem nor do they suggest an individualized treatment approach. Some labels are so broad that the individual differences and needs of a particular child may be overlooked. "Learning disabled," a currently popular label, is of that kind; it tells nothing but that the child is having some difficulty in school or in learning. Many such labels result in discrimination, decreased expectations of and for the child, stigmatization, and tracking. In the end, labels can become self-fulfilling or even have social and political implications which may follow a child through life (Hobbs, 1975). Some children are excluded from services because of rigid definitions and category requirements which determine who can be treated and where. Children who need service the most too often end up excluded from treatment resources or being sent through an endless round of diagnoses in lieu of receiving help.

It is rare that professional social workers label children. The combination of system hierarchies, allocation of roles, and mental health laws usually designate the psychiatrist as responsible for the labeling process. It is more common for social workers to use a dynamic diagnostic formulation, a more inclusive and comprehensive approach to the child's life experience. Though this may contain a clinical label, it will also contain an evaluation of the child, the situation, and the child's reaction to current as well as past experiences (Hamilton, 1963). Available facts about the child and the family's present and past history and functioning will be interpreted to understand the child and the family within a variety of contexts; strengths as well as stresses and problems will be identified. Cross-referencing the chronology of important events with the individual's age at the time of occurrence will suggest the existence of old traumas. For children these are separations from parents, maternal depression, emotional disturbance in a parent or other family member, neglect or abuse, hospitalizations or traumatic medical manipulation, illness or operations, and the deaths or illnesses of important people. Understanding of the problem is enhanced by identification of the stimuli that precipitated the problem—those that predispose the child to certain reactions, such as constitution, heredity, endowment, previous events, personality, family patterns, and parent-child relations, and those within the child and the situation that combine to perpetuate the difficulties. A dynamic diagnostic formulation is the foundation upon which treatment begins and is built. It determines timing, target, modality, and the variety of essential services that may be needed.

Treatment of Children

Beginnings. It is quite obvious that it is essential to begin with the parents or the child's caretakers because children do not bring themselves to treatment. Some adult will have complained or worried about them and their activities and will feel it necessary for them to change. But children approach treatment with different goals. They may want things to be better and for things outside of themselves to change, but they rarely wish to change themselves. There are other children who think of themselves as bad and may wish to be different, but they may feel this is impossible. Many of the children social workers see have no hope that their lives will improve. Children have very personal ideas about the aim, meaning, and function of the treatment process; these include conscious and unconscious fantasies about the purpose of treatment and the person who conducts the treatment (Blos, 1970).

Children have the right to participate in the planning that is done for them, even though their dependence on adults necessitates their doing many things they may not want to do. Seeing a social worker may be one of those things; it may also be one of the many things they do not understand. Sometimes it is helpful to clarify the difference between a social worker and other authorities such as teachers and doctors. However, very young children may not really understand; even older children may be confused.

Children will understand the difference when they are consulted about appointments and some of the mechanical details of treatment. The careful attention to the child's questions or interests, empathy with the child, and curious exploration of the child's initial responses to treatment will assist the child's understanding. A therapeutic alliance, essential for successful therapeutic work with any client, must be nurtured. Lane (1980, p. 119) suggests that the therapeutic alliance—"the axis around which turns the kaleidoscope of events and affects which make up child psychotherapy"—is initially difficult for young children. Their limited life experience and immature intrapsychic development necessitate a beginning that teaches what this is about and what the therapist will be like. As part of this initial process the child must know why he or she is being seen and why parents or others are concerned; in addition, the child needs help in thinking through his or her own concerns which may be different. Listening and accepting the child's different viewpoint will help establish the therapeutic alliance.

One cannot expect children to say in a straightforward manner that they need or want therapy. If the worker joins the child in understanding that together they are doing something mandated by parents, school, or some authority, if this is the case, then the two together can consider ways to make their sessions worthwhile. More often than not children will communicate in a roundabout fashion, in a child's way, through toys and stories; in these activities they will indicate their needs and problems.

Certainly, even seven-year-olds can talk about the meeting time that may be best for them. Perhaps a time suggested by the worker will interfere with an afterschool activity or with a school activity that is desired or important. Conferring together about a mutually acceptable time is a beginning demonstration of the nature of treatment and the respect and freedom it connotes. It is important that the child's requests be considered most seriously; indeed, when the child is engaged in an age-appropriate activity that can assist in development it is best that therapy does not interfere. After all, a child's play is a child's work and therapeutic work has as a goal releasing the child from the tensions and fears that restrict activity with peers and in the "real" world.

The goals of treatment need to be clarified with the child because the child's goals may not be the same as the parents'. The following case example illustrates this.

Lois, a twelve-year-old black child, was brought to the clinic because of school complaints. Though her work was good, her behavior and attitude were considered poor. She was reported as wanting everything her own way, easily provoked, argumentative, and attacking teachers. Her mother described her as defiant, always seeking excitement, and jealous of her mother's attention to an older retarded sister. When Lois was ten she was severely burned while using the stove; she was hospitalized for sixteen weeks. Yet, her mother reported, when Lois came home she behaved as if nothing had happened.

Lois, who had missed several initial appointments for a variety of reasons, came twenty minutes late to her first interview. She smiled and acted very carefree throughout the interview. When the worker said that she thought Lois had been reluctant to come to see her, the child said she was willing to give her a chance. In answer to the question of why she had been sent to the clinic, Lois stated it was because she went into a "trance." She explained that she "meditated" and "daydreamed" so intensely that she became unaware of what was going on around her. She joked that the neurologist and psychologist told her mother she was normal but her mother wanted her to see a "shrink." Asked her opinion, she just shrugged her shoulders.

Now Lois was saying that her mother was concerned about her strange behavior; she herself was concerned that her mother think of her as normal. The worker could recognize that this was a serious matter and together with Lois consider how to convince her mother that she was normal. In addition, since Lois had said she daydreamed and meditated so intensely, the worker could examine with her what was so good in the daydreams that they blocked out reality, and what needed blocking out in reality. When this was done, Lois explained that she meditated by concentrating on one thing. She did this to escape from the world around her, especially at school. She wasn't concerned about this. What did concern her was her temper. She had a terrible temper and would count to ten in order to control herself; otherwise, she would just lash out. The worker knew that Lois had thrown a chair at a teacher. Lois explained that the teacher had criticized her report about "Hair" and the class laughed at her. She said she threw the chair because she was upset at their laughter. She did not throw it at the teacher, but only to release tension. The worker recognized that sometimes tension can be intolerable, and just build up. She could see how Lois needed to figure out something to deal with all her tensions. What worried the worker was that the meditation wasn't helping enough; it just seemed to get Lois into more trouble. Lois nodded sadly.

In another interview Lois was a half hour late. She had left home late because she did not want any of the kids to get suspicious. No one knew she was seeing a social worker. The worker said she knew how hard it is to feel different from other kids. Lois looked sad. Lois talked about missing school because she had gone back to sleep after her mother had awakened her. She found it hard to get up in the morning because she would go to sleep late and then dream. She wouldn't talk about her dreams because her dreams were "like X-rated movies." She thought the worker would be shocked. When the worker wondered why she thought so, Lois said because she herself felt so embarrassed. She wouldn't talk about her feelings, but said that after every appointment with the worker her mother gave her the "third degree." Lois wouldn't tell her anything, saying it was none of her business. She continued that sooner or later her mother pressured people into telling her what she wanted to know. Now the worker said it sounded like Lois was worried that the worker would be pressured into telling her mother what Lois talked about. To this, Lois said yes. The worker explained about confidentiality, but remembered that once she had inadvertently told the mother when Lois had missed an appointment. Lois said that was an example of what would happen; the worker would just let something slip out. The worker said she understood why Lois needed to be careful about what she said. Lois agreed.

Lois was now well into treatment. She was establishing the ground rules, clarifying her distrust of adults who talked to each other about her, and testing to see if she could indeed trust this worker. As the worker followed her carefully, Lois began in this and later interviews to talk about other people she did not trust and said that she had no one in whom she could confide. When the worker generalized that some people would be lonely without people to confide in, Lois was quiet, then said she didn't know why she was that way. She wondered if it was because she was never able to be carefree. From the time she was very young she had to take care of her retarded sister; she hated her mother for this. Then she said she often dreamed about killing her mother but added, of course, she would never do it, she couldn't kill a fly. She had to repeat this several times.

Now Lois was no longer joking. She was trusting, slowly, and bringing appropriately her concerns to the treatment session. She was talking in a very grownup manner for a twelve-year-old and clarifying much of her behavior. Slowly her worker, who would help her to be a child as is appropriate to her age and need, would also help her to find more adaptive ego-supportive ways to meet her needs. In addition, the family situation suggested that Lois's mother needed help in finding more appropriate resources to assist her with her handicapped child.

Resistance. Children are "involuntary" clients. Therefore it is not strange that many of them are resistant or unwilling to talk or cooperate. In addition, it is appropriate for latency-age children to defend against anxiety through projection, denial, displacement, and repression. But these defenses make therapy difficult. The younger six- to eight-year-olds cannot sit still for very long and they tend to regard interpretations of their behavior as criticism. On the other hand, they also can misconstrue an understanding or permissive attitude as seductive and as permission to do forbidden things. It does not take much for them to engage in wishful thinking or to employ primary process thinking, both of which interfere with reality testing and make the therapeutic process more difficult (Lieberman,

1979). Older latency-age children are better able to evaluate reality, integrate contradictions, and abide by rules, but they also have strong defenses that shield them from their painful feelings and what they view as criticism. Preadolescents who may have more access to their uncomfortable feelings also have more elaborate defenses (Williams, 1972).

Children who have suffered a great deal attempt to defend against their pain by trying not to feel. Sometimes they engage in prolonged testing of the therapist to determine if they will be protected and properly cared for. The following example illustrates this testing; it is derived from the work of Linda Bernstein, a social worker in a child welfare agency.

Susan, a six-year-old girl, was referred because of poor school performance, poor impulse control, enuresis, and a depressed, disoriented affect. She had been living with her mother and the mother's male friend. She often was left alone in the apartment with no food and no adult supervision. Concerned neighbors reported the situation, which was being investigated by protective services.

In her first session she brought in a picture book called *The Scared Rabbit,* which she wanted read to her. In the next session she brought in a baby doll, diapers, and blanket. She insisted on the worker being the babysitter who was taking care of her baby doll. She sat in the corner and cautiously watched how the doll was cared for, making sure that it was comforted and that the worker did not drop it. She wanted the doll fed frequently and tucked into bed; then both worker and child were to sit quietly until they were certain the doll was asleep.

This play lasted for many months. Then one day Susan lay down on the floor crying like a baby. There was an extremely eerie quality to her crying; she sounded like a screaming, colicky baby. In fact, this crying had been mentioned as intolerable by the referring personnel. After the worker dealt quietly with these tantrums and said that she wanted to help, Susan began another game. She became the mother and had the worker play the child. She was a cruel and impatient mother. In addition she said the worker was the dumbest therapist she had ever met, complained she wasn't helpful, and said she should go back to school to learn how to be a good one. She said she hated coming, but continued to come regularly for her appointments. She gave the worker long, tedious homework assignments, said the answers were wrong and the dumbest things she had ever seen. "You should be ashamed of yourself," she would say. She would tear up the papers and yell, "Can't you do anything right?" Thus Susan brought her pain to the therapist; only after watching the care of her doll and acting the angry, aggressive, cruel adult was she able to become the little girl who could accept help.

It is natural for children to be frightened about treatment and to find it difficult to understand. Even those who have had a therapeutic experience with another therapist and who have learned it is not frightening will be cautious and test the new therapist. Though some children will talk and play easily and seem cooperative, their extroversion and the frequency with which they change activities may represent only a superficial friendliness. Such children will relate to the therapist as they do to their parents and other important people; how they relate will demonstrate the depth of their relationships.

Another example illustrates this superficiality in relationships:

Helene, a diminutive, thin, seven-year-old girl, lived with her twenty-six-year-old deaf, nonspeaking mother and her nine-year-old brother. She was referred by her school because she was described as an "isolate"—uninvolved academically and socially. She had great cultural deprivation, was unable to count, and was not ready for reading.

Helene was seen at her school. When she was taken from her classroom for her first session with the school social worker, she immediately took her hand. As soon as she saw the toys in the room she grabbed at them, acting as if she could not get enough, and began playing in a disorganized manner. While she played, she talked spontaneously. She said her mother couldn't talk and had to point to things. They used sign language at home. She volunteered that she didn't have a father but that she knew where he was. She said he lived in Puerto Rico and owned a hot dog stand and proudly added that he could speak two languages. She also said that no one would ever get mad at her since she was just a little girl.

Though this was a new experience for Helene, she went easily with the worker, but she was only repeating her way of managing a difficult world. She was just a little girl. She was also one who needed caring, things, and attention; who provided these vital supplies was still a matter of indifference. She was neither interacting nor relating.

Some children will seem to be loquacious and intelligent but they may be using words to avoid communicating and relating. They will be and seem unhappy, serious, or lacking humor and spontaneity. They will tend to overvalue talk and try to achieve control through words that isolate and deny affective content. They are children who are perpetually involved in a power struggle and in the issue of autonomy (Adams, 1973). Ekstein (1971) noted the wordiness of some schizophrenic children and suggested that they are repeating the acts of the small child who is still searching for the reassuring, answering echo of the parent. Because they are still struggling with the issue of differentiating themselves and the outside world, their communications are more of a monologue than a dialogue and reflect an internal discourse. They tend to be boring clients and induce a counteraction of words by their therapists who do not wish to be ignored.

The silent child who refuses to talk or play also provokes the worker to struggle with them (Kaplan and Escoll, 1973; Chethik, 1973). Children who are concerned with problems involving separation and autonomy often withhold speech, and suspicious children who are afraid to test new situations keep to themselves to feel safe (Winnicott, 1964). Depressed children may not be able to believe anything will help, and children who are afraid may try to control the situation by feigning indifference and refusing to cooperate. Severely disturbed children may use withdrawal to insulate themselves as a protection against feeling. All these children equate doing with dangerous, destructive things; therefore they do nothing (Nagelberg, Spotnitz, and Feldman, 1953). Their silence may be a form of insulation to maintain control and achieve independence from their frightening impulses. When they are less afraid they can learn to express their destructive impulses in fantasy and then in more appropriate direct ways. There are others for whom silence is an expression of a need for a person with whom they need not communicate and from whom they can withdraw (Fraiberg, 1962).

Oppositional Children. Some children are more overtly oppositional; these are called the acting-outers. They break appointments and are hostile, provocative, and disruptive; some even attempt physical attacks on the worker. However, these similar behaviors may have different causations. Some children have difficulty in maintaining control over their impulses; others act out because they have some fight in them and some hope that things can be better. Young children cannot easily tolerate unpleasant feelings; therefore they tend to repress them and choose acting instead of talking. Often children act out in response to traumatic experiences in an attempt to actively master the unpleasant things that had been experienced passively. This was the case with Susan, described earlier. Similarly, Lois, who was difficult to control at school, lost her temper quickly and violently, and was described as "defiant" at home, revealed very quickly that she was frightened about her own angry, destructive thoughts and the anger and criticism of others. Lois is representative of a large group of children who are referred for treatment because of acting-out behavior in their grade school or adolescent years. Rexford (1978) suggests that the early relationship to the mother, the nature of the oedipal conflicts, the formation of the superego, and family patterns play a key role in this problem.

The personality structures of these children are not identical; there may be varying degrees of internalization and/or externalization of conflicts. It is generally difficult for any child under stress to control impulses or to avoid the childlike tendency to erupt into action. In addition, aggressive acts are normal for young children. Only with the development of the ego and superego, and identification with parents as well as wishing to have and keep their love and approval, are temper tantrums and more overt expressions of anger channeled into constructive tasks (Buxbaum, 1970). The development of thinking and language assists the child to communicate through symbolic and more indirect ways. In fact, immaturity of verbalization skills and marked learning disabilities appear to be related to acting out. In these cases there is an observable, persistent, and continued use of behavior to discharge and express feelings.

Acting out within the treatment situation is the child's way of expressing the essence of his or her object relations and core problem. Amini and Burke (1979) suggest that such behavior repeats variations of significant themes from the past. It is the child's way of being in the world and a disguised way of telling a story about the past and the nature of the child's attachment to the most significant others. In addition, when the adults are provoked to react with controls and punishment, they are also reenacting the child's customary experiences with grownups.

Nancy, age six-and-a-half, was referred because of chronic lying that was reported to have started and continued since she was two-and-a-half. She also stole small items from her mother and schoolmates. The items she stole tended to be important to these individuals and her stealing resulted in their becoming enraged. However, Nancy seemed to anticipate being caught and never protested punishment.

She was six months old when her parents divorced. Then she and her older brother lived with their mother who went to work. Until Nancy was three, she saw her father on a regular basis. Then for a year, her mother would not permit this. Her father remarried when she was four; both children went to live with him and his new wife, and their mother, who lived in a studio apartment, was visited on weekends. All parents were educated and professional. Nancy's first two years of life included eating and bowel problems. Because of the latter, she was only permitted to have three or four kinds of foods. Little else was known of her development.

In therapy, Nancy would tell stories and talk to herself, but she rarely responded directly to the questions or conversation of her therapist and then only by telling stories about other children and animals. One of her stories was about an animal that had never eaten but grew anyway. In an early session she broke a crayon in half and looked challengingly at her worker. Another time, she made an ice cream cone out of playdoh and began licking it. When the worker said she thought many children had played with the material so it wasn't clean, Nancy proceeded to pretend to lick it. Now and then she would take a real lick, smiling into the worker's face.

For the most part Nancy played alone, ignoring the therapist. She induced in the latter feelings of helplessness because there seemed to be no way to reach her. But the worker understood this as a communication of Nancy's own feelings of helplessness and her sense of being ignored. In this active repetition of her real experience, she was trying to master a disturbing situation. It was as if she passed on the disagreeable experience to another, and therefore obtained revenge (Freud, [1920], 1955). Her defiance was also her determination to grow, even if she was never fed.

Therefore the worker sat quietly, being available but not intruding. Gradually Nancy began to test the worker by including her in her play. She began to draw pictures; sometimes she would tell the worker what to draw and then they would color them together. Nancy gave the orders, and therefore controlled the situation. After being tested in this manner for many weeks, the worker was able to ask questions about the pictures they were drawing which often were of animals and sometimes of houses. Through this medium, the child began to tell of her confusion in families, her fear of being lost, and her need for feeding and caring. With this development, she stopped stealing and her relationships with peers and her stepmother began to improve.

Communication

The silent child, the defiant child, and the compliant child all communicate in ways that are congruent with their life stories and their experiences. Their actions and nonactions, equal in meaning to their words, tell their stories, problems, and hopes. Though children are not consciously aware of the full meaning of their communications, they are touched by therapeutic responses that indicate understanding and are keyed to helping and not threatening. The children, feeling understood, will understand. Then they will respond, again through actions, nonactions, and sometimes words.

Words. Children have not acquired full mastery of language and many children do not have complete command and use of secondary process thought. This is generally true of the very young child, but also of the more disturbed child or one with intellectual or learning problems. Frequently the language and level of children's communications are in some ways similar to those of infantile, regressed clients who have weak egos, primitive defenses, and generally confused thinking. Displacement is a very common defense among children. When they talk about an animal, another child, or a storybook character, that other character will be speaking for them about the important events and issues in their lives. The character's feelings will be their feelings. Sometimes this is very transparent but at other times even this is disguised. Children will use jokes to hide their fears and anxieties and to transform painful experiences into pleasurable ones. Jokes disguise forbidden impulses, ease tension, and permit the child to talk indirectly about problems. Distortions of well-known jokes will reveal important conflicts.

The spontaneous stories that children tell—whether they are about real people and events or make-believe characters—are valuable forms of communication. The affects and the content will reveal that which is of current importance to the child. These stories are the child's metaphors. Ekstein and Wallerstein (1966) suggest that the metaphoric communication repeats the earlier preverbal communication that existed in the mother-child fusion. Use of the metaphor is common to borderline adolescents who need distance from conscious awareness of conflicts because they have poor psychic organization and ability to communicate at an abstract level. Generally, children of latency age have not developed the ability to communicate at an abstract level; for them the metaphor, expressed through stories, drawings, actions, and play, is a normal and necessary way of communicating.

Play. An action metaphor rather than a figure of speech, play is a series of actions which stand for other actions, tensions, impulses, and fears. Play is of great importance in the normal life of a child and changes in play accompany developmental growth (Peller, 1954). There is general agreement that children use play to repeat real-life experiences that have impressed them and that play often is an active attempt to master a passively endured experience. With extraordinary frequency play reproduces or proceeds from situations which were in reality devoid of pleasure (Waelder, 1976). There is an inner pressure that disposes children to attempt to assimilate disagreeable experiences through play and to abreact traumatic experiences by games. Play enables the child to divide excessive experiences into smaller quantities and to work over and assimilate in smaller doses an experience which was initially overwhelming. In addition, play permits the child to take roles ordinarily prohibited by others or by the child's own conscience. Though play is "make-believe" it differs from adult fantasy. In the latter, reality is disowned; the child's play is fantasy woven about a real object and the tangible and visible things of the real world. In this way play is a form of trial thinking and appropriate for children.

In therapy, spontaneous play is a child's natural, free-associative form of communication. Erikson (1963) suggests that play is childhood's most natural method of self-healing. In the more formal therapeutic encounter, playing permits children to verbalize safely conscious material and feelings and to act out unconscious conflicts and fantasies. In this way they are able to communicate the anxieties they may be unable to share openly. They are able to talk about fears that they know are unrealistic, but which they have anyway. The central themes of the play will elucidate the child's problems.

The activities and the materials selected are related to the child's problem and need. For example, some children choose aggressive toys, such as guns; this may suggest a preoccupation with aggression, or it may represent a phase-specific normal working through of aggressive or sexual themes. Other children may be too inhibited to even play at make-believe aggressive activities. Sometimes while playing, children may stop, change the theme impulsively, or become visibly upset. This will occur when the play becomes too real, too stimulating, and too close to the real problem. Children who have suffered many losses, particularly of parents, and those who have had inconsistent care—particularly during the first three years of life, the period of separation-individuation—often play out the wish to be looked for and found; others search for a missing object in diverse ways, through ball playing, hiding behind objects, or waiting outside the therapy room and peeking in at the therapist (Lieberman, 1979).

Helene, the six-and-a-half-year-old whose mother was deaf and mute, was discussed earlier. In the third session she showed her worker her new shoes. She said she liked them because her Mom couldn't catch her in them when she ran away from her. Then she began to play house, making a cake for the worker's birthday. When the worker asked how old she was supposed to be, Helene answered that the worker was one year old and that Helene was seven and her Mom ten because she wasn't a lot taller than Helene. She said she was saving a piece of cake for Daddy. She explained, when asked, that he was far, far away and had to take a train, bus, and another train to get here. When it was time to leave she asked if the worker ever got mad. The reply was that a lot of people get mad, and for many reasons. She said she got mad at her brother for cursing at Mom. As she was being returned to her classroom, she ran ahead, calling back, "Hurry up, try to catch me."

In her fifth session she stated she was sad because her Mom was sad, too. When asked what they were sad about, she said that the father cat had left. She then began something that became a pattern. She would hide in the closet and want the worker to find her. Sometimes she would ask to be locked in the closet until she knocked from the inside to be let out. Other times she would climb high up on the cabinets where the worker could not reach her. Once, when it was time to go she began running around the room expecting to be chased. Instead, the worker verbalized how hard it was to catch Helene. She asked if the worker was getting angry. The worker thought it was hard not to be but she had to leave now and wanted Helene to come with her. Then Helene asked the worker to help her down.

There are multiple themes in this play communication. Helene is angry at her mother; Helene runs away, but wants to be caught. Is it possible that Mother became so enraged at Helene that she locked her in the closet? Where is Daddy, whom Helene has never known? The worker felt Helene was not yet ready to have her play interpreted. It was the beginning, the listening stage. But the worker knew there were things to learn about Helene's real life at home.

Communicating to Children. Verbalization and interpretation are frequently considered essential aspects of therapeutic work. They tend to be concerned with hidden meanings and unconscious connections. Yet if one speaks directly about unconscious material to children, they will equate this with mind reading and become frightened. Though it is possible to interpret events that occur between the worker and the child in ways attuned to the child's individual needs and expressed in the child's language, the best interpretations are those the children arrive at by themselves.

Communication with children is furthered through using the metaphor of their play or stories. Ekstein and Wallerstein (1966) propose that the use of the metaphor is an essential technique for gradually establishing communication and initial insight with clients whose brittle defensive structure could not stand interpretations aimed at bringing material to conscious awareness. The therapist utilizes the client's primary process material without translating its meaning into secondary process; this provides a protective distance and time for gradual integration. Thus, though the client may need to use the metaphor, the therapist will choose to use it, deliberately and manipulatively. An empathic response to the metaphoric mode chosen by the child will permit the child to know the meaning of the communication while at the same time feeling safe because of not being forced to deal with threatening ideas or feelings. Children's play usually is an attempt to process and interpret for themselves and the worker the child's psychological concerns (Burch, 1980). When children feel understood, they will sometimes emerge from their stories or play and talk of their own feelings.

Stories address the anxieties and dilemmas of the child; they offer solutions in ways the child can grasp. Bettelheim (1976) makes particular reference to fairy tales. The motifs are experienced as wondrous because the child feels understood and appreciated deep down in his or her feelings, hopes, and anxieties without these having to be harshly and rationally investigated in a manner that may be beyond the child. That the stories are unrealistic does not concern the child; it is obvious that these tales of enchantment concern the inner processes that take place in an individual.

Concetta, a thirteen-year-old black girl, was referred by her mother who could not control her daughter's behavior. Concetta lied, stole, broke curfews, disobeyed, and was sexually promiscuous. The mother became very upset when she discovered the diary the child left lying around. In it Concetta described having intercourse at age ten with a twenty-eight-year-old man and a fifteen-year-old boy on a day when her mother had left her alone; she also included other sexual material she read about in a novel. (There is a possibility that the child was raped but this was never verified.) Her mother had immediately taken her to the gynecologist for birth control pills.

Concetta's mother had become pregnant while in the twelfth grade and a forced marriage was arranged, but the father deserted after two weeks. Concetta's maternal grandmother then disowned her daughter but Concetta spent the first four years of life with her grandmother. At age four, Concetta was taken by an aunt for a visit to her mother, who was living in a permanent relationship with a Puerto Rican man she could not marry. Concetta never returned to the grandmother. She became severely depressed and stopped eating for months; in treatment she recalled that she felt she was living with a stranger. She idealized her grandmother but at the same time was quite angry at her for not making any attempt to get her back. At the time of referral her mother was making frequent threats to either send Concetta away or to go away herself.

In the first three sessions Concetta tried to give the impression of being supersophisticated. She talked nonstop, flooding the worker with details. The themes were her inability to communicate with her parents, her pattern of "inadvertently" leaving notes for her mother to "find," the family's preoccupation with her sexuality and fear of her becoming pregnant, her identity as black rather than

Puerto Rican, and the instability of the family because both parents alternately threatened to leave. She fantasized about breaking up the marriage. In the fourth session she talked about her boyfriend and admitted being a little scared so that she postponed the physical side of the relationship. In the fifth session she talked of fighting parental rules and even provided examples of setting up situations that resulted in tighter restrictions upon her activities.

When her mother was hospitalized for a tumor on her fallopian tubes, Concetta brought a boy to the house; when her stepfather objected, she stayed out all night. This disturbed her mother who discharged herself prematurely from the hospital. When her worker took a vacation which coincided with Christmas, Concetta again brought a boy to her house. Her mother began to threaten to send her away. Concetta was embarrassed to talk about this with her worker. She admitted she was able to get things from boys that she couldn't get from her mother.

As they talked together about the similarity in the two incidents, Concetta, an intelligent and verbal child, began to see that perhaps getting into trouble was a cry for help. As she felt more confident with the worker's help and availability and as, simultaneously, work went on with mother and stepfather, both of whom cared for Concetta and wished for her to do well, Concetta became quieter and more childlike in her interests.

Concetta began to write poetry. The first poem she brought to her worker, a gift, was embellished with brightly colored flowers:

Goodnight World

Well here I am, ready for
Sleep, a deep deep sleep.
When will I wake
We have yet to see.
But I want to wake
Again, to live and see
Our world, Goodnight
World! I repeat for now.

The second, in the following week:

Here I Go Again

Here I go again,
Off to dream land.
Where I can lie in the sand
And dream sweet dreams.

Here I go again,
Just give me one more spin
In another life span
Maybe I can lead a different life.

Here I go again,
Lying in a pool of gold
Where one never grows old.

So here I go again
Where no one is a winner
Except a few.
So you say or see
Here I go again.

The worker then told her the story of Sleeping Beauty, ending with: "When the time was right the wall of thorns suddenly turned into a wall of big, beautiful flowers which opened to let the prince enter and awaken the beautiful princess from her sleep. Then they lived together happily ever after." Concetta loved this story and asked that it be told to her again. She did not talk about what it meant to her but her acting out behavior diminished; she attended school regularly and there were no more incidents with men. There were a variety of themes in this fairy tale. The most appropriate theme for Concetta was that waiting for sexual fulfillment does not detract from its beauty and a warning that sexual arousal before mind and body are ready for it is very destructive. Concetta understood in an affective and most effective way. Admonitions, lectures, and birth control advice would have missed the communication of her dream. Instead of a more formal intellectual interpretation, her worker used the child's mode of expression to communicate with her about her external and internal reality.

Words Are Not Enough. Clinical work with children demands creative communication, which may include communication without a spoken word. Anthony (1977, p. 307) suggests that "a stream of communication, both nonverbal and verbal, flows from every person at every moment as a function of self-expression, information, and interaction." Thus actual verbal exchanges are always accompanied by affective communications, on the part of the child as well as the professional. It is the affect that really communicates the caring, interest, and understanding. It is possible for the worker not to talk, when this is indicated. Yet if there is an accompanying empathic, quiet, and attentive listening, the children will understand that they are important and that this meeting is different and special. Some of the activities that are shared between the two may also communicate more meaningfully than words; these activities may be games, play therapy, and even concrete services. For many children and their families the proper use of financial assistance, help with contacts with bureaucracies, home visits, assistance in obtaining clothing or decent living quarters, visits to school, and help with schoolwork may be of deep psychological significance.

Children who have been traumatized and hurt in their relations with others are not secure about forming new relations. If they do begin to make connection, they are easily threatened by any deviation, such as vacations and certainly by having the worker leave. Green (1978) noted that children who have been abused are apprehensive about new relationships and act as if they expect violence and rejection. Therefore, helping them to feel secure often necessitates the use of a tangible, concrete object, something that can be seen and touched.

Jackie, a fifteen-year-old girl in foster care, frequently verbalized the wish to run away and to commit suicide. Once she ingested seven tablets of medication. She had never had constant care. Information about her early life was vague, but it was known that she had been shifted from one relative to another and at age thirteen she was living with her maternal grandmother. She ran away because she was beaten with a broom stick. Indeed, she needed to be hospitalized where it was also discovered that she had been exposed to tuberculosis. As a result the grandmother was charged with child abuse and while the court hearings were being arranged, Jackie was placed in a foster home. Here she was described as being unusually moody, depressed, and agitated. Her family, consisting of her remarried mother, a seventeen-year-old brother who lived in a group home, a twelve-year-old sister who was pregnant, and a twenty-one-year-old married sister who had three small children, made no attempt to contact her.

Separation and loss seemed to be a major theme in Jackie's life and therefore became the theme in the therapeutic sessions. Although the child would leave on time and without difficulty, she would return throughout the day with various excuses to see her worker. Jackie displayed a tremendous need for something tangible she could use as a transitional object (Winnicott, 1965). Therefore, at each session, she was given a letter detailing her following appointment. She always carried the appointment letters with her. During a holiday, the worker mailed an appointment letter to her. When they met again, Jackie exclaimed, "I thought you wouldn't come back, but I got your letter!" She had not only carried this letter constantly, she also slept with it.

Termination

There are many children like Jackie, who have suffered so many losses and inconsistencies that any change in time or frequency revives old memories.

Disruptions of Treatment. It is most therapeutic if treatment continues without interruptions, regularly and steadily until the child has worked through problems and both therapist and client are pleased with the result. But vacations and illness of child or therapist make this impossible. As a result, disruptions or interruptions of treatment are common in therapeutic work with children (Ekstein, 1978). Sometimes there may be parental resistance in reaction to a child's change; then the parent will abruptly remove the child or find it impossible to bring the child to the office. This often occurs when parents are not engaged simultaneously and collaboratively in the process of treatment. In other situations, a reality problem of the family such as a parent's change of employment, a relocation, or a variety of other family situations may make it impossible for treatment to continue.

There is a large group of children who rarely receive continued sustained treatment. There are poor and minority-group children whose powerlessness as children is exaggerated by their social powerlessness. They are often assigned to students who may be in any of the helping professions. Frequently the termination of service for these children will not coincide with their need; instead these are children who are left behind before they are ready to do the leaving. They are then subjected to feelings of abandonment.

In all separations, someone leaves and someone is left. These are different experiences with different consequences, affects, and meanings. In normal development, the struggle around separation and individuation involves a termination of the symbiotic oneness with the mother; the child leaves the security of this oneness and the mother enables the leaving and therefore the development of the child (Mahler, Pine, and Bergman, 1975). This initial separation is duplicated in more complicated variations throughout life. Termination involves separation. It activates struggles over dependence/independence and power/powerlessness, and it compels facing loss and ambivalence about separation and individuation. Because of children's immaturity, termination touches upon current, basic developmental needs.

Final separations are never easy. But latency-age children cannot easily understand separations and the intense feelings that accompany separations and loss are difficult for children to tolerate. As a result they use denial, fantasy, and a variety of behaviors to manage their deep emotions. Children's pain about the loss of their social workers will reflect the depth of their involvement; more caring will cause more pain. Then, to defend against these intense unpleasant feelings, regression to old patterns of behavior may occur. There may be misbehavior or broken appointments—the child leaving instead of being left. Some children become seductive with their therapists, but act out in school and at home. Others withdraw emotionally from everybody, including others who may wish to help them. Disappointed again, they become afraid to trust anyone.

Sometimes social workers who are leaving their child clients feel like deserters. This is particularly true if the therapeutic situation has mirrored a pathological life history of perpetually being left behind. This can interfere with the therapeutic task of working appropriately in the last stage of the relationship to ensure that this experience of being left will not duplicate the abandonments of the past. Therapists need to provide time for the process of listening and hearing pain and anger. Then they will know how to help the child to use the experience for development and growth.

John, age eleven, was referred because he beat up smaller children, misbehaved in school, disobeyed at home, and was seen as manipulative. His parents called him a "con artist" and complained that he fought with his seven-year-old brother. But the parents also fought with each other. John's mother disparaged her husband, complaining he wasn't a man, but a sucker who always was taken advantage of by others. John's father was quiet; he did not speak much and when he did he stuttered.

The parents were seen individually and jointly, and some family sessions were held. John was also seen individually. This intensive work lasted about six months. Initially John tried to present himself as self-sufficient, independent, and capable. He was very wary about being a "sucker." Yet it was clear that he was frightened, concerned about monsters, robbers, and violence. As he progressed in treatment he began to talk about the fighting in the house, being blamed all the time, and being angry at his parents' inconsistencies.

After a few months, John mentioned that he and his father were going to the track for John's birthday. John said he always bets on the favorite but doesn't always win, so he was considering changing his tactics. His father bets on some system that needs changing too, but John thinks his father will change. John was indicating that things were getting better. His parents confirmed that John behaved better in school and at home. Family life had improved: the father had a new job which enabled moving to a better apartment in a better neighborhood.

The termination process began with the worker explaining that she was leaving the agency but that the family was also moving. John knew this and that his father had said something about going to an office near their new home if they went to an agency again. Asked if he wanted to, he said he didn't care. Anyway, he said, it didn't matter what he wanted because his parents would decide. The worker thought it was important for his parents to know his feelings. While they played checkers, a game they had often played, John looked slyly at the worker and asked if she had ever been mugged. She said no, but guessed there were times people wanted to mug her. He looked amazed and wondered how she knew. She said she only guessed because she knew there were times people were angry at her. John played to win and called her stupid when she lost. For the next weeks John alternated between saying he was bored, acting superior to the worker when they played games, or complaining how bad things had become at home. He was also in trouble at school. The worker said she thought things were real bad and this was not the time for her to be leaving; John smiled.

In the last session John was quiet. He drew a picture of flowers. Then he wanted to play a game of dots, a game the worker usually won. He drew the dots, and he handed the paper to her, saying he wasn't sure it was right. The worker looked carefully at it, and said she thought his work was good. Leaving, he asked the worker to keep his pictures. During the last session with his parents the mother talked about her son's teachers. She said that John's brother's teacher was strict and old fashioned, giving lots of homework and demanding absolute obedience. John's teacher was progressive, warm, and nice. She said John got a lot this year from school; he learned a lot, loved his teacher, and liked to go to school. The mother said she guessed that screaming and strict rules weren't the only way to get a child to do what you want. On Mother's Day, John had presented her with a bunch of daisies and had kissed her. But he looked sad and said he had wanted to give her better flowers but could only afford daisies. She had hugged John, saying nothing could have made her happier than the daisies. The father said it had been a good year. They were moving; he had a better job. He added that he thought they would be fine, and that they knew what to do if there was trouble again.

At termination, parents were supportive of John's growth. They showed that they had learned how to be parents and to live together with more pleasure. Though John could not explain clearly that things were better for him, in the ending he repeated his beginnings problems almost as if that could keep the worker from leaving, but then showed that he had learned to change his system.

Duration of Treatment. The most optimal situation occurs when the child is able to leave treatment. Generally a child's interest in therapy will decline when his or her life becomes more satisfying and engaging (Blos, 1970). This can be age-appropriate disengagement, not resistance or flight from therapy. Children can stop treatment when they have achieved significant gains, such as symptom reduction, improved behavior, stabilized parent-child relationships, or when other evidence suggests that developmental processes have started or been renewed.

There is no such thing as a total cure. The many complex variables of living make this impossible and, in addition, latency children are in the process of development. Realistic treatment goals will be geared to freeing the child from those inner and outer influences that prevent growth and development. Thus when the initial diagnostic assessment suggests that the problems are reactive and may disappear with some clarification, planning for brief treatment may be appropriate. In some cases the progress in treatment may show sufficient advance though one may hypothesize that in adolescence or even adulthood there may be some more difficulty. However, the successful treatment of latency and a good therapeutic termination can provide a sound foundation for continued work at a later and more favorable time when the child will have greater choices and perhaps greater opportunity to make independent decisions.

Children whose lives have had great inconstancies need treatment plans that consider constancy and permanency because inconstant treatment will repeat the abandonment so typical of their lives. If such children are "terminated" and left before they are ready to leave, the process must permit for expression of old abandonments and must make some bridge to the future. This bridge may be the opening of communication with another worker; sometimes giving the child a gift provides a transitional object and a concrete reminder of the therapist.

Raphael, a ten-year-old boy, lived with both parents and a nine-year-old brother. His father drank excessively and had irregular work so the family was on welfare. His mother had a long history of psychiatric hospitalizations which at one time had resulted in both children being placed in separate foster homes for two years. There continued to be many problems at home. Raphael was evaluated as having interrelated problems of dependency, immaturity, and low self-esteem. He looked like a fragile waif and appeared to be emotionally starved. He related well in therapy, almost clutching his therapist whom he seemed to view as his savior. Intensive work was begun with parents and school, as well as with the boy.

It was quite clear that the family and child needed long-term continued work, but unfortunately the worker moved after a few months. Raphael was not happy about this and questioned where the worker was going, indicated he was jealous of her attention to other children, and generally seemed unhappy. He was not yet able to discuss his anger. But his worker introduced him to the new social worker and for a few sessions the three met together. The final meeting was at McDonalds, which was a special treat for the child. He made every effort to arrive on time even though he had no watch. From the brown paper bag he carried, he produced two gifts; one was a worn, dirty teddy bear, quite obviously his old transitional object, and the other a poster of Wonder Woman—magical woman flying in space, half-clad, curvaceous, and sexy. In turn, his worker gave him a simple but real watch so he could control his appointments and be master of his time.

In this way Raphael told his wonder worker that something had happened. Perhaps he no longer felt the need of the transitional object because in the process of their relationship his internalized self-image and object images had become more benign. Or, one might hypothesize, like the child in the subphase of rapprochement, mother (the worker) is seen as a separate person with whom one might share one's possessions and one's experiences (Bergman, 1980). The worker, in return, recognizing Raphael's growing autonomy, acted to enhance and encourage it.

Summary

This chapter has focused upon individual work with the child. It is often advantageous to use methods such as group and family therapy, either alone or in conjunction with other modes of treatment. For very deprived children the availability of multiple caretakers may mitigate termination pr blems of being left before a child is ready. However, children who have never enjoyed constancy may not be able to relate to many people because they have not yet learned to relate in a meaningful way to one important person. In any case group or family therapy call for special skills, adapted to children's needs.

Clinical social work with children is a specialized practice derived from a theoretical base and having a technique that flows from the theory rather than from a preference for a particular method or way of working. It is a distinguishable form of psychotherapy, containing all the structural elements and objectives of psychotherapy and attending to the conscious and unconscious components of behavior. It aims to bring about positive behavior change accompanied by ego growth. It reflects an integration of social work's mission and psychotherapeutic methodology, and as such it concerns itself equally with the child's inner and outer space. It is derived from the profession's system of values and purpose which focus on improvement of the relationship between individuals and their social environment. Nowhere is this more important than in work with children.

References

Adams, P. L. *Obsessive Children: A Sociopsychiatric Study.* New York: Brunner/Mazel, 1973.

Amini, F., and Burke, E. "Acting Out and Its Role in the Treatment of Adolescents." *Bulletin of the Menninger Clinic,* 1979, *43,* 249–259.

Anthony, E. L. "Nonverbal and Verbal Systems of Communication: A Study in Complementarity." *Psychoanalytic Study of the Child,* 1977, *32* (3), 307–326.

Bachrach, H. "Diagnoses as Strategic Understanding." *Bulletin of the Menninger Clinic,* 1974, *38,* 144–153.

Bergman, A. "Ours, Yours, Mine." In F. F. Lax, S. Bach, and J. A. Burland (Eds.), *Rapprochement: The Critical Subphase of Separation-Individuation.* New York: Jason Aronson, 1980.

Bettelheim, B. *The Uses of Enchantment.* New York: Knopf, 1976.

Blos, P. *The Young Adolescent.* New York: Free Press, 1970.

Briar, S. "Social Work's Function." *Social Work,* 1976, *21,* 90.

Burch, C. "Puppet Play in a Thirteen-Year Old Boy: Remembering, Repeating, and Working Through." *Clinical Social Work Journal,* 1980, *8,* 79–89.

Buxbaum, E. "The Latency Period." *American Journal of Orthopsychiatry,* 1951, *21,* 182–198.

Buxbaum, E. *Troubled Children in a Troubled World.* New York: International Universities Press, 1970.

Chethik, M. "Amy: The Intensive Treatment of an Elective Mute." *Journal of the American Academy of Child Psychiatry,* 1973, *12,* 482–499.

Cohen, N. *Social Work in the American Tradition.* New York: Holt, Rinehart and Winston, 1958.

Deutsch, M. "Happenings on the Way Back to the Forum." *Harvard Educational Review,* 1969, *39,* 523–557.

DeVries, R. "Relationship Among Piagetian IQ and Achievement Assessment." *Child Development,* 1974, *45,* 746–756.

Ekstein, R. *The Challenge: Despair and Hope in the Conquest of Inner Space.* New York: Brunner/Mazel, 1971.

Ekstein, R. "The Process of Termination and Its Relation to Outcome in the Treatment of Psychotic Disorders in Adolescence." In S. E. Feinstein and P. L. Giovacchini (Eds.), *Adolescent Psychiatry.* Vol. 5. Chicago: University of Chicago Press, 1978.

Ekstein, R., and Wallerstein, J. "Choice of Interpretation in the Treatment of Borderline and Psychotic Children." In R. Ekstein (Ed.), *Children of Time and Space, of Action and Impulse.* New York: Appleton-Century-Crofts, 1966.

Erikson, E. *Childhood and Society.* (2nd ed.) New York: Norton, 1963.

Fanshel, E., and Shinn, E. *Children in Foster Care.* New York: Columbia University Press, 1978.

Fraiberg, S. A. "Therapeutic Approach to Reactive Ego Disturbances in Children in Placement." *American Journal of Orthopsychiatry,* 1962, *32,* 18–31.

Fraiberg, S., Adelson, E., and Shapiro, V. "Ghosts in the Nursery." *Journal of the American Academy of Child Psychiatry,* 1975, *14,* 387–421.

Freud, A. *Normality and Pathology in Childhood.* New York: International Universities Press, 1965.

Freud, A. "The Symptomatology of Childhood: A Preliminary Attempt at Classification." *Psychoanalytic Study of the Child,* 1970, *25,* 19–44.

Freud, S. "Beyond the Pleasure Principle." *Standard Edition.* Vol. 18. London: Hogarth Press, 1955. (Originally published 1920.)

Green, A. H. "Psychopathology of Abused Children." *Journal of the American Academy of Child Psychiatry,* 1978, *17* (1), 92–103.

Hamilton, G. *Psychotherapy in Child Guidance.* New York: Columbia University Press, 1963.

Hobbs, N. *The Futures of Children.* San Francisco: Jossey-Bass, 1975.

Kaplan, S. L., and Escoll, P. "Treatment of Two Silent Adolescent Girls." *Journal of the American Academy of Child Psychiatry,* 1973, *13,* 344–356.

Lane, B. "Some Vicissitudes of the Therapeutic Alliance in Child Psychotherapy." In J. Mishne (Ed.), *Psychotherapy and Training in Clinical Social Work.* New York: Gardner Press, 1980.

Lieberman, F. *Social Work with Children.* New York: Human Sciences Press, 1979.

Littner, N., and Schour, E. "Special Problems of Training Psychotherapists to Work With Children." In R. R. Holt (Ed.), *New Horizons for Psychotherapy.* New York: International Universities Press, 1971.

McGowen, B. "Strategies in Bureaucracies." In J. Mearig (Ed.), *Working for Children: Ethical Issues Beyond Professional Guidelines.* San Francisco: Jossey-Bass, 1978.

Mahler, M. S., Pine, F., and Bergman, A. *The Psychological Birth of the Human Infant.* New York: Basic Books, 1975.

Nagelberg, L., Spotnitz, H., and Feldman, Y. "The Attempt at Healthy Insulation in the Withdrawn Child." *American Journal of Orthopsychiatry,* 1953, *23,* 238–251.

Peller, L. "Libidinal Phases, Ego Development and Play." *Psychoanalytic Study of the Child,* 1954, *14,* 414–433.

Rexford, E. N. "A Developmental Concept of the Problems of Acting Out." In E. N. Rexford (Ed.), *A Developmental Approach to Problems of Acting Out.* New York: International Universities Press, 1978.

Sears, R. R., Raus, L., and Alpert, R. *Identification and Child Rearing*. Stanford, Calif.: Stanford University Press, 1965.

Spitz, R. A. "Hospitalism." *Psychoanalytic Study of the Child*. 1945, *1*, 53–74.

Waelder, R. "The Psychoanalytic Theory of Play." In S. A. Guttman (Ed.), *Psychoanalysis: Observation, Theory, Application*. New York: International Universities Press, 1976.

Williams, M. "Problems of Technique During Latency." *Psychoanalytic Study of the Child*, 1972, *27*, 598–620.

Winnicott, C. "Communicating With Children." *Child Care Quarterly Review*, 1964, *18*, 65–80.

Winnicott, D. *Maturational Processes and the Facilitating Environment*. New York: International Universities Press, 1965.

22

Family Therapy: A Systematic Orientation to Treatment

Froma Walsh

Over the past twenty-five years, family therapy has developed as a major approach to the understanding and treatment of psychopathology. This approach is not simply another therapeutic method. Rather, it is a new conceptual orientation to human problems and the process of change, attending to the family context of individual functioning.

The rapid growth of the field of family therapy, with a proliferation of new ideas, techniques, and schools, can lead to confusion about what family therapy is and how it is practiced. This chapter surveys the field of family therapy, aiming to clarify basic concepts, goals, and processes.

Historical Evolution

The crucial influence of the family in individual development and psychopathology has long been recognized. What distinguishes the family therapy orientation is its view of the family as a social system, with assessment and treatment of problems of an individual member in relation to the organization and functioning of that system.

As early as 1926, the sociologist Burgess (1976) described the family as a psychosocial unity of interacting personalities. Yet over the next several decades the clinical field generally saw family members, if at all, apart from and collateral to the primary individual treatment of the patient. Based on a linear-causal model of influence, attention was primarily directed to the impact of the mother-child dyad in early childhood, with deficiencies in the mother's personality and mothering style assumed to be responsible for any disturbance in an offspring.

A shift to a social view occurred in the 1950s, with the development of general systems theory (Bertalanffy, 1969), communication theory (Ruesch and Bateson, 1951), and a cybernetic perspective of the context of behavior and adaptation (Watzlawick and others, 1967). The field of social work, with its longstanding basic commitment to a psychosocial orientation and to the provision of family services, produced some of the first and foremost family theorists and practitioners, notably Frances Scherz, Sanford Sherman, and Virginia Satir, who combined core principles from the social work tradition with communications and systems approaches developing at that time.

The transformation to a family systems orientation is well illustrated in the research developments that occurred regarding the role of the family in the etiology of schizophrenia. In the 1950s, direct observation of whole families in the study of schizophrenia led to a breakthrough in thinking about the family context of human problems and therapeutic intervention to change dysfunctional patterns of interaction.

With focus on the role and personality of the mother in the 1940s, the label "schizophrenogenic mother" came to stand for a variety of noxious and destructive traits in mothers with schizophrenic offspring. Ironically, in attempting to understand the plight of a child regarded as victimized by his or her family, another family member, the mother, was blamed and thereby scapegoated.

In the 1950s, observation and conceptualization of whole-family processes were attempted in three pioneering investigations. At Yale, Lidz and his colleagues (1965) conducted an extensive study of parents and siblings of young adult schizophrenics and found a variety of family-wide problems in the network of relationships, in family structure and boundaries, and in a "transmission of irrationality" in communication processes. At the National Institute of Mental Health, Bowen's team (1960) hospitalized whole families and observed a reciprocity in their relationship patterns over time, while Wynne and his associates (1958; Singer and Wynne, 1965) found severe communication problems in family transactions. At Palo Alto, the Bateson group (1956) formulated the double-bind theory, describing a communication pattern that would lead to behavioral responses characteristic of schizophrenia.

These investigations all attended to ongoing, repeated transactional patterns. Regardless of origin, patterns were observed to operate currently in cycles that maintained or reinforced disturbed behavior in the identified patient. A complex circular chain of causality was seen to connect the actions and reactions of all family members. From these observations it was a natural step to conceive of therapeutic intervention aimed at alteration of dysfunctional relationship patterns in sessions with whole families.

The 1960s was a period of rapid expansion of theory and experimentation with different family approaches to treat a wide range of problems. The emergence of competing "schools" or models of family therapy was, perhaps, a step in the process of differentiation in the development of the field. Currently there is a need to transcend the boundaries between "camps" in order to clarify and integrate what has been learned about families and about therapeutic change.

While the particular approaches to family therapy differ from one another in many ways, they share a common conceptual orientation based on systems theory. The approaches differ mainly in their focus and emphasis on different aspects of family systems and in different beliefs about the goals of therapy and how they can most effectively be reached.

Conceptual Orientation

The practice of family therapy is grounded in a set of basic assumptions about the interplay of individual and family processes. The assessment and treatment of psychopathology, or dysfunction, are guided by principles of family systems theory.

Family System. The basic premise underlying family therapy is the view of the family as a relational system that operates according to certain rules and principles that apply to all systems (Bertalanffy, 1969). A family system can be defined as a group of individuals interrelated such that a change in any one affects all other members and the group as a whole, which in turn affects the first individual in a circular chain of influence.

The systems principle of *nonsummativity* applies to families in that the whole is greater than the sum of its parts. Interaction is not summative—the family system cannot be described simply by summing up the characteristics of its individual members or even of various dyads. It is necessary to attend to the gestalt—the family organization and interactional patterns that involve an interlocking of behavior among members.

According to the principle of *equifinality,* the same origin may lead to different outcomes, and the same outcome may result from different origins. Watzlawick, Beavin, and Jackson (1967) refer to the genetic fallacy, the error of confusing the origin of something with its significance in determining outcome. Rather, it is asserted, the influence of initial conditions or events will be outweighed by the impact of the family organization—its ongoing interactional patterns and response to events. Thus, the same crisis may be disabling to one family while another family may rally in response.

Family Structure and Functioning. Family structural theory of Minuchin (1974) and his colleagues stresses the importance of family organization for the functioning of the group and the well-being of its members. Family structure is defined as the invisible set of functional demands organizing interaction among family members.

Boundaries, the rules determining who does what, where, and when, are crucial structural requisites in three ways. First, *interpersonal boundaries* define individual family members and promote their differentiation and autonomous yet interdependent functioning. While family organizational styles vary with cultural norms, dysfunctional families tend to be characterized by either a pattern of rigid enmeshment or disengagement. An *enmeshed* pattern limits or sacrifices individual differences to maintain a cohesive sense of unity. At the extreme of fusion, as described by Bowen (1978) and in Wynne's (1958) "pseudomutuality," members are expected to think and feel alike; differences, privacy, and separation are regarded as threats to the survival of the family. A *disengaged* pattern reinforces individual differences, separateness, and distance at the expense of family cohesion, at the extreme fragmenting the family unit and isolating individual members.

Second, *boundaries with the outside world* define the family unit, but at the same time must be permeable to maintain a well-functioning open system with contact and reciprocal exchange with the social world. Social networks are important for support and connectedness to the community (Speck and Attneave, 1973; Anderson, 1982). In a closed system, family isolation contributes to dysfunction and creates a "rubber fence" (Wynne and others, 1958) around members, interfering with peer socialization and emancipation of offspring.

Third, *generational boundaries,* the rules differentiating parent and child roles, rights, and obligations, maintain hierarchical organization in families of all cultures. They are established by the parental-marital subsystem, and in turn, they reinforce the essential leadership of the parental unit as well as the exclusivity of the marital relationship. Generational boundaries may be breached when a child assumes the function of a *parental child,* a common pattern in single-parent or large families where an elder child assumes parentlike caretaking responsibilities. A more dysfunctional breaching of generational boundaries occurs when a child assumes a sexualized *matelike* role for a parent (Walsh, 1979). Such patterns may serve to stabilize a family, but can become pathogenic for the child to the extent that expectations are identity-distorting and interfere with the child's age-appropriate developmental needs. The destructive breaching of generational boundaries in a covert parent-child coalition against the other parent has been described by Haley (1967) as a "perverse triangle."

The concept of the *triangle* and the dysfunctional process of *triangulation* has been central to the theory and practice of such diverse family therapists as Haley (1976), Bowen (1978), and Satir (1964). Each observed the tendency of two-person systems, especially in marital relationships, to draw in a third person when tension develops between the two. Three types of triangles most typically occur. In one arrangement, the couple, persons A and B, may avoid or drop their conflict to rally together in a united front of mutual concern about the third person, C, who may be scapegoated in this process. In a second kind of triangle, one member of the dyad, A, may form a coalition with C against or to the exclusion of B, as in the perverse triangle. It is important to note that the excluded member, B, supports this bargain through maintaining distance. In a third arrangement, the triangulated member, C, may assume the role of go-between for A and B, thereby balancing loyalties and regulating tension and intimacy. Triangulation of a child is a common problem presented by divorced families where parents have not emotionally separated.

It should be underscored that in each case, all three members of the triangle are active participants and each is a beneficiary in the reduction of family or marital tension. The more dysfunctional a family, the more rigid are these patterns and the more likely are there to be multiple interlocking triangles throughout the extended family system.

Communication is vital to the organization and functioning of a family system and to each member's development. Bateson (Ruesch and Bateson, 1951) noted that every communication has two functions: a *content* (report) aspect conveying factual information, opinions, or feelings, and a *relationship* (command) aspect that conveys how the information is to be taken, thereby defining the nature of the relationship. The statement "Eat your vegetables!" conveys an order with expectations of compliance, and implies a hierarchical differentiation of status or authority in the relationship between speaker and listener. All verbal and nonverbal behavior, including silence (or spitting out the vegetables in question), convey interpersonal messages ("I won't obey you!"). In every communication, each participant seeks to define the nature of the relationship. In an ongoing relationship, it cannot be left unclear or unresolved without pathological consequences or dissolution. Family units, as ongoing relationships, stabilize the process of defining relationships. These agreements are the family rules.

Family rules organize interaction and function to maintain a stable system by prescribing and limiting members' behaviors. Relationship rules, both explicit and implicit, provide a set of expectations about roles, actions, and consequences that guide family life. A redundancy principle operates, in that a family tends to interact in repetitious sequences, so that a relatively small set of patterned and predictable rules govern family operations.

Jackson (1965a) regarded family relationship rules as norms within a family, as baselines or settings on which family behavior is measured and around which it varies to a greater or lesser degree. Like a home thermostat, the range of behavior would be the temperature scale and the norm the desired setting. A marital "quid pro quo" (Jackson, 1965b) is an example of rules that are worked out by a couple, a largely implicit bargain as to how they define themselves in the relationship.

Homeostatic mechanisms are the means by which norms are delimited and enforced to maintain a steady, stable state in the ongoing interactional system. Too wide a deviation from the family norm may be counteracted in the feedback process, to regulate tension and restore the family equilibrium, or homeostasis. At the same time, some flexibility is required for the family to adapt to changing circumstances and new developmental imperatives. Through morphogenesis, change can occur by the amplification of deviations to increase the degree of permissible options, a first-order change, or, by a shift in rules, a second-order change. The transition from one family developmental stage to the next involves such a second-order change, as new norms and options are required to meet new phase-appropriate needs and tasks (Hoffman, 1982).

All family members contribute to the homeostatic balance, as in forming or shifting an alliance, rescuing a member in distress, and through silence or distancing. A child may predictably misbehave each time parents' marital disagreements escalate beyond the tolerable limits, thereby calling attention away from the marital conflict and easing the tension between parents as they focus on the child. Moreover, the devilish behavior of an "acting-out" child is typically offset by the angelic behavior of a sibling, who contributes in this complementary way to the family balance. The reciprocal interplay of these behavior patterns may become obvious only when the devilish child leaves home and the "angel" starts to misbehave in response to similar interactional cues.

The Functionality of Symptoms. Thus, behavioral symptoms can be seen to function as a homeostatic mechanism, restoring stability in a dysfunctional family system. This observation has several implications for clinical assessment and treatment.

First, diagnosis becomes an interactional assessment. The symptom bearer, or identified patient, must be assessed in the family interactional context to understand what function the symptom may serve for the system. It is assumed that the distress of the individual is also a symptom of current family dysfunction. Psychopathology is thus redefined as a relationship problem (Haley, 1970).

Second, assessment of current family maintenance of symptoms becomes more meaningful than searching for problem origins, since symptoms are presumed to be multidetermined and reinforced in a circular chain of causality. There is no victim and no villain. A scapegoating process involves all members and the "victim," or symptom bearer, participates in this reciprocal relationship bargain.

Etiological arguments over whether illness or psychopathology is *either* biologically *or* environmentally caused are irrelevant to the systems model. Each individual carries a genetic predisposition and particular strengths and vulnerabilities. Systems theory assumes that the family plays a critical role in the adaptation of its members. A child predisposed to asthma, for example, will resonate with the family's emotional wavelength such that asthma attacks tend to occur at moments of family tension, thereby serving both as a barometer and as a tension regulator (Liebman and others, 1974).

Moreover, the family's response to the symptoms (of whatever origin) may exacerbate the symptoms in two ways. First, attention to the symptom and labeling of the symptom bearer tend to reinforce the problem behavior and acceptance of "patient" role. Second, the attempt to solve the problem may itself become a problem, so that a vicious cycle can ensue: the harder the family tries to solve the problem, the worse the problem gets (Watzlawick, Weakland, and Fisch, 1974). One father, a police officer, tried to solve his son's runaway problem by locking him up in his room. The more punitive the father became, the more lenient the mother became, covertly encouraging the son to run away. After the son had escaped from his second-story window, father handcuffed the boy to a chair in his room, only to find that the son escaped again, taking the chair with him.

Furthermore, the particular presenting problem or symptom may have special meaning to the family in which it occurs. It is important to note precisely what family members say concerns them about the symptom, as it may be a projection or metaphor for similar underlying concerns elsewhere in the system, especially in the marriage or extended family (Haley, 1976; Walsh, 1980). A mother's concern about her sixteen-year-old daughter's sexual promiscuity may serve as, in large part, a displacement of anxiety about a current sexual problem in her own marriage. It may also signal the reactivation of unresolved emotional issues from parents' families of origin, as when it is learned that the mother herself became pregnant out of wedlock at the age of sixteen. It may even be that the grandmother, at the same age, gave birth out of wedlock to the mother, and a multigenerational repeated pattern of expectation is in operation. A transgenerational anniversary pattern may involve fathers as well, as in the tragic case of a young man who, at the age of fifteen, stabbed an elderly man in a dissociated episode. A family-of-origin history revealed that the paternal grandfather had been stabbed to death by a young man when the father was fifteen. The apparently irrational act by the son, at the same age, takes on additional symbolic meaning when viewed in his family context.

The question of why one family member bears symptoms when other members appear symptom-free is not fully understood, but is likely to be multi-determined, depending on such factors as an individual's biological predisposition, such as to alcohol tolerance; sibling position (Bank and Kahn, 1982), particularly as related to parents' family-of-origin sibship experiences (Toman, 1975); and a child's developmental stage or transition at the time of family stress. In studies by Walsh and Orfanidis (Walsh, 1978), 41 percent of schizophrenics were found to have been born within two years of a grandparent death. Only 13 percent of all siblings were born concurrently with a grandparent death and in all but one case, the schizophrenic offspring was born in the same time period. Such findings suggest that from birth, the identified patient may have assumed a triangulated replacement function for the family that siblings do not, thereby complicating the differentiation, separation, and launching processes with that particular child [Walsh and McGoldrick (Orfanidis), 1983].

Finally, where symptoms serve a function in a family, change in the symptom bearer will have a reverberating impact on the system. As a patient begins to improve, family members will react to preserve the homeostasis. The family may resist or counteract the improvement, or another family member may become symptomatic as the system is destabilized. Such complementarity in a marital relationship becomes overt when a recovering alcoholic finds his spouse tempting him to drink, becoming depressed at his improvement, or even getting a divorce.

Normal Family Functioning and Dysfunction. While family systems concepts and family therapy have developed primarily out of attempts to understand and treat psychopathology, implicit in theory and practice are a number of assumptions about normal family functioning. Studies of normal family processes have found that no single pattern distinguishes well-functioning families. Rather, a variety of styles are found among asymptomatic families and a number of dimensions, or aspects of family structure, communication, and dynamics, are important in family adjustment (Walsh, 1982).

An assessment of family organization and functioning must take into account the values, orientation, and objectives of a family, the tasks it has to accomplish, and its structural composition. Certain tasks are basic to all childrearing families, including nurturance, socialization, and emancipation of offspring (Fleck, 1966). Coping with stress and crises is another task critical to a family's life adaptation. The interactional process by which a family solves problems is as important as any particular solution. Both will vary with sociocultural norms and ethnic differences (McGoldrick, 1982).

The structural composition and resources of a family must also be taken into account. A single-parent household will have to organize itself differently than a two-parent family. A blended family will have not only a more complicated relational network to integrate, but it will also have additional tasks particular to the transitions and transformations required. Thus, assessment of family functioning involves the way a family organizes itself to maintain integration, to provide for the needs of its members, and to adapt to life challenges.

The dimension of time is another important consideration. Specific actions—and problems—take meaning in temporal context. First, they can be seen as embedded in the immediate sequence of events and interactions surrounding them. An apparently isolated or irrational act must therefore be viewed sequentially. Second, the family epigenesis is the evolutionary process of family formation and development over time. The transmission of family values, myths, expectations, and loyalty patterns shape family life across the generations (Boszormenyi-Nagy and Spark, 1973). Moreover, functioning must be considered within the framework of the family life cycle (Carter and McGoldrick, 1980). Families at one stage will require different tasks and organizational patterns than at another stage. Transitions from one developmental stage to the next involve a loss and require renegotiation and reorganization of relationships. Symptoms frequently occur when families have difficulty making these transitions. For instance, a young adult's separation problems, as in drug abuse and schizophrenia, should be considered in developmental context, in interaction with the family's difficulties adjusting to the developmental transition at the launching stage, when the two-generational household contracts to the marital dyad as children leave home (Haley, 1980; Walsh and McGoldrick, 1983).

For a family therapist, the question of why a problem exists has past, present, and future implications. The etiological question, first, concerns how it evolved historically out of past family experience. Second, the question "why now" leads a family therapist to look for recent or impending stressful changes in the immediate family context to understand triggering symptom appearance or exacerbation, or heightened family concern about longstanding patterns. A third question, future-oriented, seeks to understand the function of the symptom in terms of the family's catastrophic expectations: What do they fear might happen if they no longer had to worry about the problem or if it did not serve as a regulator; that is, if the problem were solved (Feldman and Pinsof, 1982)? Different approaches to family therapy vary in their temporal emphasis and in the valuing of family insight into the reasons for a problem. Nevertheless, most family therapists do assess family dysfunction and resistance to change along such explanatory lines. The process of change itself is focused on the present and immediate future in direct patient interaction with the family.

Family Therapy Approaches

Family therapy is based on the assumption that problems presented by an individual can most effectively be treated by changing dysfunctional family relationship patterns that contribute to or maintain symptoms.

Several approaches to systemic change have developed that give varying emphasis to family dynamics, structural patterns, or communication processes. They differ conceptually in their views of how symptoms occur and how change takes place. Attempts to categorize a rapidly evolving field of theory and practice are precarious. At the same time, it is useful to survey the field in order to identify and distinguish major models of family therapy.

This broad overview will focus on several models and originators that have been most influential in the development of family therapy. Growth-oriented approaches include psychodynamic-transgenerational, Bowen systems therapy, and experiential models. Problem-solving approaches include structural, strategic-systemic, and behavioral models. Other approaches, including social network intervention, multiple-family groups, and multiple-impact crisis intervention, will be described briefly. Discussion of approaches will highlight distinctions in views of pathology, goals of therapy, and processes of change.

Psychodynamic and Transgenerational Models. The psychodynamic and transgenerational models of family therapy derive from the psychoanalytic tradition and theory of object relations. The approaches of several pioneers in family therapy, including Ackerman, Boszormenyi-Nagy and Spark, Framo, and Paul, clearly reflect their psychoanalytic origins.

Symptoms are viewed as resulting from largely unconscious dynamics: attempts by parents to reenact, externalize, or master intrapsychic conflicts originating in family-of-origin relationships (Skynner,1976). Current family relationships are shaped and interpreted to fit these needs. The interlocking of projection and introjection processes between spouses and between parents and children form a shared family projection process based on a complementarity of needs (Boszormenyi-Nagy and Spark, 1973; Meissner, 1978). The symptomatic member may serve as scapegoat for unresolved family conflicts (Ackerman, 1958). In other cases, the loss of a significant relationship in the family of origin can result in an emotional upheaval for the entire family system, with unresolved grief expressed by symptoms in one or more members.

Assessment and treatment include exploration of transgenerational family patterns. The complex, multigenerational relational network is examined over time, and connected to resulting disturbances in current functioning and role relations. Extended family members may be included in family sessions, or individual members may be encouraged to work on changing relationships with the family of origin outside of sessions. In either case, the aim of therapy is for family members to confront and deal with one another directly in order to work through unresolved conflicts. Negative introjects from the past are tested out in reality and altered or brought up to date in direct contact with their sources in the family of origin, rather than by analysis of the transference patterns with the therapist (Framo, 1965). The role of the therapist is that of a catalyst, actively encouraging the family's awareness of intense conflictual emotions, interpreting their origin and consequences, as well as identifying their shared defense mechanisms. In direct confrontation, the therapist makes the family's covert processes overt and accessible to solution (Stierlin, 1980).

Boszormenyi-Nagy and Spark (1973) emphasize the importance of covert but powerful family-of-origin loyalty patterns in their transgenerational approach to family therapy, which aims toward reconstruction and reunion of relationships in the resolution of grievances. They view the marital—and therapeutic—task as synthesizing two family-of-origin systems into a new, functional whole. Similarly, Paul (Paul and Paul, 1975) accounts for most tensions and conflicts in a marital relationship by the concept of marriage as the collision of two family subcultures: patterns of behavior, memories, labels, and expectations that comprise a fundamental way of being in the world. For Paul, the resolution of marital crises involves insight and an emotional working through of those influences and resulting conflicts. Where unresolved grief issues impact on current relationships and functioning, the task becomes the resolution of grief and guilt around the past relationship and loss (Paul and Grosser, 1965). Visual stimuli, through video and photographs, are used inventively by Paul as an implosion technique, for confrontation with denied or highly defended, painful feelings. Action is encouraged to confront and resolve unfinished emotional issues, as in sending a client to visit a parent's grave. The therapist takes active charge in preparing, guiding, and processing such highly emotional work.

Bowen Family Systems Therapy. Bowen developed a theory of the family emotional system and a method of psychotherapy designed to help individuals to differentiate themselves from their families of origin.

In this model, functioning is thought to be impaired by poorly differentiated relationship patterns characterized by high anxiety or emotional reactivity. This anxiety commonly results in triangulation or cutoffs of highly charged relationships. Stresses on the family—especially birth and death—can decrease differentiation and heighten reactivity. Underfunctioning, or symptoms, may be linked with and reinforced by overfunctioning in other parts of the system in a reciprocating compensatory cycle.

The goal of therapy is to assist individuals to achieve a higher level of differentiation and reduced anxiety in contact with the family of origin. Improved functioning will result when emotional reactivity no longer dominates intellectual processes. It is assumed that current family problems or symptoms in a child will be resolved with the increased differentiation of the spouses/parents from their extended families.

The basic task is to assist adult individuals to modify their relationships with their families of origin. This process differs from other approaches that promote confrontation and sharing of feelings among family members in conjoint sessions. In the Bowen model, a client may be seen individually and coached to change self in relation to the family of origin between sessions. When spouses meet together, the focus is not on their interaction, but rather on coaching each individual to work separately on his or her own extended family relationships. In sessions the therapist assumes a cognitive stance, toning down emotional reactivity, discouraging transference reactions, and guarding against the therapist's own triangulation in the family emotional system. The therapist takes an objective role of consultant or coach, guiding each individual through carefully planned stages of intervention.

Therapy begins with a family evaluation process that surveys the entire nuclear family and extended family field. A genogram, similar in appearance to a family tree, is used as a structural framework to diagram facts (names, sibling order, dates of significant events) and complex information (triangles, cutoffs, repetitive patterns) in concrete terms (Guerin and Pendagast, 1976). Family life is sketched over at least three generations to follow the family through the time with a focus on related events in interlocking fields. The aim is to obtain a working knowledge of the entire family system before undertaking work with any individual or part of the family. A client may be asked to contact extended family members to obtain obscured or missing information and to gain new perspectives on the family.

The process of changing self directly with one's family requires long-term work in stages (Carter and Orfanidis, 1976). First, in engagement, the client is helped to shift focus to an overview of self-with-others. The genogram is used in planning steps of intervention. In the reentry stage, the client begins the process of differentiation by redeveloping personal relationships with key family members, repairing cutoffs, detriangling from conflicts, and changing the part played in emotionally charged dysfunctional cycles. The therapist encourages the client to take an "I-position," a clear statement asserting one's own thoughts and feelings without attacking, defending, or withdrawing. Humor is used to detoxify an emotional situation. Techniques of detriangling, shifting the motion of a triangle, and reversals expressing the unacknowledged other side of an issue are two of many means employed to break up rigid communication patterns and open up a closed system. Follow-through of the work is essential, given the anxiety generated and the necessity of handling system efforts to self-correct. Sessions may start at regular weekly or biweekly intervals and be spaced out as work proceeds. The work requires strong motivation and persistence to be effective.

Experiential Approaches. Experiential approaches to family therapy have been developed by Satir (1964; 1972), who blends a communication emphasis with a humanistic frame of reference; Kempler (1974), who is associated with the Gestalt movement; and Whitaker (Neill and Kniskern, 1982; Napier and Whitaker, 1978).

Current behavior and feelings are seen as the natural consequence of the experience of one's own life. Regardless of awareness or intent, old pains are propagated and made stronger by current interaction about them. To explain and change behavior, several important aspects of a family and their mutual influence must be taken into account. These ingredients—individual self-worth, communication, system, and rules—are all believed to be changeable and correctable (Satir, 1972).

The goal of these growth-oriented approaches is a fuller awareness and appreciation of self in relation to others, while providing an intense, affective experience in the sharing of feelings. Focused on the immediate experience in the present, important information is elicited in current behavior with others, emphasizing the holistic nature of human interaction in relational systems. The therapist takes a phenomenological approach to assessment and treatment of the individual in the family context. This approach is characterized by exploration, experimentation, and encouragement of spontaneity of members' responses to one another in the here and now. Experiential exercises, such as family sculpting and spacial representation of relationships, are used to facilitate this process.

The experiential approach is a highly intuitive and relatively nontheoretical form of therapy. The therapist's role is facilitative, following and reflecting the family interaction process and stimulating genuine and nondefensive relating through one's own experience with the family.

Structural Model. The structural approach to family therapy was developed by Minuchin (1974) and his colleagues at the Philadelphia Child Guidance Clinic. This model emphasizes the patterning of transactions or interrelationships between individual behavior and environmental context. Symptoms are viewed as an indication of imbalance in the family organization, particularly a malfunctioning hierarchical arrangement with unclear parent and child subsystem boundaries. Most commonly it is viewed as a maladaptive reaction to changing environmental or developmental requirements, such as an inappropriate accommodation to a life stage transition. Child-focused symptoms are seen as metaphors for systems problems, and are thought to function to detour conflict between parents, or between parent and grandparent.

The therapeutic approach centers on the structural requisites for proper family functioning, particularly the importance of an appropriate organizational hierarchy, with parents maintaining a strong leadership unit, and with clear boundaries between subsystems that are neither too diffuse (as in enmeshment) nor too rigid (as in disengagement). The aim of therapy is the repair or modification of dysfunctional family structural patterns so that the family can better perform basic tasks and cope with life stresses. Presenting symptoms, a function of family distress, will be resolved as this reorganization is accomplished.

Treatment, which is short term, involves three processes: joining, enactment, and restructuring. First, the therapist joins the family system in a position of leadership to form the therapeutic system. Joining operations are actions aimed at relating to and blending with the family to gain entry into the system in order to gain influence to bring about change. Second, the therapist assesses the family experientially by getting the family to enact its presenting problem interactionally in the interview. The therapist will confront and push them to test out their interactional flexibility and limits. Third, based on the interactional diagnosis, a structural mapping of the immediate family field, the therapist employs directives and tasks designed to restructure the family around its handling of the presenting problem. The therapist uses himself or herself actively to shift triangular patterns in sessions by blocking dysfunctional coalitions while promoting more functional alliances. Particular attention is directed to strengthening the parental subsystem and establishing appropriate generational boundaries.

Structural family therapy is action oriented, based on a belief that change in behavior occurs independently of insight on the part of members. Innovative use of live supervision was developed to facilitate the training and implementation of direct, active, therapeutic intervention in sessions. Therapists may be telephoned or called out of sessions for consultation by supervisors or colleagues observing the interview through a one-way screen. The approach grew out of early work with delinquent youth at the Wiltwyck School of Minuchin and Montalvo, and their subsequent attempts to develop a therapeutic approach useful with poor, urban, multiproblem families (Minuchin and others, 1967). More recently the approach has been applied successfully to a broad spectrum of families and problems ranging from psychosomatic disorders to anorexia nervosa (Minuchin, Rosman, and Baker, 1978; Aponte and Hoffman, 1973). It is generally used in cases of child-focused symptoms, although structural problems involving the extended family may be addressed, for example, between a single-parent mother and grandmother. Here still, the treatment focus would be not on exploring the origin of the conflict but rather restructuring the family hierarchical arrangement so that symptoms are no longer reinforced.

Strategic and Systemic Models. Strategic approaches to family therapy have been most fully developed by Haley (1976), by the Mental Research Institute at Palo Alto (Weakland and others, 1974), and most recently by the Milan associates (Selvini-Palazzoli and others, 1978). These family-oriented problem-solving approaches focus on the immediate social situation of the presenting client. Assuming that all problems have multiple origins, a presenting problem is viewed as a symptom of and a response to current dysfunction in family interaction. It is important to learn how a family has attempted to solve its problem, since the attempted solution may exacerbate the problem or become a problem itself.

The goal of therapy is to solve the particular problem that is presented. The symptom is regarded as a communicative act that is part of a repetitive sequence of behaviors among family members, serving a function in the interactional network. Therapy focuses on problem resolution by altering the feedback cycle that maintains the symptomatic behavior. The therapist's task is to formulate the problem in solvable, behavioral terms and to design an intervention plan to change the dysfunctional family pattern.

The strategic models, while sharing with experiential approaches a common origin in communications theory, are distinct in assuming that change depends more on indirect means of influence than on insight or simply improved communications. The therapist's stance is highly intellectual and remote from personal involvement. At the same time, the therapist is active and pragmatic, planning and carrying out a strategy to achieve specific behaviorally defined objectives. Innovative techniques of relabeling, reframing, directives, and paradoxical instructions are employed to this end.

Relabeling and reframing refer to the strategic redefinition of a problem or situation in order to cast it in a new light or perspective. It is useful in shifting a family's rigid view or stereotyped response, in altering an unproductive blaming or scapegoating process, and in overcoming resistance to change. A problem presented as "inside" an individual or as a character trait is redefined behaviorally in interactional context. A label of "hysteric" or diagnosis of "depression" might be redefined as a wife's futile attempt to get attention from her husband when he comes home from a hard day's work. The more she complains, the more he buries himself in a newspaper. In the reformulation of a problem or set, new solutions become apparent (Watzlawick, Weakland, and Fisch, 1974).

Directives are carefully designed behavioral tasks assigned to families to be carried out either in a session or between sessions. They have several purposes. They are used to gather direct information about the ways family members interact and how they will respond to—and resist—change. They are also useful in intensifying the therapist's relationship with the family by involvement in action outside of sessions. Well-formulated and well-timed directives are considered a highly effective way of bringing about behavior change. For Haley (1976, p. 77), the best task is "one that uses the presenting problem to make a structural change in the family."

Paradoxical instructions are a type of directive that seems to be in opposition to the goals being sought but actually serves to move the family toward them. A commonly used paradoxical intervention is to prescribe the symptom—to direct a client or family to do even more of what they are complaining about, with a rationale for doing so. After a good session, a therapist may predict that the family will have a bad week. A relabel or reframe may be used paradoxically to redefine as positive or helpful what the family has labeled as negative or destructive. Doing so makes explicit the function of a symptom and the resistance to change. While a paradoxical injunction can be an extremely powerful means of overcoming resistance, its effective use requires careful planning, appropriate timing, and skill.

The problem-solving techniques of Haley and the Palo Alto group were strongly influenced by the work of Milton Erickson and his use of hypnotic suggestion (Haley, 1973). Haley grounds his approach in a family structural frame, from his collaborative work with the Philadelphia group. The Palo Alto group attends less to structure and more to communication sequences involved in a family's futile attempts to solve a problem. Specific tasks are designed to reframe and unhook the family members from their unsuccessful efforts.

Selvini-Palazzoli and her colleagues at the Institute for Family Study in Milan, Italy, have developed an innovative team approach to systemic treatment of severe disorders such as anorexia nervosa (Selvini-Palazzoli, 1974) and schizophrenia (Selvini-Palazzoli and others, 1978). A therapist-consultant team structures each family therapy session. In the presession, the team plans the interview based on relational information about the family. The therapist then meets with the family while one or more consultants observe through a one-way screen. Next, while the family waits, the team meets to discuss the session and formulate a conclusion and recommendation. Then the therapist ends the session, introducing the recommendation, prescription, or reframing to the family. Finally, in a postsession, the team discusses the family's reactions. Therapy may be long-term, but sessions are spaced at monthly intervals.

The Milan approach emphasizes three principles for conducting family interviews and obtaining the most useful information. First, working hypotheses are formed about the connection of symptoms with family relationships, to test out and confirm or disprove. Second is the use of circularity, whereby therapists conduct their investigation based on the family feedback in response to information elicited about relationships. Paradoxical instruction is used in prescriptions that link the whole system. Interventions are made to test the hypotheses about the function of the problem in a family. Third is neutrality, the therapist's avoidance of judgment or criticism of events or of moral alignment with any part of the system in order to minimize resistance. The value of positive connotation is emphasized, reframing positively the symptom's adaptive function for the family and the good intentions of members, implicitly joining the family in order to facilitate change (Selvini-Palazzoli and others, 1980).

Behavioral Learning Approaches. Behavioral approaches to family therapy, with such proponents as Patterson and others (1975) and Liberman (1970), have developed from behavior modification and social learning traditions in clinical psychology. Symptoms or maladaptive behavior are seen, regardless of origin, as reinforced or rewarded by the family. Treatment problems and goals are specified in concrete and observable behavioral terms, as in strategic models described above. However, the emphasis of behavioral learning approaches is on guiding family members directly to learn more effective modes of dealing with one another by changing the interpersonal consequences of behavior, or contingencies of reinforcement. Family members learn to give each other approval and acknowledgment for desired behavior instead of rewarding and reinforcing maladaptive behavior with attention and concern.

Thus, the basic learning principle that underlies this family approach is that social reinforcement is made contingent on adaptive behavior rather than maladaptive or symptomatic behavior. Imitative learning, or modeling, is also an important part of the process. The therapist, within a positive therapeutic alliance, serves both as a social reinforcer and model, defining his or her role as an educator.

Other Approaches. Mention should be made of three other family approaches that organize larger group forces in a systematic way: multiple-family groups, multiple-impact crisis intervention, and social network intervention.

Multiple-family groups have been found to be an extremely valuable means of integrating the families of psychiatric inpatients in the treatment plan in order to facilitate optimal readjustment (Laqueur, 1976; Anderson and others, 1980). Groups are typically composed of four to six patients with their families, including parents, siblings, and spouses. They may meet weekly or monthly with the therapist team throughout the hospitalization or aftercare of the identified patient, dealing with issues common to the experience and to realistic planning. Objectives may include the improvement of communication and structural patterns to reduce interactional stress and to facilitate maximal functioning and problem solving.

The group context provides opportunities for families to learn from other families and support to try out new adaptive role relations. Family members can relate to the experience of their counterparts in other families, gain a cognitive frame for perspective on their own crisis situation, reduce guilt and blame, and feel less isolated with their problems. Family relationships can be changed less threateningly with the mutually supportive network the group provides.

Multiple-impact crisis intervention involves the use of an intervention team with all members of a family when one member is in crisis. The work of Langsley and Kaplan (1968) focuses on immediate contact with the family at the time of crisis, as in emergency room admission. The crisis is defined as a family problem and responsibility is placed on the family for relief of immediate tension sufficient to prevent hospitalization and regression of the member in crisis. The goal is to strengthen the family's ability to manage not only the immediate situation but future crises as well. Likewise, the multiple-impact therapy of MacGregor and others (1964) uses a team approach to mobilize healthy interpersonal processes within the family.

Social network intervention is an approach developed by Speck and Attneave (1973) from their appreciation of the value of tribal meetings for healing purposes in many cultures. In this approach, the intervention team convenes a meeting of all members of the kinship system, friends, neighbors, and everyone of significance to a family presenting a problem. It is estimated that a typical urban family has close to forty people in such a potential network, but that a dysfunctional family tends to be cut off or isolated from network involvement and support. The goal of this intervention is to stimulate and focus the problem-solving potential of the network in a shared sense of responsibility and cooperation. The approach is based on a conviction that people are better able to deal with crises when they can share coping strengths with others in their natural social networks.

Toward an Integrative Approach

Goals, Strategies, and Techniques. Table 1 presents an overview of the chief characteristics of each of the major models of family therapy in terms of: view of symptoms or pathology; goals of therapy; and process of change (strategies and techniques).

There have been several other recent attempts to compare the similarities and differences of various family approaches and to categorize them along numerous dimensions (Madanes and Haley, 1977; Feldman, 1976a, 1976b; Stanton and Todd, 1982; Levant, 1980; Chasin and Grunebaum, 1981). Such attempts reflect the current need to integrate our knowledge and beliefs about critical family variables, family therapy goals, and change processes.

Levant (1980) suggests a useful clustering of approaches according to historical, structural/process, and experiential paradigms. The psychodynamic, transgenerational, and Bowen approaches fit a historical paradigm. They are long-term, growth-oriented models that emphasize insight and working through of past family-of-origin influences on present patterns, with family history and epigenesis an important focus of assessment and treatment. The structural, strategic, systemic, and behavioral approaches are ahistorical, stressing current family structure and process. They are short-term, action-oriented, pragmatic approaches directed at immediate problem resolution by changing systems maintenance patterns. The experiential paradigm is growth-oriented and yet ahistorical, promoting communication of feelings and revealing of self with others in the here and now.

Feldman, while sectoring the family therapy field differently, offers a useful perspective on strategies and techniques. He defines a therapeutic strategy as a "careful plan or method for achieving an end" (Feldman, 1976a, p. 14), for promoting change in the family and its members. The strategy is derived from a theory of change and directed toward clear objectives. Techniques are the specific tools, or behaviors, designed to implement that strategy or rationale of therapy. Thus, following an insight/working-through paradigm (historical or experiential), strategies of change would include interpretation and confrontation of family members with aspects of their feelings and behavior. Several innovative techniques have been developed to implement these processes, such as family sculpture and choreography (Papp, 1976), spatial manipulation (Satir, 1972), and videotape feedback.

Most current teachers and practitioners of family therapy attempt to combine or integrate family therapy models. In a recent survey of 175 family therapists by the present author, the large majority described their own orientation as eclectic or integrative, with most combining psychodynamic and structural/strategic approaches in their work.

Proponents of any single model of family therapy tend to see that approach as most effective with a wide range of problems and families. Eclectic clinicians tend to view strategies and techniques as a repertoire from which to select as fitting the characteristics and demands of specific families, varying problems and resistances to change, and particular treatment settings. A separation problem involving an adolescent and parents may be handled with some families by a brief problem-solving approach, whereas other families might profit more from an insight-oriented, historical exploration of separation conflicts. As Gurman and Kniskern (1981) point out, there is a need for more outcome research to compare the effectiveness of various family approaches—and individual therapy approaches—with different types of problems and families.

An integrative family therapist may also selectively combine approaches through stages of therapy with a given family. In his problem-centered approach,

Table 1. Major Models of Family Therapy

Model of Family Therapy	*View of Symptoms or Pathology*	*Goals of Therapy*	*Process of Change: Strategies and Techniques*
GROWTH-ORIENTED APPROACHES			
Psychodynamic Ackerman Boszormenyi-Nagy Framo Meissner Paul Skynner Spark Stierlin	Symptoms due to shared family projection process stemming from unresolved past conflicts or losses in family of origin	1. Resolution of family-of-origin conflict and losses 2. ↓Family projection processes 3. Relationship reconstruction and reunion 4. Individual and family growth	1. Insight-oriented, linking past and present dynamics 2. Assist in resolution of conflicts, losses (Paul: operational mourning) 3. Facilitate healthier modes of relating
Bowen Family Systems Therapy	Functioning impaired by relationships with family of origin: (a) Poor differentiation (b) Triangulation (c) Cutoffs (d) Anxiety (reactivity)	1. Differentiation 2. ↑Cognitive functioning 3. ↓Emotional reactivity 4. Modification of relationships in family system: (a) Detriangulation (b) Repair cutoffs	1. Coach individual action outside sessions: (a) Survey multigenerational family field (use of genogram) (b) Plan focused interventions to change self directly with family 2. Therapist takes cognitive stance, minimizing transference reaction
Experiential Kempler Satir Whitaker	Symptoms are nonverbal messages in reaction to current communication dysfunction in system	1. Direct, clear communication 2. Individual and family growth	Change here-and-now interaction in conjoint session 1. Share feelings about relationships: (a) Self-disclosure (b) Confrontation (c) Concretize, using spatial manipulation or sculpture (d) "experiential" techniques 2. Therapist uses own experience with family to model, catalyze process

PROBLEM-SOLVING APPROACHES			
Structural Minuchin Montalvo	Symptoms result from current family structural imbalance: (a) Malfunctioning hierarchical arrangement and boundaries (b) Maladaptive reaction to changing requirements (developmental, environmental)	Reorganize family structure: (a) Shift members' relative positions (b) Create clear, flexible subsystems and boundaries (c) Promote more adaptive coping	1. Therapist uses power and action to shift interaction patterns: (a) Joining family (b) Enactment of problem (c) Map structure, plan stages of restructuring (d) Task assignments and paradoxical intervention 2. Live supervision
Strategic Haley Milan group Palo Alto group	Multiple origins of problems; symptoms maintained by family's unsuccessful problem-solving attempts	Solve presenting problem; specific behaviorally defined objectives	1. Pragmatic, focused, action-oriented: (a) Clear plan to change symptom-maintaining sequence to new outcome (b) Substitute new behavior patterns to interrupt feedback cycles (c) Relabeling, reframing techniques (d) Directives and paradox 2. Use of consultant-observers
Behavioral Liberman Patterson	Maladaptive, symptomatic behavior reinforced by family attention and reward	Concrete, observable behavioral goals, social reinforcement (acknowledgment, approval) of adaptive behavior	1. Therapist as social reinforcer, model, educator 2. Change contingencies of reinforcement; interpersonal consequences of behavior 3. Guide family to reward desired behavior

Pinsof (1983) begins at the behavioral level and shifts, progressively, to the marital relationship, and finally to family-of-origin relationships (and intrapsychic issues) when—and only when—resistance blocks change at the previous level.

Comparison with Individual and Group Treatment Approaches. Regardless of differences in particular strategies and techniques employed in various models of family therapy, all approaches focus on direct assessment and change of the relationships among individuals, rather than problems "inside" the individual symptom bearer or derivatives in transference phenomena. This is perhaps the major distinction of the family systems orientation from traditional individual treatment models.

The therapeutic transference, an essential vehicle for assessment and change in individual models, plays a diminished role in family therapy because the therapist can observe patterns and promote change directly among key family members. Transference reactions do occur in family therapy, but are redirected for expression and change back into the natural relationship network.

Countertransference issues are stimulated as well in family therapy. In fact, the emotional power of a family and the likelihood that some member or relationship in a family may feel too close to "home" for a therapist requires that family therapists be aware of interface issues between their own family experiences and the families they are treating. A common problem for beginning family therapists is the tendency to overidentify with a symptomatic child such that it impedes empathic joining with parents. (After all, most therapists have spent more of their lives as children than as parents.)

There is a myth that working with family members together and focusing on behavior are more "superficial" than what can occur in one-to-one psychodynamic treatment. In fact, the experience is quite powerful and lasting change frequently occurs more rapidly than in individual therapy. First, in focusing only on the individual in pain, one is only treating the symptom of a relationship problem involving others. In attending to the system, the therapist can anticipate reactions to change and has more power to alter symptom-maintaining patterns. Second, intrapsychic issues are also interpersonal; the family therapist choosing to work at the interactional level believes that change in the system is easier to bring about in behavioral terms and will also result in intrapsychic change, regardless of the origin or chronicity of a problem. Third, direct confrontation and change with significant family members, whether planned to occur in sessions or between sessions, has potential therapeutic benefit for all members, not only the current symptom bearer.

Family therapy and group therapy approaches share common elements, for instance, in attention to group dynamics, communication processes, and use of psychodrama experiential techniques. The approaches are frequently merged in training and treatment settings as distinct from individual therapy in the treatment of more than one individual together. However, family therapy differs significantly from group therapy in convening the natural relationship unit that has a shared past, ongoing interaction, and future, as well as its own values, goals, language (verbal and nonverbal), and loyalties. Family therapy is defined by its attention to that system, not by the number of people seen together. In fact, individual sessions may be used to plan systemic change, as in the Bowen model.

Treatment Decisions. The often asked question, "When is family therapy indicated?", requires reframing from a systems perspective. When problems are conceptualized at the relationship level, an individual's problems cannot be understood or changed apart from the context in which they occur and the functions they may serve. An individual cannot be expected to change or sustain change without symptoms appearing elsewhere unless the system changes. Thus, the question of "indications" becomes a question of "What is the symptom-maintaining context of a specific problem in a particular family and how can it most effectively be altered?"

An assessment of any problem should therefore include a careful assessment of the family system, preferably in most cases by convening the nuclear family or household unit for a conjoint session. At times, some therapists may be reluctant to convene a large family or include small children because of a catastrophic fear of being overwhelmed by chaos or simply outnumbered, or because of concern about the impact on the child. Paradoxically, seeing all members conjointly can be easier, when they are conceptualized as a system and when the therapist attends to the repetitive relationship patterns connecting members rather than addressing them as a collection of individuals. A small child's tantrum at a certain point in the session can be instructive, revealing what sensitive issue may have been interrupted at that moment (the homeostatic regulator) and how the parents handle the behavior (the functioning of the parental subsystem).

It is important to consider all key relationships in the assessment, in order to determine treatment objectives and to decide who to include in subsequent sessions. Treatment may selectively focus on specific problems and the parts of the system most critically involved. Different members may be brought in, according to plan, at different phases of treatment. A family presenting a child-focused problem is generally treated conjointly, including both parents, siblings, and any other significant member in the household. A problem identified by a family as one spouse's problem or as a marital problem would more likely be treated in couples' therapy, excluding children just as one would close the bedroom door. Family therapy focused on intergenerational issues may progress to marital therapy focused on the couple. The indications for whom to see include: (1) involvement in the system maintaining the problem, and (2) the structural and emotional relationships the therapist wishes to promote to achieve objectives. Likewise, a short-term contract to accomplish a specific objective may be renegotiated or extended to fit a longer-term contract with broader goals.

Thus, it can be seen that family therapy is not a single treatment approach, but rather a flexible model that can be tailored to fit specific client needs and treatment situations. At the same time, treatment plans are carefully designed: contracts and objectives are explicitly formulated with families, and strategies and techniques follow a clear direction based on a sound assessment of the family system.

References

Ackerman, N. W. *The Psychodynamics of Family Life.* New York: Basic Books, 1958.

Anderson, C. "The Community Connection: The Impact of Social Networks on Family and Individual Functioning." In F. Walsh (Ed.), *Normal Family Processes.* New York: Guilford Press, 1982.

Anderson, C., Hogarty, G., and Reiss, D. "Family Treatment of Adult Schizophrenic Patients: A Psychoeducational Approach." *Schizophrenic Bulletin,* 1980, *6,* 490–505.

Aponte, H., and Hoffman, L. "The Open Door: A Structural Approach to a Family with an Anorectic Child." *Family Process,* 1973, *12,* 1–44.

Bank, S., and Kahn, M. *The Sibling Bond.* New York: Basic Books, 1982.

Bateson, G. *Mind and Nature: A Necessary Unity.* New York: Dutton, 1979.

Bateson, G., and others. "Toward a Theory of Schizophrenia." *Behavioral Science,* 1956, *1,* 251–264.

Bertalanffy, L. In W. Gray, I. Duhl, and N. Rizzo (Eds.), *General Systems Theory and Psychiatry.* Boston: Little, Brown, 1969.

Boszormenyi-Nagy, I. "Contextual Family Therapy." In A. Gurman and D. Kniskern (Eds.), *Handbook of Family Therapy.* New York: Brunner/Mazel, 1981.

Boszormenyi-Nagy, I., and Spark, G. *Invisible Loyalties.* New York: Harper & Row, 1973.

Bowen, M. "A Family Concept of Schizophrenia." In D. Jackson (Ed.), *The Etiology of Schizophrenia.* New York: Basic Books, 1960.

Bowen, M. *Family Therapy in Clinical Practice.* New York: Jason Aronson, 1978.

Carter, E., and McGoldrick, M. (Eds.). *The Family Life Cycle: Framework for Family Therapy.* New York: Gardner Press, 1980.

Carter, E., and (McGoldrick) Orfanidis, M. "Family Therapy with One Person and the Family Therapist's Own Family." In P. Guerin (Ed.), *Family Therapy: Theory and Practice.* New York: Gardner Press, 1976.

Chasin, R., and Grunebaum, H. "A Brief Synopsis of Current Concepts and Practices in Family Therapy." In J. Pearce and L. Friedman (Eds.), *Family Perspectives on Psychotherapy.* New York: Grune & Stratton, 1981.

Feldman, L. "Strategies and Techniques of Family Therapy." *American Journal of Psychotherapy,* 1976, *30,* 14–28.

Feldman, L. "Goals of Family Therapy." *Journal of Marriage and Family Counseling,* 1976, *2,* 103–113.

Feldman, L., and Pinsof, W. "Problem Maintenance in Family Systems: An Integrative Model." *Journal of Marital and Family Therapy,* 1982, *8,* 295–308.

Framo, J. "Rationale and Techniques of Intensive Family Therapy." In I. Boszormenyi-Nagy and J. Framo (Eds.), *Intensive Family Therapy.* Hagerstown, Md.: Harper & Row, 1965.

Guerin, P., and Pendagast, E. "Evaluation of Family System and Genogram." In P. Guerin (Ed.), *Family Therapy: Theory and Practice.* New York: Gardner Press, 1976.

Gurman, A., and Kniskern, D. "The Outcome of Family Therapy." In A. Gurman and D. Kniskern (Eds.), *Handbook of Family Therapy.* New York: Brunner/Mazel, 1981.

Haley, J. "Toward a Theory of Pathological Systems." In G. Zuk and I. Boszormenyi-Nagy (Eds.), *Family Therapy and Disturbed Families.* Palo Alto, Calif.: Science and Behavior Books, 1967.

Haley, J. *Uncommon Therapy: The Psychiatric Techniques of Milton Erikson.* New York: Norton, 1973.

Haley, J. *Problem-Solving Therapy.* San Francisco: Jossey-Bass, 1976.

Haley, J. *Leaving Home.* New York: McGraw-Hill, 1980.

Jackson, D. "The Study of the Family." *Family Process,* 1965a, *4,* 1–20.

Jackson, D. "Family Rules: Marital Quid Pro Quo." *Archives of General Psychiatry,* 1965b, *12,* 589–594.

Hoffman, L. *Foundations of Family Therapy.* New York: Basic Books, 1982.

Kempler, W. *Principles of Gestalt Family Therapy.* Salt Lake City: Deseret Press, 1974.

Kramer, C. *Becoming a Family Therapist: Developing an Integrated Approach to Working with Families.* New York: Human Sciences Press, 1980.

Langsley, D. G., and Kaplan, D. *The Treatment of Families in Crisis.* New York: Grune & Stratton, 1968.

Laqueur, H. "Multiple Family Therapy." In P. Guerin (Ed.), *Family Therapy: Theory and Practice.* New York: Gardner Press, 1976.

Levant, R. "A Classification of the Field of Family Therapy: A Review of Prior Attempts and a New Paradigmatic Model." *American Journal of Family Therapy,* 1980, *1,* 3–16.

Liberman, R. "Behavioral Approachs to Family and Couple Therapy." *American Journal of Orthopsychiatry,* 1970, *40,* 106–118.

Lidz, T., Fleck, S., and Cornelison, A. *Schizophrenia and the Family.* New York: International Universities Press, 1965.

Liebman, R., Minuchin, S., and Baker, L. "The Use of Structural Family Therapy in the Treatment of Intractable Asthma." *American Journal of Psychiatry,* 1974, *131,* 535–540.

McGoldrick, M., Pearce, J., and Giordano, J. (Eds.). *Ethnicity and Family Therapy.* New York: Guilford Press, 1982.

McGoldrick, M., and Walsh, F. "A Systemic View of History and Loss." In L. Wolberg and M. Aronson (Eds.), *Group and Family Therapy 1983—An Overview."* New York: Brunner/Mazel, 1983.

MacGregor, R., and others. *Multiple Impact Therapy with Families.* New York: McGraw-Hill, 1964.

Madanes, C., and Haley, J. "Dimensions of Family Therapy." *Journal of Nervous and Mental Disease,* 1977, *165,* 88–98.

Meissner, W. "The Conceptualization of Marriage and Family Dynamics from a Psychoanalytic Perspective." In T. Paolino and B. McCrady (Eds.), *Marriage and Marital Therapy.* New York: Brunner/Mazel, 1978.

Minuchin, S. *Families and Family Therapy.* Cambridge, Mass.: Harvard University Press, 1974.

Minuchin, S., and Fishman, C. *Family Therapy Techniques.* Cambridge, Mass.: Harvard University Press, 1981.

Minuchin, S., and others.*Families of the Slums.* New York: Basic Books, 1967.

Minuchin, S., Rosman, B., and Baker, L. *Psychosomatic Families: Anorexia Nervosa in Context.* Cambridge, Mass.: Harvard University Press, 1978.

Napier, A., and Whitaker, C. *The Family Crucible.* New York: Harper & Row, 1978.

Neill, J., and Kniskern, D. *From Psyche to System: The Evolving Therapy of Carl Whitaker.* New York: Guilford Press, 1982.

Papp, P. "Family Choreography." In P. Guerin (Ed.), *Family Therapy: Theory and Practice.* New York: Gardner Press, 1976.

Papp, P. *Family Therapy: Full Length Case Studies.* New York: Gardner Press, 1977.

Patterson, G., and others. *A Social Learning Approach to Family Intervention.* Eugene, Ore.: Castalia Publishers, 1975.

Paul, N., and Grosser, G. "Operational Mourning and Its Role in Conjoint Family Therapy." *Community Mental Health Journal,* 1965, *1,* 339–345.

Paul, N., and Paul, B. *A Marital Puzzle: Transgenerational Analysis in Marriage.* New York: Norton, 1975.

Pinsof, W. "Integrative Problem-Centered Therapy: Toward the Synthesis of Family and Individual Psychotherapies." *Journal of Marital and Family Therapy,* 1983, *9.*

Ruesch, J., and Bateson, G. *Communication: The Social Matrix of Psychiatry.* New York: Norton, 1951.

Satir, V. *Conjoint Family Therapy.* Palo Alto, Calif.: Science and Behavior Books, 1964.

Satir, V. *Peoplemaking.* Palo Alto, Calif.: Science and Behavior Books, 1972.

Selvini-Palazzoli, M. *Self-Starvation: From the Intrapsychic to the Transpersonal Approach to Anorexia Nervosa.* London: Chaucer Publishing, 1974.

Selvini-Palazzoli, and others. *Paradox and Counterparadox: A New Method in the Therapy of the Family in Schizophrenic Transaction.* New York: Jason Aronson, 1978.

Selvini-Palazzoli, M., and others. "Hypothesizing—Circularity—Neutrality: Three Guidelines for the Conductor of the Session." *Family Process,* 1980, *19,* 3–12.

Singer, M., M., and Wynne, L. "Thought Disorder and Family Relations of Schizophrenics, IV: Results and Implications." *Archives of General Psychiatry,* 1965, *12,* 201–212.

Skynner, A. *Systems of Family and Marital Psychotherapy.* New York: Brunner/Mazel, 1976.

Sluzki, C. "Marital Therapy from a Systems Perspective." In T. Paolino and B. McCrady (Eds.), *Marriage and Marital Therapy.* New York: Brunner/Mazel, 1978.

Speck, R., and Attneave, C. *Family Networks.* New York: Pantheon, 1973.

Stanton, M., and Todd, T. *The Family Therapy of Drug Abuse and Addiction.* New York: Guilford Press, 1982.

Stierlin, H. *The First Interview with the Family.* New York: Brunner/Mazel, 1980.

Toman, W. *Family Constellation.* (3rd ed.) New York: Springer, 1975.

Walsh, F. "Concurrent Grandparent Death and Birth of Schizophrenic Offspring: An Intriguing Finding." *Family Process,* 1978, *4,* 457–464.

Walsh, F. "Breaching of Generational Boundaries in Families of Schizophrenics." *International Journal of Family Therapy,* 1979, *3,* 254–275.

Walsh, F. "Conceptualizations of Normal Family Functioning." In F. Walsh (Ed.), *Normal Family Processes.* New York: Guilford Press, 1982.

Walsh, F., and McGoldrick, M. "The Systemic Impact of Loss: Implications for Dysfunction at the Launching Transition." In H. Liddle (Ed.), *The Family*

Life Cycle: Implications for Clinicians. Rockville, Md.: Aspen Publications, 1983.

Watzlawick, P., Beavin, J., and Jackson, D. *Pragmatics of Human Communication.* New York: Norton, 1967.

Watzlawick, P., Weakland, J., and Fisch, R. *Change: Principles of Problem Formation and Problem Resolution.* New York: Norton, 1974.

Weakland, J., and others. "Brief Therapy: Focused Problem Resolution." *Family Process,* 1974, *13,* 141–168.

Wynne, L., and others. "Pseudo-Mutuality in the Family Relations of Schizophrenics." *Psychiatry,* 1958, *21,* 205–220.

23

Practice in Cross-Cultural Settings

Samuel O. Miller

Clinical social work practice in cross-cultural contexts has had a long tradition in our profession. Although practice involving primarily nonminority clinicians with individuals and groups of clients of ethnic and racial minority groups is extensive, only recently has there been interest in seeking to identify the distinctive nature of this practice, to examine the efficacy and effectiveness of available therapeutic techniques, and to systematically assess the implications of this practice arrangement. The process has not proceeded without controversy or conflict, nor has it captured the full support of the profession. Rather, the thrust to fully comprehend and ultimately improve clinical services to racial and other minority groups has called into question many of the most basic professional assumptions. It has also achieved only partial success in the wake of opposition, uncertainty, and defensiveness, and, occasionally raised the spectre of rampant racism and discrimination within the hallowed spheres of the profession.

There has never been any doubt that members of such populations, or cultural groups, as black Americans, Asian-Pacific Americans, Native Americans, and Spanish-speaking/surnamed Americans have been consistently and disproportionately represented among those most in need of social and clinical services. Similarly, it is a well-documented fact that they have tended to use mental health facilities at a greater rate than members of the majority group. In responding to

Some of the ideas presented in this chapter were generated by readings and discussions with colleagues at the Spanish Speaking Mental Health Research Center, University of California at Los Angeles, where I spent an internship in 1980—*Samuel O. Miller* their needs and requests for services, a majority of practitioners have assessed the problems which these clients bring, utilized clinical approaches, and evaluated the outcomes of the clinical encounters based primarily on traditional psychoanalytic/psychotherapeutic viewpoints. The result is that some clients have received, on occasion, excellent services and expeditiously accomplished the objectives which they, and presumably their clinical social worker, sought when they became involved. Further, we have learned a great deal about the strengths of ethnic-minority individuals, families, and communities, and of the contributions made by the church and selected social institutions to their health and welfare.

On the other hand, the theoretical and research literature focusing on dropouts (Urban Associates, Inc., 1974), admission rates (Burruel and Chavez, 1974), length and cost of services (Miranda, 1974), differential diagnoses (Cole and Pilisuk, 1976; Kramer, Rosen and Willis, 1972), and client expectations (Abad, Ramos, and Boyce, 1974), among other factors related to clinical practice, has raised increasing concern about the appropriateness and adequacy of traditional forms of clinical social work practice for dealing with the array and complexity of problems experienced by ethnic minority or culturally different clients. Some writers have gone so far as to question whether, in fact, clinical social work as currently practiced has not been harmful by contributing to, rather than alleviating, the oppression that most minority clients experience in their daily lives (Solomon, 1976). As stated succinctly yet forcefully by the Task Panel on Mental Health of Hispanic Americans, in their report to the President's Commission on Mental Health (1978, p. 910): "A mental health program which attempts to reduce patients' anxieties with medication or individual therapy while neglecting or assaulting their sociocultural values will defeat its own purpose and cause more damage than benefit."

Response to this expressed concern has been prompt and diversified. In certain quarters there has emerged a strong defense of traditional treatment approaches. Many professionals, on the other hand, have engaged in concerted efforts to modify existing treatment strategies and develop new approaches. Two rather promising developments, resulting from this controversy, are represented by the increasing contributions of minority professionals to the theory and research on minority issues and to providing leadership in stimulating viable changes, plus the substantive development of private and publicly funded agencies which "incorporate ethnic factors, not as problems, but as components of service delivery" (Jenkins, 1981, p. 43–44).

Despite the changes in concern, methodology, and contexts, the expansion of knowledge capable of informing practice and service delivery, and the best of intentions on the part of individuals and groups of clinical practitioners, the mental health of ethnic and racial minority groups is still in grave jeopardy and the treatment of the illnesses that occur in these populations is woefully inadequate and frequently inappropriate. Besides being bleak, the overall picture is in sad disarray. The reasons for these sad circumstances are legion. They will become obvious in the discussion to follow.

It is the intent of this chapter to (1) discuss the definitional issues related to clinical practice in cross-cultural contexts, (2) indicate the need for clinical services, (3) discuss the utilization of clinical services by ethnic-minority-group members, and (4) discuss the critical dimensions emerging in the literature on clinical practice with ethnic-minority clients.

Concepts and Problems

A definition of clinical social work which clearly distinguishes it from direct social work practice or from psychotherapy and which enjoys broad-based professional acceptance has not yet been fully achieved. Definitions offered in the literature or in professional discussions tend to depend exclusively on the point of view of the definer(s). Similarly, there appears to be limited agreement on the boundaries or essential characteristics of clinical social work among those seeking to define or describe this professional process. Clinical social workers in particular, and the professional leaders in general, have recognized the implications of the absence of an articulated definition. Efforts to correct this serious gap have expanded, as evidenced by the Symposium on Education for the Practice of Clinical Social Work at the Master's Level in 1977 (Pinkus and others, 1977) and by the National Invitational Forum on Clinical Social Work two years later (Ewalt, 1980). The contributions to our understanding and appreciation of clinical social work evolving from these efforts are informative and unprecedented. Yet the continuing absence of a universally accepted definition is a reality and inhibits the process of professional developments, including the education for competent practice, articulation with other professions, and licensing agreements.

At times, serious effort is exerted to equate or identify the process of clinical social work with all of social work practice. A small segment of practitioners are content to define clinical practice more narrowly, emphasizing the essential therapeutic functions. For example, Cooper (1980, p. 22), while noting that clinical practice is "not exclusively concerned with counseling," specifically states that she believes it to be "*that sector of social work* which takes as its primary universe the world of the mind and its behavior; how it works in social contexts and develops, adapts, copes with, and hampers achievement. Our function as clinicians primarily rests on understanding and using these processes in the service of better human adaptation and functioning" (emphasis added). Ewalt (1979, p. 29), in another context, defines clinical social work in terms of its purpose, noting that, "*as with all social work,* the purpose of clinical social work is to improve the quality of life by enhancing or maintaining interactions between people and their environments" (emphasis added).

For purposes of this chapter, clinical social work is defined as that combination of social work processes which address themselves primarily to the internal life of the client, although not overlooking the external or social aspects. The unit of attention is most often the individual, family, or small group. The aims are those of modifying maladaptive behavior, thought processes, or perceptions; increasing the client's capacity to adapt and function; and improving the client's interactions and transactions with his or her impinging social environment.

Certain assumptions underlying this definition and the discussion to follow must be made explicit. First, this definition conceptualizes clinical social work as an identifiable orientation within the broad field of social work. In contrast to the recent past, when casework, groupwork, and community organization could be compared according to their methodologies and the unit(s) of attention on which practitioners focused, or earlier, when psychiatric social work, for example, could be contrasted with medical social work, school social work, or family practice on the basis of their locus of practice, there is no current orientation comparable to clinical social work. Yet, as suggested by Strean (1978), such a practice model came into being in 1970 as a response to several professional trends, not the least of which was the "concern by direct service practitioners in social work . . . that the national social work organizations were overlooking their contributions and professional needs" (p. 34).

Irrespective of the original motivations, several actions, discrete and in tandem, have created and currently maintain such a model or entity. Some of the most critical of those actions include the formation of the National Federation of Societies for Clinical Social Work in 1971; the founding of the *Journal of Clinical Social Work* in 1972; and the publication of the *Register of Clinical Social Workers* by the National Association of Social Workers in 1976. Related activities, such as the rapid increase in the number of social workers engaging in or aspiring toward private practice and the recent publication of several books and articles on clinical social work (including this volume), appear to further legitimate this professional model.

Individuals and organizations in ethnic-minority communities, notably the National Association of Black Social Workers, have seen these efforts as creating an elite cadre of professionals and in serious conflict with the best interests of ethnic-minority communities. They have questioned whether the efforts to establish this model of practice have not superseded concern with the needs of clients and whether the objectives identified with this process represent another insidious use of euphemisms to cover belated expressions of racism.

The second assumption to be made explicit about the definition of clinical social work is that the convergence of interest in the client's intrapsychic life consistently distinguishes clinical social work from any other type of social work practice (Meyer, 1977). If the major distinguishing feature stemmed only from why, how, and when it emerged, clinical social work as a structural entity would simply be a political force within the field of social work. If, on the other hand, the distinction stemmed from educational preparation and knowledge, orientation, and special abilities (Pinkus and others, 1977), it would simply be a specialization within the field or a higher level of direct practice. Important as those features and their implications are, and since this practice model shares the skills, values, and knowledge of all of social work, the distinction to date is only one of foci. The definition postulated here is developed principally from an analysis of what clinical social workers say and write about their practice, and is a studied attempt to minimize conceptual and professional obfuscation in the discussion to follow. The predilection of clinical social workers for working with intrapsychic factors is frequently out of fit with the priorities of ethnic-minority clients. This situation is a continuing source of contention and has broad professional implications.

Third, this definition implies that a clinical social worker is not always a clinician. Social workers, irrespective of their theoretical and ideological persuasion, engage in a range of different activities and assume different roles in carrying out their professional duties—from consultation to collaboration, supervision to administration, and a variety of others in between. These activities are undoubtedly informed by the knowledge, skills, and values of social work. In addition, they are rooted in the social and behavioral sciences, centrally dependent on the professional use of relationship and communication techniques, and employ certain therapeutic strategies commonly used in direct practice. However, it is imperative that the clinical social worker not assume that he or she is always engaged in direct clinical practice, inasmuch as these roles and activities are unequivocally different from work with a client and from each other. The difference stems principally from the nature and degree of authority in the relationship, the role relationships themselves, and the defined limits of the task to be accomplished. In cross-cultural contexts the clinician assumes roles wherein the sharp distinction of responsibilities and the requisite knowledge and skill frequently determine the success or failure of the venture.

Since this discussion also focuses on "cross-cultural contexts," it is important to clarify this construct. Franz Boas conceptualizes culture as the distinctive body of customs, beliefs, and social institutions which characterize each society (Stocking, 1966). In that respect, it is posited that we have in the United States a meta-culture* consisting of the unprecedented mix of values, beliefs, traditions, customs, languages, and institutions introduced by the heterogeneous ethnic, racial, and national groups coexisting as the American populace. Since we have not achieved that homogeneous whole projected in the melting pot theory, each of the discrete racial/ethnic groups maintains to a greater or lesser degree its distinctive cultural heritage. Implicit in this discussion is the assumption that the Hispanic, black American, Asian-Pacific American, and Native American groups each has a distinctive culture which influences the development, functioning, and adaptation of individuals within the groups. Further, their respective cultures influence a range of factors and issues related to clinical social work, including their perspectives on the problems which can best be dealt with in clinical social work settings, how they should be approached, and what are the most desirable outcomes of such clinical encounters.

Although the discussion to follow considers members of the four cultural groups jointly, I do not mean to imply that they are identical in all respects. Indeed, even within groups there is tremendous diversity determined by geographical location of residence, generations, social class, and historical events. The discussion also recognizes that the nature and quality of cultural development between and among the groups is rapidly changing. Neither is there any intent to overlook the clinical needs and concerns of other ethnic or cultural groups, notably those Americans of Euro-ethnic origin. The rationale for focusing on the four ethnic groups identified stems from the unique history of oppression, racism, and discrimination which they share and which occasion the equally unique social, economic, and clinical problems which they experience. Data will be presented to confirm that their unique experiences have shaped and continue to shape their mental health status, the national and professional response to their needs, and their ultimate potential for functioning in today's society.

*I wish to express my appreciation to my colleague Robert Jones for clarifying this concept and its implications.

Need for Clinical Services

In keeping with the definitions stated earlier, the major objective of clinical social work is to improve the social functioning of clients. Ultimately, practitioners seek to reduce the number of people who bear the brunt of undue stress, to reduce stress and stressors where they can be eliminated, and to reduce the risk of individuals succumbing to stress. The activities designed to accomplish these objectives are carried out in a range of settings and fields of practice. However, clinical social work is most closely aligned with the field of mental health and its "function is similar to those of psychiatry and clinical psychology. . . . [I]ndeed the three disciplines work together in teams in the same settings and often do the same work" (Pinkus and others, 1977, p. 257). Unfortunately, specific data on the need for and the utilization of clinical social work per se is not readily available. Thus, it is instructive to review the estimates of the mental health needs of ethnic-minority groups.

Recent estimates suggest that as many as two of every ten Americans may be in serious need of mental health services (Bryant, 1977). A review of any previous or current estimate of mental health needs reveals that those individuals who are members of racial and other minority groups have been consistently and disproportionately represented among those most in need.

For example, a study (Bachrach, 1975) of mental hospital admissions throughout the country indicates that during 1972 nearly three in ten Spanish-speaking/surnamed Americans and nearly four in ten nonwhites admitted to state and county mental hospitals were given a primary diagnosis of schizophrenia. Alcohol disorders accounted for 15 percent and drug disorders for 17 percent of Spanish-speaking/surnamed admissions, and for 23 percent and 6 percent of the nonwhite admissions, respectively. The same study revealed a wide and significant variation in the legal status of admissions to state and county mental hospitals according to ethnicity. Among whites, over half of all admissions (52 percent) were voluntary, the most desirable form of admission to a mental hospital, if one has to be admitted. In contrast, voluntary admissions accounted for 43 percent among the Spanish-speaking/surnamed group and 35 percent of the nonwhites admitted.

While the average length of inpatient stay decreased significantly for all patients between 1964 and 1973, it was still greater for members of racial and other minority groups. Admission rates to hospitals for minority patients were twice as great as for whites, and blacks exceeded whites in mental hospitals by 52 percent. The study concluded that while racial minorities used more mental health facilities at greater rates than whites, they made greatest use of inpatient and publicly funded facilities as compared to outpatient and private facilities.

Recently, the members of the Task Panels on Mental Health Issues of the four ethnic-minority groups detailed for the President's Commission on Mental Health (1978) the pressing and overwhelming needs of each particular ethnic group. Their documentation is so vivid that the reader is encouraged to review them in their original details. The most impressive aspect of these data is the overwhelming repetition of negative indicators leading to the unmistakable conclusion that members of these groups are at enormous risk concerning all aspects of mental health. Briefly, the following evidence was highlighted, indicating that ethnic-minority individuals, families, and communities:

suffer the full impact of a culture of poverty to a much higher extent than the general population (Padilla and Ruiz, 1973);
have an increased prevalence of substance abuse, alcoholism, and juvenile delinquency;
have a higher number of families devastated by mental illness and alcoholism (Staples, 1976);
experience high unemployment leading to mental illness, family disruption, and alcoholism (American Indian Policy Review Committee, 1977);
have less services available;
have an increasing rate of institutionalization compared to a decreasing rate for whites, and simultaneously have low "treatment" rates (Sharpley, 1977);
are admitted, committed, or sentenced for custodial care sooner than whites;
are more disturbed than Caucasian patients on admission (Berk and Hirata, 1973);
have a higher proportion diagnosed as psychotic (Sue, 1977);
receive less accurate diagnosis (Cooper, 1973);
suffer from more nonspecific dispositions (Lowenger and Dobie, 1966);
are more likely to be seen for diagnostic purposes and less likely to be selected for insight-oriented therapy (Jackson, Berkowitz, and Farley, 1974; Rosenthal and Frank, 1958).

These findings are of recent origin, collected, analyzed, and reported by ethnic-minority professionals in the main, and, particularly in the case of the data presented by the Task Panels, developed for the specific purpose of influencing the development of a national policy on mental health. These data simultaneously confirm some and contradict other data of more distant origin regarding the level of mental health and mental illness of ethnic-minority populations. This combination of circumstances is extremely pertinent to this discussion, inasmuch as many professionals (primarily of ethnic-minority background) have questioned repeatedly and seriously the application of traditional definitions of mental health, mental illness, and social dysfunctioning to the practice with and research on the culturally different.

These professionals have posited that to develop the most effective practice with and the most relevant research on these groups, the functioning of ethnic-minority individuals, families, and communities must be approached with a dual perspective (Norton, 1978). Such a perspective involves the conscious and systematic comparison of values, attitudes, and behaviors considered to be appropriate within the larger societal system with those that are valued and deemed appropriate to the individual's immediate family and community system. Such a perspective also takes into account the social, economic, political, and institutional contexts which influence and are simultaneously influenced by the individual and his or her observed behaviors.

If we accept the viability of the dual-perspective concept, several critical issues, which have implications for how the needs of ethnic-minority groups and communities are viewed, warrant attention. Perhaps the most obvious implication is the recognition that the extent of mental health and mental illness in these communities may be more or less than officially stated and/or statistically documented at any point in time. Some of the most salient issues are outlined below.

1. *The absence of a precise definition of mental health.* The definition of mental health is as illusive as that of clinical social work. As posited in the literature, it entails some perspective of the equally ill-defined concepts of mental illness, the person's view of himself or herself, and his or her concept of the world. These essential elements—the self-concept, the individual's world view, and "the working of the mind" (which, as suggested by Cooper, 1980, is the principal universe of clinical social work)—are not readily observable, rarely measured with precision, but unquestionably determined or influenced by culture. Thus, any unilateral definition of or conclusion about the mental health, or more important, the mental illness of ethnic-minority individuals, families, or groups which is not cognizant of the definitional imprecision or which excludes consideration of the barriers to opportunity, the impact of interrupted transactions between the individual and the larger system, and the demands of his or her immediate environment, is partial at best and professionally irresponsible at worst.

2. *Prevailing myths regarding the behavioral contexts in ethnic-minority communities.* It has been suggested with considerable frequency that ethnic-minority communities are willing and able to tolerate deviant behavior. Policies, practices, and programs stemming from this assumption place ethnic-minority individuals and communities in double jeopardy. Behaviors which are indeed deviant are overlooked or minimized to the extent that the individual has to behave or appear extremely bizarre before he or she is brought to the attention of clinicians. On the other hand, some behaviors which simply do not conform to norms existing in the larger social context are automatically seen as deviant when, in fact, they may constitute the only available or appropriate response to the social, physical, and environmental trauma confronting the individual. As Meers (1980) states: "One culture venerates what another abhors. . . . While it is not difficult to document that there are clear differences between cultures which shape both the evolution and form of human behavior, it is far more complicated to distinguish which aberrant behaviors or psychobiological symptoms are an expression of unconscious, psychoneurotic conflict. With respect to the ghetto-reared black child, we know all too little to generalize on symptom formation with any degree of certitude" (p. 81).

3. *The complexity of help-seeking behaviors.* It has been documented that ethnic-minority individuals come or are brought to the attention of mental health facilities substantially later than are whites; only at the point of acute breakdown or stress, and when their symptoms are quite serious, do they finally come (Fabrega, Swartz, and Wallace, 1968; Newton, 1978). Structural barriers to the utilization of mental health services will be detailed and described below. However, under the best of circumstances, the decision-making process for seeking help is known to be complex and is compounded by various cultural factors. Newton (1978) reported, in his study of Mexican-Americans: "The factor most strongly emphasized in influencing response to emotional problems is pride.

Desiring to maintain a self-image of strength, individuals will wait and struggle with a problem by themselves and/or with the help of relatives and friends before seeking more professional help. Moreover . . . a Mexican-American will delay substantially longer than an Anglo-American before seeking help" (p. 89).

4. *The special vulnerability of ethnic-minority populations.* Two major factors, the age distribution of ethnic-minority populations and their almost uniform status as urban dwellers, appear to compound their plight and increase their vulnerability to dysfunctioning. For most of the ethnic groups, the number of children and adolescents in the total population approaches one-half. The consensus of social and behavioral scientists on the critical nature of these periods of human development for the level and quality of adult functioning does not augur well for these populations, especially when large family size and poverty multiply their vulnerability to psychological and emotional stress. Similarly, socioeconomic factors force a majority of these special populations to become urban dwellers and, in particular, residents of the inner city. The decay, crime, and other identified unhealthy features characteristic of most inner cities have tremendous consequences for the current and future mental health of these populations.

The grim reality is that, irrespective of how the comparison is made, a large majority of these special population groups exist under the most stress-producing conditions: neighborhoods with high morbidity and mortality rates; schools which are substandard in the physical structure and the quality of education provided; work settings which are unsatisfactory, even frequently dangerous; rampant unemployment; dilapidated and expensive housing; poor nutrition; low educational attainment; and an overwhelming shortage of relevant, accessible health and mental health services and facilities. These stress-producing circumstances and the resulting stress responses have historically been the target of clinical social work.

When we speak of the utilization of clinical services by racial and other minority groups, we should perhaps rephrase it as *under*-utilization. Research and experience repeatedly confirm that, while the need is extensive and clearly documented, ethnic and racial minority-group members ironically and consistently receive services in less quantity and of more inferior quality than their nonethnic counterparts. Detailed review of the research literature further indicates that this arrangement is not of recent origin, that it may have worsened during the last decade despite the most drastic upheaval on the social and professional scene, and that the explanatory hypotheses offered are contradictory and unclear. As early as 1966, Karno, after reviewing the case records of blacks, Mexican-Americans, and Caucasian patients, reported: "The prospective ethnic patients are less likely to be accepted for treatment than are the nonethnic patients. Ethnic patients who are accepted for treatment receive less and shorter psychotherapy than do nonethnic patients of the same social class. Ethnicity tends to be avoided by clinic personnel" (p. 520).

Cohen (1969) provides an early view of the intransigence of professional responses, in a graphic description of the experience of a family service agency in southern California. It was evident that the black population living in greatest proximity and most likely to utilize the services was not from the typical lower socioeconomic class, which tends to eschew institutional services. Yet service utilization by this group, minimal from the outset, decreased even further during the ten years preceding the study. A review of the case records to determine the quality of services "revealed that psychological problems presented by blacks were frequently ignored, with attention focused mainly on concrete service. . . . For example, premature judgments about the treatability of marital problems occurred frequently; referrals were made for public assistance with little attempt to deal with other concrete or emotional problems; arrangements were made by the agency for childcare placement with little attention paid to such matters as one parent's comments that her son had 'bitten a neighbor child's penis.' . . . In general, [there was] evidence of a mechanical and superficial approach to service for blacks rather than the more fully developed treatment given to others" (Cohen, 1969, p. 104).

In the decade since this report the relationships between humans and crucial societal institutions have undergone radical changes. Institutions that were previously and automatically respected have been subjected to intense scrutiny and critical assessment of their current and continuing import. In the process, few social, political, economic, religious, educational, or welfare institutions escaped challenges from their actual or potential clientele or from the disenfranchised, the disillusioned, or the dissatisfied. Groups including ethnic-minority people, previously quiescent and seemingly willing to accept a subordinate status, affirmed their identity and vociferously demanded an examination of their special circumstances as well as improved institutional responses to their particular needs and aspirations. Groups previously operating as mutual foes developed coalitions, identified their mutual concerns about the responsiveness of social and political institutions to their interests, and joined forces in demanding of these institutions greater accountability in carrying out their societal assignments. Cultural groups, among others, developed an interest in understanding and controlling the forces governing their daily lives and in participating actively in the shaping of their own futures.

During the initial years of the struggle, the demands from one or another group were for "more"—more schools, jobs, educational opportunities; more health and mental health services or personal and social services. In time, as they realized that "more" was not enough and "better" was less than optimal, these groups changed their demands, opting for "relevance"—relevance to particular individuals and groups and to the life situations shared by each. Client participation became a hallmark of this changing scene. Given the stridency and viability of these demands, and given social work's unique commitment to self-determination as an essential value, it would appear logical to have expected considerable changes in the delivery structure and the practice arrangements in clinical settings.

However, the reports of the Task Panels to the President's Commission on Mental Health (1978) clearly demonstrate that few positive changes emerged during the 1970s. In every group, even in locations where they represent a sizable portion of the population in residence, ethnic-minority patients represented a small portion of the patient population in the appropriate mental health facilities.

The subpanel reporting on Hispanics (p. 906) stated it most succinctly: "Although the social and economic conditions described . . . render them vulnerable to psychological and emotional stress, Hispanic Americans underutilize the mental health services available. Utilization rates vary from different groups and geographic locations; these rates, however, rarely exceed 50 percent; that is, Hispanic representation among recipients of services is one-half (or less) of their representation in the general population."

Hypotheses purporting to explain the documented underutilization of traditional mental health services by members of special population groups have been contradictory. Some have emphasized the various social, economic, and cultural aspects inherent in the ethnic-minority individual or community. Others have focused on certain attributes of the clinical facilities, practitioners, and services they provide.

Some theorists and researchers have hypothesized that the limited-motivation characteristic, lower socioeconomic status, perceptions of illness and treatment, and reliance on alternative resources (such as family members, curanderos, faith healers, or folk medicine) serve to explain the limited use by ethnic-minority individuals of existing mental health services. Recent data do, in fact, suggest that socioeconomic factors may be a powerful explanatory variable in decisions about continuing use of mental health services (McLemore, 1963), but the data on the existence and use of indigenous resources are less than conclusive (Keefe, Padilla, and Carlos, 1978).

Similarly, systematic studies reveal that ethnic-minority individuals and communities do indeed have different perceptions of mental illness and treatment. Their overall perceptions of treatment and its potential contributions were found to be essentially positive and the identification and acknowledgment of mental illness not essentially different from those of the majority group (Acosta, 1975). The differences that do exist are in the willingness (or lack of it) to label their psychological discomfort, perceptions of the role of mental health professionals, and attitudes toward the help available from indigenous resources. These differences, critical to the acceptance and utilization of mental health services, have many positive features. Consequently, it seems inappropriate to denigrate them, especially since they are not intransigent to professional interaction, when and if changes should be necessary.

In contrast, findings on the negative impact and influence of structural factors on utilization of mental health services by minority clients are more conclusive. These findings consistently confirm the existence and effects of institutional policies and organizational patterns which contravene all of the standards of accessibility (National Institute of Mental Health, 1972); those accessibilities include visible, physical, procedural, economic, psychological, and cultural factors which enhance or discourage availability of services. A brief discussion of each of these factors, with the relevant research which supports the concept, follows.

1. *Visible accessibility*. Edgerton and Karno (1971) found that while 80 percent of the Mexican-Americans of East Los Angeles who participated in their study felt that therapy could assist people with psychiatric disorders, an equal percentage could not name or locate a single mental health center. The Task Panel on Black Americans (1978) concludes that among the factors which mitigate against blacks and poor people in general availing themselves of health services are "lack of awareness of the availability of such services, the reliance on traditional media to inform blacks and poor people of the existence of such services,

inadequate transportation to and from health delivery agencies, and scheduled hours that are more convenient for the health delivery personnel than for the potential black consumer" (p. 836). Several other studies (Knoll, 1971; Laosa, Burstein, and Martin, 1975; Phillipus, 1971) add data which suggest that specific segments of ethnic-minority populations—the poor, ghetto residents, the aged, recent arrivals, or monolinguals (non-English speaking)—tend to be the most unaware of the services available.

2. *Physical accessibility.* The physical location of clinical services, compounded by the cost of transportation, potential loss of income or employment due to absence from work, and the lack of childcare facilities, is a well-known deterrent to the use of facilities. Historically, efforts to compensate with the development of branch offices of family service agencies and satellite clinics were made during the heyday of the community mental health movement. Two studies (Brurrel and Chavez, 1974; Torrey, 1972) confirm the current reluctance to use services on the part of those who have to travel to distant locations, frequently involving considerable time and inconvenience.

3. *Procedural accessibility.* Among the procedural factors which have been systematically correlated with underutilization are: the limited availability of ethnic-minority professionals (Olmedo and Lopez, 1977; Yamamoto, Jones, and Palley, 1968); the adherence to a traditional clinical and therapeutic orientation (Brurrel and Chavez, 1974; Martinez, 1973; Ruiz, Casas, and Padilla, 1977); and the staunch presence of formal procedures which alienate actual and potential users of clinical services (Phillipus, 1971).

4. *Economic accessibility.* Reference has been made to the impact of poverty, secondary costs (transportation, loss of income), and the ability to pay for services on the utilization and quality of services. Experience has also documented that a minimal number of ethnic-minority individuals use private mental health services. Thus members of racial-minority groups have few alternatives and those that are available are often of the poorest quality (Chu and Trotter, 1974; Firman and others, 1975). In a compelling article, Spurlock and Cohen (1969) ask, "Should the Poor Get None?" and immediately document how current policies and practices serve to provide an affirmative answer again and again.

5. *Psychological accessibility.* Perhaps the most damaging experiences occur when ethnic-minority clients finally request services only to have their expectations denied. Several authors have reported findings that the expectations of ethnic-minority clients involved in therapy may not be customarily ascertained or met. In the main, these clients approach the encounter hoping for advice rather than reflection, anticipating the resolution of social rather than intrapsychic problems. Nevertheless, many clinicians immediately and naively approach these patients with an extensive, historical review of intrapsychic experiences; this leads to confusion on the part of the patient, frustration on the part of the therapist, and frequently premature termination of the therapeutic contact. This point is fully articulated by Abad, Ramos, and Boyce (1974, p. 590), who state: "They [Puerto Ricans] expect to see a [clinician] who will be active in his relationship with them, giving advice and prescribing medication or some form of tangible treatment. The more passive . . . approach, with reliance on the patient to talk about his problems introspectively and take responsibility for making decisions about them, is not what the Puerto Rican patient expects. This discrepancy

between the patient's expectations and his actual experience may well determine whether he continues in treatment."

6. *Cultural accessibility.* The thrust of this discussion has been the clear and unquestionable need for culturally relevant and accessible services. Most of the studies mentioned have some indirect relationship to this issue. Several, however, have taken this notion as their central focus (Casas, 1976; Phillipus, 1971; Torrey, 1970) and document the correlation between underutilization and the failure to consider language and culture in the design and implementation of clinical services. Newton (1978) focuses on the overlooking of cultural differences in categorizing mental health symptoms, and Schensul (1974) reports on the absence of community input and involvement in organizing and administering mental health services.

Emerging Dimensions of Practice

Despite the criticism of clinical social work practice leveled in the preceding sections, this practice model has much to offer to ethnic-minority individuals and communities. Indeed, many more ethnic-minority individuals and families are seeking and utilizing clinical social work services as currently defined and practiced (Brurrel and Chavez, 1974; Cooper, 1973; Meers, 1980; Pinderhughes, 1973). The reasons for this change are that the congruence between the objectives and techniques of clinical practice and the needs and interests of ethnic-minority clients has experienced some corrective aspects as a result of recent social changes. Pinderhughes (1973) provides us with a picture of some of the following shifts which have occurred.

> The psychology and behavior of ethnic-minority individuals have changed to a remarkable degree as a result of the various movements to develop ethnic consciousness and pride.
>
> Many more ethnic-minority individuals are aware of the potential for developing the capacity for independent and autonomous functioning, through the medium of in-depth psychotherapy.
>
> A greater number of ethnic-minority individuals are financially capable of underwriting clinical services in private settings.
>
> The increasing number of ethnic-minority individuals seeking and using clinical services has been a catalyst for change in the modification of treatment and the development of alternative approaches.

The segments of ethnic-minority populations enjoying the greatest benefit of clinical social work are, in the main, privileged by reason of their economic status, education, and geographic location in urban settings. They must be distinguished from the large segment of ethnic-minority individuals who remain unserved or underserved. Those that are served, however, are finding the special competencies of clinical social workers increasingly applicable to their struggles to overcome longstanding patterns of self-defeating behavior and to increase self-esteem and personal power in light of insidious racism.

Among the special competencies and unique features of clinical social work which can (and do) serve the best interests of many ethnic-minority clients and communities are the following.

Knowledge about people—their limitations and strivings, as well as their capacity to function in spite of seemingly insurmountable odds. Knowledge about the stresses and stress-response characteristics of today's social scene. Knowledge of the special needs of ethnic-minority individuals as they confront normal developmental tasks as well as the special tasks brought by their minority status.

Knowledge and skills in intervening in critical psychosocial situations, including the capacity to adopt a range of practice roles—from clinician to advocate, from broker to enabler—depending on the special needs of the client.

Knowledge of social institutions and organizations—how they develop and maintain themselves, how they (all too frequently) become culturally insensitive and unresponsive to the needs of those who could benefit most from their services.

Skills of engaging clients, even those markedly unwilling and unknowing of the services clinicians have to offer. The commitment and skills in reaching out to many ethnic-minority clients and acting as intermediary between them and critical social institutions distinguish social work from other helping professions to which such clients might conceivably turn.

Skills of assessment, which take cognizance of the inexorable link between culture and personality and are particularly useful to ethnic-minority clients who are socialized to believe that personal pathology is inherently responsible for the negative responses from society.

Traditional clinical practice is changing also, by virtue of the demands placed by those very clients. One form of the change is the encouragement of ethnic consciousness, pride, and assertive behavior as essential goals of clinical practice. Another aspect of the change is an increase within the profession in the number of minority professionals and a clarification of the specific contributions which paraprofessionals can make. Finally, the most recent and cogent progression in the series of changes are the efforts to develop a coherent theory of clinical practice with minority clients. This task is evident in the innovative efforts to adapt or develop treatment modalities to fit the diverse needs which confront clinical practitioners.

Several initial efforts at developing treatment approaches have recently become available through the literature (Solomon, 1976; LeVine and Padilla, 1980). These writings are informative and inspiring. Their recent appearance precludes the requisite experimentation, research, and reformulation that will confirm (or deny) their ultimate contributions to this distinctive area of practice. The comprehensive approaches presented have much in common, and, in tandem with the numerous isolated articles, reports, and commentaries on practice with ethnic-minority clients, they are suggestive of a framework for practice.

Conceptually the perspective presented defines five critical dimensions which determine the effectiveness of clinical social workers in their activities with ethnic-minority clients. These dimensions are: (1) ideology of practice, (2) perspective on causality, (3) the context of clinical social work, (4) intervention strategies, and (5) evaluation of outcomes. The framework, for purpose of discussion, is presented here in linear fashion. However, the content areas with their specific knowledge and behavioral components become intertwined in the clinical encounter.

Ideology of Practice. Clinical practice in cross-cultural contexts is a dynamic transaction, and the process of increasing one's skills and competency in this area requires, for most clinicians, a drastic change in perspective. When fully achieved, this new professional stance reflects an integrated reorganization of previously acquired knowledge, values, and skills with emerging, relevant cultural constructs and approaches to be used for the benefit of ethnic-minority clients. The result is a strategically different use of professional self and the effective management of the clinical process and relationship.

Germain (1973) suggests the presence and limitations of a current ideology when she states: "The ideology that developed over the years to justify the preference for the medical-disease model of practice obstructed change and closed off exploration of new themes in science and culture. In that sense, the medical metaphor and its ideology inhibited the potential adaptability of casework to fit the new conditions of contemporary life" (p. 129).

The conditions of contemporary life confronting minority clients are complex and pervasive. To deal with them successfully requires a commitment by the profession and by individual clinicians to a specific, conscious ideological stance. Ideology may be defined as the ideas and objectives that influence a whole group or national culture, shaping especially its political and social procedure(s). Taken as a whole, there seems to be almost no end to the ideas, issues, information, and objectives related to culture which can and should influence clinical social workers in their activities with ethnic-minority clients. The recent literature on practice with this group is instructive in defining some of the most salient issues.

The effective clinician should have an appreciation of cultural diversity, especially the variance between cultural and personality development in ethnic-minority Americans and members of the majority group. He or she should possess a recognition of how history, economics, politics, and present and past ecological conditions exert an inexorable influence on the cultural expressions of behavior. This recognition simultaneously frees and compels the clinician to confront the specific ways in which the individual is influenced by cultural variables which have immediate relevance for the clinical process. Edwards and Edwards (1976) state this quite cogently, noting: "An American Indian maintains identity as an individual, as a member of a family, a member of a tribe (perhaps a member of a clan), and as an American Indian. There are many elements of this identity which are also complicated by such factors as traditional or reservation Indians, compared to more acculturated or urban Indians. . . . Concentrated time and effort are required to help Indians sort through the many ramifications of their feelings of self-acceptance, pride, and identity. . . . When utilizing casework with American Indians, the relationship-building aspect assumes heightened importance. Basic understanding of Indian culture is necessary" (pp. 58–59).

Another issue in this perspective is the deep appreciation of how individuals or groups of clients may use the various components of culture in problem solving, in the expression of symptoms, and in participation in the clinical encounter. Such an appreciation generates for the clinician a sense of questioning, uncertainty, and curiosity which encourages him or her to purposefully and consciously screen the data on which conclusions are based. In so doing the clinician automatically seeks alternative explanations for behavior based on a broad understanding of the cultural milieu and processes that affect the lives of individual clients.

The ideological perspective presented here requires the recognition that certain patterns of functioning and certain symptoms of maladjustment are pancultural, or universally accepted. Individuals behaving in certain ways would be considered to be functioning appropriately or inappropriately (depending on the exact nature of the behavior), irrespective of his or her cultural milieu. However, the perspective also suggests that certain behaviors are uniquely present within a cultural milieu; they may be culturally specific styles of positive adaptation rather than evidence of clinical pathology. For example, an *ataque* is a response found exclusively among Puerto Ricans, and, unless appreciated from a cultural perspective, it could be viewed as a schizophrenic response. In the black community, the frenzy, accompanied by wild gestures, wordless utterances, stomping, clapping, and frantic jumping, characteristic of some religious ceremonies may suggest pathology if viewed from a strictly clinical perspective.

One final notion regarding culture which is crucial to clinical social work practice is that while ethnic-minority individuals are influenced and affected by common cultural experiences confronting their particular group, the unique experiences which they face are also important in development and personality formation. Solomon (1976) states this point very clearly: "Despite the universality of negative valuations directed toward blacks, the experience of these negative valuations is not uniform throughout the group, so that there may be a multiplicity of individual responses to negative valuations based on the differential exposure. Furthermore, responses may be perceived as instrumental or noninstrumental, depending upon the effectiveness in protecting the self-concept and permitting effective social functioning. However, most people in black communities who come to social agencies for assistance have not escaped the more serious consequences of society's negative valuations of them as members of the stigmatized group" (p. 13).

Perspective on Causality. Perhaps one of the most important activities in clinical social work is the assessment of the client's problem, which in turn influences the subsequent process of the clinical encounter. The assessment is a process involving efforts to gain an understanding of what is troubling the client as he or she sees it initially, and as formulated (or reformulated) in the process. The worker must take into account the factors which contribute to and maintain the problem and the factors which are amenable to change through social work intervention. Assessment is also a product, inasmuch as the final outcome of the assessment process is usually a diagnostic statement or label and a design for action developed from an integrated view of the facts. All too often, untoward effects of a diagnostic assessment emerge to plague both the client and the worker. The process and the product may negatively influence how the client responds to himself or herself, and how others respond to him or her; they may also fail to convey a dynamic picture of both the inherent strengths and weaknesses or the pervasiveness of the social factors in the condition facing the client.

Arriving at a professional judgment is no simple matter, principally because of its strategic import to both client and worker, and because of the short- and long-range implications for the outcome of the encounter. As such, the process does and should take time, but for many ethnic-minority clients in severe crisis or undergoing grave stress, the time may seem interminable and may deter them from continued participation, unless hope of some relief is offered early in the contact.

An accurate and useful diagnosis depends on the client's willing provision of the "facts" and on the worker's frame of reference to guide his or her thinking about the facts. The difficulty in achieving such a diagnosis with ethnic-minority clients is multiplied severalfold for the following reasons.

1. While most clinical social workers are prepared to attribute maladjustment to psychosocial and biological factors, within ethnic-minority communities individuals frequently include supernatural and metaphysical factors as important contributors to maladjustment or mental illness. Since the client's statement of the problem and its etiology is critical to the definition of the problem, the extent to which a worker is able to accept this view conveys some preliminary acceptance and engages the client in further elaboration. Such an acceptance will determine whether in fact a mutual understanding of the problem can be achieved, or whether the worker will be left with an impressive diagnosis but no client.

2. Racism, with concomitant discrimination and poverty, and the social environment created by these factors are the main causes of the mental health problems that ethnic-minority clients face. Further, these same factors conspire to restrict the resources for dealing with these problems. Thus, clinicians who focus exclusively or primarily on intrapsychic evidence may fail to give appropriate recognition to the extent, pervasiveness, and impact of these factors. In so doing, workers will also fail to appreciate the stigma which racial discrimination causes—the utter sense of inferiority and powerlessness that it creates. They will fail to see racism as the explicit or implicit basis for symptomatology of various functional disorders observable among ethnic-minority clients.

3. Until recently it was possible to predict with considerable certainty the responses of most ethnic-minority clients to the racist and discriminatory practices which confront them daily. However, the movements within each of the minority communities, beginning in the late 1960s, have given rise to different behavioral expressions and impetus to a more adaptive psychology and approach to role relationships. Self-esteem and a sense of worth, combined with a greater respect and appreciation for one's identity and responsibility for one's life, are concomitant results for many individual residents of these communities. Action-oriented efforts to correct past injustice, establishment of alliances with members of one's own group and with other minority groups, and a direct confrontation of the larger society with strident demands for equality are characteristic of the behavior within ethnic-minority groups aimed at promoting a sense of achievement and empowerment. Appreciation of these changes and the implications for personal growth and development require a keen sense of differential diagnosis, new terminology, and a new perspective on cause and effect. Describing this process as observed in the black community, Pinderhughes (1973) states: "For many blacks, the Black Power Movement meant learning and testing new roles; learning not to capitulate and surrender themselves; and experiencing a period of dictating, setting the structure, and running the show in the important areas of their lives. For most blacks it involved a new relationship to their own emotions, especially to

their anger toward whites which they could now permit, accept, and learn to master" (p. 86).

As a result of these three major thrusts, the clinical social worker interested in developing an appropriate diagnosis of ethnic-minority clients is advised to proceed with a healthy skepticism, a basic sense of humility (particularly with respect to what is known and what is knowable), and a willingness to learn from clients and ethnic colleagues.

Context of Clinical Practice. Providing the appropriate facilities to maximize utilization by ethnic-minority clients is a task which continuously confronts the profession. Developing competent professionals with the appropriate perspective on this model of practice is necessary but not sufficient to accomplish the task. The context in which services are offered and delivered—having as it does, serious implications for the important transactional processes of clinical practice—must also be considered.

In situations where the two principal participants do not share a common heritage, there are innumerable opportunities for contextual factors to limit successful interaction within the encounter. Three contextual factors are repeatedly mentioned in the emerging literature, namely, language, cultural life-styles, and natural support systems.

1. *Language.* It does not take much to imagine the difficulty—or impossibility—of providing clinical social work services when neither the worker or the client speaks the other's language. Fortunately, in most client-worker interactions the communication problem is not that extreme. However, the number of ethnic-minority clients whose first language is not English, combined with the upsurge of pride in one's ethnic background and cultural expressions, propels the issue of language into the forefront. The problem is not obvious solely in those situations where another recognized language (such as Spanish, Chinese, Filipino, or Sioux) is operative; the communication of numerous ghetto residents in what is commonly known as black English may also preclude appropriate communication even when a common language is assumed.

The issue of language becomes extremely problematic in clinical situations when the following conditions exist:

The worker's language handicap (that is, his or her inability to communicate with the client in the latter's language) is projected and defined as the client's problem.

Bilingualism/biculturalism is denigrated and treated so as to emphasize the negative effects on psychological development (Barker, 1947).

Through misunderstanding of the nuances of the client's communication, the social and psychological reality as seen and described by the client are not appreciated; worse, a different or negative perspective may be obtained.

Nonverbal methods of communication which are culturally determined (such as touching or forms of politeness) are misunderstood, resulting in distance and mistrust, or even an evaluation as pathological.

A direct negative relationship between language and critical personality variables (as with intelligence or problem-solving capacity) is assumed and acted upon (Jensen, 1961; Rapier 1967).

Institutional efforts to cope with language problems, as when family members or neighbors are casually recruited to serve as interpreters, may themselves pose or heighten problems. The most promising solution is the systematic recruitment and training of bilingual professionals and, secondarily, increasing the capacity of clinical social workers to communicate in the language of their clients. These are solutions which are both long-range and not within the immediate province of the individual worker, but rather are a professional responsibility. Productive steps (including referrals when necessary or developing a systematic plan for the use of translators) may be taken only when and if there is appropriate recognition of this variable as an important element in cross-cultural clinical practice.

2. *Life-styles.* Within minority groups there are compelling cultural values which govern the behaviors of individuals and groups in their daily lives. These values frequently serve to define the ideal and imply culturally specific criteria for identifying the mature or well-adjusted individual. Because they are so inherently cultural, they may not be known or appreciated outside of the particular cultural group; their unique characteristics or impact on the personality structure of ethnic-minority people may not be understood and they are frequently at odds with values accepted within the larger society. When these minority values and their implications are expressed within the context of seeking and using mental health services, the limited perspective of the clinician increases the potential for miscommunication and may occasion an irreconcilable breakdown in service delivery.

A clear example of the unique value system is found among American Indians, for whom the reality of being an Indian is all-consuming. It expresses the essence of community in which there is strong identification with the clan or tribe, and the needs, pain, and joy of one member is shared by all. Within the clans and tribe, relationships and responsibilities are clearly spelled out and there are numerous positive and negative reinforcers that enhance the individual's adherence to these values.

Edwards and Edwards (1976) note that while there is great diversity in values and life-styles among Native Americans, many values do appear to be generic to the various tribes. They further emphasize the high appreciation given to individuality among Native Americans, which results in considerable freedom for individuals to assume responsibility for themselves and their actions. Edwards and Edwards further elaborate this concept, noting: "The importance of the individual . . . [is] important to Native Americans. The belief in the freedom and dignity of the individual was deeply ingrained in many Indian societies. In some tribes it was observed to such an extent that at any time, even when his people were fighting for their lives, a man could go his own way and do whatever seemed right to him. In the Pueblo society, for example, individualistic qualities, competitiveness, aggressiveness, and the ambition to lead were looked upon as offensive to the supernatural powers, and laid people open to accusations of witchcraft. The Pueblo people were taught to 'value modesty, sobriety, and inoffensiveness and to avoid conflict and violence'" (p. 31).

Another example of compelling cultural values is provided by the report of the Task Panel Subpanel on Mental Health of Asian-Pacific Americans. The report indicates that the ability to control the expression of personal problems or troubled feelings is considered to be a clear sign of maturity. In turn, this self-control is closely related to shame and pride which are also paramount values governing the behavior of Asian-Pacific Americans. The subpanel members further clarify the impact on help-seeking/help-using behavior: "Thus the Asian-Pacific American may perceive services, such as counseling, as shame-inducing processes and will undergo extreme stress when asking for or accepting help from anyone outside the family. In the case of the Japanese, who are bound up in an elaborate social system based on *giri* (reciprocal obligation), they are reluctant to take the initiative and find it difficult to make up their minds on any questions where the decision has not been predetermined by rule or precedent or by a superior. Other operative values which influence interpersonal relationships are *haji* (shame, disgrace, dishonor), *enryo* (hesitancy, restraint, lack of assertiveness, desire not to be of trouble), and *gaman* (patience, endurance, self-control, forbearance)" (pp. 791–792).

3. *Natural support systems.* The data on availability, importance, and utilization of indigenous resources by ethnic-minority individuals have not been clearly understood or appropriately interpreted by clinicians. The major assumption is that indigenous resources (including folk medicine, curanderos, and the like) and established mental health services are mutually exclusive and compete for the allegiance of ethnic-minority individuals and communities. This hypothesis, which is not supported by recent research (Keefe, Padilla, and Carlos, 1978; Farge, 1977) has led to the denigration of these resources and a lack of appreciation for their potential contribution to the mental health of individuals. Similarly, it has limited mutual cooperation between practitioners and such community resources as family, friends, relatives, teachers, and clergymen, and especially the known practitioners of folk medicine. The latter group are known to be the first sources to which many individuals turn in time of stress and conflict and their support for, or participation in, clinical efforts frequently determines success or failure. To utilize them, communication channels must be developed with these resources or, at a minimum, an effort must be made to identify their unique potential for enhancing the mental health of their respective communities; these efforts may be seen as clear indications of clinicians' willingness to understand and use various aspects of culture as an important and inherent variable in the therapeutic process.

Intervention Strategies. Ideally, clinical social work practice should be informed by a theory of personality development strategically adapted to ethnic-minority people, from which psychotherapeutic prinicples to fit that theory would be formulated. As clearly indicated throughout this discussion, such is not the case. Rather, the effectiveness of the dynamic model of practice with ethnic-minority clients is as little described in the literature as is the overall effectiveness of this approach. Positive outcomes utilizing clinical techniques have been reported with clients suffering from anxiety reactions, obsessive-compulsive and hysterical neuroses, and schizoid disorders (Carrillo, 1978).

LeVine and Padilla (1980) also report positive outcomes utilizing group counseling, family therapy, psychodrama, and assertiveness training. With each modality they discuss some of the critical practice, ethical, and research issues and provide several case examples. Solomon (1976) suggests three major therapist roles applicable to the pursuit of empowerment among blacks; they include resource consultant, sensitizer, and teacher/trainer. Similarly, she raises some of the pertinent issues related to intervention strategies, and in a brief passage speaks pointedly to the issue of self-knowledge or insight, an objective which is extremely important to clinicians.

> Self-knowledge as a goal in social work with black clients has often been criticized. However, many problems brought to agencies by black clients cannot be solved by material resources alone. Many of the power deficits they demonstrate are in the area of social and emotional resources which may be more difficult to provide or even to reach mutual agreement regarding their significance in the problem situation. On the other hand, the key that opens the door to these much less tangible resources is self-knowledge. Yet for many black clients, to identify self-knowledge as a goal for themselves is tantamount to being defined as "crazy," "sick," or some other indicator that one is flawed or deviant. . . . Thus, it is necessary not only to demonstrate that exploration of psychosocial history in search of self-knowledge is not related to negative valuation of the client but in addition it is necessary to demonstrate that such exploration is in the interest of creating new opportunities for the client to control his life situation [pp. 348–349].

Given the current gaps in our knowledge, the task confronting clinical social workers is to demonstrate the implementation of specific strategies and their effectiveness with ethnic-minority clients through systematic, replicated research (Chestang, 1980; Goldstein, 1980). A seemingly logical approach would be for clinical societies to select a series of problem situations which typically confront special population groups as the subject for a series of longitudinal, comparative studies. These studies would attempt to provide clear and vivid demonstration of the problems, how the selected interventions operated, and the outcomes achieved, observable in behavioral terms.

For example, ethnic-minority clients who are experiencing problems in identifying and exercising power to achieve their personal goals could be made aware of the alternatives available to them, the factors limiting their choices, and selective ways of overcoming these barriers. Sessions in which clients are helped to practice ways of exercising power, with subsequent experimentation in real-life situations and review with the clinician, might constitute elements of a systematic, testable approach. Ethnic-minority clients are known to assume that personal pathology, rather than societal training and other external forces, are causal to the powerlessness which they feel and which governs many of their behavioral responses. Clinical interventions which help such clients to learn to value themselves, develop the skills requisite for independent functioning, and reshape their self-image into a more assertive and self-directing stance would represent another viable approach. Previous mention was made of the import of indigenous helping resources for the therapeutic process. A major contribution could be made both to knowledge and practice if clinicians would systematically demonstrate techniques designed to enlist the cooperation and utilization of such resources. In effect, research strategies applicable to each of the situations identified, or other equally pertinent ones, would be developed and replicated with input and direction from clinicians in different locations and under similar controlled conditions, the knowledge gap would thus be considerably decreased.

Simultaneous with demonstrating the effectiveness of traditional clinical methods, it is incumbent on clinicians to make the effort to develop and assess nontraditional approaches. Some of the problems confronting ethnic-minority individuals and families are novel, and there is evidence that they will require novel approaches. Similarly, some of the problems, such as fratricide among blacks or the anger which ethnic-minority people vent on each other, are so devastating that they will require new methodology. To this end, Morales (1978) has identified the need for and the emerging effectiveness of nontraditional programs and practices to apply to barrio-police relations, riots and gang wars in ethnic-minority communities, and the increasing degree of alcohol and drug abuse, especially among adolescents. Jenkins (1981), in her study of ethnic agencies, particularly those engaged in child welfare, has contributed a beginning identification of and a systematic approach to the study of what works and what doesn't work.

Before leaving the area of intervention, it appears necessary to focus briefly on the import of workers' attitudes in practice with ethnic-minority clients. Much has been said of the inability of anyone to escape the impact of racism in our society, even with the best of intentions (Cooper, 1973). The myths and stereotypes abound about ethnic-minority people—their behavior and its rationale, and the motivation surrounding interactions with nonminority people. Thus, it would be impossible for the nonminority clinician to avoid contamination. As discussed above, recent events, including the vast changes in society stemming from the militant efforts of ethnic-minority groups toward enhanced self-expression and pride, have injected considerable uncertainty and confusion into the interactions between people. In effect, the rules of the game, which previously governed interaction and were more or less accepted by participants, are no longer valid or helpful. To cope with the current uncertainty, and influenced by their individual history of socialized responses to ethnic-minority people, clinicians tend to respond inappropriately on a subconscious level to ethnic-minority clients. This countertransference takes a variety of forms—from covertly rejecting such individuals to overidentifying with them and their experiences. Clinicians, motivated by recognized or unconscious guilt, may tend to deny the interethnic factors pertinent to the encounter or even overlook the client's essential ethnic identity, rationalized by a wish to be objective or nonbiased. At the other extreme, the clinician may so overexaggerate the ethnic component that no productive work can be accomplished. Given the current reality, it seems almost impossible to overstress differences and ethnicity or its meaning socially, psychologically, politically, and otherwise to the client. The worker is advised to raise the issue and permit the client to indicate its relative importance to him or her. As with countertransference in other client situations, it is incumbent that the clinician acknowledge the possibility of its existence and confront it fully when it appears, seeking through various mechanisms to limit the potential damaging effects.

Evaluation of Outcomes. Theorists writing about clinical practice with ethnic-minority clients acknowledge that the client's problems may be primarily social or personal in nature. In the first event, the client's needs are for skills to cope with the difficult situation confronting him or her. In the latter case, the client's identification of a specific individualized goal (with assistance from the clinician) contributes to the development of criteria by which outcomes are measured. Irrespective of the nature of the problem, evaluation utilizing identified, and, where possible, behaviorally specific, criteria is a viable component of the termination process. Evaluation seeks to develop and utilize a comprehensive view of what transpired during the clinical encounter.

Although the research and theoretical literature on outcome evaluation is woefully limited, two significant concepts are offered. In the evaluation process, the functioning of ethnic-minority clients within the worker/client context is less of a barometer of change than in typical clinical encounters. Since the client's real-life situation and the experiences and forces which assault him or her are so unlike those experienced in the clinical encounter, there is little base for assuming comparability between these systems. Obviously, it is possible to note changes in how the client uses the clinical experience, how he or she relates to the worker, and his or her stated view of the progress made. However, an appreciation of the limits to which transferability can be assumed must remain in the forefront of the clinician's thinking.

A second idea given prominence in the literature is the need to go beyond the ethnic-minority client's capacity to deal with the immediate or specific problem to assuming some responsibility for changing the social contexts which confront all ethnic-minority clients. The worker is encouraged to assume personal and professional responsibility for continuing to make such social changes, and similarly to increase the client's capacities for contributing to a changed context and exercising power over his or her own destiny (Carrillo, 1978). Theorists appear to be convinced that since racism confronts all ethnic-minority clients equally, regardless of class or other circumstances, those with increased financial or emotional resources have the responsibility to use them to benefit those who are less fortunate. More pointedly, such responses are seen as providing the ethnic-minority client who has successfully completed a course of treatment with opportunities for "demonstrating strengths and skills which reduce humiliating and crippling self-definitions" (Solomon, 1976, p. 354).

Conclusion

This discussion of clinical practice in cross-cultural settings makes no pretense at completeness but claims only to highlight some of the critical issues, discuss the current need and level of utilization of clinical services by minority individuals, and present a viewpoint. In an earlier article, written with another colleague (Kramer and Miller, 1974), I wrote: "It is virtually undeniable that the developments that have taken place in the black community constitute one of the most formidable challenges ever to face the field of social work. The profound social and ideological changes achieved to date and their ramifications represent a turning point that is partly inspiring and reassuring, and partly frustrating and discouraging. The questions yet unanswered, the barriers yet untoppled, and the challenges yet unembraced constitute the agenda for the next decades in social work" (p. 38).

The same can be said about clinical social work today. Clinical social work's beginning efforts to embrace the agenda of practice with ethnic-minority clients has been clearly documented in this chapter. The achievement is at once discouraging and reassuring. The barriers and continuing questions remain as we look to see how the profession will meet the challenge during the coming years. Recently, professionals have been concerned with issues such as professionalism, licensing and the maintenance of high standards of practice. Important as these issues are, they cannot and should not be allowed to supersede social work's essential character and its mission to work with the alienated, the poor, and the disadvantaged. A large portion of the population of ethnic-minority individuals fall within these categories and it is incumbent on clinicians to use their "special competencies to bridge the social distance, make connections, and find common ground with people of other racial, ethnic, and social backgrounds" (Hartman, 1980, p. 36).

References

Acosta, F. "Mexican-American and Anglo-American Reactions to Ethnically Similar and Dissimilar Psychotherapists." In R. Alvarez (Ed.), *Delivery of Services for Latino Community Mental Health.* Monograph no. 2. Los Angeles: Spanish Speaking Mental Health Research Center, 1975.

Abad, V., Ramos, J., and Boyce, E. "A Model for Delivery of Mental Health Services to Spanish-Speaking Minorities." *American Journal of Orthopsychiatry,* 1974, *44,* 584–595.

American Indian Policy Review Committee. Final Report, Vol. I, S/N 052-070-04165-0. Submitted to Congress, May 17, 1977. Washington, D.C.: U.S. Government Printing Office, 1977.

Bachrach, L. L. *Utilization of State and County Mental Hospitals by Spanish Americans in 1972.* (Statistical Note no. 116.) Rockville, Md.: National Institute of Mental Health, Division of Biometry, June 1975.

Barker, G. "Social Functions of Language in a Mexican American Community." *Acta Americana,* 1947, *5* (3), 185–202.

Berk, B. B., and Hirata, L. "Mental Illness among the Chinese: Myth or Reality." *Journal of Social Issues,* 1973, *29,* pp. 149–166.

Brurrel, G., and Chavez, N. "Mental Health Outpatient Centers: Relevant or Irrelevant to Mexican Americans." In H. B. Talipan, C. L. Attaneave, and E. Kingstone (Eds.), *Beyond Clinic Walls.* POCA Perspectives. Alabama: University of Alabama Press, 1974.

Bryant, T. *Preliminary Report of the President's Commission on Mental Health.* Washington, D.C.: National Institute of Mental Health, 1977.

Carrillo, C. "Directions for a Chicano Psychotherapy." In J. Casas and S. Keefe (Eds.), *Family and Mental Health in the Mexican-American Community.* Monograph no. 7. Los Angeles: Spanish Speaking Mental Health Research Center, 1978.

Casas, J. M. "Applicability of a Behavioral Model in Serving the Mental Health Needs of the Mexican Americans." In M. R. Miranda (Ed.), *Psychotherapy with the Spanish Speaking: Issues in Research and Service Delivery.* Monograph no. 3. Los Angeles: Spanish Speaking Mental Health Research Center, 1976.

Chestang, L. "Competencies and Knowledge in Clinical Social Work: A Dual Perspective." In P. L. Ewalt (Ed.), *Toward a Definition of Clinical Social Work.* Washington, D.C.: National Association of Social Workers, 1980.

Chu, F., and Trotter, S. *The Madness Establishment.* New York: Grossman, 1974.

Cohen, J. "Race as a Factor in Social Work Practice." In R. R. Miller (Ed.), *Race, Research and Reason: Social Work Perspectives.* New York: National Association of Social Workers, 1969.

Cole, J., and Pilisuk, M. "Difference in the Provision of Mental Health Services by Race." *American Journal of Orthopsychiatry,* 1976, *46,* 510–525.

Cooper, S. "A Look at the Effect of Racism on Clinical Social Work." *Social Casework,* 1973, *54,* 76–84.

Cooper, S. "The Master's and Beyond." In J. Mishne (Ed.), *Psychotherapy and Training in Clinical Social Work.* New York: Gardner Press, 1980.

Edgerton, R. B., and Karno, M. "Mexican-American Bilingualism and the Perception of Mental Illness." *Archives of General Psychiatry,* 1971, *24,* 286–290.

Edwards, E. D., and Edwards, M. E. "American Indians: History, Culture, Federal Policies and Implications for Social Work Practice." In M. Sotomayor (Ed.), *Cross-Cultural Perspectives in Social Work Practice and Education.* Houston: Graduate School of Social Work, University of Houston, 1976.

Ewalt, P. "Clinical Social Work in Community Mental Health Programs." In A. Katz (Ed.), *Community Mental Health: Issues for Social Work Practice and Education.* New York: Council on Social Work Education, 1979.

Ewalt, P. (Ed.). *Toward a Definition of Social Work.* Washington, D.C.: National Association of Social Workers, 1980.

Fabrega, H., Swartz, J., and Wallace, C. A. "Ethnic Differences in Psychopathology—II: Specific Differences with Emphasis on a Mexican-American Group." *Psychiatric Research,* 1968, *6,* 221–235.

Farge, E. J. "A Review of Findings from 'Three Generations' of Chicano Health Care Behavior." *Social Science Quarterly,* 1977, *58,* 407–411.

Firman, B., and others. "Development of Quantitative Indices of Institutional Change with Regard to Racial Minorities and Women in NIMH Extramural Programs." Unpublished report by Human Sciences Research, Inc., May 31, 1975, prepared for Center for Minority Group Mental Health Programs. Rockville, Md.: Division of Special Mental Health, National Institute of Mental Health, U.S. Department of Health, Education and Welfare.

Germain, C. B. "Social Casework." In H. B. Trecker (Ed.), *Goals for Social Welfare, 1973–1983.* New York: Associated Press,1973.

Goldstein, E. G. "Knowledge Base of Clinical Social Work." In P. L. Ewalt (Ed.), *Toward a Definition of Clinical Social Work.* Washington, D.C.: National Association of Social Workers, 1980.

Hartman, A. "Competencies in Clinical Social Work." In P. L. Ewalt (Ed.), *Toward a Definition of Clinical Social Work.* Washington, D.C.: National Association of Social Workers, 1980.

Jackson, A. M., Berkowitz, H., and Farley, G. "Race as a Variable Affecting the Treatment Involvement of Children." *Journal of American Academy of Child Psychiatry,* 1974, *13,* 20–31.

Jensen, A. R. "Learning Abilities in Mexican-American and Anglo-American Children." *California Journal of Education Research,* 1961, *12,* 147–159.

Jenkins, S. *Ethnicity and Child Welfare: The Ethnic Agency Defined.* New York: School of Social Work, Columbia University, 1977.

Jenkins, S. *The Ethnic Dilemma in Social Services.* New York: Free Press, 1981.

Karno, M. "The Enigma of Ethnicity in a Psychiatric Clinic." *Archives of General Psychiatry,* 1966, *14,* 516–520.

Keefe, S. E., Padilla, A. M., and Carlos, M. L. "The Mexican-American Extended Family as an Emotional Support System." In J. Casas and S. Keefe (Eds.), *Family and Mental Health in the Mexican-American Community.* Monograph no. 7. Los Angeles: Spanish Speaking Mental Health Research Center, 1978.

Knoll, F. R. "Casework Services for Mexican-Americans." *Social Casework,* 1971, *52,* 279–284.

Kramer, P. H., and Miller, S. O. "Eliminating Racial Barriers in Schools of Social Work: A Conceptual Framework." In *Black Perspectives on Social Work Education: Issues Related to Curriculum, Faculty and Students.* New York: Council on Social Work Education, 1974.

Kramer, M., Rosen, B. M., and Willis, E. M. "Definitions and Distributions of Mental Disorder in a Racist Society." In C. Willie, B. M. Kramer, and B. S. Brown (Eds.), *Racism and Mental Health.* Pittsburgh: University of Pittsburgh Press, 1972.

Laosa, C. M., Burstein, A. G., and Martin, H. W. "Mental Health Consultation in a Rural Chicano Community." *Crystal City Aztlan,* 1975, *6,* 433–453.

LeVine, E. S., and Padilla, A. M. *Crossing Cultures in Therapy: Pluralistic Counseling for the Hispanic.* Monterey, Calif.: Brooks/Cole, 1980.

Lowinger, P. L., and Dobie, S. "Attitudes and Emotions of the Psychiatrist in the Initial Interview." *American Journal of Psychotherapy,* 1966, *20,* 17–34.

McLemore, S. D. "Ethnic Attitudes Toward Hospitalization: An Illustrative Comparison of Anglo- and Mexican-Americans." *Southwestern Social Science Quarterly,* 1963, *43,* 341–346.

Martinez, C. "Community Mental Health and the Chicano Movement." *American Journal of Orthopsychiatry,* 1973, *43,* 595–601.

Meers, D. R. "Cultural and Traumatic Determinants of Symptom Formation." In J. Mishne (Ed.), *Psychotherapy and Training in Clinical Social Work.* New York: Gardner Press, 1980.

Meyer, C. "Social Work Practice vs. Clinical Practice." *Alumni Newsletter.* New York: School of Social Work, Columbia University, Spring 1977, pp. 4–6.

Miranda, M. R. "Acculturation and Dropout Rates Among Mexican-American Psychiatric Clients." Unpublished manuscript, 1974. (Mimeographed.)

Morales, A. "The Need for Nontraditional Mental Health Programs in the Barrio." In J. Casas and S. Keefe (Eds.), *Family and Mental Health in the Mexican-American Community.* Monograph no. 7. Los Angeles: Spanish Speaking Mental Health Research Center, 1978.

National Institute of Mental Health. *The Community Mental Health Policy and Standards Manual.* Rockville, Md.: National Institute of Mental Health, 1972.

Newton, F. "The Mexican-American Emic System of Mental Illness: An Exploratory Study." In J. Casas and S. Keefe (Eds.), *Family and Mental Health in the Mexican-American Community.* Monograph no. 7. Los Angeles: Spanish Speaking Mental Health Research Center, 1978.

Norton, D. *The Dual Perspective: Inclusion of Ethnic Minority Content in the Social Work Curriculum.* New York: Council on Social Work Education, 1978.

Olmedo, E. L., and Lopez, S. (Eds.). *Hispano Mental Health Professionals.* Monograph no. 5. Los Angeles: Spanish Speaking Mental Health Research Center, 1977.

Padilla, A. M., and Ruiz, R. A. *Latino Mental Health: A Review of the Literature.* Washington, D.C.: U.S. Government Printing Office, 1973.

Phillipus, N. J. "Successful and Unsuccessful Approaches to Mental Health Services for Urban Hispano-American Populations." *American Journal of Public Health,* 1971, *61,* 820–830.

Pinderhughes, C. A. "Racism and Psychotherapy." In C. Willie, B. Kramer, and B. Brown (Eds.), *Racism and Mental Health.* Pittsburgh: University of Pittsburgh Press, 1973.

Pinkus, H., and others. "Education for Practice of Clinical Social Work at the Master's Level: A Position Paper." *Journal of Clinical Social Work,* Winter 1977, *5,* 253–268.

Rapier, J. L. "Effects of Verbal Mediation upon the Learning of Mexican-American Children." *California Journal of Educational Research,* 1967, *18* (1), 40–48.

Rosenthal, D., and Frank, J. "Fate of Psychiatric Clinic Outpatients Assigned to Psychotherapy." *Journal of Nervous and Mental Diseases,* 1958, *127,* 330–343.

Ruiz, R. A., Casas, J. M., and Padilla, A. M. *Culturally Relevant Behavioristic Counseling.* Occasional Paper no. 5. Los Angeles: Spanish Speaking Mental Health Research Center, 1977.

Schensul, S. L. "Skills Needed in Action Anthropology: Lessons from El Centro de La Causa." *Human Organization,* 1974, *33,* 203–209.

Sharpley, R. H. *Treatment Issues: Foreign Medical Graduates and Black Patient Populations.* Cambridge, Mass.: Solomon Fuller Institute, 1977.

Solomon, B. *Black Empowerment: Social Work in Oppressed Communities.* New York: Columbia University Press, 1976.

Spurlock, J., and Cohen, R. "Should the Poor Get None?" *Journal of American Academy of Child Psychiatrists,* Jan. 1969, *8,* 16–35.

Staples, R. *Introduction to Black Sociology.* New York: McGraw-Hill, 1976.

Stocking, G. W., Jr. "Franz Boas and the Culture Concept in Historical Perspective." *American Anthropologist,* 1966, *68,* 867–882.

Strean, H. *Clinical Social Work: Theory and Practice.* New York: Free Press, 1978.

Sue, S. "Community Mental Health Services to Minority Groups: Some Optimism, Some Pessimism." *American Psychologist,* 1977, *32* (8), 616–624.

Task Panel Reports. Mental Health of Asian/Pacific Americans, Black Americans, Hispanic Americans, American Indians and Alaska Natives. Vol. 3. Submitted to the President's Commission on Mental Health. Washington, D.C.: U.S. Government Printing Office, 1978, pp. 773–873, 912–1021.

Torrey, E. F. "The Irrelevancy of Traditional Mental Health Services for Urban Mexican-Americans." *American Journal of Orthopsychiatry,* 1970, *40,* 240–241.

Torrey, E. F. *The Mind Game: Witch Doctors and Psychiatrists.* New York: Emerson Hall, 1972.

Urban Associates, Inc. *A Study of Selected Socioeconomic Characteristics of Ethnic Minorities Based on the 1970 Census.* Vol. 1: Americans of Spanish Origin (Report no. 5, HEW publication HEW-PUB-(05)-75-120). Washington, D.C.: U.S. Department of Health, Education and Welfare, July 1974.

Wesley, C. "The Women's Movement and Psychotherapy." *Social Work,* 1975, *20* (2), 120–124.

Whittaker, J. K. *Social Treatment: An Approach to Interpersonal Helping*. Chicago: Aldine, 1974.

Woody, J. D. "Preventive Intervention for Children of Divorce." *Social Casework,* 1978, *59* (9), 537–544.

Yamamoto, J., Jones, Q. C., and Palley, N. "Cultural Problems in Psychiatric Therapy." *Archives of General Psychiatry,* 1968, *19,* 45–49.

Zimmerman, C. C. "The Future of the Family in America." *Journal of Marriage and the Family,* 1972, *34* (2), 323–333.

24

A Feminist Perspective

Sophie Freud Loewenstein

My dearest son,*

Your announcement that you want to turn away from your promising computer sciences career and enter social work, a profession which, you hope, will not just engage your brain, but your heart as well, evokes in me, a feminist-oriented social work educator, many complex reactions. Let me share them with you. Let me use this occasion to reflect on the place of women in social work.

Yes, this last sentence is paradoxical. It is well documented and all too often repeated that social work is a women's profession (Scotch, 1971; Kravetz, 1976) or rather a women's semi-profession (Etzioni, 1969), in which predominantly women clients are seen by predominantly women practitioners (Kadushin, 1976). Our clients are single mothers in poverty (who are depressed); mothers of troubled children (who are depressed); depressed middle-aged housewives; abusive mothers (who are depressed) and their abused children; impregnated teenagers who need an abortion, or who want to keep their babies to meet their dependency needs; and women who have been raped or sexually molested by their fathers, or battered by their husbands. There are other clients, but it is primarily these women who come to us, out of necessity, out of courage, out of desperation.

So you, my son, with your fine brains, want to enter a "mere" women's profession. After earning, in your computer field, within two years of graduating from college, as much as I earn after thirty years of social work practice, you want to exchange your potential high-status career to enter a women's profession. In my mind I can hear you ask in an irritated voice, why do I harp so continuously on this matter of a women's profession? Why do I talk as if I despised my own

*Any resemblance to my real son is purely accidental.

profession? It is true, there are times when my feminist friends and I buy into the time-honored self-hatred of all minority-group members (Kirsch, 1974). We have contempt for a profession that is associated with the poor and helpless, that is composed of women, that is held in low esteem by the general public. No wonder we have been eager to invite men into the field; perhaps colleague contact with your superior sex will improve our self-concept, not to mention our status and financial position.

You will of course earn a few thousand dollars more than women of equal competence, just for being a man (Scotch, 1971; Fanshel, 1976). And you will be promoted with lightning speed up the professional ladder into administrative positions, just for being a man (Zitz and Erlich, 1976; Knapman, 1977). But people will think, my son, that you could perhaps not make it in the real male world, out there—that you needed to be in a women's field to achieve such rapid advancement. With all your intelligence and competence and interpersonal skills, you will be forced to wonder whether you owe your future position of leadership just to being a man. And with all your talents, "full" professional men in law and medicine with whom you will be working will look down on you. I worry how that will affect you.

I am not angry at men who have moved into our field and taken over the top agency and educational administrative jobs. Some of my best friends, favorite colleagues, and much loved students are men social workers. How could I possibly be angry at these men who are close to me? I am glad that you will get a top job and earn more money than I, since you will be able to subsidize me in my old age. It is hard to fight men who are our sons, husbands, fathers, brothers, and friends. Do you remember when I drew up a petition for a junior faculty male colleague of whom I had grown very fond? He had decided to leave our school for a higher-paid position, and I was ready to set aside my own claims for a higher salary than his, in the hope of keeping him on our faculty.

I should not complain. I myself refused to compete for the best-paid jobs because I liked direct practice, and now I like to teach, rather than administer agency or faculty personnel. It surprises me sometimes that our field of social work rewards its personnel in exactly the same way as every other organization in our society: administrators are better paid and more highly valued than practitioners in almost all agencies and schools (Scotch, 1971). It is even more surprising that few have questioned the assumption that our field must follow society's general reward system.

As women social workers we were brought up to conform to the social order. It has taken us a very long time to start to question the blatant sexism in our profession. But our courage and our anger and our feminist consciousness has been growing. Do not come into this field, my son, to take over our top jobs. We don't need you for that. Your sisters, who are quite as bright and competent as you are, can take over these jobs.

Of course, I am being unfair. If you were eager to earn much money or to attain administrative positions, you would not give up a lucrative and prestigious career to come into social work. I foresee that you will even resist your prospective school advisor's attempt to steer you into community organization (Diangson, Kravetz and Lipton, 1975). You clearly want to become a social worker because you are interested in helping people, in exploring emotions, in understanding human nature. I brought you up to be respectful of all ethnic and racial diversity, as well as sensitive and empathic toward women. I feel concerned, however, that you too will succumb to the sex discrimination and sex-role stereotyping that pervades every aspect of our society. "In a sexist society, one should expect even normal, considerate, and sensitive men to be sexist" (Longres and Bailey, 1979, p. 27). After all, the very language in which you were reared guides all your perceptions along particular channels while hiding alternate views. It is the English language which makes male the norm, while women are "other," unimportant or invisible (Miller and Swift, 1976). It is, for example, quite obvious that Bronowski did not think about women when he produced and wrote *The Ascent of Man* (1973). Among the 219 pictures in the book, there is only a single woman (a spinner) engaged in furthering the culture.

As an enlightened young man you probably realize that the racial division into white and black is a mere social designation without genetic reality. Have you also considered that the division of humanity into male and female is equally arbitrary and deceptive? We realize that fewer and fewer human beings fit the idealized female and male stereotypes, either physically, emotionally, intellectually, or erotically. Just think, we could unstigmatize thousands of currently deviant women and men if we had seven genders instead of two. But then there might be no need for transexual surgeries or segregated gay bars, no need to buy falsies, or wear elevator shoes, or smoke heavy deadly symbolic cigars. And all that would impoverish our culture and might be bad for industry.

You have learned to judge beauty and ugliness, heroism and cowardice, sin and virtue along very narrow, culturally prescribed lines. "We select and edit the reality we see to conform to our beliefs about what sort of world we live in" (Engel, 1972, p. vii). In short, my son, we are all thoroughly brainwashed and the cultural blinders we wear are sexist.

It might not matter if you remained within an unexamined framework if you stayed in computer sciences. The damage might then be limited to your future wife and children. However, social work is a value-laden enterprise. You will have to become newly conscious of many basic assumptions that have guided your life, reevaluate them, and consider alternate perspectives. If you want to become a social work practitioner you must think deeply about your values and confront them honestly.

Myths About Women

I am concerned that your prospective social work school might not be sufficiently sensitive to the feminist viewpoint. Information and theories about female development through the life cycle were very distorted for a long time. Social work curricula have only recently been revised (Schwartz, 1973) and your future readings may thus not be fully updated. Let me therefore briefly review for you some of the patriarchal myths that have pervaded women's lives and which continue to haunt your future colleagues and clients. I hope to refute those myths for you, and to show you how creative approaches to casework with women is based on the new understanding that we now have of women's development, their needs, and lives.

I am not trying to be objective. I am presenting to you a passionately biased viewpoint which many of my colleagues, women and men, might not share. Please don't think, moreover, that these myths have troubled only a few unenlightened women. I know that you respect me as an educated and liberated woman and I have therefore chosen to share with you those myths that have diminished in important ways the quality of my own life. I have been privileged in many ways, and women who have been raised and lived in poverty might emphasize different myths, probably even more destructive ones. Yet I believe that I am talking at least to some extent for all women.

It was hard for me to order these myths since they all seem interconnected. I have tried to use a framework of successive life stages and have ended with some all-pervasive myths. It might seem strange to have all these references in a letter to you, but I hope and expect that you will want to study these issues more in depth, since I can only refer to them as so many tips of so many icebergs. The references are there to guide your research. Let me start with the following.

The Myth of Cinderella and the Prince. We all cling to the belief that we live in a just society. Women, like any other minority group, therefore conclude that their low power and low status in society is due to their own deficiencies. "They develop traits typical of minority groups: dislike for their own sex, negative self-image, insecurity, self-blame, a submissive or 'shuffling' attitude, identification with males, and low aspirations" (Kirsch, 1974, p. 330). Most women I have known harbor deep self-doubts about being intelligent, attractive, loving, and lovable. The famous need to please others, which is said to be such a typical female characteristic, is the obvious result of such an insecure self-concept. Some day you must also write me a long letter and tell me whether this is true for men. But most women's entire life is dominated by their anxious need to love and be loved by men, as their one major road to happiness and perhaps self-love.

Female adolescence is overshadowed by the agony and shame of the "popularity" contest. Heartbreaking episodes of unrequited love, betrayals, and rejections sometimes leave their marks for life. Remember Anderson's little mermaid who gave up her powerful mermaid tail and her beautiful singing voice to gain the love of a man who could not love her back. Then comes young adulthood with the dreaded possibility that no suitable prince might come to the rescue to follow the fairy-tale script (Parent, 1972). Do you realize, my child, that after thirty-five years, I still remember how I was haunted, during my late adolescence, with worries that I might not find a suitable man. Why would an attractive and intelligent young woman, such as I must have been, be beset with such anxieties? Women are socialized to believe that their private nightmares are unique and deeply neurotic, and I thought for many years that I was burdened with abnormal self-doubts. Then I started to talk to other women and realized that they had similar self-doubts and that those doubts are part of our patriarchal culture. How grateful we are to men who are willing to love us with all of our imperfections!

In addition, women enter marriage with some deep conviction that their husbands will protect them from the pains and anxieties and problems of life. The reality of marriage can therefore only be a rude awakening. I felt much rage at your father when he could not meet these unrealistic expectations.

Once married, each woman continues to worry whether her husband loves her enough and she hopes that he will not beat her, nor drink, nor be unfaithful.

"I guess I can't complain. He's a steady worker; he doesn't drink; he doesn't hit me," responded working-class wives when asked by Rubin (1976, p. 93) "what they valued most about their husbands." As women age, they hope that their husbands will not leave them for a younger woman. Some aging women fall in love with younger men and experience the pain and humiliation of rejection. Remember biblical Mrs. Potiphar, wife of the king's housekeeper, who loved the young Joseph? She was a vicious and vengeful old hag, was she not? Other aging women (or the same) get divorced and are faced, once again, in the middle of their lives with the task of man-hunting, and man-finding, and man-keeping that will pursue them to their graves.

Yes, I know, things have changed. Women sometimes take the initiative in divorcing, these days, if they are economically independent. Their rejected husbands suffer deeply, but, unlike their middle-aged wives, they remarry quickly and easily.

Modern young women postpone marriage until their late twenties (Lipman-Blumen, 1976), at which time they undergo the same terror and agony that my generation did when we were younger. Let me give you an example from my counseling practice:

> I saw a young woman of twenty-eight. Both her parents had died and she felt alone in the world. Would she have to spend a lonely life without loving or being loved by a permanent mate? She was a highly accomplished young woman, and she knew exactly why she had not found a mate. No, she did not blame the shortage of interesting young men for highly educated young women, or circumstances, or the difficulty of finding an interesting man at any age. She blamed her various shortcomings.
>
> She thought she had a crooked nose and she was a bit too fat. Being a woman, she was depressed—too depressed to get her house in order, or to go on a diet, or to go out and seek a man, all projects her male counselor had urged her to pursue. I had only two major prescriptions: to stop the attempt at dieting, since she was quite attractive enough, and to live triumphantly in her messy house which she did not have to clean up for any man.

I believe in paradoxical prescriptions—but forgive me for jumping ahead.

If women felt strong and independent and confident and even ready to face, with some equanimity, life without a permanent mate, then they could relax and simply be open to the encounters with women and men that life might bring them. I believe we all feel, partly at least, so desperate about finding a man because we all believe in the next myth, below.

The Myth of the Lonely Spinster. Research on comparative life satisfaction in the last two decades has consistently shown single women as a group to be in better mental health than married women, while the opposite is true for single men (Campbell, 1975). These general statistics were reinforced by a recent study my students and I (Loewenstein and others, 1981) undertook by studying the life satisfactions of sixty never-married, divorced, and widowed women age thirty-five to sixty-five whose children, if any, no longer live at home. We found that the great majority of women in our sample were either highly satisfied (50 percent) with life, or reasonably content (30 percent). Only 15 percent (nine women) in our sample, as compared to about 10 percent of the general American population felt deep dissatisfaction with the quality of their lives. We were particularly stunned to find that life satisfaction was highly related to work satisfaction and good health, and only minimally related to a good sex life, to having a steady man friend, or to the presence of young adult children in their lives. We could only conclude from our study that neither marriage, nor sex, nor motherhood are necessary components of high life satisfaction.

So perhaps you better hurry and get married. If enough women learn about those findings and believe them, you may have to beg some woman to marry you. I look forward to your having to do that. On the other hand, I could understand your reluctance to marry. I think you have seen through:

The Myth of the Family as Haven in a Heartless World. This myth was particularly destructive to my life. It has generally been my downfall that once, long ago, I used to believe experts, and take their writings very seriously. I remember reading in a sociology book that the family was the institution from which people drew enough comfort and strength to function in the world of work. Since I had always found working less stressful than raising you children, and looked forward to work as a welcome relief from family life, I knew that something must be different and very wrong with our particular nuclear family. Later, it was almost a relief to realize that most nuclear families are a jungle of brutality (Lystad, 1975), islands of despair or breeding grounds of madness (Henry, 1965). (Actually, references for all three categories—both from social science writings and from literature—would run into many pages.) Our own family compared rather favorably, once the myth was dispelled.

Christopher Lasch (1977) blames mental health professionals for invading the family with measures of social control. There is little question that the social control is needed at this point, and that the family as an institution should be under attack, rather than the mental health professionals who are trying to keep it functioning with at least minimal safety for all its members.

At least men and women seem to be in the same miserable boat, you are probably thinking. But that is not true either. There is unquestioned documentation that women are more often the victims of violence, suffer more from depressions (Weissman and Klerman, 1977), and have more schizophrenic breakdowns (Chesler, 1972) than men. In addition, women have traditionally been held responsible, and have held themselves responsible, for the emotional disturbances that the system creates in the children. Actually, there is a great deal of evidence that both marriage (at least in its traditional style) and the nuclear family are much more destructive to women than to men. Remember the life-satisfaction research literature that demonstrates that marriage is positively a mental health hazard for women, especially nonworking women (Bernard, 1972)?

It is arresting to learn that "for every age bracket the more income a girl or woman has, the lower the rate of marriage, a sitaution just the reverse of that of men" (Bernard, 1972, p. 35), and high-status women are also the least likely to remarry after a divorce (Lipman-Blumen, 1976). I must admit, however, that the research (and my own experience) suggests that it is not marriage per se, but the housewife role and raising children that seem to create so much stress. I am sorry if you were hurt when I said that I enjoyed working more than raising you and your sisters. You were (and are) all very satisfactory children and I loved (love) you very much, but the anxiety and uncertainty, awesome responsibility, guilt, shame, and blame attached to childrearing in our society were an enormous burden for me, for many years. These thoughts bring me of course to:

The Myth of Blissful Motherhood. It is most fortunate that this myth is finally being exploded, because at least today's young mothers need not add guilt about the natural ambivalence they feel toward their children to the list of motherhood stresses. Sociologists (Bernard, 1974) and autobiographical and feminist writings (McBride, 1973; Radl, 1973; Lazarre, 1976; Rich, 1976) have clarified that the greater prevalence of depression among women as compared to men is at least partially related to their mothering role. Studies of depression repeatedly find a strong correlation between motherhood, especially young and multiple motherhood, and the incidence of depression (Weissman, 1980).

I feel bitter that the knowledge that "post-partum blues" are a commonly expected phenomenon has only recently been publicized (Weissman and Klerman, 1977). I still remember the surprise and guilt I felt as a new mother, when I found myself depressed during what I had learned would be "the happiest period of my life." My conviction that I was an unnatural mother—a conviction that pursues women throughout life (Rubin, 1979)—was a worse burden than the depression itself.

I am sure you remember vividly as I our struggles regarding who was to be in control of your life, you or I. I am relieved that you opposed my intrusiveness with your determined stubbornness and I had to give up the fight. However, please do understand, at least now that you are grown up (or nearly so), that childrearing carries responsibility without authority. The infamous Mrs. Portnoys of this world, Jewish or non-Jewish, are only trying to do a good job. They feel that since they are held responsible for their children's physical, emotional, and intellectual present and future well-being they must take charge of their children's lives.

I admit with shame and sorrow that I loved you less ambivalently and more generously than I loved your sisters. Freud thought the special love of a mother for her son is based on the finally triumphant possession of that precious penis (Freud, 1933). Others have seen the boy child as the most suitable carrier for the mother's ambition. Believe me, I did not want your penis, and I distributed my ambitions among all my children. The true reason I could love you better is that you were (are) Other, rather than Self (Chodorow, 1978). It was not upon you, a child of a different gender, that I needed to project the dislike of my female body, or the doubts about my female mind. I could even protect you better from your father's projections than I could protect your sisters. The intense symbiotic tie between a mother and a child of her own gender is very difficult to break. I do not believe in other male/female differences—an issue about to be discussed—but I do think the particular nature of the mother/daughter bond makes differentiation of self a lifelong problem for many women. It is therefore not surprising that more women than men have borderline disorders, which I believe to be above all a difficulty with differentiation of self. Patriarchal society has produced badly mothered daughters, who become badly mothering mothers, in an endless chain that we need to interrupt.

Many women are now asking their husbands or mates to participate to a much larger extent in the initial nurturing tasks. This will dilute (for better or worse?) the mother's passion for her infant and will facilitate the infant's early identification with both genders. It will protect mothers and daughters against excessive fusion and help sons to acquire an early male identification, thus freeing them from their current lifelong need to repudiate their early female identification (Stoller, 1974). Early nurturance will hopefully protect fathers from becoming outsiders who feel jealous and abandoned. Dinnerstein (1976) thinks that the suppression of women will only cease after *both* men and women take on the role of the all-powerful early caretakers which become invested with lifelong ambivalence and consequent need for devaluation.

More generally, the move from total oneness with a boy or girl infant to "letting go" not too fast and not too slowly, but exactly as dictated by cultural prescriptions, is a formidable expectation of a young, immature, inexperienced, and usually isolated young woman.

As long as children are the only outlet for a mother's life energies they are apt to be overloved. In addition, a woman's thwarted ambition makes it more likely that she will delegate the fulfillment of her dreams and hopes to her children, which once again results in binding and oppressive patterns.

It is thus quite natural that working women actually become better loving mothers. Did you know that an effective way of stopping child abuse is to send a mother to work? How ironic that mothers of my generation had been promised by Dr. Spock (and other men who teach women how to take care of their children) that we would have perfect children if we stayed at home and took care of them twenty-four hours a day. Slater (1970) was quite right when he speculated that the mothers of America were angry about these false promises and did not protect Dr. Spock when he went into politics.

These experiences are even more relevant to mothers who live in unfavorable economic circumstances. Belle (1980), conducting a large study of low-income families, describes the alarmingly high incidence of depression and other psychiatric disturbances among low-income mothers. She found that single mothers and mothers with large families and preschool children were generally apt to be exposed to exceptionally stressful lives and consequent psychiatric symptoms. Belle writes (p. 87): "It is instructive to consider the nature of some of the highly stressful life events experienced by our small sample of women (forty). These include: rape, beating by the husband, robbery, nervous breakdown, appearance in court, husband stabbed to death, children claimed by their father after many years, and desertion by the husband. Violence is not rare, and husbands and lovers are frequently the perpetrators of violence."

I worked as a young mother to preserve my emotional and intellectual equilibrium. It is interesting that Belle found that even for very poor women, employment is not only a vital economic necessity, but also a buffer against depression. She continues (p. 90): "Jobs represented a bright hope for many of these women. Research . . . suggests that employment can actually protect women's mental health when other circumstances are difficult. To several of the women with whom we worked, the future looked dismal without a job to provide some way out of poverty, isolation, and low self-esteem." However, most married and unmarried women work for sheer financial survival. It seems therefore quite bitter that for many middle-class and most working-class women working conditions are permeated by low status, low salaries, and various forms of discrimination and stress (Lemkau, 1980).

The unmitigated bliss of motherhood was not only emphasized for the young mother, but social science literature perpetuated the illusion that women could not bear to ever separate from their children. This was the creation of:

The Myth of the Empty Nest. I remember telling a (childless) woman psychoanalyst how relieved I was, when watching children's birthday parties in the neighborhood, that those days were over.

She promptly suggested that my sense of loss for the days when my children were young was so profound that I had to deny it completely. At the time I felt uncertain and confused. We have since learned that excessive sadness about the children's departure from home is confined to women who were exclusively invested in motherhood and arrive at midlife and menopause with no other available roles (Lowenthal, Thurnher, and Chiraboga, 1975). Even for these women depressive feelings focus more on a lack of alternate meaningful activities than on the loss of children or reproductive capacity. The newer research findings all suggest consistently that women tend to feel a sense of relief from the burden of motherhood (Radloff, 1975; Rubin, 1970; Loewenstein, 1980a).

Do you recall, my son, when you befriended some delinquent classmates, and when you refused, one day, to take any more examinations out of some ethical convictions, and when you had your motorcycle accident, and when you became so deeply upset because a girlfriend rejected you? The effort to get you and your sisters halfway through adolescence safely and sanely was enormous and I was glad when it was accomplished. Distress is experienced not when children leave home, which is after all a long-anticipated and encouraged event (when properly timed), but when young adult children return home during periods of unemployment, marital separation, or mental instability.

I have already elsewhere expressed my anger about the maligned midlife woman who is said "to be engaged in an active struggle against her decline," who is ridiculed for displaying "youthful" enthusiasms (Deutsch, 1945, pp. 459, 461–464), or, more recently, scolded for neglecting her grandmotherly duties in favor of more frivolous pursuits (Fraiberg, 1977).

It is a great comfort to me to hear women that I admire speak out against these stereotypes. "The most creative force in the world is a post-menopausal woman with zest," stated Margaret Mead (1977).

Midlife women have been particularly diminished in the area of sexuality. Popular writers such as David Reuben (1969) have falsely equated the capacity for reproduction with the capacity for sexual lust and enjoyment. Fortunately here again, the newer voices of women researchers have swept aside these distortions and given older women full permission to remain, or even to become, sexual beings (Huyck, 1977). Actually, the whole area of female sexuality has been particularly prone to value-laden distortions by "experts." Women of my generation grew up with the next myth.

The Myth of the Sleeping Beauty. Men have not only instructed women on how to rear their children, but, starting with Freud, they have defined women's sexuality for them. I have commented elsewhere "how uncertain women are about the nature of their own sexuality," that they don't know "what they feel, what they think they should feel, whether they are unique and therefore deviant, or whether they are (hopefully) normal" (Loewenstein, 1978a, p. 107). It is most fortunate that women in consciousness-raising groups have been willing to share their sexual experiences, and women have finally revealed themselves to women researchers (Hite, 1976; Seaman, 1972b), thus ending the pluralistic ignorance in which each woman, individually, bore the secret shame of her particular sexual inadequacy. Freud and some of his women disciples suggested that mature femininity depended on the transfer of erotic sensitivity from the clitoris to the vagina, but the vagina itself was downgraded as an organ much inferior to the priceless penis. It was not until Master's and Johnson's (1966) research that the role of the clitoris in adult female sexual functioning was restored. We now understand that women may indeed have either a vaginal orgasm or a clitoral orgasm, or the combined orgasm that Masters and Johnson studied in their laboratory, and that these diverse patterns of female sexuality are neither related to emotional maturity nor even to some ill-defined "femininity" (Loewenstein, 1978a; Singer, 1973).

While psychoanalytic literature defined "frigidity" (lack of vaginal orgasmic experience) as a neurotic rejection of the feminine role, social scientists have pointed out that "the human female's capacity for orgasm is to be viewed as a potentiality that may or may not be developed by a given culture" (Mead, quoted in Seaman, 1972a, p. 65). This capacity is said to be a learning process that involves considerable deinhibition (in our culture), sexual experience, and skillful lovers. The Kinsey (1953) researchers found that it took some women many years before they had their first orgasm and that many women were more orgasmic during their postmarital life than during their marriages (Gebhard, 1970). We grew up with the expectation that we were to wait passively until our young and probably relatively inexperienced husbands would magically awaken our sexuality and "give us" orgasms. The lesson that women must take charge of their own sexuality and communicate their needs to their lovers has been a hard one to learn.

It thus becomes very obvious that the romantic ideal of chastity and virginity until marriage is highly dysfunctional for both women and men. I know, my son, that this is one bit of news with which you are apt to be in agreement!

Feminist writers have also tried to exorcise the guilt traditionally associated with masturbation. They urge women to masturbate, both as a primary form of female sexuality (Dodson, 1974) and as a potential bridge toward vaginal orgasmic capacity (Barbach, 1975). Feminist therapists have emphasized comfort with one's own female body, responsibility for one's own sexuality, and specific technical sexual skill training. However, the importance of feelings and of the emotional aspects of the sexual relationship has not been denied.

Female sexuality is of course not confined to heterosexuality and that brings me to:

The Myth of Homosexual Pathology. When Eleanor Roosevelt's correspondence with Lorena Hickok (Carmody, 1979) was recently published, speculations about her sexual orientation were rampant. Western culture thrives on false polarities. It is very important in our society that people not only be sharply divided into men and women, but also be viewed as having either homosexual or heterosexual orientations. Harry Stack Sullivan, an important pioneer in rejecting this insidious dichotomy, wrote (1953, p. 294): "This results in seventy-two theoretical patterns of sexual behavior in situations involving two real partners. . . . From this statement, I would like you to realize, . . . how fatuous it is to toss out the adjectives "heterosexual," "homosexual," or "narcissistic" to classify a person as to his sexual and friendly integration with others. Such classifications are not anywhere near refined enough for intelligent thought; they are much too gross to do anything except mislead both the observer and the victim."

The actual frequent bisexual behavior widely documented (Kinsey and others, 1948, 1953; Bell and Weinberg, 1978; Riess, 1974) is often dismissed in the psychiatric literature as "limited" or "situational" experimentation (Saghir and Robins, 1973). Marriages of women who later identify themselves as lesbians are retrospectively defined as "doomed to failure," eschewing the alternate explanation that women who are disappointed by men may turn to other women for emotional and physical satisfaction (Loewenstein, 1980b). The myth of an early acquired "basic propensity" is no more than a value bias, like all discussions of "propensities" and "dispositions" (Salzman, 1979, p. 82). In our new, more fluid culture and somewhat more permissive life-styles, changes in sexual orientation throughout the life cycle have become not infrequent. "The evidence supports a theory of multi-potentiality of sexual expression" (Bleier, 1979, p. 55). I know women who have changed their sexual orientation, and other researchers have confirmed this finding (Blumstein and Schwartz, 1976). It is true of course that women and men in our society are almost forced to make an allegiance to a heterosexual or homosexual life-style which then binds them into a particular network of social relations which reinforces and sharpens their allegiance.

Most destructive has been the mental health professionals' insistence that homosexuality is a severe emotional problem, in spite of all the research evidence that "homosexuality is simply not a clinical entity" (Riess, 1974, p. 19) and that "there is no evidence whatsoever that homosexuality represents either a biological or an emotional aberration" (Bleier, 1979, p. 55; Klaich, 1974).

The American Psychiatric Association in 1973, perhaps under political pressure, removed homosexuality from the category of mental illness, but the stigmatization persists. As I have written elsewhere, "homosexuality has been alternately or simultaneously labeled a crime, a sin, or a sickness, three labels that have oppressive, guilt- and shame-producing consequences" (Loewenstein, 1980b, p. 31). Lesbian women have tended to avoid using traditional mental health facilities and social agencies for fear of discrimination. However, as women (and men) courageously come out of their closets, we realize that "lesbian women are everywhere" (lesbian motto). "Everywhere" includes social work faculty, social work students, and social work practitioners, and therefore lesbians will soon feel more confident about using traditional "integrated" agencies. It has become crucial for all social workers to resist stigmatization of lesbians, and to become aware of the particular life stresses of these women, such as discrimination in jobs, housing, and child custody fights; heartbreak when a love relationship ends; and all the practical hardships faced by women who are not "protected" by a man. Counselors of lesbian women need to regard their life-style as a valid and potentially gratifying choice, and separate it from the problems that the lesbian woman brings for help.

There are two last myths which I would like to discuss, and I mention them last because they pervade in subtle ways all the issues that we have discussed. One is:

The Myth of Natural Inferiority of Women. I shall count in this category all the myths of sexual differences, because the concept of "different but equal" is itself a myth. Inevitably, "when a difference is established between groups that have different positions in the social hierarchy, the attributes of the dominant group are the 'right ones' to have" (Hubbard and Lowe, 1979, p. 30).

What a relief that the famous (infamous) psychoanalytic trinity of penis envy, masochism, and narcissism, when present, has been convincingly identified as arising as a response to inferior status (Miller, 1973). We understand that unhealthy narcissism is a form of self-doubt that is quite common among both women and men. It may be particularly pronounced for women, since their early socialization and their inferior social status both suggest natural inferiority to men. Penis envy, it is suggested (Thompson, 1943), when it exists, is envy of the male position in society. Masochism might be rage turned inward, as well as a weapon of the weak (Horney, 1935). As long as our inferiority was based on "inner space" (Hopkins, 1980), it was an eternal verdict, but new interpretations of women's behavior, based on the realities of social life, give rise to optimism, since cultural conditions can be changed. Even the accusation that our superegos, and our sense of justice, were inferior (Freud, 1957) has recently been convincingly reinterpreted (Gilligan, 1977).

It is ironic, but perhaps not accidental, that we women were just recovering from these psychoanalytic insults when new curses were laid on our lives, this time in the guise of sociobiology or biosociology. Instead of an inner space, we were afflicted with evolutionary biological destiny. Our genes and our hormones, it was said, meant us to be passive, maternal, and submissive to our more aggressive and therefore more successful mates. The social organization of hordes of apes was suddenly held up to us as a cultural ideal.

Once again we read that women and men are profoundly different in other than cultural programming. Little girls are less aggressive than little boys, apparently right from the cradle. Girls have better verbal skills, but only until adolescence, while boys' better-developed visual/spatial skills are beneficiently fateful throughout life (Maccoby and Jacklin, 1974). They are connected with greater field independence, which amounts to a higher capacity for abstract, analytical thinking, nothing less than the most highly prized attribute of our culture. While nineteenth-century "craniology" was not able to prove women's intellectual inferiority (Hubbard and Lowe, 1979), modern research about differences between the right and left hemisphere of the human brain raises once again the specter of inferior female intelligence. While this research has produced highly confusing and contradictory speculations, it suggests that females think less (or more?) holistically and less (or more?) intuitively than males (Star, 1979).

Of course women did not lose out completely in this research. "Women are better than men on . . . a number of other tests of visual matching and visual search which are predictive of good performance in clerical tasks" (Buffery and Gray, quoted in Star, 1979, p. 123). That finding was a great comfort to me. My highest ambition has always been to become a file clerk.

I feel unqualified to evaluate all this contradictory research that sounds perfectly reasonable to me even though it assaults my self-esteem. Am I tempted to believe in it precisely because it confirms those deep-seated female self-doubts? I feel grateful to other women, scientists, who have accepted the task of critically examining sex-role research. They explain the biased perspective and the deficient methodology on which most of this research is based. They comment that the scientists who did the research "did not acknowledge the ways in which observations are made and, indeed, what one sees, are strongly colored by the hypotheses one uses and by the framework in which one's observations are made. If one is sure that there are innate behavioral differences and tries to demonstrate this, then facts which do not support this belief are often simply not seen or are even unconsciously distorted or misinterpreted" (Hubbard and Lowe, 1979, p. 12).

Finally, we have learned that the Cartesian duality between mind and body, nature and nurture, does not correspond to reality. Social biologists seem to neglect modern genetic wisdom which states that behavioral outcomes are the result of "processes by which traits are maintained in the transactions between organism and environment" (Sameroff, 1976, p. 21), each modifying the other in a continuously circular feedback process. Moreover, the geneticists say, two populations with different environments can simply not be compared. We have encountered the same basic methodological fallacies in the comparison of differences between the IQ of black and white children. Hubbard and Lowe (1979, p. 145) summarize this situation well: "There is no theory at present that enables one to determine the origins of behavioral differences between the two groups in two different environments. This theoretical limitation invalidates all attempts to distinguish between genetic and environmental sources of sex differences, race differences, or of any other *group* difference in behavior."

I sincerely hope that you will use your good mind to review sex-role research with these caveats in mind, and that you will come to your own conclusions. The last myth that I want to share with you is equally pervasive.

The Myth of "Inner Space" Psychology. I will end up arguing that we need the myth of inner space (Rabkin, 1970; Loewenstein, 1979) to lead productive lives, but we also need to be alert to its fallacies. We like to cling to the belief that the mainspring of our actions is within ourselves, even though ingenious social psychological experiments (Milgram, 1974; Asch, 1955), not to speak of the dramatic lessons of history, teach us that the great majority of people, including mental health professionals, are ruled by obedience to authority and conformity and act in accordance with prevalent societal expectations.

This holds true regardless of whether we consider the trivial corruptions of Watergate, the perversion of ethical principles by Russian psychiatrists, or the horrifying events of the Holocaust.

If the motivation for our actions is to be found primarily within our inner space—meaning our unconscious, critical periods in our development, or genetic and biological predispositions—it leads to the logical conclusion that the reasons for our misfortunes also lie within us.

Am I mistaken in thinking that women have been particularly prone to take responsibility for all the misfortunes and betrayals that tend to befall them, joyfully cooperating with mental health professionals in this respect? Would your first impulse be one of self-blame if you had a retarded child, if you were raped, if your mate were alcoholic, or if your mate were to beat you or leave you for a more attractive partner? Perhaps it would. Women have no monopoly on guilt, shame, and self-blame, and we are perhaps only leading the way when questioning how this entire ideological framework affects our lives. It is easier to accept self-blame than to end up with a condemnation of the entire fabric of our society; it gives us some illusory sense of control over our lives, and it preserves the concept of a just, or at least minimally meaningful, society, an idea without which we might not be able to survive.

Systems theory seems more oriented toward the blending of inner space and outer space realities. Its three basic tenets—that nothing can be understood outside its context, that everything in the world is interconnected, and that behavior happens between people rather than inside people—seems consistent with a feminist perspective of the world. However, systems theory draws our attention to the interlocking complementary functioning of different family members, while the feminist perspective emphasizes power differentials. The latter leads to a view of women as victims, trapped by their economic needs and their responsibilities for children, while the former emphasizes a more equal responsibility of all members for the functioning or usually the malfunctioning of a social system. I feel personally caught between these two perspectives, seeing validity in each.

Although the "woman-as-victim" orientation is tempting, its accuracy in terms of group inequalities indisputable, and its superior moral position comforting, it is a perspective that must ultimately be rejected. Let me explain my position.

You can understand that the impact of these multiple myths and betrayals of expectations has had the result of making each woman feel that she is deficient, inadequate, and uniquely responsible for not measuring up to the various unrealistic cultural ideals. Learning to love herself becomes a woman's lifelong struggle. I think that most women are plagued so deeply by self-doubts that they need to accept them as a life condition. Ellen Goodman recognizes very well that Joan Kennedy's "journey toward self-confidence is . . . part of that mass migration known as the women's movement" (Goodman, 1980, p. 30). I advise my women clients to do what I practice myself: pretend to love yourself better than you really do and it will serve you well enough. We need to accept the paradox that a pretense at more self-confidence, more power, and more control over our lives than we either feel or can realistically assume may become a self-fulfilling prophecy. We need to reject a victim position. Perhaps you can use the same advice. Who knows, we all might turn out to be much more similar than different!

This last thought immediately leads us to the next theme I want to develop: the implications of this new understanding of women's lives for nonsexist or feminist social work practice.

You can see that women need above all a sense of mastery and competence. They need to learn to reject a view of the self as defective, passive, powerless, and helpless. While all human beings must lead responsible and considerate lives, they must learn to avoid excessive self-blame for the misfortunes of fate and excessive responsibility for the welfare of others. They need not become self-absorbed in a negative way; self-love rather than self-doubt, and healthy rather than unhealthy narcissism (Loewenstein, 1977) should be primary therapeutic objectives. Feminists have tried to formulate casework practices that are conducive to these goals.

Although I shall advise you not to concentrate on working primarily with women, I would take it for granted that your approach to any human encounter would be a nonsexist one, and that nonsexist practice is simply equivalent to good practice. You will also notice that many of the creative techniques embodying feminist principles will be equally useful for casework with men.

Marecek and Kravetz (1977) distinguish between nonsexist and feminist therapy, the former having individual change and the modification of personal behavior as its focus, the latter concentrating on political change and on critique of society and social institutions. However, both approaches are often loosely called feminist counseling (Williams, 1976), and I believe in actual practice the two overlap. It might be more useful to differentiate individual, group, and family approaches, and emphasize the distinctive feminist perspective in each approach.

The Individual Approach

Individual counseling is probably not the preferred feminist helping method, especially not by radical feminists, but there are life situations, acute crises, severe emotional problems, and personal preferences which would call for individual counseling.

Here are some of the principles of individual feminist counseling as extracted from the literature and from my own thinking (Berlin, 1976; Marecek and Kravetz, 1977; Menaker, 1974; Thomas, 1977; Williams, 1976; Krause, 1971; Radov, Masnick, and Hauser, 1977):

1. Problems are interpreted in a sociopolitical framework without denying the individual situation of a particular woman.
2. No particular sex-role expectations are held up, but automatic submission to traditional sex roles is questioned. There is support and permission for both traditional and nontraditional life choices.
3. Emphasis is on strength rather than pathology.
4. Potential sources of strength and power, available lifestyles, and ways of having an impact on one's own life are identified.
5. Traditional feminine assets of sensitivity and interpersonal skills are acknowledged, while the learning of assertiveness and an analytic-rational approach to problems is also encouraged.
6. Encouragement is given to the development of an independent identity that is not defined in relation to others.
7. Friendships with women are held to be as important and life-enriching as relationships with men.
8. Taking some immediate action as well as making concrete long-term plans is recommended.
9. Open and honest confrontation both with the counselor and with the woman's significant others is encouraged. It is to take the place of martyrdom and psychological sabotage. The expression of rage and fury within the counseling session is permitted and expected.
10. Work is considered a natural aspect of living and the woman is helped to find some balance between work and interpersonal relationships.
11. New ways of filling traditional familial roles can be suggested with the goal of avoiding subordinate positions in love relationships.

It is important to realize that any casework orientation, be it psychodynamic, problem-solving, behavioral, transactional analysis, or Gestalt, can implement the above principles. Although long-term dependency relationships are viewed with some concern, and there is a suspicion of models that involve strong transference, with its concomitant regressive features, Menaker (1974) thinks that even psychoanalytic therapy can have a feminist perspective and thus by implication so can any other long-term therapy. Krause (1971), while aware of the danger of dependency in long-term therapeutic relationships, also suggests that some women may need extensive casework to give up their "femininity complex." She defines such a complex as: "(1) the binding of a woman's life to a man, (2) the denial of her needs in favor of serving and pleasing a man and their children, (3) the sense of abnormality if she does not marry and bear children, and (4) an internal prohibition against self-assertion and development outside the context of a family" (Krause, 1971, p. 476).

Most important is the worker's attitude, her respect and her belief in the woman's ability to forge a better life for herself. Therapeutic orientation is toward affirmation, empathy, and consensual validation of suffering. These are the values of humanistic therapies, as well; indeed, the feminist and humanistic approach have many common denominators (Heckerman, 1980, p. 196). In addition, giving information about education, providing access to needed resources during crisis situations or life transitions, and other practical assistance is a vital aspect of feminist casework, as it is of all casework. A feminist counselor will also guide women toward experiences that will enhance a sense of autonomy, mastery, and control over their lives. The choice for abortion may be such an experience (Nadelson, 1978) or, by contrast, drugfree childbirth may have similar rewards (Seiden, 1978).

Feminists have called for a symmetrical relationship between worker and client, in order to set a model of equality rather than subordination in the client's other important relationships. There is actually a stress between social work professionalism and a certain feminist mistrust of professional social workers, as well as of other "experts." It is a stress that should be acknowledged and openly discussed. I think any professional helping relationship carries some, at least temporary, asymmetry, which can be minimized through the use of clear contracts, emphasis on the commonality as women, and general therapeutic demystification. Since interpretations can easily be experienced as disconfirmation—the presentation of a different reality—they must be used sparingly and only if the client has explicitly asked for them. It is important nevertheless, I believe, that feminist therapists not give up their therapeutic power!

As an example of my form of feminist casework, I shall give you vignettes of two interviews with two different clients. I see women for one- or two-session consultations. Women sometimes call on me to seek advice about major life decisions, apparently wanting either warning or permission around risk-taking situations, or because they are in great despair about some life crisis, perhaps precipitated by a loss.

Since I see these women only for short-term encounters I make a tentative contract with them on the telephone. I then meet them with the same skills and frame of mind as I approach any other professional consultation (Kadushin and Buckman, 1978). Moreover, my stance is that of an advocate. I am not a neutral observer; rather, I deliberately view the situation from their perspective. I externalize problems with conviction and energy directed especially toward diminishing feelings of shame too prevalent in women (Lewis, 1976). I boldly give advice, believing with Reid and Shapiro (1969) that the wrong advice will make people realize what they really want to do. The following vignettes ilustrate my working style in one-session counseling situations:

A woman of forty-three wants to understand why she has not been able to find the right man. For five years she has been going out with a man whom she loves, but who is sexually incompetent. She is ashamed to have clung to this man. My message to her is that "usable" men are hard to find for a woman her age, or even for the woman she was five years ago, at thirty-eight. Since she has found no one else, she has naturally stayed with this imperfect man. She now has to decide how important sex is in her life, versus companionship, for example, and weigh what her current mate can offer her, versus potentially being on her own. We discuss her search for Mr. Right and I assure her that she will find him, but he will have diabetes and will need a great deal of caretaking, which will cut into her professional plans. We explore the possibility of extending her women friendships, making specific plans. We are two women making a cold-blooded, cost/benefit analysis of her life.

A woman comes to me a year after her divorce. She pours out numerous heartaches, mentioning suicide as a contemplated alternative. She had left an alcoholic husband (who has since remarried). One of her three children was troubled and disrespectful, but the two other children were sources of pleasure and she was careful not to exploit them to fill her loneliness. I give her permission to set limits on her daughter's rudeness; I label her general distress as a temporary, normally expected psychosocial transition. When I inform her that research has shown that the legacy of suicide on children is extremely destructive, I learn that her grandmother had committed suicide and that her mother was alcoholic. She suddenly wonders about any connection between these events. She then responds, "Well, that takes care of this idea," and settles back more comfortably. I make a derogatory comment on the (now irretrievable) ex-husband. She has a married lover who is intensely jealous and my client starts to protest her innocence. I comment that it was too bad he had no reason for jealousy, blocking the usual cycle of recriminations and justifications. We laugh together at the possessiveness and absurdity of this particular man and perhaps men in general. She clings to him because he loves her in spite of her obesity, and we end the session with specific weight-reduction plans. I refuse to pity her; rather, I enumerate her assets and point out that the quality of her life is clearly in her own hands, putting her in charge of her life.

The Group Approach

Since feminists are often suspicious of any psychodynamic approaches, they prefer practice theories that state that sex-role behavior and dysfunctional behavior in general are either adaptive to a particular situational context (Redstockings Sister, 1971), or simply learned, or the consequence of a particular cognitive set, and can therefore be changed without personality transformation. Many feminists thus prefer group approaches in which new attitudes can be discussed and new behavior can be practiced and learned.

Group approaches have the great advantage of avoiding dependency and unequal power relationships. There are many different kinds of groups for women in need of help.

Since the beginning of the feminist movement, women realized that the small group was a powerful medium for social change and perhaps personal change as well. Bequaert (1976, p. 140) comments: "Women are changing their relations to the helping professions and are beginning to seek public, collective solutions to the problems which the professions have tended to view as private, personal, and subject to solution in isolation from other women's lives. Such issues as the anxieties of separation, loneliness, grief, and depression; the problems of job discrimination, single-parenting, and legal expertise; sexuality and social roles in new life-styles—are all now becoming items of debate among women."

These are the subjects of discussion in feminist consciousness-raising (CR) groups. CR has been defined as "the attempt to bring internalized assumptions into awareness" (Hubbard and Lowe, 1979, p. 26). In our case this would mean "to expand one's awareness of what it means to be a woman in the current social and cultural context" (Kirsch, 1974, p. 342). Most women associate CR with the effort to transform the personal into the political. Through the sharing of deeply personal experiences in a warm, supportive, and accepting climate, women are gradually freed from their burdens of guilt and shame, depression, and sense of inadequacy. They "find their anger" and move toward "autonomy, activity, self-esteem, and self-acceptance as the characteristic styles of relating to the world and themselves" (Kirsch, 1974, p. 347).

Some writers characterize CR groups as forms of self-help groups (Bond and Lieberman, 1980), and although that is not the stated purpose of CR, both types of group do have similar goals. Both promote healing through self-expression, group support, mutual problem solving, and intimate sharing of difficult experiences in a peer setting. Self-help groups have proliferated in the last decade (Riessman, 1977). Feminist self-help groups are often "crisis-oriented . . . [dealing] with crises that are unique to women or that affect women in a special way: rape, unwanted pregnancies, marital crises, wife-abuse, job reentry for mature women. . . . These groups are informally constituted, grass-roots groups, working outside the mental health establishment" (Marecek and Kravetz, 1977, p. 327).

Sometimes such groups can be used as a forum where a woman can bear witness to her suffering. I believe that bearing witness in speaking, writing, in public, or even to just one significant other (who could be a social worker) is a powerful human urge. In doing so we need to be heard, nonjudgmentally accepted, and above all believed. Bearing witness should not be confused with catharsis, an emptying of inner space. It is a social act of sharing. I believe that creative forms of bearing witness account for the healing that goes on in CR groups, self-help groups, psychodrama or Gestalt groups, dynamic psychotherapy groups, and individual counseling. Here is one woman talking: "My experience and that of the women I know tells me there is no treatment for rape other than community. Therapy or consciousness raising can be helpful as long as no 'cure' for a 'condition' or 'disease' is implied. Rape is loss. Like death it is best treated with a period of mourning and grief. . . . The social community is the appropriate center for the restoration of spirit" (Metzger, 1976, p. 406).

I deeply agree with Metzger (p. 408) that women need to speak up "to break some of the silence and isolation which reinforces the personlessness of women." I have dealt with difficult life experiences in similar ways. "The private voice in the public sphere confirms our common experience through which we begin to assert ourselves" (Metzger, p. 406).

I feel such strong personal conviction about the healing possibilities of all forms of public sharing that I would like to quote yet another similar view, this one in relation to incest. "Consciousness raising has often been more beneficial and empowering to women than psychotherapy. In particular, the public revelation of the many and ancient sexual secrets of women (orgasm, rape, abortion) may have contributed far more toward the liberation of women than a restorative therapeutic relationship. The same should be true for incest. The victims who feel like bitches, whores, and witches might feel greatly relieved if they felt less lonely, if their identities as the special guardians of a dreadful secret could be shed. Incest will begin to lose its devastating magic power when women begin to speak out about it publicly and realize how common it is" (Herman and Hirschman, 1977, p. 755).

Participants in consciousness-raising groups, as well as those who join self-help groups, tend to have the same anti-professional bias that I mentioned in relation to individual counseling. However, consciousness-raising groups of various kinds have recently been adapted to social work practice as an instrument of social change (Longres and McLeod, 1980). Moreover, social work practice has managed to integrate self-help groups into community networks of helpful resources, or they have been used for particular populations at risk (Golan, 1980).

Some self-help groups are led by professionals, but the feminist viewpoint that expertise, responsibility, and power exists and should be divided among all group members should be respected (Silverman, 1978; Habib and Landgraf, 1977). Social workers know from experience that being in the helping role is one of the most effective ways of gaining strength and self-confidence.

Hotlines are a supplement to self-help groups. They may be organized by social workers and are typically staffed by volunteers who may have had similar crises, as in the Widowed Service Line in Boston (Abrahams, 1972) or the telephone peer counseling service in Baltimore (Kaplan, Lazarus, and Saidel, 1976).

More directly related to social work expertise and highly compatible with feminist principles is the whole area of psychosocial transition counseling (Loewenstein, 1978b). The method is particularly suited to women, in providing non-stigmatizing, time-limited, problem-focused educational counseling during a life-transition period. It does not involve self-definition as a client and it involves no dependency. It is truly preventive, reaching women in periods of vulnerability, and aims "to facilitate change in [their] assumptive world" (Parkes, 1971, p. 110) to fit their new circumstances. The group leader typically has a didactic plan for each session, attempting to first acknowledge that loss is involved, even in situations that are ultimately favorable; focus is then on the current state of possible turmoil and disorientation; and finally there are some sessions devoted to anticipatory guidance for the future.

The material is usually not presented in a lecture form, but elicited from group discussions, with the leader providing a guiding focus, emphasis, and a summary of what has been learned in each session. The benefits of such groups are multiple: There is reassurance that personal reactions are expected and behaviorally meaningful, rather than crazy or deviant. Practical, mutual problem solving and expressions of support are encouraged. Liking and empathy among group members lead to a sense of contributing to others, and therefore increasing competence, and a beginning of repaired self-esteem. The fact that participants are as a rule at different points along the transitional continuum facilitates group members' learning from each other. The group also provides a temporary community for dealing with those crises that involve uprooting, and new friendships are frequently formed.

I am very happy that social workers have moved into that domain and have made transition counseling an integral part of their daily practice in a great variety of settings. Social workers conduct such groups for women who have recently moved (Kaplan and Glenn, 1978), for middle-aged housewives who are ready to move out into the world (Klass and Redfern, 1977), for divorced or separated women (Pincus, Radding, and Lawrence, 1974), for widows (Toth and Toth, 1980), for mothers of children of all ages (Hayes, 1976), for pregnant and postpartum women (Turner and Izzi, 1978), and many others. Schlossberg and Kent (1979) have made a case that all women are in a continuing state of important role and identity transition. They think that the transition model of counseling women is therefore the most appropriate one.

There is another form of group counseling that is often sought by women, and which is based on behavioral principles, namely, assertiveness training. This kind of training is so important to women that it is often practiced in CR groups. Gambrill and Richey (1980, p. 223) define assertiveness training as designed "to increase the influence people exert over the interpersonal environment by increasing the appropriate expression of both positive and negative feelings." Appropriate assertiveness, which is carefully differentiated from aggressiveness, is meant to counteract feminine, passive, dependent, submissive, fearful, and emotionally impulsive behavior. Many women find it difficult to disagree in conversations (especially with men!), to refuse unfair requests, and to give and receive criticism, and they have these difficulties in some circumstances but not in others. Careful assertiveness training involves individual assessments of particular difficulties and focused skill training through modeling, reinforcement, and feedback from the group, in those areas where greatest difficulties have been identified.

Behavior therapies such as assertiveness training and cognitive therapy have been welcomed by many practitioners as an alternative to psychoanalytically based counseling (Wesley, 1975). We need to give cognitive therapy at least a small place in discussing counseling approaches to women, because it has assumed a prominent theoretical position in the treatment of depressions, the prototypical female disturbance. Cognitive therapy uses many of the same behavioral techniques as assertiveness training and its principles may be used in both individual or group counseling.

Depressed people suffer from what Beck and Greenberg (1974, p. 118) term a "cognitive triad" of negative views about themselves, the world, and the future. In addition to having selective perceptions and cognitive deficits, depressed people are said to draw arbitrary (pessimistic) inferences, make overgeneralizations (based on one unfortunate incident), magnify particular (unpleasant) events, and focus on (one unhappy) detail. The cognitive approach teaches clients to monitor their "automatic thoughts" and to recognize the type of cognitive distortions that they habitually use. In addition to teaching new thinking patterns and engaging clients in logical discussions, cognitive counselors use role playing, modeling, the creation of positive reinforcements for nondepressed thoughts and behavior, task assignments that guarantee success, and the evoking of amusement and affection (Combs, 1980).

As an educator I would also like to mention the effectiveness of education in inducing change. As you know, for a number of years I have taught classes on the "new" psychology of women, both in a large lecture format and in small seminars. Many students have told me that their learning about women as potentially strong and competent human beings gave them the strength to take charge of their lives in new ways. I believe that social workers might want to move into this whole area of adult and even late-adulthood education which is currently evoking so much interest.

I am pleased to see that mental health centers for women tend to offer all the different helping modalities that I have discussed, from individual counseling, to a variety of group meetings, to practical and educational services. Here is the description of one such center: "Services offered include counseling by a psychiatric social worker, and information on career development, employment, education, and child care is available. Referrals are made to and received from a variety of vocational settings, as well as social agencies and treatment facilities. The center conducts symposiums and group discussions on combining roles, reentry to work and study, and career decisions" (Pincus, Radding, and Lawrence, 1974, p. 188).

The Family Therapy Approach

Most family therapy now conducted is based on systems theory, a thought system that, I have already mentioned, is at least theoretically respectful of the total context of a patriarchal society to which women must adapt in order to survive and function. Initially it looked as if systems theory, and family therapy, would relieve women of having to bear sole responsibility for their children's pathology, and it is true the responsibility becomes somewhat more spread out. Yet, subtly, family therapy has become a male-dominated enterprise, and traditional male values have crept in. Systems theory has been used, in my opinion, to justify the myth of equal responsibility of at least the two parents, with minimal discussion of the effect of the power differential between a wage-earning husband and a (usually) lower-income-earning wife. There is little analysis, in the mainstream family therapy literature, on the constraining effect that the wish to preserve a father for her children has on a woman's behavior and her freedom to fully assert herself.

There is currently a thrust in some methods of family therapy to strengthen the father's executive role (Hare-Mustin, 1978). When the question arose, during my one-month internship at the Philadelphia Child Guidance Clinic, why initial alliance was usually formed with the father, it was explained that fathers are generally more reluctant to engage in therapy, that they are (usually) already dominated by the wife, and that men are apt to be more vulnerable and need more support. I actually agree with all these statements, but it leads once again to an unfavorable, often shameful, therapeutic position for women. It is true that some male family therapists are extremely sympathetic to the feminist viewpoint and I have personally observed their sensitive work with women, but "the client's emotional reactivity solely to the sex of the therapist may override the experience, talent, and warmth that the therapist brings to bear" (Hare-Mustin, 1978, p. 192). I think family therapy is a creative technique which, instead of reinforcing traditional values, could be an agent for promoting healthier, more egalitarian, less sex-role-bound family constellations. I know that you are too wise to protest that family therapy should not be a political tool. You have understood that all therapy is inevitably political and the question is merely "whose politics?"

Cross-Gender Counseling

I can see you becoming more and more uneasy, anxious, and angry as you read this long letter, especially since I casually mentioned that women might not be your most suitable clients. I know that you, along with most young people who are going into clinical social work, are fascinated by the challenge and promise of family-oriented casework. I do not want to dissuade you from that specialty, but I think cotherapy with a woman who is either your peer or your senior (in ability, age, or status) might be a fairer approach to the women (mothers and daughters and grandmothers) in the family.

And what do I think, finally, about your working with women clients? It is rather curious that the social work literature has tended to ignore the issues raised by cross-gender casework (Schwartz, 1974). I have come to share the profound doubts about the possibility of a creative encounter between a professional man and a woman client that other feminists have voiced (Chesler, 1972; Fabrikant, 1974; Stevens, 1971; Wesley, 1975; Kravetz, 1976; Marecek and Kravetz, 1977; Kirsch, 1974). These women have rejected men counselors, because, at least in the past, men had expected from their women clients (or more often women patients) adaptation to traditional sex-role definitions. Men counselors have also been accused of operating from an outmoded psychoanalytic model of women's development, although, to be fair, so did women caseworkers. Chesler has been concerned lest the male-counselor/female-client relationship reproduce the unequal power relationship already existing in marriage and other social institutions, with the accompanying unhealthy dependency feelings that such relationships encourage.

Most serious, I think, is the accusation that men counselors have seduced their women clients (usually patients), openly or covertly, sexually (Freeman and Roy, 1976; Davidson, 1977; Volth, 1972) or emotionally (Mitchell, 1973; Ferguson, 1973). It is true that most accusations have been made against male psychiatrists, rather than social workers. However, similar dangers exist for male caseworkers, as Kadushin's research has demonstrated (1976), although his research questions to male caseworkers project all seductive impulses on female clients.

I trust that you will be well trained, and that your consciousness has now been properly raised, so that you will not fall into any of the traps outlined so far. However, boundaries between different kinds of intimate or pseudo-intimate relationships are very difficult to maintain and I have seen even skillful therapists stumble in this area. An intensive counseling encounter is very similar in its projective transference elements to a passionate love experience, and even Freud ([1915], 1957) admitted the similarity between "real" love and transference love. In my research on passionate love experiences in women's lives (Loewenstein, 1980c), I found that many women seek counseling help after a disappointing love relationship, and the therapeutic encounter, especially when it is a cross-gender one (for heterosexual women), has the potential of evoking once again those elements of unrequited yearning, passion, dependency, masochism, and intense ambivalence from which they are trying to recover, both at the time they seek help and perhaps permanently in their lives.

Your women clients will fall in love with you, because you are exceptionally handsome, well educated, and, unlike the infamous "inexpressive American male," you are emotionally expressive (otherwise you would have continued playing with your computers). What chance is there that your woman client will not compare you with the man in her life and find him wanting; and if she is without a man, that she will not fall in love with you? As a matter of fact, she will fall in love with you because the men in her life do not take time to listen to her, affirm her, connect with her pain, or encourage her strivings, all of which you will have learned to do in your training. You think you will therefore offer her a better model of male/female relationships than she has ever had—a corrective emotional experience and an example of what she deserves? It is useless.

What she needs to learn is not to love you, as a man, but to love herself, to become strong and independent and self-respecting, and then—if she still wants a man—she might find one whom she can love and who treats her well.

There are still other reasons why I am dubious about your seeing women clients. It is inevitable that women in our society feel inhibited in talking to men about a whole variety of issues important to them, and here again we have confirmation from Kadushin's research (1976). Masters and Johnson were wise to insist on a male/female cotherapy team for sexual counseling. There are other issues related to women's intimate lives that may cause embarrassment, humiliation, or shame when shared with a man.

Another important matter in cross-gender counseling, which has rarely been discussed, bears mentioning here. I have noticed that women are afraid to overwhelm men with their rage—either murderous fantasies against the men in their lives, or rage against the male caseworker himself, for whatever reason, rational or irrational. When I have encouraged women to confront their male therapist (of any discipline) about some major complaint, they have been unwilling to do so. They respond: "He is very well-meaning and I don't want to hurt his feelings." "He is just not the kind of person who could tolerate much anger." "He might stop seeing me if I told him how much I sometimes hate him." Women look up to men, but, paradoxically, they also perceive them as weak, vulnerable, and in need of protection, especially from women's rage. Women have learned to bolster men's egos, not to attack them. They know that they should be good and loving little girls, preferably obedient—not castrating bitches.

I know that many women, expressing typical minority-status self-contempt, prefer male therapists (Schwartz, 1974), male pediatricians, and male obstetricians who will deliver their babies, rather than assist the woman to do so (Seiden, 1978), but times are changing in this area as well.

I want to admit that some people generally find it easier to talk to a very different "other" and that the effort to explore and understand differences can be a creative act. I think, however, that it is time- and energy-consuming and a casework encounter during a time of stress might not be the right medium or moment for such personal enrichment. Yes, there will be times when it is important for women to see a male counselor, and I will leave it to you to argue the case. On the whole, however, I suggest that you let women caseworkers work with women clients. They can be models of competence and assertiveness, and such same-gender counseling will avoid the destructive and defeating male/female interactions that I have outlined.

Women social workers, in their very roles as women identified with their women clients, must also avoid certain traps. There is the danger of the "yes, I know how it is" syndrome, which blocks careful exploration. Overidentification might also lead to premature reassurance (indirect reassurance of self) and fear of exploring some of the more frightening aspects of certain experiences such as rape or incest. McCombie (1975, pp. 156, 157) warns: "In an effort to reduce stress, the counselor may inadvertently . . . [offer] reassurance [and] without giving the victim the opportunity to explore and master conflict, the counselor can end up fostering regression. . . . The counselor needs to be sensitive to feelings of shame and guilt. If left unattended, such feelings may lead to self-punitive acting out in an unconscious effort to expiate guilt or to bolster claim to legitimate victimization."

Another possible temptation for women caseworkers is getting angry in behalf of the client. Women must be allowed to feel and express their own rage, even if it is not directed at the "true enemy," but, for example, at other women. A feminist counselor may be "distressed by the frequent histories of indifference, hostility, and cruelty in the mother-daughter relationship. She may find herself rushing to the defense of the mother, pointing out that the mother herself was a victim" (Herman and Hirschman, 1977, p. 755).

Both Menaker (1974) and Nichols (1977) comment on the frequently deeply distorted relationship between mother and daughter in our society, and they suggest that some women may need substitute mothering that is neither hostile nor suffocating, and that allows for the experience of both nurturance and gradual differentiation. Women social workers can perhaps be such new kinds of mothers who give their client/daughter permission to be autonomous and strong.

It might be similarly painful for a feminist counselor to listen to and give credibility to mutual betrayals among straight and lesbian women. They do happen. Political ideologies must not be allowed to pervert therapeutic needs.

"So you don't want me to enter the field of social work?" you ask. "You want to recreate a sex-segregated profession that will ultimately be held in even lower esteem than social work's current position." No, that is not my message after all. I do welcome you, with your generous spirit and your fine mind and your vitality, into the profession. I want you to help us in our fight for more equitable wages. We need you, but as a peer, not as a boss.

What I want you to do is work with the men who oppress women. I would like you to work with the adolescent boys who irresponsibly impregnate their girlfriends; with other adolescents (or the same) who beat up their mothers, like their fathers used to do; with the men who rape women; or with husbands who beat their wives because they feel weak and inadequate and need to assert their domination and vent their rage. Higgins (1978, pp. 269, 270) says this well in discussing services for battered women: "The weakest feature of the existing wife abuse services concerns the small number of men requesting help. Because most men refuse to participate in conjoint counseling, individual counseling continues to be provided to the women. This unintentionally reinforces the traditional error of focusing on the victim rather than on the husband or on the relationship. . . . This victim orientation also diverts energy from innovative efforts to provide services for battering men."

I am very happy to see that services for battering men are finally being initiated on significant and imaginative scale (Dullea, 1980). You need to work with fathers who sexually molest their daughters; with divorced men who neglect to stay in touch with children and neglect to contribute to their support (Brandwein, 1977); with bosses who sexually harass their women employees; with police and judges who take the man's side in cases of rape and wife beating. You need to teach fathers to share early childrearing with their wives; to give up their compulsive sex-typing and help their sons and daughters develop androgynous personalities; and to encourage the development of children who can both think and feel, who can be active and passive, logical and intuitive, assertive and tender. We need your help with the multiple issues pertaining to advocacy and legislation that is favorable and fair to women. There is lots for you to do in here, in our social work world. I hope you will join us. I welcome you.

Your most loving mother

References

Abrahams, R. B. "Mutual Help for the Widowed." *Social Work,* September 1972, *17* (5), 54-61.

Asch, S. "Opinions and Social Pressure." *Scientific American,* November 1955. In *Frontiers of Psychological Research. Readings from Scientific American.* San Francisco: W. H. Freeman, 1948-1966.

Barbach, L. G. *For Yourself: The Fulfillment of Female Sexuality.* Garden City, N.Y.: Doubleday, 1975.

Beck, A. T., and Greenberg, R. L. *Cognitive Therapy with Depressed Women.* In V. Franks and V. Burtle (Eds.), *Women in Therapy.* New York: Brunner/Mazel, 1974.

Bell, A. P., and Weinberg, M. S. *Homosexualities.* New York: Simon & Schuster, 1978.

Belle, D. "Mothers and Their Children: A Study of Low Income Families." In C. L. Heckerman (Ed.), *The Evolving Female.* New York: Human Sciences Press, 1980.

Bequaert, L. *Single Women, Alone and Together.* Boston: Beacon Press, 1976.

Berlin, S. "Better Work with Women Clients." *Social Work,* Nov. 1976, *21* (6), 492-497.

Bernard, J. *The Future of Marriage.* New York: World, 1972.

Bernard, J. *The Future of Motherhood.* New York: Dial Press, 1974.

Bleier, R. "Social and Political Bias in Science." In R. Hubbard and M. Lowe (Eds.), *Genes and Gender.* New York: Gordian Press, 1979.

Blumstein, P., and Schwartz, P. "Bisexuality in Women." *Archives of Sexual Behavior,* 1976, *5* (2), 171-181.

Bond, G. R., and Lieberman, M. A. "The Role and Function of Women's Consciousness Raising: Self-Help, Psychotherapy, or Political Activation?" In C. L. Heckerman (Ed.), *The Evolving Female.* New York: Human Sciences Press, 1980.
Brandwein, R. "After Divorce: A Focus on Single Parent Families." *The Urban and Social Change Review,* 1977, *10* (1), 21-25.
Bronowski, J. *The Ascent of Man.* Boston: Little, Brown, 1973.
Carmody, D. "Letters by Eleanor Roosevelt Detail Friendship with Lorena Hickok." *The New York Times,* October 21, 1979, p. 34.
Campbell, A. "The American Way of Mating." *Psychology Today,* May 1975, *9* (5), 37-43.
Chesler, P. *Women and Madness.* Garden City, N.Y.: Doubleday, 1972.
Chodorow, N. *The Reproduction of Mothering.* Berkeley: University of California Press, 1978.
Combs, T. D. "A Cognitive Therapy for Depression: Theory, Techniques, and Issues." *Social Casework: The Journal of Contemporary Social Work,* July 1980, *61* (6), 361-366.
Davidson, V. "Psychiatry's Problem with No Name: Therapist-Patient Sex." *American Journal of Psychoanalysis,* 1977, *37* (1), 45-50.
Deutsch, H. *Psychology of Women.* Vol. 2. New York: Grune & Stratton, 1945.
Diangson, P., Kravetz, D. F., and Lipton, J. "Sex-Role Stereotyping and Social Work Education." *Journal of Education for Social Work,* Fall 1975, *11* (3), 44-49.
Dinnerstein, D. *The Mermaid and the Minotaur.* New York: Harper & Row, 1976.
Dodson, B. *Liberating Masturbation.* New York: Betty Dodson, 1974.
Dullea, G. "A Center Where Wife Batterers Are Counseled—Man-to-Man." *The New York Times,* September 16, 1980, p. A24.
Engel, M. Preface. In G. Bateson, *Steps to an Ecology of Mind.* New York: Ballantine Books, 1972.
Etzioni, A. (Ed.). *The Semi-Professions and Their Organizations—Teachers, Nurses, Social Workers.* New York: Free Press, 1969.
Fabrikant, B. "The Psychotherapist and the Female Patient: Perceptions, Misperceptions, and Change." In V. Franks and V. Burtle (Eds.), *Women and Therapy.* New York: Brunner/Mazel, 1974.
Fanshel, D. "Status Differentials: Men and Women in Social Work." *Social Work,* Nov. 1976, *21* (6), 448-454.
Ferguson, S. *A Guard Within.* New York: Pantheon, 1973.
Fraiberg, S. *Every Child's Birthright: In Defense of Mothering.* New York: Basic Books, 1977.
Freeman, L., and Roy, J. *Betrayal.* New York: Stein & Day, 1976.
Freud, S. "The Psychology of Women." In *New Introductory Lectures on Psychoanalysis.* Lecture 33. In J. Strachey (Ed.), *Standard Edition of the Complete Psychological Works of Sigmund Freud.* Vol. 22. London: Hogarth Press, 1957. (Originally published 1933.)
Freud, S. "Observations on Transference Love." In J. Strachey (Ed.), *Standard Edition of the Complete Psychological Works of Sigmund Freud.* Vol. 12. London: Hogarth Press, 1957. (Originally published 1915.)

Gambrill, E. D., and Richey, C. A. "Assertion Training for Women." In C. L. Heckerman (Ed.), *The Evolving Female.* New York: Human Sciences Press, 1980.

Gebhard, P. "Postmarital Coitus among Widows and Divorcees." In P. Bohannon (Ed.), *Divorce and After.* New York: Doubleday, 1970.

Gilligan, C. "In a Different Voice: Women's Conceptions of Self and of Morality." *Harvard Educational Review,* November 1977, *47* (4), 481–518.

Golan, N. "Intervention at Times of Transition: Sources and Forms of Help." *Social Casework. Journal of Contemporary Social Work,* May 1980, *61* (5), 259–266.

Goodman, E. "Portrait: Joan Kennedy." *Life,* May 1980, *3* (5), 29–30.

Habib, M., and Landgraf, J. "Women Helping Women." *Social Work,* November 1977, *22* (6), 510–512.

Hare-Mustin, R. T. "A Feminist Approach to Family Therapy." *Family Process,* June 1978, *17* (2), 181–194.

Hayes, L. S. "A YWCA Program for Groups." *Social Work,* November 1976, *21* (6), 523–524.

Heckerman, C. L. "Introduction to Part III: From Traditional Psychoanalysis to Alternatives to Psychotherapy." In C. L. Heckerman (Ed.), *The Evolving Female.* New York: Human Sciences Press, 1980.

Henry, J. *Pathways to Madness.* New York: Random House, 1965.

Herman, J., and Hirschman, L. "Father-Daughter Incest." *Signs,* Summer 1977, *2* (4), 735–756.

Higgins, J. J. "Social Services for Abused Wives." *Social Casework,* May 1978, *59* (5), 266–271.

Hite, S. *The Hite Report.* New York: Macmillan, 1976.

Hopkins, L. B. "Inner Space and Outer Space Identity in Contemporary Females." *Psychiatry,* February 1980, *43* (2), 1–12.

Horney, K. "The Problem of Feminine Masochism." *Psychoanalytic Review,* 1935, *12* (3), 157–241.

Hubbard, R., and Lowe, M. (Eds.). *Genes and Gender.* New York: Gordian Press, 1979.

Huyck, M. H. "Sex and the Older Woman." In L. E. Troll, J. Israel, and K. Israel (Eds.), *Looking Ahead.* Englewood Cliffs, N.J.: Prentice-Hall, 1977.

Kadushin, A. "Men in a Woman's Profession." *Social Work,* November 1976, *21* (6), 440–447.

Kadushin, A., and Buckman, M. "Practice of Social Work Consultation: A Survey." *Social Work,* September 1978, *23* (5), 372–379.

Kaplan, M. F., and Glenn, A. "Women and the Stress of Moving: A Self-Help Approach." *Social Casework,* July 1978, *59* (7), 434–436.

Kaplan, M. F., Lazarus, E., and Saidel, B. H. "A Self-Help Telephone Service for Women." *Social Work,* November 1976, *21* (6), 519–520.

Kinsey, A. C., and others. *Sexual Behavior in the Human Male.* Philadelphia: Saunders, 1948.

Kinsey, A. C., and others. *Sexual Behavior in the Human Female.* Philadelphia: Saunders, 1953.

Kirsch, B. "Consciousness-Raising Groups as Therapy for Women." In V. Franks and V. Burtle (Eds.), *Women in Therapy.* New York: Brunner/Mazel, 1974.

Klaich, D. *Woman Plus Woman.* New York: Simon & Schuster, 1974.

Klass, S. B., and Redfern, M. A. "A Social Work Response to the Middle-Aged Housewife." *Social Casework,* February 1977, *58* (2), 101–102.

Knapman, S. K. "Sex Discrimination in Family Agencies." *Social Work,* November 1977, *22* (6), 461–465.

Krause, C. "The Femininity Complex and Women Therapists." *Journal of Marriage and the Family,* August 1971, *33* (3), 476–482.

Kravetz, D. "Sexism in a Woman's Profession." *Social Work,* November 1976, *21* (6), 421–426.

Lasch, C. *Haven in a Heartless World: The American Family Besieged.* New York: Basic Books, 1977.

Lazarre, J. *The Mother Knot.* New York: Dell, 1976.

Lemkau, J. P. "Women and Employment: Some Emotional Hazards." In C. L. Heckerman (Ed.), *The Evolving Female.* New York: Human Sciences Press, 1980.

Lewis, H. B. *Psychic War in Men and Women.* New York: New York University Press, 1976.

Lipman-Blumen, J. "The Implications for Family Structure of Changing Sex Roles." *Social Casework,* February 1976, *57* (2), 67–79.

Loewenstein, S. F. "An Overview of the Concept of Narcissism." *Social Casework,* March 1977, *58* (3), 136–142.

Loewenstein, S. F. "An Overview of Some Aspects of Female Sexuality." *Social Casework,* February 1978a, *59* (2), 106–115.

Loewenstein, S. F. "Preparing Social Work Students for Life-Transition Counseling within the Human Behavior Sequence." *Journal of Education for Social Work,* Spring 1978b, *14* (2), 66–73.

Loewenstein, S. F. "Inner and Outer Space in Social Casework." *Social Casework,* January 1979, *60* (1), 19–29.

Loewenstein, S. F. "Toward Choice and Differentiation in the Midlife Crises of Women." In C. L. Heckerman (Ed.), *The Evolving Female.* New York: Human Sciences Press, 1980a.

Loewenstein, S. F. "Understanding Lesbian Women." *Social Casework,* January 1980b, *61* (1), 29–38.

Loewenstein, S. F. "Passion as a Mental Health Hazard." In C. L. Heckerman (Ed.), *The Evolving Female.* New York: Human Sciences Press, 1980c.

Loewenstein, S. F., and others. "A Study of Satisfactions and Stresses of Single Women in Midlife." *Sex Roles: A Journal of Research,* November 1981, *7* (11), 1127–1141.

Longres, J. F., and Bailey, R. H. "Men's Issues and Sexism: A Journal Review." *Social Work,* January 1979, *24* (1), 26–32.

Longres, J. F., and McLeod, E. "Consciousness Raising and Social Work Practice." *Social Casework,* May 1980, *61* (5), 267–276.

Lowenthal, M. F., Thurnher, M., and Chiraboga, D. *Four Stages of Life.* San Francisco: Jossey-Bass, 1975.

Lystad, M. H. "Violence at Home: A Review of the Literature." *American Journal of Orthopsychiatry,* April 1975, *45* (3), 328–345.

McBride, A. B. *The Growth and Development of Mothers.* New York: Harper & Row, 1973.

Maccoby, D., and Jacklin, C. *The Psychology of Sex Differences.* Stanford, Calif.: Stanford University Press, 1974.

McCombie, S. L. "Characteristics of Rape Victims Seen in Crisis Intervention." *Smith College Studies in Social Work,* November 1975, *46* (1), 137–158.

Marecek, J., and Kravetz, D. "Women and Mental Health: A Review of Feminist Change Efforts." *Psychiatry,* November 1977, *40* (4), 323–329.

Masters, W. H., and Johnson, V. *Human Sexual Response.* Boston: Little, Brown, 1966.

Mead, M. Comment made during a talk at the Harvard School of Public Health, April 7, 1977.

Menaker, E. "The Therapy of Women in the Light of Psychoanalytic Theory and the Emergence of a New View." In V. Franks and V. Burtle (Eds.), *Women in Therapy.* New York: Brunner/Mazel, 1974.

Metzger, D. "It Is Always the Woman Who Is Raped." *American Journal of Psychiatry,* April 1976, *133* (4), 405–412.

Milgram, S. *Obedience to Authority.* New York: Harper & Row, 1974.

Miller, C., and Swift, K. *Words and Women.* Garden City, N.Y.: Anchor Press/Doubleday, 1976.

Miller, J. B. (Ed.), *Psychoanalysis and Women.* New York: Brunner/Mazel, 1973.

Mitchell, S. *My Own Woman.* New York: Horizon Press, 1973.

Nadelson, C. C. "The Emotional Impact of Abortion." In M. T. Notman and C. C. Nadelson (Eds.), *The Woman Patient.* New York: Plenum Press, 1978.

Nichols, B. B. "Motherhood, Mothering, and Casework." *Social Casework,* January 1977, *58* (1), 29–35.

Parent, G. *Sheila Levine Is Dead and Living in New York.* New York: Putnam's, 1972.

Parkes, C. M. "Psycho-Social Transitions: A Field for Study." *Journal of Social Science and Medicine,* 1971, *5,* 101–115.

Pincus, C., Radding, N., and Lawrence, R. "A Professional Counseling Service for Women." *Social Work,* March 1974, *19* (2), 187–194.

Rabkin, R. *Inner and Outer Space.* New York: Norton, 1970.

Radl, S. *Mother's Day Is Over.* New York: Charterhouse, 1973.

Radloff, L. "Sex Differences in Depression: The Effects of Occupation and Marital Status." *Sex Roles,* 1975, *1* (3), 249.

Radov, C. G., Masnick, B., and Hauser, B. B. "Issues in Feminist Therapy: The Work of a Women's Study Group." *Social Work,* November 1977, *22* (6), 507–511.

Redstockings Sister. "Brainwashing and Women." In J. Agel (Ed.), *The Radical Therapist.* New York: Ballantine Books, 1971.

Reid, W. J., and Shapiro, B. "Client Reaction to Advice." *Social Service Review,* June 1969, *43* (2), 165–173.

Reuben, D. *Everything You Always Wanted to Know About Sex but Were Afraid to Ask.* New York: Bantam Books, 1969.

Rich, A. *Of Woman Born.* New York: Norton, 1976.

Riess, B. "New Viewpoints on the Female Homosexual." In V. Franks and V. Burtle (Eds.), *Women in Therapy.* New York: Brunner/Mazel, 1974.

Riessman, F. *Self-Help in the Human Services.* San Francisco: Jossey-Bass, 1977.

Rubin, L. B. *Worlds of Pain.* New York: Basic Books, 1976.

Rubin, L. B. *Women of a Certain Age.* New York: Harper & Row, 1979.

Saghir, M. T., and Robins, E. *Male and Female Homosexuality.* Baltimore: Williams & Wilkins, 1973.

Salzman, F. "Aggression and Gender: A Critique of the Nature-Nurture Questions for Humans." In R. Hubbard and M. Lowe (Eds.), *Genes and Gender.* New York: Gordian Press, 1979.

Sameroff, A. J. "Early Influence on Development: Fact or Fancy?" In S. Chess and A. Thomas (Eds.), *Annual Progress in Child Psychiatry and Child Development.* New York: Brunner/Mazel, 1976.

Schlossberg, K., and Kent, L. "Effective Helping with Women." In S. Eisenberg and L. E. Patterson (Eds.), *Helping Clients with Special Concerns.* Chicago: Rand McNally, 1979.

Schwartz, M. C. "Sexism in the Social Work Curriculum." *Journal of Education for Social Work,* Fall 1973, *9* (3), 65–70.

Schwartz, M. C. "Importance of the Sex of Worker and Client." *Social Work,* March 1974, *19* (2), 177–185.

Scotch, B. C. "Sex Status in Social Work: Grist for Women's Liberation." *Social Work,* July 1971, *16* (3), 5–11.

Seaman, B. "The Liberated Orgasm." *Ms.,* August 1972a, pp. 65–69, 117.

Seaman, B. *Free and Female: The Sex Life of the Contemporary Woman.* New York: Coward, McCann & Geoghegan, 1972b.

Seiden, A. M. "The Sense of Mastery in the Childbirth Experience." In M. Notman and C. C. Nadelson (Eds.), *The Woman Patient.* New York: Plenum Press, 1978.

Silverman, P. *Mutual Help Groups: A Guide for Mental Health Workers.* Rockville, Md.: National Institute of Mental Health, 1978.

Singer, I. *Goals of Human Sexuality.* New York: Norton, 1973.

Slater, P. *The Pursuit of Loneliness.* Boston: Beacon Press, 1970.

Star, S. L. "Sex Differences and the Dichotomization of the Brain: Methods, Limits and Problems in Research on Consciousness." In R. Hubbard and M. Lowe (Eds.), *Genes and Gender.* New York: Gordian Press, 1979.

Stevens, B. "The Psychotherapist and Women's Liberation." *Social Work,* July 1971, *16* (4), 12–18.

Stoller, R. J. "Facts and Fancies: An Examination of Freud's Concept of Bisexuality." In J. Strouse (Ed.), *Women and Analysis.* New York: Grossman, 1974.

Sullivan, H. S. *The Interpersonal Theory of Psychiatry.* New York: Norton, 1953.

Thomas, S. A. "Theory and Practice in Feminist Therapy." *Social Work,* November 1977, *22* (6), 447–454.

Thompson, C. "Penis Envy in Women." *Psychiatry,* May 1943, *6* (2), 123–125.

Toth, A., and Toth, S. "Group Work with Widows." *Social Work,* January 1980, *25* (1), 63–65.

Turner, M. F., and Izzi, M. H. "The COPE Story: A Service to Pregnant and Postpartum Women." In M. T. Notman and C. C. Nadelson (Eds.), *The Woman Patient.* New York: Plenum Press, 1978.

Van Hook, M. "Female Clients, Female Counselors: Combating Learned Helplessness." *Social Work,* January 1979, *24* (1), 63–65.

Vattano, A. J. "Power to the People: Self-Help Groups." *Social Work,* July 1972, *17* (4), 7–15.

Volth, H. "Love Affair Between Doctor and Patient." *American Journal of Psychotherapy,* 1972, *26* (3), 394–400.

Weissman, M. M. "The Treatment of Depressed Women." In C. L. Heckerman (Ed.), *The Evolving Female.* New York: Human Sciences Press, 1980.

Weissman, M. M., and Klerman, G. L. "Sex Differences and the Epidemiology of Depression." *Archives of General Psychiatry,* 1977, *34* (1), 98–111.

Welsey, C. "The Wo's Movement and Psychotherapy." *Social Work,* March 1975, *20* (2), 120–122.

Williams, E. F. *Notes of a Feminist Therapist.* New York: Dell, 1976.

Zietz, D., and Erlich, J. L. "Sexism in Social Agencies: Practitioners' Perspectives." *Social Work,* November 1976, *21* (6), 434–439.

Section IV

New Applications of Research in Clinical Practice

Stuart A. Kirk
Section Editor

with *Aaron Rosenblatt*

Social workers practice their profession in a changing environment. Changes in social policy at the federal and state levels alter the nature of the social services to be delivered at the local level, influencing the structure of the local service delivery system and determining the target populations to be served. Furthermore, changing social and demographic trends produce different kinds of human problems. Social workers are expected not only to be fully aware of such changes but also to participate actively in bringing about social change. Research serves two important functions in this regard. Studies generate new knowledge about the factors affecting human problems, and the results of studies present information on the most effective and efficient means of responding to these problems

Social work accepts certain assumptions about the possibility and desirability of change—change in society, in individuals and groups, and within the profession itself. Change in social work practice results from shifts in government policies, court decisions, developments in other human services professions, and the response of the profession to social and environmental changes. In this introduction to the research section of the *Handbook,* we address the following issues in order to examine how research methods and findings produce change in social work practice: the role of knowledge and research; the uses of research; and different models of research.

Role of Knowledge and Research in the Social Work Profession

Professions have two essential characteristics. The first is possession of a body of abstract knowledge that forms the basis of professional authority over the selection and training of candidates, prescribes the terms under which the profession is practiced, and identifies the services clients receive. Although many occupations require substantial skill, professions derive their skills directly from a body of abstract knowledge.

The second essential characteristic is the commitment of professionals (often embodied in a code of ethics) to use their knowledge and skill in rendering services to clients. Whether a physician, lawyer, or social worker, the professional strives to be a scholar-servant (Goode, 1969).

All professionals were once trained "in the field." In the seventeenth and eighteenth centuries, apprenticeship was the normal model used to train physicians in the United States. Similarly, lawyers were once apprenticed in a law office as clerk-copyists (Thorne, 1973). In most professions, practice was relatively simple compared to the standards of today. Physicians relied heavily on prayer and placebo; lawyers settled small quarrels; ministers purged minor sins from their parishioners; social workers offered moral uplift to the wayward.

Today, professional education is university-based and is distinguished from other training programs primarily by the requirement that students master a body of abstract knowledge. In addition, members of professions are trained to participate in basic and applied research, to design studies, and to assume responsibility for reporting results that can enhance practice.

Tradition and precedent, cherished principles and ethics, practice and practice wisdom contribute to professional knowledge. Further, this knowledge is increasingly derived from scientific research, a source that grows in importance as the development and evaluation of social policies and programs are subjected to systematic examination (Austin, 1978; Turem, 1979). Today, social workers are frequently challenged to document the effectiveness of their services. Lacking not only a strong research tradition but also well-established mechanisms for translating knowledge into practice, they often have difficulty defending their practices.

Despite the crucial importance of research, an uneasy relationship has existed between social work practitioners and researchers since social work founded its first national professional organization about one hundred years ago (Rosenblatt, 1981). Recognizing the significant contribution of science to industry and medicine, leaders of the charity organization movement hoped that a scientific approach to social welfare would yield similar advances. As scientific knowledge about society became available, they expected that rapid progress would be made in solving social problems (Zimbalist, 1977).

During the 1870s, social workers and social scientists attended meetings together at the American Social Science Association, but their major interests differed: the reform-minded social workers manifested a zeal for action that clashed with the social scientists' scientific objectivity. A few years later, social workers left the association to found a new organization, the National Conference on Social Welfare, more in keeping with their emphasis on reform.

These early strains between the world of practice and the world of science persist today. The social work profession continues to maintain an interest in science and research, seeking to use research to achieve its goals. Nonetheless, disagreement and ambivalence still characterize exchanges between practitioners and researchers.

Although professing the importance of research, practitioners use it sparingly (Eaton, 1962). When they confront a difficult practice problem, they seldom look for solutions in research studies (Rosenblatt, 1968). Students also are unlikely to draw on knowledge generated by research studies (Casselman, 1972; Kirk and Rosenblatt, 1977).

Perhaps social workers seldom read research reports because their knowledge of statistics is limited (Weed and Greenwald, 1973; Witkin, Edleson, and Lindsey, 1980). In a recently completed survey of 1100 social work students (Kirk and Rosenblatt, 1981), the students report that the most frequent barrier they encounter in reading research is their inability to understand the statistics. In another study, M.S.W. students record only small increments in research learning during their training (Rosenblatt, Welter, and Wojciechowski, 1975).

Most clinical practitioners keep their distance from research once they complete their graduate training (Kirk, Osmalov, and Fischer, 1976). Few consult research studies when they face difficult practice situations, and the journal articles they read rarely report on, review, or analyze research. The attitudes of practitioners who make use of research are more positive. Typically, they complete more research courses and are engaged in macro-practice, rather than micro-practice.

Social work authors are less likely than authors from several related professions to cite reports of empirical research. After conducting a study of research citations, Simpson (1978) concludes that the research orientation of the social work profession is weak. His conclusion gains support when one examines the empirical studies available in the literature of clinical social work. In preparing for this introduction, we asked graduate assistants to identify every article published in *Social Work, Social Service Review,* and *Social Casework* from 1970 to 1979 that presented some form of systematic data about the practice of clinical social work. Instructed to be liberal in their definitions of what constituted research and clinical practice, the researchers classified only 5 percent of the articles as "clinical research."

Use of Research in Practice

Establishing the use of research in social work is complicated, since social work research seeks both to explain and to change phenomena. What actually constitutes the use of research? Must a recommendation be adopted intact before it qualifies as an instance of research use? Or is it sufficient that a study merely be consulted and considered, even though the decision finally arrived at fails to reflect the course of action recommended by the investigators? Obviously, the degree of use varies. In one sense, a study read is a study used. A more restrictive definition would require that the recommendations in a study be put into effect, in which case the consequences of the study determine the definition of use.

Data generated by research methods can be used to test theory (Polansky, 1977), the most important use of research in those academic fields in which theory development is of primary importance. By contrast, social work theories are often so global that it is difficult to test them. However, to the extent that social interventions and programs are based on or guided by explicit theoretical assumptions about social phenomena, the scientific evaluation of those programs constitutes a testing of theory.

The use of research methods to develop social-intervention strategies is of growing importance in social work, as exemplified by the emergence and development of single-subject research in clinical social work (discussed in the chapters by Martin Bloom, Rona Levy, Edwin Thomas, and Wallace Gingerich). No clear parallel for this use of research exists in academic disciplines.

In the social sciences, research findings are used to validate, reject, or modify theory. To validate theory, many relevant studies must be conducted, or research conducted for another purpose can often be used to test hypotheses derived from theory through secondary analysis of existing data or the comprehensive review of existing research findings (Shyne, 1977).

A potentially important use of research in social work is to help guide social intervention. This requires social workers to become consumers of research findings (Tripodi, Fellin, and Meyer, 1969). Reviewing the research literature becomes a method of identifying problems and selecting the most effective and efficient interventions for ameliorating them (Rothman, 1974).

Perhaps the most general motive for the use of research is that it provides information needed to improve practice. Many of those who accept this motive assume a linear, rational approach to problem solving. First, a social problem is identified. Next, information is sought to determine the best solution to the problem or to select the best existing alternative. Thus, research is used to generate information needed to arrive at a solution. Often a single study is expected to perform this function. When it is acquired for that purpose, the single study on the topic of concern affects the choice of decision makers (Weiss, 1977).

A somewhat more restricted use of research is to sensitize therapists, managers, or policy makers to the various dimensions of a problem. The research information need not always provide an answer to the problem, but the resulting discussion of the data helps to specify the locus of the problem for potential users. One previously reported example discussed a decision to support large-scale programs designed to treat alcoholics. Research showed that the effects of alcoholism had more serious and lasting social consequences than the use of such drugs as marijuana and heroin. In this instance, the social science data were of key importance in rethinking the entire issue of substance abuse and the appropriateness of policies and programs to deal with it (Caplan, Morrison, and Stambaugh, 1970).

In considering the uses of research, one must also be aware of its several misuses (Weiss, 1972, 1977; Suchman, 1967; Tripodi, 1974). The motives for conducting research or using its results are not always praiseworthy, and research and the trappings of research are sometimes used to hide other than noble intentions.

For example, research can be used primarily to gain political objectives. Adversaries in a debate often use evidence from a research study "in an attempt to neutralize opponents, convince waverers, and bolster supporters." According to Weiss (1977, pp. 14–15), this use is neither "unimportant" nor "improper." Research gives partisans "confidence, removes lingering doubts, and provides an edge in the continuing debate."

The political use of research is similar to the informational function presented earlier. The partisan use of a study also provides information to users, with the difference that the information is now being used as political ammunition. The problem for political partisans is to overcome their adversaries, not to promote a fuller understanding of the issue at hand.

Research is put to a number of other well-established political uses. One is to delay taking action. The skilled politician who wishes to postpone making a decision may decide instead to appoint a committee to study the problem, hoping that by the time the study is completed the controversy will have died down. Or policy makers may use research as a means of shifting responsibility for unpopular decisions away from themselves and onto objective research data. Some executives or politicians fund a study because they have strong reason to hope that the results will prove embarrassing to their adversaries, or they may commission a study because they expect the results to enhance their own reputation as well as that of the program they direct.

Research can also be used symbolically to legitimate the organization sponsoring the research to groups that are imporatnt for its survival. Organizations that wish to gain support and approval strive to incorporate the dominant values of a society. Since research is fair-minded and forward-looking and represents progress and accomplishment, research is often used to boldly advertise the legitimacy of an organization and underscore its claim for continued support (Meyer and Rowan, 1977).

Finally, research is used to generate further research. Someday a graduate student may be persuaded to scan the research literature and count the number of times investigators report that the results should be accepted with caution and that further research on the subject is needed. In the first case, replication of the study is in order; in the second, a new study is recommended that builds on the previous one. In both cases, the investigators have issued a call for additional research.

Different Models of Research

Social work practitioners are currently presented with five major models of research utilization (Rosenblatt, 1981a, 1981b). Some models use research *methods* to conduct practice; and some use research *findings* to guide practice. At one extreme, research is peripheral to most social work activities. At the other, it is an essential, integral element. Between these two extremes are a number of possible approaches.

Direct Practice as Research Project. Approximately sixty years ago, Mary Richmond stressed the centrality of research for social work practice. As Martin Bloom indicates in Chapter Twenty-five, Richmond outlines in her book *Social Diagnosis* the manner in which direct service is guided by the careful gathering and analysis of evidence about individual cases (Richmond, 1965). Thus, even in the earliest days of the profession, individual clinical research was recognized as an important part of social work practice. The case-study approach received additional support from the psychoanalytic movement, which stressed the detailed study of clinical evidence as an integral part of intervention.

The same orientation still prevails in the profession. Both practice and research are based on verifiable information. Practitioners use research methods to obtain and process information and rely on scientific procedures to interpret information, make decisions, and report findings (Thomas, 1975). Several authors have recently argued that every case should be a research project for the practitioner and that the processes of practice and research are similar (Wood, 1978; Minahan, 1979).

Research Techniques as Therapy. In this book, the integration of research into direct practice has been extended one step further. Certain basic techniques of research—counting, measuring, and graphically representing change—can themselves become an essential part of the practitioner's stock in trade (Hudson, 1978). In fact, as Fischer and Hudson argue in Chapter Thirty, the use of measurement in clinical practice is inescapable. Any time a social worker notes a client's progress, stability, or deterioration, an act of measurement is being performed. They contend that an important aspect of good clinical practice is the accurate measurement of the client's problem and the outcome of treatment.

Often clinicians ask clients to monitor their own behavior and record critical events in their lives. This involvement of the client in the measurement process may be an essential aspect of the therapeutic strategy. Although, as Fischer and Hudson indicate, the act of measurement itself, rather than the treatment, may induce behavioral change, such measurement reactivity may in some cases be therapeutically helpful.

Clinical Scientists. Despite its claims to be scientifically based, social work has produced few clinical scientists (Briar, 1979). The clinical scientist model seeks to heal the split between researchers and practitioners and to unite good practice and good research in the same person.

Clinical scientists are practitioners who do much more than use the techniques of research in practice and go considerably beyond the use of normal case studies and routine practices. They continuously and rigorously evaluate their practice, using only those methods and techniques empirically known to be most effective.

Untested or unvalidated methods are used cautiously and only with adequate control and evaluation. Through the use of a variety of research strategies described by Levy in Chapter Twenty-six, the clinical scientist participates in the discovery, testing, and reporting of more effective ways of helping clients (Briar, 1979).

One of the anticipated advantages of this blend of practice and research is the accelerated development of knowledge utilization within social work. Ideally, clinical scientists are to undertake small studies of practice, with results that have direct, immediate utility for practitioners. A second advantage is the "evaluation of practice that could be incorporated into the routine practice of social work clinicians generally" (Briar, 1979).

To capitalize on these advantages, clinicians must be knowledgeable about the available research designs for use in practice. Levy in Chapter Twenty-six describes the variety of single-subject methods that may be employed, cautioning that single-subject research is not a fixed procedure, but rather a collection of procedures from which clinicians may choose to meet their needs within each case.

In Chapter Twenty-nine, William Reid extends this discussion by illustrating how experimental designs can be used creatively to develop effective practice interventions. He contends that experiments should not be conceived of as narrow, controlled, equivalent group designs but argues instead for a broad conception of experimental social work, one in which a wide variety of experimental approaches can be used to build practice technology.

Consumers of Research. Taking a radically different tack from the other three models mentioned, the research-consumer model makes no attempt to incorporate the methods of research into practice. Its advocates expect direct-service practitioners to become consumers of research, not research practitioners.

At present, most social work graduates learn only the most elementary knowledge about research and its methods. Graduates of some schools of social work have completed only one course in research and, when they become practitioners, are ill equipped to conduct a research study. Few employers of these graduates harbor any expectations about their research capabilities. Nor are graduates of many schools equipped to "consume" research—that is, to read a report intelligently. Consequently, it is difficult for practitioners to derive any of the benefits presumed to result from reading research studies that bear upon clinical practice.

A major goal of the consumer model is to raise the research sophistication of social workers. Those trained in accordance with this model should learn to read studies intelligently and to make appropriate applications of research findings. Tripodi, Fellin, and Meyer (1969) have attempted to set forth principles and guidelines that facilitate research utilization.

Edward Mullen, in Chapter Twenty-eight, takes the process one step further and describes one method by which clinicians can use research and other sources of information in developing practice guidelines to be integrated into personal practice models. His discussion highlights the complexities of the research-consumer model, demonstrating that the use of research is an interactive, creative process, rather than a mechanical application of findings.

Research Specialists. The research specialist model accepts research as a basic method of social work practice. Years of education and practice are required for a social worker to become proficient in research. As evident in Wallace Gingerich's chapter on testing for statistical significance, assessing client change—so basic for all clinicians—requires substantial knowledge of both applied and experimental significance. Becoming proficient in clinical measurement, design, and significance testing may indeed be as complex and as demanding as acquiring expertness in any clinical method of social work.

From this perspective, it is appropriate for schools of social work to train research specialists. In 1972, however, most schools of social work generally assigned a low priority to such training (Zimbalist, 1974). Also, comparatively few students choose to specialize in social work research at the master's level. Although some changes have occurred since then, a 1978 survey reported that only 29 percent of graduate social work programs rated production of research as of high importance for M.S.W. students (Rubin and Zimbalist, 1979). The research specialist model appears to foster a division between research and practice. If some are to become research specialists, then clinicians specializing in practice can reduce their commitment to this aspect of the profession. Similarly, those electing to become research specialists often reduce their commitment to clinical practice.

Conclusion

All five of the models identified in this Introduction acknowledge the contribution of scientific research but differ in the extent to which research is viewed as an essential part of practice. The first three models propose the almost total interpenetration, as well as the complete congruence, of research and practice. As Wood (1978, p. 455) argues, "Every case can and should be a research project for the practitioner." Indeed, according to these models, the ideal professional career consists of research, practice, and teaching. In fact, however, most clinical practitioners are unlikely to become well grounded in both research and practice.

Some years ago, Robert Merton (1963) identified three components of the social roles assigned to persons engaged in scientific research: "The role of workers in basic research has distinctive characteristics: (a) it provides them with relative autonomy in selecting the problems on which they will work; (b) it gives them . . . latitude . . . to shift from these initial problems to others turning up in the course of the inquiry, which they find more interesting or promising; and, (c) in this role, the primary 'reference groups' . . . are made up primarily of fellow scientists, with nonscientists entering only at a distant remove" (p. 87).

The role of clinical practitioner was never designed to meet these criteria. It makes little sense to talk of clinicians having autonomy to make decisions over the problems they choose to study, since these clinicians are usually available to all clients needing help at a social agency. Clinicians have no power to refuse service to clients because they prefer to investigate other problems. To pose such alternatives is to show a lack of familiarity with the role of the clinical social worker, whose essential purpose is to help those in need, not to study them. Following Merton, we distinguish between study for the purpose of helping and study for the purpose of contributing to knowledge. For this reason, researchers and clinical social workers arrive at separate, often conflicting priorities.

In Chapter Twenty-seven, Edwin Thomas elaborates on some of these potential research–service conflicts as they relate to objectives, criteria of change, independent variables, phases, target responses, and professional roles. More importantly, he outlines some of the alternative strategies for minimizing these conflicts.

Researchers are enjoined by the norms of science to engage in organized skepticism. "The temporary suspension of judgment and the detached scrutiny of beliefs in terms of empirical and logical criteria have periodically involved science in conflict with other institutions. Science which asks questions of fact, including potentialities, concerning every aspect of nature and society may come into conflict with other attitudes toward these same data which have been crystallized and often ritualized by other institutions" (Ben-David, 1971, p. 24). Researchers must remain skeptical. "They do not preserve the cleavage between the sacred and the profane, between that which requires uncritical respect and that which can be objectively analyzed" (Merton, 1959, pp. 537-549). This stance often brings them into conflict with clinicians and administrators. The goal of researchers is to extend knowledge and to certify its truth. Clinicians must suspend the organized skepticism of the scientist in order to adhere to the practices of their profession.

Professions such as medicine and law have little expectation that most practitioners will conduct practice research. This expectation is probably affected by the structure of service delivery in these professions, which is predominantly private. Salaried professionals employed in the public sector have a greater stake in the development of practice, given their dependence on public funding, as well as a greater opportunity to assist in the development of knowledge, given their organizational base.

Certifying truth and helping those in need are both noble pursuits. Yet scientists and clinicians within the same profession make invidious comparisons. Which should command higher respect? Which, greater resources? The strain between them results in part from such unnecessary competition. This long, inglorious struggle is best avoided in the future. Society needs the contributions of both clinicians and scientists. The time has come for both sides to recognize the contributions of each one to the profession and to bend their efforts to establishing ways of working together. Clinicians should respect their own ability to alleviate pain and restore lost capacity, and researchers should value their own ability to certify truth—without in any way demeaning one another's capabilities. Society needs the contributions of both scientists and clinicians.

References

Austin, D. "Research and Social Work: Educational Paradoxes and Possibilities." *Journal of Social Service Research,* 1978, *2* (2), 159-176.

Ben-David, J. *The Scientist's Role in Society: A Comparative Study.* Englewood Cliffs, N.J.: Prentice-Hall, 1971.

Briar, S. "Incorporating Research into Education for Clinical Practice in Social Work: Toward a Clinical Science in Social Work." In A. Rubin and A. Rosenblatt (Eds.), *Sourcebook on Research Utilization.* New York: Council on Social Work Education, 1979.

Caplan, N., Morrison, A., and Stambaugh, R. *The Use of Social Science Knowledge in Policy Decisions at the National Level.* Ann Arbor: Institute for Social Research, University of Michigan, 1970.

Casselman, B. L. "On the Practitioner's Orientation Toward Research." *Smith College Studies in Social Work,* 1972, *42,* 211-233.

Eaton, J. W. "Symbolic and Substantive Evaluative Research." *Administrative Science Quarterly,* 1962, *6,* 421-442.

Goode, W. "The Theoretical Limits of Professionalism." In A. Etzioni (Ed.), *The Semi-Professions and Their Organizations.* New York: Free Press, 1969.

Hudson, W. "Research Training in Professional Social Work Education." *Social Service Review,* 1978, *1,* 116-121.

Kirk, S., and Rosenblatt, A. "Barriers to Students' Utilization of Research." Paper presented at annual program meeting of the Council on Social Work Education, Phoenix, Ariz., 1977.

Kirk, S., and Rosenblatt, A. "Research Knowledge and Orientation Among Social Work Students." In S. Briar, H. Weissman, and A. Rubin (Eds.), *Research Utilization in Social Work Education.* New York: Council on Social Work Education, 1981.

Kirk, S., Osmalov, M. J., and Fischer, J. "Social Workers' Involvement in Research." *Social Work,* 1976, *21,* 121–124.

Merton, R. K. "Science and Democratic Social Structure." *Social Structure and Anomie.* Glencoe, Ill.: Free Press, 1959.

Merton, R. K. "Basic Research and Potentials of Relevance." *American Behavioral Scientists,* 1963, *6* (9), 86–90.

Meyer, J. W., and Rowan, B. "Institutional Organizations: Formal Structure as Myth and Ceremony." *American Journal oj Sociology,* 1977, *83* (2), 340–363.

Minahan, A. "Specifying Curriculum Goals for Research in Social Work Education." In A. Rubin and A. Rosenblatt (Eds.), *Sourcebook on Research Utilization.* New York: Council on Social Work Education, 1979.

Polansky, N. "Theory Construction and the Scientific Method." In N. Polansky (Ed.), *Social Work Research.* (Rev. ed.) Chicago: University of Chicago Press, 1977.

Richmond, M. *Social Diagnosis.* New York: Free Press, 1965. (Originally published 1917.)

Rosenblatt, A. "The Practitioner's Use and Evaluation of Research." *Social Work,* 1968, *13,* 53-59.

Rosenblatt, A. "The Utilization of Research in Social Work Practice." In N. Gilbert and H. Specht (Eds.), *Handbook of the Social Services.* Englewood Cliffs, N.J.: Prentice-Hall, 1981a.

Rosenblatt, A. "Models of Research Utilization in Social Work Education." In S. Briar, H. Weissman, and A. Rubin (Eds.), *Research Utilization in Social Work Education.* New York: Council on Social Work Education, 1981b.

Rosenblatt, A., Welter, M., and Wojciechowski, S. *The Adelphi Experiment.* New York: Council on Social Work Education, 1975.

Rothman, J. *Planning and Organizing for Social Change: Action Principles from Social Science Research.* New York: Columbia University Press, 1974.

Rubin, A., and Zimbalist, S. "Trends in the M.S.W. Research Curriculum: A Decade Later." New York: Council on Social Work Education, 1979.

Shyne, A. "Exploiting Available Information." In N. Polansky (Ed.), *Social Work Research.* (Rev. ed.) Chicago: University of Chicago Press, 1977.

Simpson, R. "Is Research Utilization for Social Workers?" *Journal of Social Service Research,* 1978, *2* (2), 143–157.

Suchman, E. *Evaluative Research.* New York: Russell Sage Foundation, 1967.

Thomas, E. J. "Use of Research Methods in Interpersonal Practice." In N. A. Polansky (Ed.), *Social Work Research.* (Rev. ed.) Chicago: University of Chicago Press, 1975.

Thorne, B. "Professional Education in Law" and "Professional Education in Medicine." In E. Hughes and others (Eds.), *Education for the Professions of Medicine, Law, Theology, and Social Welfare.* New York: McGraw-Hill, 1973.

Tripodi, T. *Uses and Abuses of Social Research in Social Work.* New York: Columbia University Press, 1974.

Tripodi, T., Felling, P., and Meyer, H. *The Assessment of Social Research.* Itasca, Ill.: Peacock, 1969.

Turem, J. "Research Priorities in Social Work Education: A Communication to Colleagues." In A. Rubin and A. Rosenblatt (Eds.), *Sourcebook on Research Utilization.* New York: Council on Social Work Education, 1979.

Weed, S. P., and Greenwald, S. R. "The Mystics of Statistics." *Social Work,* 1973, *18,* 113–115.

Weiss, C. *Evaluation Research.* Englewood Cliffs, N.J.: Prentice-Hall, 1972.

Weiss, C. "Introduction." In C. Weiss (Ed.), *Using Social Research in Public Policy Making.* Lexington, Mass.: Lexington Books, 1977.

Witkin S., Edleson, J., and Lindsey, D. "Social Workers and Statistics: Preparation, Attitudes and Knowledge." *Journal of Social Service Research,* 1980, *3* (3), 313–322.

Wood, K. "Casework Effectiveness: A New Look at the Research Evidence." *Social Work,* 1978, *23* (6), 437–459.

Zimbalist, S. E. *Historic Themes and Landmarks in Social Welfare Research.* New York: Harper & Row, 1977.

Zimbalist, S. E. "The Research Component of the Master's Degree Curriculum in Social Work: A Survey Summary." *Journal of Education for Social Work,* 1974, *10* (1), 118–123.

25

Empirically Based Clinical Research

Martin Bloom

This chapter will review some of the major concepts and assumptions of empirically based clinical research in order to present a frame of reference for subsequent discussions in this section of the book. This will be a bringing together of many of the threads of past efforts that led to the present fabric of our scientific endeavors in clinical research, and these, in turn, may perhaps offer a hint of fashions to come.

Definitions of Terms

The genre of evaluative procedures discussed in this chapter has many labels: "single-case experimental designs" (Hersen and Barlow, 1976); "single-subject research" (Kratochwill, 1978); "quasi-experimental time-series designs" (Campbell and Stanley, 1963; Cook and Campbell, 1976); "intensive research designs" (Chassan, 1967, 1979); "N=1 research designs" (Davidson and Costello, 1969); "practitioner-researcher designs" (Broxmeyer, 1978); "within-subject designs" (Mahoney, 1978); "idiographic studies" (Jayaratne and Thompson, 1977). Bloom and Fischer (1982) recommend the general term "single-system designs" as more suitable for the evalutive research conducted by helping professionals dealing with a wide array of concerns, including individuals (Levy and Olson, 1979), groups and families (Witkin and Harrison, 1979; Mutschler, 1979), and organizations or other collectivities (Tripodi and Harrington, 1979). Although these designations of evaluative procedures imply some differences, the similarities among them are more relevant, in contrasting them with the dominant research model, the experimental control-group design. Table 1 presents some distinguishing differences, as well as some similarities, between single-system and group designs.

Single-system designs most commonly involve the repeated collection over time of objective information on a single system, as well as a plan for the logical comparison of data between intervention and nonintervention phases. This chapter will attempt to explicate the meaning and usefulness of these attributes of the single-system design, in comparison with those of the classical experimental control-group design. This group design ordinarily consists of the collection of objective information on a large number of subjects on a small number of occasions, as well as a comparison between a randomly selected experimental group that has received some special intervention and a control group that has received none.

Examining the history of social-psychological research may prove helpful in highlighting the issues and assumptions in the development of single-system designs, a major alternative to the classical approach to research. Yet the objective of this chapter is not to emphasize the conflict between these two approaches but to facilitate their coordinated use (Jayaratne, 1977).

The terms used to refer to practitioners of single-system designs—including such labels as "empirically guided practitioner" (Thomas, 1975), "clinical scientist" (Briar, 1977), "clinical researcher" (Jayaratne and Thompson, 1977), and "caseworker-researcher" (Howe, 1974)—are also important, for they provide insight into the philosophy of empirically based clinical research. I have chosen the term "scientific practitioner" (Bloom, 1975). These many labels clearly imply the unity of the two roles in the integral scientific practitioner, who is committed to both the understanding/knowledge-building aspect of science and the understanding/knowledge-using aspect of practice. Such a practitioner places equal emphasis on values and evaluation and shows a balanced concern for the particular (this client-system, here and now) and the general (this type of client-system, whenever the need arises).

This dual allegiance is not without its problems (Thomas, 1978), but the scientific practitioner concept accepts these potential conflicts and adapts creatively to their challenge. The ultimate goal of the scientific practitioner is effective, efficient, and humane practice through the application of the scientific method in the ongoing evaluation of intervention.

Historical Review of Issues and Accomplishments in Clinical Research

The past 100 years have witnessed the alternating ascendancy of two main approaches to understanding human behavior and to assessing the effects of therapeutic interventions. On the one hand, the individual—idiographic (Allport, 1961), intensive (Chassan, 1967, 1979)—approaches have sought to characterize the unique variations in human development and behavior, with particular emphasis on intrapersonal reactions to various stimuli, including therapeutic effects. Chassan (1967, p. 181) emphasizes the statistical aspects of symptom fluctuation within a given client: "Such variability is the basis of defining the patient-state in terms of statistical distributions, or probabilities, estimated from sequences of observations of a given patient and consequently provides the framework for the applica-

Table 1. Comparison Between Single-System Designs and Experimental Control Group Designs

Characteristic	*Single-System Designs*	*Experimental Control Group Designs*
1. Number of client systems involved	One individual, group, or collectivity. Data may reflect interpersonal involvements, for example, number of arguments with spouse.	At least two groups involved. Ideally, these groups are randomly selected from a common population and possibly stratified to control for intersubject variability.
2. Number of attributes measured	Limited to a number feasibly collected by the client, worker, or others. Usually a large number of issues are assessed before selecting the specific targets, which are few in number.	Variable, depending on purpose of the study. Usually a medium-to-large number of items are asked of a large number of persons by research interviewers.
3. Number of measures used for each attribute	Variable. Ideally, multiple measures of the same attribute would be used (cf. Cook and Campbell, 1976).	Variable. Ideally, multiple measures of the same attribute would be used (cf. Campbell and Fiske, 1959).
4. Number of times measures are repeated	Data are collected frequently in regular intervals before, during, and sometimes after the intervention. Assumes variability in behavior (cf. Chassen, 1967, 1979)	Data are collected only a few times, usually once before and once after intervention. Assumes relative staticness in human behavior, which may be representatively sampled in research.
5. Duration of research	Variable, depending on whether time-limited services are provided, wherein the duration is fixed, or an open-ended service is given.	Fixed time periods are usually used.
6. Choice of goals of research	Goals usually chosen by the client, and agreed to and made operationally clear by the worker.	Goals usually chosen by the researcher, occasionally in consultation with funding agency or community representatives; rarely by the participants themselves.
7. Choice of research design and its review by others for ethical suitability	The worker usually selects the particular design and receives no professional review, except perhaps by the practice supervisor.	The researcher chooses the design but usually has to submit the design and instrumentation to peer review (for example, by a human subjects review committee).

8. Feedback	Feedback is a vital ingredient of single-system designs; it is immediately forthcoming as progress is monitored, and the service program be modified accordingly. This permits the study of process as well as outcome. Systematic recording opportunities are present (Chassan, 1967, 1979).	There is almost no feedback in the group design until the entire project is completed, lest such information influence events under study. Little information is given about process in studies of outcome.
9. Changes in research design	Changes are permitted, albeit with risks. Any set of interventions can be described as a "design," but some designs are logically stronger than others. Flexibility of design is a major characteristic of single-system designs.	Changes in research design are not permitted. Fixed methods are used as exactly as possible across subjects. Standardized instruments and trained interviewers are often employed.
10. Use of theory as guide to practice	Variable. In ideal form, some clear conceptual rationale is used to give meaning to the set of operational procedures.	Variable. In ideal form, some clear hypotheses are derived from a theory that gives direction to the entire project.
11. Use of comparison groups in arriving at the evaluation	It is assumed that the relatively stable baseline period would continue were the intervention not made. Therefore, the single-system design serves as its "own control" by comparing outcomes from the intervention period with the preintervention baseline.	Ideally, a control or contrast group is randomly selected from a common population on the assumption that such a group would represent what would probably have occurred to the experimental group had the intervention not been made.
12. Reliability	Usually achieved by having a second observer make ratings, where possible. Internal consistency used with self-report measures, along with conventional tests where standardized instruments are used.	All the basic methods of measuring reliability can be used, including reliability of tests (test-retest, alternative forms, split-half) and observer agreements.
13. Validity	The closeness of the measures, especially direct measures, to the ultimate criteria increases the opportunity for validity; various pressures toward distortion in reporting decrease that opportunity.	All basic methods of measuring validity can be used; including face validity; context validity; criterion (concurrent) validity (Kerlinger, 1979).
14. Utility of findings for intervention	Direct and immediate; may include involvement of client as well as worker in collecting and interpreting data and modifying intervention.	Indirect; probably will not affect subjects of the present project but may be useful for the class of subjects (or problems) involved.

Table 1. Comparison Between Single-System Designs and Experimental Control Group Designs *(Continued)*

Characteristic	*Single-System Designs*	*Experimental Control Group Designs*
15. Targets of intervention and measurement	Ideally, should be important life events, but single-system designs are susceptible to trivialization in choice of targets. Emphasis is on knowledge for use, but some efforts concern knowledge-building issues.	Variable, depending on the purpose of the study. Can include important life events or targets of theoretical interest (and low practice utility). Emphasis is more likely to be on knowledge for knowledge building, but with some concern with knowledge for use.
16. Kinds of data obtained	a. Descriptive data on the system in question, providing norms for that system b. Change scores for that system c. If the design permits, inferences of causal or functional relationships between independent and dependent variables (but susceptible to many alternative explanations for given outcomes) (cf. Kratochwill, 1978)	a. Descriptive data, providing normative information b. Change scores, grouped or averaged, thus masking individual patterns of change (Chassan, 1967, 1979) c. Experimental designs provide strong logical bases for inference of causality (cf. Campbell and Stanley, 1963; Cook and Campbell, 1976)
17. Costs	Relatively low. A small amount of time and energy must be expended in designing the evaluation and carrying it out, but this may be routinized as part of the empirically guided practice itself. Essentially a do-it-yourself operation.	Relatively high. Most group designs require research specialists separate from the practitioners involved, as well as expenses for data collection, analysis, and report writing. Computers are often involved.
18. Relationship of values in the research	Clients' values are incorporated in the choice of targets and goal-setting procedures. Workers remain "agents of society" in accepting or modifying these goals and helping clients to attain them.	Researchers or funders control the values expressed in the research—the goals, instruments, designs, and interpretations.
19. Limitations	Statistical and logical considerations and limitations (such as generalization) are not yet well explicated; indeed, there are many differences of opinion among specialists in the field. A large body of exemplary research is not readily available for social work practitioners to model.	Problems remain with social workers' reading, understanding, and using scientific information from group designs (cf. Kirk, 1977). Ethical issues (for example, withholding treatment from controls) are still not resolved among practitioners, and minority resistance to large-scale

		research is increasing. The findings of therapeutic-effectiveness studies involving group designs are ambiguous (Wood, 1978; Fischer, 1978; Smith, Glass, and Miller, 1980; Reid and Hanrahan, 1982)
20. Prospects	Optimistic. The literature on single-system designs is expanding rapidly (see Hersen and Barlow, 1976). Freedom from major funding needs and the relative simplicity of the task—and the teaching of the task—may stimulate more clinical research and evaluation with the single-system design. It is not potentially possible for every social worker to evaluate every case situation on every occasion.	Optimistic. Greater care in selecting populations and problems seems likely. Funding of large-scale research suffers in times of economic scarcity. The new social work research journals should stimulate communication of current social work research, as well as the rediscovery of relevant research in other literatures.

tion of statistical inference and experimental design to the data of the individual patient."

On the other hand, collective—nomothetic (Allport, 1961), extensive (Chassan, 1967, 1978)—approaches use group comparisons to test hypotheses across persons and assume that randomization of large numbers of persons into groups makes them more or less homogeneous with respect to the outcome variables (Campbell and Stanley, 1963). However, the larger the number of persons involved in the research, the greater the likelihood for increasing the variation in the attributes under study (Chassan, 1967, p. 109), making homogeneous groupings less probable. Exactly at this point—when the experimenter cannot control all events—complex designs are necessary to permit the use of powerful statistical methods for the analysis of data.

Although a history of the alternation of individual and collective approaches to clinical research in psychology is the context for the present discussion, a full description of this history is beyond the scope of this chapter. (See a brief summary in Table 2, in which the major events in psychological research and critical thinking are listed.) However, the developments in clinical social work research may be usefully described to highlight current trends and issues.

Early Theory and Research. Social work has always had its individual and collective perspectives on the nature of its professional purpose. The Charity Organization Society of the late nineteenth century was established in part as a means of bringing order to the chaos into which charity had fallen, with special emphasis on ways to determine who was to be eligible for the limited assistance—hence, an individual perspective was needed. This was to be "scientific charity," a combination of humanitarian impulses and a deep trust in scientific and rational solutions to complex social problems (Zimbalist, 1977). Schools of social work emerged as places to train workers to ask the kinds of questions that would enable them to understand the individual client through a detailed investigation of his or her background. The answers to these questions stimulated ideas about the best way to rehabilitate the client, which were then subjectively and privately tested in practice and revised as needed, until some workable or pragmatic solution was achieved. Mary Richmond's *Social Diagnosis* (1917) codified this multiple-causation approach, reflecting a medical/disease model combined with a legal emphasis on evidence. Thus, both a fledgling practice and a nascent individual clinical research began to emerge from a common matrix. They were not without their early critics, however, as social reformers with a collective perspective objected to petty and subjective calculations of individual characteristics that seemed irrelevant and biased.

Marx and other social theorists began to delineate the social forces that produced the poverty and misery in the industrial towns of Western Europe and America. Charles Booth's studies of the London working classes documented the extent of this poverty and demonstrated once again (Chadwick had marshalled epidemiological statistics in his sanitation reform efforts a generation earlier) that research data could have an impact on society. But perhaps most important in the long run was the impact of these data on theorists and practitioners dealing with collective forms of individual misery. The settlement house movement took shape as the results from early social surveys filtered back into society through its intellectual elites. The Fabians and other social philosophers began speculating on the

Table 2. Major Trends In Clinical Research in Psychology over the Past One Hundred Years

1800s:	Rechner, Wundt, Titchener, and Ebbinghaus initiated a variety of scientific approaches to the study of the single organism (Boring, 1950). At the same time, group comparison studies derived from work on individual differences (Quetelet, Darwin, and later, Galton and Pearson) and epidemiology (Farr, Snow, and Simon) generating descriptive statistics proved to be socially important. (See, Susser, 1973.)
1900–1910:	In the early years of this century, Galton, Pearson, Binet, and J. M. Cattell expanded the group-comparison approach with continuing developments in statistics.
1910–1920:	Binet's intelligence tests were used during World War II with millions of military inductees. The popularization of statistical techniques followed.
1920–1930:	Psychoanalysis became the predominant psychotherapy in the 1920s and resisted the application of contemporary research methods. Experimental clinical behaviorism began.
1930–1940:	Fisher developed sophisticated statistical procedures (inferential statistics) for group comparison designs. Learning theories and behavioral research continued to develop, but with little clinical application.
1940–1950:	The scientist-practitioner model emerged, stemming from clinical psychologists who were also trained in research (Chassan 1967). Comparative outcome studies of psychotherapy began.
1950–1960:	Rogerian therapy was developed, with research incorporated. Clinical behaviorism also began, with single-subject designs as the major evaluation tool (Shapiro, 1957). Critics of psychotherapeutic effectiveness began to raise questions about practice methods (Eysenck, 1952; Levitt, 1957), and professional conferences were held on the evaluation of psychotherapy. Allport called for idiographic research, and naturalistic studies began at the Menninger Clinic (Wallerstein, 1963).
1960–1970:	Scientist-practitioner split occurred, leading to the "flight-to-process" research (as contrasted with outcome research). Behavior modification and the experimental analysis of behavior became increasingly popular, and specialized journals and conferences were generated. Campbell and Stanley's (1963) seminal book on experimental and quasi-experimental research designs included a discussion on threats to internal validity and to generalizability. Sidman's (1960) text on experimental methodology made single-system designs creditable in psychology; Chassan (1967) developed intensive designs within a psychotherapy and drug context. Dukes (1965) reviewed some two-hundred single case studies that had appeared over a quarter of a century.
1970–1980:	Bergin and Strupp (1970, 1972) called for the cessation of comparison-group outcome studies in favor of single-system designs. Sophisticated statistical procedures for single-system designs were developed (Box and Jenkins, 1970; Glass, Willson, and Gottman, 1975; Kazdin, 1976). Kratochwill identified threats to internal validity and to generalizability for single-system designs explicitly. Major books of review and analysis appeared, including Hersen and Barlow (1976) and Kratochwill (1978).

etiology of the documented conditions and offering solutions to them. The social reformers, often emerging from among the settlement workers themselves, dominated the social work scene, taking collective approaches to social problems and, on occasion, using collective indicators of the scope of problems and reforms. Once again, collective practice and large-scale research emerged, in their beginning stages, from a common ground. However, the great upheaval of World War I and its aftermath turned back social reforms in favor of more conservative, individualistic policies and practices. The ascendancy shifted as the use of psychoanalytic theory, with its emphasis on the individual's unconscious conflicts, began to spread among social workers.

Case-Study Approach. The 1920s was the era of the case-study approach. Social work became casework, and casework became psychiatric casework. The case approach merits careful study, because it involves some of the problems, as well as the promise, of single-system designs. First, it was a study, a careful and sensitive appraisal of the complex problems of a human being within numerous psychological and, to some extent, social contexts. This type of study derived from the best empirical traditions—after all, Freud was a neurophysiologist and a first-rate empiricist. It recognized the enormous number of active variables in human affairs and sought to find underlying patterns that made them comprehensible, if not predictable and potentially controllable. Second, the case-study approach was changeable—at least in the hands of a scientifically minded practitioner like Freud, who modified major portions of his conceptualization and his methods over time, as new observations required. Third, case study methods generated ideas for conceptual and practical speculation, dealing with rare events in unfettered (experimental) ways, trying always to grasp the underlying configurations that were the key to understanding and control.

However, the very lack of control over the variables being observed, the types of observations being made, the lack of precise measures, the nonlogical arrangements of observations and interventions, and the subsequent analysis of resulting information made the case study a haven for biased practice that offered almost no opportunity for rigorous or logical determination of client change, let alone of the causation of problems. Often several interventive techniques were occurring simultaneously, so that, if any initial measures of the presenting problems were taken, the practitioner could at best distinguish only gross differences based on global impressions of a more than casually interested observer. Neither the state nor professional organizations exerted significant quality control on performance, so that case studies grew to predominant, though precarious, ascendancy.

Yet clear voices were calling for reconsideration. For example, Dr. Richard Cabot, in his presidential address to the National Conference of Social Work in 1931 (pp. 21–24), stated:

> I appeal to you, social workers of the country—(1) . . . measure, evaluate, estimate, appraise your results . . . in some form, in any terms that rest on something beyond faith, assertion, and "illustrative cases." State your objectives and how far you have reached them. . . . (2) Let time enough elapse so that there may be some reasonable hope of permanence in the results which you state. . . . (3) The greatest value of [evaluation of

> practice] will not be a comparison of worker with worker or agency with agency but an evaluation of one method against another, of one's own present work with one's past and one's hoped-for future. Out of such evaluations will come, I believe, better service to the client [by getting attention focused on at least a fair proportion of attainable goals and by finding better means of knowing when we are off the track that we meant to follow] but, still more, a better courage and confidence in the soul of each worker who will see better what she is about, wherein she is succeeding or failing, how she can do better.

Cabot's speech could be given today, nearly a half century later, with equal validity. Discussing not survey research or large-scale experimental designs but scientific study of single-case situations, he calls for the statement of specific client objectives; stability in the effects of intervention; comparisons between past and present work, which could be conceived in terms of preintervention and postintervention measures on one client-system, as well as earlier and later work with different clients; use of feedback by comparing case progress with defined goals; continuing education of the practitioner based on effectiveness of given techniques; and a concern for accountability in the broadest sense. This list also applies as a philosophy for using contemporary single-system designs in clinical research.

Reemergence of Collective Research. But Cabot's message did not arouse the profession into concerted efforts in individually oriented evaluation, not simply because the methodological procedures were lacking but also because the Great Depression obscured all other concerns. Along with this enormous social trauma came the reemergence of collective research, not only in the social surveys used earlier in the century but also in the collection of social statistics and indexes, as well as in evaluative research projects (Zimbalist, 1977). The social surveys began as attempts to gauge the needs of the community and of the relevant interest groups involved, but they evolved into partisan attempts to publicize these findings and to stimulate social change by means of one large-scale study of the social welfare needs of a community. The scientific basis of these surveys took second place to their value objectives and hence were the subject of much criticism inside and outside the profession. Eventually the large-scale studies were replaced with more focused projects, often with community participation (self-studies) (Zimbalist, 1977).

Social indexes had unintended effects in the collecting of uniform sets of social statistics for administrative and planning purposes. Zimbalist (1977) describes their checkered development, in which such indexes were used in an attempt to reflect "social breakdown" through official records of divorce, delinquency, and so on. He points out technical weaknesses in these data-collection procedures, including the arbitrary selection of items and their subjective weighting, the heterogeneity of the demographic areas studied, and the subjective conceptualization of social need (Zimbalist, 1977). However, indexes continue to be developed and expanded—social indicators are the latest version of such indexes—as the need for administrative and planning information continues.

Of particular interest from the perspective of collective research is the emergence of large-scale evaluative research during the Depression and its continuing increase in our own day. For example, Reed's (1931) problem-centered approach—akin to contemporary Goal Attainment Scaling (Kiresuk and Sherman, 1977; Seaberg and Gillespie, 1977)—applied a rating system to case summaries, including such items as "accomplishment—extent to which the objectives of treatment were achieved (on a scale from −100 to +100)" (Zimbalist, 1977, p. 253). The Cambridge-Somerville Delinquency Prevention Project, originally conceived by Cabot but carried out by others following his death in 1939, was a model of experimental control-group design, although the exigencies of the war years necessitated modifications. However, the results were largely negative—the service program did not prevent the experimental youth from having higher rates of delinquency than the controls, even though the control group committed more serious crimes, on the average (cf. McCord, 1978).

Research at the Community Service Society. After the war, large-scale projects continued to be developed, but an important individually oriented research effort also took place. In the early 1940s, about a half century since its inception, the Community Service Society of New York (CSS) (a metamorphosed Charity Organization Society) initiated a study "to determine and express how casework is carried on, at what cost, and with what success" (Klein, 1968, p. 188). These efforts, stemming from the work of a sociologist-psychologist team (Dollar and Mowrer, 1947), led to the development of a new quantitative procedure—the Distress-Relief Quotient—to measure reduction of client tension during the course of intervention. This tool was based on the learning principle that the reduction of tension aids learning because it is rewarding; hence, the client-worker context could be monitored by assessing the levels of client tension over time (Zimbalist, 1977). Although this instrument had high interjudge reliability, its validity was doubtful, and methodological and conceptual problems were soon pointed out—for example, the measure was applied to a given page of case recording, assuming that client tension is suitably and representatively displayed in this fashion.

Such weaknesses led to another approach by psychologists at CSS, termed the Movement Scale (Hunt and Kogan, 1952), which became the most soundly developed and widely used instrument to date, a landmark in methodology in social work research (MacDonald, 1960). This instrument emerged out of attempts by caseworkers to assess four kinds of global movement or change in the individual client or his or her environment: changes in adaptive efficiency (such as in a client's ability to get along with other people or in his or her efficiency at work); changes in habits and conditions (such as those that involve a disabling personality trait or state of health); changes in attitudes and understanding (for instance, if a client verbalizes that he or she has come to accept other persons); and changes in environmental circumstances (such as moving to new living quarters) (Hunt and Kogan, 1952). Eventually detailed instructions were developed for the use of this instrument, including anchoring illustrations for each of the degrees of change from −2 through 0 to +4. (More degrees of positive change were used, as iatrogenic effects were not widely recognized in the helping professions at this time [cf. Stuart, 1970].) The elaborate training required to use the instrument reliably meant that its applications were mainly in research, rather than everyday practice, although interjudge (reliability) agreements on the movement scale were as high as 0.8 (Shyne, 1963).

Other Measures of Client Movement. Other measures have tended to replace the Movement Scale, which was limited to individuals and, even then, was still an indirect measure of client change—that is, workers' judgments were the actual data being manipulated by the scale. Moreover, no logical basis existed for inferring that the worker's efforts were the cause of observed differences in the client's situation from opening to closing.

Developments in the measurement of client movement continued. For example, Hetzler (1963) developed another type of evaluation scale for measuring case severity and case movement in public assistance, postulated on the idea that objective criteria are preferable to subjective ones and that specific topics should be considered, rather than broad classes of evidence. This scale contains fifty-seven items under seven headings: family environment, family health, physical and mental functioning, family sexual stability, employment, school progress, financial management, and home integration. The very completeness of this scale guides workers to gather systematic information and provides more nearly objective baseline information, but the scale is limited to public assistance settings and has a family focus; its annual or semiannual application provides limited information on the direction and degree of movement.

The more widely used Scale of Family Functioning developed by Geismar (1971) involves ratings of family functioning by pairs of judges using a seven-point scale ("totally inadequate" to "adequate"—thus skewed, four degrees out of seven, in the direction of pathology) on nine dimensions: family relationships, individual behavior, care and training of children, social activities, economic practice, household practices, health conditions, relation to worker, and community resources. Work on this instrument was intricately tied to practice concerns with the multiproblem family. Zimbalist (1977) reviews the history of this topic, including one critical turning point for single-system designs: Because of methodological and practical difficulties in conducting an experimental- and control-group design using the Scale of Family Functioning with multiproblem families, Geismar argued that the treatment group itself might be considered its "own control" because cases exhibit an extended history (or baseline) of various problems prior to treatment and then often improve noticeably during the intervention period (Zimbalist, 1977, p. 344). This is a statement of basics on single system design.

Like pieces in a large puzzle, many of the previous experiences in evaluation came together in the "Chemung County Evaluation of Casework Service to Dependent Multiproblem Families" (Wallace, 1967), subtitled "Another Problem Outcome." This large-scale investigation assessed the effects of intensive casework on a group of fifty multiproblem families. In comparison with a control group, the demonstration group had better trained workers, lower caseloads, greater access to community resources, and more frequent contact on the initiative of workers (Wallace, 1967, p. 384), yet the results did not significantly favor the experimental sample. This study was followed in turn by a study by Mullen, Chazin, and Feldstein (1972) that attempted to intervene with families earlier than in the Chemung County study, but again produced no significant evidence that the experimental service was more effective than the existing services provided to controls.

Apart from the problematic outcomes of these and other major social work projects, the important point for present purposes is that, in the Chemung County study, both the Hunt-Kogan and the Geismar scales were used with the same clients; indeed, two sets of rating judges were employed, and the results compared case by case. The results were very similar: "In more than 40 percent of the cases, the ratings were the same, while, in another 40 percent, the differences were no greater than one degree" (Wallace, 1967, p. 387). These results may mean that researchers had gone as far as possible in obtaining reliable observer ratings without involving clients directly in their own evaluation or using other approaches to clinical research. However, the validity of these social work research instruments, as well as the effectiveness of the practice, was not clearly demonstrated.

Critical Reaction. Just as major evaluative studies in psychology, sociology, and social work were appearing in great numbers, a critical reaction began. Eysenck's (1952) early controversial paper on the lack of effectiveness of psychotherapy with neurotic adults was followed by Levitt's (1957) paper indicating similar findings with neurotic children. These findings were later expanded upon by many others, including Bergin (1966); Gurman (1973); Luborsky, Singer, and Luborsky (1976); Meltzoff and Kornreich (1970); and Smith, Glass, and Miller (1980), as well as, in the social work field, Fischer (1973, 1976, 1978); Mullen, Dumpson, and Associates (1972); Geismar (1972); Wood (1978); Stuart (1970); and Reid and Hanrahan (1982).

More than simply a critical reading of outcomes, this reaction involved reconsideration of the group design as an appropriate tool for analysis of interventions. For example, Bergin and Strupp (1972, p. 440) wrote: "Among researchers as well as statisticians, there is a growing disaffection from traditional experimental designs and statistical procedures which are held inappropriate to the subject matter under study. . . . The exaggerated importance accorded experimental and statistical data cannot be blamed on the techniques proper, . . . but their veneration mirrors a prevailing philosophy among behavioral scientists which subordinates problems to methodology." These same writers called for a cessation of classical process and outcome studies and suggested "new directions in psychotherapy research" (Bergin and Strupp, 1970)—namely, what I am here terming single-system design. Only a few social work researchers have responded to this call for new approaches to evaluation of clinical practice.

These criticisms suggested that the best social-work practice did not produce significantly more favorable outcomes than standard practice across a range of client settings (Mullen, Dumpson, and Associates, 1972; Fischer, 1976)—although others argued strongly that these results were misleading (for example, Geismar, 1972; Wood, 1978). The "best practice" referred to was, at core, dynamically oriented (Simon, 1970). Two interesting implications emerged from these professional discussions. First, social workers began to pay increasing attention to the history and promise of behavioral approaches to intervention as generating a more respectable outcome record. Participants in these early efforts were few but significant, from Reynolds's (1925) involvement in the behaviorally oriented "habit clinics" of the mid-1920s to the important contributions of Thomas, Stuart, Carter, and others in the 1960s. The behaviorists were using single-organism studies from the beginning, and it was relatively easy to transfer these single-system designs to other content areas (cf. Hersen and Barlow, 1976; Kratochwill, 1978).

The second implication derived from the problematic outcomes of large-scale social work research projects was a feeling, voiced as early as the Cambridge-Somerville study, that workers thought they were successful whether the results from group designs supported their perceptions or not. This disillusionment with classical research results and the concomitant sense that something works in some cases readied the profession to consider single-system designs, perhaps as one more step in the professional quest to demonstrate solid empirical credentials of effectiveness and efficiency.

Analysis of the Historical Review in the Light of Single-System Designs

The basic theme underlying all of the efforts described in the previous section is the concern for constructing better ways to evaluate practice. Because of the complexity of human behavior, human values, and social events, perfect or final evaluation tools will probably never be found. It is as if each generation of researchers will identify what it takes to be of paramount importance in the study of human affairs and how these should be translated into, and out of, systems of mathematics. What tend to persist are the issues for which new (or rediscovered) solutions are proposed.

Randomization. Among the enduring issues of the recent past are several to which single-system designs offer new approaches. Whether one considers these approaches to be solutions depends on one's value judgments more than on any clear scientific criteria. One such issue concerns randomization in the classical research framework, in which each subject, with his or her unique life history and attributes, has an equal chance to fall into an experimental or a control group. With large samples, randomization is a vital and fundamental principle that has proved to be most fruitful for researchers. But, within small samples, a problem emerges: controls—from stratification of attributes to matching—are needed to ensure that randomization provides homogeneous samples prior to intervention. Otherwise, though randomly assigned, small experimental and control groups become divergent and therefore unworkable. But the more such controls are used, the less true randomization is permitted to operate. What is ideally needed is to have perfectly homogeneous small groups that are randomly assigned to treatments.

Single-system designs solve at least one part of this problem and offer a potential solution for the other part. By having the client act as his or her own control, researchers establish perfect homogeneity. And, to the degree that treatments can be assigned randomly to individual clients during the period of time when such interventions may be assumed to be equally effective, the other feature of the ideal measurement situation is achieved. But using one client as the focus of evaluation violates the spirit of randomization of large numbers of persons and the empirical structures built on this principle. Whether researchers will accept single-system designs as offering a complement to randomized research designs is unknown, not because the empirical credentials are lacking but because the dominant paradigm of research demands other approaches.

The classical research design uses randomization in order to compare averaged scores of groups of subjects, as if the central tendencies expressed in the data represent normative events—what happened to the typical person under defined conditions. Such information is very useful for administrators and planners, since typicalness is exactly what is needed in developing institutions serving ranges of people. The variability expressed around measures of a central tendency are also important to planners in designing the scope of services—what structured services can feasibly be made available to a given population. However, for the individual client, grouped or averaged data present a ready-made suit that is, more often than not, ill fitting. What, then, is the individual practitioner to do with normative data? Sarbin, Taft, and Bailey (1960) have offered some provocative advice (see also Bloom [1975] for a translation of this advice into social work terms) involving the formal syllogism: If all persons have *x* disease show symptoms *a, b,* and *c,* then a particular person *y* showing symptoms *a* and *c* fits the general class in two out of three ways, a probability of .67 that *y* will also respond to treatment devised to deal with disease *x*. As intriguing as this method may be, it still leaves many subjective decisions in the hands of the practitioner—weighting of symptoms, definition of disease *x*, identification of symptoms in client *y*, and so on—problems that have plagued evaluators from the Movement Scale to Goal Attainment Scaling.

Ideally, what is needed is a calculus of small numbers. The issue is to identify patterns of behaviors and characteristics in one client-system, including what is normative for that person—that is, his or her own norms of typical behaviors. These individual norms can be compared with group norms for applicability of interventions devised in relation to classes of persons, but the focus of clinical service is ultimately on the particular client-system, not on clients in general. Single-system design provides such a mathematical view of single client-systems, although it makes a critical assumption (most clearly articulated by Chassan, 1967) that what is being considered is a *population of attributes of one client-system over time,* as contrasted to a population of persons. This population idea allows the machinery of scientific probability to be applied. Thus, we arrive at the same point that Sarbin, Taft, and Bailey (1960) sought to reach, but without the elaborate set of assumptions needed to make their probability system work.

Classical group research usually deals with a once-before and a once-after measurement of a large number of persons as the basis of its logical, mathematical decisions. Single-system designs belong to the time-series approach that requires frequently collected baseline data in place of the control groups of the classical designs. Baseline becomes a mathematical equivalent of control groups and has to attain stability and clarity as the comparison point for later evaluation. If baseline data fluctuate wildly, if there are marked trends in the data before intervention begins, or if there are missing or suspicious (fraudulent) data, the potential for comparison is greatly reduced. In some cases, mathematical procedures, such as transformations of autocorrelated data (see Gottman and Leiblum, 1974), may attempt to compensate for these difficulties. But, as with any other research, one cannot make more of the data than the data contain. Assuming that reasonable baseline data are available—and no consensus exists on what is reasonable—the single-system design may be used with precise effect.

Precision in Single-System Designs. Precision is an important assumption in the employment of these single-system designs. The assumption is that one client-system can be precisely targeted—that is, that it is possible to explore a client situation and to identify a finite set of targets that the client wants changed in socially approved directions. The selection of targets is a critical juncture in single-system design. What is important and central to client problems should be the chosen targets, but they may not be amenable to change, especially the change that a worker can effect. Therefore, the set of targets must be chosen on the basis of theoretical meaningfulness and practical feasibility (Reid, 1978). This approach is no different than in group research, except that each individual client potentially has a unique set of such targets.

Likewise, each individual client-system may respond to a unique set of interventions. Classical group-evaluation projects have set interventions with clients—albeit often vaguely defined ones, such as "social work." The specificity of targets in single-system design makes it more feasible to require detailed interventions suitable for particular targets. Therefore, the independent variable tends to be more clearly delineated—though not as clearly as the operational definitions of dependent or target variables, which form the ordinate of the typical graph. A similar operational definition of interventions is needed, as well as a way to scale those interventions.

Just as the dependent or target variable must be specified, single-system designs can also require specification of the independent variable. I would recommend a simple scheme requiring specification of the *extent* of the intervention—what particular actions are taken across what range of environmental situations—and the *intensity* of the intervention—how much of each action is taken, defined in some terms of magnitude of effort. Intensity is equivalent to the scale of magnitude used to describe target events, and extent is equivalent to an operational definition of each of the particular acts taken.

Experimental control-group designs vary with regard to fulfilling the logical requirements to make inferences of causality, just as do single-system designs. However, there is presently a wider array of defined and categorized group designs than single-system designs. Campbell and Stanley (1963) and Cook and Campbell (1976) illustrate these with considerable richness and diversity. Hersen and Barlow (1976) do an equally adequate analysis of single-system designs (see also Bloom and Fischer, 1982), but their work is not as well known at this time. Some single-system designs are essentially descriptive and exploratory, whereas others supply rigorous bases for causal inference. The educational task involves explicating not only the designs themselves but also the circumstances in which they may be used to best advantage. For some practice situations, it is sufficient to describe changes in client behavior over time; for other circumstances, it is necessary to know with great precision whether a given intervention caused a given outcome. Single-system designs can potentially supply an array of information to fit the needs of practitioners.

Generalizability of Research Results. Another persisting issue concerns the generalizability of research results. Campbell and Stanley (1963) discuss threats to external validity in classical group designs, that is, the capacity of a design to have its results generalized to other populations, settings, and practitioners. Kratochwill (1978, pp. 28–29) presents a similar analysis for time-series research designs and concludes that all such designs are susceptible to threats. Research that is not clearly and safely generalizable cannot provide cumulative evidence for the empirical generalizations on which science is built. However, generalizability is a matter of some dispute. Some writers suggest that replicability of the same intervention by the same practitioner over several clients is sufficient to provide a basis for practical generalization (Hersen and Barlow, 1976). Others have argued that it is possible to explicate a set of rules for making sound statistical inferences from single-system design research (Kennedy, 1979; Tripodi, 1980). Although this issue remains subject to vigorous discussions in the literature, practitioners will probably continue to do what they have always done—generalize from one set of their own experiences to other cases. What single-system designs provide is a medium to make these natural transfers of experience clearer and more unambiguous.

Developments in Research Methodology. In developments regarding single-system designs, the past is the present, that is, the history of this enterprise is so brief that almost all of the major contributors are still currently at work refining existing approaches and constructing new methods. The landmark volume on "single-case experimental designs" by Hersen and Barlow (1976) summarized more than a decade of extensive research and practice in behavioral approaches with this experimental model. Later books, such as Kratochwill's (1978), provide greater depth in specific areas, and journal articles in the logic and operation of single-system designs are proliferating.

This basic methodology is slowly being translated into simple forms for widespread use. Jayaratne (1978) succinctly describes two rule-of-thumb methods—a proportion-frequency approach (Bloom, 1975) and a two-standard deviation approach (by Shewart, 1931, as described by Gottman and Leiblum, 1974)—as well as two "true statistical procedures"—an analysis of variance and a t-test procedure—within the single-system design approach. Although he makes important critical observations about their limitations (see also Jayaratne and Levy, 1979), such as the problem of autocorrelated data, Jayaratne (1978, p. 35) concludes with these remarks: "[The two rule-of-thumb procedures are] extremely simple to compute, thus enhancing [their] heuristic value. Together, these two rules of thumb provide the clinician with predictive analytic methods that are easy to use and also provide clinical direction by establishing a statistical basis for considering treatment to be a success or failure. In fact, this author believes that these procedures alone will suffice for the vast majority of clinicians, leaving more sophisticated procedures to those interested in writing reports and publications." Likewise, Gingerich and Feyerherm (1979) note other important limitations in these two rule-of-thumb methods and offer another simple approach—the celeration-line technique—that may overcome some of their weaknesses. The important point is that developments in creating and critiquing practical designs are proceeding rapidly, offering the hope that out of these discussions and empirical investigations will emerge some sound and usable evaluation tools (see also Hudson, 1977, 1982).

Potential Conflicts Between Research and Practice. One additional discussion deserves special note, Thomas's (1978) observations on the potential conflicts between experimental research and human services. Since each has its own requisites that appear to interfere with the carrying out of the other's program,

Thomas (1978, p. 21) raises the "fundamental question . . . as to whether *any* within-subject experiment, given present design alternatives and service requirements, can be carried out without posing at least some threat to either the service or the research." Thomas emphasizes that evaluation of practice, as contrasted with research experimentation, is fully possible, given its less restrictive design requirements. Perhaps what is necessary at this time is to clarify that, when practitioners assess pragmatic effects on clients' target behaviors, they are doing scientific evaluations, not, strictly speaking, research that identifies the functional relationships between variables.

However, this distinction can be overdrawn. Research in human behavior appears to be conducted on a continuum—a bimodal one at present, to be sure, but bimodality is not an essential attribute. At the one extreme is pure experimentation, with its emphasis on tightly controlled analyses of functional–causal relationships between variables, and at the other extreme is pure pragmatic inquiry to determine whether some defined goal has been attained in the course of using some systematic intervention. In between are the countless times when the purposes of the activity overlap, such as when a practitioner seeks to learn how to help a particular client but at the same time attempts to generalize this experience to other clients. Experimentation and practice overlap in the types and phases of activities each involves, as many writers have pointed out (Mahoney, 1978; Briar and Miller,1971). It is as true to say that behaviorists can find their heart (Wolf, 1978) as it is to suggest that practitioners can find their head.

But Thomas's (1978) cautions are worth noting. On certain occasions, collecting an elaborate baseline may needlessly delay the start of the service program, as Thomas suggests. But collecting a solid baseline may also provide the clear knowledge that a practitioner needs before embarking on any less informed intervention. At times, as Thomas describes, the phases of the tightly logical experimental design will part company with good practice. But ongoing monitoring of client data may also be the only sound basis for deciding when to change an intervention, to identify iatrogenic effects, or to ascertain when goals have been objectively attained. In short, Thomas provides good examples of problems that might arise in using single-system designs for practice evaluation, but these examples would be improperly interpreted at this stage of development as universal limitations.

Nevertheless, these very limitations may be viewed from an ethical perspective as providing important strengths for social work research or, more properly, social work evaluation. Single-system designs enable the practitioner to involve clients directly in definitions of target behaviors, in the collection of data before and after intervention, and in the interpretation of graphs of these data. In other words, research has been brought back to the participant for his or her immediate use and has been employed to monitor long-term maintenance of the effects of intervention (Fischer,1978). The involvement of clients in their own evaluation breaks down the barriers of secrecy in research and the numerous problems that such secrecy breeds. Openness of evaluation increases opportunities for accountability (Bloom, 1978), an enduring issue not only for the worker on a given case situation but also for the social service agencies and the professions that staff them.

Conclusion

The following remarks by Mahoney (1978, p. 671) summarize the spirit of this chapter: "We must recognize . . . that all of our scientific efforts fall along a continuum of fallibility. There is no investigation that can be totally lacking in its potential informativeness, nor will there ever be one that is perfect in its attainment of internal, external, and theoretical validity. Our goals, then, should be to strive toward conducting the least fallible inquiries, to cautiously interpret our experiments in accordance with their logical warrant, and to guard against the paralysis of complacency regarding the adequacy of current research methods." Single-system designs, in which practitioners as well as clients are the major participants, are rapidly becoming a major vehicle for objective evaluation in clinical research. Their futures lies in the hands of many, including the readers of this book.

References

Allport, G. W. *Pattern and Growth in Personality.* New York: Holt, Rinehart and Winston, 1981.

Bergin, A. E. "Some Implications of Psychotherapy Research for Therapeutic Practice." *Journal of Abnormal Psychology,* 1966, *71,* 235–246.

Bergin, A. E., and Strupp, H. H. "New Directions in Psychotherapy Research." *Journal of Abnormal Psychology,* 1970, *76,* 13–26.

Bergin, A. E., and Strupp, H. H. *Changing Frontiers in the Science of Psychotherapy.* New York: Aldine-Atherton,1972.

Bloom, M. *The Paradox of Helping: Introduction to the Philosophy of Scientific Practice.* New York: Wiley, 1975.

Bloom, M. "Challenges to the Helping Professions and the Response of Scientific Practice." *Social Service Review,* 1978, *52,* 584–595.

Bloom, M., and Fischer, J. *Evaluating Practice: Guidelines for the Accountable Professional.* Englewood Cliffs, N.J.: Prentice-Hall, 1982.

Boring, E. G. *A History of Experimental Psychology.* (2nd ed.) New York: Appleton-Century-Crofts, 1950.

Box, G.E.P., and Jenkins, G. W. *Time Series Analysis: Forecasting and Control.* San Francisco: Holden-Day, 1970.

Briar, S. "Incorporating Research into Education for Clinical Practice in Social Work: Toward a Clinical Service in Social Work." Paper presented at the Conference on Research Utilization in Social Work Education, New Orleans, 1977.

Briar, S., and Miller, H. *Problems and Issues in Social Casework.* New York: Columbia University Press, 1971.

Broxmeyer, N. "Practitioner-Research in Treating a Borderline Child." *Social Work Research and Abstracts,* 1978, *14* (4), 5–10.

Cabot, R. C. "Treatment in Social Casework and the Need of Criteria and of Tests of Its Success or Failure." *Proceedings of the National Conference of Social Work,* 1931.

Campbell, D. T., and Fiske, D. W. "Convergent and Discriminant Validation by the Multitrait-Multimethod Matrix." *Psychological Bulletin,* 1959, *56,* 81–105.

Campbell, D. T., and Stanley, J. C. *Experimental and Quasi-Experimental Designs for Research.* Chicago: Rand McNally, 1963.

Chassan, J. B. *Research Design in Clinical Psychology and Psychiatry.* New York: Appleton-Century-Crofts, 1967; New York: Irvington Press, 1979. (Also see 2nd ed.)

Cook, T. D., and Campbell, D. T. "The Design and Conduct of Quasi-Experiments and True Experiments in Field Settings." In M. Dunette (Ed.), *Handbook of Industrial and Organizational Psychology.* Chicago: Rand McNally, 1976.

Davidson, P. O., and Costello, C. G., (Eds.). *N = 1: Experimental Studies of Single Cases.* New York: Van Nostrand Reinhold, 1969.

Dollard, J., and Mowrer, O. H. "A Method of Measuring Tension in Written Documents." *Journal of Abnormal Psychology,* 1947, *42* (1), 3–32.

Dukes, W. F. "N = 1." *Psychological Bulletin,* 1965, *64,* 74–79.

Eysenck, H. J. "The Effects of Psychotherapy: An Evaluation." *Journal of Consulting Psychology,* 1952, *16,* 319–324.

Fischer, J. "Is Casework Effective? A Review." *Social Work,* 1973, *18,* 5–20.

Fischer, J. *The Effectiveness of Social Casework.* Springfield, Ill.: Charles C. Thomas, 1976.

Fischer, J. *Effective Casework Practice: An Eclectic Approach.* New York: McGraw-Hill, 1978.

Geismar, L. I. *Family and Community Functioning: A Measurement for Social Work Practice and Policy.* Metuchen, N.J.: Scarecrow Press, 1971.

Geismar, L. I. "Thirteen Cumulative Studies." In E. M. Mullen, J. R. Dumpson, and others (Eds.), *Evaluation of Social Intervention.* San Francisco: Jossey-Bass, 1972.

Gingerich, W. J., and Feyerherm, W. H. "The Celeration Line Technique for Assessing Client Change." *Journal of Social Service Research,* 1979, *3* (1), 99–113.

Glass, G. V., Willson, V. L., and Gottman, J. M. *Design and Analysis of Time Series Experiments.* Boulder: Colorado Associated University Press, 1975.

Gottman, J. M., and Leiblum, S. R. *How to Do Psychotherapy and How to Evaluate It.* New York: Holt, Rinehart and Winston, 1974.

Gurman, A. S. "The Effects and Effectiveness of Marital Therapy: A Review of Outcome Research." *Family Process,* 1973, *12,* 145–170.

Hersen, M., and Barlow, D. H. *Single Case Experimental Designs: Strategies for Studying Behavior Change.* New York: Pergamon Press, 1976.

Hetzler, S. A. "A Scale for Measuring Case Severity and Case Movement in Public Assistance." *Social Casework,* 1963, *44* (8), 445–451.

Howe, M. "Casework Self-Evaluation: A Single-Subject Approach." *Social Service Review,* 1974, *48,* 1–23.

Hudson, W. W. "Elementary Techniques for Assessing Single-Client/Single-Worker Interventions." *Social Service Review,* 1977, *51,* 311–327.

Hudson, W. W. *The Clinical Measurement Package: A Field Manual.* Homewood, Ill.: Dorsey Press, 1982.

Hunt, J. McV., and Kogan, L. S. *Measuring Results in Social Casework: A Manual on Judging Movement.* New York: Family Service Association of America, 1952.

Jayaratne, S. "Single-Subject and Group Designs in Treatment Evaluation." *Social Work Research and Abstracts,* 1977, *13* (4), 35–42.

Jayaratne, S. "Analytic Procedures for Single-Subject Designs." *Social Work Research and Abstracts,* 1978, *14* (4), 30–40.

Jayaratne, S., and Levy, L. *Empirical Clinical Practice.* New York: Columbia University Press, 1979.

Jayaratne, S., and Thompson, J. V. "The Clinician-Researcher: The Core for Progress in Social Work Intervention." *Le Travailleur/The Social Worker,* 1977, *45* (1), 39–44.

Kazdin, A. E. "Statistical Analyses for Single-Case Experimental Designs." In M. Hersen and D. H. Barlow (Eds.), *Single Case Experimental Designs: Strategies for Studying Behavior Change.* New York: Pergamon Press, 1976.

Kennedy, M. M. "Generalizing from Single Case Studies." *Evaluation Quarterly,* 1979, *3* (4), 661–678.

Kerlinger, F. N. *Behavioral Research: A Conceptual Approach.* New York: Holt, Rinehart and Winston, 1979.

Kiresuk, T. J., and Sherman, R. E. "Goal Attainment Scaling: A General Method for Evaluating Comprehensive Community Mental Health Programs." *Community Mental Health Journal,* 1968, *4* (6), 443–453.

Kiresuk, T. J., and Sherman, R. E. "A Reply to the Critique of Goal Attainment Scaling." *Social Work Research and Abstracts,* 1977, *13* (2), 9–11.

Kirk, S. "Understanding the Utilization of Research in Social Work and Other Applied Professions." Paper presented at Conference on Research Utilization in Social Work Education, New Orleans, 1977.

Klein, P. *From Philanthropy to Social Welfare: An American Cultural Perspective.* San Francisco: Jossey-Bass, 1968.

Kratochwill, T. R. *Single Subject Research: Strategies for Evaluating Change.* New York: Academic Press, 1978.

Levitt, E. E. "The Results of Psychotherapy with Children: An Evaluation." *Journal of Consulting Psychology,* 1957, *21,* 189–196.

Levy, R. L., and Olson, D. G. "The Single-Subject Methodology in Clinical Practice: An Overview." *Journal of Social Service Research,* 1979, *3* (1), 25–49.

Luborsky, L., Singer, B., and Luborsky, L. "Comparative Studies of Psychotherapies: Is It True That 'Everybody Has Won and All Must Have Prizes'?" In R. L. Spitzer and D. F. Klein (Eds.), *Evaluation of Psychological Therapies: Psychotherapies, Behavior Therapies, Drug Therapies, and Their Interaction.* Baltimore, Md.: Johns Hopkins University Press, 1976.

McCord, J. "A Thirty-Year Follow-up of Treatment Effects." *American Psychologist,* 1978, *33,* 284–289.

MacDonald, M. E. "Social Work Research: A Perspective." In N. A. Polansky (Ed.), *Social Work Research.* Chicago: University of Chicago Press, 1960.

Mahoney, M. J. "Experimental Methods and Outcome Evaluation." *Journal of Consulting and Clinical Psychology,* 1978, *46* (4), 660–672.

Meltzoff, J., and Kronreich, M. *Research in Psychotherapy.* New York: Atherton, 1970.

Mullen, E. J., Chazin, F. M., and Feldstein, D. M. "Services for the Newly Dependent." *Social Service Review,* 1972, *46* (3), 309–322.

Mullen, E. J., Dumpson, J. R., and others (Eds.). *Evaluation of Social Intervention.* San Francisco: Jossey-Bass, 1972.
Mutschler, E. "Using Single-Case Evaluation Procedures in a Family and Children's Service Agency: Integration of Practice and Research." *Journal of Social Service Research,* 1979, *3* (1), 115–134.
Reed, E. F. "A Scoring System for the Evaluation of Social Casework." *Social Service Review,* 1931, *5,* 214–236.
Reid, W. *The Task-Centered System.* New York: Columbia University Press, 1978.
Reid, W., and Hanrahan, P. "Recent Evaluations of Social Work: Grounds for Optimism." *Social Work,* 1982, *27* (4), 328–340.
Reynolds, B. C. "Environmental Handicaps of 400 Habit Clinic Children." *Hospital Social Service,* 1925, *12,* 329–336.
Richmond, M. *Social Diagnosis.* New York: Russell Sage Foundation, 1917.
Sarbin, T. R., Taft, T., and Bailey, D. E. *Clinical Inference and Cognitive Theory.* New York: Holt, Rinehart and Winston, 1960.
Seaberg, J. F., and Gillespie, D. F. "Goal Attainment Scaling: A Critique." *Social Work Research and Abstracts,* 1977, *13* (2), 4–9.
Shapiro, M. B. "Experimental Method in the Psychological Description of the Individual Psychiatric Patient." *International Journal of Social Psychiatry,* 1957, *3,* 89–102.
Shewart, W. A. *Economic Control of Quality of Manufactured Product.* New York: Van Nostrand, Reinhold, 1931. (Also see Gottman and Leiblum, 1974.)
Shyne, A. W. "Evaluation of Results in Social Work." *Social Work,* 1963, *8* (4), 26–33.
Sidman, M. *Tactics of Scientific Research: Evaluating Experimental Data in Psychology.* New York: Basic Books, 1960.
Simon, B. K. "Social Casework Theory: An Overview." In R. W. Roberts and R. H. Nee (Eds.), *Theories of Social Casework.* Chicago: University of Chicago Press, 1970.
Smith, M. L., Glass, G. V., and Miller, T. I. *The Benefits of Psychotherapy.* Baltimore: Johns Hopkins University Press, 1980.
Stuart, R. B. *Trick or Treatment: How and When Psychotherapy Fails.* Champaign, Ill.: Research Press, 1970.
Susser, M. *Causal Thinking in the Health Sciences: Concepts and Strategies in Epidemiology.* New York: Oxford University Press, 1973.
Thomas, E. J. "Uses of Research Methods in Interpersonal Practice." In N. A. Polansky (Ed.), *Social Work Research.* (Rev. ed.) Chicago: University of Chicago Press, 1975.
Thomas, E. J. "Research and Service in Single-Case Experimentation: Conflicts and Choices." *Social Work Research and Abstracts,* 1978, *14,* 20–31.
Tripodi, T. "Replication in Clinical Experimentation." *Social Work Research and Abstracts,* 1980, *16,* 35.
Tripodi, T., and Harrington, J. "Uses of Time-Series Designs for Formative Program Evaluation." *Journal of Social Service Research,* 1979, *3* (1), 67–78.
Wallace, D. "The Chemang County Evaluation of Casework Service to Dependent Multiproblem Families: Another Problem Outcome." *Social Service Review,* 1967, *14* (4), 379–389.

Wallerstein, R. S. "The Problem of the Assessment of Change in Psychotherapy." *International Journal of Psycho-Analysis,* 1963, Part i, *44,* 31–41.

Witkin, S. L., and Harrison, D. F. "Single-Case Designs in Marital Research and Therapy." *Journal of Social Service Research,* 1979, *3* (1), 51–66.

Wood, K. M. "Casework Effectiveness: A New Look at the Research Evidence." *Social Work,* November 1978, pp. 437–458.

Wolf, M. M. "Social Validity: The Case for Subjective Measurement or How Applied Behavior Analysis Is Finding Its Heart." *Journal of Applied Behavior Analysis,* 1978, *11,* 203–214.

Zimbalist, S. E. *Historic Themes and Landmarks in Social Welfare Research.* New York: Harper & Row, 1977.

26

Overview of Single-Case Experiments

Rona L. Levy

The design methodologies variously labeled single-subject, single-case, time-series, single-system, and clinical-research have received considerable attention in the social work literature in recent years, as the clinical research section of this book clearly indicates. One might very reasonably ask, Why is there this much enthusiasm? What do these designs offer to social workers that has resulted in their being so popular?

These designs (which, for simplicity, will be referred to here as single-subject) provide clinicians and researchers with the tools to answer many questions that are important in clinical practice. Depending on which components of the single-subject methodology are utilized, social workers may answer such questions as: What is the outcome of this case? How is this client progressing through the course of treatment? Am I (or is my agency) providing service that can be demonstrated to be effective? Which techniques work with which kinds of clients? Is treatment *x* better than treatment *y*? Is this intervention producing the change I see in the client? In a profession such as social work, which is both service oriented and increasingly called upon to be accountable for the services it provides, the ability to answer such questions is of critical importance.

Single-Subject and Case-Study Methodologies

The single-subject methodology enables social workers to address these questions by providing a framework for the integration of clinical practice and research techniques (Thomas, 1975). In many ways, it may be viewed as a refinement of the case study (Bolger, 1965), a method indigenous to social work (Richmond, 1917). But the differences are clear. In the typical case-study method, a clinician who has worked with a client and determined that the client has improved will share treatment information with some audience. The goal is to provide information that other practitioners can incorporate into their own practice. Unfortunately, typical case conduct and reporting methods limit the contributions these studies are able to make to the common knowledge base of the field. First, a case report may not specify the particular components of the intervention clearly enough for a reader to accurately replicate the procedure described. Second, the evidence presented for client change may not be reliable or valid. A reliable measurement procedure is consistent. With direct observation, two or more observers looking at the same event must have a high likelihood of agreeing on what has occurred. A measurement method is generally said to be valid to the extent that the information it provides is the same as information produced by another selected method. For example, in a case study, if the measurement method is simply client report, this measure may not be in agreement with the information produced by other methods, such as family or spouse observations. A third and final problem with the case-study method is the limited attention often given to experimentally controlling for extraneous variables—variables that may in fact be more responsible than the intervention for observed client change. This lack of control for extraneous factors, coupled with unreliable data, weakens the reader's confidence that utilization of the same intervention—even if it could be replicated—would produce desirable effects on particular clients.

Single-subject strategies offer an improvement over this approach by providing a set of procedural guidelines for the empirical measurement of clinical intervention with a single client or group of clients. The evaluation occurs over a period of time and provides repeated measures of at least one problem or goal throughout the treatment process. Although overt behaviors are the problems or goals typically studied in the single-subject literature, any thought pattern, feeling, or other experience subject to change through clinical intervention can be measured within this framework.

Addressing the problems of the case-study methodology, the model first requires clear specification of the intervention to the extent possible within the constraints of the clinical situation. Second, the model requires—again, to the extent possible—that the data collected be reliable and valid. Finally, the model provides a set of design options that allow the clinician to control for many extraneous factors.

One concern that has been raised regarding this methodology is that research and practice goals are simply different (Thomas, 1978): "The purpose of research with single-subject designs is to demonstrate that an intervention provides experimental control over a given target behavior. . . . The purpose of service, in contrast, is to achieve a practice criterion of change and thereby improve some aspect of human well-being" (pp. 21–22). This dichotomy might lead one to conclude that there should be two models—a single-subject research model and a single-subject practice model (the former including only situations where a primary goal is the demonstration of "experimental control of an intervention over a given target behavior" (p. 21).

Unfortunately, although it certainly is true that the techniques of the single-subject model may at times be used to serve different ends, this point by

Thomas may be incorrectly interpreted by some as evidence for once again reestablishing the traditional gap in social work between clinical research and clinical practice (Lawrence, 1979). This gap serves neither practice nor research. Research in social work will benefit from the opportunity to receive input from on-line clinicians, and clinical practice will benefit from the use of research techniques as additional tools in the promotion of human well-being.

Much of the concern with the use of the single-subject methodology results from the (accurate) belief that the single-subject model, as traditionally presented in texts by Sidman (1960), Chassan (1967), Hersen and Barlow (1976), and Kratochwill (1978), is too intrusive for clinical settings. These presentations, written primarily for researchers, do stress the demonstration of experimental control of the intervention above all other goals and do present standards that are often difficult to attain in many social work settings. Recognizing these problems, this chapter (as well as Jayaratne and Levy, 1979) presents an alternative view of the single-subject model that seeks to utilize what the model has to offer to clinical practice while recognizing the very real constraints in social work practice.

Toward this end, the reader is advised to view the single-subject methodology not as a fixed procedure but *as a collection of procedures from which the clinician may pick and choose components to meet the needs of each case.* Whatever the clinician's priorities in a particular case, knowledge of an empirical single-subject approach to practice adds two important potential benefits to a practice repertoire. First, it may enhance the clinician's effectiveness. Second, it may provide the opportunity for each case to make a useful contribution to a professional or personal body of knowledge on the effect of clinical interventions. Subsequent sections of this chapter will discuss these two benefits in more detail and outline some of the more common procedures and some of the questions currently being raised regarding single-subject practice.

Contributions of the Single-Subject Design to Clinical Effectiveness

The single-subject approach can be used to clarify treatment procedures—for clients, clinicians, and any other relevant persons with a legitimate right to this information—putting relevant problems and goals in clearly specified and measurable terms. This process provides a framework for both the client and clinician to consider the reasons for treatment, the intended goals, and possible desirable or undesirable side effects. Different types of problems and goals will be specified in different ways, depending on client needs and clinician practice style.

Practice effectiveness is also enhanced by repeated empirical feedback that allows both clinician and client to monitor the client's ongoing progress or lack of progress and to respond appropriately. Continuous data feedback to the clinician before intervention begins can provide useful information about the extent of the problem. For example, it may be determined during this early period that the originally designated problem is not as severe as first described and that intervention on another problem may be more appropriate.

Data feedback after intervention has been in effect for a period of time can provide information that the clinician can use to make judgments about continuing, discontinuing, or in some way altering the intervention. For example, the circumstances in a client's life might change, affecting the value of continuing a once successful intervention.

Feedback to the client on case progress can also be a key ingredient leading to a desirable outcome (Drabman and Lahey, 1974; Hayes and Cone, 1977). For example, providing clients with a graphic demonstration of progress can encourage continuation of treatment when perceived change is slow, help the client discriminate instances of positive change, and lead to the information necessary to repeat such change.

Contributions to a Knowledge Base

The model also contains components that allow the clinician working with a single client to systematically examine the effect of different interventions. Many single-subject designs allow clinicians to examine the effect of an intervention by controlling extraneous factors, allowing the clinician to have a fair degree of confidence that observed changes are due to the intervention.

Classical group experimental designs, traditionally taught in most graduate clinical training programs, provide one method to address this control issue while providing inputs to a clinical knowledge base. However, the prototypical control-group design requires a fairly large number of subjects who are randomly separated into two groups, with one group receiving and the other group not receiving a particular intervention. This structure presents a number of practical problems. First, potential investigators often cannot assemble a large group of clients with similar characteristics and further go on to assign some of the clients to an equivalent control group. Second, even if this were possible, creating a no-treatment control group is often considered unethical. Third, information provided by group research may not, in some circumstances, be useful for clinical practice. Group designs are often aimed at determining differences between the average change in two or more groups. The clinician, however, is usually not concerned with average change but with change in a particular client possessing unique characteristics. Furthermore, the practitioner is not only interested in overall effect at the end of treatment but in the specific course of that change over time. The usual way of calculating change in groups by a single posttreatment change (or difference) score does not provide such information. As Strupp and Bergin put it so well (1969), we need to know "what treatment, by whom, is most effective for this individual with that specific problem, and under which set of circumstances" (p. 111). The single-subject approach involves the collection of data on relevant treatments and problems and under specified circumstances from only one client or client group at a time. Thus, the clinician does not need to ponder how much this client is like the "average" client—or even what the average client looks like. Instead, clinicians can compare the information presented on the single reported case in a single-subject design to their particular clients and make their judgments accordingly. (However, the rules for making such judgments are still being developed, as mentioned in the concluding section of this chapter.)

The point here is not to criticize the use of group-design research. On the contrary, group designs will continue to play an important role in increasing our clinical knowledge base. In some cases, group designs are more appropriate than single-subject designs. Administrators, for example, may prefer group research when addressing change across a large number of clients or generalizability of treatment effects from one situation to another. In a comparison of single-subject and group research, Jayaratne (1977) notes: "It could be that the therapy rendered and the effects obtained are particular to that therapy and client-system" (p. 41). Therefore, research relevant for clinical practice may sometimes need to be conducted as group research and sometimes as single-subject research, depending on the questions asked and the particular constraints of a given situation.

Parallels with Group Research

As mentioned earlier, the single-subject methodology provides a framework for the incorporation of scientific methods into the clinical practice setting. As such, the processes and logic of a single-subject case closely parallel the group experimental research process.

Component 1—Specification of the Independent Variable. Any research process begins with a specification of the independent variable, or the factor whose effect will be tested. In the single-subject methodology, this independent variable is the clinical intervention. At a minimum, this methodology requires that clinicians be able to clearly specify, in a way that makes it replicable, what they are doing to try to help their client improve.

Component 2—The Collection of Data on the Target Problems or Goals. Research designs, both group and single-subject, require that data be collected from which conclusions can be drawn. As mentioned earlier, data collection procedures should be reliable, and the data should be a valid representation both of what they are supposed to measure and of change important to the clinical process. A number of measurement methods are available, each with its own strengths and weaknesses (Ciminero, Calhoun, and Adams, 1977; Cone and Hawkins, 1977; Jayaratne and Levy, 1979; Keefe, Kopel, and Gordon, 1978; Mash and Terdal, 1976). For example, although interviews are often more convenient than *in vivo* observation, they are often subject to therapist bias and influence (Thomas, 1973). The clinician should be aware of these potential problems and try to correct for, or at least be aware of, limitations in the information obtained. One strategy available to the clinician to correct for limitations with any one data collection method has been labeled multifactorial measurement (Bergin, 1971; Fiske and others, 1970; Jayaratne, Stuart, and Tripodi, 1974; Kazdin and Wilson, 1978). Multifactorial measurement may involve measuring more than one problem or goal and/or using more than a single method to measure a particular problem or goal. A more extensive discussion of the various methods for collecting clinical data is presented in Chapter 30 by Fischer and Hudson.

Component 3—The Selection of an Appropriate Design. In the classical group-design paradigm, measures are taken on clients in both the experimental and control groups before and after the intervention has been applied. Extraneous factors are controlled by reasoning that, although some persons may improve due to factors other than the intervention, this should occur in roughly equivalent proportions in both groups if both groups are indeed equal due to random assignment. (After random assignment, many studies measure equivalence to determine if the assignment actually was random.) A significantly greater improvement in the experimental group on the measure of interest is said to be probably due to the influence of the intervention.

The single-subject approach uses no control group, only one subject or group of subjects. To control for the effect of extraneous factors, the basic logic of all single-subject designs is the same: Compare the data collected from the subject during a period of time (called a phase) when intervention *B* is in effect to the data collected during a period of time when no intervention, a different intervention, or a different variation of intervention *B* is in effect. Thus, the client serves as his or her own control or standard of comparison. A corollary to this basic principle is: The more of these comparisons demonstrating the effect of *B*, the stronger is the case for *B*. In other words, if *B* is repeatedly introduced and the client improves each time *B* is introduced and does not improve (or does not improve as much) when *B* is not present, one can have greater confidence that *B* is in fact the agent of change than if change is demonstrated only once, after a single introduction of *B*. Robert Carter (1972) has called this the principle of unlikely successive coincidences. One change in the data at the time an intervention is introduced or withdrawn may be due to coincidence. Two changes are less likely to be coincidental, and so on. Since some designs allow for only one change and others for two or more, some designs are stronger than others in demonstrating experimental control—the control of the intervention over the outcome measure. These designs are said to have stronger internal validity. To repeat an important point made throughout this chapter: Clinicians should choose designs that are consistent with their goals for each case and with their clinical constraints. If the constraints of the case permit, and if the clinician is interested in determining the effect of the intervention, designs with stronger internal validity should be chosen.

Component 4—The Data Collection Process. Again, in the typical group experimental design, data are collected before treatment begins and after treatment is terminated. This procedure provides information on overall change but not on the progress of change throughout treatment. The recommendation with the single-subject methodology is therefore that data be collected frequently throughout the intervention process. This more complicated data collection process requires that the clinician consider the following issues:

BASELINE. As noted earlier, the basic process of the single-subject framework involves the comparison of data collected when the intervention is in effect and when the intervention is not in effect. Often no treatment is given when the intervention is not in effect; these no-treatment phases, often the first phase of the design, are called baseline. Thomas (1979) accurately points out that an adequate baseline may be one of the components of the single-subject methodology that the practitioner less interested in demonstrating experimental control of the intervention may wish to forgo: "Taking an adequate baseline might delay intervention and also impose on the client an otherwise extraneous measurement task, an activity that could be aversive and produce negative client reactions" (p. 22).

Several solutions to the baseline problem are available. For example, rather than jump to conclusions that no baseline is possible for the crisis worker on a telephone hotline, we may say to that worker: You do in fact have some criteria on which you are measuring that client's state. Based on these criteria, you decide when the call, and therefore your intervention, may be terminated. First, specify these criteria. Then determine the client's rating on these criteria at the beginning phase of the call, and call this baseline. After your intervention has begun, you should continue your measurement until the call ends.

Such an approach might raise the question of where baseline ends and treatment begins. Hayes (Hayes and Nelson, 1979; Hayes, 1981) suggests one design currently labeled the periodic treatment design, which, in summary, allows the clinician to consider as baseline any time that he or she either is not intervening in some way or is not present. Client responses to the therapist's repeated actions over time would then be measured. Repeated improvement each time a client visits a therapist, for example, with deterioration or stabilization between visits, would provide evidence for the effects of visits.

Another option might be to rely on archival data collected prior to the client's entering treatment. However, these data present several problems (Jayaratne and Levy, 1979), such as the inability to determine their accuracy or even get the kind of information that may be needed. Or attempting to construct a retroactive baseline may be the best alternative possible in some cases. For example, a client may be asked to remember which days over the past week were good days (however "good" has been defined). This method also presents problems, such as reliance on client memory, which may be inaccurate.

Statistical procedures have been suggested for comparing baseline and intervention phases. In one such procedure, Bloom and Block (1977) recommend that the researcher can even assume one occurrence of a problematic event during baseline phases that have not been long enough to provide any occurrences of that event. (See brief discussion below on data interpretation, as well as the chapter by Gingerich in this handbook.) The basis for such assumptions has, however, been questioned (Loftus and Levy, 1977).

CONSISTENCY. Hersen (1973) notes that, whenever possible, all measurements should be standardized "with respect to measurement devices used, personnel involved, time or times of day measurements are recorded, instructions to the subject, and the specific environmental conditions (e.g., location) where the measurement sessions occur" (p. 1). A clinician would be ill advised to compare, for example, a client's report on the extent of depression on two no-treatment–phase weekend days to two treatment-phase weekdays. The data collection situation in the client's life may be totally different between the weekend days and the weekdays and thus could affect any conclusions made from such comparisons.

FREQUENCY OF DATA COLLECTION. According to the ideal time-series model, data should be collected repeatedly over time within each phase. Jayaratne and Levy (1979) have allowed for those situations in clinical practice where only a single measure is taken within each phase. This they call single-point measurement and note that it may occur when the only outcome measure in which a clinician is interested would not typically be taken frequently, such as an MMPI test. However, they strongly caution that single-point measurement be recognized as a compromise with several drawbacks. Data collected only once before and once after intervention would seriously limit one's ability to draw conclusions about the effect of the intervention or even about whether the problem had actually changed, because it is difficult to determine clearly to what extent a few data points are representative of a complete picture. For example, let us consider a clinician and client working together to improve the client's overall mood. Let us further assume that they have worked out some system or scale for the client to measure his moods. If the clinician sees the client weekly and asks him to record his mood only once during the following week, that one data point may only be an indication of how he felt on a particularly "down" or "up" moment and might not give the clinician an accurate picture of such dimensions as frequency or proportion of bad moods.

No formal rules are available for the exact frequency of data collection, as this frequency is in part determined by the dictates of the guideline on the need to attain stability. Barlow and Hersen (1973) note that at least three data points are needed to determine a trend. This guideline suggests that the clinician should ideally choose problems or goals that occur frequently enough to allow collection of treatment data points in a reasonable period of time. Alternate measures sensitive enough (Jayaratne and Levy, 1979) to provide sufficient data points may be needed to replace or augment the measurement of rare-occurrence phenomena. For example, although a final problematic event might be quite rare, other events earlier in the problematic chain might occur more frequently. In the example of a client with suicidal behavior, the client may actually make a suicidal gesture rather infrequently but much more often have negative thoughts in which he or she puts herself down. Sometimes these thoughts may escalate and lead eventually to suicidal gestures, but much more commonly they do not. In this case, the clinician might choose to ask the client to collect data on negative self-statements. In cases where extreme rarity is not a problem, frequency of data collection would be determined by the frequency at which the behavior (problem or goal) being measured is likely to occur and the nature of the problem or goal. For example, if the problem involves something that happens to the client immediately after a weekly paycheck is received, weekly measurement over many weeks might be the logical choice. On the other hand, a child's behavior of hitting a sibling may need to be monitored daily or even hourly.

LENGTH OF PHASES. In the ideal form of the model, Barlow and Hersen (1973) recommend that all phases be of equal length. One advantage to keeping phases as equal as possible is that both treatment and no-treatment phases can be equally exposed to cycles in the client's life pattern. Thus, in the depression case cited above, alternating phases of one week of no treatment with one week of treatment might circumvent potential problems presented by weekend cycles of depression.

DATA INTERPRETATION. The clinician should display the data in a manner that helps in the determination of patterns. This chapter will utilize methods of visual inspection of graphed data to discuss the client's level of performance under different phases. An alternative method of interpretation uses statistics. The strengths and weaknesses of various statistical techniques are described in this section by Gingerich, as well as elsewhere (Baer, 1977; Bloom and Block, 1977; Gingerich and Feyerheim, 1979; Glass, Wilson, and Gottman, 1975; Hudson, 1977; Jayaratne, 1978; Jones, Vaught, and Weinrott, 1977; Kazdin, 1979; Loftus and Levy, 1977).

The most common method of visual inspection utilizes the line graph, in which some dimension of time is usually represented along the horizontal axis and the dependent measure along the vertical axis. By plotting data on such a graph, clinicians can make a judgment regarding characteristics of the data pattern across time, such as the data's stability.

STABILITY. Whenever possible, data within each phase should attain stability before the clinician moves on to the next phase. A stable data pattern permits clear comparison across treatment phases. A roughly stable data pattern is indicated in Figure 1.

Three other common patterns, known as increasing, decreasing, and variable, are shown in Figures 2, 3, and 4, respectively.

Although stability is the ideal, Kazdin (1978) notes that a trend in one phase opposite to the direction one would expect in the next phase should not seriously affect the ability to draw inferences about the treatment. For example, during a baseline period, a depressed client may be getting progressively worse. After a successful intervention, the client would be expected to improve. This situation would produce a clear change in the data pattern and would probably not cause serious interpretive problems. In contrast, if the client were already improving during baseline, it might be difficult to attribute any postintervention changes to the intervention. (This is one case where statistical techniques may be useful; see Kazdin, 1978.)

Single-Subject Designs

As noted earlier, the interpretive logic of the single-subject methodology rests on comparisons between phases when a particular intervention is and is not in effect. The clinician interested in contributing to a cumulative body of knowledge on the effect of an intervention should consider how the different designs control for extraneous variables—that is, the designs' internal validity. The strength of a design's internal validity is measured by the confidence one can have in answering this question: "Did the treatment cause the change in observed behavior, or is there another plausible explanation?" (Jayaratne, 1977, p. 38). If alternate explanations can be offered as potential causes of observed changes, the internal validity of a study is compromised (Campbell and Stanley, 1963).

Kratochwill (1978) presents a thorough discussion of validity threats in single-subject research. He notes that most of the sources of invalidity discussed by Campbell and Stanley are possible threats to validity with all the common single-subject designs. Investigators should consider these threats in their interpretations of the designs. All of the following threats identified by Kratochwill (1978) may produce change in the measured problem or goal: (1) *History*—events in the client's natural environment other than intervention; (2) *Maturation*—physical or psychological developmental changes in the client; (3) *Testing*—effects of being tested, particularly when a reactive (change-producing) measurement method is used (Nelson, 1977); (4) *Instrumentation*—confounding when unreliable measurement devices are used; (5) *Multiple-intervention interference*—when two or more interventions are introduced sequentially with one client, the effect of subsequent interventions may be related to the client's exposure to prior ones; (6) *Instability*—natural variation in the data.

It should be stressed again that these are only possible threats to validity that the researcher should consider. When conducting single-subject research, evidence can be gathered to reduce concern over these threats and increase confidence that observed changes were in fact caused by the intervention. For example, a radical change in the frequency of a problem after intervention has been intro-

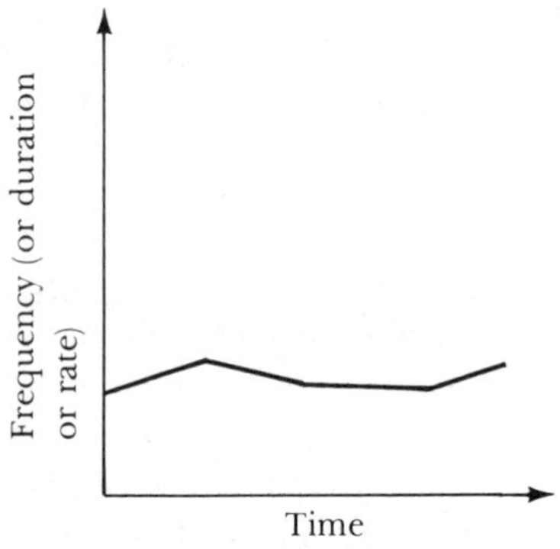

Figure 1. A Hypothetical Stable Data Pattern

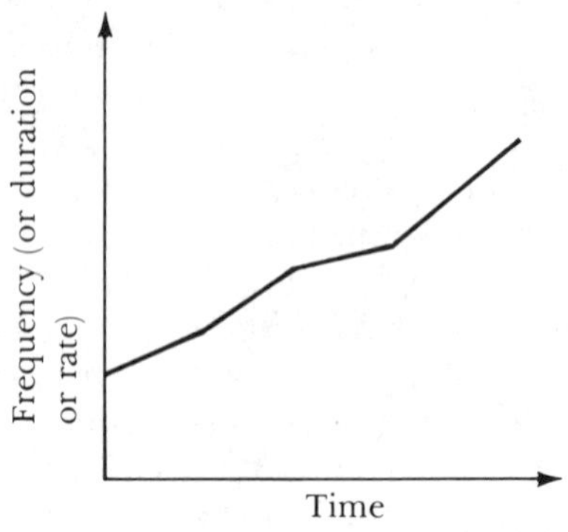

Figure 2. A Hypothetical Increasing Data Pattern

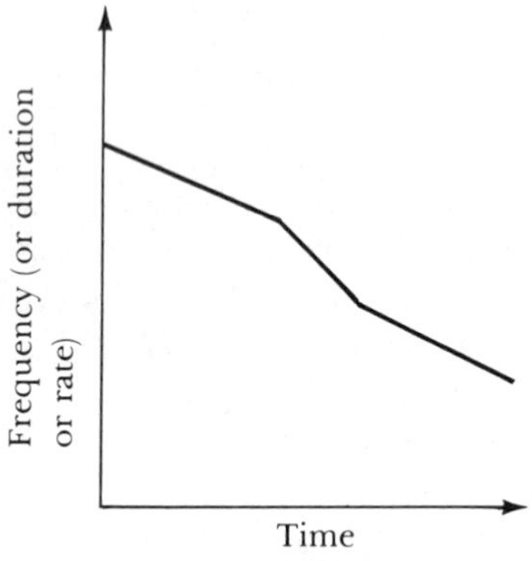

Figure 3. A Hypothetical Decreasing Data Pattern

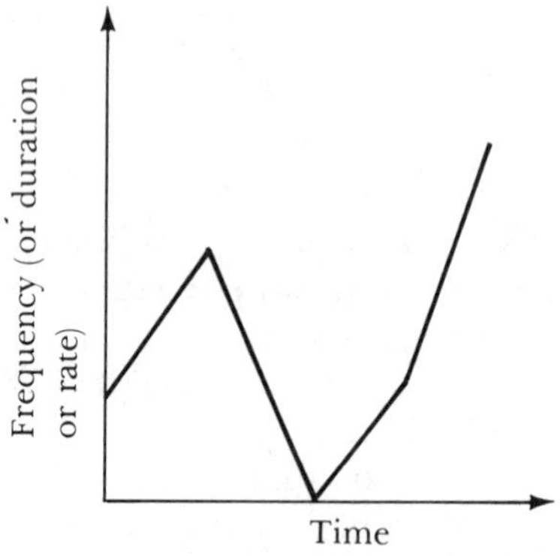

Figure 4. A Hypothetical Variable Data Pattern

duced, in a case in which multiple data points have been obtained over a long period of time prior to intervention, would reduce some validity concerns. Also, the extent to which a design is planned in advance, as opposed to evolved in response to client behavior, will also reduce validity concerns. The use of some single-subject designs rather than others will also reduce such concerns, as some designs are stronger than others in controlling threats to validity.

Hayes (Hayes and Nelson, 1979; Hayes, 1981) makes a useful distinction between the within-series, between-series, and combined-element designs. In the within-series designs, conclusions are drawn from a single series of data points across time; in the between-series designs, comparisons are made between two or more series of data points across time, with each series spanning the same period of time. Combined-series designs utilize both procedures to draw conclusions. These distinctions will become clear in the following discussion of the specific series.

Within-Series Designs. AB DESIGN. The most common form of single-subject design is the *AB* design. *A* usually stands for the baseline, or no-treatment level, of measured client behavior. All subsequent interventions are given different letters of the alphabet. If an intervention or intervention program is repeated, it

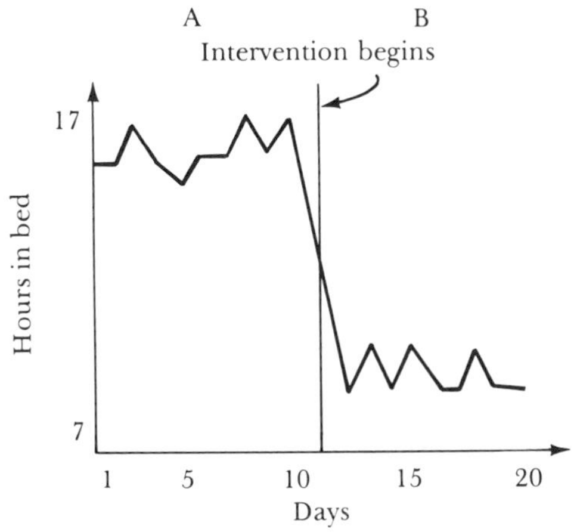

Figure 5. An *AB* Design Showing Hours in Bed for a Depressed Client

keeps the same letter. For example, a clinician may decide to use the number of hours in bed as a measure of a client's depression. (The clinician may use other measures as well, but only one will be identified for the purposes of this illustration.) The client agrees to collect data on this measure. Days of the week are graphed along the abscissa and hours in bed along the ordinate.

Before treatment begins, the client is asked to record the number of hours spent in bed per day. This number is indicated in the baseline phase (the first *A*) and looks fairly steady. We will assume that it is about sixteen hours. Then the client begins treatment; the beginning of intervention is represented by the vertical line, and the intervention period is represented by the letter *B*. The hours of time in bed go down to about nine.

When we allow our M.S.W. students an option, the *AB* is by far the most common design they implement in their clinical settings. They find this design fits best with the way they naturally conduct clinical practice. In most clinical practice, they would take some measure of the client's level of functioning before treatment and then continue to monitor the client throughout the treatment period.

In one example, a client complaining of low self-esteem and periodic depression worked with the therapist to help create a five-point scale as a dependent measure. Each of the points on the scale was given specific thought-referents. After the client then recorded her moods for eight hours each day over a twelve-day baseline period, an intervention was implemented. This intervention basically consisted of a procedure in which the client reminded herself of her positive attributes. The graph for this case is presented in Figure 6. In this graph, the data can be seen as increasing from a mean of 0.42 per day during baseline to a mean of 1.03 after baseline.

Strengths of the *AB* design are that it allows for a comparison of the outcome measure between periods of time both before and after intervention and that it is fairly easy to implement in most treatment settings. The major disadvantage is that it is very weak in controlling for threats to internal validity, such as history. This is due to the information from which the clinician draws to conclude that the intervention caused any observed change. In both the hypothetical and

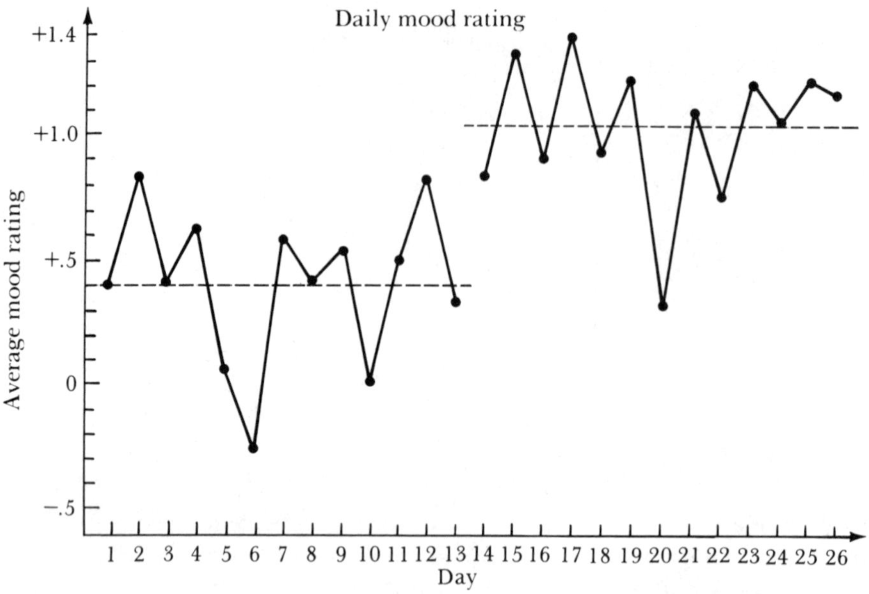

Figure 6. An *AB* Design Showing an Alteration in Mood Rating

actual cases reported earlier, high levels of undesirable behavior fall to reasonable levels after intervention is introduced. However, only one alteration of the data patterns is in evidence, occurring at the one point in time that the intervention is introduced. History is a potential threat, since some other factor in the client's life may have coincided with this one alteration and have been responsible for the change. However, for the clinician primarily interested in assessing whether and how much the behavior has changed, this design is still very useful and may be the design of choice when the determination of intervention effect is not a primary concern.

ABA AND ABAB DESIGNS. In order to demonstrate more forcefully the relationship between the treatment and the in-bed pattern of our hypothetical depressed client, the clinician could use a withdrawal or reversal design, withdrawing the intervention after it has been implemented for a period of time and thereby producing a graph resembling the one in Figure 7.*

The *ABA* design provides greater confidence in determining the effect of the intervention based on the principle of unlikely successive coincidences. An obvious disadvantage of the *ABA* design is that, if the design patterns go as planned, the client is left in an undesirable state. Therefore, the client may then have positive treatment effects restored by adding a final *B* phase, creating the *ABAB* design represented in Figure 8.

Although both the *ABA* and *ABAB* designs do provide the practitioner with greater confidence in ruling out threats to validity, these designs often pre-

*Leitenberg (1973) provides a useful distinction between the withdrawal and reversal designs. In the withdrawal design, treatment is actually withheld, whereas in the reversal design it is reversed. Thus, for example, in a reversal design a behavior might be rewarded during treatment (the first *B* phase) and a behavior incompatible to it rewarded during the second *A* phase.

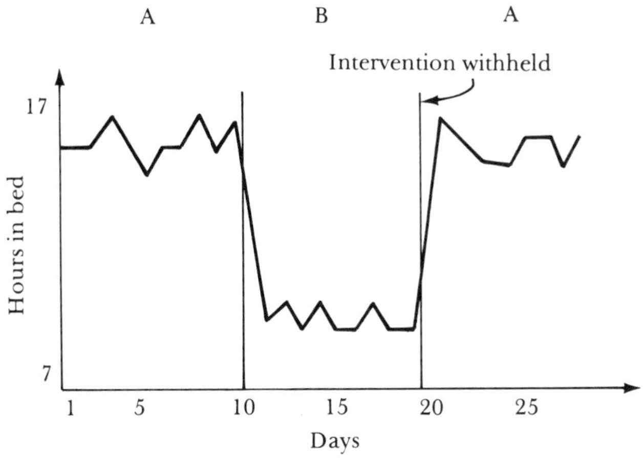

Figure 7. An *ABA* Design Showing Hours in Bed for a Depressed Client

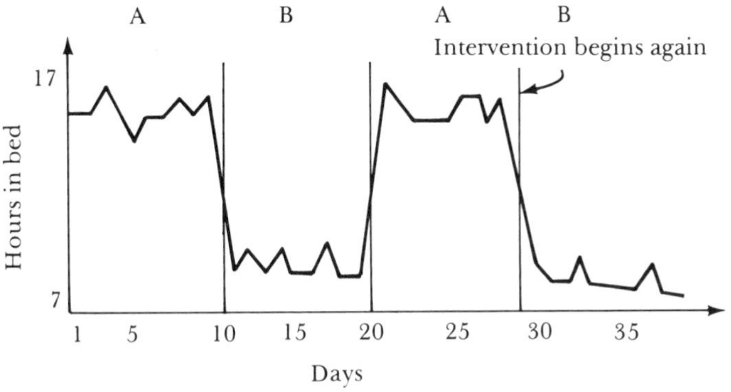

Figure 8. An *ABAB* Design Showing Hours in Bed for a Depressed Client

sent serious problems in implementation. One major problem involves the ethics of trying to get the client to return to a baseline level of functioning. The client and others in his or her life may find this "regression" aversive. Although this objection can be met by ensuring that the return is brief (Browning and Stover, 1971) and by providing good rationales to relevant persons for return to baseline, returns may still be undesirable. Also, the client is learning how to retrieve maladaptive patterns, and the bad effects of this behavior may be difficult to determine. Another problem is whether or not the client's data pattern actually will return to baseline levels by a withdrawal of intervention. For example, consider the case of a depressed woman whose intervention consisted of the therapist encouraging her to become involved in new, rewarding activities. She may stay involved with these activities even when therapist support is withdrawn, and these activities may continue to reduce or eliminate her level of depression. The intervention has, in a sense, become self-sustaining and cannot be withdrawn. Another case where reversal of the data pattern may be unlikely is when new skills and learning occur during treatment. Withdrawal may not mean a loss of these skills.

The intended return to baseline levels to demonstrate the control of the intervention is another example of a procedure cited by Thomas (1979) that is primarily useful to the clinician interested in a demonstration of the controlling effect of the intervention. On the other hand, the clinician focusing on producing permanent change in the client may hope the effect of the intervention has been strong enough to maintain even if clinician-administered treatment must be withdrawn. From such a perspective, a return to baseline levels would not be planned, and the intervention would probably not be withdrawn if such a return seemed probable. For this reason, many clinicians often do not choose to perform a withdrawal or reversal design.

The strength of this design, then, is that it permits greater demonstration of treatment control by means of two or three planned alterations of the data pattern. Its weaknesses include the clinical undesirability of a return to baseline levels and the difficulty of achieving such a return if the intervention has been particularly powerful.

CHANGING CRITERION. The changing criterion, a design used less frequently than the others mentioned, usually involves a behavioral program focused on shaping a client's performance by systematically altering the criteria for reward. Kratochwill (1978) describes this design as requiring "initial baseline observations on a single target behavior. Subsequent to baseline, an intervention program is implemented in each of a series of intervention phases. A stepwise criterion rate for a target behavior is applied during each intervention phase" (p. 66). A changing criterion would be useful if the treatment with our depressed client involved her agreeing to give herself some reward contingent on only fifteen hours in bed on day 1, fourteen hours on day 2, thirteen hours on day 3, and so on. If her behavior met the criterion, the graph might resemble the one in Figure 9.

This design is useful only when the goal to be attained can be broken down into such successive, quantifiable steps and criteria for change can be specified.

OTHER WITHIN-SERIES DESIGNS. The clinician should use creativity to construct designs to meet the needs of varied clinical situations. The periodic treatment design is a within-series design. Another the clinician may conduct when no baseline is possible but a reversal is desired is called a *BAB* design. To determine whether intervention *B* works better than intervention *C*, the clinician might do a *BCBC* design. To determine whether the component *C* of the *BC* package is really the only component causing the change, the clinician might do a *B-BC-B* design, and so on. In creating other designs, however, the clinician should recognize again that some designs may increase potential threats to validity and others may not. For example, an *ABC* design is not suitable for comparing the effects of *B* and *C* because of multiple intervention interference. That is, in observing a change that occurs along with *C*, a skeptic might question whether such a change would have occurred had *C* not been preceded by *B*. In other words, *B* may have "primed" the client for *C*.

Between-Series Designs. Barlow and Hayes (1979) attempted to clarify the previously existing confusion in the literature between designs variously labeled multiple-schedule, multi-element baseline, randomization, and the simultaneous-treatment design (which has also been called a concurrent-schedule design). They suggest instead the label "alternating-treatments design" for any designs involving "the fast alternation of two different treatments or conditions, each associated with a distinct and discriminative stimulus" (p. 200). The simultaneous-treatment design, in contrast, requires "the concurrent or simultaneous application of two

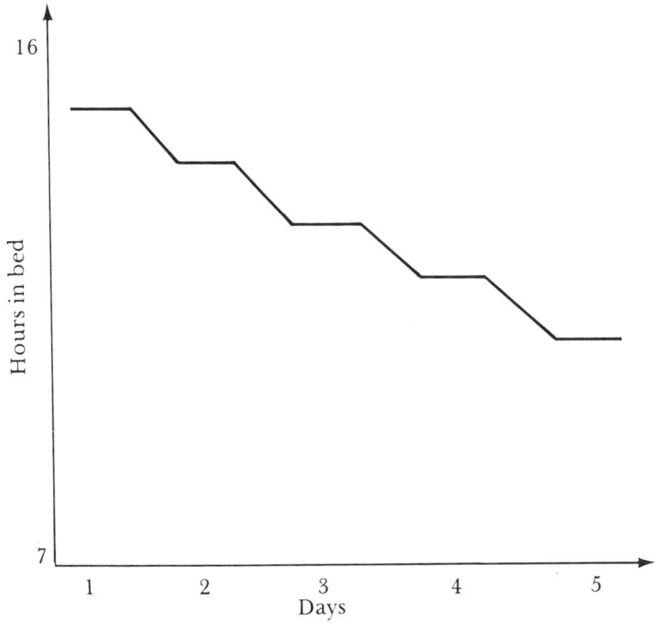

Figure 9. A Changing-Criterion Design Showing Change in Hours in Bed for a Depressed Client

or more treatments in a single case where the subject actually demonstrates a preference for one of the available treatments" (p. 202). As this latter design occurs extremely rarely (Barlow and Hersen, 1973, note only one example in the literature), only the alternating-treatments design will be discussed. The reader interested in the simultaneous-treatment design is referred to Browning (1967), Browning and Stover (1971), or the discussion in the Barlow and Hayes articles.

As an example of the alternating-treatments design, consider the case of the clinician who is interested in working with a teacher to determine if reprimanding an inappropriate behavior or praising desirable behavior is a more effective strategy in controlling a disruptive child. The teacher may begin by using praise in morning sessions and reprimands in afternoon sessions, then switch to praise in the afternoons and reprimands in the morning, monitoring the child's cooperative behavior at all times. A graph of this hypothetical example is presented in Figure 10. After a baseline period, it can be seen that the child is more cooperative in phase 2, when the praise is in effect. Praise is thus the treatment which has been selected for phase 3. An important feature of this design is that all conditions are counterbalanced. That is, in this case, if praise is presented in the morning, it must also be presented in the afternoon, and the introduction of reprimands is similarly switched. This helps to demonstrate that it is the praise, and not something about the morning, that produces a difference in behavior.

The alternating-treatments designs can be used to address all the questions raised by the within-series designs, with the clinician either alternating a no-treatment condition with one or more treatments or alternating two or more interventions, as in the present example.

Combined-Series Designs: The Multiple-Baseline Design. The most common combined-series design is the multiple-baseline design. A multiple-baseline

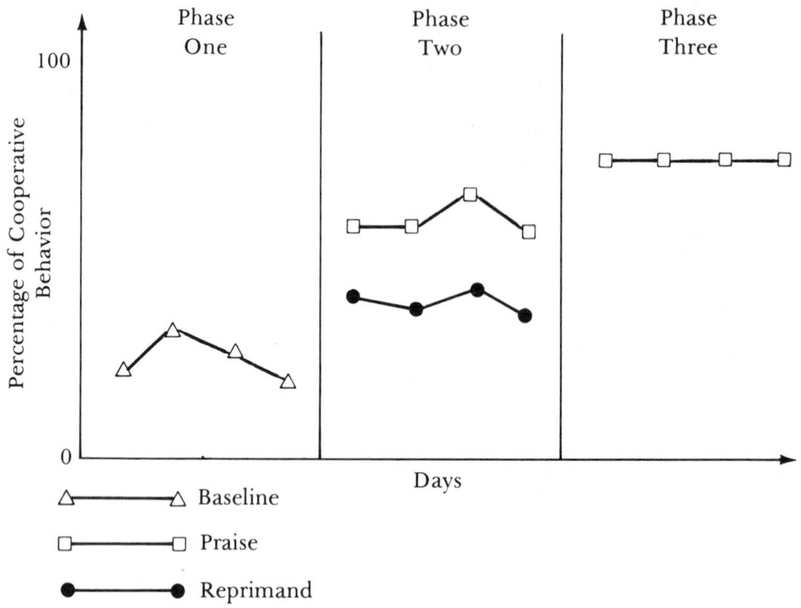

Figure 10. A Simultaneous-Treatment Design Showing the Superiority of Praise over Reprimand in Improving Cooperative Behavior

may be conducted by taking at least two separate problems (some argue at least three are needed for a strong demonstration; see Hersen and Barlow, 1976) and applying the same intervention to one at a time. If change occurs when the intervention is introduced, the clinician can say with some assurance that the intervention caused the change.

An M.S.W. student used a multiple-baseline design to show the effects of an intervention to help parents improve the behavior of their child in going to bed, setting the table, and staying quiet once in bed. By first beginning a baseline on all behaviors, the intervention (having the parents reward appropriate behavior with praise and allowance) was sequentially introduced for each problem. Corresponding changes in these problems were shown after the intervention was introduced.

Another social worker used a multiple-baseline design to demonstrate the effect of a social worker's training of dental students in appropriate interactional skills with children. The dental student was observed and baseline measures taken on three separate behaviors (such as using age-appropriate language and providing procedural explanation). The social worker then sequentially trained the dental students in more desirable alternatives and measured change on each behavior after the training.

Multiple-baseline design can be done in several ways. Those discussed earlier introduced an intervention sequentially to multiple problems for a single client in a single setting. A multiple-baseline can also test the effect of an intervention on different clients in the same setting and with the same problem. In this situation, the clinician would then begin to baseline the problem in all clients at the same time, and intervention would be introduced to these clients one at a time. Finally, a multiple-baseline could sequentially introduce an intervention across settings to the same client and with the same problem or goal. In all of these

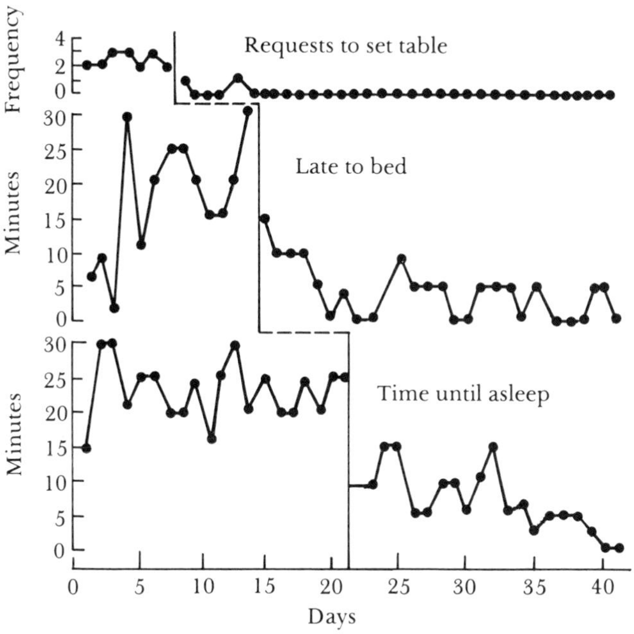

Figure 11. A Multiple-Baseline Design Showing Change in Compliance Across Three Separate Behaviors

versions of the design, the point is to sequentially introduce an intervention to one person, setting, or problem at a time and determine if the measured problem or goal changes only at the point in time that the intervention is introduced.

One disadvantage of this design is that it requires that, to demonstrate the controlling effect of the intervention, each problem change only when the intervention is introduced. If two problems change when the intervention is introduced, the demonstration of the effect is weakened. Independence of the problems, people, or settings is necessary for this design to be useful. For example, if compliance with going to bed on time changed when intervention began, and the client's compliance with being quiet changed as well, the design's usefulness is reduced. Often such independence is not possible.

Advantages to this design are that no reversal of treatment effects is necessary to demonstrate the experimental control of the intervention. Another advantage is that this design also often fits into good clinical practice, with sequential intervention across problems, for example, being a logical activity.

This chapter will conclude its introduction of specific designs with the multiple-baseline design. At this point, the reader should have the necessary skills to construct a variety of new designs, label designs that have already been conducted, and recognize many of the internal validity threats present in these designs. For more detailed information, one of the texts mentioned earlier on single-subject designs should be consulted.

Final Comments

Although the single-subject methodology has deep historical roots, many of the methods discussed here have only recently been applied in clinical practice, and many unresolved issues and techniques are still being developed. The labeling of the simultaneous-treatment and alternating-treatment designs and the introduction of the periodic-treatment design are examples of the continuous evolution of the field.

Among the numerous unresolved issues is the question of the generalizability of the findings where the single-subject study is used to look at the effects of an intervention. In research, the ability to generalize from the results of a study is referred to as the study's external validity. One argument for generalizability is that, if subjects are in fact randomly drawn from a population, other persons also randomly drawn from that same population should react to the intervention in much the same way as the clients in the study. Obviously, this argument cannot be made with a single subject. The answer that has been given to this problem in single-subject research is replication—the repeated testing of the same intervention across relevant domains, such as client, therapist, and setting. But the rules for determining the number of successful replications necessary to have confidence in an intervention simply do not exist. The field has yet to address the question of whether such rules are even necessary.

Another concern that has been raised relates to the implications of altering the original model for presentation and utilization in clinical practice. Thomas addresses this issue in the next chapter, and Hayes (in press) has raised several valuable questions along this line in a review of a book by Jayaratne and Levy (1979). Although this paper takes the position that we should continue to think in terms of one single-subject model with several components, many key questions are still unanswered. For example, at what point might clinicians be making so many compromises in the model that information derived from their efforts has no clinical usefulness (Levy, 1978)?

The single-subject model allows us to begin to bridge the gap between clinical practice and research. But, as already mentioned, the model is far from complete, and only if on-line practitioners are centrally involved in finding answers to key questions will those answers be meaningful in practice.

References

Baer, D. M. "Perhaps It Would Be Better Not to Know Everything." *Journal of Applied Behavior Analysis,* 1977, *10,* 167–172.

Barlow, D. H., and Hayes, S. C. "Alternating Treatments Design: One Strategy for Comparing the Effects of Two Treatments in a Single Subject." *Journal of Applied Behavior Analysis,* 1979, *12,* 199–210.

Barlow, D. H., and Hersen, M. "Single Case Experimental Designs: Use in Applied Clinical Research." *Archives of General Psychiatry,* 1973, *29,* 319–325.

Bergin, A. E. "The Evaluation of Therapeutic Outcomes." In A. E. Bergin and S. L. Garfield (Eds.), *Handbook of Psychotherapy and Behavior Change.* New York: Wiley, 1971.

Bloom, M., and Block, S. R. "Evaluating One's Own Effectiveness and Efficiency." *Social Work,* 1977, *22,* 130–136.

Bolger, H. "The Case Study Method." In B. B. Wolman (Ed.), *Handbook of Clinical Psychology.* New York: McGraw-Hill, 1965.

Browning, R. M. "A Same-Subject Design for Simultaneous Comparison of Three Reinforcement Contingencies." *Behavior Research and Therapy,* 1967, *5,* 237–243.

Browning, R. M., and Stover, D. O. *Behavior Modification in Child Treatment: An Experimental and Clinical Approach.* Chicago: Aldine-Atherton, 1971.

Campbell, D. T., and Stanley, J. C. *Experimental and Quasi-Experimental Designs for Research.* Chicago: Rand McNally, 1963.

Carter, R. D. "Internal Validity in Intensive Experimentation and Designs"; "Designs and Data Patterns in Intensive Experimentation." Unpublished course monographs, School of Social Work, University of Michigan, 1972.

Chassan, J. B. *Reseasrch Designs in Clinical Psychology and Psychiatry.* New York: Appleton-Century-Crofts, 1967.

Ciminero, A. R., Calhoun, K. S., and Adams, H. E. *Handbook of Behavioral Assessment.* New York: John Wiley, 1977.

Cone, J. D., and Hawkins, R. P. (Eds.). *Behavioral Assessment.* New York: Brunner/Mazel, 1977.

Drabman, R. S., and Lahey, B. J. "Feedback in Classroom Behavior Modification: Effects on the Target and her Classmates." *Journal of Applied Behavior Analysis,* 1974, *7,* 591–598.

Fiske, D. W., and others. "Planning of Research on Effectiveness of Psychotherapy." *American Psychologist,* 1970, *25,* 727–737.

Gingerich, W. J., and Feyerheim, W. H. "Celeration Line Techniques for Assessing Client Change." *Journal of Social Service Research,* 1979, *3,* 99–110.

Glass, G. V., Wilson, V. L., and Gottman, J. M. *Design and Analysis of Time-Series Experiments.* Boulder: University of Colorado Press, 1975.

Hayes, S. C. "Review of Empirical Clinical Practice." *Behavioral Assessment,* 1980, *2,* 306–308.

Hayes, S. C. "Single Case Experimental Design and Empirical Clinical Practice." *Journal of Consulting and Clinical Psychology,* 1981, *49,* 193–211.

Hayes, S. C., and Cone, J. D. "Reducing Electrical Energy Use: Payments, Information, and Feedback." *Journal of Applied Behavior Analysis,* 1977, *10,* 425–435.

Hayes, S. C., and Nelson, R. O. "Realistic Research Strategies for Practicing Clinicians." Workshop presented at the annual meeting of the Association for the Advancement of Behavior Therapy, San Francisco, 1979.

Hersen, M. "Different Design Options." Paper presented at the Association for the Advancement of Behavior Therapy, 1973, Miami Beach, Fla.

Hersen, M., and Barlow, D. H. *Single Case Experimental Designs: Strategies for Studying Behavior Change in the Individual.* New York: Pergamon Press, 1976.

Hudson, W. W. "Elementary Techniques for Assessing Single Client/Single Worker Interventions." *Social Service Review,* 1977, *51,* 311–326.

Jayaratne, S. "Single Subject and Group Designs in Treatment Evaluation." *Social Work Research and Abstracts,* 1977, *13,* 35–42.

Jayaratne, S. "Analytic Procedures for Single-Subject Designs." *Social Work Research and Abstracts,* 1978, *14,* 30–40.

Jayaratne, S., and Levy, R. L. *Empirical Clinical Practice.* New York: Columbia University Press, 1979.

Jayaratne, S., Stuart, R. B., and Tripodi, T. "Methodological Issues and Problems in Evaluating Treatment Outcome in the Family and School Consultation Project." In P. O. Davidson, F. W. Clark, and L. A. Hamerlynck (Eds.), *Evaluation of Behavioral Programs in Community, Residential, and School Settings.* Champaign, Ill.: Research Press, 1974.

Jones, R. R., Vaught, R. S., and Weinrott, M. "Time-Series Analysis in Operant Research." *Journal of Applied Behavior Analysis,* 1977, *10,* 151–166.

Kazdin, A. E. "Data Evaluation for Intra-Subject Replication Research." *Journal of Social Service Research,* 1979, *3,* 79–98.

Kazdin, A. E. "Methodological and Interpretive Problems of Single Case Experimental Designs." *Journal of Consulting and Clinical Psychology,* 1978, *46,* 629–642.

Kazdin, A. E., and Wilson, G. T. *Evaluation of Behavior Therapy: Issues, Evidence, and Research Strategies.* Cambridge, Mass.: Ballinger, 1978.

Keefe, F. J., Kopel, S. A., and Gordon, S. B. *A Practical Guide to Behavioral Assessment.* New York: Springer, 1978.

Kratochwill, T. R. (Ed.). *Single Subject Research: Strategies for Evaluating Change.* New York: Academic Press, 1978.

Kratochwill, T. R. "Foundations of Time-Series Research." In T. R. Kratochwill (Ed.), *Single Subject Research: Strategies for Evaluating Change.* New York: Academic Press, 1978.

Lawrence, H. "Message from the President." *Newsletter of the Social Work Group for the Study of Behavioral Methods,* 1979, *3,* 1–3.

Leitenberg, H. "The Use of Single Case Methodology in Psychotherapy Research." *Journal of Abnormal Psychology,* 1973, *82,* 87–101.

Levy, R. L. "Clinical Conclusions from Compromised Data Sources." Paper presented at the annual meeting of the Association for the Advancement of Behavior Therapy, Chicago, 1978.

Loftus, G. R., and Levy, R. L. "Statistical Evaluation of Clinical Effectiveness: A Reply to Bloom and Block." *Social Work,* 1977, *22,* 504–506.

Mash, E. J., and Terdal, L. G. *Behavior Therapy Assessment.* New York: Springer, 1976.

Nelson, R. O. "Methodological Issues in Assessment via Self-Monitoring." In J. D. Cone and R. P. Hawkins (Eds.), *Behavioral Assessment.* New York: Brunner/Mazel, 1977.

Richmond, M. *Social Diagnosis.* New York: Russell Sage, 1917.

Sidman, M. *Tactics of Scientific Research: Evaluating Experimental Data in Psychology.* New York: Basic Books, 1960.

Strupp, H. H., and Bergin, A. E. "Some Empirical and Conceptual Bases for Coordinated Research in Psychotherapy: A Critical Review of Issues, Trends, and Evidence." *International Journal of Psychiatry,* 1969, *7,* 18–90.

Thomas, E. J. "Bias and Therapist Influence in Behavioral Assessment." *Journal of Behavior Therapy and Experimental Psychiatry,* 1973, *4,* 107–111.

Thomas, E. J. "Research Methods in Interpersonal Practice." In N. A. Polansky (Ed.), *Social Work Research.* Chicago: The University of Chicago Press, 1975.

Thomas, E. J. "Research and Service in Single-Case Experimentation: Conflicts and Choices." *Social Work Research and Abstracts,* 1978, *14,* 20–31.

27

Problems and Issues in Single-Case Experiments

Edwin J. Thomas

Although case studies have been conducted in behavioral and clinical research for over a century, until recently such studies have generally not involved systematic measurement or experimental manipulation. However, the advent of single-case experimentation has done much to change this situation. Such experimentation combines some of the advantages of the old-fashioned nonexperimental case study (for example, flexibility and individualization) with the advantages of experimentation, in which selected variables or conditions are intentionally altered for purposes of drawing inferences about possible causal factors. Because of these advantages, within-subject experimentation represents one of the most important methodological developments in clinical research. More generally, single-case experimentation complements the use of the conventional between-group designs consisting of experimental and control groups, and, when systematically replicated, single-case experiments may be superior to group designs.

First employed in the experimental analysis of animal behavior in the laboratory, single-case experimentation has since been widely used in applied behavior analysis for at least two decades and is now being actively considered for purposes of research and outcome evaluation in clinical and other types of direct service with individuals, families, and groups. The rapid spread of this methodology has been accompanied by such developments as new within-subject experimental designs, novel design applications, and further codification and explication of the methodology. Nevertheless, single-subject experimentation is still new and rapidly evolving, and the rules of the game are not all that clear, even for research carried out in nonapplied settings.

Applications of the single-subject methodology in clinical research and in service settings raise special issues and problems, many of which are just now being identified and recognized. Advocates of single-subject experimentation in social work and related fields have, until recently, been mainly concerned with describing this new methodology and touting its promise, giving little attention to the many methodological problems and remaining relatively insensitive to possible research–service conflicts. I have long been among the advocates of single-case experimentation and have employed such experimentation for some time in my clinical research. The emphasis in this chapter on problems and issues in single-subject experimentation is thus not intended to discourage such experimentation or to detract from its great promise, but rather to encourage a discerning use of this methodology and to highlight directions for further development.

Common Methodological Problems

Although recognition of methodological problems associated with single-case experimentation is increasing (for example, see Hartmann and Atkinson, 1973; Kazdin, 1973, 1978; Kazdin and Kopel, 1975), the discussions presently available tend to address only a restricted range of difficulties, and, to my knowledge, no comprehensive exposition of methodological difficulties exists, nor is one likely to be available soon. In the meantime, the discussion that follows is intended to provide a selected, contemporary review.

Altering Phases of Conditions During the Experiment. Single-case experimental designs consist of phases, or periods, of relatively uniform activity during which measurements are taken. Each design generally involves one or more control phases, such as baseline, in which there is measurement without experimental intervention, and one or more experimental phases consisting of measurement combined with experimental intervention. The different experimental designs are defined by particular, sequential arrangements of control and experimental phases for one or more subjects. Unlike traditional research designs, which are preplanned and are generally carried out without modification, single-case experimental designs involve a number of important decisions that are made only as the data are gathered. Thus, the investigator generally makes decisions as the data are gathered concerning the length of the baseline, when to introduce the intervention, and how long the intervention is to remain in effect. As Kazdin (1978, p. 631) has observed: "A fundamental design issue is when to change phases to maximize the clarity of the data interpretation. . . . There are no clear rules for altering phases."

Problems may derive from trends in the data, intrasubject variability, and the duration of phases. The following presentation on phases is based in part on Kazdin's (1978) discussion of these problems, to which the reader is referred for additional details. Thus, in regard to trends in the data, the trend in baseline may not be stable, may progress in a direction opposite from that of the intervention, or, most perplexingly, may be in the same direction as that of the intervention. There are several alternatives if the data show a trend toward improvement, which is the most problematic trend for interpretation. In the first alternative, an *A-B-A-B* design may be employed for changing behavior in the direction opposite to the data trend. Thus, if the trend is toward improvement, the intervention can be directed toward reducing the behavior. This, of course, may be experimentally sound but clinically inappropriate. A second solution would be to select designs in which trends in the results are unlikely to affect each of the baselines, such as a multiple-baseline design, or in which trends are not relevant to evaluate the different treatments, such as simultaneous-treatment design. A third solution would be to employ statistical techniques, such as time-series analyses, to assess the effectiveness of the intervention.

In regard to intrasubject variability, great variability in the data may interfere with drawing conclusions about treatment. When stability of the data, as in the baseline condition, cannot be achieved through continued data collection, and when variability persists, the investigator endeavors to look for the controlling variables that affect the variability in order to bring about greater stability or endeavors to redefine the behavior or conditions of assessment to reduce variability. As Kazdin (1978, p. 683) has observed: "Continuation of the program in the face of excessive variability eliminates the possibility of drawing inferences about treatment."

The duration of phases are generally not specified in advance of the research, and their length is ordinarily determined on the basis of the data as they are collected. The investigator must avoid altering phases before a clear pattern emerges, as in the case of introducing an intervention while the data are continuing to progress in a given direction and have not yet stabilized. Hersen and Barlow (1976) have advocated that the length of phases, in any event, should be equal. This may be most appropriate when the data cooperate and reach satisfactory levels of stability, but, when they do not, the use of arbitrarily equal phase lengths could lead to ambiguity rather than clarity in interpretation. As Kazdin (1978) has indicated, there are no agreed-upon, objective rules for choosing alternating phases in single-case experimental designs. Although he indicates that investigators may occasionally be able to specify objective criteria in advance concerning the conditions under which baseline and experimental conditions will be alternated, such preset rules may not be able to address complications that derive from emerging trends and erratic data patterns. Researchers would be well advised, other factors being equal, to endeavor to maintain phases as long as possible until the data have stabilized or until the pattern, if not stable, is evident.

Checking the Intervention. Researchers very often introduce an intervention as part of an experimental design and fail to determine whether or not it was carried out as intended. Thus, if the intervention involves the client's carrying out specific homework assignments, it would be important to determine the extent to which these assignments were carried out as directed by the intervention plan. If the intervention is not carried out as intended, an experiment involving this intervention may not be a fair test. It is important to recognize that any given intervention in an experiment may be carried out not at all or only partially as intended or may result in totally unanticipated consequences that nonetheless may greatly influence measured outcome.

Comparing Alternative Interventions. Kazdin (1978), as well as others (Hersen and Barlow, 1976), has observed that single-case designs in which alternative interventions are carried out in sequence, as in an *A-B-C-B-C* design, run the risk of sequential multiple-treatment interference. That is, there may be multiple-treatment interference in which the effects for an intervention (such as *C*) are not independent from those produced by another (such as *B*) but rather are a combined interactive effect of both. The multiple-treatment effect can be a significant threat to validity (Campbell and Stanley, 1966), and designs in which this type of interference may occur should generally be avoided. There are alternative single-case designs, including the multiple-schedule design and the simultaneous-treatment design, that are suited to making comparisons of different treatments.

Meeting Basic Design Assumptions. Like inferential statistics, the designs of single-case experimentation involve basic assumptions that, if violated, raise questions about the validity of conclusions that may be drawn from the experimentation. Each single-case experimental design has one or more basic assumptions that should be met if the logic of the design is not to be violated. For example, a critical assumption in the *A-B-A-B* design involving the phases of baseline (*A*), intervention (*B*), return to baseline (*A*), and reinstitution of the intervention (*B*) is that the intervention is reversible. If the intervention is irreversible, it will not be possible to return to baseline or, at a later point, to reinstate the intervention. The logic of the *ABAB* design calls for demonstrating the effect of the intervention when it is introduced and removal of that effect with the withholding or withdrawal of the intervention. An irreversible intervention in a design calling for reversibility produces ambiguity in the interpretation of the results. Thus, one interpretation is that the intervention was ineffective inasmuch as it could not be demonstrated that the intervention could be turned on and off and on again with appropriate changes in measured effects. In this interpretation, the original effect might be seen as the result of some extraneous causal factor. Another interpretation might be that what seemed a reversible intervention was in fact irreversible. However, this is but a post hoc interpretation that cannot be sustained short of replication.

Part of the problem with interventional reversibility is, of course, that it is not always possible to determine in advance what interventions may be reversible. Further, from the point of view of service, an irreversible intervention is highly desirable to the extent that it leads to enduring change when that intervention is removed. It has been suggested that one increases the likelihood of keeping interventions reversible by keeping their application short and, if reinforcement is involved, by making use of a schedule (such as a continuous schedule of reinforcement) that has lower resistance to extinction (for example, see Bijou and others, 1969; Hartmann and Atkinson, 1973; Kazdin, 1973; and Hersen and Barlow, 1976). In general, the manipulation of consequences (such as reinforcement) and of antecedent stimulus conditions for interventions have the greatest likelihood of reversibility because they may be readily turned on and off, whereas interventions involving more enduring organismic changes, such as cognitive restructuring or acquisition of skills through training, cannot ordinarily be directly removed or turned off, once introduced.

Multiple-baseline designs likewise have their basic assumptions, which can only be briefly mentioned here. For example, the multiple-baseline design over behaviors presupposes that the behaviors are independent, such that if one changes, the others will not; that the likelihood of achieving change with one behavior is approximately the same as with the other behaviors; and that the independent variable is equally relevant to all of the behaviors that serve as dependent variables in the design. The multiple-baseline design over different situations assumes that a change in one situation will be independent from and will not generalize to changes in other situations. Likewise, the multiple-baseline design over persons presupposes that there is an independence among the persons, such that change for one will not result in change for another. This design involves the additional assumption that the individuals to whom the intervention is applied are roughly equally changeable, such that a change demonstrated for one can as readily be achieved with another.

Other designs also have their assumptions. For example, the multiple-schedule design presupposes that there will be no stimulus generalization between and among the conditions differing in discriminative conditions. For further details, the reader is referred to such sources as Hersen and Barlow (1976), Kazdin (1973, 1978), Kazdin and Kopel (1975), and Leitenberg (1973).

The researcher's task is clearly to determine in advance of conducting the experiment that the design assumptions can be met. Guidelines for checking on assumptions before conducting an experiment presently involve mainly the experience and good judgment of the researcher. When one or more critical assumptions involved in a design cannot be met, a more suitable alternative design should be selected that does not rely on that assumption. For example, if the assumption of reversibility cannot be met, alternatives to the *A-B-A-B* reversal design might include a series of replicated *AB* designs or a multiple-baseline design over behaviors, persons, or situations.

Other Common Problems. Among other methodological problems are interpretation of data in the light of different change criteria (for example, the experimental in contrast to the therapeutic criterion); rules for improvising designs in order not to capitalize on chance occurrences or to realize a design to fulfill one's own treatment–outcome prophesies; the proper number of baselines to obtain in multiple-baseline designs involving persons, situations, or settings; the extent to which the investigator should rely on visual inspection of data presented graphically or should employ statistical procedures; the extent to which interventions should be fully specified and described before conducting experimentation that has the promise of being replicated by others; and the appropriate names for designs and proper notation to capture design intricacies.

Single-Subject Research and Service: Potential Conflicts and Choices

In their endeavor to persuade practitioners and researchers that single-subject experimentation has great promise for conducting research on clinical and applied problems, writers have placed primary emphasis on the nature and requirements of the single-subject research methodology and have muted or glossed over possible research–service conflicts. If proper attention is not given to possible conflicts between single-subject experimentation and service, researchers and practitioners run the risk of conducting experiments that violate the requirements of single-subject experimentation or service. Researchers and practitioners should have a clear understanding of some of the important differences between single-subject research and service, should be sensitive to the ways in which each may threaten the adequacy of the other, and should be prepared, in the light of differences and possible conflicts, to design the research or service in such a way that possible conflicts are reduced or eliminated.

The following discussion of service emphasizes direct service involving one or more helping persons and their clientele but also largely applies to service in general. It is based on and extends an earlier discussion of possible conflicts between research and service in single-case experimentation (Thomas, 1978). The term *research* is used to refer to single-case experimentation only.

Differences Between Single-Subject Experimentation and Service. Although almost everyone would acknowledge that differences exist between single-case experimentation and service, the extent and variety of such differences are generally not highlighted. There are in fact major differences involving the objectives, criteria of change, independent variables, types and sequence of phases, target responses, and the role of researcher versus practitioner. Differences in these areas have been summarized in Table 1, which reveals that, in each area of difference, the dissimilarities between single-subject research and service create potential conflicts for the research, the service, or both.

Consider the differences in objectives, for example. The research and service objectives have different implications for the activities of intervention and, depending on which takes precedence, can result in conflicts that have unfortunate effects for the service, for the research, or for both. In a situation in which the service objectives are primary, one can ask how within-subject experimentation might be affected if it were carried out concurrently with service. If the service objective were to increase client assertiveness to a clinically satisfactory level, there would generally be no baseline, since establishing one could interfere with service requirements. If a single intervention (*B*) was used successfully in producing the desired level of assertiveness, the resulting design is simply *B*, intervention only, which is an essentially useless design for demonstrating experimental control because it does not rule out the large number of threats to internal validity (see, for example, Campbell and Stanley, 1966).

If *B* increased assertiveness a little but not enough, the practitioner would typically try another intevention (*C*) and if that too failed to increase assertiveness sufficiently, still another intervention (*D*) would be tried until the service criterion were achieved or the effort abandoned. The resulting *B-C-D* design lacks a baseline or other control condition and is otherwise weak because it has, among other threats to validity, multiple-treatment interference and because it has no reversal or other means of demonstrating experimental control.

However, if, in contrast, *B* and *C* were ineffective and *D* was effective, we then have a design that Hersen and Barlow (1976) believe could be rendered, after the fact, as a baseline intervention (*A-D*) on the grounds that *B* and *C* were ineffective and functionally equivalent to an initial baseline. Such an *A-D* design is among the weakest because it protects against few of the threats to internal validity. There are, of course, other "service-controlled" designs that could be used as illustrations. When designs are controlled exclusively by service considerations, they are generally incomplete, confounded, or weak.

If, on the other hand, the research requirements for the experimental designs predominate, they might interfere with the service. For instance, taking an adequate baseline might delay intervention and also impose on the client an otherwise extraneous measurement task, an activity that could be aversive and

Table 1. Some Characteristic Differences Between Single-Subject Research and Service

Area of Difference	*Single-Subject Research*	*Service*
Objectives	To determine the possible causal relationship between an independent and dependent variable (Baer, Wolf, and Risley, 1968, p. 94).	To achieve, by whatever appropriate helping method, a practice criterion of change relating to the human-services objective.
Criteria of Change	Sufficient change to demonstrate experimental control, which may or may not be sufficient to meet a service objective.	Sufficient change to meet a service objective, which may or may not be sufficient to demonstrate experimental control. objective.
Independent Variables	Consist of one variable (or a "package" of variables), generally preselected, manipulated one at a time when proceeding from one phase to the next (Hensen and Barlow, 1976), and administered in only the experimental phase of the experiment, often in a standardized, nonvarying manner.	Consist of any of a large variety of helping methods given, as clinically appropriate, in response to individual client needs and administered in an individualized, generally nonstandardized fashion at any point in the helping process, from initial contact through termination.
Types and Sequences of Phases	Phases are relatively uniform periods during which measurements are taken in a design consisting of an arrangement of one or more control phases (such as a baseline) in which there is no experimental intervention and one or more experimental phases during which the experimental intervention is in operation—all determined by the logical requirements of the research design.	Phases may consist of assessment, treatment, maintenance, and termination, each of which may not correspond to the control and experimental phases of experimentation, and each of which may overlap and vary in length and practitioner activity—all as determined by service objectives to improve client well-being.
Target Responses	Generally, only one target response is involved, the dependent variable (or sometimes a restricted set) addressed in the experiment.	Generally, many target responses are involved as desired outcomes, and these are addressed flexibly and may shift, given changes in outcome and treatment objectives.
Role of Researcher versus Practitioner	Role of researcher is to be unbiased, impartial, and objective in presiding over the administration of experimental procedures and in gathering and processing data.	Role of practitioner is to be warm, compassionate, sensitive, and empathetic in providing help, which in some cases may implicate the helper in highly involved relationships with the client, including serving as a partisan and advocate.

For further details, see Thomas (1978).

produce negative client reactions. If, following baseline (*A*), the first intervention (*B*) had the good fortune of turning out to be fully effective, without the necessity of adding other interventions later, the result would be an *A-B* design—a weak design for purposes of demonstrating experimental control. Most researchers would therefore prefer to add a reversal and reinstatement of the intervention, thus yielding an *A-B-A-B* design. However, as several researchers have observed, the intervention must not be carried out for a long period of time if is reversal is contemplated, because it may then lose its reversibility and generalize (Hartmann and Atkinson, 1973; Kazdin, 1973; and Hersen and Barlow, 1976).

To avoid these problems and maintain the integrity of the research, the intervention should probably be carried out for a shorter period of time than it ordinarily would be for service purposes. Reversing the intervention would stop it at a time when service considerations would require either continued intervention or a maintenance program. All service of any kinds has to stop during the period of reversal to avoid confounding the design.

If the reversal fails to return the data to baseline because the intervention has been exceptionally successful, such an outcome is good for service, which is generally directed toward achieving enduring change, but awkward for the research because it raises questions about the possible role of extraneous factors in producing the change (Hartmann and Atkinson, 1973). However, it is possible that the client will learn to discriminate between the conditions under which the intervention is and is not operating if the reversal produces a return to baseline. This reduces the possibility of generalizing the target behavior to conditions that are not the same as in the experiment (Hartmann and Atkinson, 1973; Kazdin, 1973; O'Leary and Kent, 1973).

With the completion of an *A-B-A-B* design, the research would be finished, if this were the design planned at the outset. However, considerations of service would typically call for continued intervention to maintain the intervention already applied, to introduce other target behaviors, or both.

Such a "research-controlled" design may produce such adverse effects on service as delayed service, incomplete service, or the imposition of extra service requirements, in addition to producing needless adverse effects on the client. The *A-B-A-B* design is a relatively intrusive design because of the problems it generates for service; nevertheless, the other single-case experimental designs pose analogous difficulties for service when the strict requirements of the design are met.

There can also be mixed dominance of objectives, in which the interventions are first guided mainly by service and then largely by requirements of research. An example of this is the *A-B-C-D-C-D* design reported by Liberman and others (1974). The *B* intervention was not effective, and therefore interventions *C* and *D* were introduced, with *D* being the intervention that finally produced the desired change. The design wandered, as it were, in search of effective intervention. As the authors put it: "In treatment settings, many contingencies have to be tried before one is found to be effective" (p. 114). Had the objective initially been to examine the efficacy of a given intervention—*B*, for example—then, after discovering that *B* was not successful, one research alternative would have been simply to return to baseline and reinstate the intervention, yielding an *A-B-A-B* design.

The first part of the design, *A-B-C-D,* provides no demonstration of experimental control. To demonstrate experimental control, the researchers then carried out a reversal to *C* and a reinstatement of *D,* both of which were successful—thus completing the *A-B-C-D-C-D* design. The wandering design wanders first in search of effective intervention and then to demonstrate experimental control. As I have stated elsewhere (Thomas, 1978):

> Although the wandering design appears to resolve conflicts between the objectives of research and those of service, it really compromises both. Many interventions carried out sequentially in the search for an intervention that produces a service criterion of success increase the likelihood of multiple-treatment interference, a threat to validity described by Campbell and Stanley (1966). There may also be order and contrast effects such as those reported by Kendall, Nay, and Jeffers (1975) for a successive-treatments design of two durations of time out.
>
> Moreover, successive interventions, if sufficiently numerous or highly individualized, make it difficult, it not impossible, to replicate the experiment. The last part of the design, in which there is an effort to demonstrate experimental control, involves substantial interference with service, such as the delay or interruption of service and the imposition of research requirements extraneous to the service [p. 23].

Contrasts and implications deriving from objectives are only one area of difference between single-subject research and service. Each of the others—criteria and change, independent variables, types and sequences of phases, target responses, and role of researcher versus practitioner—also have important implications for the conduct of research and service and may be sources of conflict. For further details, see Thomas (1978).

Threats to Service. Differences between research and service discussed earlier and summarized in Table 1 indicate that the requirements of research can limit or interfere with service. When the effects of single-case experimentation in a setting of direct service adversely affect service, it is appropriate to refer to research intrusiveness. Threats to the adequacy of service include delayed service, incomplete service, imposition of extraneous requirements, and adverse client reactions.

Any of these research-imposed threats to service may adversely effect the length and quality of the service relationship, the service objectives achieved and the effectiveness with which they are attained, and the costs in time and effort incurred by the clients. Disrupting service for the sake of single-case experimentation may be seriously harmful in extreme cases or little more than an inconvenience in others. The threats, however, cannot be dismissed as inconsequential or unworthy of attention; they pose ethical problems and constrain us to address alternatives and accommodations that would reduce their likelihood.

Threats to Single-Case Experimentation. The differences mentioned earlier between research and service make it clear that the requirements of service may interfere with single-case experimentation in numerous ways. When the effects of service reduce or limit the internal or external validity of single-case experimentation, it is appropriate to refer to service intrusiveness. Threats to the validity of single-case experiments include extraneous causal variables, inadequate data, defective experimental designs (for example, broken, disordered, or confounded designs), restriction of design options, biased experimentation, biased data analysis, biased data interpretation, misrepresented interventions, idiosyncratic interventions, and nonreplicable interventions.

Alternatives and Accommodations. With greater recognition and understanding of the potential conflicts between single-subject experimentation and service, researchers will need to develop alternative approaches and methods of resolution that will permit single-subject research to be carried out with minimal interference with service. New methods of collecting data, designing experiments, and conducting service will be among the innovations that can be expected to make this possible.

At present, however, there are no ideal resolutions. The differences outlined earlier are real and impose difficult choices on researchers and practitioners. Fortunately, available alternatives can help reduce the strains between experimentation and service, but each has its own preconditions before it can be effectively adopted. Further, each alternative is to some extent a less than ideal accommodation inasmuch as some modification of the experimental regimen or the service format is required in order to reduce potential conflict.

ALTERNATIVE 1: CONDUCT SERVICE AS THE EXPERIMENT. By treating service as an experiment, the practitioner can meet most, if not all, of the requirements of the research while still conducting the service. Since the purpose of the service is unequivocally experimental, with the focus primarily on determining the effectiveness of the intervention, procedures that reduce service intrusiveness are more easily justified, and the experiment can be conducted with fidelity to the research requirements.

Before this alternative is adopted, it is important that prior interventions of established service techniques have failed or that established procedures do not appear to be applicable. If the focus of the experimentation is on analysis of components of the intervention assemblies, prior research should have shown these intervention packages to be effective. Further, it is particularly important for clinicians to observe the proper ethical safeguards when conducting service as experimentation in this way.

ALTERNATIVE 2: REDUCE MEASUREMENT INTRUSIVENESS. The reduction or elimination of measurement intrusiveness may eliminate an important source of strain between the service and single-case experimentation. For example, baselines may be reconstructed from case records (Bloom and Block, 1977; Bloom, Butch, and Walker, 1979); archival data may be used for the baseline (Webb and others, 1972; Jayaratne and Levy, 1979); or short baselines (Azrin, 1979), unstable baselines (Jayaratne and Levy, 1979), and single data points may be used for preintervention and postintervention comparisons (Jayaratne and Levy, 1979). The researcher may also make use of less intrusive methods of gathering data. Thus, the client may be interviewed to obtain data on selected behaviors or events instead of requesting that systematic records be kept, or client ratings of aspects of interaction in the home may be employed instead of actual observations by the researchers in the client's living room and kitchen. Most of the examples just given involve weakened measurement; and hence, the alternative of reducing measurement intrusiveness is only viable if it does not leave the researcher with data that are insufficiently reliable or valid to pursue the research objectives.

ALTERNATIVE 3: REDUCE DESIGN INTRUSIVENESS. Selection of a less intrusive design may reduce, although not necessarily eliminate, the conflict between research and service. It has long been recognized, for example, that multiple-baseline designs over behaviors or persons may be ethically or practically more suitable than a design calling for a reversal of an intervention (Baer, Wolf, and Risley, 1968; Franks and Wilson, 1976; Hartmann and Atkinson, 1973; Hersen and Barlow, 1976; Kazdin, 1973, 1978; and Kazdin and Kopel, 1975). Instead of reversing and reinstating the intervention in an *A-B-A-B* design, one may apply the intervention successively to one or more target responses for which baselines were previously taken, using a time-lagged multiple-baseline design over responses. Other methods of reducing design intrusiveness have been described elsewhere (Thomas, 1978).

Reductions in design intrusiveness are frequently accomplished at the expense of the power of the design to rule out threats to validity—for example, moving from an *A-B-A-B* design to an *A-B* design. The challenge is to reduce design intrusiveness without losing design power. Researchers should try to select an alternative design that is less intrusive but not appreciably less powerful. If there is a loss of design power, it should ideally be adequately offset by a reduction in threats in service.

ALTERNATIVE 4: SELECT A MULTIPLE-N DESIGN. Some between-subject designs, in contrast to strict single-subject designs, afford additional opportunities to reduce research–service conflicts. For example, subjects volunteering for research on a new intervention method may be assigned at random to the new experimental treatment or to the best-established alternative treatment, if one exists. Some participants in Azrin's research on toilet training were assigned to his new method or to the approved pad-and-buzzer treatment (Azrin, 1977). In my research on unilateral family therapy, similar spouses of uncooperative alcohol abusers were treated as "yoked dyads," one of which was assigned at random to the experimental condition of unilateral family therapy and the other to Al-Anon, the self-help counterpart. Other clinically relevant, between-subject multiple-N designs have been discussed by Azrin (1977) and Kratochwill (1978), among others.

ALTERNATIVE 5: CONDUCT ASSESSMENT EXPERIMENTATION. Most diagnostic data are gathered by nonexperimental methods; however, on certain occasions, systematic experimental manipulation of clinical conditions would yield more definitive conclusions. In an assessment experiment, the hypothesized maintaining conditions are experimentally manipulated during some portion of the diagnostic or assessment phase. In this approach, the research objective of isolating possible independent variables is entirely consonant with the service objectives of determining the maintaining conditions for the purpose of formulating an intervention plan. Such assessment experiments may take the form of a formal single-case experiment suitable to the problem or of a more modest experimental probe (Thomas, 1977a).

ALTERNATIVE 6: CONDUCT EXPERIMENTATION FOR PERSUASIVE CORROBORATION. Clients sometimes remain unconvinced of what occasioned their progress, even when the intervention employed by the practitioner is well established and prior research indicates that it is the probable basis for the client's progress. It may be appropriate in such cases to conduct a formal experiment with the client to determine whether the intervention was responsible for the positive changes observed, especially if the client's scepticism either makes it unlikely that the client will continue to use the intervention or is otherwise countertherapeutic. Because such experimentation is carried out for purposes of persuasive corroboration and thus serves service objectives, clear justification exists for establishing the conditions for an appropriate single-case experiment.

ALTERNATIVE 7: CONDUCT SINGLE-CASE EXPERIMENTATION AS A COMPONENT OF SERVICE INTERVENTION. In this alternative, single-subject experimentation is carried out in a separate segment in which research objectives are foremost and the requirements of service are not allowed to interfere with the research. Likewise, the service segment gives service objectives priority and includes no experimentation involving research. Strict separation of these segments helps to ensure that mutual threats are minimized and that the activities of each are carried out properly. Although the research segment may come at any point, it is generally best introduced just before the service proper, thus reducing the threat to validity posed by multiple-treatment interference.

ALTERNATIVE 8: CONDUCT EVALUATION WITHOUT SINGLE-CASE EXPERIMENTATION. Given the many potential conflicts between single-case experimentation and service and the intrusiveness of most single-case experimental designs at this stage of methodological sophistication, single-case experimentation may be inappropriate for purposes of service evaluation. Liberman, King, and DeRisi (1976) have published one of the few accounts of the use of single-case experiments for evaluation—in their case, evaluation of a service program. Every sixth patient who entered a day-treatment center was designated as one whose treatment program would be experimentally analyzed. The sample included a total of fifteen patients; for only five was it possible to complete a design involving such features as withdrawal, reversal, or multiple baseline. These authors indicated that they had difficulties with single-case experiments because of the openness of the setting and that they encountered problems in obtaining repeated measurements and adequate baselines.

In addition to such practical difficulties, the reader is reminded of the differences in objectives between single-subject research and service (see Table 1). Whereas the purpose of within-subject experimental research is to isolate possible causal conditions, with focus particularly on the effects of given independent variables, outcome evaluation in service is generally directed toward the simpler question of appraising outcomes. In service evaluation, attention is given to whether the dependent variables, such as the target responses of service, have changed or attained some criterion.

The concept of single-case evaluation, as distinguished from single-case experimentation, seems to be appropriate here. In an endeavor to integrate practice and research in a family and children's service agency, Mutschler (1979) employed single-case evaluation procedures, which she describes as follows: "Thus, the term 'single-case evaluation' in the project refers to a time-series model: to repeated measures of a client-unit's target behavior rated independently by the client(s) and social worker, allowing a systematic evaluation as to whether and to what extent the treatment goals are achieved. A client-unit can consist of one person, a couple, a family, or any other combination of relatives or friends who are receiving services as a unit. The advantages of focusing on repeated measurements of target behaviors were that they were less obtrusive than experimental designs and were more acceptable to the clients and workers as an integral part of the presently used interventive procedures at this agency" (p. 120). This study found that the practitioners tested and selected a number of single-case evaluation procedures applicable to their clientele. Although still preliminary, the findings suggest that the evaluation instruments that met the requirements of practice were the most regularly used and tended to become an integral part of the workers' treatment interventions. For further details, the reader is referred to Mutschler (1979).

For purposes of evaluation, a simple design consisting of preintervention and postintervention measurement is often sufficient to shed light on the question of how much change has occurred. Such a design, of course, would generally be inadequate for drawing inferences about what was responsible for any given change; such inferences usually require stronger and more intrusive designs, including single-case experimental designs proper. Among the presently available methodologies for service evaluation are time-series analyses (for example, Jones, Vaught, and Weinrott, 1977) and methods oriented toward measuring goal attainment (for example, Kiresuk and Sherman, 1968). Design frameworks for evaluation include classical experimental group designs, as well as quasi-experimental designs, such as a time-series experiment and multiple–time-series design (Campbell, 1969; Campbell and Stanley, 1966).

ALTERNATIVE 9: ADOPT AN EMPIRICAL (OR SCIENTIFIC) MODEL OF PRACTICE. Models of practice are changing, and there is increasing emphasis on conceptions of empirically and scientifically oriented practice (for example, see Bloom, 1975; Briar, 1977; Fischer, 1978; Jayaratne and Levy, 1979; Thomas, 1975, 1977b; Tripodi and Epstein, 1978). In one version of this approach, I have indicated the following (Thomas, 1975): "The empirically oriented practitioner . . . makes strategic use of the ways of thinking and procedures of behavioral science research, along with the particular practice procedures of his method of helping, to help attain clinical and practice objectives" (p. 254). In addition to the substantive content, the contributions to practice of behavioral science research methods include the research methods per se, as well as the components of a scientific perspective, practices of data processing and interpretation, and the conventions of research reporting (see Thomas, 1975, for further details).

Unfortunately, one can too easily reach the conclusion from reading the writings in this area that few or no conflicts would arise if only the practitioner would adopt an empirically and scientifically oriented mode of practice. Unquestionably, the activities of measurement, monitoring, and evaluation may be more readily justified and carried out in the context of an empirical model of practice that endeavors to integrate these activities into the case management regime. However, defining such activities as service requirements does not reduce their intrusion on service or eliminate the differences between research and service or the threats that each may pose to the other.

An empirical model of practice is highly desirable but need not necessarily include the requirement of single-case experimentation as a constituent feature of practice. (For an approach that emphasizes a data-based, accountable, and empirical practice that does not necessarily depend on single-case experimentation, see Thomas, 1977b). As indicated, single-case evaluation may be more appropriate than single-case experimentation for the evaluation of routine practice (Thomas, 1975; Mutschler, 1979). In general, an empirical model of practice should enhance the possibilities of making use of one or another of the conflict-reducing alternatives outlined earlier (for example, conducting service as the experiment, conducting experimentation as a component of service, conducting experiments for persuasive corroboration, and conducting single-case evaluation in contrast to single-case experimentation).

Generalization

Results of single-case experiments frequently raise questions about the representativeness of the findings. A finding does not a generalization make. Or does it? The problem of generalization has been particularly significant in single-subject experimentation because the results of these experiments typically involve one or a very small number of persons. A critical question is, To what populations of clients or individuals, as well as to what different ecological conditions, such as therapists or settings, may the findings from single-case experiments be generalized?

In his discussion of the basic principle of single-case experimentation, Chassan (1979) has said the following: "Once a true process or effect has been established as having occurred in one person, it can reasonably be inferred that there will be other persons as well in which the process or effect will occur" (p. 403). The question then arises, under what conditions may such generalization be extended? In other words, when is it possible to generalize results involving only a small number of experimental subjects? Dukes (1965) has given attention to the special occasions when the sample of one would be likely to provide valid results. Among the conditions identified were the following: when between-individual variability for the phenomena under investigation is known to be negligible, making results for a second subject redundant; when one case in depth exemplifies many; when negative results from one case are sufficient to demand revision or rejection of an asserted or assumed universal relationship; when the behavior studied is very unusual and opportunity to study it is limited; or when the practitioner wants to focus on a problem by defining questions and variables that may lead to more refined approaches.

Additional conditions have been identified that would appear not to call for extensive aggregation of results over situations or occasions. In his approach to studying the stability of behavior, Epstein (1980) has indicated that intrinsically robust phenomena; potent, ego-involving events; and single ratings following multiple or extended observations constitute the kinds of events from which replicable results can be expected without aggregating over stimulus situations or occasions. Notably, the first two of these conditions (robust variables and potent, ego-involving events) apply to the majority of single-case experiments, especially those involving therapy and clinical research. As also noted by Baer (1977) and Parsonson and Baer (1978), single-subject experiments in the tradition of applied behavior analysis have focused expressly on powerful variables having applied implications for which the effects may be discerned clearly by visual inspection without the necessity of statistical analysis. In this context, Kazdin (1978) has further observed: "Investigators who use single-case designs have made a special point to look for interventions that produce dramatic changes in behavior. Interventions with such effects for the single case are likely to generalize more broadly than are interventions that meet the relatively weaker criterion of statistical significance based on group averages that characterize between-group research" (p. 640).

When a sample of one or just a few is insufficient, researchers in single-case experimentation typically turn to replication, as opposed to between-group experimentation. Between-group experimentation, however desirable otherwise, has certain limitations from the point of view of clinical research: the behavior change of individuals often tends to be obscured; data are averaged across subjects, emphasizing mean differences between groups; there is generally a search for statistical significance; and behavior tends to be assessed on relatively few occasions (for example, through before- and after-intervention assessments). Replication with single-case experiments has the advantage of being flexible, individualized, clinically relevant, and less costly than conventional between-group experimentation.

Sidman (1960) has identified two types of replication relevant to single-case experimentation. The first, called direct replication, involves repetition of the given experiment by the same investigator. Sidman further divides direct replication into two types: repetition of the experiment on the same subject (within-subject replication) and repetition on different subjects (between-subject replication). Although both types increase the investigator's confidence in the generalizability of the results, intersubject replication has more relevance to generalization across subjects.

Hersen and Barlow (1976) have identified the following guidelines for a direct replication: "(1) therapists and settings should remain constant across replication; (2) the behavior disorder in question should be topographically similar across clients, such as a specific phobia; (3) client background variables should be as closely matched as possible, although the ideal goal of identical clients can never be attained in applied research; (4) the procedure employed (treatment) should be uniform across clients, until failures ensue . . . ; (5) one successful experiment and three successful replications will usually be sufficient to generate systematic replication on topographically different behaviors in the same setting or the same behavior in different settings . . . ; and (6) broad client generality cannot be established from one experiment and three replications" (pp. 334–335).

The second type identified by Sidman is systematic replication, which involves replication to help establish the generality of findings over a wide range of conditions, such as therapists, clientele, and settings. Systematic replication is fundamentally a search for exceptions. Following the successful completion of direct replication in at least several experiments, systematic replication is conducted by the successive replication of the experiment with systematic variation of such conditions as clientele, therapists, or settings. In her discussion of criteria that might be employed in replication to extend the generalizability of results, Kennedy (1979) has suggested the following criteria for sampling attributes: (1) a wide range of attributes across the sample cases; (2) many common attributes between sample cases and the population of interest; (3) few unique attributes in the sample of cases; and (4) relevance of the attributes to the treatment. Systematic replication should ideally be extended to only a few, rather than many, new conditions, thus retaining the essential integrity of the conditions for direct replication. This allows for the possibility of incremental extension of findings if the replications are successful, and for determining the bases for failure when replications do not succeed.

Hersen and Barlow (1976) identify still another type of replication that they call clinical replication: "We would define clinical replication as the administration of a treatment package containing two or more distinct treatment procedures by the same investigator or group of investigators. These procedures would be administered in a specific setting to a series of clients presenting similar combinations of multiple behavioral and emotional problems, which usually cluster together. Obviously, this type of replication process is advanced in that it is the end result of a systematic 'technique-building,' applied research effort, which would take years" (p. 336).

The basis of generalization through replication is an important concept. In this view, each successive positive replication, whether direct, systematic, or clinical, increases plausibility multiplicatively, because a chance occurrence of such events becomes much more improbable with each additional replication. The same may be said, of course, for replicated failures. The results involving mixed positive and negative outcomes pose special action alternatives. As Sidman (1960) has noted, "Successful replications . . . cannot be balanced out by any number of failures to replicate" (p. 94). The researcher's purpose in such instances is not to try to draw conclusions about some sample of clientele but rather to develop a more reliable intervention for those cases where the initial intervention failed. According to Sidman, "if a datum fails to achieve consistent replication, the scientist cannot afford to ease his conscience with the rationalization that we live, after all, in a probabilistic world, where truth is only a relative matter. The proper inference to be drawn from variability is that one's control techniques are inadequate" (p. 94). Mixed outcomes and negative results should encourage the researchers to identify and achieve some control over the sources of variability. As Sidman has further observed: "Tracking down sources of variability is then a primary technique for establishing generality. . . . Experience has taught us that precision of control leads to more extensive generalization of data" (p. 152).

Human Subjects Protections

Like all research, inquiry involving single-case experimentation should provide proper protections for the research participants. A critical problem posed by single-case experimentation conducted in service settings involves possible research–service conflicts that may serve to increase risks or decrease benefits for research participants. Many, if not all, of the threats of single-case experimentation to service outlined earlier may, under certain conditions, raise ethical issues for which protections are required. In general, at least three important factors are involved in the protection of participant rights: making provisions for informed consent; determining that any risks involved for the participant are generally outweighed by the benefits; and ensuring that information provided by the participant will be kept confidential.

The first of these factors is particularly important because consent, in order to be legally effective, must be informed. As stated in the Department of Health, Education, and Welfare (DHEW) regulations on this matter (*Federal Register,* 1974):

> "Informed consent" means the knowing consent of an individual or his legally authorized representative, so situated as to be able to exercise free power of choice with undue inducement or any element of force, fraud, deceit, duress, or other form of constraint or coercion. The basic elements of information necessary to such consent include: (1) a fair explanation of the procedures to be followed and their purposes, including identification of any procedures which are experimental; (2) a description of any attendent discomforts and risks reasonably to be expected; (3) a description of any benefits reasonably to be expected; (4) a disclosure of any appropriate alternative procedures that may be advantageous for the subject; (5) an offer to answer any inquiries concerning the procedures; and (6) an instruction that the person is free to withdraw his consent and to discontinue participation in the project or activity at any time without prejudice to the subject [p. 18917].

In addition to informed consent, the researcher is expected to have made reasonable efforts to assure that consent is voluntary and that the subject at risk is competent. Provisions should be made for the subject to withdraw from the experiment if so desired, and a method of appeal to a third party should be specified (Schwitzgebel and Schwitzgebel, 1980). In work with voluntary clients who are research participants in clinical research, the DHEW guidelines for work with human subjects referred to earlier may provide adequate protection for such areas as informed consent. However, additional protections may be required in work with special populations—for example, children where parents or other legally responsible representatives are required to provide consent for minors (*Federal Register,* 1978), or alcohol and substance abusers where special, additional measures have to be taken to protect the confidentiality of records (*Federal Register,* 1975).

In addition to assuring the protection of the participants as research subjects, research with clientele involved in treatment must give attention to client rights. Court rulings like *Wyatt* v. *Stickney,* ethical guidelines proposed by professional organizations (for example, the Association for the Advancement of Behavior Therapy), and articles on ethical issues and client rights help to suggest and to define more clearly special protections for clients (see Begelman, 1975; Davison and Stuart, 1975; Schwitzgebel and Schwitzgebel, 1980; Thomas, 1977c; Wexler, 1973). For example, it is increasingly being emphasized that provision should be made for clients, whether or not they are researcher subjects, to make informed choices about entering and continuing in therapy. As stated by Hare-Mustin and others (1979), such choices involve knowledge in the following three areas: (1) the procedures, goals, and possible side effects of therapy; (2) the qualifications, policies, and practices of the therapist; and (3) the available sources of help other than therapy. Clinical researchers also need to give attention to the right to treatment, the right to decline treatment, and, if the client is confined or committed, rights to the least-restrictive alternative of confinement (Ennis and Friedman, 1973).

The protections that may be most appropriate for conducting single-case experimentation in service settings must take into account degrees of risk and benefit for the participants. As Davison and Stuart (1975) suggest, the protections involved in the consent-giving process may be thought of as a hierarchy ranging from minimal to maximal protection. For example, if there is a low risk to the subject and high potential benefit promised, participant consent should be obtained without necessarily providing full disclosure of objectives and methods of research. However, when there are experimental rather than established procedures involved in the research, these authors recommend that, in addition to consent, there be full disclosure of objectives and procedures. Further, if there are greater risks and little potential benefit for the participant but high potential benefits for society, such additional protections as witnesses and independent review by an internal and external human subjects committee are recommended. Despite these suggestions, much more work needs to be done to develop proper subject protections when there are potential risks and different blends of subject and societal benefits.

When single-case experimentation involves clinical practice in an agency or research setting, it is strongly recommended that a human subjects review committee be established to provide oversight for the protection of subject and client rights and to review procedures in the light of these protections.

References

Azrin, N. H. "A Strategy for Applied Research: Learning Based but Outcome Oriented." *American Psychologist,* 1977, *32,* 140–149.

Azrin, N. H. "The Present State and Future Trends of Behavior Therapy." In P. O. Sjoden, S. Bates, and W. S. Dockens (Eds.), *Trends in Behavior Therapy.* New York: Academic Press, 1979.

Baer, D. M. "Perhaps It Would Be Better Not to Know Everything." *Journal of Applied Behavior Analysis,* 1977, *10,* 167–172.

Baer, D. M., Wolf, M. M., and Risley, R. R. "Some Current Dimensions of Applied Behavior Analysis." *Journal of Applied Behavior Analysis,* 1968, *1,* 91–97.

Begelman, D. A. "Ethical and Legal Issues in Behavioral Modification." In M. Hersen, R. M. Eisler, and P. H. Miller (Eds.), *Progress in Behavior Modification.* Vol. 1. New York: Academic Press, 1975.

Bijou, S. W., and others. "Methodology for Experimental Studies of Young Children in Natural Settings." *Psychological Bulletin,* 1969, *19,* 177–210.

Bloom, M. *The Paradox of Helping: Introduction to the Philosophy of Scientific Practice.* New York: Wiley, 1975.

Bloom, M., and Block, S. "Evaluating One's Own Effectiveness and Efficiency." *Social Work,* 1977, *22,* 130–137.

Bloom, M., Butch, P., and Walker, D. "Evaluation of Single Interventions." *Journal of Social Service Research,* 1979, *3,* 301–311.

Briar, S. "Incorporating Research into Education for Clinical Practice in Social Work: Toward a Clinical Service in Social Work." Paper presented at the Conference on Research Utilization in Social Work Education, New Orleans, La., Oct. 1977.

Campbell, D. T. "Reforms as Experiments." *American Psychologist,* 1969, *24,* 409–430.

Campbell, D. T., and Stanley, J. C. *Experimental and Quasi-Experimental Designs for Research.* Chicago: Rand McNally, 1966.

Chassan, J. B. *Research Design in Clinical Psychology and Psychiatry.* (2nd ed., rev. and enlarged) New York: Irvington, 1979.

Davison, G. C., and Stuart, R. B. "Behavior Therapy and Civil Liberties." *American Psychologist,* 1975, *30,* 755–763.

Dukes, W. F. "N=1." *Psychological Bulletin,* 1965, *64,* 74–79.

Ennis, B. J., and Friedman, P. R., (Eds.). *Legal Rights of the Mentally Handicapped.* Vol. 1 and 2. New York: The Mental Health Law Project, Practicing Law Institute, 1973.

Epstein, S. "The Stability of Behavior: II. Implications for Psychological Research." *American Psychologist,* 1980, *35,* 790–807.

Federal Register. "Protection of Human Subjects." 1974, *39* (105), 18914–18920.

Federal Register. "Confidentiality of Alcohol and Drug Abuse Patient Records." 1975, *40* (127), 27802–27821.

Federal Register. "Protection of Human Subjects: Research Involving Children." 1978, *43* (141), 31786–31794.

Fischer, J. *Effective Casework Practice: An Eclectic Approach.* New York: McGraw-Hill, 1978.

Franks, C. M., and Wilson, G. T., (Eds.). *Annual Review of Behavior Therapy: Theory and Practice.* New York: Brunner/Mazel, 1976.

Hare-Mustin, R. T., and others. "Rights of Clients, Responsibilities of Therapists." *American Psychologist,* 1979, *34,* 3–17.

Hartmann, D. P., and Atkinson, C. "Having Your Cake and Eating It Too: A Note on Some Apparent Contradictions Between Therapeutic Achievements and Design Requirements in N=1 Studies." *Behavior Therapy,* 1973, *4,* 589–592.

Hersen, M., and Barlow, D. H. *Single-Case Experimental Designs: Strategies for Studying Behavior Change.* Elmsford, N.Y.: Pergamon Press, 1976.

Howe, M. W. "Casework Self-Evaluation: A Single-Subject Approach." *Social Service Review,* 1974, *48,* 1–24.

Jayaratne, S., and Levy, R. L. *Empirical Clinical Practice.* New York: Columbia University Press, 1979.

Jones, R. R., Vaught, R. S., and Weinrott, M. "Time-Series Analysis in Operant Research." *Journal of Applied Behavior Analysis,* 1977, *10,* 151–167.

Kazdin, A. E. "Methodological and Assessment Considerations in Evaluating Reinforcement Programs in Applied Settings." *Journal of Applied Behavior Analysis,* 1973, *6,* 517–532.

Kazdin, A. E. "Methodological and Interpretative Problems of Single-Case Experimental Designs." *Journal of Consulting and Clinical Psychology,* 1978, *46,* 629–643.

Kazdin, A. E., and Kopel, S. A. "On Resolving Ambiguities of the Multiple Baseline Design: Problems and Recommendations." *Behavior Therapy,* 1975, *6,* 601–609.

Kendall, P. C., Nay, W. R., and Jeffers, J. "Time-Out Duration and Contrast Effects: A Systematic Evaluation of a Successive Treatments Design." *Behavior Therapy,* 1975, *6,* 609–616.

Kiresuk, T. J., and Sherman, R. E. "Goal Attainment Scaling: A General Method for Evaluating Comprehensive Mental Health Programs." *Community Mental Health Journal,* 1968, *4,* 443–453.

Kratochwill, T. R. "Foundations of Time-Series Research." In T. R. Kratochwill (Ed.), *Single-Subject Research: Strategies for Evaluating Change.* New York: Academic Press, 1978.

Leitenberg, H. "The Use of Single-Case Methodology in Psychotherapy Research." *Journal of Abnormal Psychology,* 1973, *82,* 87–102.

Liberman, R. P., and others. "Behavior Measurement in a Community Mental Health Center." In P. Davidson, E. Mash, and W. Handy (Eds.), *Evaluating Social Programs in Community Settings: Proceedings of the Fifth International Banff Conference on Behavior Modification.* Champaign, Ill.: Research Press, 1974.

Liberman, R. P., King, L. W., and DeRisi, W. J. "Behavior Analysis and Therapy in Community Mental Health." In H. Leitenberg (Ed.), *Handbook of Behavior Modification and Behavior Therapy.* Englewood Cliffs, N.J.: Prentice-Hall, 1976.

Mutschler, E. "Using Single-Case Evaluation Procedures in a Family and Children's Service Agency: Integration of Practice and Research." *Journal of Social Service Research,* 1979, *3,* 115–134.

O'Leary, K. D., and Kent, R. "Behavior Modification for Social Action: Research Problems and Tactics." In L. A. Hamerlynck, L. C. Handy, and E. J. Mash (Eds.), *Behavior Change: Methodology, Concepts and Practice.* Champaign, Ill.: Research Press, 1973.

Parsonson, B. S., and Baer, D. M. "The Analysis and Presentation of Graphic Data." In T. R. Kratochwill (Ed.), *Single-Subject Research: Strategies for Evaluating Change.* New York: Academic Press, 1978.

Schwitzgebel, R. L., and Schwitzgebel, R. K. *Law and Psychological Practice.* New York: Wiley, 1980.

Sidman, M. *Tactics of Scientific Research.* New York: Basic Books, 1960.

Thomas, E. J. "Uses of Research Methods in Interpersonal Practice." In N. A. Polansky (Ed.), *Social Work Research: Methods for the Helping Professions.* (Rev. ed.) Chicago: University of Chicago Press, 1975.

Thomas, E. J. *Marital Communication and Decision-Making: Analysis, Assessment, and Change.* New York: The Free Press, 1977a.

Thomas, E. J. "The BESDAS Model for Effective Practice." *Social Work Research and Abstracts,* 1977b, *13,* 12–17.

Thomas, E. J. "Social Casework and Social Group Work: The Behavioral Modification Approach." *Encyclopedia of Social Work.* Vol. 2. Washington, D.C.: National Association of Social Workers, 1977c.

Thomas, E. J. "Research and Service in Single-Case Experimentation: Conflicts and Choices." *Social Work Research and Abstracts,* 1978, *14,* 20–31.

Tripodi, T., and Epstein, I. "Incorporating Knowledge of Research Methodology into Social Work Practice." *Journal of Social Service Research,* 1978, *2,* 65–79.

Webb, E. J., and others. *Unobtrusive Measures: Nonreactive Research in the Social Sciences.* Chicago: Rand McNally, 1972.

Wexler, D. B. "Token and Taboo: Behavior Modification, Token Economies, and the Law." *California Law Review,* 1973, *61,* 81–109.

28

Personal Practice Models

Edward J. Mullen

This chapter examines the nature of personal practice models and the process of their development. Personal practice models are presented as orienting conceptual schemes developed and used by individual practitioners for guiding their work with clients. Model building is seen as an ongoing process involving the critical use of information derived from examination of experience, theory, and research. (For extension discussions of the model concept, see Brodbeck, 1959; Kaplan, 1964; and Kuhn, 1970.)

What Are Personal Practice Models?

Personal practice models are explicit conceptual schemes that express an individual social worker's view of practice and give orderly direction to work with specific clients. Personal practice models are not the product of simple scholarly curiosity but rather are motivated in their development by pragmatic interests. Such models are the product of serious, critical consideration of multiple information sources by individual social workers. Once developed, personal models put forth summary generalizations and practice guidelines that give general direction to the practitioner's subsequent practice. These summary generalizations explicate the practitioner's understanding and perspective on important practice dimensions; practice guidelines provide prescriptive practice principles derived from the generalizations. Because such models are explicit and specific, they can

Note: Special appreciation is expressed to my students who have contributed so much to our work in model development. The developments discussed in this chapter are especially based on the creative and hard work of Gerald Bostwick, Nancy Kyte, Susan Anderson-Ray, and the students in SSA 301-304 during the 1978-1979 and 1979-1980 academic years. The earlier support of the Ittleson Foundation is appreciated for making much of this work possible.

serve as a basis for evaluating practice. Guidelines can be tested against practice experience, and that experience can serve as a basis for model revision.

The term *personal* is used to denote two ideas (Mullen, 1981). First, the process is meant to be rational and self-conscious. Second, it is meant to reflect the idiosyncracies of the individual social worker. Therefore, such models reflect both the science and art of practice.

Why Are Personal Practice Models Needed?

A number of concerns might be raised about the idea of personal practice models. First, it might be argued that the profession already has a number of general practice models developed by social work scholars after considerable thought and study. Therefore, effort expended in the development of personal models might be viewed as redundant and wasteful. Second, it might be considered unrealistic to expect individual social workers to engage in such an activity, given the amount of time and effort required. Finally, concern might be expressed about the subjectivity such an approach might bring to practice.

Each of these concerns in fact presents an argument in favor of personal practice models. The assumption underlying the argument for personal models is that social work professionals are personally accountable to their clients, agencies, profession, and society for the nature of their own practice. This accountability results in personal and individual responsibility for the nature, quality, and effects of practice. Given this assumption, it would seem risky to advocate that individual social workers simply adopt one or another of the general practice models readily available in the literature without critically studying alternatives. In addition, consideration of additional information that may not have been available at the time the general model was developed is particularly important, given the rapid expansion of knowledge. To simply adopt a general model or models without such critical thought would seem to be to skirt personal accountability, just as imitation differs from responsible creativity.

The second concern—the feasibility of individual social workers expending the time and effort required to develop personal practice models—is problematic, as is the acquisition of the skills of information utilization and model development. The art of social work practice is difficult and complex, and development of a conceptual scheme for use in practice and continual revision of that scheme in light of new information will also be a difficult and complex undertaking, particularly at its inception. The ongoing revision of an established personal practice model is manageable, however, and information utilization and model development will become easier as further resources and methods are developed.

The final concern is the subjectivity of personal models. The fear is that such models could be simply the illusory product of a particular practitioner's subjective views. In fact, personal models are being advocated precisely as an attempt to avoid such situations. While incorporating the idea of individual practitioner variation, the term *personal* is intended to denote the use of a rational and self-conscious approach. Information is to be considered from a range of sources, including those external to the individual's practice experience (for example, theory, research). By emphasizing personal accountability and the use of multiple information sources, practice should become increasingly reality-oriented.

What Are the Dimensions of a Model?

Personal practice models face the same requirements faced by general models regarding the direction they must give to practice.

Social Welfare and the Profession. First, the practitioner should articulate a working understanding of the field of social welfare and the place of social work practice within that field, including, if necessary, a conceptualization of his or her practice specialization (for example, clinical social work) and its relationship to the social welfare field. The implications of these conceptualizations for directing practice should then be specified in the form of practice guidelines.

Social Work. Having mapped the general practice territory, a personal practice model should also specify at least five subdimensions: the general mission and objectives of practice; the source and nature of practice sanctions and accountability; the guiding philosophy, values, and ethics of the personal model; the general types of knowledge considered relevant for practice; and the general types of practice roles, activities, and skills required for practice within the framework of the personal model. The practitioner's goal as this dimension is considered would be to critically consider varying conceptions of social work practice and to explicate a working personal orientation to each of these subdimensions, including the implications of this orientation for an approach to practice.

Although the first two dimensions are quite broad, the remaining involve specific consideration of practice elements: the client, the worker, their relationship, the agency, intervention techniques, and monitoring and evaluation plans.

Clients. Although clients are clearly the recipients of social workers' services, it is not always clear how particular workers involve their clients in practice or which client characteristics they consider significant in choosing an intervention. Does it matter whether the client is rich or poor, motivated or unmotivated, old or young, an individual or a family unit, depressed or manipulative, and so on? Personal practice models should include a specification of the place and significance of the client in practice, as well as client qualities to be considered in planning intervention. The practitioner's goal in developing this dimension of the model would be to critically consider information concerning client qualities related to the use of, continuance in, and outcome of social work intervention, including specification of practice guidelines.

Practitioner. Just as practice always involves a client, individual practitioners, too, are ever present, with all their idiosyncracies. What characteristics of the practitioner are relevant to practice? Does practitioner style, expectation, theoretical orientation, training, experience, age, race, or sex have any relevance to planning intervention? As this dimension is developed, the goal would be specification of practitioner characteristics considered relevant to the client's use of, continuance in, and benefit from intervention, including specification of those practice guidelines implied.

Relationship. Since social work intervention occurs within the context of specific practitioner–client interactions, the relationship dimension of the personal model also needs to be addressed. The practitioner should specify an understanding of the place of the relationship in practice and of the relationship qualities considered relevant. Does it matter how the client experiences the practitioner's expression of warmth, empathy, or genuineness? Are the phenomena of transference and countertransference to be considered? Do similarities or differences of practitioner–client cognitive styles, race, age, sex, or personality styles have any relevance? As this dimension of the model is developed, the goal would be specification of relevant relationship qualities thought to be associated with the use of, continuance in, and outcome of intervention and the development of practice guidelines.

Agency. Social work is generally practiced in organizations. Whether these organizations are voluntary or public agencies or organized forms of private practice, practice normally takes place in an organizational context. Does the organizational environment, structure, or climate have any relevance to the nature, quality, and outcome of practice? Does it matter whether the practitioner is functioning in an agency whose source of funding is fluid and uncertain? Whether the agency is large and centralized or small and decentralized? Whether the supervision is authoritarian or supportive? Whether the agencies' goals are clear and generally accepted or ambiguous and unacceptable? Addressing this dimension of the model, the practitioner would specify organizational characteristics considered relevant for planning intervention and would describe how these characteristics might be affected by or affect the practitioner's practice.

Techniques. At the core of the personal practice model would be specification of intervention techniques. The range of options available to the practitioner is wide and increasing. To a considerable extent, the relevance of various techniques will be constrained by resolution of previously mentioned model dimensions. If a practitioner's general view of social work places high value on environmental work, psychological techniques might be less significant; if relationship qualities are considered of particular importance, techniques designed to manipulate the relationship might be sought; or, if particular importance is placed on client self-determination, techniques might be valued that facilitate the client's problem-solving skills.

In addition to the constraints operating as a consequence of earlier decisions made in model development, selection of techniques for inclusion will also be limited by the range available. Currently, a wide spectrum of techniques is available for consideration by the clinical social worker from among such specialized theoretical approaches as client-centered, psychodynamic (and its many variations), operant and respondent conditioning, observational learning, cognitive, family, and small-group theories. In addition, numerous techniques are available for consideration from sources not theory-based, including a range of structuring approaches and environmental methods. As the clinical social worker expands the personal model to neighborhood, community, and organizational levels of intervention, additional techniques are available, including those recommended for promoting innovations, changing organizational goals, fostering client participation, dealing with organizational conflict, and providing staff supervision, to name only a few. As the range of techniques are considered in model development, the practitioner's initial goal would be to become familiar with the major techniques available for use in clinical social work. Ultimately, the practitioner would specify those to be included in the model and delineate practice guidelines for their use (such as the conditions under which a particular technique would be relevant).

Monitoring and Evaluation. The model should address the nature of monitoring and evaluation strategies to be used. A strategy should be devised for collecting and considering information about the results of guideline implementation. Without systematic plans for such feedback, the relevance and effectiveness of the practitioner's approach would remain uncertain. Techniques for monitoring and evaluating the various guidelines within the model could include structured use of supervision, focused and structured recording, audiotaping or videotaping of interventions, use of client feedback, and more highly controlled single-subject designs (see Levy and Thomas in this volume). As this dimension is developed, the goal would be to specify monitoring and evaluation strategies and techniques and plans for their implementation. Such feedback strategies then become systematic sources of information for further model refinement.

What Sources of Information Are Considered in Model Development?

Central to model development is critical consideration of information potentially relevant to practice. To an extent, the selection of information sources thought to be potentially relevant is a subjective decision made by each practitioner. Yet professional ethics and accountability place considerable responsibility on the individual practitioner for consideration of information from a number of sources, including practice wisdom, personal experience, theory, and research. To ignore any of these sources as potential channels of useful information for personal model development would seem myopic and unethical.

Taken together, these sources provide an information base for the individual practitioner's critical consideration in model development. Specific sources will be found more relevant and informative than other sources for each of the model dimensions. Table 1 presents a cross-partitioning of sources of information and model dimensions. Each cell represents an "information space." The contribution of each source to the overall model would depend on the amount of useful information available from that source, the value placed on the information source, and the amount of valued information available from other sources.

For purposes of illustration, the author surveyed a group of seventeen second-year master's degree students who had been engaged in the process of model development during their first year of study. The survey sought to determine student perception regarding the relative contribution of the four sources to their personal models and was restrictetd to the microsystem practice model developed during the first year of graduate study. The students were presented with the model dimensions illustrated in Table 1 and asked to rank the contribution of each information source to each dimension in their own model using the rating scale illustrated in Table 1.

Of the seventeen students, nine returned the questionnaire in time for inclusion in this analysis. Additional student response was not pursued since the data are presented simply by way of illustration and no attempt is made to claim validity or generalizability.

Table 2 illustrates student response regarding the contribution made by each of the four sources to their summary generalizations. On the average, these students considered all sources to have made a modest contribution to their model's summary generalizations. However, the perceived contribution of each source

Table 1. Potential Sources of Information for Model Development

MODEL DIMENSION	*INFORMATION SOURCE*							
	Practice wisdom[a]		*Personal experience*[b]		*Theory*		*Research*	
	S.G.[c]	*P.G.*[d]	*S.G.*	*P.G.*	*S.G.*	*P.G.*	*S.G.*	*P.G.*
The social welfare field								
Social work's								
Mission								
Sanction and accountability								
Philosophy, values, ethics								
Goals								
General nature of knowledge base								
General nature of skill requirements								
Client qualities								
Worker qualities								
Relationship qualities								
Agency-organizational qualities								
Technologies and techniques								
Monitoring and evaluation strategies								

[a] "Practice wisdom" refers to the collective experiential learning of the profession transmitted through published authoritative materials. Practice wisdom is distinguished from theory and research in that it is based on less systematic methods and is usually presented with less precision or organization. To some extent, it appears as professional common sense.
[b] "Personal experience" refers to direct experiences in both professional and personal roles.
[c] S.G. = summary generalization.
[d] P.G. = practice guideline.

Rating Scale
0 = no contribution to summary generalizations or practice guidelines in student's model for the particular dimension rated
1 = slight contribution
2 = moderate contribution
3 = great contribution

Table 2. Contribution of Information Sources to Summary Generalizations: Student Self-Report Based on First-Year Study

RATING	*SOURCE*			
	Practice wisdom	*Personal experience*	*Theory*	*Research*
Mean[a]	2.3	2.3	2.3	2.1
Range[b]	1.5–3	1.5–3	2–3	1–3

[a]A model rating for each of the thirteen dimensions was calculated (see Table 1). Reported are the mean ratings across the thirteen model dimensions.
[b]Reported are the range of modal ratings across the thirteen model dimensions.

varied considerably across model dimensions. As indicated by the range, each source reportedly made, on the average, a great contribution to at least one of the model dimensions (an average rating of 3). In no instance was a source viewed, on the average, as having made no contribution (an average rating of 0). If both the average and range are considered, this group of students perceive theory to have made the strongest general contribution, research the least, and the remaining two sources, practice wisdom and experience, a contribution of intermediate value.

Table 3 presents a breakdown of these data for each of the thirteen model dimensions. Noteworthy is the differential contribution of the sources to the various dimensions. Practice wisdom, on the average, is perceived to have made a great or moderate contribution to all dimensions with the possible exception of monitoring and evaluation strategies.

The contribution of personal experience is more variable. As might be expected, some students have more experience to draw on than others. In addition, the variation may also be partly due to the differing values placed on experience by the students. Taking into account this individual student variation, one can see that for this group of students personal experience most consistently contributes to an understanding of social work's mission, sanction/accountability, philosophy/values/ethics, worker characteristics, and technologies/techniques.

Considerable student variation is also apparent regarding the perceived contribution of theory to the model dimensions. There is general agreement that theory contributed either moderately or greatly to the general nature of social work knowledge, as well as to practice technologies/techniques. In every dimension except the understanding of social work's mission, at least one student viewed theory as having made a great contribution to summary generalizations.

Research is perceived to have made its greatest contribution to summary generalizations regarding client characteristics, worker characteristics, the relationship, practice technologies/techniques, and monitoring/evaluation strategies. Attesting to individual student variation, at least one student reported research to have made a modest contribution to summary generalizations in every dimension. Conversely, in six of the dimensions, at least one student reported research to have made no contribution.

Table 3. Contributions of Information Sources to Summary Generalizations: Student Self-Report Based on First Year

MODEL DIMENSION	INFORMATION SOURCE			
	Practice wisdom	*Personal experience*	*Theory*	*Research*
The social welfare field	Great (1–3)[a]	Slight, moderate, and great (1–3)[c]	Moderate (0–3)	Moderate (0–2)
Social work's Mission	Great (2–3)	Moderate and great (1–3)[b]	Moderate (1–2)	Moderate (0–2)
Sanction and accountability	Great (2–3)	Moderate (1–3)	Slight, moderate, and great (1–3)[c]	None, slight, and moderate (0–2)[c]
Philosophy, values, ethics	Great (2–3)	Great (1–3)	Slight, moderate, and great (1–3)[c]	None and moderate (0–2)[b]
Goals	Moderate and great (1–3)[b]	Moderate (0–3)	Slight, moderate, and great (1–3)[c]	Moderate (0–3)
General nature of knowledge base	Moderate (2–3)	Great (0–3)	Great (2–3)	Slight (1–3)
General nature of skill requirements	Moderate (1–3)	Great (0–3)	Moderate (1–3)	Slight (1–3)
Client qualities	Moderate (0–3)	Slight and great (1–3)[b]	Moderate (1–3)	Great (2–3)

Worker qualities	Moderate (1–3)	Moderate (1–3)	Moderate (0–3)	Great (1–3)
Relationship qualities	Moderate (2–3)	Slight and moderate (1–3)[b]	Moderate and great (1–3)	Great (2–3)
Agency-organizational qualities	Moderate (1–3)	Moderate (0–3)	Moderate (1–3)	Moderate (0–3)
Technologies and techniques	Moderate (1–3)	Great (1–3)	Great (2–3)	Great (2–3)
Monitoring and evaluation strategies	Slight and moderate (1–3)[b]	Moderate (0–3)	Great (0–3)	Great (2–3)

[a]The modal rating is reported. Ranges are reported in parentheses.
[b]Bimodal
[c]Trimodal

Student report regarding the contribution of the four sources to practice guidelines is illustrated in Table 4. The contribution of practice wisdom and personal experience remains nearly the same as for summary generalizations. Theory and research are reported to have been somewhat less useful in their contribution to practice guidelines. Theory, on the average, is perceived to have made a modest contribution. Again, however, considerable variation across dimensions is apparent. Every source is reported, on the average, to have made a great contribution to at least one dimension.

Table 5 presents the student ratings of contributions to practice guidelines for each of the dimensions. The contribution of practice wisdom is essentially the same as previously reported regarding summary generalizations. Personal experience is reported as contributing more significantly to practice guidelines than to summary generalizations regarding the field of social welfare, social work's mission, and its sanction/accountability. Little difference of opinion is evident for these dimensions.

The decrease in the perceived contribution of theory to practice guidelines results from less relevance to social work's mission, sanction/accountability, philosophy/values/ethics, and general practice skills. However, student variation is apparent, and at least one student reports theory to be a great contribution for every dimension.

The marked decrease in the perceived contribution of research is accounted for by a decrease in its impact on guidelines regarding the field of social welfare, social work's mission and goals, and the client, worker, and relationship dimensions. However, in spite of these decreases, research continues to be seen, on the average, as having made a modest to great contribution to guidelines regarding client, worker, and relationship dimensions. Research's perceived contribution to guidelines is greatest regarding monitoring/evaluation strategies and practice technologies/techniques.

Although the reported data are of questionable validity and representativeness, they illustrate the major point of this section. The various information sources available for model development will be judged as more or less relevant to each of the model dimensions according to the practitioner's personal criteria. Since students and practitioners engaged in personal modeling will usually find themselves drawing from a range of information sources, they will require skill in information analysis.

What Process Is Used to Develop Personal Models?

The process for developing personal practice models is a special case of information utilization for application purposes. Elsewhere, I have delineated processes for using both research and theoretical information in model development (Mullen, 1978, 1981). However, the process of using information from practice wisdom or personal experience has not been systematically considered within the context of personal model development, and no process of information utilization for modeling has yet been developed that includes all these sources.

At the outset, it should be acknowledged that using information in practice is a complex process, and a comprehensive approach to this process would need to take into account political, organizational, socioeconomic, and attitudinal com-

Table 4. Contribution of Information Sources to Practice Guidelines: Student Self-Report Based on First Year

RATING	*SOURCE*			
	Practice wisdom	*Personal experience*	*Theory*	*Research*
Mean[a]	2.3	2.3	2	1.7
Range[b]	2-3	1-3	1-3	1-3

[a]Reported are the mean ratings across thirteen model dimensions.
[b]Reported are the range of mode ratings across the thirteen model dimensions.

ponents, in addition to the specific information involved. It should also be expected that, for the most part, the process will result in "conceptual utilization," rather than "instrumental utilization" (Caplan and others, 1975). Most often instrumental utilization, in which single pieces of information are used directly, does not occur. Rather, as is the case in conceptual utilization, multiple sets of data from a range of sources are blended and indirectly affect practice. In this form of utilization, it should further be expected that information will usually be used in modified form, or partially, and that adaptation of the information to the practice situation will require practitioner innovation. At times after information is considered, the practitioner may justifiably decide not to use it. Direct and complete adoption of information for practice can be anticipated to be the exception. At times, using a particular piece of information for practice can even be inappropriate (Larsen, 1980).

Information used for the development of personal practice models has an indirect effect on specific case situations and will not necessarily translate directly into specific case applications. Rather, in the context of model development, information serves an "enlightenment" function (Weiss, unpublished). It is not usually used for specific decision making or problem solving in identifiable cases but rather may influence the practitioner's general thinking for future utilization in a general set of case situations, "creeping" into future decision making by a process of "accretion" (Weiss, 1980). Information is translated into practice guidelines of generalizable value.

Further, it should be anticipated that information utilization for personal model development will involve a process distinct in many ways from utilization by groups. Larsen (1980, p. 433) notes: "To what extent are there differences in knowledge utilization by individuals concerned with direct implications for practice on the personal level and utilization by decision-making groups concerned with defining national policy? It is obvious that knowledge utilization in which one individual considers his or her personal options is drastically different from knowledge utilization involving many special interest groups, each of which may be in opposition with the others and even with the utilization process. There are certainly differences between knowledge utilization in practice and policy, but there are similarities as well" (Larsen, 1980, p. 433). While the study of knowledge

Table 5. Contributions of Information Sources to Practice Guidelines: Student Self-Report Based on First Year

MODEL DIMENSION	*INFORMATION SOURCE*			
	Practice wisdom	*Personal experience*	*Theory*	*Research*
The social welfare field	Great (2–3)	Great (2–3)	Moderate (0–3)	Slight (0–2)
Social work's Mission	Great (1–3)	Great (2–3)	Slight and moderate (1–3)[b]	None, slight, and moderate (0–2)[c]
Sanction and accountability	Great (0–3)	Great (2–3)	Slight (0–3)	None, slight, and moderate (0–2)[c]
Philosophy, values, ethics	Great (2–3)	Great (1–3)	Slight (1–3)	None and moderate (0–2)[b]
Goals	Moderate (1–3)	Moderate (1–3)	Moderate (1–3)	Slight and moderate (0–3)[b]
General nature of knowledge base	Moderate (1–3)	Moderate (0–3)	Great (1–3)	Slight (1–3)
General nature of skill requirements	Moderate (1–3)	Moderate and great (0–3)[b]	Slight (1–3)	Slight (1–3)
Client qualities	Moderate (0–3)	Slight and great (1–3)[b]	Moderate (0–3)	Moderate (2–3)

Worker qualities	Moderate (1–3)	Moderate (1–3)	Moderate (0–3)	Moderate and great (1–3)[b]
Relationship qualities	Moderate (2–3)	Moderate (1–3)	Great (0–3)	Moderate (2–3)
Agency-organizational qualities	Moderate (1–3)	Slight (1–3)	Moderate (1–3)	Moderate (0–3)
Technologies and techniques	Moderate (1–3)	Moderate and great (1–3)[b]	Great (2–3)	Great (1–3)
Monitoring and evaluation strategies	Moderate (1–3)	Slight, moderate, and great (1–3)[c]	Moderate and great (0–3)[b]	Great (2–3)

[a]The modal rating is reported. Ranges are reported in parenthesis.
[b]Bimodal
[c]Trimodal

utilization is relatively young, its vigor has resulted in the development of a considerable literature descriptive of the way in which decision makers, professionals, and others use the results of research and formal expertise. For further information, the reader is referred to the works of Davis (1973), Rothman (1974, 1980), Fairweather, Sanders, and Tornatzky (1974), Blum (1974), Lippitt (1973), Rogers and Shoemaker (1971), and Zaltman (1979) in the fields of organizational innovation and planned social change and to the works of Hovland and others (1953), Janis and Mann (1977) and Rosenthal and Bandura (1978) in the fields of social psychology and cognitive learning.

A Process for Consideration. Although an examination of the information-utilization literature indicates the complexity of the process, relatively little is known about how to facilitate that process, particularly in creating personal practice models. Yet, over the past several years, my associates and I have developed a rudimentary process, which is briefly outlined here. The proposed process is not without its problems, however. The adaptation of what has been generally learned about information utilization to the process of utilization for personal practice model development remains problematic and assuredly will require considerable ingenuity and effort.

The proposed process, similar to one used generally in research and development and adapted from a framework developed by Rothman and his colleagues at the University of Michigan, is illustrated in Figure 1 (Rothman, 1980). Over the past six years, my associates and I have developed a working conceptualization, consisting of six stages and five steps, of what seems to be the flow of activity in personal model development. The various parts of the process have been implemented over the past four years, and the illustration given includes proposed revisions in that process based on these experiences.

The process begins with the goal of developing a personal practice model that will be useful for assisting clients. The goal can be to develop a general model or a model specific to particular need or problem areas. For those beginning their work as professional social workers, the more general goal is recommended to establish a general basis for practice. For more experienced workers, the development of a need- or problem-specific model could be more useful. Following goal specification, the relevant literature is examined for information giving direction to development of a conceptualization for practice. Personal experience is also considered at this stage. The process moves along a continuum culminating in broad application of the model in practice with clients. The five steps located within the arrows result in corresponding stages consisting of products for subsequent use in the process. These products are summary generalizations, intervention guidelines, and monitoring/evaluation guidelines.

Stage 1: The information for use in stage 1 includes relevant practice wisdom, theory, and research reported in the profession's literature, as well as relevant literature from allied disciplines and professions. Less organized sources of information are also relevant at this stage, including one's own experiences and those of one's colleagues. Step 1: Students beginning their studies depend, for the most part, on their instructors for relevant references, although new sources are also sought. Especially useful are review articles that critically consider specific model dimensions using contrasting perspectives, theory, and research. More knowledgeable practitioners will already be alert to relevant sources. This step

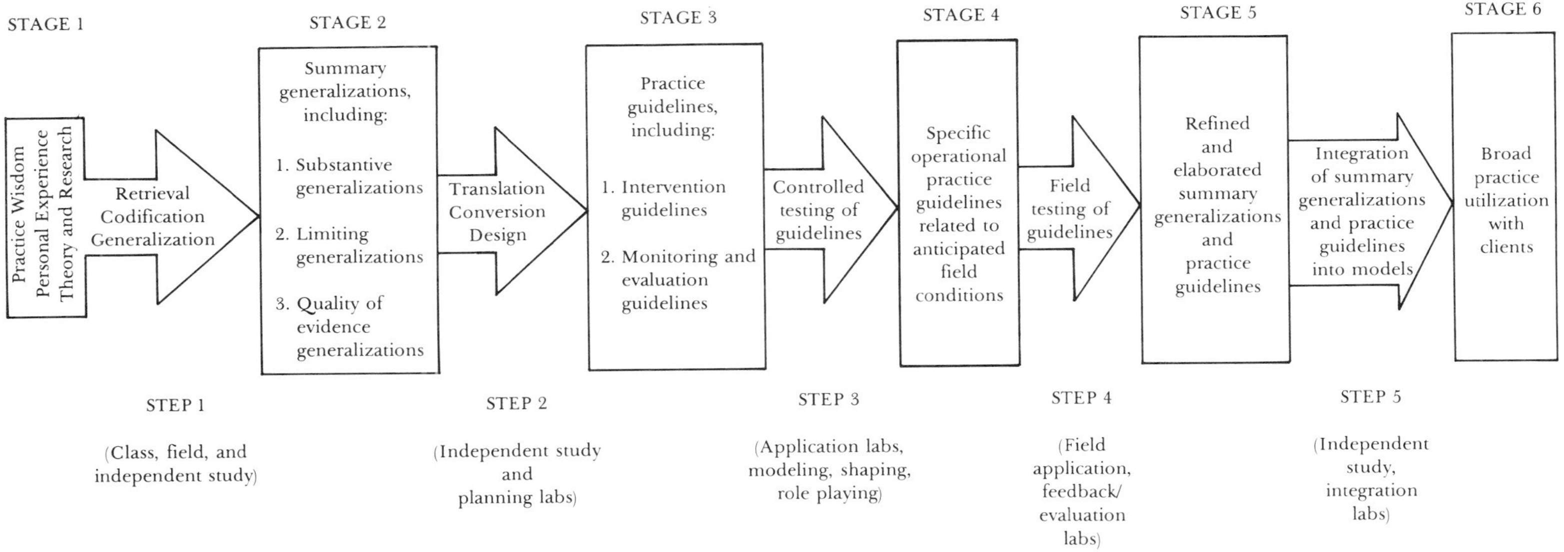

Source: Adapted from Rothman, 1980, p. 23.

Figure 1. Illustration of Modeling Process

involves retrieval of relevant information sources, however they are located, including literature and informed opinion. Both primary and secondary sources can be used, including abstracted material and information systems. The process is similar to that used by students engaged in library and field research for the development of an academic paper.

From the range of information sources located, those most germane to the particular dimension at hand are selected for intensive study. Given the vast literature available and the range of perspectives normally encountered, some degree of discrimination is required; however, significant sources usually become quite readily apparent.

Information is then placed into some classification system for use, a step normally requiring consolidation of material and the development of a system for codification. Consensus findings are sought, including regularities in authoritative opinion, consistency (or lack of consistency) in research findings, and so on. The nature of the grounding for the consensus findings is examined, and the reliability, validity, applicability, and limitations of the information are considered. Summary generalizations are then formed that bring together the substantive conclusions drawn regarding the dimension in question, specification of limitations in applicability, and quality of the grounding for the conclusions.

Stage 2: Based on the analysis conducted in step 1, one or more summary generalizations are produced in stage 2. Summary generalizations can take the form of paragraph statements bringing together apparent consensus in the information examined regarding the dimension under review or, if appropriate, addressing the lack of consensus. These summary generalizations would also include statements concerning applicability and limitations of the findings, as well as statements of the quality of the grounding.

To illustrate this process, three examples are presented. The first illustrates use of research findings as the primary source for summary generalizations and guidelines. The second illustrates use of practice wisdom. A third example illustrates use of a combination of sources, including practice wisdom, experience, theory, and research.

Research as Source. All forms of clinical practice in social work emphasize the relationship between worker and client. A clinical worker wishing to address this dimension of the model would review a rather large body of literature on relationship both in social work and in allied professions, noting specific qualities descriptive of the relationship. The considerable literature on accurate empathy, for example, is both theoretical and research-oriented. In order to illustrate the use of research as a source in model development, this discussion will limit itself to the research literature.

A first task is the location of research reports dealing with accurate empathy. Since the goal in model development is ultimately the development of guidelines that will enhance the effectiveness of intervention, research reports would be sought that examine the effects on clients of variation in the worker's expression of accurate empathy. In this case, the practitioner would soon discover that extensive research is available and that the study of review sources would be a more efficient approach. Research on the effects of accurate empathy has been critically examined in a number of secondary reviews, including Truax and Mitchell (1971), Chinsky and Rappaport (1970), Gurman and Razin (1977), and Parloff, Waskow, and Wolfe (1978). (The practitioner will find that research reviews are increasingly available for many aspects of model dimensions.)

A second task involves the codification of the information provided in the reviews. Based on experience, I have found it useful to record the substantive information (nominal and operational definitions of accurate empathy and its reported effects); the limiting conditions under which the studies were conducted that might limit the generalizability of the results reported (for example, qualities of the interveners, clients, organization, technologies used, and focus of the intervention); and the level of evidence supporting the asserted findings (for example, realism of studies, type of design, extent and nature of controls, consistency and replication of the findings).

A final task in step 1 is specification of summary generalizations, which are usually of three types: substantive generalizations (here specifying the nature of the relationship between accurate empathy and its effects on clients); limiting generalizations (here specifying relevant environmental, organizational, client, and technical conditions under which the relationship was found to occur); and quality-of-evidence generalizations (here specifying the soundness of the research grounding).

In the case of accurate empathy, a practitioner might form the following summary generalizations (Mullen, 1978, pp. 56–57):

> 1. *Substantive generalization.* An intervener's sensitivity to the moment-to-moment feelings of the client and the intervener's verbal facility to communicate this understanding in a language attuned to the client's current feelings (as measured by the Accurate Empathy Scale, Truax, 1961) are positively associated with the client's depth of self-exploration (as measured by the Self-Exploration Scale, Truax and Carkhuff, 1967) and are frequently associated with attitudinal, cognitive, and behavioral improvements in clients. A low level of empathic responses (as defined above) is associated with low levels of client self-exploration and is frequently associated with deterioration in attitudinal, cognitive, and behavioral areas. Although associated with intervention outcome, this quality does not appear to be either a necessary or sufficient condition, nor does it appear to be among a set of necessary and sufficient conditions for successful outcomes. Empathy accounts for a relatively small amount of variance in intervention outcomes, yet this amount is often statistically significant.
>
> 2. *Limiting generalizations.* Since most of the research has been based on interventions using interveners trained in a client-centered approach, it is not known to what extent the substantive generalization would be valid for other types of interveners. Since most studies incorporated as techniques nonpossessive warmth and genuineness, it is unknown to what extent the substantive hypothesis would be valid independently of warmth and genuineness. Limiting conditions concerning client characteristics and organizational contexts are of unknown relevance, based on the available information.
>
> 3. *Quality-of-evidence generalizations.* The substantive generalization is based on a relatively small number of uncontrolled field studies involving a relatively small number of investigators. The reliability and validity of the Accurate Empathy Scale is questionable, and the subject of much disagreement. It is unclear to what extent accurate empathy is inde-

pendent of client qualities and the extent to which the qualities are reciprocal (interactive). It is not clear to what extent the reported association between accurate empathy and intervention effects is a function of the particular scales used to measure empathy and its assumed effects and the interdependence of the scales. Since the research is relatively uncontrolled, little is known about the extent to which empathy and the effects are causatively associated. Although the findings favor the substantive generalization, some inconsistency is evident, especially in more recent reports.

Practice Wisdom as Source. Practice wisdom is most frequently the source for a number of model dimensions, most notably, in the survey reported earlier, the dimension of practice sanction. Taking practice sanction as the example, a first task in step 1 would be to locate relevant sources in the literature for discussion of what authorities in the profession have considered the source and nature of the professional social workers' sanction. Especially useful would be review sources contrasting varying perspectives, as well as selected sources dealing with the matter in greater depth. In the example used, the practitioner located a review source contrasting varying perspectives of established authorities in the profession (*Social Work,* vol. 22, no. 5) and selected two authoritative sources that examine sanction in greater depth (Siporin, 1975; Pincus and Minahan, 1973).

A second task in step 1 involves codification of the information. Unlike the research example, this task may be less systematic when practice wisdom sources are used. Practitioners will need to take good notes and perhaps develop a codification system that fits both their style and the material examined.

The third task in step 1 involves specification of summary generalizations. Again, unlike the research example, the summary generalization drawing on practice wisdom as a source will be less detailed. Using the example of sanction, one practitioner developed the following summary generalization.

> *Substantive generalization.* The specific tasks and actions that social workers undertake to carry out their objectives are legitimized by two major types of sanction: official and negotiated. Official sanction gives an individual the authority, or right, to offer services and engage in certain activities as a social worker. Official sanction (also referred to as public sanction) derives from (1) society, as expressed through social customs and legislative mandates; (2) the profession, as communicated through educational requirements and the code of ethics; (3) the community, as expressed through legislation, licensure/certification, and resource allocation; and (4) the agency, as defined by official policies and procedures. In contrast, negotiated sanction (also referred to as private sanction) derives from worker–client transactions in specific planned change efforts. This type of sanction represents collaborative agreement, as opposed to authoritative permission. Its primary sources are the client and the others with whom the social worker interacts. To these might be added another type of sanction, personal sanction, which is based in the knowledge, skills, values, and convictions of the individual social work practitioner.
>
> This conceptualization of sanction raises two important implications. First, if social workers regard their sanction as coming only from employing agencies, governmental organizations, and the profession, they may tend to see themselves as being accountable only to them. If, however,

they view their clients as an essential—if not primary—source of sanction, they must hold themselves accountable to their clients as well. This in turn means they must be explicit about the goals that are set, the tasks each will perform, and the conditions under which they will work together. A second implication is that these multiple sources of sanction can never be fully resolved; the existence of different sanctioning sources does provide the social worker with opportunities to use one source as leverage in dealing with another. Finally, it should be emphasized that sanction—regardless of its nature or origins—is not only granted but also evolves cumulatively as the profession demonstrates commitment and competence to undertake responsibility in various areas of social concern [Bostwick and Kyte, 1980].

Combined Sources. In some instances, information for model development is drawn from more than one source. As an example, many intervention technologies and techniques have been developed from information derived from experience, theory, and, at times, research. Practitioners involved in modeling may decide to use only one of these sources when considering a particular technique or technology, but, for a more complete base, all sources may be of interest. A system my students and I have developed and used with some success is applied here to cognitive learning technologies for purposes of illustration. The illustration is based on an analysis conducted by a first-year master's student (Anderson-Ray, 1980).

As with the other sources, a first task in step 1 is location of relevant reference material, including published reviews written from the perspective of practice wisdom, theory, or research. Regarding cognitive learning technologies, the student located a comprehensive review of theory and research (Mahoney and Arnkoff, 1978), a relevant behavioral text (Rimm and Masters, 1979), and specialized references for particular techniques (Beck, 1976; Ellis, 1970; Meichenbaum, 1977). In addition to the published material, the student's personal practice experiences were also considered for analysis.

A second task in step 1 is codification of the information. As in the research example, my students and I have found it useful to record the substantive information (definitions of the technology or technique and its reported effects); the limiting conditions reported to affect the generalizability of the application of technology and techniques and the level of evidence supporting the reported substantive effects (including the soundness of the experiential, theoretical, and empirical base).

A final task in step 1 is specification of summary generalizations, which, in this combined example, are of three types: substantive generalizations specifying the nature of the relationships between the cognitive techniques and their effects on clients; limiting generalizations specifying the relevant environmental, organizational, client, and technical conditions under which the cognitive techniques reportedly have an effect; and quality-of-evidence generalizations specifying the nature of the experiential, theoretical, and empirical grounding.

In the case of the cognitive learning technologies, the student (Anderson-Ray) developed the following generalizations.

1. *Substantive generalization.* The cognitive learning therapies are considered by Mahoney and Arnkoff (1978) to be of three general types:

> cognitive restructuring techniques; coping skills techniques; and, problem-solving techniques. Each of these general types are composed of more specific techniques. Cognitive restructuring includes rational-emotive therapy, self-instruction, and cognitive therapy. Coping skills techniques include covert modeling, coping training, anxiety management, and stress inoculation. The problem-solving techniques include behavioral problem solving, problem-solving therapy, and personal science. The general class of cognitive learning therapies are seen by Mahoney and Arnkoff (1978) as related to and sharing some similarities with behavioral self-control and covert conditioning.
>
> In general, these techniques share a common goal—to increase social functioning by assessing and modifying maladaptive cognitions by means of teaching new, more realistic patterns of thought, feeling, and/or behavior.
>
> These various techniques share a common set of intervention principles, as well as principles specific to each technique. The common principles are that the human organism responds primarily to cognitive representations of its environment, rather than to the environment per se; that the cognitive representations are fundamentally related to processes and parameters of learning; that most human learning is cognitively mediated; and that thoughts, feelings, and behaviors are causally interactive.
>
> Derivations include the following. (1) In attempting to predict behavior, phenomenology is a better predictor than external reality, and a weighted prediction based on phenomenology and external variables will often be best. (2) Beliefs, attitudes, and other cognitive representations should be modified by procedures that parallel those of the learning laboratory. (3–4) There is causal circularity—an interactive (or reciprocal) determinism between cognitive representations on the one hand and feelings, actions, and consequences on the other hand. Cognitions are both the process and product of learning [Anderson-Ray, 1980].

In those instances where a practitioner wished to develop a summary generalization for a particular cognitive technique, this could be done by summarizing that technique's specific nature, its goal, and its process.

> 2. *Limiting-conditions generalization.* Concerning the characteristics of the intervener relevant to the cognitive learning techniques, it is reported that such techniques can be and have been used by a wide range of professional helpers with no particular limitations specified. Interveners are generally required to play an active role in structuring and controlling the direction of the session. Teacher and enabler roles are seen as important in helping the client clarify thought patterns and learn new patterns and behaviors. The relationship is of obvious importance, and the relationship effects appear central, especially manipulation of expectancy. Relatively little training is required to learn these techniques.
>
> The techniques are proposed for and reportedly have been used with a wide range of clients with diverse problems, including depression, obesity, smoking, alcohol abuse, stress, sexual problems, phobias, and avoidance patterns. A client limitation is that the client must be able to distinguish between external reality and internal experiences and be able to test hypotheses and try alternative behavior, accepting them as valid.

The *organizational* or agency contexts appropriate for the use of these techniques have not been specified, nor has their use in social work settings [Anderson-Ray, 1980].

3. Quality-of-evidence generalization. When assessing the quality of evidence, drawing from multiple information sources, we have found it useful to develop summary generalizations regarding the quality of the evidence or grounding for each source. In this example, three sources were used by the student—theory, research, and personal experience. The approach to consideration of theoretical information has been discussed in detail elsewhere (Mullen, 1981). In summary, the assessment of theoretical information includes a consideration of the usual formal criteria—derivability, clarity, logical consistency, simplicity, coherence, generality, and verifiability (see Mullen, 1981; Fischer, 1978; Bloom, 1975). In addition, the criterion of relevance is considered (relevance to professional and personal values and relevance to prescriptive knowledge). Finally, the functions the theory can potentially serve are addressed—heuristic, instrumental, or technological (Mullen, 1981). Concerning grounding in personal experience, we have found it useful to consider the extent to which techniques are used, the perceived relevance to clients served, perceived effectiveness, perceived efficiency, and the practitioner's personal comfort with the techniques. Using the cognitive learning technologies, examples of these three sources follow drawing from the student's work (Anderson-Ray, 1980):

Theory as source of evidence. Cognitive learning principles are based on a combination of psychodynamic and behavioral theories. A well-developed cognitive learning theory has not been devised. Although each of the subtypes has its own set of principles and propositions, a more general, overarching theory is not evident. Mahoney and Arnkoff (1978) have outlined four principles and several derivations, cited earlier, that reflect the foundation of cognitive learning theory at its present state of development. Although the theory in its present state of development is too skeletal to merit high marks on the formal criteria, it does appear to be developing favorably in terms of derivability, clarity, logical consistency, simplicity, and generalizability. Its potential cohesiveness or fit with the larger body of theoretical development is less clear. Its verifiability also appears to be somewhat problematic, especially due to the theories concerned with internal, cognitive events. Concerning relevance to personal and professional values and to prescriptive knowledge, the general theory seems highly congruent, to the extent of its development. The theory appears to be based on humanistic assumptions. Of some concern is the idea of restructuring the client's cognitions. Because of this idea, special consideration of client consent and involvement of the client in goal formation seems ethically important. Finally, it does appear that this theoretical base lends itself to a heuristic function in model building (stimulating further development of the theoretical system), as well as an instrumental function (providing guidance to the practitioner and client because of the believability of the ideas included in the theory). However, because of a lack of empirical support, it would be premature to consider it as serving a technological function (being used because of its demonstrated validity).

> *Research as source of evidence.* Largely untested, coping skills techniques are without an adequate research base from which to draw meaningful conclusions regarding their effectiveness. Cognitive restructuring and the problem-solving therapies are also not well grounded in research evidence, although the small amount reported tends to be favorable. Research in this area has generally failed to control for limiting conditions (qualities of the interveners, clients, relationship factors, or organizational contexts), and the quality of the designs and research methods is poor.

Experience as Source of Evidence. The student mentioned earlier (Anderson-Ray, 1980) reported the following summary generalization based on experience.

> While I have used techniques associated with cognitive therapies, I initially did not identify them as such. Frequently used techniques include disputing irrational beliefs, teaching problem solving and coping skills, teaching and practicing new behaviors, and so forth. Overall, I see the applicability of these techniques to my field work to be high. Their relevance to my clients is good. When I have used these approaches, they have appeared to be effective and efficient. I am generally comfortable with these approaches, and they do not appear to require much training.

A broad summary generalization might even be attempted as a general conclusion, as in the following example for cognitive learning technologies (Anderson-Ray, 1980).

> *Concluding summary generalization.* Because interest in cognitive therapy has developed relatively recently, neither cognitive learning principles nor intervention techniques have been fully developed or adequately researched. In spite of this, the principles give the practitioner a new way to understand the client that unites the psychodynamic and behavioral perspectives. In addition, many of the techniques hold potential for increasing the efficiency and effectiveness of interventions. Among the most promising of these are self-monitoring, covert counterconditioning, and the entire set of cognitive learning techniques.

Step 2: Here the summary generalizations are critically and creatively examined with an eye toward implications for practice. Given the nature of the substantive findings, the application limitations, and the nature of the grounding, the practitioner examines possible practice implications. Inferences made from the summary generalizations to practice guidelines at times require considerable subjective assessment and often involve numerous assumptions. At times, this is not the case, and the practice guidelines flow rather directly from the summary generalizations.

This stage also involves consideration of the reality of application, including such matters as feasibility of interventions based on the prescriptive practice guidelines, desirable and undesirable consequences of such interventions, and possible alternatives.

This step also involves a consideration of methods and strategies for monitoring and evaluating the consequences of interventions based on the practice guidelines. Although standardized designs and methods are sometimes available for consideration, ad hoc procedures will often need to be devised, with attention to practice guidelines for monitoring and evaluating.

This step requires personal study, and we have also found that group discussion in the form of "planning labs" can be useful, especially if conducted within the context of a field setting.

Stage 3: Practice guidelines are the result of step 2 and the product at this stage. Prescriptive statements giving general direction to intervention and to monitoring and evaluation of the intervention are specified and are now available for use in practice. However, these prescriptive statements are generally abstract, and their workability and effects remain questionable.

Following the model of earlier examples, three illustrations of practice guidelines are provided.

Research as Source. As in the previous example of accurate empathy, the following are examples of practice guidelines that might be derived from the summary generalizations presented earlier:

> 1. In practice situations where client self-exploration is desirable, intervener responses that reflect accurate empathy should be used to facilitate client self-exploration.
> 2. Expression of low levels of accurate empathy should be avoided, especially with more fragile and vulnerable clients, to avoid harming clients.
> 3. Since expression of accurate empathy appears, to a large extent, to be reciprocal, interveners should be aware of how they are empathically relating to their clients and should exert control over their expression of empathy.
> 4. Since accurate empathy at best appears to account for only a small portion of variance in intervention effects, other intervention qualities should be used to enhance effectiveness.
> 5. Since research evidence supporting the efficacy of accurate empathy is of questionable validity, interveners should closely monitor and evaluate the effectiveness of this response when applied in practice and should use this feedback to rethink the substantive generalization. Similarly, new research findings should be monitored and utilized to rethink the substantive hypothesis [Mullen, 1978, p. 58].

Practice Wisdom as Source. Examples follow of practice guidelines derived from the earlier summary generalization regarding sanction. These examples were developed by the same students who formulated the summary generalizations (Bostwick and Kyte, 1980).

1. Always make sure that my activities as a social worker do not exceed the sanctions that have been "granted" me.
2. In any given situation, obtain sanction from all parties concerned.
3. When different sources do not sanction the same actions, give priority to what best meets the needs of my client.
4. Establish a contract, either formal (written) or informal (verbal), with every client.

5. Be accountable and responsive to the source(s) from which I have received sanction to function as a social worker.
6. Keep abreast of relevant policies that, either directly or indirectly, sanction my work with clients.
7. Develop skills I need to competently discharge the responsibilities I undertake.
8. Monitor the effectiveness of the interventions I provide.
9. Know what I can and cannot do—give my clients an honest appraisal of any limitations (stemming from my own personal skills or imposed on me by my employing agency) that may impede the accomplishment of the goals of our working relationship.
10. Master the competency required for professional licensure/certification.

Combined Sources. Practice guidelines regarding cognitive learning technologies developed by the first-year master's student mentioned earlier are presented as examples (Anderson-Ray, 1980). Among the guidelines are the following:

1. I will use cognitive learning principles to better understand and assess clients by considering the effect of maladaptive cognitions on behaviors.
2. Under relevant conditions, I will develop a treatment plan including an assessment of maladapative cognitions; use techniques to dispute or disrupt the maladaptive thought process; develop means to help the client understand and control maladaptive thoughts and resulting inappropriate behaviors; provide for teaching of appropriate skills and behaviors, as necessary, including problem-solving and/or coping skills; and provide for practice and rehearsal of new skills and behaviors, as needed.
3. Cognitive techniques will not be used exclusively in my model, but rather they will be combined with other approaches, as relevant.
4. I will be alert to counterindications for the use of cognitive techniques.

In addition to these intervention guidelines, this student also specified guidelines concerning the monitoring and evaluation of the intervention plans. The monitoring/evaluation plan was simply an intent to collect information on the extent to which the intervention guidelines were in fact used and the apparent effects of the intervention. The plan called for the use of process recording (periodic), regular tape recording, specific consultation with supervisor regarding guideline implementation, and periodic discussion with clients to secure client feedback regarding the progress of the intervention.

Step 3: To move directly ahead with the implementation of practice guidelines at this stage of development would be risky without pilot testing in simulated or experimental settings to give the guidelines the necessary specificity and support. This step involves such pilot testing. Specific types of practice settings, clients, and other situational factors need to be considered and, as much as possible, included in some form of pilot testing exercise. In addition, the practitioner needs to develop some proficiency in the intervention and its monitoring and evaluation. The question examined in this step is: Can the necessary skill be acquired to implement the intervention and monitoring/evaluation guideline, and what are the effects of such implementation in a controlled field setting?

My students and I have found that application labs are a useful setting for completion of the tasks in this step. If acquisition of skills is required, the use of specialists to model the interventions can be most useful. Modeling, shaping, role playing, and repeated practice are all useful devices to be considered in the pilot phase.

Stage 4: As a result of step 3, practice guidelines are further refined and operationalized for both intervention and monitoring/evaluation. More detail and precision is provided, essential or particularly significant components are determined, and limitations and possible desirable and undesirable consequences are specified. In addition, the fit with other guidelines and dimensions of the model is clarified. Finally, the practitioner develops a degree of confidence and skill in implementing the guidelines, and their relevance to more specific field settings and clients is clarified.

Step 4: Although the activities of step 3 provide an opportunity for some skill development and result in tested guidelines, what will in fact happen under real field conditions remains uncertain. Step 4 assumes that the details of the implementation plan have been recorded and are included in the working model. Field implementation and evaluation of the results remain, with the expectation that the guidelines will be modified in the process. The intent of the field test is to implement the intervention based on the guideline in order to test and further refine the guideline under actual conditions. Fairly detailed specification of the conditions, constraints, and procedures of application are sought, involving a number of clients and applications. Especially important at this step is evaluating the implementation and effects of the intervention, as well as the utility of the monitoring/evaluation strategy itself.

Stage 5: As a consequence of previous steps in this process of model building and especially of the field test, the soundness and general applicability of the practice guidelines involved can now be determined. Based on step 4, revised guidelines are developed for both the intervention and the monitoring/evaluation strategy. Additional field tests would normally be conducted until some degree of confidence and generalizability is reached. Additional clients and agencies may be engaged.

Step 5: Here the guidelines are integrated into the practice model for subsequent use as appropriate situations require. The relationships of the new guidelines to those already in the model are detailed. Further training may be sought in the use of guideline-related skills.

Stage 6: The end product of what must appear to be a long and tedious process is a set of practice guidelines that are integrated into a personal practice model that provides a basis for ongoing evaluation. Revisions are made as feedback is received and new information is considered. When queried as to one's approach to practice or as to what one can offer clients, the response is documented and readily available for review.

References

Anderson-Ray, S. "Personal Practice Model: Technologies and Techniques for Microsystem and Mezzosystem Interventions." Unpublished paper, School of Social Work Services, University of Chicago, 1980. (Mimeographed.)

Beck, A. *Cognitive Therapy and the Emotional Disorders.* New York: International Universities Press, 1976.

Bloom, M. *The Paradox of Helping.* New York: Wiley, 1975.

Blum, H. L. *Planning for Health.* New York: Human Sciences Press, 1974.

Bostwick, G., and Kyte, N. "Notes on Summary Generalizations and Practice Guidelines." Instructional memo developed for a social work practice course (SSM 301-04) at the School of Social Service Administration, University of Chicago, 1980. (Mimeographed.)

Brodbeck, M. "Models, Meaning, and Theories." In L. Gross (Ed.), *Symposium on Sociological Theory.* New York: Harper & Row, 1959.

Caplan, N., and others. "The Use of Social Science Knowledge in Policy Decisions at the National Level." Ann Arbor: Institute for Social Research, University of Michigan, 1975.

Chinsky, J. M., and Rappaport, J. "Brief Critique of the Meaning and Reliability of 'Accurate Empathy' Ratings." *Psychological Bulletin,* 1970, *73* (5), 379–382.

Davis, H. R. "Change and Innovation." In S. Feldman (Ed.), *Administration and Mental Health.* Springfield, Ill.: Thomas, 1973.

Ellis, A. *The Essence of Rational Psychotherapy: A Comprehensive Approach to Treatment.* New York: Institute for Rational Living, 1970.

Fairweather, G. W., Sanders, D. H., and Tornatzsky, G. *Creating Change in Mental Health Organizations.* New York: Pergamon Press, 1974.

Fischer, J. *Effective Casework Practice: An Eclectic Approach.* New York: McGraw-Hill, 1978.

Gurman, A. S., and Razin, A. M. *Effective Psychotherapy: A Handbook of Research.* New York: Pergamon Press, 1977.

Holzner, B., and Fisher, E. "Knowledge in Use: Considerations in the Sociology of Knowledge Application." *Knowledge: Creation, Diffusion, and Utilization,* 1979, *1* (2), 219–244.

Hovland, C. I., and others. *Communication and Persuasion.* New Haven: Yale University Press, 1953.

Janis, I., and Mann, L. *Decision Making.* New York: Free Press, 1977.

Kaplan, A. *The Conduct of Theory.* San Francisco: Chandler, 1964.

Kuhn, T. *The Structure of Scientific Revolutions.* Chicago: University of Chicago Press, 1970.

Larsen, J. K. "Knowledge Utilization: What Is It?" *Knowledge: Creation, Diffusion, Utilization,* 1980, *1* (3), 421–442.

Lippitt, G. L. *Visualizing Change: Model Building and the Change Process.* Fairfax, Va.: NTL-Learning Resources, 1973.

Mahoney, M. "Reflections on the Cognitive-Learning Trend in Psychotherapy." *American Psychologist,* 1977, *32,* 5–13.

Mahoney, M., and Arnkoff, D. "Cognitive and Self-Control Therapies." In S. L. Garfield and A. E. Bergin (Eds.), *Handbook of Psychotherapy and Behavior Change: An Empirical Analysis,* 2nd ed. New York: Wiley, 1978.

Meichenbaum, D. *Cognitive Behavior Modification.* New York: Plenum Press, 1977.

Mullen, E. "The Construction of Personal Models for Effective Practice: A Method for Utilizing Research Findings to Guide Social Interventions." *Journal of Social Science Research,* 1978, *2* (1).

Mullen, E. "Use of Information from Theories and Research in Personal Intervention Models." In R. M. Grinnell, Jr. (Ed.), *Applied Social Work Research and Evaluation.* Itasca, Ill.: Peacock, 1981.

Parloff, M. B., Waskow, I. E., and Wolfe, B. E. "Research on Therapist Variables in Relation to Process and Outcome." In S. L. Garfield and A. E. Bergin (Eds.), *Handbook of Psychotherapy and Behavior Change.* (2nd ed.) New York: Wiley, 1978.

Pincus, A., and Minahan, A. *Social Work Practice: Model and Method.* Itasca, Ill.: Peacock, 1973.

Rimm, D., and Masters, J. *Behavior Therapy.* New York: Academic Press, 1979.

Rogers, E. M., and Shoemaker, F. *The Communication of Innovations.* New York: Free Press, 1971.

Rosenthal, T., and Bandura, A. "Psychological Modeling: Theory and Practice." In S. L. Garfield and A. E. Bergin (Eds.), *Handbook of Psychotherapy and Behavior Change: An Empirical Analysis.* New York: Wiley, 1978.

Rothman, J. *Planning and Organizing for Social Change.* New York: Columbia University Press, 1974.

Rothman, J. *Social R and D: Research and Development in the Human Services.* Englewood Cliffs, N.J.: Prentice-Hall, 1980.

Siporin, M. *Introduction to Social Work Practice.* New York: Macmillan, 1975.

"Special Issue on Conceptual Frameworks." *Social Work,* 1977, *22* (5).

Truax, C. B., and Mitchell, K. M. "Research on Certain Therapist Interpersonal Skills in Relation to Process and Outcome." In A. E. Bergin and S. L. Garfield (Eds.), *Handbook of Psychotherapy and Behavior Change.* New York: Wiley, 1971.

Weiss, C. H. "The Many Meanings of Research Utilization." 1978, *10.* Unpublished, cited by J. K. Larsen, "Knowledge Utilization: What Is It?" *Knowledge: Creation, Diffusion, Utilization,* 1980, *1* (3), 425.

Weiss, C. H. "Knowledge Creep and Decision Accretion." *Knowledge: Creation, Diffusion, Utilization,* 1980, *1* (3), 381–404.

Zaltman, G. "Knowledge Utilization as Planned Social Change." *Knowledge: Creation, Diffusion, Utilization,* 1979, *1* (1), 82–105.

29

Developing Intervention Methods Through Experimental Designs

William J. Reid

The emphasis given to experimental approaches in the clinical research section of this handbook reflects their central importance in the study and improvement of the methods of clinical social work. While naturalistic research may be the primary source of knowledge about the human problems targeted by clinical social work, experimentation provides the most direct and powerful means of building methods to affect those problems.

Varieties and Functions of Experimentation

The importance of experimentation in clinical social work may be difficult to perceive if the experiments are viewed only as elaborate undertakings requiring sizable samples, control groups, and statistical analysis. Such experiments, although of considerable importance, make up only a fraction of a broad range of activities that might properly be called experimental social work. A social work activity becomes an experiment if it is carried out with a realized intent to study the characteristics and effects of that particular activity. At a simple level, an experiment may take the form of a trial of an intervention approach in one or a few cases, accompanied by careful observation of what takes place. Measurement may be qualitative, and procedures to control for extraneous factors may not be used. Single-group experiments, perhaps in the form of demonstration projects, may involve quantitative data but may lack control or comparison groups. In short, the essence of experimentation is to do and then to study what is done. How the study is carried out reflects different varieties and grades of experimentation.

For purposes of analysis of experimental design in a social work context, experiments can be divided into two general classes, controlled and uncontrolled. A controlled experiment is a study in which intervention is manipulated for research purposes in order to control or rule out extraneous factors that might influence the apparent outcome of the intervention. Such factors include the tendency of clients to improve with the passage of time or through their own devices (maturation), the influence of events in the client's life that are not produced by intervention (history), and protreatment biases in assessing change (instrumentation). See Campbell and Stanley (1963) or Cook and Campbell (1979) for a comprehensive listing. To sort out extraneous factors, sometimes referred to as alternative explanations, controlled experiments employ manipulative strategies. Thus, intervention may be withheld from one group, varied between two or more groups, or withheld or varied within a single case.

In an uncontrolled experiment, intervention is not specifically manipulated to increase the power of the design to detect intervention effects, aside from the degree of manipulation inherent in the introduction of the intervention itself. That is, an intervention may be introduced for study purposes but is not accompanied by procedures that attempt to isolate its effects.

The designation "uncontrolled" refers only to the absence of specific features of research design, not to the intervention. The intervention itself may be systematic and well planned; in fact, it may be better put together—or better controlled, if you will—than an intervention in a controlled experiment. Uncontrolled experimentation is often hard to distinguish from ordinary practice, which may in itself involve innovation and monitoring of practitioners' activities and outcomes. An experiment can be distinguished, however, by an attempt to define and study a particular kind of intervention or set of interventions. One is interested not simply in determining case outcomes but rather in determining outcomes in relation to specified experimental variables.

This conception of experimentation runs counter to certain traditions about experimental design in social work and social research. Center stage has been given to the equivalent-group experiment, in which a group receiving a particular experimental intervention is compared with one receiving something else—for example, a different intervention, a lesser intervention, or no intervention at all. Generally, random assignment ensures equivalence of the groups. Although this design provides a very powerful tool for the testing of treatment effects in a definitive way, it is not for everyday use. One recent review suggests that only two or three published tests of social work interventions using this design are produced each year (Reid and Hanrahan, 1982). The great bulk of experimental work makes use of uncontrolled designs (Reid, 1979a).

In view of these considerations, the tendency to restrict the term *experiment* to controlled designs is indeed unfortunate. One expression of this tendency is the use of the misleading and certainly ambiguous term *true experiment* to refer to controlled designs, with the term *quasi-experiment* used to describe designs that do not conform to that standard. The fallacy in limiting a fundamental strategy in science to a particular methodological refinement (equivalent groups) becomes apparent when one examines the variety that experimentation may take in different sciences. For example, consider the well-known imprinting experiments of Konrad Lorenz (1970), who trained mallard ducklings to follow him as if he were a mother duck. Lorenz, as far as I know, did not have an equivalent group of ducklings quacking along after their real mothers. In clinical research itself, it is difficult to maintain the fiction of the true experiment in the light of such recent developments as the single-subject design (see Chapter Twenty-six). Some of these designs, such as the reversal design, achieve a high degree of control over extraneous factors without equivalent groups, and others, such as the *AB* design, achieve less control but are generally referred to as experiments nevertheless.

Another facet of the primacy given controlled experiments has been the tendency to downgrade anything less. Undertakings with "poor controls" are likely to be dismissed as having "inadequate designs" and hence little value. Thus, Kerlinger (1973), in a widely used research methods text, calls an uncontrolled design in which a program is tried and evaluated "scientifically speaking . . . worthless" (p. 318).

Kerlinger's subsequent equivocation on this matter obliquely points to the value of lesser designs but at the same time shows why they are not given much weight. He goes on to say that such designs are not "universally worthless" and cites "Freud's brilliant observations" as apparent evidence that they do have some value after all. Their value notwithstanding, "when such a paradigm is labeled as scientific or believed to be scientific, . . . difficulties arise" (p. 318). It is curious that Freud, who viewed himself and has been viewed by others as a scientist, could make "brilliant observations" that turn out to be "scientifically worthless."

If a broader and more realistic conception of science is adopted, Freud's observations do have scientific value, in large part because of the uncontrolled single-case experiments that gave rise to his observations. These experiments helped Freud generate conceptions, hypotheses, and theories about the properties and possible effects of psychoanalysis, as well as about the role of unconscious processes (among other things) in human behavior. Furthermore, they provided some tentative evidence that his intervention could bring about change in human functioning. The result was a profoundly influential system of practice and behavioral theory that has, over the past half century, spawned a large amount of research quite respectable by the usual standards of behavioral science (Fisher and Greenberg, 1977).

The scientific contribution of Freud's experiments lay largely in their heuristic value: they generated a dazzling array of possible truths. It is important to recognize, however, that his case studies provided no definitive proof of either the effectiveness of his therapy or the validity of his theories. The design of his studies makes it impossible to factor out the contribution of his interventions from his biases and selective perceptions, as well as from expectancy effects, spontaneous remissions, and many other confounding factors, and the lack of objective measures makes it difficult to calibrate the amount of change that may have occurred. In short, his studies lack a strong verifying function. Failure to appreciate this limitation is as shortsighted as failure to appreciate the significance of what they do in fact contribute. As Freud's case studies suggest, an experiment does not require controls in order to be of value. An experiment employing primitive research methodology may produce a conceptualization of a promising intervention, show how the method can be used, and provide suggestive evidence on how well it worked. This process of creation, trial, and feedback can not only serve to guide the direction of more rigorous experimentation but also contribute directly to the profession's supply of intervention methods.

This last statement raises the enduring issue of premature utilization of methods that have not been definitely tested through more rigorous designs. Almost any experiment provides at least some clues as to what appears to be effective. At a primitive level of design, the evidence may be impressionistic and open to a variety of interpretations and may well be misleading, particularly in the direction of attributing change to treatment when in fact other factors may be responsible. If there were no pressures for action, the evidence might be simply converted into hypotheses for further and more rigorous testing. In social work, however, action is a continuing necessity; further, little tested knowledge may be available to inform the practitioner's intervention. In the face of such uncertainty, there is some justification for action based on suggestive or equivocal evidence about the effects of an intervention—the kind of evidence yielded by the uncontrolled experiment. The risks of being misguided must be taken into account and balanced against the risks of using methods even less well tested or of doing nothing at all. However, the risks of being misled by the results of an uncontrolled experiment vary considerably according to the characteristics of the experiment. The discriminating user of uncontrolled studies, as I will subsequently attempt to show, can minimize the risks of buying the wrong product.

My promotion of the uncontrolled experiment should not be interpreted as a rejection of its controlled counterpart. My intent is rather to develop a broad conception of experimental social work, one in which a wide variety of experimental approaches can be used creatively to build practice technology.

Developmental Research Strategy

To attain that objective, experimental social work can most profitably proceed within the framework of developmental research (Thomas, 1978; Reid, 1980). (See also Chapter Twenty-seven.) From this perspective, the focus of research is not the generation of knowledge about intervention methods but rather the development of intervention methods themselves. Thus, the main product of developmental research is not the usual report of findings but a service approach in the form of practice procedures or practice models. Practitioners need not understand the empirical bases of the approaches they use in order to put the results of research to work; research utilization is accomplished when the practice methods themselves are used.

A developmental research strategy can take the form of a continuing program. A preliminary practice model may be devised from existing research, theory, clinical trial and error, or other sources. The model or its elements are shaped through one or more uncontrolled tests in which data are collected on the operations of the model and its apparent outcomes. Data from each test are used to revise the model prior to subsequent testing; in this way, the model can be progressively improved in the light of research data. Controlled experiments can then be introduced to provide more definitive evidence on the model's effects.

Different (and not necessarily mutually exclusive) patterns may be followed. One may begin by testing and perfecting a single practice method; a second method is then added and tested to determine if it improves on the effects attained; and so on (McFall and Lillesand, 1971). Methods may be developed and tested separately, and those proving to be effective may then be combined. Alternatively, one may begin with a package of interventions and, by subsequently varying and testing components, attempt to replace those that do not contribute to the effectiveness of the package and to maximize the role of those that do. Development may take the form of testing a model with different and perhaps progressively more challenging clinical problems, or the focus may be on developing the most effective way to treat a particular type of problem. The starting point may be a laboratory analogue of an intervention: the analogue is first developed and tested under highly controlled conditions, then applied to actual clinical situations.

Although developmental research may be most productive when part of a continuing program, a developmental research perspective can guide single experiments that may not be a part of such a program. An experiment could be conducted to develop interventions for immediate use or to test adaptations of methods such as those produced by research and development programs for use in particular settings. A one-time experiment, such as a single case study or a small demonstration project, is given a developmental character if its findings can be used to modify the intervention tested. Key interventions themselves must be carefully described and considerable attention given to their immediate consequences. Thus, global evaluation of a complex program may tell little about the workings of its components; at a minimum, developmental research must obtain data about particular aspects of an intervention so that the data can be used to modify the intervention in specific ways.

Developmental research, then, makes use of a "formative evaluation" strategy (Scriven, 1969) and, in many respects, parallels approaches—such as those proposed by Fairweather (1967), Suchman (1970), and Gottman and Markman (1979)—in which programs are developed in stages in response to feedback from a continuing process of evaluation. Perhaps the key distinction—if indeed there is one—is that developmental research calls for a fuller integration between program innovation and evaluation. Developmental research does not usually make a clear division between developers and evaluators of an intervention model. These roles may be combined in the same person or shuttled back and forth within a team of workers. Also, developmental research makes more use of tentative findings or good ideas generated by research.

Selected Designs

This section will present selected experimental designs that may be used in the development of intervention methods. Since this chapter, like the *Handbook* itself, is oriented toward the needs of social work clinicians, and since basic, controlled, single-case experiments have been reviewed in a previous chapter, the selection has been guided and limited by considerations of simplicity, feasibility, and economy of design, with a good deal of attention given to uncontrolled studies. Uncontrolled and controlled designs will be covered in turn and, within each major division, the discussion will move from the simpler single-case experiments to more complex group designs. Partially controlled (nonequivalent) group designs will be included in the discussion of controlled designs. For illustrative purposes, I will draw heavily on the developmental research efforts in which I have participated, particularly those involving task-centered practice (Reid and Epstein, 1972, 1977; Reid, 1978; Reid and Hanrahan, 1982).

Basic Single-Case Experiment. For the most part, the single-case designs covered in Chapter Twenty-six fell in the controlled category, as defined in the present chapter. Even simple time-series, or *AB*, designs (in which an observation or baseline period is followed by intervention) has an element of control, since intervention is withheld until baseline data are obtained.

In the uncontrolled single-case experiment, baseline data are obtained retrospectively during the initial or assessment phase of the case, which is not extended for research purposes. From interviews with the client and collaterals and from available data, the practitioner-researcher obtains data on problem frequency and severity prior to the beginning of contact. The length of the retrospective baseline depends on the nature and frequency of the problem. For specific problems that have a high rate of frequency, one can obtain counts of problem occurrences for the preceding week, as has been done in several studies of task-centered methods (Reid, 1978; Reid and Hanrahan, 1982). For problems occurring less frequently, the baseline period can be extended further back in time. For any chronic problem, data on the problem manifestations for the previous six months to a year are generally useful in evaluating subsequent change. When the assessment period may be prolonged for service reasons, retrospective baselines can be supplemented with short prospective baselines on problem occurrence taken between initial contact and the actual beginning of intervention.

At the close of the assessment period, an experimental intervention is defined and subsequently carried out. Although the intervention may consist of a complex set of methods, it should have conceptual coherence—that is, it should consist of a specified way of dealing with a particular problem and should be adhered to, unless, of course, there are compelling clinical reasons for departing from it. If intervention becomes too idiosyncratic, it may be difficult to learn much of value from the experiment. Not that a rigid plan must be followed: improvisations can certainly occur, but they should be in the form of improvements on the original conception.

Data on change in the target condition can be gathered during the course of the intervention or at termination only, and a postintervention follow-up can be added. Although the specifics of data collection and measurement procedures are beyond the scope of this chapter, procedures in this type of design generally tend to be relatively simple and well fitted to service requirements and may include brief interviews with collaterals, practitioner observation, and client self-reports obtained as part of clinical interviews or in the form of completion of brief standardized instruments (Levitt and Reid, 1981).

Although it is difficult to draw definitive conclusions about the effects of intervention from an uncontrolled case study, the design may still provide valuable evidence on such effects. Extraneous variation is, of course, not ruled out by control procedures, but informed judgment can be made about the likelihood of its occurrence. By assessing how the problem has varied prior to intervention, the practitioner-researcher can evaluate the extent to which spontaneous remission (maturation) might complicate interpretation about the effects of intervention. For certain problems, it may be possible to establish that little fluctuation has occurred. Thus, through an interview with a teacher or through records, one might determine that a child's classroom academic performance has been relatively stable for the past several months. If the child's performance shows improvement when treatment is begun, the case for a treatment effect receives some support. However, if the baseline pattern reveals considerable variation in the problem or a trend toward alleviation, an uncontrolled design may provide little information about treatment effects. Although current environmental influences cannot be completely controlled, data on the occurrence of particularly obvious events that might affect problem change can be collected and evaluated.

The specificity, directness, and explicitness of the intervention are also important considerations. If the intervention is aimed at general changes that are difficult to delineate, if it operates in an indirect manner, and if its processes are not clearly demonstrable, then alternative explanations become more attractive or competitive. Thus, to attribute a change in a mother slapping her son to participation in an unstructured parents' discussion group would require a chain of inferences connecting supposed values derived from the group experience—such as emotional support from other parents—to the change in question. Although a plausible explanation linking the group treatment to change could be constructed, a certain amount of speculation would be required. For this reason, the explanation may not prove much more convincing than others based on speculation about changes in the mother's motivation, family circumstances, or other factors not necessarily the result of intervention.

By contrast, an intervention consisting of direct, specific, and explicit efforts to change the problem—for example, having the mother rehearse and practice other responses when her son cries—could be more plausibly connected to the change. The link between intervention and change requires fewer assumptions than in the first case cited, since the process by which intervention may produce change is more readily apparent. The plausibility of the connection can, of course, be further strengthened through documentation of the intervention-change process. For example, one might be able to provide evidence that a problem changes immediately following an intervention and in a way specifically suggested by the intervention: the mother in our example might agree, in response to the practitioner's suggestion, to have one of her older children attend to the infant if she feels as if she is losing control. If it could be shown that she in fact then behaves in this manner, the value of the intervention becomes more persuasive.

As Cook and Campbell (1979) observe, a cause may operate with such specificity that it leaves a unique "signature" in its effects. Thus, the identity of a criminal may be revealed by the modus operandi of the crime, or characteristics of a trainee's performance may tell us who the trainer was. Social work intervention may likewise resemble such "signed causes," as perhaps in the example just cited. In such cases, plausible alternative explanations may not arise, and controls may not be necessary to rule out such alternatives in order to establish the effectiveness of the intervention.

An instructive example of an uncontrolled single-case experiment is provided by Rossi (1977). The client, Daniel, was a seven-year-old boy who had not spoken in class during the previous year and a half. Evidence for the history of mutism was based on interviews with Daniel's teacher and parents. Additional evidence that the problem showed little variation was obtained through four hours of direct observation of the child in different classroom situations over a three-day period. The child did not speak and would answer questions only through head shakes. Rossi's intervention program, which took six sessions, consisted primarily of reinforced, graduated practice in a simulated classroom situation. Since Daniel was willing to talk outside the classroom, Rossi first saw the child alone and was able to engage in a limited dialogue. He then met with Daniel and a classmate selected by Daniel. Gamelike conversational exercises plus candy reinforcement were used to stimulate Daniel to talk in this small group. Then additional children selected by Daniel were incrementally added until a miniature classroom was created. The conversational requirements of the exercises were progressively increased but were temporarily relaxed if Daniel did not respond. An assistant teacher was then asked to visit the group; Daniel continued to talk. At this point, Daniel was "tested" in his regular classroom: when his regular teacher called on him to read aloud, read aloud he did. Follow-ups indicated that he continued to speak appropriately in the classroom during the rest of the school year.

Although the experiment lacked both quantitative measures and controls, the evidence strongly suggested that the intervention program was responsible for the change. Since mutism had been a problem for some time prior to the intervention, maturation was probably not a cause of the change. The problem may have been positively affected by contemporaneous events, such as a shift in teacher attitudes toward the child that may also have been responsible for the referral, but there were no indications that she treated Daniel differently. The specific character of the intervention, its graduated structure, and the child's stepwise progress made the connection between intervention and change rather clear. (The logic of the changing-criterion design presented in Chapter Twenty-six applies here.) Finally, the brevity of the intervention limited the influence of extraneous factors.

Single-Case Micro-Experiment. An experiment need not involve an entire case. At any point in the life of a case, an intervention can be introduced and its apparent effects assessed (Nelson, 1978). As in the basic design, a specific problem is identified, and baseline data are collected. Retrospective methods of obtaining baseline data can be used, or, in many cases, the raw data will already have been gathered in the course of treatment and need simply be organized. A specific intervention addressed to the problem is applied, perhaps in a single interview, and immediate changes that may be associated with the intervention are studied. (See discussion of group micro-experiment below.)

Uncontrolled Single-Group Experiment. Perhaps the most frequently used evaluative design in social work (Reid, 1979a), the uncontrolled single-group experiment, may range from a modest test of a specific intervention with a handful of cases to a study of hundreds of cases exposed to a multifaceted program. The logic of design, however, is no different from that of the uncontrolled single-case study. A program of intervention is administered without manipulation, that is, without delay, interruption, witholding, or other procedures for control of extraneous variation.

In the better of these designs, a target is measured at least before and after intervention, as in the uncontrolled single-case study, and change is assessed accordingly. In weaker versions, premeasures are not obtained, and change is evaluated ex post facto. When they are used with relatively stable targets and involve tests of well-explicated models of practice, such designs can provide valuable evidence on intervention effectiveness but tend to be less useful in that respect than their single-case counterparts. A measurement of change lacks the focus and precision that is possible in the single case, and evaluation of the possible role played by extraneous factors is more difficult if one must deal with a number of cases.

Testing an intervention over a group of cases has particular advantages, however, when an experiment is conducted largely for purposes of rapidly accumulating experience with the intervention in the early stages of development. Such an experiment, referred to as an exploratory experiment, consists essentially of a preliminary trial of an intervention on a small scale—with perhaps a half dozen to a dozen cases (Reid, 1979b). First, guidelines explicating the model are developed. Practitioners are trained in its use, and a data-collection plan is devised. Particular emphasis is given to securing data on what practitioners do and on what follows their actions. The practitioners themselves, who may include the model developers, supply data through such devices as structured recording forms, ratings, audiotapes, and reports of critical incidents. Clients or other actors in the practice situation may be interviewed.

The main purpose of the experiment is to fill out and correct the rough map laid down in the preliminary formulation of the model. Some questions concern feasibility: Are practitioners able to carry out the suggested operations? If not, why not? Other questions concern the range and variation of expected events: What kinds of case situations will be encountered? What methods, of those suggested, will be used most frequently, and what will they look like in actual use? Still other questions are related to possible effects. Because design controls are not used, it is not possible to obtain definitive answers to questions concerning the effectiveness of the practitioners' activities. Nevertheless, one can gather evidence that permits tentative judgments. For example, is the use of an intervention followed by expected changes in the client's behavior? How do practitioners, clients, and collaterals assess the effectiveness of a particular intervention? In addition, problems and events not anticipated by the model are bound to occur. It is assumed that some of these occurrences will be revealed in the data and will help form subsequent model development.

A secondary, though still important, purpose of the experiment is to test and refine data collection and measurement procedures. Through this process, one hopes to devise research methods that are maximally sensitive to the practice operations and outcomes of interest in the model.

Data analysis, which makes use of both quantitative and qualitative methods, has two objectives: (1) the identification of variables and hypotheses for further research and (2) model revisions. The first purpose is a conventional product of exploratory research. Analysis directed toward the second purpose focuses on understanding, distilling, and ordering the mass of events that occurred during the field test. This base can then be used to flesh out the initial formulation of the model. Thus, what practitioners and clients actually did across a range of problems and situations can be used to make judgments about what is to be expected and perhaps what should be done. Innovative work, perhaps stimulated by the model but not specified as a part of it, can be identified, evaluated, and, if the work seems promising, incorporated into the next version of the model. Unanticipated problems can be described and new guidelines written. As noted, the data may well generate hypotheses for further research, and some of these hypotheses may be translated into tentative model guidelines. For example, correlational evidence may suggest that a certain procedure does not work well with a particular type of client. Pending a more definitive test of this hypothesis, the model might be revised to suggest that the procedure in question be used cautiously with this type of client and discontinued should adverse effects appear. Through this process of analysis and application of findings, the developer puts together a revised version of the initial model.

An example of an exploratory experiment at the micro-practice level is provided by Ronald Rooney (1978). The model to be developed was a task-centered approach for helping natural parents secure the return of their children from foster care or to prevent such placement. The model design called for a special unit of practitioners to work with child welfare staff, the court, natural and foster parents, and children to identify and alleviate psychosocial problems that were causing children to be kept in foster care or were likely to precipitate placement. Intervention was to be short-term, focused on specific, agreed-upon target problems, and to be organized around problem-solving actions or tasks carried out by clients and practitioners.

The test of the model consisted of its use with eleven families referred by a cooperating public child welfare agency. Six cases were carried by master's students supervised by Rooney and five by Rooney himself. Primary sources of data were structured narrative recordings; practitioner ratings of task progress and outcome; tape recordings of selected sessions; and postproject interviews with clients, student practitioners, child-welfare workers, and family court judges.

Of particular interest is how data were used to inform model development. The use of data to fill gaps in the initial model formulation is well illustrated by observations gathered on family court judges' reactions to specific evidence of parents' having accomplished constructive tasks or actions. It was not known at the outset how judges would react to the evidence or how it could best be presented. Data from the cases indicated that such evidence was viewed favorably; in addition, the data provided numerous leads as to how it might be used more effectively in the future. Although this information may have been obtained by other means, such as interviews with judges or experienced childcare workers, the test-and-observation approach used seemed particularly direct.

The exploratory experiment can provide a fruitful means of using empirical methods to facilitate the early development of crudely formulated practice models. It is an attempt to make more systematic and rigorous the kinds of trial-and-error processes long employed by practitioners to improve their efforts. Consequently, there is justification for arguing that its central product, a practice model, can be put to immediate use while further testing and development are being undertaken—if, of course, there is evidence that the model is capable of achieving desired results. Granted, the model will not yet have been subjected to a rigorous test of effectiveness—but few models have been. Given limited alternatives, a practitioner might sensibly choose to use a well-explicated model that has received some testing, rather than poorly formulated methods that may never have been touched by research.

Multiple-Baseline Designs. Although the simple time-series (*AB*) design is the most commonly used of the single-case controlled designs, it provides, as Levy and Olsen have noted in a previous chapter, relatively weak control, particularly for contemporaneous events and offers only a slight improvement over the uncontrolled single-case experiment considered at some length in the preceding section. Reversal and withdrawal designs, in which intervention is systematically interrupted, provide a greater amount of control but have a limited range of application in clinical social work. Often practitioners and clients object to the withdrawal of intervention after initial gains have been made. Moreover, in order to use such a design, one must have an intervention whose effects will not persist after it is withdrawn or whose effects can be readily undone. Frequently this criterion cannot be met; in fact, practitioners usually hope for the opposite. For example, forms of intervention designed to bring about change through cognitive methods are expected to have effects that are persistent and irreversible. One does not expect insight or altered beliefs to vanish when treatment stops.

Of the single-case controlled designs, those employing multiple baselines have perhaps the most value in more definitive tests of social work intervention. In the multiple-baseline design, one attempts to attain control through replication. By staggering the inception of intervention across a series of targets, a researcher can demonstrate that change occurs only when intervention is introduced and hence is the result of the intervention. The pattern could theoretically, of course, be produced by a series of coincidences, but such an explanation begins to sound implausible when predicted change consistently follows the introduction of intervention.

The strategy is illustrated by Figure 11 in Chapter Twenty-six. The targets, which could be behaviors (as in the figure), problems, situations, or clients, are monitored over time with intervention introduced successively in each. When the targets consist of clients, the design, technically speaking, is no longer a single-case experiment, although it is convenient to present it within this general category of design.

Because its range of application in social work is perhaps broader than other multiple-baseline designs, the across-clients design will be considered first and in greater detail. Clients are selected who are as closely matched as possible—preferably clients who share the same type of problem and are similar in respect to other important characteristics, such as age, that might influence the characteristics of the intervention. With a group of similar clients, an intervention program can be expressly designed; baselines are more likely to be similar, thus making it easier to detect changes associated with treatment; and generalizations are easier to make.

Baseline data on a target behavior or problem are obtained for each client, and intervention is introduced in staggered fashion. Each time-series is expected to show systematic improvement over its own baseline only after intervention is introduced.

The across-clients design, as noted, has a broad range of applications in tests of social work intervention. It can be used with "nonreversible" methods, and clients can be treated in a holistic manner, that is, one does not need to concentrate on one problem or situation at a time. For these reasons, this design may be more suitable than other controlled single-case designs for studies of the effects of nonbehavioral forms of social work practice.

Generally, the across-clients design can be used to evaluate any intervention that is amenable to testing through an *AB* design. The only additional constraint is that the treatment to be tested must be able to generate measurable effects rather quickly; otherwise, the waiting (or baseline) period for the last client to be treated might become excessively long. Many varieties of social work intervention meet this requirement. The multiple-baseline designs can also be used to assess the effects of intervention as a social system, such as a family, ward, or class. For example, Hubek and Reid (1982) studied the effects of a self-management program with children excluded from the regular school system because of behavior problems. They selected four classrooms of such children and, using an across-groups, multiple-baseline design, sequentially introduced a self-management training program in each group. In this program, pupils were taught how to control their in-class behavior problems; the pupils recorded, evaluated, and reinforced their own behaviors. The training program was evaluated by observing the behavior of randomly selected children in each classroom at repeated points. From these observations, measures of inappropriate behavior for each classroom were constructed. It was then possible to document the changes that occurred in the classrooms (not individual pupils) following introduction of the program.

Among other forms of multiple-baseline design, the across-behaviors, or across-problems, design merits comment. In this design, one tests the efficacy of an intervention method with different problems of the same client-system. In other respects, the design is equivalent in structure to the across-clients multiple baseline. That is, baselines are taken on different problems, and the timing of intervention is staggered across the set of problems.

The principal advantage of this design over its across-clients counterpart is that an experiment requires only one client, rather than several concomitantly. Clients do not need to be kept waiting lengthy periods in baseline conditions before service starts. The interdependency that usually exists among different problems in the same client is almost always a matter of concern. Treatment of one problem is likely to affect another, or spontaneous recovery may occur in all problems simultaneously. If all problems show positive change during baseline, one cannot determine whether treatment or extraneous factors were responsible. If carry-over effects are to be avoided, the intervention must be problem-specific. Behavioral treatment meets this criterion better than most other modalities that social workers use, but any approach that permits highly focused work on specific problems can conceivably be tested through this type of design. In one application of the across-problems design, Tolson (1977) tested a set of methods used in task-centered practice, including homework assignments and in-session practicing of tasks, with a married couple. Target problems consisted of three communication difficulties—interrupting, manipulating, and tangential speech. The problems were treated sequentially and, despite some carry-over effects, Tolson was able to demonstrate a treatment effect.

Equivalent-Group Design. In the equivalent-group design, control is achieved by comparing variation in change targets between similar groups. Equivalence between groups is achieved basically by random (chance) assignment of cases to the different groups. When samples are small, cases may be matched on variables thought to influence outcome and then may be randomly assigned. This procedure, which ensures greater equivalence on key variables, should not be confused with attempts (discussed later) to fashion equivalent groups through case matching alone.

In the basic, or classical, form of the equivalent-group experiment, which will be considered first, one group (the experimental group) receives the intervention; another group (the control group) does not. The function of the control group is to provide an estimate of change caused by influences other than intervention.

In thinking about control groups, one should distinguish between two types of clients: those who are actively seeking service and those who are not in the market for service but who would be willing to accept it if offered. With help-seeking clients, a no-intervention control group is especially difficult to achieve. Agencies are reluctant to withhold services from clients, and assigning clients to control groups is no guarantee that they will remain isolated from experiences that may compete with the intervention program. Some may seek comparable forms of service elsewhere; others may obtain informal help from friends, clergy, physicians, and the like.

Nevertheless, some workable solutions are possible. Perhaps the msot satisfactory is to use a control condition in which clients are requested to wait for service. This solution works best, of course, if the agency has some form of waiting list and if the waiting period for clients assigned to the control group is relatively brief. While waiting for regular service, control clients can be given some form of placebo treatment not only to keep them connected with the agency but also to determine what changes might be produced by such minimal interventions as sympathetic listening. This variation has its difficulties, however. It is often hard to draw a line between placebo and genuine treatment. In addition, practitioners may have qualms about having clients participate for any length of time, if at all, in a pseudotreatment.

The situation is somewhat different when clients are not seeking help. The experimenters offer to provide a possibly useful program to a population that would ordinarily not receive it on condition that they be permitted to conduct a controlled study. Under such circumstances, the complaint that service is being unnecessarily withheld from the control group is less likely to arise, and control clients are less likely to feel deprived or to seek alternative forms of service. Usually such groups are found in settings—such as schools, hospitals, courts, welfare agencies, or residential institutions—that can facilitate recruitment of potential clients and can help avoid exposure of controls to competing programs.

There are, of course, certain drawbacks in soliciting the participation of clients in tests of social work interventions. Since they have not sought help, clients may not be motivated to receive it, a factor that may weaken the effectiveness of social work services, which are usually based on the assumption that clients are genuinely interested in receiving them. This explanation has in fact been used to account for failure of casework intervention to show demonstrable effects with such possibly unmotivated groups as predelinquent youngsters and families receiving public assistance (see reviews by Mullen, Dumpson, and others, 1973; Fischer 1976; and Wood, 1978). In some situations, the population to be offered the experimental program may be already receiving some form of "lesser" service, such as routine supervision by a probation officer. The control group may then consist of clients so served. In fact, often such services are mandatory, that is, required by law or regulation, and cannot be withheld. A number of experiments in social work have used some form of lesser treatment as a control under the assumption that clients in the control group were receiving little real help—at least not enough to compete with the experimental program. The failure in a number of such studies (for example, Wallace, 1967; Mullen, Chazin, and Feldstein, 1972) to demonstrate the superiority of experimental programs over such routine-service control groups has raised questions about this assumption. Although their negative findings might be explained on the basis that neither experimental nor control clients were helped, the evidence in some of the studies, such as those just cited, is consistent with the possibility that both types of clients received comparable benefit. Although there are studies in which the experimental clients have surpassed routine-service controls (Stein and Gambrill, 1977; Jones, Neuman, and Shyne, 1976), it may usually be more appropriate to view lesser programs as alternate forms of service, as in a comparative design (discussed later in this chapter), rather than as something equivalent to no-service controls. If lesser programs were viewed in this way, then more attention would be paid to the content of the lesser service and to its strengths relative to the experimental program. It is probably generally true that "captive" control clients—even children in ordinary school settings—are likely to receive help that may be competitive with an experimental program. Close attention must be paid to inputs of this kind.

Fundamentally, a no-treatment control group, whether it consists of help-seeking or specially recruited clients, gives a picture of what can be expected to happen in the lives of a group of clients who do not receive a systematic intervention with goals and methods similar to that of the experimental program. This form of control is not necessarily invalidated if clients occasionally receive help of the kind being tested, but it is useful to know the extent of this help in order to make a valid assessment of the accomplishments of the experimental service.

Certain variations of the classical design may be particularly useful in social work applications, given problems inherent in using no-treatment control groups. The variations to be considered here should be seen as only illustrative of ways in which the classical design may be shaped to fit the exigencies of practice situations.

As indicated earlier, some of the objections to use of no-treatment control can be answered by providing clients assigned to a control condition with the treatment at a later point. In a partial crossover design, the control clients can be made a part of the experiment by providing them with the experimental intervention following the control period and then measuring their progress once again after they have received the intervention. In its simplest form, the design can be schematized as shown in Figure 1.

This design not only assures that control clients will receive the benefit of the experimental treatment but also provides an additional test of the intervention. Changes in the control clients during the no-treatment condition (T_1-T_2) can be compared with changes in these clients during the intervention period. In this kind of comparison, the control clients' rate of problem change would be expected to increase after their crossover into the treatment condition. Although

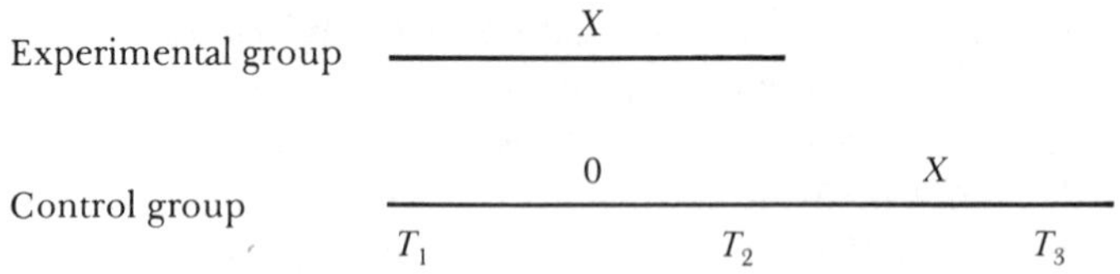

X = Intervention provided
0 = Intervention withheld
T_1–T_3 = Measurement points

Figure 1

this use of clients as their own controls does not rule out maturation and other extraneous factors as possible causes of change, it does provide a useful supplement to the more definitive comparisons between experimentals and controls (T_1-T_2). It can also provide evidence confirming that an intervention effect has occurred, as well as additional data on the nature of this effect.

A key consideration in using this design with help-seeking clients is the length of the first phase (T_1-T_2). Ideally, this phase should be kept as short as possible to minimize the time that control clients need to be kept waiting. The longer this period, the greater will be the objections to the design and the greater the attrition from the control group. If this period is kept reasonably brief—for example, no more than a few weeks in length—the experimental intervention must be able to demonstrate results quickly, even though subsequent results may also be achieved. (Experimental cases can continue "off the study" after T_2.) Even with a brief initial phase, attrition from the control group may limit the usefulness of the crossover comparison (T_1-T_2-T_3). It must also be kept in mind that any follow-up after T_3 can only involve cases that have received the experimental treatment. This limitation is less serious than it appears for help-seeking controls, who will usually have obtained some form of help by the time of a posttreatment follow-up. Examples of studies using a partial crossover design may be found in Bandura, Blanchard, and Ritter (1969) and Reid (1978).

As noted, a controlled experiment need not involve the entire life of a case; nor need it examine the full effects of an intervention. These principles are more fully exploited in what I have referred to as a micro-experiment. The purpose of this design is to assess the immediate effects of a specific intervention method. In a group experiment, cases are paired and randomly assigned to experimental and control conditions, with the same practitioner carrying both cases. The cases are handled in a similar fashion until the experimental phase, which may consist of a single interview, is terminated. The experimental cases then receive a specific method of intervention withheld from the control cases; the control cases may, for this brief period, receive no treatment at all or a continuation of the form of treatment they had been receiving. Both experimental and control cases are assessed before and after the experimental intervention, with the second assessment taking place within about a week after the intervention. Assessment is focused on specific changes expected to result from application of the intervention: experimental and control cases are compared on this variable, with a check for related changes or side effects. Following the experimental or control phases, both cases are treated in ordinary fashion, although they may be followed up at a later point to determine the persistence and longer-term influence of the experimental variables.

An example of this design is provided by an attempt to assess the effectiveness of a set of experimental activities devised to help clients plan out, justify, and rehearse problem-solving actions or tasks (Reid, 1975). In brief, thirty-two clients (largely children from a school setting) were randomly assigned to experimental and control conditions. Sixteen student practitioners each carried one experimental and one control case. Experimental and control clients received the same form of task-centered treatment until approximately the fourth interview in each case. (The practitioners were not informed of the assignment plan until just prior to the fourth interview.) At this point, the two cases were treated differently: in the experimental case, a task was formulated with the client, to which the experimental activities were applied. In the control case, a task was formulated in a similar fashion, but nothing further was done in this regard. No systematic differences were found in the characteristics of the experimental and control tasks. Progress on each task was reviewed by the practitioner in the next session with the client. On the basis of tape recordings of these reviews, judges independently made ratings of task progress, not knowing which cases were experimental or control. Almost 70 percent of the experimental tasks, in contrast to only 20 percent of the control tasks, were substantially or completely achieved—a statistically significant difference.

As can be seen, the service phase of the experiment took only a week and affected only a single interview. Although the design yields data on only short-term effects of the method tested, such data can be useful in model development, as in the example given.

In the comparative, or contrast-group design, two or more experimental interventions are assessed. The purpose of this design is to test the relative effectiveness of the interventions, that is, to determine which is the more (or most) effective.

As in the classical experiment, clients are randomly assigned to different conditions. However, each condition consists of some form of intervention. (To simplify discussion, we shall assume that two interventions are being compared, which is the usual case; the same design principles apply to comparisons of several interventions.) The interventions compared are considered to be alternative means of achieving common goals in respect to client outcome. Although experimenters may hypothesize that one intervention is superior to the other, it is not assumed—as it is when an experimental intervention is compared to a "lesser" treatment program—that one approach will be more successful. Recent examples of the use of this design in social work include comparison of structured communication training and conjoint marital therapy (Wells, Figurel, and McNamee, 1977); comparison of behavioral role play, problem solving, and social group work (Toseland and Rose, 1978); and comparison of behavioral counseling programs of different lengths (Stuart and Tripodi, 1973).

The comparative strategy has several advantages but also some shortcomings. One of its most attractive features is the elimination of the various problems that accompany a no-treatment control—a particularly compelling advantage with help-seeking clients, none of whom need to be deprived of service. Concerns about untoward effects on clients are not necessarily eliminated, however. Some agency personnel may regard one program as inferior to the other and may therefore have reservations about shortchanging clients. Some may also argue that assignment to a service should be based on diagnostic criteria: assigning clients at random may produce mismatches between client and service. But there are solutions for these difficulties. Many possible comparisons involve services neither of which is regarded as clearly superior. Or the design may permit clients assigned to the presumably inferior service to be given, if needed, the superior program after the experiment has been completed. Criteria for selection of project cases can be adjusted to exclude cases determined to be inappropriate for either of the services being compared; then the argument that professional judgment is needed to assign cases has less force.

A comparative experiment provides data on the relative effects of different interventions, a feature with both advantages and disadvantages. On the positive side, the findings are more likely to be utilized than findings from classical designs. If practitioners are already using some form of the interventions tested, they probably consider both to be effective. In such cases, a classical experiment testing one of the interventions may not alter a practitioner's use of it, regardless of outcome: positive results may not affect practice behavior, since practitioners had already assumed the intervention to be effective; negative results may be discounted, since practitioners would otherwise be forced to conclude that their practice had been ineffective. By contrast, an experiment comparing the two interventions would not necessarily challenge the practitioner's convictions that both were effective but would present evidence that one was more effective than the other. Such findings are more readily accepted and may influence practitioners to make greater use of the methods found to be more effective.

Given the lack of no-treatment control, the comparative design does not provide an estimate of the absolute effects of either intervention, that is, what either can achieve in comparison to what clients can accomplish on their own or through unsystematic helping efforts. The seriousness of this limitation largely depends on the outcome of the comparative study. If one intervention proves to be relatively more effective than the other, it can be argued that the more effective intervention had some degree of absolute effectiveness. In other words, the group receiving less effective intervention can then be used as a control group in a classical design, unless, of course, there is reason to suppose that the less effective intervention hindered solution of the clients' problems.

The risk of obtaining null findings in comparative tests is high. For example, in reviewing a large number of experiments testing different forms of psychotherapy with one another, Luborsky, Singer, and Luborsky (1975) found few studies that showed significant differences. Several recent comparative tests of social work intervention have also failed to find differences between alternative types of service (Reid and Hanrahan, 1982). As Luborsky, Singer, and Luborsky suggest, this "tie-score effect" may reflect the work of generic helping processes. If these processes exert a strong effect relative to the more specific effects of an intervention, it may be difficult to demonstrate clearly that one method is better than the other. Nevertheless, one cannot claim that positive but similar outcomes from competing forms of intervention are the result of such helping processes.

Maturation and other forms of alternative explanation are hard to rule out. Thus, the risk of "tie scores" becomes a limitation of the comparative design.

The advantages of both the classical and the comparative designs can be realized if a no-treatment control group is added to the latter. The result is a powerful hybrid that permits a comparison of the relative efficacy of two or more interventions and provides an estimate of the absolute effects of each (see, for example, Sloan and others, 1975; Berger and Rose, 1977). Thus, if the interventions have similar outcomes, it is possible to say that both were effective (or ineffective).

Like most things that are elegant, this design is difficult and costly to create. Problems in obtaining an adequate no-treatment control must be resolved, and there must be sufficient numbers of clients for at least three groups, as well as the wherewithal to collect data for these groups and resources to engineer and oversee this elaborate design's many facets.

Nonequivalent-Group Designs. When clients cannot be randomly assigned to equivalent groups, experimental designs may still be used to compare different nonequivalent groups. A nonequivalent group may either be used as a no-treatment control or be given an alternative form of intervention. (For illustrative studies, see Craig and Furst, 1965; Geismar and Krisberg, 1967; Larsen and Mitchell, 1980.)

The preferred strategy is to use natural groups, if they can be located—classes, wards, residential units, caseloads of different practitioners, and so on. Ideally, the researcher hopes to find groups that are more or less alike, even thought their equivalence cannot be assured. Thus, two sixth-grade elementary school classes may have been formed in a manner that approximates random assignment.

The possible influence of between-group differences in outcome is the primary concern of the researcher. The groups may differ in initial charcteristics or may be exposed to different external events during the course of the experiment, and any of these differences may affect outcome. Initial differences affecting outcome can sometimes be dealt with through statistical controls, but, no matter how sophisticated the analysis, all statistical control procedures are fundamentally limited by the scope and quality of the data to which they are applied (Reid and Smith, 1981). Groups not randomly assigned may differ in ways not measured; thus, critical data needed for control purposes may be missing, or critical variables may be crudely measured. One can go through the motions of statistically controlling for differences, but little control may occur if measurement is fraught with error.

Another means of reducing the influence of extraneous variables in nonequivalent-group designs is to utilize some form of matching. For example, an innovative marital counseling program may be tested in one office of a family agency. Comparison cases may be drawn from another office in which the agency's usual counseling program is offered. Experimental and comparison cases may be matched on two variables thought to have an important influence on outcome: socioeconomic level and degree of marital disturbance (as rated by judges). Thus, each working-class, severely disturbed couple in the experimental group would presumably have its working-class, severely disturbed counterpart in the comparison group.

The major limitation of this procedure is that one cannot assure equivalence on other variables that may also be important: for example, regardless of their social class or degree of marital disturbance, couples in the experimental office may be younger and better motivated than those in the comparison office. Without random assignment, such differences cannot be equalized. Although matching does not need to be limited to one or two variables, matching for several is often impractical because of the large number of cases needed to find correct matches.

Nonequivalent groups are generally less useful as control devices if the experimental group was formed for the purpose of receiving the intervention. For example, in a study of the effects of a voluntary, extracurricular program designed to improve the communication skills of high school students, the students will have selected themselves into the experimental group. Any group that might be found or formed for purposes of comparison will necessarily differ on motivational and other variables that could, of course, have a strong influence on outcome.

In general, the interpretation of results of nonequivalent-group designs needs to be guided by the kind of logic that can be applied to evaluate the findings of uncontrolled studies. The crucial question is this: What plausible alternative explanations need to be ruled out? If the evidence for an intervention effect in the experimental group is in itself quite persuasive, a nonequivalent group may need only supply limited data to help rule out a rival hypothesis of questionable plausibility.

Design Sequences. The designs presented in the preceding section can be used in various sequences in programs of developmental research. As indicated, a logical progression would be from uncontrolled (single-case or exploratory) studies to more highly controlled designs. This sequence is particularly desirable, if not essential, when an attempt is being made to develop an innovative approach. For example, in the task-centered developmental research program, several uncontrolled single-group experiments (Reid and Epstein 1972, 1977) were followed by two small-scale controlled designs: a micro-experiment (Reid, 1975), in which the immediate effects of key methods of the task-centered model were examined, and an across-problems single-case experiment, in which the immediate and longer-range effects of these methods were tested in a single case (Tolson, 1977). Then a large-scale experiment was conducted to test longer-range effects of the model as a whole. The same logic applies to the extension of a tested model into unknown territory. In Rooney's (1978) exploratory experiment, the task-centered model was applied to problems of separation of parents and children in a complex child-welfare setting; a controlled across-clients design (Rzepnicki, 1981) was then undertaken with the same kinds of problems in the same kind of setting.

A different form of sequencing may be used—a succession of controlled single-case experiments is the most feasible—if new applications of a tested intervention involve only limited variations in problem or method. Additional studies can be used to gradually extend the range of demonstrated effectiveness of a model with different types of clients, problems, and so on. This strategy, sometimes referred to as systematic replication, is discussed and illustrated by Hersen and Barlow (1976). This form of sequencing may also be used if the intent is to determine if an additional component will improve the effectiveness of a model or achieve additional effects. For example, Brown (1980) used a controlled design to ascertain the effects of giving clients problem-solving instructions as a component of the task-centered approach. Brown's design also illustrates how developmental research lends itself to economy in design: he was able to make use of completed cases from a prior experiment as controls for his study.

Still another kind of sequence may be used if the goal is to apply, with minimal variation, a method whose effectiveness has been well demonstrated through prior controlled studies. Through an uncontrolled or partially controlled experiment, one can obtain evidence that the method previously tested was applied in the prescribed manner and achieved apparently similar effects. One then has a good basis for arguing that the effects are genuine, in view of the prior evidence attesting to the method's effectiveness.

The sequences presented comprise only a few possibilities among many. This form of research is itself too new to permit a definitive mapping of different ways of ordering designs. Although the sequences discussed either begin or terminate with controlled studies, developmental research need not necessarily lead to or depart from controlled research; methods can be developed by means of a succession of uncontrolled studies.

Building a Developmental Research Program

This chapter will conclude with some comments about planning and implementing programs of developmental research in both academic and agency settings. Regardless of setting, a primary consideration is continuity: ideally, a program of developmental research should have the kind of continuity accorded most educational or service programs. It should not depend on external funding but rather should receive at least survival support from the setting itself. External funding can be sought and more readily obtained after the intervention methods and the means of evaluating them have been reasonably well developed.

Details of program structure will differ according to type of setting, with the most important differences dependent on whether the program is based in an academic setting—a school of social work, for the purposes of the present discussion—or a social agency. School-based programs are usually led by faculty members who work collaboratively or with master's and doctoral students to design and implement specific projects. The projects may be carried out in agencies, with agency staff or students serving as practitioners. Such programs can be run at minimal cost, since they are shaped around normal research, instruction, and service activities. Research and practice courses, student projects, field work, and ongoing agency services can be adapted to the needs of the research program, often with gains for both instruction and service. For example, in the task-centered developmental research program, a year-long integrated course package consisting of field work, classroom methods instruction, and a research practicum provided the structure and opportunity for a series of research projects to be carried out at field-work sites (Reid, 1978).

Perhaps for the reasons just considered, developmental research programs have thrived more under academic than under agency auspices. Lack of resident research expertise and pressure to devote maximum resources to immediate service demands have been major impediments to developmental research in the agency setting. This situation is unfortunate, since developmental research is a potentially powerful means of enabling agency staff to perfect their own promising innovations. Moreover, an agency can use a developmental research capacity to adapt newer methods from whatever sources to its own particular needs.

Although only very large or very affluent agencies might be able to establish a well-staffed and well-financed developmental research program, most agencies should be able to allocate enough time for at least one staff person. An increasing number of graduates, many with doctoral training, are interested in positions combining research and clinical practice. Moreover, developmental research can be integrated with in-service training; in fact, learning through active application and evaluation may be much more effective then passive participation in workshops and the like. A modest investment in a continuing program of developmental research can pay for itself in many ways, but its most important contribution over the long term will be the increase in effective services.

References

Bandura, A., Blanchard, E. B., and Ritter, B. "The Relative Efficacy of Desensitization and Modeling Approaches for Inducing Behavioral Affective and Attitudinal Changes." *Journal of Personality and Social Psychology,* 1969, *13,* 193–199.

Berger, R. M., and Rose, S. D. "Interpersonal Skill Training with Institutionalized Elderly Patients." *Journal of Gerontology,* 1977, *32,* 346–353.

Brown, L. "Client Problem-Solving Learning in Task-Centered Social Treatment." Unpublished doctoral dissertation, School of Social Service Administration, University of Chicago, 1980.

Campbell, D. T., and Stanley, J. C. "Experimental and Quasi-Experimental Designs for Research on Teaching." In N. L. Gage (Ed.), *Handbook of Research on Teaching.* Chicago: Rand McNally, 1963.

Cook, T. D., and Campbell, D. T. *Quasi-Examination: Design and Analysis Issues for Field Settings.* Chicago: Rand McNally, 1979.

Craig, M. M., and Furst, P. W. "What Happens After Treatment? A Study of Potentially Delinquent Boys." *Social Service Review,* 1965, *39,* 165–171.

Fairweather, G. W. *Methods for Experimental Social Innovation.* New York: Wiley, 1967.

Fischer, J. *The Effectiveness of Social Casework.* Springfield, Ill.: Charles C. Thomas, 1976.

Fisher, S., and Greenberg, R. P. *The Scientific Credibility of Freud's Theories and Therapy.* New York: Basic Books, 1977.

Fortune, A. E. "Communication in Task-Centered Treatment." *Social Work,* 1979, *24,* 390–397.

Geismar, L., and Krisberg, J. "The Family Life Improvement Project: An Experiment in Preventive Intervention: Part II." *Social Casework,* 1967, *47,* 563–570.

Gottman, J. M., and Markman, H. J. "Experimental Designs in Psychotherapy Research." In S. L. Garfield and A. E. Bergin (Eds.), *Handbook of Psychotherapy and Behavior Change.* New York: Wiley, 1979.

Hersen, M., and Barlow, D. H. *Single Case Experiment Design.* Elmsford, N.Y.: Pergamon Press, 1976.

Hubek, M. M., and Reid, W. J. "Components of Self-Management in Special Education Classes." In R. T. Constable and J. P. Flynn (Eds.), *School Social Work: Practice and Research Perspectives.* Homewood, Ill.: Dorsey Press, 1982.

Jones, M., Neuman, R., and Shyne, A. W. *A Second Chance for Families: Evaluation of a Program to Reduce Foster Care.* New York: Child Welfare League of America, 1976.

Kerlinger, F. N. *Foundations of Behavioral Research.* (2nd ed.) New York: Holt, Rinehart and Winston, 1973.

Larsen, J., and Mitchell, C. T. "Task-Centered, Strength-Oriented Group Work with Delinquents." *Social Casework,* 1980, *61,* 154–163.

Levitt, J. L., and Reid, W. J. "Rapid Assessment Instructions for Social Work Practice." *Social Work Research and Abstracts,* 1981, *17,* 13–20.

Lorenz, K. *Studies in Animal and Human Behavior.* Vol. 1. Cambridge, Mass.: Harvard University Press, 1970.

Luborsky, L., Singer, B., and Luborsky, L. "Comparative Studies of Psychotherapy." *Archives of General Psychiatry,* 1975, *32,* 995–1008.

McFall, R. M., and Lillesand, D. B. "Behavioral Rehearsal with Modeling and Coaching in Assertion Training." *Journal of Abnormal Psychology,* 1971, *77,* 313–323.

Mullen, E. T., Chazin, R., and Feldstein, D. "Services for the Newly Dependent: An Assessment." *Social Service Review,* 1972, *46,* 309–322.

Mullen, E. T., Dumpson, J. R., and others. *Evaluation of Social Intervention.* San Francisco: Jossey-Bass, 1973.

Nelson, J. C. "Use of Communication Theory in Single-Subject Research." *Social Work Research and Abstracts,* 1978, *14,* 12–19.

Reid, W. J. "A Test of the Task-Centered Approach." *Social Work,* 1975, *20,* 3–9.

Reid, W. J. *The Task-Centered System.* New York: Columbia University Press, 1978.

Reid, W. J. "Evaluation Research in Social Work." *Evaluation and Program Planning,* 1979a, *2,* 209–217.

Reid, W. J. "The Model Development Dissertation." *Journal of Social Research,* 1979b, *3,* 215–225.

Reid, W. J. "Research Strategies for Improving Individualized Services." In D. Fanshel (Ed.), *Future of Social Work Research.* New York: National Association of Social Work, 1980.

Reid, W. J., and Epstein, L. *Task-Centered Casework.* New York: Columbia University Press, 1972.

Reid, W. J., and Epstein, L. (Eds.). *Task-Centered Practice.* New York: Columbia University Press, 1977.

Reid, W. J., and Hanrahan, P. "Recent Evaluations of Social Work: Grounds for Optimism." *Social Work,* 1982, *27,* 328–340.

Reid, W. J., and Smith, A. *Research in Social Work.* New York: Columbia University Press, 1981.

Rooney, R. H. "Prolonged Foster Care: Toward a Problem Oriented Task-Centered Practice Model." Doctoral dissertation, School of Social Administration, University of Chicago, 1978.

Rossi, R. B. "Helping a Mute Child." In W. J. Reid and L. Epstein (Eds.), *Task Centered Practice.* New York: Columbia University Press, 1977.

Rzepnicki, T. "An Adaptation of Task Centered Intervention to Foster Care Cases." School of Social Service Administration, University of Chicago, 1981.

Scriven, M. "Logical Positivism and the Behavioral Sciences." In P. Achinstein and S. F. Barker (Eds.), *The Legacy of Logical Positivism.* Baltimore, Md.: Johns Hopkins University Press, 1969.

Sloane, R. B., and others. *Psychotherapy Versus Behavior Therapy.* Cambridge, Mass., and London: Harvard University Press, 1975.

Stein, T. J., and Gambrill, E. D. "Facilitating Decision-Making in Foster Care: The Alameda Project." *Social Service Review,* 1977, *51,* 502–503.

Stuart, R. B., and Tripodi, T. "Experimental Evaluation of Three Time-Constrained Behavioral Treatments for Pre-delinquents and Delinquents." In R. D. Rubin, J. P. Brady, and J. D. Henderson (Eds.), *Advances in Behavior Therapy.* New York: Academic Press, 1973.

Suchman, E. A. "Action for What? A Critique of Evaluative Research." In R. O'Toole (Ed.), *The Organization, Management, and Tactics of Social Research.* Cambridge, Mass.: Schenkman, 1970.

Thomas, E. J. "Mousetraps, Developmental Research, and Social Work Education." *Social Service Review,* 1978, *52,* 468–483.

Tolson, E. "Alleviating Marital Communication Problems." In W. J. Reid and L. Epstein (Eds.), *Task-Centered Practice.* New York: Columbia University Press, 1977.

Toseland, R., and Rose, S. D. "Evaluating Social Skills Training for Older Adults in Groups." *Social Work Research and Abstracts,* 1978, *14,* 25–33.

Wallace, D. "The Chemung County Evaluation of Caseworker Service to Dependent Multi-Problem Families: Another Problem Outcome." *Social Service Review,* 1967, *41,* 379–389.

Wells, R. A., Figurel, J. A., and McNamee P. "Communication Training Versus Conjoint Marital Therapy." *Social Work Research and Abstracts,* 1977, *13,* 31–39.

Wood, K. M. "Casework Effectiveness: A New Look at the Research Evidence." *Social Work,* 1978, *23,* 437–459.

30

Measurement of Client Problems for Improved Practice

Joel Fischer
Walter W. Hudson

During the past few years, clinical social work practice and the way it is taught in the classroom have been changing in at least four important ways. First, social work practitioners are making greater efforts to be more specific in defining the problem to be treated and in identifying the specific treatment or intervention techniques to be employed. Second, they are becoming more eclectic in their use of theory, knowledge, and technique as a basis for planning and directing change efforts (Fischer, 1978). Third, they are making better use of some of the tools of science in order to monitor and evaluate intervention efforts and client problems for the purpose of increasing the likelihood of a more positive outcome for the client (Hudson, 1978b). Finally, as a consequence of these innovations, social work practitioners are increasingly using the tools of measurement as a basis for detecting, recording, and assessing the nature and degree of client problems and the extent of change or stability.

Whereas other chapters of this book present discussion, direction, and guidelines for understanding and using the first three practice innovations or directions, this chapter provides an introductory level of instruction and guidelines for the productive use of measurement for improving practice. It is intended to help social workers who want to practice more effectively to more accurately detect and report the consequences of their treatment or intervention efforts and to more accurately monitor, assess, and reflect the nature and degree of client problems and problem changes.

What Is Measurement?

What, then, is measurement? A good formal definition is that "measurement consists of rules for assigning numbers to objects in such a way as to represent quantities of attributes" (Nunnally, 1978, p. 3). In order to be useful, however, this definition requires some elaboration.

The rules for assigning numbers to objects can be very simple or very complex, and a thorough understanding of their variety, scope, and effective use requires specialized study and training. Good sources for such training and study include Grinnell (1981, chaps. 7–9) Nunnally (1978), Helmstadter (1964), and Allen and Yen (1979). Although social workers do not have to become experts in psychometric theory, study in this area can be very helpful and is encouraged.

The essential point of Nunnally's definition of measurement is that numbers are assigned to objects in a consistent manner. For example, in measuring client problems, it is important to use the simple rule of assigning a large number to any problem the therapist or client considers serious and smaller numbers to problems considered less serious.

The mechanism used to apply the rule is called a measurement tool or instrument. If an expert is asked to rate the seriousness of a client's problem, the person doing the rating is the measurement instrument. If an orange is weighed on a balance scale, the balance is the tool of measurement. However, people rarely are regarded as measurement tools; more commonly, the tool is the device on which they record their measurement judgments. Therefore, the recording document used by an expert to rate the seriousness of a client's problem is considered the measurement tool, and such recording documents can be constructed in hundreds of different ways: single-item rating scales, open-ended questions, true–false items, forms for making behavioral observations, multiple-choice items, essay questions, category-partion scales (which include Likert-type scales, Osgood semantic differential scales, ladder scales, multi-item scales, unidimensional scales, multidimensional scales, and so forth).

Some of these different tools of measurement are described later in this chapter so that they can be used in practice, and several references are given to enable readers to locate, study, and then use various measurement devices.

Why Measure?

Many people complain about the use of measurement in social work practice. Some feel it dehumanizes the client, the worker, and the profession. Others feel that measurement in the "soft" sciences is generally so weak and flawed that it should not be used with clients or taken seriously as a guide for directing or even influencing the conduct of practice. Others feel that it is not necessary, because "good clinical judgment" is sufficient. Still others simply do not understand measurement, and some say that formal measurement is sometimes useful but is so complex and technical that it must be left in the hands of experts.

All of these arguments need to be addressed. Many of the things workers do can be dehumanizing, and measurement can be used in a dehumanizing way. However, it can also be used with intelligence and warmth for the purpose of better helping the client to cope with very serious problems. Some measurement tools are indeed quite crude and misleading and should not be used. However, many are highly accurate and dependable. One must never forget that, in all forms of measurement involving human judgment, the accuracy of the final measurement is a direct function of human discrimination and perceptual ability. In many cases, such abilities are nothing short of impressive. One must also never forget that "good clinical judgment" is an act of measurement. Those who claim that measurement must be left to experts are avoiding the issue. Some types of measurement do require specialized training, but a wide variety of measurement applications are available with very modest amounts of training and are well within the abilities of nearly all social work practitioners.

But why measure? The simplest answer is that we must and that we do so routinely, without knowing it. When a worker places a note in a client's record to indicate that the client's marital relationship has improved, the worker has performed a crude act of measurement. Anytime one observes progress, stability, or deterioration, acts of measurement are being performed. In short, the use of measurement in social work practice is inescapable and inevitable.

But, if workers are already using measurement, why formalize it? The answer is that the advance of any science or profession is clearly marked by its increased use of precision and control. Modern surgery has its roots in the barber shop, and, by analogy, workers must decide whether they will operate in the barber shop or in the modern surgical amphitheater. The use of measurement will be a major determinant in this choice.

If increased precision and control are basic to the improvement of social work practice, then the use of measurement must be a fundamental ingredient of such practice. If a client suffers from fear, anxiety, depression, or pain, it is important, for a number of reasons, to know how often and how much. Is the disorder frequent and severe enough to warrant treatment? Is the frequency or intensity of the problem great enough to imply one form of treatment or another? Does the problem occur at times and places that suggest either its cause or a possible solution? Once treatment or intervention begins, can the worker determine whether and at what rate the problem is abating or worsening? Can that knowledge be useful in making decisions about treatment: to retain or drop the treatment techniques being used or to add others? The extent to which such questions can be answered depends on the precision of the worker's information about the client's problem, and that level of precision has a marked impact on the extent to which the worker is able to control the problem.

What Can Be Measured?

Since anything that exists can be measured, all types of client characteristics can be measured. For example, measuring immaturity may be impossible because "immaturity" itself does not exist. But immaturity is manifested in behaviors that do exist (for example, a child not following instructions in a classroom), any of which could be measured as an indicator of immaturity. Thus, the way one defines the problem is crucial to whether or not it can be measured.

Of course, if workers do not set some limits of their own, they will be so busy measuring characteristics of the client that they will never get around to treatment, and the client will drop out in disgust or dismay. Therefore, a better question might be, What should be measured?

At a very minimum, the worker should measure two things: the problem to be changed and the change agent, or treatment. There are powerful advantages to measuring the client's problem and the treatment. By measuring the client's problem, workers can often determine what type of treatment and what types of resources are needed to deal with the problem; they can also make a prognosis concerning how long it will take to resolve the problem. Most important, by measuring the client's problem repeatedly over time on a regular basis, the worker can determine whether any progress is being made, information vital in helping to decide whether to continue or change the treatment.

Measurement is crucial for demonstrating whether treatment exists and whether it has the desired effect on the client's problem. Just as the problem that is not measurable does not exist and cannot be treated (Hudson, 1978a), the treatment that cannot be measured does not exist and cannot be administered (Gingerich, 1978).

Measurement for Single-System Designs

If some feel it is difficult enough to measure client problems, others will no doubt claim it is impossible to measure treatment. Actually, however, treatment is rather simple to measure. But, first, it is important to ask, What is treatment? Is it psychoanalysis, Gestalt therapy, supportive therapy, behavior modification, rational-emotive therapy? Decidedly not. These are theories of behavior and intervention, the treatment is the worker's behavior, what the worker does to create change in the client's problem.

If the behavior of the social worker is seen as the principal ingredient of treatment, that provides a simple basis for measuring treatment in a very useful way. Consider the total period of time during which the worker will have contact with a single client, and divide that period into two phases, or periods, *A* and *B*. During phase *A*, the worker will deliberately exhibit no treatment behavior and, during period *B*, the worker will exhibit professional behaviors specifically designed to have an impact on the client's problem. If the worker's behavior during period *A* is compared with that during period *B* and if one cannot detect any difference in those behaviors, it must be concluded that treatment does not exist. If, however, behavior during period *B* is distinctly different from behavior during period *A*, the worker has successfully measured treatment and, in the process, has demonstrated its existence.

The client's problem is the second factor that should be measured. If the client's problem is measured regularly during both time periods (*A* and *B*), the client problem measures taken during period *A* are called baseline measures, and those taken during period *B* are called treatment-phase measures. If treatment is really not present during the baseline period, one would expect the client's problem to be fairly stable—nothing is being done to change it. Also, if an effective set of treatment behaviors is selected, one would expect the client's problem measurements to change during the *B* period, or treatment phase—something is being done during that period that is intended to change the client's problem.

What has been described thus far is the simple *AB* design. Many other designs are described elsewhere in this text, but the *AB* design represents the fundamental design strategem used to help monitor and evaluate treatment: measure the treatment, and measure the client's problem on a regular or intermittent basis.

Basic Characteristics of Measurement

Although measurement applies to both the worker's treatment and the client's problem, the measurement of treatment is largely included in the research design. Because the issues of research design are discussed in detail elsewhere in this text, the remainder of this chapter will focus mainly on the task of measuring client problems.

Any strategem or device used to quantify a client's problem is called a measurement tool, and, if measurement tools are to have any utility in practice, they must possess several desirable characteristics. They must be reliable and valid; easy to administer, score, understand, and interpret; and brief. Clinical measurement tools should also be sensitive to change, and they should be fairly immune from reactivitiy (for those who want a more technical discussion of measurement charcteristics, see Grinnell, 1981, chaps. 7–9).

If a measurement tool is not both reliable and valid, it is useless and should be discarded. Unfortunately, most practitioners are not in a position to make this determination for themselves. Even so, there are two good rules that can be followed: use specific measurement tools that have previously been shown to be reliable and valid, and use types or classes of measurement devices that have been shown to be reliable and valid. A number of these devices are described later in this chapter.

Often workers, in attempting to measure a client problem, will discover that little or no change can be observed. The problem could be that change does take place but the measurement tool is not sensitive enough to record it. For example, it is always possible to measure whether a client problem is present (a score of 1) or absent (a score of 0); in many cases, however, it is possible to do more. Suppose a problem of enuresis is defined as being present or absent (scored as 1 or 0). After working with the client, the worker notices real change taking place (the client has eighteen dry nights per month, as compared to only seven before treatment), but, because the problem is still present at some level, the client continues to obtain a score of 1. Insensitivity to change is often reflected in one or both of two ways: no change in obtained scores and low reliability. Clinician judgments concerning the amount of client change are notoriously unreliable (insensitive) and should be avoided.

Measurement tools vary considerably with respect to whether they are direct or indirect measures of some construct. At one extreme are the so-called projective tests, which are very indirect measures of some construct; at the other extreme are the behavioral measures, which are usually very direct measures of some construct. As a general rule, the more indirectly one measures some variable, the more one must depend on subjective interpretation of the results. In such cases, it is very difficult to establish the validity of the measure. The Rorschach, TAT, and Draw-a-Person tests are examples of indirect measures; after years of research, their validities are still in doubt (Hersen and Barlow, 1976).

Although behavioral measures are usually very direct measures of some construct, they can be abused. For example, temperature, respiration, pulse rate, and galvanic skin response are all excellent measures of the level of physiological activity, but do they also represent anxiety or fear? Sleeplessness is often associated with depression; nonetheless, some people who are not troubled with sleeplessness are very depressed.

As a general rule, the more directly a construct is measured, the more confidence the worker can have in the measurement results, and the easier it will be to establish the validity of those results. Consider, for example, the complex syndrome called depression. Depression can be measured in terms of behavioral symptoms, affects, relationship patterns, perceptions, and cognition. It can be measured directly by using a self-report, self-anchored scale, by behavioral observation, by self-reports of affects and cognitions, or by self-reports of behavioral symptoms. All of these measures tend to have very high validities.

Another desirable characteristic of measurement tools is that they be relatively nonreactive. A measurement tool that has high reactivity is one that causes the client's problem to change as a result of having the problem measured. One of the authors, for example, had a client who deliberately falsified her responses to the Generalized Contentment Scale (GCS) described later in this chapter. She candidly reported that, when she was honest with the scale, her score was higher and she felt worse. When she was dishonest, her scores were smaller and she felt better. In other words, this client was deliberately manipulating her own reactivity to the measurement tool as a means of coping with and managing her own depression.

Reactivity is a serious problem for the scientist who is trying to isolate the true effects of experimental variables. In some cases, it may seem to be an aid to the clinician who is trying to help the client reduce or eliminate a personal or social problem. However, if observed improvement turns out to be purely reactive, it is doubtful that the gains will be sustained following termination of treatment. In assessing client problems and the effects of treatment, nonreactive gains are the most desirable and are more likely to be obtained when one uses measurement tools that are relatively nonreactive.

Defining Problems and Goals

In order to make good use of measurement in clinical practice, it is important to recognize that social work is a practice-based, problem-solving profession. In working with a client, one must define the problem to be solved in both measurable and treatable terms. In all of social work, social workers encounter and deal with only five broad classes of problems: (1) to provide concrete personal services (that is, clean the client's house); (2) to increase the capacity of the environment to provide positive supports for clients; (3) to decrease impediments and obstacles in the environment that retard or interfere with the client's functioning or welfare; (4) to increase or enhance client strengths and capacities for personal and social functioning; and (5) to decrease or eliminate client deficits in relation to personal and social functioning.

Although these broad classes of problems or goals describe the scope of all social work practice, they are of little use to the worker beyond the initial stage of case planning because they do not define any problem in either measurable or treatable terms. For example, a worker may initially decide that a specific client has clear deficits in social functioning, and the problem therefore becomes one of reducing or eliminating those deficits. But what are they, specifically? Suppose the worker further specifies the problem as an inability to get along with the boss at work. This description is more precise, but the problem is still not defined in sufficient detail to enable the worker to either measure or treat it.

Suppose the client is a technical writer for an advertising agency, and he resents the fact that his boss makes repeated changes in his work. He sees such changes as a criticism of his work; he feels the boss does not like him, and he feels resentment toward the boss, which he is now taking out on his wife through quarreling and irritability at home. The client feels that, if this situation continues, he will lose his job and possibly his marriage. Suppose it is the worker's diagnosis that the client severely misperceives his boss's attitudes and does not know how to discuss and negotiate conflict. The worker further decides that the best choice of treatment is cognitive restructuring or rational-emotive therapy. What needs to be measured? What needs to be changed? By the choice of treatment, the worker has decided what needs to change, and the measures that may reflect whether that change occurs certainly include (1) the number of times the boss makes changes in the client's work, (2) the number of times the client sees these as positive criticisms, (3) the number of times the client sees these as negative criticisms, (4) the number of times the client feels resentment, (5) the number of times the client quarrels with his wife, (6) the number of times he feels irritable at home, (7) the number of times he attempts to clarify with his boss the nature of and reason for the changes in his work, and so on.

Each of these measures can be defined as a problem for the client, and, by monitoring them at regular intervals, the worker can determine whether progress is being made in helping the client. However, the major point of this example is that the worker has progressed from a more general to a more specific and detailed definition of the problem. If the worker stops short of identifying one or more specific ways of measuring the client's problem, the worker will probably not be able to select an appropriate treatment technique. In other words, workers must select a specific intervention because they have good reason to believe that it will bring about change in the specific problems being measured. The definition and the measurement of the client's problems have a significant bearing upon finding a way to solve those problems.

Unfortunately, social workers are often taught in introductory research courses that it is difficult to prove one thing to be the cause of another. From a scientific point of view, the proof of causal relationships is indeed difficult, but that by no means dictates that causal thinking must be avoided. Quite the contrary, it is essential that social workers think, plan, and intervene from a strict causal frame of reference. If the client is anxious, what can the worker do to cause a reduction of anxiety? If the client is a thief, what can the worker do to cause him to stop stealing? If the client has a poor relationship with a spouse, what can the worker do to cause the marriage to improve? If a client is abused because of his passivity, what can the worker do to cause a reduction in that abuse?

These are difficult and, at the same time, extremely important questions that encourage the practitioner to consider what specific treatment techniques or services can be used to enhance the likelihood of a positive outcome. The chief merit of such causal thinking is that it is most productive when it is also very specific—specificity in planning and intervention is the hallmark of good practice. Specificity requires that workers address and at least tentatively answer several important questions: (1) What is the specific problem that should be changed? (2) What should not be changed? (3) What specific treatment techniques can be used that are known to be effective with this particular type of problem? (4) Who will use what technique with, to, or in behalf of whom?

In order to illustrate how these questions and ideas can and should be applied, let us consider a couple of examples. Suppose a diagnostic statement found in a case record says, "This is an inadequate mother who is trying to cope with three unruly children." Are any specific treatment techniques known to be effective in reducing "mother inadequacy"? Of course not. This diagnostic statement is inappropriate because it tells the worker nothing. Such statements should never be allowed in case records because labels such as "inadequate" provide no information about the problem or about what can or should be changed (Wodarski and Hudson, 1976). Who knows what the worker really meant? Perhaps the woman in question did not know how to use adult authority in the regulation of her children's behavior. Or perhaps the worker meant something entirely different.

The use of labels can be misleading or even dangerous. Many do not have real-world referents (Chase, 1938; Korzybski, 1933), and many represent a form of circular reasoning or illogic called reification (Hudson, 1976). If the mother in this example was referred to as inadequate because she was unsuccessful in coping with her children's unruliness, a more productive approach would be to focus on what specifically is meant by unruly and what specifically the mother was or was not doing in her efforts at parenting. If the worker can identify the specific ineffectual parenting behaviors, these can be partially or completely extinguished and then replaced by other behaviors that are more effective in controlling the children. Behavior can be treated but labels cannot; problems must be defined in measurable and treatable terms.

Suppose a client says he wants to experience everything he can—including killing someone. Calling this a "character disorder" does not tell the worker anything about the problem or how to go about solving it. Then why clutter up records with labels? Are there specific treatment techniques known to be effective in treating character disorders? Probably not, because the term is so broad that it can be used to describe a number of different problems. Suppose, on the other hand, that the worker has observed that the client's affective responses are cold, logical, and insensitive. Perhaps the client is starving for affection and for recognition of his real talent and is outraged at being treated by his mother as a fool, a child, and an incompetent. What can the worker do to help? The worker might give him an IQ test to discover how bright he really is. Or the worker might try to retrain the client and his mother to argue more productively and less destructively; teach the client to have and enjoy emotion; acknowledge that his boredom in school has a basis in reality; help the school to better assist the client with his education; and so on. The major point is that, the more specific one can be about the nature and cause of the problem, the more productively one can think about how to change it.

The forgoing discussions may seem rather removed from the issue of measurement, but the point is that, if the components of the client's problem are enumerated in considerable detail, an available measurement device can be selected to assess and monitor the client's problem or can be created on the spot to suit the client's unique situation. If the worker develops a treatment plan based on solid causal thinking ("What must I do to cause an improvement in each problem area?"), the worker will have automatically stated the goals of treatment, which can be used to guide the measurement and assessment of the client's problem.

Consider the case of the cold, logical, brilliant adolescent. The limited description of this case (a real one treated successfully by one of our students) provides enough details to enable the worker to construct an assessment scale. The worker, for example, could ask the client once every two weeks to give these ratings—1 = never, 2 = rarely, 3 = occasionally, 4 = frequently, and 5 = very frequently—to the items in the following chart:

1.	I feel bored in school.	______
2.	My mother treats me like a child.	______
3.	Arguments with my mother seem to be rather destructive.	______
4.	I feel like I get a lot out of school.	______
5.	I feel strong emotion.	______
6.	I feel detached from my emotions.	______
7.	I would like to know what it feels like to kill someone.	______
8.	My mother has no respect for my intellectual ability.	______
9.	I feel affectionate and loving toward my mother.	______
10.	I prefer logic to emotion when I relate to others.	______

If the worker reverse-scores items 4, 5, and 9 (by subtracting the client's rating from 6, so that 1 becomes 5, 2 becomes 4, and so on) and then adds up all ten item responses, the total score will provide a rough index of the magnitude of the client's problem. More important, the total score, plotted on a graph over time, will provide a relatively good description of the extent to which the client is or is not making progress in treatment.

Methods of Measurement

In comparison to social workers of the past, today's social workers increasingly have available to them a wide range of measurement tools that can aid in objectifying and systematizing practice. These tools are a major resource for operationalizing problems and goals, as described earlier, and, perhaps even more important, for monitoring and evaluating progress with every case. Not that some of these tools have not been available for several years (although some have been developed rather recently). Rather, social workers are becoming more aware of the need for such measurement tools, the clinical literature is increasingly reflecting their use, and more resources are being published (see References) that include collections of measurement procedures, thereby enhancing their accessibility to social workers.

This section of the chapter presents a review of the most basic available measures of clinical problems. These measures include: direct observation of behaviors, standardized measures, simple self-anchored scales that one can construct oneself, client logs, and unobtrusive measures (particularly the use of archival records). Of necessity, this chapter only reviews the use of these measures; in-depth discussions are available in Bloom and Fischer (1981), Jayaratne and Levy (1979), and in the other references cited.

A major set of measures—the electromechanical, or physiological, measures—has not been included here because they are generally expensive and complicated to use, require specialized training, are often unavailable to practitioners, and seem to have more narrow applicability than the other measures. Relatively few references examine in detail the use of such measures (see, for example, Pugh and Schwitzgebel, 1977; Lang, 1977; Epstein, 1976; Haynes, 1978). Such other devices as Goal Attainment Scaling (Kiresuk and Sherman, 1968; Kiresuk and Garwick, 1979) and Problem-Oriented Recording (Kane, 1974; Martens and Holmstrup, 1974) are not included here because, although they are extremely useful, they focus more on case planning, organization, and recording than on measurement per se.

Before proceeding with this section, try this exercise. Think of all the practice problems you have ever faced, or imagine some you might encounter one day. Write down those you think might not be measurable, and put that list aside until you have finished this chapter. At the conclusion of the chapter, there will be a suggestion as to how this list can be used.

The remainder of this section of the chapter consists of a review of the key measures available for use in clinical practice.

Direct Observation of Behavior. Direct observation refers to the counting and recording of behaviors as they actually occur. *Behavior,* as used in this context, refers to anything people do. Thus, a behavior could be overt (hitting, walking, crying) or covert (thinking, feeling). The key here is measurability. To be considered a behavior, it must be observable by someone—the client, the practitioner, a relevant other, or an independent observer. (Some good references on direct observation are Ciminero, Calhoun, and Adams, 1977; Haynes, 1978; Hersen and Bellack, 1976; Cone and Hawkins, 1977).

Observing behavior is one of the most important ways of evaluating whether problems really do change, because behavioral measures involve the actual functioning of the client. They can therefore provide at least as good a picture of real changes in the client or client-system as any other method of evaluation. That is, in line with the discussion earlier in the chapter, behavioral measures are often the most valid measures because they are the most direct expression of the problem to be solved. In addition, since behaviors lend themselves well to clear, specific definition, they can be recorded reliably. Finally, precisely because behaviors can be clearly pinpointed and the events affecting their occurrence detailed, use of behavioral measures add a great deal to the practitioner's assessment capabilities.

INSTRUMENTS FOR RECORDING BEHAVIORS. Questions that arise in deciding how to record behavior through direct observation include: Is the method portable enough to be used? Is it unobtrusive enough not to be distracting or embarrassing? Is the method likely to be used? Is the method pleasant or enjoyable to use?

Several different methods of direct observation are available. Some of the more complicated methods involve the use of codes—symbols or phrases used to represent specific categories of behavior (Haynes, 1978). Perhaps the simplest to use is a form—a prepared checklist with spaces or boxes for checking whether or not a behavior does occur. Other methods include small 3 in. x 5 in. cards to note when and where a behavior occurs; coins moved from pocket to pocket or from one compartment in a purse to another each time a behavior occurs; inexpensive wrist golf-score counters; necklaces or bracelets made of lanyards or rawhide with beads strung tightly on them and moved each time a behavior occurs; soap or a large rubber eraser kept in a pocket and an indentation made with a fingernail each time a behavior occurs. As you can see, the methods for recording behavior are limited only by the imagination of the practitioner.

TYPES OF BEHAVIOR. There are two basic ways of recording behaviors: frequency counts and duration measures. (A third, interval recording, combines frequency and duration; measurement of intensity or magnitude will be described under self-anchored scales.)

Frequency measures involve simply counting how often a target behavior occurs during a given period of time. Frequency measures are used when the target problem occurs too often and has to be decreased or does not occur often enough and has to be increased. No special equipment is usually necessary. All that is required is that the behavior has a relatively clear beginning and end and that each occurrence takes a relatively constant amount of time.

Frequency counts, then, entail a simple tally of how many times a behavior occurs. A variety of behaviors can be assessed using frequency counts, including number of positive (or negative) thoughts, number of cigarettes smoked, number of mistakes, number of times a conversation is initiated, number of dates, number of times a child follows instructions, number of aggressive phrases used, and so on.

As with any measure, the behavior must be clearly and specifically defined. If the practitioner is not doing the recording, he or she will have to train someone else to do it, possibly the client or someone in the client's environment. To establish just how reliable these observations are, two observers are needed—for example, the primary observer and the practitioner or two people in the family. The two observers record the number of times a behavior occurs during a given time period. Then their observations are compared, and a percentage of agreement is determined—the interobserver reliability. Simply divide the larger number of behaviors into the smaller and multiply by 100. The result, in a percentage form, will tell the extent of agreement. For example, if observer 1 records ten behaviors as occurring and observer 2 records twelve behaviors, 10 would be divided by 12 and the result multiplied by 100 (10/12 x 100), yielding 83 percent reliability. As a general guideline, 80 percent agreement or better is an indication of adequate reliability.

These reliability checks should be used frequently during training and occasionally once intervention has started just to be sure that the observers are being consistent. However, high reliability does not necessarily mean that two observers are recording the same behaviors all the time, only that they agree on total frequency. Thus, this figure should be interpreted cautiously.

Duration measures, the second key type of direct observation, are used when the problem concerns time: that is, when the problem or target behavior lasts too long or not long enough. The main logistical problem in using a duration measure is determining the length of time between the beginning and end of a behavior. Thus, some form of timepiece is necessary.

The main considerations in using duration measures are to be absolutely clear about defining when a behavior begins and ends and to be clear about the time period recorded. A wide range of behaviors can be recorded using duration measures, including studying, exercising, period of time of obsessive thoughts, insomnia, length of tantrums, periods of feeling depressed, and so on.

To establish interobserver reliability for duration measures, one would follow basically the same procedures as with frequency measures. Two observers record how long the behavior lasts over the same time period, and then the smaller duration is simply divided by the larger duration and multiplied by 100. It is important that the observers begin and end their total period of observation at the same time.

Standardized Measures. A standardized measure is one that has uniform procedures for scoring and administration and has certain types of information available about it (Anastasi, 1976). This information includes at least five areas: the purpose and interpretation of the measure; validity; reliability; administration and scoring; and norms (for comparison). All standardized measures do not address each of these areas equally well, but, to the extent that a measure does, one can be assured that it is standardized.

Standardized measures have a number of advantages. They are generally rather simple and inexpensive to use, take fairly little time or energy, are relatively available, and often provide a good deal of information about the problem of concern. Perhaps most important there is a standardized measure for just about any problem the practitioner might face.

However, there are certain disadvantages to the use of standardized measures. Some do not provide all the information needed to clearly evaluate them (for example, information on validity). Since most research on standardized measures is done on large groups, error is always possible when the measures are applied to an individual. Since standardized measures deal only with predetermined questions and problems, they may not be exactly suited to all the specific characteristics of the problems faced. In addition, most standardized measures, especially questionnaires, surveys, and nonbehavioral checklists, tend not to be very direct measures of a problem.

One of the advantages of standardized measures noted earlier—that so many are available that one can measure just about any clinical problem—could also prove to be a problem by making it difficult to choose among them. The following criteria, described in Anastasi (1976) and Bloom and Fischer (1981), are helpful in making such a choice: be sure the purpose of the measure relates to the problem with which you are dealing; try to select one that is as direct a measure of the problem as possible; look for data on reliability, validity (the more types of validity addressed, the better), and sensitivity to change; make sure the measure will be useful for your purposes (possible, practical, and so on); be sure the measure can be used repeatedly (high test-retest reliability indicating stability); and be sure it is short enough not to become aversive to the client.

Since there are so many standardized measures available—literally thousands, measuring most forms of human social functioning—it would be impossible to describe them all here. Therefore, the interested reader is referred to the following references, each of which reviews and evaluates a number of measures appropriate for particular uses: Levitt and Marsh, 1980; Comrey and others, 1973; Buros, 1972; Lake and others, 1973; Andrulis, 1977; Arkava and Snow, 1978.

One set of measures, the Clinical Measurement Package (CMP), will be described in this chapter, not only because it exemplifies what is available but also because it meets most of the criteria noted earlier, is suitable for use in single-system research (that is, as repeated measures), and forms an integrated package with the same format, scoring methods, and administration.

The CMP is a package of scales developed by Hudson and his coworkers (Hudson, 1977; Hudson and Glisson, 1976; Hudson and Procter, 1976a, 1976b; Giuli and Hudson, 1977; Hudson, Harrison, and Crosscup, 1980; Hudson, Acklin and Bartosh, 1980; Hudson, Wung, and Borges, 1980; Cheung and Hudson, 1980; Hudson and others, 1980). All of the work on these scales is available in a new volume entitled *The Clinical Measurement Package: A Field Manual* (Hudson, 1982).

The Clinical Measurement Package consists of nine twenty-five-item scales designed specifically for clinical practice and single-system research to monitor and evaluate the magnitude (extent, degree, intensity) of the client's problem through periodic administration of the same instrument. The first six scales are: (1) the Generalized Contentment Scale (GCS), a measure of the degree or magnitude of nonpsychotic depression, (2) the Index of Self-Esteem (ISE), which measures the degree or magnitude of the client's problem with the evaluative component of self-concept; (3) the Index of Marital Satisfaction (IMS), designed to measure the degree or magnitude of problems spouses have in their marital relationship; (4) the Index of Sexual Satisfaction (ISS), which is designed to measure the degree or magnitude of discord or dissatisfaction that partners experience with their sexual relationship; (5) the Index of Peer Relations (IPR), designed to measure the degree or intensity of a problem in the ability to relate to peers; and (6) the Index of Family Relations (IFR), designed to measure the degree or intensity of intrafamilial stress as seen by the client. Three other scales were designed to measure the degree or magnitude of parent–child relationship problems: (7) the Index of Parental Attitudes (IPA), completed by the parent, is designed to measure the degree of magnitude of a relationship problem a parent has with a child; (8) the Child's Attitude Toward Father (CAF) measures the degree or magnitude of relationship problems children have with their father; and (9) the Child's Attitude Toward Mother (CAM) measures the degree or magnitude of relationship problems children have with their mother. The latter two scales, CAF and CAM, are completed by the child. One of these instruments, the ISE, is reproduced as an example in Figure 1.

All of the scales have internal consistency reliabilities and test–retest reliabilities (stability) of 0.90 or better. They all have high content, concurrent, and construct validity. In addition, the scales appear to discriminate well between people known or admitting to have problems and people known or claiming not to have problems in each area. In other words, the scales clearly appear to be measuring what they are intended to measure.

INDEX OF SELF-ESTEEM (ISE) Today's Date ______________

NAME: ______________________

This questionnaire is designed to measure how you see yourself. It is not a test, so there are no right or wrong answers. Please answer each item as carefully and accurately as you can by placing a number by each one as follows:

1 Rarely or none of the time
2 A little of the time
3 Some of the time
4 A good part of the time
5 Most or all of the time

Please begin.

1. I feel that people would not like me if they really knew me well ____
2. I feel that others get along much better than I do ____
3. I feel that I am a beautiful person ____
4. When I am with other people, I feel they are glad I am with them ____
5. I feel that people really like to talk with me ____
6. I feel that I am a very competent person ____
7. I think I make a good impression on others ____
8. I feel that I need more self-confidence ____
9. When I am with strangers, I am very nervous ____
10. I think that I am a dull person ____
11. I feel ugly ____
12. I feel that others have more fun than I do ____
13. I feel that I bore people ____
14. I think my friends find me interesting ____
15. I think I have a good sense of humor ____
16. I feel very self-conscious when I am with strangers ____
17. I feel that, if I could be more like other people, I would have it made ____
18. I feel that people have a good time when they are with me ____
19. I feel like a wallflower when I go out ____
20. I feel I get pushed around more than others ____
21. I think I am a rather nice person ____
22. I feel that people really like me very much ____
23. I feel that I am a likable person ____
24. I am afraid I will appear foolish to others ____
25. My friends think very highly of me ____

Figure 1. The Index of Self-Esteem (ISE)

All of the scales are scored in the same way, a distinct advantage when using several instruments. Following are the instructions for scoring; reverse-score every positively worded item. (The items to be reverse-scored are listed at the bottom of each scale.) For example, if the client scored one of these positively worded items as 1, rescore it as 5; 2 is rescored as 4; 3 is left unchanged; 4 is rescored as 2; and 5 is rescored as 1. After all the positively worded items have been rescored (all negatively worded items are left unchanged), add up all of the scores, then subtract 25 from the total. (Consult the references for scoring procedures to be used when clients fail to complete one or more items.) This method of scoring produces a minimum score of 0 (lower scores are interpreted as absence of problems or minimal problems) and a maximum score of 100 (higher scores are interpreted as presence of problems).

On all scales, the higher the score, the greater the magnitude of the problem. Each of the scales has also been designed to have a "clinical cutting score" of 30, the idea being that people who score over 30 generally have been found to have clinically significant problems in the area being measured, whereas people who score below 30 do not. This guideline is potentially an important one for use in practice. However, this cutting point should be interpreted with caution, pending validation by further research. At present, it probably would be safe to view the 30 level as a very rough guide to the existence or absence of problems. A score of 29 does not mean complete absence of problems, and a score of 31 does not mean clinical intervention is obviously necessary. The point, though, is that higher scores deserve attention, and the goal of intervention is to reduce those scores to at least below 30.

Although these scales can be used to measure the severity, intensity, degree, or magnitude of a problem, they are not intended to be used to determine its source, locus, or origin. Thus, to that extent, they do not provide all the diagnostic or assessment information necessary prior to beginning an intervention program.

Further, it is assumed that, despite the high reliability of each scale, there will still be some measurement error. None of the scales is perfect. As a rough guide, then, assume that changes in score of five points or less over repeated administrations may be a result of this error, and that changes of more than five points in either direction probably reflect real changes in the client's problem or situation.

These scales are recommended for use approximately once per week both to evaluate change and to provide a basis for discussion between client and practitioner. Research by Hudson and his colleagues reveals that the scales do appear to be stable and reasonable measures of change when administered repeatedly over several weeks. Of course, if the client does express dissatisfaction with the use of these scales, they may have to be administered less frequently or dropped altogether and less aversive measures found.

Self-Anchored Scales. In some situations, direct observation of overt behaviors may be difficult or impossible, and standardized measures dealing with the problem of concern may not be available or practical. Does that mean that the client's problem can not be measured? Not at all. There is a type of measure that can be used in a range of situations and is so flexible that it has been called an "all-purpose measurement procedure" (Bloom, 1975). This procedure consists of actually developing one's own scale to measure whatever it is practitioner and client have decided to focus on. This do-it-yourself procedure is called a self-anchored scale (Bloom, 1975; Gingerich, 1979).

Self-anchored scales are simple self-report scales that can be constructed in an individualized fashion to measure a given problem. In essence, practitioner and client simply identify a particular problem area and establish a sliding scale—say, from zero to ten points—to measure that problem. These scales have numerous advantages. They are very flexible, and therefore can be used to tap a whole range of problems. Self-anchored scales can be used to measure the intensity of problems (for example, the intensity of pain in migraines) or the intensity of negative thoughts. Related to this, self-anchored scales can be used to measure internal thoughts and feelings—everything from fear to sexual excitement or self-esteem. Self-anchored scales are also very easy to construct and easy for the client to use; they therefore have the virtue of being highly efficient. Indeed, they can readily be used as repeated measures one or more times per day.

Self-anchored scales tend to have high face validity. That is, on the face of it, they appear to be measuring what they are intended to measure. That is, they can be used to measure things that only the client can report on and therefore often represent a fairly accurate portrayal of the client's circumstances, thoughts, or feelings. As self-reports, they may provide the primary focus for intervention—changing what a client thinks about himself or herself. Self-anchored scales can be used as primary or sole measures, if no other measures are available or appropriate, or as secondary measures to supplement other information (for example, data on overt behavior). Finally, the scores on self-anchored scales, like the scores on standardized measures or the frequency or duration data of behavioral measures, can be charted to provide a visual display of changes in the problem over time.

Several simple steps can be used to develop these scales:

1. Prepare the client. Help the client become as specific as possible about the problem. Help the client think of the need for a social or psychological thermometer (Bloom, 1975) with the high point the highest, best, most intense description of the problem and the low point the lowest description.
2. Select the number of points for the scale. Although these scales can run up to 100 points, for purposes of simplification, eleven-point scales are suggested. Thus, 5 (midpoint on the scale) could be neutral or moderate (compared with the two extreme poles); 0 would always be low and 10 always high. However, if the client has trouble discriminating between points on the scale, use fewer points.
3. Use equal intervals. Try to clarify that there is not a bigger jump between points 1 and 2 than between any other two points, say, 7 and 8.
4. Use only one scale per dimension, and try to limit each scale to measuring only one dimension. Instead of having two different dimensions at each pole (for example, happy on one end, depressed on the other), because people can and do experience contradictory feelings at the same time, it is clearer to use each scale to measure only one dimension at a time (for example, degree of sadness from low to high).
5. Anchor the scale points. The last step is attempting to use concrete examples to clearly define the points on your scale. At the most general level, you would want to identify the end points—for example, level 0, "Don't experience the problem at all," and level 10, "Feel the problem all the time." In addition, it is very helpful to try to develop examples of thoughts, feelings, and behaviors that might be occurring at those points to help the client recognize that level of intensity. Thus, the client might know to rate himself or herself as severely depressed (level 10) when he or she cannot sleep or work and has suicidal thoughts.

An example of a scale measuring severity of feelings of anger would be:

0	1	2	3	4	5	6	7	8	9	10
Not at all angry					Moderately angry					Furious (want to scream and hit)

An example of a scale measuring intensity of cognitions of sadness would be:

0	1	2	3	4	5	6	7	8	9	10
No cognitions of sadness					Moderate sadness					Extremely intense sadness (crying most of the day)

Client Logs. The client log is essentially a journal kept by clients of events that they consider to be relevant to their problem situation. The use of the log helps the client take systematic and objective notes on such events in an attempt to avoid distortions when presenting information to the practitioner. The log, consisting of a more or less formal record of events that occur but may somehow be forgotten or overlooked, represents an attempt to help the client "tell it like it is" (Schwartz and Goldiamond, 1975; Bloom and Fischer, 1981).

The client log has two basic purposes or uses. The first and most important is an assessment device. Client logs help pinpoint target problems. They serve as sources of hypotheses for intervention and help in planning by allowing practitioner and client, in discussing the problem situation, to examine the log to determine which events appear to be related to the occurrence of the problem.

The second use is for evaluation purposes: the log provides an ongoing record of the client's activities in relation to the problems being worked on. The log often shows changes in these activities and problems as the client experiences them.

Overall, client logs are not to be construed as precise scientific instruments; their accuracy is based on the client's perceptions. Thus, questions of reliability and validity suggest that they probably should not be used as the primary source of assessment or evaluation information. On the other hand, logs do appear to be excellent sources of secondary or supplementary information. All client logs use basically the same format, a prepared form that lists across the top of the page the type of information to be collected. The information varies with the nature of the problem but, at the least, might include a brief description of some event or behavior that occurred and what the client did, thought, or felt about it. On the left-hand side of the page, the client lists the time each event occurred.

Client logs can be constructed according to two major variables, time and category of client problem. Clients can be asked to record any event that occurs that they consider to be important (critical-incident recording), or they can be asked to summarize, at preestablished intervals (for example, every hour or two), the key events that occurred during that interval (see Bloom and Fischer, 1981).

The categories of client problems can also vary in their specificity. The practitioner can leave the categories open and suggest that the client record any event that is "critical," or the categories can be highly specific—for example: Who did what to whom? What was your reaction? What events preceded and followed the problem situation? and so on. Examples of different types of client logs and forms are available in Schwartz and Goldiamond (1975) and Bloom and Fischer (1981).

Unobtrusive Measures. One of the concerns of many practitioners is that somehow the measurement process will affect practice in some presumably negative fashion. Indeed, that concern bears a grain of truth. Earlier in this chapter, we described the potential for one such effect, reactivity—changes in the problem due to the act of measurement itself. For many of the measurement procedures described thus far, however, reactivity can be either overcome or accounted for (see Nay, 1979; Bloom and Fischer, 1981).

But some methods of measurement, called unobtrusive measures, avoid the problem of reactivity: the client "is not aware of being [measured] and there is little danger that the act of measurement will itself serve as a force for change or elicit role playing that confounds the data" (Webb and others, 1966, p. 175).

Many of these unobtrusive measures are indirect ways of measuring problems and therefore should serve in most instances as secondary sources of data. These measures include physical traces (evidence left by an individual or group with no knowledge that it will be used for other purposes), behavior products (measurement of the effects of behaviors—for example, items left on a floor—rather than the behaviors themselves), and simple observations (where the observer observes a problem without being seen or noticed). All of these are described in detail in Webb and others (1966).

One type of unobtrusive measure that is often readily available to social workers is the archival record, data that are available from records kept for various purposes but not originally intended to be used in an intervention program. Because these records are often available from a variety of sources and can be used to measure the effects of an intervention program, they are probably the most important and useful type of unobtrusive measure.

In some instances, archival records may directly reflect the problem to be worked on and can therefore serve as primary measures. An example might be school records: attendance data, test scores, grades, and so on. Other forms of records, including agency record data, recidivism notes, actuarial data, and government data, may be used as primary or secondary sources, depending on the goals of a specific intervention program.

Of course, archival records do present some problems, including inflexibility, limited accessibility, incompleteness or inconsistency of available data, and systematic bias of content. However, since these data do overcome the effects of reactivity, they can prove to be a particularly valuable resource, especially in allowing evaluation of activities that otherwise might not be accessible to evaluation.

Selecting a Measure

Once familiar with the range of measures available, the practitioner needs to consider several factors in making a selection (see also Nay, 1979). The first involves the characteristics of the measure, in particular its reliability, validity, utility, and directness, as well as its suitability for single-system research. To the extent that a measure can be positively evaluated on each dimension, it should be considered as a prime candidate for use. The second factor to consider is the nature of the problem. Even though a measure is valid and reliable, it must accurately reflect the problem it is intended to measure. A behavioral measure would not be appropriate when the goal is to change an attitude, and vice versa. The third factor relates to the characteristics of the client and the resources available. Someone (the client or relevant other) must be willing and able to use the measure selected and be trained in its use, if necessary.

The last guideline for selecting measurement procedures is one of the most important: whenever possible, use more than one. Changes in clients are often multidimensional and often do not even correlate with each other. Not that several measures should be used merely in the hope that one will show change. Rather, systematical selection and use of more than one measure will increase the chances of identifying change if change really occurs. More specifically, use of more than one measure offers the opportunity to provide a balanced measurement package—that is, one that measures two different aspects of the same problem, taps internal and external change, uses both a direct and an indirect measure, or uses different vantage points to evaluate change (for example, client and practitioner).

Conclusion

Earlier in this chapter, it was suggested that you list some of the problems you have encountered in your practice that you consider to be immeasurable. In reviewing that list now, note whether any of those problems can in fact be measured by the procedures described in this chapter. Once you have clearly specified the problem, you should find it amenable to measurement by one or more of the instruments presented.

As noted earlier, measurement is at the very heart of the process of integrating research and practice and provides the opportunity for social workers to be clear about what they are doing and where they are going with every case or situation. Use of the measurement procedures described in this chapter provides the basis for assessment and evaluation processes that can be more systematic, more objective, and more helpful to clients and practitioners.

References

Allen, M. J., and Yen, W. M. *Introduction to Measurement Theory*. Monterey, Calif.: Brooks/Cole, 1979.

Anastasi, A. *Psychological Testing*. (4th ed.) New York: Macmillan, 1976.

Andrulis, R. S. *Adult Assessment*. Springfield, Ill.: Thomas, 1977.

Arkava, M. L., and Snow, M. *Psychological Tests and Social Work Practice*. Springfield, Ill.: Thomas, 1978.

Bloom, M. *The Paradox of Helping: Introduction to the Philosophy of Scientific Practice*. New York: Wiley, 1975.

Bloom, M., and Fischer, J. *Evaluating Practice: A Guide for the Helping Professional.* Englewood Cliffs, N.J.: Prentice-Hall, 1981.

Buros, O. K., (Ed.). *The Seventh Mental Measurements Yearbook.* (2 vols.) Highland Park, N.J.: Gryphon Press, 1972.

Chase, S. *The Tyranny of Words.* New York: Harcourt, Brace, 1938.

Cheung, P.P.L., and Hudson, W. W. "Assessing Marital Discord in Clinical Practice: A Revalidation of the Index of Marital Satisfaction." *Journal of Social Service Research,* 1982, *5* (1/2), 101–118.

Ciminero, A. R., Calhoun, K. S., and Adams, H. E. (Eds.). *Handbook of Behavioral Assessment.* New York: Wiley, 1977.

Comrey, A. L., and others. *A Sourcebook for Mental Health Measures.* Los Angeles: Human InterAction Research Institute, 1973.

Cone, J. D., and Hawkins, R. P., (Eds.). *Behavioral Assessment.* New York: Brunner/Mazel, 1977.

Epstein, L. H. "Psychophysiological Measurement in Assessment." In M. Hersen and A. S. Bellack (Eds.), *Behavioral Assessment: A Practical Handbook.* New York: Pergamon Press, 1976.

Fischer, J. *Effective Casework Practice: An Eclectic Approach.* New York: McGraw-Hill, 1978.

Gingerich, W. "Measuring the Process." *Social Work,* 1978, *23* (3), 251–252.

Gingerich, W. "Procedure for Evaluating Clinical Practice." *Health and Social Work,* 1979, *4,* 104–130.

Giuli, C. A., and Hudson, W. W. "Assessing Parent-Child Relationship Disorders in Clinical Practice." *Journal of Social Service Research,* 1977, *1* (1), 77–92.

Grinnell, R. M., Jr. (Ed.). *Social Work Research and Evaluation.* Springfield, Ill.: Peacock, 1981.

Haynes, S. N. *Principles of Behavioral Assessment.* New York: Gardner Press, 1978.

Helmstadter, G. C. *Principles of Psychological Measurement.* New York: Appleton-Century-Crofts, 1964.

Hersen, M., and Barlow, D. H. *Single Case Experimental Designs: Strategies for Studying Behavior Change.* Elmsford, N.Y.: Pergamon Press, 1976.

Hersen, M., and Bellack, A. S. (Eds.). *Behavioral Assessment: A Practical Handbook.* New York: Pergamon Press, 1976.

Hudson, W. W. "A Measurement Package for Clinical Workers." Paper presented at the 23rd annual program meeting of the Council on Social Work Education, Phoenix, Ariz., March 1977.

Hudson, W. W. "First Axioms of Treatment." *Social Work,* 1978a, *23* (1), 65–66.

Hudson, W. W. "Research Training in Professional Social Work Education." *Social Service Review,* 1978b, *52* (1), 116–121.

Hudson, W. W. *The Clinical Measurement Package: A Field Manual.* Homewood, Ill.: Dorsey, 1982.

Hudson, W. W. "Guidelines for Social Work Practice." School of Social Work, University of Hawaii, 1976. (Mimeographed.)

Hudson, W. W., Acklin, J., and Bartosh, J. C. "Assessing Discord in Family Relationships." *Social Work Research and Abstracts,* 1980, *16* (3), 21–29.

Hudson, W. W., and Glisson, D. H. "Assessment of Marital Discord in Family Relationships." *Social Service Review,* 1976, *50,* 293–311.

Hudson, W. W., Harrison, D. F., and Crosscup, P. "A Short-Form Scale to Measure Sexual Discord." *Journal of Sex Research,* 1981, *17,* 157–174.

Hudson, W. W., and Procter, E. K. "A Short-Form Scale for Measuring Self-Esteem." School of Social Work, University of Hawaii, 1976a. (Mimeographed.)

Hudson, W. W., and Procter, E. K. "The Assessment of Depressive Affect in Clinical Practice." School of Social Work, University of Hawaii, 1976b. (Mimeographed.)

Hudson, W. W., Wung, B., and Borges, M. "Parent-Child Relationship Disorders: The Parent's Point of View." *Journal of Social Service Research,* 1980, *3,* 283–294.

Hudson, W. W., and others. "A Comparison and Revalidation of Three Measures of Depression." School of Social Work, Florida State University, Tallahassee, 1980.

Jayaratne, S., and Levy, R. *Empirical Clinical Practice.* New York: Columbia, 1979.

Kane, R. A. "Look to the Record." *Social Work,* 1974, *17,* 412–419.

Kiresuk, T. J., and Sherman, R. E. "Goal Attainment Scaling: A General Method of Evaluating Comprehensive Community Mental Health Programs." *Community Mental Health Journal,* 1968, *4,* 443–453.

Kiresuk, T. J., and Garwick, G. "Basic Goal Attainment Scaling Procedures." In B. R. Compton and B. Gallaway (Eds.), *Social Work Processes.* (Rev. ed.) Homewood, Ill.: Dorsey Press, 1979.

Korzybski, A. *Science and Sanity: An Introduction to Non-Aristotelian Systems and General Semantics.* Lakeville, Conn.: The Institute of General Semantics, 1933.

Lake, D. G., and others. *Measuring Human Behavior: Tools for the Assessment of Social Functioning.* New York: Teachers College Press, Columbia University, 1973.

Lang, P. J. "Physiological Assessment of Anxiety and Fear." In J. D. Cone and R. P. Hawkins (Eds.), *Behavioral Assessment.* New York: Brunner/Mazel, 1977.

Levitt, J. L., and Marsh, J. "A Collection of Short-Form Repeated Measurement Instruments Suitable for Practice." Chicago: School of Social Service Administration, University of Chicago, 1980. (Mimeographed.)

Martens, W. M., and Holmstrup, W. "Problem-Oriented Recording." *Social Casework,* 1974, *55,* 554–561.

Nay, W. R. *Multimethod Clinical Assessment.* New York: Gardner, 1979.

Nunnally, J. C. *Psychometric Theory.* New York: McGraw-Hill, 1978.

Pugh, J. D., and Schwitzgebel, R. L. "Instrumentation for Behavioral Assessment." In A. R. Ciminero and others (Eds.), *Handbook of Behavioral Assessment.* New York: Wiley, 1977.

Schwartz, A., and Goldiamond, I. *Social Casework: A Behavioral Approach.* Chicago: University of Chicago Press, 1975.

Webb, E. J., and others. *Unobtrusive Measures: Nonreactive Research in the Social Sciences.* Chicago: Rand McNally, 1966.

Wodarski, J., and Hudson, W. W., and Buckholdt, D. R. "Issues in Evaluative Research: Implications for Social Work." *Journal of Sociology and Social Welfare,* 1976, *4* (1), 81–113.

31

Significance Testing in Single-Case Research

Wallace J. Gingerich

The ultimate goal of a clinical evaluation study is to be able to demonstrate that client change occurred as a consequence of a particular intervention. To demonstrate effectiveness, however, three steps in the evaluation process must be achieved. First, the client's problem must be correctly identified and a suitable measure developed. Without a reliable and meaningful measure of the problem, it is impossible to assess the severity of the problem or the amount of change, if any, during intervention. The second step in clinical evaluation is to determine whether the observed client change was significant, a matter of direct concern to both client and worker, since such change was presumably the initial reason for the client's seeking help. In the final step in clinical evaluation, an inference is made about whether client change was due to the intervention. Although it is probably enough for the client to know that he or she has improved, the worker will want to know whether the observed change can be attributed to the intervention. The new knowledge that accrues from clinical evaluation studies is crucial to development of the worker's personal expertise, as well as to the general effectiveness of the profession.

This chapter will address issues and techniques pertaining to the second step in clinical evaluation. Although client change will appear obvious in many cases, a number of judgment guides and statistical aids will be useful at times. In earlier chapters, Fischer and Hudson cover the theory and techniques measurement, and Levy and Olsen provide a thorough discussion of the issues involved in inferring causality in single-subject research and present a number of practical design alternatives. In conjunction with the present chapter, those two chapters provide a complete discussion of the process of conducting clinical evaluation studies.

This chapter begins with a discussion of applied significance and experimental significance, two different approaches for assessing client change. Subsequent sections present guidelines and techniques for determining the applied significance of client change and experimental criteria for assessing such change. The characteristics of clinical time-series data sets are discussed along with the types of change commonly observed in clinical practice. Then a number of approaches to assessing experimental significance are outlined, including visual inspection, the Shewart chart, the celeration line, and time-series analysis. The final section of the chapter suggests guidelines for selecting and using the various techniques for assessing client change.

Criteria for Assessing Client Change

Assuming the worker has developed a suitable measure of the problem and has monitored it over a period of time, the question arises as to whether the problem has really changed. Although this question appears to be a simple and straightforward one, closer examination reveals that it is actually rather complex. Significance, in a general sense, refers to the importance or worthwhileness of an event. Different individuals may disagree, however, about the criteria of importance. The client may have one set of standards or expectations against which he or she evaluates the importance of the change, the spouse or another family member may have another set of standards, and the worker may have still a different set. Finally, an outside evaluator, knowing little about the clinical and social aspects of the client problem, may apply an altogether different set of criteria for judging the importance of the observed client change. In actual practice, it is not uncommon for the client, family member, worker, and supervisor to disagree about the significance of the change. This disagreement arises out of a lack of agreement on the criteria for evaluating change or what constitutes a realistic or reasonable amount of change.

Most clients and many workers evaluate the significance of client change in relation to a predetermined goal that had been set for the client—that is, did the client achieve the level of change initially thought to be desirable, necessary, or within the ability of the client and worker to achieve? Researchers, on the other hand, usually evaluate the significance of client change by comparing the client's present level of functioning with the level prior to intervention—in other words, has there been a noticeable, reliable change? The first of these sets of criteria has been referred to variously as clinical significance (Kazdin, 1976), therapeutic significance, (Risley, 1970), or social or applied significance (Kazdin, 1977). The general term *applied significance* will be used throughout this chapter, since it subsumes the other terms and suggests that practical considerations form the criteria for assessing significance. The second set of criteria, that of comparing current client performance to the preintervention level, has usually been referred to as statistical significance (Kazdin, 1976); however, the term *experimental significance* (Risley, 1970) will be used here, since it conveys the notion that significance is based on observed changes in the client. Accordingly, visual analysis as well as statistical techniques will be considered under the topic of experimental significance.

Applied Significance. In a general sense, applied significance means that the change in the client problem has been of sufficient magnitude to be clinically or socially important. More specifically, Risley (1970) defines applied significance as the comparison between the amount of client change that has occurred and the amount of change thought necessary for adequate functioning in society. This definition goes beyond the purely individual concerns of the client and acknowledges the expectations of society at large. Wolf (1978) and Kazdin (1977) refer to this as the social validation of client change. According to Kazdin, social validation can be accomplished through social comparison methods or subjective evaluation methods. In social comparison, the performance of the client is compared with the performance of "normal" peers. In subjective evaluation, the client's performance is evaluated by others in the client's environment, who are asked whether the degree of client change has been socially important.

Assuming that a realistic goal has been set for the client, applied significance is relatively easy to evaluate. One simply notes whether the client's performance has reached the desired goal. In practice, however, applied significance is often difficult to assess. Realistic and appropriate goals for the client are difficult to establish because norms or criteria for adequate change are often ambiguous and subjective. Further, incomplete knowledge about the severity of the client's problem, the client's capacity for change, and the potency of the intervention all contribute to the difficulty of setting realistic goals. Yet applied significance is an important and useful method for evaluating client change and is certainly the most commonly used criterion. Thus, the process of goal setting must be as objective and systematic as possible. A number of useful goal-setting techniques have been developed and will be presented in the section on assessing applied significance.

Experimental Significance. In contrast to applied significance, which compares the client's performance to a predetermined goal, experimental significance compares the client's performance to what it would have been if treatment had not been implemented (Risley, 1970). In single-subject research, the client's functioning during treatment is compared with his or her functioning prior to treatment. If the client's behavior during treatment is a continuation of his or her behavior during baseline, no significant change has occurred. If, on the other hand, the level of the client's behavior during treatment clearly differs from the level during baseline, the change may be termed experimentally significant. More precisely, experimental significance assesses the probability that the pattern of client behavior observed during treatment may be viewed as an extension of the behavior pattern prior to treatment. Occasionally statistical procedures are used to help arrive at such a determination. If the probability is sufficiently low—less than 5 percent, for example—the baseline and treatment behavior may not be interpreted as manifestations of the same behavior pattern. Thus, the change in client behavior is said to be statistically (or experimentally) significant, that is, not due to chance. Although this judgment appears to be simple and straightforward, the characteristics of clinical time-series data sets and the variety of intervention effects sometimes complicate the process. These issues will be discussed in more detail in the section on assessing experimental significance, and specific techniques for making assessments will be provided.

Applied Versus Experimental Significance. Considerable controversy has arisen in recent years over the relative merits of applied and experimental criteria for assessing the significance of client change (Michael, 1974; Kazdin, 1976; Baer, 1977; Carver, 1978; Kratochwill and Brody, 1978; and Kratochwill, 1978). The tradition, at least in behavioral research, has been to identify potent interventions, interventions whose effects are so strong and clear that their significance is unquestionable. Little attention has been paid to small or ambiguous intervention effects, since they provide too little evidence of effectiveness to be of value. Further, as one anonymous manuscript reviewer has said, "The development of sensitive statistics appropriate for the research designs of applied behavior analysis would be bad for the field . . . because they would result in the development of more and weaker principles. . . . The field needs basic effects, that is, effects that are large, reliable, powerful, clear, and durable" (Gottman and Glass, 1978, pp. 197–198). Thus, according to this argument, experimental criteria for judging significance are needed only when client change is small or ambiguous, and, when that is the case, the intervention should be discarded because it is too weak to be of practical importance.

There seems to be little disagreement with the importance of applied criteria for judging significance or with the goal of developing interventions whose effects on client behavior are strong and clear. The major point of disagreement focuses on whether small and ambiguous changes in client behavior should be pursued further or ignored. When client change is so strong and clear that its presence is unmistakable, statistical significance testing is unnecessary. Only when change is unclear do statistical aids become potentially useful. A complicating factor is that what appear through visual analysis to be significant effects may not be statistically significant, and vice versa (DeProspero and Cohen, 1979). Jones, Weinrott, and Vaught (1978, p. 280) found, for example, that visual and statistical (time-series analysis) inferences "agreed better when the statistical test indicated nonsignificant changes in level than when significant changes in level were indicated." In other words, visual analysis is unreliable when compared with statistical analysis. As a precaution, statistical analysis should perhaps be performed even when effects seem to be significant through visual inspection.

Kazdin (1976) identifies three such situations in which statistical significance testing may be of value: (1) failure to establish a stable baseline, (2) desire to tease out new or subtle treatment effects, and (3) need to control statistically for extraneous factors in naturalistic studies. It is not always possible to get a stable baseline of the client problem before treatment—the client's behavior may fluctuate widely or may show a consistent trend upward or downward. In these cases, statistical techniques sensitive to variability and trend may be helpful. Second, some interventions, particularly new ones, do not have immediate and dramatic effects. Effects that appear ambiguous to the eye may nevertheless be reliable and statistically significant (Gottman and Glass, 1978; Jones, Weinrott, and Vaught, 1978; DeProspero and Cohen, 1979). In such cases, a new treatment may be retained and refined further, rather than thrown out for lack of dramatic effects. Of course, the opposite may also happen—that is, what appears to the practitioner to be a potentially useful, albeit weak, intervention may turn out to be statistically insignificant. Finally, since clinical evaluation studies usually take place in the natural environment, it is often not possible to achieve the desired level of control over extraneous variables. Consequently, the data are likely to contain more variability, and, therefore, intervention effects are less easily detected. In these cases, too, statistical techniques may aid in assessing the experimental significance of client change.

Another issue in the controversy over significance testing concerns which statistical tests are appropriate for use in single-case studies (Michael, 1974; Kratochwill and Brody, 1978; Glass, Willson, and Gottman, 1975; Kazdin, 1976; Gottman and Glass, 1978; Elashoff and Thoreson, 1978; Berger and Witkin, 1978; Loftus and Levy, 1977; Bloom and Block, 1977b, 1978; Jayaratne, 1978). Clinical time-series data often do not meet the assumption of independence of observations required by standard parametric tests (Glass, Willson, and Gottman, 1975; Huitema, 1982); consequently, the results of common statistical procedures may be misleading (Gottman and Glass, 1978; McCain and McCleary, 1979). Also, standard inferential statistics that evaluate comparisons between groups of subjects are generally inappropriate for evaluating change in a series of repeated observations of a single subject.

Both approaches to assessing the significance of client change appear to have value. Applied criteria are almost always relevant, since most client problems have personal (to the client) and social consequences. Yet practical criteria for assessing the significance of client change are often vague and unnecessarily subjective. The techniques described in the following section assist in making applied criteria more explicit and objective. Experimental criteria are also of value, not only because they help determine whether change has occurred but also because experimentally significant change becomes the basis for inferring the effectiveness of interventions. The techniques presented in the section on assessing experimental significance are simple, straightforward procedures that can assist the worker in determining whether significant client change has occurred.

Techniques for Assessing Applied Significance

As noted earlier, applied significance compares the amount of client change that has occurred with the amount of change deemed necessary for adequate functioning. Applied significance is often difficult to assess because it is difficult to specify exactly what degree of client change is necessary or desirable. In many cases, different individuals will disagree. A school-age client may believe a reduction in truancies from ten per month to five per month is adequate, the worker may believe that such a rapid reduction is an unrealistic short-term goal, and the school principal may insist on no more than one truancy per month. Often this lack of consensus is left unresolved, with the consequence that the applied or clinical significance of client change is in dispute. Social comparison and subjective evaluation are two methods that have been used by a number of clinical researchers to establish applied significance (Kazdin, 1977). Goal Attainment Scaling, developed by Kiresuk and his associates (Kiresuk and Lund, 1978), is a technique that specifies in advance the goal for client change that will presumably have applied significance. Finally, White (1977) has proposed a graphing technique using an "aim-star" that also specifies in advance the criterion of applied significance. Each of these methods and techniques is presented in the remainder of this section.

Social Comparison. In social comparison, peers of the client are identified who are similar in social and demographic characteristics but do not exhibit the target problem that is the focus of intervention (Kazdin, 1977). The level of functioning of the peer group in the target-problem area then serves as the criterion of applied significance. If, with intervention, the functioning of the client falls within the range of the "normal" peer group, the change can be said to have applied significance. In one of the examples cited by Kazdin, Patterson (1974) evaluated the applied significance of change in the disruptive behavior of deviant boys. Behavioral observation before treatment in the homes of the boys and in the homes of "normal" boys (matched on socioeconomic status and age) showed the deviant boys had higher rates of disruptive behavior. After treatment and during the following year, the disruptive behavior of the deviant boys had decreased to within the range of the "normal" boys. In this example, the social significance of the change in the group of clients was evaluated directly by empirically determining the necessary or normative level of functioning in the community.

A similar approach can be used to evaluate the personal significance of client change; in fact, this approach is often used informally in clinical practice. Rather than comparing the client's performance with normal peers, performance can be compared with the client's own level of functioning before the problem occurred. Particular attention should be paid to documenting the prior level of functioning through reliable data sources. Once established, the criterion of personal significance for the client becomes specific and concrete. This approach is of particular relevance when the goal of intervention is to restore client functioning to an earlier level; it would be inappropriate when teaching new skills.

Kazdin (1977) notes a number of precautions when applying the criterion of social comparison. In some situations, the normative level of functioning of the peer group may not be an adequate criterion. In some programs, for example, the goal is to change the normative level, as when training for energy conservation. In other cases, the level of functioning of the peer group may be too high or too low a standard of significance for a given client, considering his or her personal resources. Another potential problem in the use of social comparison is in identifying an appropriate peer group. For a retarded individual, should nonretarded or similarly retarded individuals serve as the comparison group? Similarly, for a minority child, should minority or nonminority children serve as the normative group? What are the relevant factors on which the comparison group sould be matched with the client? Although the answers to these questions are still largely unknown, the comparison with a peer group can often assist in judging the social or applied significance of client change.

Subjective Evaluation. Subjective evaluation refers to judgments of the importance of observed change by qualified individuals who know the client (Kazdin, 1977). The judgments made are qualitative and usually address overall improvement in the client. They may be made by expert observers, such as teachers, social workers, or probation officers, or by others in a special position to evaluate the client's behavior change, such as ward staff, houseparents, or fellow students. In a study cited by Kazdin, adults of lower socioeconomic status were trained to engage in effective problem-solving skills on a community board (Briscoe, Hoffman, and Bailey, 1975). Videotapes of board meetings were made before and after intervention. To evaluate change in problem-solving ability, several professionals and community leaders were asked to rate the tapes. The postintervention tapes were rated higher in problem-solving ability, providing a subjective evaluation of the applied significance of client change.

In contrast to social comparison, subjective evaluation provides no standard or norm by which client change is evaluated. It merely asks for a global, subjective evaluation as to whether the client has demonstrated improvement. The feature that distinguishes subjective evaluation from typical clinical practice is that the evaluation is made by someone other than the client or worker. In this sense, subjective evaluation is probably more unbiased and reliable than evaluation by the worker alone. Some evidence suggests that evaluations by significant others or by trained observers are more reliable than the evaluations of the worker directly involved with the client (Sloane and others, 1975).

As with social comparison, a number of considerations limit the applicability of subjective evaluation (Kazdin, 1977). Subjective evaluations are based on perceived change in the client; thus, they may indicate just noticeable differences, rather than truly important change. In other words, although the client may have changed noticeably, the level of functioning may still be inadequate. A second consideration pertains to the methodology used to measure subjective evaluation. Usually Likert-type scales have been used to make global ratings on a named client problem. When such traditional measurement procedures are used, the reliability and validity of the scale become relevant issues that have rarely been addressed thus far.

Goal Attainment Scaling. Goal Attainment Scaling is a technique developed in the 1960s by Kiresuk and his associates at the Hennepin County Mental Health Center in Minnesota to measure the effects of service for individual clients (Kiresuk and Lund, 1978). It is a goal-oriented evaluation procedure in which, prior to intervention, one or several goals are identified for the client and criteria for measuring each goal are specified. Then the expected outcome (level of goal attainment) is specified, based on what the worker judges to be the most probable level of client functioning at the end of intervention. When the client completes treatment, his or her functioning is compared to the expected outcome on the goal attainment follow-up guide. If the level of functioning is as expected, one can say that the client change has clinical or applied significance. Although not originally conceived as a technique for assessing applied significance, Goal Attainment Scaling operates in much the same way in making such assessments as in measuring the effects of service. A goal or standard of adequate performance is established before treatment, and client performance after treatment is evaluated in terms of the goal. If the goal is achieved, the client change has attained a level of applied significance.

Like other techniques for assessing applied significance, however, Goal Attainment Scaling is still a somewhat subjective procedure. Workers are instructed to set as the expected level of goal attainment the level thought most likely to occur. The factors that contribute to making the expected outcome prediction are usually unstated but probably include the current level of client functioning, the presumed capacity and motivation of the client for change, the worker's (or agency's) track record of success in working with similar problems in the past, and the presence of any inducements or obstacles to change in the client's environment. In other words, the expected outcome stated by the worker is the result of "clinical judgment." Although such judgment may at times be highly subjective, Goal Attainment Scaling provides the benefit of specifying beforehand the clinical goal for the client and has the practical advantage of being standard operating procedure in many social agencies. Also, many materials have already been developed to assist the worker in identifying and stating useful goals.

One limitation of the technique for assessing the applied significance of client change is that the criteria for establishing the goal are mixed. The procedure specifies that the most likely client outcome six weeks from now be set as the goal. This prediction is based not only on a personally or socially desirable outcome but also on what is clinically possible within six weeks. In a pure test of applied significance, the criterion of significance would be independent of the present level of functioning of the client, the worker's success rate, and the likely outcome in six weeks.

Aim-Star Technique. A graphing technique for displaying applied significance has been suggested by White (1977). This technique, similar in concept to Goal Attainment Scaling, was originally proposed as a means to evaluate the progress of the client toward a predetermined goal, but it implicitly evaluates applied significance as well. The technique requires that the worker draw a graph on which the client's behavior can be plotted (Figure 1). Then the worker simply draws an "aim-star" on the graph at the level of performance targeted for the client and on the day that level of performance should be reached. The worker then monitors client performance on a daily basis to see if the desired level of performance has been reached within the time frame established. If it has, client change can be said to have attained a level of applied significance. In settings where the worker is already graphing the client's behavior, the aim-star technique is a convenient and explicit way to display the criteria for judging clinical significance.

Like the other techniques for evaluating applied significance, the aim-star is subjective. As in Goal Attainment Scaling, the factors that determine where the goal is set are often implicit and undefined. Yet this technique has the important advantage of stating the criterion of applied significance before intervention has begun and client change has occurred.

Although the criteria for judging it remain largely subjective, applied significance is still viewed by most clients and workers as the most important means of judging the significance of client change. Nevertheless, the methods and techniques just described may aid in evaluating applied significance because they provide an empirical basis for setting goals (social comparison), an independent and informed evaluation of client change (subjective evaluation), or an explicit and a priori statement of the goal of client change (Goal Attainment Scaling, aim-star) and therefore a more rigorous assessment of applied significance.

Techniques for Assessing Experimental Significance

Whereas applied significance compares the level of client performance with a criterion of adequate functioning, experimental significance compares client performance during or after intervention with performance prior to intervention.

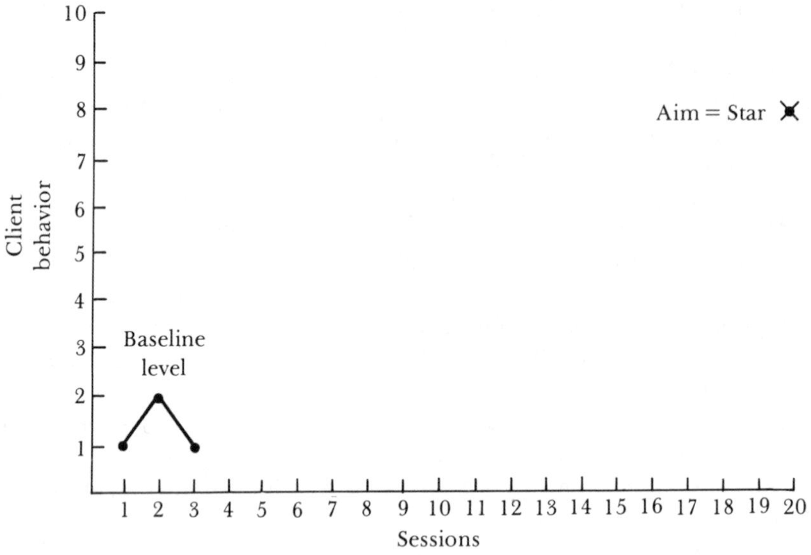

Figure 1. The Aim-Star Technique

If the client's performance during intervention changes sufficiently, the change is said to be experimentally significant. The various visual and statistical techniques that have been developed to assess experimental change provide logical and statistical guidelines for determining what constitutes significant change.

The assessment of experimental significance always requires that client performance be monitored during a period of no intervention (baseline) and an immediately adjacent period of intervention. The purpose of the baseline period is to establish the level and pattern of client performance in order to predict the client's performance during intervention if there is no change. Thus, the assessment of experimental significance requires a series of repeated measurements of client performance over time, both prior to treatment and during or after treatment.

Clinical time-series data contain several characteristics, all of which should be taken into account when making a determination of experimental significance. These properties, including level, trend, variability, and autocorrelation, are defined and illustrated in the following section. Then four techniques for assessing experimental significance in clinical settings are presented, and a number of other statistical techniques are mentioned, along with considerations for their use.

Properties of Time-Series Data. At least four characteristics of time-series data can be identified: level, trend, variability, and autocorrelation (Jones, Vaught, and Weinrott, 1977; Kratochwill, 1978). *Level* refers to the central tendency or location of a set of time-series data. When there is no upward or downward trend in the data, as in Figure 2a, level is equivalent to the mean of the observations in the baseline or treatment. When there is trend in the data, level is somewhat more difficult to define. As in regression analysis, level is usually described by the value taken at a specified point in time—for example, in Figure 2b, the level of the baseline data would be defined by the value of the trend line on the

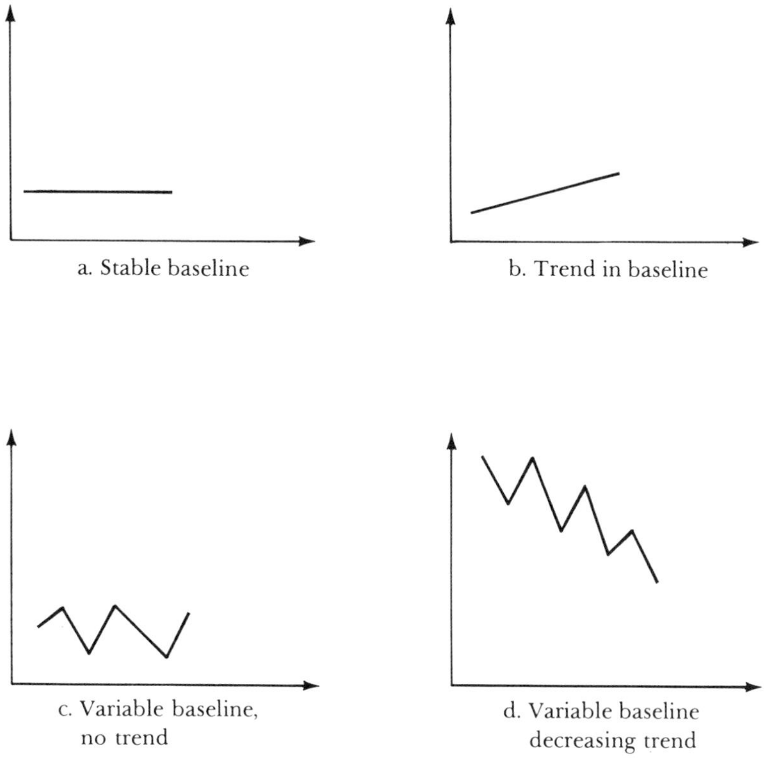

Figure 2. Characteristics of Time-Series Data

first observation. Likewise, change in level is defined as the difference in the two trend-lines at the start of treatment (see Figure 3d).

Trend refers to a deterministic change in the level of the data over time. Figures 2a and 2c reveal no trend in the baseline data, whereas Figures 2b and 2d show nonzero trends. Trends in time-series data can be linear (straight trend-line) or nonlinear (curved trend-line). Although nonlinear trends may occur in clinical time-series data sets, this discussion assumes that most trends will be linear. Examination of actual data sets shows that this assumption is appropriate in about nine out of ten cases (Glass, Wilson, Gottman, 1975).

Variability refers to the extent to which data points vary around the trend-line. When the data contain little variability, the actual observations will be on or very close to the trend-line, as shown in Figure 2c. If the data contain greater variability, they will fluctuate more widely around the trend line, as in Figure 2d.

Autocorrelation refers to correlation among successive data points; that is, the value of an observation at one point in time is predictable from previous observations (Glass, Willson, and Gottman, 1975; McCain and McCleary, 1979). Autocorrelation may be due to nonstationarity (deterministic trend or stochastic drift) in the data, an autoregressive component (the value of one observation is directly related to adjacent observations), a moving-averages component (one observation is related to the persistence of a random stock from previous observations), and a seasonal component, in which a cyclical pattern repeats itself

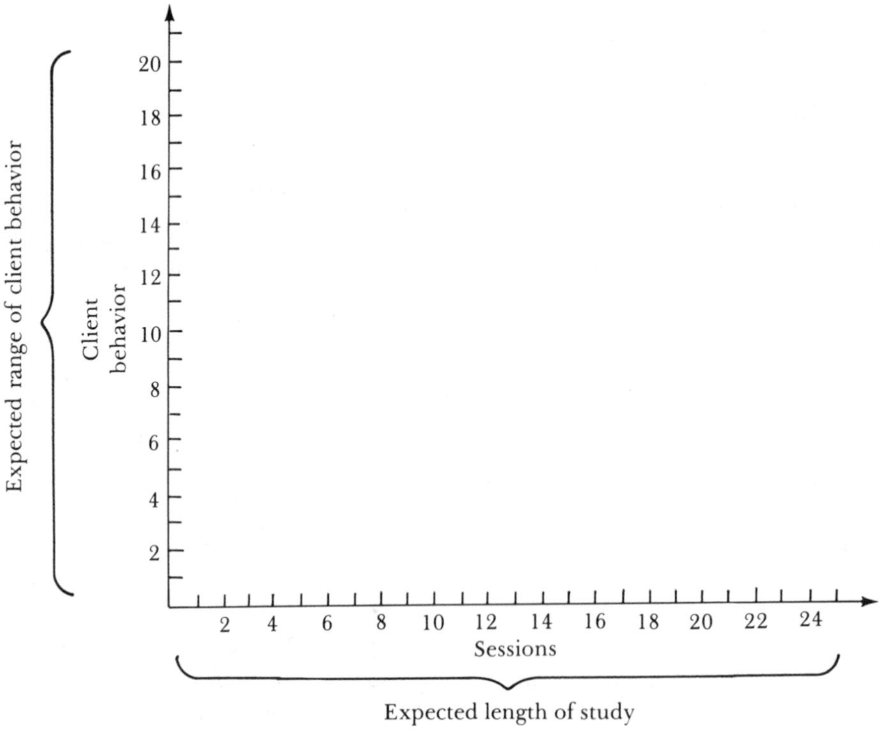

Figure 3. A Simple Time-Series Graph

throughout the time-series. The presence of autocorrelation in time-series data produces erroneous conclusions when using conventional statistical significance tests (Gottman and Glass, 1978; Michael, 1974; Jones, Weinrott, and Vaught, 1978). Unfortunately, the presence of autocorrelation in time-series data is visually undetectable. Since any given set of clinical time-series data can be described by their level, trend, variability, and autocorrelation, change in the client due to intervention could conceivably be reflected in any one or a combination of these four properties. Thus, the reliable detection of change in client performance can become a highly complex task. Most of the techniques designed to assess experimental significance are sensitive only to changes in level or perhaps trend. None of the techniques are specifically designed to assess change in variability. Only the ARIMA (autoregressive integrated moving-averages techniques) technique is able to control satisfactorily for the various sources of autocorrelation when reaching conclusions about the significance of client change.

Visual Analysis. Visual analysis is by far the most common procedure for assessing experimental significance in clinical time-series applications. Often a change in the client is so dramatic that visual inspection leads to unequivocal conclusions. The standard of significance in visual analysis is "clearly evident and reliable," that is, the difference in client performance between baseline and intervention has to be clearly evident before a reliable conclusion can be reached regarding experimental significance (Parsonson and Baer, 1978, p. 112). Parsonson and Baer (1978), Jayaratne and Levy (1979), and Kazdin (1979) give an excellent, detailed discussion of visual analysis of clinical time-series data. Much of the following discussion is based on their suggestions.

The first step in visual analysis is to construct a graph and plot the client data (see, for example, Figure 3). The horizontal axis is used to represent time in minutes, hours, days, weeks, or treatment days. The vertical axis is used to represent client behavior in frequency, rate, duration, or rating on a scale. Both the horizontal and vertical axes should be drawn on a scale that approximates the expected range of client behavior and the duration of the study.

Once the graph has been drawn, the data points should be plotted and connected with a solid line. Changes in experimental phases (such as from baseline to treatment) are usually shown with a dotted vertical line.

Once the data are graphed, visual analysis of experimental significance can begin. The ideal criterion for concluding that a change in level of client behavior has reached experimental significance is that there is no overlap in data points between phases (Figure 4a). When little or no overlap between phases occurs, experimental significance has clearly been achieved. Change in level can be characterized by its magnitude, its immediacy, and its permanence (Glass, Willson, and Gottman, 1975). Ideally, client change will be evidenced in a strong, immediate, and permanent change in behavior. However, it is not unusual for changes to be of lesser magnitude (Figure 4b), to be delayed in their impact (Figure 4c), or to be temporary and eventually die out (Figure 4d). In each case, the conclusion of significant change is more ambiguous.

On occasion, the preintervention data will appear to show a trend. When this occurs, it is always sound practice to attempt to control the trend by analyzing whether other controlling influences are present or by continuing to collect the baseline data until the trend gradually levels off. If neither of these approaches succeeds and the baseline continues to show a trend, special care must be taken in visual analysis of experimental significance. A trend in baseline away from the treatment goal poses only a minor problem in judging significance. However, if baseline trend is in the direction of desired client change, conclusions regarding client change during intervention will be ambiguous. If the baseline trend is at all large, it is advisable, from a clinical standpoint, to withhold treatment, since the client may reach the desired state without intervention. If the direction of the baseline trend is away from the goal (Figure 5a) or is relatively small (Figure 5b), conclusions about client change can be made with somewhat more certainty. Also, if client performance during treatment appears to reverse the direction of trend (Figure 5c) or produces a large change in level (Figure 5d), it may also indicate experimentally significant change.

Like trend, variability in clinical time-series data increases the difficulty of detecting client change. Again, the first strategy should be to try to control or reduce the variability of the client behavior during baseline. Generally speaking, the more variability contained in the data, the greater must be the change in level before the conclusion of experimental significance can be reached. If the baseline data are highly variable, encompassing the entire range (Figure 6a), then a conclusion of significant change will be impossible to reach based on visual analysis. When the effect of intervention is to reduce the variability such that the client behavior seems to come under greater control (Figure 6b), this reduction may

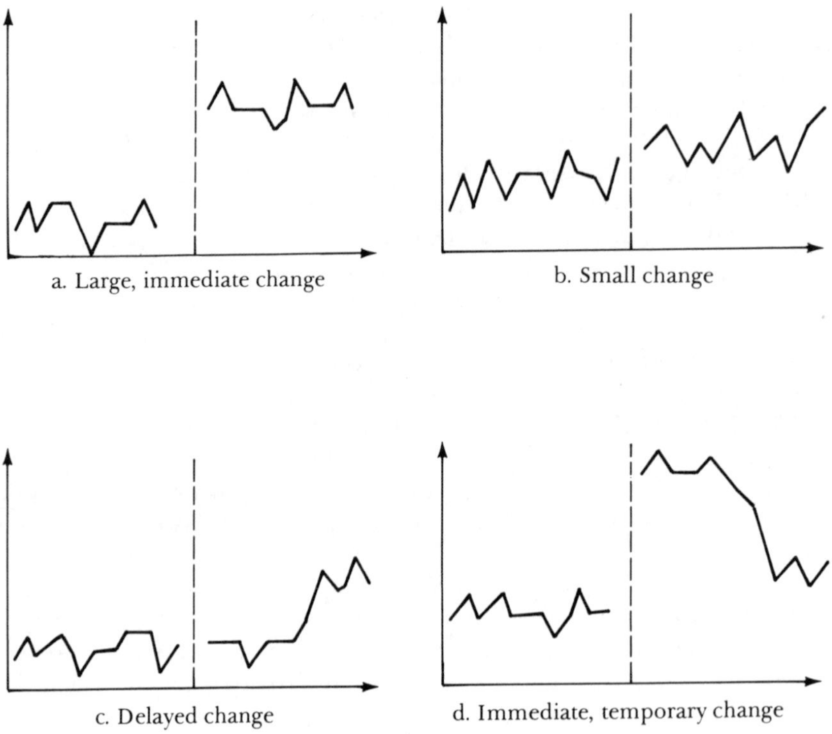

Figure 4. Illustrative Changes in Level

nevertheless be experimentally significant. Although the intervention goal is often to reduce the variability in highly variable data, the goal may occasionally be the opposite. For example, in a client with flat affect the treatment goal may be to increase the variability in emotional expression rather than change its level (Figure 6c). When treatment is intended to change the variability of client behavior, the experimental significance of client change is difficult to determine. There are no established criteria for assessing the significance of such change other than a test of the homogeneity of variance (Kirk, 1968), but this procedure will lead to an invalid conclusion if the data contain autocorrelation (Hartmann, 1974).

To the extent that the data show a small change in level, a trend, or unusual variability, it is necessary to collect more observations. As the number of observations in all phases is increased, the pattern of client performance during baseline can be described with more certainty, and, therefore, any departures from the predicted performance during treatment can be more reliably assessed.

Although the ideal situation is characterized by minimal trend and variability in baseline and a marked, immediate, and permanent change in the level of client behavior, the ideal situation does not always obtain. Further, it is quite possible for clinical data to show changes in several parameters at the same time. For example, change during intervention could involve an abrupt change in level, as well as a reversal of a downward trend (Figure 7a). Another common occurrence

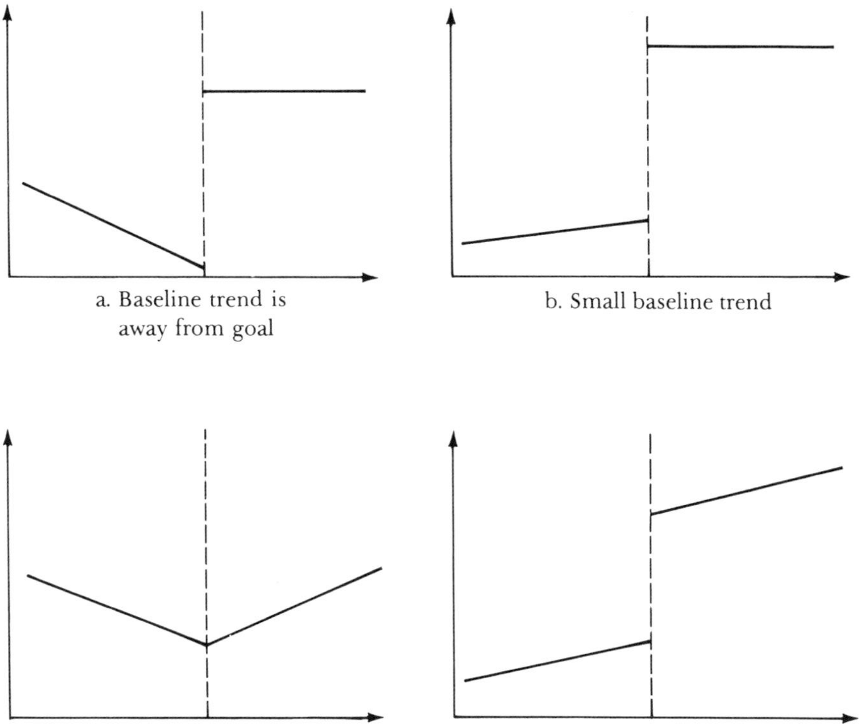

Figure 5. Illustrative Changes in Trend

is for client performance to show an immediate change in level in the desired direction but then deteriorate back to the baseline level over time (Figure 7b).

It will often be impossible to conclude, based on a comparison of only two phases, that a significant change in client behavior has taken place. In such cases, Parsonson and Baer (1978) recommend that data be collected during several additional baseline and treatment phases. The most convincing evidence of significant client change would be where client behavior during the first baseline and treatment phases is replicated during subsequent baseline and treatment phases. To the extent that subsequent phases fail to replicate the initial baseline and treatment phases, evidence of significant client change is diminished.

Several precautions are in order when using visual analysis to assess experimental significance. First, if the standard "clearly evident and reliable" is not met, conclusions based on visual analysis should not be trusted. As noted earlier, a more rigorous statistical analysis of client change will sometimes show conclusions based on visual analysis to be incorrect. Unless visual analysis shows client change to be completely unequivocal, statistical aids should be used.

A second precaution is that the length of the treatment phase should be no longer than the length of baseline (Herson and Barlow, 1976; Gingerich and Feyerherm, 1979). The reliability of visual analysis depends on the immediacy of client change. The more that client change is delayed (further removed in time

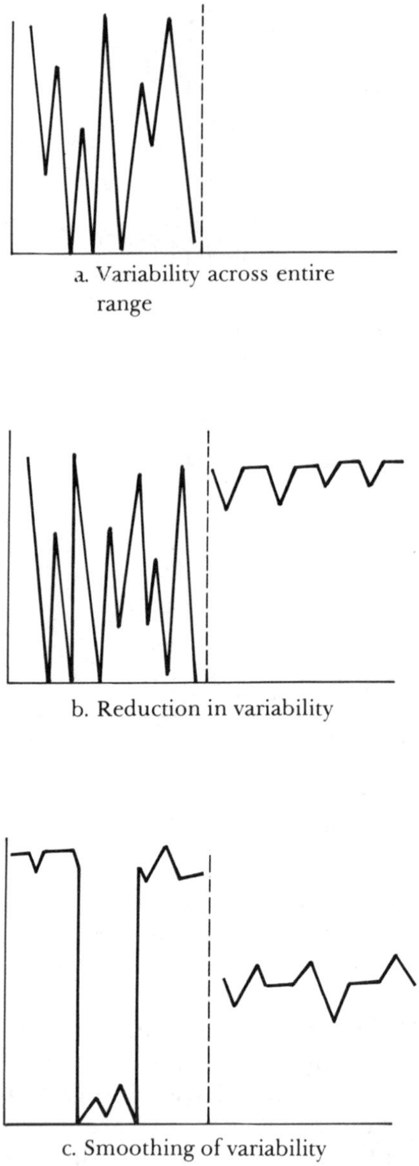

Figure 6. Illustrative Changes in Variability

from baseline), the more difficult it is to detect such change from visual analysis. In such cases, the worker should observe client change over several additional phases or use a statistical aid.

Shewart Chart. Gottman and Leiblum (1974) suggest the Shewart Chart, a well-known industrial quality-control procedure, for assessing the significance of client change. The procedure assumes that the baseline observations are distributed normally and do not contain autocorrelation. If two successive treatment observations fall outside a band drawn two standard deviations on either side of

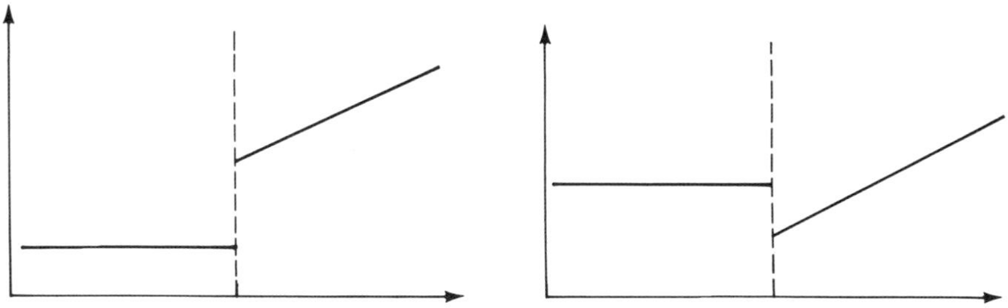

a. Change in level and trend, both in desired direction

b. Immediate drop in level, change in trend in desired direction

Figure 7. Complex Change Patterns

the mean of baseline, significant change is said to have occurred. The Shewart Chart procedure is relatively easy to use; the steps for applying it are as follows.

Step 1: Plot the baseline observations (Figure 8).

Step 2: Compute the mean of the baseline observations.

$$\text{Mean} = \bar{x} = \frac{\sum x}{n}$$

where $\sum x$ = the sum of the observations
n = the number of the observations

Step 3: Compute the standard deviation of the baseline observations.

$$\text{standard deviation} = \sigma = \sqrt{\frac{\sum x^2 - \frac{(\sum x^2)}{n}}{n-1}}$$

where $\sum x^2$ = the sum of the squared observations
$(\sum x)^2$ = the square of the sum of the observations

Step 4: Compute and plot the Shewart band.

$$\text{Shewart band} = \bar{x} \pm 2\sigma$$

Step 5: Plot the treatment observations.

Step 6: Determine whether significant change has occurred. Have two successive treatment observations fallen outside the Shewart band? If YES, significant change has occurred. If NO, change is not significant.

Since the Shewart Chart (Figure 8) assumes that no trend or other correlation is present in baseline data, its usefulness is limited primarily to small sample baselines (less than ten observations). Longer baselines permit the use of other techniques, such as the celeration line or ARIMA model, which will produce more reliable results. When the baseline appears to contain a trend, additional observations should be collected and the celeration-line technique used. Although Gottman and Leiblum (1974) provide transformations for dealing with autocorrelation, the procedure is conceptually complicated, and conclusions based on transformed data are indirect and difficult to interpret.

A second precaution, as with visual analysis, is that the length of the treatment phase should not exceed the length of baseline. Over an extended period

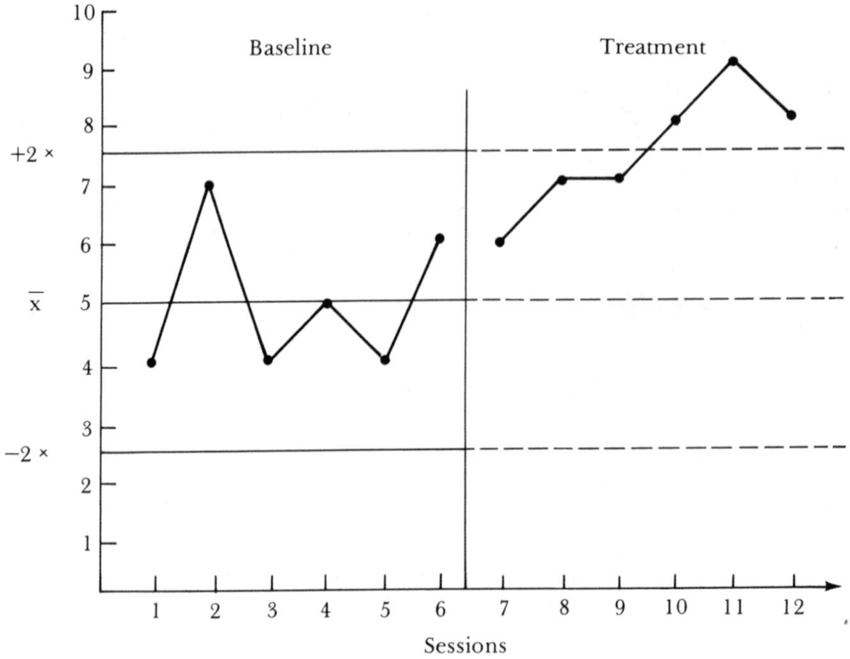

Figure 8. Shewart Chart

of time, it is not unlikely that client behavior would eventually "drift" outside of the Shewart band, but this would not be a reliable indication of client change due to intervention.

Celeration Line. Gingerich and Feyerherm (1979) propose the celeration-line technique as a quasi-statistical procedure for assessing the experimental significance of client change. This technique is based on earlier work by White (1974, 1977), Bloom (1975), Kazdin (1976), and Parsonson and Baer (1978). Conceptually, the celeration line uses a shorthand procedure to fit a trend-line to the baseline data and then projects this trend-line into the treatment portion of the graph to predict client behavior in the absence of change. If there is a change in the client's behavior, the proportion of treatment observations above or below the extended celeration line will be significantly different (using the binomial) than during baseline.

STEP 1. Plot the baseline observations (Figure 9). A minimum of ten baseline observations is recommended for use in the celeration-line technique.

STEP 2. Divide the baseline period in half by drawing a solid vertical line separating the first half of the observations from the second half (Figure 9a). When the baseline period contains an odd number of observations, draw the vertical line through the middle observation. Divide each of the halves in half again by drawing dotted vertical lines. Again, when there is an odd number of observations during each half of the baseline period, draw the dotted lines through the middle observations.

STEP 3. Determine the mean ($\bar{x}$) level of behavior for each half of the baseline data. Draw a cross-mark at this value intersecting the dotted vertical line

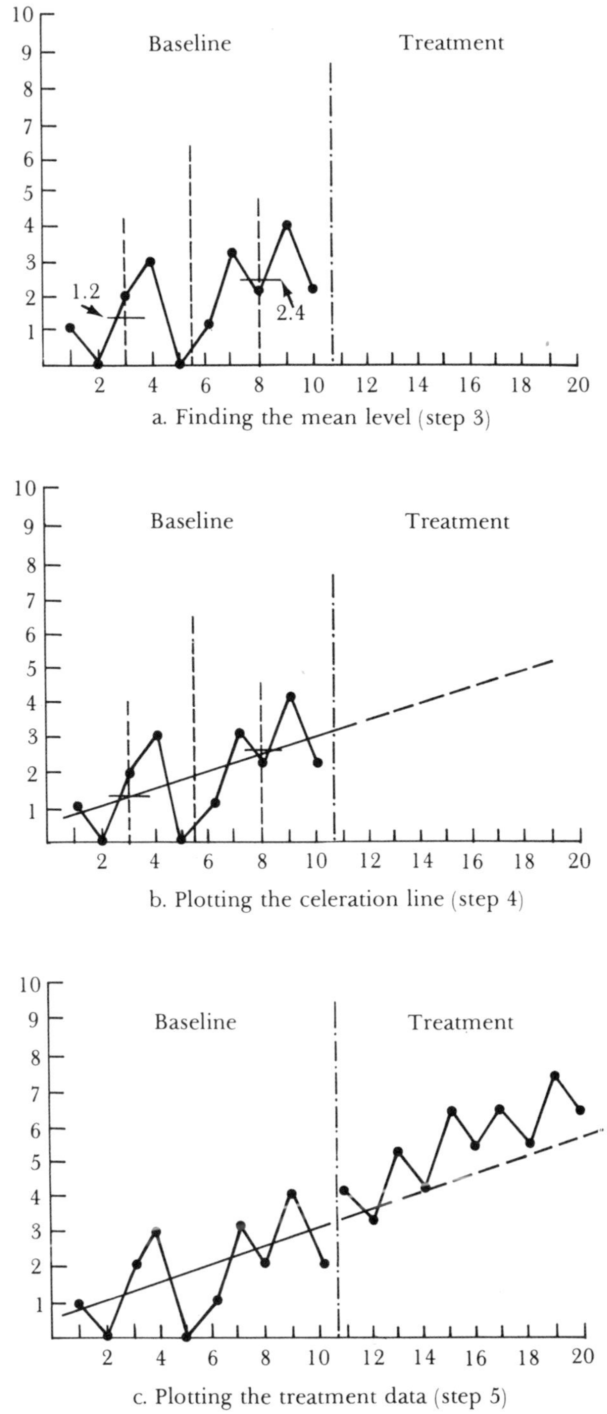

Figure 9. The Celeration-Line Technique. (Reprinted by Permission of The Haworth Press, publisher of *Journal of Social Service Research, 1979, 3,* 106–108.)

drawn in step 2 (Figure 9a). Repeat this process for the second half of the baseline data.

STEP 4. Draw a straight line connecting the two intersects created in step 3 and extend it with a dotted line into the treatment portion of the graph (Figure 9b). The extended portion of the line is dotted to indicate that it is an estimation of what the client behavior will be if its present pattern continues.

Next, determine what proportion of baseline observations fall in the desired zone. For example, if the goal is for client behavior to increase, divide the number of baseline observations on or above the line by the total number of baseline observations. Use this proportion to enter the corresponding row of Table 1.

STEP 5. Plot the treatment data (Figure 9c). Count the total number of treatment observations and enter the corresponding column of Table 1. Now identify the cell in Table 1 where the row selected in step 4 and the column selected in step 5 intersect. The cell entry indicates the number of treatment observations that must be in the desired zone in order for there to be a statistically significant change at the 0.05 level (one-tailed test).

The celeration-line test as presented is a directional (one-tailed) test of significance of client change. The directional test is appropriate because the worker will almost always have a desired direction for client change.

The celeration technique is recommended for use with time-series data sets where the baseline contains ten or more observations, particularly when the baseline data appear to contain trend. With baselines of less than ten observations, the Shewart Chart is recommended.

A number of cautions are in order when using the celeration line (Gingerich and Feyerherm, 1979). The celeration-line technique will detect significant change in most situations where real change has occurred. However, it will not be sensitive to client change when a change has occurred in both level and trend such that the proportion of treatment observations in the desired zone is still roughly equivalent to the proportion of baseline observations in the desired zone. Such a situation would occur when implementation of treatment brings about an immediate decrease in desired behaviors but is followed by a steady increase in behaviors up to the desired level. Although the pattern of client behavior during treatment is clearly different from the baseline pattern, the celeration-line test would not be sensitive to this particular combination of changes. Secondly, the celeration line is not sensitive to autocorrelation in the data other than deterministic trend. Hence, if the baseline data contain an autoregressive or moving-averages component, conclusions based on the celeration-line technique will be misleading. Unfortunately, there is no way to assess this short of collecting a substantially larger number of observations (50–100) and using the ARIMA technique (Glass, Willson, and Gottman, 1975). Although the celeration line appears to be useful in detecting client change (Feyerherm and Gingerich, in press), it should be considered a quasi-statistical test.

ARIMA Model. The autoregressive integrated moving-averages (ARIMA) model has been suggested as the most sensitive and methodologically sound approach to detecting change in time-series data (Glass, Willson, and Gottman, 1975; Jones, Vaught, and Weinrott, 1977; Gottman and Glass, 1978; McCain and McCleary, 1979; McCleary and Hay, 1980). The time-series analysis techniques are

Table 1. Number of Treatment Observations Required Above (or Below) the Celeration Line to Show Statistically Significant Change at the .05 Level

	Total Number of Treatment Observations															
	4	*6*	*8*	*10*	*12*	*14*	*16*	*18*	*20*	*24*	*28*	*32*	*36*	*40*	*60*	*100*
Proportion of baseline observations in desired zone[b]																
.10	3	3	3	4	4	4	5	5	5	6	7	7	8	8	11	16
.20	3	4	5	5	6	6	7	8	8	9	10	11	12	13	18	28
.30	4	5	6	6	7	8	9	10	10	12	13	15	16	18	25	39
.40	4	5	6	8	9	10	11	12	13	15	16	18	20	22	31	49
.45	4	6	7	8	9	10	11	13	14	16	18	20	22	24	34	54
.50	-	6	7	9	10	11	12	13	15	17	19	22	24	26	37	59
.55	-	6	8	9	10	12	13	14	16	18	21	23	26	28	40	64
.60	-	6	8	9	11	12	14	15	17	19	22	25	27	30	43	69
.70	-	-	-	10	12	13	15	17	18	21	24	28	31	34	49	78
.80	-	-	-	-	-	14	16	18	20	23	27	30	34	37	54	87
.90	-	-	-	-	-	-	-	-	-	-	-	32	36	40	58	95

[a]One-tailed test. Adapted from Bloom, 1975, p. 203. Reprinted by permission of the Haworth Press, *Journal of Social Service Research*, 1979, *3*, 109.
[b]If the proportion of baseline observations above (or below) the celeration lines does not appear in the table, use the next-larger proportion.

based on earlier work by Box and Jenkins (1976) and, until recently, have been applied primarily to the field of economic forecasting. Time-series analysis is based on the observation that many time-series data sets contain autocorrelation—that is, the value of one observation is partially known from the values of preceding observations. Because time-series observations are sometimes autocorrelated, standard statistical techniques may be inappropriate. Depending on the nature of the autocorrelation present, statistical techniques assuming independent observations will lead to underestimates or overestimates of the significance of client change (Gottman and Glass, 1978). Although the application of the ARIMA model is too complex to describe completely here, the major steps in using the approach will be outlined in order to provide an introduction to the technique. The reader is referred to McCain and McCleary (1979) for an excellent introduction to time-series analysis and to Box and Jenkins (1976) and Glass, Willson, and Gottman (1975) for a more detailed mathematical treatment.

The first step in time-series analysis is to identify the appropriate model for the data by determining whether the data contain trend or stochastic drift, an autoregressive component, a moving-averages component, or several components together. Identification of the correct model is based on the computation and analysis of the autocorrelation and partial autocorrelation functions of successive lags in the data. Once the correct model is identified, the weights of the autoregressive and moving-averages components are estimated using a computer program. Then the model identification and weights are verified by checking to see if the residuals, after the model is fitted to the actual data, behave as random-error components. The next step is to add an intervention component to the ARIMA model to determine whether the model's predictability increases to a statistically significant degree. If the inclusion of the intervention component makes a statistically significant improvement in the ability of the ARIMA model to fit the observed data, a statistically significant change is concluded to have occurred in the client's behavior. For computer programs to apply the model, the reader is referred to Gottman and Leiblum (1974), Box and Jenkins (1976), Glass, Willson, and Gottman (1975), and Gottman and Glass (1978).

A number of considerations are relevant when using the ARIMA model to assess change in client behavior. Perhaps most important, the ARIMA model requires fifty or more observations in order to accurately identify the correct model and estimate the necessary parameters (Glass, Willson, and Gottman, 1975). Unfortunately, it is often not feasible to collect so many observations in applied settings. When the ARIMA model is applied to data sets of less than fifty observations, it increasingly degenerates into a standard t-test, and its advantage over other available techniques rapidly diminishes (Feyerherm and Gingerich, in press). A second consideration involves the mathematical sophistication required for proper application of the ARIMA model, as well as the accessibility of computer facilities and programs for carrying out the mathematical operations. Clearly, most practice settings do not have such resources available; hence, the ARIMA model is of limited practical utility. In instances where fifty or more observations are available, however, the ARIMA model offers substantial advantages over other approaches in being sensitive to small but significant changes in the client that may not be noticeable through visual analysis or other techniques.

Other Statistical Tests. Three other statistical techniques have been suggested for use with clinical time-series data; however, because of limited applicability, they are presented only briefly. These include randomization tests, the R_n statistic, and Markov chains.

Randomization tests have been proposed by Edgington (1967, 1980), Kazdin (1976), and Levin, Marascuilo, and Hubert (1978). These tests require that baseline and treatment conditions be assigned on a random basis over a number of phases. The average performance of the client during each phase is computed and evaluated to see if the differences between baseline and treatment phases are significantly different from those that would have occurred due to chance alone.

Randomization tests have the advantage of being unaffected by serial dependency and of being distribution-free. The tests require, however, that treatment effects are reversible and also require a large number of different phases in order to show significant change. Kazdin (1976) indicates, for example, that it would be impossible to show significant change at the 0.05 level with only five phases. Further, because randomization tests ignore the structure or pattern of client change within phases and require a large number of phases, these tests are perhaps too conservative for use in many clinical settings (Elashoff and Thoresen, 1978).

Revusky (1967) and Kazdin (1976, 1979) have proposed the R_n statistic for use with clinical time-series data. This statistic requires a multiple-baseline design where data are collected across at least four different individuals, behaviors, or situations. Treatment is then introduced at random to each individual or behavior at a different point in time, and the performance of each individual or behavior that receives treatment is ranked with the other individuals or behaviors that have not yet been exposed to treatment. These ranks are then summed across all individuals or baselines, yielding the R_n statistic. The significance of R_n is evaluated by consulting the appropriate tables (Kazdin, 1976; Revusky, 1967).

Like randomization tests, the R_n statistic appears to be unaffected by autocorrelation or assumptions of normal distribution. Its applicability is limited, however, by the requirement of a multiple-baseline design containing at least four different individuals, behaviors, or situations. Since R_n is also influenced by the absolute levels of each of the baselines, a transformation of the raw data is often necessary (Kazdin, 1976; Revusky, 1967). Further, R_n is sensitive only to client change that occurs on the first day of intervention; all other data are ignored. Thus, the R_n statistic would be inappropriate when client change is delayed or gradual.

Markov chains have been proposed by Gottman and Notarius (1978) for analyzing sequential dependency and cross-sequential dependency in clinical time-series data. In Markov analysis, the client is observed continuously over time, resulting in a set of codes indicating the behavior or state observed each time. The observed probability of each type of behavior, given the occurrence of each other type of behavior, is then noted, and, on the basis of this history, client performance can be predicted into the future. Markov analysis appears to have a great deal of relevance for the study of human interaction, since it can take account of the sequential patterning of behavior over time and is not limited to static analysis of frequency or rates of behavior. However, the feasibility of Markov chain analysis in practice settings is limited by the mathematical complexity of the technique and the level of sophistication required to interpret the results.

Several other statistical techniques have been proposed for assessing the significance of client change but are not recommended here either because they are not appropriate for data containing autocorrelation or because they have not performed well in comparison with other statistical tests. The t-test (Hudson, 1977) and conventional analysis of variance (Gentile, Roden, and Klein, 1972) have both been suggested for use with time-series data, and both assume that observations are independent, that is, that the data do not contain autocorrelation. This assumption can be tested (Hudson, 1977; Gottman and Leiblum, 1974); if it is met, both the t-test and the analysis of variance appear to be valid. However, the assumption of independence is frequently not accurate, particularly with relatively short baselines, and these statistical tests are then inappropriate (Michael, 1974; Kratochwill and others, 1974; Hartmann, 1974; and Thoresen and Elashoff, 1974).

A relative-frequency procedure proposed by Bloom (1975) and Bloom and Block (1977) is roughly analogous to the Shewart Chart procedure in that a band is drawn to encompass the middle two-thirds of the baseline observations. Treatment observations are then examined to see if enough of them fall outside this typical range of client behavior to achieve statistical significance based on the binomial test. However, like the Shewart Chart, the relative-frequency procedure ignores trend in the baseline, one source of autocorrelation, and is subject to uncertainty in the computation of the middle two-thirds of the baseline observations (Loftus and Levy, 1977; Berger and Witkin, 1978). Further, on a purely empirical basis, it appears that the relative-frequency procedure is less successful than the Shewart Chart or the celeration line in identifying significant client change when the ARIMA model has indicated that such change has actually occurred (Feyerherm and Gingerich, in preparation).

Guidelines for Selecting a Technique

In any clinical evaluation study, the worker will always be interested in the significance of client change. This chapter has discussed two sets of criteria for assessing significance: applied criteria, in which client performance is compared to a predetermined goal, and experimental criteria, in which client performance is compared to its preintervention level. Applied significance will almost always be relevant, since the client, the worker, and significant others always have implicit, if not explicit, goals for how the client should change. Experimental significance will also often be useful, particularly when the amount of client change is small and therefore difficult to detect or when the worker wishes to infer that intervention made a significant impact on the client (client performance changed significantly from baseline). The following set of guidelines is meant to assist the worker in selecting techniques for assessing client change. Although these suggestions are based on practical, empirical rationale, they are still somewhat tentative and will probably change as new techniques are developed and present ones more thoroughly tested.

Applied Significance. Since workers almost always assess applied significance implicitly, they are strongly urged to apply some of the following techniques for assessing it directly. At the minimum, the practitioner should specify, before intervention, the goals for client performance based on the client's wishes, the interests of significant others and the community, and the worker's own judgment. The goal can be stated narratively or shown graphically, as in the aim-star technique or goal attainment scaling.

Beyond this minimum, applied significance can often be further substantiated through the technique of subjective evaluation. Ideally, one would use a standardized rating instrument of some sort, such as a Likert Scale or a criterion-referenced scale, to document subjective evaluations. When this is not feasible, the informal reactions of others in a position to know are still useful in more objectively assessing the importance of client change. The opinion of someone other than the client or the worker should routinely be sought, since the client's evaluation of change is sometimes colored by his or her participation in the treatment process and the worker sometimes overestimates client change.

Finally, social comparison is probably the most rigorous and objective assessment of applied significance. Empirical evidence of the level of performance of the client's "normal" peers provides a strong basis for goal setting for the client. Unfortunately, the procedures required to establish social comparison data are often beyond the worker's means. On the other hand, if clients with similar problems are regularly seen by the worker, the efforts involved in gathering social comparison data may be justified. Further, social comparison data are already available on a number of instruments and observation procedures that have been standardized for normal populations. Some psychological tests (Buros, 1980) and some behavioral assessment systems (Ciminero, Calhoun, and Adams, 1977) also provide these data. When the purpose of intervention is to restore normal social functioning, social comparison techniques seem particularly relevant.

Experimental Significance. Experimental significance should always be assessed first through visual analysis of graphed data. Often visual analysis will be sufficient to establish experimental significance, but, even if it is not, the worker will know the amount and nature of client change in graphic detail, information that will subsequently be useful when selecting a statistical aid for assessing significance. When conducting visual analysis, the worker must be careful not to stretch the guidelines for concluding that significant change has occurred. If the "clearly evident and reliable" standard is not met, one of the statistical aids should be used in the judgment process.

If visual analysis is insufficient, the worker should make every effort to obtain at least ten baseline observations and then apply the celeration-line technique. This technique has the capacity to take baseline trend into account and thus appears to be more valid than the other quasi-statistical procedures (Feyerherm and Gingerich, in press).

In situations where it is impossible to obtain ten or more baseline observations, the Shewart Chart procedure is recommended as a useful judgment aid that is easily applied and directly interpretable. The Shewart Chart is also useful with longer baselines, providing there is no trend.

If the requirements of a large number of observations and a high level of mathematical sophistication can be met, the ARIMA model is the preferred method of assessing experimental significance. The only available technique that is strictly suitable for autocorrelated data, this model can be used to examine the process of client change throughout a study. Unfortunately, the requirements of the technique appear to make it impractical in most practice situations. The R_n, randomization, and Markov techniques are useful primarily in research or more highly controlled settings.

A special word of caution is in order when attempting to assess experimental significance. None of the quasi-statistical techniques, such as the celeration line or Shewart Chart, is strictly appropriate for time-series data containing autocorrelation, and the validity of these techniques is still unknown. Accordingly, they should be used as guides or judgment aids and not be interpreted with the same level of certainty one normally associates with statistical analysis. Unless the ARIMA model can be applied, the worker, for the time being at least, may have to accept some uncertainty about the experimental significance of client change.

References

Baer, D. M. "Perhaps It Would Be Better Not to Know Everything." *Journal of Applied Behavior Analysis,* 1977, *10,* 167-172.

Berger, R. M., and Witkin, S. "Comment on Evaluating One's Own Effectiveness and Efficiency." *Social Work,* 1978, *23,* 253-254.

Bloom, M. *The Paradox of Helping: Introduction to the Philosophy of Scientific Practice.* New York: Wiley, 1975.

Bloom, M., and Block, S. R. "Evaluating One's Own Effectiveness and Efficiency." *Social Work,* 1977a, *22,* 130-136.

Bloom, M., and Block, S. R. "Reply to Loftus and Levy's Comment." *Social Work,* 1977b, *22,* 506.

Bloom, M., and Block, S. R. "Reply to Berger and Witkins' Comment." *Social Work,* 1978, *23,* 254.

Box, G.E.P., and Jenkins, G. M. *Time-Series Analysis: Forecasting and Control.* San Francisco: Holden-Day, 1976.

Briscoe, R. V., Hoffman, D. B., and Bailey, J. S. "Behavioral Community Psychology: Training a Community Board to Problem Solve." *Journal of Applied Behavior Analysis,* 1975, *8,* 157–168.

Buros, O. K. *The Eighth Mental Measurements Yearbook.* Highland Park, N.J.: Gryphon Press, 1980.

Carver, R. P. "The Case Against Statistical Significance Testing." *Harvard Educational Review,* 1978, *48,* 378–399.

Ciminero, A. R., Calhoun, K. S., and Adams, H. E. (Eds.). *Handbook of Behavioral Assessment.* New York: Wiley, 1977.

DeProspero, A., and Cohen, S. "Inconsistent Visual Analyses of Intrasubject Data." *Journal of Applied Behavior Analysis,* 1979, *12,* 573–579.

Edgington, E. S. "Statistical Inference from N = 1 Experiments." *Journal of Psychology,* 1967, *65,* 195–199.

Edgington, E. S. *Randomization Tests.* New York: Marcel Dekker, 1980.

Elashoff, J. D., and Thoresen, C. E. "Choosing a Statistical Method for Analysis of an Intensive Experiment." In T. R. Kratochwill (Ed.), *Single Subject Research: Strategies for Evaluating Change.* New York: Academic Press, 1978.

Feyerherm, W. H., and Gingerich, W. J. "An Empirical Comparison of Statistical Techniques for Assessing Client Change." University of Wisconsin–Milwaukee, Milwaukee, Wisc., in press.

Gentile, J. R., Roden, A. H., and Klein, R. D. "An Analysis of Variance Model for the Intrasubject Replication Design." *Journal of Applied Behavior Analysis,* 1972, *5,* 193–198.

Gingerich, W. J., and Feyerherm, W. H. "The Celeration Line Technique for Assessing Client Change." *Journal of Social Service Research,* 1979, *3,* 99–113.

Glass, G. V., Willson, V. L., and Gottman, J. M. *Design and Analysis of Time-Series Experiments.* Boulder: Colorado Associated University Press, 1975.

Gottman, J. M., and Glass, G. V. "Analysis of Interrupted Time-Series Experiments." In T. R. Kratochwill (Ed.), *Single Subject Research: Strategies for Evaluating Change.* New York: Academic Press, 1978.

Gottman, J. M., and Leiblum, S. R. *How to Do Psychotherapy and How to Evaluate It: A Manual for Beginners.* New York: Holt, Rinehart and Winston, 1974.

Gottman, J. M., and Notarius, C. "Sequential Analysis of Observational Data Using Markov Chains." In T. R. Kratochwill (Ed.), *Single Subject Research: Strategies for Evaluating Change.* New York: Academic Press, 1978.

Hartmann, D. P. "Forcing Square Pegs into Round Holes: Some Comments on 'An Analysis-of-Variance Model for the Intrasubject Replication Design.'" *Journal of Applied Behavior Analysis,* 1974, *7,* 635–638.

Hersen, M., and Barlow, D. H. *Single-Case Experimental Designs: Strategies for Studying Behavior Change.* Elmsford, N.Y.: Pergamon Press, 1976.

Hudson, W. W. "Elementary Techniques for Assessing Single-Client/Single-Worker Interventions." *Social Service Review,* 1977, *51,* 311-326.

Huitema, B. E. "Autocorrelation in Behavior Modification Data: Wherefore Art Thou?" Paper presented at the Association for Behavior Analysis Annual Meeting, Milwaukee, Wisc., May 1982.

Jayaratne, S. "Analytic Procedures for Single-Subject Designs." *Social Work Research and Abstracts,* 1978, *14,* 30-40.

Jayaratne, S., and Levy, R. L. *Empirical Clinical Practice.* New York: Columbia University Press, 1979.

Jones, R. R., Vaught, R. S., and Weinrott, M. "Time-Series Analysis in Operant Research." *Journal of Applied Behavior Analysis,* 1977, *10,* 151-166.

Jones, R. R., Weinrott, M. R., and Vaught, R. S. "Effects of Serial Dependency on the Agreement Between Visual and Statistical Inference." *Journal of Applied Behavior Analysis,* 1978, *11,* 277-283.

Kazdin, A. E. "Statistical Analyses for Single-Case Experimental Designs." In M. Herson and D. H. Barlow (Eds.), *Single-Case Experimental Designs: Strategies for Studying Behavior Change.* New York: Pergamon Press, 1976.

Kazdin, A. E. "Assessing the Clinical or Applied Importance of Behavior Change Through Social Validation." *Behavior Modification,* 1977, *1,* 427-452.

Kazdin, A. E. "Data Evaluation for Intrasubject-Replication Research." *Journal of Social Service Research,* 1979, *3,* 79-97.

Kiresuk, T. J., and Lund, S. H. "Goal Attainment Scaling." In C. C. Attkisson, W. A. Hargreaves, M. J. Horowitz, and J. E. Sorensen (Eds.), *Evaluation of Human Service Programs.* New York: Academic Press, 1978.

Kirk, R. E. "Experimental Design: Procedures for the Behavioral Sciences." Belmont, Calif.: Brooks/Cole, 1968.

Kratochwill, T. R. "Foundations of Time-Series Research." In T. R. Kratochwill (Ed.), *Single Subject Research: Strategies for Evaluating Change.* New York: Academic Press, 1978.

Kratochwill, T., and others. "A Further Consideration in the Application of an Analysis-of-Variance Model for the Intrasubject Replication Design." *Journal of Applied Behavior Analysis,* 1974, *7,* 629-633.

Kratochwill, T. R., and Brody, G. H. "Single Subject Designs: A Perspective on the Controversy Over Employing Statistical Inference and Implications for Research Training in Behavior Modification." *Behavior Modification,* 1978, *2,* 291-307.

Levin, J. R., Marascuilo, L. A., and Hubert, L. J. "N = Nonparametric Randomization Tests." In T. R. Kratochwill (Ed.), *Single Subject Research: Strategies for Evaluating Change.* New York: Academic Press, 1978.

Loftus, G. R., and Levy, R. L. "Statistical Evaluation of Clinical Effectiveness." *Social Work,* 1977, *22,* 504-506.

McCain, L. J., and McCleary, R. "The Statistical Analysis of the Simple Interrupted Time-Series Quasi-Experiment." In T. D. Cook and D. T. Campbell, *Quasi-Experimentation: Design and Analysis Issues for Field Settings.* Chicago: Rand McNally, 1979.

McCleary, R., and Hay, R. A., Jr. *Applied Time Series Analysis for the Social Sciences.* Beverly Hills, Calif.: Sage, 1980.

Michael, J. "Statistical Inference for Individual Organism Research: Mixed Blessing or Curse?" *Journal of Applied Behavior Analysis,* 1974, *7,* 647–653.

Parsonson, B. S., and Baer, D. M. "The Analysis and Presentation of Graphic Data." In T. R. Kratochwill (Ed.), *Single Subject Research: Strategies for Evaluating Change.* New York: Academic Press, 1978.

Patterson, G. R. "Interventions for Boys with Conduct Problems: Multiple Settings, Treatments, and Criteria." *Journal of Consulting and Clinical Psychology,* 1974, *42,* 471–481.

Revusky, S. H. "Some Statistical Treatments Compatible with Individual Organism Methodology." *Journal of the Experimental Analysis of Behavior,* 1967, *10,* 319–330.

Risley, T. R. "Behavior Modification: An Experimental-Therapeutic Endeavor." In L. A. Hamerlynck, P. O. Davidson, and L. E. Acker (Eds.), *Behavior Modification and Ideal Mental Health Services.* Calgary, Canada: University of Calgary Press, 1970.

Sloane, R. B., and others. *Psychotherapy Versus Behavior Therapy.* Cambridge, Mass.: Harvard University Press, 1975.

Thoresen, C. E., and Elashoff, J. D. "An Analysis-of-Variance Model for Intrasubject Replication Design: Some Additional Comments." *Journal of Applied Behavior Analysis,* 1974, *7,* 639–641.

White, O. R. "The 'Split-Middle': A 'Quickie' Method of Trend Estimation." (3rd rev.) Working paper available through the Experimental Education Unit, University of Washington, Seattle, 1974.

White, O. R. "Data-Based Instruction: Evaluating Educational Progress." In J. D. Cone and R. P. Hawkins (Eds.), *Behavioral Assessment: New Directions in Clinical Psychology.* New York: Brunner/Mazel, 1977.

Wolf, M. M. "Social Validity: The Case for Subjective Measurement, or How Applied Behavior Analysis Is Finding Its Heart." *Journal of Applied Behavior Analysis,* 1978, *11,* 203–214.

Section V

Policy Issues in Clinical Practice

Harry Specht
Section Editor

All social work is practiced in a sociopolitical context. The primary purpose of social work is to help individuals, families, and groups deal with their problems by utilizing the resources in their social environment—friends, family, schools, public and voluntary social services, income-maintenance programs, the correctional system, and the like. In addition, social workers may act as psychotherapists to help individuals resolve intrapersonal conflicts, but this is not the primary function of professional social work. Other professionals may help individuals, families, and groups to utilize social resources: psychiatrists, for example, may enable their patients to use social agencies; lawyers sometimes do family counseling. No profession but social work, however, has taken as its primary function that of enabling individuals to utilize all their social resources to solve problems of living.

It is focus on the social environment that makes social work "social," identifies the uniqueness of the profession, and represents its historical mission, which distinguishes it from related professions. This mission has not been fully embraced by all social workers. The social environment has often occupied a less important place in defining and training for practice than the psychodynamic aspects have, especially in the United States. For this reason, it is appropriate that we begin this section on professional issues with a discussion of the sociopolitical context of practice.

The sociopolitical context of social work requires the capacity to understand and deal with the organizational, communal, governmental, and political aspects of social services. The term *social services* carries a special meaning: It implies that the help to be given is socially sponsored. It is this expression of the community's desire to use itself as an instrument of help, as manifested in an infinite variety of agencies and organizations, that provides social work with its unique mission. The social/communal nature of these services requires that the profession be attentive to the organizational, political, and structural features of the social services.

The term *social environment* evokes images of social agency manuals that catalogue the different kinds of services offered in communities, along with other mundane information such as eligibility requirements and office hours. *Sociopolitical context* is a more dynamic term, which communicates the interaction of the law, government, organizations, and family and informal social networks that regulates the various components of the social services system. The interaction of these sociopolitical elements determines who will be served by social workers, the nature of those services, and the conditions under which they will be given. Because social service programs are established by public laws or voluntary agency charters, they must be approved by legislatures or boards of directors. Professional practitioners are educated in universities, and their activities are regulated by government and professional associations.

On a local level, social networks and community groups and organizations play a significant role in these sociopolitical processes. Sometimes these local entities are immediately involved as part of an intervention; and sometimes they are involved with other sociopolitical elements to regulate the intervention. Surprisingly, relatively little is known about the role and the utilization of natural social networks and community groups in the helping processes of social work (Collins and Pancoast, 1975). Yet friends, relatives, and neighbors constitute the single most important source of help available to people who are physically or socially handicapped or disabled. As Moroney (1976) stated: "The overwhelming majority of the handicapped are in the community and are being cared for by their families with varying degrees of support from public and voluntary agencies. . . . Many families, often with the help of friends and neighbors, have provided what can only be described as a staggering amount of care. . . . If the state were to pay families who cared for their handicapped members a sum equal to the cost of care in institutions, or even the current rate paid to homemakers, the costs to the public sector would be staggering" (pp. 1, 11).

Social Work in the Twentieth Century

Social work is a twentieth-century profession. It is essentially a response to the positive and negative effects of industrialization, the dominating social force of this era. Fragmentation of the family and kinship group, alienation, and anomie are the bitter fruits of a highly individualistic, mobile, and technically oriented civilization. The benefits of industrialization—increased leisure, greater longevity, and society's greater capacity to provide goods and services—also cause problems.

Social work and other human service professions exist because society needs them and can afford them. They are needed to deal with complex problems that cannot be handled by the family or individuals alone: counseling and support for the mentally ill, the handicapped, the frail and dependent aged, dependent and abused children, and so forth. And despite the debate about the proper balance between the public-service economy and the goods-producing economy, we can afford to provide basic health and social services for all.

The roles of professional social workers overlap those of family members. This redundancy can be irksome, particularly when using public funds to provide professional services to those in need sometimes further weakens the bonds of kin and community. Our great dilemma is that we would prefer a society that did not need these armies of professional caretakers, but we do not want the reduced standard of living of a simpler, more intimate society. One of the most challenging problems we face is that of balancing the resources of primary groups with those of professionals and formal institutions. The growth of self-help groups and demands for citizen and consumer participation in planning and policy making are, in part, manifestations of that problem.

The professionalization of the human services is, historically, a new phenomenon. Only in this century has society had small armies of social workers, public health nurses, marriage counselors, and others to meet common human needs that, for most of human history, have been met by the family and kinship group, and perhaps by an occasional specialist like a shaman or a priest. Therefore, it is no surprise that the community's perceptions of relationships with professionals are often ambivalent, confused, and perplexing. Questions about how to educate, regulate, and compensate them for activities that are difficult to understand and measure have been, and will continue to be, difficult to answer.

Neglect of Primary Groups

For a profession that has the primary mission of helping people to utilize their social environment in problem solving, social work has focused a surprising amount of attention on the development of technologies for working with individuals. In the United States, this can be understood in the context of prevalent social values. Professional social workers are the bearers of social values that are reflected in social welfare policy, while at the same time they carry major responsibility for changing and reforming the institution of social welfare (Gilbert and Specht, 1976). Thus, human-service professionals are responsible for implementing the very policies and programs they may be attempting to change. Implementors will inevitably be socialized to some degree to the values of the systems in which they work. The initial screening into professional schools and the socialization that takes place in professional education are followed by the screening of these professionals into the social welfare bureaucracies (Haug and Sussman, 1969).

The values of greatest significance that professionals carry into their work are those of individualism and respect for technical expertise. These values are mutually supporting. Technical expertise is the sine qua non of the professional (Greenwood, 1957). The claim that professionals make to the perquisites and privileges of their positions rests on the belief (which in varying degrees may correspond to fact) that only the professional intervenor is capable of helping the client. As Pruger and Specht (1968) stated: "(The professional imagination) has much to recommend it. It permits those who are to be helped to spurn the help offered without any weakening of the professionals' desire to help; it returns disciplined understanding for impulsive rancor; it demands hard working conditions. Indeed, it embodies the finest in civilized behavior, holding no thing in the human experience foreign to it, save one . . . the notion that the helped, except in certain prescribed, professionally approved ways, can or should be the helpers" (p. 25).

One would not expect it to be difficult for the human-service professions to integrate the notion that some of the major resources for helping lie, not in the professional, but in the client. This notion views part of the professional's expertise as the knowledge and skill that is required to help the client to make best use of resources such as relationships with family, friends, and voluntary associations. However, the value that is placed upon individualism in American life frequently constrains a professional from maximizing the use of a client's own resources. This occurs for several reasons.

First, most professionals are of middle-class origin. Those professionals who come from working-class backgrounds become socialized to middle-class values, which they frequently embrace with even greater fervor than others do. Therefore, professionals may denigrate the life-styles and values of their lower-class clients (Sjoberg, Brymer, and Farris, 1966). This value difference may result in professionals placing greater value on individual achievement, initiative, and independence than they do on the more communal and noncompetitive behaviors of some client groups.

Second, the majority of human-service professionals work in bureaucratic systems that, for the most part, are not organized to deal with clients as groups, whether in family units or extended kinship systems. Bronfenbrenner (1976) puts it succinctly: "That the family is the core institution in every society may startle and annoy many contemporary Americans. For most of us it is the *individual* that is the chief social unit. We speak of the *individual* versus the state, *individual* achievement, support for disadvantaged *individuals,* the rights of *individuals,* finding ourselves as *individuals.* It's always the *individuals,* with 'the government' a weak second. The family is not currently a social unit we value or support" (p. 4, emphasis in original).

Third, most professionals receive their education and are socialized into the human-service professions at a time of life when they themselves are disengaged from their families of origin, have not yet started their own families, and do not live in communities in which most families live. Most professionals are trained and educated at a life stage in which they are emotionally and socially divorced from the major concerns of family life. This aspect of education has important consequences. For example, at the master's level, all schools of social work in the United States have one or more required courses that deal with human growth and development. These courses are usually organized to focus on the development of the individual through the life cycle. However, schools of social work have no required courses on the family, a curious situation for a profession that is committed to helping people make use of their social resources.

Over the last two decades, social acceptance of a wider variety of social bonds has increased. For example, homosexuality, single-parent families, and communal living arrangements are coming to be recognized as significant and perhaps socially useful for individuals who express preference for them. And, increasingly, society is coming to recognize as acceptable a wider range of social role behaviors for women and men. One regrettable feature of these current social innovations is that the major claim of these various movements is not for new ways to establish social commitment, communality, and caring. Rather, they are concerned with self-realization and self-expression; they are popular expressions of the value of individualism (Novak, 1976).

The Current Sociopolitical Context of Social Work

Early in this century, the relevant sociopolitical context of the newly developing social work profession was much less complex and comparatively easier to understand than is the case today. Social work was practiced almost exclusively on a rather small scale in voluntary charitable organizations, hospitals, and schools. Social welfare has evolved into a mainline institution involving thousands of federal, state, and local agencies and programs, serving hundreds of thousands of clients, and financed by public and voluntary organizations with annual expenditures of hundreds of billions of dollars. Social welfare expenditures constitute the largest item in the federal budget and cover a wide range of programs, such as social services, public assistance, Social Security, Medicare, and so forth. If state and local government allocations and those of voluntary agencies are included, national expenditures for social welfare in 1976 came to approximatley $443.5 billion (Skolnick and Dales, 1977).

Expenditures for social services alone represent only about 5.5 percent of these social welfare costs, but that comes to a quite significant sum, approximately $24 billion. It covers such programs as the Older Americans Act of 1965; the food stamp program; vocational rehabilitation; services for children, the aged, and the mentally ill; and those included under Title XIV and Title XX (McMillan, 1979). The 1975 Title XX amendments to the Social Security Act allocate resources to the states to enable them to provide a very wide range of social services, from foster care to education and training services (Social and Rehabilitation Service, 1975, p. 7). All of these programs have organizational subunits that operate on a state and local level and interpret federal policy and delivery services. For example, under the Older Americans Act each state is required to have a State Unit on Aging to implement the act. Within the states there are over 500 Area Agencies on Aging that assume varying kinds of responsibility in planning and delivering services for the aged.

In the United States today, social services are no longer perceived to be "for the poor alone." Such services—child care and protection, relocation, job counseling, assistance with developmental disabilities, care of the aged—are coming to be considered necessary to meet the normative needs of all citizens throughout the life cycle. As Gilbert (1977) has stated with respect to the "quiet revolution" that Title XX represents in the social services:

> Unlike the War on Poverty and related federal reform initiatives of the 1960s, this new legislation is not aimed at encouraging the poor and minor-

> ities to struggle for a redistribution of power or a larger share of local resources. The issues of redistribution at stake under Title XX concern changes in eligibility standards that provide the middle class with entitlement to services previously reserved for the poor. . . . In 1975 the doors to an array of public social services began opening to a middle-class clientele. At the same time, that clientele has become more favorably disposed toward utilization of these services. . . . Even the most cautious interpretation of the eligibility categories in the Title XX plans leaves no doubt that large numbers of people now qualify for public social services who are not poor and would not have qualified for these services just twelve months earlier under the previous social service programs [p. 63].

Social workers help people from all social classes to deal with a wide range of social problems in an environment that places many legal, ethical, and political constraints and requirements upon both the worker and the client. For that reason, the functions of referral, advocacy, consulting, coordinating, providing information, contracting with other service providers, organizational management, program evaluation, and work with community groups and organizations have become increasingly important in modern social work practice. They have come to be as significant (although not as happily embraced by many social workers) as traditional social casework.

Social Policy Issues

This part of the book highlights some of the major social policy issues that arise in the sociopolitical context of social work practice. The purpose of these introductory remarks is to give an overview of the sociopolitical terrain. Although only a few issues can be discussed in depth in this volume, it will be useful to the reader to be familiar with the large range and variety of questions that abound in the sociopolitical context.

Who Shall Receive Services? The poorest? The most infirm? Those who are most likely to respond to treatment? Those who have contributed service? Those who have suffered most? Issues related to the basis of allocation frequently generate great controversy because they reflect conflicts in our social values. Affirmative action programs, for example, stir debates about social justice and the appropriateness of compensation for past injuries inflicted by society. Shirley Jenkins, in her chapter entitled "Social Service Priorities and Resource Allocation," deals with two major aspects of this large set of issues. First, she discusses a taxonomy of social needs. She describes the differences among "normative" need (as identified objectively by professionals), "felt" need (as stated by consumers), "expressed" need (as reflected in service-use statistics), and "comparative" need (as measured by examining services offered in two or more communities). Second, she introduces readers to the concept of *social triage.* This term, adapted from the medical military, means "to sort" in situations of overwhelming need and limited resources. Jenkins applies the notion of triage to social services, pointing up the variables social workers utilize in selecting priorities and allocating resources.

What Types of Services Will Be Given? Psychotherapy or counseling? Thanksgiving baskets or food stamps? Child allowances or child daycare? Community action or recreation? Questions about the nature of the social provision are, of course, related to the first set of questions about who will be served. However, decisions about the types of social benefits offered to meet social needs are based upon theories about individuals and society that are more or less explicit: "If we increase (or decrease) X, we can expect an increase (or decrease) of Y." Thus, all of the various psychotherapeutic procedures, such as behavior modification and psychoanalysis, are based upon a given set of interactional theories about human behavior; some of these theories are conflicting (for example, Freudian versus behaviorist theories). Other modes of intervention, such as social group work, community organization, and social planning, are based on sets of theories from other disciplines, such as sociology and political science.

In addition to values and theories, issues of choice regarding the basis of allocation and social provision are affected by political factors. One of these factors is the financial cost of providing a specific service for a particular group. Another factor is the varying ideological meaning of the service for different groups. For example, some perceive family planning programs to be "black genocide"; and some see psychotherapeutically oriented counseling as a means of "blaming the victim." In her chapter, "Clinical Social Work Practice Models," Carol Meyer analyzes the many different concepts of social work practice. Meyer has developed a paradigm that is useful in identifying the salient variables in analysis of practice models. The paradigm includes such variables as ideology, values, knowledge, and the unit of attention. She notes that there is a high degree of consistency in the patterning of these variables among different models of practice. And she suggests that methodological preferences that prevail at any given time are significantly related to prevailing social and economic trends.

How Shall the Delivery System Be Structured? Centralized or decentralized? Multiservice or specialized function? Bureaucratic or collegial? With citizen participation or by professional experts? The ways we organize service-delivery systems significantly affect the nature of social provisions and the composition of user populations. It has been demonstrated that a variety of delivery-system attributes have an impact upon the nature of services and composition of user populations (Gilbert and Specht, 1974). For example, in highly bureaucratized systems there is a tendency to minimize professional discretion (Street, Martin, and Gordon, 1979). On one hand, regulations and routines are likely to be considered of great importance; the professional value of individualizing clients and treating them on the basis of their particular needs may be viewed as disruptive to the bureaucratic organization. On the other hand, organizations that operate on more collegial, democratic, and informal bases may prove to be less efficient and more costly than bureaucracies.

The field of social services has developed in this century in part as a result of a continuous series of experiments, innovations, and social change movements spearheaded by voluntary groups. These efforts often originate as challenges to the established service-delivery system. Henry Miller and Connie Philipp in their chapter, "The Alternative Service Agency," present a provocative perspective on the relationship of the alternative services agency to the established service system. Alternative agencies, they say, tend to support "criminal" objectives and to be radical, atheoretical, and based on bonds of intimacy. These same qualities also make them valuable, sometimes as prods to change existing agencies and sometimes as harbingers of new forms of social assistance and service delivery.

How Are Services to Be Financed? With categorical grants or revenue sharing? By social insurance or from tax revenues? Based on fee-for-services payments or capitation? According to means-tested or universal criteria? The means of financing social services affect all of the other choices we have discussed so far. Even social workers in private practice will be able to provide only certain types of services to particular clients, depending on the mode of finance. Payments based on social insurance, third-party, or purchase-of-service schemes, for example, will allow for a wider range of clients to be served but may introduce more restrictions regarding the types of interventions that will be paid for, length of treatment, and reporting requirements. The stigma of means-tested programs may discourage some potential users and create negative attitudes toward the service among both users and the public. However, if a service is exceedingly expensive or in short supply, there is likely to be strong support to limit its availability to the neediest and the poorest, or to those who are most likely to make the best use of it. Thus, social values and social theory affect this set of decisions, too.

In his chapter, "Financing Social Services," Paul Terrell analyzes the derivation and allocation of funds to pay for social services. His analysis strongly supports his contention that the social work profession is strongly influenced by changes in funding. Social workers, he says, must know enough to promote tax reform alternatives that can address legitimate grievances of the middle class without undermining the basic tax equity or condemning the poor.

Social Work Education: What Kind and for Whom? Generalists or specialists? Paraprofessionals, "new careerists," B.S.W.s, or M.S.W.s? Workers who are theoretically or practically oriented, responsive to the sociopolitical context or to professional scholarship? Faculties of schools and departments of social work frequently disagree about the extent to which they should insulate themselves against the sociopolitical context of practice. Because social work practice is, by definition, immediately concerned with the sociopolitical context, it is not possible for social work educators to eschew entirely involvement in the issues of social choice. Part of the studies and fieldwork of social work students requires that they learn to grapple with such problems as racism, sexism, poverty, poor service-delivery systems, and unresponsive bureaucracies. Not surprisingly, the subject matter of social work and the university itself frequently become the focal point around which these issues are argued. Schools of social work, for example, have been more concerned than other units in colleges and universities with minority recruitment and affirmative action, and they have dealt more actively with many social issues.

However, position in the university is achieved on the basis of scholarship, research, and publication. The awards of prestige and status (and the accompanying university resources) are not made on the basis of sociopolitical good works. The time and energy that must be devoted to scholarly work, and the orientation of scientific objectivity that it requires, create conflicting demands for the social work educator. The preferred values of the university are intellectual excellence, scientific objectivity, and academic freedom to pursue knowledge unfettered by prevailing sociopolitical beliefs and values. The preferred values of practice are responsiveness to social need and concern for social justice.

In his chapter, "Values and Ideological Dilemmas in Professional Education," Gary Lloyd explores the ways in which these conflicting values emerge in education for social work. He points out, for example, that even though few clinical social workers may work with poor and oppressed people, professional education consistently focuses on work with the poor, the disabled, and the disenfranchised.

How Shall Social Work Activities Be Regulated? By registration, certification, or licensing; by self-regulation through one or several professional associations; or through accredited academic institutions?

In his chapter on this subject, "Certification, Licensure, and Other Forms of Regulation," David Hardcastle analyzes various forms of regulation and assesses social work's current capacity to utilize them. Clinical practice, he says, lacks sufficient specificity to meet the requirements of legal regulation. Hardcastle believes that the fundamental problem in regulating any variety of social work is the difficulty in distinguishing social work as a professional activity from social work as an occupational area.

Professionals base their claim to their position on their mastery of an identifiable body of knowledge and skills that can be communicated and tested. A large part of that knowledge should consist of tested theories dealing with the major issues of choice outlined here. Social work skills should include the demonstrated capacity to apply that knowledge in resolving social problems.

Although social work is an emerging profession, it has grown rather quickly into a large and diverse enterprise with a significant institutional mission. There is much room in the profession and the institution for diverse interests, perspectives, and specializations. That room allows a high degree of flexibility and choice in the profession; and one of the reasons the profession has been able to thrive is that things have been so wide open. But with all that openness, the profession suffers for lack of boundaries. There is not yet any consensus among social workers about what social work practice is or about what its mission should be. A distinctive and significant mission for the profession lies in the planning, management, and implementation of the goals and objectives that inhere in a communally sponsored system of personal social services. In the United States, Title XX provides the legislative framework that could, if properly financed and implemented, allow the states to develop programs to provide a comprehensive range of social services on a universal basis. One of the important elements that will determine the fate of a system of personal social services is the profession that provides leadership and direction for it. That profession could be social work. But this task will require social workers to address the sociopolitical issues arising in the context of practice.

References

Bronfenbrenner, U. "The Disturbing Changes in the American Family." *Search,* 1976, *21,* 2–8.

Collins, H., and Pancoast, D. L. *Natural Helping Networks: A Strategy for Prevention.* Washington, D.C.: National Association of Social Workers, 1975.

Gilbert, N. "The Burgeoning Social Service Payload." *Society,* 1977, *14,* 21–30.

Gilbert, N., and Specht, H. *Dimensions of Social Welfare Policy.* Englewood Cliffs, N.J.: Prentice-Hall, 1974.

Gilbert, N., and Specht, H. *The Emergence of Social Welfare and Social Work.* Itasca, Ill.: Peacock, 1976.

Greenwood, E. "Attributes of a Profession." *Social Work,* 1957, *2* (3), 45–55.

Haug, M. R., and Sussman, M. B. "Professional Autonomy and the Revolt of the Client." *Social Problems,* 1969, *17,* 153–161.

McMillan, A. "Social Welfare Expenditures Under Public Programs, Fiscal Year 1977." *Social Security Bulletin,* 1979, *42* (4), 6–20.

Moroney, R. *The Family and the State: Considerations for Social Policy.* London: Longman, 1976.

Novak, M. "The Family Out of Favor." *Harpers,* April 1976, pp. 37–46.

Pruger, R., and Specht, H. "Establishing New Careers Programs: Organizational Barriers and Strategies." *Social Work,* 1968, *4* (3), 21–32.

Sjoberg, G., Brymer, R. A., and Farris, B. "Bureaucracy and the Lower Class." *Sociology and Social Research,* 1966, *50,* 325–337.

Skolnick, A., and Dales, S. "Social Welfare Expenditures, Fiscal Year 1976." *Social Security Bulletin,* 1977, *40* (1), 4–18.

Social and Rehabilitation Service. *Social Services U.S.A.* Washington, D.C.: National Center of Social Statistics, 1975.

Street, D., Martin, G. T., Jr., and Gordon, L. K. *The Welfare Industry: Functionaries and Recipients in Public Aid.* Beverly Hills, Calif.: Sage, 1979.

32

Selecting Appropriate Practice Models

Carol H. Meyer

Professional clinical social workers must puzzle at times over their chosen work: What is our purpose? What is the situation before us? What knowledge and values influence what we do? What are the consequent interventions? When clinicians ask these questions, it indicates that they are consciously using themselves and their knowledge to achieve an explicit purpose. This sense of purpose differentiates the work of a clinician from the efforts of an indigenous worker, family member, friend, or member of a helping network.

Social workers in clinical practice are not notably theoretical. They tend to do what "seems indicated" or what they intuit as the right thing to do. This atheoretical stance is indicative of the limited utility of many practice models. Such models, approaches, or ways of defining problems and interventions have a long history in social work. If practitioners are not aware of them or do not use them, then questions should be raised about the professional quality of practice or the credibility of the models.

Some social work practitioners consciously use theory or models of practice that are behavioral or psychological, for example, existential, Gestalt, Rogerian, and psychoanalytic models. The use of such models raises questions about how their clinical practice fits social work theory and, once again, about the credibility of social work practice models.

Still other practitioners seem to misunderstand the use of social work practice models. Assuming the models have no consistency or integrity, they adopt a mix-and-match attitude: a pinch of problem solving here; a dash of psychosocial theory there; a sprinkling of behavioral, life-model, and task-centered practice; and the net result—confusion instead of coherence.

We begin our exploration of clinical social work practice models with a working definition. The term *clinical* poses a complicated definitional problem that we will discuss fully later. The National Association of Social Workers' (NASW) Clinical Registry definition of the clinical social work practitioners is used here for the time being: "A clinical social worker is by education and experience, professionally qualified at the autonomous practice level to provide direct, diagnostic, preventive, and treatment services to individuals, families, and groups where function is threatened or affected by social or psychological stress or health impairment" (National Association of Social Workers, 1978, p. viii). This definition is sufficiently broad and ambiguous to get us started.

Purposeful Practice

Professional social work practice involves consciously and deliberately carrying out skillful, appropriate interventions that are informed by knowledge and influenced by purpose and values. This definition is one of those "truths" that rests on a high level of generality and is useful for all occasions. The art of translating ideas into doing, or theory into practice, is like all art highly dependent upon illusive and idiosyncratic factors. Yet the struggle must continue to make practice purposeful, to relate actions to concepts and principles, to analyze meanings, and to evaluate outcomes. Without an intellectual framework and an awareness of purpose, values, and knowledge used, practice has to be viewed as accidental and not reliable or replicable. The essential difference between the nonprofessional (or lay helping person) and the professional is that the humane and intuitive responses of the professional are governed by consciousness of the "who, what, why, how, where, and when context" in which those responses take place. Social work educators are familiar with the beginning students' protest over loss of authenticity in their response to clients. Later, when thinking and self-control become as automatic as their muscles, practitioners can respond authentically to their clients.

It is the purpose of this chapter to analyze the implications of the conscious use of social work practice models. Most clinical social work practitioners do what they do without thinking too much about the models they use (Jayaratne, 1978) and without being interested in other models that might challenge them to rethink their commitments. The demands for authenticity, for freedom to be eclectic, for license to "do what is needed" can assume professional legitimacy. To be legitimate, these demands must be made within some framework that seeks to describe and explain professional purposes and the uses of knowledge and values. Without such a framework, practitioners are as undependable and inconsistent as the next-door neighbor who tries to help people solve their personal problems.

Eclecticism appears to be a popular way to avoid the use of theory. "There is . . . an underlying condition as far as being eclectic is concerned, and that is that eclecticism requires the critical consideration and understanding of the available theories before a decision is made about what should be used, and this casts doubt upon . . . (the) claim to being genuinely eclectic" (Carew, 1979, p. 354). To practice professionally is to practice critically, not on the basis of habit, hearsay, personal experience, or imitation. The following exploration of clinical social work models is undertaken in the service of critical, eclectic practice.

The literature cautions against worshiping a theoretical hegemony (Bloom, 1978; Fischer, 1978) instead of relying on empirically based evidence of effectiveness. Today's social work practitioners almost universally rely upon accumulated "practice wisdom" and learning from elders and colleagues, much as in the transmission of folklore. Both of these approaches to conscious practice—empirical and experiential—are significant in the development of practice theory. Nevertheless, practice models are proliferating, and practitioners need to understand their social and professional implications.

Embarking upon a theoretical exploration in an atheoretical professional sea may be a foolish voyage. Still, this chapter offers a Baedecker for that voyage, a guided tour of practice models that will enable readers to choose which model to use or reject, entirely or partially. Personal values always play a part in the choice, but it is after all, a professional matter that social workers become aware of their values and of the role they play in practice. Social work's tenuous credibility in our society may have more to do with lack of clarity and articulation among social workers than with what they actually do or intend. An exploration of the status and purposes of current clinical practice models is necessary to develop clarity and to achieve internal professional coherence, if not concurrence. An analytic framework helps social workers understand the implications of the use of these multiple models for practice.

How to Look at Social Work Practice Models

Over a dozen practice models are currently in use. While it is somewhat presumptuous to refer to all of them as "models" (Meyer, 1973), they all have authors, texts, and followers, as others have described (Turner, 1979; Roberts and Nee, 1970; Roberts and Northen, 1976). This chapter seeks analytic ways of viewing those approaches, a framework for comparing and contrasting practice models. For this analysis, the purpose of social work clinical practice is assumed to be to "improve social functioning" (Bartlett, 1970). The choice of framework depends upon the viewer's predelictions (Kettner, 1975). Let us dabble a moment in the exercise of selecting a useful framework.

The Myth of Holistic Theoretical Consistency. Because social work is a practicing profession, it is unlikely that any practice model will achieve absolute consistency in the integration of the theories upon which it draws. That is, it is unlikely that a model based upon a holistic theory of (biological, social, and psychological) man and woman will produce the practice principles to carry out the dictates of the theory. Let us grant that the knowledge drawn from the pertinent basic sciences is derivative. Once these disciplines are applied in the real world of social work practice—which deals with such vast differences in biological, social, and psychological clientele—the search for holistic concepts across knowledge boundaries appears unrealistic. Nonetheless, the search to develop incremental, interdisciplinary knowledge must continue. The need for principles by which to apply knowledge remains; holistically pure models usually suggest overgeneralized, abstract practice principles. The aim of holistic theoretical consistency should remain an academic pursuit. At this time, it is not useful in a framework for analyzing clinical practice models.

The Myth of Immediate Usefulness. This idea is the opposite of the myth of theoretical consistency. Clinicians always need help in knowing what to do and always seek skills applicable to the moment in practice models. However (and this is bad news for the clinician, who may not want to read on), no practice model that is intended to generalize beyond a single case can prescribe the skill required under particular circumstances. Cases differ, practitioners differ, and the conditions of practice differ. Skills have to be cited in a viable practice model, but they have to be viewed as integral to or flowing from the whole thrust of the model, or there would be no purpose for the use of models at all. Here, we can refer back to the empirical and experiential interests whereby "what works" is the model for practice. This criterion merits credence, but the purpose in this chapter is to explore the implications of use of current (theoretical) practice models. These ordinarily suggest principles for action or skill repertoires; they seldom prescribe what to do under particular circumstances.

Clinical Practice Models

An analytic framework to assess clinical practice models has its limitations as well as utility. Complex as it is to decide which variables are significant, the development and the use of such a framework are relatively simple when compared to other ways of looking analytically at models. Any general overview would be purely descriptive, and in fact the models can be studied directly in the current literature.

Other approaches to viewing or comparing social work practice lead us into a conceptual morass. Social work practice models have evolved without plan since 1917, building accidentally upon experience and knowledge. Methods were developed by the leading casework practitioner-theorists of the time. They wanted to build a social work practice theory based upon particular personality theories. We can examine these theoretical roots by reading the history of casework methods (Germain, 1971; Hartman, 1972) and by identifying the "family tree" of social work practice theorists according to their commitments to Freud, Rank, Skinner, and the neo-Freudian ego theorists. This task is not made easier when one reviews recent practice models that are almost totally derived from psychological theories without integration into a social work perspective. The analytical problem becomes almost insurmountable when clinical practice with families and groups is included in an exploration of practice models.

Today clinical practice deals with individuals, families, and groups. Therefore, it is necessary to look at three streams of method and model development. At the risk of oversimplifying the task, we will first present a straightforward chart (Table 1) of the major or most commonly used "models," listing the approaches by their names in the order of their origin. The presentation is chronological because there has been overlapping. It is beyond the scope of this chapter to deal with the historical subtleties of theorists at a particular moment in history. Many theorists knew each other and practice models sometimes derived from their debates and thus became consensus models. In other instances, they were incrementally developed.

This table suggests that historical sequence, knowledge building, and theory development have occurred in clinical social work practice; only to a limited

Table 1. Most Commonly Used Clinical Social Work Models

	Social Work (Clinical) Practice Methods	*Major Theorists*	*Decade of Origin*
I.	*Casework*		
	A. *Diagnostic Casework*	Richmond, Reynolds, Hamilton, Lowry, Austin	1917
	Crisis Intervention	Parad, L. Rapoport	1950
	Psycho-social Therapy	Hollis, Turner	1960
	Clinical Social Work	Strean, Turner	1970
	B. *Functional Casework*	Robinson, Taft, Smalley	1930
	C. *Problem-Solving Casework*	Perlman	1950
	D. *Socio-Behavioral Casework*	Thomas	1960
	E. *Task-centered Casework*	Reid and Epstein	1970
II.	*Group Work*		
	A. *"Democratic Service"*	Wilson, Ryland, Coyle, Kaiser	1930
	B. *Psycho-social* (therapeutic)	Vinter	1950
	C. *Mediating-Reciprocal*	Schwartz	1960
	D. *Developmental*	Tropp	1970
	E. *"Group Therapy"*	Rose, Scheidlinger	1950
III.	*Family Treatment*	Scherz, Satir, Sherman	1950
IV.	*General Social Work Practice*	Barlett, Meyer, Pincus-Minahan, Middleman-Goldberg, Goldstein	1970
V.	*Life Model*	Germain-Gitterman	1980
VI.	*Miscellaneous* (drawn from psychological/behavioral theorists)		
	Psychoanalytic		1920
	Rogerian		1950
	Gestalt		1960
	Existential		1960

extent is this so, possibly because the theorists listed have had different views of humanity and the ways of the world and because practitioners in social work have been notably atheoretical. Theory has not governed their practice. Thus, this listing probably has little to do with what actually happened in practice.

Today, "clinical" has come to mean almost whatever an individual or practitioner or interested group wants it to mean. Derived from the Greek, clinical originally meant "at the bedside." That idea has been expanded to include direct attention to people, and the practitioner is no longer restricted to the bedside or to one person at a time. Today's clinician is a practitioner (in the art of healing, helping, treating, or intervening) who works with (directly or in behalf of) individuals, families, and groups with the goal of solving problems (via psychological change or psychosocial adaptation). The options in parentheses suggest some differences in emphasis that might be debated endlessly among clinical practitioners. If the terms of the clinical debate were confined to these options, the professional atmosphere in social work would be less charged than it is.

Serious consequences for the profession, for practice formulations, and for clients result from social workers' persistent overuse and misuse of the term *clini-*

cal. The ambiguity in the use of imprecise and unresolved definitions has a political utility and allows practitioners to use the term to serve many masters and to avoid confrontation with the underlying problems. Assigning the word clinical to a method, task, problem, type of practitioner, or setting obscures its meaning. Let us deal first with the political uses of the term and then with more substantive matters. To start, we will consider the time in which clinical social work became a contender for status as a practice model.

Clinical Practice as Backlash. Some of the assaults on professional social work practitioners during the 1960s, when attention was directed to community and social change, were specifically directed to caseworkers. Not only were they accused, often unjustly and unreasonably, of being "irrelevant" and "uninterested" in the environment, but they were also derided for being white and middle-class in their orientation. In reaction to these attacks, the term *casework* went underground. It resurfaced in two forms. Some caseworkers integrated the individualizing process into *social work practice,* which implied a broader knowledge base plus new interventions, multiple units of attention, and an open system for the use of practice models. But all caseworkers did not resurface as social work practitioners; others came back as clinical social work practitioners. The term *clinical social work practice* swept the field and developed as both "model" and mystique. If it is indeed a model, it can be subjected to the framework for analysis that will be suggested here for other practice models.

It is the mystique that contains political characteristics and has professional and social implications. Clinical has been associated with psychiatric social work and psychotherapy. Why? Is it so that clinical practitioners can gain greater power on interdisciplinary clinical teams? Or access to third-party payments? Or a rationale for private practice? These are all political purposes for using the term *clinical,* and they appear to be politically sensitive to circumstances. The medical analogy can be found in the upgrading of the general practitioner to internist or family medicine specialist. The change in term led to change in status from generalist to specialist, with an increase in professional and community respect and financial reward.

The only contentiousness involved in the political use of the term *clinical social work* rests in its exclusivity. The appropriation of the title had implied that direct practice in social work that is not confined to the clinical social worker's interests—that is, clinical team, third-party payments, private practice—is not clinical practice. In other words, *clinical,* being a term denoting direct attention, can just as well define the social work practitioner who is not in private practice. The alternative assumption, that it is a discrete model, can be put to a rational test against a framework for analysis. The appropriation of a clinical mystique by clinical social workers competes on vague and political grounds with the clinical work of those who practice social work but who do not define what they do as a particular clinical model of practice.

The Use of "Clinical" as a Code Word. Beyond the mystique, there may be other purposes served by use of the term *clinical.* The entrance of the BSW worker on the social work scene has had an impact upon graduate (MSW) practitioners, graduate schools of social work, and "manpower" strategies in social work agencies, hospitals, and clinics. The extent of the impact is still unclear, but the threat of the BSW upon the domain of the MSW is obvious, especially in an era of diminishing funds and declassification of social work positions. Could clinical social workers be a euphemism for graduate as distinguished from undergraduate social workers? Unquestionably, there are problems and issues yet to be addressed, much less resolved here, but it will be more productive to deal directly with these problems and issues, rather than to mask the difficulties through the misuse of the term *clinical.*

The use of *social work practice* as an umbrella term for multiple services, interventions, and tasks has made it difficult to differentiate direct from indirect services. Thus, social work intervention in community processes (on behalf of individual clients) has so broadened the concept of practice, that clinical social workers have felt compelled to identify specific, direct, one-to-one practice as clinical so as to differentiate it from social change. As distinguished from social change, policy planning, and administration, this use of the term *clinical* is probably appropriate. It is unclear when the term is used to distinguish the clinical practitioner from other direct social work practitioners who happen to include ecosystems rather than linear perspectives in their practice.

Another use of clinical as a code word, stemming from its association with private practice, indicates some conceptual confusion. Private practice is a setting, a "house" in which practice takes place that is sanctioned by the profession. That practice can take place in voluntary, proprietary, and public settings, as well as in profit and nonprofit work sites. The association of clinical practice with private practice has distorted the generally understood meaning of the term *clinical.* Private practitioners, in fact, sometimes carry out tasks of consultation and service provision that have no clinical intentions.

These imprecise uses of the term *clinical* can distort practitioners' goals. There are three tasks in demystifying and decoding the term. First, the problems and issues underlying the (felt) necessity to mask them with the term *clinical* have to be addressed head-on. Second, the appropriation of clinical for political purposes has to be faced as a problem for direct (clinical) social workers who do not share those political concerns. Third, a clinical model has to be evaluated in some analytical framework. The following is a suggested framework.

A Framework for Analysis. The answers to the questions posed in this framework can be grouped in a variety of ways. Apart from yes and no answers, which are sometimes helpful in determining whether or not certain information is there, it is possible using this framework to identify profiles of models along the continua of one's choice. The proposed framework analyzes the following elements:

- Ideological biases
- Values
- Knowledge base
- Unit of attention
- Problem definition
- Congruent and explicit interventions
- Uses of the professional relationship
- Desirable outcome
- Structure of time
- Options for use of differentially trained staff

- Options for work with social services
- Evaluation of effectiveness

This framework may provide clinicians with a compass for finding their way through the various models.

What Are the Ideological Biases? Ideology has come to have a bad reputation in the face of scientific evidence. Ideology means commitment to a particular system of ideas, and science means empirical discovery of ideas. Yet, ideology plays a part in scientific discovery, if only in the choice of what is to be studied. As clinical social work practice is hardly value-free, all one can do is to ask of theoreticians and idea investigators to make their ideological commitments clear so that clinicians can take the inevitable biases into consideration when they make choices among models.

The major ideological competition in social work results from differing emphases on the person and the environment. Other, subsidiary ideologies have been found in different commitments to various processes, to uses of particular knowledge, to uses of differential manpower, to concerns regarding specialization, but many of these subsidiary conflicts in ideology rest upon the major ideological context of the emphasis on person or environment in practice.

An analytic framework is not supposed to take sides in an ideological contest, but it can, and probably must, raise this question: Is the ideological bias articulated? The answer to this question, when found in the explication of any model, will indicate whether or not the purposes of the model are clear and will offer an explanation for its selection of knowledge base, use of differential manpower, and tilt toward a particular kind of specialization commitment. Of course, the description of relevant skills will also be better understood in the light of its expressed emphasis on person or environment. New practice models are attempting to bridge the separation between emphasis on the person and the environment. This effort at integration requires the same attention to the articulation of ideology.

Traditional models were highly reflective of ideology, but in recent years empirical investigation has played a more powerful role in model development. Obviously, a method of practice governed by ideology would be a creator of, if not a captive of, the ideology of its time. It is possible to trace the ideological purposes of casework—that is, the person/environment emphases in the last sixty years—in relation to expectations of social change. Figure 1, for example, illustrates how in times of low social expectation of social change practice models turn inward, and in times of high expectation of social change they turn outward.

Figure 1 depicts the entrance of practice models into social work with *Social Diagnosis* (Richmond, 1917) and the beginning influence of Freudian psychoanalytic ideas during a period of post–World War I prosperity illustrate this shift in ideological emphasis. In the Depression, methods development was overcome by events, to reappear in the World War II period in full force when diagnostic and functional casework struggled for dominance. The Eisenhower/McCarthy era dampened expectations, and practice methods like problem-solving appeared. When the civil rights and peace movements raised expectations, practice methods again reached toward an environmental emphasis, as in the newly defined social work approaches. In the post-Vietnam era, interest in clinical practice models was

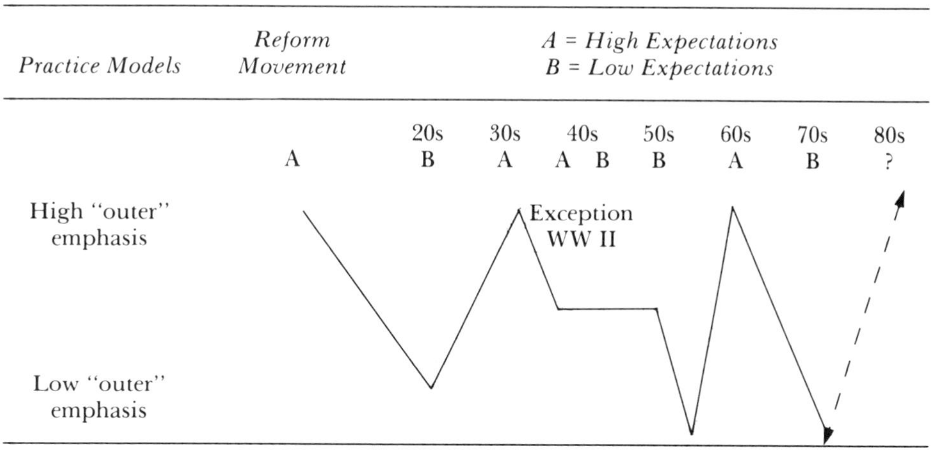

Source: Based on ideas proposed in 1969 by Bo Seabury, then a doctoral candidate at Columbia University.

Figure 1. Levels of Expectation of Social Change

renewed. If the patterned trajectory were allowed to take its course, and if social change expectations were to rise as the economic swing lowers, then practice models governed by ideology would continue to follow the arc of the pendulum, and turn outward once again in the 1980s.

However, a shift was evident beginning in the 1970s. Empirically minded clinicians (Bloom, 1978; Reid and Epstein, 1977; Fischer, 1978; and others) sought to build clinical practice models by undertaking scientific investigation of effectiveness, or by asking, "What works?" It will be interesting to observe the trajectory of clinical social work practice to determine whether it continues to rise and fall in future decades or develops an empirical base and becomes more independent of social and economic cycles.

What Is the Real Value System? Professional social workers hold closely to an articulated value system that is not sexist, racist, ageist, or classist. In other words, these and other structural and unchangeable conditions of life are never to be viewed as eligibility factors in a means test for determining help, treatment, or service. If one takes at its word the NASW Code of Ethics and the verbal commitment of professional social workers that these "ists" and their resultant "isms" are always excluded from practice models in social work, then the framework for analyzing practice models need not question whether the model is sexist, racist, ageist, or classist. Another way to state the question is: Who is left out of the model? With the rising "ethnic practice," "feminist practice," "aging practice," and "poverty practice," the negative attitude toward these groups has been turned around toward an affirmative practice, which is also not value-free. There may be as little hope for developing a "general clinical practice model" for people in all conditions and statuses of life as there is for developing a holistic knowledge base.

Jenkins' (1981) work on ethnic minority agencies and Solomon's (1976) *Black Empowerment* are recent examples of affirmative ethnic practice. The materials by feminists and by poverty workers are not dissimilar in that there is growing interest in defining the special needs, services, and practices applicable to special groups in our society. Clinical practice defined as ethnic, feminist, or poor is not incipiently racist, sexist, or classist, because it is practice borne of necessity. Their adherents perceive these practice models as responses to racism, sexism, and classism. Whether these developing models are phasic or will become permanent features of the clinical repertoire remains to be seen. The "melting pot" was not hot enough; the War on Poverty was lost; and women have not achieved equal rights. Whether defensive or affirmative, the felt necessity to develop an ethnic, feminist, and poverty clinical practice has to be recognized as a reflection of the failure of the existing general clinical practice models.

If clinical social work practice models are avowedly not sexist, racist, ageist, or classist, why have there been efforts to develop special clinical practices? It is quite possible to hold certain social values dearly and at the same time be unaware of the properties of one's clinical practice model. For example, all clinical models rely heavily on talking. Therefore, they operate upon assumptions that the client will possess cognitive ability, emotional readiness, and social accessibility to words, thoughts, and ideas. Consider the structural barriers of language. Differences in language (culture) and different meanings of the same language (class) inevitably influence clinical encounters between practitioners and clients of different cultures and classes. Where attention is not paid to this barrier in the practice model, the poor and ethnic minorities can be found ineligible solely on the grounds of ascribed and acquired characteristics. This then becomes a social value as well as a substantive issue to be addressed by the clinician in search of an appropriate practice model.

Another example of the way a practice model might be viewed as discriminatory is in the degree to which it expects clients to depend upon resources other than the clinician for physical, social, economic, and emotional sustenance. There are recognized limits to the capacities of clinical practitioners, and it would be beyond their role and function to "fill in" for clients' deprivation of family, housing, income, child care, health care, employment, and so on. Yet, clients must have these resources, and if a clinical practice model does not propose ways of intervening in the client's environment to help with this kind of deprivation, then the clinician has to expect the client to take care of his external problems himself—or not to have these problems. Too much deprivation can make one ineligible for clinical help, and the grounds may then be poverty, sex, ethnicity, and age.

These examples of characteristics of clinical practice models—the requirement of talking and the need to deal with deprivation—suggest reasons some models are in effect sexist, racist, ageist, or classist despite contrary affirmations to an open value system of practice. Of course, it is possible to modify these obstacles through creative use of manpower, direct attention to environmental factors, and a host of indirect actions. What is important to include in our framework for analysis of practice models is the question of (fewer) eligibility criteria. To what extent does the model exclude people by virtue of their status, cultural characteristics, and condition of life?

What Is the Knowledge Base? We mentioned that the selection of knowledge as the basis of informed practice has something to do with one's ideological commitments. Thus, in a practice model concerned with the person over the environment (that is, in real emphasis; no model of social work practice—no matter how intrapersonal—actually admits to lack of emphasis upon environment), the primary knowledge base will be drawn from the biological and psychological sciences. In models more concerned with environmental emphases, knowledge will be sought from areas of social science concerned with social change, social systems, anthropology and so on. More recent models that adopt ecosystems perspectives have sought bridging concepts through use of some aspects of ego psychology with less emphasis upon internal psychological processes. Apart from the articulation of ideology or purpose, one must ask for the nature of knowledge explicitly used because this will serve as the basis for viewing the person and/or the environment.

All clinical practice models rely upon some psychological theory, and some models identify certain aspects of social science theory. There may be a "knowledge" explanation here of the different inner and outer ideological emphases in clinical social work practice. The two kinds of theory are not matched in the level of their coherence. One can appropriate Freudian or behavioral theory and find an explanation of why or how people act in certain ways. However, social science has not produced any comparable single theory that explains why society acts in certain ways. Thus, it is impossible to determine theoretically why or how people will act in relationship to how society will act; there is no holistic concept of this reciprocity. Furthermore, compared to the comfort with which any given psychological theory can be drawn upon for use in clinical practice, it is very complicated to confront the multiple social science theories to explain social phenomena. It is necessary to be selective, to use social role theory, organizational theory, deviance theory, political science, anthropology, and so on for help in explaining the whys and hows of stratified events. In this psychological and social science seesaw, the power of a single unitary (psychological) theory outweighs that of fragmented (social science) theory. This may partially explain why clinicians have relied more on psychological than on social science knowledge.

The imbalance in this knowledge base, a difficult problem for a profession that is psychosocially oriented to solve, is not made easier by the interdisciplinary barriers in American education. Theorists on either side of the psychological-social science divide tend to view the other side in simplistic terms, because they do not understand it. So they say: There are subtle differentials in psychological theory, but (erroneously) there is a definitive social science theory—or vice versa (Bendix, 1968).

Efforts to find bridges, as in the sociobehavioral model and the life model, are salutory, but at their present stage of development these efforts are selective in the choice of those aspects of both psychological and social science theory that are to be joined. Emphasis on knowledge of selected behaviors or on ego effectiveness and competence relates "outer" aspects of ego to social events and the necessary emphasis upon impinging environments. Use of partial knowledge is, at this stage of knowledge building, a trade-off in the search to bridge psychological and social science theory.

The articulation of the knowledge base used in clinical social work practice models helps in determining the appropriateness of the model to social work. Some clinical practice models in use should not be viewed at all as containing social work psychosocial purposes. The use of Freudian, Gestalt, Rogerian, existential, or whatever psychologies or philosophies without balanced use of social science theories suggests a distortion of social work purpose. Of course, the same can be said of use of social science theory without psychological theory, which also tilts the knowledge base away from the profession's purpose. But in the latter case, it is clear that the emphasis would not be defined as clinical knowledge anyway. The clinical debate in social work seems to be focused on the extent to which psychological knowledge is used exclusively, without reference to social science theory. At the least, a model of practice has to identify its knowledge base and expect it to be used as informative of clinical practice carried out in the name of that model.

What Is the Unit of Attention Addressed by the Model? The profession listened when Bartlett (1970) observed that social work practice was preoccupied with methods-skills development and insufficiently interested in the search for knowledge as its unifying base. Soon after, practice models developed that included as their unit of attention various sizes of systems: the individual, the family, and the group viewed as phenomena rather than as methods. The historical themes that guided casework, group work, and family treatment are beyond the scope of this chapter. But some theorists are interested in developing generalist models of practice that include common processes applicable to all of these units of attention. Some theorists, while accepting all these units of attention as appropriate for clinical practice, view the interventive or treatment processes as differential. What is important in analyzing a practice model is to determine whether or not the model encompasses different sizes of systems for attention. The analysis of interventions will indicate whether the model proposes a general or specific (to individual, family, group) set of interventive processes. In addition to these sizes of systems, the breadth of the unit of attention, as mentioned earlier, is dependent upon the perspective used.

How Are Problems Defined? The way problems are defined in each practice model has enormous power as a guide to intervention. In social work practice, a simple description of the observable factors in a case may call forth various definitions, depending upon the nature of the model. For example, a single case can conceivably be described as anxiety hysteria, poverty, a problem of role transition, alcoholism, child abuse, marital conflict, alienation, psychosis, or an enmeshed family. Each definition says something about the direction of intervention in a case. The direction is largely determined by the ideological commitment and the choice of knowledge base. A model that emphasized personality change might rely heavily upon psychoanalytic theory and consequently might define a case in psychodynamic terms, an environmentally oriented practice model might emphasize social deprivation, and a transactional model might select problem-solving issues or problems in living as the definitional construct. In other words, the mind set of practitioners who utilize one practice model or another is such that they define problems in the terms of the model's structure. The unit of attention is also governed by the way problems are defined. A case defined as "an enmeshed family" calls for different interventions (family treatment) than "an isolated family in a housing project" (group intervention) or than "a wife who is depressed because her children are grown and her husband has a mistress" (treatment of the individual or the marital pair). Each unit of attention elicits different interventive treatment processes.

The way problems are defined offers clues to the intent of the model. There is usually some inner consistency if the model is tightly drawn, for example:

Framework	*Problem Definition*		
Ideological commitment:	personality change		environmental emphasis
Knowledge base:	psychoanalytic		socioeconomic
Unit of attention:	individual	or	group of isolated people
Problem definition:	hysteria		social isolation
Intervention:	psychotherapy		development of group cohesion; use of self-help group

Are Interventions Congruent and Explicit? The practice of social work is defined by what is actually done in a case situation. Purpose, knowledge and values, problem definition, and unit of attention chosen have but one direction, and that is toward the explication of interventions. In this connection, the repertoire may be narrow or broad. It can be narrow in the sense of attention to the person only or environment only or to the unit of attention of individual, family, or group adaptation only. The interventive repertoire can be broad to encompass interventions on both the person and environment sides of the equation (for example, organizations and communities, as well as individual, family, and group practice). When it comes to precise skills, what one says in an interview or what one does with a social institution, it is the author's (unpopular) opinion that skills cannot be prescribed, because at this level of conceptualization they are too "distant" from the model's theoretical orientation and indeed totally iconoclastic and dependent upon the often not replicable circumstances of client, problem situation, and worker.

Fern Lowry (1939) pointed out that if a practitioner understands that a person needs reassurance (a key assessment question), the worker might say, "That must be hard for you" or "Gee, that's tough" (skill). The choice depends upon the worker's style; when we consider this aspect of clinical practice, style, words, and specifics cannot be prescribed. All that can be theoretically suggested by models is the purpose, knowledge base, values, unit of attention, definition of problem, and assessment and skills repertoire. The model's theoretical integrity can only suggest skills. If, after using all of these constructs, a practitioner still does not know what to say or do, then we are beyond professional practice. We are at the level of manuals, apprenticeship, and rote response.

Alternatively, practice research that is not model-oriented is moving toward the empirical study of well-defined problems to determine with increasing specificity "what works" under particular, replicated circumstances. This movement toward empirically determined interventions will probably be the next stage in the development of clinical theory, but it will have little to do with practice models discussed here.

How Is the Professional Relationship Used? All professional practitioners—in all professions—aim at a controlled, client- or patient-centered use of the practitioner-client relationship. In social work practice, two kinds of relationship have always been used as a tool in "treatment" with individuals, families, and groups. On the simplest level, a benign, considerate, and positive relationship has been viewed as the basis for all interventions. After all, help has to be offered in a supportive manner that is universally understood. At one extreme, models of practice use the professional relationship as a backdrop to the service provided, while at the other extreme the relationship is used as the major tool of practice. In the case of psychodynamic psychotherapy, the relationship is raised to the theoretical level of transference, wherein change is expected to occur through the transference experience. In the sociobehavioral model, therapeutic decisions are made as one aspect of the professional relationship—whether or not to use reinforcement, for example. The emphasis placed upon the relationship as a tool or as a backdrop is a differentiating factor among some practice models. All models make explicit the way the relationship is used, and a clinician's choice inevitably is based upon awareness of this factor.

What Is the Desirable Outcome: Cure/Resolution or Adaptation/Maintenance? Even though clinical social work practice models differ in so many ways, practitioners' choices are often most influenced by desired outcome or goal. The decision to work for cure/resolution or adaptation/maintenance is heavily value-based. The source of the value commitment may lie in the practitioner's view of his or her own life or of personal treatment experiences. Or the value commitment may derive from experiences with favorite teachers, supervisors, or colleagues in which identification has played a role. Clearly, one can choose to ally oneself with one or another practice outcome and be "correct" in either choice. Some practice models seek cure/resolution of conflict and others explicitly seek adaptation/maintenance, but that is not to say that use of the models always proves to be effective. For purposes of the analytic framework being developed here, one caution has to be mentioned: all aspects of the framework have to be considered in a wise choice. For example, to choose a cure goal could contradict the value of nonracist or nonclassist practice. It will always be a cost-benefit decision. Also, the choice of a goal, to be effective, has to be well rooted in knowledge and skill.

In the psychoanalytic view, for a clinical practitioner to set out to cure a condition or resolve a conflict is to go beyond the presenting situation—beyond in the sense of the client's history. In that view, the clinician must ask the question "Why?" or "How did this come about?" to attempt to remove the cause, and thus to allow the cure. In a behavioral view, symptomatic cure can be sought without history but with careful manipulation of environmental reinforcement.

The notion of adaptation or maintenance permits the clinician to focus on "here and now" events, eliciting and developing such ego functions as coping, mastery, and competence, and working with stress-producing envrionmental factors so as to ameliorate their effects and permit adaptations.

The choice is not as clearly implied as are the clinical interventions. Extraclinical questions inevitably have to be answered simultaneously with the planned intervention. Such questions arise as: Is this client old enough (or young enough), sick enough (or well enough), to warrant the choice of either goal? Is the client verbal, intelligent, and capable of the insight necessary for psychological cure? Is the client strong enough, free enough of psychological, cognitive, or social deficits to be able to benefit from a maintenance approach? Are there sufficient resources within the person, family, community, or organization to support clinical interventions of either type?

The decision to choose a goal of practice has to derive from real as well as clinical considerations. The more explicit the conditions to make either approach effective, the more informed is the clinician's choice.

How Is Time Structured? Some clinical practice models prescribe time limits as integral to the models. Direct and indirect use of time is one of the significant descriptive factors to be understood in choosing a model. Direct use of time as a clinical issue means that time is used as an expectation, dynamic, and control in the clinical experience: time-limited contacts, measured in minutes, amount of contacts, number of days or weeks, and so forth. When used in this direct way, the models seek the pressure and focus that time limits bring. The functional model's use of time as a necessary structure, like the agency's function or its fee scale as posed against the negative will, has fallen into disuse. Nonetheless, the explicit use of time to speed up the treatment process or to deal with resistance, passivity, and lack of focus remains prominent in some models of practice.

Indirect uses of time are more common in all practice models. The reality of time limits in crises, the acknowledgment that time sometimes is "short," is increasingly taken into consideration. The old idea that "open-ended treatment" is clinical and "planned short-term treatment" is not clinical no longer serves as a differentiating factor. The differences are important, however, when one seeks to know why and to root out causes so as to achieve (psychoanalytically oriented) cure and resolution. In such an approach, open-ended time is needed. Beyond this requirement, planned short-term treatment, crisis intervention, time-limited clinical services, and so on are used alternately, depending upon the client, the problem, the setting, financial resources, and the availability of clinical staff. The use of a time orientation as a condition of clinical practice is only one aspect of the analytic framework; it depends upon purpose, perspective, knowledge base, and all other components of the framework.

What Options Exist for Use of Differentially Trained Staff? Clinical social work practice does not take place in a socioeconomic or political vacuum. Private practice is of course the area in which clinical practice is not affected by staffing issues because the choice to practice alone closes the issue. However, clinical social work practice takes place in all organizational settings that can be even faintly presumed to have a connection with social work, social services, and social welfare. Once having agreed upon a definition of clinical social work practice—or direct social work practice with individuals, families, and groups—it is important to include staffing issues in the framework for analyzing practice models, for these determine whether the clinical practice can be delivered.

These issues assume increasing importance in areas of social work practice where there is a heavy client demand for professional, clinical attention; where there is a true shortage of graduate professionals; and where the clinical assessment determines that certain tasks might be best carried out by differentially trained types of personnel. This last idea, that clinical outcomes may be best served by use of an array of helping types, makes manpower issues relevant for the private practitioner's consideration as well. The criterion of nonexclusion of clients in need is linked with the previously mentioned value position of social work. Clinical practitioners in all settings (except private practice) cannot for long shut down services because of lack of available staff and still maintain credibility in the community being served and in the public funding offices. This is a political reality, for we already know that if social work clinicians do not do the necessary job, it will be declassified and other professionals or human service practitioners will be called upon to do it. The example of nurse practitioners carrying the hospital discharge function instead of social workers comes to mind. In geographical or organizational areas where there are insufficient or unwilling graduate social work clinicians, a criterion of a useful model of practice is: Can it be delivered at all? This consideration assumes priority over whether or not the model is effective.

The clinical assessment may suggest certain (therapeutic) tasks that need to be carried out, that are "doable," and that are perhaps more appropriately doable by others than graduate social work clinicians. Depending upon the case and the problem at hand, families in treatment might also need advocacy in schools and other bureaucracies; aged people coming to terms with the ache of their children not visiting might also need a "friendly visitor"; adolescents going through identity crises might also need camping, trips, or special help in developing certain skills. Every case problem has multiple entry points where planned interventions can reinforce each other. Of course, the more systematically one views a case, the more entry points are evident, and the more narrowly or linearly one views the same case, the more limited the entry points and the less one sees the necessity for wider use of manpower.

The options offered by a practice model for use of differential (clinical and nonclinical) staff to carry out case-related tasks are part of the framework for analysis. A frank psychoanalytic-psychotherapeutic purpose where treatment relies totally upon the transference offers no manpower options (except for menial, arranger, and "go for" tasks). A life, problem-solving model in a systemic framework offers options for a panoply of differentially trained staff. The model must be chosen in keeping with the immediate economic realities of practice.

To What Degree Does the Model Permit Use of Social Services? It may seem odd to inject social services (including self-help groups) into a framework for analysis of clinical social work practice models. Yet clinical practice has to be responsive to social forces as well as to social indicators. One might extrapolate from social services to any groups or institutions outside of the direct clinical encounter, for that is what is at issue here. We are still confining our analysis to what the clinician does directly, one-on-one (or multiples of one, depending on the size of the unit of attention), but the client lives a life outside of the encounter. The increasing use of self-help groups, for example, is a potential therapeutic dynamic of no mean importance (McGowan, 1979). In today's world, even the classical psychoanalyst will encourage a patient to join a weight reduction group or to use a supportive network or social institution. Classical psychoanalysis being the extreme example of one-on-one direct clinical practice, it would not seem to be impertinent to include the potential for use of "services" or groups external to the clinical encounter as an aspect of the framework for analysis of practice models.

Can the Model Be Evaluated for Effectiveness? Just as modern clinical practice increasingly is understood in its political context—that is, resources available, sanction, consumer demand, and so forth—so its effectiveness is being evaluated. On the surface, clinicians may see no problem with clinical research, but experience thus far has not demonstrated a great interest, willingness, or developing expertise in actually doing research. The practice model's explicitness in each category of the framework will determine how readily it can be evaluated. Until now, behavioral models have been those most easily and therefore most often evaluated precisely because of the behavioral explicitness within all parts of the model, as defined by our framework. The practice models that rest upon practice wisdom, belief, conviction, and "hidden," inexplicit processes are less subject to objective research. In the selection of a practice model, this researchability factor might be particularly significant in some instances. For example, "evidence" might be necessary in developing a teaching lab, an experimental clinical program, or a demonstration for seeking funds. The professional interest in knowledge development and refinement of clinical practice that really works should serve as ongoing pressure to subject practice models to objective investigation through research. The elite clinical practitioner someday might become the research clinical practitioner. As far as practice models are concerned, there is room for explication in every category of the framework. If these models are to persist, work will have to be done to show evidence of their validity and reliability. The eighties are too late for belief and conviction alone.

A Summary of the Framework. Barring criteria of theoretical purity and immediate usefulness, there is much to be examined in the analysis of clinical social work practice models. There is no higher authority than informed choice to tell the professional what model to use, and there is powerful logic and reason on the side of informed choice.

What do we look for in our search? What aspects of the model are important to clinicians, depending upon their location and other factors? No clinical social work practice model defines a particular client group, (psycho) social problems, and condition or status of life as its domain. Perhaps, in coming years, clinicians will determine what model works best for whom and under what specific conditions. However, if this determination is to be made, it is necessary for practitioners to know how to look at and evaluate models of practice.

"Since a single unitary theory of clinical practice is unfeasible, we combine things eclectically in order to meet the diverse and differential needs, objectives, and dimensions of interventive action, with regard to many different types of problems, persons, and situations" (Siporin, 1979, p. 84). It is the professional's task to know what is to be combined to master the various bases of knowledge in eclectic clinical practice.

A Model for Use in Clinical Social Work Practice

Clinical practice models have substantial limitations when they are examined against the framework suggested in this chapter. No practice model meets all criteria for preferred knowledge, values, purposes, or skills. Yet, even if they are not used very much in their entirety, models are considered to be useful or necessary.

Harriet Bartlett (1970) broke through the mystique of model use by pointing out the limitations of the methodological model development. Judith Nelsen (1975) commented upon the narrow view of problems that derived from the narrow perspective of methods. Social work models have been methodological models;

approaching cases, problems, or psychosocial phenomena through a predilection for any model is unscientific, as well as biased. Models may determine the way to view clients, to use processes, and to explain outcomes—no matter who the client or what the problem. How does one find a way to choose among models? What values, purposes, and commanding circumstances shape a clinician's choice?

The overriding necessity is to make an assessment of the situation in which the clinician is to intervene. The wider the psychosocial perspective, or the more clinicians allow into their perspective, the more numerous the significant variables will be. Difficult though it is to consider complexity—be the factors inner or outer—the greatest scientific validity is achieved through the most realistic perspective. Thus, to view a child who fails in school only as a child with a fear of achievement or only as a failure of the school is to fail to appreciate the real complexity that can be found only in a psychosocial (or ecosystems) perspective. Use of the psychosocial perspective will require an assessment of variables to account for the inner and outer situations. The exploration and assessment will tell it all. It will tell who and what is involved in the case at hand, and—given a clinician informed by an appropriately broad range of knowledge—an assessment will indicate what intervention is needed. Upon contracting with the client as to desired outcome, the clinician will have a conception of the professional task ahead.

Only after this process of assessment is accomplished is it possible to know what is needed, what the client wants, and what is possible to do. Then—and only then—is it useful to select a practice model. The use of a model prior to the assessment can narrow the vision and predetermine the outcome. That may be the most serious limitation in using particular models, but this limitation can be mitigated by the practitioners' knowledge of a repertoire of models from which can be derived a true eclectic practice of "doing what is needed."

Practice theorists will continue to develop models, although it is unlikely that in the future there will be increasing empirical evidence to support the use of any particular model. Even when evidence of effectiveness is presented, it is unlikely that a single overriding, holistic practice model can be devised to meet all requirements of all situations. Thus, as the clinical social work practitioner assesses the case and selects an appropriate model, it is the repertoire that matters. The most knowledgeable practitioner will know more and have a broader repertoire from which to choose. But all clinicians should know how to look scientifically at cases, how to assess the problem, and how to decide upon interventions most likely to work within the idiosyncratic circumstances thrust forward by the case and its demands. The case—problem, situation, and condition of life—is the phenomenon that needs empirical attention. What works for whom under what circumstances? Future models should derive from investigations of these differences; the phase of development of models from the wisdom and genius of theorists is over.

References

Bartlett, H. M. *The Common Base of Social Work Practice.* New York: National Association of Social Workers, 1970.

Bendix, R. "The Pitfalls of Reductionism." In N. J. Smelser and W. T. Smelser (Eds.), *Personality and Social Systems.* New York: Wiley, 1968.

Bloom, M. "Challenges to the Helping Professions and the Response of Scientific Practice." *Social Service Review,* 1978, *52* (4), 584–595.

Carew, R. "The Place of Knowledge in Social Work Activity." *British Journal of Social Work,* 1979, *9* (3), 349–364.

Fischer, J. *Effective Casework Practice.* New York: McGraw-Hill, 1978.

Germain, C. "Casework and Science: A Study in the Sociology of Knowledge." Unpublished doctoral dissertation, School of Social Welfare, Columbia University, 1972.

Hartman, A. *Casework in Crises 1932–1941.* Unpublished doctoral dissertation, School of Social Welfare, Columbia University, 1972.

Jayaratne, S. "A Study of Clinical Eclecticism." *Social Service Review,* 1978, *52* (4), 629–642.

Jenkins, S. *The Ethnic Dilemma in Social Services.* New York: Free Press, 1981.

Kettner, P. M. "A Framework for Comparing Practice Models." *Social Service Review,* 1975, *49* (4), 629–642.

Lowry, F. (Ed.). *Readings in Social Casework.* New York: Columbia University Press, 1939.

McGowan, B. "Self-Help and the Provision of Family Services." *Cross-National Studies of Social Services and Family Policy.* New York: School of Social Welfare, Columbia University, 1979.

Meyer, C. H. "Practice Models—The New Ideology." *Smith College Studies in Social Work,* 1973, *43* (2), 85–98.

National Association of Social Workers. *NASW Register of Clinical Social Workers.* (2nd ed.) Washington, D.C.: National Association of Social Workers, 1978.

Nelsen, J. "Social Work Fields of Practice, Methods, and Models: The Choice to Act." *Social Service Review,* 1975, *49* (2), 264–270.

Reid, W., and Epstein, L. *Task-Centered Practice.* New York: Columbia Press, 1977.

Richmond, M. E. *Social Diagnosis.* New York: Russell Sage Foundation, 1917.

Roberts, R., and Nee, R. (Eds.). *Theories of Social Casework.* Chicago: University of Chicago Press, 1970.

Roberts, R., and Northen, H. *Theories of Social Work with Groups.* New York: Columbia Press, 1976.

Siporin, M. "Practice Theory for Clinical Social Work." *Clinical Social Work Journal,* 1979, 7 (1), 75–87.

Solomon, B. *Black Empowerment.* New York: Columbia University Press, 1976.

Turner, F. J. *Social Work Treatment: Interlocking Theoretical Approaches.* (2nd ed.) New York: Free Press, 1979.

33

Values and Ideological Dilemmas in Professional Education

Gary A. Lloyd

This chapter is fugal in nature. Themes are introduced, discussed, and assessed only to disappear and be reintroduced later in conjunction with other themes. The musical fugue is taxing to create and to comprehend. Its composer must bring out recurring themes so that they can be heard and at the same time blend them into a sonorous whole. Any writer on the subject of clinical social work education must reach for a similar accomplishment. Issues of theory development, practice specializations, and curriculum structure are complex and must be examined from several vantage points. Clinical social work itself cannot be simplified and discussed as a single or unified component of professional social work.

If for no other reason, lack of integrative theories and varying ideological positions on the "best" way to educate for clinical practice create problems of boundary and scope that cannot be resolved or understood within a single perspective. To complicate the analytic task further, clinical social work is a distinct practice (with its internal themes and variations) and is also an integral part of the social work profession (which has its own complementary and sometimes dissonant themes). As a body of knowledge, mode of practice, or world view, clinical social work, can be perceived as different from policy, planning, administration, and community organization or—to use the current jargon—"macro-social work." It can be perceived as one of several social work methods or as a specialization or as the central form of social work practice and the major emphasis of social work education. Each of these points of view has been ascendant in social work education at different times, and all exist simultaneously today.

Because of the varied ways in which clinical social work is perceived, problems of definition and boundaries are dealt with extensively here. For the moment, Meyer's (1979) point of view that all direct practice with individuals is clinical will serve as a defining statement. Clinical methods are those used to help individuals (qua individuals, or as members of groups or families) fulfill concrete, intrapsychic, and interpersonal needs. Clinical social work educators strive to prepare graduates with knowledge and skill sufficient to support practice aimed at helping people resolve, ameliorate, or prevent problems and at fostering interpersonal and self-development.

Clinical social work can be understood only in the context of the profession of which it is a part. A contextual orientation to education for clinical social work will be evident in this chapter, at the admitted risk of blurring focus and turning a fugue into a round. Several questions are addressed at varying levels of detail:

- How are changing definitions of the purposes and scope of clinical social work reflected in curricula?
- How are theories supportive of clinical social work practice developed and evaluated?
- What is the influence of the continuing debate about the balance of knowledge (theory) and skill on curriculum development for clinical social work education?
- What are the curricular issues related to education for clinical social work with respect to the structure of professional education, the purposes of the
- What are the implications of generalist and advanced generalist practice models for educating clinical social workers?
- What are the effects of multilevel professional education on the development and organization of curricula for clinical social work?
- How is clinical social work education affected by emerging human services programs and highly specialized clinical training programs, for example, in marriage and family therapy?

Definitions and Purposes

Although educators and practitioners increasingly use the phrase clinical social work, it is as much a euphemism for social casework, social treatment, or direct practice as it is a distinctively new practice field. While the term *clinical* is repugnant to some social work educators because it connotes a medical model or approach to practice based upon assumptions about individual pathology, its use is increasing. For other educators, the clinical prefix strengthens definition and public understanding of social work treatment or casework with individuals, families, and groups. As Goldstein's (1980) work indicates, a centrist position is possible. She notes that the term *clinical* "either evokes an image of people in white medical garb, diagnosing diseases and prescribing medication or surgical cures, or it suggests the status, roles, practices, and theories associated with dynamic psychiatry in general and with private, insight-oriented, individual psychotherapy or family treatment of white, middle-class heterosexuals or intact families" (p. 175). She concludes, however, that clients "do not have to be sick or pathological to benefit from services directed toward enhancing their ability to cope" and that social work practice "does not have to be narrowly conceived of as psychotherapeutic in nature of treatment in order to be therapeutic in outcome" (p. 175). As will be seen, the pull is strong toward rather narrow definitions of clinical social work treatment as therapy, but a broader view of practice taken by Goldstein and others also is reflected in clinical social work curricula today.

If clinical social work is not synonymous with circumscribed definitions of therapy, what is it? What differentiates a clinical social worker and clinical social work education from clinicians and education for other professions? Clinical social workers (and all social workers, for that matter) have for many years concerned themselves not only with individual functioning but also with the interaction of human beings and their social environments. The concept of *social environment* is as central to defining, teaching, and practicing clinical social work as are ideas about personal coping and motivation. According to a recent Council on Social Work Education (CSWE) National Association of Social Workers (NASW) Task Force on Specialization, social workers practice in the "transaction zone": the "fundamental zone of social work . . . where people and their environment are in exchange with each other. Social work historically has focused on this transaction zone, where the exchange between people and the environments which impinge on them results in changes in both" (Council on Social Work Education, 1979b, p. 2).

Clinical social work curricula reflect this dual focus on individual and environment. A major theoretical task yet to be accomplished in clinical social work is to place this interactional view less simplistically within the context of complex systems of multiple actors and environments of varying dimensions. As more adequate, encompassing theories are developed, the student/practitioner will be better equipped than is now possible to make sense of disparate data coming from different sources and to deal with idiosyncratic personal problems within a social context. Social work educators have understood the nature of their theoretical problem for generations, but have not moved far in developing theory, nor substantially beyond Hamilton's (1951) description thirty years ago of a social case as a living event "within which there are always economic, physical, mental, emotional, and social factors in varying proportions" (p. 304).

Devising curricula that combine the interactional focus with attention to internal and intrapsychic phenomena has been difficult for clinical social work educators. Even if, as will be seen, contemporary meta-theories were more helpful than they are, judging how best to intervene in the transaction zone would be difficult. The question of how to develop practice-based theory and theory-based practice, particularly with regard to the interactional perspective, is nettlesome.

Existing issues and difficulties are succinctly summarized by Minahan (1980) in six provocative questions. When social workers do clinical work, she asks:

- Is the environment merely a backdrop or stage set that affects individual emotions, cognition, and behaviors and thus should be understood by the social worker but not viewed as a legitimate target of change?
- Should the social worker always focus on unconscious drives and fantasies of clients?
- Are people in the many environments impinging on individuals viewed by the social worker as legitimate targets for social work intervention?
- Should the social worker focus on the conscious coping behavior of people and their aspirations and life choices?
- Is the professional relationship between social worker and clients the major tool in helping clients?

- Should and can social workers manage productive relationships to achieve a professional purpose, on behalf of clients, with people in clients' immediate environment and with other people whose actions are needed to assist clients in achieving their needs and aspirations? [p. 171]

Such questions are undoubtedly familiar to clinical social work educators attempting to devise curricula based on interactional (or transaction zone) concepts. In both education and practice, the dual focus of social work has led to polarization within the profession (and thus to diffuse boundaries) and to sometimes erratic borrowing of theory. Education for clinical social work reflects the profession-at-large, with its theoretical eclecticism, uncertainty and focus, common and conflicting values, competing ideologies, and diverse methodological orientations. Beginning with the first training programs for "friendly visitors" (caseworkers) in the late nineteenth century and continuing to the present, professional education has encompassed study of both personality and the social environment. *Social environment,* it should be noted, has been defined as narrowly as a client's immediate family or reference group and as broadly as social institutions. However defined, until rather recently students were usually prepared to assess the impingement of the social environment from the restricted vantage point of the professional social worker's office. Social work students were oriented more to intrapsychic than to interpersonal phenomena. Whether environmental manipulation required professional skills was an open question. Today, educators strive to broaden the clinical curriculum to include resource location and development, and understanding of sociocultural and ethnic influences on individual and family behavior. Significantly, educators have reached consensus in that their curriculum objectives and teaching must encompass study of theories and interventions related to interacting individuals and environments.

Similar agreement does not exist about the particular knowledge, values, and skills that are fundamental to remedial or preventive practice within the interactional frame of reference. To confound the situation, clinical social work education—again reflecting the profession—lays claim to functions of enormous scope and conceptual ambiguity: socialization, social action, policy analysis, advocacy, and the development and provision of social services. Students of clinical social work usually study in some, if not all, of these areas. Given the breadth of knowledge to be mastered and the lack of integrative theories, it should not be surprising that students (and faculties) of clinical social work seek anchors in particular and circumscribed methods and roles. Tension exists within education between broadly stated social goals and aspirations and more limited, individualistic, and allegedly realistic practice curricula.

Whenever tentative agreement about purposes, definitions, and theories appears imminent, social realities seem to shift, and the fit between what is taught and what are considered to be the realities of practice is again loosened. Thus, the "right" curriculum for clinical social work is as changeable as changing human needs. That being so, the desire to keep practice curricula relevant often encourages the indulgence of fads, inattention to systematic theory development, and, as Rein (1970) has noted, efforts to derive legitimacy from clients served rather than from demonstrated competence (p. 14).

The problematic relationship of curricula to changing human needs militates against clear-cut definitions either of purposes or of a knowledge base. The interactional world view, which brings to social work much of its richness and diversity while guaranteeing irresolution, continues to serve as bedrock. Harry Lurie's (1954) comment a quarter of a century ago holds true today: "Social work, whether it focuses its attention on an individual, a family, a group of people, or an entire community is socially oriented" (p. 31).

That social work educators have understood the centrality of the social and interactional orientation is clear through definitions of methods and statements or purposes formulated over several decades. Those definitions and statements were reflected first in training programs and then in higher education for social work, which for a considerable period of the profession's history was virtually synonymous with social casework, the precursor of clinical social work.

Curricula for training friendly visitors testified to a view that individual character defect was a major cause of distress. Direct contact and influence by someone wiser and more experienced was seen as a necessary corrective. Expectations were high for the volunteers and paid agents who participated in the training programs, which had been inspired by desires for scientific philanthropy founded on tested and transmittable principles rather than on sentiment. C. R. Henderson (1901) wrote, for example, that the friendly visitor was expected to be a "walking encyclopedia of knowledge about nutritious and economical foods, hygienic dress, the best fuel and stoves, and must also be an electric storage battery of cheerfulness, courage, hope, and inspiring sympathy, with all these resources on draft as required by the neighbors" (p. 161). Individually oriented methods were taught. In those early years, environmental conditions were not ignored entirely, but the training programs dealt with them mainly by cataloguing the incidence of poor housing and disease.

Considering environmental forces secondary to character defect as the source of distress and individual example and inspiration as major methods of intervention became difficult in the midst of the economic panics and depressions that characterized the formative years of social work. Awareness grew during the closing years of the nineteenth century, and continued to develop in the Progressive Era, that certain needs were basic to human dignity and survival. That awareness required modification of traditional and doctrinaire pronouncements about self-reliance and character defects. Slowly it was learned that even the most scientific philanthropy was inadequate if it did not pay heed both to subjective human needs and values and to the sometimes devastating impact of social forces beyond the control of a person, family, or community. As training programs evolved into schools of social work in the first decades of the twentieth century, the new awareness was reflected in curricula that, while retaining emphasis on individual problems and causation, included courses in "social diagnosis" and political economy. In the Progressive Era, some social work educators turned their attention to modification of the environment through research and education programs about slums, illness and public health measures, and poverty and nutrition; it was hoped that by providing wholesome places to live and work, people's lives would be changed.

Not every caseworker was a convert to this point of view. The dichotomy between individual and social orientation, therapy and social action, was drawn very early. Curricula to educate social workers were influenced at the outset by two points of view, which taken at their extremes are: (1) that individuals have only themselves to blame for their problems and (2) that the environment shapes and determines individual character. The methodological corollaries of these principles are: (1) practice to change character and (2) practice to modify social environments. The pioneers of social work brought both points of view—described by Mary Richmond (1917) as retail and wholesale reform—into the same frame of reference (pp. 214–221). By so doing, they laid the groundwork for casework to develop a variety of activities, which in later years would be called *clinical* and *therapeutic,* and established precedents for both family therapy and community organization.

A doctrine of self-help that had emerged along with the character defect theory remained in casework in modified form as a point of philosophy and guidance for intervention. Students were taught to work toward a goal of client independence. As Cannon and Klein (1933) put it, casework was practiced to put clients into "a position which would enable them to achieve the fullest possible nature of self-help" (p. 3). Almost a half century later, Crouch (1979) defined social work (the interchangeability of the terms remains apparent) as "the attempt to assist those who do not command the means of human subsistence in acquiring them and in attaining the highest possible degree of independence" (p. 46). Self-help gradually became defined as both means and end, depending upon clients' circumstances, and was incorporated as an ideology into curricula, thus broadening definitions of social work practice with individuals, families, and groups. The self-help philosophy was placed within the person-environment perspective. That is, casework students were taught during the first quarter of the twentieth century that environmental forces might diminish or obviate possibilities for self-help. As in many other areas of teaching about practice, maintaining balance was difficult, not only because of conceptual weaknesses, but because the traditional linking of self-help and a "blaming the victim" outlook remained strong.

As these perceptions of self-help were emerging, educators were emphasizing casework goals of individual or personal change within a context of a social environment, but an individualistic orientation persisted. For example, five years after her exhaustive review of the initial phase of social casework and of the uses of social evidence in *Social Diagnosis,* Mary Richmond (1917) offered a concise definition of social casework in *What Is Social Casework?* "Social casework," she wrote, "consists of those processes which develop personality through adjustments consciously effected, individual by individual, between men and their social environment" (1922, pp. 98–99).

Although maintaining balance was arduous, Richmond and others in education and practice did attempt to develop a holistic view. Devising curricula that incorporated that holistic perspective was difficult because by the 1920s social work practice, services, and curricula were fragmented and organized around populations in need (families and children), social control agencies (schools, probation), and specializations linked to other professions (medical and psychiatric social work). In the decade of the 1920s, moreover, all aspects of social work were deeply affected by the introduction of psychodynamic theories and Freudian concepts. Social workers, particularly psychiatric social workers, eagerly adopted the Freudian canon, finding in it both conceptual usefulness and a means of forging stronger ties to psychiatry. Ready acceptance of psychodynamic theory and the development of psychiatric social work as a discrete practice field closely aligned (at least in the developmental years) with psychiatry somewhat attenuated the process of elaborating the person-environment paradigm. As noted in a survey conducted by the American Association of Psychiatric Social Workers, as early as 1925 family welfare agencies "were employing psychiatric social workers or were providing means whereby their own staff might add mental hygiene and social psychiatry to their equipment" (French, 1940, p. 26). The same study found that "psychoanalysis has had in the last several years a marked influence upon the whole field of social work. Courses offered to social workers by leaders representing the field of psychoanalysis have been very popular, resulting in a tendency to accept generally and perhaps uncritically psychoanalytic interpretations of behavior" (p. 10). Nevertheless, the psychoanalytic focus had not wholly obliterated the social orientation of social work. French, for example, described the psychiatric social worker's functions as follows: "First, she . . . analyzes the patient's social situation in relation to his present difficulty; such analysis is based upon a study of conditions in his home, family, and neighborhood, and his attitude toward them. . . . Second, she interprets to the family the patient's problem . . . always keeping in close touch with changing conditions in the home and family life, which may cause an adaptation in plans. Third, she aids the patient and family to work out a program for a more adequate social adjustment. . . . And, last, she interprets the diagnosis and plans for treatment to her coworkers or to members of other social agencies. . ." (p. 17).

Attention to the social orientation was also indicated by the assertion in the report of the survey that "the years of the depression have resulted in a general swing of interest from intensive treatment of individual problems to a general program of social welfare, from adjustment of an individual to his environment to the establishment of social conditions that will prevent burdens of insecurity and fear so great that adjustment is impossible" (p. 21). While it is difficult to separate rhetoric from fact in this observation, the comment itself indicates the ways in which practice (and doubtless education) had lost the person-environment balance; the focus on the individual is clear.

Curricula in many schools of social work between 1930 and 1955 strongly emphasized psychodynamic theories and ego psychology. Despite efforts to hold attention on environmental factors and influences, those years were the "age of psychiatry" for social work education, during which almost everything was defined in psychological terms. Riessman and Miller (1964)—writing in a period when many social workers challenged the psychodynamic approach—remarked that the psychodynamic world view had been costly to social work in two ways: "It deflected analysis and action from nonpsychodynamic (for example, social) approaches and it often contaminated the original problem by introducing inappropriate modes of attack" (pp. 29–38).

Analyzing early developments in social work, Brieland (1975) noted that "eventually a marriage with psychiatry was consummated, and casework developed a medical model that emphasized personality change through psychosocial treatment" (p. 253). He argues however, that not all social workers were influenced by the medical model. "They continued their concerns with helping a person get more marketable skills and a better job, reducing family conflict by talking with other family members, trying to provide childcare, and improving housing. Those activities, however, *were usually considered secondary to treatment, which was centered directly on a better self-concept or an increase in ego strength*" (p. 253 [emphasis added]). While some social workers may have held to the concerns mentioned by Brieland, they found variable or minimal class and field support in the schools—regardless of whether they studied psychiatric or school social work—for environmental manipulation. Here again, the survey by the American Association of Psychiatric Social Workers is instructive. Curricula of eight schools of social work were scrutinized in 1940. With no significant exceptions, those schools offered specialized course work for psychiatric social work students in human behavior, psychopathology, behavior problems of children, clinical demonstration, advanced psychiatry, and social implications of mental testing. Such curriculum offerings seem to support critics who maintain that the medical model and psychiatric orientation did in fact dominate; indeed, many of the courses were taught by psychiatrists. If a contextual view is taken, however, the impression changes slightly. Social work educators never abandoned the social orientation entirely. Each of the eight schools required additional content for the training of psychiatric social workers, which included courses in social casework, social statistics or social research, health and disease or public health, community organization, and child welfare. All but one required fieldwork in family or child welfare agencies (French, 1940).

Clearly, psychological theories (and related curricula) were characteristic of social work education for a long time. The broader or more holistic outlook endured, however, and is evident in influential texts that began to appear in the 1950s, as well as in papers and speeches of the 1940s. Hamilton's (1951) observation on the social case, alluded to earlier, is typical: "A social case is composed of internal and external or environmental factors. One does not deal with people in a physical sense or with environment in a physical sense, but treats individuals in relation not only to their social experiences but also to their feelings about their experience. So when one thinks of a social case, one must always consider it in terms of both inner and outer interacting factors" (pp. 3–4).

In her widely used text, Perlman (1957) defined social casework as "a process used by certain human welfare agencies to help individuals to cope more effectively with their problems in social functioning" (p. 4). Hollis (1964) observed that casework had always been a psychosocial treatment method. In her influential book, she developed the point that psychosocial treatment "recognized both internal psychological and external social causes of dysfunctioning and endeavors to enable the individual to meet his needs more fully and to function more adequately in his social relationships" (p. 9). In their more recent application of systems concepts to defining social work practice, Pincus and Minahan (1973) state that the "focus of social work practice is on the interactions between people and systems in the social environments" (p. 3). In his text focused more directly on clinical social work, Turner (1974) defines psychosocial therapy in a way that summarizes many previous definitions of social casework and points to a not unfamiliar but nevertheless changed and broadened approach to clinical social work education and practice.

In Turner's (1978) view, psychosocial therapy is: "that form of psychotherapeutic practice in which the bio-psychosocial knowledge of human and societal behavior; skills in relating to individuals, families, groups, and communities; and competence in mobilizing available resources are combined in the medium of individual, group, and familial relationships to alter their personality, behavior, or situation in a manner that will contribute to the attainment of satisfying, fulfilling human functioning within the framework of their own values and goals and the available resources of society" (p. 5). An internal-external perspective is also brought out in Whittaker's (1974) definition of social treatment as "an approach to interpersonal helping which utilizes direct and indirect strategies of intervention to aid individuals, families, and small groups in improving social functioning and coping with social problems" (p. 49).

Closely correlating enduring themes and changing definitions with modification in curriculum philosophy and content is impossible. Definitions nevertheless provide evidence of longstanding interest in, and attention to, environmental influences on human behavior. To reiterate, maintaining in curricula a balanced outlook on the transaction zone has been difficult. The interactional frame of reference implies compelling need for theories and paradigms to aid students in understanding and dealing with extremely complex relationships and situations. In the absence of such, social work educators have frequently reduced and simplified their field of interest. Incongruence between definitions, aspirations and rhetoric, and what actually was taught is evident. Today, efforts are made continuously to develop concepts and frames of reference that will help students of clinical social work learn about and cope with complex, interacting systems. Simultaneously, a more traditional method of handling complexity is at work. A tendency to narrow the field through methods orientations or dichotomizing social work functions and concerns is discernible and strong. Three major problems identified by Cannon and Klein in the 1930s are still in evidence: "the determination of the character and scope of the subject matter in the field; the selection of material from the subject matter, and its organization into courses comprising the curriculum; and the development of teaching methods which will contribute most effectively to the development in students of proficiency as practitioners" (1933, p. 7).

Dichotomies and Curricula

From the beginning of professionalization to the present, tension and friction have existed between the wholesalers and retailers, the people-changers and systems-changers. Currently, even as social work educators work on generalist curricula and some speak of social work as a generalist profession, dichotomies persist. Despite consensus on the need for a social orientation, the ways in which that orientation are best presented in curricula are subjects of debate. Social work remains divided like some disputed territory. Partisans of "micro" practice look askance at advocates of the "macro" areas. The contentious sentiment is as often as not fully reciprocated. Such ideological divisiveness has often had negative impact on curriculum development for clinical social work. It militates against a contextual examination of the curriculum objectives and content needed to prepare clinical practitioners who are also social workers. Energies that might go into developing theories of intervention are frequently displaced by a perceived need to defend a particular mode of practice. At some times (such as in the 1960s) clinical social workers have responded to attack by withdrawing; at other times (such as the present) they have responded by narrowing purposes and expectations and expanding the domains from which to borrow theory. In either instance, the consequences of drawing dichotomies of the kind Parad (1958) once defined as "deceptive" continue to support confusion about professional means and ends. Parad's dichotomies included those which social workers have drawn (and have reflected in curriculum design) between the conscious and unconscious, individual and environment, research and practice, generic and specific, and treatment and prevention.

Dichotomizing is one way of dealing with complexity; another is to narrow focus. The narrowing approach is discernible in some educational programs today that direct minimal attention to environmental issues and that graduate students whose primary aim is to "do therapy." The resulting paradox is that the profession, which espouses the goal of transforming social systems or at least mitigating social injustice, trains many of its practitioners to engage in the narrowest kind of therapeutic practice.

The social-environment orientation of clinical social work is also reduced and made more manageable through a methods orientation. Clinical social work educators have attuned themselves as much to method as to theory. A desire for replicable technique coexists with the valued, idiosyncratic use of self on behalf of others. Science and art compete, and to art goes the victory. Clinical social workers struggle with all of the so-called helping professions to find a workable balance between intuitive artistry and empirically based theory. Although increasing numbers of educators attempt to evaluate clinical social work practice with systematic methods of research, resistance to measuring is strong both in academe and in the practice field. Methods of intervention, often bereft of solid theoretical support, develop into ideologies. The methodological orientation helps social workers draw boundaries and select theory, but at a risk of restricting vision and displacing goals. Although social circumstances, nomenclature, and curriculum goals and designs have changed over the years, Younghusband's (1968) acerbic comment about social work in general can still be applied to clinical social work: "For reasons which could themselves constitute a paper, American social work now finds itself possessed by rather than being the designer of its methods of providing services" (p. 18).

During most of social work's history, social casework was viewed as its primary method, which was practiced within various settings and specializations. Even though the methods orientation has always been strong, it has not gone unchallenged. During the early professionalization period, for example, teachers and practitioners of social casework expressed concern about the proliferation of specializations and the meaning of that for the profession's identity. The Milford Conference of 1923 to 1929 was the first major effort to define common elements within social casework that had to be mastered by the student, irrespective of field of practice or specialization. While the deliberations of the conference did not have immediate consequence for abridging dichotomies or diminishing emphasis on methods per se (because it was focused on casework), a precedent was set for systematic search for elements of generic practice. Particularly during the 1960s, that search was extended to finding concepts, theories, values, and practice modes that were common to all social work practice, regardless of methods employed. Concern about the attractions of a limited vision of therapy, discontent with the individual focus of much social treatment, and, finally, vociferous criticism of social casework during the War on Poverty era led clinical social work educators to participate in a search for a meta-theory that would integrate fragments of social work practice wisdom, social and behavioral science theories, and the myriad tasks assumed by the clinical worker. Introduction and acceptance of social science concepts in the 1950s and of social systems theories in the 1960s exemplified this search. Although social workers generally tended to oversimplify the systems framework (particularly when trying to adapt general systems theories to social work uses), it had heuristic value and was congruent with the interactional perspective. But, as Meyer (1970) observed, the "theory has so many attractive possibilities as a scheme for organizing knowledge and as a framework for action that one must be careful to avoid overdetermining its value and thus ironically creating a closed system of the theory itself" (p. 125).

While general and social systems theories provided an analytic approach to understanding the dynamic interplay of people and their environments, they did not—despite expectations of some educators—guide the practitioner toward more effective intervention into interactional and interpersonal problems. Systems theories provided a useful set of metaphors and may have ameliorated somewhat problems arising from dichotomizing and methods orientations. Education for clinical social work now includes and applies systems concepts to both individual and organizational behavior. Systems theories have joined those of Freud, the ego psychology and role theorists, symbolic interactionists, and behaviorists in the theoretical jambalaya of clinical social work.

By 1970 two polar impulses were discernible within the profession and within clinical social work education. Some educators (probably a minority) wished to hold to the traditional methods orientation while at the same time acknowledging its limitations and overcoming them through such compromise courses as "Group Work for Caseworkers." Others sought to redefine practice within the systems framework and to develop a curriculum that broke free, at least in part, of particular methods in favor of more generalized or generic study. Although the latter point of view gained popularity, the urge toward unification through theory coexisted with forces tending toward specificity in practice.

Curricula of the traditional vein placed heavy emphasis on individual and family functioning. Distinct methods courses were taught, often accompanied by courses organized around fields of practice. Curricula included content on interviewing and casework techniques, theory of human growth and development (usually Freudian and psychodynamic), and direct experience with clients in field practice. Concern about environmental and social influences led to inclusion of courses on social policy and (sometimes) community organization and administration. Research was included in many curricula but often viewed as an unnecessary subject area for clinical social work students.

While those traditional curriculum areas are still reflected in the official *Curriculum Policy Statement* of the Council on Social Work Education (1969), the content and structure of social work curricula have changed. After revisions of the *Policy Statement* in 1969, educators were free to experiment with curriculum design and to offer nontraditional courses. Curriculum objectives in many schools began to reflect the search for unifying principles and theories. Social workers moved through the 1970s with a hope of unity, if not about general purposes, about the objectives and techniques of intervention with individuals, families, and groups. Led by Meyer, Minahan, and Pincus, social work educators increasingly adopted a systems framework and a broadened definition of clinical social work. Curricula were expanded to include more specific attention to ethnic/minority concerns and cross-cultural perspectives. Social work's traditional, if downplayed, role of developing social resources was accentuated. As social workers evaluated their curricula in the context of the status revolutions of the 1960s and 1970s, methodological fragmentation appeared insupportable when so many people needed so many kinds of services provided by an enormous, erratically funded, and barely coordinated service network.

To some social work educators, this direction was alarming; for others it was an indication that social work education was returning to origins, to the social (and hence broadened) orientation that deemphasized individually and psychologically oriented methods and accentuated environmental and systemic forces.

Clinical Social Work Curricula

As clinical social work educators participated in the search for unifying theories and processes, critical decisions about curriculum format and content were made, centered in part about the balance between micro- and macro-content to be mastered by the student of clinical social work. Curricula have been organized in almost every conceivable structure and combination of theories to reflect the interactional imperative, to mirror and counter the complexities of social work's general purposes, and to provide knowledge for specific practice within a general framework.

Although clinical social work educators have evaluated and broadened the scope of their curricula, they have not found consensus about knowledge and theory, which is absolutely essential for competent and autonomous practice of clinical social work. While currently there is disaffection with traditional psychodynamic approaches, courses in human behavior and social environment, for example, are as likely as not to include traditional ego psychology theories of human development, alongside social science notions about culture and ethnicity, and behavioral science concepts of collective and organizational behavior. To take up an earlier point, students often react to such diversity by seeking security and certainty in a method, field of practice, or restricted definition of therapy. Paradoxically, the movement toward general, unifying theory may now be culminating in a return to methodological fragmentation, preoccupation with specific skills, and narrowing conceptions of clinical social work practice. Because there is no single definition to give form to clinical social work curricula, structure and content are extremely variable. The academic and practice components often march to different drums as faculties try to teach a unifying set of principles or generalist conceptions of practice, while practice-based field instructors teach "relevant," particularized, methods-oriented techniques and skills.

It is possible that in many schools, students will graduate poorly prepared for clinical practice beyond the therapeutic function. Goldstein (1980) states the result bluntly: "Practitioners have an incomplete, oversimplified, and overgeneralized view of what effective coping means, how it develops, and what environmental conditions and interventive strategies foster it. For those social work practitioners who, within social work's overall mission, are compelled and challenged by the need for an individualizing direct practice role with clients—that is, by a need for working directly with people and environments rather than engaging in social action—there is a necessity to define the knowledge base that will give sufficient life and depth to the notion that human beings are individuals in transaction with their environment. Defining this base is the profession's challenge" (p. 175).

In the absence of clear definition of "an individualizing direct practice role," clinical social work may be returning to a field of practice and methods orientation. Clearly, educators today are bereft of the quiet confidence of Harriett M. Bartlett (1959) writing that "Social work has now arrived at a point of a unified profession where the relation between the whole and its parts can be understood clearly" (p. 159). Precisely because unity does not exist, despite two decades of efforts to identify unifying theories, a tendency toward narrowing definitions of practice domain is resurgent. Where at one time the narrowing had been accomplished by selecting one theory and applying it to all sorts of problems regardless of appropriateness, the process today seems to be more in the direction of defining the therapeutic role as being synonymous with clinical social work and the generalist model as being antithetical to clinical social work. The therapeutic role, ambivalently defined within the medical model, is juxtaposed with the individual-environment-interaction or transaction zone model. Problems of theory-practice and academic-field congruence are critical. Although the clinical social work conception of therapy has been extended beyond that of psychiatry and psychology to include attention to resource development, linkage, and utilization of social support networks, a more restricted view of *clinical* is still reflected in curriculum development, teaching, role modeling, and field practice in many graduate programs in social work.

In sum, conflicting goals and an eclectic theoretical framework are characteristic of most clinical social work programs. Although a few may select one theory or set of related theories, most teach and seek to apply a variety of theories additively, binding them together somewhat tenuously with systems theories. This approach has the advantage of a broadened perspective on people and their problems; a disadvantage is a reduced demand for theoretical rigor because there is so much to be scanned and no one theory to be mastered as an essential basis for practice. Although it can be argued that adherence to Freudian theory over a long period of the profession's history had negative consequences for clinical social work education and practice, mastering that theory placed upon students intellectual and personal demands that are absent in much education for clinical social work today.

As clinical social work educators have moved from concentration on one body of theory to eclecticism, boundary problems have been accentuated. When a broadened definition of "clinical" work is accepted, many of the tasks and functions now to be learned and practiced by the clinical social worker may appear to differ little from those used by social workers in other roles and settings. To those educators who want to foster social work as a generalist profession, that is an encouraging direction. For educators who believe that there is a place for the individualizing role, such development indicates weakened practice skill and professional identity.

Early development of an integrative meta-theory is unlikely. That being so, arguments are heard that knowing how to assess and apply theories selectively and differentially is itself a legitimate and essential professional skill to be acquired through formal education and practicum experience. From that vantage point, a general theory underlying clinical social work or unifying the theoretical base of practice is a chimera. For those of different persuasion, the conviction stands that without more clearly defined theory, students will not have a frame of reference with which to develop interpersonal skills. Perhaps, in view of the present state of the clinical social work art, the opposition of an "application" focus and a "framework" focus creates yet another false dichotomy. For the foreseeable future, it is probable that social work educators will be developing and changing curricula according to both perspectives. The current range and diversity in theory and approaches to teaching clinical practice will be maintained. As a consequence, at one end of the spectrum some teachers of clinical social work are applying psychodynamic theories, helping their students identify problems of id and superego, and concerning themselves about transference. At the other end are clinical social work educators teaching social treatment with individuals, families, and groups; preoccupied with systems theories, communications patterns, and social roles; and adapting action therapies eclectically to social work practice. At all points along that continuum, the probability is high that environmental factors will be to a greater or lesser degree attended to, and the focus on intrapsychic and interpersonal aspects of human behavior will vary. Within a social orientation, be it explicitly or implicitly conveyed, some clinical educators help their students explore their clients' past, while others keep their focus with equal vigor on the here and now. In brief, contemporary curricula for clinical social work education reflect all kinds of practice modes and theoretical orientations. That situation is likely to hold for a long time to come, given the array of available theories, absence of integrative paradigms, boundary problems, lure of the therapeutic image and status, and uncertainty about the nature of environmental interventions in clinical practice.

Teaching Skills for Clinical Practice

Skills necessary for clinical social work practice include: interviewing; forming and working with problem-solving, task, and developmental groups; intervening into various family systems and subsystems; engaging persons on their own behalf in developing and strengthening resource networks; providing information and direct access to resources needed by individuals, families, and formed groups; linking people and services; instructing in human development and dysfunction; interpreting the impact of environment (including political and economic) on the behavior of individuals and families; and participating in team approaches to treatment and change.

This is by no means an exhaustive listing of skills expected of the beginning level graduate of a clinical social work program. In part because of the various problems discussed in this chapter and in part because of the range of content that must be included to develop and support even a minimal range of skills, concern is now frequently expressed about the degree of clinical skill a student is likely to acquire in the usual course of study. There is growing doubt about the expertise of the graduate clinical social worker. That doubt emanates from convictions of some educators and practitioners that the social orientation has been too broadly defined. Others gladly accept reinforcement of the social orientation but are bothered nevertheless by the resultant need to master many disparate skills in a relatively brief period of time. Because most graduate programs provide a generalist foundation before moving students into a clinical track, specialization, or concentration, educators must consider time limitations and scope of content as critical variables in planning curricula that provide both special knowledge about intervention with individuals, families, and groups and general knowledge about other forms and methods of social work intervention. Whether this issue is dichotomized into depth versus breadth, or generalist versus specialist, boundary problems related to skill development are as acute as those relative to theoretical support for practice. Employers of new graduates lament that the neophytes lack specific skills and need immediate in-service training. Some teachers insist that emphasizing skills development encourages a technician mentality, which is even more deleterious to professional practice than being methods-bound. Students complain that they have not had sufficient, specific grounding in particular methods of interpersonal helping.

Few, if any, schools attempt to restrict skills development to the area of intrapsychic phenomena. Curriculum for clinical practice includes courses in social welfare policy and services, research, and so-called macro-electives designed to develop within clinical social workers skill in resource utilization and policy assessment. At times, curriculum objectives include development of research skills in analyzing, for example, caseloads for trends in service and communicating those findings and needs to allocating and decision-making agencies. Curricula include practice courses to prepare students for more specific work with individuals and families. Electives in human functioning and dysfunctioning, theories of change and development, and new approaches to interpersonal helping are often included. Because the *Curriculum Policy Statement* of the Council on Social Work Education is not prescriptive, it would be possible for a clinical program to exclude all policy courses, for example, in favor of a sequence of skills-oriented study providing highly specialized and technical training focused on practice with individuals, families, and groups. Given the growing consensus about the transaction zone as the nexus of social work practice, it is unlikely that any school of social work would make such a radical exclusion. Nevertheless, there are perceptible pressures to reduce the so-called nonclinical content for students of clinical social work and to increase attention to development of specific skills. Arguments are heard that expert clinicians cannot be prepared in a two-year period if a significant amount of time is devoted to generalist study. Students often take courses in social research, administration, and policy under duress, deeming them impractical and unrelated to skills needed for clinical practice.

Questions about skill development bear an obvious relationship to questions about theory. They also bring to the fore the recurring problems of assessing the fit between class and field, theory and practice, breadth and depth. Such concerns are neither new nor confined to educational settings. Edith Abbott (1942) diagnosed the situation as early as 1931: "There can be no question that the social workers need a broad, liberal, disciplinary, professional education in preparation for the important work that is to be undertaken. But when those of us who are in the schools press for a broader curriculum, we are met with the objection on the part of some of our friends representing important social agencies, that such courses as, for example, social statistics, or social politics, are 'not practical.' It is, in fact, made very clear to us that nothing is to be considered 'practical,' and therefore professionally useful, except a limited vocational course" (p. 35). While the vision of clinical social work educators now extends far beyond a limited vocational course, the issues and tensions identified by Abbott endure.

To bring a familiar theme back into the fugue, if professional education is to transcend the vocational course, considerable attention must be given to supporting professional skills with generalizable and verifiable knowledge or theory. Articulation of knowledge and skill is always difficult. In social work, that task is complicated, as indicated above, by the scope and domain of practice claimed by social workers. If, as the Commission on Educational Planning stated in *A Framework for the Explication of Base in Social Work Education,* "skill involves the integration of knowledge and value in practice, is learned through the actual experience of practice, and, as practice integration, needs to be seen as an individualized process for each learner" (Council on Social Work Education, 1979a, p. 10), the task of the clinical educator can only be viewed as awesome. Each of the knowledge areas identified by the Council on Social Work Education/National Association of Social Workers Task Force on Specialization, for example, requires a concomitant skill component. The following list of the knowledge areas prescribed by the task force indicates the enormity of the educator's task in integrating knowledge and value and translating them into skills:

- "Knowledge about the structure of services, public and private, funding arrangements, and the nature of community sanction of the services provided
- Knowledge about the legal framework (laws, codes, rules), which influences or governs the services provided
- Knowledge about the population served (age, epidemiology, populations at risk, class differences, and so forth)
- Knowledge about human and environmental factors, which cause problems at the point of interface between people and institutions
- Knowledge about boundary issues as they relate to the delivery of services (such as the overlapping in specializations, for example, health, mental health)
- Knowledge about problem classification and labeling regardless of the field of practice (mental health and illness, child neglect and abuse, and so forth)
- Knowledge about manpower issues, both interdisciplinary and within social work (for example, B.S.W./M.S.W. issues)
- 'Choreographic ability,' meaning the ability to borrow or use knowledge and put it together for intervention purposes" [Council on Social Work Education, 1979b, Appendix A].

The final area is interesting in the way it summarizes the problems of skill definitions discussed here. Clinical social workers, in this schema, must not only derive and apply skills in myriad areas of theory and fact but must also develop skills in borrowing and using knowledge for intervention purposes. That is the enduring conundrum for clinical educators and all other social work educators as well.

Clinical Social Work Education and Specialization

Trends in social work education toward providing generalist foundation or base knowledge supportive of a broad range of social work practice have raised questions about specialized practice. Lack of consensus about whether social workers should be specialists and, if so, what definition of specialization will be used has many ramifications for curriculum development and teaching in clinical social work.

Historically, social work education developed around methods and fields of practice—such as psychiatric social work—which were in turn linked to some other profession (psychiatry, medicine), to populations (children), or to institutions (social welfare). Until the creation of the National Association of Social Workers (NASW) in 1955, several professional organizations represented the interests of the respective fields. Within schools, curricula were organized usually around the specific requirements and goals of a field of practice. As Kahn (1965) has pointed out, "most of the period prior to the mid-1940s saw a social work profession involved in an intensive, productive, and probably quite necessary effort to cultivate individual fields of practice. A corollary was the limited attention to the whole, the general, the underlying, the common core" (p. 750). Once the Milford Conference had concluded that there were generic or common components of social casework practice, irrespective of the specific practice setting, the resulting generic-specific concept referred to "(1) a body of common concepts and methods—the *generic* aspects of social casework and (2) their application in practice, in a wide range of different settings—the *specific* aspects of social casework" (Bartlett, 1959, p. 162). Such conclusions related to the dominant method were extended in various forms. The NASW Commission on Social Work Practice (1962) decided in 1961 to retain and build upon the fields of practice model, despite inherent problems with it. Both the generic concept and the fields of practice model coexisted in social work curricula from the mid-1950s onward.

Within an often implicit framework of generic knowledge and values, fields of practice continued to serve as means for organizing practice specializations, although ties to particular settings and methods were loosened. Beginning in the late 1950s, social work educators were increasingly concerned with devising curricula that would support both generic practice and specialization. In reaction to stinging criticism of specific, individualized methods, efforts to broaden the scope of practice increased in the 1960s. Generic methods courses were found in many places, paving the way both for today's generalist curriculum model and debate about the place of—or need for—specialized study and practice. Early efforts to devise generic curricula usually went in one of two directions. Some such curricula were put together additively; that is, every student was required to take courses in casework, group work, and community organization. The other major effort was to identify concepts or processes (such as communication) that would inform social work practice irrespective of the size or type of system served. Both approaches had limitations. While each had its defenders, widespread support for generic social work practice did not develop until the work of Meyer (1970) and of Pincus and Minahan (1973) focused attention on tasks and processes common to all of social work practice. Generic gave way to generalist, still leaving open questions about specialization in social work. For clinical social workers, who had viewed their practice area as a unique and dominant specialization, this state of affairs was troublesome. Efforts to prepare for both generalist and specialized practice have not pleased partisans of either persuasion.

Social work education continues to attempt preparation for generalist and specialized practice. Many educators, however, are uncertain about the appropriate mix of theories and learning experiences; some see inherent conflict in the two models. Consensus is lacking on what are the truly general tasks and skills needed by all social workers. Even less consensus exists about the generalist practice role of the holder of the M.S.W. While some would argue that the social orientation requires a mixture of generalist/specialized expertise, others see graduate-level social work education as education for specialization. Although the conclusions of the American Association of Psychiatric Social Workers would not hold today, some problems and processes still obtain. According to French (1940), "It is unfortunate that so much emphasis has been placed on the fact that courses in mental hygiene and social psychiatry, once regarded as preparation for a specialized field, are now an accepted part of training for all social work. As a matter of fact, as early as 1918, leaders in the field of psychiatric social work not only predicted but recommended this very development. However, increasing similarity of academic courses need not mean the disappearance of the basis for training for a special field. Such a field is after all best defined in terms of its functions in relation to a special area of activity. Similarly, the distinguishing characteristics of specialized training for any field of social work should lie not in the content of the basic courses but in the fieldwork and seminars closely related to it" (p. 13).

Whether called a generic or generalist approach—or simply social work—perceived need to expand the scope of practice and the varieties of systems into which social workers intervene led in some places to virtual abandonment both of the field of practice notion and of strong support for specialization. But educational goals and patterns varied widely. Some schools developed advanced generalist curricula in lieu of specialization, or as one of several specializations. Some constructed curricula that had a generalist foundation, followed by a period of specialization in a method, practice field, or social problem. Still others organized curricula according to micro- and macro-tracks that, within respective tracks, combined both generalist and specialist orientations.

By the mid-1970s, educators and practitioners were expressing renewed concern about boundary and identity issues related to the generalist/specialist issue. Teachers and students alike were perplexed about definition and balance of specialization content (and related issues of the educational continuum). Concerns can be summarized in such questions as: Is clinical social work a specialization within social work? Is clinical social work synonymous with social work, or a subsystem of it? Is clinical social work a clustering of knowledge, value, skill, and methods that differs little from other helping professions? Is clinical social work a concentration within a specialization organized around a substantive area or target population?

Because of the negative consequences of such irresolution about generalist and specialist issues, the CSWE and the NASW formed a joint Task Force on Specialization in 1977. Their 1979 report on *Specialization in the Social Work Profession*, published in slightly different versions by the two sponsoring organizations, provided "A Conceptual Framework and Principles for Organizing Specializations." As already indicated, the task force focused attention on "the fundamental zone of social work . . . where people and their environment are in exchange with each other" (Council on Social Work Education, 1979b, p. 2). Having identified the transaction zone as essential, the report continued that it "is the duality of the focus on people and their environments that distinguishes social work from other professions and that permeates the organizing principles and criteria which follow." Members concluded that the most useful way of defining social work practice areas vis à vis specialization was "in relation to institutions which society has evolved to meet common human needs," and "corresponding service-providing health, education, legal and economic, and religious/familial institutions which social work has, throughout its history as a profession, tried to make humane and workable in the context of societal mandates" (p. 2). Three criteria for specialization were offered:

- Within an environment, a population experiencing a common condition to be altered or nurtured must be identified in some critical number.
- It must be demonstrated that there exists within social work, competence for work with and on behalf of this population. The skills and other elements of this competence must be identified, related to the unique needs of the population and the condition of their situations or environments. It must be shown that the use of this competence would be effective in altering or supporting the condition.
- The conditions which characterize the population and the competence required of social work specialists to deal with them must be sufficiently complex to require the guidance of a substantial body of knowledge. Such knowledge must be clearly related to the areas of transaction between people and their environments and must be translatable into effective intervention [p. 3].

The task force recommended that "specializations in social work be organized around sectors of the environment which follow closely the institutions designed to meet human needs, in areas such as: health; justice; education; economics; family, child, and adult development" (p. 4). In their schema, the specialist practices at the level of the particular service-delivering institutional structure and should be educated within the context of educational concentrations developed around the need-institutional rubric. "Thus, rather than developing educational concentrations in hospital social work or long-term care, a health concentration might be developed which would focus more broadly on the health-serving system; rather than courts or corrections, an educational concentration might be built around the justice system" (p. 4).

While the task force report begins to address complex and emotionally charged issues, it can serve as only a tentative first step toward defining the nature and place of specialization in social work education. That is particulary true with respect to clinical social work. The section on implications for the profession, for instance, opens for clinical social work educators more questions than may be resolved in the rest of the report taken altogether: "It can be expected that educators, for example, will want to be certain that a specialization model does not lead to undue fragmentation of students' learning experiences. Social workers who identify themselves with *particular methods, such as clinical workers* or administrators, may be concerned about how this approach will affect them, as may advanced practitioners who do not view themselves as specialists" (p. 6 [emphasis added]).

Whether the institution-need framework is a useful one for specialization will be debated by social work educators for a long time to come. Whether this formulation is sufficient will certainly be widely discussed. For clinical social work educators, the report and its particular view of specialization pose many interesting questions and dilemmas: How does the introduction of the concentration idea fit with and clarify an already confused issue? What are the curriculum and educational planning implications of defining clinical social work as a method that would be subsumed under a specialization and supported, in turn, by a concentration? How does the proposed framework dovetail with the existing individual, family, and group focus of many clinical social work programs? Are there theories and concepts within the specialization areas designated by the task force that would be unique to, or defining for, clinical social work? Would this particular view of specialization actually increase the numbers of roles and extent of general knowledge required of all social work students? How would specialized knowledge about individual or group behavior be applied in, say, a specialization in economics?

Implicitly, the report reinforces the fact that practice areas and boundaries of clinical social work and social work in general have been expanding over the past two decades. In large part because of that expansion, the clinical social worker today accepts multiple role performance as a requisite for practice in a way that would have been unthinkable in the methods-bound era. Whittaker (1974), for example, has stressed that "the professional may operate within the framework of a number of complementary roles, the most prominent of which are the treatment agent, the advocate-ombudsman, the teacher-counselor, and the broker of services and resources" (p. 56). Except for the treatment agent (therapeutic) role, each of these roles is claimed by social workers in all areas of practice.

Whether defined as a specialization or as a method, clinical social work continues to flourish in schools of social work. Clinical social work programs attract most of the students enrolled in graduate schools of social work. In the absence of any professionally agreed-upon definition of clinical social work, curriculum development in the schools proceeds idiosyncratically, influenced by faculty predilections, availability of practicum resources, the needs of the professional community, or particular definitions of specialization. It is entirely possible that consensus will ultimately emerge in support of the notion of several acceptable definitions of specialization. If that were to occur, the diversity so evident in curricula and educational expectations today would still exist but the range of curricular designs would be limited and the variability of outcomes (perhaps) decreased. For the moment, however, clinical social work educators are left to struggle with definitions of specialization that are intrinsically linked to dilemmas about balance of theory and skill orientations in clinical social work curricula.

Issues of the Educational Continuum

The corollary to inadequate definitions of specialization is an inadequate definition of core or (to use the currently favored term) base knowledge. These inadequacies make it difficult to resolve the generalist/specialist issue and to place clinical social work education appropriately within the assumed continuum of social work education.

Social work has three levels of professional education leading to the baccalaureate degree in social work, the M.S.W., and the doctorate. Students may enter professional education at either the B.S.W. or M.S.W. level and receive base or core knowledge at either level. Consequently, there is some confusion about differential practice and competency for varying tasks. Some have sought to lessen such confusion by stating that the B.S.W. programs prepare for *generalist* practice and M.S.W. programs prepare for *advanced* practice. While there is some consensus about the meaning of generalist, there is less about the definition of advanced. The situation is obfuscated further by a tendency to use advanced and specialized interchangeably and by the existence of some master's programs educating students for *advanced generalist* practice.

In theory, a social work student moves along a continuum of professional education. In light of uncertainty about the missions, capacities, and differentiating characteristics of each level, however, students may find themselves studying content that in one program might be defined as baccalaureate and generalist but in another as advanced and specialized. Although social work educators have talked about the continuum at length, discontinuity, gaps, or overlapping between the three educational levels is apparent.

After the Council on Social Work Education (1974) established its accreditation process for baccalaureate programs, such programs had to demonstrate that the "primary stated educational objective [was] preparation for beginning professional social work practice" (p. 1). Because of the "beginning professional" practice objective, some educators concluded that the baccalaureate degree should be oriented to general practice and the M.S.W. degree to specialized practice. As has been seen from another vantage point, consensus is lacking on that point of view. There has been, however, perceptible movement within baccalaureate programs toward generalist curricula (however defined). That movement was given considerable impetus by the activities and publications of an Undergraduate Social Work Curriculum Development Project sponsored by the Council on Social Work Education. The project's reports included this definition of the *generalist approach:* "All efforts in the generalist, unitary approach to practice are based on the premise that all of a person's needs involve a variety of systems and the social worker functions at the interface of people and social systems or societal institutions. Social systems theory is the basis for all efforts to explicate the generalist approach to practice" (Baer and Federico, 1979, p. 155).While supporting the generalist conceptualization, the authors of the report remarked upon the "difficulty of operationalizing this conceptualization in terms of action guidelines. . . ." (p. 156). While the generalist terminology has replaced the generic designations totally, the report's observation about operationalizing was well taken. No single definition or format informs generalist curricula at any level of professional education. Generalist curricula are often developed additively. In some respects, the generalist approach suffers from weaknesses similar to those of the generic perspective with regard to its tenuous theoretical support for practice and from a weakness identified within the generic framework by Constable (1978). As he observed, "the most serious problem of the generic curriculum was that it did not develop workable links either to specializations or a practicing profession" (p. 24).

If preparation for generalist practice were clearly the domain of baccalaureate programs, there would not be any need for discussion in this chapter. As in many other areas of social work education, however, a middle course has been taken, with generalist study offered at both baccalaureate and graduate levels, which has direct consequences for defining and teaching clinical social work practice.

As the generalist rubric suggests, the B.S.W. practitioner is expected to perform many professional tasks within numerous systems. Although never adopted as policy by the national professional organizations, the tacit assumption is that the B.S.W. practitioner will not conduct autonomous or specialized practice and will work primarily in the public social services. Yet some baccalaureate programs include within their curricula courses on family therapy and new action therapies, which suggests that the cachet of specialized practice (now presumably reserved for M.S.W. and doctoral levels) is desired by some at the entry level as well. Furthermore, some educators (and employers) now see the B.S.W. practitioner as a "front-line" clinical worker in the public services, with M.S.W. degree holders providing supervision, consultation, or other "nonclinical" support.

Because the baccaulaureate degree has been accepted as the first professional degree, it might be assumed that there would be tight connections with the master's level (which in turn would be carefully articulated with doctoral study). Logically sequenced, nonrepetitive progression of learning might be expected. While progression does occur, it may not be smooth, logical, or sequenced. Complications arise, as previously noted, when core or base knowledge is taught at both the baccalaureate and master's levels. Irresolution about specialization also is a factor in educational discontinuity. The prevailing situation is one in which progression may start at different points and arrive at approximately the same end. Here is equifinality at work, indeed, with often problematic curriculum consequences.

A student arriving at a graduate school of social work already having completed a B.S.W. degree may or may not be given advanced standing. If not, most of the core or base knowledge taught in the first semester or first year of the M.S.W. program may be in large part redundant for that student. Impatient to try new ideas and to learn new or specialized methods, such a student may understandably press for more specialized curricula. The B.S.W. student hoping to become a skilled clinical social worker wants to give immediate attention to work with individuals and groups.

Students who enter graduate professional social work education without previous education in social work take the same core curriculum at the graduate level as other students had completed at the baccalaureate level. Even if unfamiliar with the base, those students often react in the same fashion as the B.S.W. students and press for focused clinical study.

The existence of two entry levels into social work education and practice virtually guarantees problems of redundancy, uncertainty about the length of time that should be devoted to generalist and specialized study, and confusion about appropriate placement of base and specialization knowledge within the curriculum. Because base knowledge can be taught at both B.S.W. and M.S.W. levels, the credibility of graduate social work education for clinical practice is threatened when a graduate student may take courses akin to or exactly like those taken by undergraduate students. In addition, this circumstance results in a shortened period of graduate study, although most educators assume that M.S.W. study requires two academic years. The first semester or year of graduate work is usually generalist in nature, leaving fifty-four weeks or less in which to absorb theory, test oneself, and become an advanced clinical practitioner.

If social work is to be true to its historic missions and its values, it can be argued that all social workers must be provided with a generalist education. That proposition seems to be accepted. Little recognition seems accorded to unresolved issues pertaining to relationship of educational levels and definitions of specialization that have resulted in shortened periods of time for specialized graduate study focused on by fields of practice, social problems, or combinations of approaches. At the moment, problems of the continuum and specialization are inextricably related, and raise important questions about the breadth and depth of knowledge acquired by the person leaving graduate school with a degree in social work and a desire to enter clinical practice.

If a central problem of articulation between B.S.W. and M.S.W. programs is redundancy, the issue with respect to M.S.W.-D.S.W. linkage is sharp discontinuity. Doctoral programs are frequently focused on research and preparation of academicians. They can become increasingly isolated from social work practice. Indeed, some doctoral educators encourage students to "unlearn" practice skills that might contaminate research learning. This situation has particular meaning for clinical social workers who find few programs established to prepare students for advanced clinical practice and evaluation of practice techniques and programs. Siporin (1979) has commented that clinical social work education's continuing dilemmas about theories and their integration are not apt to be systematically addressed until more "clinical doctoral" programs are in place. Although frequently discussed since the Council on Social Work Education's Task Force on Structure and Policy Report of 1974 (Dolgoff, 1974), few schools of social work have moved to establish clinical doctorates. Research-oriented doctoral programs (clearly more respectable in universities) continue to be the norm. They provide education in research that can be valuable to the clinical social worker, but usually very little to extend the clinician's skill as a practitioner and theory builder.

Although not directly related to the educational continuum, another articulation issue must be addressed. Early in its history, professional social work entered the university. By moving from the original training-course format, early teachers of social work hoped to develop more rigorous knowledge and create higher status for an emerging profession. Overall, the consequences of that move have been positive. Within the university setting today, however, some trends militate against preparation of skilled clinical social work practitioners. Although social workers pioneered the field instruction format later adopted by other disciplines, experiential learning (central to teaching and developing skills for clinical practice) is generally not valued by academic faculty. The lot of the faculty-based field instructor, for example, is not a happy one. Problems of tenure and status are intense for people who are recruited to faculties because of their practice expertise but lack the doctorate and motivation for research needed for advancement. Pressures upon all faculty to publish may result in some expansion of knowledge, but may also deflect faculty members away from maintaining and extending their own practice skills because practice activities do not figure prominently—or in some places, at all—in the reward system of the university. As a result, it is possible for teachers of clinical social work to have little experience in practice or current relationship to it. Although some educators argue that capacity to analyze practice is as important as continuing practice experience, that point of view seems most often advanced by people who are skeptical of clinical methods and goals. It is doubtful that the same reasoning would be applied, for example, to teachers of research who are expected to be skilled in research methodology and design (that is, practice) and whose everyday work places them securely within the university reward system. Clinical teachers clearly need substantial theoretical knowledge. Because of constantly changing social conditions and problems presented by clients, ongoing practice experience is also essential for effective teaching of clinical social work.

Another area where articulation is often at issue is the relationship between classroom and field instruction. School-agency relationships are of critical importance for sound clinical social work education. Social agency directors and staff members involved in practicum instruction often voice dissatisfaction about curriculum developments and preparation of students entering the practicum. Faculty and agency supervisors, because of differing environmental contexts and reward systems, look at the same practice phenomena or service needs from different perspectives. A fragmented or poorly supervised practicum experience can be one result.

A pronounced trend during the 1960s and 1970s toward faculty-based field instruction (which developed from the assumption that faculty-based instructors could ameliorate the persistent incongruence between classroom curriculum and field learning experience) is now being reversed by reductions in federal funding and the pressures of university reward systems. Agency-based field instruction once again dominates, with corresponding increases in problems of articulation and integration. The apprenticeship model with which the profession began is resurgent. The outlook for a carefully devised internship (with clearly established educational goals, objectives, and learning experiences) for clinical social work students is bleak.

Clinical Social Work and Other Helping Professions

For the past several decades, clinical social workers have assumed that they practiced within a core discipline in the mental health field and were central to service delivery in almost all other social services. Curricula in schools of social work reflected that assumption through offerings in mental health practice and administration, the various fields of practice, and specialized interventions.

At present, clinical social work, and the profession in general, is confronted by emerging human service professions. Relatively new, specialized programs at Associate of Arts, baccalaureate, and graduate levels now challenge social work's hegemony. Hokenstad's (1977) observations on this development are useful: "Speech departments have become communications departments. Departments of school guidance and personnel have become departments of counseling. Academic departments in the social and behavioral sciences have placed emphasis on applied sociology and applied political science, and in some cases, are providing fieldwork as a part of the educational process" (p. 54).

As such transformations occur, it is inevitable that these modified disciplines will compete with clinical social work within both academic and practice settings. Curricula will be at least in part duplicative. Existence of briefer courses of study in the human services and duplication of some content may create pressures on social work from within the university to reorganize or shorten professional clinical social work education. Students may find social work education less attractive than a shorter program of study in the human services. Some institutions now offer highly specialized thirty-six-hour master's degree programs, for example, in counseling, gerontology, and long-term care administration. The onus is therefore on social work education to demonstrate that its present format of two academic years and sixty credit hours of graduate study is needed to master the knowledge, skills, and values of the profession. To reiterate an earlier point, such pressures will be felt particularly by clinical social work programs, which must demonstrate that their graduates have attained specialized knowledge from programs that include considerable generalist content.

Emerging human service programs and reexamination of social work's assumptions about length of study and nature of curricula must be viewed in the context of shifting demographic patterns that affect all of higher education and of general questioning about the length of time needed to prepare for entry into the marketplace. With regard to the latter point, in 1970, 12.6 percent of the work force had sixteen or more years of schooling, but only 10.1 percent of jobs required that much schooling (O'Toole, 1979).

Many clinical social work educators resist the notion of shortening the duration of professional education yet are fearful of competition from the newer, specialized disciplines. Turf concerns are apparent. Beyond those concerns, however, are more serious problems associated with the boundary and purpose issues discussed at intervals in this chapter. The emerging "clinical" disciplines such as applied sociology and family ecology tend to define their domain in terms of problem areas or methods related to a particular segment of the social service network. While eclectic in their theoretical base, they may maintain a more consistent and discrete focus on the problem or population of interest and on developing specific skills than is often true in clinical social work education.

Professional education for marriage and family therapy is a prominent example of competition with clinical social work education. Now accredited in some states through a national accrediting body analogous to the CSWE's Commission on Accreditation, these programs tend to focus directly upon problems of families and theories related to treatment of families. While concerned with policy issues related to family life, they do not devote significant curriculum coverage to them. Tending toward strong comparative theory and practice courses, these programs graduate specialized practitioners who may not have the breadth of understanding of the clinical social worker (particularly about resource networks). Nevertheless, they possess a depth of knowledge and skills with respect to intervening in family systems.

If social work is to hold its own in light of such developments, clearer choices must be made about content to be taught, the depth and breadth issues must be resolved, and the historical purposes of the profession must be reexamined and perhaps redefined. With respect to the last point, both social work educators and clinical social work practitioners are caught on the horns of a painful dilemma. Historically, social workers have served poor and oppressed people. Today, social workers continue to serve those groups but in different ways than in the past. In his extensive survey of emerging human service educational programs, Brawley (1980) cites data gathered by Hardcastle and Katz about the employment status of members of the NASW. Less than 2 percent of employed social workers surveyed were engaged in "the field of poverty and its elimination, a long-standing concern of social work and one of the priorities of NASW. . ." (pp. 85–86). Yet curricula are still devised to prepare students to work directly with poor people or, in the policy arena, on their behalf. The rhetoric and history that is reflected in curricula is often incongruent with the realities of clinical social work practice methods and agency goals. Perhaps because of separation of the realities of practice from the broad social mission of the profession, clinical social workers may tend to designate themselves by some other title, such as psychotherapist. In sum, curricula of schools of social work contain core or foundation courses to prepare students for work with populations with which many will have little association. Clinical social workers in particular usually have only peripheral relationships with poor or oppressed people. Social workers in the public social services are more apt to be supervising or directing than providing clinical services. Social workers who offer direct services or social treatment in the private sector most often work with clients above the poverty line.

All this is not to say that social workers' commitments to the poor and underserved are not genuine, but rather they are discrepant with much of practice and education today. This problem is one for the entire profession to resolve, but it is perhaps felt most keenly in the clinical realm, particulary now that new therapeutic disciplines are emerging.

Toward the Future

In view of the plethora of available interventions, the range of activities claimed as central to clinical social work, emergence of competitive human service programs, lack of clarity about areas of (or necessity for) specialization, and the eclectic theoretical base for practice, it is almost certain the boundary problems of clinical social work will intensify. A blurring between clinical social work, marriage and family therapy, and counseling is already discernible. That blurring of boundaries is affecting curriculum development and is an important influence on defining clinical social work in rather narrow terms of therapeutic activity. Boundary issues lead schools of social work to stress "uniqueness" of clinical practice and search for professional identity. The search for uniqueness and identity warrants special comment on a theme already introduced into the fugue.

Social work now, as in the past, is under attack. Unable to conquer poverty or diminish racism and sexism (avowed goals of the profession), social workers have retained their rhetoric while scaling down expectations. Even though there are probably few clinical social workers practicing with poor and oppressed people, professional education is consistently focused on work with the poor, disabled, and disfranchised. Young clinicians are taught theories and facts that are relevant to the historical purposes and mission of the profession but not supportive of current practice. The rhetoric of social justice and study of social policy provide useful and essential perspectives for clinical social workers. Courses in those areas, however, subtract time available for specialization for the 60 percent to 80 percent of social workers and students studying in the clinical area. Consequences of this incongruity are frequently reiterated laments about the profession's withdrawal from the poor, professional guilt, and loss of purpose and meaning. Because particular populations originally served by social workers shaped the purposes and values of social work and social work education and because those populations are minimally served by clinical social workers, there is not a "good fit" between curriculum and practice. In the author's own experience, serious discussion of this perceived incongruity is almost impossible without generating charges of racism, sexism, or lack of concern for poor people. Until this issue is examined fully, clinical social work will experience continuing irresolution about its base of knowledge and its purposes.

Education for effective clinical social work practice is problematic because of the boundary and mission problems presented throughout this chapter from various perspectives. Professional education for clinical social work will continue to be difficult because of the constraints and pressures of the environment, most importantly the university and agency networks to which graduate programs are related. Competition with other clinical programs within universities will increase. For the foreseeable future, social work educators can be expected to be hardpressed to defend (as sufficiently clinical) curriculum and assignments given to students in field practice. Given declining enrollments, stress on part-time and on continuing education programs, and the financial straits of many universities, clinical teachers will almost certainly feel greater pressure to conform to university reward systems, which themselves are constricting. The number of clinical social work students taught by professors who hold a research doctorate, but who have had little hands-on practice experience will very likely increase. One result will be continuation of a tendency for social work educators and practitioners to place themselves in adversarial positions.

Greatly expanded research programs exploring and comparing clinical social work interventions and outcomes are essential. Almost total separation—if not alienation—from practice on the part of clinical educators, however, may impede vitally needed research. The false dichotomy of practice and research has had persistent, negative consequences for theory development and practice in clinical social work. Perhaps the few newly developing programs offering the clinical doctorate will play a significant role in softening this dichotomy, focusing attention on the need for research-based practice, and validating practice experience as necessary preparation for teaching clinical practice.

Within the context of the total profession, the future of clinical social work is problematic. There is already a noticeable trend for social workers to seek doctoral work in other fields or to enroll in professional training programs that augment skills gained in graduate work. The tension between micro- and macropractice is apparent. Conceivably, those clinical social workers who identify most closely with the traditional therapeutic function will leave the profession. If that happens, the nature, structure, and knowledge base of social work education will undoubtedly change, and a generalist profession would result.

References

Abbott, E. *Social Welfare and Professional Education.* (Rev. Ed.) Chicago: University of Chicago Press, 1942.

Baer, B., and Federico, R. C. (Eds.). *Educating the Baccalaureate Social Worker: A Curriculum Development Resource Guide II.* Cambridge, Mass.: Ballinger, 1979.

Bartlett, H. M. "The Generic-Specific Concept in Social Work Education and Practice." In A. Kahn (Ed.), *Issues in American Social Work.* New York: Columbia University Press, 1959.

Brawley, E. A. "Emerging Human Service Education Programs." Unpublished paper, 1980.

Brieland, D., and others. *Contemporary Social Work: An Introduction to Social Work and Social Welfare.* New York: McGraw-Hill, 1975.

Cannon, M. A., and Klein, P. (Eds.). *Social Case Work: An Outline for Teaching.* New York: Columbia University Press, 1933.

Constable, R. T. "New Directions in Social Work Education: The Task Force Reports." *Journal of Education for Social Work,* 1978, *14,* 23–30.

Council on Social Work Education. *Curriculum Policy Statement.* New York: Council on Social Work Education, 1969.

Council on Social Work Education. *Standards for the Accreditation of Baccalaureate Degree Programs in Social Work.* New York: Council on Social Work Education, 1974.

Council on Social Work Education. *A Framework for the Explication of Base in Social Work Education.* New York: Council on Social Work Education, 1979a.

Council on Social Work Education. *Specialization in the Social Work Profession.* New York: Council on Social Work Education, 1979b.

Crouch, R. W. "Social Work Defined." *Social Work,* 1979, *24,* 46–48.

Dolgoff, R. *Report to the Task Force on Social Work Practice.* New York: Council on Social Work Education, 1974.

French, L. M. *Psychiatric Social Work.* New York: Commonwealth Fund, 1940.

Goldstein, E. G. "Knowledge Base of Clinical Social Work." *Social Work,* 1980, *25* (3), 173–178.

Hamilton, G. *Theory and Practice of Social Casework.* (2nd ed., rev.) New York: Columbia University Press, 1951.

Henderson, C. R. *Introduction to the Study of Dependent, Defective, and Delinquent Classes.* (2nd ed.) Lexington, Mass.: Heath, 1901.

Hokenstad, M. C., Jr. "Higher Education and the Human Service Professions: What Role for Social Work?" *Journal of Education for Social Work,* 1977, *13,* 52–59.

Hollis, F. *Casework: A Psychosocial Therapy.* New York: Random House, 1964.

Kahn, A. "Social Work Fields of Practice." In *Encyclopedia of Social Work.* Issue 15. Washington, D.C.: National Association of Social Workers, 1965.

Lurie, H. "The Responsibilities of a Socially Oriented Profession." In Kasius, C. (Ed.), *New Directions in Social Work.* New York: Harper & Row, 1954.

Meyer, C. H. *Social Work Practice: A Response to the Urban Crisis.* New York: Free Press, 1970.

Meyer, C. H. "What Direction for Direct Practice?" *Social Work,* 1979, *24,* 267–273.

Minahan, A. "What Is Clinical Social Work?" *Social Work,* 1980, *25,* 171.

National Association of Social Workers, Commission on Social Work Practice, Subcommittee on Fields of Practice. "Identifying Fields of Practice in Social Work." *Social Work,* 1962, *7,* 7–14.

O'Toole, J. "Education Is Education, and Work Is Work—Shall Ever the Twain Meet?" *Teachers College Record,* 1979, *81,* 5–21.

Parad, H. (Ed.). *Ego Psychology and Dynamic Casework.* New York: Family Service Association in America, 1958.

Perlman, H. H. *Social Casework: A Problem-Solving Process.* Chicago: University of Chicago Press, 1957.

Pincus, A., and Minahan, A. *Social Work Practice: Model and Method.* Itasca, Ill.: Peacock, 1973.

Rein, M. "Social Work in Search of a Radical Profession." *Social Work,* 1970, *15,* 13–28.

Richmond, M. E. *Social Diagnosis.* New York: Free Press, 1917.

Richmond, M. E. *What Is Social Casework?* New York: Russell Sage Foundation, 1922.

Riessman, F., and Miller, S. M. "Social Change Versus the 'Psychiatric World View'." *American Journal of Orthopsychiatry,* 1964, *34,* 29–38.

Siporin, M. "Practice Theory for Clinical Social Work." *Journal of Clinical Social Work,* 1979, *7,* 75–89.

Turner, F. J. (Ed.). *Social Work Treatment: Interlocking Theoretical Approaches.* New York: Free Press, 1974.

Turner, F. J. (Ed.). *Psychosocial Therapy: A Social Work Perspective.* New York: Free Press, 1978.

Whittaker, J. K. *Social Treatment: An Approach to Interpersonal Helping.* Chicago: Aldine, 1974.

Younghusband, E. (Ed.). *Social Work and Social Change.* New York: Council on Social Work Education, 1964.

Younghusband, E. (Ed.). *Education for Social Work: Readings in Social Work.* London: Allen & Unwin, 1968.

34

The Alternative Service Agency

Henry Miller
Connie Philipp

When certain social conditions give rise to new clients groups, the existing network of social agencies cannot possibly be a source of help for some of these groups. In these instances, the alternative service agency may arise outside of the conventional network and act as gadfly to the profession.

In the context of clinical practice, the alternative service agency becomes a stimulus for change and innovation. These changes occur not only in regard to the organization of service delivery but also in regard to the theory and technique of intervention. In the long run, the alternative service agency becomes an important factor in the way the profession of social work grows and amends its practice. This is not to say that in the short run the alternative service agency is not a source of considerable stress for the enterprise of social work and social welfare.

In its skeletal form, this argument presumes a tension between special and emergent client groups and the established professional community. But why does this tension sometimes exist? What aspects of conventional agencies seem to preclude certain kinds of services to certain kinds of client groups? And what aspects of these services and clients make their inclusion problematic?

Certain special conditions underlying social work practice affect the answers to these questions. Perhaps the most critical condition is operating under the aegis of a sponsor. That sponsor is a community of interest that may be as large as a federally funded program or as small as a private and parochial social agency. But whatever the size of the sponsor, the service agency is beholden to some larger entity that is always concerned with the legitimacy of the particular service in question. The patron is ever present, even though usually invisible (Galper, 1975).

Legitimation of Clienthood

Funding, whether from the public coffers or from private sources, always implies that the target of service, if not the service itself, has legitimacy. That is to say, the client group served by the agency and financed by the sponsor has an acknowledged need for the service. The legitimacy of a client group thus derives from the funding source rather than from professional judgment or client need, a rather simple observation that nonetheless has rather momentous consequences for potential agency clients. Intake procedures attempt to match a client's self-definition with the legitimated definition of the patron; a mismatch results in the denial of service.

The legitimation of clienthood may or may not have anything to do with objective need if "objective need" means the claims of clients. Disbursers of monies for social services have their own ways of determining need and, hence, of determining client groups. When the monies derive from the public at large, the determination—an act of public policy—must stem from some modicum of general consensus as to a hierarchy of social problems. This hierarchy is, by nature, unstable and subject to the vagaries of social and political exigencies. The history of the last several decades of governmental concern for particular social problems is instructive: delinquency, mental illness, poverty, child abuse, aging, the handicapped, and drug abuse were all found worthy of public attention and intervention. Some of these various legitimations of need and clienthood may have been seen as rather faddish and even quite irrational, but they had a tremendous impact on services and practice. Indeed, specialties and subspecialties within the profession of social work were created, in some part, as a response to the definition of client groups by public legitimation. Witness, for example, the street worker, community mental health as a social work specialty, aging as a specialty, grass-roots organizing, drug counseling, and the like. Similar developments occurred in other disciplines—community psychiatry in medicine and community psychology in clinical psychology.

Because public sponsorship of service requires some agreement within the public domain, the legitimation of certain client groups is quite problematic. Unpopular groups of people, unpopular problems, and unpopular services—all a function of the climate of the times—are not likely to become accepted as legitimate activities by public policy. In the not too distant past, for example, the mentally ill, alcoholics, drug addicts, the disabled, and single parents, to name a few, were not perceived by public patrons as "worthy" clients. Indeed, the early professional diagnostic task—to differentiate the worthy poor from the unworthy poor—was essentially a clinical problem defined by patrons rather than by practitioners and was certainly not a clinical process thought essential by clients (Leiby, 1978; Lubove, 1965). Public sponsorship, hence, has certain inevitable conservative tendencies although these are not always self-evident in a modern welfare state, which may even go so far as to make innovation a priority of public policy. But the innovation must be within boundaries of daring and legality. Because of this, the private agency is thought to have considerably more freedom in its ability to legitimate client groups' services.

Private agencies are beholden to patrons of a more parochial nature. These patrons, unlike their public counterparts, do not necessarily embrace a wide consensus of opinion or value. Indeed, they may choose to legitimate a client group that is unpopular among the broader citizenry. The history of social services provides many examples. The benefit to the spectrum of social services that derives from such a freedom, however, is attenuated by what may often become eccentricities among some private patrons. The fact that the private agency is not beholden to a broad public sponsorship allows for the possibility of extreme parochiality and/or archaic mandate. Times change; a social need that is clear at one moment may disappear at a later time. The patron who addressed the earlier and real client group may not be able, for a variety of reasons, to accommodate to new circumstances. A well-known example is what happened to the National Foundation for Infantile Paralysis after the discovery of the Salk vaccine (Sills, 1957).

Whether the sponsorship be public or private, however, the agency service is still a function of the mandate that descends from the sponsor. The mandate refers not only to the type of client who is to be helped but also to how the client is to be helped. Some childcare agencies, for example, support institutional or foster care not because of objective treatment considerations but, rather, because of the predilections of sponsors (Wolins and Piliavin, 1964). The congregate orphanage with a long history and a roster of distinguished and generous alumni may continue to survive simply because of the sentiment and nostalgia of its patrons and in spite of an array of alternative placement strategies.

But even existing private agencies, no matter what their freedom in terms of defining meritorious client groups, are not absolutely free. They must exist within a broader social and organizational climate, as Gilbert, Miller, and Specht (1980) discuss at length. What happens when social conditions are such that neither public nor private agencies will respond to newly emergent needs?

Instigation of Need and Emergence of Client Groups

To begin with, the enterprise itself, both social welfare as an institution and social work as a profession, was born as a result of cataclysmic changes in the wider social context. Prior to the pervasive social changes wrought by industrialization and urbanization, there was neither a social work profession nor an institution of social welfare. In a literal sense, then, social work was conceived as an alternative to other elements in the social fabric that were found to be lacking or otherwise insufficiently able to respond to new social needs. These other elements, until the catastrophe of the industrial revolution, had served humankind well for several millennia: the religion, the family, and the economy of feudal society were found to be adequate to the task of meeting the vicissitudes of the human condition. But this was not so after the upheavals of the nineteenth century. Slowly, haltingly, and with much external criticism and opposition, the profession of social work grew to be an alternative social structure when the more conventional elements of society failed (Leiby, 1978; Wilensky and Lebeaux, 1965).

New social conditions thus give rise to new structural arrangements. In the context of social welfare and social work, the new social conditions generate new "needs" and new client groups. When the existing network of social agencies cannot or will not respond to emerging client groups (and this can occur for a variety of reasons), conditions exist for the establishment of new and alternative service agencies.

New social needs and client groups are, in truth, new. The chaos of industrialization gave birth to something never before witnessed by human beings: industrial poverty. There had always been individual and aggregate disaster that resulted from insufficiencies, of course. Famine, hunger, and exposure were ubiquitous to human history. But a system that tied survival to wage labor rather than to the more traditional reciprocities between family and feudal lord brought forth the distinct and stunning problem of industrial poverty. In contemporary times, new social problems may be somewhat less dramatic, and in some cases they achieve a novelty that derives only from a visibility not previously obtained.

Let us consider how new client groups emerge. Although changes in the social fabric may be so profound as to produce an entire profession from the resultant cauldron of need, the consequence need not be that spectacular. Social change may result in adaptations of the profession itself, either by the construction of new appendages in the form of agencies or new subprofessions in the form of specialties.

Thus, the wave of immigrants to the United States during the decades before and after the turn of the century resulted in the rise of the settlement house and the birth of social group work as a new professional service. The fledgling profession lacked the knowledge and resources to help enormous numbers of immigrants experiencing problems with poverty, language, acculturation, and ghettoization. The social service response to immigration was a settlement house movement, and the fact that it was a movement as well as an organizational and professional innovation signals a second feature of the instigation of need. In addition to social change, political climate generates need and characterizes emergent client groups. The new agencies become political creatures, which helps explain why they are often met with hostility by the establishment. Hull House, for example, was seen by the contemporary establishment as a hotbed of political radicalism, intrigue, and subversion. It was none of these, of course. Jane Addams was hardly a wild revolutionary, but she did fight city bosses and she did pinprick the system. In their own time and in their own way, the settlement houses and their clients were a deliberate, self-conscious political force that greatly discomfited the establishment, both lay and professional.

The Great Depression of the 1930s is an important instance of social change that had a profound impact on the profession, the nature of its service organizations, and the clinical thrust of practice. This social event gave rise to the relentless growth of public social services; what had once been a "neglected" alternative to the dominant private agencies relatively quickly became the mainstream of service provision. It was the enormity of the need, far beyond the fiscal capacity of private philanthropy, which required the growth of public services. Again, the explosive growth of public services under the New Deal administration was, in spite of overwhelming need, not met with enthusiasm by the established social service community. The innovation of governmental involvement in the domain of charity on a massive scale was received with suspicion and alarm by many well-meaning social workers (Leiby, 1978).

Just as the settlement house movement gave rise to the specialty of social group work, so did the Depression give rise to technical changes in practice.

Notions of economic dependency changed. It was no longer comfortable to view financial need as the consequence of individual deficit. In the face of such generalized need, the locus of economic distress moved from the individual to the external environment. Briar and Miller (1971) claim that the shift in explanatory theory brought with it a shift in treatment technology: characterological and moral uplift was replaced by a more secular "treatment" plan based on financial planning and occupational possibilities.

Finally, the 1960s, a time of great social change and political ferment, gave rise to a proliferation of alternative service agencies. Indeed, the very concept of an alternative agency was brought into concrete awareness during this tumultuous decade. The new client groups that arose during these times consisted of two very large and heterogeneous demographic entities: alienated youth and racial minorities.

The events of the 1960s that led to the spawning of new social needs and of new client groups are too complex to deal with in this chapter. In essence, they consist of an unprecedented burgeoning of population brought on by the post–World War II baby boom; a civil rights movement; a serious, divisive, and unconscionable war; a curious mixture of economic affluence and economic anxiety; and a unique increase in postsecondary school enrollment. Whatever the cause of the events of the 1960s, the consequences in terms of the social work enterprise were clear: drug abuse and drug counseling agencies, runaway and residency centers, free medical clinics, draft counseling agencies, community action programs, and a variety of agencies devoted to the needs of particular minority groups. Some of these agencies are now in the mainstream of the established network of social services. At the time, however, these agencies were almost all outside of the orthodox structure—they clearly were alternatives to a social service structure found wanting.

An important point deserves reiteration here: a combination of social change and political climate instigates need and the emergence of new client groups. The 1970s brought with them their own brand of change and politics, with women's issues and the concerns of gay population groups in the forefront. A current generation of alternative agencies now serves the needs of these newer clients, and both the theoretical conceptions and treatment technologies employed to meet these needs are changing.

To say that new social services derive from the emergence of new social needs may be a statement of the obvious. But what may not be obvious is why these alternative services often arise outside of the orthodox service structure. Because the remainder of this chapter will devote itself to this case, it is important to remind the reader that not all innovations occur outside the system. Indeed, new agencies, new programs, and new techniques and theories frequently arise from the inside. They are planned, deliberated, and calculated by the existing network of organizations and professionals. But some changes cannot possibly occur from the inside.

The Alternative Service Agency as Criminal

Some client groups manifest service needs and/or political credos that are beyond the pale insofar as the service orthodoxy is concerned. This must be so by the very nature of established agency patronage; the existing agencies are constrained by law and by public tolerance. Consider a very extreme example:

During the last half of the 1960s, service agencies arose that were designated by the euphemism "draft-counseling agencies." These agencies should more properly have been called "draft evasion agencies"; their essential service was to help young men avoid being drafted under the selective service act through means that were sometimes legal and sometimes clearly illegal. To many of the clients of these organizations, the service was absolutely essential. They needed help of a complicated and technical nature; the decisions they were facing were momentous, the alternatives varied, and the emotional support and clarification involved in the process required skilled and empathic counselors. It would have been quite out of the question for the established social service community to have provided such a service, if for no other reason than the illegality or quasi-illegality of the endeavor. As a result, young men experienced in the possibilities of avoiding selective service joined with volunteers—attorneys, social workers, and others—in providing an ad hoc counseling service. The early draft counseling services were provided by various branches of the American Friends Service Committee. Gradually the more unorthodox types of counseling centers emerged. It is not surprising, given the quasi-legal nature of what was done, that there is no professional literature left behind by those agencies. The extreme case of the draft counseling agency points to an important feature of many alternative service agencies and explains why some must arise outside of the system: These agencies flirt with illegalities.

The early drug counseling services found themselves in a similar context. Much drug abuse, when it first appeared as a widespread phenomenon among white, middle-class youth, was not only a problematic behavior but an illegal activity as well. Because of that, and because of the social opprobrium attached to the activity, the social service orthodoxy could not immediately respond. Services arose alternatively—generated by clients in collaboration with some professionals who acted independently of agency sponsorship (Glasscote and others, 1975; Dupont, Goldstein, and O'Donnell, 1979). We must remember that the concern of some of these agencies, in part, was with a corrupt marketplace. Bad drugs, adulterated drugs, and misrepresented drugs were and continue to be a fearsome problem within the drug culture, and these agencies attempted to somehow police what was a clearly illegal market.

Drug abuse agencies did much more than chemical analysis and consumer protection, of course. But the moral stigma that initially attached to drug usage was powerful enough to cause most medical and social agencies to avoid dealing with the new and burgeoning population of needy clients. It was not until there was a change in perception of the problem—in essence, a legitimation of the problem—that the conventional social service system could deal directly and openly with issues of drug abuse. That change in perception was brought about, in large measure, by the alternative agencies that were dealing with the problem.

One final example from the 1960s might be helpful: the case of runaway centers. The phenomenon of thousands of young adolescents fleeing their homes presented childcare workers and police with a peculiar problem. The traditional response to the phenomenon of runaways—apprehension, notification of parents, and return home—was governed by law, habit, and theory and was clearly counterproductive. It tended to drive runaways underground and to compound their fugitive status. Alternative agencies, operating under different philosophical and theoretical principles, arose that promised help to these needy youth under a guarantee of confidentiality (Beggs, 1969). Such a guarantee could not have been offered by existing agencies.

We see, then, one feature of the alternative service agency: It is often engaged in activities that are not only unorthodox but also on the edge of legality. It is only after a period of time, when the legal issues are clarified, that the establishment can engage with the new clientele in a more meaningful way. That clarification, to reiterate, comes about through the very existence of the alternative.

The Alternative Service Agency as Radical

The quasi-legal character of alternative services is not the only important feature that makes them unpalatable to the orthodoxy. Equally troublesome is their frankly political posture. The new client groups are frequently dissident groups and most outspokenly so. The political statement made is often a very broad and sweeping condemnation of established society and what is seen as its handmaiden, the social service agencies themselves.

The civil rights movement made a clear political statement that indicted the entire society; its attack on social service delivery did not occur in the absence of that statement. Social services were claimed to be discriminating against their clientele, in their policies, treatments, and personnel practices. More than that, the indictment continued, even when the established services were not discriminatory, they were dilatory. They were passive, complacent, timid, and otherwise unwilling to do battle on behalf of their oppressed clientele. In the presence of this recalcitrance, the alternative was alternatives. Hence, the rise of ethnically oriented agencies, at first outside and antithetical to the establishment. Later, when the political message and purpose of these agencies lost their stigma, they gradually began to merge into the mainstream of interorganizational life.

More recent examples that illustrate the political character of new client groups and their discomfiting impact on established agencies concern the women's movement and the gay rights movement. Notice again, that like the settlement house movement, the phrase that identifies them explicitly describes their political essence. Like the case of civil rights, the indictment is broad and pervasive: The society is oppressive, discriminatory, wrong, unfeeling, and sick. The social services being part of that society—indeed, being its instrumentality—suffer from the same inadequacies. A proliferation of agencies devoted to women's issues and problems and gay issues and problems are currently responding to the need for alternatives.

The important feature of many of these alternative services is that they are openly political. They proselytize their clients. This is done frankly and unashamedly; part of the "treatment," it is claimed, is consciousness raising. Fitzgerald (1978) underscores that only when women become cognizant of their plight, their oppression, and their status can they be helped. This aspect of alternative service agencies deeply troubles the established network of services. Operating under a different set of premises, which consists of ideas of neutrality and of political transcendence, the conversion of a clientele falls outside the realm of acceptability.

The fact that many alternative service agencies operate under the proposition that effective individual treatment includes political awareness and action is a recurrent phenomenon in social work. Such awareness and action was an essential part of the settlement house movement; in a more vitiated form, it underlies much of the treatment occurring in mental health settings under the guise of patient government and organization. And of course, it is implicit in the contemporary treatment strategy of advocacy. Nonetheless, when the political awareness called for or the political action that follows has not yet been absorbed by the profession and its sponsors, there is no recourse other than the alternative service agency.

The Alternative Service Agency as Theoretician

To the service establishment and especially its professionals, probably the most troubling aspect of alternative service agencies concerns the theoretical critique embodied by their existence. The critique argues that the practitioner has been blind to the problem or at least to the extent and dimensions of the problem. Thus, it took a bitter struggle by the civil rights movement to explicate the nature of racial oppression in this country, and social workers were not necessarily more attuned to the issues than were other members of the majority society (Goodman, 1973).

In essence, then, the alternative service agency points to serious gaps in the diagnostic taxonomy of the profession. More important than these lacunae, however, are the theoretical errors to which the new client groups attend. The most blatant example can be seen in regard to gays. For many decades, homosexuality was viewed by mental health professionals as a pathological behavior. By legislative fiat, this perception, supposedly based on theory and empirics, was changed as a result of the political efforts of the gay movement. The theory, it was argued, was in error; professionals had been wrong, unscientific, and, by implication, incompetent. The elimination of homosexuality from the American Psychiatric Association *Diagnostic and Statistical Manual* (1980) was a correction of faulty theory. (Or it was an implicit admission that the classification system was based on premises that had little to do with theory.)

New and dissident client groups almost always challenge the profession on theoretical grounds. The case of the women's movement is also quite straightforward in this regard. Theories of human development, of psychotherapy, of interpersonal relations are, it is claimed, governed by fallacious conceptions created by men who live and think and feel in the context of a male-dominated experience. The critique adds that it is almost futile to expect a theoretical correction from the inside of the service entity. Thus, there is need for an alternative organization without the encumbrance of an antiquated and erroneous theoretical perspective.

Similar statements of theoretical inadequacy and error can be found among many other alternative service organizations. The professional legacy of knowledge is challenged by the mentally ill and their advocates, such as Laing (1967) and Szasz (1961); the criminal, who constructs and designs halfway houses embracing a wide range of vocationally oriented services as well as innovative psychotherapies; the physically handicapped, who, through their own initiative, have opened up previously unheard-of opportunities for full participation; health clinics and collectives; free medical clinics; switchboards; houses of refuge. The list can be extended.

The very wide spectrum of new and radically different psychotherapies that exist today can be viewed as alternatives to a mental health establishment that has been found wanting on theoretical grounds. Est, rolfing, biofeedback, massage, dance, a multitude of group experiences—all offer competitive theoretical positions that challenge not only social work but also orthodox medicine. The critique can be all-embracing: The new agencies offer radically different explanations as to the nature of humankind, the causes of physical and mental distress, and the appropriate therapeutic responses to such disturbances. More than that, they offer an organizational response that is different. Instead of an allegedly cold, dispassionate, partial, and bureaucratic reception, they claim to offer a warm, sympathetic, holistic, and essentially more humane response.

The attack on theory can be quite devastating or it can be mild, but it is understandable that the continually emerging new client groups will, at first, be met with suspicion and even distaste by professionals. Gradually, however, whatever is legitimate in the critique becomes incorporated into the body of "knowledge," and the alternative service agencies achieve respectability and are incorporated into the service establishment. But one further attribute of the alternative agency remains to be swallowed before this can be accomplished: the inevitable antiprofessional stance of the new client groups.

The Alternative Service Agency as Gemeinschaft

All of the factors described so far converge to make the professional orthodoxy a very real encumbrance to the satisfaction of these new client groups and their attendant needs. The professional and the mystique of professionalism become, for the subject, enemies: They are perceived as standing outside, with self-interests, with fallacious and demeaning theories, with authority, with antagonism, and with no compassion.

The division made between "outsiders" and "insiders" leads to the conclusion that the only people able to comprehend fully the new problems are the clients themselves. Thus, another special feature of the alternative service agency emerges: It is staffed, in large measure if not entirely, by lay people, many of whom were once or still are clients of the agency they serve. In essence, the critique is phenomenological. Its most extreme version makes the statement that: "Not being one of us, you cannot possibly help us." To continue the criticism: "You have not had the same experience we have had with our problem, and you cannot possibly understand us or what we feel like."

This argument, whatever its merit, is very familiar to the social work profession and has had throughout its history a profound impact on agency programs and policies. In more recent times, the impact has resulted in a very direct participation by "the community" in the directorate of social agencies and in the formulation of agency policy. The community in this regard consists of recipients or consumers, and the major rationale for such inclusion consists of some version of the phenomenological critique. Consumers, it is argued, have some unique and special insight into the business of the social agency.

For the insiders, the alternative service agency provides much more than a platform from which to assault the orthodoxy of professionalism. The agency provides a very real community of interest, activity, and mutual support. By its very nature, this community provides an opportunity for mutual help and self-help that the professionally staffed and general agency cannot possibly provide.

Ex-felons help themselves while they help other felons; the same is true of drug abusers, alcoholics, delinquents, battered women, gays, the handicapped, the aged, parents without partners, widows, parents of handicapped children, and so on (Philipp, 1979; Philipp, forthcoming; Silverman, 1978). Whatever else they might be, alternative service agencies of this type are clearly therapeutic communities and as such fulfill a serious therapeutic purpose. And when the purpose becomes acceptable to the professional establishment, it is embraced and made part of the armamentarium of recognized service.

The Alternative Service Agency as Harbinger

We have seen how alternative service agencies become part of the existing network of social agencies. In the first instance, when the clientele becomes legitimized, it can be incorporated into the caseloads of the establishment, and the alternative agency can be accepted into the family of social agencies. Thus, drug abusers are not now the anathema to many treatment facilities that they once were. The stigma and the moral opprobrium attached to such a clientele has fallen away. At the same time, the legal confusion surrounding service to drug abusers has been clarified or otherwise become of less concern.

By the same token, much of the political thrust of civil rights groups, the women's movement, and gay movement has lost its rankle. A good deal of the political commentary is now part of a more general and respectable discourse. Because of that, "ordinary" social agencies find it somewhat more comfortable to attend directly to these concerns, which formerly were the preemptive domain of the alternative organizations.

In short, one end state of the alternative service agency is cooptation. When they truly succeed in their mission, when the message has been gotten across and it "takes," the end result is an acceptance of both clientele and of structure. What is found to be "good" survives; what is not so viable, is in time, sloughed off. Further, for a variety of reasons the antiprofessional edge of these newly arrived agencies becomes blunted. For reasons of acceptability, respectability, and, not the least, funding, experienced alternative groups find it felicitous to reach for a professional image with its attendant features of education and credentials.

But not all alternative service agencies evolve such that they become part of the establishment. Some disappear simply because their client groups no longer exist. Draft counseling agencies represent the clearest illustration of this case. With the end of the Vietnam War and, subsequently, of the draft itself, the need for this type of service evaporated. Other agencies linger on for a while before their demise becomes obvious. Thus, during the heyday of the hippie movement, a network of switchboards, emergency food centers, and shelters grew up across the country and particularly around the campuses of several of the major universities. With the subsidence, over several years, of that movement, many of these services were liquidated. The need either disappeared or lost its visibility or its acceptability.

Another end to the evolution of the alternative service agency is much rarer but has an important and serious consequence. The "agency" becomes so radical in purpose and so impervious to the shaping forces of the community that it essentially goes "haywire." It becomes more militant and more demanding, begins to take on a mystical coloration, and basically transforms itself into a total political or religious entity. Examples of this type of outcome are subject to some debate because the ones that come to mind are, to begin with, somewhat unusual. For example, the People's Temple, although ostensibly a religious organization was hardly distinguishable in its beginnings from a religiously sponsored service organization and therapeutic community. Over time, it became more encapsulated, less permeable to moderating forces, and more politically strident, ultimately leading to the catastrophe at Jonestown. Less extreme examples may be found in the histories of such organizations as the Black Panther Party, Synanon, and the Church of Scientology. Some of these started off as purely political or religious entities, but all had an explicit and important service function that was unabashedly therapeutic. And, over time, because of the unyielding nature of the establishment, the new organizations' hyper-radicalism, and their relentless critique, they became more extreme in their mission and unyielding in their organizational structure. Of course, these agencies gone haywire had other characteristics that set them apart from the mainstream of alternative service organizations. One of these characteristics seems to be the presence of a charismatic personality who singlehandedly dominates the organization. But the alternative service agency that goes haywire is a possible outcome that should be of concern.

In sum, then, alternative service agencies do not remain fixed in their relation to the establishment. Whether they are eventually absorbed by that system or die out or become more radicalized depends not only on the nature of the alternative but also on the nature of the orthodoxy's response. The phenomenon is, in short, dialectical.

This discussion has, by implication, taken the position that the phenomenon of the alternative service agency is a powerful and positive dynamic in the evolution of social services and of social treatments. New social conditions, in the context of new political forces, give rise to new social needs and new client groups. Many times, the established social service system quickly adapts to these conditions with innovations in service and its delivery. Indeed, there are times when the system can even anticipate the generation of new client groups and meet the needs as they arise. Frequently, however, this cannot be done, for all the reasons previously discussed. If the theoretical critique is too extreme, if the clients are too stigmatized, if the issues are too unpopular or divisive, and if the political statement is too radical, then the establishment cannot immediately respond.

The alternative service agency arises to meet the novel conditions. Very often this happens with the help of professionals who operate, however, as individuals rather than as functionaries. It is the very existence of the alternative service agency that helps to generate a new climate for the client groups and their needs. Although they are opposed in some fashion by the more conservative elements within the profession, alternative service agencies must also serve to change the atmosphere of public and professional opinion. Out of this dialectic of conflict, the issues will eventually become clear, the struggle will slowly subside, and the alternative service agency will become reputable. (Other alternatives of demise or of extreme radicalization fall outside of the dynamic.)

Without this dialectic, social service systems would be much less capable of change than they currently are. The alternative service agency itself is a threat to the profession, and sometimes it is responded to as such. But in the long run, it is a salvation. Without it, social services would stultify. With it, the opportunities for change, evolution, innovation, and experimentation are greatly enhanced.

It is always foolish to prophesy about the future, particularly in the present climate of uncertainty within social work. But there might be some clues in the current social structure as to the new client groups that will emerge in coming decades.

First, the demography of American society is such that a tremendous increase in the aged population, relative to other population groups, is almost certain. The youth of the 1960s will become the aged of the 2010s, and given the low birthrate of the last decade, they will be economically dependent on a proportionately smaller labor force. What this will mean is hard to say, but if there is any carry-over at all among that aged population from their militancy of the 1960s, we can expect a group that far surpasses the Grey Panthers in activity.

Second, the phenomenal increase in the labor force participation of women is likely to bring social problems of a sort never before experienced. The implications of this phenomenon already appear in regard to such things as daycare, changes in household structure, and marital patterns. Further, and as a corollary to the entire women's movement, there will be a substantial increase in the number of childless women. It would not be unreasonable to predict, then, that new client groups will emerge that consist of women with unique problems in regard to their employment, families, and other needs contingent upon the process of growing older.

Finally, there is the general economy—not nearly as expansive as it has been for the two and a half decades following World War II. We have already seen an unemployment rate of some 9 to 10 percent, which has existed for several years; the rate, of course, is much higher for young people and for minority members of the labor force. If the economy continues to be sluggish—and some predict that it will be for a long time to come—hard times are sure to spawn larger groups of people unwilling to settle for the services currently provided by the welfare system. Further, with a constricting welfare system, there will be fewer services available to meet the needs of larger client groups.

But whatever the current state of affairs, we can be fairly confident that new alternative agencies will arise. Changing conditions require their existence. If we are wise, we will learn from them; indeed, we will learn whether we are wise or not. Their existence is a lesson in and of itself.

References

American Psychiatric Association. *Diagnostic and Statistical Manual of Mental Disorders.* (3rd ed.) Washington, D.C.: American Psychiatric Association, 1980.

Beggs, L. *Huckleberry's for Runaways.* New York: Ballantine Books, 1969.

Briar, S., and Miller, H. *Problems and Issues in Social Casework.* New York: Columbia University Press, 1971.

Dupont, R., Goldstein, A., and O'Donnell, J. (Eds.). *Handbook on Drug Abuse.* Rockville, Md.: National Institute on Drug Abuse and Executive Office of the President, 1979.

Fitzgerald, L. E. "Women's Changing Expectations: New Insights, New Demands." In L. W. Harmon and others (Eds.), *Counseling Women.* Belmont, Calif.: Wadsworth, 1978.

Galper, J. H. *The Politics of Social Services.* Englewood Cliffs, N.J.: Prentice-Hall, 1975.
Gilbert, N., Miller, H., and Specht, H. *An Introduction to Social Work Practice.* Englewood Cliffs, N.J.: Prentice-Hall, 1980.
Glasscote, M., and others. *The Alternative Services: Their Role in Mental Health.* Washington, D.C.: American Psychiatric Association, 1975.
Goodman, J. A. (Ed.). *Dynamics of Racism in Social Work Practice.* Washington, D.C.: National Association of Social Workers, 1973.
Laing, R. D. *The Politics of Experience.* New York: Pantheon Books, 1967.
Leiby, J. *A History of Social Welfare and Social Work in the United States.* New York: Columbia University Press, 1978.
Lubove, R. *The Professional Altruist.* Cambridge, Mass.: Harvard University Press, 1965.
Philipp, C. "A Study of Maternal Participation in Preschool Programs for Handicapped Children and Their Families." *Social Work in Health Care,* 1979, *5* (2), 165–175.
Philipp, C. "A Support Group for Adults with Severe Physical Disabilities." *Social Casework.* (Forthcoming.)
Sills, D. *The Volunteers.* New York: Free Press, 1957.
Silverman, P. R. *Mutual Help Groups: A Guide for Mental Health Workers.* Rockville, Md.: National Institute of Mental Health, 1978.
Szasz, T. *The Myth of Mental Illness: Foundations of a Theory of Personal Conduct.* New York: Hoeber-Harper, 1961.
Wilensky, H. L., and Lebeaux, C. N. *Industrial Society and Social Welfare.* New York: Free Press, 1965.
Wolins, M., and Piliavin, I. *Institution or Foster Family, A Century of Debate.* New York: Child Welfare League of America, 1964.

35

Financing Social Services

Paul Terrell

In 1978, the last fiscal year for which information is available, spending for social welfare in the United States totaled $548.9 billion (McMillan and Bixby, 1980, p. 3). About 95 percent of this outlay represented health, education, housing, and income-security programs operated through the agencies and institutions of the public and private sectors. The remaining 5 percent of the outlay funded mental health and social-service programs—programs like child welfare, psychotherapy and counseling, family planning, home-delivered and congregate meals for the aged, daycare, and information and referral.

Every dollar spent for social welfare—for the programs mentioned above—creates a monetary obligation. Each dollar spent has to be paid for, and the fashion in which this payment is organized powerfully influences the character of services, as well as their magnitude. As its basis, then, the organization of welfare finance in this country has two major components—derivation and allocation. Derivation refers to the measures through which welfare revenues are generated. While the burden of support can be conceptualized in a variety of ways, it is individuals who ultimately pay for welfare, either through their taxes, their contributions to charitable causes, or their direct expenditures for services rendered. Allocation refers to the process through which collected revenues are funneled to social welfare providers. Although private individuals foot the final bill for the welfare state, it is the various allocation mechanisms that define its fiscal character. Channeling taxes, charity, and fees into program resources, these mechanisms link those who pay for services with those who actually produce and provide them.

The national government, for example, allocates billions of federal aid dollars annually to service programs run by state and local government agencies. In the voluntary sector, fund-raising federations such as the United Way promote community and corporate giving to support the programs of member agencies. In the commercial sector, third-party health insurance programs use subscriber premiums to reimburse the services of authorized care providers.

The sources of welfare revenue and the character of the funding streams transforming revenues into programs are topics of importance for social work. Because services cannot be provided without budgets, resource development is the essential prerequisite for securing the personnel, space, and supplies necessary to organize programs. Because the structure of financial arrangements is hardly a neutral "given" in the social welfare enterprise, the nature of the revenue system, its consequences, and its potential for alteration are all vital issues for examination.

The purpose of this chapter, then, is to explore some of the important connections between services and revenues, giving special attention to the "who, what, why, and with what result" issues that have an impact on the nature of clinical services. In a period in which resources are increasingly scarce, and in which welfare is a major target of cost cutters, it is urgent for human services workers and students to understand the fiscal workings of the welfare system and to be able to engage that understanding for action.

Deriving Revenue

The monetary basis of social welfare originates in taxes, charity, and consumer spending. Of the three, taxes provide by far the greatest sum. As compulsory levies—levies imposed in accordance with law—taxes are used to support the general functions of the public sector. U.S. tax collections in 1979 provided $661 billion—roughly 38 percent of the GNP—for this purpose (Advisory Commission on Intergovernmental Relations, 1980). Nearly two thirds of this total supported social welfare activities.

Although the primary function of taxation is to finance governmental budgets, taxes serve other purposes as well. In uncertain times such as our own, the economic function is especially important. Tax cuts, for example, provide an important instrument in efforts to stimulate the economy, while tax increases can cool an overheated period of growth. A considerable body of recent economic theorizing, in addition, addresses the fashion in which tax policies can counteract inflation.

Tax policies can also be employed to advance social needs. As Richard Titmuss (1959) has argued, the tax system can be viewed as a basic form of welfare, along with "regular" welfare expenditures and "occupational" welfare embodied in employee-related fringe benefits. There is no doubt that the American tax system incorporates a multitude of components directed toward antipoverty, redistribution, and health objectives, as well as toward the provision of specific types of social services for vulnerable population groups.

The Federal Income Tax. The federal personal income tax, the largest single source of government revenue, accounts for 48 percent of federal taxes and 33 percent of all taxes. The salient characteristic of the income tax is its progressive rate structure—in contrast to most other forms of taxation, it is levied in accordance with ability to pay. As income rises, in other words, so does the tax rate. Poor families, for the most part, are exempt from the income tax.

Crossing over the tax threshold, the rate begins at 11 percent. As income increases, so does the rate, through fifteen incremental brackets to a maximum of 50 percent.

While the federal income tax imposes heavier overall and marginal burdens on heftier incomes, the relationship between total income and taxes paid is not as simple or as direct as suggested by the progressivity model. A variety of complicating factors make total income, in and of itself, a very poor indication of tax obligation. Rather, type of income, family size, spending patterns, and charitable behavior combine to determine an individual's tax liability.

The type of income is critical because different income is taxed differently. Many forms of income, like public assistance, are exempted entirely from taxation. Other forms, such as capital gains, are taxed at a fraction of the normal rate. Family size is important because it is inversely related to taxable income.

The character of one's spending is critical because many expenditures can be subtracted from taxable income or from actual taxes owed. These special deductibles and credits include spending for education, health, interest on loans, and local taxes.

Philanthropy is important because federal tax law permits contributions to charitable and other nonprofit organizations to be deducted from one's tax liability. Individuals can reduce their tax burden, in other words, in proportion to the value of their gifts. Corporations can also deduct philanthropic giving from their taxable income.

Tax exemptions, deductions, and credits have been characterized as "tax expenditures" because they provide subsidies to certain kinds of taxpayers. Although the overall distribution of tax expenditure benefits is regressive, many clearly address the welfare of populations with special needs. Working parents can subtract a portion of their childcare expenses directly from their tax liabilities. Income maintenance benefits—"transfer," like public assistance—are exempt from taxation. Families adopting hard-to-place children can deduct up to $1,500 of the fees involved. The earned income tax credit provides rebates to working people with poverty-level earnings. The blind (but not the deaf or other handicapped populations) are granted double personal exemptions, as are the elderly. Medical costs are cushioned by their deductible status. Spending for health insurance is similarly promoted. Voluntary agencies are assisted in their attempts to address social needs because charitable contributions are deductible. These and other special credits, deductions, and exemptions provide roughly $102 billion annually for broadly defined welfare purposes (Minarik, 1981, p. 275).

The elderly are especially assisted by tax expenditures. People over sixty-five get double personal exemptions, meaning $2,000 for an individual and $4,000 for a couple. Their Social Security income is tax-free. They are covered by the standard deduction of $3,400 for a joint return. Assuming a couple receives Social Security benefits of $5,200 a year and has other income from part-time work or employer pensions or stock earnings, they can make up to $12,600 and not be obligated for a single penny in federal taxes. Additional income from public programs or private insurance would also be tax-free.

The rationale behind these preferences, of course, is one of need. It is generally the case that the aged have less ability to pay taxes relative to their expenses than do other groups. Because all the elderly are eligible for these allowances, however, many people who are financially well-off are aided.

Social components in taxation are nothing new or revolutionary. One of the oldest antipoverty programs of all is the personal exemption, through which federal income tax obligations are varied according to family size. In the pre-Depression period, the exemption was large enough, compared to average family earnings, to relieve lower-income people of all income tax liabilities. This was Congress's intention, the prevailing view being that people with family responsibilities should not be subject to income taxes until their income ensured at least a modest standard of living (Eisenstein, 1961).

While the personal exemption is still part of the tax code, it is now at best a marginal antipovery measure. Standing at a low level in comparison with average income, it removes only the very poorest from the tax rolls. While relief is still provided—especially to the elderly, who get double exemptions—the amount is hardly sufficient to exempt even a small fraction of the proportion aided over sixty years ago.

In addition to directly affecting the level of disposable income, tax policies can promote or discourage different kinds of behavior. A variety of income tax credits exist to promote corporate social responsibility, such as the hiring of welfare recipients. Other taxes discourage "undesirable" individual behavior. A primary purpose of sumptuary taxes, in this vein, is to penalize the consumption of cigarettes and alcohol.

Social policies advanced through the tax code can be every bit as important as policies implemented through direct spending. In many cases, both tax and spending policies address similar objectives. Daycare, for example, is a major area of federal and local activity under spending programs such as Title XX, the Elementary and Secondary Education Act, the Work Incentive Program, and Head Start, as well as under revenue programs such as the childcare credit. While spending programs generally provide revenues directly to agency providers, tax credits give consumers additional purchasing power for use in the marketplace.

Although tax benefits have the potential to be as "redistributive" as regular spending programs, in actuality they are not. In general, indeed, they provide an "upside down" system of subsidies, with major advantages going to the rich, modest help going to the middle class, and no help at all going to the poor. Daycare spending under Head Start and Title XX, for example, is focused on eligible low-income populations, while childcare credits provide subisidies primarily to middle- and upper-income groups. A full 85 percent of federal childcare spending in 1977 was aimed at segments of the population with incomes below $10,000 annually; yet tax expenditures provided only 14 percent of their benefits to those under $10,000 (U.S. Congressional Budget Office, 1978, p. 27). Paying little or no income taxes, low-income families received little advantage from the credit. Households earning over $20,000, on the other hand, derived virtually no benefit from direct spending programs while receiving 43 percent of the tax expenditure benefits.

The regressive nature of the childcare credit is representative of the tax expenditure system in general. Tax expenditures are regressive because income tax rates are progressive. A $100 deduction or exemption saves taxpayers in the 50 percent bracket $50 in taxes while providing only $11 in savings for taxpayers in the 11 percent bracket. It is not surprising, therefore, that the wealthiest 5 percent of all taxpayers garner roughly two thirds of all tax expenditure benefits (Wisher, 1980, p. 31).

Such "welfare for the rich" substantially diminishes the overall progressivity of the income tax. While still the most redistributive form of taxation, the burden of its real ("effective") rates—taxes measured as a proportion of overall income—varies only moderately among income groups. Despite the presumed 50 percent tax bite on the marginal income of the rich, even the top 1 percent of taxpayers rarely pay more than one third of their total income to Uncle Sam. Medium earners pay 11 percent and low earners pay under 3 percent (Pechman, 1977, pp. 349–350).

Social Security, Sales, and Property Taxes. Despite the magnitude of tax expenditures—$267 billion in 1982—the federal income tax remains modestly progressive (Minarik, 1981). Although the rate progression may not be as steep as many would desire, higher income groups do pay higher rates.

This is not the case for the second-largest source of tax revenue—the Old Age, Survivors, Disability, and Health Insurance (OASDHI) tax, commonly known as Social Security "contributions." More than almost any other source of revenue, Social Security taxes bear heavily on those least able to pay.

Social Security is regressive because it levies a fixed tax rate on a fixed amount of earnings. The fixed rate—6.7 percent for both employees and employers in 1982—means that Uncle Sam takes the same proportion from everyone's covered earnings. Rates are not scaled to income, family size, or any other factor associated with ability to pay.

The fixed rate, in addition, is applied only to earnings up to a certain point. In 1982, for example, the taxable base was $31,800, and those with earnings within this limit paid their 6.7 percent share into the Social Security Trust Fund. Those with higher earnings, however, faced no obligations on the excess. The individual earning $63,600, for example, paid just 3.35 percent overall—6.7 percent of the first $31,800 and nothing on the second $31,800.

Other factors compound Social Security's regressivity. First, the tax is levied only on "payrolls," that is, earned income. This is in line with the program's character as insurance against interruptions in work-related income, but it results in full taxation for working people and dispensation for those wealthy enough to compose their income in other ways. Those who depend on nonwork income—capital gains and dividends, for example—have zero earnings in the Social Security sense of the term, and therefore pay no taxes. Social Security taxation is regressive for another reason—it is levied on individual rather than family income. This results in households with identical total earnings having very different tax liabilities. A family with a single earner making $50,000 in 1982, for example, paid Social Security taxes of $2,130.60—6.7 percent of $31,800. A family with both spouses employed, each earning $25,000, however, paid $3,350.00—$1,675.00 apiece. Since multiworker households are more common among lower-income groups, it is the poor and near-poor groups that once again are disproportionately burdened.

The Social Security tax, finally, differs from most other tax programs in that it is earmarked for specific spending. In contrast to income taxes, which provide general funds for the support of federal activities, Social Security revenues can be used only to support OASDHI benefits.

A third major tax form, the excise tax, is based on consumption rather than on income. One is taxed, in other words, according to what one buys. Sales taxes, the most common excise and the largest source of state revenue, are levied on the sale of goods. Ranging in magnitude from 2 to 7 percent, state sales taxes cover most products, although food, medicine, and medical care are often exempted, while certain "offensive" products, like alcohol or cigarettes, are taxed at especially high levels. While all residents in a given jurisdiction are subject to the same percentage sales tax, the burden is regressive because the items taxed absorb a higher proportion of the income of lower-income households.

Property taxes, the major local source of city, county, and school district revenue, are usually levied at a given dollar amount per $100 of assessed value. Whether its incidence is regressive or progressive, however, is a matter of considerable debate among economists, and others. Historically, property taxes have been viewed as regressive for two reasons. First, in any given community a fixed rate tax of this sort takes proportionately more from the poor than it does from better-off groups. Second, homeowners in poor communities must be assessed at rates higher than those in effect in richer areas in order to produce a given level of tax revenues. The new view, however, sees property taxes as one of the few means that exist for taxing wealth. In this sense, the levy concentrates its burdens in relation to property ownership, falling heavily on owners of commercial, agricultural, and apartment property, less so on single homeowners, and hardly at all on nonowners (Aaron, 1973).

Like other forms of taxation, the property tax is often modified to further welfare objectives. "Circuit-breaker" mechanisms, for example, are commonly employed to exempt the low-income elderly (and occasionally other needy groups) from prevailing tax rates (Advisory Commission on Intergovernmental Relations, 1977).

Tax Burdens. What is the distribution of the overall burden of the federal-state-local tax system in the United States? The definitive volume on the issue, Pechman and Okner's (1974) *Who Bears the Tax Burden?*, puts it this way: "There is little difference in effective rates over most of the income distribution [so] the tax system has very little effect on the relative distribution of income. . . . The tax system is virtually proportional for the vast majority of families in the United States. Under the most progressive set of assumptions, taxes reduce income inequality by less than 5 percent; under the least progressive assumptions, income inequality is reduced by only about 0.25 percent (pp. 6, 64).

In general, the American tax system is hardly the instrument of progressiveness it is often touted to be. For this reason, a critical priority on the liberal agenda must be tax reform and a fairer burden of tax payments. The equity considerations inherent in choosing alternative tax methods should be as clear to welfare advocates as the alternatives that exist in spending policy. Social welfare requires the strengthening of progressive tax forms such as the income tax, the reduction of tax expenditures not clearly justified by social considerations, and the containment or reconstitution of regressive taxes such as Social Security.

Use Fees and Charges. Although social welfare is occasionally defined as a system separate and distinct from the institutions of the private economy, an important and growing range of welfare services is purchased by consumers much like any other goods offered for sale. Education, for example, especially at the higher levels, is rarely free. While tuition costs may be relatively modest in public universities, few institutions are entirely supported by tax funds and philanthropy. The situation in the health field is even more "commercial." Fees constitute a major source of funding for physicians, hospitals, and nursing homes, and public policy in support of health care often takes the form of reimbursements for services offered eligible populations. Pension plans similarly rely on charges to consumers. Clinical social workers in private practice, much like other professional service providers, also depend on fees for their income.

Social welfare charges serve a variety of functions. The basic one, of course, is to provide financial support. Social welfare organizations, whether commercial or not, need revenues to survive, and a primary source of revenue in many instances is the user—especially when he or she seeks out the service and is able to pay for it. Fees generated in this fashion are paid voluntarily, borne by those who directly benefit from the services they purchase. In most instances, of course, the revenue raised covers only part of the total expenses of provision, with fees supplementing sources of income such as taxes, foundation grants, and community fund raising. Very few welfare organizations—whatever the economic status of their clientele—exist primarily on fees, although many could scarcely survive without such revenues. Private practitioners, on the other hand, are highly dependent on fee income.

Beyond providing program revenue, fees serve to ration benefits. Expensive programs, such as health services, occasionally rely on charges to reduce utilization. The intention in this situation is less to generate dollar support (fee administration costs often exceed the amounts raised) than to discourage unnecessary use. A modest charge, it is argued, deters those with superficial problems without acting as a barrier to those with legitimate needs.

Fees serve a variety of other functions. On the one hand, charging those able to pay can provide the revenues necessary to subsidize poorer clients. Fees may reduce the stigma attaching to charity or welfare efforts. In the mental health field, some have ingenuously argued that client behavior with respect to fees offers an important opportunity for diagnosis (Lohmann, 1980).

Critics, on the other hand, view fees as antithetical to the philosophy of welfare, a philosophy based on "unilateral transfers" rather than on exchange. It is certain that fees are inequitable in the sense of imposing criteria on services beyond that of need alone.

Fees for social welfare can be paid either directly, at the time of purchase, or indirectly, through third-party funding arrangements. Direct payments represent the most basic form of market transaction. Individual A pays counselor B for one family therapy session. In this instance, and others, charges may be adjusted to account for the economic circumstances of the consumer. Both public and private agencies, for example, often employ fee scales that vary according to income. Under Title XX of the Social Security Act, over forty states provide homemaker and daycare services gratis to low-income clients, while charging individuals and families in the income range immediately surrounding the state median (U.S. Department of Health and Human Services, 1980). And the National Association of Social Workers (NASW) Code of Ethics requires social workers to set fees in a way that is "fair, reasonable, considerate, and commensurate with the service performed and with due regard for the clients' ability to pay" (National Association of Social Workers, 1980, Section I).

Indirect finance, by contrast, separates funding and service, client and provider, by involving a third party in the transaction. Employed typically in the health field, third-party organizations provide insurance protection against a range of unpredictable, and possibly costly, medical eventualities. Rather than facing steep, potentially ruinous, physician or hospital bills, an individual may elect the insurance option, remitting monthly premiums to Blue Cross or some comparable firm in return for insurance protection. In this fashion, expenses are largely manageable, whatever illness or accident may ensue.

Medical services frequently are funded through both direct and third-party means, because the latter rarely cover all charges. While policies vary considerably, insured consumers must usually bear both deductibles and copayments, charges that represent the difference between total medical costs and the portion paid by the insurance company. Deductibles are out-of-pocket payments that must be paid by the consumer before insurance payments go into effect. In the standard Blue Cross policy, the deductible is $200, meaning that Blue Cross will not reimburse any part of the first $200 in charges in a given year. Copayments are out-of-pocket payments paid for by the consumer on charges above the deductible. The Blue Cross copayment is typically 20 percent, meaning that the subscriber pays 20 percent of the expenses above $200.

While these supplemental fees are customary in private health insurance, they are not absent in public policy. Medicaid programs in several states require beneficiaries to carry a portion of their hospital bills and a share of "optional" services such as hearing aids and drugs (Spindler, 1979). Medicare Part B is a voluntary program that covers physician and other medical costs in exchange for a monthly fee. Part B also requires a deductible payment annually for medical services and hospitalization and a 25 percent copayment for medical services above the deductible.

With respect to the overall balance of spending in the United States, governmental funds provide 41 percent of all health and medical care expenditures, a figure that has remained stable since the mid-1970s. Medicare and Medicaid are the two largest components of public spending on health. The 59 percent provided by the private sector is divided between direct out-of-pocket payments by patients (34 percent) and private insurance benefits (25 percent) (McMillan and Bixby, 1980, pp. 12–13).

In the mental health area, direct payments by clients are even more important, making up 42 percent of all spending. Subscriber premiums cover just 15 percent of mental health costs, though the trend is toward increasing third-party use (President's Commission on Mental Health, 1978, p. 533).

Private financing systems, finally, are frequently promoted by public policy. Employee health insurance and pension plans, for example, have grown in large measure through favorable tax treatment. Since World War II, major federal tax expenditures, most notably the deduction for employer contributions to health and pension plans, have encouraged private businesses to establish and fund welfare-oriented programs as part of the benefit package available to their workers.

Charity. In 1978 charitable organizations—organizations operated on a nonprofit basis to improve, in one way or another, the general welfare—received $37 billion in gifts from individuals. Provided through donations, bequests, and fund-raising campaigns such as the United Way, as well as indirectly through charitable foundations, the $37 billion composed nearly 2 percent of the nation's disposable personal income—a proportion that has not changed significantly in recent years (American Association of Fund Raising Council, 1979, p. 10). Given the great expansion in public funding since 1960, the maintenance of private giving has been an important achievement.

Charitable contributions function to support a wide variety of "quality of life" organizations benefiting the entire range of the population. Private charitable support, for example, is a major source of support for the students attending private colleges and universities, who are largely from the middle class. Charity is also a main source of support for health research, symphonies, museums, and hundreds of thousands of churches and synagogues.

Only about 10 percent of private giving funds traditional social-service programs. While this 10 percent is composed of everything from spare change for free clinic panhandlers to raffle tickets for the Leukemia Society, the increasing bureaucratization of "organized" charity is resulting in an ever greater dominance of "intermediary" fund-raising organizations. Of the nearly $4 billion contributed to the social services in 1978, for example, $1.32 billion went to local United Ways, largely through corporate gifts and the monthly payroll deductions of employees, $475 million supported Jewish Federations, and $280 million went to the United Jewish Appeal, chiefly for refugees and overseas aid (American Association of Fund Raising Council, 1979, pp. 36–37).

Most of the funds contributed to charity federations and other nonprofit organizations come from living individuals, and, as might be expected, individuals with the highest incomes give the most. Nearly one charitable dollar in five, indeed, comes from the richest 1 percent of all households (American Association for Fund Raising Council, 1979, p. 56). The motivations of the wealthy for giving are mixed, but one dominant factor is clearly the "upside-down" nature of tax subsidies. Rich people simply receive the greatest tax savings per dollar contributed.

The relationship between giving and tax gains is sufficiently powerful that for several years a major legislative priority of organized philanthropy has been the liberalization and extension of the charity deduction. A major victory toward this end was achieved in 1981 when federal tax law for the first time permitted taxpayers receiving the standard deduction to derive additional benefits from their contributions. Such "over the line" deductions are expected to generate roughly $5 billion annually for charities (United Way of America, 1979). The additional giving, of course, will produce a nearly equivalent reduction in federal tax revenue. Uncle Sam's loss, in this sense, is charity's gain. The interest of the charity industry in extending "their" deduction, moreover, conflicts with the desire of tax reformers to limit the use of regressive tax expenditures of all sorts.

While direct giving accounts for 83 percent of all philanthropic activity, considerable sums are also generated through posthumous bequests, foundation grants, and corporate charity. Just 16 percent of the $2.16 billion in charity distributed by foundations in 1978 supported the social services, but many foundations focus their aid entirely on such activities. Private corporations, for their part, provide nearly one quarter of their philanthropic expenditure to United Ways and other federated drives (American Association of Fund Raising Council, 1979, p. 14). Under the provisions of Reagan's Economic Recovery Tax Act of 1981, corporate deductions for charitable contributions were increased to 10 percent of taxable income, double the previous limit.

Intermediary Mechanisms

A key feature of welfare finance in the United States is complexity, a complexity reflecting both our federal system of government and the existence of a large, varied, and well-supported network of nongovernmental welfare institutions. Federalism creates a multi-tiered system of local, state, and federal governments, with units at each level possessing important discretionary powers in raising and spending funds. Both commercial and nonprofit organizations, moreover, play major roles in funding, organizing, and delivering welfare benefits, and their scope and importance is likely to grow in the future, especially in the pension, health insurance, and community social service areas.

Another aspect of complexity in the American welfare state is the frequent separation of the fund-raising and expenditure functions. The institutions that have developed in this country to generate money for welfare purposes are only occasionally the institutions that are responsible for operating services. This is true in both the public and private sectors. A variety of "intermediary mechanisms" connect the fund-raising and fund-spending functions. These mechanisms translate the revenues supplied by taxpayers, charity givers, and program consumers into usable resources for service delivery.

Intermediary mechanisms are not new, nor are they limited to specific welfare functions. In the public sector, federal and state governments play critical "banker" roles, raising funds for distribution to other organizations. More than ever before, indeed, taxes paid to governments at one level support welfare activities at other levels. Tax funds, in addition, are frequently contracted out to nongovernmental providers of service, or are used to subsidize the service choices of eligible populations in program areas such as health and developmental disabilities. Legislation like Medicare and Medicaid, for example, provides entitlements to services from existing community networks.

In the commercial sector, of course, private insurance companies have long acted as third-party intermediaries for health care. In the nonprofit sector, finally, philanthropic intermediaries like United Way operate to funnel the contributions of many thousands of individual and corporate givers to a limited number of human service agencies.

Grants-in-Aid. Federal aid, promoted in one fashion or another from the very founding of the American Republic, is a primary mechanism for tying together national revenues and local social welfare activities. Currently providing over $90 billion annually for state and local programs, aid payments are generally made for specified program purposes, and typically require some degree of local financial matching.

Federal aid programs are voluntary—states and localities are not required to participate in them. Once federal money is accepted, of course, the receiver is obligated to abide by prescribed standards and requirements. While states and localities ceaselessly lament the debilitating burdens and hindrances of federal "strings," few countries in the world have as much genuine sharing of fiscal and political power between their central and local governments as the United States. There are three forms of federal aid: categorical grants, block grants, and general revenue sharing.

CATEGORICAL GRANTS. Still the predominant form of aid, categorical grants are characterized by their specificity of purpose—funds can be used only for narrowly defined activities. While the administration of categorical aid is left to local and state authorities, the character and intent of the funding is congressionally precise. The Social Security Act of 1935, for example, provided aid not for public assistance in general but rather for particular at-risk groups: the blind, the aged, and dependent children. Similarly, the Juvenile Justice and Delinquency Prevention Act of 1974, rather than providing funds for social services in general, or for young people more narrowly, extended assistance to encourage a specific federal priority: removing juveniles from adult jails and lockups.

Public assistance, juvenile justice grants, and the approximately 500 other categorical programs currently in effect are all premised on the axiom of central direction. Reflecting the belief that detailed federal controls were required to protect programs from local mismanagement, parochialism, and lack of social commitment, categorical grants as they developed first in the 1930s under Franklin Roosevelt, and then in the 1960s under Lyndon Johnson, were structured with built-in protections to ensure efficient service delivery and targeting of the poor. Planning, personnel, citizen participation, and nondiscrimination provisos, for example, were regularly included in grant legislation, as was the nature of program activities and the populations eligible to be served.

BLOCK GRANTS. The second form of federal aid, block grants, were a manifestation of the "new federalism" theme of the Nixon-Ford-Reagan administrations, which was formulated in response to the categorical tradition of the New Deal and the Great Society. At the heart of the new federalism is a philosophy of decentralizing authority to states and localities.

Operationally, the new federalism is redefining the balance of grant policy making. Block grants, for example, promote decentralization by restricting the national role to funding and setting broad legislative goals and procedures, while state and local officials are left the task of actually defining the character of programs. Overall "policy," in other words, remains in federal hands while "program" substance becomes the responsibility of recipient governments.

Block grants promote decentralization in two ways. First, they provide funds for use in a broad functional area at the discretion of the recipient government. Uncle Sam doesn't dictate how the funds have to be applied. Second, block grants allocate funds according to a statutory formula. This gives the aid an automatic nature, limits the power of federal agencies, and provides a greater sense of control and certainty to recipient units.

Block grants have generally been created through the consolidation of categorical programs. The Comprehensive Employment and Training Act (CETA) of 1973, for example, aggregated over a dozen specific manpower enactments into one general grant authorizing localities to provide "comprehensive manpower services." Within this mandate, recipient "prime sponsors" have considerable discretion for establishing the optimal "mix" among program efforts. These include (but are not limited to): on-the-job or classroom training, remedial education, work experience, and "supportive social services."

In addition to CETA, several other block grant programs have been enacted: the Partnership for Health Act (1966); the Omnibus Crime Control and Safe Streets Act (1968), also known as the Law Enforcement Assistance Act (LEAA); the Housing and Community Development Act (1974, 1981); Title XX of the Social Security Act (1975, 1981); and a series of Reagan enactments in the health, mental health, and education areas.

Among the block grant programs, Title XX provides the most substantial degree of support for the social services. In the spirit of the block grant idea, Title XX does not define eligible social services. It does, however, establish five policy goals to guide program formulation by the states. These goals are:

- To achieve or maintain economic self-support to minimize dependency
- To achieve or maintain self-sufficiency
- To prevent or remedy the neglect or abuse of children or adults who are unable to protect themselves, and to preserve, rehabilitate, and reunite families
- To prevent or reduce inappropriate institutionalization by supporting community and home-based care
- To support institutional services, when such are necessary

The states are given almost full authority to reach these objectives as they wish, although they cannot use funds for land acquisition, construction, cash assistance, medical care, or regular educational services. The act provides an extensive list of service examples: childcare, protective services for children and adults, family planning, training and employment, preparation and delivery of meals, services to populations with special needs, and so forth. Like other block grants, no matching share is required of the states, and no state plan is necessary to qualify for funds, although a statement of "intended use" must be submitted. The new Title XX, finally, abolishes federal limitations on income eligibility. In a sharp reversal from pre-Reagan arrangements, the 1981 amendments eliminated all targeting of low-income populations.

Title XX expresses the principles of CETA and other block grant enactments in other basic fashions. All are appropriated on a formula basis, with federal funds divided among eligible units on the basis of population and other factors. All are focused on general-purpose governments rather than on special districts, neighborhoods, or independent agencies. All deemphasize the idea of national direction and priorities in favor of local flexibility. And while reporting, audit, and civil rights requirements remain, block grants—especially the newer ones—place little stress on citizen participation and the idea that social aid should be focused on those in greatest financial need.

Unconditional aid as provided for in general revenue sharing legislation was the second noteworthy manifestation of the new federalism. Revenue sharing involves the automatic and unrestricted distribution of federal aid to states and localities. In contrast to all other grant legislation, revenue sharing establishes no programmatic objectives. While recipient governments must abide by certain procedural rules in the administration of the program (there must, for example, be public hearings, completion of "use reports," and civil rights compliance), the "no strings" posture of the program is unimpaired with respect to program use.

Revenue sharing is special as a grant program in other respects. First, it is 100 percent aid—no matching is required. Second, all governmental jurisdictions, from the smallest township to the largest state, are enrolled in the program. Four times a year, federal entitlements are mailed automatically to some 40,000 units of "general government." Applications or plans aren't necessary, and monitoring is minimal. Finally, revenue sharing supports elected officials. While other aid revenues are typically funneled to particular administrative agencies, unconditional aid provides opportunities for city, county, and state chief executives and legislative bodies to decide themselves how aid support can best be structured to benefit their communities.

For advocates of federal priorities and tight accountability, revenue sharing represents a dangerous principle. For one thing, decentralizing program authority violates one of the oldest precepts of fiscal accountability—that only the level of government raising revenue should control its spending. Separating tax-raising and tax-spending responsibilities, it is argued, encourages irresponsible outlays. Why should local governments exert care in spending somebody else's dollars?

A more general objection stems from apprehensions concerning the "social mindedness" of states and localities. The American grant system has generally been in the vanguard of social innovation. While states and localities have been, on occasion, "laboratories" of social progress, it has been the national government that has historically responded to social problems and needs. Unconditional aid abdicates specific federal initiatives in favor of the questionable intensions and capacities of local decision makers.

Critics also attack revenue sharing's "you are there" eligibility formula. If all jurisdictions, no matter how small or inefficient or wealthy, receive aid, less remains for funding high-need problems and areas.

The Current Grant System. From the categorically focused and fiscally modest grant system of the 1950s and 1960s, federal aid has evolved into a tripartite arrangement of great magnitude. In 1980 federal aid provided $90 billion to states and localities, some 31 percent of state and local source receipts. Big cities are even more dependent on intergovernmental assistance, with federal aid making up 47.5 percent of the total budgets of the fifteen largest municipalities. Because most states provide aid of their own to their localities, counties and cities wind up receiving 78 percent as much revenue from outside as from local sources (Advisory Commission on Intergovernmental Relations, 1980, pp. 161–165). Clearly, the fiscal "middlemen" in the public sector are of enormous importance.

The degree to which banker governments restrict the freedom of aid recipients is a perennial social policy concern. Even with the new federalism, grant controls are pervasive. Categorical grants still provide more than three quarters of all aid dollars, and while block and unconditional grants have loose federal strings, a great number of mandates have become permanent, general features of the grant process as a whole. All recipient governments, for example, no matter how much or how little they receive in aid, are held to certain "cross-cutting" standards with regard to civil rights, nondiscrimination, environmental protection, wage rates, and accounting procedures.

Yet "local control" remains a tangible reality in some of the most critical areas of social decision making. States and localities are the implementors of social welfare policies, organizing programs, hiring staffs, and delivering benefits to people in need. While each of these operations occurs largely within a context specified in federal legislation, the grant system, like the federal system as a whole, retains genuine powers for local citizens and policymakers.

Third-Party Mechanisms. Governments can structure social welfare provisions in three fundamental ways: They can organize and deliver services thmselves, they can fund other governmental units to provide service, or they can act to promote service delivery by nongovernmental bodies. The federal government, on the one hand, operates the Social Security system—especially the social insurance components—almost entirely on its own. Federal aid, on the other hand, is organized intergovernmentally, with services delivered by local governmental jurisdictions. Governmental contracts with the voluntary sector, finally, permit public agencies to engage private organizations suitable for operating given types of programs.

The nongovernmental sector is also promoted by public policies that stimulate consumer social welfare purchases. Income maintenance strategies give individuals resources for making their own spending decisions. Tax subsidies similarly promote consumer spending in certain areas, as do "earmarked" income transfers such as food stamps.

Another "market mechanism" built on the principle of consumer choice is third-party financing. While third parties operate in a variety of service fields, health-care arrangements are of particular importance for social work.

Health care is the area in which third-party programs have the longest history and the greatest magnitude. Commercial insurance carriers are vast enterprises serving many millions of subscribers. Insurance firms, like government units, play a banker role. Whereas governments secure their revenues through tax or social insurance levies, however, private companies raise their funds through premiums priced to reflect the costs of coverage as defined in the insurance policy.

In public third-party programs, coverage is defined in legislation. The major public programs such as Medicare and Medicaid "subsidize demand" for large numbers of people in special need. In Medicare, the population served is the elderly; in Medicaid, it is the poor. In both cases, public tax dollars ensure access to health services by paying health "suppliers" for the services they render. In both cases, as under private plans, beneficiaries can seek care from any authorized provider participating in the program.

Both public and private systems limit their coverage to certain health services, health providers, and levels of expenses. Third-party programs differ, for example, in their comprehensiveness. Some cover dentistry, speech therapy, and cosmetic surgery while others do not. Roughly 90 percent of private employee plans have some mental health coverage (President's Commission on Mental Health, 1978, p. 506). With respect to providers, medical doctors are generally the approved "vendors." Finally, few policies pay all the expenses involved in health services. In both public and private programs, indeed, considerable consumer copayments and deductibles are often required.

Much of the social work dilemma in third-party arrangements results from the fact that state-licensed social work professionals are not generally recognized as legitimate—and therefore reimbursable—providers of mental health services. Despite the virtual absence of evidence indicating the effectiveness of any particular type of mental health intervention or profession, the dominant payment model favors physicians. Blue Cross, the largest third-party firm, is illustrative. Mental disability, generally covered as a supplementary benefit, often can only be treated by, or under the supervision of, an M.D. with the supervision requirement frequently interpreted to require the physical presence of a physician in the facility where service is provided. Except in a few states, such as California, social workers operating "solo," or independently within a counseling or mental health agency, cannot be reimbursed (Kurzman, 1973).

The public system funds mental health care in an even more restrictive fashion. Under state Medicaid programs, mental health services for the poor can be provided by physicians, and, in some states, by psychologists and Christian Science practitioners. In no states are social workers authorized as independent providers. Under CHAMPUS (Civilian Health and Medical Program of the Uniformed Services), social workers can be reimbursed for mental health services given retired servicemen and other eligibles if a referral is made by a physician who then provides ongoing supervision. About 4 percent of CHAMPUS billings fund licensed social workers (U.S. General Accounting Office, 1980, p. 8).

Because of the varying roadblocks to reimbursement, community mental health centers—which rely heavily on nonphysician professionals such as social workers, psychologists, and psychiatric nurses—have not been able to secure significant third-party funding. In 1973, indeed, 69 percent of Community Mental Health Center (CMHC) support was from categorical aid, just 2 percent from Medicare, 9 percent from Medicaid, and 8 percent from commercial insurance (President's Commission on Mental Health, 1978, p. 508).

The role of nonphysician providers in future health and mental health legislation, of course, is of considerable interest to several human services professions. The American Psychological Association has been fighting for years to get Congress to include psychological care within Medicare and Medicaid. The National Association of Social Workers has "vendorization" as one of its chief legislative priorities. While these professional groups have attained a measure of success through the judicial system and state legislatures—state "freedom of choice" laws increasingly are eroding the psychiatric monopoly—liberalized enactments at the federal level are unlikely in the near term. The issue of who should be sanctioned for reimbursement, for how long, and under what kinds of arrangements, however, is of considerable concern to federal agencies, such as the National Institute of Mental Health (NIMH), that are charged with planning for improved services. In an effort to address questions of who should be paid for what kinds of mental health services, NIMH has undertaken an extensive program of "clinical trials" to test different modes of treatment and different types of therapists. These empirical studies are intended to determine safety and effectiveness and serve as a basis for constructing the mental health payment policies of the future.

While public third-party arrangements are best known in the health care field, other services are similarly organized. Vendor payments are frequently used to promote or protect the welfare of population groups with clear and generally recognized human care needs—populations such as dependent children, the mentally disabled, and the indigent elderly. Under federal developmental disabilities legislation, for example, state agencies certify a broad spectrum of providers for services to developmentally disabled clients. Local regional centers providing case management to these clients can purchase goods and services only from those individuals, agencies, and institutions "vendorized" by the state.

Under Title XX of the Social Security Act, many states act as third-party funders of daycare services. Eligible vendors may include individual, group, or agency providers. The client makes his or her own service arrangements, and the supplier is compensated for service in accordance with predetermined rate schedules.

Whereas daycare tax credits are provided for most any and all service arrangements, third-party funding under Title XX generally limits payments to providers meeting certain standards. In some states, only licensed daycare centers are eligible for reimbursement. In others, suppliers must meet certain conditions related to staffing and physical facilities. Occasionally, only nonprofits are eligible under the program.

Contracting Out. Governments are increasingly calling on private organizations, especially nonprofit community agencies, to deliver tax-funded social welfare services. Contracting, for example, is the major service delivery model under the Older Americans Act and Title XX and accounts for nearly one third of all job-training expenditures under CETA (Terrell, 1979, p. 64). States have vastly expanded their use of service contracting to bolster community-based residential services for deinstitutionalized mental patients. Local governments, more than ever before, are relying on voluntary services as an alternative to traditional public administration.

Contracting differs from public third-party programs in being production- rather than consumption-oriented. Instead of extending entitlements to specific population groups and paying for their market choices, contracts directly finance particular program operators. A municipality seeking "nonbureaucratic" alternatives to the juvenile justice system, for example, may contract with a local diversion project for counseling and other services to young people. A state seeking to strengthen at-risk families may purchase a broad range of counseling, family planning, and homemaker services.

Like market-oriented programs, contracting advances public objectives through nonpublic means. Private agencies often have a special competency absent in the public sector, and their use enables governments to provide services they could not otherwise. Community agencies, for example, may be acceptable to marginal populations—the mentally ill, drug abusers, the minority aged—unwilling to seek assistance from public bureaus. Private agencies, because of their reliance on volunteers or nonunionized labor, may be able to provide services at a lower cost than their public counterparts. Contracting may also be an expedient way of avoiding personnel or budget limits on the public sector.

Contracting, finally, is often an easier way of implementing new programs, since it avoids the start-up problems of public services.

Contract finance, of course, can be a hazardous undertaking. Independent of the public line of command, private agencies may use public funds to advance their own, rather than public, purposes. Private agencies, more than public ones, are often small and lacking even rudimentary management and fiscal skills. And private agencies, backed up by powerful boards of directors and militant consumers, can coerce governments into ever larger and more flexible delegations of money and power. A recent Massachusetts report, indeed, argues that the state has been the victim of "a provider-dominated purchase system which contributes to [a] lack of effective fiscal and program control. Providers have become such an important part of the service organization that some state agencies fear the repercussions if stricter controls are imposed. Thus, the impasse has become self-perpetuating: The larger the role of the providers, the less control the state can exert over them; the less control the state exerts, the larger the providers' role in the system becomes" (Massachusetts Taxpayers' Foundation, 1980, pp. i–ii).

Federated Fund Raising. Federated fund raising developed rapidly in this country after World War I as a means of coordinating the charity drives of social agencies. By conducting a single annual community-wide solicitation, the federations sought to reduce the annoyance and inefficiency of multiple fund-raising efforts. Federations also sought, generally without any great degree of success, to "rationalize giving" by using "scientific allocation" techniques to balance community problems and resources, promote coordination and planning, and advance needs studies and other services research.

The United Way of America, the largest of the federations, is composed of approximately 2,300 local organizations, each of which is governed by a board of directors representing member (that is, supported) agencies, labor unions, businesses, and other civic organizations. Like governments, local United Ways perform two basic functions: fund raising and fund allocation. Under the slogan "one gift for all," the campaign proceeds house-to-house, business-to-business, institution-to-institution on behalf of constituent agencies. Unlike governments, of course, the United Way relies on contributions rather than compulsion.

In 1979 $1.32 billion was collected by local campaigns—roughly one quarter from corporations and three quarters from employees through payroll deductions and contributions. While these funds benefited many thousands of local social efforts, by far the largest portion went to finance the local affiliates of the major nationwide charities—the Boy Scouts, Girl Scouts, YMCA, YWCA, Salvation Army, Red Cross, Urban League, Family Service agencies, Travelers' Aid, and so forth. The Red Cross alone received 15 percent of all outlays. Though allocation patterns have been shifted somewhat in recent years, the United Way remains under heavy fire for alleged racism, sexism, and corporatism. While many local independent agencies are part of the United Way network, funds continue to be concentrated on old-line, uncontroversial services.

Despite its position as the "IBM of the charity business," the United Way funds only a small portion of the local human services enterprise, even for its own affiliate agencies. On the average, member agencies receive about 25 percent of their budgets from the United Ways. In many metropolitan areas, member agencies receive a far greater portion of their support from government contracts.

Welfare Finance in an Era of Austerity

Social welfare agencies and institutions, as Peter Drucker (1973) has noted, are budget-based enterprises. Generally unable to price and sell their products in order to secure fiscal support from consumers, nonprofit and governmental organizations must, of necessity, be concerned with maintaining and expanding their budgets. In the 1980s, this revenue task will be increasingly difficult. After two decades of rapid growth in the magnitude of available resources, powerful counterforces have set in. Welfare allocations from tax dollars are no longer increasing as a proportion of GNP. Private spending for welfare has leveled off. Philanthropic giving is barely holding its own. The welfare state, if not in decline, is clearly in a period of slowdown.

Increasing resistance to the cost of welfare, however, should not be misread as a rejection of the human services. Opinion surveys consistently attest to a high degree of satisfaction with the existing level of services in most all welfare areas except public assistance (Lipset and Raab, 1978). The recent abatement of voter support for tax and expenditure limitation initiatives also indicates a genuine fear on the part of many voters that further cuts might substantially damage important programs.

It is difficult, nevertheless, to be sanguine about the implications of the current fiscal austerity. With respect to tax burdens, spending patterns, and government employment, fiscal trends promise increasing hazards for social programs and the constituencies they serve.

First of all, most pressures now on the tax system are pushing toward regressivity. Property tax reductions, for example, provide their greatest benefits to those whose wealth is in land and buildings, particularly agribusiness, large corporations, and owners of residential property. Single homeowners receive moderate benefits from property tax reductions. Renters receive few if any benefits. In the first year after Proposition 13 in California, for example, only 24 percent of the $7 billion tax cut benefited individuals living in and owning their homes; fully 40 percent of the savings went to the owners of commercial, industrial, agricultural, and rental property ("Proposition 13: Who Really Won?" 1979, p. 546).

Efforts to reduce income taxation, of course, clearly steer toward regressivity, lowered rates providing disproportionate savings to the wealthy. And while efforts to limit "tax creep" by indexing income taxes can address the hidden tax burdens built into inflation, they also eliminate one of the few tax mechanisms for extracting greater revenues from highest income groups.

In addition to altering the overall progressivity of the tax system, fiscal austerity threatens social spending. The Reagan cutbacks clearly focus on social spending. Because the poor and handicapped are most dependent on government services, revenue reductions directly affect their well-being. In the wake of Proposition 13, for example, most all income maintenance and social service programs run by state and local governments in California lost revenues in spendable-dollar terms. A recent NASW study, indeed, determined two-year losses to have ranged from 14 percent in Aid to Families with Dependent Children (AFDC) budgets to 42 percent in the case of revenue sharing funds designated for community-based services (Terrell, 1981, p. 276).

Faced with fewer real dollars, elected policymakers and administrators are concentrating cutbacks in program areas where they have reduction discretion and where direct on-the-line public services are not immediately affected. In California, therefore, the major reductions have occurred in contracted services with the voluntary sector and in "ancillary" program areas such as outreach, community education, and staff development (Terrell, 1981, p. 279).

A third implication of fiscal austerity is likely to be at least a partial loss in the public-sector job gains made in the past ten years by minority groups and women. Slowdowns in the growth of government employment endanger progress toward affirmative action goals because it is through new hiring that disadvantaged groups increase their work force proportion. When job cutbacks are implemented, minority employees—who tend to be most recently hired—are most likely to be targeted for dismissal. When New York City reduced its payroll by 13 percent after its near-bankruptcy in the early 1970s, it lost half of its Hispanic and 40 percent of its black male work force (Menchik and Pascal, 1980, p. 19).

Many of the social services instituted in the recent past are particularly jeopardized by the new austerity. As two Rand Corporation researchers have stated: "Newer programs have not yet developed strong and vocal constituencies; it can be argued that the last-instituted activity is the least urgent—otherwise, it would have been instituted earlier. The very fact that many services for the disadvantaged, ethnic-oriented services, community development activities, and innovative programs for children are not traditional functions of state or local government put them at particular risk. Programs with a poorly organized clientele—perhaps because the programs are new, perhaps because their clients are impoverished or demoralized—may also suffer. Where clients lack well-organized employee groups to team up with, their services are even more vulnerable. Most police and teacher organizations, for instance, are much more powerful at both the local and state levels than employees who work in libraries and human service agencies (Menchik and Pascal, 1980, p. 18).

The social work profession, of course, cannot escape being powerfully affected by changes in the source, nature, and magnitude of welfare receipts. One fundamental lesson of the current austerity, indeed, is that all social workers have a major stake in issues of finance. If human services workers are not to be continually buffeted in the years ahead by tax "reform" measures à la Howard Jarvis, Jack Kemp, and Ronald Reagan, welfare advocates must be able to understand the workings of the finance system, the fashion in which revenues are raised, and how allocations are determined. Social workers should know enough at the very least to be able to promote meaningful tax reform alternatives that can address the legitimate grievances of middle-class taxpayers without undermining the basic principles of tax equity or condemning the poor.

Human service workers in the "indirect" services, of course, have special responsibilities for guiding programs through the fiscal thickets ahead. Confronted by a tighter revenue environment, administrators will be subject to increasing pressures for spending cuts, efficiency, and evidence of "results." Creative responses, in my judgment, will require program managers to directly confront and plan for retrenchment. Rather than ad hoc approaches, professional administrators need considered strategies for survival, new means for securing revenues, and better methods for mobilizing constituencies. Perhaps most of all, managers will have to be increasingly adept at justifying the value of their efforts.

Welfare officials, unfortunately, have traditionally been weak at proving program effectiveness. To quote Drucker (1980): "Services institutions are not *want*-oriented; they are *need*-oriented. By definition they are concerned with 'good works' and with 'social' or 'moral' contributions rather than with returns and results. The social worker will always believe that the very failure of her efforts . . . proves that more effort and more money are needed. She cannot accept that her failure means that she had better stop doing what she is so valiantly failing in" (p. 44).

Drucker's point is timely. Welfare advocates have long been accustomed to thinking in terms of programs rather than outcomes. In an era of mounting skepticism, however, such "moral" approaches are not likely to be successful. Managers arguing for support on the basis of intentions rather than performance will increasingly find themselves losing in the competition for resources.

Fiscal austerity, if it is to be managed and survived, demands the assessment of both organizational strengths and weaknesses. Accommodating fund reductions by spreading them "across the board" ignores the tangible certainty that in every organization some activities are more critical than others. "Sharing the pain" out of some mistaken notion of equity means that inessentials (or less essentials) will not be pared in favor of productive units. Such approaches abdicate the responsibility that every manager has to concentrate funds where they can best address organizational goals.

Austerity, then, requires the assessment of activity in terms of results, the clarification of purposes, and a plan to strengthen those program and practice components having the greatest potential for success. It requires, also, the ability to slough off what doesn't work, for only by abandoning the least promising activities can the important efforts be sustained.

For the casework practitioner, fiscal austerity will mean greater job demands and fewer job rewards. In the aftermath of Proposition 13, public service work loads have increased throughout California, lowering morale and, in areas where private job opportunities exist, leading to an exodus of talented people from government. This trend is not going to disappear. Demands for accountability, for example, will escalate the paperwork of line workers as new systems for gauging activity and results are tested and applied.

In addition, if the California situation is illustrative, lessened resources will result in reduced support services. The NASW report on Proposition 13 found significant reductions in the human services work force in those positions backing up direct service employees with supervisory and technical assistance and training (Terrell, 1981).

For social program consumers, finally, austerity threatens decreased service levels and lessened service quality. Lower budgets and fewer workers result, in most cases, not in greater program efficiency but rather in the deterioration of services. The environment of restraint severely limits efforts to address currently unmet needs, no matter how severe they may be. With program maintenance the new sine qua non of planning and budgeting, there are but infrequent opportunities to establish new services or to initiate long-term commitments. Fiscal conditions, in this sense, have clearly brought a new conservatism to the welfare sector, along with a new caution in tackling social problems.

References

Aaron, H. J. *Who Pays the Property Tax?* Washington, D.C.: Brookings Institution, 1973.

Advisory Commission on Intergovernmental Relations. *Property Tax Circuit Breakers.* Washington, D.C.: Advisory Commission on Intergovernmental Relations, 1977.

Advisory Commission on Intergovernmental Relations. *Significant Features of Fiscal Federalism, 1979–1980.* Washington, D.C.: Advisory Commission on Intergovernmental Relations, 1980.

American Association of Fund Raising Council. *Giving U.S.A., 1979 Annual Report.* New York: American Association of Fund Raising Council, 1979.

Drucker, P. "Managing the Public Service Institution." *The Public Interest,* 1973, *33,* 43–60.

Drucker, P. *Managing in Turbulent Times.* New York: Harper & Row, 1980.

Eisenstein, L. *The Ideologies of Taxation.* New York: Ronald Press, 1961.

Kurzman, P. "Third-Party Reimbursement." *Social Work,* 1973, *18* (6), 11–23.

Lipset, S. M., and Raab, E. "The Message of Proposition 13." *Commentary,* 1978, *66* (3), 42–46.

Lohman, R. *Breaking Even.* Philadelphia: Temple University Press, 1980.

McMillan, A., and Bixby, A. "Social Welfare Expenditures, Fiscal Year 1978." *Social Security Bulletin,* 1980, *43* (5), 3, 12–13.

Massachusetts Taxpayers' Foundation. *Purchase of Service: Can State Government Gain Control?* Boston: Massachusetts Taxpayers' Foundation, 1980.

Menchik, M., and Pascal, A. *The Equity Effects of Restraints on Taxing and Spending.* Santa Monica, Calif.: Rand Corporation, May 1980.

Minarik, J. J. "Tax Expenditures." In J. A. Pechman (Ed.), *Setting National Priorities, the 1982 Budget.* Washington, D.C.: Brookings Institution, 1981.

National Association of Social Workers. *Code of Ethics.* Section I. Washington, D.C.: National Association of Social Workers, July 1980.

Pechman, J. *Federal Tax Policy.* (3rd ed.) Washington, D.C.: Brookings Institution, 1977.

Pechman, J. A., and Okner, B. A. *Who Bears the Tax Burden?* Washington, D.C.: Brookings Institution, 1974.

President's Commission on Mental Health. *Report of the Task Panel on Cost and Financing.* Vol. 2 Appendix. Washington, D.C.: President's Commission on Mental Health, 1978.

"Proposition 13: Who Really Won?" *Consumer Reports,* September 1979, p. 546.

Spindler, A. *Public Welfare.* New York: Human Sciences Press, 1979.

Terrell, P. "Private Alternatives to Public Human Services Administration." *Social Services Review,* 1979, *53* (1), 56–74.

Terrell, P. "Adapting to Austerity: Human Services After Proposition 13." *Social Work,* 1981, *26* (4), 275–281.

Titmuss, R. "The Social Division of Welfare: Some Reflections on the Search for Equity." *Essays on the Welfare State.* New Haven, Conn.: Yale University Press, 1959.

U.S. Congressional Budget Office. *Childcare and Preschool: Options for Federal Support.* Washington, D.C.: U.S. Congressional Budget Office, September 1978.

U.S. Department of Health and Human Services. *Annual Report to the Congress on Title XX of the Social Security Act, Fiscal Year 1979.* Washington, D.C.: Office of Human Development Services, U.S. Department of Health and Human Services, February 1980.

U.S. General Accounting Office. *Extent of Billing by Non-Psychiatric Specialty Physicians for Mental Health Services Under CHAMPUS.* Washington, D.C.: U.S. General Accounting Office, 1980.

United Way of America. *Fisher-Conable/Moynihan-Packwood Fact Sheet.* Alexandria, Va.: United Way of America, February 2, 1979.

Wishner, J. *The Government Subsidy Squeeze.* Washington, D.C.: Common Cause, 1980.

36

Social Service Priorities and Resource Allocation

Shirley Jenkins

It is an axiom of social welfare that needs will always outrun resources. And even if it were possible to satisfy today's needs, tomorrow's would be greater because of rising expectations. Decisions on allocations of resources in every country, whether the economy is planned or unplanned, emerge from compromises among a variety of interests and demands of public, professional, and client groups with reference to competing problems requiring attention. Given this process, how do priorities emerge in determining who shall get what? The aim of this chapter is not to say what should be, but rather to examine the components of decision making.

With such a wide berth, however, some reference should be made to the different ways in which the term *priority* can be used. *Webster's* (1960) definition, "precedence in time, order, or importance" is not helpful (p. 1159). Each of the three factors may be in conflict with the others. What should be done first may not be the most important, and the most important thing need not necessarily be done right away. In general usage, priority is often taken to be a value term, a broad ideological concept without empirical referents. More specifically, in the programmatic sense, the term priority can be used operationally to refer to a policy backed by resources and administrative measures. Both the general and the specific usages are incorporated in the discussion that follows, and the context should reveal which is applicable.

The analysis of how priorities emerge can take place at two levels. At the national level, decisions are made that affect what proportion of the national budget is allocated to the social services. Although precise intercountry comparisons are difficult—because of differences in definitions, inclusions, exclusions, subsidies, and controls—discrepancies can be identified among countries with regard to what proportion of the gross national product is allocated to social welfare. Among the factors affecting these differences are the levels of national economies, political ideologies, internal struggles, and the history, unique characteristics, and social institutions of each country.

The second level of analysis is to look within the social service system of any one country to see how the pie is cut. Given the total budget allocation for human resources, what accounts for the distribution of funds among the various programs and interest groups?

Although these are different levels of analysis, they are not unrelated, since both are affected by economic and social developments and ideological commitments. It is ironic that there often appears to be an inverse relationship between social needs and resources available for social welfare. Social needs always exist, but when times are prosperous and budgets are not as tight, there may be fewer demands for social services than in periods of depression and unemployment. During hard times, however, funds for service are usually constricted. Thus, a corollary to the axiom that needs will always outrun resources might be, "there is more when needs are less, and less when needs are more."

What is the relevance for clinical social workers of a discussion of policy priorities? Clinicians continue to make case decisions, whether explicit or implicit, on treatment goals and modalities. But the illusion may persist that their field of decision making is bounded by the treatment situation, with the clinician at one pole and the client at the other. Such is not the case. Priorities, even in treatment, cannot be abstracted from the social context in which they are determined.

There are many ways in which the social polity of the treatment milieu affects worker priorities. At the simplest level, the patient's decision to enter treatment, and the therapist's decision to accept the patient, depends in part on income level, insurance coverage, reimbursement, and fee scales for treatment. And part of the decision on the therapeutic plan may depend on whether coverage is available for short- or for long-term treatment.

At a second level, the practice model of the clinician may affect treatment priorities. If the clinician sees interaction between the individual and the environment as part of the client's problem, priorities in treatment will be ordered differently than if the problem is seen as purely an intrapsychic phenomenon. One example of a reordered set of priorities is found in the growing field of industrial social work, where services are offered in the work setting, often under trade union auspices. A clinician in such a setting must be aware of both work issues and union policy issues and order priorities accordingly.

A third level exists where policy decisions to treat specific client groups require altered or new treatment modalities, and these may lead to the development of new theoretical constructs. Clinicians have often bemoaned the "inaccessibility of the poor" to treatment, for example, and the problems of working with the "hard-to-reach." Some of the difficulties may be because psychological help may not be effective in the face of overwhelming economic need, but the other explanation is that the policy decision on whom to treat needs to be backed up by clinical decisions on how to treat, given the particular needs of the client group.

Two examples will illustrate how clinicians may alter treatment modalities in view of policy priorities. Work with women who have experienced mastectomies, for example, might best be undertaken in the form of self-help and association with others who have had the same experience. The role of the clinician is an altered one. Another example of clinicians' adapting modes of treatment to help a group of people in need is the work of Robert Jay Lifton and others (1973) with veterans of the Vietnam War. Because of the singularity and intensity of their experience, and the fact that veterans suffered not only from battlefield exposure but from conflicts engendered by being involved in an unpopular war, Lifton and his colleagues developed ways of treatment in "rap" sessions. They remained clinicians, but the way they worked, the materials they used in therapy, and the ways they adapted old theories to new situations and generated new theories were all outcomes of the particular client group they treated.

Finally, the place of clinical work in the broad spectrum of human services is itself a priority issue. The cost-effectiveness of psychotherapy is a subject for lively debate in Washington, in both congressional and executive branches. This debate should engage clinicians because they, more than policy specialists, will be called upon to provide evidence to support their current training, research, and treatment budgets. If this defense cannot be adequately made, clinical work itself will have low priority in the national ordering of social service programs.

How do priorities in social services emerge in the United States, with the many competing demands, sectors, and needs? It is suggested that four areas relate to decision making and affect "who gets what" in social service benefits. These areas are social needs, social issues, social and political pressures, and social triage. These are not mutually exclusive categories, and there is overlap for each. But they provide a handle for approaching different dimensions of the priorities issue, and each will be discussed in turn.

Social Needs

It is both valid and simplistic to say that social needs affect the priorities for social services. It is valid because just about every service will respond to some need and simplistic because beyond absolute life-and-death decisions (and even for some of those), social needs are culturally determined and subject to a variety of interpretations. Thus, the search for absolute priorities with universal application is not likely to be fruitful. It is more useful to analyze the factors that enter into the determination of policy.

As Eveline Burns (1956) pointed out in her definitive work *Social Security and Public Policy*, a variety of features of contemporary society will be relevant to social security planning, and these factors also apply to social service delivery. Included are the general level of productivity of the country, national perceptions of an appropriate standard of living, available technology, level of employment, demographic characteristics of the population, changing roles of the family system, and technical and administrative inventiveness. Thus, Burns concludes that it is unwise to generalize about the impact of new programs without knowing the social configuration in which they will be played out, and it is also unwise to assume that any one set of value assumptions should prevail: "intelligent policy formation, that is, the attainment of the best possible compromise between conflicting objectives, can be expected only if people know what they are choosing between. And the choice is not of an 'either-or' character but between relatively more and relatively less. There are no absolutes" (p. 279).

Within this frame of reference, however, decisions are made, and the concept of social need influences the process. Bradshaw (1972) presents a useful categorization of the different concepts of need used in the social planning process at the regional or local level of administration. His definitions clarify the categories according to normative need, felt need, expressed need, and comparative need.

Normative need is defined by professional or expert assessment in any given situation. Nutritional standards or inoculation procedures would be examples of normative needs. These are not absolute for all times and places and are subject to value judgments. Nonetheless, for a given time and place, a relatively large area of agreement can be reached on services falling into the normative need category.

Felt need is equated with want. It may be a consideration in developing social service programs, but as Blenkner, Jahn, and Wasser (1964) showed in a study of the elderly, it can open a Pandora's box of demands beyond the system's capacity to fulfill. In a program designed as a "saturation study," research workers asked the elderly what they felt they needed. The more they were asked, the more needs they felt. So felt need is presumably a less reliable priority factor than normative need.

Bradshaw (1972) defines expressed need as "felt need turned into action," (p. 641). One criterion for use in priority determination is the existence of waiting lists, such as for daycare or nursing home entry. Another is in the area of social action, which will be discussed later under the general subject of social pressure.

Finally, comparative need refers to situations in which people with similar characteristics may not be receiving similar services. Examples might be related to the question of "take-up" of entitlements, to people eligible but not applying for welfare, or to situations in which people at risk are identified and preventive services are appropriate.

What Bradshaw suggests is a taxonomy of social need as a basis for priority determination with a plus or minus allocation for each of the four categories. Thus, if a single-parent working mother (normative need) wants daycare for her child (felt need), registers at the daycare center (expressed need), and has a neighbor similarly situated with a child at the center (comparative need), she would have clear priority for service over another applicant who might not be single or working, not feel the need, might not register, might not show a comparable situation, or any combination thereof. This taxonomy is particularly useful in determining priorities among applicants. There is an implicit assumption, however, of equal values for each of the need categories, which may not be warranted by the facts of the case. But as Burns (1956) has noted, choices cannot be made unless people know the alternatives, and some way to develop precision in describing the categories of need can be a useful tool.

A more rigorous approach to the development of priorities has been attempted by the social indicators movement. The goal is to utilize a range of statistical measures that, in combination, can provide indicators of social development and social need, and give a quantitative base for social planning. This movement has had a varied history, first promising more than it could deliver, and then being utilized less than its technology warrants. A brief review of the indicators movement can be found in Rossi and Gilmartin (1980).

The publication of *Toward a Social Report* was an ambitious effort of the Department of Health, Education and Welfare, now Health and Human Services (1969), to suggest development of measures of social change comparable to the widely used set of national economic indicators. It was anticipated that such measures would be useful to policy makers in assessing change, in program evaluation, and in indicating priority areas. A social indicator, according to the report, was defined as "a statistic of direct normative interest which facilitates concise, comprehensive, and balanced judgments about the conditions of major aspects of society. It is in all cases a direct measure of welfare and is subject to the interpretation that, if it changes in the 'right' direction, while other things remain equal, things have gotten better, or people are 'better off'" (p. 97).

This formulation was sharply criticized by other workers in the field. Sheldon and Freeman (1970) saw indicators as quantitative descriptive measures, rather than as normative, value-laden devices. The limitation of needing a continuum from right to wrong, or better or worse, restricts the variables subject to analysis. In addition, some data sets measure natural phenomena, others measure administrative or programmatic outcomes. Admissions to psychiatric facilities, for example, may decline when the population becomes more healthy, when facilities are closed for lack of funding, or when the philosophy of treatment changes from institutional to community care. The data themselves will not tell if things are "better" or "worse." Furthermore, social indicators tend to be composites of a range of statistics, gathered over time, and this is another limitation to their use in evaluation of specific programs or in setting goals and priorities.

Even though they may have limited value in program evaluation or priority determination, social indicators, which include both direct and indirect measures of relevant variables, have an important role in descriptive, analytical, and forecasting work. A study by Kogan and Jenkins (1974) that sought to identify factors associated with the need for child health and welfare programs illustrates the use of social indicators. The goal was to develop a single "quality of life" measure, and twenty-four variables representing key aspects of child conditions and family context were included. Data were collected for two time periods, 1960 and 1970, and for three sets of geographical units—the fifty states plus the District of Columbia, the sixty-two counties of New York State, and the sixty-two community districts of New York City. When factor analytic procedures were applied to the twenty-four normative variables, five showed high loadings (above a criterion of .60) on the first principal factor in all six independent analyses. This factor was interpreted to represent an underlying dimension associated with poverty. The variables included dependency (Aid to Families with Dependent Children), incomplete families, premature births, out-of-wedlock births, and juvenile venereal disease. Together they indicated the level of "quality of life."

In a follow-up study in two contrasting counties in upstate New York, each of which represented the "best" and the "worst" of the poverty indicators, a carefully designed probability sample was selected, and families were visited in a home interview to study children's problems (Kogan, Smith, and Jenkins, 1977). The findings showed that, for the primary sampling units, the aggregate social indicators data could successfully predict a considerable proportion of both child and parent variables derived from the interview data. These studies show that to determine broad categories of need, aggregate social data can be used and expensive and time-consuming sampling studies may not be necessary. For specific program efforts, however, aggregate data may not suffice.

In summary, social needs, normative needs in particular, can be measured by aggregate data, and these findings feed into but do not necessarily determine the priority for programs. Social need, especially normative need, appears to be more relevant in defining the field and setting the boundaries than in establishing specific priorities.

Social Issues

Social issues and social problems have direct impact on determining social-service priorities. The issues may arise from social needs, but they tend to peak and fade in a cycle of public attention and concern. In the last two decades, for example, major attention has been given, in turn, to juvenile delinquency, drug addiction, and child abuse. The shift in priorities does not mean that the earlier problem is solved, but rather that it is no longer popular. Senator Moynihan was quoted in the *New York Times* (1980) as stating to the National Urban League Conference, "For reasons that I do not entirely understand, therefore cannot fully explain, welfare reform is no longer high on the agenda of the groups and organizations that tend to define the national social policy agenda" (Sec. A, p. 10).

To what can we attribute this fadlike quality of priority attention? Some of it reflects surfacing of real needs and important issues. Some of it is political, in that the concern may be not only for the clients but for a victimized group. Some of it may be diversionary from underlying problems and ways of meeting partial need. The way in which our social service system funds programs, and the categorical rather than universal approach to services, reinforces the tendency to give priority to special issues with popular appeal, rather than to an integrated system of personal social services.

The current attention to child abuse—the proliferation of programs in this area and the special funding that has been made available—is a case in point. In a recent national study of public social services, Jenkins, Schroeder, and Burgdorf (1981) found that child neglect and abuse together accounted for 52 percent of all primary problems in children for a client population of 1.8 million people (p. 22).

Anthony Downs (1972) refers to the phenomenon of the "issue attention cycle," describing a sequence in which a social problem is discovered, attention is paid, hope is high, and then commitment falls as the difficulties of solution emerge and new issues arise. Concern that child abuse has entered a new phase in this "issue attention cycle" was expressed by the executive director of the New Jersey Protective Services Resource Institute. Writing in their *P.S.R.T. Report,* Frank Schneiger (1970) states, "In part, this change is a result of the fact that it has been around for a while and is no longer new and exciting. As is the case for most issues, its potential competitors for public attention are visible on the horizon. While this competition can hardly be characterized as a zero-sum game, there are winners and losers, with the prize being funding for programs. Thus, if we are likely to hear more and more about wife battering and problems of the elderly, it will probably be, at least to some extent, at the expense of abuse and neglect" (p. 2).

Reference to child abuse as an overstated issue is not to be interpreted as expressing a minority position in its favor. Its relevance is rather as an illustration of how a phenomenon that is a partial indication of a larger problem can emerge as a priority issue, expand because of the system of categorical funding, then face decline in part because answers are not directly forthcoming. The same cycle would apply to "surrender and adoption" or "permanency in planning," which could be cited as alternative illustrations.

One factor not recognized by these categorical programs is that every solution presents a problem. Antler (1978) expresses concern that the medical model of treating child abuse as a disease creates problems of fragmentation and unreal expectations of cure through professional treatment. In addition, the stigma of identification as an "abusing parent" can only be dysfunctional. The real danger is that the priority on child abuse diverts and detracts from a comprehensive approach to family and community services, wherein probably lies the most viable approach to the problem itself.

In summary, social issues build on social need in the development of priorities for services. Attention must be paid to the concerns of the times, but they are unreliable as a base for shifting directions in service delivery, developing new modalities, training new cadres, teaching new courses, developing new theories. When attention fades, it may be because the approach hasn't worked, not because the problem has been solved. Priority issues can and should be identified, but each issue does not call for categorical programming or a separate service system.

Social and Political Pressures

Social issues generate pressure to specify priorities, but social and political pressure in itself represents a somewhat different dimension in determining the direction of services. Priorities arising from such pressures may be blatant and explicit, such as the opening of a senior citizen center on the eve of an election campaign or a clean-up of the Times Square area in New York City just before a national convention. Political pressure may also arise in response to the concerns of a victimized group, such as a priority on arrests following a street mugging of a prominent person or a check on housing violations after a fire in a nursing home. In addition, political priorities emerge in relation to issues that cut across program lines, such as budget, accountability, management, and professionalism. Administrative priorities of the welfare bureaucracy are not always directed to meeting client needs. For example, a recurrent theme in recent years has been priority attention to reduction of welfare rolls. The national attention to case management does not arise from the discovery of a significant new practice model, but rather from the priority given to efficiency, economy, and accountability.

Other social and political pressures arise from the organized groups who, as Bradshaw (1972) said, turn felt needs into social action. These groups include the more vocal and visible social movements, such as welfare rights, organized special-interest groups (for example, those concerned with particular handicaps), and professional lobbies who campaign for priority attention on their own behalf.

The importance of interest-group influence on priority determination can be inferred from the way in which Title XX funds have been allocated by the various states. With a predetermined ceiling on overall expenditures, the states were given responsibility under Title XX of the Social Security Act to develop a

Comprehensive Annual Social Service Plan. In New York City, for the program year 1977–1978 a total expenditure of $193 million was projected. Of this total, $102.7 million or over 53 percent was to go for daycare for children (New York City Human Resources Administration, 1977). Although an important service, questions can be raised about whether it warrants over half of the social service budget. The effectiveness of the daycare lobby, however, and the public appeal and visibility of the enterprise all help strengthen the priority status.

Reimbursement formulas constitute a further strong pressure on priority allocations under federal legislation. For example, family planning is reimbursable at 90 percent federal, 5 percent state, and 5 percent local match (Title I); Head Start at 100 percent federal; Location and Support (by parents under Title IVD) at 75 percent federal and 12.5 percent each state and city; Work Incentive Program (Title IVC) at 90 percent federal and 5 percent each state and city; Child Welfare (under Title IVB) at 50 percent federal and 25 percent each state and city; and Home Relief at 50 percent each state and city (New York City Human Resources Administration, 1977). It is no wonder, then, that hard-pressed executives at different levels of government seek to tailor programs into those areas where maximum reimbursement may be obtained, thus unwittingly subverting the legislative intent.

One way to comprehend the issues of social service priorities is to examine the legislative process from which the body of law governing the programs emerges. The poor have been a less valued group in our society, and within their numbers the distinction between "deserving" and "undeserving" persists. In a study of families who place children, Jenkins and Norman (1975) found a series of issues on which distinctions could be drawn between situations where children were placed for reasons deemed "socially approved" or "socially unacceptable."

The impact of uneven distribution of legislative benefits, an important aspect of priority determination, has been reviewed by Howe (1978) in an analysis of 414 bills submitted to the New York State legislature from 1970 to 1973 by six agencies of the New York City government. Areas covered included human services, housing, pensions, police, transportation, and consumer affairs. Outcomes included passage of 63 percent of pension bills but only 18 percent of those concerned with human services (pp. 173–188). Although not evaluating individual legislation on its particular merits, Howe's analysis suggests the trimming and direction of the Human Resources Administration's proposals to favor the politically popular groups, such as children, and avoid the stigmatized poor, such as employables.

In summary, political and social pressures affect priority determination in a variety of ways. Social action may occur by a client group or a victimized group; political popularity may be sought to get elected, to stay in office, or to turn the rascals out. It is important to look at not only what gets pushed but also what gets neglected. Almost any cause will reflect some social need; the policy analysis required is to ask why that cause rather than another, and whose interests are served.

Social Triage

In addition to the categories of needs, issues, and pressures, another approach to priority determination in the social services deserves consideration.

This ideological approach can be identified as *social triage,* a term suggested as an adaptation of the medical concept, which relates to allocation of resources in the face of overwhelming need. In an emergency situation, for example, with five injured persons and one surgeon, a preliminary appraisal might show that all five were in critical condition. But if the most severely injured needed one hour of surgery and the other four needed fifteen-minute procedures, a calculated decision would be to save not the most severely injured, but the four who could be saved in the time it would take to help the one. Such is medical triage—a hard decision made necessary by a crisis situation.

How does the concept of triage relate to that of priorities? Both may be based on the same assumptions and work out the same way if undertaken within a comprehensive planning operation that examines alternatives, options, and trade-offs. But comprehensive planning is not widely engaged in in the United States, and policy determination in social services rests heavily on the three factors already discussed: needs, issues, and pressures.

With an approach that stresses priorities, attention is focused on what is most important and/or what to do first. With an approach that encompasses triage, more attention may be given to subsequent considerations—that a decision to do "this" also means a decision not to do "that." Thus, the trade-off becomes more explicit, and the attendant risk more visible. The planning process may be the same, but the decision makers are forced to acknowledge that attention to priority services leaves a residue in the nonpriority areas.

The argument may be made that there should be enough for both, and this analysis is not a justification for a constricted social services budget. But every planning process involves decisions and limited resources, from the treatment plan for the individual case to a United Nations scheme for international development. The comprehensive plan is more reasoned if it incorporates consideration of what is not being done as well as justification of what is being done. The "benign neglect" of today may become the backlash of tomorrow.

In social welfare, the differences between the triage and the priorities concepts surface in several ways. For example, the remedies for the problems faced by many clients of social workers are outside of the scope of the social welfare system. Poverty, poor housing, racism, and unemployment are among the factors that affect clients. Social workers may concern themselves with those factors but be essentially powerless to affect them. In response, many professionals decide that with the resources at hand they will maximize their effectiveness by working with people who have enough of their own capacities to attain a successful outcome. This pattern has been noted not only in selection of clients for treatment but also in the dispositional outcomes related to institutional care.

The situation of adolescents in trouble is a case in point. In New York State, for example, children found to be delinquent or in need of supervision may be dealt with in different ways. They may be placed in voluntary childcare agencies, state training schools, or city shelters, or they may be returned home. One study that did case sampling of the dispositional pattern of the family court (National Council on Crime and Delinquency, 1972), reported that 76 percent of black and 66 percent of Puerto Rican children were placed in training schools and public shelters, whereas 78 percent of white children were placed in voluntary agencies. The report stated, "We found discrimination by voluntary agencies against children who lack 'cooperative' families. We found discrimination against children with the most serious emotional problems, low IQ levels, and low reading levels. We found discrimination against children who are seriously involved with drugs, and we found discrimination against adolescents" (pp. 22–23).

It is not unreasonable for a professional to decide to do what he or she can do best, and it is understandable that some people derive greater job satisfactions in a particular kind of effort. Although generalizations are risky, it is hard not to notice preferences on the part of many workers for the voluntary sector over the public sector—for example, for the treatment center over the state hospital or for private practice over the community mental health center. These preferences often are reactions to differences in treatment resources, case loads, and growth potential of clients, as well as worker job satisfactions, both professional and personal.

But regardless of motivation, such a direction of resources is bound to affect many aspects of the profession, including research, theory building, and social work education. In medical research, much attention is paid to the currently incurable diseases; comparable effort in social work research is sparse. Geismar and La Sorte (1964), who studied the "multiproblem family," came closest to trying to reach the unreachable, but this is not a current trend. Thus, in giving priority to clients with the greatest chance of success, in helping those most able to accept help, we ignore what happens to the others. We differ from the medical model, however, in that our neglected clients—the "unworkable," "hard-to-reach," "unworthy," or "resistant"—do not die like unattended critically injured patients. The "nonclients" are not in the orbit of the social service delivery system, but they comprise a growing number of untreated and currently unreachable people, on or off welfare rolls, in or out of psychiatric institutions or training schools, deficit in social functioning or social contribution.

There are valid questions about whether it is ethical to redirect limited resources from the treatable good prospects for success to the hard-core problem clients. This is a question in which the dimension of time must be included in priority determination. Triage as a model needs to go beyond emergency care and crisis to consider long-term implications. Although resources will never be sufficient, our goal should be a social policy comprehensive enough to encompass different levels of need, and the time dimension is critical. In the social service field, the piling up of unmet needs will not be diminished without a direct approach. Help will not "filter down," and the generational aspects of failure mean there can be a geometric progression of problems as more children are born into troubled and dependent families.

This is not to suggest that there are known methods and resources being deliberately withheld from the "untreatable" groups. It is more likely that the techniques are not known, the diagnoses not appropriate, and the resources not available under the present ordering of national priorities. In addition to social action, there is need for research, experimentation, trials, and allowable errors.

To suggest that priorities should be identified only at a crisis level is not a fruitful approach. A comprehensive social service policy would need to consider both the short run and the long run, the easy-to-reach and the hard-to-reach, the impact of what is to be done and what is not to be done, and it should eschew the avoidance of failure in the search for success.

Perhaps the fourth leg of the priority base—in addition to social needs, issues, and pressures—should be the social responsibility of the profession in the utilization of social triage. This would mean continuing to help those who can be helped, but directing a greater effort to those most in need, including the search for more effective and appropriate modalities of service.

References

Antler, S. "Child Protection: A Critique of Current Trends." *P.S.R.I. Report,* 1978, *3* (1), 16–17.

Blenkner, M., Jahn, J., and Wasser, E. *Serving the Aging: An Experiment in Social Work and Public Health Nursing.* New York: Institute of Welfare Research, Community Service Society of New York, March 1964.

Bradshaw, J. "The Concept of Social Need." *New Society,* March 30, 1972, pp. 640–643.

Burns, E. M. *Social Security and Public Policy.* New York: McGraw-Hill, 1956.

Downs, A. "Up and Down with Ecology—The Issue Attention Cycle." *The Public Interest,* Summer 1972, pp. 38–50.

Geismar, L. L., and La Sorte, M. A. *Understanding the Multi-Problem Family.* New York: Association Press, 1964.

Howe, E. "Legislative Outcomes in Human Services." *Social Service Review,* June 1978, pp. 173–188.

Jenkins, S., and Norman, E. *Beyond Placement: Mothers View Foster Care.* New York: Columbia University Press, 1975.

Jenkins, S., Schroeder, A., and Burgdorf, K. *Beyond Intake: The First Ninety Days.* Washington, D.C.: Administration for Children, Youth, and Families; Office of Human Development Services; U.S. Department of Health and Human Services, 1981.

Kogan, L. S., and Jenkins, S. *Indicators of Child Health and Welfare: Development of the DIPOV Index.* New York: Columbia University Press, 1974.

Kogan, L., S., Smith, J., and Jenkins, S. "Ecological Validity of Indicator Data as Predictors of Survey Findings." *Journal of Social Service Research,* 1977, *1* (2), 117–132.

Lifton, R. J. and others. *Home from the War: Vietnam Veterans, Neither Victims nor Executioners.* New York: Simon & Schuster, 1973.

National Council on Crime and Delinquency. *Juvenile Justice Confounded: Pretensions and Realities of Treatment Services.* New York: Committee on Mental Health Services Inside and Outside the Family Court in the City of New York, National Council on Crime and Delinquency, 1972.

New York City Human Resources Administration, *Funding Sources for HRA/DSS Social Services.* New York: New York City Human Resources Administration, January 1977.

Rossi, R. J., and Gilmartin, K. J. *The Handbook of Social Indicators.* New York: Garland STPM Press, 1980.

Schneiger, F. *P.S.R.I. Report,* 1978, *3* (1), 2.

"Senators Call on Urban League to Help Reform Welfare System." *New York Times,* August 6, 1980, Sec. A., p. 10.

Sheldon, E. B., and Freeman, H. E. "Notes on Social Indicators: Promises and Potential." *Policy Sciences,* 1970, *1,* 97–111.

U.S. Department of Health and Human Services. *Toward a Social Report.* Washington, D.C.: U.S. Government Printing Office, 1969.

Webster's New World Dictionary. New York: World, 1960.

37

Certification, Licensure, and Other Forms of Regulation

David A. Hardcastle

Social work, at least since the formation of the National Conference on Social Work in 1874, has sought to achieve status as a profession. Since the Flexner (1915) report of the 1915 National Conference on Charities and Corrections, "Is Social Work a Profession?" the professionalization of social work has been one of the major goals of the profession. To become members of a profession, social workers need not satisfy their internal critics or even develop a coherent knowledge base. Essentially, the public must sanction social workers' exercise of professional authority. Professional authority "refers to the client's belief in the superior knowledge of the professional regarding the particular activities in which the profession is engaged" (Gilbert and Specht, 1976, p. 282). A profession, according to Johnson (1972), is not an occupational activity, "but a means of controlling an occupation" (p. 45). A profession exercises authority over an occupation, and the public recognizes the right of the profession to exercise that control. The rationale for this arrangement, instead of relying upon marketplace authority, stems from other attributes of a profession: a definable, systematic body of knowledge and specialized skills; a regulatory code of ethics; a professional culture or community; and most basically, a service ethic or commitment. This last attribute provides the justification for professional authority and peer regulation.

The history of professions and professionalization has been a history of efforts by practitioners and vendors to gain occupational control, whether the basis for the control emerged from the normative sanctions of the church for the priesthood and related service practitioners or from guilds, with their more economically directed motivation. Wilensky (1970) traces a natural history of professional development that begins with the emergence of a full-time occupation and moves through the establishment of training schools and professional associations to political agitation and efforts directed toward the establishment of the profession's control and authority over its occupational territory by force of law. The efforts of the profession to gain control are intended to obtain monopolistic power over the service or practice area.

Professional control differs from labor union control. Labor unions strive to obtain control over workers. They attempt to influence wages and working conditions for their memberships. Professions, in contrast, attempt to control the occupational activity itself, not just the conditions of labor. Control can extend beyond determining those who may engage in the occupation, the working conditions, and the compensation, to determining the ways in which the work is done. Professional association and control, according to Horowitz, is more akin to a cartel that represents the organization of service providers to many customers.

In the professional cartel, many sellers or providers of service attempt to act as one in selling their services to many independent buyers. The buyer gains no economic advantage by turning from one vendor to another. The price and quality of the professional service are not responsive to the supply or number of professional service providers. The assumptions of marketplace competition do not hold. The task of the professional cartel is to convince the public that the cartel serves the public interest, that the price of its services is fair and reasonable, and that the cartel is more beneficial to the public than a professional service would be if it were left to unencumbered marketplace competition. In other words, the profession through its systematized body of knowledge, professional culture, and service ideal as embodied in its regulatory codes will provide better mechanisms for quality service than independent consumer preferences and judgments on the price and quality of services offered by truly competing vendors.

Social work has passed through several stages of development. Earlier, it represented a guild model that required formal education, fieldwork training and supervised practice. Social work has moved beyond internal professional credentialing and is now seeking formal public sanction for its authority. Licensure, or legal regulation, is a priority of most national professional social work organizations such as the National Association of Social Workers (NASW) and the National Federation of Societies of Clinical Social Work (NFSCSW). The intent of this chapter is to examine licensure and other forms of credentials for the practice of clinical social work.

Credentialing

Credentialing is designed to protect the public by assuring the competency of practitioners. This it does by setting minimum standards of education and training for entry into the occupation and, often, standards of competency for continued practice. Enforcement of the standards can be assured by the threat of revoking an individual's credential to practice. The attraction of credentialing, therefore, comes from the increased economic, political, or social well-being the practitioner gains from obtaining the credential. Conversely, withdrawal of the credential can detrimentally affect a person's economic, social, and political well-being.

Private Credentialing. In private credentialing, a private organization or association, such as NASW, establishes requirements for professional activity and certifies that the practitioner meets the requirements and standards. Private credentialing is of two broad types: registration and certification.

Registration is a listing or registry of persons identifying themselves with the occupational activity. Registration can require specified qualifications, such as the possession of a certain educational degree, post-master's training, years of experience, and the payment of fees. A private association issuing such a register does not have police powers and must call upon the state for enforcement. The unregistered practitioner does not draw penalties from the state for engaging in the occupation unless the practitioner claims to be registered. Registration provides few restrictions on the practitioner, but does provide the client or consumer with a listing of vendors who have met certain standards.

Certification involves the issuance of credentials when the professional association attests that a person has obtained a specific level of knowledge and skill. Similar to registration, certification does not prohibit uncertified practitioners from engaging in the occupational activity, but it does prevent their use of the term *certified.* Certification goes beyond registration in that it lists vendors according to the certification criteria and makes a more finite judgment as to the practitioner's competency. Certification provides the public with an a priori judgment of the competency of certified practitioners. The certifying group defines competency, and practitioners must pass examinations established by the certifying group. However, the certifying group cannot enforce its definition of competency over all who work in the occupation; it can only enforce the definition over practitioners choosing to be certified. Consumers, clients, and practitioners have the choice as to whether they wish to use or to meet the certifying group's definition of competency. Uncertified practitioners can engage in the occupational activity, generally without restrictions other than the prohibition on using the certifying title. Certification is title protection. NASW provides certification through the Academy of Certified Social Workers (ACSW).

Social work, especially in the clinical practice of social work, has various forms of private professional credentialing. NASW and NFSCSW maintain clinical registries that require similar standards of education and experience. The standards for inclusion in NASW's *Clinical Registry* are: a master's from a Council on Social Work Education (CSWE) accredited graduate social work program; two years or 3,000 hours of post-master's clinical social work practice under the supervision of an M.S.W. social worker or "if social work supervision . . . [is] unavailable, supervision by mental health professional with the added condition of [the applicant] giving evidence of continued participation and of identification with the social work profession"; membership in the Academy of Certified Social Workers; or a license in a state with licensing at ACSW standards (National Association of Social Workers, 1976, p. xi). While the NASW register requires supervised practice experience, the supervision need not be from social work nor from practitioners engaged in the clinical practice of social work. The registry, as NASW points out, is a voluntary process. NASW holds that the registry makes no judgment that the review for inclusion or exclusion "did in any way examine, determine, or establish the competency of any Clinical Social Work Practitioner" (p. xii). The register, therefore, is a listing of persons who meet certain specified credentials of education and/or experience. It is an information document and not a mechanism for directly controlling the occupation. NASW also maintains another registry of NASW members for its full membership called the *Professional Social Workers' Directory* (National Association of Social Workers, 1978a). Its purpose, again, is public information, and it has very limited, if any, occupational control.

Certification has greater occupational control implications. NASW's certification program, the Academy of Certified Social Workers, has as its goals to:

- Secure national recognition and acceptance of social workers with ACSW certificates as independent, self-regulated practitioners
- Have individual states with legal regulations statutes accept ACSW membership as an alternative to their examination process
- Gain acceptance of ACSW standards in the federal and state merit system and in social services
- *Promote ACSW membership as an employment criterion for key social service* positions in organizations and private practice [emphasis added]
- Create, in recognition of testing competence, salary differentials for those who have gained admission to the academy (National Association of Social Workers, 1979)

ACSW's aim is to increase the professional, social, and economic influence of the ACSW social worker.

ACSW requires, in addition to the criteria specified for inclusion in the *NASW Register of Clinical Social Workers,* regular membership in NASW and successfully passing an examination. ACSW makes a judgment about practice competency and knowledge through the examination. The examination is an objective test involving multiple choice questions that cover the basic elements of social work practice knowledge, principles, and values as defined by NASW. Both the *NASW Register of Clinical Social Workers* and ACSW attempt to capture professional ethics through NASW membership and its code of ethics. Both are voluntary for clinical social workers.

Private association credentialing has obvious limitations. It is done by private parties and carries with it little enforcement power. It depends on the voluntary acceptance or compliance by the professionals, employers, consumers, and clients. Few sanctions can be imposed. The major sanction of withdrawal of the credential does not prevent the social worker from engaging in the occupation unless third-party vendors, employers, fellow professionals, and clients choose not to use or refer to the uncredentialed practitioner.

Public Credentialing. Public credentialing is done by the public sector. Professions generally seek public credentialing because it takes on the attributes of public regulation. The public or legal regulation of a profession occurs when the state, through formal legislation, utilizes its police powers to define and regulate an occupational activity. It is the police powers of the state that determine the professional parameters. Public or legal regulation of the occupational activit of a profession indicates that the profession has received the sanction and mandate of the public to engage in the occupational activity. It represents public recognition, if not protection, of the profession's job territory, sustaining code of ethics, and professional culture. Depending on the degree of police power utilized in the public regulation, it holds the potential for enhancing professional status, protection of jobs, and protection of the public from incompetent practitioners. Public regulation implicitly recognizes peer judgment and provides explicit community sanction for the exercise of professional authority. But, as will be elaborated on later, public regulation guarantees neither professional status nor authority.

Public regulation as a form of credentialing can be parsimoniously classified into three categories according to the state's use of the police powers to enforce its definitions and prohibitions: It includes licensure in addition to registration and certification. Licensing can only be done by the public sector.

For registration and certification, the state essentially performs the same functions as do voluntary associations. The state's use of its police powers in registration and certification is minimal and generally limited to imposing sanctions for the unauthorized use of the titles of "registered" and "certified" by practitioners.

The third and strongest form of credentialing and legal regulation is licensure. Registration and certification, whether done by the state or private associations, essentially perform the same functions. Licensure, however, represents a quantum leap over registration and certification. It captures the functions of registration and certification and carries with it restrictions. Licensure's essence is restriction and control in that it prevents the unlicensed practitioner from engaging in the occupational activity. Licensing, in effect, grants the profession a monopoly over the occupational activity. According to Shimberg and Roederer (1978), licensing is a "process by which an agency of government grants permission to an individual to engage in a given occupation upon finding that the applicant has attained the minimal degree of competency required to ensure that the public health, safety, and welfare will be reasonably well protected" (p. 1). The essential element of licensing is a legislative function involving the stipulation of the circumstances under which permission to perform an otherwise prohibited activity is granted by the state. The actual granting of permission to specific individuals is an administrative function (Council of State Government, 1952).

Under licensure, the state decrees that people may engage in particular economic activities or occupations only under specific conditions set forth by the state. Licensing states explicitly the requirements for knowledge and skills, describes how these are to be obtained and demonstrated, and uses the state's regulatory or police powers to enforce the definition of standards and behaviors. Licensing protects both the title and job activity. It limits the occupation only to those who meet its definitions. For example, individuals may use an uncertified accountant to monitor and record their fiscal affairs or an unregistered architect to design their homes, but their surgery, whether gratis or for a fee, must be performed by a state-approved practitioner.

Criteria for Professional Licensure. Occupations seeking licensing as a profession, to distinguish professional licensing from other occupational licensing, need to meet the following four criteria:

- Perform a relatively specific, socially necessary function upon the regular performance of which the practitioner depends for livelihood and social status
- Require competence in special techniques based on a body of generalized knowledge requiring theoretical study
- Possess a generally accepted ethic that subordinates private interests to performance

- Have formal professional associations that foster ethics and standards of competency [Council of State Governments, 1952, p. 58]

A general rule in licensing, especially professional licensing, is the welfare criterion. The welfare criterion, according to the Council of State Governments, is that only those occupations which "directly affect the public health, safety, morals, and general welfare and which can distinguish themselves from the other occupations should be licensed" (1952, p. 59). The reason for the need for clarity of definition and the distinction of the profession's occupational activity from other occupations is that licensing or legal regulation is government regulation and restriction of an activity that was previously permissable and unrestricted. It may deny some people opportunity for a livelihood. Restriction without a clear definition of the need for restriction can be unfair and an unreasonable restraint of trade.

Licensing to regulate the right to practice an occupation, profession, or trade has long been accepted as a proper exercise of the police powers of the state (Council of State Governments, 1952, p. 6). While licensing and public regulation grew out of two major historical trends—(1) mercantilism, nationalism, and the state's taxing power and (2) the guild movement, with its control over occupations and the state's enforcement of the occupation's control—its major justifications are found in the "welfare criterion." The two primary elements of the welfare criterion are the protection of the public and the development and protection of the profession.

Public Protection. The need for public protection by statute and its deviation from marketplace regulation is based on the assumptions of consumer ignorance, externalities or the "neighborhood effect," and equity considerations. The consumer ignorance assumption holds that the occupation is extremely complex and that an independent evaluation requires knowledge, skill, and technology for judgment beyond that which can reasonably be expected of a consumer. The state makes a judgment of practitioner competency for the consumer. However, if consumer satisfaction with the service is to be used as a major criterion of successful service—that is, whether or not the consumer is happy with the service—then consumer ignorance is not relevant. In addition, as some economists ask, are human services more complex in terms of the consumer's ability to make a judgment than are other types of professional services such as the utilization of sophisticated computers and other hardware (Blair and Rubin, 1980)?

Related to consumer ignorance is the argument of "irreversibility." By irreversibility is meant that the impact of inadequate goods and services on the consumer is not remediable through other mechanisms such as economic restitution, compensation, and restoration. If the impact of inadequate service is not severe or the client or consumer has access to restoration, then the need for a priori regulation independent of the consumer and marketplace is reduced. However, the notion of irreversibility and restitution is complex. While the courts can compensate a client or consumer for shoddy goods and services, they may not be able to restore physical and mental health and well-being. Arthur Okun (1970) states, "Some situations cry out for public intervention. For example, it is cold comfort that, without food and drug regulation, any customer who is fatally poisoned by a medication will never buy that product again" (p. 21). But, as the

Virginia Board for Registration of Social Workers (1975) puts it, the use of the consumer ignorance and irreversibility argument requires that "the potential for harm is recognizable and not remote or dependent on tenuous arguments" (p. 1).

Externalities refer to the "neighborhood effect" or the impact that the service or economic activity has on its environment beyond those directly involved in the economic or service transaction. The argument of externalities for professions is relatively weak, although there may be externalities similar to air and water pollution for industrial and agricultural activity. Zoning or land use regulations address "social externalities" as well as physical externalities. Shoddy or improper counseling might have detrimental impacts on others beyond the counselor and client, such as family, neighborhood, and community. Certain communicable diseases have obvious externalities or "neighborhood effects."

Equity arguments address the rationing of certain goods and services to consumers without regard to economic ability to consume in order to meet the public good as well as private interests and preferences. For example, a minimum level of health services has generally been accepted as part of public policy, although the definition of "minimum level" is still being debated. Public regulation of a profession ensures the consumer that the professional will meet the minimum standards regardless of the consumer's purchasing power.

Development and Protection of the Profession. The development and protection of the profession is inherent in the protection of the public. Through its police powers, the state can impose or enforce the profession's entry requirements and standards for maintaining competency. Tests of continued competence and the updating of knowledge and skill can be required. Although these standards are designed to protect the public, they also protect the competent professional from the deleterious neighborhood impact of charlatans and incompetents practicing under the umbrella of the profession.

Legal regulations generally provide regulatory boards with the following powers: development and administration of examinations, issuance of licenses, suspension and revocation of licenses, enforcement of licensing standards, and approval of or specification of schools necessary for professional training. These powers obviously give the regulatory boards substantial influence over the profession. The powers extend beyond the individual professional to professional institutions such as professional schools and their curriculum designs and employers. These powers include sanctions of the codes and rules formulated by private professional associations. With the exception of the growing use of sunset reviews, regulatory boards tend to operate with little state executive or legislative oversight. Sunset reviews and sunset laws require the regulatory board to demonstrate its utility and accountability to the state legislatures. The sunset laws hold that at the end of a specified period of time, the regulatory board ceases to exist unless specific legislative action is taken for continuation of the board. The board must walk a tightrope between setting entry standards and standards of continuing education that are not so prohibitively high as to reduce the supply of professionals and standards so low as to be meaningless in ensuring competency and protecting the public.

The profession has the potential for development of control and influence, if not always its competency and expertise, through the administrative structures used in regulation. The potential of legal regulation to provide the profession with control over service providers and practitioners is dependent on the degree to which the profession controls the regulatory boards that set and monitor credentialing standards. Friedman (1962) cites a 1956 study indicating that 75 percent of the regulatory boards were controlled by people who had a direct economic interest in the regulated activity (p. 139). Indeed, a hallmark of full professional status is when the profession controls the licensing process and utilizes the regulatory powers of the state. It represents public sanction of the profession. The regulatory board's authority comes from its vested powers and its major advisory role to the state's executive and legislature for the regulated profession. While its structure and composition should promote accountability and public confidence, a fundamental question is whether the regulatory board is responsive to public needs or operates as an arm of the profession to meet professional interests first? Although there has been a movement toward greater public control of regulatory boards, they remain largely controlled by the regulated professions. As Rubin and Haig emphasize, the attempts of regulatory boards to improve performance have been piecemeal and without apparent impact (Blair and Rubin, 1980).

The legal regulatory boards for social work are generally comprised of social workers (Hardcastle, 1977). However, this should be read with caution. The boards in some states are changing so that social workers will no longer hold a majority, or the boards will fall under an amalgam of a legal regulation superstructure. The NASW, to its credit, has generally supported boards composed of professionals and strong public interest representation (National Association of Social Workers, 1978b). The state's judgment of public protection is generally expressed through the judgments of the regulatory board. It is for this reason that public representation and accountability of the regulatory board are important.

While a prime motive by a profession for seeking licensing is protection of its occupational arena and enhancement of its social status, licensing itself doesn't ensure professional status. The state can license both occupations and businesses, such as pharmacists, pharmacies, social workers, and social agencies. Licensing is not limited to the classic professions, and licensing does not transfer an occupation into a classic profession. Licensed occupations include physicians and surgeons and in some states, detectives, barbers, pest controllers, egg graders, and well diggers, among others. The 1974 Kansas legislature considered the original social work licensing legislation along with a bill to license timber harvesters (Kansas Statewide Health Coordinating Council, 1978).

Licensure and Professional Authority. The growth and development of social work has created a professional culture with professional associations, professional education, professional meetings and conferences, a code of ethics, and so forth. The professional associations, such as NASW and the NFSCSW, provide peer support to their members. They also provide a vehicle for community sanction and status. The licensing efforts and compulsory regulation are often accompanied by tightened professional control and authority. The motivation for public regulation, especially of social work, appears to be from the profession rather than from the public. The profession gains authority through the establishment of the standards for entry into the profession, maintenance of licensing, and control or influence on the regulatory boards. Eligibility in the twenty-three states with social work licensing, certification, or registration in 1980 generally required, depending on the level of regulation, a social work degree from a CSWE-accredited social work education institution and for specialties such as clinical social work, supervision by a licensed specialty practitioner (National Association of Social Worker, 1978b).

Legal Regulation and Codes of Ethics. Most professional organizations, such as NASW, have professional codes of ethics to provide a normative base for professional behaviors. However, the professions are limited in their ability to impose sanctions for violations of the professional codes of ethics by practitioners. The professional association codes do not have the weight of law, and the professional associations are dependent upon the good will and cooperation of their membership, other professionals, employers, and clients to enforce any sanctions. For example, NASW can publicly censure, admonish, expel from membership, or terminate from ACSW, a professional social worker who violates its code of ethics, but NASW can only recommend the termination of employment to prevent the social worker from engaging in the practice of social work. It cannot directly prevent the social worker from practicing social work. As the preamble to the NASW code of ethics states, "The ethical behavior of social workers results not from edict, but from a personal commitment of the individual. This code is offered to affirm the will and zeal of all social workers to be ethical and to act ethically in all that they do as social workers" (National Association of Social Workers, 1980, p. 3).

The code emphasizes that professional social workers should strive to become and remain proficient in professional practice and in their professional functioning. But NASW does not have police powers. When codes of ethics are incorporated into legal regulation, they are no longer "personal commitments" but are edicts backed by police power. The legal regulation provides enforcement power and legal sanctions for violations of the code. Legal regulation is not dependent on the good will of the professional, clients, colleagues, or employers for enforcement but has, especially in the case of licensure, the ability to prevent the professional from engaging in the occupational activity. The legal regulation can take requirements for maintenance of professional proficiency from a "should" admonition of a professional association to a "must" requirement of law. Legal regulation can require professional education, periodic retesting, and other mechanisms to facilitate the maintenance of professional competency.

The enforcement power of licensing for the code of ethics contributes to the development of the profession and to client protection. For example, while the NASW code of ethics and professional tradition emphasize confidentiality, without licensing it has no force of law. As pointed out by Wilson (1978), "The duty to keep matters confidential is governed by ethics. The right to disclose is governed by law" (p. 97). Therefore, while social work tradition and ethics emphasize confidentiality, without privileged communication, either established by case law or through legal regulation, the ethic of confidentiality carries no legal protection. In order for the professional to have confidentiality, the client must have privileged communication. A social worker must be licensed to practice in the state that has a licensure statute on its books declaring that communication is privileged between a social worker and client. The right and protection of privileged communication relates to the client or patient rather than to the professional. All legal regulation of social work statutes do not contain privileged communication clauses, nor is the regulation of privileged communication absolute in those state statutes that do contain it; but over half of the states' legal regulation statutes have some safeguards for privileged communication (National Association of Social Workers, 1978b).

Costs of Legal Regulation. Legal regulation has costs. Some of the costs are a result of the benefits of regulation. It is designed to protect the public by ensuring competency through establishing minimum entry standards and enforcing standards through the threat of revoking an individual's credential. Many economic theorists believe that due to this labor market limiting effect, legal regulation drives up the price of services and limits vertical and horizontal mobility within the professional labor market. Upward mobility can be limited if differing credential requirements are used for different vertical levels of the profession. Horizontal mobility is limited if different entry requirements exist for different geographic areas. By intent, licensure restricts open entry into the professional labor market. The more stringent the licensing requirements, the more restrictive is the entry into the professional market. In general, the more stringent the licensing requirement, the lower the quantity of potential service vendors available to a given consumer. If the supply of labor, goods, or services is limited relative to demand, the cost of the goods or services increases to a point where the increased costs reduce the demand to an equilibrium point. If increasing costs cannot be met by additional entry into the professional marketplace, because of the entry restrictions by legal regulation or long lead time to meet educational and training requirements for entry, other potential professionals cannot make rapid entry into the occupation to take advantage of the increased cost of services. The restrictions make the supply side of the equation inelastic, depending on the lead time necessary for education and experience. Depending on the consumer's ability to substitute another good or service, the consumer may be limited to a choice between high-cost services or no services, which has been referred to as the "Cadillac effect." Low-income consumers may have to do without or rely on unlicensed or substitute providers. The consumer does not have the option of lower quality of professional service at a lower price.

The social work licensing is opposed by some social workers because of these potential cost effects. If licensing results in the substitution of other types of professionals, it may not protect the public. For example, a study reported in *Business Week* on the licensing of electricians and death rate found that there was a positive correlation across the fifty states between death rates and licensing of electricians ("How Licensing Hurts Consumers," 1977). The assumption was that given the increased cost of licensed electricians, some consumers either used nonelectricians or provided their own wiring. Both led to detrimental results. The review reported other studies that indicated while there were fewer malpractice suits among dentists when licensing standards were raised, costs increased and states with strong licensing standards discriminated against out-of-state dentists.

Horizontal professional labor market or interstate mobility is affected by restricted or high standards for entry into the profession. If licensing reciprocity between states does not exist, each state becomes a separate labor market with separate entry requirements. The interstate mobility of professionals is limited, and the profession cannot respond to changing population patterns. This necessarily limits the potential supply of professional labor within a given state and may drive up costs of professional services. While professions in particular states may seek to restrict the supply of the occupation, such as restrictions on "ski and sunshine doctors," this limitation and the increased costs are not in the public interest. Although reciprocity exists in approximately half the states with social work licensure, reciprocity can be more apparent than real. Each state licensing board independently determines the equivalency of the licensing of the other states, and the licensing board can limit the number of reciprocal states.

A second contribution to the potential increased cost is the human capital approach and the ability of the occupation or profession to pass forward to the consumer all costs of education, development, and licensing. Because of the entry restrictions due to the legal regulation, the occupational grouping in effect has a monopoly. The human capital costs include the cost of the original entry requirements (such as education, training, and experience) and the costs of the legal regulation itself (such as licensing fees to cover issuing credentials, maintaining credentialing boards, and the costs of continuing education). The alternative to passing the costs on to the consumer is for the licensed professional to suffer a reduction of real income to offset the additional costs or to increase production to meet the increased costs. The increased costs to the consumer or client can be justified insofar as the impact of licensing increases productivity, the quality of the services, and gains in the public's health, safety, and welfare. However, the increased quality may produce the "Cadillac effect."

Public Regulation, Social Work, and Clinical Social Work Practice

Public credentialing and regulation are and have been for the past decade a major priority of the social work profession in its efforts to obtain full professional status and authority. NASW has made public regulation a priority of the professional association since its 1969 Delegate Assembly, as illustrated by the following resolution: "Resolved: That the various combinations of chapters, working in concert at a state level, be authorized to pursue licensing of social work practice within each state. . ." ("New Policy Statement on Licensing Issues," 1974, p. 12). The NFSCSW shares NASW's ardor for public regulation of social work, although it generally limits its efforts to the licensing of the clinical practice of social work.

As of June 1980, twenty-five states had some form of legal regulation of social work. Thirteen states call their legal regulation licensing, and the remaining twelve states can best be classified as registration or certification, which offer some form of title protection. Social work's legal regulation does not meet in any state all of the criteria required for licensure (Hardcastle, 1977). No state uses its police powers to enforce its definition of social work practice for people engaging in the economic activity and behaviors if they do not call themselves social workers.

As already stated, legal regulation, especially licensing, has the two fundamental rationales of (1) protection of the health, safety, or welfare of the public and (2) the development of the profession. In their pursuit of licensing, social workers and clinical social work practitioners must be prepared to explain how legal regulation is in the public's interest. Questions such as those posed by the Council of State Governments (1952) and also contained in much of the current sunset legislation primarily address issues of public good rather than professional interest (Shimberg and Roederer, 1978). Questions generally relate to:

- Cost of the regulation: Does the regulation by the state directly increase the costs of goods and services involved, and to what extent is the increased cost more harmful to the public than the harm that could result from the absence of regulation?
- Potential impact of nonregulation: Will the absence of regulation significantly harm the public's health, safety, and welfare, and, as the Virginia legislation points out, is the relationship between the harm and the absence of regulation clear or nebulous?
- Utilization of police powers: Is there a reasonable relationship between the utilization of the state's police power and the protection of the public's health, safety, and welfare, or is the police power being used to benefit primarily those regulated?
- Alternative methods of regulation: Are there less restrictive methods of regulation available that could adequately protect the public?

These questions have special merit for social work as its occupational situs is largely as a public and agency-employed profession. Should the state regulate social work, or should it regulate the delivery system of agencies? What is the minimum level of regulation required for agency-employed social workers: licensure, certification, or registration? Does the regulation, in fact, provide protection to the public beyond that provided by the social agency? Does social work legal regulation contain entry requirements and requirements for continued competency beyond those required for maintaining employment? Does the frequent and extensive use of "grandfathering" ensure competency? Grandfathering brings into the profession all practitioners at the point of the introduction of the regulation without a meaningful entry test of competency. Grandfathering with lifetime certification means that grandfathered practitioners will be afforded all the protection and gains of licensure without having their competency judged during their professional lives. The public will pay any increased service costs brought about by the legal regulation without receiving any increases in the standards and performances of professionals.

A most fundamental question for regulation of social workers is who should be regulated and at what level? If an occupational activity requires or is conducted under close supervision, should the supervisee or only the supervisor be licensed and regulated? With the social work apprenticeship model, which strongly advocates supervision of all but the most advanced practitioners, should all social work practitioners be licensed or regulated? For example, the NASW's standards for social service manpower define "levels" of social work practice and specify supervision for social service aides, social service technicians, B.S.W. social workers, and M.S.W. social workers. It exempts certified social workers and social work fellows from supervision (National Association of Social Workers, 1973b, pp. 14–19). NASW's licensing law calls for supervision of social workers. The supervision requirement of the profession seems to be an inherent problem as it seeks "multilevel" regulation of B.S.W.s, M.S.W.s, and specialist-clinical practitioners (National Association of Social Workers, 1973a).

Indeed, the requirements and emphasis on supervision in social work, as contrasted with consultation, have been a recurrent issue in social work and have led many scholars of the professions to classify social work as as semiprofession rather than as a profession. Both Toren (1972) and Scott (1967) hold that social work is a semiprofession, along with nursing and elementary and high school teaching. Their position largely is based on social work's emphasis on supervision. According to Scott, the supervision of social workers, especially within agencies, differs from consultation in that the worker is not free to reject the supervisor's professional directive when the worker believes that the directive is contrary to the professional relationship or the client's best interests. The issue is not a question of agency supervision for accountability, but whether the profession should have a built-in requirement of supervision as an inherent element of professional practice, and still argue the need for an alternative and additional form of public regulation.

The National Federation of Societies for Clinical Social Work in its promotion of licensing does not face the same dilemma as NASW. The federation does not advocate multilevel licensure or the licensing of supervised practitioners. Its position is to license clinical social workers who generally function as autonomous clinical professionals. NFSCSW holds that the multilevel licensing, especially of baccalaureate-level social workers, represents a "deprofessionalization" of social work (Jett, 1974; Summers, 1976). The disagreements between NFSCSW and NASW on the issues of supervision, levels of practice, and what constitutes needed professional licensure have led some state clinical societies to deprofessionalize social work by dissociating themselves from social work and developing amalgamated licensure approaches with other related clinical professions, such as the "social psychotherapists" licensure in Texas.

Many states adhere to the NFSCSW position. The Kansas Post-Legislative Audit Committee's 1979 sunset report called for licensing only those social workers operating an autonomous practice, essentially the clinical social work specialists. Many other states' legal regulations exclude supervised practice or practice within agencies. For example, in 1978 ten of the twenty-three regulated states excluded public employees and five states excluded private-agency employees (National Association of Social Workers, 1978b).

Social Work Licensure and Standard Setting. The extensive use of grandfathering in legal regulation raises questions about whether legal regulation extends public protection. Public protection might be enhanced through the utilization of examinations both at the entry point and at periodic times through the professional life of the practitioner and through continuing education requirements to keep professionals abreast of new knowledge and skill. Unfortunately for social work licensing, few states use examinations either for entry into the profession or for the maintenance of the license. Seven of the twenty-three states in 1978 required no entry examination. While sixteen states did require entry examinations, the extent of examination is suspect. For example, in Kansas, legal regulation required examination for all levels but in 1981 the state had an examination only for the licensed clinical specialty level. The rationale has been that the examination of such credentials as academic degrees was sufficient for the licensed B.S.W. and licensed M.S.W. levels. During the first four years of operation, the clinical specialized examination did not exclude anyone from practice who met the other requirements of education, references, and experience. No state requires examination of knowledge or skill to maintain the license (National Association of Social Workers, 1978b; Hardcastle, 1981).

Continuing education also holds some potential for the maintenance of professional competency. Again, as with entry examinations, continuing education for social work is nonexistent in some states and irregular in others. In 1978 only ten of the twenty-three states with some form of legal regulation required continuing education. In the ten states, the definition of continuing education was left to the discretion of the regulatory boards. In some states, for example Kansas, the continuing education did not have to be focused on or defined within the social work arena. Frequently agency staff development can meet the continuing education requirements.

It is unlikely that the continuing education and examination standards for improving, upgrading, and ensuring competency will improve as social work licensing is expanded and there is an accumulation of experience with social work licensing. The motivating force for social work licensing has been the social work profession. The profession has developed, designed, and advocated the existing legal regulations. If state licensing standards are currently weak, there is little reason to assume that the profession in these states unilaterally will promote stronger standings unless the public itself through legislatures and other organized groups advocates stronger standards. Licensure or legal regulation bills most recently passed do not appear stronger than those passed earlier, although the more recent bills have the experience of the earlier licensing states. In a study of a related profession, psychiatry, Feigelson and Frosch (1977) found that psychiatrists in private practice, direct practitioners most analogous to the most broadly covered clinical social workers, were the most resistant to meeting continuing education standards or other recertification requirements such as practice audits and continuing-competency examinations.

Legal Regulation and the Clinical Practice of Social Work. A fundamental question is whether social work, especially clinical social work, is a valid and distinct occupational activity with its own professional culture and a defined, definable, and transmittable body of theory and technique. Social work is generally recognized as a professional activity. The Department of Labor estimates that there are over 300,000 social workers (Hardcastle and Katz, 1979, p. 607). In addition, there are a number of professional organizations of social workers with substantial memberships. Professional schools exist and have existed for nearly a century. A nationally recognized accrediting body exists for social work education. Professional literature abounds. On the face of it, there is a profession of social work.

Within social work, the clinical practice of social work under its various nomenclatures forms the substantial core of the profession. Studies by Hardcastle and Katz (1979) and others indicate that the direct-service methods constitute the single largest methodological area of social work practice. Approximately half the membership of the National Association of Social Workers indicates that they utilize direct-service methods. For purposes of the Hardcastle/Katz study, direct-service methods were defined as casework, group work, generic social work, and psychotherapy. Direct-service methods have also been the primary service methods utilized by social workers for the past decade. A 1971–1972 National Association of Social Workers (1977) survey reported in the *Encyclopedia of Social Work* indicates that over 40 percent of social workers responding to the survey were direct-service social workers (p. 1028). A 1973–1975 survey of new NASW members, also reported by the *Encyclopedia of Social Work,* indicates that approximately 65 percent of new members were direct-service social workers (p. 1028).

Social work's continuing existence appears to be well ensured because schools and departments of social work exist. While enrollment in schools of social work has declined since 1979, the number of graduates per year still exceeds 9,000. With the inclusion of undergraduate social workers, the number of new entrants into the profession will increase significantly over the next decade. Clinical or direct-service methods remain the methods of choice for graduate social work students. For full-time, second-year, degree-seeking students in social work graduate schools in November 1979, over 60 percent were specialized in direct-service methods: generic, casework, micro or clinical, and group. Concentrations or specializations designated specifically as "clinical" comprised 30 percent of all second-year degree-seeking students (Rubin, 1980).

A fundamental problem in regulating social work is not to demonstrate that it exists but to distinguish social work as a professional activity from related professions also seeking regulation. Social work suffers from multiple definitions and utilization of the term social work as a job title regardless of the occupational activity or professional preparation (Hardcastle, 1981). Richan and Mendelsohn (1973) argue that a strength of social work has been its broadness. Social workers may not be the most expert in any particular body of theory or area of technology, but they have expertise in bringing to bear a broad range of knowledge and skills on behalf of their clientele and in the meeting of human needs. This strength is also a weakness in developing public regulation and licensure. The need for the licensure must be demonstrated to a legislature who may not understand that the gestalt or configuration of social work's broad range of knowledge and skill itself may be a unique function deserving of licensure and regulation. Indeed, legislators tend to view social work as a job title rather than as a profession requiring specialized preparation, knowledge, and skill.

Although the clinical practice of social work as a subset or speciality within social work should have a more specified set of theory and technique, unfortunately clinical practice of social work also lacks specificity. For example, a recent conference sponsored by NASW to develop a definition of clinical social work produced multiple definitions (Ewalt, 1980). Chestang, a participant at the conference, defined clinical social work as "a helping activity aimed at assisting individuals, families, and groups in dealing with problems of social functioning, whether these are caused by internal or external factors. Such problems may be manifested in intrapsychic or interpersonal functioning or they may be reflected in the person's transaction with the environment" (p. 2). The broadness of this definition is attractive, but it cannot be used to distinguish social work from several other professions such as psychology, psychiatry, and even certain functions of law ("person's transaction with the environment"). Another participant, Frank, defined clinical social work as "a process of treatment which addresses itself to the support, promotion, and increase of internal resources (psychic equipment) in people" (p. 14). Other definitions, by Cohen, Lurie, and Ewalt, all tend to emphasize the social functions and concerns of clinical social work or the interaction of the individual with the social environment. With the possible exception of Frank's definition, according to Ewalt, "the forum participants firmly decline to take the position that intrapsychic change is the primary focus of clinical social work or that knowledge sufficient for autonomous practice in this area is a prerequisite for all clinical social workers" (p. 89). Clinical social work, perhaps all social work, suffers not from a dearth of knowledge and technique in general, but from the lack of specific knowledge and techniques of practice. As Eda Goldstein (1980) states, "Social workers paradoxically have too much theoretical knowledge from which to draw at the same time that they have a paucity of specific types of knowledge needed in specific situations to achieve specific goals" (p. 174). For purposes of legal regulation and licensing, this is a significant paradox. The question remains: Is there a suitable definition that can form the basis for licensing and distinguish the clinical practice of social work from related professional practice? Or is title protection the basis for regulation?

Conclusions

Credentialing, especially legal regulation, is a complex issue and represents costs and benefits to the profession and to the public. While the profession generally supports legal regulation, it has its critics. The critics include legislatures and economists as well as some social workers. The National Association of Black Social Workers in the past has opposed licensure as premature for the profession and primarily a bogus status-accruing device that holds the potential for excluding minorities from the profession and for reducing services to the minority community. The potential for service reduction is inherent in the "Cadillac effect" of licensing discussed earlier. The arguments of the Association of Black Social Workers must be considered in the development of credentialing and legal regulation.

Credentialing and legal regulation, however, must be prudently pursued. Sound credentialing and legal regulation represent an advancement of the profession. The profession must develop and exercise professional authority if it is to impose the self-discipline necessary to develop and validate the knowledge and competencies necessary for it to fulfill its service ethic. Legal regulation holds the potential for enforcement of the profession's definition for ethical and competent practice.

Credentialing and legal regulation will become more critical in the future with the expansion of autonomous clinical social work practice. Given the broadness of the definition of social work, can the profession afford to have all who want to engage in autonomous practice do so under the umbrella and name of the profession regardless of their knowledge, skill, or ethical stance? Without minimal title protection, anyone can hold himself or herself forth publicly as a social worker. The standards for regulation cannot be capricious. But they must hold the potential for exclusion. If they do not exclude, then there is no need for restriction or regulation. The exclusion must be based on the essential knowledge, skills, and ethical imperatives necessary for the public protection. As demonstrated by Hardcastle (1977), much current legal regulation fails to meet the necessary prudent tests outlined in this chapter.

There are some pragmatic arguments for advocating legal regulation of clinical social work. It may reduce the costs of some human services. If legal regulation leads to third-party reimbursements to social workers for mental health services, for example, costs should be reduced. Social workers are significant providers of mental health services and generally cost less than psychiatrists and psychologists (Fishman and Kasser, 1976). While the costs of social work services should increase with meaningful legal regulation, the costs should remain less than those charged by psychiatrists and psychologists. The inclusion of social workers as eligible third-party vendors will increase competition. If the economic arguments against licensing are valid, the expansion of the potential numbers of service providers should have a positive cost effect. It is unlikely from an economic or professional point of view that psychiatrists will drop their legal regulation requirements. The inclusion of additional service providers, such as social workers, benefits the public by increasing competition. It is hoped that the increasing number of state sunset laws that require a profession to maintain its arguments for licensing relative to the public good will lead to greater accountability from the profession and legal regulatory boards to see that regulated professions, in fact, meet the public need.

References

Blair, R. E., and Rubin, S. (Eds.). *Regulating the Professions.* Lexington, Mass.: Lexington Books, 1980.

Council of State Governments. *Occupational Licensing Legislation in the States: A Study of State Legislation Licensing Practice of Professional and Other Occupations.* Chicago: Council of State Governments, June 1952.

Ewalt, P. L., (Ed.). *Toward a Definition of Clinical Social Work: Papers from the NASW Invitational Forum on Clinical Social Work, June 7–9, 1979, Den-ver, Colorado.* Washington, D.C.: National Association of Social Workers, 1980.

Feigelson, E. G., and Frosch, W. "Continuing Education, Recertification, and Examination Anxiety." *American Journal of Psychiatry,* 1977, *34* (8), 869–873.

Fishman, B., and Kasser, J. "Third Party Reimbursement for Mental Health Care Delivery by Clinical Social Workers: The Case for Its Expansion." *Clinical Social Work Journal,* 1976, *4* (4), 302–318.

Flexner, A. "Is Social Work a Profession?" *Proceedings of the National Conference on Charities and Corrections.* Chicago: Hildmann Printing, 1915.

Friedman, M. *Capitalism and Freedom.* Chicago: University of Chicago Press, 1962.

Gilbert, N., and Specht, H. (Eds.). *The Emergence of Social Welfare and Social Work.* Itasca, Ill.: Peacock, 1976.

Goldstein, E. G. "Knowledge Base of Clinical Social Work." *Social Work,* 1980, *25* (3), 173–178.

Hardcastle, D. A. "Public Regulation of Social Work." *Social Work,* 1977, *22* (1), 14–20.

Hardcastle, D. A. "The Profession, Professional Organizations, Licensure and Private Practice." In N. Gilbert and H. Specht (Eds.), *Handbook of Social Services.* Englewood Cliffs, N.J.: Prentice-Hall, 1981.

Hardcastle, D. A., and Katz, A. J. *Employment and Unemployment in Social Work: A Study of NASW Members.* Washington, D.C.: National Association of Social Workers, 1979.

"How Licensing Hurts Consumers." *Business Week,* November 28, 1977, pp. 127-131.

Jett, B. L. "News of the Societies." *Clinical Social Work Journal,* 1974, *2* (2), 158-160.

Johnson, T. J. *Professions and Power.* London: Macmillan, 1972.

Kansas Statewide Health Coordinating Council. *Report on Credentialing of Health Care Personnel in Kansas.* Topeka, Kans.: State Department of Health and Environment, December 1978.

National Association of Social Workers. *Legal Regulation of Social Work.* Washington, D.C.: National Association of Social Workers, 1973a.

National Association of Social Workers. *Standards for Social Service Manpower; Professional Standards.* Washington, D.C.: National Association of Social Workers, 1973b.

National Association of Social Workers. *NASW Register of Clinical Social Workers.* (1st ed.) Washington, D.C.: National Association of Social Workers, 1976.

National Association of Social Workers. *Encyclopedia of Social Work.* Issue 17, Vol. 2. Washington, D.C.: National Association of Social Workers, 1977.

National Association of Social Workers. *The 1978 NASW Professional Social Workers' Directory.* Washington, D.C.: National Association of Social Workers, 1978a.

National Association of Social Workers. *State Comparison of Laws Regulating Social Work; July 1978.* Washington, D.C.: National Association of Social Workers, 1978b.

National Association of Social Workers. *Academy of Certified Social Workers Information Bulletin, 1979-80.* Washington, D.C.: National Association of Social Workers, 1979.

National Association of Social Workers. *Code of Ethics.* Washington, D.C.: National Association of Social Workers, 1980.

"New Policy Statement on Licensing Issues." *NASW News,* 1974, *19,* 12.

Okun, A. M. *The Political Economy of Prosperity.* Washington, D.C.: Brookings Institution, 1970.

Richan, W. C., and Mendelsohn, A. R. *Social Work: The Unloved Profession.* New York: New View Points, 1973.

Rubin, A. *Statistics on Social Work Education in the United States: 1979.* New York: Council on Social Work Education, 1980.

Scott, W. R. "Professional Employees in a Bureaucratic Structure: Social Work." In A. Etzioni (Ed.), *The Semiprofessions and Their Organization: Teachers, Nurses, Social Workers.* New York: Free Press, 1969.

Shimberg, B., and Roederer, D. *Occupational Licensing.* Lexington, Ky.: Council of State Governments, 1978.

Summers, G. M. "Public Sanction and the Professionalization of Social Work," *Clinical Social Work Journal,* 1976, *4* (1), 48-57.

Toren, N. *Social Work: The Case of a Semi-Profession.* Beverly Hills, Calif.: Sage, 1972.

Virginia Board for Registration of Social Workers. *Regulations.* Richmond, Va.: Department of Professional Occupational Regulation, Commonwealth of Virginia, September 30, 1975.

Wilensky, H. L. "The Professionalization of Everyone?" In O. Gursky and G. A. Miller (Eds.), *The Sociology of Organizations.* New York: Free Press, 1970.

Wilson, S. J. *Confidentiality in Social Work: Issues and Principles.* New York: Free Press, 1978.

Section VI

Values, Ethics, and Legal Issues

John Allen Lemmon
Section Editor

This introduction reflects the section editor's view of the practice principles to be derived from each of the chapters in this section. The authors provide the information necessary to begin implementation of these guidelines.

One theme implicit in a number of these topics is the extent to which clinical social workers actually believe in and act according to the values and ethics espoused by their profession. Stewart (1981) notes that social work increasingly serves the middle class rather than oppressed groups and suggests that one reaction to the recent rollbacks of social welfare legislation may be to revise the value base, ethical code, and training of the profession to delete references to a commitment to such groups.

Another theme in this section involves resolution of competing obligations. The profession has been accused of silently sacrificing one member of a family under the guise of a systems approach, especially regarding children in custody disputes and old people facing a nursing home if they move out of their children's homes. Clinicians have been criticized by their more radical colleagues for not being sufficiently advocacy-oriented. Advocacy is not difficult when the issue is clear, or if the advocate either adopts a hired-gun mentality or sees the world in absolute terms. For most of us, however, our curse as well as our skill is the ability to see several sides of a given conflict. These chapters are intended to provide information that will aid clinical social workers in resolving ethical dilemmas.

Ethical and Legal Issues in Clinical Social Work

The goal of the first chapter is to provide background information to serve as a general introduction for subsequent topics in this section. Trends in values and ethics in society are noted. Next, social work ethics are reviewed, with particular attention to the 1980 National Association of Social Workers (NASW) Code of Ethics. Clinical social work values and ethics are then examined for their congruence with those of the profession as a whole. Areas that may be added to both codes are considered in terms of the American Psychological Association's (APA) latest revisions of their code (1981), as well as recent legal mandates. The broader concerns of legal regulation of clinical social work practice are addressed. The most effective means of teaching values and ethics to social work students are debated. Practice principles derived from this chapter include:

- Giving a high priority to visibly ethical practice due to increased societal concern with the topic and rising expectations for and increased suspicion of professionals generally
- Encouraging the ethic of commitment for clients when they express such a goal
- Becoming knowledgeable about the NASW Code of Ethics and remaining aware of continuing clarification and interpretation of its standards
- Contributing to the evolution of the profession's values and ethical code by noting emerging dilemmas and recommending solutions whenever possible
- Learning the Code of Ethics of the National Federation of Societies for Clinical Social Work and participating in the debate about points where clinical values and positions concerning licensing and other issues diverge from the rest of the profession
- Knowing clinical practice and conforming it to relevant law in order to provide the most effective service and avoid malpractice charges
- Teaching values and ethics by modeling for colleagues, students, clients, and society as to what constitutes appropriate clinical social work practice

Value Issues in Clinical Social Work with Oppressed Minority Clients

A major controversy concerns the extent to which clinical social workers have the motivation and ability to work with oppressed groups, particularly minorities of color who have a low income or values other than those of the dominant culture.

After reviewing dominant values in the United States, Barbara Solomon concludes that "American core culture values the individual personality over collective identity and responsibility. It is ironic that despite this value, oppressed minorities are stigmatized precisely because of the widespread belief that the individual is incapable of transcending some set of inferior characteristics inherited from his endless line of ancestors."

Do clinical social workers alleviate such racism by their attitudes and actions? What are guidelines for effective practice with a client who is a member of an oppressed group, especially when the clinician is neither a member of that minority nor familiar with the possible experiences of the client? Practice principles that emerge from Solomon's chapter regarding oppressed minorities of color include:

- Values reflect the clients' behavioral expectations of self and others and so are vital to assessment.
- Oppressed groups may not share the values of the dominant culture.
- An attempt to change the client's values should only be made if he or she agrees that such a change is needed to reach a personal goal.
- A client belonging to an oppressed group should not be assumed to believe in the values attributed to that group.
- The importance of membership in an oppressed group must be assessed for each client.
- The influence of living in a neighborhood where the client's group constitutes a majority should be evaluated in terms of intervention strategies.
- The significance of religion to the client should be explored.
- Relationship patterns in oppressed groups may reflect views of interdependency, consensus, expression of emotion, and beliefs in human nature that vary from United States core culture.
- Provision of services to oppressed groups should emphasize the possible need for a personal approach, the availability of clinicians who are members of that group, and consideration of the impact of family, culture, and social institutions on the client's problems, rather than an assumption of intrapsychic causation.
- Preferences regarding structuring the helping process, expectations about the roles of client and clinician, and preferred problem-solving approaches of a number of oppressed groups may differ from one another as well as from the dominant culture.
- Sensitivity to these potential value differences by clinicians should lead to increased professionalism, practice guided by rational knowledge, as well as the impartial and responsible use of power.

Commitment to the Disenfranchised

Jerald Shapiro reviews the debate about the disparity between the stated commitment of the social work profession to the disenfranchised and the numbers actually served, especially by clinical social workers. Broadly defining disenfranchisement as deliberate exclusion and denial of resources of one group by another through societal institutions, he suggests impoverishment, discrimination, and bureaucratization as processes through which it is reached. Shapiro then considers the relationship between clinical methodology and commitment to those most in need. Resulting practice principles include:

- Awareness of the social construction and maintenance of human environments
- Analysis of the interpersonal and organizational rules, regulations, and processes that comprises the micro-policies of disenfranchisement
- Negotiation between clients and societal institutions as a multirole practitioner
- Complementarity between client and worker, so that the former sets goals and the latter suggests strategies to achieve them
- Utilization of a variety of worker roles in working with the client
- Movement toward empowerment of the client through shared decision making

Shapiro contrasts these guidelines with traditional descriptions of essential methodology in clinical social work, which emphasize the ability to conduct individual or family interviews or lead groups. He attributes the latter approach to a psychodynamic and biopsychosocial perspective. For clinical social work work to date, he says, "the underlying dynamic guiding the worker is that of treatment, and the generalized goal is the adaptive functioning of the client; for the methodological commitment to the disenfranchised, the dynamic is one of facilitation, and the generalized goal is empowerment. The former perspective relies heavily upon diagnosis to structure the treatment relationship; the latter combines an understanding of the client's environment, the nature of the client's immediate goal, and the emergent character of the working relationship to arrive at the particular progression of exchanges between the client and the client's environment that the worker will facilitate. The former focuses upon the client's command over him- or herself as the means for structuring life experience, and the latter upon the process of gaining command over the environment as a means for gaining skill and direction in structuring the totality of life experience."

Shapiro recommends that in working with disenfranchised clients, psychodynamic intervention be subordinated to environmental concerns unless the request is specifically for a psychotherapist. He also sees a secondary role for diagnosis and treatment unless, once again, the client is seeking individual, family, or group psychotherapy.

Client Self-Determination

Charles Levy, who has long considered ethical questions in social work practice, takes an extensive look at client self-determination. After noting that the professional literature has often urged social workers to overrule this principle, not only when it conflicts with societal interest, but also when the client's choice for a course of action will apparently harm him or her alone, Levy states the following practice principles:

- In terms of professional ethics, "the social worker always has the ethical responsibility to honor, to preserve, and to facilitate the client's self-determination."
- Any variation from this standard should be clearly justifiable to peers.
- "Certain professional behaviors are intrinsically valued, and therefore they are done; not certain results are attained in certain ways and therefore those ways are preferred."
- It has not been demonstrated through research that self-determination is essential to effective social work intervention.
- Self-determination is a basic social work value that leads to the realization of other values of the profession.
- The 1980 NASW Code of Ethics specifies a number of principles predicated upon client self-determination.
- Social workers should enable clients to exercise the most self-determination possible, even given the realities of involuntary service.
- "The client's autonomy (and hence self-determination) is inversely related to the social worker's autonomy."

Levy concludes his comments by maintaining that even when breaching confidentiality because of a client's threat to harm another, a case where not only other values but also legal constraints such as the *Tarasoff* ruling apply, this action should be viewed as clearly a violation of the principle of client self-determination, although a compelling and justifiable one. His intent is that rather than "many considerations require review before client self-determination can be honored . . . it should be the other way around: client self-determination may have to be honored unless and until other considerations compellingly and imperatively dictate otherwise."

Consumerism in the Social Services

After reviewing the movement toward sharing knowledge with an increasing percentage of the population as well as a trend toward greater equality than in the past, Burton Gummer proposes consumerism as a strategy for further reform of the social services. He notes that such an approach has appeal for conservative and liberal policy makers, because of the replacement of the notion of a client with the concept of a consumer in the market model sense. Gummer moves beyond facile labels to point out that a true consumer has:

- "Comprehensive knowledge of the kind and quality of goods and services available in the market
- The ability to freely choose among those goods and services so as to maximize one's self-interests
- A nondependent relationship with the producers of these goods and services, secured by one's control over personal expenditure decisions (that is, producers and consumers are mutually dependent because each controls resources the other needs)"
- The financial wherewithal to purchase what one wants

After reflecting on how this idea reinforces many national values such as individuality, freedom to choose, and the responsibility to absorb any negative consequences of decisions, Gummer proceeds to identify problems that might be alleviated by consumerism, suggests conditions that must obtain before this approach will work, and makes specific recommendations.

Professionalism is at odds with consumerism to the extent that the service to be provided is defined by the professional. The need to be ultimately answerable only to peers is often reflected in ethical statements, as Levy points out. This issue is complicated further for clinicians who work in bureaucracies. Residual services, funding sources other than the consumer, and the need for organizational maintenance also mitigate against the consumer concept.

Gummer also traces the decline of an American governing class and the gradual empowerment of various oppressed groups. However, it is the potential hindrance by professionalism to the sharing of knowledge that may be most problematic for clinical social workers. Because an essential feature of a profession is a specialized body of knowledge, and attempts to deregulate or downgrade the importance of credentials have been vigorously rebuffed by social workers, how can a true consumer model be advocated?

Practice principles that may promote consumerism include:

- Support for vouchers or cash transfers to move power from funders and providers to users

- Definition of the consumer-clinician relationship as consultative
- Movement toward empowerment of the consumer as a goal of professional relationships

At present, private practice may meet more of the criteria of consumerism than agency-based work, but not as a reform strategy in the absence of income redistribution, national health insurance, or a voucher system because the poor are excluded. Vouchers have exclusionary hazards of their own, even when addressing a universal service such as education. Whatever the vehicle, Gummer makes a compelling case that consumerism can balance the power between users and providers and make social services more responsive than in the past.

Children's Rights

It is difficult to find someone who is not in favor of children's rights, which may account for the widespread perception that court cases and legislation have corrected any potential abuses in this area. Donald Brieland reviews the rights of children in terms of legal enforceability in the courts, the family, the schools, and mental health services. He examines current policy and practice to determine what choices are available for children, rather than simply what protection has been assessed as necessary by others. Practice principles that may be inferred from Brieland's review include:

- Bills of rights proposed for children to date are not appropriate vehicles for social change, as they list needs rather than legally enforceable rights and offer few choices to be exercised by children.
- The Supreme Court of the United States has been the most influential source of decisions balancing the rights and responsibilities of parents, children, and the state.
- Clinical social workers should combine their knowledge of the needs of children with familiarity with family law in order to best aid children and their families.
- Such needs may receive legal attention in custody disputes or in the form of allegations of dependency, neglect, need for supervision, or delinquency.
- Schools are a vital aspect of the rights of children because that is where they are or ought to be for many of their waking hours, and the schools have had considerable discretion to ignore their rights or to exclude them.
- The rights of mentally ill or retarded chidlren have been slighted recently by court decisions in favor of parental judgment and state freedom to decide the appropriate level of care.
- It is the responsibility of the clinician to act as advocate for children. This does not mean full self-determination for them, but rather a balancing of the power of parents and the state by raising the stated and implicit needs of children as a issue.
- Children should be given progressively more responsible rights as they approach the age of majority, with emancipation an option where appropriate.

This last point has been most difficult to achieve in services to children. There may be a presumption that the course of action that is in the child's best interest is obvious, and he or she is too young to add relevant information. As an overreaction to this view, a number of legally oriented child advocacy groups consider only the child's stated wishes, treating him or her as an adult capable of living with the consequences of any mistaken decisions. Here the need for clinical social workers who know developmental principles, how to interview, and legal options is apparent. Children are the best guide to their feelings, so they should be asked about issues that affect them. They may be helped to state their needs and to participate in arriving at a solution that respects their rights.

Legal Dilemmas of Confidentiality

Suanna Wilson has previously undertaken an exhaustive review of confidentiality in social work. In her chapter, she focuses on three topics from a legal perspective; consent for the purpose of disclosure of information, privileged communication, and subpoenas. She provides a number of specific practice guidelines:

- Discuss confidentiality expectations with clients and document them in the record.
- Obtain informed consent in writing from clients for each request for release of confidential information.
- Caution clients against signing blanket consent forms.
- Learn the definition of privileged communication, its exceptions, and alternatives to prevent disclosure.
- Take responsibility for determining if a subpoena has been properly issued and if the information sought should be divulged, rather than either ignoring it or simply complying.
- Stay informed about changing legal requirements, ethical standards, and practice skills.

A number of Wilson's recommendations, such as arguing that a professional code of ethics or case law creates privileged communication in the absence of a statutory provision, have seen increasing success in the courts. She has continued to emphasize the relationship between legal developments and ethical practice. Her previous admonition (Wilson, 1978) that privileged communication is riddled with exceptions and brings problems rather than simply being an unqualified hallmark of the professional clinician deserves study by every social worker.

Each of the authors in this section addresses hard questions concerning certain aspects of values and ethics that are considered to be cherished in social work. Who is not for compliance with ethical codes and the law, respect for the values of oppressed minority clients, commitment to the disenfranchised, and self-determination and a consumer role for clients? However, a knowledgeable review of the complexity of trying to balance these concepts with other values demonstrates that ethical behavior in clinical social work requires an assessment of each unique situation. An understanding of the values and ethics subscribed to by the profession as well as relevant law is a starting point from which to begin individuation.

References

"Ethical Principles of Psychologists." *American Psychologist,* 1981, *36,* 633–638.

National Association of Social Workers. *Code of Ethics.* Washington, D.C.: National Association of Social Workers, 1980.

Stewart, R. "Watershed Days: How Will Social Work Respond to the Conservative Revolution?" *Social Work,* 1981, *26,* 271–273.

Wilson, S. J. *Confidentiality in Social Work: Issues and Principles.* New York: Free Press, 1978.

38

Legal Issues and Ethical Codes

John Allen Lemmon

You are a supervisor at a residential institution for adolescents. As licensed clinical social worker, you are particularly concerned with confidentiality both from a legal and ethical point of view. In your work with adolescents, you have attempted to promote an alliance that is in part dependent upon your respect for them as individuals apart from their families, teachers, childcare workers, and others. This afternoon you received a call from your part-time medical director who also works at the public health clinic. A fifteen-year-old girl who is on runaway from your setting is at the clinic seeking treatment for venereal disease. While working there he recognized her and called so that you could send one of your staff members to pick her up.

You are relieved at first, because you know that she is safe. You also remember that she has a court hearing on Thursday and suspect that if she is not there the judge will order her to a more restrictive juvenile justice placement, which you think would not meet her needs. However, you also realize that the public health clinic is one of the few places in the city that young people freely attend for the treatment of venereal disease and for contraceptive information because it has a reputation for confidentiality. Would your staff's institutional car swooping down to nab this young woman there damage that availability? What is legally correct? What guidance is provided by the National Association of Social Workers (NASW) Code of Ethics? What is best for the girl on runaway? For her peers? What would the doctor and the board of the institution expect you to do? Why did the doctor have to call when you are on duty?

You have established a part-time private practice in addition to your agency job. This evening a young man, legally and psychologically in the midst of a bitter divorce, is delivering a tirade about his estranged spouse. "I'm going to kill the bitch!" he says. "Now what do I say?" you think. You have heard about the duty to warn of the dangerousness of clients to others. Should you see if he gets more specific about how he might bring about her demise, stop him now and tell him if he mentions that idea again you have to call the police and his wife, or call them without saying anything to him? A number of your clients have made such statements in graphic detail in the past, and you have encouraged them to express their anger. None of them has ever carried out the threats. Yet now there is a legal obligation that may be in conflict with your previous clinical approach. How do you decide what to do next?

Throughout their careers as therapists, employees, and supervisors, clinical social workers face dilemmas such as those just described. This chapter examines the changing values in our society and the values and ethics of the social work profession, with its considerable range of roles. Next, it identifies clinical social work values and ethical standards and reviews legal regulation of clinical social work practice. Finally, it recommends methods for teaching values and ethics to social work students.

Ethics in Society

Ethics, "the study of the specific moral choices to be made by the individual in . . . relationship with others" (Morris, 1969, p. 450), is enjoying a resurgence in both professional and personal life today. The subject of ethics is appearing in a variety of contexts. *Esquire* magazine has a regular column so named. *Psychology Today* recently surveyed readers concerning everyday ethical dilemmas (Hassett, 1981). Harvard University's new core curriculum includes "understanding of and experience in thinking about moral and ethical problems" as one of six basic characteristics of educated men and women (Scully, 1981, p. 1).

One benefit of the political and professional scandals of the past few years has been an increased concern about ethics. Some of our most cherished institutions have been sullied. After a president of the United States resigns in disgrace, congressional officials are convicted of taking bribes, and the Pulitzer Prize is returned by a major newspaper when its reporter admits fabricating the award-winning story, the trust necessary for our society to function has been called into question. More rigorous ethical codes and more specific requirements to disclose information or verify references are being sought as a means of restoring this trust.

Human service professionals as well as lay persons recognize that the family, rather than individuals, composes the core of society (Hartman, 1981). Recent research and social commentary suggests a movement from an individual supremacy notion in this country toward serious consideration of commitment to others (Yankelovich, 1981). A comparison between attitudes in the United States in 1957 and in 1976 (Veroff, Douvan, and Kulka, 1981) shows that: "Americans have shifted their concerns from outer, superficial qualities to inner, more personal ones. People now talk more about their problems and worries than before; they are less status-conscious, more sensitive to interpersonal relationships, place more value on friendship, and, in general, have happier marriages" (Rubenstein, 1981, p. 78).

Yankelovich (1981) sees an ethic of commitment emerging in the United States in two ways: increased attention to continuing personal relationships, including friends as well as lovers, and a willingness to exchange instrumental values such as money or status for saced/expressive ones like consideration of the past and future through religion or a relationship with nature. Schnall (1981) also notes a search for new values following the cultural narcissism that a number of writers have maintained describes the past decade (see especially Lasch, 1978). Schnall argues that: "we can create a new climate in which human needs and values can be nurtured . . . a parent-oriented society that supports the family as the mainstay of the community; a responsible society that values excellence and the common good over money and power; a caring society that promotes decency and reciprocity in our relations with others and balance between the opposing but inseparable aspects of the self; a communal society that encourages the individual to make a connection with something larger than one's own life—a social issue, a political movement, a cultural matter—and through one's commitment to it find a sense of purpose" (p. 319).

A large percentage of the current U.S. population, the children of the baby boom, are now reaching their late twenties and early thirties. The renewed cultural interest in personal commitment, family, and societal ethics may reflect their predictable psychosocial development (Erikson, 1950), just as the rebellion of the sixties and the narcissism of the "me generation" of the seventies may have paralleled the earlier developmental stages of this group.

Ethical issues have traditionally been a central part of the social work profession. As this larger shift toward commitment and concern for others becomes more apparent in society, these professionals working with people directly or for agencies designed to meet social needs are expanding their range of ethical responsibilities.

Social Work Ethics

In addition to the societal attitudes about right and wrong behavior, ethics are also "rules or standards governing the conduct of the members of a profession" (Morris, 1969, p. 450). Levy (1976), who has written about social work ethics for almost twenty years, says that ethics generally consist of expectations regarding others that stem from a responsibility toward them. Professional ethics involve "that which ought to be done . . . in an occupational capacity because of the responsibility assumed to be carried by virtue of occupational capacity" (p. 25). Social work ethics are our profession's values in operation. Ethical and legal issues are related because the general obligation to act in a trustworthy manner, attributed to any profession, whether codified formally in a statement or not, offers a recourse to a wronged client. The most recent codification of these professional standards is available as the NASW Code of Ethics (1980), which describes the social worker's conduct as a professional and responsibility to clients, colleagues, employers, the profession, and society. The code is intended to provide guidelines to influence professional behavior as well as to serve as the authoritative reference in alleged ethical violations that are to be adjudicated.

This code has emerged after a decade of comment that the previous version no longer reflected the values of the profession adequately. As Keith-Lucas (1971) says, "emphasis had shifted, often in reaction against values overstressed by the previous generation. New social problems and new roles for social work demanded reformulations and guidelines for new situations" (p. 325). Keith-Lucas also states that contemporary social work ethics both mirror the values of society in part and are in conflict with aspects of them. "While rejecting many capitalist-puritan values, social work ethics are deeply rooted in Judeo-Christian principles, especially those that emphasize justice, equality, and concern for others" (p. 325).

The 1980 code "is based on the fundamental values of the social work profession that include the worth, dignity, and uniqueness of all persons as well as their rights and opportunities" (National Association of Social Workers, p. 3). How should members of the profession promote the general welfare of society? The NASW Code of Ethics states that:

1. The social worker should act to prevent and eliminate discrimination against any person or group on the basis of race, color, sex, sexual orientation, age, religion, national origin, marital status, political belief, mental or physical handicap, or any other preference or personal characteristic, condition, or status.
2. The social worker should act to ensure that all persons have access to the resources, services, and opportunities which they require.
3. The social worker should act to expand choice and opportunity for all persons, with special regard for disadvantaged or oppressed groups and persons.
4. The social worker should promote conditions that encourage respect for the diversity of cultures which constitute American society.
5. The social worker should provide appropriate professional services in public emergencies.
6. The social worker should advocate changes in policy and legislation to improve social conditions and to promote social justice.
7. The social worker should encourage informed participation by the public in shaping social policies and institutions [p. 9].

In addition, the code attempts to be specific enough to serve as a guide to practice situations. It considers confidentiality and privacy, aspects of the social work's ethical responsibility to clients that often present dilemmas:

1. The social worker should share with others confidences revealed by clients, without their consent, only for compelling professional reasons.
2. The social worker should inform clients fully about the limits of confidentiality in a given situation, the purposes for which information is obtained, and how it may be used.
3. The social worker should afford clients reasonable access to any official social work records concerning them.
4. When providing clients with access to records, the social worker should take due care to protect the confidences of others contained in those records.
5. The social worker should obtain informed consent of clients before taping, recording, or permitting third-party observation of their activities [pp. 5–6].

These are clear and operable principles, especially for recordkeeping. But what are "compelling professional reasons" for sharing the revelations of clients? Greater specificity is still needed to make clear to practitioners exactly what actions they should take, especially in light of recent legal mandates. In cases such as *Tarasoff* v. *Regents of the University of California* (17 Cal. 3d 425, 1976), which create a duty to warn of dangerous clients, law has preceded incorporation of an ethical standard into a code.

Clinical Social Work Values

Concern is often expressed about the extent to which there is communality between clinical social workers and the rest of the profession. Fortunately, Jackson (1979) recently studied a national sample of clinical social workers, asking them to define themselves and describe their values. His results revealed that this group is identified with social work: ". . . despite their frequent involvement with postmaster's continuing education and training outside the profession. They are committed to participation in the solution of social problems. These practitioners perceive their values, knowledge base, and practice as well within the social work rubric" (p. 82).

However, this study does reveal some differences that concern clinical social workers. They refer to themselves as "clinical," as do members of the National Association of Social Workers Register of Clinical Social Work and the National Registry of Health Care Providers in Clinical Social Work. Yet the social work literature, written primarily by professors rather than practitioners, seldom uses this term, using instead titles such as the direct service worker. This is seen as reflecting a preference for a generic model in schools of social work rather than the specialization in psychotherapy sought by clinicians. Further, the Council on Social Work Education (CSWE) as well as schools of social work are seen as developing the B.S.W., whereas clinical social workers seek post-master's continuing education and the opportunity for doctoral study with a clinical concentration. Finally, most of the clinical social workers in this study prefer psychoanalytic theory. Moreover, eight of the nine programs advertised in the *NASW NEWS* in April of 1981 for a course of study longer than a weekend in psychotherapy described themselves as psychodynamically or psychoanalytically oriented. The sole exception was also the only program located in a university, and the theoretical orientation of this postgraduate program in advanced clinical social work was not specified. A psychoanalytic framework for practice may provide a different perception of such values as maximum self-determination for clients or the manner in which the general welfare of society is to be promoted than do other perspectives such as social action advocated within the social work profession.

Additional clinical social work values may be inferred from the ethical standards developed for this specialization. The California Society for Clinical Social Work Code of Ethics (1975) assumes privileged communication and possession of a clinical license:

1. The clinical social worker shall be committed to serve the needs of the individual or group receiving services. Services are based on sound diagnostic skills and respect for the integrity and dignity of each person. This must include respect for differences in race, religion, and ethnic background.

2. The clinical social worker is identified with and upholds the concept of improving the mental health and social functioning of individuals.
3. The clinical social worker is responsible for the quality of the services offered.
4. The clinical social worker is responsible for special self-awareness so as to prevent the intrusion of personal needs into the professional relationship.
5. The clinical social worker will continually strive to increase professional knowledge and skills.
6. The clinical social worker is committed to function within the legal requirements of the license for clinical social workers.
7. The clinical social worker shall not misrepresent his professional qualifications and associations.
8. The clinical social worker holds as privileged all communications obtained in the course of the therapeutic relationship.
9. The clinical social worker shall not solicit patients through public advertisements.
10. The clinical social worker is responsible for following the rules and regulations of the employing agency and will use appropriate channels to effect improvements.
11. The clinical social worker shall make clear whether public statements are made as an individual or as the representative of an organization [p. 111].

A number of these statements appear to be intended as a guide to private practitioners. However, others specifically refer to organizational affiliations, while the remaining principles apply to clinicians regardless of their setting. There may be similarities between private and agency practice. In one study, three groups of licensed clinical social workers were surveyed: solely private practitioners, solely agency workers, and those working in both settings (Borenzweig, 1981). None of the groups was significantly involved in social change. Post-1967 graduates had little supervision but were more secure in their identification with social work than earlier cohorts. All three groups based their practice on Freudian theory rather than social work formulations, but few had sought additional clinical training at psychoanalytic or other centers past the M.S.W.

However, differences that prompt criticism of private practice were also found. Agencies served those most in need, while private practitioners saw people with more money who were labeled as neurotic. More innovative treatment methods were in use in agencies, while the traditional interview characterized private practice. Private clinicians spent more time with clients, possibly both because of the bureaucratic nature of agency practice and the seldom-acknowledged fact that a private practice is a business in which the therapist is paid only for seeing clients directly, rather than for attending meetings or taking coffee breaks.

Legal Issues for Clinical Social Workers

Clinical social workers have increasingly specific levels of ethical responsibility to their clients. First, they share with lay persons a general moral obligation to others. Next, professing expert knowledge conveys additional duties to respect the trust given by clients. The social work profession has a general Code of Ethics that addresses the range of roles performed by social workers, which is difficult because many problems implicit in the regulation of the profession arise from the diversity of roles that social workers take (Brieland and Lemmon, 1977). The specialization of clinical social work has produced an ethical code as well. Finally, laws mandating certain behaviors and proscribing others for clinical social workers exist in a number of states and are lobbied for by NASW and clinically oriented practitioners in the remaining states. Certain aspects of practice may be considered especially sensitive for clinicians, both ethically and legally. In particular, Van Hoose and Kottler (1977) see group work, behavior therapy, and assessment as posing potential problems.

Professional Licensing

Clinical social workers have led the drive for legal recognition of social work as a profession with exclusivity of function, the limitation of certain activities to holders of a state license. Such licensing tends to describe direct practice with an emphasis on privately provided psychotherapy. These laws create formal sanctions for failing to do what ought to be done in an occupational role, a violation of professional ethics. According to Erikson (1980), "ethics and the law must define the bearable limits of exclusional rejection . . ." (p. 218).

Incompetent practice has been distinguished from unethical behavior, which assumes a minimal level of competence (Levy, 1976). The promotion of both competent and ethical practice is the goal of licensing of social workers. A number of state clinical social work societies oppose legislation that would license at each level of practice—such as an A.A. in human services or a B.A. in an unrelated field, B.S.W., M.S.W., and postgraduate experience—believing that to do so would lower professional standards. However, the National Association of Black Social Workers questions the relation of state licensure in any form in terms of the profession's commitment to social change, fearing that entry by nonwhites into the field may be limited by laws that stress degrees and examinations rather than clinical effectiveness in the community.

Data showing that successful application for the Academy of Certified Social Workers (ACSW) is related to race bear out their concern. From 1973 to 1978, the certification was determined by a multiple-choice examination and, if necessary, augmented by references. Only 55 percent of black applicants were certified during these years, compared with 93 percent of Caucasian candidates. The procedure was then changed so that three factors—an examination, three references, and the number of years of professional experience beyond the two postgraduate years required for application—were weighted equally. The number of successful black applicants rose to 72 percent, while the rate for Caucasians remained about the same as before, 94 percent (1981).

Those arguing for state licensing for clinical social work might respond with situations such as the plight of one social worker who, despite ACSW certification and listing in the NASW Register of Clinical Social Workers, was charged with practicing psychotherapy without a certificate from the appropriate state board in Ohio, which does not have licensing for social workers ("Association, Chapter Submit Briefs. . . ," 1981). Such court cases may be prompted by professional groups in psychiatry and clinical psychology who are acting to prevent competition in the absence of state legislation affirming the right of clinical social workers to provide psychotherapy.

Confidentiality and Privileged Communication

Confidentiality is a professional standard to treat client information responsibly. Privileged communication is the right of a client involved in court action to keep the therapist from testifying, a right that must be created by state statute in order to apply to social workers. Wilson (1978) states that there are twenty-nine exceptions to privileged communication, a concept that many social workers confuse with confidentiality. What is ethical behavior when a client being seen for psychotherapy says that she is the one who has badly beaten her child? Should the clinical social worker whose client says that he is going to kill his lover tell the police and/or the potential victim?

In one such situation, a clinician did inform police, but the client was questioned and released. He subsequently did kill the woman whose life he had threatened. Her parents sued the therapist's employer, and the California Supreme Court ruled that the victim herself should have been warned (*Tarasoff* v. *Regents of University of California*). Reasonable care must be exercised by therapists to protect potential victims if, under prevailing professional standards, they believe that the threats might result in harm to others. What are those standards? The National Association of Social Workers Code (1980) does not offer guidance other than "compelling professional reasons" and "informing clients fully about the limits of confidentiality in a given situation" (pp. 5-6).

A study of California therapists after this court decision found that they had reacted by discussing confidentiality more often with clients, by either focusing more on content indicating dangerousness or avoiding this information altogether, by increasing consultation with other professionals, and by limiting the records they kept to avoid legal charges ("California Therapists. . . ," 1979). This research revealed that therapists lacked adequate criteria to determine when warning potential victims was indicated. Yet the duty to warn established by *Tarasoff* has been successfully cited in other states in cases against therapists who have argued that it is not possible to accurately predict dangerousness. The ruling in *McIntosh* v. *Milano* (48 *L.W.* 2039, 1979) confirmed that a "therapist may have a duty to take whatever steps are reasonably necessary to protect an intended or potential victim of his patient when he determines, or should determine, in the appropriate factual setting and in accordance with the standards of his profession established at trial, that the patient is or may present a probability of danger to that person" (p. 2040). Neither court cases nor detailed ethical codes can compel knowledge to be exercised that simply does not exist. The definition of malpractice in any profession is a failure to follow established standards.

However, the American Psychological Association (APA) addresses this issue directly in the June 1981 revision of its ethics code ("APA Releases Major Revisions. . . ," 1981) by permitting psychologists to breach confidentiality without the client's consent if failure to do so "would result in clear danger to the person or to others" (p. 3). Other emerging concerns are reflected in additions to the code: sexual harassment—the "deliberate or repeated comments, gestures, or physical contacts of a sexual nature"—is condemned; students are added to the group of those not to be exploited, "sexually or otherwise"; minors and others who may not be able to give informed consent are to be given extra care; when a consumer is not benefiting from clinical or consulting assistance, the psychologist is to "offer to help the consumer locate alternative sources of assistance" (p. 3). These are sound recommendations that may aid clinical social workers seeking guidance in these areas.

Written ethical standards have proven useful in court situations. A therapist with an M.S.W. persuaded the judge in a child custody hearing that since she did not have a signed consent from her client to testify, the NASW Code of Ethics as well as that of the American Association of Marriage and Family Therapy to which she also belonged precluded breaching confidentiality. The judge excused her even though she was not covered by the privileged communications law of the state, setting an important precedent for social workers who are not protected by such statutes ("Judge Upholds Professional Ethics Code. . . ," 1981).

Such cases underscore the need for clinical social workers to know the laws that affect their practice, as when privileged communication is limited to social workers holding a state license as well as in regard to whether a duty to warn is imposed in their state. Legal regulation of social work practice varies by state, despite attempts at universal standards such as the ACSW and the clinical register. A number of states either have licensing, which restricts certain activities, most often characterized as clinical, to the class of the holder, or certification, which is merely title protection. In the absence of a clear statutory privilege, it has been recommended that therapists: (1) obtain a written agreement of privilege from all clients involved in therapy, including both husband and wife (which is especially important if a subsequent divorce occurs); (2) secure from clients written permission to testify or divulge information to their attorneys; and (3) consult an attorney, who may know about state legislation that extends privileged communication to situations such as the provision of mental health services (Gumper, 1981).

Teaching Values and Ethics in Clinical Social Work

Simmons College, which in 1904 became the first academically affiliated school of social work in the United States, at first provided a joint program in which male students registered in the graduate Department of Social Ethics at Harvard ("A Retrospective. . . ," 1980). This demonstrates the former prominence of ethics in the general curriculum as well as its affiliation with social work.

There has been a resurgence of interest in applied and professional ethics in the past decade. The Institute of Society, Ethics, and the Life Sciences, also known as the Hastings Center, was established in 1969 to encourage research on ethical issues and to promote teaching in this area, with social work among the professions represented. This need arose because the replacement of ethics with the scientific method as central to curriculum had not provided adequate guidance for increasingly complex issues faced by professionals. Familiar dilemmas—"conflicts of interest, whistle blowing on corruption, obligations to clients or patients versus duty to society, and the consequences of deception versus truth telling" ("Applied Ethics. . . ," 1980, p. 2) were being exacerbated by technological advances. The Hastings Center was concerned that professions had become too limited in focus, doing a good job technically without regard for the larger issues involved. Their goals in teaching ethics are to help students (1) realize that professional decisions have moral consequences; (2) recognize ethical issues; (3) develop skill in analysis from an ethical point of view; (4) develop moral responsibility that is reflected in behavior; and (5) learn when to tolerate and when to resist ambiguity and disagreement.

The Council on Social Work Education now requires as a condition of accreditation that "a dean or director of a school of social work shall bring to the post demonstrated . . . commitment to the ethical values of the social work profession" and that "the focus of examination of a program of basic professional social work education shall include an assessment of adherence to the ethical values of the profession of social work" (Gross, Steiner, and Rosa, 1980, p. 21).

Educational programs may be characterized as either allegedly value-free, emphasizing cognitive analysis of facts and concepts, or value-laden, emphasizing specific allegiances (Gross, Steiner, and Rosa, 1980). In one research study, four values—equal rights, service, psychodynamical-mindedness, and universalism—were considered to be essential for socialization into social work (Varley, 1963). A pre- and posttest found that of these four values a graduate education in social work increased only students' commitment to equal rights. Students entering social work school have reported more interest in social and religious values than in personal economic concerns (Hayes and Varley, 1965). Social work faculty have stated that they teach values and adhere more closely to values identified with social work than a comparable sample of arts and sciences professors (Rosa, 1978). Being openly value-laden may explain the low regard with which other departments hold social work in some research universities, as well as the increased pressures on social work faculty at those programs, due to value conflicts among the faculty.

Assuming that core social work values are agreed upon, and that faculty openly espouse them, what is the best way to teach this content? While presenting moral dilemmas to illustrate ethical choices is relatively easy, it is naïve to expect student behavior to change in the future as a result of classroom exercises. Modeling a sense of morality may be the most powerful teaching strategy, which is another reason for universities to employ social workers who exemplify the profession's values by their actions.

Case examples are useful in a number of professions to develop ethical reasoning. This is certainly a familiar method in social work education. Such teaching might begin with a dilemma of virtue, or a "good-bad" dilemma (Keith-Lucas, 1977) in which the correct behavior is clear but the temptation is great, as when a clinical social worker facing tremendous medical bills for her sick child is offered money to lie in court by a client facing criminal charges for child abuse. Keith-Lucas believes that only situations in which one action is generally accepted as correct are controllable by a code of ethics. He states that these good-bad dilemmas can be resolved by reference to "the principles of nonexploitation, nondiscrimination, the preservation of legal and constitutional rights, and the general concept of accountability . . . possibly the nearest to being absolutes for social work practice" (p. 35).

Dilemmas of principle, or "good-good" situations, present more difficult ethical problems because they involve competing obligations. Consider the common practice by clinicians of listing a less serious diagnosis on insurance forms than is their true assessment. Here integrity as a professional is in conflict with avoiding harm to the client who has sought help. Violations of confidentiality by personnel departments at the client's place of employment and through insurance company data banks have occurred often enough to inhibit honest disclosure. Keith-Lucas (1977) maintains that good-good situations are resolvable only by analysis of the unique circumstances involved and the values of the clinician. No general rules can aid in reconciling:

1. The tension between the obligation to reform the social structure and the obligation to help people cope with the social structure in which they find themselves. This is sometimes presented as a tension between two different time scales, the immediate and the more distant future.
2. The tension between responsibility to the consumers of service and responsibility to those who pay for it, who are not usually the same group in society
3. The tension between the good of the individual and the good of the group or community of which he (she) is a part
4. The tension between the client's right to freedom of choice and what is perceived as good for him (her)
5. The tension between equity (treating everyone evenhandedly) and the fulfilling of individual needs [p. 352]

Even in these complex and conflicting situations, guidance is available. Ethical codes are becoming increasingly explicit concerning certain behaviors. Legislation and court cases have spoken to a number of these issues. Both ethics and law will continue to change, however, and the direction of this change can reflect the actions of clinical social workers who rely on their values in exercising professional judgment.

Field placement would seem to be critical to the teaching of ethics and the development of professional judgment in social work. It is there that modeling for clinical practice rather than for university teaching takes place. An opportunity to examine ethical dilemmas that have confronted clinicians in the practice setting could be included in the student's fieldwork contract. The student and supervisor could also review the NASW Code of Ethics, the ethical codes of cognate professions, and relevant law. The selection of a fieldwork supervisor who has demonstrated knowledge of and commitment to the NASW Code of Ethics in the course of clinical practice may be as important as concern for the skills that students may acquire and practice in a given setting. Indeed, with the rapid changes in information, demonstrating an ethical reaction to such changes in terms of social work values is more important in influencing the course of student careers than any other aspect of socialization into the profession.

References

"A Retrospective on the Occasion of the Diamond Jubilee: An Historical Monograph." Boston: School of Social Work, Simmons College, 1980.

Academy of Certified Social Workers. "Report on Certification by the Academy of Certified Social Workers, 1973–1980." *NASW NEWS*, 1981, *26*, 10–12.

"APA Releases Major Revisions in Psychologist's Ethics Code." *Behavior Today,* 1981, *12,* 3.

"Applied Ethics: A Strategy for Fostering Professional Responsibility." *Carnegie Quarterly,* 1980, *28,* 1–7.

"Association, Chapter Submit Briefs Supporting Clinical Practice Rights." *NASW NEWS,* 1981, *26,* 12.

Borenzweig, H. "Agency vs. Private Practice: Similarities and Differences." *Social Work,* 1981, *26,* 239–244.

Brieland, D., and Lemmon, J. *Social Work and the Law.* St. Paul, Minn.: West, 1977.

California Society for Clinical Social Work. *Code of Ethics.* Los Angeles: California Society for Clinical Social Work, 1975.

"California Therapists Say Court Ruling Has Brought Changes to Their Practice." *Chronicle of Higher Education,* 1979, *18,* 6.

Erikson, E. *Childhood and Society.* New York: Norton, 1950.

Erikson, E. "On the Generational Cycle." *International Journal of Psycho-Analysis,* 1980, *61,* 213–223.

Gross, G., Steiner, J., and Rosa, L. "Educational Doctrines and Social Work Values: Match or Mismatch?" *Journal of Education for Social Work,* 1980, *16,* 21–28.

Gumper, L. "Must Pastoral Counselors Reveal Confidential Information?" *Marriage and Divorce Today,* 1981, *6,* 3–4.

Hartman, A. "The Family: A Central Focus for Practice." *Social Work,* 1981, *26,* 7–13.

Hassett, J. "Is It Right? An Inquiry into Everyday Ethics." *Psychology Today,* 1981, *15,* 49–56.

Hayes, D., and Varley, B. "Impact of Social Work Education on Student Values." *Social Work,* 1965, *10,* 45.

Jackson, J. "How Do Clinical Social Workers Define Themselves and Describe Their Values, Knowledge, and Practice?" Unpublished doctoral dissertation, Institute for Clinical Social Work, Sacramento, Calif., 1979.

"Judge Upholds Professional Ethics Code: Excuses Therapist from Testifying." *Marriage and Divorce Today,* 1981, *6,* 1.

Keith-Lucas, A. "Ethics in Social Work." *Encyclopedia of Social Work,* 1971, *1* (16), 324–328.

Keith-Lucas, A. "Ethics in Social Work." *Encyclopedia of Social Work,* 1977, *1* (17), 350–355.

Lasch, C. *The Culture of Narcissism.* New York: Norton, 1978.

Levy, C. *Social Work Ethics.* New York: Human Sciences Press, 1976.

Morris, W. (Ed.). *The American Heritage Dictionary.* Boston: Houghton Mifflin, 1969.

National Association of Social Workers. *Code of Ethics.* Washington, D.C.: National Association of Social Workers, 1980.

Rosa, L. "Personal and Advocated Values of Faculty Members." Unpublished baccalaureate independent study, School of Social Work, Syracuse University, Syracuse, N.Y., 1978.

Rubenstein, C. "The Revolution Within." *Psychology Today,* 1981, *15,* 78–81.

Schnall, M. *Limits: A Search for New Values.* New York: Potter, 1981.

Scully, M. "New 'Core' Curriculum Working Well, Harvard Dean Says; Critics Less Vocal." *Chronicle of Higher Education,* 1981, *22* (1), 13.

Van Hoose, W. H., and Kottler, J. A. *Ethical and Legal Issues in Counseling and Psychotherapy.* San Francisco: Jossey-Bass, 1977.

Varley, B. "Socialization in Social Work Education." *Social Work,* 1963, *8,* 103–105.

Veroff, J., Douvan, E., and Kulka, R. *The Inner-American: A Self-Portrait.* New York: Basic Books, 1981.

Wilson, S. J. *Confidentiality in Social Work: Issues and Principles.* New York: Free Press, 1978.

Yankelovich, D. *New Rules.* New York: Random House, 1981.

39

Value Issues in Working with Minority Clients

Barbara Bryant Solomon

The English language is not particularly rich in constructions that differentiate the subtle variations of meaning among similar concepts. For example, the term *minority group* fails to inform whether the group is racially, ethnically, or numerically defined; whether its status is based on voluntary self-identification or imposed by a dominant group; or whether it has been formally recognized in the legal, economic, or political systems of the community. The focus of this chapter is on members of minority groups in American society that not only have been negatively valued but have been the target of legislative as well as administrative politics placing them at severe, societally condoned disadvantage. This has been reflected in slavery, segregation laws, exclusion laws, confiscatory policies, and less protection against punitive and discriminatory practices of governmental agencies than has been accorded other citizens. These oppressed minorities—black, Hispanic, Asian-Pacific, and American Indian—are perhaps most clearly differentiated from other disadvantaged groups by their intense racial, ethnic, and political consciousness, which enhances their appreciation of themselves and their relationship with each other and often binds them together under the term *Third World* (Morales, 1981).

The identification of certain groups as "oppressed minorities" only has significance for the clinical social worker to the extent that the individuals or families who belong to that group and who seek help are influenced by factors uniquely associated with membership in the group. Among the most powerful such factors is the value system. Although values have been used synonymously with such other terms as likes, duties, moral obligations, goals, needs, aversions, and attractions, a core phenomenon to which all these terms refer is "criteria or standards of performance" (Williams, 1979, p. 16). When explicit and clearly conceptualized, values become criteria for judging one's own social functioning as well as the social functioning of others, for identifying preferences in regard to problem-solving activities, and for choosing among alternative activities. Thus, the value orientation or value system of any client—but particularly of those who are members of oppressed minority groups—is an important variable to be assessed. It would be a serious mistake to assume that these clients share the core values of American society and therefore will utilize the same criteria in judging the behaviors of themselves and others as any middle-class, Anglo-American.

Because oppressed minorities are themselves negatively valued by the larger society, it is obvious that distinctive values they hold are also likely to be negatively valued. Rokeach (1968) has stated that "Belief congruence will override racial or ethnic congruence except when the perceived cost is too great" (p. 80). Thus, value differences would be perceived as more powerful determinants than racial differences. Whether or not one accepts this proposition unconditionally, the point may be moot since racial differences and value differences are so highly correlated. Therefore, racial conflicts may be based more on perceived value differences than on racial differences. More relevant to the concerns of this chapter is the fact that value differences may similarly account for obstacles encountered by clinical social work practitioners in their efforts to implement problem-solving activities with clients from an oppressed minority group.

Basic Assumptions

Consideration of the influence of a value system on clinical social work practice must flow from a set of assumptions that serves as a framework of organizing principles. Those assumptions that appear to be most relevant for the development of a perspective on clinical social work with clients from oppressed minority groups will be discussed.

Assumption: Values are capable of different structural arrangements. These arrangements constitute a value system that will be similar for those who belong to the same cultural group and will vary among different cultural groups.

Differences among individuals may not appear so much in the presence or absence of particular values, as in their hierarchies or priorities (Rokeach, 1973). Certainly differences in values across different ethnic populations do not consist for the most part of a complete absence of some values in one case and their presence in another. The difference may be in the relative importance given to the value when one group is compared with another. This notion of differential value arrangements also incorporates the concept of "value specialization" (Williams, 1970, p. 39). This refers to a phenomenon occurring in highly differentiated modern societies, such as in the United States, where diverse values are compartmentalized in the major specialized institutions (kinship, stratification, economy, polity, education, science, and religion). To the extent that an institution is the more powerful—for example, science or religion—its values will have the greater priority within individual value systems. Many of the traditional societies from which the oppressed minorities in this country have come have vested more power in certain institutions (for example, kinship, religion) than have members of the dominant culture. Furthermore, contradictions and incongruities are often assigned to a specialized collective or social status, such as those specialized in adjudication, mediation, suppression, therapy, or diversion (Williams, 1979). Again, in different societies, different collectivities or statuses may be given particular responsibilities. The curing of a mental disorder, for example, may be a responsibility of a spiritualist or a priest or a psychiatrist, depending on the society.

Assumption: Values are capable of undergoing change as a result of clinical social work intervention.

The clinical social worker has a responsibility to choose with exceeding care those times when values will become a target for change. The risk is that his or her own values may be imposed on the client. For example, as a helping professional, the social worker may value highly ethnic diversity and multicultural activities. A member of an oppressed minority, however, may find so much comfort and security in the selective association with other members that he will repel any effort to broaden his associations to members of other ethnic groups. Or an individual whose culturally salient religious orientation may include practices harmful to the individual's personal health may find religious conformity a higher value than personal health or vice versa. Imposing values can be avoided, however, to the extent that clients are involved in setting the change objectives. Hardman (1975) suggests that only when the values of a client conflict with the welfare of others or with the client's achieving agreed-upon goals, should values themselves become a target for change.

Assumption: In considering whether an individual member of an ethnic group will adhere to a particular value system, it is important to avoid the "ecological fallacy."

The ecological fallacy occurs when inferences are made about behavior, attitudes, and so forth of individuals by examining measures made on groups. For example, we may find a correlation between the percentage of blacks in a neighborhood and the rate of hospitalization for schizophrenia or the number of homicides. It would be an error, however, to infer that an individual who is black is more likely to be schizophrenic or a murder victim. Similarly, the evidence that oppressed minority groups tend to place higher value on kinship structures, religion, or primary-group relationships than the majority group should not lead one to directly infer that an individual who belongs to the oppressed minority group will have the same value priorities. For example, if 40 percent of the members of the oppressed minority group hold traditional religious values as compared with only 10 percent of the majority group, the difference will be significant. Yet, in each instance most members do not hold those values. This suggests that assessment of clients still must place primary emphasis on individual indicators rather than on group indicators. In other words, taking into account one's cultural values is not synonymous with the creation of cultural stereotypes.

Assumption: American society is an ethnosystem comprising groups or collectivities of individuals whose ethnicity serves to define them and their relationship to the whole—either by self-determination or by determination of others in the system (Solomon, 1976, p. 45).

Perhaps the most pervasive characteristic of the ethnosystem is the centrality of both race and ethnicity in almost every aspect of social interaction within it. Thus, one's ethnic identity is developed through time and takes on varying degrees of importance in the course of one's life experience as one contrasts one's own group along some dimension with the dominant culture and with other groups in the ethnosystem as well. From the perspective of clinical social work, the individual's value system is not merely a reflection of the individual's membership in a cultural group but a product of his interaction with all other groups in the ethnosystem. Furthermore, the salience of the value system is likely to be greatest at points of challenge or choice when the individual's personal and social functioning is threatened. These are also the points at which the individual is most likely to encounter the helping professional.

Comparing Value Systems

Values and value orientations have been favored subjects for scholarly analysis in a variety of disciplines, ranging from philosophy and comparative literature to anthropology, psychology, and sociology. The following discussion of dimensions along which value positions of majority and minority cultures in American society may be compared has drawn heavily from the works of Kluckhohn and Strodtbeck (1961), Rokeach (1968, 1973), Williams (1970 and 1979), Arensberg and Niehoff (1971), De Vos (1975), and Turner (1963).

Williams (1979) identified fifteen major themes of value-belief orientations considered to be salient in American society, including humanitarianism, science and secular rationality, and external conformity. On the basis of his analyses of these themes, he concluded that the core culture tends to emphasize active mastery rather than passive acceptance of events, an external view of the world, the perception of society and history as open-ended rather than static, rationalism as opposed to traditionalism, orderliness, a universalistic social ethic, egalitarian rather than hierarchical social relationships, an individual rather than a collective identity, and an extremely strong emphasis on an instrumental rather than an expressive society.

In regard to the source of these values and their "spread" in the society, Arensberg and Niehoff (1971) state: "There is a national core usually characterized as that of the middle class having its origin in Western European culture. The language is English, the legal system derives from English common law, the political system of democratic elections comes from France and England, the technology is solidly from Europe, and even more subtle social values, such as egalitarianism (though modified) seem to be European-derived. Thus, it seems justifiable to characterize the middle-class value system of the United States, as derived originally from Europe but modified to suit local conditions, as the core of American culture. All people born and raised in this country will have been conditioned by the national culture although obviously the middle class will be most strongly marked" (p. 364).

These core values appear to express particular value positions or orientations that may be expressed in particular arenas (such as religion and interpersonal relationships). These arenas may be conceptualized as value dimensions along which various groups in the society may be placed according to the positions taken. For example, "economic system" may be a value dimension along which different cultural groups may take different positions, some preferring a socialist economic system and others preferring a capitalistic system. Because there has been no documentation of significant differentiation of oppressed minorities in this country on this dimension, it will not be discussed here in more detail. However, five dimensions have particular relevance for comparison of value systems of majority and minority groups in our society.

Racial-Ethnic Uniqueness. As already indicated, American core culture values individual personality over collective identity and responsibility. It is ironic that, despite this value, oppressed minorities are stigmatized precisely because of the widespread belief that the individual is incapable of transcending some set of inferior characteristics inherited from his endless line of ancestors. It is as if the core values are accepted as criteria for performance in the "in-group" but do not hold for the "out-groups." Oppressed minorities are therefore more likely to perceive a significance in their membership in the collective than are members of the majority.

De Vos (1975) suggests that minority groups in American society differ in the extent to which some sense of genetically inherited differences, real or imagined, is an accepted part of their ethnic identity as well as a factor in the dominant group's belief system. Thus, if an empirical study were undertaken to determine the extent to which members of the black, Hispanic, Asian-Pacific, or American Indian groups perceived themselves as racially unique when compared to the white majority, we would expect to find differential perceptions among the groups; blacks might be more likely to perceive themselves as racially unique than would Hispanics, for example. There may also be differential value placed on this uniqueness from extremely negative to extremely positive.

Regardless of the propensity for any individual in an oppressed minority group to value racial uniqueness, the message to the clinical social worker is that this is an important dimension to measure in the process of assessment. For some individuals, their identity as black, Hispanic, Asian-Pacific, or American Indian is a necessary component of a positive self-image; for others, it is the major aspect of their negative identity; and for still others, it is an irrelevant facet of a self that has been constructed from other, more personally salient characteristics, such as occupation, educational level, or religious affiliation. A logical (although untested) proposition flowing from this formulation is that the congruence of individual and core American value systems will be inversely related to the individual's perception of the racial/ethnic uniqueness of the group to which he or she belongs.

Territoriality. De Vos (1975) has indicated that "territory may be central to maintain ethnicity, or it may be minimal, or even nonexistent . . . the degree to which some territorial concept is necessary to the maintenance of ethnic identity, symbolically or actually, must be considered in relation to the use of nonterritorial definitions of ethnic uniqueness . . ." (p. 12). There is considerable differentiation among the minority groups in this country in regard to the value placed on those "territories" or neighborhoods in which their group is at least numerically dominant. In fact, a major characteristic differentiating the oppressed minority groups and other minority groups such as the "white ethnics" may be the higher value placed by the latter on their ethnic enclaves. The neighborhood for these groups is more likely to be perceived as a comforting, secure environment than as a trap from which there is no escape. Individuals in minority groups will, therefore, tend to measure their life satisfaction to some extent by their ability to either maintain or sever territorial ties with their group depending on their particular value position on this dimension. From the perspective of the clinical social worker, an assessment of the significance of territorial ties for the individual will influence the extent to which the neighborhood may be seen as a context in which the helping process should be embedded.

Religious Orientation. Arensberg and Niehoff (1971) project the religious orientation reinforced by core cultural values as one of puritanic morality that has become generalized and secularized, part of the total culture rather than any single religious sect. "Religion can hardly be considered a particularly unifying institution in American life. The spirit of the country is secular and rationalistic. Most people are not antireligious but merely indifferent" (p. 366). The more recent rise in the power of the "moral majority" and the increase in religious affiliation among middle-class and working-class Americans may be perceived as a minority reaction to the secularization of society, which may or may not be a harbinger of change in a basic societal value orientation.

In any event, the secular orientation in American society is in marked contrast to the religious orientation of many oppressed minority groups in this country. For example, instead of indifference to religion, the Puerto Rican minority group members often "hedge all bets" by moving among several religious orientations simultaneously—calling on the Roman Catholic clergy for weddings and baptisms while looking for cures for illness or assurance of good luck from "spiritualist" technicians.

The significance of the individual's religious orientation for mental health professionals is amply demonstrated in Tyler and Thompson's (1965) account of a Navajo woman's return to the reservation after years of hospitalization in a mental institution: "Her family had arranged for some ceremonies to be performed that were designed to cure Mrs. Y of her illness. . . . These ceremonies are the Basic Navajo method of curing illness, including illness caused by witchcraft . . . the most efficacious reassurance for victims of witchcraft is provided, therefore, by the unusual, complicated, and costly prayer ceremonials, with many relatives and friends in attendance, lending their help and expressing their sympathy" (p. 219).

Patterns of Interpersonal Relationships. In their discussion of primary and secondary relationships in American core culture, Arensberg and Niehoff (1971) identified certain value positions that are different when compared to positions taken by some oppressed minority groups within the ethnosystem. For example, autonomy is highly valued in the American core culture. Frankel (1976) has defined autonomy as "doing only what we consent to do, being one's own master, accepting no obligations except those freely taken" (p. 358). Yet ethnic groups often value interdependency more; for example, group members are expected to supply help and comfort in times of need. A member will not only expect sociability or brotherhood, he will expect to be able to express his dependency needs to other members and to have these needs met.

Kluckhohn and Strodtbeck (1961) advanced a theory of variation in value positions based on a set of assumptions about value dimensions that were classified on the basis of "common human problems" that all societies must confront:

time dimension, relational dimension, activity dimension, man-nature dimension, and the basic human nature dimension. Value positions along each of these dimensions have strong implications for the management of interpersonal relationships. The Group for the Advancement of Psychiatry (1970) has used the Kluckhohn and Strodtbeck formulation as a basis for contrasting interpersonal relationships in the American core culture and in Puerto Rican culture.

Turner (1963) used the Kluckhohn-Strodtbeck formulations as a framework for comparing value orientations of Anglo, French-Canadian, and Slovakian clients of a large Canadian family service agency. Even though differences were not found in the value profiles of the three ethnic groups, Turner concluded that (1) practicing social workers do not seem to be oriented to the concepts of ethnic differences and value differences; (2) future development of variation in value-orientation theory should enable a description of people and their values that has been impossible due to the high degree of abstraction currently existing; (3) rather than continue to emphasize the dominant patterns, it is important that discussions of value systems consider the idea of variation within groups; (4) a variation in value orientations within behavior spheres would influence to a great extent the type of difficulties and problem areas that persons at variance with their culture would meet; and finally, (5) information about such problems and difficulties should lead to more efficient use of treatment methods.

In Puerto Rican families, the traditional preference has been for the present time orientation, whereas the American middle-class culture places a heavy emphasis on the future. The relational dimension has three major positions determined by the manner in which decisions are made within social groups, including the family: (1) the collateral position accents decision making by consensus; (2) in the individualistic position, decisions are optimally made by each person, freely and independently of the group; and (3) in the lineal position, decisions are made by top authorities and passed down the chain of command. The American middle class emphasizes the individualistic position whereas the collateral position is the dominant one in Puerto Rican families. The activity dimension has three major positions: (1) the being position, in which the preference is for spontaneous and expressive activity; (2) the doing position, in which the preference is for instrumental activity judged "in the eyes of others"; and (3) the being-in-becoming position, which accents the well-rounded personality incorporating a balance of doing and being. Puerto Rican culture emphasizes being; the individual is expressive and airs feelings, usually with dramatic flair. The preference for doing in American life is obvious.

Kluckhohn's man-nature dimension refers to the relationship between man and nature or supernature, yet it strongly influences man's relationships with other men. On the one hand, if one adopts the dominant-over-nature position on this dimension, there is an assumption that man can solve most of his problems by planning, hard work, and the application of scientific principles, including, one assumes, problems in psychosocial functioning. On the other hand, if one adopts the subjugated-to-nature position, it is necessary to appeal to a stronger deity for the solution to any problem. In the harmony-with-nature position, man is expected to fit himself into the ways of nature and not attempt to overthrow the natural order of things. Clearly, American core culture emphasizes the dominant-over-nature position, whereas some American Indian groups would prefer the harmony-with-nature position. A report of the Group for the Advancement of Psychiatry (1970) points out that individuals and family groups within the Puerto Rican culture move about all three positions with remarkable ease.

Finally, with respect to the basic-human-nature dimension, the first-order preference in Puerto Rican culture is for the position that man is born in a state of sin and has a large component of evil in his nature; therefore, one must watch out carefully for the intentions of others. Middle-class Americans tend to see man as either a mixture of good and evil or as neutral. It would not be surprising, however, to find that helping professionals who subscribe to the American core culture's position on this dimension might be more likely to find "paranoid" personality orientations among members of minority cultures who have a more pessimistic view of man's basic human nature.

Patterns of Giving and Receiving Help. Ethnic group membership for some people provides a field for the expression of benevolence. Ethnic groups in plural societies often set up benevolent programs for their members. Although humanitarianism has been identified as one of the core values in the dominant American culture, it is usually highly organized and impersonal. This is in contrast to the more personal "folk-helping" that is valued among many minority groups, including the ones discussed here.

Traditional approaches to the provision of professional help for those persons encountering problems in psychosocial functioning have been most consistent with American core-cultural values and most inconsistent with the values held by many oppressed minority groups, for example, emphasis on individual versus collective responsibility. Furthermore, many people in distress see the detachment that is deliberately cultivated by professional helpers as an aid to impartial, rational analysis of facts as aloof, cold, or uncaring.

Lenrow (1978) has examined the criticisms of professional helping and has concluded that there is nothing inherent in the professional helper's role that would lead inevitably to value conflicts and ineffectiveness in work with poor and oppressed people. There is a core of "classical values" of professions—impartiality, rationality, empirical knowledge, and ethics committed to the dignity of the individual and to the public welfare. Although these values may not be entirely consistent with "folkways," they are not the source of the criticism that has been leveled against professionals, particularly by oppressed minority groups. Rather, the source of this criticism lies mainly in institutionalized practices that corrupt the expression of professional ideals, namely bureaucratic organization, economic self-interest, narrow preoccupation with "techniques," defensive self-aggrandizement that ignores potential sources of help outside the profession, and ethnocentrism.

Lenrow's implication is that rather than "deprofessionalizing" their roles, members of the helping professions should be more professional by greater adherence to "classical values" that define the professional role with less involvement in dysfunctional institutional practices. "There is a need for some combination of (a) being accountable to clients in a way that acknowledges one's limitations in understanding and helping in their life situations, (b) promoting structural conditions that can support ongoing helping relationships with a minimum of dependency on outsiders and professional specialists, and (c) practicing what one preaches about the importance of helping networks by working in collaborative teams rather than alone. Although such roles will no doubt be as stressful as present ones, they would be more faithful to the concept of help" (p. 287).

Value Issues and the Clinical Social Work Process

Clinical social workers, psychologists, psychiatrists, and other mental health practitioners are required to implement a helping process incorporating objectives and behaviors that represent a socially institutionalized version of "folk helping." For the dominant culture, the help is "marketed" as surely as are bread and automobiles. In contrast, oppressed minorities are characterized by their limited access to the marketplace. Moreover, residual institutions developed to provide services to those unable to purchase them on the open market have done so with a clear message that it is a system to serve "losers." Yet it is in these residual institutions that oppressed minorities are most likely to be served by clinical social workers.

A major difference between folk helping and professional helping is the personalizing style of the former and the bureaucratic style of the latter. Thus, social control is exercised in the form of regulations by the bureaucratic organizations that license, insure, and pay the professional helper rather than by ongoing networks of enduring mutual obligations. It has been argued that private practice is a more effective way of structuring help in order to empower powerless people because it makes the helper more directly accountable to the client. While this does make the private practitioner more directly accountable than the agency staff person, the private practitioner is still less accountable than the folk helper, who is often involved with the client in that network of mutual obligation. Furthermore, as Lenrow (1978) points out, the potential for a "no strings" involvement with the poor and/or minority person seeking help may never be realized if economic self-interest is given higher priority: "When a professional chooses his clientele primarily on the basis of their ability to pay high fees and when the continuation of services is heavily dependent on the client's continuing ability to do so, these priorities also conflict with the priority given in folk helping to the interests of the individuals to be helped or to the well-being of the community, rather than to the aggrandizement of the helper" (p. 280).

The need for nonbureaucratic approaches to work with clients from oppressed minority groups is one of several themes that emerged in the past decade of belated concern on the part of scholars in the field. Other themes have been the need for a more balanced focus on intrapsychic and extrapsychic forces in the determinants of problem behavior as exhibited by Third-World clients and the need for more helping professionals who are themselves members of the oppressed minority groups. Actually, these themes are interrelated and represent particular points of emphasis in the conceptualization of a helping process in which persons who have experienced powerlessness as a consequence of membership in a stigmatized collective can be empowered to take more control over their lives. More specifically, issues have been raised as to the influence of cultural values held by members of oppressed minority groups on various aspects of the helping process—for example, client motivation, target problems, the client/social worker relationship, and problem-solving activities.

Client Motivation. The following vignette demonstrates how a clinical social worker's knowledge of the value system held by a black client made it possible for that client to remain engaged in the helping process rather than leave with the possible label of "unmotivated."

Mr. W. is a sixty-nine-year-old, black, retired construction worker who has lived alone since the death of his wife approximately three years ago. He has a married daughter thirty-eight years old and a forty-one-year-old son who is also married. Both children live in the city and frequently visit their father. However, his relationships with them have been deteriorating recently. Since his wife's death, Mr. W. has been moderately depressed. "Every time I think about doing something, I remember that Ella and I had planned to do it together. I just lose my interest." He has been treated by his physician for a variety of mild, somatic complaints for which the physician had been unable to find an organic basis. Now, Mr. W. has become more and more argumentative with his son and daughter, accusing them of wanting to put him into an institution so that they can get his property. They have responded by avoiding him so that his isolation is increasing.

Mr. W. attended church regularly before his wife's death but has attended infrequently since then. After one of his infrequent visits, the minister came to see him in his home to encourage him to become involved again. Mr. W. was noncomittal but shared with the minister his problems with his son and daughter and again accused them of conspiring against him. The minister advised him to see a counselor in a special counseling program located at the church.

Mr. W. arranged to see the social worker and again described his problems with his children and his fears about institutionalization. He cried in the intake interview and as it was ending, he said to the worker that it was the first time he had really cried since his wife died. When he returned for the second interview, however, he told the social worker that he had "prayed a lot" after the last visit and that the night before he had had a dream in which God came to him and said, "Keep faith and I will see to it that your problems are solved." He thought that this was a sign from God that he should trust only in him. "I won't be coming back to see you again," he said. "I'm going to let God take care of everything!"

At this point, the worker, who was familiar with the role that religion plays among black older persons, replied: "God works in mysterious ways. Have you considered, that I may be the instrument he will use to help you solve your problems?" Mr. W. was silent for a while and then said, "I never thought about that but you could be right." He then decided that he would continue to come in to see the social worker and "work together on the problems."

The tendency of Third-World clients to place a higher value on the man-subjugated-to-nature position—and thus the supranatural rather than the rational, scientific world view—meant in this case that the client's perception of the social worker's expertise and therefore the motivation to make use of that expertise was determined not by her university credentials but by the possibility that she was chosen by God, who would be the source of her expertise. In this instance, it was not necessary for the social worker to be religious but only to be able to relate to the client's religious belief that God may "use" persons (even the devil himself) for His purposes.

It was also important here that the services were located in a mediating structure—between the individual and the wider social environment. The services could be offered in a more personalized, nonbureaucratic manner although delivered by a profession. This validates the view that there is nothing inherently inconsistent in the professional role when compared to the folk-helper role; problems arise because of societal pressures that twist the process into a constricting, alien experience.

It is necessary to admit, however, that in some instances, value differences can be so great that motivation for psychosocial help from professionals is unlikely to exist. For example, in reference to the American Indian, Good Tracks (1973) has written: "The explanation for the social worker's initial uselessness is easily given. His professional function is generally performed from within the Indian culture, and no foreign interference is desired or contemplated. If a man's problems seems to be a result of his having been witched, for example, he will seek out the properly qualified person to help him alleviate the condition. He will have no need of any outside diagnosis or assistance. Should a personal or family problem be of another nature, it is addressed again to the proper individual, an uncle (mother's brother) or a grandfather—not to a foreigner, such as the social worker. In every case, the people utilize the established, functional, culturally acceptable remedy within their own native system" (p. 33).

Other authors have recognized the varying points at which an individual American Indian may be along the dimension of "racial uniqueness" or as more commonly phrased "acculturation." Thus, the acceptance of Indian values may not be complete. Perhaps this accounts for the more hopeful posture of some authors when identifying strategies for creating or increasing the motivation of American Indians to become clients in a psychosocial problem-solving process (Lewis and Ho, 1975; Edwards and Edwards, 1980; Tyler and Thompson, 1965). However, the theme that is reiterated by all of these authors is that the social worker can come to be perceived by the American Indian client as an appropriate link between the family (including any identified client) and the resources of the larger society. At the next level of working relationships, the social worker would be perceived as a teacher of principles for use by the individual and the families themselves to improve their relationships with that external world. Finally, when the social worker has practically become one of the family and is therefore no longer an alien, the social worker may be permitted a role in helping the family members themselves to relate to each other in more effective ways.

Assessing the Target Problems. Assessment is a major step in any of the therapeutic systems utilized by clinical social workers (Strean, 1978; Hollis, 1972; Roberts and Nee, 1970). Heavy emphasis has been placed on the recognition of internal, intrapsychic processes and family relationships as determinants of problem-producing behavior. Less attention has been paid to the significance of relationships between individuals and families and their cultural ties, as well as their relationships with larger social institutions, as factors in the etiology of social dysfunction. Yet theorists and practitioners have identified overemphasis on intrapsychic determinants of behavior as a major source of ineffective problem-solving strategies with black (Thomas and Sillen, 1972; Jones and Jones, 1970) and Hispanic (Alvarez, 1975; Padilla, Ruiz, and Alvarez, 1975; Diaz-Guerrero, 1977) clients.

The emphasis on intrapsychic rather than external or "extrapsychic" determinants of behavior has been blamed on the strong commitment to Freudian psychoanalytic theory and its derivatives, which focus on the individual and have the primary treatment objective of "insight." However, there is evidence to support the notion that the strong value placed on the individual and individual responsibility in the American value system has been responsible for making psychoanalytic interpretations of the human condition so popular in this country.

Hollis (1972) has pointed out that "Because Freud elaborated more upon the needs and responses of the individual than upon the impact of the environment, it has become popular to regard Freudian theory as a theory of the instincts or biological theory and to accuse it of disregarding environmental influences. . . . But the truth is that Freud strongly emphasized the influence of both intra- and extrafamilial life experiences . . . the person with a hysterical paralysis, for example, is using this symptom to protect himself from something he fears in his relationships with other people" (p. 18). Yet even if individual behavior were influenced by extrafamilial forces, the "cure" was seen as greater understanding of the unconscious so that the irrational fears residing there would no longer govern the individual's behavior. The example of hysterical paralysis demonstrates this admirably, for the issue with many clients from oppressed minority groups is not irrational fears directing from the unconscious but rather fears based on real environmental threats, such as loss of a job or eviction from housing. In other instances, it may not be personality structure but environmental pressures that create problems for people in a client group. The following example demonstrates the difficulties that arise for the helping professional who misinterprets the significance of personality factors relative to extrafamilial and environmental factors in a presenting problem situation.

When Emilio first began to toy with the wish to drop out of school, his parents, particularly his father, became concerned. They took the boy to a clinic where the psychiatrist found them "able to accept responsibility for the boy's behavior." He described the parents as understandably "frightened about the possibility that Emilio would drop into the neighborhood's growing drug scene upon leaving school." He was impressed with Emilio's insistence that he could succeed, but the psychiatrist was even more impressed with the father's loud, defensive, and rigid counterinsistence, "You are not going out to work yet!"

The mutual intimidation between father and son and the wife's rather soft attitude toward the son's wishes appeared to the therapist as classical signs of an oedipal entanglement, hinging chiefly on the father's machismo. The concept of machismo found its way into the next session. The father was gently confronted with the well-meaning and presumably culturally attuned inquiry, "Are you afraid that if your son goes out to work, there will no longer be just one head of the house?" This question was received with silence, and the psychiatrist followed with another question, "Would you be threatened if not only your son, but your wife went out to work?" The family dropped out of treatment.

A Puerto Rican teacher who had taught Emilio years before and who was sympathetic to the family was asked if he could find out why the family had dropped out of the clinic (in the same way that Emilio wanted to drop out of school). To this teacher, the mother proclaimed: "They don't understand city Puerto Ricans. Look, many of our relatives, on my side as well as my husband's side, started out here by the woman going out to work during the beginning years, while the men stayed home and did some drinking between whatever little jobs they could get here and could not keep. Our families are not built only around the man. Instead of holding us away from jobs, many of our men easily and quickly let us out to get jobs. There is as much hembrismo (a term pertaining to the significant role of women, its centrality and power in the culture) as machismo in them. Matter of fact, many of them are concerned we won't go out fast enough. If you ask me, they count on it. . . ."

The power of machismo in explaining the father's strict reaction toward his son's rebellious attempts to drop out and go to work was then reconsidered. His reaction was seen as quite natural. It was not only protective of his masculinity. It was also genuinely protective of his son, of the meaning of work, and of his wife. Work was for him a hard-won productive function. He had waited long to reciprocate for the years in which he was disoriented and unable to get a steady job while his wife stabilized the family through emotional and financial support.

The family returned to the clinic, and, through mutual apologies, the intercultural misunderstanding was cleared. The sessions then moved to engage the parents and Emilio in discussions of the circumstances under which they would allow him to work. They agreed that they would allow him to work as long as he agreed to eventually return to school, perhaps in a year. It was easier then to deal with the fact that Emilio had felt about his situation in school the same way the parents had felt about their situation in the clinic: "They are unable to understand."

As the situations of the son and the parents were transformed into a larger and shared situation, other steps became possible. The sessions could move into how school was pushing Emilio out through boredom and discouragement, and they could also deal with the extraordinary pulls Emilio felt coming from the bright boys in his peer group, who were also leaving school to take jobs.

In this situation, it was necessary to assess the target problem without the strangling commitment to the value position of individualism and with recognition of the strong value placed on interdependence and primary group relationships.

The Client/Social Worker Relationship. Egalitarianism is a major component of the core value system of American society. Although this value is more of a moral imperative than a fact of life, the legal and institutional heritage of this country prescribes equal rights, condemns special privileges, and demands fair representation for every citizen. Oppressed groups, however, are characterized by the failure of the society to accord them these desiderata. Arensberg and Niehoff (1971) suggest that the American attitude toward equality of treatment really means that within the major value system people are, or should be, treated equally if they accept the basic beliefs and behaviors of the social majority. In this sense, the American idea is similar to that of the Muslims who have always taught that all men are equal under Allah—as long as one is dealing with acceptors of the faith. However, to unbelievers no rights are accorded.

The contrasts between egalitarian values on the one hand and respect for authority on the other and between collateral relationships on the one hand and linear relationships on the other hold for some Third-World groups but not others. For example, De Vos (1975) describes the traditional Japanese and their attitudes relative to their American experience: "The Japanese communities accorded status to their members which had little or no correspondence to their jobs outside. They did not evaluate themselves on the basis of American attitudes toward them as peasants or immigrant workers or 'yellow' Asians. . . . A traditional Japanese does not feel it socially or personally demeaning to be in a subordinate position *while he is learning*. His sense of integrity is not destroyed by adversity. Japanese immigrants imparted to their Nisei children a respect for authority, even the authority of an alien society—they were to become loyal citizens. This was not inconsistent with Japanese concepts of loyalty to organizations once one became a success. This pattern is less understood by some third-generation or Sansei youth who are impatient with what they considered the complacency and conformity with which their parents met social discrimination" (pp. 35–36; emphasis added).

Keeping in mind the ordinal character of adherence to traditional norms and values in the Japanese-American group, it can still be seen that Japanese-Americans are more likely than other oppressed minority groups to prefer a social worker or other helping professional who provides structure, gives advice, and is generally more authoritative (not authoritarian) in the role (Kitano, 1969). Other Asian-Pacific cultures, such as Chinese, Philipino, and Samoan, also have traditionally valued authority to a greater degree than Americans so that clients from these cultural backgrounds would also be likely to prefer a more structured helping process than would middle-class American clients.

As indicated earlier, not all oppressed groups in the ethnosystem place the same relative value on authority. As the only group whose descendants came to this country as slaves, black Americans place particular emphasis on the relevance of equality. Egalitarianism as expressed in collateral rather than lineal relationships has become an almost necessary condition for the experience of self-esteem and positive self-concept. Thus, structuring the worker/client relationship with black clients has as a major objective the reduction of social distance and of the client's sense of powerlessness. Although this does not ignore the fact that some inequality is inherent in the relationship, that inequality can be reduced by the extent to which at least some power is perceived in the client role and the sharing of power is made a part of the helping process. It has been suggested that the client must take initiative in order to perceive himself or herself as a causal agent in achieving the solution to the problem. The emphasis is not on the worker as the authority who leads the client to the solution but rather on both as peer collaborators or partners in the problem-solving effort. The following example demonstrates how such a collaborative contract could be negotiated:

Client: Are you going to be the one to decide whether I get my child back or not?

Worker: The court will ask my opinion about how you and your child will get along if he is returned.

Client: How will you know anything about that?

Worker: I hope you will let me know something about that.

Client: O.K. I'll tell you. It's going to be great, so you can go tell the court to let him come back.

Worker: But I don't know that it will be great.

Client: I just told you, didn't I? You said that if I let you know . . . didn't I?

Worker: Just listening to what you say is all I need to do to understand what happens with you and Jimmy.

Client: Yes.

Worker: Then I think you need to say a good deal more.

Client: I still don't understand what good talking is going to do. I told that other social worker who did the investigation for the protective services people that I didn't mean to hurt Jimmy. I wouldn't hurt him either if he hadn't tried to pull away from me so hard. That's why his arm got dis . . . dis. . . .

Worker: Dislocated.

Client: Yeah. Dislocated. But I caught him stealing from next door. He could grow up to be an armed robber and what would the court think about that? They'd throw him in jail for life, that's what! But they'd rather pick on parents who're just tryin' to make kids grow up decent!

Worker: It sounds as if you feel that you're damned if you do and damned if you don't.

Client: Damned right!

Worker: Are you also wondering what *I* can do to change all that?

Client: Damned right!

Worker: Well, I guess the answer is not much—not nearly as much as you can.

Client: What d'ya mean? You can tell the court to give me back my child! I can't get him back by myself!

Worker: I can tell the court that I think you know how you got into a situation where the court thought it necessary to remove your child from your home and I can also tell the court that I am convinced that because of that knowledge, it won't happen again. But I can only say that if I really am convinced and that can only come from what you tell me.

Client: You want me to say that I lose my temper sometime with Jimmy and I have learned how to control it?

Worker: I don't want you to say anything that is not true. I am only saying that it has to be true that you know how you got into this situation and that you have figured out how to prevent it from happening again.

Client: (suspiciously) Suppose I say that I got into it because that no-good, used-to-be friend of mine called the protective service people and lied on me because I wouldn't loan her money. And suppose I say it won't happen again because I'm going to beat her ass for her if I ever catch her!

Worker: Then I would want to talk about that plan of yours to see how workable it is. For example, how do you know some other "no-good friend" won't call the protective service people on you the next time you accidentally hurt Jimmy? Can you be sure that you won't accidentally hurt him again? How can you deal with his behavior so that you won't need to punish him or maybe not so often? How can you deal with trying to raise a kid in a neighborhood where so many things can go wrong? How can you deal with friends who hit on you for money and then do you dirty first chance they get?

Client: I sure hope you got the answers to all that cause I sure don't.

Worker: I think that you do! And maybe if I can help you get at your answers, maybe you'll find out that you can prevent what has happened from happening again.

Client: That's a pretty big order. (Silence) But I think that I would like to try. I want my kid back and I don't want to lose him again.

Worker: Can you tell me what it is that you're saying you want to try?

Client: Well, I guess I'm saying that I'm going to try to talk about all those problems I'm having and maybe if I can understand what's happening, I'll know how to handle Jimmy better . . . because, if it seems that I can, then you'll let the court know it so I can get him back.

Worker: That sounds like a good place to start . . . maybe we can start with whatever problem of the many you mentioned you think is the most important in terms of what happened between you and Jimmy [Solomon, 1976, pp. 335–337].

The client initially perceived herself as powerless to deal with the powerful court system. At the same time, she perceived the worker as having a great deal of influence with the court, enough in fact to extract her son from its control if she wished to. Thus, the worker's influence was considered to be discretionary, that is, to be wielded on the basis of arbitrary, subjective, or even capricious response to the client. The worker was able to obtain the client's commitment to a mutual problem-solving effort, the success of which would determine whether the social worker's influence would be utilized to have the child returned.

Problem-Solving Activities. Perhaps as much attention has been given to the influence of values on choice of appropriate problem-solving activities as to any other aspect of clinical social work with Third-World clients. To avoid stereotyping, it is important to remember that although we are talking about individuals who belong to groups, the differentiating attitudes, behaviors, and value orientations have been group-determined and represent probability statements. Thus, the identification of the phenomenon "Indian time" based on natural phenomena (morning, days, months, years) rather than on the clock is important to know in working with Indian clients. Yet the adherence to Indian time may vary from individual to individual based on a variety of other variables, both personal and societal. The incorporation of a probabilistic frame of reference in the development of practice strategies has been described elsewhere (Solomon, 1976).

An inordinate emphasis on the individual as the focus of change efforts may lead to ineffective practice with Third-World clients. The objectives of clinical social work intervention have been described as "maximizing the potential of the individual for effective social functioning" or "helping the client cope with some currently incapacitating or stressful situation." These are value-laden objectives. Most importantly, the issue is how one perceives the actual behavioral manifestations of successful achievement of these objectives; for example, what constitutes fulfilling one's potential or optimal social functioning.

Clearly, these judgments may be colored by the value positions taken along such dimensions as activity (doing versus being) and man-nature (with the value position dominant-over-nature taking precedence over the subjugated-to-nature position). Thus, a client who spends his days studying obscure Eastern philosophies as he struggles with his own search for identity may be identified as failing to achieve his potential for using his superior intellect to become a computer scientist or lawyer or doctor and therefore be able to lead a more "productive" life. Similarly, a client who continues to believe that the negative forces that appear to govern his life have been willed by a supranatural being instead of being under the control of his own actions will be likely to be evaluated as not functioning at optimal level or maximizing his capacities for social functioning.

Helen was a twenty-three-year-old Chippewa mother with three children. Helen left high school following pregnancy at sixteen. She was bright and motivated and eventually earned a high school diploma through a Graduate Equivalency Diploma program. Helen had drifted into several household situations following the birth of her first child. Initially, she lived with her mother. She then established a household with a boyfriend and had two more children. She later lived with a sister, then a cousin at her home reservation, and then again with her mother.

During this seven-year period, Helen always contributed as a family member. She had been gainfully employed since leaving high school. She simply indicated a preference to be close to her mother's home or in it. She sensed a responsibility to maintain relationships with kin and to be available for family duties.

One day Helen shared the news of her independence from her mother with a human service professional. Helen had rented an apartment and was going to live away from her mother permanently. The professional inquired of Helen where the new apartment was located. Helen beamed brightly and said, "Next door to my mother's." During subsequent visits, the professional always saw mother and daughter visiting each other's home. Helen's mother continued to care for the grandchildren daily.

Helen's definition of independence is refreshing. Her behavior typifies self-reliance guided by family interdependence.

The constant awareness that we are dealing with probabilities can serve to lessen the frustration at finding differing opinions or even contradictory ones regarding the appropriateness of specific practice modalities when working with specific Third-World clients. For example, Toupin (1980) suggests: "Many Asians have found groups especially traumatic in themselves. To share one's problem with *one* person was shameful enough; to share with a group was overwhelming. Also, work in a group seemed to require more expression of verbal aggression than Asians find worth the emotional effort. One student described her experience in these terms: 'As soon as I had convinced myself that what I had to say was important or as important as everyone else's problem, the session was over'" (p. 85).

Ho (1976) suggests, however, that Asian-American group members usually welcome participation in a group atmosphere that allows them the opportunity to share problems and help each other with them rather than requiring members to compete with each other. The concept of mutual aid and reciprocity is a part of the core values of most Asian cultural traditions so that group members operating in this context are no longer conscious of the inhibitions and defenses prohibiting social worker intervention with their problems. Ho gives the following example of inhibitions in a group being transformed into a constructive interchange on the basis of "group sharing":

> Long silences, which are usually indicative of group resistance, had plagued a group of Asian Americans. After one such silence, the worker commented that because he did not feel comfortable with the silence, he imagined the members generally felt the same way. He asked the members to identify what was happening so that more could be accomplished within the alloted time for group interaction. One member immediately said that he no longer could afford to waste time sitting in a group in which the members did nothing but stare at each other. He asked the worker if he could share with the group the reason behind his silence. Would that, he added, be answering the worker's concern? The worker thanked him and said that the members' input was most needed for the group to head in the direction that was most beneficial to all members [p. 200].

The appropriateness or nonappropriateness of a modality obviously relates as much to "how it is done" as to "what is done." For example, several authors have recognized that Third-World clients are more likely to require a personalized basis for granting expertise (for example, personal knowledge of the worker) than a bureaucratic basis (such as university credentials or a license). Professional practice theory indicates that when clients ask personal questions, it is most often a form of resistance that should be handled by the social worker by another question, such as: "Why do you have a need to know this about me?" In some instances, however, the client may need to know in order to get a better "feel" for the kind of person the social worker is and what kind of experiences he may have had that are relevant for his problem situation. In such cases, it may be important to answer the question. In the following example, the question was not answered, apparently without undue consequences for the problem-solving process; however, this was probably due to a response that at least suggested an answer to the question and therefore some empathic understanding of the client.

We talked a while longer, and I had to leave. As I stood up she said, "That's a nice dress; you look good today. Are you gonna meet your boyfriend?" I thanked her but must have appeared embarrassed. She said, "Why do you always get embarrassed when I ask about your boyfriend?" I was silent a few seconds, and then said that she was right in sensing that I did get embarrassed. I said that I was not sure why, but thought it might be because I did not feel I should share my personal life with her since I was there to help her. She said maybe if she knew I had problems, she wouldn't think about her own so much. I said maybe that was true but it wouldn't help her work on her own problems to think about mine. She said, "You have problems? Don't kid me." I asked, "Do you believe I don't have problems as you have?" She agreed.

I said that I knew she thought I had a better life than she had and was more fortunate, and in many ways it was true. I said that sometimes I guess she'd resent me for it because I was in a position to help her, and she might wish that the tables were turned. She smiled a knowing smile and said that such a situation would be nice. Then she asked, "You do have some problems, don't you?" I said that I did and I guessed all people had problems, although they might be of a different nature. She said that she sometimes felt life was bad only for her and that she wished others had their share, too. I said it was natural to feel that way, especially when things were going bad for her. I said it was all right even when she wished I would find life a little difficult.

Clearly, all Third-World client groups do not have the same value orientation, and therefore preferences in regard to problem-solving approaches are not always the same. For example, Acosta (1977) has suggested the following approaches: "An eclectic approach with low-income Spanish-speaking patients has proved to be the most effective and has resulted in significant levels of improved functioning for many patients. Combined use has been made of the following approaches: (a) evaluation of degree of acculturation, which identifies the relative probability that traditional rather than core American values will guide expectations and behaviors, and (b) approaches which emphasize experiencing present feelings and dealing with present problems, for example, crisis intervention, role playing, client-centered listening, and behavioral approaches such as teaching techniques for relaxation or assertiveness" (p. 227).

Summary and Conclusions

This chapter has sought to consider the challenges and opportunities inherent in cross-cultural counseling from the perspective of cultural values. Although the significance of values is usually acknowledged in the literature, it rarely moves from the fact that values influence the problem-solving or therapeutic process to an analysis of when and how that influence is operational. Toward that end, the focus here has been on the identification of specific value dimensions along which different cultural groups—particularly those which have been identified as "oppressed" in the American ethnosystem—may be expected to hold different value positions. Case examples have been utilized to illuminate the relationship between a client's value position and the implementation of specific stages in the problem-solving process, such as identification of the problem, motivation to seek help, selection of the target problems, and implementation of the helping process. Finally, it has been underscored that a preference for a more personalized, nonbureaucratic helping process does not require a "nonprofessional" approach. A reduction in the institutional practices that serve to reinforce feelings of alienation in clients who belong to oppressed minority groups should in fact lead to increased professionalism, that is, practice guided by the classical values of the profession, which emphasize rationality, knowledge and skills relating to human capacities and problems, and responsibility in the use of the power residing in anyone possessing such knowledge and skills.

If values permeate every aspect of human life, we can begin to ask whether a value perspective is essentially different from anything else. Some aspects of practice with minority clients that have been emphasized in other literature were not addressed here. For example, differences in language and communication style are clearly important in any cross-cultural encounter. It has led scholars in the field to press for the development of more practitioners for minority cultures, not with the futile goal of a minority clinician for every minority client but rather for the development of bicultural—minority group and professional—staff. They would be expected to hasten the development of necessary bridging concepts and behaviors and contribute to a process whereby such knowledge could be infused into training programs for all practitioners. This is a matter of values only to the degree that the society places value on or appreciates cultural diversity. Beyond that, it is a technical issue that would have to be dealt with in regard to each cultural group with its different history and place in the ethnosystem.

We have also not discussed the consequences of oppression for the personality, aspirations, or opportunity for social mobility that differentiates the oppressed minority groups from each other and from the dominant majority. Again, these are essential issues in counseling with minority-group clients. However, since these are more directly related to the power and influence of the environment, which shapes values rather than being created by them, they did not constitute central issues for this chapter. It has been noted that those cultural groups in which there is a strong future time orientation and an acceptance of adversity in the present with the expectation that it will be compensated for in the future are less vulnerable to the "slings and arrows" of discrimination than those groups whose orientation is firmly rooted in the present. However, since the individual client who belongs to an oppressed minority group is likely to represent a wide range of value positions as well as responses to oppression, and since much of the research on responses to oppression has not measured ethnicity except as a nominal variable, it appears that much work must be done before a great deal of the literature linking specific personality orientations with specific cultural groups can be trusted.

The plea for more rigorous and more culturally sensitive research in the area of counseling minority-group clients is so time-worn that it may be considered as belaboring the obvious. Yet the significance of an emphasis on value differences is that it provides a mechanism for operationalizing that vague exhortation. For example, if research is being done on the outcome of specific problem-solving strategies, it would be important to disaggregate clients from minority ethnic groups and to determine whether the groups so constructed differ in regard to outcome. However, it may be more important to determine whether they differ in regard to relevant value orientations and whether value orientation is a more or less powerful predictor of outcome than group membership. Empirical knowledge so obtained will move us away from considerable risk of racial or ethnic stereotyping and much closer to understanding the dynamic interrelationship of race, ethnicity, social class, value orientations, and, perhaps most of all, the times in which we live.

References

Acosta, F. "Ethnic Variables in Psychotherapy: The Mexican-American." In J. L. Martinez, Jr. (Ed.), *Chicano Psychology*. New York: Academic Press, 1977.

Alvarez, R. (Ed.). *Delivery of Services for Latino Community Mental Health.* Monograph No. 2. Los Angeles: Spanish Speaking Mental Health Research and Development Program, University of California, 1975.

Arensberg, C., and Niehoff, A. H. "American Cultural Values." In C. Arensberg and A. H. Niehoff (Eds.), *Introducing Social Change.* Chicago: Aldine-Atherton, 1971.

De Vos, G. "Ethnic Pluralism: Conflict and Accommodation." In G. De Vos and L. Romanucci-Ross (Eds.), *Ethnic Identity: Cultural Continuities and Change.* Palo Alto, Calif.: Mayfield, 1975.

Diaz-Guerrero, R. "A Sociocultural Psychology." In J. L. Martinez, Jr. (Ed.), *Chicano Psychology.* New York: Academic Press, 1977.

Edwards, E. D., and Edwards, M. E. "American Indians: Working with Individuals and Groups." *Social Casework,* October 1980, pp. 498–506.

Frankel, C. "The Impact of Changing Values on the Family." *Social Casework,* 1976, *57* (6), 355–365.

Good Tracks, J. G. "Native American Noninterference." *Social Work,* November 1973, pp. 30–35.

Group for the Advancement of Psychiatry. *Case History Method in Study of Family Process.* Report No. 76, Vol. 6. New York: Group for the Advancement of Psychiatry, 1970.

Hardman, D. G. "Not with My Daughter You Don't." *Social Work,* July 1975, pp. 278–285.

Ho, M. K. "Social Work with Asian Americans." *Social Casework,* March 1976, pp. 195–201.

Hollis, F. *Casework: A Psychosocial Therapy.* (2nd ed.) New York: Random House, 1972.

Jones, M. H., and Jones, M. C. "The Neglected Client." *The Black Scholar,* March 1970, pp. 35–42.

Kitano, H. H. "Japanese-American Mental Illness." In S. G. Plog and R. B. Edgerton (Eds.), *Changing Perspectives in Mental Illness.* New York: Holt, Rinehart and Winston, 1969.

Kluckhohn, F., and Strodtbeck, F. L. *Variations in Value Orientations.* New York: Harper & Row, 1961.

Lenrow, P. "Dilemmas of Professional Helping: Continuities and Discontinuities with Folk Helping Roles." In L. Wispe (Ed.), *Altruism, Sympathy, and Helping: Psychological and Sociological Principles.* New York: Academic Press, 1978.

Lewis, R. G., and Ho, M. K. "Social Work with Native Americans." *Social Work,* September 1975, pp. 379–382.

Morales, A. "Social Work with Third World People." *Social Work,* January 1981, pp. 45–51.

Padillo, A. M., Ruiz, R., and Alvarez, R. "Delivery of Community Mental Health Services to the Spanish Speaking and Surnamed Population." In R. Alvarez (Ed.), *Delivery of Services for Latino Community Mental Health.* Monograph No. 2. Los Angeles: Spanish Speaking Mental Health Research and Development Program, University of California, 1975.

Rokeach, M. *Beliefs, Attitudes, and Values: A Theory of Organization and Change.* San Francisco: Jossey-Bass, 1968.

Rokeach, M. *The Nature of Human Values.* New York: Free Press, 1973.
Roberts, R., and Nee, R. (Eds.). *Theories of Social Casework.* Chicago: University of Chicago Press, 1970.
Solomon, B. B. *Black Empowerment: Social Work in Oppressed Communities.* New York: Columbia University Press, 1976.
Strean, H. S. *Clinical Social Work: Theory and Practice.* New York: Free Press, 1978.
Thomas, A., and Sillen, S. *Racism and Psychiatry,* New York: Brunner/Mazel, 1972.
Toupin, E.L.W.A. "Counseling Asians: Psychotherapy in the Context of Racism and Asian-American History." *American Journal of Orthopsychiatry,* January 1980, pp. 76–86.
Turner, F. "Social Work Treatment and Value Differences: An Exploration of Value Differences and Specific Use of Casework Techniques with Clients from Three Ethnic Groups Receiving Treatment in Family Agencies." Unpublished doctoral dissertation, Columbia University, 1963.
Tyler, I., and Thompson, S. D. "Cultural Factors in Casework Treatment of a Navajo Mental Patient." *Social Casework,* April 1965, pp. 215–220.
Williams, R. J. *American Society: A Sociological Interpretation.* (3rd ed.) New York: Knopf, 1970.
Williams, R. J. "Change and Stability in Values and Value Systems: A Sociological Perspective." In M. Rokeach (Ed.), *Understanding Human Values: Individual and Societal.* New York: Free Press, 1979.

40

Commitment to Disenfranchised Clients

Jerald Shapiro

A commitment to serving the poor, the disadvantaged, and the oppressed has been central to the characterization of social work as a helping profession. As part of the profession's heritage and value base, it has encouraged the specification of a domain of practice meant to encompass both environmental and personal aspects of human needs. The resulting practice perspective has been distinctive in its recognition of social forces as determinants of life experience and in its responsiveness to the diverse circumstances in which helping efforts are accordingly understood to be embedded. Consistent with this special awareness of the complexity and scope of the process of determining the quality of life, social work has come to identify itself as a profession concerned "with human beings, where there is anything that hinders or thwarts their growth, their expanding consciousness, their increasing cooperation" (Reynolds, 1935, p. 235). It has accepted therein a broadly based responsibility for purposeful change in a wide range of conditions, conditions which it was uniquely prepared to view as not only presenting immediate complication and distress, but as also introducing needless compromise to the realization of individual and collective potential. Significantly, social work has been the only helping profession with the vision and practice base sufficiently expansive to work with people around their aspirations as well as their needs.

As a dimension of actual practice, however, social work's commitment to individuals and populations collectively viewed as disenfranchised has been a subject for considerable difference of opinion. Despite the profession's claim to an ongoing commitment to serving this population, formidable questions have been raised about the role of social workers as agents of social control and perpetuators of an unjust status quo (Galper, 1975; Hampden-Turner, 1975; Ruzek, 1973); the predominance of a deviance and social pathology perspective in the shaping of worker-client relationships (Mills, 1943; Rein, 1970; Ryan, 1971); and the relevance of services provided with regard to the social, cultural, and economic experience of those clients with the greatest need (Miller, 1969; Morales, 1977; Richan and Mendelsohn, 1973; Solomon, 1976). Concern has been expressed about the apparent distancing of social workers from disenfranchised clients (Cumming, 1968; Cloward and Epstein, 1965; Meyer, 1977) and the decline of social work's involvement in social reform and social action endeavors (Dean, Jr., 1977; Howard, 1954; Kallen, Miller, and Daniels, 1968).

For social workers whose style or context of practice involves a clinical perspective on intervention and purposeful change, this questioning of social work's commitment to the disenfranchised has taken on its own set of issues. Having identified so long with a psychosocial framework for practice, clinical practitioners are now increasingly being called upon to expand and upgrade the social component of this practice framework (Grinnell, Jr., 1973; Hollis, 1980; Meyer, 1979; Perlman, 1952 and 1974). At a time when significant advances are occurring in the therapeutic areas of practice (one thinks of the work of Blanck and Blanck [1974 and 1979], of Kohut [1971 and 1977], Kernberg [1975 and 1976], Mahler [1975], and a number of family, behavioral, and humanistic therapists), the attention of clinical social workers is being drawn to a variety of basic practice matters pertaining to ethnocentrism (Brooks, 1974; Lopez, 1977; Ruiz, 1977), homophobia (Gochros, 1977; Tully and Albro, 1979), sexism (Kravetz, 1976; Miller, 1974; Perlmutter and Alexander, 1978), and the unmet needs of "unattractive" populations such as the aged (Berkman 1978; Brody and Brody, 1974; Meyer, 1973b) and the mentally retarded (Horejsi, 1979; Scanlon, 1978). Clinical social workers are being asked to justify labeling and dispositional activities (Case and Lingerfelt, 1974; Cumming, 1967; Rees, 1975), use of a medical model perspective for interpreting human behavior (Briar and Miller, 1971; Meyer, 1973a; Pearson, 1975), and what many have deemed to be an excessive emphasis upon intrapsychic and unconscious dynamics (Briar, 1968; Gronjberg, Street, and Suttles, 1978; Toren, 1972). In short, social work's avowed commitment to the disenfranchised is no longer being taken for granted. It is, in fact, being seriously questioned, and clinical social work appears to be an area of practice where this questioning has been particularly focused.

At the center of this challenge to social work's claim to a commitment to serving the disenfranchised is the issue of social work's methodology. Beyond expressions of concern and statements of values, the critical question appears to be, what do social workers do to prevent, ameliorate, or modify disenfranchisement as it touches individual lives? Further, in terms of the actual exchanges between and among worker, client, and environment, which courses of action constitute a commitment to addressing the needs and aspirations of the disenfranchised? What are the principles guiding such actions, and what are the conceptual and interpersonal skills through which these principles can be actualized? This chapter examines the nature of a methodological commitment to the disenfranchised in clinical social work practice. In considering the circumstances that structure disenfranchisement, the chapter moves toward the specification of a practice framework that bears a clear and direct relevance to intervention in the process of determining the quality for disenfranchised clients. The implications of this framework for clinical social work practice are then discussed.

Disenfranchisement

In a formal sense, disenfranchisement refers to the loss or absence of voting privileges (Black, 1979). It represents a deliberate divestment of influence and an exclusion from decision-making processes. Importantly, it also reflects an underlying power relationship in which one party possesses some measure of institutionalized control over another, and chooses to exercise this control to deprive that party of specific rights and privileges.

Within the social, cultural, and political framework of the United States, disenfranchisement has come to be understood as a broader and more oblique phenomenon. It is increasingly being viewed as a pattern of exclusion and marginalization. The origin and perpetuation of this pattern appears to be complexly locked into the structure of societal institutions. It is being understood as a fundamental disjuncture between specific individuals/populations and the material, social, and psychological resources from which the course and quality of life experience is derived. The resulting awareness of highly distinctive patterns in the distribution of individual and collective *life chances* (Dahrendorf, 1979; Levin, 1975) has underscored the socially structured inequality of American society and supported a closer examination of the institutions and mechanisms that perpetuate this inequality. Schools, hospitals, courts, public service agencies, and various other points of social and economic exchange have been shown to employ a variety of means for controlling the allocation of rights and privileges within their domains (Baratz and Baratz, 1970; Goffman, 1961; Hasenfeld, 1972). Attention has been drawn to IQ testing, creaming (selection of only the very best prospective clients by an agency), tokenism, budgetary shortfalls, cooptation, redlining, and attitude and motivational assessment as mechanisms that limit the client's access to resources that determine quality of life. Without the power to change the operation of institutions from above, the knowledge and skills to countermand agents and mechanisms encountered in daily life, or the opportunity to obtain goods and services from alternative providers, the disenfranchised face the continuous challenge of meeting basic life needs in a hostile and manipulative environment. They must watch their lives unfold within a societal framework in which they have little or no influence upon the decision-making processes directly affecting them.

The precariousness of this position, as well as the very real material and psychological deprivation, creates a set of conditions for undertaking personal development that in fact discourages growth and actualization. It imposes an atmosphere of purposelessness and ineffectuality, which constitutes an added burden in the pursuit of both short- and long-term life goals. For many, these circumstances foster a state of personal oppression. As characterized by Goldenberg (1978), this state of oppression has a far-reaching impact upon the individual's life perspective: "Oppression is, above everything else, a condition of being, a particular stance one is forced to assume with respect to oneself, the world, and the exigencies of change. It is a pattern of hopelessness and helplessness, in which one sees oneself as static, limited, and expendable. People only become oppressed when they are forced (either subtly or with obvious malice) to finally succumb to the insidious process that continually undermines hope and subverts the desire to 'become.' The process, which often is both self-perpetuating and self-reinforcing, leaves in its wake the kinds of human beings who have learned to view themselves and their world as chronically, almost genetically estranged. The end product is an individual who is, in fact, alienated, isolated, and insulated from the society of which he nominally remains a member. He and his society are spatially joined, but psychologically separate: they inhabit parallel but nonreciprocal worlds" (pp. 2–3).

For others, the circumstances of their disenfranchisement serve as the context for a personal and/or communal struggle toward some degree of change, toward some degree of control over the means through which autonomy and influence can be achieved. The physical and emotional cost of such efforts is substantial. All too frequently the gains are limited, leaving the individual with a sense of bitterness and frustration. Other individuals choose to encapsulate themselves and assume an essentially defensive posture toward the outside world. Still others fatalistically accept their situation. Whichever course of response the disenfranchised individual undertakes, the actual disenfranchisement represents a tragic waste of human resources and a serious compromise of the human spirit.

Measuring the extent and degree of disenfranchisement in the United States has proven difficult (Matza, 1966; Waxman, 1977). Perhaps this is due to the magnitude and complexity of the phenomenon and the resulting barriers to quantification. Qualitative studies, in contrast, have provided a number of compelling portrayals of the impact that disenfranchisement has upon the structuring of the individual's life experience (Edgerton, 1967; Ladner, 1972; Lewis, 1966; Minuchin and others, 1967; Rainwater, 1970a; Shapiro, 1971). These studies have presented agents and mechanisms associated with particular instances of disenfranchisement and the quality of life experiences that follow. They offer ample documentation of the influence that disenfranchisement bears for the ongoing determination of the individual's life experience. They also suggest distinctive dynamics or pathways through which individuals are led into, and maintained in, a position of disenfranchisement. The dynamics appearing with the greatest frequency have been impoverishment, discrimination, and bureaucratization. Each of these represents a pathway, or line of focused experiences, that brings individuals to a common state of powerlessness, exclusion, and deprivation.

Impoverishment, the first of these dynamics, is a progressive experience drawn from the accumulated impact of poverty upon the course and quality of the individual's development. Whether or not this process constitutes a culture of poverty (Lewis, 1963; Valentine, 1968; Waxman, 1977), it is most certainly reflective of both an immediate state of being and a prospective course of life. In this regard, impoverishment is meant to suggest a life perspective. This life perspective emerges from a particular relationship that society imposes upon the poor, a relationship that in each transaction between the poor and societal institutions bears the message that the poor "are not included in the collectivity that makes up the 'real' society of 'real' people" (Rainwater, 1970b, p. 9).

From this position of marginality, the impoverished individual is presented with two areas of experience that take that individual beyond the concrete demands of not having enough money. The first of these is a pervasive sense of containment, immobility, and restriction. In contrast to the vague and frequently misleading promises of societal opportunities for change in the personal circumstance of poverty, societal institutions present impoverished individuals with clear statements of what is expected of them. These expectations often take the form of contingencies in which the provision of a particular material, social, or psychological resource is tied to the impoverished individual's performance of the "appropriate" behavior or attitude. In classrooms, personnel offices, housing authorities, and hospital clinics, the impoverished are tacitly admonished to recognize the nature of their position within the operation of the established social system. Both the motives and means of change become lost in the struggle to survive in the face of the "real" world's power and self-interest. The second area of experience is the significant depletion of the individual's developmental resources. Poor physical and/or mental health, nonproductive patterns of adaptation (such as resignation, isolation, negativism—all understandable responses to the given conditions, but not contributing to the individual's realization of developmental potential), and life-space management (tedious and time-consuming exchanges with building superintendents, food stamp workers, eligibility technicians, hospital clinic personnel, and so forth) turn the individual's attention away from the pursuit of developmental goals. Having already been removed from the mainstream of society's processes for the distribution of developmental opportunities and resources, the disenfranchised individual's time and energy is drained away in efforts to achieve some measure of security in a hostile and impersonal world of clerks, supervisors, and administrative functionaries. It follows, therefore, that disenfranchisement results from impoverishment in two ways: the "disinheritance" (Rainwater, 1970b) of the individual in terms of status, dignity, and opportunities accorded other human beings and the purposeful preoccupation of the individual in what may be deemed second-order life tasks.

The second pathway to disenfranchisement is that of discrimination. Historically, poverty and discrimination have been closely connected impediments to the expression and realization of human potential. This connection is still very much in evidence in the United States. There has, however, been an expanded recognition of other individuals and groups subject to discrimination. While race, culture, nationality, and religion continue to be recognized as major bases for discrimination, there has been a growing awareness of characteristics such as age, sex, sexual identity, and degree of physical and/or intellectual functioning as other sources of discriminatory actions. In addition, discrimination has come to be understood as an institutional as well as an interpersonal phenomenon.

Discrimination represents a fundamental rejection of an individual based upon one or more characteristics of that individual's being. It is a special manifestation of prejudice, an "applied prejudice in which negative social definitions are translated into action and political policy through the subordination of minorities and deprivation of their political, social, and economic rights" (Kinlock, 1974, p. 54).

This prejudice may arise from fear, irrational beliefs, or self-interest. Whatever its origin, discrimination establishes a framework of exchange between individual and individual, and between individual and institution, which denies the subordinate individual fair treatment. At the interpersonal level, this denial might take the form of overt or covert invalidation, abuse, stereotypic depreciation, depersonalization, or deliberate neglect. Institutionally, similar experiences are directed against individuals and populations through the structure and operating policies of the organization (Feagin, 1977; Hamilton and Carmichael, 1967; Jones, 1974; Knowles and Prewitt, 1969). At both levels, disenfranchisement results from the dispossession of the individual or population from rights, privileges, and benefits accorded those not discriminated against. This inherent devaluing of an individual based upon the presence of a particular characteristic reduces access to resources determining quality of life and undermines the individual's sense of self-worth. It steers the individual toward a prescribed set of inferior experiences in education, housing, and employment and confronts the individual with a variety of psychological challenges ranging from a questioning of personal competency and self-esteem to the constructive channeling of frustration and rage drawn from the unreasonable circumstances of the discrimination.

The third dynamic is the bureaucratization rooted in the operation of public service organizations in the United States. It is directly tied to the movement of organizations such as hospitals, schools, and welfare agencies toward a greater degree of bureaucratic operation (Gronjberg, Street, and Suttles, 1978). The organization's heightened concern with documentation, lines of authority, and procedural matters has been noted to actually compromise the quality of service provided (Prottas, 1979; Rosengren and Lefton, 1970). In many instances, an organization's preoccupation with its internal operation has resulted in the displacement of the organization's original goals and has made the meeting of the original goals more cumbersome. In other instances, bureaucratization has provided a facade of order used by employees to mystify and more easily control the client. This particular aspect of bureaucratization has been evident in the proliferation of the "street-level bureaucrat." According to Weatherly and Lipsky (1977), these governmental employees, police officers, welfare workers, legal-assistance lawyers, lower-court judges, and health workers operate under conditions in which "personal and organizational resources are chronically and severely limited in relation to the tasks that they are asked to perform." As a result, "the demand for their services will always be as great as their ability to supply these services. To accomplish their required tasks, street-level bureaucrats must find ways to accommodate the demands placed upon them and confront the reality of resource limitations. They typically do this by routinizing procedures, modifying goals, rationing services, asserting priorities, and limiting or controlling clientele. In other words, they develop practices that permit them in some way to process the work they are required to do" (p. 172).

In both instances the client is confronted with the complexity and formality of the organization's operating procedures. Without benefit of "inside" knowledge about the organization's rules and loopholes, the client searches for some line of rational design and personal relevance in attempting to negotiate the system. At the same time, the client is expected to know all the rules of the organization and to abide by them. Failure to follow the rules and regulations often leads to a denial or delay of service. These circumstances frustrate the consumer's use of the organization and often promote a nonproductive, adversary relationship. Although the bureaucratization of public service organizations ostensibly works toward the smoother and more efficient operation of the organization, it minimizes individualization in an area of providing services where it is a major consideration.

Bureaucratization minimizes client participation and subtly promotes the type of hierarchical, discretionary decision making with which disenfranchised individuals are all too familiar. For the client who lacks the choice of alternative service providers, bureaucratization can in fact be viewed as a "multiplier of disadvantage" (Gronjberg, Street, and Suttles, 1978, p. 141).

Disenfranchisement, then, is imposed upon individuals through impoverishment, discrimination, and bureaucratization. Each of these dynamics, in turn, is understood to involve its own distinctive processes for bringing individuals to a common state of powerlessness, marginality, and deprivation. These processes are not only highly complex in nature, but are also often obscured in multiple levels of social, economic, and interpersonal exchange. Moreover, these processes have a powerful impact upon individuals' views of themselves and their relationships with others. Quite simply, disenfranchisement is a multifaceted phenomenon touching individuals' lives at a number of different points in a variety of different ways. Individuals seeking to promote or undertake modification in the nature and circumstances of disenfranchisement must therefore be prepared to address its complexity and expansiveness. For social workers, this preparedness involves a deliberate particularization of practice methods.

Methodological Commitment

In social work, methodology pertains to the design and the designing of practice. It refers to "the 'how' of helping, to purposeful, planned, instrumental activity through which tasks are accomplished and goals are achieved" (Siporin, 1975, p. 43). This "purposeful, planned, instrumental activity" embodies an integrated set of values, principles, and skills that constitutes a framework for practice. This framework provides guidelines for the worker's "choice of how to give service" (Nelsen, 1975, p. 266), guidelines that influence the shaping of the client-worker relationship and determine the focus of activities associated with particular tasks and goals. At a very general level, these guidelines have been tied to the "responsible, conscious use of self in a relationship with an individual or group" (Bartlett, 1958, p. 7). Beyond this level, however, guidelines for practice have emerged from specific methods of practice, such as casework, group work, community organization, generic practice, and methodologies fashioned for particular fields of practice. Each of these practice frameworks reflects its own distinctive perspective on practice.

The idea of a methodological commitment to the disenfranchised, then, suggests the designing of practice guidelines that focus upon disenfranchisement as a primary context for practice. As either a central theme or an adjunctive component of the worker's practice framework, this focus directs the structuring of goals, working relationships, and change processes in line with the conditions of the client's disenfranchisement. The "how" of helping is specially crafted to address both the immediate circumstances of the disenfranchisement and the client's general experience of powerlessness, marginality, and deprivation. The provision of service is therefore undertaken in a manner that is not only relevant to the actual service being provided but also consistent with an underlying concern for the expansion of the client's participation in the determination of life experiences and realization of developmental potential.

One essential element of such a practice perspective is a directed awareness of how human environments are socially constructed and maintained (Berger and Luckmann, 1966; Strauss and others, 1963). Such an awareness reaches beyond the formal and overt operation of societal institutions to identify and examine the agents and mechanisms structuring specific instances of disenfranchisement. It views environments as marketplaces of human resources (psychological and social, as well as physical) in which the complex, and often institutionalized, patterns of exchange selectively deprive individuals of resources central to meeting basic needs and addressing personal aspirations. Much as a social policy analysis examines the "system of interrelated, yet not necessarily logically consistent, principles of action that shape the quality of life or the level of well-being of members of society" (Gil, 1971, p. 413), this directed environmental awareness is meant to explicate the immediate circumstances through which impoverishment, discrimination, and bureaucratization are imposed upon individuals. Essentially, it constitutes an ongoing analysis of the interpersonal and organizational rules, regulations, and processes that comprise the micro-policies of disenfranchisement. Within this framework, societal institutions are understood to be direct agents in the distribution and allocation of resources determining quality of life. The operation of these institutions (hospitals, schools, courts, and so on) and the actions of their employees serve as powerful determinants of specific instances of disenfranchisement. As such, they represent a critical arena for worker activity and influence.

Beyond understanding the agents and mechanisms structuring disenfranchisement, social workers must also be able to intervene in this arena effectively. They must be able to successfully negotiate with institutional agents for both the resources needed by the client and the modification of the disenfranchising micro-policies. As drawn from the particular conditions of specific exchanges between clients and resource-providing settings, this negotiation process can take a variety of different forms. A successful renegotiation of the exchange between client and provider might, for example, result from advocacy, coordination, conflict resolution, mediation, litigation, or a combination of these and other possible worker activities. Accordingly, the social worker must be prepared to undertake that particular role or combination of roles which most directly addresses the circumstances presented. In this regard, the worker must serve as a multirole practitioner (Baker, 1976), prepared to offer the client conceptual and interpersonal skills that are broad, specialized at the point of individual practice roles, versatile, and effective. A particular line of practice is understood to emerge with each instance of disenfranchisement, and the worker is ready to exercise specific skills and assume those roles deemed most relevant to each practice situation.

A third element of a methodological commitment to the disenfranchised is that of a complementary working relationship. As suggested by the use of the term complementary, it is a working relationship characterized by a special effort to recognize and be responsive to the immediate set of circumstances under which the client and worker have come to work together, and a comparably special effort to continuously evolve the working relationship in line with client specifications. This perspective on the development of a working relationship is meant to convey the centrality of the client as a participant in decision-making and goal-achieving processes. Readily distinguishable from the relationships clients experience in other exchanges with resource-providing settings, this complementary working relationship encourages the client to use the worker in a manner that makes sense to the client and that proceeds from the client's perspective on timing and purpose. Having acknowledged that the client is the ultimate decision maker in setting goals and that the client has the most relevant knowledge as to how the personal dimensions of these goals can be addressed, the worker functions as an individual facilitator. The worker offers knowledge about the environment and how it operates, identifies options and alternatives associated with the client's specified goals, and provides an interpersonal setting for the client's reflection and introspection.

Drawing upon another dimension of the idea of a multirole practitioner, the client is presented with the choice of a variety of possible worker roles. In terms of direct contact with the client, these roles might be those of problem solver, educator, counselor, psychotherapist, confidant, or supporter. As previously noted, worker roles directed toward facilitating the exchange between client and environment might encompass those of advocate, coordinator, conflict resolver, or mediator. With regard to the selection of roles and the possibility of differences of opinion at this and other points in the working relationship, the worker maintains a responsive posture but does not unquestioningly follow the requests of the client. Hesitancies and refusals are presented and subsequent feelings discussed as part of an ongoing consideration of the advantages and disadvantages associated with particular ways of pursuing the client's specified goals. Every effort is made in the working relationship to acquaint the client with the challenges as well as the benefits of franchisement and direct involvement in decision making.

This complementary working relationship is also meant to work toward the empowerment of the client. Its emphasis upon the worker providing information and cultivating a framework of shared decision making underscores an underlying process "whereby persons who belong to a stigmatized social category throughout their lives can be assisted to develop and increase skills in the exercise of interpersonal influence and the performance of valued social roles" (Solomon, 1976, p. 6).

As a principle for practice, empowerment establishes a basic concern for client autonomy and mastery. Whether the client comes to the worker voluntarily, involuntarily, or ambivalently, and whether the focus of this first contact is a request for a particular service, a request for assistance in solving a problem, or an expectation by a societal institution that the client's behavior be changed in a specified manner, the worker's regard for the client's active and purposeful determination of life experience serves as a primary influence upon the definition and development of the client-worker relationship. The worker's skill in recognizing client strengths and competencies, and in successfully utilizing these resources toward realizing the client's specified goals assumes the position of a central dynamic of practice. Without either totally doing things for the client or pushing the client to do everything for him- or herself, the worker carefully individualizes the joint-planning and decision-making processes to guarantee the client options and alternatives that promise to place the client into a variety of possible action roles. In line with the client's own sense of priorities and timing, these roles can be chosen and prepared for in a manner that increasingly extends the client's command of environmental transactions and that provides a natural context for discussing feelings associated with such efforts. Empowerment, then, seeks to incorporate the meeting of immediate client needs into a more expansive task of drawing the client into a position of initiative and leadership in structuring the course and quality of life experience.

These four elements of a methodological commitment to the disenfranchised cannot be properly taken as constituting a comprehensive model for social work practice. In fact, together they hardly go beyond the statement of a general framework for practice. They do, however, represent an integrated methodological core for either developing a practice model with a specialized focus upon addressing the needs and aspirations of the disenfranchised or for shaping already specialized practice methodologies for possible applicability to disenfranchised individuals and populations. Within this integrated methodological core, an awareness of the complex, socially structured nature of human environments is combined with the worker's multirole action base and a reflexive working relationship with the client to promote the development of social and conceptual skills through which the client can attain a purposeful structuring of his or her life experience. Moreover, this is accomplished in a manner that affirms a primary respect for the client's dignity, individuality, and potential. From this perspective, therefore, practice with the disenfranchised is understood to necessarily entail involvement in those immediate circumstances of the client's life through which some degree of franchisement can be achieved. This deliberate subordination of methodology to specific, environmentally connected goals raises a number of apparent implications for clinical social work practice.

Implications for Clinical Social Work

In a recent position paper on clinical social work education at the master's level (adopted as the official position of the National Federation of Societies of Clinical Social Work), Pinkus and others (1977) present the thesis that "clinical social work is a specialization within the field of social work drawing on social work values and encompassing a particular body of knowledge which leads to therapeutic interventions on behalf of the individual, both in his own right and as a member of a family, a group, and a society; it is not viewed as comprehensive or all-encompassing and is open to change, revision, and modification" (p. 253).

They go on to identify health as the focus of clinical practice and to characterize the objectives of practice as being both preventive and remedial. They observe the specific goals in working with a client to "emerge from the constantly shifting action within the helping process, and these are determined by client and worker in collaboration. . . . The unconscious components of the client's behavior and the client's reality experiences are of equal importance. The individual, family, and group and social, cultural, and economic realities are included in the diagnostic understanding and assessment of their relationship to the individual's need and problem" (p. 258).

Based upon such an understanding of the client's needs, one or more specific methods are employed to achieve designated ends. These methods range from individual psychotherapy to the provision of concrete services, though "where the worker is not skilled in a particular approach that diagnostically appears necessary, referral is made to the appropriate source" (p. 259). The basic skill of clinical social work is identified to be "the ability to conduct an interview in the one-to-one context" (p. 259), with possible supplementation in the areas of family interviewing and group leadership. Similar characterizations of the methodological framework of clinical social work are found in works by Sackheim (1974) and Strean (1978).

As presented earlier, a methodological commitment to the disenfranchised involves a somewhat different set of emphases. Primary concern is given to an examination of the circumstances structuring individual instances of disenfranchisement, and to the client's and worker's ability to negotiate with the environment for a modification of these conditions. The worker-client relationship is characterized as a reflexive one, distinguished by its consistent regard for the client's self-determination and active participation in the change process. Both client and worker undertake a variety of different action roles, with the worker utilizing the client's involvement in the change effort as a natural context for the client's consideration of the personal dimensions of disenfranchisement and the process of pursuing planned change. Finally, the methodological commitment promotes the empowerment of the client toward the autonomous determination of the course and quality of life experience.

In comparing the two practice perspectives, it becomes apparent that each has adopted a different set of organizing principles. Clinical social work, on the one hand, has derived much of its actual methodology from a psychodynamic understanding of the individual and a biopsychosocial appreciation of the individual's experience of meeting basic needs in a complex world. The methodological commitment to the disenfranchised, on the other hand, has focused upon the circumstances, from which disenfranchisement emerges and the processes through which individuals can act to change these circumstances. For clinical social work, the underlying dynamic guiding the worker is that of treatment, and the generalized goal is the adaptive functioning of the client; for the methodological commitment to the disenfranchised, the dynamic is one of facilitation, and the generalized goal is empowerment. The former perspective relies heavily upon diagnosis to structure the treatment relationship; the latter combines an understanding of the client's environment, the nature of the client's immediate goal, and the emergent character of the working relationship to arrive at the particular progression of exchanges between the client and the client's environment that the worker will endeavor to facilitate. The former focuses upon the clients command over him- or herself as the means for structuring life experience, and the latter upon the process of gaining command over the environment as a means for gaining skill and direction in structuring the totality of life experience. And, whereas the former tends to be analytic and scientific in its conceptual methodology, the latter is synthetic and phenomenological.

The prospect of a methodological commitment to the disenfranchised in clinical social work practice, then, appears to be inextricably bound to a reconciliation of at least some of the major elements of these contrasting practice perspectives. The first area of possible reconciliation would be the psychodynamic versus the environmental context for intervention. The challenge here is not the rejection and exclusion of one or the other, but rather the purposeful subordination of one to the other. In psychotherapy, and in-depth psychotherapies in particular, the subordination of environmental to psychodynamic intervention is quite clear. In clinical social work, this relationship is less clear. Generally, it is understood to vary with the nature of the client and the practice situation. In working with the disenfranchised client, however, the connection between the environment and the client's quality of life is recognized to be so routinely significant that the worker appears compelled to subordinate psychodynamic to environmental intervention. With the exception of instances in which the client comes to the social worker expressly requesting the services of a psychotherapist, the clinical social worker would seem obligated to begin with a consideration of the manner in which both the client's stated need and the disenfranchising circumstances surrounding this need can be addressed.

Similarly, the guidelines for working with the disenfranchised client, the goals of this interaction, and the actual interventions would seem to emerge from the nature of the client's requested service and the relationship of this requested service to the client's disenfranchisement. Other than in instances in which the client requests it, there does not appear to be a basis for maintaining that all service for the disenfranchised client should be "related to individual need as determined through the clinical process and as derived from a dynamic, diagnostic understanding of rational and irrational, conscious and unconscious behaviors and attitudes reflected in interaction with a variety of systems: the family, the group, or the larger society" (Pinkus and others, 1977, p. 258).

On the contrary, the sensitivity of social workers to the nature and processes of disenfranchisement should magnify the importance of the client's involvement in the planning and action phases of meeting a stated need. This second area of possible reconciliation draws the worker's attention and skill to the highly particularized process of formulating with the client, and undertaking, courses of action that bear a direct relevance to the client's goals and immediate experience. This formulation process serves as a medium through which (1) the worker provides information about the nature and modification of specific environmental conditions, (2) the client clarifies his or her goals and expands the consideration of the personal circumstances under which those goals are being addressed, and (3) the worker and client achieve a working relationship based upon the client acting as a decision maker and the worker serving as a facilitator. To the extent that the client perceives the worker's efforts to be of value, the client may be expected to extrapolate the worker's activities to other areas. These extrapolations may or may not lead to the type of treatment relationships in which diagnostic evaluation would be an appropriate directive for practice.

A third consideration in the relationship of a clinical social work practice perspective to a methodological commitment to the disenfranchised is the actual setting of service. In community mental health centers, family service agencies, and child guidance clinics, clinical social workers can expect to draw heavily, if not predominantly, from the clinical framework presented earlier. These settings bear a clear identification with psychotherapeutic processes and much of the clientele come to the agency seeking such processes. In these settings, it follows that the methodological commitment to the disenfranchised is subordinated to a clinical knowledge and skill base. This does not rule out the use of the methodological commitment to the disenfranchised but instead puts this framework and its use into a perspective that reflects both the nature of the setting and the client's initial request for service. For many other settings in which clinical social workers provide services, this perspective is not present. Much of the contact that disenfranchised clients have with medical care facilities, schools, protective service agencies, and case management settings is not for psychotherapeutic experiences. In these instances, the clinical social worker might have to begin with a methodological commitment to the disenfranchised and move cautiously to incorporate clinically based exchanges as sanctioned by the client. It seems apparent therefore, that guidelines need to be established for the balanced and selective use of clinical processes with disenfranchised clients that reflect a regard for the nature of the agency setting and the expectations that clients bring to such a service setting.

This discussion of possible areas of reconciliation between clinical social work and a methodological commitment to working with disenfranchised clients suggests the intricacies of theory and technique that remain to be addressed. A real reconciliation of these two important dimensions of social work practice will undoubtedly involve a more intensive and detailed consideration of underlying issues and concerns. This chapter has sought to encourage such a consideration. It has identified and examined some of the major processes of disenfranchisement and has offered a methodological core for a social work practice response. Further, it has briefly explored the relationship of clinical social work to this practice response. Above all, it has worked toward assuring that whatever reconciliation is reached, it will be a methodological one.

References

Baker, R. "The Multirole Practitioner in the Generic Orientation to Social Work Practice." *British Journal of Social Work,* 1976, *6* (3), 327–349.

Baratz, S., and Baratz, J. C. "Early Childhood Intervention: The Social Science Base of Institutional Racism." *Harvard Educational Review,* 1970, *40* (1), 29–50.

Bartlett, H. "Toward Clarification and Improvement of Social Work Practice." *Social Work,* 1958, *3* (2), 3–9.

Berger, P., and Luckmann, T. *The Social Construction of Reality.* Garden City, N.Y.: Doubleday, 1966.

Berkman, B. "Mental Health and the Aging: A Review of Literature for Clinical Social Workers." *Clinical Social Work Journal,* 1978, *6* (3), 230–245.

Black, H. C. *Black's Law Dictionary.* (5th ed.) St. Paul, Minn.: West, 1979.

Blanck, G., and Blanck, R. *Ego Psychology, Theory and Practice.* New York: Columbia University Press, 1974.

Blanck, G., and Blanck, R. *Ego Psychology II, Psychoanalytic Developmental Psychology.* New York: Columbia University Press, 1979.

Briar, S. "The Casework Predicament." *Social Work,* 1968, *13* (1), 5–11.

Briar, S., and Miller, H. *Problems and Issues in Social Casework.* New York: Columbia University Press, 1971.

Brody, E., and Brody, S. "Decade of Decision for the Elderly." *Social Work,* 1974, *19* (5), 544–554.

Brooks, C. M. "New Mental Health Perspectives in the Black Community." *Social Casework,* 1974, *55* (8), 489–496.

Case, L. P., and Lingerfelt, N. B. "Name-Calling: The Labeling Process in the Social Work Interview." *Social Service Review,* 1974, *48* (1), 75–86.
Cloward, R. A., and Epstein, I. "Private Social Welfare's Disengagement from the Poor: The Case of Family Adjustment Agencies." In M. Zald (Ed.), *Social Welfare Institutions: A Sociological Reader.* New York: Wiley, 1965.
Cumming, E. "Allocation of Care to the Mentally Ill, American Style." In M. Zald (Ed.), *Organizing for Community Welfare.* Chicago: Quadrangle Books, 1967.
Cumming, E. *Systems of Social Regulation.* New York: Atherton Press, 1968.
Dahrendorf, R. *Life Chances.* Chicago: University of Chicago Press, 1979.
Dean, W. R., Jr. "Back to Activism." *Social Work,* 1977, *22* (5), 369–373.
Edgerton, R. B. *The Cloak of Competence.* Berkeley: University of California Press, 1967.
Feagin, J. R. "Indirect Institutionalized Discrimination." *American Politics Quarterly,* 1977, *5* (2), 177–199.
Galper, J. H. *The Politics of Social Services.* Englewood Cliffs, N.J.: Prentice-Hall, 1975.
Gil, D. "A Systematic Approach to Social Policy Analysis." *Social Service Review,* 1971, *44* (4), 411–426.
Gochros, H. L., and Gochros, J. S. (Eds.). *The Sexually Oppressed.* New York: Association Press, 1977.
Goffman, E. *Asylums.* Garden City, N.Y.: Anchor Books, 1961.
Goldenberg, I. I. *Oppression and Social Intervention.* Chicago: Nelson-Hall, 1978.
Grinnel, R. M., Jr. "Environmental Modification: Casework's Concern or Casework's Neglect?" *Social Service Review,* 1973, *47* (2), 208–220.
Gronjberg, K., Street, D., and Suttles, G. D. *Poverty and Social Change.* Chicago: University of Chicago Press, 1978.
Hamilton, C., and Carmichael, S. *Black Power.* New York: Random House, 1967.
Hampden-Turner, C. *From Poverty to Dignity.* Garden City, N.Y.: Doubleday, 1975.
Hasenfeld, Y. "People Processing Organizations: An Exchange Approach." *American Sociological Review,* 1972, *37,* 256–263.
Hollis, F. "On Revisiting Social Work." *Social Casework,* 1980, *61* (1), 3–10.
Horejsi, C. R. "Developmental Disabilities: Opportunities for Social Workers." *Social Work,* 1979, *24* (1), 40–43.
Howard, D. S. "Social Work and Social Reform." In C. Kasius (Ed.), *New Directions in Social Work.* New York: Harper & Row, 1954, 158–175.
Jones, T. "Institutional Racism in the United States." *Social Work,* 1974, *19* (2), 218–225.
Kallen, D., Miller, D., and Daniels, A. "Sociology, Social Work, and Social Problems." *The American Sociologist,* 1968, pp. 235–240.
Kernberg, O. F. *Borderline Conditions and Pathological Narcissism.* New York: Aronson, 1975.
Kernberg, O. F. *Object Relations Theory and Clinical Psychoanalysis.* New York: Aronson, 1976.
Kinlock, G. C. *The Dynamics of Race Relations.* New York: McGraw-Hill, 1974.
Knowles, L. L., and Prewitt, K. (Eds.). *Institutional Racism in America.* Englewood Cliffs, N.J.: Prentice-Hall, 1969.

Kohut, H. *The Analysis of the Self.* New York: International Universities Press, 1971.

Kohut, H. *The Restoration of the Self.* New York: International Universities Press, 1977.

Kravetz, D. "Sexism in a Woman's Profession." *Social Work,* 1976, *21* (6), 421–426.

Ladner, J. A. *Tomorrow's Tomorrow.* Garden City, N.Y.: Anchor Books, 1972.

Levin, H. M. "Education, Life Chances and the Courts: The Role of Social Science Evidence." *Law and Contemporary Problems,* 1975, *39* (2), 217–240.

Lewis, O. "The Culture of Poverty." *Trans-Action,* 1963, 17–19.

Lewis, O. *La Vida.* New York: Random House, 1966.

Lopez, S. "Clinical Stereotypes of the Mexican-American." In J. L. Martinez, Jr. (Ed.), *Chicano Psychology.* New York: Academic Press, 1977.

Lowy, L. *Social Work with the Aging.* New York: Harper & Row, 1979.

Mahler, M. S., Pine, F., and Bergman, A. *The Psychological Birth of the Infant.* New York: Basic Books, 1975.

Matza, D. "Poverty and Disrepute." In R. K. Merton and R. A. Nisbet (Eds.), *Contemporary Social Problems.* (2nd ed.) New York: Harcourt Brace Jovanovich, 1966.

Meyer, C. H. "Direct Services in New and Old Contexts." In A. J. Kahn (Ed.), *Shaping the New Social Work.* New York: Columbia University Press, 1973a, 26–54.

Meyer, C. H. (Ed.). *Social Work with the Aging.* New York: Columbia University Press, 1973b.

Meyer, C. H. "Discussion." *Clinical Social Work Journal,* 1977, *5* (4), 289–292.

Meyer, C. H. "What Directions for Direct Practice?" *Social Work,* 1979, *24* (4), 267–272.

Miller, D. "The Influence of the Patient's Sex on Clinical Judgments." *Smith College Studies in Social Work,* 1974, *44* (2), 89–100.

Miller, H. "Social Work in the Black Ghetto: The New Colonialism." *Social Work,* 1969, *14* (3), 65–76.

Mills, C. W. "The Professional Ideology of Social Pathologists." *American Journal of Sociology,* 1943, *49* (2), 165–181.

Minuchin, S., and others. *Families of the Slums.* New York: Basic Books, 1967.

Morales, A. "Beyond Traditional Conceptual Frameworks." *Social Work,* 1977, *22* (5), 387–393.

Nelsen, J. C. "Social Work's Fields of Practice, Methods, and Models: The Choice to Act." *Social Service Review,* 1975, *49* (2), 264–270.

Pearson, G. *The Deviant Imagination.* New York: Holmes & Meier, 1975.

Perlman, H. H. "Putting the 'Social' Back in Social Casework." *Child Welfare,* 1952, *31* (7), 8–9, 14.

Perlman, H. H. "Confessions, Concerns, and Commitment of an Ex-Clinical Social Worker." *Clinical Social Work Journal,* 1974, *2* (3), 221–227.

Perlmutter, F. D., and Alexander, L. B. "Exposing the Coercive Consensus: Racism and Sexism in Social Work." In R. C. Sarri and Y. Hasenfeld (Eds.), *The Management of Human Services.* New York: Columbia University Press, 1978.

Pinkus, H., and others. "Education for the Practice of Clinical Social Work at the Master's Level: A Position Paper." *Clinical Social Work Journal,* 1977, *5* (4), 253–268.

Prottas, J. *People-Processing*. Lexington, Mass.: Lexington Books, 1979.
Rainwater, L. *Behind Ghetto Walls*. Chicago: Aldine, 1970a.
Rainwater, L. "Neutralizing the Disinherited: Some Psychological Aspects of Understanding the Poor." In V. Allen (Ed.), *Psychological Factors in Poverty*. Chicago: Markham, 1970b.
Rees, S. "How Misunderstanding Occurs." In R. Bailey and M. Brake (Eds.), *Radical Social Work*. New York: Pantheon, 1975.
Rein, M. "Social Work in Search of a Radical Profession." *Social Work*, 1970, *15* (1), 13–28.
Reynolds, B. C. "Social Case Work: What Is It? What's Its Place in the World Today?" *The Family*, 1935, *16*, 235–241.
Richan, W. C., and Mendelsohn, A. R. *Social Work, the Unloved Profession*. New York: New Viewpoints, 1973.
Rosengren, W. R., and Lefton, M. *Organizations and Clients*. Columbus, Ohio: Merrill, 1970.
Ruiz, R. A. "The Delivery of Mental Health and Social Change Services for Chicanos: Analysis and Recommendations." In J. L. Martinez, Jr. (Ed.), *Chicano Psychology*. New York: Academic Press, 1977.
Ruzek, S. K. "Making Social Work Accountable." In E. Freidson (Ed.), *The Professions and Their Prospects*. Beverly Hills, Calif.: Sage, 1973.
Ryan, W. *Blaming the Victim*. New York: Random House, 1971.
Sackheim, G. *The Practice of Clinical Casework*. New York: Behavioral Publications, 1974.
Scanlon, P. L. "Social Work with the Mentally Retarded Client." *Social Casework*, 1978, *59* (3), 161–166.
Shapiro, J. H. *Communities of the Alone*. New York: Association Press, 1971.
Solomon, B. B. *Black Empowerment: Social Work in Oppressed Communities*. New York: Columbia University Press, 1976.
Siporin, M. *Introduction to Social Work Practice*. New York: Macmillan, 1975.
Strauss, A., and others. "The Hospital and Its Negotiated Order." In E. Freidson (Ed.), *The Hospital in Modern Society*. New York: Free Press, 1963, 147–169.
Strean, H. S. *Clinical Social Work: Theory and Practice*. New York: Free Press, 1978.
Toren, N. *Social Work: The Case of a Semi-Profession*. Beverly Hills, Calif.: Sage, 1972.
Tully, C., and Albro, J. C. "Homosexuality: A Social Worker's Imbroglio." *Journal of Sociology and Social Welfare*, 1979, *6* (2), 154–167.
Valentine, C. A. *Culture and Poverty*. Chicago: University of Chicago Press, 1968.
Waxman, C. I. *The Stigma of Poverty*. Elmsford, N.Y.: Pergamon Press, 1977.
Weatherly, R., and Lipsky, M. "Street-Level Bureaucrats and Institutional Innovation: Implementing Special Education Reform." *Harvard Education Review*, 1977, *47* (2), 171–197.

41

Client Self-Determination

Charles S. Levy

Strange as it may seem, the Code of Ethics of the National Association of Social Workers (NASW) in the version adopted in 1960 (National Association of Social Workers, 1960 and 1967a) and amended in 1967 contains no reference whatsoever to self-determination or to its analogue, autonomy—either that of the client or anyone else—although many of the provisions in both versions evidently required a considerable degree of initiative on the part of the social worker. Now this observation would not be especially noteworthy were it not for the reflection in social work literature of a preoccupation, if not an obsession, with the concept and ramifications of client self-determination. It is odd that a concept that had for years been regarded as basic to social work practice would be omitted in a set of moral prescriptions designed to guide and influence that practice.

This omission may be an index to the conflicts and ambiguities that have been associated with the concept of self-determination. Indicators of such conflicts and ambiguities include the entry in the 1960 and 1967 versions of the NASW Code of Ethics: "I regard as my primary obligation the welfare of the individual or group served, which includes action for improving social conditions." It is very difficult for a practitioner to honor this principle of professional responsibility and at the same time to feel free to honor a principle that ostensibly leaves to the practitioner's clientele the option not to have its welfare served—an option rather clearly consistent with the idea of self-determination, notwithstanding the numerous limitations with which it has been encumbered in social work as well as political and philosophical literature.

Similarly, it is often difficult for the practitioner to reconcile what has been ascribed to social workers as responsibility to society with the priority implicitly accorded in the code to the practitioner's clientele, particularly if it is the clientele's self-determination that represents the risk to the interests of society. The social worker, in other words, is not likely to be inclined to maximize a client's freedom of choice if the action the client chooses offends a societal norm—for example, by insisting on rearing an illegitimate child and going on welfare despite all the provisions that might be made available to the client to avoid the necessity of either having the child or accepting welfare in the first place.

Perhaps more dramatic is the implication that has been drawn from the conflict between a client's own choice of action as it might coincide with the concept of self-determination and the negative consequences for the client of that choice. In such a case, the conflict is not one of client interest versus societal interest, when the social worker has a professional commitment to both but can only accommodate one. Rather, the conflict is between the client's self-determination and the client's welfare.

Felix P. Biestek, who has given the matter constant and scrupulous attention for many years, took a position on the conflict this represented for the social worker and, interestingly enough, tied that position to the social worker's responsibility to society: "*Because of their responsibility to society,* social workers realized that, even though dedicated to the spirit of human freedom, the clients had to be protected from making decisions that potentially or actually would be injurious to the client himself or to others" (National Association of Social Workers, 1967b, p. 22; emphasis supplied).

Although conflict and a modicum of personal agony are inevitable in the attempt to resolve issues in social work ethics, the nature of the difficulties that have been experienced in both the formation and operation of the concept of client self-determination in social work practice is a function primarily of the analysis of the concept in political, cultural, and historical terms rather than in ethical terms. Not that the task is easier when approached from the point of view of professional ethics, for it is not. Rather, the difference is that when approached politically, culturally, and historically, the task is primarily to understand the meaning and ramifications of the concept of self-determination, and both its meaning and ramifications are beset by conceptual contradictions and dilemmas. When approached from the point of view of professional ethics, however, the task is primarily to understand the premises of the application of the concept of self-determination as a matter of professional responsibility. If dilemmas emerge in the application of the concept in social work practice situations, they are a function not so much of what self-determination is, but whether it applies in given cases and, if so, how it applies, especially when the social worker is faced with conflicting responsibilities, to clients, to others, or to both.

Viewed from the perspective of professional ethics, the concept of self-determination is never open to question—as a concept. The social worker always has the ethical responsibility to honor, to preserve, and to facilitate the client's self-determination. Whether the social worker fulfills that responsibility or not is something else again. But when the social worker does not—assuming professional intention—an accounting for the failure is required, and the failure must be regarded as a deviation from an ethical expectation.

This does not mean that the deviation is never justifiable. This means only that, as with any other principle of professional ethics, client self-determination may, as a matter of professional discretion, have to succumb to other value priorities. But both when an action is contemplated in professional practice and when an action is actually taken, reasons for any deviation from the principle must be eminently clear, sufficiently clear, in fact, to meet the test of unbiased and systematic professional peer judgment.

Although it has been accorded rather intensive analytical and historical attention, the concept of self-determination merits examination (McDermott, 1975; Biestek and Gehrig, 1978). Biestek (1967) claimed that "The conviction of social workers concerning the high value of client self-determination developed inductively, from observation and experience, rather than deductively and philosophically" (p. 22). My purpose is not so much to question that judgment as to emphasize a major premise of professional ethics, namely that it is precisely deductive and philosophical: certain professional behaviors are intrinsically valued, and therefore they are done; not certain results are attained in certain ways and therefore those ways are preferred.

The Concept of Self-Determination

In order to separate the task of understanding what self-determination means from the task of identifying the behavioral obligations and expectations that flow from the meaning of the term, the concept should be distinguished from the principle. This distinction applies especially to the social workers' behavioral obligations and expectations in relation to self-determination.

As the literature on the subject indicates, self-determination has represented, among other things, an end or a process or both, in that it has been described as an activity in which human beings engage in order to arrive at choices of actions or goals in relation to their own lives and circumstances. The following definitions underscore the ultimate relevance of self-determination to the relationship between social workers and their clienteles: "(1) determination by oneself or itself, without outside influence; (2) freedom to live as one chooses, or to act or decide without consulting another or others; (3) the determining by the people of the form their government shall have, without reference to the wishes of any other nation . . ." (1967).

Because the word autonomy is often used as a synonym for self-determination, it seems pertinent to refer to the same dictionary's definition for that term. It emphasizes a critical dimension of the concept, namely the will, which is also of great ultimate relevance to social worker–client relationships: "(1) independence or freedom, as of the will, one's actions . . . (2) the condition of being autonomous; self-government, or the right of self-government . . ." (1967).

Charles Frankel (1976) reinforced this dimension of self-determination in his description of autonomy as "being one's own master, doing only what we consent to do, accepting no obligations except those freely undertaken" (p. 358).

Each of these definitions of self-determination is phenomenological in that it simply identifies what self-determination is, when it is, if it is. The concept is rarely viewed simply because so many doubts and limitations are applied to it that one wonders whether self-determination or autonomy exists in the natural state that the cited definitions imply. Such doubts and limitations caused Helen Harris Perlman (1965) to wonder whether self-determination was not, in fact, an "illusion." Salzberger (1979) takes issue with her and with others who have expressed doubt about self-determination as a phenomenon of human existence, insisting that what is lost when a social work client does not have access to self-determination is only the opportunity to exercise it. He does, however, seem to allow for what he considers an acceptable degree of therapeutic influence in social work practice, without conceding that to be an edging away from self-determination as a reality toward self-determination as something of an illusion. Salzberger is primarily concerned with self-determination as a "right."

Thus, some writers claim self-determination exists, at least as a possibility, although it apparently is rarely expected to exist in a pure state. For other writers, of course, it is hardly expected to exist at all, and for not a few it cannot or should not. Perhaps Albert Camus said it all most clearly through Caligula (in Stuart Gilbert's translation): "Well, tomorrow there will be a catastrophe, and I shall end it when I choose. After all, I haven't so many ways of proving I am free." And Caligula adds as an acknowledgment of manifest reality what other writers have proposed as a prescriptive constraint, "One is always free at someone else's expense." But more about this in a moment. What is important here is what client self-determination would look like if it did exist; and, if it were to be conceded as a social work value or a social work responsibility, it would also represent a professional objective.

Self-Determination as a Right

Self-determination has been conceived of as a right. Politically and philosophically it is acknowledged as a value without a necessary connection to professional responsibility except, of course, for the legal profession. This has been as true of social work literature as it has been of the literature of political science and political philosophy. McDermott (1975) says, for example: "Far from being a mere means to any goal, the individual's right to make his own decisions and choices affecting him has long been regarded as one of the cornerstones of the moral framework to which democratic western societies are committed, a framework determining both the goals that may be justifiably pursued and the means that may be chosen to attain them" (pp. 1–2).

And Biestek (1951) characterizes the right of self-determination as a self-directed responsibility for the person who has that right: "As a human being he has the responsibility of living *his* life in such a manner as to achieve *his* life's goals, proximate and ultimate, as *he* conceives them. Corresponding to this responsibility, he is endowed with a fundamental, inalienable right to choose and decide the means for the prosecution of his own personal destiny" (p. 370; emphasis supplied).

The right of self-determination presumably belongs to all, but its particular significance lies in the process of receiving and giving the kinds of help that social workers have a professional responsibility to make available to clients.

On the one hand, self-determination is a right easily and readily, sometimes necessarily, compromised and constrained, because it is bounded by the rights of others, the capacity of clients to make choices, legal limitations, societal norms, and so on.

Or as William Graham Sumner put it in "The Forgotten Man": "If there were any such liberty as that of doing as you have a mind to, the human race would be condemned to everlasting anarchy and war as these erratic wills crossed and clashed against each other. True liberty lies in the equilibrium of rights and duties, producing peace, order, and harmony" (Larson, 1977, p. 89).

On the other hand, the right of self-determination becomes a keystone for other rights and privileges, both legal and civil, that figure prominently in the social worker–client relationship, among them confidentiality and privacy. Though usually cast as values in social work literature, these may also be regarded as rights to which clients as well as others are entitled, sometimes with safeguards provided for in law. And self-determination is one of the major premises upon which they rest. This is made quite evident in *Price* v. *Sheppard* (239 N.W.2d 905), in which the decision of the court stated:

> At the core of the privacy decisions, in our judgment, is the concept of personal autonomy—the notion that the Constitution reserves to the individual, free of governmental intrusion, certain fundamental decisions about how he or she will conduct his or her life. Like other constitutional rights, however, this right is not an absolute one and must give way to certain interests of the state, the balance turning on the impact of the decision on the life of the individual. As the impact increases, so must the importance of the state's interest. Some decisions, we assume, will be of little consequence to the individual and a showing of a legitimate state interest will justify its intrusion; other decisions, on the other hand, will be of such major consequence that only *the most compelling state interest* will justify the intrusion. But once justified, the extent of the state's intrusion is *not unlimited.* It must also appear that the means utilized to serve the state's interest are *necessary* and *reasonable,* or, in other words, in light of alternative means, *the least intrusive.* [Brieland and Lemmon, 1977, pp. 762–763; emphasis supplied].

To anticipate my consideration of client self-determination from the point of view of social work ethics, it should be evident that if there are requirements for the state in relation to the self-determination of clients—which represents a foundation for other rights and opportunities, a client's access to which requires safeguarding and preservation—no less should be required of social workers who serve those clients.

Self-Determination as Therapeutic and Developmental Necessity

Whatever its political and philosophical connotations, the concept of self-determination has been viewed as a practical necessity in relation both to human growth and development and to therapeutic interventions. Thus, it represents not merely a right to be exercised by the human being without unwarranted intrusion or deflection (this being a function of the limitations to that right upon which many writers have insisted), but also a human need, as explicated by Charlotte Towle (1957). For example, Biestek (1951) asserted that the social work client, "like every human being, can achieve his proximate goals, the perfection of his personality, intellectually, emotionally, socially, and spiritually, *only* through the exercise of his basic freedom. The client, specifically as a client, *needs* freedom to make his own choices of the available means in order to make casework help effective. Caseworkers, throughout the thirty years of casework literature, have given abundant practical testimony of the *futility of casework* when plans are superimposed upon the client" (p. 370; emphasis supplied). And a few years later, in the now classic *The Casework Relationship,* Biestek affirmed his convictions on this score by alluding to the "pragmatic observation that casework treatment was truly effective only when the client made his own choices and decisions" (McDermott, 1975, p. 18).

Both observations are subject to argument and require empirical testing, although they are widely supported on ideological grounds. Self-determination may justifiably be valued on such grounds, but it remains to be demonstrated that self-determination works so well either developmentally or therapeutically. On the contrary, to honor the concept of self-determination is often to defeat the purposes of social work intervention. Its confirmation as a guide to efficient social work practice, therefore, must be otherwise founded.

Self-Determination as a Social Work Value

Referring to "the innate dignity and value of the human person" as the "supreme value" of the social work profession, Biestek and Gehrig (1978, p. 1) go on to say that "client self-determination is the first logical consequence and test of the supreme value" (p. 4). They suggest that the concept has usually been accorded "second place in the hierarchy of social work values" (p. 4), not so much to assign it a lower ranking among the imperatives that guide and influence social work practice as to stress the significance of the value of human dignity and worth. As they put it, the value of client self-determination "declares that the human person has an innate right to make choices and decisions in those things that affect his life. To deprive him of that right is to deny his dignity and worth" (p. 4).

The keystone nature of self-determination extends beyond its indicative connotation in relation to human dignity and worth—which is indeed a fundamental value in the social work value system. It also functions as a kind of independent variable for social workers in that it may be viewed as the means to the realization of other social work values. In fact, Biestek and Gehrig suggest as much when, though acknowledging the controversial nature of the concept of self-determination, which they say has long endured, nevertheless describe it as "the focal point of the value system in social work" (p. 4). In this sense, the client's self-determination is, or should be, the determinant of whether or not the client receives treatment (Redlich and Mollica, 1976, p. 132), whether or not the client's confidences are shared (Blaine, 1964), whether or not a client's consent is informed and voluntary (Biklen, 1978).

As a social work value, client self-determination has its ethical significance for social work practice. That is, if client self-determination is truly valued by social workers as a group, it is reasonable to expect that social workers will act in their practice in such a manner as to preserve the self-determination of their clients. They will choose courses of professional action clearly and scrupulously designed to ensure the voluntariness and the intentionality of the choices, decisions, and actions of their clients. In Talcott Parsons's frame of reference, as Larson (1977) has characterized it: "Action as opposed to behavior is viewed essentially as the intervention of the element of decision making . . . between stimulus and response. The unit of analysis is an actor. An actor may be an individual, a group, or a society. A situation may be thought of as a stage, an arena, or a setting in which an actor is *obliged to decide between alternative* roles to play. The situation includes a variety of potential stimuli . . . for example objects, . . . norms, . . . and values" (p. 132; emphasis supplied).

For the social worker, an action premised on client self-determination as a value is an ethical action, an action in response to ethical responsibility, and an action derived from an analysis and weighing of alternatives. Included among the alternatives considered by the social worker are alternatives affecting other social work values, other ethical responsibilities, and the interests of others besides the social worker's client to whom the social worker's responsibility dictates or modifies the choice of action.

Decisiveness is a cultural counterpart to self-determination, which may explain in part the valuation of self-determination in social work. Indecisiveness may not always be "cured" in social work practice, but it is invariably judged, whether it is an affliction of social work clients or of social workers themselves. And of course one person's decisiveness may be another's indecision. "Scarcely anything will offend one so much as the charge that he is indecisive. The truer the charge, the more prompt and definite the reaction. Call a man wife beater, embezzler, pervert, liar, loafer, knave, and expect a disappointed pout. Say he is indecisive, and seismographs quiver. Accuse him of being insipid, dull, tedious, overbearing, arrogant, egotistical and with a condescending smirk he will ask if you aren't being just a trifle petty. Tell him he can't make a decision and he will turn blue with rage. A premium is placed on decisiveness in our culture" (Levy, 1962, p. 10).

Client Self-Determination as Ethical Responsibility in Social Work Practice

Despite its omission in earlier versions of the Code of Ethics of the National Association of Social Workers, client self-determination is given considerable emphasis in the version of the code adopted by the NASW Delegate Assembly in San Antonio, Texas in 1979 (National Association of Social Workers, 1979), either explicitly or by implication in other provisions in the code. To begin with, the code assigns primacy to the interests of clients: "The social worker's primary responsibility is to clients" (IIF), which indicates that the social worker who works with a client must be ever cognizant of the primary duty to the client, regardless of concurrent duties to others. This hardly means that the social worker is ethically free to ignore responsibilities to others. However, it is equally clear that duties to others cannot be favored over those to the client without good and sufficient, and perhaps compelling, reasons—reasons that can be substantiated, as the preamble to the code states, to the satisfaction "of an unbiased jury of peers," a test that every professional action is required to meet in confrontations with ethical issues in social work practice.

More specifically, the code confirms the rights and prerogatives of clients with the principle that "the social worker should make every effort to foster self-determination on the part of clients" (p. ii, G). The code, moreover, leaves entirely to social work clients discretion regarding any effect on their privacy and any sharing of confidences revealed in the course of their relationship with the social worker. From the social worker's point of view, "The social worker should respect the privacy of clients and hold in confidence all information obtained in the course of professional service" (p. ii, H).

Additional principles are specified that detail ethical responsibilities for the social worker affecting client self-determination, and other principles are included in the code that have bearing on the same ethical expectation. All are quite compatible with the concept of self-determination as it stands, without the cloud that has been placed upon it by the various restrictions and limitations on its operation. Thus, one entry states that "The social worker should under no circumstances engage in sexual activities with clients" (p. ii, F5), suggesting thereby that the client's response, even when collaborating in a sexual act, may not be entirely free and self-determining in view of the influential role that a social worker may play in the social worker–client relationship. In another context, but nevertheless one within which the risk to client self-determination may be similarly based, a provision in the code admonishes, "The social worker should not engage in any action that violates or diminishes the civil or legal rights of clients" (p. ii, G3).

The code also requires that the social worker afford clients reasonable access to records concerning them (pp. ii, 1, 3), with a caution affecting the confidences of others that may be contained in the records (pp. ii, 1, 4). And the code requires clients' informed consent before their activities are observed, taped, or recorded for use by others besides the social worker (pp. ii, 1, 3). In each case, the essential consideration is that what belongs to the client, or represents a risk or exposure for the client, becomes a matter for the client to decide and an ethical responsibility for the social worker to ensure for the client as a function of the client's self-determination.

These principles, as the preamble to the code states, are "intended to serve as a guide to the everyday conduct of members of the social work profession and as a basis for the adjudication of issues in ethics when the conduct of social workers is alleged to deviate from the standards expressed or implied in this code." The preamble also states that "in subscribing to and abiding by this code, the social worker is expected to view ethical responsibility in as inclusive a context as each situation demands and within which ethical judgment is required. The social worker, moreover, "is expected to take into consideration all the principles in this code that have a bearing upon any situation in which ethical judgment is to be exercised and professional intervention or conduct is planned" (National Association of Social Workers, 1979).

Now this may reflect the scope of considerations within which particular action choices must be made by the social worker in contending with the right to, and opportunities for, the exercise of self-determination by clients. But it may also explain some of the difficulty that social workers face in honoring client self-determination in social work practice. The expectation seems to be that many considerations require review before client self-determination can be honored. Perhaps it should be the other way around: Client self-determination may have to be honored unless and until other considerations compellingly and imperatively dictate otherwise. A brief review of some conflicting considerations, and some of the intrusions on client self-determination in which social workers may be inclined to participate, should indicate the bases for this assertion.

The Social Worker–Client Relationship

Social workers deal with a variety of clienteles in a variety of professional relationships. They also carry a wide range of professional responsibilities, some of which do not explicitly require the kind of relationship associated with the helping function usually characteristic of the social worker's professional role. It is to the helping function that client self-determination is especially relevant, since it is in, and as a consequence of, the performance of that function that issues affecting client self-determination arise.

These issues arise out of the very nature of the goals by which the social worker's helping function is guided, since the decision of whether to be treated or not, as well as the goals to aim for, are matters of critical concern to the social worker's clients. As such, therefore, they become matters of critical professional concern to the social worker, both because they represent a general focus of attention for the social worker in work with any clientele and because the social worker is required to walk a tight line between making decisions that affect clients and making sure that clients make those decisions for themselves to the maximum extent possible. That thin line between the two generally marks the distinction between the social worker's responsibility for competent and effective professional practice, and the social worker's responsibility for ethical professional practice.

The component of social work practice that affects the operation of client self-determination is present wherever and whenever the social worker is engaged in the performance of the social work helping function. It applies therefore to the full range of professional responsibilities that social workers carry. This includes so-called clinical practice, the broader meaning of which is direct work with individuals and groups, and the purpose of which is to assist them in the achievement of personal and group goals to which the social work helping function is relevant. It also includes administrative roles within the framework of which social workers assist boards, committees, and staff to implement institutional and service functions. In both, as in other social work relationships, self-determination is a significant consideration for the social worker as far as ethical responsibility is concerned, although its operation and application differs from relationship to relationship.

These variations in the operation and application of client self-determination are dramatically evident in the different ways in which social work clients become social work clients. Not all social worker–client relationships are voluntary in the sense that clients, on their own initiative and for purposes of their own design, seek out the assistance of social workers and make their own contractual arrangements with them. Many do, of course, but many do not. Even when some clients do look for and find the social work help that they feel or decide they need, they may not have the freedom or the capacity to decide the form of help that they will get—public welfare, for example, and free social service in hospitals and voluntary, nonprofit institutions.

Some become clients at the insistence of others—children who are brought to agencies to receive one form of treatment or another, for example, or court-assigned clienteles. And, finally, some become clients in spite of themselves—those, for example, who are "committed" to social work treatment as an alternative to incarceration or institutionalization or some other fate that they dread more than social work treatment, like persons convicted of sex offenses, child abuse, or mate battering.

The primary concern in this book is with "clinical" social work practice. However, notwithstanding all of the practical and philosophical variations in the operation and application of client self-determination, its basic concepts of professional ethics remain the same. Its essence still lies in the rather categorical conclusion that social work ethics—certainly as codified—requires the highest possible priority in the right and opportunity of clients to make their own choices and decisions in matters affecting their own lives and fate. If modifications in client self-determination are essential—and short of being essential, they cannot be justified on ethical grounds—then as the great Talmudist Hillel said, what is done is a function of commentary on the concept of client self-determination and not of its substance.

In this spirit, it is interesting to refer once again to an early notion of Biestek's (1951) regarding the social work client: "When he applies for the services of a social agency he has no intention, under ordinary circumstances, of surrendering either his basic right to freedom or any of its derivatives. . . . The client wants to know what choices are available to him and will welcome the caseworker's evaluation of each alternative, but he wants to remain free to make his own decisions" (p. 370).

Again, this observation is subject to dispute. It may apply to some clients but by no means all. Some clients skillfully manage to avoid the opportunity to make their own choices and may even resort to treatment in quest of a guarantee that they will not have to (compare with Levy, 1963b). Just as the proposition has been offered to the effect that the exercise of client self-determination may lead to failure without invalidating the concept of self-determination (Soyer, 1963), the proposition may be offered to the effect that clients may choose to exercise their self-determination by relinquishing jurisdiction over it. Giving up the right to choose is, in effect, a choice. This may require an arbitrary limit to client self-determination, which does not seem as excessive as some of the limits currently in operation in social work practice—namely, that client self-determination is not to be encouraged, in social work practice, to be used to give up self-determination. This paraphrases an old dictum in political theory to the effect that freedom cannot be used to give up freedom.

However, this is quite irrelevant to my immediate purpose, for the primary consideration is the ethical responsibility of the social worker—what it is incumbent upon the social worker to do or not to do in the interest of client self-determination.

This responsibility should be framed in terms reasonably reflective of the social worker's social responsibility and yet duly cognizant of the primacy of the ethical duty owed to clients:

> The objective of the principle of respect for the client's autonomy is to allow the client to make his own choices to the maximum extent that the situation and his competence permit. The social worker, in fact, must do

> all he can to make the situation as permissive as possible and to help the client to equip himself as well as he can to exercise his own judgment and initiative whenever and wherever practicable. This principle makes it incumbent on the social worker to "enable" the client to make his own decisions and to act for himself within the framework of existing laws and policy—although the worker may also help him attempt to change them—and any other reasonable boundary within which the client, like any other free and responsible citizen, is obliged to stay. Enabling implies that the practitioner should provide or illuminate the facts the client will need to make intelligent and realistic decisions. He should clarify the available alternatives as well as the anticipated consequences—to the extent that the client needs his help to do so [Levy, 1976, p. 144].

As problematic as the social worker's ethical responsibility is in relation to client self-determination affecting clients in a voluntary social worker–client relationship, it is obviously more problematic for professional relationships with assigned or involuntary clients, particularly clients in "total" institutions and correctional facilities. Nevertheless, the principle of ethical practice affecting client self-determination applies with the necessary differences introduced by the boundaries of third-party initiative and interest (parents of children who are clients, for example), and the boundaries of institutional restrictions and authority. Psychiatric patients and prisoners are hardly free to roam about at will or to choose their own courses of action at will, but whatever the boundaries of free choice to which they have access or to which persons are normally entitled, social workers' ethical responsibility is to so act and so conduct themselves as to stretch the self-determination of their clients to the most outer reaches of those boundaries. It may be that the test of client self-determination, as far as the social worker's relationship to it is concerned, is greatest when clients are not voluntary. The test is greatest when both social worker and client are severely limited by the setting, for then the social worker needs a good deal of imagination and a great deal of restraint to make client self-determination maximally possible and yet as effective as it can be in relation to the professional purposes to which the social worker's skill and intervention are addressed.

Elliot Studt (1954) put this point into helpful perspective when she drew an interesting parallel between the authority of the social worker in an authoritarian setting, like a prison, and the social worker in a voluntary agency—a family service agency, for example:

> Social work has long recognized that helping by means of the casework relationship depends upon the acknowledgement by the client that the caseworker is superior to himself for the *purposes of the problem at hand,* and so is able to help. . . . A formal authority relationship has always been able to secure certain external conformities in behavior, depending on the client's need to secure services. But a more meaningful influence relationship is achieved only when the client genuinely joins with the caseworker in dealing with a commonly acknowledged problem and gives to the caseworker temporary leadership responsibilities in this process. The caseworker accepts the temporary dependency implied in this relationship and attempts to encourage in the client whatever capacities for solving the problem exist within him. In this process, the particular authority relation-

> ship moves toward dissolution as the client becomes stronger and more able to deal independently with his situation. . . . Every casework relationship starts with a formal authority relationship [p. 233].

There is a tendency among social workers to justify intrusions on client self-determination on the basis of limitations of capacity or rationality perceived in clients and on the basis of what social workers regard as contravening or superseding values or interests—those of community and society, for example, or even of agency. They tend also to justify such intrusions on the basis of the interests and welfare of clients themselves—a justification that is acted upon with particular vigor because there is relatively little risk, as social workers see it, of the workers' satisfying an interest or preference of their own, not as long as they can demonstrate that what they do or neglect to do is for the good of the clients. In all of these cases, there is an imminent danger to client self-determination.

And the danger is a real one, with client self-determination giving way much too easily to other considerations, despite the priority that is acknowledged to be accorded to clients, who after all are the ones to whom professional responsibility is owed, the ones who subject themselves to all manner of risk because of their need for social work help, the ones to whom the loyalty and devotion of social workers are due and to whom specific commitments for service are made.

Speculation on the validity of a mathematical formula affecting the relationship between the social worker's autonomy as a professional practitioner and the client's autonomy as a client yields the following tentative formulation: The client's autonomy (and hence self-determination) is inversely related to the social worker's autonomy. Because in this respect the social worker is generally, though not invariably, in an advantageous position as compared with the client, the hazard to client self-determination would be quite real according to such a formula.

There is some empirical basis for this judgment, especially as it affects institutional settings, as Haug and Sussman (1969) have suggested: "Given bureaucratic delivery systems for professional services, the client is faced not only with the authority of the professional as practitioner, but also as administrator, armed with the regulations and rules of the institutional setting . . . the professional . . . in effect . . . draws upon organizational power as well as the power of his expertise to control the circumstances under which service is given. This aspect of professional autonomy is a function of the structural links between practitioner and administrator in any institutional setting" (pp. 154–155).

This hardly deprives clients of recourse to means for safeguarding their options. From the point of view of social work ethics, however, it seems clear that the social worker must be ever sensitive to the likelihood of relatively greater practitioner autonomy, based on the factors operating in the social worker–client relationships, to reduce if not deprive the client of opportunities for self-determination. From the point of view of social work ethics, moreover, it would appear that the greater part of the responsibility to avoid this consequence lies with the social worker.

Unfortunately, there is much in some concepts of social work practice to militate against the kind of practitioner sensitivity and initiative necessary to avoid this effect on client self-determination. Perlman encapsulates this observation in her penetrating comment on the "new controlling trends and intents" (National Association of Social Workers, 1967b, p. 52), which have cluttered the social work vocabulary recently and which carry rather subversive connotations as far as client self-determination is concerned. She does not mean to cast aspersions on the good will of social workers and the social work profession, for the aggressiveness of both in relation to the social injustices that continue to be heaped upon poor and innocent victims is quite well taken and justified. Still, if client self-determination is as much the value that it is purported to be for social workers, and if social workers are charged with ethical responsibility to nurture it, then a degree of constraint even on this score is indicated (compare with Levy, 1972).

A similar concern must attach to a kind of persevering dread of client resistance that is regarded as antithetical to the noble purposes of social work practice, although resistance is not infrequently one of the more noble manifestations of client self-determination (compare with Michaels, 1956). It may be appropriate to question social workers' apparent validation and facilitation of compliance on the part of clients when a treatment plan or procedure is jointly arrived at in relation to the treatment goals for the clients or to question the concern social workers express when clients do not comply (compare with Levy and Carter, 1976). According to Etzioni (1975), "Compliance is . . . a major element of the relationship between those who have power and those over whom they exercise it. . . . *Compliance* refers both to a relation in which an actor behaves in accordance with a directive supported by another actor's power, and to the orientation of the subordinated actor to the power applied" (p. 3). Implied is a kind of disappointment in the clients or in the practice if treatment does not proceed according to the social worker's plan, and yet that would appear to be what client self-determination is for. This should not appear to be inordinately easy. Client self-determination is a supreme test of the social worker's art as well as competence and philosophy. However, it hardly suggests a predetermined and social worker–preferred end.

It seems unnecessary, in the light of the literature on client self-determination and on social work practice in general, to explore any further the ways in which—even despite intentions to the contrary—social workers contrive, conspire, or otherwise manage to avoid the need or the compulsion to live up to the ethical requisites of client self-determination. Frieda Fromm-Reichmann's (1950) discussion of the tendencies and inclinations of psychiatrists that might stand in the way of patients' self-determination (among other things) is generally applicable to social workers. It also suggests the reaches and intensity of the intrusion on client self-determination.

Conclusions: When Is the Social Worker Exempt from Ethical Responsibility for Client Self-Determination?

The answer to this question, strictly speaking, is "never." If this seems harsh, categorical, and arbitrary, it is only because it must be. Another answer would be unreasonable. There can be no sensible reason for depriving clients of that which they would have if they had not sought, or been required to undergo, social work treatment.

The social worker's ethical responsibility in relation to client self-determination is no more absolute than a client's right to self-determination. Some limitation is essential, whether because of law, custom, the rights and immunities of others, or whatever, but these are limitations by which client self-determination may have to be guided rather than limitations to be imposed by the social worker to limit the client.

The social worker does have professional responsibility and opportunity to afford access of clients to all of the considerations affecting them or others, and the social worker does need skill in effecting such access. But that is only for the purpose of providing the grounds and foundation for the exercise by the client of self-determination. One caution in this connection is the need for awareness on the part of the social worker that there are ways of communicating relevant considerations to clients that amount to influence if not pressure. Social workers must be sensitive to the innuendos of certain gestures and intonations that belie spoken words, that amount to instruction and intimidation more than guidance, especially in relation to clients of the social worker and the social worker's role.

To disavow the social worker's responsibility in relation to law and social norms is not to imply collaboration or conniving with a client in the contravention of either—or even the facilitation of either. Nor does such a disavowal negate the freedom as well as professional responsibility to represent values with which the social work profession is associated, but again with the caution regarding the possibility of moving inadvertently and perhaps intentionally beyond guidance toward influence and pressure, more for compatibility with the social worker's vested interests than with the client's preferences (Wessel, 1961; Foot and Russell-Lacy, 1973).

The client's capacity sets some limit on the social worker's approach to effecting client self-determination. So do the boundaries and restrictions of authoritarian settings. But these limitations speak more for what the client is free and able to do than what the social worker does or does not do in relation to the client's self-determination.

Inevitably, in the contemplation of the ramifications of client self-determination, and of the social worker's responsibility, the questions arise: What if the client chooses to destroy himself or threatens to kill another person or to commit other serious offenses to self or to others—what is the social worker's responsibility? How does the social worker cope with ethical responsibility in relation to client self-determination? First of all, there are reasonable differences of view regarding a client's right to commit suicide so that it is not possible to assert with any definitiveness that it cannot be permitted by the social worker if there is any opportunity at all to intercede. Social workers as a group are not that sure that the client does not have that right, whatever they may be able to do to discourage action upon it. It is an option that a client might be privileged to exercise if not engaged in a social worker–client relationship. Why, therefore, should it not be available to a person who is so engaged?

But for those social workers who feel that they cannot condone such an act and feel moved to avert it, does their intervention constitute an alternative principle of ethical practice or the obviation of the principle of client self-determination? The argument in this chapter suggests that it is the latter, with the failure to honor the principle of client self-determination being justified on the basis of priority being accorded to what is regarded as a higher value—that of life. It is still a violation of a principle of ethical practice, but one based on compelling considerations. Interference with a client's threat to another's life would be similarly justified—not merely with respect to the social worker depriving the client of self-determination, but also, perhaps, with respect to the social worker's betraying of the confidence that the client may have shared in expressing the intention to commit the murder. Neither is ethical, but both may be justified on the basis of contravening value considerations, and put as such to peers for review. Again, the major criterion would be whether the considerations militating against the social worker's honoring the principle of client self-determination are so compelling and so amenable to substantiation on value grounds that even the principle of client self-determination must fall. But it would still be violated.

This represents a rather different starting point for the comprehension of client self-determination than has been customary. Let us leave it as such in the hope that the concept may be differently, and perhaps better, understood.

References

Biestek, F. P. "The Principle of Client Self-Determination." *Social Casework,* 1951, *32* (9), 369–375.

Biestek, F. P. "Basic Values in Social Work." In National Association of Social Workers, *Values in Social Work: A Re-Examination.* New York: National Association of Social Workers, 1967.

Biestek, F. P., and Gehrig, C. C., *Client Self-Determination in Social Work: A Fifty Year History.* Chicago: Loyola University Press, 1978.

Biklen, D. "Consent as a Cornerstone Concept." In J. S. Mearig and Associates, *Working for Children: Ethical Issues Beyond Professional Guidelines.* San Francisco: Jossey-Bass, 1978.

Blaine, G. B. "Divided Loyalties: The College Therapist's Responsibility to the Student, the University and the Parents." *American Journal of Orthopsychiatry,* 1964, *34* (3), 481–485.

Brieland, D., and Lemmon, J. *Social Work and the Law.* St. Paul, Minn.: West Publishing, 1977.

Etzioni, A. *Comparative Analysis of Complex Organizations: On Power, Involvement, and Their Correlates.* (Rev. ed.) New York: Free Press, 1975.

Foot, H. C., and Russell-Lacy, S. P. "The Imposition of Values in Social Casework." *Social Casework,* 1973, *54* (9), 511–518.

Frankel, C. "The Impact of Changing Values on the Family." *Social Casework,* 1976, *57* (6), 355–365.

Fromm-Reichmann, F. *Principles of Intensive Psychotherapy.* Chicago: University of Chicago Press, 1950.

Haug, M. R., and Sussman, M. B. "Professional Autonomy and the Revolt of the Client." *Social Problems,* 1969, *17* (2), 153–161.

Larson, C. J. *Major Themes in Sociological Theory.* (2nd ed.) New York: McKay, 1977.

Levy, C. S. "Decisions! Decisions!" *Adult Leadership,* 1962, *2* (1), 10–12, 26.

Levy, C. S. "Decision-Making and Self-Determination." *Adult Leadership,* 1963a, *12* (3), 68–69, 90.

Levy, C. S. "Social Worker and Client as Obstacles to Client Self-Determination." *Journal of Jewish Communal Service,* 1963b, *39* (4), 416–419.
Levy, C. S. "Values and Planned Change." *Social Casework,* 1972, *53* (8), 488–493.
Levy, C. S. *Social Work Ethics.* New York: Human Sciences Press, 1976.
Levy, R. L., and Carter, R. D. "Compliance with Practitioner Instigations." *Social Work,* 1976, *21* (3), 188–193.
McDermott, F. E. (Ed.). *Self-Determination in Social Work.* Boston: Routledge & Kegan Paul, 1975.
Michaels, R. "Giving Help to Resisting Patients." *Social Work,* 1956, *1* (4), 76–83.
National Association of Social Workers. *Code of Ethics.* Adopted by the Delegate Assembly. New York: National Association of Social Workers, October 1960.
National Association of Social Workers. *Code of Ethics.* Amended by the Delegate Assembly. New York: National Association of Social Workers, April 11, 1967a.
National Association of Social Workers. *Values in Social Work: A Re-Examination.* New York: National Association of Social Workers, 1967b.
National Association of Social Workers. *Code of Ethics.* Adopted by the Delegate Assembly. Washington, D.C.: National Association of Social Workers, November 18, 1979.
Perlman, H. H. "Self-Determination: Reality or Illusion?" *Social Service Review,* 1965, *39* (4), 410–421.
Redlich, F., and Mollica, R. F. "Overview: Ethical Issues in Contemporary Psychiatry." *American Journal of Psychiatry,* 1976, *133* (2), 125–136.
Salzberger, R. P. "Casework and a Client's Right to Self-Determination." *Social Work,* 1979, *24* (5), 398–400.
Soyer, D. "The Right to Fail." *Social Work,* 1963, *8* (3), 72–78.
Studt, E. "An Outline for Study of Social Authority Factors in Casework." *Social Casework,* 1954, *35* (6), 231–238.
Towle, C. *Common Human Needs.* (Rev. ed.) New York: National Association of Social Workers, 1957.
Wessel, R. "Implications of the Choice to Work for Mothers in the Aid to Dependent Children Program." *Training for Service in Public Assistance.* Washington, D.C.: Department of Health, Education and Welfare, 1961.

42

Consumerism and Clients' Rights

Burton Gummer

Of the many social processes at work in our society, two often singled out as important in promoting major social changes are the increase in society's "knowledgeableness" and the movement toward greater equality. Knowledgeableness refers to both the total amount of knowledge (how much is known) and the number of people who have that knowledge (how many know what is known). As is often pointed out, the total amount of knowledge is increasing at an exponential rate. The library holdings of major American universities, for example, have doubled approximately every twenty years since the early nineteenth century. Similarly, significant increases in educational levels have paralleled the increasing number of people attending schools of all sorts, and the opportunities for access to advanced (college and graduate) education have opened up (Bell, 1973).

While the amount of equality in a society is more difficult to document, there are indications that the norm of equality has become more firmly fixed in the social, political, and economic philosophies of the American people. Recent public policies have attempted to promote the equalization of the conditions of all citizens. Examples include the extension of the vote to disenfranchised groups, progressive taxation schemes, extensive social welfare benefits and services, and programs for normalizing the social lives of heretofore excluded and stigmatized individuals. While there is debate over whether these policies have been successful in producing increases in the actual amount of equality, there appears to be agreement about the norm of more equality as a central tenet of America's public philosophy.

These general social processes have had an important effect on the social services in terms of how the providers and recipients of services should deal with each other. As the knowledge differentials between provider and recipient have declined, and the legitimacy of all kinds of inequalities has been called into question, the mechanisms for the provision of services have undergone major criticisms, and a number of alternatives have been proposed. Charles Reich's (1964) ground-breaking analysis of the social services as a form of "new property" can be taken as the approximate starting point of the contemporary attack on the traditional approaches to the provision of services. The decade of the 1960s saw both an increase in criticisms of established ways of providing services and a number of experiments with new forms (Rubin, 1967; Gilbert, 1969; Kaufman, 1969; Kramer, 1969; Vosburg and Hyman, 1973).

This chapter will examine one approach to reforming the provision of social services that has attracted a fair amount of attention in the past few years and may receive even greater attention in the future because of its special appeal to conservative policy makers. This is the notion of treating the recipient of social benefits and services as a "consumer," as distinct from a client (in the professional-client sense) or from the object of public or private charity. Given the social forces at play in contemporary life, the attraction of this idea is readily understandable. In the classic, free-market context from which the concept derives its primary meaning for most Americans, a consumer is a person who has: comprehensive knowledge of the kind and quality of goods and services available in the market; the ability to freely choose among those goods and services so as to maximize self-interests; and, a nondependent relationship with the producers of these goods and services, secured by control over personal expenditure decisions (that is, producers and consumers are mutually dependent because each controls resources the other needs). The ideal consumer is a knowledgeable, equal, and self-directing actor in whichever marketplace he or she chooses to enter.

The notion of the social service recipient as consumer is appealing for at least two reasons. This role has intrinsic appeal for Americans because it embodies so many strongly held national values. Individual competency to choose and act, freedom from restraint, the latitude to establish one's own life directions along with the responsibility for personally assuming the consequences of bad choices—all are central to the American dream. In addition, the consumer role has a special appeal to planners of social service systems who see it as a device for correcting some of the major shortcomings of those systems (Piliavin, 1968; Feldstein, 1971; Reid, 1972; Pruger and Miller, 1973; Perlman, 1975). The purposes of this chapter are to (1) examine the problems in our service systems that might be corrected by the introduction of consumerism; (2) identify the conditions that must be present in order for consumerism to work in the social services; and (3) assess the potential worth of consumerism as a strategy for service reform.

The Structure of the American Welfare System

While it is difficult to characterize something as complex as the American welfare system, certain features can be critical in shaping the form it takes and the way it operates. These same features, moreover, are also the source of its major shortcomings. American welfare programs are, by and large, residual, professionalized, bureaucratized, and outside the market. Wilensky and Lebeaux (1965) introduced the term *residual* to describe welfare systems exclusively for the very poor. (The opposite of a residual system according to their scheme is an institutional system, in which services are universally available regardless of one's income.) In a residual system, the recipients are extremely dependent on the providers because of their dire financial and personal straits. Having to be impoverished in order to qualify for services, one must approach the system as a supplicant. This situation has great potential for abuse unless legal and administrative safeguards are created to curtail arbitrariness and cavalier treatment (Handler and Hollingsworth, 1969; Handler, 1973; Gummer, 1979a).

Another feature of our welfare system is that many who work in it aspire to professional status. For social workers, the leading occupation in the system, the enhancement and legitimization of their professional status is a major concern. An important characteristic of a professionalized service system, or one aspiring to be recognized as such, is that the professional must retain the final prerogative for deciding on the nature of the presenting problem and the most appropriate strategies for dealing with it. A professionalized activity is one in which, as Boulding (1968) points out: "the activity originates from the profession rather than from the client, from the supplier rather than the demander. In its extreme form it takes the form of, "What you need is what I as your professional advisor have to give you; what you want is quite irrelevant" (p. 204).

While there are attempts to temper the nondemocratic and authoritative character of a professionally provided service, in the last analysis a professional must act on the basis of his or her own judgment, answerable only to colleagues. In this context, Eulau (1973) argues that "Client participation in decisions appropriately within the province of the professions violates the constitutional basis of the professional-client relationship. This basis cannot be democratic if professional service is to have any meaning" (p. 185).

As the American welfare system has grown in size and scope since the 1930s, the standard organizational form for the agencies comprising it, both in the public and voluntary sectors, is the complex bureaucracy. Bureaucratization, like professionalism, has many consequences for the ways in which service recipients encounter providers (Freidson, 1970a). The strength of bureaucracy as an organizational form stems, in part, from its ability to deal with situations so large in magnitude (number of people, mix of technologies, extensiveness of operations) that they overwhelm other types of organizations. Bureaucracies are able to deal with complex situations because of their capacity to develop internal structures as complex and differentiated as the environments they confront. This process, specialization through the division of labor, is both its strength and, from the recipient's perspective, its major weakness.

The problems people bring to social agencies are the problems of everyday living. These are the problems that arise from the struggle to maintain a suitable income; physical and mental health; satisfying relationships with family, friends, and neighbors; and feelings of worthwhileness, purpose, and meaning. These facets of our lives are connected in a "seamless web" such that when one part breaks down, the consequences for the others are immediate and direct. But bureaucratically organized service systems cannot deal with seamless webs. They have specialized functions to perform, and potential users of their services must somehow redefine their overall life problems into terms that can be understood and encoded by these organizations. The resulting problems to service recipients—fragmentation, discontinuity, and inaccessibility—in bureaucratic service systems have been extensively documented (Robb, 1965; Gilbert, 1972; Kahn, 1976).

Another characteristic feature of bureaucracies is what has come to be known as "organizational maintenance." As an organization develops, it acquires characteristic ways of doing things. It settles on a primary mission (its major service objectives), a distinctive way of pursuing those objectives (its service technologies), and a way of organizing its internal operations (its administrative style). As the organization becomes an ongoing concern, its members develop commitments to the maintenance of these arrangements (Selznick, 1948). The major motivation for doing so is based in the benefits (jobs, incomes, statuses, prerogatives) derived from existing arrangements. If the process of organizational maintenance proceeds unchecked, a form of "organizational pathology" develops where resources are increasingly directed to satisfying the interests of organizational members rather than to producing services for recipients (Blau, 1963; Rein, 1964). To the extent that service recipients are not considered members of the provider organization, and therefore have little opportunity to make their preferences known concerning how resources should be distributed, there will be few obstacles to the allocation of those resources in ways that primarily satisfy the interests of those able to exercise the greatest power in the system.

A last characteristic of the service system to be addressed here is that the social services, as Titmuss (1968) remarked, lie "outside or on the fringes of the so-called free market, the mechanisms of price, and the tests of profitability" (p. 20). The absence of a market is for some the distinctive feature of the social services. Drucker (1973), for instance, details the consequences of the absence of a market for the structure and operations of social service organizations: "The one basic difference between a service institution and a business is the way the service institution is paid. Businesses (other than monopolies) are paid for satisfying the customer. They are only paid when they produce what the customer wants and what he is willing to exchange his purchasing power for. Satisfaction of the customer is, therefore, the basis for performance and results in a business. Service institutions, by contrast, are typically paid out of a budget allocation. Their revenues are allocated from a general revenue stream that is not tied to what they are doing, but is obtained by tax, levy, or tribute. . . . Being paid out of a budget allocation changes what is meant by 'performance' or 'results.' *'Results' in the budget-based institution means a bigger budget. 'Performance' is the ability to maintain or to increase one's budget*" (pp. 49–50; emphasis in original).

This results in managers of service organizations being primarily concerned with anticipating and satisfying the interests of funders, with a consequent lessening of the attention they can give to the interests of service recipients. In its most extreme form, the budgetary process can totally undermine the autonomy of service organizations as they become "captives" of budget officers, as Sarri and Hasenfeld (1978) observe, and "thus come to serve their interests rather than the interests of the population they were established to serve" (p. 4). The social service system, in short, becomes dominated by funders, rather than providers or users. Moreover, because of the fiscal orientation of funders, their primary interests lie in promoting program efficiency (reduced costs per unit of service) rather than program effectiveness (services that actually solve or ameliorate recipients' problems).

These features of social service systems produce many undesirable consequences for recipients. Since they must be very poor in order to qualify for most social services, recipients can only gain access to the system when they are in a weakened and powerless condition. While professionalism and bureaucratization involve very different ways of organizing work, from the recipients' perspective the consequences of both are the same in terms of reducing, or eliminating, their voice in determining the nature of the service. Both processes produce service providers with a marked tendency to ignore the concerns of recipients. Their orientations are elsewhere. For bureaucrats, on the one hand, the primary concern can easily become the protection and enhancement of the role of their offices and functions in the overall operations of the organization. Professionals, on the other hand, are often preoccupied with the "state of the art" in their areas of practice, and their opportunities for acquiring and mastering new techniques. These techniques, moreover, may or may not be responsive to client problems, but their acquisition is essential for enhancing one's professional reputation with colleagues. Finally, because of the nonmarket nature of the service system, funders have a disproportionate role in determining the nature and operations of social programs.

The Consumer Model: Prerequisites

Advocates of consumerism argue that the service delivery problems just discussed can be dealt with by enabling recipients to function as consumers. This claim will be examined from two perspectives. The first concerns the question of whether the consumer model can, in fact, be applied to the social services. Are the assumptions underlying consumerism and social services sufficiently congruent to allow a blending of the two? The second line of inquiry will address the desirability of doing so. Assuming that consumerism can be applied to at least parts of the service system, is this a good thing?

In the ideal model of consumerism, one must have the following things: the freedom to choose one's purchases (a basic assumption of a free-market society is that people are free to dispose of their incomes as they deem proper, within the constraints of civil order); knowledge of what's available in the market (the kind and quality of goods and services and their potential utility for satisfying one's needs); and the financial wherewithal to purchase what one wants. The following discussion will examine the extent to which these requirements can be accommodated within the existing framework for social services.

Freedom of Choice. Are the users of social services free to choose which services they want? This question raises fundamental issues about the nature of social welfare in this society. One approach to the question is to disaggregate the general social welfare field into its major functional areas and analyze each separately. At least three distinct functions are performed under the name of social welfare: (1) providing a minimum standard of living for all members of society; (2) maintaining conformity to established codes of social behavior; and (3) promoting the general welfare. (The following discussion draws upon ideas presented in Rimlinger, 1966; Beck, 1967; Shlonsky, 1971; Carrier and Kendall, 1973.)

Ours is a market society in which the basic way of acquiring income is through remunerated work. If one is unable to work, various forms of transfer payments are made to maintain the person at what society considers an acceptable minimum level of living. The form and amount of these payments are roughly correlated with the reason the individual is not working. Regardless of the form, however, all such payments carry with them varying degrees of social opprobrium and behavioral requirements to which the recipient must conform. Failure to perform adequately in the economic market is a basic failure in this society and is treated with official harshness. "We are brutal in the giving of money we define as relief." Schorr (1966) observes: "We are sweetly charitable only when we have succeeded in defining the gift as something else—social security, urban renewal, business deduction" (p. 24).

The act of receiving public aid puts one in the degraded status of being poor. This degradation stems from the almost universal assumption in this society that the poor are less-than-adequate and are culpable in promoting their own poverty (Coser, 1965; Alston and Dean, 1972; Matza and Miller, 1976). One form this degradation takes is the reduction in the aid recipient's freedom to choose. As Coser points out: "When monies are allocated to the poor, they do not have free disposition over their use. They must account to their donors for their expenses and the donors decide whether the money is spent 'wisely' or 'foolishly'" (p. 142).

Depending upon the state of the economy and the political mood of the country, the degree of official control and harassment will vary (what one wag calls the "hassle factor"), but even under the best of circumstances the condition of the official (welfare) poor is kept "less eligible" for minimum standards for decent treatment, in the historic tradition of the Poor Laws. The poor as consumer, within the American context, is a poor joke at best and, at worst, a distraction from the realities of the situation. As long as our public aid system remains for the very poor only—and there are no indications that this will change in the foreseeable future—it will continue to perform, in addition to its stated function of providing a minimum level of financial aid, its unstated but equally important function of the "overseer of the poor," where its primary role is to monitor, sanction, and control the behavior of its charges (Perrow, 1978).

While sanctioning of undesirable behavior operates at a covert level in financial assistance programs, there is a second area of the social services where this is the explicit mission. Every society has a system of roles and statuses in which its members are expected to function. Traditionally, the preparation of individuals for the assumption of these roles has been left to the primary social units of family, friends, neighbors, locally controlled schools, and religious and civic associations. An important social change in this century, however, has been the decline in the influence of these socializing agents and a consequent rise in the amount of deviant and anomic behavior. Social welfare organizations are increasingly called upon to augment the work of these groups, and social programs currently play a major role in promoting conformity to established patterns of individual, familial, and community behavior (Lasch, 1977; Janowitz, 1978).

An individual who seriously deviates from prescribed social patterns is, much like the recipient of public aid, viewed as a failure in one of life's major roles. We should therefore expect similar limitations on the amount of choice or influence such an individual can exercise over social programs aimed at promoting acceptable social behavior. This is not, however, the case. There is a growing amount of political and social enfranchisement of individuals who, a mere decade ago, were subjected to varying degrees of coercive, authoritarian, and punitive treatments. Inmates of all kinds, such as prisoners, psychiatric patients, delinquents, physically and mentally disabled; homosexuals and other proponents of alternate personal and family styles; nonnative and nonwhite minorities—all are acquiring, or have acquired, a degree of political and social power that enables them to successfully resist attempts to restrict their freedom to choose on issues affecting their lives.

One of the factors contributing to this phenomenon is the decline in the ability of established social and political elites to maintain the allegiance of the general population to patterns of behavior prescribed by them. Pfaff (1980, p. 70) identifies some possible reasons for this:

> The American experience since the nineteen-fifties has been of dismantled hierarchies. . . . In our time, the Protestant ascendancy has lost its force. It has included a national political elite, but that "establishment" made its last stand during the Second World War, when its members oversaw, among other things, the creation of the modern American foreign-policy and intelligence organizations. Vietnam finished them off as a coherent and confident governing elite. Our surviving government apparatus of international affairs no longer possesses a recognizable class character, and this circumstance marks only one dramatic development in a national situation. Conservatives call our condition twilight, in which, according to Robert Nisbet, "the loss of confidence in political institutions is matched by the erosion of traditional authority in kinship, locality, culture, language, school, and other elements of the social fabric." Certainly we are in a situation we could not have expected even twenty-five years ago, when American life and government were still dominated by a Protestant gentry certain of its values. . . . [I]t is only now that the United States has really discovered what it is to be a society without a recognizable governing class, and thus without that consensus on political values which is implicit in the existence of such a class.

While this development troubles those concerned with decline in our social and moral order, it has provided a serendipitous gain in the civil and social rights of members of groups long outside the mainstream of American life. This development increases the possibilities of introducing consumer mechanisms since potential service recipients are now in a much stronger position to make their preferences about services known and acted upon. The American Psychiatric Association's declassification of homosexuality from a pathological to a nonpathological category is but one example of the break-up in the dominance of established groups and the empowerment of those recently considered social outcasts.

Because of these developments, this second category of services is starting to overlap with the third, the promotion of the general welfare. This is the sector of the social services that deals neither with the poor nor with the deviant, but addresses the social and psychological problems of the population at large. These are individuals not classified as failures in any of their major life roles, but instead are seen as needing help in dealing with social and psychological stresses attendant upon the normal conduct of those roles. Whereas the function of the social services in the first two categories is to control behavior, in this category the goal is to provide support so as to enhance an individual's ability to function. The differences between support and control are spelled out by Cumming (1968): "Support has the diffusely positive quality of encouragement or reward. . . . Control always has at least the overtones of punishment; it is meant to suppress or isolate disruptive behavior or to enforce prescribed behavior in the interest of the common good. . . . The agent is supporting the client when he recognizes the requirements that the client expresses, or when he responds affirmatively to the behavior of the client's own choosing. The agent controls the client when he expects behavior that conforms to standards that the client does not understand or does not subscribe to, and can enforce his expectations with sanctions" (pp. 6, 9–10). It is here that recipients come closest to meeting the assumption in the consumer model about freedom of choice. These services deal with the discontent rather than the deviant and disreputable and are thus relatively free from societal prescriptions.

The extent to which the freedom of choice requirement is met, then, is a function of the degree to which the recipient is seen as having failed to perform in one or more major life roles. Moreover, failure to perform in economic roles is treated more harshly than failure to perform in social roles where, because of the growing delegitimization of traditional authorities, there is a decline in the established mechanisms for social control and a growing empowerment of the socially disaffiliated.

Knowledge of Available Services. The second requirement in the consumer model is access to information about available services and their utility for satisfying one's needs. There are at least two obstacles to the free flow of this information: intrinsic obstacles arising from the nature of the material itself and extrinsic obstacles placed around a body of information. Intrinsic obstacles occur primarily when information is so technical it requires special training for its comprehension and application. Much of medicine falls in this category, along with large parts of law and the more arcane psychotherapies such as psychoanalysis. Extrinsic obstacles refer to situations where, while the information itself can be readily understood by the average person, there are considerations of a political, administrative, or professional nature that prevent its free flow. Obstacles to information flows in the social services, moreover, tend to be primarily of this kind.

If politics is the art of "who gets what, when, and how," political obstacles to the flow of information arise when the distribution of services is such that different groups want to keep it a secret. Psychiatric and counseling services, for example, tend to be distributed along economic and social class lines. Poor patients are far more likely to receive custodial care in institutions, while the affluent more often receive psychotherapy on an outpatient basis (Hollingshead and Redlich, 1958; Purvine and Ryan, 1969; Gruber, 1980). The bureaucratic harassment that recipients of public assistance are routinely subjected to is justified in the public mind by the presumption that alternative sources of income are available in the job market. If information about the actual distribution of employment opportunities for this group of people were widely disseminated, it would seriously challenge the conventional wisdom about why people need public assistance (Rein, 1977; Garfinkel, 1978). The political approach to information, as Burke (1945) shrewdly observes, strives to "sharpen up the pointless and blunt the too sharply pointed" (p. 393).

Similarly, administrative obstacles to information arise when what might be considered excessive shares of social service budgets are absorbed in administrative and personnel costs. A social agency's legitimacy is questioned when its members are suspected of benefiting at the expense of recipients. Thus, the debate over New York City's financial crisis follows quite different lines if one views it as an excess of greediness on the part of municipal employees rather than an excess of humanitarianism on the part of the city's leaders (Piven, 1973). Other kinds of information administrators have an interest in suppressing include evaluative studies questioning the efficiency or effectiveness of a program; procedures for determining eligibility and the assignment of clients to different kinds of services; criteria for hiring, retaining, and promoting staff (Noble, Jr., and Wechsler, 1970; Piliavin and McDonald, 1977; Rossi, 1978)—in short, the kinds of information that, if widely known, would seriously interfere with the ability of organizational leaders to operate with what they consider to be a sufficient amount of discretion and autonomy (Gouldner, 1963).

A third source of interference with the flow of information comes from the various professional groups employed in the social services. One of the hallmarks of a profession is its command of a body of esoteric knowledge. The literal meaning of esoteric is something known only to a few. The reason only a few are presumed to have professional knowledge is that its intrinsic difficulty requires special training for its comprehension. For many of the human service professions, however, the knowledge that forms the basis of practice—knowledge derived primarily from the social and behavioral sciences—can be acquired without a great deal of specialized training (Lindblom and Cohen, 1979). Because of this, there is an unfortunate tendency on the part of human service professionals (and others, for that matter) to create obfuscating smokescreens around what they know as a way of protecting and promoting their claims to professional status. In the most extreme case, this takes the form of what Freidson (1970a) calls the "imperialism of knowledge": "The [professional] . . . does not see his work as merely different than another's. He develops around it an ideology and, with the best of intentions, an imperialism which stresses the technical superiority of his work and of his capacity to perform it. . . . The pathology arises when outsiders may no longer evaluate the work by the rules of logic and the knowledge available to all educated men, and when the only legitimate spokesman on an issue relevant to all men must be someone who is officially certified" (p. 92).

Considering the number of obstacles to the dissemination of information about the social services, the interesting thing is the dramatic increase in the amount of information about them currently available to the public at large, including service recipients. It has been said that information is to the twentieth century what land was to the nineteenth as a basis of power. Beginning in the 1960s with the successful efforts of the Welfare Rights Organizations, the consumer advocacy groups formed by Ralph Nader, and other advocacy and client-rights organizations, the importance of access to information as part of reform strategies has been stressed. Affirmative action guidelines, Sunshine Laws, informed consent, and truth-in-lending are some of the formal expressions of the efforts of those outside professional and bureaucratic organizations—both in the nonprofit and profit sectors—to gain legal access to information previously considered the exclusive preserve of professionals, bureaucrats, and owners.

While one should not be overly sanguine about the ease with which previously restricted information will continue to be made available to the general public, there are indications that social service systems will move toward more, rather than less, openness. This would be in keeping with what appears to be a climate in this country opposing secrecy in government, business, and the professions. A society that permits information about its espionage activities to appear in the newspapers and requires its highest-ranking public officials to disclose their personal financial holdings and dealings will certainly be one that will also require its social welfare professionals and administrators to "eschew obfuscation" when presenting how and why they arrive at their decisions and what the probable consequences of those decisions will be.

Financial Resources for Recipients. The third thing one needs to function as a consumer is the financial wherewithal for acquiring the goods and services one wants. This, interestingly, might prove the least difficult of the three to accomplish. Since the mid-1960s, there has been a shift in social policy from what is called the "services strategy" toward a "cash" or "incomes strategy." The arguments advanced from various disciplines and political perspectives converge on several points. Social services, usually taken to mean personal services such as individual and family counseling, vocational counseling, and the like, have not proven effective in dealing with the problems of the poor and the near poor. They are labor-intensive, proceed from shaky theoretical and empirical bases, are difficult to administer, and have had either indiscernible or negative effects on recipients' problems (Gilbert, 1966; Fischer, 1973; Hoshino, 1973; Rein, 1975). Services should be replaced as much as possible with cash provided through transfer mechanisms with the least deleterious effects on work incentives (Hefferman, 1972; Garfinkel, 1978; Worcester, Jr., 1980). Proponents of the incomes strategy argue, as Rabinovitz, Pressman, and Rein (1976) point out, that the following considerations will produce better social policies:

(1) We should design simple, straightforward programs that require as little management as possible.
(2) Programs predicated on continuing high levels of competence, on expeditious interorganization coordination, or on sophisticated methods for accommodating diversity and heterogeneity are very vulnerable.
(3) Policy designers should prefer to operate through manipulated prices and markets rather than through substantive regulations, through delivering cash rather than services, through communicating by means of smaller rather than larger units of social organization, through seeking clearances from fewer rather than more levels of consultation and review [pp. 414–415].

Both liberal and conservative policy analysts see in cash transfers a mechanism for dealing with social problems that: (1) has a strong common-sense appeal (the problem of the poor is no money); (2) is relatively easy to administer (the Social Security Administration is a model of efficient public management); (3)

reduces professional and bureaucratic interference into the personal lives of recipients (a concern among "rights" advocates of the left and the right); and (4) brings market forces to bear since recipients will have income to dispose of in ways they deem appropriate (the preferred strategy of conservatives).

To summarize, of the three preconditions for consumerism in the social services—freedom of choice, knowledge of options, and financial resources—the most problematic is the first, and that only when considering recipients experiencing economic as opposed to personal or social difficulties. In general, there is enough convergence between the requirements of a consumer approach and the current framework for social services to make it a feasible strategy for service reform. This leaves the question of whether consumerism is a desirable strategy.

Consumerism and Service Reform

This chapter began with a discussion of the kinds of problems in our service systems that any reform strategy must address. These problems, moreover, have one common element: They arise from a structured power imbalance between service institutions and service recipients. A critical criterion for assessing any reform strategy, then, is the extent to which it can reduce this imbalance. Power imbalances in social life are created, according to Emerson's (1962) scheme, when a person is dependent upon another for needed resources under the other's control and for which there are no alternative sources of supply. The extent of the imbalance is a function of the degree of one's dependence on the resource and the ease with which one can gain access to alternative sources. This framework provides a guide for judging the efficacy of consumerism as a reform strategy.

Of the two factors in the framework, degree of dependency and availability of alternatives, the first will be largely unaffected by changes that would come about through consumer mechanisms. As noted earlier, the American welfare system is primarily a residual one. The vast majority of its services and benefits are available only to the very poor, with the result that recipients are extremely dependent on these services. The only rational strategy for reducing dependency on welfare services and benefits is to establish institutionalized financial supports through fiscal and employment policies (for example, significantly increased minimum wages, family allowances, full employment), which would provide a minimum level of support for all citizens that was well above the poverty line. This, in turn, would require radical changes in our national economic and social policies along aggressively redistributional and egalitarian lines, changes that are obviously not in the offing. So as regards a major source of power imbalance in our system—its residual nature—consumerism cannot be expected to have any impact. Nor, for that matter, will any reform strategy because the very nature of reform is to modify existing arrangements rather than replace them with entirely new ones.

Consumerism can be expected to have an impact, however, through its reputed ability to increase the number of alternative service suppliers and thus to redress power imbalances by increasing the options open to recipients. A typical scenario for a consumer-based service system starts with the provision of financial resources—in the form of cash, vouchers, or credits—to potential service users. Proponents of consumerism in education, for instance, suggest that the equivalent of the government's per pupil expenditure be made available in the form of special-purpose vouchers to parents, who would then be free to spend them on educational programs of their own choosing. Because the needs for and consequently the cost of social services are not as predictable as education for a given family, the financing of consumer-based social services would more appropriately employ credit mechanisms or third-party payments along the lines of existing public health insurance programs (Medicaid and Medicare).

Once they have the financial wherewithal, consumers would then explore the "market" to see what kinds of services are available for the problems they have. It is at this point that knowledge of the service system is crucial. Pruger and Miller (1973) present the kind of information-processing system a consumer-oriented service organization would have to install so that appropriate information would be provided to consumers, along with the necessary technical assistance of how to put the information to best use. In addition to knowledge of service options, this stage of the scenario assumes that options do, in fact, exist. That is, the service system cannot be organized along monopoly lines if the consumer approach is to work.

Critics of consumerism in the human services frequently point to American medicine as an example of a situation where market mechanisms predominate, the patient is a consumer (in name, at least), and yet the system is as unresponsive and inefficient and falls as far short of its goals of promoting the health of all the population as any other service system in this country (Titmuss, 1968 and 1971). However, it is difficult to tell to what extent this is a shortcoming in the consumer approach and to what extent a function of other characteristics of our medical system, most notably the monopoly position of physicians in that system. For a consumer model to work, the consumer must have choices as well as be able to make choices. Medical care in the United States offers practically no alternatives to the putative consumer except hospital-based, physician-controlled, high-technology, aggressive physical-chemical treatments (Illich, 1976). The lack of alternatives, moreover, is attributed to the near-monopoly control that the medical professional exercises over the entire health-care system (Freidson, 1970b). The "consumer" of medical services today is in pretty much the same position as the "consumer" of a Model T Ford when Henry Ford, the leading force in that industry, said: "You can have any color you want, as long as it's black!"

This, however, is not the case in the social services. In fact, as the influence and control of professional social work has lessened in the past decade and a half, particularly in the public sector, there has been a marked increase in the number of alternative approaches for dealing with the problems service users present. While this has become a serious challenge to the social work profession in terms of redefining its place and role in the social service system, it can prove salutory for recipients who now have real options, provided they have the wherewithal and opportunity to exercise them (Reid, 1977; Gummer, 1979b; Meyer, 1979). Reid (1972) details the kinds of advantages that would accrue to recipients in a truly consumer-based service system: "Use of vouchers [the financing mechanism he recommends] would make agencies directly accountable to clients since their continued existence would depend on their collection of vouchers. If competition was real, agencies would quickly adapt services to the changing interests of clients and have full regard for their power to choose among competing agencies. . . . Such a system would provide a ready measure of the most obvious dimension of agency success: client satisfaction. . . . A competitive social service market would require innovative, enterprise-minded social workers who always consider the needs and interests of clients. Client focus, rather than agency focus common at present, should be relatively easy to maintain" (pp. 52–53).

A major strength of the consumer approach, then, is its ability to reduce the power imbalance between service providers and recipients by providing the latter with alternatives to choose from. While such a reform could go a long way toward correcting some of the problems in the service system—particularly the orientation of the system away from users and toward funders and providers and its lack of responsiveness to the realities of the recipient's situation—as with any solution to a problem, factors contained within it can become the source of new problems. The consumer model might prove most problematic when applied to those sectors of the service system which are highly professionalized due to the advanced state of knowledge and technique that form the bases of the service. (For the sake of argument, it will be assumed that such areas exist, although there is an active debate about whether the social services, because of their intrinsic nature, lend themselves to professionalization at all [Feldstein, 1971; Specht, 1972; "Special Self-Help Issue," 1976; Epstein and Conrad, 1978; Street, 1978].)

In its most basic form, the professional-client encounter is a kind of consultative relationship, the main features of which are put forth by Eulau (1973): "The relationship is entered voluntarily for the purpose of deliberation or consideration because one party, the seeker of advice, is ignorant or in need of help, while the other party, the consultant, is a skilled or learned person who gives advice diligently and intelligently. But the consultant is not just an expert but also a compassionate person who cares for and worries about the matter brought to him for counsel, and he has the gift of accurate diagnosis and wise prognosis" (p. 169).

The relationship, thus, is an unequal one. The more important question, however, is whether the relationship must be unequal in order for professional help to occur. Eulau seems to think this is so: "Much of the current crisis in professional services turns on the nature of client participation in decisions concerning these services. . . . If professionals fail to persuade clients of what constitutes proper service, they leave themselves open to client demands of what proper services should be. They allow themselves to be pressured into conformity with client expectations, even if it violates professional criteria of service" (pp. 177–178).

Bidwell (1970) offers a different, more sanguine view of the effects of reducing inequalities in professional-client relationships: "If . . . clienteles become more knowledgeable, and more confident of their knowledge, professional authority may tend toward a rational, technique-centered base and away from moral mystique of the secret. Perhaps, then, the relation of professional and client will become more an instrumental collaboration between equals—a matter of convenience of a specialist division of labor among members of a knowledgeable community—and less that of trusting subordination to the esoteric" (p. 39).

It is beyond the scope of the present discussion to pursue this debate further. However, where one comes out on the question of the relationship between professional services and inequality in the professional-client relationship will determine, to a large extent, one's attitudes toward proposals for reforming service delivery systems along the lines of consumerism or other strategies aimed at power equalization. It is clear, however, that the professions no longer have the option of "business as usual." The attack on the shortcomings of the social service system is as much an attack on what many see as the self-serving behavior of professionals as it is on the repressive social policies of an achievement-obsessed, acquisitive society, or the distortions produced by bureaucratic pathologies. Bledstein (1976), in summing up his history of the growth of professionalism in twentieth-century America, puts the issue well: "Perhaps never before within the last century have we Americans been so aware of the arrogance, shallowness, and potential abuses of the vertical vision of venal individuals who justify their special treatment and betray society's trust by invoking professional privilege, confidence, and secrecy. The question for Americans is, How does the society make professional behavior accountable to the public without curtailing the independence upon which skills and the imaginative use of knowledge depend?" (p. 334).

Conclusions

The purpose of this chapter has been to examine one proposal for improving our social services. Consumerism obviously is not the panacea for all service-delivery problems; they are complex problems and require complex, multiform responses. As a realistic alternative, consumerism can only be considered if certain very specific conditions are present in a service system. Aside from its feasibility, there are important philosophical and political issues surrounding it that raise basic questions about the nature of welfare services in a modern, affluent society: the distribution of power and privilege between the rich and the poor, the educated and the ignorant; the possibilities for authentic mutual aid in a society so committed to individual striving. On balance, however, the advantages seem to outweigh the disadvantages, and consumerism should be given a prominent place on the agendas of advocates of reform.

There are two arguments for supporting consumerism. The first is that it would deal directly with two major deficiencies in existing systems: the imbalance of power between providers and recipients and the difficulty recipients have in making service systems responsive and accountable to them. One reason for this is that recipients currently command very few resources needed by providers. By giving the recipient some control over agency financing—either through the actual transfer of cash or through cash surrogates like vouchers—the recipient of service would become, for the first time, part of the political economy of the service organization and be able to exercise influence over organizational policies and procedures.

Obviously, the amount of influence and power consumers will be able to exert will increase with the extent to which they act collectively rather than individually. It is here that consumerism can be joined with other reform strategies, notably the creation of recipient organizations and the decentralization and devolution of decision-making power in service organizations. A major weakness with recipient organization and participation strategies is that they ignore the "golden rule" of organizational decision making: The person with the gold makes the rules. The opportunity to take part in internal agency deliberations, to vote on committees and boards, proved illusory victories when recipients quickly learned that unless they controlled resources, unless they were a real part of the constituencies of organizational decision makers, their votes and recommendations were easily ignored, distorted, or nullified as "compelling problems of implementation and/or financing" arose. "Cooptation," once an esoteric sociological concept, has become part of the patois of the service reformer.

Consumerism, because it involves the real transfer of resources to recipients and not just opportunities to participate in discussions, could, in combination with other reform strategies, become the keystone of an overall approach to service reform that can have real impact on these systems. In much the same way, industrial workers in Europe and America have learned that without control of significant factors of production participation in management decisions becomes, as Sennett (1979) calls it, "the boss's new clothes."

A second advantage to consumerism is that it appeals to a range of ideological and political interests. There is currently a convergence of people from the left, right, and center of the political spectrum into a band of critics of the welfare state that Starr (1978) calls the "renegades": "renegade lawyers and intellectuals who have, so to speak, deserted the professional's camp; radical champions of the movements on behalf of the prisoners, patients, and the poor; conservatives long suspicious of the welfare state; and liberals . . . who now believe that the programs set up by Progressive reformers early in the century deny the dependent their liberties and yield little in improved well-being" (p. 9). Consumerism can have a broad-based appeal and can reach many of these groups, an essential prerequisite to the coalition building without which reform in our political system cannot realistically be considered.

Consumerism, of course, would not be without its problems. Social agencies could engage in the same underhanded practices in their competition for consumer-clients as businesses do in their competition for consumer-buyers. Misrepresentation, unnecessary services, "doctored" program evaluations and success stories, and a caveat emptor cynicism on the part of administrators and workers can all develop if competition is left unchecked. These excesses would have to be anticipated and regulatory devices—hopefully more effective than those currently in use in the private market—would have to be part of any service reform along consumer lines.

But the excesses do not appear as great a threat to the well-being of recipients, and the quality of services they receive, as the perpetuation of increasingly powerful and unresponsive bureaucratic and professional systems. Unless our service systems can be made to operate primarily on behalf of the interests and needs of their users, their legitimacy will continue to wane, and they will increasingly have to resort to aggressive political and bureaucratic strategies to maintain their positions in society. Consumerism offers a way that, in combination with other strategies for equalizing the power and control between givers and receivers of services, can revitalize and relegitimize our social welfare institution.

References

Alston, J. P., and Dean, K. I. "Socioeconomic Factors Associated with Attitudes Toward Welfare Recipients and the Causes of Poverty." *Social Service Review,* 1972, *46,* 13–23.

Beck, B. "Welfare as a Moral Category." *Social Problems,* 1967, *14,* 258–277.
Bell, D. *The Coming of Post-Industrial Society: A Venture in Social Forecasting.* New York: Basic Books, 1973.
Bidwell, C. E. "Students and Schools: Some Observations on Client Trust in Client-Serving Organizations." In W. R. Rosengren and M. Lefton (Eds.), *Organizations and Clients: Essays on the Sociology of Service.* Columbus, Ohio: Merrill, 1970.
Blau, P. M. *The Dynamics of Bureaucracy.* Chicago: University of Chicago Press, 1963.
Bledstein, B. J. *The Culture of Professionalism: The Middle Class and the Development of Higher Education in America.* New York: Norton, 1976.
Boulding, K. E. "The Concept of Need for Health Services." *Milbank Memorial Fund Quarterly,* 1968, *44,* 202–225.
Burke, K. *A Grammar of Motives.* New York: Prentice-Hall, 1945.
Carrier, J., and Kendall, I. "Social Policy and Social Change: Explanations of the Development of Social Policy." *Journal of Social Policy,* 1973, *2,* 207–224.
Coser, L. A. "The Sociology of Poverty." *Social Problems,* 1965, *13,* 140–148.
Cumming, E. *Systems of Social Regulation.* New York: Atherton Press, 1968.
Drucker, P. "On Managing the Public Service Institution." *The Public Interest,* 1973, *33,* 43–60.
Emerson, R. E. "Power-Dependence Relations." *American Sociological Review,* 1962, *27,* 31–41.
Epstein, I., and Conrad, K. "The Empirical Limits of Social Work Professionalization." In R. C. Sarri and Y. Hasenfeld (Eds.), *The Management of Human Services.* New York: Columbia University Press, 1978.
Eulau, H. "Skill Revolution and the Consultative Commonwealth." *American Political Science Review,* 1973, *67,* 169–191.
Feldstein, D. "Do We Need Professions in Our Society? Professionalization Versus Consumerism." *Social Work,* 1971, *16,* 5–11.
Fischer, J. "Is Casework Effective? A Review." *Social Work,* 1973, *18,* 5–20.
Freidson, E. "Dominant Professions, Bureaucracy, and Client Services." In W. R. Rosengren and M. Lefton (Eds.), *Organizations and Clients: Essays in the Sociology of Service.* Columbus, Ohio: Merrill, 1970a.
Freidson, E. *Professional Dominance: The Social Structure of Medical Care.* New York: Atherton Press, 1970b.
Garfinkel, I. "What's Wrong with Welfare?" *Social Work,* 1978, *23,* 185–191.
Gilbert, C. E. "Policy-making in Public Welfare: The 1962 Amendments." *Political Science Quarterly,* 1966, *81,* 196–224.
Gilbert, N. "Maximum Feasible Participation? A Pittsburgh Encounter." *Social Work,* 1969, *14,* 84–92.
Gilbert, N. "Assessing Service Delivery Methods: Some Unsettled Questions." *Welfare in Review,* 1972, *10,* 25–33.
Gouldner, A. W. "The Secrets of Organizations." *Social Welfare Forum, 1962.* New York: Columbia University Press, 1963.
Gruber, M. L. "Inequality in the Social Services." *Social Service Review,* 1980, *54,* 59–75.
Gummer, B. "On Helping and Helplessness: The Structure of Discretion in the American Welfare System." *Social Service Review,* 1979a, *53,* 214–228.

Gummer, B. "Is the Social Worker in Public Welfare an Endangered Species?" *Public Welfare,* 1979b, *37,* 12–21.

Handler, J. F. *The Coercive Social Worker.* Chicago: Markham/Rand McNally, 1973.

Handler, J. F., and Hollingsworth, E. J. "The Administration of Social Services and the Structure of Dependency: The View of AFDC Recipients." *Social Service Review,* 1969, *43,* 106–120.

Hefferman, J. "Negative Income Tax Studies: Some Preliminary Results of the Graduated-Work-Incentive Experiment." *Social Service Review,* 1972, *46,* 1–12.

Hollingshead, A. B., and Redlich, F. C. *Social Class and Mental Illness: A Community Study.* New York: Wiley, 1958.

Hoshino, G. "Social Services: The Problems of Accountability." *Social Service Review,* 1973, *47,* 373–383.

Illich, I. *Medical Nemesis: The Expropriation of Health.* New York: Pantheon, 1976.

Janowitz, M. *The Last Half-Century: Societal Change and Politics in America.* Chicago: University of Chicago Press, 1978.

Kahn, A. J. "Service Delivery at the Neighborhood Level: Experience, Theory, and Fads." *Social Service Review,* 1976, *50,* 23–56.

Kaufman, H. "Administrative Decentralization and Political Power." *Public Administration Review,* 1969, *29,* 3–14.

Kramer, R. M. *Participation of the Poor: Comparative Community Case Studies in the War on Poverty.* Englewood Cliffs, N.J.: Prentice-Hall, 1969.

Lasch, C. *Haven in a Heartless World: The Family Beseiged.* New York: Basic Books, 1977.

Lindblom, C. E., and Cohen, D. K. *Useable Knowledge: Social Science and Social Problem Solving.* New Haven, Conn.: Yale University Press, 1979.

Matza, D., and Miller, H. "Poverty and Proletariat." In R. K. Merton and R. Nisbet (Eds.), *Contemporary Social Problems.* New York: Harcourt Brace Jovanovich, 1976.

Meyer, C. H. "What Directions for Direct Practice?" *Social Work,* 1979, *24* (4), 267–272.

Noble, J. H., Jr., and Wechsler, H. "Obstacles to Establishing Communitywide Information Systems in Health and Welfare." *Welfare in Review,* 1970, *8,* 18–26.

Perlman, R. *Consumer and Social Sevices.* New York: Wiley, 1975.

Perrow, C. "Demystifying Organizations." In R. C. Sarri and Y. Hasenfeld (Eds.), *The Management of Human Services.* New York: Columbia University Press, 1978.

Pfaff, W. "Aristocracies." *The New Yorker,* January 14, 1980, pp. 70–78.

Piliavin, I. "Restructuring the Provision of Social Services." *Social Work,* 1968, *13,* 34–41.

Piliavin, I., and McDonald, T. "On the Fruits of Evaluative Research for Social Services." *Administration in Social Work,* 1977, *1,* 63–70.

Piven, F. F. "The Urban Crisis: Who Got What and Why." In R. P. Wolff (Ed.), *1984 Revisited.* New York: Knopf, 1973.

Pruger, R., and Miller, L. "Competition and the Public Social Services." *Public Welfare,* 1973, *31,* 16–25.
Purvine, M., and Ryan, W. "Into and Out of a Child Welfare Network." *Child Welfare,* 1969, *48,* 126–135.
Rabinovitz, F., Pressman, J., and Rein, M. "Guidelines: A Plethora of Forms, Authors, and Functions." *Policy Sciences,* 1976, *7,* 399–416.
Reich, C. A. "The New Property." *The Yale Law Journal,* 1964, *73,* 732–787.
Reid, P. N. "Reforming the Social Services Monopoly." *Social Work,* 1972, *17,* 44–54.
Reid, W. J. "Social Work for Social Problems." *Social Work,* 1977, *22,* 373–381.
Rein, M. "The Social Welfare Service Crisis: The Dilemma—Success for the Agency or Service to the Needy?" *Trans-action,* 1964, *1,* 3–8.
Rein, M. "Social Services as a Work Strategy." *Social Service Review,* 1975, *49,* 515–538.
Rein, M. "Equality and Social Policy." *Social Service Review,* 1977, *51,* 565–587.
Rimlinger, G. V. "Welfare Policy and Economic Development: A Comparative Historical Perspective." *Journal of Economic History,* 1966, *26,* 556–571.
Robb, J. H. "Family Structure and Agency Coordination: Decentralization and the Citizen." In M. N. Zald (Ed.), *Social Welfare Institutions.* New York: Wiley, 1965.
Rossi, P. H. "Some Issues in the Evaluation of Human Services Delivery." In R. C. Sarri and Y. Hasenfeld (Eds.), *The Management of Human Services.* New York: Columbia University Press, 1978.
Rubin, L. "Maximum Feasible Participation: The Origin, Implications and Present Status." *Poverty and Human Resources Abstracts,* 1967, *2,* 5–15.
Sarri, R. C., and Hasenfeld, Y. "The Management of Human Services—A Challenging Opportunity." In R. C. Sarri and Y. Hasenfeld (Eds.), *The Management of Human Services.* New York: Columbia University Press, 1978.
Schorr, A. L. "Alternatives in Income Maintenance." *Social Work,* 1966, *11,* 22–29.
Selznick, P. "Foundations of the Theory of Organization." *American Sociological Review,* 1948, *13,* 25–35.
Sennett, R. "The Boss's New Clothes." *The New York Review of Books,* February 22, 1979, pp. 26, 42–46.
Shlonsky, H. R. "Welfare Programs and the Social System: A Conceptual Examination of 'Social Services' and 'Income Maintenance Services'." *Social Service Review,* 1971, *45,* 414–425.
Specht, H. "The Deprofessionalization of Social Work." *Social Work,* 1972, *17,* 3–15.
"Special Self-Help Issue." *Social Policy,* 1976, *7* (entire issue).
Starr, P. "The Helpers and the Renegades." *New York Times Book Review,* May 21, 1978, p. 9.
Street, D. "Bureacratization, Professionalization and the Poor." In K. Grønjberg, D. Street, and G. D. Suttles, *Poverty and Social Change.* Chicago: University of Chicago Press, 1978.
Titmuss, R. M. *Commitment to Welfare.* New York: Pantheon, 1968.
Titmuss, R. M. *The Gift Relationship: From Human Blood to Social Policy.* New York: 1971.

Vosburg, W. W., and Hyman, D. "Advocacy and Bureaucracy: The Life and Times of a Decentralized Citizen's Advocacy Program." *Administrative Science Quarterly,* 1973, *18,* 423-448.

Wilensky, H., and Lebeaux, C. N. *Industrial Society and Social Welfare.* New York: Free Press, 1965.

Worcester, D. A., Jr. "Blueprint for a Welfare State that Contributes to Economic Efficiency." *Social Service Review,* 1980, *54,* 165-183.

43

Children's Rights

Donald Brieland

The United States has been considered a model for human rights, but unfortunately rights do not extend broadly enough to children and youth. Children study the Constitution to learn about freedom but are significantly restrained in major decisions by parents, school officials, and other adults.

Children's rights recently have received more attention from lawyers, judges, and social workers. The Supreme Court has overcome its reluctance to rule on cases involving children's rights. It has extended due process to children and youth and has ruled on freedoms related to the schools and consent for abortion, but it has not dealt with many other critical topics. The Supreme Court has restricted rights of children about as often as it has extended them.

Children's rights differ in various places because they are derived from fifty sets of state laws as well as local ordinances. No state gives the unemancipated minor the right to choose a place of residence over parental objections. Child labor laws restrict economic opportunities, especially for the younger school dropout. Control of income of children is the legal right of the parent, and children cannot obtain credit. If they run away, they are returned home. At the bidding of parents or school officials, children can be given drugs to modify behavior. School lockers may be searched without notice. Corporal punishment may be administered by school personnel with no right to appeal or review.

Conflicts over rights and responsibilities of children often help to involve them in treatment. Rights are especially important for children who need special protection, including those who are considered mentally ill or developmentally disabled. Many children who are placed arbitrarily outside the family home because of their own behavior, parents' behavior, or both, also need legal protection.

This chapter will review the general bills of rights that try to define children's needs. It will then examine the status of rights in the legal system, the family, the school, and the mental health services. Rights in these settings affect the role of the therapist because conflicts in basic relationships lead children to seek treatment or lead society to impose it on them.

Bills of Rights

The bills of rights of most professional organizations encourage parents and children to expect protection from harm rather than increasing the power of the individual to choose.

The United Nations (1960) Declaration of the Rights of the Child was publicized again twenty years later for the International Year of the Child. It specifies children's needs but gives little freedom to the child. One article, for example, stresses the right to a free and compulsory education: "The child is entitled to receive education, which shall be free and compulsory, at least in the elementary stages. He shall be given an education which will promote his general culture, and enable him on a basis of equal opportunity to develop his abilities, his individual judgment, and his sense of moral and social responsibility, and to become a useful member of society. The best interests of the child shall be the guiding principle of those responsible for his education and guidance; that responsibility lies in the first place with his parents" (p. 19).

The Joint Commission on Mental Health of Children (1970) provided a succinct statement on rights of interest to mental health practitioners:

- The right to be wanted
- The right to be born healthy
- The right to live in a healthy environment
- The right to satisfaction of basic needs
- The right to continuous loving care
- The right to acquire the intellectual and emotional skills necessary to achieve individual aspirations and to cope effectively in our society
- The right to receive care and treatment through facilities which are appropriate to their needs and which keep them as closely as possible within their normal social setting [pp. 3–4]

The Joint Commission's report proposed a federal cabinet-level post to represent children's interests and official state and local councils, but this advocacy structure was not seriously pursued.

In its bill in 1975, the National Association of Social Workers ("Bill of Rights. . . ," 1975, p. 28) included three topics of special relevance to children's rights: legal processes, social work services, and advocacy.

> *The Right to Legal Status, Legal Protection, and Legal Redress.* Children shall have all the safeguards and protections of due process as guaranteed to adults by the Fourteenth Amendment, Bill of Rights, and statutory law. This includes the right to protection from physical and psychological violence and cruel punishment. Children have the right to redress of grievances against both parents and social institutions that are damaging or interfering with their welfare or rights. Children have a right to appropriate representation in judicial and quasijudicial proceedings in

> which their interests may be directly affected. This includes custody proceedings.
>
> Children should have: freedom from incarceration for offenses which, if committed by an adult, would not be considered criminal acts; freedom from incarceration with adult offenders; and freedom from incarceration beyond minimum length and conditions necessary for their safety and the safety of others.
>
> Children have the same right to privacy and confidentiality afforded to adults, in addition to special provisions to protect minors.
>
> *The Right to Service.* Children, who are dependent upon society for care and protection or who have special needs, must be given the opportunity to achieve the highest level of social functioning of which they are capable. Service must be legislatively mandated, with input from knowledgeable citizens and professionals, and must establish a comprehensive integrated system of services for families with children and for children separated from their families.
>
> *The Right to Advocacy.* The professional social worker must advocate for all clients, especially those who cannot advocate for themselves. Therefore, we as a professional association must reaffirm our professional responsibility of advocating for children to insure that the rights of children herein defined become a reality. Children must have the right to advocacy services to provide assurance that they will be guaranteed full benefit of the legal rights established by our society for the protection and well-being of all citizens.

Foster and Freed (1972), experts in family law, emphasize the moral and potential legal rights of the child in their bill of rights to enhance children's sense of responsibility. Until the Supreme Court decision in 1967 *In re Gault* (387 U.S. 1) giving juveniles due process guarantees in court, children had infrequently been recognized as persons under the law. Foster and Freed conclude: "[C]hildren are people; they are entitled to assert individual interests in their own right, to have a fair consideration given to their claims, and to have their best interests judged in terms of pragmatic consequences" (p. 346).

The bill provides:

> A child has a moral right and should have a legal right:
>
> 1. To receive parental love and affection, discipline, and guidance, and to grow to maturity in a home environment which enables him to develop into a mature and responsible adult
> 2. To be supported, maintained, and educated to the best of parental ability, in return for which he has the moral duty to honor his father and mother
> 3. To be regarded as a *person,* within the family, at school, and before the law
> 4. To receive fair treatment from all in authority
> 5. To be heard and listened to
> 6. To earn and keep his own earnings
> 7. To seek and obtain medical care and treatment and counseling
> 8. To emancipation from the parent-child relationship when that relationship has broken down and the child has left home due to abuse,

neglect, serious family conflict, or other sufficient cause, and his best interests would be served by the termination of parental authority

9. To be free of legal disabilities or incapacities save where such are convincingly shown to be necessary and protective of the actual best interests of the child
10. To receive special care, consideration, and protection in the administration of law or justice so that his best interests always are a paramount factor [p. 347].

The Child's Legal Status

In the eyes of the law, the child is an infant who has no status to approach the court as a plaintiff on his or her own behalf. Suit must be brought through an adult "next friend" or a court-appointed lawyer—a guardian ad litem. Adults control the litigation and may take positions opposite to those of the child.

The child generally cannot give legal consent since he or she is not considered competent to enter into binding contracts. Here, too, the parent or guardian who consents for the child may not necessarily act in the child's best interest. The Supreme Court, for example, denied the right to a precommitment hearing to children committed by their parents for mental treatment. This case will be discussed in the final section of the chapter.

In establishing an age of majority, the law provides an overnight transformation from legal infant to legal adult. For most purposes, age eighteen is clearly more satisfactory than twenty-one, but responsibility develops gradually at highly individual rates. Many youth well under eighteen are already fully independent of their families by choice or by parental default.

Legal emancipation is one way to convey rights to older children. Increasingly, states provide means for emancipation through petition to the court. This means that a child may divorce the parents or vice versa. Emancipation is usually sought by the parent who finds the child to be beyond control, but the adolescent may also take the initiative. With handicapped children, however, the trend has been to extend parental responsibility beyond the age of majority. Eighteen, then, is not always an adequate dividing line between childhood and adulthood. It may delay adulthood unjustly or impose it too soon.

Children may face legal difficulties because of parents' actions. The illegitimate child receives a legal label as a consequence of the parents' behavior and is often punished because of societal disapproval. Proposed uniform laws relating to children's rights in this area have had relatively little success. For example, the Uniform Parentage Act drafted a decade ago to eliminate the legal concept of illegitimacy has been adopted in only eight states.

Homosexual behavior of parents provides another illustration of value conflict. In 1981 the Supreme Court left intact a Kentucky Appeals Court ruling that a lesbian mother had to give up custody of her six-year-old daughter. She had taken a lover into her home. Testimony of a psychologist indicated that the mother's lifestyle might lead to internal conflicts and difficulties in the daughter's achieving a heterosexual identity (*Stevenson* v. *Stevenson,* 606 S.W. 2d 64, 49 L.W. 3781). Custody was given to the father because of possible threat to the "physical, mental, moral, or emotional health" of a child.

Parental nonconformity has led to legal proceedings. Two cases serve as illustrations. In *Painter* v. *Bannister* (284 Iowa 1390) a father lost custody of his son because of an unconventional style of living. *In re Burus* (recounted in *McKeiver* v. *Pennsylvania*, 403 U.S. 528) involved juvenile defendants who were arrested because of parentally approved picketing against racially segregated schools. In these cases, as in others, assessment of moral environment is a matter of values.

Special groups of children have been particularly disadvantaged by laws and regulations. For example, several states permitted children to remain on the AFDC rolls after age eighteen if they chose trade or technical school but not if they went to college. The Supreme Court outlawed this practice in *Townsend* v. *Swank* (404 U.S. 197) in 1971.

Most readers will already be familiar with changes in juvenile court procedure to guarantee rights of alleged offenders. As a result, the informal counseling atmosphere in the court has given way to a formal adjudication procedure specified in 1967 under *Gault* (387 U.S. 1) to extend due process rights to juveniles. The standard of evidence required in adult criminal actions—proof beyond a reasonable doubt (*In re Winship*, 397 U.S. 358)—also was held to apply to juveniles. Under *Kent* v. *U.S.* (383 U.S. 541), the juvenile is also entitled to a fair hearing before his or her case may be transferred to an adult court. While the juvenile may waive due process rights to counsel (*West* v. *United States*, 399 F.2d 467), no one else can do it.

Except for trial by jury, an adjudication hearing for the alleged delinquent comes to resemble an adult criminal proceeding. However, every attempt is usually made to provide probation or other diversionary means.

Under the 1966 *Miranda* decision (384 U.S. 436), the court specified that the accused had the right to remain silent during interrogation or to consult an attorney. Any statement obtained from him during interrogation thereafter may not be used against him at his trial. Recently *Miranda* rights were restricted in a decision that drew a sharp distinction between the function of a lawyer and of a probation officer for juveniles in *Fare* v. *Michael C.* (442 U.S. 707 [1979]).

The police officer interrogating Michael C. about a murder told him that he had the right to an attorney but denied his request to call the probation officer: "Well I'm not going to call Mr. Christiansen tonight. There's a good chance we can talk to him later, but I'm not going to call him right now. If you want to talk to us without an attorney present, you can. If you don't want to, you don't have to. But if you want to say something, you can, and if you don't want to say something you don't have to. That's your right. You understand that right?" (442 U.S. at 711). Michael C. answered questions the officers asked. His statements and sketches incriminated him in the Yeager murder. Michael C. alleged that his request to see his probation officer constituted a violation of his Fifth Amendment rights, just as if he had requested the assistance of an attorney. Because a probation officer is not in a position to advise the accused of his legal rights and does not have the right of privileged communication, the Supreme Court ruled that Michael C.'s request was properly denied by the juvenile court. The accused was denied access to the person who was probably in the best position to serve as an advocate.

The courts show little uniformity in processing age-status offenders who are charged with no crime but are considered beyond the control of adults. Courts often refer these juveniles to the public child welfare authority, which lacks both the resources and the knowledge to deal with them successfully.

Child custody in divorce is most often handled outside of juvenile court. Traditionally, custody has been awarded to the mother, usually as a function of the "tender years" presumption. Recent trends will be discussed later in this chapter.

The role of the juvenile court with the child victim is to intervene in cases of inadequate parenting. It will find the child dependent if the fault is not clearly that of the parents. Poverty or mental retardation are major contributing factors. The child is declared to be neglected if the problem involves knowledge and intent. Child abuse is often legally classified as neglect. If the children are victims of inadequate parenting, the court may leave them in the home with supervision or other special services, remove them temporarily while the parents are seeking help, or remove them permanently by terminating parental rights. Such termination generally requires clear and convincing evidence and is usually imposed only after attempts at remediation.

How much should the state have to say about child welfare and how successful is its intervention? Courts and child protection agencies have proclaimed what is good for children. Juvenile delinquents often have not been rehabilitated and status offenders have fallen somewhere between the boundaries of the correctional, the mental health, and the child welfare systems. In dealing with child victims, the courts and agencies have terminated parental rights without replacing the family of origin with an adequate substitute. Thus, agencies have been considered child snatchers. In child abuse programs, the privacy of the family can be invaded with termination based on flimsy evidence, and minority group members have complained that cultural norms are disregarded by child protection agencies.

Elise Boulding (1979) criticized the courts:

> The fact documented extensively in the records of court proceedings on behalf of children against their parents, that some families are not good for their children; that they may prevent them from receiving economic aid, welfare services, and health and educational opportunities that children are entitled to by law; and that they may further abuse and neglect them and contribute to their delinquent behavior suggests that there needs to be continual rethinking of legislation on the subject of child welfare. Court procedures for intervention "in the best interests" of the child are far from satisfactory. "The best interests" standard, initially followed in most state interventions and explicitly used as the standard for adjudicating children's interests in proceedings evaluating parental care, is not properly a standard. Instead, it is a rationalization by decision makers justifying their judgments about a child's future, like an empty vessel into which adult perceptions and prejudices are poured. It does not offer guidelines for how adult powers should be exercised. Seductively, it implies that there is a best alternative for children deprived of their family. Often there is no "best alternative." It would however be appropriate to make careful provision for children to seek a guardian as an alternative to inadequate parents if they are too young to live alone, and for children to be legally emancipated if they have demonstrated the capacity to live independently and be self-supporting [p. 84].

Children's Rights in the Family

Children's rights to family life are moral and ethical. Parents are expected to provide the child adequate food, shelter, and clothing. They are expected to give emotional support and to send the child to school. In a negative sense, they must refrain from inflicting physical or emotional injury on the child, although emotional injury is not well defined.

Criteria for *neglect* are often challenged on grounds of vagueness because they give parents no adequate way to determine what behaviors constitute neglect. In *Alsager* v. *Polk County* (406 F. Supp 10) in 1975, the Iowa trial court found the parents unfit "by reason of conduct detrimental to the physical or mental health or morals of their children." This standard was considered vague by the appellate court. The evidence was insufficient to give the state "a child protection interest" clear enough to require termination. The performance of social agencies when rights have been terminated are often notably unsuccessful. In six years, the Polk County Department of Social Services had placed the four sons in the Alsager family in twenty-three foster homes.

The source of the abuse or neglect report affects processing by an official protective agency. Reports of a physician are usually considered objective and trustworthy, but those of a social worker less so. Reports from a noncustodial marital partner are regarded more skeptically then those of a close neighbor. An adolescent who is both reporter and victim may be seen as provoking abuse through defiant behavior.

Adolescent unmarried mothers who keep their children and other single parents are often the subject of child abuse reports. The concurrent demands of making a living and of parenting complicate child rearing. If the custodial parent stays home, welfare benefits provide a marginal standard of living at best. As the child gets older, constant pressure is put on the parent to seek employment. The parents' own needs for autonomy and acceptance by other adults, as well as economic stress, may encourage neglect or abuse.

Foster care ordered by the court or entered into voluntarily has become the popular solution to serious problems in the natural family. Such care is intended to be temporary but typically involves several placements over several years. Because of some hope of reconciliation, great reluctance is shown to terminate the rights of natural parents. Also, placing a child out of state is illegal in some jurisdictions because it destroys the link with the natural family.

Permanency planning attempts to modify the strong emphasis on the rights of the natural family by freeing children in long-term care for adoption. Formerly the foster and adoptive parent roles were considered mutually exclusive, but recently the foster parents have more often been given first chance at adoption—sometimes with help of subsidies from public funds. The Supreme Court, however, denied foster parents the right to an adversary court hearing when an agency removes a child (*Smith* v. *Organization of Foster Families for Education and Reform*, 431 U.S. 816 [1977]). In this case, the foster parents were given the status of next friends of the children but the court-appointed counsel for the children opposed hearings for foster parents because they were contrary to the children's best interest. Children's rights to request a hearing were not even considered.

Institutional care for children without severe emotional problems has been generally rejected as damaging to personality. Especially for the young child, multiple care figures are considered undesirable even though institutional treatment programs may be devised to simulate a family situation. Diagnostic skills have not been developed well enough to predict accurately the children who will profit from residential treatment. The number of children and rapidly rising costs have also made intensive treatment programs difficult to finance.

Much more common than foster care is custody of children following the divorce of their parents based on the best interests of the child. This standard is specifically elaborated in section 401–406 of the Uniform Marriage and Divorce Act. In applying "best interest," the tender years presumption leading to the award of the child to the mother has been questioned as a sexist bias. Also, four practices have become more common: a court-ordered social study, the appointment of a guardian ad litem to represent the child's interests, considering the wishes of the child as a guide to custody, and award of joint custody to try to assure continuation of the relationship with both parents.

Legal emancipation is important to a consideration of the family because it provides the means to establish the reciprocal rights and responsibilities of parents and children. Traditionally its major purpose was to relieve the parent of responsibility for support. Physical maturity at an earlier age has apparently accelerated the need for legal emancipation. The issue arises commonly in response to parental abandonment, ejecting the child from the home, the child's running away and staying away, or the child's moving out of the home voluntarily because of pregnancy, marriage, or enlistment into the armed forces.

Although parents generally have the responsibility for support and the right to claim the earnings of minor children, when the child is economically self-sufficient and lives outside the home, the traditional parental relationship no longer exists. Emancipated children should generally be allowed to make their own decisions independent of parental veto, and parents should have no claim on their earnings. If children are abandoned, they may be emanicapted without relieving the parent of the legal responsibility for support. Clearer provisions for legal emancipation are important to social service agencies that are called on to make independent living arrangements for older adolescents.

Children's Rights in School

Recent Supreme Court decisions on legal rights in school seem to create more problems than they solve. Historically, the public schools have had considerable freedom to disregard children's rights. The Court held that the federal Constitution does not guarantee free public education (*San Antonio* v. *Rodriguez,* 411 U.S. 1), although the right is set forth in state constitutions.

In *Wisconsin* v. *Yoder* (406 U.S. 205), the Supreme Court decided that parents of old-order Amish children did not have to send their children to school beyond the eighth grade, but the child's preference was given no attention.

Personal freedom of students is often ambiguous because the school is authorized to act in loco parentis. For example, school officials may examine students' lockers without their permission and may impose dress codes in the interests of sanitation and protection of property.

The Supreme Court accorded students the right to express peaceful sentiments of protest in a case involving the wearing of black arm bands to protest the Vietnam War (*Tinker* v. *Des Moines,* 393 U.S. 503). Supreme Court decisions also provide for due notice and a hearing in the case of suspension (*Goss* v. *Lopez,* 419 U.S. 565), although the distinction between repeated suspension and expulsion is unclear. Students expelled illegally have the right to sue school officials for damages (*Wood* v. *Strickland,* 420 U.S. 308).

The Supreme Court, however, gave school officials broad discretion for use of corporal punishment without the need for due notice. The recourse has to be a civil suit against the school official administering the punishment (*Ingraham* v. *Wright,* 430 U.S. 651). Some states restrict corporal punishment but most do not. Only three outlaw it completely. The *Ingraham* decision is unfortunate in view of the vastly different philosophy of child-abuse legislation. Providing legal due process for suspension but not for corporal punishment is an absurdity.

Pregnancy and marriage no longer disqualify a student from attending school, but the pregnant female may receive instruction at home or in segregated classes at the discretion of the school.

Rights of children with behavior problems are often limited by the school. Schools may restrict the freedom of choice of children and their parents by setting special conditions for children to remain in attendance. A child may be required to seek a physician to obtain medication to reduce hyperactivity. A child who is a discipline problem may be given the choice of outpatient treatment or expulsion from school. From the school's point of view, attendance is more a privilege than a right. While truancy as an age-status offense can lead to a finding of delinquency, many schools no longer seek to compel problem children to attend school because school personnel are not unhappy when such children are absent.

The courts do not want to emphasize the rights of students because of fear of violence against other students or teachers or damage to school property. Apparently neither school officials nor citizens see a great need for increased student rights.

The schools have also traditionally restricted children's rights by withholding information. Children and parents were not given the legal right to examine school records until the Family Educational Rights and Privacy Act of 1974.

A court decision in 1971 in Pennsylvania mandated providing education at public expense for all retarded children (*Pennsylvania Association for Retarded Children* v. *Pennsylvania,* 334 F. Supp. 1257). In 1975 the Education for All Handicapped Children Act (Pub. L. 94–142) significantly clarified the rights of children. Handicapped children are entitled to a free and appropriate education in the least restrictive environment. The handicapped label can no longer exclude a child from educational services.

The act defines as handicapped those children who are: "mentally retarded, hard of hearing, deaf, speech impaired, visually handicapped, seriously emotionally disturbed, orthopedically impaired, other health impaired, deaf-blind, multihandicapped, or who have specific learning disabilities, who because of those impairments need special education and related services" (20 U.S.C. 1402). It provides for active participation of the parent in a program plan, as well as due process rights to assure that the program fits the child. Protection is provided in evaluation procedures and confidentiality of information. Inclusion of the child in educational planning is encouraged.

Mainstreaming in regular classes usually provides the least restrictive environment. The act does not require mainstreaming for all but does imply that education be provided using the least restrictive educational option. The act puts excessive emphasis on "place" as an answer to educational needs while neglecting the relationships between the teachers and the child. An emphasis on educational slots does not necessarily lead to the realization of a child's rights. Important rights are also extended through acts to eliminate architectural barriers that restrict the mobility of physically handicapped children.

Some of the problems have included overuse of special classes for children with behavior problems and those who need bilingual instruction, but mainstreaming is not a simple solution. Sometimes parents insist that severely handicapped children be kept in regular classes, thereby infringing on the rights of nonhandicapped children.

Funding of services under Public Law 94-142 has always been a problem, but the Reagan administration expects the effort to come from state revenues. After an analysis of the implications of Public Law 94-142, Frances P. Connor and Dennis M. Connors of Teachers College, Columbia University conclude (1979): "Handicapped children, as with most people, do not need to be respected in order to be granted basic rights. They do, however, need to be respected as persons so that they may become, as they are entitled, fully functioning members of our human community" (p. 82).

The school is an appropriate target for child advocacy efforts. We have seen that the official status of corporal punishment is especially repressive, but parents have not rebelled. They often consider corporal punishment as a means to assure adult respect. In some instances, school officials have been reported as child abusers.

Mental Health Services

Mental health services for children involve either institutional or outpatient care. Legal issues have been better defined for the institutionalized child whose liberty is restricted. Outpatient services must be considered mostly in terms of moral and ethical principles because of the paucity of legal findings.

The last decade has clarified the status of the adult hospitalized patient. One who is involuntarily committed generally has the right to a court hearing to assert his or her rights and to be placed in the least restrictive environment necessary to protect the patient and society. If the person's liberty is curtailed, treatment must be provided or the patient may demand to be released. With these rights has come both less frequent and briefer hospitalization. However, apparently the number of children in inpatient care has increased (Beyer and Wilson, 1976).

What behaviors of children lead to hospitalization? Many times the same precipitating problems—incorrigibility, running away, sexual misconduct, or theft—lead to a finding of delinquency.

The relation of mental health and delinquency and appropriate diagnosis and treatment were issues in *In re M.* (354 N.Y.S.2d 80). David M. was diagnosed as a schizophrenic at age eight, hospitalized for five months, and then referred to a child guidance clinic. A year and a half later, he began a three-and-a-half-year stay in a state hospital. Eight days after discharge, he was readmitted to the psychiatric division of the city hospital. In six years, he was out of the hospital one month, and his IQ dropped from 95 to 77.

David was referred to a children's hospital for long-term psychiatric care and escaped a few months later. Then at age fourteen, he was taken into custody as a juvenile delinquent. He spent time in a service detention facility but was rereferred to the city hospital. He was discharged to the juvenile center and then rehospitalized. A competency hearing concluded that David was mentally ill and also that he was mentally ill when he came before the juvenile court. Therefore, the State Commissioner of Mental Hygiene should not have discharged a mentally ill youngster to the family court.

The decision concluded:

> It would seem, based on testimony herein, that David is not a proper subject for treatment in an ordinary mental hospital, nor an appropriate subject for placement in an institution for ordinary juvenile delinquents. The experts are at a loss to know what to do with David and say the courts must not bear the responsibility of planning for him. It seems that David's case is not unique, and other children are, and have been, in a similarly unfortunate state of limbo. The courts are not an executive agency with power to provide the services required by mentally ill children. That is the exclusive province of the executive branch and specifically the Department of Mental Hygiene. The Commissioner of Mental Hygiene is provided with authority to service a child such as David and a remand to the Commissioner's custody is the most appropriate disposition of this case at this time [354 N.Y.S.2d 80, 85].

Some states do accord the minor the right to seek hospitalization. The Illinois Mental Health and Developmental Disabilities Code in section 3–502 provides: "*Voluntary admission on minor's application—notice to parents or guardian:* Any minor sixteen years of age or older may be admitted to a mental health facility as a voluntary patient under Article IV of this Chapter if the minor himself executes the application. A minor so admitted shall be treated as an adult under Article IV and shall be subject to all of the provisions of that Article. The minor's parent, guardian, or person in loco parentis shall be immediately informed of the admission (p. 85)."

The minor apparently finds it easier to seek hospitalization than to avoid it. Can the child demand a judicial review before admission? Most children are admitted voluntarily but are "volunteered" by their parents, who consent for them. According to the Supreme Court in *Parham* v. *J. R. et al.* (442 U.S. 584 [1979]), such a review is not required since both parents and hospital staff generally act in the child's best interest. With a scarcity of mental health resources the court held that hearings would divert attention and resources from the treatment tasks. The court stressed that mental health officials who participate in admissions decisions and review each other's conclusions are neither indifferent to the child's welfare nor incompetent. The independent examination by the hospital staff was declared to adequately protect the "liberty interest" of the child. According to the decision, an adversary hearing would not preclude medical specialists acting against the child's interest.

In *Parham,* the children had no substantive constitutional right not to be hospitalized for psychiatric treatment. The decision provides no protection for the retarded and mentally ill children railroaded into inpatient treatment by parents, guardians, or hospital examiners.

An earlier lower federal court decision, *Bartley* v. *Kremens* (402 F.2d 1039 [1975]), set forth more acceptable procedures to protect the child: a probable cause hearing with seventy-two hours, a postcommitment hearing within two weeks, written notice of the hearing and a statement of its grounds, the right to counsel, and the right to be present, including the offering of evidence and the cross-examination of witnesses. Unfortunately, Pennsylvania legislation enacted during the appeal process led the U.S. Supreme Court to find the original issue moot.

The right of the institutionalized child to receive treatment rather than mere custody has not been fully tested, although the Federal Court of Appeals did not agree the courts could impose detailed staffing requirements to help ensure the capability to provide treatment in two Alabama institutions (*Wyatt* v. *Stickney,* 344 F. Supp. 373, [1972]).

Rather than a formal court hearing, an advocacy commission may be preferable to review the conditions at admission, during hospitalization, and at release. A commission is probably more likely to assure specialized competence in the protection of individual rights. Appeal to the courts may still be made from the decisions of the commission.

Most of the concern has centered on the rights of the older adolescent, who is especially likely to be in conflict with parents and guardians. Congruent with the need to consider the adolescent's wishes, protections for patients who refuse admission or demand release from the hospital should be available to all persons over age sixteen.

Rights of the retarded received a setback in 1981 when the Supreme Court held that a Federal Bill of Rights for them enacted six years earlier did not oblige the states to provide any particular level of care and training in state institutions (*Pennhurst State School* v. *Halderman,* 49 L.W. 4363).

Litigation related to hospitalization has concerned psychosurgery (generally prefrontal lobotomy), the use of electroconvulsive therapy, or sterilization. Use of psychosurgery has decreased markedly, so that it presents little threat to patients' rights, but electric shock and sterilization are still common. Sterilization now requires informed consent.

A Minnesota Supreme Court appeal in *Price* v. *Sheppard* (239 N.W.2d 905) dealt with twenty electric shock treatments given to a minor against the wishes of his mother. While the defendant's actions were found by the court to have been proper, three steps were established for future cases of psychosurgery or electroshock: (1) in the face of objection of parent or guardian, obtain a court order, (2) appoint a guardian ad litem to represent the interests of the patient, and (3) empower the court to determine the necessity and reasonableness of the procedure. The court can then balance the need for treatment against the intrusiveness of it.

The U.S. District Court decision in *Wyatt* v. *Aderholt* (30 F.Supp. 1383 [1974]) set standards for sterilization, restricting the operation to persons over twenty-one except in cases of medical necessity. Previously, written informed consent had become required of all individuals to be sterilized in federally funded programs (42 C.F.R. 50.204 [1973]). Safeguards must include an instruction that the individual may withhold or withdraw consent to the procedure at any time prior to the sterilization without prejudicing future care and without loss of other project or program benefits to which the patient might otherwise be entitled. However, there is no mention of informed consent for minors on their own behalf. Both *Wyatt* and the federal guidelines include processing by a special review committee.

The improper use and the overuse of psychotropic drugs with children both in hospital and outpatient treatment has led to concern from children's advocates. Drug research projects have often used the children as subjects but provided no other services. The most popular drugs are tranquilizers that reduce hyperactivity. Critics underscore that hyperactivity may result from the child's situation—therefore factors in the situation should be modified to improve behavior. The teachers who may cause the stress are called on to make judgments about a child's hyperactivity. The unacceptable behavior may be intepreted as a problem of the child independent of the input of the school environment. Drugs usually do not lead to permanent improvement. The objectionable behavior too often returns when the drugs are discontinued. Side effects of long-term use of the drugs are still unclear.

In the case of drugs as well as electroshock, the doctrine of informed consent is often considered a safeguard, but the child's consent comes from the parent or guardian acting as legal agent. As with adults, the emotional state of the patient may make it impossible for a minor to become informed.

Stewart (1976) asserts that drug treatment short-circuits children's learning through experience and their own efforts to control behavior and master stress. Drugs tend to make children dependent, undermine their self-respect, and prevent them from building strength of character.

Stewart highlights the need for active participation in problem solving and the issue of consent: "It would not be realistic to make drug treatment contingent on a child's consent, but the child should at least be told why the medicine is being prescribed, what is to be gained from taking it, and what side effects the drug can produce. Children should be encouraged to ask questions and to express their feelings about a plan of treatment, because they may not fully grasp the situation or they may be overawed and too anxious to talk naturally. With patience and encouragement, a child's assent to treatment can be obtained, so that s(he) will not feel like a pawn in the hands of adults. No one knows whether most physicians deal with children as openly as they should, but it is a fact that few articles written on drug treatment say anything about children's feelings and opinions on the subject" (pp. 230–231).

Drug experiments in Massachusetts led to a law in 1973 prohibiting the use of psychotropic drugs in school without certification of the commissioner of public health that the administration of such drugs is a "legitimate medical need of the pupil" (Mass. Gen. Laws C. 71 Section 54 B).

With outpatients, treatment depends more on principles than on court cases. Questions such as "Who should be the patient?" become important.

Koocher (1978), in the case of Paula P., presents the conflict between parents' desires and the needs of a seven-year-old child as seen by the therapist.

> Paula is an active, attractive, physically healthy youngster with a two-year-old brother. Her parents are college-educated. The father works as a computer programmer, and the mother is a housewife and part-time bookkeeper. Both parents have somewhat rigid personalities, are members of a fundamentalist religious sect, and consider themselves to be pillars of the community. They have brought Paula for outpatient evaluation and "therapy" because she is "overactive" and have expressed the hope that medication and/or psychotherapy can help her. Specifically, they note that she has recently tended to contradict them in conversations at home, that she cannot sit still in church, and that she is running around with some "very fresh children" in the neighborhood from whom she has learned "rather foul language." They hope she can again become the "little lady" she was just a year or so ago.
>
> School reports suggest good academic progress and no particular behavior problems but the parents present the latter information with a verbal aside regarding the low standards of acceptable social behavior exemplified by Paula's divorced teacher. A professional evaluation reveals an essentially normal youngster whose social development is reasonably appropriate to her age level, although clearly in conflict with parental values.

Koocher asks whether Paula ought to be accepted as a psychotherapy case and with what frames of reference and therapeutic goals. "If we are to truly respect the rights of children who come to us for diagnostic evaluation, consultations, or psychotherapy, we must first recognize that divided loyalties and conflicts of interest are valid issues to be attended to. Perhaps the best approach to take with the P. family is to meet with all concerned, recognize the nature of differences that exist, and attempt to work toward a solution by mutual accommodation in treating the family unit. It is the professional's duty in such situations to raise the issues that the child is unable to. It is necessary that the child, as well as the parents, get appropriate feedback on the results of the evaluation and have input in the treatment planning process" (pp. 89–90).

For older children, the right to obtain mental health services is as important as the right to obtain treatment for veneral disease or to obtain an abortion. To seek outpatient mental health treatment is accorded to patients over age fourteen in Illinois and to adolescents in Virginia, but the payment problem remains unsolved.

The Illinois Mental Health and Developmental Disabilities Code [Ill. Rev. Stat. Chap. 91 1/2, paragraph 3-501 (1979)] provides:

> (a) Any minor fourteen years or older may request and receive counseling services or psychotherapy on an outpatient basis. The consent of his parent, guardian, or person in loco parentis shall not be necessary to authorize outpatient counseling or psychotherapy. The minor's parent, guardian, or person in loco parentis shall not be informed of such counseling or psychotherapy without the consent of the minor unless the facility director believes such disclosure is necessary. If the facility director intends to disclose the fact of counseling or psychotherapy, the minor shall be so informed. However, until the consent of the minor's parent, guardian, or person in loco parentis has been obtained, outpatient counseling or psy-

> chotherapy shall be limited to not more than five sessions, a session lasting not more than five minutes.
>
> The minor's parent, guardian, or person in loco parentis shall not be liable for the costs of outpatient counseling or psychotherapy which is received by the minor without the consent of the minor's parent, guardian, or person in loco parentis.

A proposed Uniform Medical Consent Act (Wilkins, 1975) removes restriction of age and marital status and provides for emergency treatment. For minors, parental notification is required if the rendering of services would create a substantial risk of harm to the physical or mental well-being of such persons but a positive duty is established to maintain the confidentiality of treatment to protect the privacy of minors when the observance of confidentiality would not be detrimental to the physical or mental well-being of the person, the family, or the public. Persons receiving the service are also responsible for payment. Wilkins also has drafted a proposed Uniform Minor's Capacity to Borrow for Medical Purposes Act.

Honoring children's confidences also presents difficulty. Although privileged communication is intended to encourage a person to enter into treatment, parents often insist that they have the right to know everything that transpires since they are sponsoring and paying for the treatment. A confidential relationship between the therapist and the child may make them feel that they don't get their money's worth. A therapist should not avoid discussing the therapeutic process with parents but must ascertain from the child the content that he or she considers confidential and honor that wish.

Confidentiality cannot be maintained, however, when the patient makes threats to the safety of others. In *Tarasoff* v. *Regents of the University of California* (17 Cal. 3d 425), the California Supreme Court in 1976 ruled that when a patient presents a probable danger to a third party, the therapist assumes a duty to take reasonable steps to protect the potential victim. Disclosure is considered necessary to avert danger to others.

The New Jersey Superior Court extended the Tarasoff principle to minors in *McIntosh* v. *Milano* (403 A.2d 500). A fifteen-year-old patient had fired a B.B. gun at a woman in her car and had expressed violent fantasies involving anxiety and jealousy when the woman dated other men. The court held that under the circumstances the therapist's duty to warn involved weighing the relationship of the parties, the nature of the risk involved, and the public interest.

The therapist may be perceived by the child as only an agent of the parent, but the child cannot have the right of full self-determination. The treatment situation is somewhat analogous to marriage counseling, in which there is a common endeavor involving both partners but the therapist must also respect the privacy rights of both. The therapist must teach the parent(s) how to accept the right of privacy of the child, except for threats that endanger the safety of others.

Conclusion

Rodham (1973) has indicated two general approaches to children's rights: extending adults' rights to children and seeking legally enforceable recognition of children's special needs and interests. Adults' rights are usually qualified before they are extended to children, as in the case of contracts for "necessaries," which are binding.

The second approach is usual. Emphasis on the child's needs and interests often puts the adult in the role of advocate for the child's well-being. Advocacy may focus on all children in a given geographic area, all children with a particular status or characteristic, or a combination of the two. Strategies may include any or all of the following: case advocacy, class litigation, monitoring of existing services, and legislative advocacy.

Knitzer (1976) concludes that "for too long, and with severe consequences to children and families, we have relied upon the description that adults with power to intervene in the child's life care about children and inevitably make the right decision" (p. 204).

Youth participation may be obtained through membership on community boards and bodies that determine youth's destiny, but this approach is used infrequently. When it is used, young people who have had few problem behaviors are usually selected. Such participation is not appropriate for an elite but for those from client groups. It takes great skill to sustain the interest of youth, because adults must accept them and their suggestions as valid and important.

The legal route seems to have only limited promise. Recent decisions of the Supreme Court on corporal punishment and on *Miranda* rights should discourage youth advocates from seeking judicial review at the highest level. We may have to wait for some time for changes in the composition of the Court that will facilitate significant extensions of children's legal rights. Meanwhile the clinician must be guided by a combination of legal precedents and moral and ethical principles on behalf of the child.

References

Beyer, H. A., and Wilson, J. P. "The Reluctant Volunteer: A Child's Right to Resist Commitment." In G. P. Koocher (Ed.), *Children's Rights and the Mental Health Professions.* New York: Wiley, 1976.

"Bill of Rights for Children and Youth." *NASW News,* 1975, *20* (7), 27–28.

Boulding, E. *Children's Rights and the Wheel of Life.* New Brunswick, N.J.: Transaction Books, 1979.

Connor, F. P., and Connors, D. M. "Children's Rights and Mainstreaming of the Handicapped." In P. A. Vardin and I. N. Brody (Eds.), *Children's Rights: Contemporary Perspectives.* New York: Teachers College Press, 1978.

Foster, H. H., Jr., and Freed, D. J. "A Bill of Rights for Children." *Family Law Quarterly,* 1972, *6,* 322–375.

Joint Commission on Mental Health of Children. *Crises in Child Mental Health: Challenge for the 1970s.* New York: Harper & Row, 1970.

Knitzer, J. "Child Advocacy: A Perspective." *American Journal of Orthopsychiatry,* 1976, *204,* 200–216.

Koocher, G. P. "Child Advocacy and Mental Health Professionals." In P. A. Vardin and I. N. Brody (Eds.), *Children's Rights: Contemporary Perspectives.* New York: Teachers College Press, 1978.

Rodham, H. "Children Under the Law." *Harvard Educational Review*, 1973, *4*, 487–514.

Stewart, M. A. "Treating Problem Children with Drugs." In G. P. Koocher (Ed.), *Children's Rights and the Mental Health Professions*. New York: Wiley, 1976.

United Nations. *Official Records of the General Assembly*. 14th Session, Supplement No. 16, 1960.

Wilkins, L. P. "Children's Rights: Removing the Parental Consent Barrier to Medical Treatment of Minors." *Arizona State Law Journal*, 1975, *31*, 73–81.

44

Confidentiality

Suanna J. Wilson

Confidentiality was once a very simple social work ethic, understood and accepted by nearly everyone. Many social work texts mentioned the concept, and Felix Biestek (1957) gave it special attention by listing confidentiality as one of seven basic casework principles. Unfortunately, the passing years have increased the subject's complexity to an almost overwhelming degree. The average clinician must now consider the impact of many different factors in order to comply with confidentiality principles: state and federal laws, court rulings on specific cases that interpret the law, regulations mandated by licensing and accreditation bodies, the National Association of Social Workers (NASW) Code of Ethics, disclosure demands of third-party payers, specific agency policies (which may be vague or nonexistent), the data-hungry computer, client rights (including consumer access to records), the litigious consumer, and old-fashioned common sense. These various factors often conflict with one another in their philosophy and demands, leaving the practitioner in the uneasy position of being "damned if he does and damned if he doesn't."

Prevention of confidentiality difficulties begins with the initial client contact. Clinicians generally recognize that confidentiality of client information is basic to the helping relationship; however, the client needs a similar awareness. Should the practitioner or his records be subpoenaed, in order to convince the courts that disclosure would constitute a violation of confidentiality, it might be necessary to prove that the consumer shared the information in question with an expectation that it would be kept confidential. For example, in *Minnesota v. Lender* (266 Minn. 561 [1963]) the records of several social service agencies were subpoenaed in a paternity proceeding. Minnesota had no privileged communication statute, and the agencies attempted to convince the courts that their records were "confidential and privileged." The court found the evidence presented to support their contention inadequate. A number of issues were involved, but the court pointed out that "proof that conferences illegitimate child's mother had with Welfare Department caseworker, Legal Aid Society employee, and priest were private and intended to be kept secret would be required to establish privilege . . ." (pp. 355–356). The professionals failed to provide the required proof, and the court ruled that the data had to be disclosed. Had legal counsel been better informed on relevant issues, including legal precedents and social work ethics, he might have presented a stronger defense on behalf of agency staff. In any case, some discussion of confidentiality rights, protections, and limitations is desirable as part of the initial contracting phase of a treatment relationship. A number of settings are also developing printed flyers describing confidentiality policies for distribution to all consumers.

Most clinicians consider intake an integral part of the overall treatment process. However, in at least one instance, the courts have raised the question whether, for confidentiality purposes, an application for services is subject to the same protections as records maintained after the client moves past the intake phase. In the case of *Community Services Society* v. *Welfare Inspector General* (398 N.Y.S.2d 92 [1977]), a welfare recipient in New York State applied for participation in counseling through the Community Services Society (CSS). The Welfare Inspector General suspected fraud against his department and subpoenaed the CSS records to try to get information regarding employment and marital status. Since New York grants privileged communication to social workers, the CSS used the statute to obtain a ruling in its favor that the records did not have to be disclosed. However, New York State appealed the decision, claiming, among other things, that "the information sought was given on 'application forms' acquired before the social worker–client relationship came into being" (p. 92). Since only that information which is generated through the professional relationship could be considered "privileged," the question arose whether data supplied during an application process is generated before, or as part of, the relationship between social worker and client. Thus, to avoid difficulties of this nature, the astute practitioner or agency may want to document evidence of discussion of confidentiality expectations and establishment of a formal professional relationship as part of the initial contact.

This chapter will examine three problematic areas from a legal perspective and discuss them in sufficient depth to provide some practice guidelines: blanket versus informed consent for disclosures, the right of privileged communication, and techniques for contesting subpoenas (Wilson, 1978).

Blanket Versus Informed Consent for Disclosure

The concept of *informed consent* has been applied traditionally to consent for medical/surgical procedures and, more recently, to consent for certain innovative treatment approaches used in psychiatry. According to the American Medical Association (AMA): "The patient has the right to reasonably informed participation in decisions involving his health care. To the degree possible, this should be based on a clear, concise explanation of his condition and of all proposed technical procedures, including the possibilities of any risk of mortality or serious side effects, problems related to recuperation, and probability of success. The patient should not be subjected to any procedure without his voluntary, competent, and understanding consent, or that of his legally authorized representative. Where medically significant alternatives for care or treatment exist, the patient shall be so informed. The patient has the right to know who is responsible for authorizing and performing the procedures or treatment" (Joint Commission on Accreditation of Hospitals, 1979, pp. xiv–xv).

This concept is now being applied to consent for disclosures of confidential information. For example, the American Medical Record Association (AMRA) has taken a strong stand on this issue: "Informed patient consent means that the patient should know about the existence of all information in his health record (subject to legal or medical restrictions), have access to it, and be able to exercise maximum control over its dissemination in any given situation" (National Commission on Confidentiality of Health Care Records, 1978, p. 2). The AMRA goes one step further, advocating client access to records as a requirement for informed consent: "Without the opportunity to review the contents of his health record, a patient is placed in the untenable position of consenting to the release of information of which the patient has no knowledge. This situation is incompatible with the rationale of informed consent. Further, many patients sign blanket prospective consents to release of medical information as a condition of participation in both private and public health insurance programs. Here, again, the patient is required to consent to the release of information which does not yet exist, and therefore it cannot be considered *informed* consent" (American Medical Record Association, 1977, p. 10). This policy statement currently reflects a professional ethic held by members of the AMRA; however, the association hopes it will one day become mandatory as an accreditation requirement of the Joint Commission on Accreditation of Hospitals.

Individuals who agree to the release of confidential information must know: (1) who wants the data (name, title, employer, and address); (2) why the data are desired; (3) how the receiving party plans to use the data; (4) if the receiving party may pass them on to yet a third party without the client's consent; (5) exactly what information is to be disclosed; (6) the repercussions of giving consent or refusing permission for the disclosure; (7) the expiration date of the consent; and (8) how to revoke the consent. The client's consent must be in writing on a proper consent for release of information form, which specifies the eight items listed. A new consent form must be signed each time different information is to be disclosed or a different party requests the data or whenever a consent form expires or has been revoked by the client. Copies should be retained by the agency, the client, and the party who is receiving the data (Wilson, 1978).

Except in unusual, emergency situations, the client's consent for disclosure of confidential information should be in writing. Verbal consents are undoubtedly obtained and acted upon daily by practitioners across the country without significant reprisals. However, in *Doe* v. *Roe* (400 N.Y.S.2d 668 [1977]), a therapist's failure to obtain written rather than verbal consent caused her considerable inconvenience, professional embarrassment, and a $20,000 fine. A psychiatrist with over fifty years of practice experience had been treating a married couple for many years. During treatment, she discussed with the couple her desire to publish a book one day regarding their therapeutic experiences, and allegedly obtained permission to proceed. Some ten years later (eight years after the couple had terminated treatment), the book was completed and several hundred copies sold. It gave an extensive and verbatim account of details shared by the patients while in therapy. Even though the identities were disguised, others recognized the wife and she sued for violation of privacy. In addition to the damages awarded, the court ordered the book removed from the market. Had the psychiatrist obtained a highly specific written consent (and disguised the patient's identity more adequately), the court might not have ruled against her.

Many practitioners are not required to grant client access to records in the absence of state or federal laws requiring access. However, it has been argued that in order for a client to give informed consent, he needs to see the material in question and perhaps even correct or amend it before he can determine whether he wants to permit its disclosure. For example, many states have statutes requiring and governing the maintenance of medical and/or mental health records. A few laws clearly specify that patients should have access under certain conditions; however, many simply omit reference to client access or state that access can be granted only "at the discretion of the physician." Tennessee's *Medical Record Legal Handbook* (Tennessee Medical Record Association, 1977) describes a typical statute: "Information should not normally be given to the patient. The patient should be referred to his attending physician, and hospital policies should be developed in regard to this. The Medical Record Act of 1974 (T.C.A. Section 53-1322) states, however, that the patient should have access to the information in the medical record if he can show good cause for needing the information" (pp. 29-30).

However, a little-publicized case in Florida (*Sullivan* v. *State of Florida*, 352 S.2d 1212 [1977]) set a precedent that uses the concept of informed consent to mandate client access to records. A patient in a state mental hospital asked for "the right to receive a copy of the most recent clinical summary of his mental condition as prepared by staff of the Florida State Hospital" (p. 1212). The lower court denied his request, and he appealed. The District Court of Appeals ruled that "Where the legislature, in its wisdom, placed with patient the right to designate a person and agency, named in the statute, who may have access to the record of his mental condition, it followed that, in order to properly exercise that right, the legislature clearly intended that the patient have access to the record in order to determine whether and to whom he wished the report to be released. . . . Any ambiguity in the statute as to whether the report should be released to the patient should be resolved in favor of the patient" (pp. 1212-1213). Thus, consumer access may not be optional when concepts of informed consent are implemented fully.

Blanket consent forms, which are in widespread use, constitute a significant problem as few consumers hesitate to sign them, and they are often completed as part of an application process. The clinician who is in private practice or associated with a mental health facility may exercise great care in the frequency and kind of consent consumers are asked to give for disclosures from their records. However, unbeknownst to the therapist, her patient may also be a recipient of financial aid or involved with a program using blanket consent forms. In an effort to establish eligibility, some agencies have developed forms authorizing the release of "any and all medical and psychiatric information. . . ." The client may not be receiving mental health services at the time he signs the form. When he subsequently enters into a therapeutic relationship, the other agency will have its blanket consent form on file and could potentially use it to force the therapist to reveal highly sensitive information.

This actually happened in the case of *In the Interest of Penny Annie Helen Hochmuth et al.* (251 N.W.2d 484 [1977]). Ms. Hochmuth was seeking custody of her children after the juvenile court had ordered her parental rights terminated. She had a long history of alcoholism and had been in various treatment facilities. Just prior to the court hearing, a social worker had Ms. H. sign a routine consent form authorizing the psychologist/director of a treatment facility where she had stayed for an extended period, to "discuss information concerning me with any judges, attorneys, social workers, etc., and to release any and all information contained in records to the Family and Children's Service of Davenport, Iowa" (p. 490). Even though a state statute existed that could have prevented the psychologist from testifying, the court ruled that the consent form waived the client's right to claim confidentiality, and the psychologist's resulting testimony was a key factor in the court's decision not to return the children to Ms. Hochmuth.

Consider the following examples of blanket consent forms:

> I, ________________________, give my permission for ABC Agency to release general information on my condition to the following individual(s). (Space is provided to fill in the name, relationship, address, and phone number).

> I, ________________________, give my permission for XYZ Hospital to release and receive medical, social, and financial information from my records to the following agencies listed below as necessary for the purpose of assisting me to return to community living. [Space is provided to fill in the name, organization, and the period of time for which the release is valid].

The following form was fabricated by a secretary in response to repeated inquiries for information and was adopted subsequently by a large number of eligibility workers:

> I hereby authorize release of any and all information or reports pertaining to me, my history, or my physical or mental condition, by any hospitals, agencies, physicians, psychologists, and other persons to the PQR Residential Home.
>
> I further authorize the release of any such information or reports by the PQR Home to such agencies and persons as they may deem appropriate. [Space is provided for signature, witness, and date.]*

Note that the last form gives the facility the right to pass on any information it receives to anyone it desires, at any time, without informing the client of this process or seeking his permission. Most clinicians quickly respond to such examples with, "But those forms aren't used by trained professionals—*I'd* never have my client sign that kind of form." Of course not. But such a form could force a therapist to supply confidential data to agencies who sponsor the form and to the courts in legal actions. And "trained professionals" do indeed develop such forms. Some might argue further, "But any person dumb enough to sign such a form . . ."

Are our "clients" the only "dumb" consumers? How many clinicians belong to the National Association of Social Workers and subscribe to their group

*The sources of these forms shall remain anonymous for obvious reasons.

insurance program? Consider the following statement, which appears on the NASW insurance application form (Bankers Life Insurance Company):

> I hereby authorize any licensed physician, medical practitioner, hospital, clinic or other medical or medically related facility, insurance company, the Medical Information Bureau or other organization, institution or person, that has any records or knowledge of the proposed insured or of their health, to give to the Bankers Life Company any such information. Bankers Life Company is given the authority to use such records and knowledge for underwriting and claims administration purposes and may release such information only to the Medical Information Bureau or to an organization or entity under authority of its own signed authorization.
>
> A photographic copy of this authorization shall be as valid as the original.
>
> Information regarding your insurability will be treated as confidential. . . .

The applicant is waiving privacy rights to nearly all information. Furthermore, Bankers Life is one of over 700 insurance companies belonging to the Medical Information Bureau (MIB), which maintains information on over twelve million Americans (Wilson, 1978; Baskin, 1978). All information disclosed to Bankers Life can be submitted to the MIB. Several lawsuits have attempted to claim that the sharing of information with the MIB constitutes a violation of privacy rights, but the courts have ruled consistently in favor of the insurance companies, especially in view of the fact that each applicant for insurance signs a waiver authorizing such disclosures.

For an example, see *Senogles* v. *Security Benefit Life Insurance Co.* (217 Kan. 438 [1975]), where an applicant for health insurance signed a consent form very similar to that of the first sentence in the Bankers Life application and was rejected based on information secured from the MIB. The consumer sued, claiming privacy invasion. The court ruled that the applicant had authorized the disclosure, and that information exchange between the MIB and member insurance companies was not improper. The court reached a similar conclusion in *Millsaps* v. *Bankers Life Co.* (311 App.3d 735, 342 N.E. 2d 329 [1976]). Thus, once information is disclosed to an insurance carrier, the practitioner can assume that it will receive subsequent and perhaps widespread distribution among a variety of insurance companies. Confidentiality of data gathered by insurance carriers is of such concern that the American Psychiatric Association has published a special report documenting damages to patients resulting from unauthorized or problematic disclosures between insurance companies and employers (American Psychiatric Association, 1975).

Many clinicians are fighting for the privilege of third-party reimbursement from Blue Cross, Blue Shield, and similar insurers in spite of the pocketful of confidentiality problems accompanying this process. For example, both the insured's application form and his ID card from Blue Cross/Blue Shield of Michigan contain the following blanket statement: "Acceptance or use of this card acknowledges . . . consent to the examination by Blue Cross and Blue Shield of Michigan of all medical, hospital, and other records pertaining to treatment rendered to the subscriber or members using this card." Furthermore, the insurance company requires that their utilization review auditors have "full" access to patient records during on-site visits and "Provider compliance with this requirement must be adhered to because failure to comply will be adequate basis for withdrawing participating status and possible withholding of future benefit payments. This requirement applies to all sites where patient records are maintained, whether in physician offices or facilities in which professional services are rendered" (Kent County Community Mental Health, 1980, p. 5). Thus, the applicant for insurance coverage consents to the release of information that may not even exist at the time his application is made, directly affecting the clinician who may subsequently render professional services.

Fortunately, some consent forms are so blanket that they fail to specify each individual form of data involved. For example, a blanket consent to disclose "all medical records" could be interpreted to exclude psychiatric or mental health records, since they are not mentioned specifically. In fact, in the case of *Roberts* v. *the Superior Court of Butte County* (508 P.2d 309, 9 Cal.3d 330 [1973]), the court determined that an applicant for insurance coverage had not authorized disclosure of psychotherapeutic records, since the consent form (signed and dated by the patient) made no reference to these data. It read as follows:

> TO WHOM IT MAY CONCERN:
>
> You are hereby authorized to furnish to General Adjustment Bureau or Western Casualty & Surety Company any reports or information whatsoever they may request regarding the medical history, physical condition and treatment rendered ________, and, if requested, to permit them or any person appointed by them to examine any and all x-ray pictures or records regarding the physical condition of or treatment rendered to ____________. Photostatic copies of this Authorization carry same Authority as original [p. 317].

In its ruling, the court expressed its concern over blanket consent forms, stating that "The waiver of an important right must be a voluntary and knowing act done with sufficient awareness of the relevant circumstances and likely consequences. . . . Accordingly, a form consent by the patient-litigant waiving her privilege is to be strictly construed against the insurance company supplying the form so that the waiver encompasses only that which clearly appears on its face" (p. 317). Thus, the precedent set by the court opinion expressed in this case could prove helpful in challenging the validity of blanket consent forms. This case also demonstrates some lack of information on the part of the plaintiff's attorney, who initially failed to even object to the production of the psychotherapist's records.

In summary, clinicians need to (1) avoid the use of blanket consent for release of information forms in their own practice, (2) caution clients against signing such forms for other parties, and (3) perhaps assist the consumer to make otherwise blanket forms more restrictive. The individual can request that a more specific form be prepared for his signature; he could submit a written statement to the agency in question retracting or modifying his former consent; he might write in a description of exactly what he will and will not consent to disclose and include any other restrictions he wishes be observed. The client may need to realize, however, that such actions could affect his eligibility for services from the program sponsoring the blanket consent form.

The Right of Privileged Communication

The great majority of social workers do not know what privileged communication is and do not know if they or their clients have the coverage. Many assume their information is "safe from the courts," when in reality they are practicing in a state providing no such protection. A preliminary review of raw data gathered by the author from several thousand questionnaires completed by practitioners across the country suggests that greater than 80 percent of respondents cannot define the concept of privileged communication, including those practicing in states granting social workers the coverage.

The right of privileged communication is a highly complex subject. The mere adherence to a professional ethic called "confidentiality" will not guarantee confidentiality in the courtroom. The right of privileged communication is an attempt to control legally the confidentiality of a practitioner's information. Very simply, the right of privileged communication (often referred to as "the privilege") gives a client the right to prohibit his social worker from disclosing in court in response to a subpoena information gathered in the course of their professional relationship. Psychiatrists, psychotherapists, psychologists, physicians (general M.D.s and/or psychiatrists), and social workers are among the professionals covered by privileged communication statutes in some states. Privileged communication coverage for social work–client communications currently exists in fifteen states: Arkansas, California, Colorado, Delaware, Idaho, Illinois, Kansas, Kentucky, Louisiana, Massachusetts, Maine, Michigan, New York, South Dakota, and Virginia. Two additional states—Utah and Maryland—make reference in their statutes to the confidentiality requirements of the NASW Code of Ethics, but have not enacted privileged communication statutes per se (National Association of Social Workers, 1980). Only licensed or certified practitioners are covered in all states. There are many loopholes in privileged communication statutes, permitting the courts to rule that the information must be supplied regardless of the existence of the statute. As a result, some authors have questioned the validity of privileged communication as a means of protecting the confidentiality of mental health data (Slovenko, 1973 and 1974; Wilson, 1978).

Practitioners functioning in states without privileged communication statutes for social workers are virtually at the mercy of the courts should their information become of interest in a legal action. Even the private practitioner cannot promise absolute confidentiality to clients, and the absence of records has proven ineffective as a game to convince the courts that "I don't remember" (Landis, 1980). Indeed, the practitioner may need certain records to defend his actions or diagnostic assessments when faced with malpractice litigation.

Thus, clinicians must (1) become thoroughly familiar with privileged communication as a concept and with specific statutes in their own state, including those of other disciplines; (2) become individually licensed or certified to practice in the state if necessary in order to acquire the privilege; (3) inform clients of the implications of the privilege to ensure that the consumer claims it, should he wish to prevent the professional from testifying; (4) guide one's attorney in researching state statutes and cases where the courts have upheld the privilege for social workers, psychotherapists, and related disciplines (Barbre, 1973; Bockrath, 1973; Best, 1972); and (5) be aware of arguments that can be used to prevent courtroom disclosures if privileged communication statutes are nonexistent or are overruled by the court.

The Subpoena—Can Disclosure Be Avoided?

A subpoena may request the personal appearance of the clinician in a legal proceeding or demand that he send or bring his clinical records. Unfortunately, many practitioners comply blindly with the subpoena, not realizing that various arguments can be used to challenge it. Consider Maurice Grossman's (1973) description of a subpoena:

> If the recipient knew how easy it was to have a subpoena issued; if he knew how readily the subpoena could demand information when there actually was no legal right to demand the disclosure of information; if he knew how often an individual releases information that legally he had no right to release because of intimidation—he would view the threat of the subpoena with less fear and greater skepticism. A lawyer may merely attest that he believes a certain individual has certain information that is relevant to the issue at court to get a subpoena issued. These forms are transmitted to the office of the clerk of the court routinely and the clerk of the court has a staff that routinely makes out the subpoena to be served by organized processors. No one reviews the request for the subpoena. No one examines the basis for the request. No one discusses with anyone else whether there is a legal right for disclosure. No one raises the question whether information is protected by law against disclosure before the subpoena is issued. The subpoena is requested and routinely issued on the principal of law that there is a right for discovery of any and all facts relative to the issue at court [p. 245].

Thus, it is up to the professional receiving a subpoena to determine if it is properly issued and if the information it seeks should be produced. Obviously, there are situations where it would be desirable and in the client's best interest to disclose data, as in child custody proceedings and protective service actions. However, there are times when the clinician and/or client may want to challenge the subpoena by presenting legal arguments defending a position that the information should not be disclosed. In this instance, the court will consider the practitioner's arguments (presented through his attorney) and render a decision mandating disclosure, ruling that disclosure need not occur or modifying the nature of the disclosure.

This chapter cannot attempt to address all the specific arguments a clinician might use to challenge a subpoena; however, a few guidelines and case examples are presented to aid the practitioner and his attorney in ferreting out data and preparing arguments to contest subpoenas.

First, all state statutes covering privileged communication can be researched and the privilege claimed by the client if appropriate (note that the client actually holds the privilege in most states; thus, it is the consumer who must waive or claim the coverage). Privileged communication statutes for other disciplines often will declare all communications to persons who are acting as their "agents" as privileged. Thus, social workers can sometimes claim the privilege for specific communications through their role as professionals working closely with psychiatrists, psychologists, and others.

In the absence of relevant privileged communication statutes, a social worker can argue that the court should treat the particular information in question as if it were privileged, thereby creating a privilege by "case law." Unfortunately, past efforts have not been very successful, and usually issues other than privileged communication have determined the court's ruling (*State* v. *Lender*, 266 Minn. 561 [1963]).

Clients may waive their right to claim the privilege and sometimes do so to the consternation of their treating professional. Thus, practitioners need to become familiar with the various ways in which clients may intentionally or unintentionally waive the privilege so as to avoid accidental actions that could allow the courts access to the data in question. Clients may intentionally waive privilege by simply giving the professional permission to testify. A rather common waiver occurs when clients sign both specific and/or blanket consent forms or introduce otherwise confidential information into their own testimony. The latter action has forced disclosure in several cases, the most well-known and significant being that of *In re Lifschutz* (2 Cal.3d 415 [1970]). An individual sued someone over an alleged assault, complaining that the assault caused severe mental and emotional distress. During a deposition, the plaintiff revealed that he had received psychiatric treatment from Dr. Lifschutz. The psychiatrist refused to provide his records when subpoenaed, claiming privileged communication (a specific statute existed in California providing this coverage). A complicated series of events evolved, with the therapist spending some time in jail for his refusal to comply with the court's demands, and he eventually obtained a hearing before the Supreme Court on the matter. A number of complex issues were involved, but part of the court's decision that Dr. Lifschutz must produce all relevant records was based on its conclusion that the client had waived the right to claim privilege by introducing the fact that he had been in treatment with Dr. Lifschutz. Thus, even when a professional feels that the client's waiver of privilege is not in the client's best interests, the client's actions to invoke or waive the privilege are final—the therapist cannot override them or act in his behalf except in most unusual circumstances (California Evidence Code, section 1012–1015, 1965) or when specifically permitted by state law, as in Illinois (Mental Health and Developmental Disabilities Confidentiality Act, Public Act 80–1508, State of Illinois, Effective January 1, 1979). Once again, the *Lifschutz* case is of interest in demonstrating to the critical reader several instances in which it would appear that a more informed attorney might have presented a more effective case on behalf of the clinician.

An in-depth search of state statutes will often produce a list of information that must be treated as privileged or confidential. States vary in the kinds of restrictions imposed on the disclosure of various kinds of data, but the following topics are encountered frequently: parole and probation client data; information concerning drug abusers in evaluation and treatment centers; records of state tuberculosis facilities; protective services records for children, the aged, and the developmentally disabled; alcohol and substance abuse treatment records; home health agency records; reports on mentally disturbed sex offenders, adoption, and matters before nursing home ombudsman or other consumer rights committees; birth records (in specific situations only); information received by hospital licensing and accrediting bodies; the identity of victims of sex offenses; rape, abortion, and juvenile arrest records; police investigative reports regarding criminals, and so forth.

Federal regulations may affect the data in question. If an agency is federally funded and administered, the Federal Privacy Act of 1974 (Pub. Law 93–579) will mandate confidentiality procedures, including consumer access to records. Private programs receiving federal grant monies for the treatment of substance abusers may be subject to very strict provisions governing disclosures (Department of Health, Education and Welfare, 1975). These regulations even forbid staff to indicate whether a given individual is known to the treatment program. Many general hospitals treat substance abusers as a primary presenting problem or secondary to other illnesses and injuries and, in some instances, are required to comply with these federal regulations; yet many facilities appear unaware of the existence of the regulations or of the fact that their compliance may be required. Records of students at the secondary and collegiate level are subject to the regulations of the Buckley Amendment (the Family Educational Rights and Privacy Act of 1974), which grants students and parents access to most records and governs certain types of disclosures. Several proposed revisions to the Federal Privacy Act of 1974 (Pub. L. 93–579) were pending before Congress until recently would have extended its basic provisions, with some modifications, to both medical and psychiatric records in a wide variety of nonfederal settings. For example, see the Federal Privacy of Medical Information Act, H.R. 5935, introduced into the House of Representatives on March 10, 1980. It would have mandated the concept of informed consent for disclosures from medical records and required patient access to records under specified conditions. The Congressman supporting this particular bill was swept out of office with Reagan's election; however, interest in privacy legislation remains high and many feel it is only a matter of time before similar legislation is passed.

It is important to determine the relevancy of all information requested by a subpoena. The court will not require disclosure of excess or irrelevant data. It is a very common practice for subpoenas to request the "entire record" or "any and all records," when in reality only a small portion of the record(s) may be pertinent to the issue at court. If a subpoena is contested based on relevancy issues, the client or clinician may need to reveal sufficient details about the information in question to enable the court to determine if the data are relevant. Such disclosures should take place in the privacy of the judge's chambers rather than before the entire court. There are a number of instances in which courts have had to rule on the relevancy issue, and it has proved effective in preventing disclosures. For example, see the analysis by Zupanec (1977) for a discussion of specific cases in which record material was declared relevant and admissible in court and other situations in which the material was found irrelevant, and therefore safe from disclosure. The decision in *Re Kryschuk and Zulynik* (25 West Week N.S. 77, 14 D.L.R.2d 676 [1958], Saskatchewan, Canada), for example, reflects a consideration of this principle.

The clinician's attorney can conduct a thorough study of legal cases to determine if prior court rulings set a precedent that would help the practitioner fight disclosure in the current situation. It is obvious that state and federal laws govern what can and cannot be done; however, the courts are constantly interpreting the laws through their rulings on specific cases. Courts often quote prior cases in reaching decisions so that these cases may have as great an impact on the court's ruling as do the laws themselves. (For serious inquiry into the subject, consult Barbre [1973] and Best [1972] for cases on which to conduct followup research.)*

State laws sometimes require that various professional groups adhere to specified confidentiality standards, and social workers may be mentioned. There are often specific statutes pertaining to financial assistance records, mental health or medical records, and the employees who handle them. Professional ethics often regulate confidentiality practices as do the requirements of some licensing and accrediting bodies (Joint Commission on Accreditation of Hospitals, 1979 and 1980). Arguments may be postulated that it would be in violation of the practitioner's code of ethics to disclose confidential information in court. The revised NASW Code of Ethics (National Association of Social Workers, 1979) contains an expanded section on confidentiality, reflecting the association's awareness of the increasing complexity of this ethic:

> The social worker engaged in research should ascertain that the consent of participants in the research is voluntary and informed, without any implied deprivation or penalty for refusal to participate and with due regard for participant's privacy and dignity.
>
> The social worker who engages in the evaluation of services or cases should discuss them only for professional purposes and only with persons directly and professionally concerned with them.
>
> Information obtained about participants in research should be treated as confidential.
>
> The social worker should respect confidences shared by colleagues in the course of their professional relationship and transaction.
>
> The social worker should respect the privacy of clients and hold in confidence all information obtained in the course of professional service.
>
> 1. The social worker should share with others confidences revealed by clients, without their consent, only for compelling professional reasons.
> 2. The social worker should inform clients fully about the limits of confidentiality in a given situation, the purposes for which information is obtained, and how it may be used.
> 3. The social worker should afford clients reasonable access to any official social work records concerning them.
> 4. When providing clients with access to records, the social worker should take due care to protect the confidences of others contained in those records.
> 5. The social worker should obtain informed consent of the client before taping, recording, or permitting third party observation of their activities [pp. 5–6].

**State ex rel. Haugland* v. *Smythe,* 1946, 25 Wash 2d 161, 169 P2d 701, 165 *ALR* 1295; *State* v. *Driscoll,* 1972, 53 Wis 2d 699, 193 NW2d 851, 50 ALR3d 554; *State* v. *Lender,* 1963, 266 Minn 561, 124 NW2d 355; *People* v. *Bridgeforth* (1972) 51 Ill 2d 52, 281 NE2d 617, 54 ALR3d 757, app dismd 409 US 811, 34 L Ed 2d 66, 93 S Ct 100, 190; *State* v. *Driscoll* (1972) 53 Wis2d 699, 193 NW2d 851, 50 *ALR*3d 554; *Lindsey* v. *People* (1919) 66 Colo 343, 181 P 531, 16 *ALR* 1250, error dismd 255 US 560, 65 L Ed 785, 41 S Ct 321; *Saucerman* v. *Saucerman* (1969) 170 Colo 318, 461 P2d 18; *Re Kryschuk & Zulynik* (1958, Sask) 25 West Week NS 77, 14 DLR2d 676 are examples of cases testing the principle of privilege by case law and related issues.

Unfortunately, a significant case has been decided against two psychiatric social workers who attempted to prevent disclosure on the basis of adherence to the code (*Belmont* v. *California State Personnel Board,* Cal. App. 3d 518 [1974]). They were required by their employer to submit mental health information to a computerized data bank system and refused, claiming that their clients had no control over the process, the data-bank system had inadequate safeguards to protect confidentiality, and to do as ordered would violate the NASW Code of Ethics. They also maintained that the agency was keeping excess, unnecessary information. The social workers received five days suspension for refusing to comply with their employer's mandate and took the issue to court. Unfortunately, the court negated each argument and ruled against the social workers. The court's ruling contained two especially disturbing conclusions: "In case of conflict between allegiance by psychiatric social workers employed by Welfare Department to code of ethics and social worker's duties as employees of State, social workers were legally bound to fulfill duties of their employment or suffer disciplinary action" (p. 607). In addition, the court observed "no reason why the Department [of Social Welfare] is legally or constitutionally restricted to the use of such information as is *necessary* to its functioning; some *relevancy* to the agency's administrative functions would reasonably be sufficient" (p. 610; emphasis in original). Is the court maintaining that agencies have unlimited freedom in directing the professional activities of staff, even if the demands force employees to violate professional ethics? Is the court saying that agencies may keep any and all information they wish regardless of necessity?

The precedent set by this case ruling represents a real step backward for the social work profession, and its implications are most frightening, especially considering that California had, at the time of the decision, some of the country's most progressive privileged communication legislation on its books for psychiatric social workers. Yet, the courts have recognized the importance of the American Medical Association's Code of Ethics, which forbids physicians (including psychiatrists) to reveal patient confidences, and in several cases have not required disclosure in apparent recognition of "the control which the American Medical Association's Code of Ethics and the American Medical Association itself exerts over the conduct of its members, to the extent that such 'privilege' could be considered a de facto law governing A.M.A. members. . . ." (Best, 1972, p. 46). Why is the NASW Code of Ethics not accorded similar respect?*

The client can be consulted to determine his wishes regarding disclosure, even in the absence of privileged communication statutes. Does he want the data disclosed, and what adverse effect might this action have upon him? The practitioner may choose to argue that damage to the client would be sufficient to warrant nondisclosure. Several cases have been decided in a clinician's favor based on this point. In *Perlman* v. *Perlman* (Index No. 5105, N.Y. Sup. Ct. Bronx Cty. [June 20, 1930]), a social worker argued the merits of confidentiality and the court

*As this book is going to press, a social worker in New York State won the right not to disclose some data based on the NASW Code's confidentiality restrictions. Perhaps this will set a precedent in a more positive direction. See the following cases for court deliberations recognizing the American Medical Association's Code of Ethics requiring maintenance of confidentiality: *Re Cathey* (1961), 55 Cal2d 679, 12 Cal Rptr 762, 361 P2d 426, infra 36, and *Ritt* v. *Ritt* (1968) 98 NJ Super 590, 238 A2d 196, infra [6 a, rev'd on other grounds, 52 NJ 177, 244 A2d 497.

did not require disclosure; unfortunately, the ruling was later reversed by a higher court (*In the Matter of the City of New York,* Sup. Ct., Bronx Cty. 91 N.Y.L. [Feb. 1, 1934]). In *Simrin* v. *Simrin* (43 Cal. Rptr. 376, Dist. Ct. App. [1965]), a rabbi was not forced to testify based on the court's feeling that the importance of preserving marriages and the necessity of confidentiality to effective counseling approaches outweighed the need for disclosure. Unfortunately, there are many more cases in which the courts have taken the opposite view and required disclosure. This occurs when the court decides it must have the information to render a just decision in the matter under consideration because the damage resulting from an improper decision due to inability to get at relevant data would be greater than any damage resulting to the client through disclosure of confidential material. Such a ruling has even forced the disclosure of information covered by privileged communication statutes. *Lindsey* v. *People* (16 A.L.R. 1250 [1919]), *State ex rel. Haugland* v. *Smythe* (165 A.L.R. 1295 [1946]), *Re Clear* (296 N.Y.S. 184 [1969]), *State* v. *Driscoll* (50 A.L.R.3d 554 [1972]), and *Humphrey* v. *Norden* (359 N.Y.S.2d 733 [1974]) all illustrate application of this principle.

The ruling in at least one case suggests that disclosure may not be required if a practitioner can prove that a formal agreement occurred between counselor and client in regard to nondisclosure of confidential information. In *Simrin* v. *Simrin,* communication between a husband, wife, and rabbi did not have to be revealed because "at the time the husband and wife sought the rabbi's advice, they agreed that he would not reveal his conversations with them" (Barbre, 1973, p. 571). Furthermore, "The husband and wife should be held to an agreement which they had made with the rabbit at the time they sought his counseling services, that the communications made to him would be confidential and would not be used in the event of an action between the parties" (Barbre, 1979, p. 574). In the Canadian case of *Re Kryschuk,* an employee of a department of social welfare and rehabilitation resisted disclosure on a number of grounds and submitted evidence that "every employee of the department had to take an oath of secrecy, and that the work of the department . . . would be handicapped if people who need the service thought that statements made to agency representatives would not be kept confidential" (Barbre, 1973, p. 572). Since *Belmont* v. *California State Personnel Board* has already established that allegiance to an employer is of greater priority than allegiance to the social work Code of Ethics, would the ruling in *Kryschuk* suggest that courts might not force disclosure if doing so would cause an employee to violate a written agreement with, or a mandate issued by, the employer? Perhaps such written agreements, with disciplinary measures built in for violators, should become a part of every social worker's personnel file.

The manner in which a clinician's record is maintained can affect its admissibility in court. The nature of the record itself, the way in which the data are recorded, and other factors can cause a record to be inadmissible and some material should not be recorded because it could prove problematic should the become involved in legal action (Wilson, 1980; Zupanec, 1977).

The informed clinician will also recognize those situations in which confidentiality cannot be maintained, due to state and federal laws. For example, many states require the reporting to various authorities of abuse to children, the elderly, and the developmentally disabled; abortions; deaths; births; gunshot wounds; venereal disease; stabbings; certain kinds of drug usage; the legally blind and those with seizure disorders (to the Driver's License Bureau); and fraud against or within financial assistance programs. Medical social workers encountering physicians resistant to reporting child abuse may find "Annotation: Civil Liability of Physicians for Failure to Diagnose or Report Battered Child Syndrome" (Roberts, 1980) of interest since it discusses physician negligence and suggests several pertinent references for additional study.

In addition, it may be necessary and desirable to violate normal confidentiality provisions in life-saving emergencies or to arrange involuntary commitment. Most of the federal regulations concerning confidentiality contain a number of loopholes and have received criticism because of tight controls on one hand and, on the other, free access permitted by government officials to ordinarily sensitive data (Federal Privacy Act of 1974, Pub. L. 93-579). Furthermore, many state privileged communication statutes specify exceptions under which the professional "may" or "must" violate confidentiality. The most frequent and most troublesome concerns the "duty to warn" when a client threatens a harmful or criminal act (Wilson, 1978). In fact, failure to violate confidentiality and disclose certain data in order to protect society and other parties could be cause for action against a social worker. For example, in *Schneider et al.* v. *Vine Street Clinic, Fenton Drake and Jay Mogerman* (Ill. 4th Dist. App. Ct., 1979) and in *Tarasoff* v. *Regents of University of Cal* (17 Cal3d 425, 1976) families of persons murdered by a patient receiving treatment from a social worker and a psychotherapist, respectively, brought suit against the professional for failure to take adequate action to try and prevent an intended crime from occurring. In *Tarasoff,* the ruling went against the clinician and the much-publicized and controversial "duty to warn" mandate was issued by the court. In *Schneider et al.,* similar issues appeared to be at stake. The trial court dismissed the case because, very simply, the plaintiffs did not appear to have a case. They appealed the decision, but missed a deadline in the legal proceedings and the appeal was never heard. In *People* v. *O'Gorman* (392 N.Y.S.2d 336 [1977]), a social worker was forced to disclose financial assistance records under the New York State privileged communication statute, which contained the following exception: "A certified social worker should not be required to treat as confidential a communication by a client that reveals the contemplation of a crime or harmful act" (N.Y.S. Statutes, C.P.L.R. section 4508). This rather common phrase has traditionally been interpreted to mean bodily harm; however, in *O'Gorman* the case involved investigation of possible fraud against the Welfare Department and the court ruled that since fraud constituted a crime or harmful act, the information in question had to be disclosed. It is also interesting to note that the applicant for financial assistance had signed a consent form agreeing to "any investigation made by the Department of Social Services to verify and confirm the information I have given or any other investigation made by them in connection with my request for Public Assistance" (p. 339). The court found that the signing of this consent form waived the client's ability to claim the right of privileged communication.

Thus, it would be foolish for a clinician to argue that certain data should not be disclosed if exceptions to state statutes, well-known prior cases, and other data clearly indicate that the nature of the information and the situation is such that maintenance of confidentiality is inadvisable (Williams, 1978).

Conclusion

It is evident that ethics, legal issues, client rights, and practice skills all blend together as the clinician struggles with confidential dilemmas. The ill-informed practitioner who violates his client's confidentiality out of ignorance or carelessness often does not get caught. However, litigious, informed consumers are increasing in numbers, and careful attention to client rights, legal issues, and professional ethics is no longer a luxury to be indulged in only by the academician and the attorney. An informed clinician can prevent confidentiality and privileged communication abuses, alert legal counsel to key areas of research and defense, and serve as an effective advocate for the client in both ethical and legal matters pertaining to privacy. The frank sharing of rights, limitations, treatment approaches, and assessments treats the client as an active partner in the treatment relationship and many supposed confidentiality nightmares can be avoided. Can social work meet the challenge of the ethical and legal dilemmas posed by the confidentiality issue?

References

American Medical Record Association. *Confidentiality of Patient Health Information: A Position Statement of the American Medical Record Association.* Chicago: American Medical Record Association, 1977.

American Psychiatric Association. *Confidentiality and Third Parties.* Task Force Report 9. Washington, D.C.: American Psychiatric Association, 1975.

Barbre, E. "Annotation: Communication to Social Workers as Privileged." *American Law Review,* 50 A.L.R.3d, 563, 1973, and The August 1979 supplement.

Baskin, F. F. "Confidential Medical Records: Insurers and the Threat to Information Privacy." *1978 Insurance Law Journal,* October 1978, *5,* 590–610.

Bernstein, B. E. "The Social Worker as a Courtroom Witness." *Social Casework,* 1975, *56* (9), 521–525.

Bernstein, B. E. "The Social Worker as an Expert Witness." *Social Casework,* 1977, *58* (7), 412–417.

Best, B. W. "Annotation: Privilege, in Judicial or Quasi-Judicial Proceedings, Arising from Relationship Between Psychiatrist or Psychologist and Patient." *American Law Review,* 44 A.L.R.3d, 1972, pp. 24–162.

Biestek, F. *The Casework Relationship.* Chicago: Loyola University Press, 1957.

Bockrath, J. T. "Annotation: Confidentiality of Records as to Recipients of Public Welfare." *American Law Review,* 54 A.L.R. 3d 768, 1973.

Re Clear. 1969, 58 Misc2d 699, 296 NYS2d 184, rev'd on other grounds *Re Klug,* 32 App Div2d 915, 302 NYS2d 418.

Department of Health, Education and Welfare. "Confidentiality of Alcohol and Drug Abuse Patient Records—General Provisions." *Federal Register,* 1975, *40* (127), Part 4.

Department of Health, Education and Welfare. "Privacy Rights of Parents and Students." Part II. Washington, D.C.: Department of Health, Education and Welfare, Office of the Secretary. "Final Rule on Education Records." *Federal Register,* June 17, 1976, pp. 24662–24675.

Family Educational Rights and Privacy Act of 1974, amending Public Law 93-568, effective November 19, 1974.

Grossman, M. "The Psychiatrist and the Subpoena." *Bulletin of the American Academy of Psychiatry and Law,* 1973, *1* (IV), 245–253.

Humphrey v. *Norden,* Sup. Court 1974, 359 NYS2d 733.

Joint Commission on Accreditation of Hospitals. *JCAH Consolidated Standards for Accreditation of Psychiatric Facilities.* Chicago: Joint Commission on Accreditation of Hospitals. April 1979.

Joint Commission on Accreditation of Hospitals. *JCAH Standards for General Medical Hospitals.* Chicago: Joint Commission on Accreditation of Hospitals, 1980.

Kent County Community Mental Health Office of Recipient Rights supplied copy of quoted material, February 1980.

Re Kryschuk and Zulynik (1958, Sask) 25 West Week NS77, 14DLR 2d 676.

Landis, D. T. "Annotation: Denial of Recollection as Inconsistent with Prior Statement so as to Render Statement Admissible." 99 A.L.R.3d, 934–959; 1980.

Lindsey v. *People* (1919) 66 Colo 343, 181 P 531, 16 *ALR* 1250, error dismd 255 US 560, 65 L Ed 785, 41 S Ct 321.

National Association of Social Workers. *Code of Ethics.* Adopted by the Delegate Assembly. Washington, D.C.: National Association of Social Workers, November 18, 1979, effective July 1980.

National Association of Social Workers. Telephone conversation with national office staff, Washington, D.C., August 9, 1980.

National Commission on Confidentiality of Health Care Records. *RX Confidentially,* 1978, *1* (IV), p. 2.

Roberts, M. "Annotation: Civil Liability of Physician for Failure to Diagnose or Report Battered Child Syndrome." 97 A.L.R.3d, 338–340; 1980.

Schneider et al. v. *Vine Street Clinic, Fenton Drake and Jay Mogerman.* Dismissed by the Trial Court and appealed in 1979 to the 4th District Appellate Court in the State of Illinois. The case was subsequently dropped without being heard.

Slovenko, R. *Psychiatry and Law.* Boston: Little, Brown, 1973.

Slovenko, R. "Psychotherapist-Patient Testimonial Privilege: A Picture of Misguided Hope." *Catholic University Law Review,* 1974, *23,* 649–673.

State ex rel. Haugland v. *Smythe,* 1946, 25 Wash 2d 161, 169 P2d 701, 165 *ALR* 1295

State v. *Driscoll,* 1972, 53 Wis2d 699, 193 NW2d 851, 50 *ALR* 3d 554.

Tarasoff v. *Regents of University of Cal,* 1976, 17 Cal3d 425, 131 Cal Reptr 14, 551 P2d 334, 83 ALR3d 1166.

Tennessee Medical Record Association. *Medical Record Legal Handbook,* Nashville: Tennessee Medical Record Association, 1977.

Williams, J. C. "Annotation: Liability of One Treating Mentally Afflicted Patient for Failure to Warn or Protect Third Persons Threatened By Patient." 83 A.L.R.3d, 1201–1205; 1978.

Wilson, S. J. *Confidentiality in Social Work: Issues and Principles.* New York: Free Press, 1978.

Wilson, S. J. *Recording: Guidelines for Social Workers.* New York: Free Press, 1980.

Zupanec, D. M. "Annotation: Admissibility Under State Law of Hospital Records Relating to Intoxication or Sobriety of Patient." 80 A.L.R.3d, 456–487; 1977.

Section VII

Practice Settings

Kay L. Dea
Section Editor

Social work is conducted primarily within the context of formal organizations that have been sanctioned and developed by society to address diverse problems. Clinical practice within this context requires that social work clinicians understand the institutional structures and policies that facilitate or impede services to clients. The effectiveness of practice depends on the knowledge and skills of individual practitioners and the flexibility and responsiveness of institutional structures to meet client needs.

Historically, social work has used unique combinations of problem, population, service, and organization to define specialized fields of practice. Traditionally, these fields have included family welfare, child welfare, medical social work, psychiatric social work, school social work, and corrections. Additional fields have been recognized at various stages in the development of the profession, and new fields are currently competing for professional recognition.

Although the concept "fields of practice" has been useful in developing specialized skills, organizational structures, and regulatory bodies to serve particular populations and to address special problems and human needs, the profession ironically has no clear definition of what constitutes a field of practice. Fields of practice have been defined individually or in combination by social problems addressed, by client groups served, by agency structure, and by clinical methods deployed in service. In recent years, major efforts have been made by the National Association of Social Workers and the Council on Social Work Education to articulate specialization in practice. The most recent model proposed by a joint task force representing these groups emphasizes specialization within basic institutional structures of society. William Gordon's chapter in this section discusses the historical development of this model and identifies problems and issues related to specialization in social work practice.

A major concern in defining specialization through fields of practice is that of maintaining a generic base of knowledge and skill to provide for common professional identity across diverse fields. Without a common base, efforts to diversify and to develop focused competencies within different fields could lead to professional fragmentation and dissolution, with each field competing for separate professional identification. The model proposed by NASW provides for a common definition and structural framework for professional practice.

The chapters in this section have been written to articulate issues in defining and developing fields of practice, to identify major trends in traditional and emerging fields of practice, and to describe the status of clinical work in each field. The chapter by Beulah Compton discusses traditional fields of practice. It has been organized to describe and contrast fields of practice across areas of common concern. Included are the social functions and responsibilities of each field; the professional tasks confronting practitioners; the organizational structures, methods, and programs in each field; clinical trends; funding patterns; and issues in practice and program evaluation. Compton suggests that fields of practice are characterized by three elements: (1) specialized delivery systems organized to focus on defined social problems, (2) special competence within these delivery systems, and (3) a unique constellation of professional disciplines working in collaborative relationships.

The chapters by Mary Waring and Nancy Neale focus on emerging fields of practice and private clinical practice as areas that have taken on characteristics similar to traditional fields of practice. Each author presents useful information to assist practitioners to understand issues in the field and professional trends in practice. This section is intended to provide knowledge sufficient to understand the special delivery systems, methodological approaches, and interprofessional networks that constitute the fields of practice in social work.

45

Development of Areas of Specialization

William E. Gordon

Social casework and, later, *social work practice* are terms that encompass a variety of different practices whose differences may exceed their similarities. When social work clearly became more than casework, these different practices were categorized by their different methods—casework, group work, community organization, and, later, administration and research. Still later, when it became evident that methods could no longer describe the increasing variety of practices, the "fields of practice" concept became the way of describing practice. This concept was aided substantially by the report of a workshop (Carter, 1965) that combined all the so-called methods and techniques into the idea of an "interventive repertoire" and attempted to define the fields by identifying the characteristics, problems treated, and knowledge and skills peculiar to different places of practice, sometimes called settings. Although the "fields of practice" were far more numerous than the old "methods" categories, they were far from distinct, clear-cut, or logically organizable, and they had seemingly no limits to their proliferation.

A separate and countertrend also existed, namely, to find out what was common (generic) to all fields. As early as the 1920s, the Milford Conference (American Association of Social Workers, 1929) sensed the two-pronged problem involved in subdividing social casework into its different practices (specializations or fields). One problem was the identification and description of the specializations, and the other was to identify what base those specializations came from or what they shared. "At the first meeting of the Milford Conference an attempt was made to define the several fields of social case work. The discussions made it clear that the group were [sic] not able at that time to define social case work itself so as to distinguish it sharply from other forms of professional work nor the separate fields of social case work so as to differentiate them sharply from each other" (AASW, 1929, p. 3). However, the Conference drew an important conclusion that was often ignored in subsequent years. "Their most important result, perhaps, was the emergence of a strong conviction unanimously held by the members of the Conference that a fundamental conception which had come to be spoken of as *generic social case work was much more . . . significant in its implications for all forms of social case work than were any of the specific emphases of the different case work fields*" (emphasis supplied).

Nevertheless, before the formation of a single social work organization—the National Association of Social Workers (NASW)—in 1955, these different fields had formed six formal groups in addition to the American Association of Social Workers—the American Association of Medical Social Workers, the American Association of Psychiatric Social Workers, the National Association of School Social Workers, the American Association of Group Workers, the Social Work Research Group, and the Group for the Study of Community Organization. There remained, however, some effort to find or define the commonalities among the various practices. "In the late 1950s the Council on Social Work Education (CSWE), as part of its movement away from 'specialization,' requested the fields of social work practice to examine their practice and report what content in terms of knowledge, skills, and attitudes they considered basic for all social workers, and what in addition they considered essential for social workers practicing in the specific field" (Bartlett, 1971).

Perhaps the greatest impetus was given to the idea of a common base, a question inseparable from that of specialization, by the Commission on Practice, the first Commission formed by the newly established (1955) National Association of Social Workers. Since the various fields of social work practice had been put together organizationally by the formation of NASW, it seemed imperative to try to put the practice fields together conceptually. This first effort resulted in the only officially sanctioned working definition of social work practice, published by NASW in an article by Harriet M. Bartlett, the first commission chairperson (Bartlett, 1958). This definition was not entirely definitive and provided no ready basis for establishing specializations, but it stimulated other attempts over two decades, which resulted in a series of papers, presentations, and a book that led to the current attempt to define specializations around a common base of social work practice, thus partially meeting the expectations of the Milford Conference over a half century earlier (Bartlett, 1970; Gordon, 1962, 1969; Gordon and Schutz, 1977).

In the meantime, the NASW Board of Directors was pursuing its own path after its Commission on Practice became inactive for lack of funds in the mid-1960s. In 1974, it "acted to move the profession toward the achievement of a critical objective . . . to develop and establish a rational, flexible, implementable model of specialization for the profession" (National Association of Social Workers, 1975). Prior to this, in autumn 1972, the NASW Division of Professional Standards recognized that "the continuing geometrical advancement of social work knowledge, the frequent emergence of new practice areas and techniques . . . pointed loud and clear to the additional need, possibly the overriding need, for definitive development of social work specialization" (National Association of Social Workers, 1974, p. 2). In September 1973, the Practice and Knowledge Cabinet (then made up of the chairpersons of the ten NASW councils) received the request from the Division of Professional Standards and agreed to have each of the ten councils in one meeting in the next 90 days to "name its specialization, develop a definition including a list of essential practice elements for its specialization, and recommend a set of appropriate standards. . . . The full Division will [then] meet for two days to develop the system of specialization, specialization definitions, and recommended standards" (1974, p. 4).

This effort resulted in a document that indirectly reflected a parallel question that had not been addressed, namely, what were the common characteristics of the profession? The report proposed an organizing concept for specialization called "methodological conglomerate" (National Association of Social Workers, 1974, p. 16). This unfortunate and unfruitful term should probably be erased from NASW records. It was the result of trying unsuccessfully to develop specializations by method, social problem, social institution, social work field, population group, and so forth (p. 4). The resulting document was circulated to a select group of social workers (the present writer not included) and was soundly, often vituperously, criticized. Unfortunately, the group of hard-working and conscientious social workers who produced this document ignored the previously determined futility of using social work methods as a way of defining social work as well as the unfortunate connotation of the term *conglomerate.* It is to their credit, however, that they recognized the need for a common organizing concept to underlie specializations, but they apparently did not recognize the difference between a term and a concept. The document was later revised around "methodological function," which was not semantically offensive but was largely empty of meaning (1975, summary). To this writer's knowledge, both of these documents are awaiting a professional historian's evaluation of where this effort fits in the evolution of the social work profession.

These earlier efforts of the NASW were the precursors of the NASW-CSWE Task Force on Specialization. The joint NASW-CSWE Board Committee authorized this joint Task Force on Specialization, consisting of three representatives of NASW and three of CSWE, "to begin to develop a conceptual base and organizing principles for a specialization model" (National Association of Social Workers-Council on Social Work Education, December 1978). This was a more modest, more fundamental approach to the problem. It began with a conceptual base rather than letting one emerge, as did the "methodological conglomerate" idea. (Representing CSWE were Ralph Garber, Carol Meyer, and Constance Williams. Representing NASW were William Gordon, Bernice Harper, and Harold Lewis.)

This six-member task force, with staff assistance and high-level staff participation, met four times until early 1978, when a final report was submitted to the parent organizations. This task force was well aware of previous efforts, including those of NASW mentioned above. It rejected the methodological approach and sought to start over with what it thought was a clearer conception of the essence of social work as an anchor point for describing and identifying specializations. To this writer's knowledge, this was the first time specializations in social work were approached from "the inside out," that is, from a generic social work base from which specializations stemmed. In a sense, the task force reverted to the much earlier conclusion of the Milford Conference, namely, that what was in the 1920s referred to as "generic" was far more important to identify than any of the specializations.

The task force commissioned one of its members (Gordon) to produce a brief historical report from his experience in working since 1955 on the problem of defining the distinguishing characteristics of social work. The repot included the basic historical assumption that "social work . . . is centered and primarily focused where person and environment make direct and active contact, at the interface between people and whatever they confront in living their lives moment by moment, hour by hour, and day by day" (National Association of Social Workers–Council on Social Work Education, February 1978, p. 4 of attachment). This definition can be elaborated on slightly to recognize that, at this interface, social work is concerned with matching the coping capacities of the person and the impinging environment both to enhance the growth and development of the person and to ameliorate the negative impact of the environment.

If this general notion is accepted, a "natural basis" of specialization becomes (1) the segments of environment (home, school, job, and so on) that are connected with a mismatch between person(s)' coping capacities and those segments of their environment, and (2) the nature of a personal disability (retardation, physical handicaps, aging, and so on) and its imposition of coping limitations across the whole range of environmental sectors. The idea of social work's central focus as the interface between person and environment seems to have been generally acceptable to the task force; this idea is gaining some recognition as the ecological or the systems approach in the literature (Germain, 1979).

Problems arose, however, in the task force in deciding how to sector the environment. School and job seemed to be obvious and clear-cut sectors of the environment. Health care and correctional institutions, in which there have historically been specialized social workers, were similarly easily defined. Serious questions arose, however, about whether families, groups, and organizations also have interfaces with their environments and whether they should also be helped, like individuals, to improve their transactional relationship to their environments. For example, was the family to be regarded as primarily the environment for each of its members or as an entity with its own environment? Some argued (the writer included) that, whenever a unit larger than the individual is considered with respect to characteristics that are similar to those of individuals, such as growth and development, there is great danger of losing sight of some individuals in that group. Certainly, knowledge of the dynamics of families, groups, and communities can be used in a practice devoted to the welfare of each individual. The task force ultimately selected social needs and the social institutions formed to meet those needs as the major sectoring device, using the manifest organizations representing them as the environments with which individuals must cope and carry on transactions to meet basic human needs. "The use of these institutions, in which social work has always been anchored, as the rubric for organizing social work specializations assures continuity with historical precedent. It relates ends (needs to be met and rights to be achieved and safeguarded) and means (institutional resource providers), and it responds to societal and professional concerns. It allows for use of all social work methods within any specialization and provides a broader context than a methodological basis for specialization. The interface between human needs and the institutions to meet them represents a positive view of social work" (National Association of Social Workers–Council on Social Work Education, December 1978, attachment, p. 4).

Somehow, that part of the specialization basis dealing with personal limitations on coping did not receive the attention given to the environment. Perhaps this reflects social work's old problem of swinging between one side of the person-environment dualism and then the other. This tendency appears throughout the history of social work, such as in Jane Addams' focus on the social solution side (settlement house) and Mary Richmond's focus on the person side (Charity Organization Society) (Germain and Hartman, 1980). Later, there followed the focus on the psychoanalytic (person side) and, more recently, on the social structure side (environment).

The task force, however, did suggest some of the criteria for specialization. There must be a critical number (not specified) of people in a dysfunctional relationship to some part of their environment. There must exist a body of knowledge applicable to successful intervention to relieve the dysfunctional relationships and the complexity of the dysfunction. And, knowledge of the intervention must be sufficiently great to require a mastery that calls for specialized training over and above the basic knowledge to practice social work in general.

There remain many questions and much work to be done before this general conceptual approach can be translated into a mechanism for defining a social work specialization and developing the criteria for certification in it. A major question is whether all social work specializations should have, as part of their base, some specialized knowledge of a segment of the environment and the nature of coping behavior required of people to make a functional match with this segment, even though the practitioners may be practicing supervision, administration, planning, or research. This way of defining a specialization would permit an interface-defined specialist to choose to further develop knowledge and to practice supervision, administration, planning, or research in the specialization. Are supervision, administration, planning, and research *social work* practice without some specialized knowledge about people and environments? This is not the old question of whether a supervisor, administrator, planner, or researcher should have first been a direct service practitioner in the area in which he supervises, administers, or does research, but rather the question of his having specialized knowledge about the interface on which the specialization is based. When the knowledge required to practice comes predominantly from another field—such as statistics or administration—we may need to distinguish between some specialization *in* social work and a *social work* specialization (Gordon and Schutz, 1977, p. 426). Another question is how this approach, if adopted, relates to education, since it is clearly a practice-oriented form of specialization. Another and crucial question is the extent to which the fields of practice and education will accept it. Some will insist that, as in medicine, there does not have to be a "natural" or logical basis for specialization. Medicine specializes around different parts of the body (heart, lungs, blood, bones), or, methodologically, around techniques (surgery, radiology), or around protection against disease (immunology, epidemiology). Specializations in social work may continue to form wherever there are enough social workers with common concerns who wish to get together and exchange views (renal social workers, perinatal workers, hospital social service administrators, and so on). Others argue that the unguided and more or less spontaneous formation of specializations will hopelessly fragment the profession and give it no basis for systematically developing and interpreting its practice, encouraging support of research, and, in general, growing in an organized way.

There are those who would still follow the traditional methodological basis for specialization, which currently must somehow be accommodated in the specialization system adopted until time brings social work to the recognition that it is its perspective on the social scene, not its way of proceeding, that gives the profession its uniqueness and social utility that ultimately sustains it.

It can be fairly said that, for the first time, however, the two central questions plaguing the field over the years have been tackled together by the task force: What are the distinguishing characteristics of social work practice in general, and how can specializations be recognized that share this common base yet permit more extensive development of knowledge about the characteristics and modifiability of some segment of the environment and about the characteristics and modifiability of persons coping with that segment that may be required to develop a satisfying and fruitful transaction between the two.

It would appear to this writer that this definition of specializations would equally well fit practice and education. If one accepts the idea that practice is based on knowledge, then specialization requires knowing more about either a particular environment or about the nature of coping with that environment. As we develop more knowledge about coping and about the similarities and differences in demands of different environments, education may become broader and more general than the present specialization around some specific mismatching combination of person and environment. The task force may have had something like this in mind when it concluded that "educational concentrations would be developed around the need-institutional rubric. . . . They should be at a somewhat broader level than the particular service-delivering institutional structure where the specialist practices" (National Association of Social Workers–Council on Social Work Education, December 1978, attachment, p. 6).

Some will argue strongly that abandonment of the present system of specialization may inhibit the free expansion and development of social work. Those who cling to the method and technique approach to social work will wonder where they fit in. It appears difficult to think of any method or technique in the broad sense that would not be applicable to the relationship of people to some environment, or to think of any method or technique that could be applied with complete disregard of the person's coping behavior and his or her environment. As Eda Goldstein (1980, p. 173) points out about the knowledge base of clinical social work, "It becomes necessary for each practitioner to be expert in understanding individuals, their environments, . . . and the transactions that take place between people and environments. One might well ask, what else is there?"

No one can confidently predict the course of specialization in social work, except that it will continue as opportunities for new areas of practice arise and as knowledge continues to grow. In general, specializations are generated when there is a spurt in the growth of knowledge applicable to some problem or when new opportunities arise to apply previous knowledge and techniques. If this new knowledge arises from research and experience concerning a person's more effective transactions with the environment, either through modification of his or her own coping behavior or induced changes in the impinging environment, then these specializations will truly be *naturally occurring* social work specializations because they will have grown from the major focus of social work's concern. We shall then be less concerned about controlling them organizationally or legislatively—they will truly be a natural basis for specialization. This must, however, largely await an increase in our knowledge about the environment and people's coping and transactions with this environment, and then the specializations will rest on a solid social work base (Gordon and Schutz, 1978).

At this writing, the report of the NASW-CSWE Task Force on Specialization has been circulated to NASW members through publication in the *NASW News* (April, 1979, pp. 20ff) for their reactions, and it has been circulated in separate and slightly modified form by CSWE to its membership for reactions of educators, in particular. Additional questions and suggestions will probably be forthcoming from these sources, and it is hoped that ultimately some policy decisions will be made about this essential and challenging problem.

References

American Association of Social Workers (AASW). *Social Casework, Generic and Specific: A Report of the Milford Conference.* New York: 1929. (This conference is so called because it held its first meeting in October 1923 in Milford, Pennsylvania, but actually submitted its final report in 1928.)

Bartlett, H. M. "Toward Clarification and Improvement of Social Work Practice." *Social Work,* 1958, *3,* 3-9.

Bartlett, H. M. *The Common Base of Social Work Practice.* New York: National Association of Social Workers, 1970.

Bartlett, H. M. "Social Work Fields of Practice." In *Encyclopedia of Social Work.* New York: National Association of Social Workers, 1971.

Carter, G. W. "Fields of Practice: Report of a Workshop." New York: National Association of Social Workers, 1965. (Mimeographed.)

Germain, C. B. (Ed.). *Social Work Practice: People and Environments.* New York: Columbia University Press, 1979.

Germain, C. B., and Hartman, A. "People and Ideas in the History of Social Work Practice." *Social Casework,* 1980, *61,* 323-331.

Goldstein, E. G. "Knowledge Base of Clinical Social Work." *Social Work,* 1980, *25,* 173-178.

Gordon, W. E. "A Critique of the Working Definition." *Social Work,* 1962, *7,* 3-13.

Gordon, W. E. "Basic Constructs for an Integrative and Generative Conception of Social Work." In G. Hearn (Ed.), *The General Systems Approach: Contributions Toward an Holistic Conception of Social Work.* New York: Council on Social Work Education, 1969.

Gordon, W. E., and Schutz, M. L. "A Natural Basis for Social Work Specialization." *Social Work,* 1977, *22,* 422-426.

Gordon, W. E., and Schutz, M. L. "Catching Up on Conceptualizations of the Environment." Paper presented at the Authors' Forum, Annual Program Meeting, Council on Social Work Education, New Orleans, 1978.

National Association of Social Workers. "Memo to Deans of School of Social Work re: 'Specialization in Social Work Profession.'" (Second working draft). January 20, 1975. (Mimeographed.)

National Association of Social Workers. "Developing a System of Social Work Specialization." (The 1963 reorganization of NASW listed nine Councils made up of fields of practice and methods. Later, a Council on Private Practice was added.) *Encyclopedia of Social Work*. Vol. 2. Washington, D.C.: National Association of Social Workers, 1977.

National Association of Social Workers and Council on Social Work Education. "In-House Memorandum and Attachments from NASW and CSWE Staff to CSWE–NASW Task Force on Specialization." February 3, 1978. (Mimeographed.)

National Association of Social Workers and Council on Social Work Education. "Task Force on Specialization Memorandum and Attachments to Board Committee." December 4, 1978. (Mimeographed.)

46

Traditional Fields of Practice

Beulah R. Compton

Historically, the concept of fields of practice has been used in social work to mean practice within a particular organizational environment developed to meet some particular socially identified human need. Three elements were central to the concept: (1) specialized delivery systems, (2) specialized knowledge and skill, and (3) specialized intraprofessional and interprofessional collaborative relationships. Each of these elements was focused to facilitate coordinated and comprehensive services to address the special problems commonly associated with clients seeking services in each field.

Although common values, concepts, and methods developed among the various fields of practice sufficient to allow social workers to identify themselves as belonging to a common profession, during the first fifty years, the advancement of professional knowledge and skills was made largely by practitioners who worked intensely within their own agencies and programs to clarify the nature of their practice. By the 1930s, five fields of practice were recognized—family welfare, child welfare, medical, psychiatric, and school social work. Corrections was included in the earliest meetings of social workers, but it was not until the 1950s that a significant literature related to social work practice in corrections began to appear. Today, there is considerable ambivalence within and outside the profession as to the relationship between social work and corrections.

While still not recognized as a traditional field of practice in the early 1930s, another field of practice that developed later involved the social settlements, forerunners of the community centers. Settlement houses were begun by groups of university-educated persons who settled in disadvantaged neighborhoods to assist the poor in overcoming poverty. Whereas other fields originally practiced a one-to-one method of helping, settlement houses developed group work methods.

The rapid development of social work activities within separate fields of practice alarmed many persons, who were concerned that the profession might lose the common elements that held it together. In its quest for professionalism, social work had to be concerned not only with the definition of a special skill but also with the development of a community of persons who would share a common sense of professional identity. In the search for a common professional practice, a group of social work leaders met regularly from 1923 to 1929. They issued a report that held social casework to be generic in its basic purposes and methodology regardless of where it was practiced. However, the issue of special practice was not resolved, and it was not until the 1950s that this concern swelled into a larger movement to recognize the generic aspects of social work practice and to see differences in setting as important to practice but as essentially external to it. There was a strong effort to identify the common elements of practice from one setting and one method to another. This effort to develop a common base was needed if social work was to become a unified profession (Bartlett, 1970, pp. 21–30). This issue has continued to be important within the profession, and today we are concerned with both "core" and specialized practice competence. We have not, however, returned to the fields of practice concept. Rather, we speak of specialization, without being able to define the parameters of specialized practice.

Recognizing the problems in defining what is meant by specialization either within the profession as a whole or within clinical practice, we chose, for the purposes of this chapter, to use the traditional fields of practice concept to describe clinical practice in different delivery systems. Without doubt, social workers who work within a particular field of practice develop special competence relative to the specific practice tasks, responsibilities, and interactions of that system, and they may use certain approaches and methodologies more than do practitioners in other fields. It is a task for the future to determine whether specialization relates to special and different methodologies or to the impact and interaction of delivery systems. At some point we must determine if specialization is best defined by problem, by agency setting, or by population.

This chapter will discuss seven central traditional fields of practice—family services, child welfare, health, mental health, school corrections, and neighborhood services. Each of these fields will be approached from a common outline that will include the social functions and responsibilities assigned to the specific field both historically and currently; the organizational and professional tasks associated with practice in the field; general status of the field in terms of structure, methods, and programs; issues in methodology, program priorities, and directions in clinical practice; issues in the interaction of clinical practice, policy, and service delivery, including resources and funding patterns in the field; and issues of accountability, regulatory standards, and standard-setting bodies.

Family Services

Social Functions and Responsibilities. The organized beginning of family social work as a field of practice is usually traced to the founding in Buffalo in 1877 of the Charity Organization Society (COS). This agency was founded in the belief that poverty was a condition that could be remedied by proper methods of prevention and rehabilitation, including the control of indiscriminate giving, which might encourage poverty. The agency responsible for controlling indiscriminate giving through the careful organization of charity and for the strengthening of the family as a "civic unit" through protecting and strengthening the home (Rich, 1956, p. 13). It sought to carry out its responsibilities through (1) the promotion of legislation to limit and control public relief and to organize private charities establishing methods of evaluation and accountability; (2) the development of new resources for poor families, such as the promotion of health care, the establishment of sewing rooms, and the organization of day nurseries to care for the children of poor working mothers; (3) the development and perfection of methods of personal treatment, which involved investigations by paid agents, careful determination of what approach should be attempted with any individual family, and the assignment of a volunteer "friendly visitor" to work with the family. The visitor so assigned was to use "personal influence" to bring about the desired changes in the family's functioning (Rich, 1956, pp. 11–13).

In the next forty years, there were to be two major changes in the responsibilities assumed by the COS that were also to have a major impact on the structure of family practice. From the beginning, the COS had difficulty reconciling and interpreting the dual responsibilities of organizing other charities and of offering direct services to individual families. In 1908 in Pittsburg, there was an organized effort to separate these two functions. A new agency was formed (which came to be called the Council of Social Agencies in most communities) to organize the social agencies of the community and to establish and improve standards of service. The COS retained its responsibility for direct services and relief to troubled families (Bruno, 1957, pp. 193–206). This was a major step in clarification of the nature of family service as a field of practice, and it furthered the beginning of a new method in social work—that of community organization.

The second major change in COS was internal to the field of practice. The responsibility for meeting the economic needs of poor families began to be lodged in public agencies rather than in the voluntarily supported COS. Although forced by the expectations of society into granting funds to destitute families, the COS had opposed giving money to the poor in the belief that financial aid only increased dependency and that the only effective way to combat poverty was through counsel and guidance. A reluctant giver itself, the COS also opposed the giving of financial relief by public agencies, on the premise that acceptance of public funds was even more corrupting than acceptance of voluntary funds. However, in the early 1900s, there was a gradual acceptance of public relief with voluntary cooperation from family agencies.

The development of public welfare agencies could have led to the establishment of a separate field of practice, but it did not. Instead, most activities of public welfare agencies were conceptualized as belonging in the family or the child welfare fields of practice.

Initially, the public assistance worker was charged both with the administration of the financial support of the family and the responsibility to offer help with psychosocial difficulties. This approach had its roots in the COS notion that poverty was a problem of individual social functioning. Over the years, there came pressure for the recognition that financial need did not necessarily mean that the family had psychosocial problems. Consequently, efforts emerged to separate financial aid from other helping activities. The Social Service Amendments of 1974, commonly known as Title XX, consolidated service provisions as a separate component of the social security system rather than an adjunct to public assistance. Under this act, public agencies have been able to provide services themselves or to contract with other agencies to provide such services.

A parallel development in the family field was the development of the Catholic and Jewish sectarian social agencies. In many ways, these agencies assumed responsibilities similar to those of the COS. For example, in the 1870s, many Jewish leaders questioned indiscriminate giving. Out of this concern, the United Hebrew Charities of the City of New York was established to investigate family need and to offer appropriate service. Catholic charitable organizations were often organized as large umbrella agencies with a division of family services. The model for the development of the Catholic agencies was the Catholic Charities of the Archdiocese of New York (CCANY). In this organization, as in COS and the Jewish agencies, the division of family services was initially established as a supervisory and relief-giving agency. But, by the 1920s, it was actively supporting public relief and operating primarily as a family counseling agency. The sectarian family agencies, however, have historically and currently assumed some additional responsibilities not assumed by the COS. One of these critical responsibilities over the years has been the resettlement of immigrants of their faith in this country. This responsibility has involved the financial support of these immigrants as well as helping them to find new homes, to learn English, and to face other difficulties of resettlement.

Social work practice as a whole, including social work with families, was strongly affected after World War I by the shift from a search for objective reasons for family problems in behavior and environment to a search for solutions in the largely subjective area of individual emotions and feelings. There came a shift from seeing people in need as essentially rational beings who could be helped by rational exhortation to seeing much of human behavior as irrational and stemming from hidden emotions developed through early life experiences. The impact of this new knowledge and the changes it brought to thinking about human beings and their functioning can hardly be overestimated. With its acceptance, and perhaps also as a result of the conflicts and changes within society at the time, a new population began to seek help through voluntarily supported family agencies and other helping resources of society. The educated middle class, able to be open for the first time about their emotional needs, sought counseling services for self-understanding. With the changes in the client population, material aid and direct advice were no longer seen by the leaders in family practice as central to the helping process, and, in fact, family agencies began to charge fees for service when clients were able to pay. The central responsibility of the voluntary family agency became to assist individuals and families to resolve emotional and relational stress largely through psychological counseling and family life education. The demand for such services on the private family agency grew so rapidly that there was a tendency to assign the indigent and those less able to respond to psychological counseling to the public agencies. Social workers have often been highly self-critical about this movement. However, it may be good to remember that this new type of helping activity took hold and became primary to social work as much because it makes sense to the people who sponsored and financed the agencies as because it was accepted by social workers. This new knowledge and its wide acceptance among social workers in all settings undoubtedly contributed to the development of a common professional identity. A further push toward a professional identity came as social workers found they shared common knowledge with other psychological helping professions and felt a need to differentiate social work from these groups.

However, as the concerns of the turbulent 1960s refocused attention on the plight of the poor and minorities in our society, the voluntary family agency began to reach out once again to these populations, but in a new way. In the late 1960s, the national board of the Family Service Association of America approved the concept of family advocacy and called upon family agencies to intervene on behalf of families who needed social and economic succor as well as emotional or psychological services. It appeared as though family social work was finding some balance between working with social and psychological needs.

Organizations and Professional Tasks. Current practice in the family field involves professional help for individuals and families with problems of individual behavior, family and social relationships, emotional and mental functioning, sexual functioning, physical disabilities, or disturbances at work or in school. Practitioners offer help to individuals and families with developmental tasks of life transitions, with the emotional pain of grief and loss, with marital or intergenerational conflict, and with preventative services. In addition to services given within an organizational structure, in recent years, social workers from the family field have engaged in the private practice of social work, primarily family therapy. These practitioners support their individual practice by fees for service. They are responsible to their clients and to the profession, rather than to an agency structure, for effective practice.

Community sanction of social work practice in the field of family services, as within all other fields of social work practice, derives from two sources—the profession itself and its organizational structure. Social work organizations can be roughly categorized as governmental agencies, organized by legislation, and voluntary or private agencies, organized under articles of incorporation. From the earliest days, the voluntary family agencies have strongly emphasized the importance of the professional competence of the practitioner as a basis of authority to practice. This emphasis is illustrated by the early professional responsibilities that were assumed by the voluntary agencies.

Beginning in the late 1890s, whenever COS workers met, they discussed the need for a national organization of agencies as a means to share policies, programs, and experiences. On June 8, 1911, the National Association of Societies for Organizing Charities was launched. In 1912, the word *American* was substituted for the word *National* in order to include Canadian agencies. The name was changed to American Association for Organizing Family Social Work in 1919, to Family Welfare Association of America in 1930, and to Family Service Association of America in 1946. This Association still functions as the national parent body of local family agencies, such as Family Service, Family and Children's Services, Jewish Family Service, Lutheran Social Service, and Catholic Social Services. Most of the sectarian family agencies that belong to this national body also belong to a national body within their own sectarian identification. It is interesting that the first agencies beyond the voluntarily supported nonsectarian founders that were admitted to the Association were public welfare departments, in 1921, and units of Mother's Aid Funds, in 1928. The Jewish agencies joined in 1929, and the Catholic agencies, in 1930. The responsibility of the Association was to form a "united program for the protection of family life" (Rich, 1956, p. 91). A later committee on the future scope of the societies recommended that the family be seen as the unit of service and that local agencies should use the name *family social work* in their titles when they adopted new names (Rich, 1956, p. 100).

The tasks of the organization were to set standards of membership, to serve as an avenue of sharing and education, and to support research efforts. These responsibilities have remained an important part of the tasks of both the FSA and of each local agency since the beginning. Even before the Association was founded, the leaders of COS were calling for the establishment of courses in "philanthropic training," and, in 1897, Mary Richmond presented a well-developed plan for a "training school in applied philanthropy." Richmond believed strongly that the development and support of professional standards was a task of the field of family service and that a school was necessary for the new profession to set and maintain standards of service. In 1898, the New York COS established the first school of social work. This school continued to be supported by the family agency until 1950; it was the last independent school of social work (Compton, 1980, pp. 383–384). However, the family agencies have continued to see the support of social work education as a professional and organizational responsibility. Many family agencies provide field instruction for students in schools of social work. In the mid 1960s, 6 percent of the family agencies were involved in such training; by 1974, 42 percent of the agencies were offering such opportunities to social work schools. Family service agencies and the Association also participate in professional education by direct communication with schools and through the Council on Social Work Education, the accrediting body of schools of social work (Ambrosino, 1977, p. 433).

From the beginning, family agencies have felt a responsibility to engage in research and to share these findings as a way of advancing the profession. One of the earliest efforts at fact-finding was the collection of basic statistics about the agencies' operations and the services given. There has been a constant increase in the number of research efforts undertaken and in the sophistication of the research. It is reported that, in 1974, 39 members of the Association undertook, or participated in, 65 research studies that involved such areas as client's evaluation of services, demonstration programs, and various training or educational activities (Ambrosino, 1977, p. 432). There may be some concern that there is not enough research conducted by family agencies, but studies in this field compare favorably both in numbers and sophistication with those from other fields of practice.

One criterion of a profession is emphasis on the creation and sharing of knowledge through the professional literature. The staff of the COS agencies early accepted the sponsorship of professional literature as a professional task. There were several early journals sponsored by individual agencies, and in 1920 the Association began the publication of *The Family*. The journal has continued publication to the present under the title *Social Casework* (Compton, 1980, pp. 390–391).

Since practice in the field of family services is largely carried forward within agencies, one of the most basic organizational tasks is simply that of organizing and ensuring the ongoing life of the agency. Voluntary agencies usually operate under the general policy directives of a board of directors. Such a board has three primary tasks—it establishes the right of the agency to carry on its program, sanctions the agency's overall policy, and raises funds. As a part of its task of carrying on the agency program, the board usually hires the executive of the agency and charges him with the day-by-day operations. The public or tax-supported agency will usually operate under legislation and will be dependent on some legislative body for its broad policy and the appropriation of funds for its support. Working within governmental organizations can be much more complex than working within the voluntary agency because workers find it necessary to understand three different levels and three different branches of government. The problem of reconciling the organizational tasks required by the agency and the professional responsibilities to which the worker carries a commitment may be extremely difficult for individual practitioners and often is a cause of conflict.

Structure, Methods, and Programs. In the early history of the development of clinical social work, the private family agency played a leading part. Much of the literature of social work practice was produced by those whose practice experience was in the urban family agency. Many teachers of practice in schools of social work were recruited from these agencies, and they were of central influence in the development of a social work curriculum. The executives of such agencies were central figures in community councils. However, the family agency is a part of the community in which it finds itself and is affected by the shifting community needs, the changes in family life, and the resources available to it. The turbulent political and social atmosphere of the 1960s, changing demographic trends of the 1970s, the nontraditional family forms that developed during these years, recent problems of inflation and increased unemployment, and changes in patterns of federal funding of human service programs have all had a significant impact on the family field of practice. In the 1960s, the private family service agency entered a period of transition that is still in process.

Although the field has attempted to respond with flexibility to changing social conditions and changes in organizational structure, policy, programs, and methods of practice during these years, the family agency has been the focus of much recent criticism. One of the most important areas of change for the family agency was the loss of its position of influence in the development of the curriculum of schools of social work in the 1960s. Feeling strongly that the trends of curriculum development of the late 1960s and early 1970s weakened the preparation of graduates of schools of social work for competent practice in family settings, the Board of Directors of the Family Service Association of America adopted a statement that set forth expectations for the beginning MSW practitioner. Concern was expressed regarding growing deemphasis on work with individuals, families, and groups. Support was given to the position that social work education had a responsibility to ensure the availability of graduates with the basic qualifications for beginning practitioners as defined in current agency practice.

Although family agencies had traditionally maintained a policy that services were available to anyone, the impact of new psychological knowledge and the movement toward psychotherapy mentioned previously may have discouraged many people who needed other kinds of help from applying to family agencies. This concern came to the fore as a part of the political climate of the 1960s; attention was focused on the special needs of minorities, the poor, and the aged, and family agencies were criticized for not doing enough to help these populations. In an attempt to be more responsive, family agencies began to develop special programs and to reach out to act as an advocate for such families. There has been a new and increased interest in the social problems affecting family life and an active development of a greater diversity of services. In 1950, the average number of programs reported by member agencies of FSAA, in addition to family therapy, was 2.1 per agency. By 1974, this number had increased to 4.4. In addition to this increase in programs, there were significant changes in basic counseling service. Group therapy, planned short-term treatment, co-therapists in group or family treatment, and newer and more experimental forms of treatment programs of family life education, programs aimed at marriage enrichment and improvement of communication skills (Ambrosino, 1977, pp. 432–434), were reported by family agencies.

These changes in programs and policies have resulted in many changes in the staff of voluntary family agencies. In 1957, 85 percent of the professional staff of FSAA member agencies had master's degrees in social work. In 1965, only 3 percent of the staff had professional certification in areas other than social work. However, by 1975, the number of MSW staff had decreased to 74 percent, and allied professionals, such as nurses, teachers, lawyers, and psychologists, made up 16 percent of the staff. Volunteers also began to be used by 48 percent of the agencies. Another significant change in the voluntary agency organization has been the efforts of the agencies to obtain boards that are more representative of the client population. In the five years from 1970 to 1975, minority representation on boards of FSAA member agencies increased from 10 percent to 16 percent (Ambrosino, 1977, pp. 331–333).

Four factors have brought significant changes in public agencies. The separation of the general counseling services from the administration of financial assistance has already been discussed. Another factor has been the unifying of child welfare and family welfare under one administrative structure. To many, this change has caused a reduction in the level of services to children without really aiding families. The public agency has never had more than a token percentage of workers with the MSW degree, particularly at the practitioner level. Currently, this small number may be decreasing because of the deprofessionalization of positions in the public services. The adequacy of social services offered to families through the public agencies remains very problematic, although certain family support programs, such as homemaker service, now are offered substantially by governmental agencies. A fourth factor has been the growing use of contracts in which the service is given by the voluntary agency and paid for by the public agency.

Issues in Methodology, Program Priorities, and Clinical Practice. Of all the helping professions, social work has been concerned the longest with the family and its welfare. Social work as a profession and the field of family work emerged together through the development of the family agencies. This relationship between agency services and methods of clinical practice may be a source of confusion. It is not so much the clinical practice methodologies that distinguish social work in the family field but rather the fact that "family casework is performed by a social worker within the boundaries of an agency whose stated concern is with the family and its individual members" (Sherman, 1977, p. 435). In the beginning, social work with families really involved a one-to-one working relationship with an individual member on behalf of the family's welfare. Certainly, one-to-one family treatment did have a broader concern than the individual alone; it was concerned with the functioning of the entire family and often changed focus from one family member to another as needed. With time, the services offered by the family agency expanded to include financial relief, homemaker services, family life education, and advocacy services, among others, and the clients were individuals of all ages, groups, families, and their collateral resources. Perhaps more critical to our concern here is not the wide-ranging services and programs found within the family agency but the wide-ranging modalities of practice that may be subsumed under the terms *casework, counseling, treatment,* and *therapy.*

As discussed earlier, the term *family social work* can cover anything done in a family agency by a social worker. In the 1940s, the Family Service Association of America supported the use of the term *family counseling* in an attempt to better define and differentiate the work that was aimed at changing or supporting psychosocial functioning from other activities, especially from financial assistance. However, *family counseling* proved to be a very broad term that has come to be used by social workers in other fields of practice and by many other professionals. Family practitioners engaged in work focused on the psychosocial functioning of the family now often use the terms *family treatment* or *family therapy* to define and label their activities. However, these terms are not easily distinguishable from each other or from *family counseling.* All of these terms are generic indicating nothing about the professional identification of the practitioner; they may cover work based on such widely differing theoretical orientations as behavior therapy and psychoanalytic treatment.

Given the confusion as to what is meant by *family practice,* it seems necessary to identify three directions in family work. There is a growing interest in treating the family as a whole; there is an increasing eclecticism found within the field; and the basic professional identification of family therapists may be any one of the helping professions. In recent years, a flood of new concepts related to the family and its treatment from many diverse sources has threatened to overwhelm those who work in this area. These concepts are poorly integrated, and there is little guidance as to their effective use in family social work. Practitioners interested in family work find that they may select and synthesize diverse concepts from many sources to construct as theory of practice, and they may adapt interventive modalities from a wide range of suggested techniques.

All these different approaches to family practice, however, rest on three common assumptions: individual dysfunction is supported by family dysfunctional patterns; effective therapy of individual dysfunction requires an assessment of the patterns of family interaction; and some type of alteration of this pattern is necessary for individual change. Among family therapists, the worker's involvement in the interaction of the family in the "here and now" is seen as enabling the worker to intervene much more effectively than is the case for approaches that are based upon one or more clients reporting family troubles. In practice, there are differing views about who constitutes the family for purposes of treatment and whether these individuals must always be treated in a group. There are also few guidelines as to which problems and families respond best to which forms of treatment.

Interaction of Practice, Policy, Resources, and Funding Patterns. In her work *The Common Base of Social Work Practice* (1970), Harriet Bartlett held that the early failure to distinguish between social welfare and social work had been an obstacle to developing a professional identity based on the practice activities of the social worker. She stated that "failure to make the distinction between agency and profession has been one important obstacle to the clarification of professional practice." She pointed out that the first discussion of the professional aspects of child welfare practice was found in the first volume of the *Encyclopedia of Social Work* (1965) and that, at that time, the article on family services was still written from the standpoint of agency services (Bartlett, 1970, p. 30).

Certainly, social work began within the structure of agencies. Certainly, the relationship and distinctions between social welfare, social agency, and social work have been continuously blurred and confused. This problem is most troublesome in the family and child welfare settings. Social workers in the early years were very concerned with the standards of service, and they established national agencies to monitor services. However, national agencies did not distinguish between standards for the operation of programs and standards for practice. Thus, we have no definition of *family social work practice* apart from the agency setting in which the practice is done. The terms *family therapy* and *family treatment,* which are labels for private practice, obscure what is unique to social work practice. For many practitioners, the problem of the interaction of clinical practice and agency program may not seem to be critically important. However, one cannot but wonder if this lack of distinction affects funding patterns and resources available to the field and hinders the development of a strong professional identification. We are in a time of shrinking resources, expanding costs, and an ever-increasing need for professional services. If a case is to be made for well-funded programs, it may be necessary for the social work profession to become more highly visible as a profession that has some competence and expertise of its own to offer the community. One method of becoming more visible is to define our practice and to engage in some viable research relative to our practice. But this research cannot come until we have made a further effort to define our practice and our problems.

Every social work practitioner working within an agency structure is constantly aware of the impact of policy on the way the client's problem is defined and on practice. We may not always be aware of the impact of our practice on policy matters. However, it is important in every setting to recognize the reciprocal nature of the policy–practice relationship. This may be of particular importance in family work, where the range of programs and practice modalities is so broad and ill defined.

Originally, family social work was funded by voluntary contributions from wealthy contributors. Beginning during World War I and continuing afterward, efforts toward centralized fund-raising and coordination among the privately supported welfare agencies began to develop. As a part of these activities, there came a growing emphasis on the methods of collecting and accounting for money.

From these concerns, there developed a plan for joint fund-raising for many agencies. This movement became known as the Community Chest Movement. An important result of this movement was the change in the identity of the givers. Over the years, almost year employed person in the community has become a contributor to this centralized fund, from which voluntary family agencies receive much of their support. Thus, the support of voluntary family agencies is no longer largely in the hands of wealthy patrons but represents many interests of the community. In addition to such funding, family agencies have established a fee for service based on ability to pay. A third important source of support that has grown in recent years is the purchase of service agreements, under which the public family or child welfare agency typically pays the voluntary agency for service to families meeting certain standards of need. Obviously, it is uncertain at this time how this source of funding will develop, given the cutbacks in federally supported social programs. Also, the splintering of community interests and the concern of many people with support of their special interests have resulted in many recent attacks on the Community Chests agencies and their manner of collecting funds. It may be that, as special interests grow, the family agency with its broad approach may suffer a loss of support.

Issues of Accountability. From their beginning, family agencies have been concerned with standards of service as well as with efforts to support an increasingly effective practice. As already discussed, national agencies were established to assist in regulating and coordinating services to clients. The Association continues to serve as the primary national standard-setting body for the field of family practice, and it continues to provide educational, research, and administrative services to improve the quality of family services.

Perhaps the major problem related to standard setting is the problem of assessing the outcome of work with individuals and families. The Association has long collected information about services and the characteristics of clients served. This type of information can be very helpful in giving the field an understanding of client problems, of changes in family life, and characteristics of families seeking assistance. Such findings are of considerable value when used to generate changes in the agency program. In 1970, Beck and Jones found that counseling activities consumed three-fourths of the agencies' time and effort, while such activities as advocacy and family life education each received no more than 3 percent of time and effort. An important finding of this study was that the practices of the agencies had changed very little from 1960 to 1970.

However, the issue of standard setting raises the question of standards for what? Is the principal concern of the agency the need for effective service to clients? If so, then we move into the questions of accountability for outcome. There is little research on outcomes in family and marital therapy. Before outcome research designs can be developed, we need much more explicit and measurable descriptions of practice procedures. What is it that practitioners in family therapy really do? What are the differences in techniques from one modality to another? And what are the results that such techniques are expected to produce? Perhaps one of the major requirements that creates problems for those attempting to develop measures of outcome is the fact that in such helping processes the intervention goals must be individualized for each family or each client. Some solutions to these problems may be found in some of the "single-subject" or "single-case" designs, such as Goal Attainment Scaling, which attempts to measure outcome against the individual client goals established at the beginning of the work. However difficult this task may seem, we must do a more competent job of identifying and testing our practice actions if social work with families is to advance practice knowledge and be accountable.

Child Welfare

Social Functions and Responsibilities. Child welfare emerged as a field of social work practice from the very beginning of the profession, and yet, there appears to be no common definition of child welfare services. In 1935, the Social Security Act defined such services as "services for the protection and care of homeless, dependent, and neglected children and children in danger of becoming delinquent." In 1958, Richman (p. 1) defined child welfare as a "field of practice concerned with children whose circumstances within themselves, their family, or community may jeopardize their normal developments." The Child Welfare League of America, the national association concerned with social work services in this field of practice, stated in 1959 that child welfare services are those social services provided to families unable to fulfill their childcaring responsibilities without help. The interesting difference between this statement and the two earlier statements is that the Child Welfare League statement speaks of service to families, whereas the other two statements speak of services to children. Certainly, the earlier practice in child welfare put primary emphasis on approaches to the care and protection of children, with little concern for the parents. In recent years, however, there has been a growing concern with the importance of family interaction and the family as the target of service. The question is often dichotomized as "does one help the child most effectively through the direct approach to, and concern with, the child or does one help the child most effectively through an approach to the family?" A further question that follows from this issue is whether there are differences between the work of child welfare workers and family service workers in their approaches to the family.

Kadushin (1980, pp. 6–7) states that child welfare services "as a field of social work practice are those services comprising a field of social work practice that engage in those activities concerned with preventing, ameliorating, and remedying of social problems related to the functioning of the parent–child relationship through the development and provision of specific child welfare services, such as adoption, foster care, institutional care, protective services, daycare, homemaker service, supportive services, and so on." In this definition, Kadushin very neatly addresses the target of intervention as the parent–child relationship, thereby using the social work concept that our concern in social work is probably more productive when addressed to the interaction between systems. He also distinguishes between family work and child welfare work by specifically stating the services the child welfare worker provides. However, in essence, this definition emphasizes practice in child welfare as the administration of certain specific social services. The question for the profession is, how do the methods used in the delivery of such services in child welfare differ from services provided by other social workers? Are practice actions and their knowledge base different, or are the services different? What is the interaction between services and the professional knowledge and skill with which they are delivered?

One of the interesting facts about child welfare service is how little they have changed over the past one hundred years. Kadushin points out that there have been changes in emphasis as to which services are seen as preferable for which clients, and there have been changes in the boundaries of the field, but the core services have remained stable (Kadushin, 1980, p. 7). A 1976 review of child welfare delivery systems in twenty-five states found that all offered the following services: adoption service, foster family care, emergency shelter care for children, institutional care for children, group home service, homemaker service, protective service, social services for unmarried parents, and social services for children in their own home. Most but not all offered residential treatment and daycare; and a few states included delinquency services as part of child welfare services (Peat, Marwick, Mitchell, and Company, 1976, p. 111.90).

Child welfare services have been affected by the American cultural values of individual independence and the sanctity of the family as a relatively closed social system in which authorities have little right to interfere. Thus, historically, the earliest type of service to children involved substitute care, either institutional care or apprenticeship of children to foster families when children were without parental care either because of the absence of the parents or because of the poverty of the parents. In 1790, the first public orphanage in the American colonies was established in South Carolina. The institution was to care for and educate both orphan children and children whose parents were destitute and unable to maintain them. The matron of the orphanage was also the schoolteacher, and she was to educate the children as well as offer them maintenance and maternal care (Compton, 1980, p. 200). Although we usually think of a supervised foster home service as developing somewhat later, apprenticeship was perhaps a crude beginning. Apprenticeship was primarily used for the purposes of education, training into a work role, and socialization of children. It was largely used privately by families seeking supplementation of their ability to educate and train their children, but it was also used by the court for children without parental care. Between 1646 and 1769, Virginia enacted a series of eight laws dealing with the power of the courts to apprentice certain groups of children, particularly illegitimate, mulatto, and poor children. These laws required that the church wardens be responsible for the standards of care received by such children in their foster homes and that records be kept of their activities. Were these the first child welfare workers?

The placement of children outside their own homes has always been a central child welfare service and probably will continue to be. There always seem to be homes where the strengths of the parents and the needs of the child are so mismatched that the child cannot safely remain at home. However, the form of the placement has changed continually over the years. The undifferentiated orphanage has disappeared, and we now have specialized placement of children in varying types of care. There are residential treatment centers and halfway houses for disturbed children. There are various types of group home care—some are publicly operated, some are privately operated. The idea of placing children to prepare them to assume productive adult roles in apprenticeship has given way to the notion that children should be placed in foster homes for purposes of nurturance and care. Also, we have moved from free foster homes to paid foster care.

Until the middle of the nineteenth century, children were seen as small adults but without adult rights. The father was considered to have an absolute right to their custody and control. However, in the late 1880s, the view of children and childhood began to change as the result of three factors: (1) adult life was no longer so precarious, so there began to be more adults in proportion to children in society, and thus children received more individual attention; (2) knowledge about the growth, development, and needs of children as a special population began to grow; and (3) there was a general growth of concern for the rights of all human beings (Compton, 1980, p. 292). Some of these concerns were seen in the increased challenge to the rights of the father to the child, in the courts' willingness to give the rights of the mother some consideration, and in the concern with the welfare of the child in disputes over the custody of children. There was also a growing concern with the importance of offering the child protection from abuse, neglect, and immoral influences, although it was not until 1875 that a legal precedent was established for removing children from such situations. In most states, the laws to protect children from abuse followed by a decade the laws to protect animals from similar treatment. Protecting children from physical abuse by their parents or other family members who may have control over them has been a very difficult issue because of the widespread belief that physical punishment is a necessary part of the effective discipline of children and that parents have the duty to control their children. As an example of this belief, we have had the Supreme Court decision of 1977, which holds that teachers have the right to use reasonable physical punishment to control children in school. There are scattered efforts in various states today to remove child abuse laws from children's codes on the basis that they allow the state to interfere with the right of parents to discipline children as they see fit.

Beginning in the 1960s, with the identification of the battered child syndrome, we have had a growing community and professional interest in abuse and a rapidly expanding range of available services for help. This interest has broadened from concern with the beaten child to concern with children as victims of familial incest or other adult exploitation. A greater understanding of the dynamics of violence toward the child and its incidence in society has resulted in the development of crisis services, usually staffed at least in part by paraprofessionals, including emergency hot-lines, drop-off centers, and such self-help groups as Parents Anonymous. Over the past decade, there has developed a new and growing literature on child abuse and considerable work toward the development of increasing professional skills in this critical and conflicted area of practice. At present, we do not seem to be as concerned about the neglected child as the abused one, although many more children are affected by neglect than by abuse.

The concern with the welfare of neglected children and the movement to protect such children developed concurrently with the child abuse laws. Neglect has been even more difficult for the courts to define than has physical abuse. Is it neglect if the parent is unable to care for a child's physical needs because there is no employment or income in the home? In the nineteenth century, many children were removed from parents, particularly from widowed mothers, and institutionalized because the parents had inadequate financial resources to care for their physical needs. Not until the early 1900s did social workers take the position that children should not be removed from parents for reasons of poverty alone. It may be that there is still dispute about this concept in society. Although the neglect laws vary from state to state, the statutes and practice today usually define the following as indication of neglect: (1) inadequate physical care, (2) the absence of adequate medical care, (3) cruel or abusive treatment, (4) improper supervision and control, (5) exploiting the child for monetary purposes, (6) unlawfully keeping the child out of school, (7) exposing the child to criminal or immoral influences that might endanger morals (Compton, 1980, pp. 295–296).

Adoption services and services to unmarried parents have been closely related throughout the history of child welfare. Adoption laws began appearing in American states in the early 1800s, although these procedures were largely a matter between private citizens, in which the only legal issue involved was the right of inheritance and control of the child. The laws merely provided for legal transfer of a child by the natural parents and required that such a transfer be recorded. Services to unwed mothers began somewhat later and were initially centered around maternity homes that provided counseling and care for the unwed pregnant woman. Currently, these areas of child welfare services are the focus of considerable concern because of the changing culture and demographics. There has been a rapid increase in teenage pregnancies over the past decade. However, the change in laws relating to abortion has enabled unwed women to choose to terminate the pregnancy. In addition, as a result of changing mores, many teenage mothers are keeping their children. This change has resulted in a decrease in the use of maternity homes by unwed mothers and an expansion of other services. The growth of such services is supported by findings of the vulnerability of the young unwed mother and her baby to neglect, poor health practices, and troubled relationships. Because of these changes, the number of white infants available for adoption has decreased markedly. Adoption workers are concentrating less on selecting the best home for normal white infants and more on the placement of older children, handicapped children, and biracial children.

Two major child welfare services, homemaker and daycare, were developed to supplement maternal childcare in the 1920s and 1930s. The homemaker service originally developed in the family agencies as a way of meeting the needs of the family in which the mother was temporarily unable to fulfill her role. Social workers also found that homemakers can be valuable in supporting, educating, and developing maternal skills in inadequate mothers. At the time of its development, such social work services were clearly directed at the welfare of children. Today, health personnel vie with social workers for control and administration of these programs, and the aged as well as children receive such services.

Daycare developed originally under a number of auspices to care for children of working mothers. In the 1930s, it became an integral part of child welfare but daycare services are no longer defined as social work services. Daycare is once again being offered in industry, in hospitals, in universities, in various community centers, and by private persons for profit. The services themselves have become diversified. They no longer serve only the preschool child of working parents but may serve children of working parents of any age. Daycare is also offered for special children who may be difficult to care for at home or who need broader socialization experiences. Also, daycare serves other special populations, such as the mentally ill and the retarded.

Two other areas that are generally included among child welfare services are services to children in their own homes aimed at support or change of parental functioning and services for children that help them to function more adequately within the family. These services are more amorphous than other child welfare services and generally involve counseling or therapy, perhaps supplemented by other services. Therefore, these services may overlap with those offered by family agencies and mental health clinics. In fact, child welfare workers often refer clients to those agencies. In spite of the lack of clarity about these services, there is a growing interest in them as an effective way of offering services to children. The unification of child welfare services and family services under Title XX may be one indication of this trend. Many child welfare workers question the integration of child welfare and family services within the public services, as they believe that they have developed a special expertise that will be diluted or lost in this movement.

Organizations and Professional Tasks. The first task of child welfare services is the protection and development of children. Social workers know that they cannot respond effectively to the needs of children without involving the family and the parents, nor can social workers effectively perform daily family tasks for any period of time for parents and family. This means that, in the interests of the child, social workers engage in some type of intervention in family life. Thus, they are faced with the difficult task of performing both protective and helping functions. Social workers recognize that, although they have access to certain resources that enable them to offer protective services, these services are always substitutes for or supplements to those of the family.

Most people are concerned with the welfare of children and are troubled by the thought that helpless and vulnerable children suffer abuse, neglect, and exploitation. The availability of child welfare services offers reassurance that the community is acting to prevent or remedy such situations. Since much of our concern with children is stimulated by our identification with them, we all have values concerning the care of children, and we may become angry and punitive toward those who fail to meet our standards. Thus, social workers often have to deal with community value systems that may be rigidly prescriptive regarding parental behavior and sexual norms, and social workers in child welfare practice often find themselves at a point of intense conflict between parent and community. The fundamental values of our society are assured through adequate family functioning in conformance with community values. Child welfare services validate societal norms by changing or supporting parental and child behavior to accord with these norms; child welfare services thereby protect and assure community stability.

The field of child welfare, probably more than any other field of practice, is dependent on the availability and organization of tangible resources and services. Frequently, resources are inadequate to the demands of the client situation. Thus, the practitioner often finds the tasks of practice expanded by the necessity of securing necessary resources. In this difficult and ambiguous practice, an often neglected task of the organizations in the field is to develop various supportive mechanisms for the practitioners. The child welfare worker is constantly confronted with conflict and failure in the most basic and meaningful areas of human life. This is demanding and stressful, and workers need organizational support for their activities. Both the organizations and the profession need to examine the question of preparation for practice in this field. This complex service is offered largely by practitioners with the BSW degree. Is this a responsible use of professional people?

Structure, Methods, and Programs. Child welfare services are at a critical point in development. Currently, four emerging practices have become controversial. The first of these is the growing tendency for certain services, especially daycare and homemaker service, to be offered through proprietary agencies for profit. Second, other professions, such as nursing and law, are developing definitions of child welfare that place their profession rather than social work at the center of the services to be provided and the programs to be developed. Third, there is a movement toward deprofessionalization as the field moves increasingly to the use of nonprofessionals to deliver some central services. Additional services have been developed by lay groups and individuals who question the necessity of social work expertise. Fourth, as a part of this deprofessionalization, there is a growing tendency to substitute specific legal directives and legislative requirements for discretionary professional decisions. Thus, the flexibility of social work has been reduced, and the central role of social work is being eroded.

The conviction that the best life for children is life within their own family has grown over the years, until today most social workers would accept and support this notion. An unfortunate result of this conviction, taken together with the lack of professional expertise on the part of child welfare workers in the public services, has been the indiscriminate use of referral of troubled families with problems of child care to mental health centers, family agencies, and specialized counseling services. In some agencies, there is a policy that workers must refer families with certain problems to certain resources. Often, these referrals result in a redefinition of the problems to focus upon individual pathology rather than parent–child relationships. Frequently, confused parents terminate treatment.

In his review of child welfare literature, Kadushin (1980, p. 41) found that certain central criticisms of child welfare services had been prevalent for several decades. Included are criticisms that "access to service is difficult and discouraging; that service is fragmented, poorly coordinated vertically and horizontally, and discontinuous; that there is an overuse of substitute care services and an underuse of supportive services; that the service offered is often not appropriate to the problem presented or to the client presenting the problem; that the approach to clients is unnecessarily authoritarian and coercive, and the worker's decisions are often arbitrary and made without regard to a systematic diagnostic assessment of the situation; that children get lost in the system, temporary care becomes permanent care, systematic review of case planning is often neglected, and there is a studied indifference to parental needs once the child has been removed; that the system operates against the achievement of permanence for many children; that large groups of children, particularly the nonwhite and the poor, are not adequately served by the system; that the system is unresponsive and inequitable."

Kadushin agrees that many of these charges are true, but he believes the system has provided an acceptable level of nurturance and care for hundreds of thousands of children, that child welfare services do have public support and recognition as necessary services, and that the large sums of money flowing into the program have been responsibly used for the purposes intended. Perhaps the important thing about the present status of the field is not that the community would abolish the system but that it would strengthen and expand services to assure greater competency and effectiveness.

Methodology, Program Priorities, and Clinical Practice. Perhaps the greatest challenge to clinical practice in child welfare services comes from the interaction of the growing conviction that children should be served in their own homes if at all possible and the growing complexity and difficulty of the situations faced by practitioners as they attempt to secure the welfare of children. Practitioners in child welfare need to recognize the real difficulty of the situations in which they work. They need to develop a far more realistic notion of the pace of change in such situations as well as the investment that the practitioner must make if any change is possible. Few of these situations are going to yield to short-term treatment or to monthly visits, nor are they readily responsive to referral to other systems, some of which may have been unsuccessfully involved with a family before it came to the attention of the child welfare system. This difficulty demands that clinical practitioners develop a clearer and more precise identification of the specialized demands and characteristics of the field and that they develop a greater understanding of the stresses of family life and the struggle that many parents face as they try to meet the daily demands of family life, often with poor preparation, inadequate skills, and little knowledge of their task.

It is generally recognized that social work practice rests upon an integration of values, knowledge, and skill and that clinical practice involves the worker's effective use of self and resources. Child welfare practice tests the worker's capacity in all these areas. There are not enough good foster homes, group homes, homemakers, residential treatment facilities, or adoptive homes for special children. There are not enough practitioners to meet the need for professional services, and many of the available staff are poorly trained.

There are equally critical issues in clinical practice itself. Child welfare practice impinges upon the values of the practitioners, upon their personal and professional beliefs about the basic relationships of life. For many in clinical practice, it is difficult to avoid anger and subtle moral judgments of parents who have abused children. Yet, such feelings effectively block offering unconditional care and support to parents. The problem of congruency and honesty in the social work relationship is a significant one. There is a demand for practitioner self-awareness in working with parents that is presently being ignored in our literature. The profession must develop ways to develop and support self-awareness and the disciplined use of self in the interests of client service. Although our knowledge base about human change may be limited, we do have some practice knowledge that has been tentatively tested and found helpful in work with neglectful and abusive parents. All these approaches involve patience, time, the ability to work with minute details, a clear commitment to families, and an ability to negotiate between family and other systems. The further development of these tentative approaches seems to be systematically neglected by the field, while attempts are made to adopt practice modalities from other fields of practice that may not be appropriate to child welfare practice. There must be a far more judicious use of referral, with careful study of which referrals are successful and which fail. Above all, there needs to be a recognition that other professions or other fields of social work practice have even fewer resources to deal with problem families than does the child welfare field.

Interaction of Practice, Policy, Resources, and Funding Patterns. The number of children in the population is declining, and the median age of the population is increasing. Thus, in actual numbers, there are fewer children at risk, which suggests less need for community support. However, there are other factors that appear to be increasing the risk of children's exposure to abuse. Infant mortality is declining, and more children are saved by treatment in utero or at birth. As more children who are fragile, vulnerable, or otherwise have special health needs survive birth and infancy, it may be that this population will need both more service and a different service. The number of out-of-wedlock pregnancies among teenage mothers is increasing, and more such mothers are keeping their children. Both these mothers and their children appear to have more problems—physically, economically, psychologically, and socially—than do older mothers. This population may require some reshaping of the types of services offered. We may need more in-home, parent–child supportive and educational services. There presently is less need for maternity homes and more need for walk-in health clinics and drop-off centers. There is an increasing divorce rate, which, added to the growth of numbers of teenage mothers, will mean a greater percentage of single parents in our society. Children of single parents are more at risk than children living in a two-parent household. Single parenthood requires that one person fulfill two roles in managing family tasks and meeting the relational demands of children. In addition, if there is only one parent in the home, there is no back-up or reinforcement when that parent is under stress, physically ill, or emotionally exhausted. Also, most single parents work out of the home, and the incomes of most single-parent families are significantly lower than the incomes of two-parent families. These two facts mean an increasing demand for subsidized daycare and, perhaps, supportive self-help groups. There also will be an increase in the number of children living in poverty. The uncertain economic climate may add further stress to both the single-parent family and the two-parent family. The stress of unemployment and lack of security may result in an increase in the amount of violence in the family and thus result in an increased need for services for the children at risk.

All these factors point to the possibility of an increased demand for child welfare services. At the same time, there is currently a growing disenchantment with the ability of either government or the professions to solve social problems and an increasing belief that people should solve their own family problems and that professional intervention in families is wrong. It may be likely that financial support for such services will decrease just as more services are needed. Likewise, certain services, such as contraceptives for the unwed, abortion counseling, and daycare for employed single mothers, may face significant cuts in public budgetary support. These cuts may support the growing movement toward private service programs for profit. Daycare has led this movement but now is joined by homemaker services and foster care.

During the past few years, there has been a growing concern about clients' rights and the growing amount of litigation between family members. These factors have increased the complexity of the practitioner's work and accelerated change in practitioner–client relationships. The ruling of the courts that the unwed father must give his permission for adoption has not only added to the tasks of the worker but has increased the complexity of the relationship between the rights of the child and the unwed mother. The controversy over the right of the adopted child to know the identity of the birth mother, who was promised complete secrecy and a closing of the books when she signed the adoption papers, has brought to the fore questions not only of the child's rights but the rights of the two sets of parents involved in adoptions. The family no longer conforms to the model of the two-parent family with two children, in which the father's role centers around financial support and the mother's around child care, but the community has not abandoned the older family form as the correct model. Thus, child welfare workers may increasingly find themselves the center of the controversy between a censorious community and a vulnerable family.

The problems of racial segregation and discrimination impinge heavily on child welfare. Minority children appear to be at greater risk than white children: more of them live in central cities where life is more difficult; more of them die at birth or in the first year of life; more of them are born to unwed parents; the percentage of black children living with single parents is higher; a greater number of minority children are placed for adoption. The question of the responsibility of child welfare work to be actively concerned with social justice and equality is an urgent one.

If the field is to confront these issues successfully, there will be an increasing demand for expansion and innovation in services at a time of decreasing resources. Initially supported by voluntary funds, child welfare services today are almost entirely supported by federal funds administered through state and federal channels. One way of making a credible demand for better support of services is to develop an increasingly effective practice skill and to demonstrate that social work is indeed competent to meet the demands imposed upon it. Thus, policy and service delivery systems call upon clinical practice to furnish the evidence needed for further development. However, in a frustrating circular way, clinical practice cannot demonstrate expertise or develop further knowledge and skill without the support of the policies of the delivery system. A social worker's right to make professional assessments and intervention plans in the best interests of clients and to deploy resources to implement plans must be supported by policy if the profession is to be held responsible for the results of intervention.

Issues of Accountability. The various states have each set standards for the licensing and regulation of certain programs found within child welfare services, such as daycare, foster care, and institutional care. Generally, these standards set adequate agency safeguards of the physical care of children and qualifications of staff. The Child Welfare League of America, a national voluntary standard-setting body, was founded in 1921 to improve standards of care and service in child welfare agencies. It has worked toward the improvement of standards and practices in the field, has been effective in promoting legislation, and has been a leader in research in the field. The issue of accountability is a very pressing one in the field since we do not have sophisticated methods to evaluate the effectiveness of intervention. A further problem is the lack of definitive statistics. We have no accurate notion of the number of children needing services or the number of children under care. We do know the extent of certain childhood problems, such as mental retardation. We know the number of working mothers, but we do not know how many of their children need care. The Child Welfare League has tried to collect meaningful statistics on services, but their data remain spotty. Until we have a more accurate accounting of the need for services, the field will be pressed to meet other questions related to accountability.

Social Work in Health Care

Social Functions and Responsibilities. When we speak of the historical roots of social work in health care, we usually think of Dr. Richard C. Cabot, who became interested in the idea of social adjustment as a part of medical treatment. In 1905, Cabot employed the first hospital social worker to help patients to deal better with their illnesses and to make better use of what the hospital had to offer. In 1907, social service was established at Johns Hopkins Hospital, but the hospital did not welcome the social workers with open arms. Helen Brogden, the second worker to be employed at Johns Hopkins, was surprised to learn shortly after her employment that no department in the hospital was willing to take responsibility for her department and that Helen Wilmer, the first social worker, had paid her own departmental expenses out of her own pocket. Massachusetts General refused to assume any responsibility for the department for many years after it began. At both these hospitals there was considerable resistance to their employment.

However, social workers were also involved at this same time in two other aspects of health care, public health and clinics. Many social agencies as well as settlement houses were concerned with the investigation of the causes of major communicable diseases, especially tuberculosis. Social workers and public health workers formed early public health teams for study and prevention. Social workers also contributed to the early struggles toward better health by the establishment of clinics in many settlements, by working toward physical examinations for all school children, and by applying their skills to public educational campaigns. Social workers in hospitals became concerned with the question of education for their practice shortly after they entered the institution. In 1921, a two-year training course (which lasted only a brief time) was initiated at Johns Hopkins Hospital.

Social work practice in health settings could be said to have become mature with the development of medical–social consultants following the passage of the Social Security Act. During the 1940s and 1950s, social workers became recognized as health care professionals participating in health teams and comprehensive health projects. During the 1970s and 1980s, social work in the health field has been expanding rapidly. Neighborhood health centers and outreach programs have involved social workers. The Joint Commission on Accreditation of Hospitals has supported the necessity of social work in hospitals. Social worker consultation has become required in nursing homes. Social work has been involved in Medicaid and Medicare programs. Social services reimbursement is already established under major federal insurance plans, and services are now required in health maintenance organizations.

Organizations and Professional Tasks. The literature on practice in the health field generally lists four central functions of the professional social worker: (1) individual practice focused on the social needs and social functioning of individual patients or their families; (2) the development of coordinated community resources that may be needed for health care; (3) providing linkages between the patient, the patient's family, and other supportive community resources; (4) consultation and teaching activities in relation to other professionals in the setting. A fifth function could well be added: exploration of need and other research efforts.

Social work in health care occurs in a setting in which other professionals, who are usually in the majority, are generally considered to be the primary service deliverers. The primary function of the setting is not the delivery of social services but the delivery of health care. Social work is seen as making a valued contribution to this function.

Structure, Methods, and Programs. Health is an interest of most citizens, and social work in the health field enjoys a certain support and status that many other social service systems do not enjoy. Social workers employed in the health field have consistently made up one-third of the membership of NASW for two decades. Most practitioners in the health field possess M.S.W. degrees. The health field is developing challenging new tasks for social workers as medicine makes dramatic advances in technology. The critical areas in health today are conquering the diseases that seem related to life-style and the need for people who develop these diseases to comply over long periods of time with a regimen of medication and living that may limit their usual ways of functioning. Infectious and communicable disease and accidents are no longer the principal problems of health care. It would seem that social workers are uniquely qualified to offer service in these developing areas, which are so closely related to social functioning. Helping patients to cope with the transition in life-style would appear to be a particularly important area for social work.

Social workers in the health field have differed somewhat from social workers in the family or child welfare fields in their central concerns. Not being as involved in the issue of the administration of services, and working in a situation where they have constantly been required to differentiate their professional responsibility and competence from the health professionals around them, they have concentrated more on the definition and differentiation of practice methods.

Social workers in the health field today are found as regular faculty members of medical schools and schools of nursing, dentistry, public health, and other health care departments. The largest number of clinical practitioners are working in hospital social service departments. Many are working in such highly specialized medical areas as regional burn centers, pain clinics, sickle-cell diagnostic centers, hospital intensive-care and coronary-care units, genetic counseling, renal disease units, and chemotherapy units.

Issues in Methodology, Program Priorities, and Clinical Practice. The prime influence on the practice of clinical social work in the health setting is the fact that it is practiced within a host setting and its work supplements the principal goal of the health agency. This setting imposes a dual goal on workers in the health field. They must attain the goals of the health agency and the primary professional staff of that agency and maintain their own identity and practice within their own profession. The effectiveness with which they carry this out depends on two groups of skills—the ability to work effectively with other members of the health team and the ability to work effectively with the other social services of the community.

Social workers also have become increasingly involved in consultation. Although they have always carried teaching and consulting roles, these roles are becoming more formalized in the effective delivery of health care. Social workers contribute knowledge about individual and family dynamics and community resources and help plan and shape treatment.

Two qualities mark clinical practice in the medical setting; one is the episodic and crisis-oriented nature of client problems, and the other is the fact that the treatment plan is shaped by and must be integrated with the medical regimen. Social workers in health care must possess crisis skills and use various short-term treatment modalities. The practitioners in this area need to be flexible and especially skilled at consideration of treatment alternatives. Previously, social workers in health care were primarily concerned with counseling and supporting the ill person. However, today the worker needs a much more sophisticated understanding of systems theory, which is moving away from the person–environment dichotomy to an understanding of the patient in interaction with his family, community, and the medical system. There is a growing use of group work and of various types of family counseling and therapy in these settings. Although most health care social workers function in hospital settings, there is a movement into extended care facilities, nursing homes, and community health centers. This trend supports the growing autonomy of the medical social worker. It also involves the worker in preventive activities and family education.

The advancement in the medical treatment of formerly hopeless conditions involves the social worker in many complex ethical issues. In addition, an important area of concern is the issue of client rights and "informed consent." These issues may put the worker in conflict with the setting in the interests of the client. However, the values of social work call for concern with the self-determination of the client. In this regard, it is noteworthy that research findings indicate that compliance with a difficult medical regimen depends on the client's feelings of responsibility for his regimen, which in turn depends on the client feeling a sense of control over what is happening to him.

Interaction of Practice, Policy, Resources, and Funding Patterns. Probably no other area of social work practice is in the midst of so much change as social work in health care. There have been significant changes in the method of payment for medical services. The increase in third-party payments has placed a demand on social workers to be clear about what they contribute to health care and to move toward nationwide licensing of medical social work personnel. The development of new programs in the area of thanatology demands that workers increase their skill in this area. The growing notion of consumer participation in medical care planning both expands and changes the nature of social work practice. It means that workers need to be active in support of patient's rights and informed consumers in any policy matters; it involves social work professionals in the education and training of other health professionals as to the importance and impact of services to support these movements; and it involves social workers to a much greater extent in supportive and facilitative services to family members.

Group medical practice, health maintenance organizations, and other new medical delivery systems put the health care worker in contact with clients who may never have previously used social work services. The expansion of extended care facilities and nursing homes will bring several new dimensions to practice. The aged will demand an expansion of services and may require a change in interventive methods. There will be an increased demand for skills in long-term care rather than crisis work. The involvement of families in treatment will demand more knowledge about families and more work with families.

Expenditures for health care are rising rapidly. These costs are paid by some combination of patient resources, voluntary health insurance, and the various levels of government through a wide variety of plans, ranging from the charity hospital to Medicare. Government support and voluntary insurance usually cover hospital expenses and most physician's services but few other health care expenses. Since the 1920s, there have been repeated efforts to increase government's role in covering the costs of health care, and there have been some gains. But the costs of medical care continue to rise as the result of inflation, the expense of the many complex methods of care, and the fact that people live longer and use more medical services. One of the time-consuming and demanding tasks of the medical social worker is helping the patient to find financial support or resources to pay the cost of illness. One of the greatest fears of the elderly patient centers on the cost of medical care. The health maintenance organizations that have developed in the past two decades with the support of federal funds are one attempt to meet the cost of care. In this plan, the patient pays in advance for almost complete medical care, and the organization furnishes other health needs, such as glasses and medication, at reduced cost.

Issues of Accountability. Social workers in health care may be more aware of the issues of accountability and regulatory standards than workers in any other setting. Many and various systems of state licensing and certification have developed to assure the quality of health care. Such attempts focus on the ability of those giving professional service in health settings to pass an examination at a certain minimal level. Certain voluntary associations certify special competencies of professionals. Voluntary hospital accreditation has a long history. Such accreditation standards have formed the basis of in-hospital control of physicians and the maintenance of standards of in-hospital medical and surgical practice. There have been recent attempts on the part of the federal government to assure quality of care through a process of peer review in institutions that participate in federally reimbursed services. Bess Dana (1977, pp. 548–549) identifies seven movements that support self-examination and accountability in the health field: (1) the spread of peer review from required to voluntary programs involving all professionals in the health field, (2) reforms in record keeping, growth in skills in evaluative research, and uniform standards of diagnosis following from peer review efforts, (3) the linkages between the structure of delivery systems and efforts at cost control, (4) increasing concern to protect the patient through professional concern with quality control, (5) mandated requirements for the protection of persons as subjects of scientific research, (6) consumer participation, (7) medical schools' participation in developing education, research, and service linkages.

Mental Health

Social Functions and Responsibilities. In a 1978 report, the Council on Social Work Education identified fourteen different types of agencies involved in the mental health delivery system and classified them into four major types: (1) community mental health centers, (2) hospital settings, (3) freestanding clinics and components of other center services, (4) agencies providing indirect services, such as planning and education (Harm, 1978, p. 51).

This classification includes all organizations that deliver mental health services, but it does not specify what services these organizations actually deliver. Hill, Lehmann, and Slotkin (1971) made a study for the Family Service Association of America and listed the following as major problems served by mental health clinics: disturbance of feeling, disturbance of thought, disturbance of behavior, sexual problems, physical difficulties, psychophysiological difficulties, disturbance of family and social relationships, disturbance of school or work, and environmental problems. In this study, disturbances of feeling and behavior accounted for 26 percent of the applications, and disturbances of family and social relationships accounted for another 25 percent (Hill, Lehmann, and Slotkin, 1971, p. 21).

Some see the responsibilities of the mental health field of practice very broadly as including all those professional and organizational services that contribute in any way to the maintenance and improvement of the emotional and mental health of citizens. Although it is possible to define the field of mental health to include all aspects of living, the focus of the field, both historically and currently, has been the direct treatment of identified problems of mental, emotional, or social disturbance as presented by the individual applicant. The past and the present orientation of most mental health services is that of medical practice aimed at curing, or at least alleviating, identified individual (or in some cases, family) pathology. Early definitions of responsibilities assigned to the field would have been much simpler and more limited in scope. Early mental health organizations were only hospitals admitting the demonstrably insane who could not function in the community. Later, outpatient clinics of various types offered services to acting-out and highly disturbed persons and their families while they remained in their own communities. Only recently have organizations—the comprehensive mental health centers—attempted the dual charge of treatment and prevention of mental illness.

The history of concern for the mentally ill in America may be traced to colonial times. The first public hospital for the insane was established at Williamsburg, Virginia, in 1773. In the 1840s, Dorothea Dix was active in seeking reform of the care of the mentally ill, becoming perhaps the earliest advocate for the use of federal funds for social welfare in her request for ten million acres of federal lands to support the care of the indigent insane. Social workers first became involved in the mental hygiene movement when members of the Conference of Charities organized the National Association for the Protection of the Insane and the Prevention of Insanity. The goals of the Association were initiating better policies for the care of the insane and assuring better hospital conditions. This early society dissolved after about ten years, as it was unable to interest the public in its concern with the mentally ill. It was opposed by the medical superintendants of the state hospitals, and it became caught in the battle between psychiatrists and neurologists for dominance in treatment of mental illness (Compton, 1980, pp. 243–247, 406–410).

The entry of clinical social work into the field of mental health came in 1904, when Dr. Adolph Meyer, Director of New York State Psychiatric Institute, asked his wife, a social worker, to visit his patients both in the hospital and at home to secure complete case histories. Meyer believed that insanity was a maladjustment of the whole personality rather than a disease of the brain and that complete information about the patient's social interactions was needed for treatment. Gradually, institutional psychiatrists came to appreciate the value of social data secured and assessed by social workers in their decision making, and the social worker became a recognized member of the mental health team. A new wave of concern with mental health services developed during and following World War I, as the federal government recognized the need for mental health assessments of recruits, for treatment of persons becoming mentally ill while in service, and for care of those who continued to suffer disabilities after their return to the community. In 1914, Mary C. Jarrett, Chief of Social Services at the Boston Psychopathic Hospital, with the support of Dr. E. E. Southard, began conducting training courses in psychiatric social work for six or seven students at a time. In 1918, as a result of her work, the Training School for Psychiatric Social Work was opened at Smith College.

Another important development for social work practice in mental health was the development of the child guidance clinics, through the efforts of such social workers as Jane Addams and the Abbott sisters, to help prevent juvenile delinquency. In 1921, the Commonwealth Fund supported the establishment of seven child guidance clinics as a demonstration program. These clinics were designed to influence other agencies and schools toward preventive services supporting mental health in children. Once established, the clinics quickly spread and quickly changed their purpose from preventive service and community reform to dealing with individual children and their mothers who came seeking treatment. Their contacts with community agencies were minimized, and the population they served changed from a predominantly lower-class population to a predominantly middle-class population (Compton, 1980, pp. 408–409; Levine and Levine, 1970, pp. 231–277).

In many ways, the history of the present comprehensive mental health centers parallels that of the earlier child guidance movement. The duality of purpose between direct treatment versus prevention that appeared sixty years ago has never been resolved. In fact, it was heightened with the introduction of the publicly supported, comprehensive mental health center approximately twenty years ago. In spite of the duality of purpose, most centers have chosen to concentrate on the single focus of psychotherapy for the individual. In 1972, Berg, Reid, and Cohen studied social workers in mental health. They found that those practitioners in agencies with a "high" investment in the concept of community mental health spent 46 percent of their time in diagnosis and treatment and 18 percent in community work; those in agencies with a "low" interest spent 60 percent of their time in diagnosis and treatment and 5 percent in community activities (Berg, Reid, and Cohen,1972, pp. 62–63). The two recent movements in the mental health field have been the movement toward the comprehensive mental health center and the movement toward the deinstitutionalization of long-time mental patients. Both of these movements would seem to require that clinical social work adapt or develop some new approaches.

Organizations and Professional Tasks. Perhaps the most important organizational task confronting mental health agencies, particularly the community mental health center, is to address the question of the organizations' responsibility to participate in activities relating to community change and prevention. The second major task is to seriously consider the full meaning of the charge for continuity of care for deinstitutionalized persons—to consider the needs of this group of neglected people and how the present organizational structure serves their needs. Social workers in mental health settings of all types provide individual, group, and family treatment and serve as case consultants to other staff members and agencies. They may be involved in the supervisory and group processes instrumental to the development and management of effective team relationships, and they may be active in community organizational services. In some settings, the worker serves as the patient's liaison with families and community. In working with the deinstitutionalized patient, the worker needs teaching and modeling skills and other supportive skills. The worker also needs to be expert in problem definition, data collection, and assessment. Workers need to be able to use certain diagnostic tools that are particularly setting related, such as the DSM III.

A wide variety of psychological helping techniques are used by workers in counseling in mental health settings. Certain agencies may focus more on one modality of treatment than another. Behavioral therapy, family therapy, group therapy, and crisis intervention all have become important modalities in mental health. It is important that social workers in mental health settings be alert to the rights of patients and possess both commitment to the role of advocate and skillful use of conflict-management and negotiating techniques.

Structure, Methods, and Programs. The field of mental health appears to be struggling with a variety of ideological issues, methodological conflicts, and problems in program diffusion. There are concerns that new programs that were meant to point bold new directions of service have not fulfilled their promises. The methods and structure of practice have not changed in ways to effectively implement the new programs. There has been a rapid influx into the field of new groups of personnel, such as nurse practitioners, pastoral counselors, and mental health aides, which has contributed to the diffusion and overlapping of functions as the boundaries and linkages among the various groups have not been articulated. The increase in the types of staff has resulted in the increased conflict and competition over various turf issues, while the least trained of the personnel are frequently left to provide direct services to the patients. As a way out of conflict over professional boundaries, some agencies have taken the position that there are no real differences between staff competencies.

Beginning in the 1960s, with an emphasis on making treatment immediately accessible to those in need of help, there was a rapid growth in crisis centers, walk-in neighborhood centers, suicide prevention centers, and the like. Emphasis was put on crisis intervention designed to give an immediate response to the call for help and to narrow the gap between the professional and those who sought help. These programs have been of great and life-saving help to many, but for many this service is not enough; they live from crisis to crisis in need of consistent supportive help. Also, in the 1960s, the use of the tranquilizing drugs to treat certain mental states became widespread. Their use helped many patients to become less violent and agitated and thus more open to many additional forms of intervention. These drugs also made it possible for patients to leave the hospital, and the movement toward deinstitutionalization has reduced the population of mental hospitals by approximately 50 percent. Various programs were developed to aid in this transition. The day hospital, or day treatment center, was one such program. These facilities have helped some patients to manage their lives and function better in the community, but the need in this area is vast and unfilled. The day-by-day detailed work of helping such patients to function in the community has not attracted any great numbers of professional people or created any great advocacy. Consequently, a huge group of marginally functioning people drift vaguely through an uncertain life, leaving concerned professionals to question whether life is more satisfying for them in the community than it was in the hospital. In the same decade, there was an accelerated trend toward the establishment of community mental health programs with emphasis on community and prevention as well as treatment. However, the centers have not been able to free themselves from the medical leadership that has characterized mental health services through the years. Thus, practice within these centers has changed little in form and structure.

Other questions have been raised about the relationship between mental health centers and other community agencies that primarily employ social workers, such as family service agencies. Do communities need both agencies? Can valuable manpower be saved by merging the existing family agencies and mental health centers? Various studies over the years have indicated that the centers and the agencies do seem to provide similar services. One study found that clients of the center were somewhat more affluent than those of the agency and that women predominate as clients of family agencies, whereas children, particularly boys, made up a large proportion of center patients. More clients come to the family agency of their own volition than do center patients. The family agency relates more closely to the social agencies of the community, whereas the center relates to medical facilities and personnel. There are few referrals between family agencies and mental health centers. One-fourth of all clients made no use of the services after application, one-third used services well, and forty percent used them partially in both cases. Both the agencies and the centers used individual therapy almost exclusively, although the centers also used drug therapy (Hill, Lehmann, and Slotkin, 1971).

Issues in Methodology, Program Priorities, and Clinical Practice. Perhaps the most important issue in clinical practice is its definition. The tendency among some working in the field of mental health to limit their practice to psychotherapy alone is not enough. It is not that social workers in mental health are not justified in practicing as psychotherapists but that their practice should clearly reflect the social work concern with a systematic and interactive perspective. Their practice should not be limited to what is often seen as the psychotherapeutic function of individual change alone. The social work focus on helping clients to develop internal problem-solving and coping capacities should not be lost to the notion of the cure of illness. Clinical practice in mental health settings should include teaching and modeling life skills, facilitating interactions between people and their social environment, and actively negotiating and changing the environment of clients when that appears to be the need. This prescription includes the development of skills in teamwork, not only in the interests of smooth interprofessional relationships but in the interests of using these relationships to provide the best service to clients, which may include advocacy within the team for client rights and adequate treatment plans.

Katz (1979, pp. 56–58), in an article discussing social work practice in community mental health, states that one set of choices in the field is between the medical model and the human services model. The human services model emphasizes linking and integrating various care-giving agencies in the interests of the client, being concerned with problems in living (especially regarding the fit between the individual and the nurturant environment), and comprehensiveness and accessibility of service. Certainly, if social work practice is to make its potential contribution to mental health, social workers need to develop activities in consultation and negotiation with the community on behalf of a better life for all members of that community. These activities should include "work with natural groups in the community to provide consultation to community caretakers, to provide mental health information to the public, and to help other community based programs develop mental health resources" (Berg, 1979, p. 8).

Interaction of Practice, Policy, Resources, and Funding Patterns. As in all fields we have examined, it is impossible to separate the practitioner's work with clients from the policy and procedures within which that work takes place. One cannot but wonder if the focus of the practitioners is ambiguous and uncertain with patients because of the lack of direction of the field in which they practice. Mental health is in a state of ideological conflict and confusion as to its direction and focus. It would appear that social workers have the right and obligation to take some leadership in working toward some clarification of the primary function of mental health and resolution of the ideological issues. It is important for social work to recognize that its contribution to the mental health delivery system is undeniably a substantial one. Social work has a significant stake in the direction and focus of mental health, and it also possesses the power to have a considerable impact on that system. In the comprehensive mental health centers, it is the social worker who should have the greatest understanding and knowledge about the day-by-day life tasks and struggles of the individual patients. The individual clinical practitioner should understand that social work has the power and the responsibility to determine what its role should be in mental health. Certainly, it would appear that the resources available to the mental health practitioner, and the flexibility of their use, could be greatly increased if the social work practitioner established linkages between resource systems. At present, there appear to be few transactional linkages between the mental health system and other systems. A state-wide look at mental health centers in one state revealed that the centers' approach to the other community agencies was one of offering as the "knowing authority" to educate the workers of the other systems in understanding the dynamics of their clients. There was no acknowledgment on the part of the centers' staff that other agencies might have some contribution to make to them or to a joint issue of helping people function better. This may be one by-product of the medical model adopted by most of the centers. There is an inherent assumption that the knowledge and skill that matter most are found in the medical authority. This moves the focus from the social work concern with the better social functioning of clients to a focus on the issue of mental illness.

Mental health services are primarily funded from public funds in some combination. All states have public hospitals for care of the mentally ill that operate under state auspices with the support of state funds. The federal role in the support of mental health services has expanded markedly and is primarily used to support the outpatient services. However, federal reimbursement for privately rendered service through Medicaid and Medicare programs is substantial. In addition, the federal government supports inpatient services of the Veterans Administration. However, with the present movement toward revenue sharing or block grants, decisions as to the level of funding for mental health services, if not the actual necessity to find the funds through local efforts, will be shifted back to the states. This shift in funding patterns makes it increasingly crucial that mental health define its focus. It would appear important that mental health become a part of the human services group and that this group present a united front as to funding priorities to the state government decision makers rather than competing for funds against other human services.

Issues of Accountability. As in other health settings, there are numerous state licensing bodies and professional membership associations that attempt to set at least minimal standards of competence for the individual practitioner. In the field of mental health, there have been active consumer groups that have pressed for accountability to the consumer for many years. State and federal governments have been interested in establishing standards of evaluation and accountability. The Professional Standards Review Organization as a nationwide network was established by 1972 amendments to the Social Security Act. Reimbursement through Medicaid and other federal programs require certain specific accounts of the services offered. All federally funded mental health centers are required by law to provide for a continuing review of the equality of service offered and the effectiveness of that service. Many mental health facilities have been developing their own approaches to the evaluation of their services to their patient group.

School Social Work

Social Functions and Responsibilities. School social service, or the visiting teacher program, as it was known at the beginning, began about 1906 as a way of providing a link between school, family, and community. Undoubtedly, one of the important forces leading to the development of the field originated in settlement house work with children. Located in the community, the settlement house workers could use their relationship to the child and the family to help teachers understand the child and to serve as a link between school, community, and family. As result of their attempts to help individual children and families work with the school, several settlement houses took on the assignment of working with the families of school children who presented special educational, social, or medical problems. The spread of the program was encouraged by the support of the Commonwealth Program and by the establishment of an educational program for school social workers by the Columbia University School of Social Work. The early programs defined their responsibilities as (1) dealing with the needs of individual school children, (2) interpreting the individual child to the school in order to modify the school's response to the child, and (3) dealing with general problems of relationship between school and community. School social workers are employed by and accountable to local school districts, although state departments of education are becoming increasingly involved in defining both the necessary competencies of the school social worker and the job they will be asked to do.

School social work grew rapidly during its early years as an effort by the community to prevent increases in juvenile delinquency. During the Depression, the ability of the school systems to support the programs was severely impaired. However, in the 1940s, services began to expand rapidly again, and there developed a shift in focus from delinquency prevention and attendance to the individual child's use of the school environment. The concern with neighborhood conditions and family problems gave way to concern with the personality of the individual child, and individual counseling techniques began to be of primary interest to the practitioner. With the social upheaval of the 1960s, school social workers again began to examine their purposes and goals. New methods of work, such as work with groups, began to be more widely used. There was a new emphasis on the impact of school policies and community conditions on the ability of youth to learn and develop. Greater attention began to be given to student's rights and to the culturally, physically, mentally, or behaviorally different child. Parents began to be more active in their children's education. These years saw the growth of many student services in the schools, and confusion about the roles of the various specialists within the school system grew apace. School social work received significant support with the passage of the Education of Handicapped Children Act of 1975, which provided for school social work service. Today, the responsibilities of school social workers are generally seen as (1) service to pupils and their families, (2) consultation with school personnel, (3) work with parents to help them understand and support their child in school, and (4) acting as a liaison between the family and other community services needed by the child and change efforts with the community.

Organizations and Professional Tasks. The primary responsibility of the school system is the effective education and socialization of the child. School social workers are in many ways guests in the house of another. One of the difficulties that school social workers face is the lack of understanding of what they can offer the school, and individual school social workers often must interpret their role and their contribution to the school. A number of years ago, the College of Education at the University of Minnesota offered a new course in working with family and community to support the educational endeavor with children. The course was a doctoral level course limited to persons who were school principals. It was taught by a social worker assisted by a very knowledgeable member of the College of Education faculty. This course—offered at an advanced level, taught by authorities, away from daily job activities, and strongly supported by the College of Education—had a tremendous impact on the use of social workers in the schools. At one point, the School Social Workers Association in the community requested to meet with the teachers of the course in order to understand how one course could make such a difference in the way they were perceived and used in the system. It would appear that one of the primary organizational tasks is the understanding of what the school social worker can offer; achieving this understanding requires more than individual interpretation.

The clinical tasks of the school social worker are many. School social workers need all the usual skills of social work—the ability to treat the emotional and social distress of individual children; the ability to work in groups of children or families; the ability to work with families, although they may use other resources for family treatment; consultation skills in work with other school personnel and other agency and community people; skills in family life education and the interpretation of the needs of children and the work of the profession; and advocacy skills both with community agencies and within their own school system. School social workers may offer children advice, guidance, and counsel; emotional support; help in controlling behavior or feelings appropriately; and help in developing an identity and life goals, among other things. They may offer parents help in finding necessary resources and securing access to them; help in understanding children and child development; and guidance in setting appropriate expectations for their child. Within the school system, school social workers may serve as a source of knowledge about neighborhoods and cultural influences in children's lives; they may consult with teachers and furnish information about individual children; they may help in evaluating progress on a problem that has been referred; they may consult with administrators about the effects of school procedures and policies on the children; they may help administrators to understand and use community resources; they may initiate committee work to advance the work of the school.

Structure, Methods, and Programs. As schools are basically locally administered and state supervised systems, it is difficult to discuss the state of school social work in general terms. There is wide diversity among school social workers in job titles, resources, characteristics of the schools within which they work, and even credentials required. Schools are often under community attack in today's world, and school social workers may be deeply affected by these attacks. Not only may the school system be criticized, but their ability to help may be circumscribed by the defensiveness of the school administrators. Principals may find it difficult to entrust the school social worker to engage in certain advocacy actions in situations of threat.

Issues in Methodology, Program Priorities, and Clinical Practice. As with other settings in which social workers interact with other professional personnel, a major problem of school social work is the clarification of roles. It often appears to the observer of school social work that social workers are in conflict with many other professionals in the area of individual treatment of emotional or behavioral disorders of children. At the same time, the overwhelming need of the community and the family to interact with the social system in the interests of the child may suffer for lack of attention.

School social workers have a unique position in the array of helping services. They are a part of a wide social system that touches the lives of most families. Their clients do not come to them on referral from other authorities. School social workers and children are in interaction in a culturally prescribed system in which there are many common concerns. Thus, the school social worker can act as a natural bridge between child, family, and community through parental visiting programs, parental groups, parent education efforts, services to minority families, and advocacy for other community services.

Interaction of Practice, Policy, Resources, and Funding Patterns. As in all other social work fields, clinical practice is shaped by the policy and service delivery procedures. However, in this field, it is important for social workers to offer leadership in examining these policies and procedures from the vantage point of the specialized knowledge they possess. Social workers are unevenly distributed in the school systems of all states. Many school systems have no social workers. One of the responsibilities of clinical social workers is to work with the education department of their state to examine what social workers can contribute, how they can be evenly distributed, and their credentials. The ratio of social workers to school population also needs to be considered. In many systems, there may be one social worker per 1,000 pupils. The full range of clinical work cannot be done when the practitioners are so thinly spread.

Issues of Accountability. The organizations concerned with standard setting and accountability in school social work are as diverse as the local school systems. The national professional associations in social work and education should be interested in this problem, as should schools of education and social work. State and local professional associations should be concerned with the issues of regulation of practice and standards of employment and classification. Some state educational systems are moving to develop these associations at the state level in cooperation with professional social workers. In this field, these issues are only beginning to be addressed.

Social Work Practice in Corrections

Social Functions and Responsibilities. Corrections has been defined as "a social process by which modern society deals officially with identified lawbreakers." It is that part of criminal justice which is responsible for administering penalties assigned by the judicial process (Studt, 1959, p. 6). Social work and corrections have had a very long and very ambivalent relationship. It may be that in corrections we have the best example of the early social work interests in both policy change and reform and change in individuals. In 1821, John Augustus began probation by persuading the court to continue the offender's case and allow him to post bail to guarantee good behavior while counseling the offender and making periodic reports to the court as to the progress of the offender. Isaac Hopper about the same time began a system of parole by helping prisoners find jobs upon discharge. There also began two major efforts at institutional reform—the establishment of institutions for juvenile offenders, commonly known as houses of refuge, and the attempt to develop more humane policies within the adult institutions. In 1885, at the meeting of the National Conference of Charities and Corrections, William T. Harris presented a paper in which he held that crime was the result of the failure of society to effectively socialize the individual. This was followed in 1886 by a paper in which the Conference was told that delinquent children were those whose characters were weakened by the influence of poor and evil surroundings. These various approaches all represented a change from concern with the punishment of wrongdoers to concern with their reform and their return to society as productive members. Part of this change was concern with understanding the needs of children as distinct from those of adults. Leading Chicago social workers concerned with the protection of children brought about a fundamental change in the handling of delinquent children when the first juvenile court met in 1899. The juvenile court represented a radical change, in that by its very nature it was assumed to be a noncriminal court of equity acting in the best interests of the child. The court acquired its right to intervene in children's lives from the right of the state to exercise parental power over children. Acting as a good parent within a child-parent relationship, the new court did not need to be as concerned with due process or legal rights as the criminal courts, whose primary purpose was protection of the public. The concept of child need replaced laws of evidence. Given the fact that every child in our society is subject to the jurisdiction of the juvenile court, this institution begun by social workers interested in helping and protecting the child can well be perceived as the most powerful agent of behavior control that our society has constructed (Compton, 1980, pp. 311–312).

Clinical social work formally became a part of the juvenile court system with the appointment of Alzina P. Stevens, a member of the Hull House staff, as the Illinois court's first paid probation officer. But, in spite of its early association, work within corrections has not always been accepted by clinical social work as an appropriate field of practice. The correctional process has come to mean the administration of the penalty assessed for law-breaking in such a way that the offender is corrected—that is, current behavior is kept within acceptable limits at the same time that general life adjustment is modified. Thus, correction is a social process by which society maintains legally identified offenders in a temporarily handicapped status, which includes control over the behavior of the offender during the period of the penalty and services designed to change the relationship to and behavior toward the community (Studt, 1959, p. 7). While recognizing that the central task in corrections involves activities that affect the offender's attitudes and relationships with others—a central social work charge—many clinical social workers are concerned with the notion of carrying the responsibility for legal control, aspects of punishment, and involuntary treatment that are an inevitable part of the offender's relationship to the legal system. Some social workers in corrections are attempting to recast the profession's role in such a way that the responsibility for social control and work with the involuntary client is eliminated. This notion would require that social workers accept as clients only those offenders who request such help, that social work's role be seen as that of "negotiator" and conflict resolver, and that the primary tasks center around working with client and community to come to some mutual definition of acceptable behavior. The present programs of restitution, in which offender and victim meet with a social worker and negotiate a contract that sets forth the responsibilities of the offender to reimburse the victim for losses suffered is an example of this new focus. This attempt to approach social work in corrections as a problem-solving process rather than as an individual change process is just beginning. It represents the first effort since Studt's work in the 1950s to reexamine work in corrections as a field of social work practice.

Organizations and Professional Tasks. Social workers in corrections practice under a bewildering array of organizational forms and at all government levels. It is difficult to speak with any certainty about these forms and how they operate because they are, by and large, state and local, with many different patterns. Certainly, there are few practitioners in the field who would not agree that many offenders are sent to prison because of the lack of staff, resources, and sound decision making at the local level. We have, for instance, little reliable statistical knowledge of the numbers of offenders, how they are processed through the system, what kinds of staff in what numbers are operating in the system, and the pattern of sentencing. In addition to reliable knowledge of the system and the services offered, the organizational tasks in corrections include the recruitment and retention of an adequate staff, providing educational opportunities for the staff presently employed, assigning appropriate caseloads, appropriate utilization of staff and the use of new categories of personnel, assigning resources to meet certain needs of the offender and the family, and designing alternative programs so that assessment can be of use in diversifying opportunities for growth and change. The tasks of the practitioner include working with clients to stimulate conforming behavior, providing opportunities for self-development, linking the client with social groups and the community, working with other appropriate criminal justice staff, and reporting to the court assessments of offender and situation.

Structure, Methods, and Programs. There is no lack of programs aimed at the prevention and treatment of delinquency in the United States; in fact, some form of intervention exists wherever there is a separate judicial process for dealing with offenders, and almost everybody has some notion of how offenders should be treated. The problem is that most such notions as well as the programs of intervention are based on beliefs and values rather than objective knowledge. *Crime* and *delinquency* are not precise terms but cover a very wide spectrum of human behavior. Most of us violate the law at some point in our lives. What distinguishes most of us from those in the corrections system and how becoming a part of that system affects offenders are matters of dispute. We know little of what causes delinquent behavior, and we have little expertise in relating the indiviual delinquent to one or another cause. Is a delinquent presumed to be sick, bad, weak, or antisocial? Are there significant differences between offenders as to cause? The prominence in our society of notions of revenge and retribution, and the conviction that punishment corrects, makes it difficult to construct programs aimed at rehabilitation and social living. The public is highly critical of any programs that seem to "coddle" offenders or are "soft on crime" or that return the offender to the community before punishment has been administered. Shireman estimates that, on any one day in the year, about 1.25 million persons are in some way affected by correctional programs (Shireman, 1977, p. 214). Yet, social work seldom has been in a position to influence the basic programs in this field.

There are, however, major changes happening in correctional programs. There is an increased concern with the ineffectiveness of institutionalization as a rehabilitation measure, which has resulted in some states in decreasing use of large institutions. This trend is accompanied by many programs aimed at decriminalization of offenses and diversion of offenders in situations in which there appears to be no serious danger to persons or property. Thus, people are not labeled as offenders, and other methods of treatment are substituted for institutionalization. There is also a movement toward shorter sentences, based on the assumption and certain studies of recidivism that, while short institutional stays may have some value in impressing the offender with the community's disapproval and power, long institutional stays do not correct. Another trend in the field is seen in the growing number of programs aimed at community-based treatment of one kind or another, based on the assumption that offenders are helped by staying close to their social roots and learning to interact productively with the community. One of the promising programs requires the offender to negotiate a restitution contract with the victim and to make some effort to reimburse the victim for the damage done. Work furloughs, home visits, halfway houses, and night and weekend incarceration are other programs that move in this direction. In addition to these programs, there is an increasing effort to develop programs within the institution that will lead to setting goals and preparing for release, such as programs of work training, college classes taught by outside instructors, use of creative skills for art work or writing, and various experiments in inmate governance. In addition, there are a growing number of programs aimed at protection of the rights of offenders and access to legal services.

The programs developing in the field could perhaps be classified as those aimed at prevention through reducing the social factors that provoke antisocial actions, those aimed at controlling actions of identified offenders, those aimed at working through emotional conflict, and those aimed at developing social responsibility and self-direction. One of the problems in advancing such programs in the field is the structure of adminstration. Shireman (1977, p. 215) describes four organizational forms found in corrections: "decentralized, locally administered departments at the county or city level; county or city operation with some degree of state financing, supervision, or consultation; operation by a single state agency; or a combination of local and state services with the local departments serving the more populous centers and the state agency serving the rural and small town areas." With few bridges between levels, it is difficult for a promising program to move beyond its originating source. Also, small local offices seldom have the staff, resources, or support to start innovative programs.

Issues in Methodology, Program Priorities, and Clinical Practice. A central issue for practitioners entering the field of corrections is administration of an assigned penalty. Social workers are more likely to think of themselves as opening opportunities and encouraging growth than setting and administering penalties. They are very aware of clients whose suffering is attributable to controls by parents and other authority figures in the past; social workers often offer supportive experiences so the client can deal with these hurtful experiences. Controls and authority are often seen as punitive, and they tend to produce distance between worker and client. As Studt (1959, pp. 19–28) points out, the distinction between the person who uses controls and the person who gains satisfaction through controlling is not always clear. The meaning and use of authority in nurturing and helping relationships need to be further studied by clinical workers. Many of our assumptions about the use of authority came from work with certain populations and may need to be reexamined in new populations. Social workers may dislike the responsibility for decision making and the visibility of such activities in corrections. Correctional workers often are involved in decisions that are of major importance to client and community, that cannot be avoided, and that involve certain calculated risks to the position of the worker, in that workers are often highly visible and are accountable to other societal authorities.

A second major problem in practice in corrections is the lack of any definitive view of what causes and supports the behavior that led the offender to the justice system in the first place. Should the offender be viewed as emotionally ill, as the victim of either a frustrating or a provocative social climate, or as having a problem in the interaction between self and social systems? Methods and programs in corrections usually are developed in response to one or more of these notions of cause—for example, community programs aimed at increasing the social opportunities of youth who might be especially vulnerable to delinquent behavior. The notion that emotional disturbance and illness cause such problems results in programs of counseling and psychotherapy. The notion that the problem is one of self-control results in such programs as behavior modification based on principles of operant learning. Such programs are often difficult to implement in correctional settings because the reward system may be very inadequate. In addition, the ability to generalize and transfer such programs into the community to offer support after the offender is free to pursue his own life is greatly limited.

Other programs aimed at building individual social controls are group programs in which the offenders interact with peers. Essential to these group programs is the power of the group in determining the group agenda and individual privileges. The restitution programs are designed primarily to teach social responsibility.

Family treatment is beginning to be used in offender programs. These programs assume that family malfunctioning contributes to antisocial behavior. Such programs are found most often in juvenile work, but such efforts are beginning to find their way into work with adult offenders in which the offender is married or has children.

One of the common obstacles to such programs is the tendency to assign responsibility for the problem to the offender alone, especially in the case of adult offenders. Some efforts to evaluate these programs have given some evidence of promise. Many of the programs and methods aimed at establishing interval social controls or those requiring conflict negotiation are uncomfortable for social workers who see themselves primarily as psychotherapists. These programs require that the worker be much more active in intervention, work more actively with social and community networks, and be able to handle the present realities of the client's life in an active way.

Interaction of Practice, Policy, Resources, and Funding Patterns. One of the primary sources of frustration for the clinical practitioner is the lack of clarity within the correctional field as to the purpose of such practice. Is it to help the offender or to protect the community? Is it to punish or rehabilitate?

Social workers coming into the field assume that their purpose is to help and rehabilitate and that to lend themselves to certain controlling efforts is a violation of professional values and purposes. The recent efforts to define the purpose of social work in corrections and to separate the social work effort from the nonvoluntary client may help to reduce some of the conflict between clinical social workers and the correctional administration. In addition, corrections is characterized by the involvement of personnel from many different professional backgrounds who function toward many different ends within the system. The police officer, the prison administrator, the judge, and the attorneys are all represented on the correctional decision-making team. In addition, therapeutic psychiatrists, psychologists, and nurses have direct contact with the client and may make decisions that are independent of the treatment plans of the social worker and the client. The difficulty of communication among members of the team and lack of clarity of roles and responsibilities results in considerable frustration and ambiguity for the clinical social worker.

There has recently been an increase in federal grants supporting certain correctional programs and innovations. However, correctional programs are basically public, local, or state efforts and thus depend on local or state public financing. This pattern of funding, together with the ambivalence about helping efforts in corrections, has resulted in inadequate financing and support for social work practitioners in the field. Caseloads are high, and support for competent professional functioning may be very low.

Issues of Accountability. There are several national voluntary associations in the field of corrections, such as the National Council on Crime and Delinquency, the National Prison Association, and the Osborne Society, whose purposes include raising the standards of correctional service and humanizing the system. However, there is no regulatory body that operates under the force of law. Accountability for protection of the public in decision making in corrections is high, but there is less interest in accountability toward the offender. Evaluative research in the field is still in its infancy.

Settlements and Community Centers

Social Functions and Responsibilities. Originally, the settlement movement could be described as the movement of a group of middle-class and upper-class people who believed in the "reciprocal relationship of classes" into poor working-class neighborhoods with the aim of "being of service and assistance to their neighbors." The residents of the settlement wanted to live among, learn from, and help their neighbors to develop for themselves a better way of life. Generally, such a purpose meant to help socialize immigrants and their children to the way of life of their new country by education, support, and advocacy. Seeing for themselves the exploitation and the struggles of their neighbors, early settlement workers became a force for reform. Out of their concern with the exploitation of children came the push toward compulsory school attendance and school social work as well as the first juvenile court and child labor laws. Out of their concern with the exploitation of women came the various labor laws limiting hours of work and improving working conditions. Much of the work of the settlements was carried on through groups, as neighborhood residents came to the settlement in groups to learn and consider neighborhood problems. Thus, the settlement movement originated work with groups as a part of social work. The method was to grow and expand in two ways, as a clinical method aimed at helping individuals and as an effective method of social change. As a part of the professionalization of social work, settlements began to hire trained social workers, who preferred to live outside the community, and the settlement as a building in which the staff lived gradually disappeared. From the beginning, settlements offered services and advice to those who lived around them. Childcare, outpatient clinics and other health services, sewing and cooking classes, various educational groups, and recreational and educational groups for children and youth were all part of their programs. From these efforts developed the community center, a center serving a particular ethnic or religious group and supported by that group to enrich the group life as well as serve as an agency to aid in child development and socialization. Then, in the 1960s, came the War on Poverty and the development of community action agencies in almost all counties in the United States. These agencies, in spite of their early purpose to serve as community action agencies, soon became dispensers of services similar to the settlements and community centers.

Professional Tasks. Settlements and other neighborhood and community centers continue to offer a variety of services and employ a wide variety of staff. Their work can be classified into tasks of social brokerage or advocacy, tasks aimed at upward mobility and assimilation, tasks aimed at human growth and development, and reform efforts.

Structure, Methods, and Programs. There is a wide diversity of services offered by these centers today and a wide variety of methods and programs found within them. Social group work originated within this structure and spread to other fields of practice, so that today clinical social work practice includes work with groups as well as individuals and families.

Issues in Methodology, Program Priorities, and Clinical Practice. The quality and emphasis of service are very different among settlements. Thus, it is difficult to discuss with any meaning the directions in clinical practice within the field. Perhaps the important thing to recognize is that the practice of work with groups has not remained within this original field and is currently developing new methodologies within other fields of practice, which may in turn be imported back into the settlements. Practice in groups now includes therapy groups aimed at reworking early life experiences, groups aimed at self-development, and groups aimed at social control. Methodology in groups has become as varied as that with practice with individuals. The basic theories upon which work with groups is now developing are also as varied as those in any other practice methodology.

Interaction of Practice, Policy, Resources, and Funding Patterns. The settlements and centers today depend primarily on the United Fund of the communities in which they operate. In addition, there is considerable public support and some foundation funds. It is difficult to assess with certainty, but it may be that the source of funding has tempered the reform movement of the settlements. Obviously, issues of policy and funding affect clinical practice in this setting as in all others. Are boards of directors representative of the neighborhood served? Does policy require the opening of the building as a place of service and help for all residents in the area, or are certain people of color or culture excluded? What about the various neighborhood gangs and groups? Are they welcome, and under what conditions? Does the Center see itself as reaching out to unsocialized youth and isolated aged? Does it see itself as primarily a tool for socialization into and preserving unity of particular groups? All these questions must be answered, and the answers determine the tasks and actions of the clinical social worker. If the center reaches out to serve the isolated, the alienated, and the unsocial, practice will be more active and more time consuming, involve greater risks, and require a different methodology than if the purpose of the center is to offer self-development and integration services to a homogenous group.

Issues of Accountability. Both public sources of funds and the United Fund are increasingly concerned with the type and quality of service given to particular population groups. There is a new wave of concern with overlapping and duplication of services. These concerns are resulting in a new demand for accountability and new emphasis on management controls. There are no legal standards of service, but, as in other fields of practice, there are voluntary bodies that serve to upgrade service, develop standards and directions of service, and aid in planning for the future, such as the National Federation of Settlements and Neighborhood Houses, and city-wide federations, such as the United Neighborhood Houses in New York.

Summary

As Bartlett (1970, p. 31) points out, "practice in separate fields and practice in agencies were among the earliest influences shaping the growth of the profession." The practice of social work has been traditionally carried on through health and welfare agencies and programs as legally established structures for administering and delivering services. These agencies and programs have been organized by fields of practice as defined by the central problems with which the agencies were concerned. It has been difficult for social work as a profession to separate itself conceptually from the notion of agency and agency services; in the real world, it has been impossible, since our traditional practice cannot exist without some supporting structure. The question that social work faces today is a question of what constitutes a specialized practice. Is it to be a practice within a certain field of practice, or with certain problems regardless of where they are found, or with certain population groups regardless of where they are found? Undoubtedly, at the level of individual clinical practice, social workers are guided in important and quite appropriate ways by the policies and structures of the field. But what in their practice marks them as social workers? What damage is done to the profession when social workers, identifying primarily with the setting and the other disciplines within it, call themselves therapists or counselors? What are the common professional values, methods, and skills of social work that make social work practice unique and thus worthy of social support in maintaining and sanctioning the professional right to practice? Obviously, no one clinician can be highly knowledgeable and skilled in all fields of practice. How can we select what is special and what is general in clinical practice and determine appropriate use of specialized methodology? The future of social work will be determined by the way we respond to these questions.

References

Ambrosino, S. "Family Services and Family Service Agencies." In J. B. Turner and others (Eds.), *Encyclopedia of Social Work, 1977.* New York: National Association of Social Workers, 1977.

Bartlett, H. *The Common Base of Social Work Practice.* New York: National Association of Social Workers, 1970.

Beck, D., and Jones, M. *Progress on Family Problems: A Nationwide Study of Client's and Counselor's Views on Family Agency Services.* New York: Family Service Association of America, 1973.

Berg, L. K. "Coordination of Services: The Interdisciplinary Team and Social Work Practice in Community Mental Health." In A. J. Katz (Ed.), *Community Mental Health: Issues for Social Work Practice and Education.* New York: Council on Social Work Education, 1979.

Berg, L. K., Reid, W. J., and Cohen, S. Z. *Social Workers in Community Mental Health.* Chicago: University of Chicago School of Social Service Administration, 1972.

Bruno, F. J. *Trends in Social Work, 1874–1956.* New York: Columbia University Press, 1957.

Compton, B. *Introduction to Social Welfare and Social Work.* Homewood, Ill.: Dorsey Press, 1980.

Dana, Bess. "Health Care: Social Components." In J. B. Turner and others (Eds.), *Encyclopedia of Social Work, 1977.* New York: National Association of Social Workers, 1977.

Harm, M. G. (Ed.). *A Report of the Community Mental Health Practice–Education Project.* New York: Council on Social Work Education, 1978.

Hill, W. G., Lehmann, J. B., and Slotkin, E. *Family Services and Mental Health.* New York: Family Service Association of America, 1971.

Kadushin, Alfred. "Child Welfare Strategy in the Coming Years: An Overview." In U.S. Department of Health, Education and Welfare, Office of Human Development Services, Administration for Children, Youth and Families, Children's Bureau, *Child Welfare in the Coming Years.* Washington, D.C.: U.S. Government Printing Office, 1980.

Katz, A. J. "An Approach to Social Work Practice in Community Mental Health." In A. J. Katz (Ed.), *Community Mental Health: Issues for Social Work Practice and Education.* New York: Council on Social Work Education, 1979.

Levine, M., and Levine, A. *A Social History of the Helping Services.* New York: Appleton-Century-Crofts, 1970.

Peat, Marwick, Mitchell, and Company. *Child Welfare in 25 States—An Overview.* New York: Peat, Marwick, Mitchell, and Company and Child Welfare League of America, 1976.

Rich, M. E. *A Belief in People: A History of American Social Work.* New York: Family Service Association of America, 1956.

Richman, L. H. "Differential Planning in Child Welfare." *Child Welfare,* 1958, *58,* 1–9.

Sherman, S. "Family Services: Family Treatment." In J. B. Turner and others (Eds.), *Encyclopedia of Social Work, 1977.* New York: National Association of Social Workers, 1977.

Shireman, C. H. "Crime and Delinquency, Probation and Parole." In J. B. Turner and others (Eds.), *Encyclopedia of Social Work, 1977.* New York: National Association of Social Workers, 1977.

Studt, E. *Education for Social Workers in the Correctional Field.* New York: Council on Social Work Education, 1959.

47

Emerging Domains of Practice

Mary L. Waring

In the early 1980s, emerging domains of practice offer new challenges for clinical social workers. Yet, at the outset, it must be conceded that developing a clear definition for emerging domains—that is, newly recognized social problem areas—is a difficult task. First, some of the social problem areas with which the profession has been concerned throughout its history are cyclical in nature. That is, they appear, recede, and reappear, depending on such factors as political climate, the extent of economic resources that are available throughout society, the types of social problems that make the societal agenda, and the profession's perception of what may be consonant with its purposes, values, knowledge, and methods. Second, some social problem areas appear as consequences of technological advances, which may lead to the expansion of an existing or traditional domain. Therefore, *emerging domains* may be a less than accurate designation for the social problem areas that present current opportunities for expanding clinical social work practice. Given this perspective, health is an expanding traditional domain, whereas industry and criminal justice are areas in which the profession has had a long though intermittent and partial involvement.

Industrial social work has a long history. In the early part of this century, social work, consonant with its social activist values, worked in the labor movement toward the founding of unions. A pioneer in planning and providing an array of services in unions was Reynolds (1951). Some others have continued this tradition. However, social work has had lesser involvement with industry, that is, with the work site and employers. Industry has been viewed by social work as exploitative of employees (for example, by knowingly injuring their health) and of natural resources for profit. However, there have also been signs recently of corporate responsibility to employees. One sign is the concept of a "human contract . . . developed by labor and management around the conference table in a climate of cooperation . . . and administered by a professional tribunal in industrial social work" (Perlis, 1977). In 1978, the first National Conference on Social Work Practice in Labor and Industrial Settings was held in New York City. This three-day conference brought together one hundred social workers with master's degrees in all aspects of industrial social work, thereby signaling a confirmation of the expansion of this practice domain.

Within criminal justice, social work and corrections parted company in 1915 when probation officers withdrew from the National Conference on Charities and Corrections, partly to protest social workers' intentions to formalize educational training (Chute and Bell, 1956). In 1945, at the National Conference of Social Work, Prey opened a debate by suggesting that social workers who are holding to a theory of self-determination might also have an important role in trying to motivate people to accept help and that this could be done even within authoritarian settings. By 1959, the National Association of Social Workers had developed a corrections curriculum (Studt, 1959a). However, until recently, the profession still limited its participation to juvenile justice and to adult probation. Today, there is evidence that professionals are moving in noticeable numbers into other parts of the system, such as police departments (Burnett and others, 1976; Collingwood, Douds, and Williams, 1976; Woolf and Rudman, 1977).

The health field is one in which social work has played a long and consistent professional role since 1904, when the first medical social service department was founded by Dr. Richard Cabot and training for this specialty was offered at what was to become the Simmons College of Social Work (Trattner, 1979). In 1981, according to the National Association of Social Workers National Office, nearly one third of its social worker members practiced within the health domain. However, as a result of new technological developments in medicine, an economic climate of concern over any increased expenditures within the health field, and continuing demographic shifts, new roles for clinical practice are developing. An example is the rising importance of independent referral and early discharge, made possible by advances in medical diagnosis and treatment and made expedient by tightening health budgets. Because of demographic trends that include a slow, steady population increase and a steady rise in the average age, the overall demand for health care and for social work services within it should continue.

Issues and Dilemmas in Emerging Domains

Although health is an old, familiar, and expanding domain, industry is relatively new, and corrections is one in which the profession has a long involvement but not in all parts of the system. Entering new or unfamiliar areas, even within established domains, does pose certain foreseeable issues and dilemmas.

One issue is that social workers must come to understand how the new or unfamiliar host setting is structured or organized, its language and customs, its demands and strains, and its resources. In industry, for instance, the social worker needs to become knowledgeable about the profit economic sector and the industrial structure, which includes both management and unions, each with their own perspective. For instance, management's focus is on employee job performance, and it is only with regard to problems in this area that management has the right to refer for social services.

A second issue is that the profession must come to understand the different functions of the various actors and disciplines in the host setting. Potentials for rivalry must be identified and a division of labor worked out based on functions that do not overlap but enhance each other's goals. Management's role in industry is to oversee production; the policeman's primary role is to maintain social control. Their roles are not to meet personal needs. Each discipline makes its particular contribution within interdisciplinary collaboration, whose strength comes from mutual respect for the reciprocal nature of their professional relationship. Thus, the disciplines must explain themselves to each other both through a case-by-case involvement and through more formal training mechanisms.

A third issue is the importance of the point of entry. For instance, within corrections, whether the clinical social worker goes out with the police as an equal member of the team or sometime later accepts a referral from them will influence how the clinician defines his role and how the client perceives him.

Yet another issue is that, when any program is small, the social worker may experience a feeling of professional isolation. This feeling is compounded by the fact that in new domains the profession is often less knowledgeable and may be practicing with very few resources. Participating in the professional association, building contacts with social workers in other organizations, and developing the program to the point that it can provide field instruction for social work students may all help to alleviate this feeling of isolation.

Finally, social workers in new programs will be faced with having to demonstrate the effectiveness of their presence. In part, this is accomplished by functioning well as a social worker. Helping clients and their families achieve a worker–client contract, interdisciplinary collaboration, identifying needs, and thorough evaluation and documentation will all help to produce sound evidence for the continuance and expansion of social work services.

Having reviewed some of the issues and dilemmas, let us turn to the emerging domains.

Industry

Certain conditions have developed that now make the reemergence and growth of industrial social work feasible. One is the passage of a series of laws that effect the world of work. Among these are the Occupational Health and Safety Act, Employee Retirement Income Security Act, Age Discrimination in Employment Act, Affirmative Action under Title VII of the Civil Rights Act and Title V of the Vocational Rehabilitation Act, all of which established certain requirements for employers and for unions.

Another very important condition is that the labor force—nearly 100 million Americans—and over 100 of the country's nearly 200 trade unions have identified as legitimate issues the quality of work life as experienced by workers and the behavior of the world of work as it affects society and social welfare (Akabas, 1977). Some evidence for this is that labor has been negotiating for and obtaining benefits that provide for services relating to mental health. At the same time, employer responsibilities have been increasing as a result of court rulings that extend the benefits of workmen's compensation to cover emotional disabilities (Meyers, 1970).

Industrial Settings. Industrial social work has been practiced within unions, at the work site, or in social agencies. Social workers have been employed directly by the union or by the work site employer or by a social agency that in turn has contracted its services to one or the other of these organizations.

At the work site—that is, within industry—there is a history of occupational health programs staffed mainly by physicians and nurses (Austin and Jackson, 1977). More recently, during the decade of the 1970s, Employee Assistance Programs (EAPs) have grown rapidly and are often staffed by social workers. Although originally developed to counter the problems of alcoholism, EAPs have been broadened to include comprehensive mental health programs (Roman, 1977). In 1974, as reported by the American Manufacturing Association, some 2,000 companies had some form of EAP.

An outstanding example is the INSIGHT program at Kennecott Copper Corporation in Salt Lake City, Utah. Directed and staffed by social workers who collaborate with community agencies, it covers all forms of absenteeism and most personal and social problems of employees and their dependents. The main problems for which help was given were, in descending order, family, alcohol, legal, marriage, finances, and drug abuse. A study of the program's effectiveness showed that, after using INSIGHT for an average of 12.7 months, work attendance improved 52 percent, weekly indemnity costs were cut 74.6 percent, and hospital and surgical costs fell 55.4 percent (Skidmore, Balsam, and Jones, 1974).

Another interesting example of an industry-sponsored social service program is that offered by Xerox in Rochester, New York, through a purchase of service agreement with the Family Service of Rochester. Over a period of time, on-site social workers offered help with family and work problems, not only to the large number of minorities that the company had hired but eventually to all levels of personnel, from hourly plant workers to technical and management personnel (Mills, 1972).

Unions also employ social work services and often locate these in their union halls. Some examples are the program offered by the Personal Service Unit, District 37 of the American Federation of State, County, and Municipal Employees of New York City; that offered by District 65, the Distributive Workers of America, New Jersey; and the program of the National Maritime Union, New York City. These programs have been developed under the leadership of the faculties of Rutgers, Adelphi, Columbia, and Hunter Schools of Social Work. Services include assistance with housing, the garnishing of wages, preretirement planning, and the consequences of inadequate pension and social security benefits (Helenbrand and Yasser, 1977; Keizer and Habib, 1980).

Some other industrial problems for which social work services are deemed appropriate according to Ginzberg (1967) are isolation, anonymity, tight supervision, technological dislocation, leisure with insufficient income, and the replacement of older workers by younger workers. Others include the urgent need for a particular community resource, adjusting to a disability or handicap, pressure generated by dual careers, and relocation.

New Practice Areas. There will probably be an increasing need within industrial social work practice for relocation services and for preretirement planning. Two major demographic trends appear to be contributing to this trend, both of which are documented in the 1980 United States census data. One is that the population is maintaining a pattern of geographic mobility in moving both south and west. The other is that the population continues to age (Los Angeles Times News Service, 1981).

On the issue of relocation, in 1977, the number of salaried employees transferred by their companies was 22 percent ("Employee Transfers," *Wall Street Journal,* 1977). Such relocation often produces stress for all family members, including the spouse and children, who give up friends, community, and contacts with relatives. So far, corporations have ignored the problem. However, over the past two decades, relocation management firms, on a fee basis, have provided corporations with services in finding appropriate homes in a desired community for those who are transferred (Gaylord, 1979). These services clearly fall short of meeting the needs of employees for recreating their social support system and for adapting to what may often be a very different cultural environment.

Somewhat analagous problems may be faced by retirees, some of whom relocate. Whether retirees move or remain in their home communities, the new retired status may bring with it a sense of isolation and depression. Marital difficulties may arise when couples begin to be together twenty-four hours a day. Some unions have developed social service programs to respond to these needs (Keizer and Habib, 1980).

In responding to many work problems, models of interaction that can be applied quickly and for short time periods appear to be appropriate. Some of these are task-centered interventions, planned short-term treatment, and crisis intervention (Kurzman and Akabas, 1981). Also appropriate are self-help groups and the traditional models of individual and group counseling.

The Future. Although it is evident that the human problems within industry are those that social work might be prepared to intervene with, whether the domain of industrial social work does expand and become firmly established may well depend on several factors. One is the willingness of social work to approach industry, the corporate world, and unions—that is, its willingness to develop and market a viable service (Jorgensen, 1979). A second factor is that social work needs to qualify under law, public policy, and administrative regulations for third-party payments because social work services are often defined as health services that are reimburseable through a variety of insurance plans held by employers, employees, and union workers (Kurzman, 1978). A third factor is that few schools of social work—only fourteen in 1979—offer a specialized curriculum in industrial social work (Akabas, 1978).

Broad outlines for professional skills for effective practice training in industrial social work might be inferred from a statement that addressed the skills needed in staffing Employee Assistance Programs. The U.S. Department of Health, Education and Welfare (1974, pp.173–174) concluded that diagnosis, counseling, consulting, training, and organizational skill were specifically needed. "These skills are somewhat similar to those used in the speciality of industrial social work, a profession well recognized in Europe, but rarely included in professional social work training in the United States."

Corrections

A second emerging, or perhaps reemerging, domain in social work is corrections. Irrespective of the role that social work decides to play, this entire field is destined to expand due to a combination of societal conditions. The population continues to grow, even though its rate of increase has slowed. The accelerating pace of technological change, unstable economic patterns, and a changing correctional philosophy are all contributing to a need for more social control (Fox, 1977).

Since the 1960s, the correctional field has been in a state of philosophical uncertainty. Until recently, there has been an emphasis on reintegrating offenders into the community and diverting as many juveniles as possible from incarceration. However, coinciding with a nationwide move toward conservatism that gained momentum during the 1970s, a new correctional philosophy of "just desserts," that is fitting the punishment to the crime rather than to the individual, has resulted in a greater application of mandatory sentences and, in many instances, a return to the use of incarceration (Fogel, 1975). This trend is resulting in the overcrowding of prisons, which will eventually bring about a need to decide whether to spend money on expanding prisons or on expanding community-based facilities, whether these be jails or less-restrictive forms of control. Historically, professional social work has maintained a visible involvement with juvenile justice and with probation and parole (Keve, 1967). It has also played a much smaller role throughout the criminal justice system in correctional institutions. Rising rates in all crime, including juvenile crime, suggest that the juvenile system, local courts, local police departments, and victim-oriented settings or these services that are within the community are the ones in which clinical social work will most likely increase its participation.

Courts. Juvenile courts usually have an intake section staffed by probation officers who often have social work training (Coffey, 1975). Frequently, successful probation that avoids institutionalization involves close collaboration between the probation officer and counseling agencies, such as child mental-health facilities and schools. Thus, the recent emphasis on diversion as a preferred alternative to institutional care for juvenile offenders has resulted in such programs as those located in Dade County, Florida, that offer individual and group counseling to youths and their parents (Mullen, 1975). Other types of juvenile programs traditionally staffed and often administered by clinical social workers are camp–ranch farms, group homes, halfway houses, and daycare centers that offer educational, vocational, and treatment programs. When juveniles are released from these programs, they are often supervised by a social worker functioning as a parole officer (Abadinsky, 1979).

Within the adult correctional system, clinical social workers also function as probation and parole officers. Probation, following an arrest, is an alternative to court and is a diversion based within the community. In cases where the decision is court appearance and trial, there is increasing recognition that this, at least for a first offender, is a traumatic experience. Thus, some public defender agencies are providing social services to support the first offender's ability to aid in his or her own defense and to work with family members on any problems that might have preceded and contributed to the court involvement. The social worker also prepares a presentence memorandum for the court, based on extensive knowledge of the offender's background. This memorandum may include recommendations for alternatives to institutionalization. In cases where the offender has a previous criminal record and needs supervised release prior to coming to trial, social workers provide an array of services, which may include locating housing, supervising attendance at vocational training programs, applying for food stamps, or arranging for alcohol and drug-abuse treatment (Abadinsky, 1979). When the offender is female, often other assistance may be necessary, such as child-welfare services (Fishman and Alissi, 1979).

Police Departments. One of the newer settings in which clinical social workers practice is police departments. This has come about as the police have broadened their human service role, not only in crisis intervention, such as in cases of abuse and family disruptions, but also in diverting persons with social and personal problems from criminal justice into social service areas. In the Illinois communities of River Forest and Oak Park, it was believed that police could easily become overburdened with social service work to the detriment of carrying out their law enforcement responsibilities. Out of this concern grew the Police–Social Service Project in cooperation with the Family Service and the Mental Health Center. Features of this program include immediate social service intervention on a twenty-four-hour-a-day, seven-day-a-week basis and a closely linked system of referral and case assignment. A liaison social worker is responsible for informing the police of progress; police officers retain full authority in deciding how and to whom referrals will be made (Woolf and Rudman, 1977).

In Pawtucket, Rhode Island, a police department–social agency project was set up in cooperation with the Family Service Society. It was geared to help families who call the police when they really have family and social problems—for instance, domestic disputes of crisis proportions. Crisis teams of plainclothes police and social workers receive referrals from the uniformed police who responded to the initial request for help with family disturbances. The teams intervene immediately. Referrals also come from desk sergeants and patrolmen on their beats. The teams cover such situations as juvenile shoplifting, first runaways, school problems, and neighborhood disturbances. In working together, police discovered that social workers have an invaluable knowledge of the service delivery system and of working with other professionals as a team. The presence of social workers conveyed to clients the idea that their problems were not strictly a police matter, but also involved patterns of family difficulties. Similarly, social workers learned that police authority can immediately quell tense feelings, that police can gain entry where they could not, and that police facilitate client cooperation (Burnett and others, 1976).

Victim-Oriented Settings. Victim-oriented settings are also among the newer locations for clinical social work practice, although a concern for compensation and restitution to the victim can be found in the *Old Testament.* In modern times, this program came into existence in Switzerland in 1937 and in the United Kingdom in 1964. The first victim program in the United States was established by California in 1965. By 1973, eleven states had enacted victim legislation (Brodyaga and others, 1975).

By far the largest program response to victimization has been for victims of rape. An exemplary program is that of the Polk County Rape/Sexual Assault Center in Des Moines, Iowa. Social workers intervene to lessen the victim's trauma during the immediate postrape period, to ease the victim's resumption of a normal life, and to provide support for her and her family during the criminal justice proceedings (Bryant and Cirel, 1977). Programs offering care to abused wives and to the abused elderly have also begun to appear. The increased importance of this area is further evidenced by the founding of a new journal, *Victimology: An International Journal,* first published in 1976.

Newer Practice Approaches. Although social workers in corrections continue to apply traditional individual and group counseling methods, three of the newer and more widely used approaches in working with juveniles are reality therapy, counseling based on Carkhuff's theories, and behavioral contracting.

Behavioral contracting establishes goals and assigns responsibilities for which privileges (rewards) are exchanged. It may supplement other interventions (Weathers and Liberman, 1975). Reality therapy, developed by William Glasser (1975), resembles behavior modification but acknowledges the importance of the relationship. It deals exclusively with the present and future; it uses several principles that include "planning responsible behavior" and "no excuses." Developed at the Ventura School for Girls in California, it has been the only method treatment taught in Maryland's state training program for probation and parole officers (Maryland Correctional Training Academy, 1976). Counseling based on Carkhuff's training in problem-solving skills and the interpersonal skills of empathy, warmth, and genuineness has been used effectively with juveniles in the Dallas Police Department Youth Service Program (Carkhuff, 1971; Collingwood, Douds, and Williams, 1976). Family therapy with the goal of promoting the social adjustment and acceptance of an individual or group of individuals who has been in trouble with the law is also viewed as effective (Fox, 1977).

The Future. Although the field of corrections is beckoning the profession, on the whole, social workers continue to maintain their distance from this "dirty work" (Studt, 1977). However, no matter what the profession decides, corrections as a domain will continue to expand if present social trends continue. Currently, preparation for employment within this domain is largely the bachelor's degree in the social sciences. However, by the mid 1970s, there were five Ph.D. programs in criminal justice or criminology, and several other programs offered doctorates in this field within sociology or public administration (Galvin, 1968).

Statistics are not available at this writing from the Council on Social Work Education concerning the number of schools offering specialized training in corrections. However, a report on manpower from the National Association of Social Workers (1975) indicates that 2.3 percent of its membership practice in courts and prisons. These figures do not include the newer areas of practice, such as police departments and victim settings. Additionally, some of those noted as practicing in child welfare are probably in the juvenile justice system.

Preparation for practicing in corrections should cover the important issue of authoritarianism, the way in which the criminal justice system is structured and organized, and the role functions of the professional within it.

Health

The health field, as discussed earlier, is one of the historical bases of the profession. It has been and continues to be an expanding domain for clinical social work practice. Since other chapters have discussed the role of clinical social work in this domain, this section will be limited to a discussion of some of the factors that contribute to its continuing growth and to those components in which social work is most likely to play a larger role.

The health field continues its steady growth for several reasons. The population continues to increase. Americans value maintaining their health. Medicine, as one of the older professions, has made extraordinarily rapid technological advances, especially since the 1920s. Nationwide legislation, particularly the Social Security Act of 1935 and its amendments (Titles XVIII and XIX) that aid the medically indigent, those with chronic renal disease, and the long-term disabled, has also contributed to the growth of this domain. In 1977, 18.5 percent of the membership of the National Association of Social Workers were employed in health (Bracht, 1974). Some 29,800 social workers were employed in health in 1971, making the profession the second largest in the field among the sociobehavioral professions (U.S. Department of Health, Education and Welfare, 1971).

Hospital Settings. Even though clinical social workers are now used in a variety of medical settings, they are still predominantly under the aegis of hospital social service departments of all categories—federal, state and local; government and private; long term and short term; chronic, general, or psychiatric. In 1970, 66 percent of the federal hospitals and 23.2 percent of nonfederal hospitals had social service departments. In fact, 92 percent of all federal hospitals with over 500 beds had such departments (American Hospital Association, 1970).

Within hospital-based clinical social work, there are important recent developments that may lead to an increase in the employment of social workers and also shift the focus of their practice. One innovation is preadmission service. It is a consequence of the continuing emphasis on shortening hospital stays. This service necessitates an assessment of psychosocial factors that may complicate or prolong hospitalization. As hospitals continue to move some of their services into the community, the definition of preadmission activities may also change. For instance, outreach by social workers to the poor, who remain medically underserviced, may help to reduce use of the hospital emergency room and the number of missed outpatient appointments (Bracht, 1978).

Another important development is a new method of early case finding or independent referral and screening. Mount Sinai Hospital in New York City pioneered this procedure in a program that identified patients whose own distress was seen as interfering with their ability to meet the needs of their chronically ill children. This type of early intervention leads to social worker–initiated involvement with more families toward the goals of facilitating their use of medical and hospital services and community resources. Independent screening also shifts the delivery of medical social services away from a crisis-intervention model, often induced by late referrals from other disciplines, toward a comprehensive and continuous service-delivery model that reaches greater numbers of those who need help (Berkman, 1977).

A role that also has as one goal an avoidance of blockages to services that result from breakdowns in hospital organizational procedures is that of ombudsman, also known as social health advocate or patient service representative. This role emerged during the 1960s. It is often filled by social workers, some of whom may also have legal training (Rehr and Ravick, 1974).

As the trend continues to ever-shorter periods of hospitalization and to ambulatory health care, there will be an increasing demand for discharge planners. Although nurses have been involved in this function and may, to a certain extent, retain some of it, such as posthospital care, the medical social worker is often more suited to performing it. It often requires an extensive knowledge of and a capacity to gain the cooperation of community resources, particularly the personal care services. This source also may involve having to establish alternative living arrangements for those who cannot live independently or with their families. Thus clinical social workers will need community organization skills.

Yet another growing trend is twenty-four-hour service by social workers. This trend partly reflects a recognition by the medical staff and by social workers of the complex social problems that often precede and accompany the need for crisis services (Krell, 1976).

Primary Care Settings. Another newer area for practice is the primary-care setting, which includes offices of family practitioners, pediatricians, and general internists as well as health maintenance organizations and neighborhood health centers. Many nonmedical problems are identified in these settings—for instance, those associated with well-child care (Brockway and others, 1977). The emerging role of social work is somewhat uncertain here, however, because physicians have a better understanding of the roles of the nurse practitioner and of the clinical psychologist (Hookey, 1978). Furthermore, social work is still struggling to obtain third-party payments.

Genetic Counseling and Family Planning Settings. Many recent developments indicate that clinical social workers may practice increasingly in the areas of genetic counseling and of family planning. Some of these developments are the application of new biomedical discoveries on chromosomal and genetic functioning, new approaches to fertility problems, and such procedures as amniocentesis. The practice of genetic counseling involves the transformation of medical genetic research findings and theories into easily understandable information so that clients can make informed decisions both about having children and about guiding the development of their afflicted children (Schild, 1977). By 1974, 389 genetic counseling units were located in the United States, according to the International Directory of Genetic Services. Some 82 units provided social work service through hospital social service departments, and another 53 units employed social workers or were training master's and doctoral level social work students.

Family planning—that is, fertility regulation and control—is also termed *planned parenthood* or *responsible parenthood.* This area is destined to continue growing due to a worldwide concern about overpopulation, the impetus of the women's movement, greater sexual activity on the part of adolescents, and a climate of economic uncertainty.

Presently, social workers are involved in counseling married couples, teenagers, and career women on issues of contraception, fertility, pregnancy, and abortion. Again, there are many indications that opportunities for social work practice in these areas will continue to increase (Meier, 1977).

The Future. Given that health is a firmly established domain in social work, and assuming that it will continue to expand for reasons that were discussed earlier, certain steps need to be taken to assure that social work is adequately prepared. It has been observed that both baccalaureate and master's degree programs are deficient in content related to the health field and that few students take the initiative or are encouraged to seek out supplementary courses in other disciplines (Bracht, 1974). Yet, if the profession is to remain competitive in this domain, then schools of social work need to make the necessary curriculum modifications, perhaps in joint relationships with other disciplines. It appears that bachelor's level social workers will be providing direct services to clients, and master's level graduates will be doing more supervision along with some administration and evaluation. Doctoral level graduates prepared both in health and in current management technologies are likely to become hospital administrators or directors of large social service departments.

References

Abadinsky, H. *Social Services in Criminal Justice.* Englewood Cliffs, N.J.: Prentice-Hall, 1979.

Akabas, S. "Labor: Social Policy and Human Services." In *Encyclopedia for Social Work.* Vol. 1. (17th ed.) Washington, D.C.: National Association of Social Workers, 1977.

Akabas, S. "Fieldwork in Industrial Settings: Opportunities, Rewards and Dilemmas." *Journal of Education for Social Work,* 1978, *14* (3), 13–19.

American Hospital Association. *Report of Annual Statistics.* New York: American Hospital Association, 1970.

Austin, M. J., and Jackson, I. "Occupational Mental Health and the Human Services: A Review." *Health and Social Work,* 1977, *2* (1), 93–118.

Berkman, B. "Innovations for Social Services in Health Care." In Francine Sobey (Ed.), *Changing Roles in Social Work Practice.* Philadelphia: Temple University Press, 1977.

Bracht, N. F. "Health Care: The Largest Human Service System." *Social Work,* 1974, *19,* 532–542.

Bracht, N. F. "Health Care Delivery: Issues and Trends." *Social Work in Health Care: A Guide to Professional Practice.* New York: Haworth Press, 1978.

Brockway, B., and others. "Social Work in the Doctor's Office." In Francine Sobey (Ed.), *Changing Roles in Social Work Practice.* Philadelphia: Temple University Press, 1977.

Brodyaga, M. G., and others. *Rape and Its Victims: A Report for Citizens, Health Facilities and Criminal Justice Agencies.* Washington, D.C.: Law Enforcement Assistance Administration, National Institute of Law, 1975.

Bryant, G., and Cirel, P. *Polk County Rape/Sexual Assault Care Center, Des Moines, Iowa.* Washington, D.C.: U.S. Government Printing Office, 1977.

Burnett, B. B., and others. "Police and Social Workers in a Community Outreach Program." *Social Casework,* 1976, *59,* 41–46.

Carkhuff, R. R. *The Development of Human Resources.* New York: Holt, Rinehart and Winston, 1971.

Chute, C., and Bell, M. *Crimes, Courts and Probation.* New York: Macmillan, 1956.

Coffey, A. R. *Juvenile Corrections.* Englewood Cliffs, N.J.: Prentice-Hall, 1975.

Collingwood, T. R., Douds, A., and Williams, H. "Juvenile Diversion: The Dallas Police Department Youth Services Program." *Federal Probation,* 1976, *40,* 23–27.

"Employee Transfers." *Wall Street Journal,* July 28, 1977.

Fishman, S. H., and Alissi, A. S. "Strengthening Families and Natural Support Systems for Offenders." *Federal Probation*, 1979, *43* (3), 16–21.

Fogel, D. *We Are the Living Proof: The Justice Model of Corrections.* Cincinnati: Anderson, 1975.

Fox, V. *Introduction to Corrections.* (2nd ed.) Englewood Cliffs, N.J.: Prentice-Hall, 1977.

Galvin, J. J. "Issues for the Seminar." In *Counseling and Corrections.* Washington, D.C.: Joint Commission on Correctional Manpower and Training, U.S. Government Printing Office, 1968.

Gaylord, M. "Relocation and the Corporate Family: Unexplored Issues." *Social Work*, 1979, *24* (3), 188–191.

Ginzberg, E. "Technological Change and Adjustment to Work." *Journal of Occupational Medicine*, 1967, *9*, 232–238.

Glasser, W. *The Identity Society.* (Rev. ed.) New York: Harper & Row, 1975.

Hellenbrand, S., and Yasser, R. "Social Work in Industrial Social Welfare." In F. Sobey (Ed.), *Changing Roles in Social Work Practice.* Philadelphia: Temple University Press, 1977.

Hookey, P. "Social Work in Primary Health Care Settings." In N. F. Bracht (Ed.), *Social Work in Health Care.* New York: Haworth Press, 1978.

Jorgensen, L. A. "Social Work in Business and Industry." Unpublished doctoral dissertation, Graduate School of Social Service, University of Utah, 1979.

Keizer, J., and Habib, M. "Working in a Labor Union to Reach Retirees." *Social Casework*, 1980, *61* (3), 180–183.

Keve, P. W. *Imaginative Programming in Probation and Parole.* Minneapolis: University of Minnesota Press, 1967.

Krell, G. I. "Hospital Social Work Should Be More Than a 9 to 5 Position." *Hospitals*, 1976, *50* (10), 99–104.

Kurzman, P. A. "Third Party Reimbursement." *Social Work*, 1978, *18* (6), 11–22.

Kurzman, P. A., and Akabas, S. H. "Industrial Social Work as an Area for Social Work Practice." *Social Work*, 1981, *26* (1), 52, 54.

Los Angeles Times News Service. "A Dramatic U.S. Population Shift." *New Jersey Record*, May 20, 1981.

Maryland Correctional Training Academy, The State of Maryland. *The Revised Entrance Level Training Program for Parole and Probation Agents.* Maryland Correctional Training Academy, The State of Maryland, 1976.

"Manpower Data Bank Frequency Distributions: February 1975." *National Association of Social Workers News*, February 1975.

Meier, G. "Family and Population Planning." In *Encyclopedia of Social Work.* Vol. 1. (17th ed.) Washington, D.C.: National Association of Social Workers, 1977.

Meyers, E. S. "Insurance Coverage for Mental Illness." *American Journal of Public Health*, 1970, *10*, 1921–1930.

Mills, E. "Family Counseling in an Industrial Job-Support Program." *Social Casework*, 1972, *53* (11), 587–592.

Mullen, J. *The Dilemma of Diversion.* Washington, D.C.: U.S. Government Printing Office, 1975, 105–112.

Perlis, L. "The Human Contract in the Organized Work Place." *Social Thought*, 1977, *3*, 31–32.

Rehr, H., and Ravick, R. "Ombudsmen Program Provides Feedback." *Hospitals,* 1974, *48* (16), 62–67.

Reynolds, B. C. *Social Work and Social Living: Explorations in Philosophy and Practice.* Washington, D.C.: National Association of Social Workers, 1975. (Reprint of 1951 edition.)

Roman, P. A. "Dimensions of Current Research in Occupational Alcoholism." New Orleans: Tulane University, 1977. (Mimeographed.)

Schild, S. "Health Services: Genetic Counseling." In *Encyclopedia of Social Work.* Vol. 1. (17th ed.) Washington, D.C.: National Association of Social Workers, 1977.

Skidmore, R. A., Balsam, D., and Jones, O. F. "Social Work Practice in Industry." *Social Work,* 1974, *19* (3), 280–286.

Studt, E. *Corrections of the Curriculum Study Committee Report.* New York: Council on Social Work Education, 1959a.

Studt, E. *Education for Social Workers in the Correctional Field.* New York: Council on Social Work Education, 1959b.

Studt, E. "Crime and Delinquency: Institutions." In *Encyclopedia of Social Work.* Vol. 1. (17th ed.) Washington, D.C.: National Association of Social Workers, 1977.

Trattner, W. *From Poor Law to Welfare State.* (2nd ed.) New York: Free Press, 1979.

U.S. Department of Health, Education and Welfare. *Health Resources Document.* Washington, D.C.: U.S. Government Printing Office, 1971.

U.S. Department of Health, Education and Welfare. *Alcoholism and Health: New Knowledge.* Washington, D.C.: U.S. Government Printing Office, 1974.

Washington Post News Service. "The Median Age Has Gone to 30, U.S. Census Says." *New Jersey Record,* May 26, 1981.

Weathers, L., and Liberman, R. P. "Contingency Contracting with Families of Delinquent Adolescents." *Behavioral Therapy,* 1975, *6,* 356–366.

Woolf, D. A., and Rudman, M. "A Police Social Service Cooperative Program." *Social Work,* 1977, *22* (1), 62–63.

48

Private Practice

Nancy K. Neale

Social work has been privately practiced in the United States for most of the twentieth century. It has been recognized as a legitimate form of social work practice by most clinicians and by the national professional organizations of social workers for some time. Yet, curiously, in this most comprehensive of the helping professions, private practice has continued to meet with questions and suspicion rather than with respect from some of its members.

Other forms of practice, such as school, medical, and industrial social work, have emerged, survived, and grown to be accepted by members of the profession. Independent clinical practice, however, has continued to be, for some, a contradiction in terms. For these social workers, social work practice cannot be—even "should not be"—both "private" and "social" at the same time. For them, the first commandment for social workers has been to be "social," that is, related to society as a whole, most particularly to the poor and disadvantaged.

This exclusive attitude generally ignores two important facts about the private practice of social work. The first is that, by definition, private practice can and does include social work with any population or with any social/psychological problems with which the practitioner can demonstrate competence, regardless of the economic status of the client or the nature of the problem. The second is that, to a profession that claims to be responsive to client needs and well-being, a growing number of clients have spoken through their choice of the practitioner in a particular setting, their need for help, their presence and persistence, and their dollars. These clients have chosen to seek services from social workers in private practice sometimes because of the social workers' reputation for competence, sometimes because they have happened upon a name in the yellow pages of the telephone directory under "clinical social workers," and sometimes because they have wanted privacy. These clients have spoken with their continuing and growing demand for the variety of services that private social workers can provide. Private practice offers benefits, liabilities, and special challenges of its own, which have drawn an increasing number of members of the profession to it.

Definition

Social workers are accustomed to seeking and developing structure and authority in order to function effectively. Where structure has not existed in workable form, social workers historically have created structure. Yet, often in agency practice, structure has come to mean both security for and dehumanization of both client and worker. The strong supports of professionalism have often not been sturdy enough to prevent the stifling aspects of bureaucracy from undoing the worker's efforts to be practical, competent, and creative. Many social workers have turned to private practice, part time or full time, to create their own structure and to become their own authorities, responsible and accountable directly to themselves, their profession, and their clients.

The basic definition of private practice remains that specified by the Board of Directors of the National Association of Social Workers (NASW) in 1961: "A private practitioner is a social worker who wholly or in part, practices his profession outside the aegis of a governmental or duly incorporated voluntary agency, who has responsibility for his own practice and sets up his own conditions of exchange with his clients and identifies himself as a social work practitioner in offering his services" (NASW, 1974).

Several tests are included in this definition that deserve special attention: (1) the social worker sets up the terms of the working relationship together with the client; (2) it must be clear that the social worker is professionally defined as a practicing member of the social work profession, *not* in terms of a specific function as marriage and family therapist, Gestalt therapist, divorce counselor, feminist therapist, psychotherapist, child development specialist, or other titles that have been used by some social workers for a variety of reasons. By this definition, the clearly professed source of the worker's knowledge and skills must be openly declared and acknowledged to be the profession of social work. Some practitioners, because of this feature of the definition, cannot be included in the group of social workers in private practice because they use other titles to identify themselves and their practices.

A second definition that is critical to the discussion of clinical private practice was offered by the NASW Council on Private Practice in 1975: "Clinical practice is that aspect of social work which is carried out in a one-to-one or one-to-group situation by a practitioner exercising special skills in a self-directed manner. It encompasses assessment, diagnosis, and treatment of problems of intrapsychic and interpersonal conflicts and their effects on the self and others. It involves utilizing community resources and providing help in coping with illness, both medical and psychiatric. It develops psychological readiness to function more effectively in relation to family, peers, associates, and the community, and in relation to employment, education, and other goals. Clinical practice involves the knowledge and treatment of definable psychopathology through psychosocial and psychotherapeutic skills in which the practitioner is both qualified and competent" (Gabriel, 1977). For some social workers in clinical private practice, this definition has major limitations because of its use of the medical or psychiatric model, incorporating the terms *psychiatric illness* and *psychopathology* rather than other more inclusive terms, such as *psychosocial distress* and *dysfunctional behavior*. Despite these limitations, the definition remains a useful one for both professional and societal consideration.

Jerome Cohen (1979), in his article "Nature of Clinical Social Work," presented a tentative definition of *clinical social work* on behalf of the NASW Task Force on Clinical Social Work Practice: "[The] purpose [of clinical social work] has been identified as the maintenance and enhancement of psychosocial functioning of individuals, families, and small groups by maximizing the availability of needed intrapersonal, interpersonal, and societal resources." This definition, more abstract than the earlier one, clarifies the focus of clinical social work practice and avoids the pitfalls of the earlier definition. It does omit reference to the qualifications of the clinician.

Minimum Standards for Private Practice

Minimum standards for social workers in private practice have evolved over the past several decades. At present, the profession's basic standard for independent practice is membership in the Academy of Certified Social Workers (ACSW), a program available through NASW. For a social worker to be eligible for membership in ACSW, he or she must have a master's degree from a graduate school of social work accredited by the profession's national educational organization, the Council on Social Work Education (CSWE). In addition, the social worker must have two years of full-time or three thousand hours of part-time postgraduate experience in social work practice. To qualify for membership in ACSW, the social worker must be a regular member of NASW and, since 1970, must pass the national ACSW certification examination as well as be endorsed by colleagues who are already members of ACSW or who are advanced in social work practice. Acceptance by the Academy indicates the profession's certification that the social worker is deemed qualified for independent and self-regulated practice, whether in agency practice or private practice.

One limitation in this minimum standard of ACSW encountered by clinicians and by NASW is its very comprehensiveness. Insurance companies and members of other professions as well as our own have questioned whether the ACSW membership is valid indication of a practitioner's *clinical* competence, since the ACSW examination includes all aspects of social work knowledge, values, and skills. In response to this concern, NASW's Council on Private Practice has recommended that private practitioners be required to have their supervised experience in a clinical setting before qualifying for the ACSW (Kurzman, 1973). Several problems arise from this modification, however. For example, an ACSW social worker may decide, after years of agency practice, that she is ready for part-time or full-time private practice. Although trained primarily as a clinician, her pre-ACSW experience was nonclinical (community center program director and group worker), but her post-ACSW experience has included clinical agency practice. What adjustments can be made in this example that will not deter a clinician from this decision, which is usually considered to be an individual's professional right? Another problem for some members of the profession is, what constitutes a "clinical setting"? The setting may not be clinical (as in a YWCA), but some of the practice in such a setting may be quite clearly clinical or clinically therapeutic in form, content, and process.

An additional aid for clinicians has been the publication of the *NASW Register of Clinical Social Workers.* To qualify for listing, the MSW social worker must have two or more postgraduate years of full-time or three thousand hours of part-time supervised clinical experience in a clinical setting during the prior ten years. The *NASW Register* can and has been used to aid in negotiations with insurance companies and governmental bodies to obtain third-party payment. However, again we see the need for some clarification of settings and elements of practice to be considered clinical or psychotherapeutic in goal, content, and result.

An additional complication occurs in that, whereas the minimum standard exists for purposes of ACSW certification, it can be ignored by some social workers who practice privately in states that have no legal restrictions in the form of licensing or certification. Here, the question remains unanswered whether such practice is performed ethically if it fails to meet the profession's stated standards. The private practice of social workers who may not be members of NASW, who may not qualify for ACSW, and who may not meet requirements of a state board of examiners for licensure continues to be a problem for the profession of social work. Only those clinicians who annually renew their membership in NASW and ACSW subscribe publicly to the NASW Code of Ethics (revised, 1979). Of course, this problem exists for agency personnel as well.

Historically, as social work has evolved, new structures on a variety of levels have been developed by the profession and its members to try to ensure practitioner competence in specific kinds of practice. These efforts developed to protect and inform clients, the profession, and the society at large. The increasing number of states that license social workers or at least restrict use of the title is an indication of one kind of evolving structure.

History

Private practice in social work was in evidence at least as early as the 1920s (NASW, 1974), shortly after Richmond's *Social Diagnosis* was published in 1917. According to Estelle Gabriel, former chairperson of the NASW Council on Private Practice, Division of Practice and Knowledge, and author of the article on private practice in NASW's *Encyclopedia of Social Work* (1977), many charter members of NASW were private clinicians. Many had received help in several ways from psychiatrists, who endorsed such a development. "In the beginning, agencies did not accept, support, or promote the private practice of social workers because they feared they would lose their experienced agency staff members. Thus in the early history of private practice strong feelings of sincere support and convinced opposition were aroused" (Gabriel, 1977).

So it is that the history of private practice has been essentially a defensive history, chronicling efforts to define, describe, justify, extinguish, and generally control this form of social work practice, particularly in its clinical emphasis. We have little information on the development or evolution of this form of practice over the years. Levenstein's (1964) work is one of the few early sources of information in this regard.

The record of the National Association of Social Workers on this matter began in 1958 with the acknowledgment that private practice was to be included within the definition of social work practice and was indeed a legitimate professional activity. In February of 1959, NASW's Commission on Social Work Practice accepted the following position statement in reference to the Working Definition of Social Work Practice (NASW, 1974): "Most of the committee believes that *as the Working Definition stands today, the private practice of social work is encompassed in it.* They believe that in social work, as in other professions, new developments must be allowed to unfold within a framework of evolving standards and tested through experience and/or research. They subscribe to the urgency of the need for NASW to arrive at policy decisions with regard to private practice in order to protect the profession, its individual members, and the public, but, in addition, believe endorsement of private practice to be important if the profession is to claim its full professional status [italics in original]."

The supporters and opponents of private practice for social workers took increasingly firm stands as the national concern both for competence of the clinician and for the social conscience of the profession became focused on private practice. Supporters endorsed the nature of the informal and direct contract between client and social worker, the opportunity to continue direct service to clients, the satisfaction of establishing only essential and minimum structure for the practice, and the sense of autonomy and self-direction available to the private practitioner. Much discussion took place on the local and national level of the need for standards for private practice, and those social workers in private practice began to request that the profession grant recognition on a national level, specifying the particular knowledge and skills required for private practice.

Opponents of the private practice of social work believed that the commitment of the profession was inextricably tied to the economic status of client groups. Social workers, it has been held, should serve *only* lower-income, socially deprived, or physically limited clients, and this service should be performed only in agencies. It was also a serious concern that, if experienced clinicians were increasingly attracted to private practice, personnel shortages in agencies would be seriously increased. Rather than noting the attractions of private practice to social work clinicians, improving agency practice, and accepting the legitimacy of private practice, the solution was seen to be the removal or disgrace of the temptation itself; it could only be a shameful activity pursued to the disadvantage of the already disadvantaged poor (Gabriel, 1977).

In March of 1960, NASW created a national committee to focus on the private practice of social work. A workshop held in the fall of that year developed a definition of private practice and recommendations for minimum standards. In the spring of 1961, the NASW Board of Directors approved the minimum qualification of membership in the Academy of Certified Social Workers of the NASW for all independent practitioners, whether in agency or private practice. This minimum standard was adopted by the Delegate Assembly in December of 1962.

In December of 1964, the Delegate Assembly adopted the report of an Ad Hoc Committee on the Profession and Private Practice. This report recommended that NASW (1974) "recognize private practice as a legitimate area of social work practice in meeting human needs but [affirm] that practice within socially sponsored organizational structures must remain the primary avenue for the implementation of the goals of the profession."

One issue debated vigorously was whether private practice ought to be specially regulated or whether such emphasis would create a special status—an elite group—where none was desired. The larger question was, how should all advanced clinical practice be regulated and monitored by the profession for competency?

The 1964 position statement further addressed these questions:

> NASW devotes its major energies to improving the quality and quantity of social work manpower, establishes areas of critical need for professional manpower, and avoids any action that will set apart or establish a special status, negative or positive, for private practice.
>
> NASW continues its efforts to define competence to practice on any level and under any auspices and that any plan to establish levels of competence should include private practitioners as part of the total range of practice, not separate from it [NASW, 1974].

This position statement inherently suggests that community organizers and social policy workers as well as private clinicians should be subject to standards of competence and regulation of their practice.

In May of 1971, the Delegate Assembly asked the NASW Division of Professional Standards to develop criteria for eligibility to practice privately, to establish procedures for monitoring those in practice (including due process for appeal), and to regulate those who did not adhere to the standards set by the profession (NASW, 1974).

In October, 1972, the Cabinet of the Division of Practice and Knowledge recognized that private practice of social workers who meet the minimum specified standards "is an integral and essential part of the professional practice of social work" (NASW, 1974). National professional acceptance continued to grow.

Another major question facing the profession during these years had to do with third-party payments for services. If social work clinical services could be covered in private and public health insurance plans, more individuals and families who had insurance coverage for mental health services by qualified providers could elect to consult social work clinicians. The economic circumstances of social workers' potential clients would not necessarily limit their options for treatment to subsidized agencies, and therefore greater freedom of choice for the clients in choosing providers of services would be available.

Recognizing these issues as vital to the profession, the Delegate Assembly in May of 1973 passed a resolution requesting the NASW Board of Directors to include vendorship coverage of qualified social workers in private practice in the insurance plans offered to NASW members. This move was a start in bringing to the attention of more social workers the social and economic implications and power issues involved in the policies of private and public health insurance.

In 1973, the Council on Private Practice was established in the NASW Division of Practice and Knowledge. Since that time, private practice councils have been formed in several states, often attached to the NASW state chapters.

Perhaps the most important recent development in the standards affecting private clinical practice is the previously mentioned *NASW Register of Clinical Social Workers.* First published in 1976 and periodically updated, the *Register* lists those clinical social workers who meet the specified standards. For some professionals, these standards are too lax, and, for some, too strict. Nevertheless, the *Register* offers clinicians who wish to practice privately a national standard and an opportunity for a national listing in a reference that has been used by some insurance companies and government bodies as a criterion for eligibility for third-party reimbursement.

If the social work profession is to continue to be as inclusive as it was at the time of the merger of so many different organizations in 1955 into NASW, it must acknowledge that different environments attract different people. Some social workers are more comfortable and satisfied with and committed to agency practice, public or private; some are more comfortable, satisfied with, and committed to private practice. Most private practitioners, in fact, practice a blend of the two.

The historical question about the social work profession's commitment to social action is indeed an important one, but just as all community organizers or social policy makers cannot be able clinicians, neither can all clinicians be able communty organizers. The psychology and sociology of occupations and professions provide important reminders for us of the uniqueness of the person-in-the-situation concept, a particular understanding of the locus for professional intervention that social work has long espoused.

This understanding must be applied to the profession's members as well as to its clients. Perhaps the primary place to develop commitment to social action and beneficial social change is at the undergraduate and graduate school level. Here is opportunity for the profession's educators to impress on would-be clinicians and community organizers alike the knowledge, values, and skills essential to social commitment expressed through social action. When graduate schools of social work offer courses in private practice, such a component can be basic to the curriculum. The best hope of the profession in this regard may lie in the design of this curriculum in schools and in continuing education offerings.

Characteristics of Private Practice and Practitioners

Both the *Handbook on the Private Practice of Social Work* (1974) and the *Encyclopedia of Social Work* (1977) include some discussion of these characteristics. In addition to Levenstein (1964), Cohen (1966), Golton (1963), and Koret (1958) contributed to the literature in this area during the 1950s and 1960s.

Private practice has included all forms and methods of social work, including social group work, social casework, community organization, community and organizational development; social welfare administration and development; consultation with agency staffs, administrators, and program directors; social and organizational planning; and teaching and research. Clinical casework which concentrates on individuals, couples, families, and groups continues to be the primary method used by private practitioners.

Most private practice is part time, which indicates a combined practice, both in agencies and on one's own. Private practitioners may be found in a number of practice arrangements in addition to the traditional form of solo practice. Some are in group practices and some are in partnerships. Increasingly, social workers have developed practices in conjunction with physicians or other professionals. In these arrangements as well as in solo practice, as long as all procedures and processes—including fees, frequency and length of appointments, therapy models, and related matters of practice—are determined between social workers and their clients, private practice does exist. When another professional controls or determines the fees or office arrangements of the social worker, the worker then operates at the direction of that professional person and no longer qualifies as a private social work clinician.

Use of an office in one's home sometimes is the locus of the private practice, particularly for those who work full-time for an agency. Many social workers rent, lease, or buy space in professional buildings in areas readily available to clients. The growth of the practice depends in large part on the developing reputation of the clinician and therefore on referral sources, which must be carefully tended and nourished in a professional manner. Many of these sources will be other professionals. Eventually, many will be satisfied clients who want others to know about their effective social worker therapist.

Clinical sessions with individuals and couples or dyads usually last for fifty minutes; group sessions, including those with families, frequently last about one and one-half or two hours. The number of sessions may range from several weeks to several years, depending on the seriousness of the problem and the kinds of change sought by the clients.

Clients generally are in middle-income groups but may also be in upper- and lower-income groups. Many clinicians will see students and other financially stressed clients for less than the standard fee or gratis. The number of clients in this category at any one time will be limited by the clinician's ability and willingness to absorb this loss.

Practitioners may specify the age groups and types of problems on which they want to focus their practice. Client problems may include marriage and divorce difficulties; consistently low self-esteem; depression; nonassertiveness; difficulty with decision making and problem solving; inadequate communication skills; isolation; suicidal and other destructive tendencies; problems with peer relationships; family relationship difficulties; problems with anger, fear, and grief management; problems with working conditions and work life; authority problems; severe identity crises; role stress and strain; and so on. Some of these problems lead to moderately and sometimes severely dysfunctional behaviors.

Borenzweig, in an article that recently appeared in *Social Work* (1981), reported on research with private clinicians in Los Angeles. Because a nonprobability accidental sample was used, Borenzweig pointed out that the study's results could only be suggestive in its application to other clinical social workers. The sample included 33 workers in combined agency–private practice, 51 workers in agency practice only, and 50 workers in private practice only, a total of 134. Characteristics of the sample included (1) at least twice as many women as men in the total sample; (2) more Anglo-Americans in agency practice, more Jewish-Americans in private practice; (3) more clinicians in combined practice and in private practice who received degrees before 1967; more than twice as many in agency practice as in private practice who received degrees after 1967.

Some of the findings of this research were as follows:

1. All respondents felt similar to other social workers in professional identification, interests, and practice.
2. The one-to-one clinical interview was the primary approach.
3. All three groups reported low involvement in social action—33 percent of the total sample did participate.
4. Most respondents reported that the primary theoretician influencing their work was not a social worker (most often Freud or Erik Erikson).
5. Clients of private practitioners tended to be middle class and upper class; clients of agency practitioners tended to be minority members of color and people of lower income.
6. Diagnoses of agency practitioners included more people labeled as psychotic; diagnoses of private practitioners labeled more people as psychoneurotic.
7. Private practitioners treated fewer children as clients but treated more young adults than did agency clinicians.
8. Private clinicians tended to spend more of their time in direct practice with clients.
9. Agency clinicians appeared to make greater use of community resources than did the private clinicians.
10. Agency workers used social work titles (such as, *clinical social worker*) with clients but changed to other titles (such as *psychotherapist*) when identifying themselves to friends and when thinking of themselves. Private practitioners were more apt to use other titles with clients and to use social work titles when identifying themselves to friends and when thinking of themselves.
11. Borenzweig concludes that "overall, . . . agency practitioners identified more strongly with social work than private practitioners did."
12. Fifty-five percent of the total sample received no supervision.
13. Earlier graduates (before 1967) were more likely to refer to people as patients than as clients.
14. Recent graduates were more reluctant to approve the absorption of social work, along with psychology and psychiatry, into "psychotherapy."
15. More innovative approaches seemed to be used by agency clinicians than by private clinicians.

It is difficult to understand, from the data presented, how Borenzweig concludes that "overall, . . . agency practitioners identified more strongly with social work than private practitioners did" (see #11). He appears to base this conclusion on the use of titles with clients rather than on the use of titles with friends and self. It can be as easily argued that one's identification is clearer through the latter situations than through the former, given the history and status of clinical private practice in the profession and the lack of information about it among potential clientele. One conclusion of this research was that graduates after 1967 were more secure about their social work identity and status than graduates before 1967, so the profession may have made progress in its educational and affiliative systems.

A second conclusion, which was viewed with alarm by Borenzweig, was that 75 percent of the graduates after 1967 were receiving little or no supervision. Surely, the validity of this concern is questionable since the minimum standard of the profession for beginning independent practice is the ACSW and two years of supervised clinical practice. Many private clinicians may use peer consultants in their practices but may believe after their beginning years are past that traditional supervision is no longer appropriate or necessary.

A third major conclusion and a second cause for alarm for Borenzweig was the involvement of only 33 percent of the total sample of clinicians in social action. It can be agreed, as stated earlier, that this commitment is essential to the profession and practice of social work, but other issues relevant to this question remain untouched by this research. For example, it would be useful to have comparisons to this sample with other samples of clinicians, social work educators, and administrators of social welfare agencies; comparisons of clinicians, educators, administrators, and community organizers in volunteer activities in civic and professsional study and action groups; and comparisons of incomes and income needs among members of the profession. More women are clinicians; more men are community organizers. Are higher salaries a differentiating factor?

What is the responsibility of the graduate schools of social work in the curriculum of private practice courses to foster the knowledge, skills, and motivation of potential private clinicians toward appropriate social action? There are important issues to be addressed in this regard in terms of the accepting, nonjudgmental attitude needed by the clinician toward clients and positions social workers take in social action on social issues. The private clinician who takes public stands on controversial issues does so with no institutional protections.

Few graduate schools offer private practice courses to second year or doctoral students. The unfortunate attitude has sometimes seemed to be, "If we teach it, they may *do* it. If we don't teach it, maybe they *won't* do it!" This exclusionary approach to private practice shows some signs of fading, but, when evidenced, it tends to leave those students or practitioners interested in private practice with the option of seeking out more sympathetic private professionals from other disciplines for assistance, knowledge, and support.

Does the tracking of graduate student education into clinical practice and community organization, one of which has traditionally attracted females and the other males, foster the disparity in graduates in terms of social action commitment? The traditional assumption has been that community organization and social planning are clearly associated with social action; clinical students typically have received less shaping and modeling for such behavior. It would appear that the tracking approach could bring even greater division. In using such an approach in its educational system, perhaps the profession fosters the very attitudes and behaviors about which it then complains.

Borenzweig's research is useful in showing that the gap between the agency and private practitioners in his sample is not as wide today as once believed. Such studies should be undertaken on a wide scale. They should be designed by both educators and clinicians familiar with both agency and private practice. Several factors should be kept in mind when considering such research—the interrelatedness of social work training and education (including effects of tracking); admission criteria in schools of social work (evidence of broad commitment to beneficial social change?); curriculum content of clinical and private practice courses in graduate schools and continuing education courses; agency salaries for direct service and administrative positions; working conditions in agencies and in private practice; the possibilities for professional autonomy and self-regulated practice in either form of practice; comparative incomes for caseworkers, group workers, community organizers (distinguished by primary emphasis and job content), administrators, and educators; and personality strengths, limitations, and personal preferences of social workers. The need for research is great, and the possibilities for its use in our educational and professional practice systems are boundless.

Current Status. The early 1980s are a time of flux, uncertainty, and change in the power of social attitudes. From the rapid development in the 1960s of humanistic concerns and legislation favorable to social work values and principles, we have entered a period of inflation, recession, and negative political attitudes toward those in lower social, economic, and political statuses and those with differing social values. Social service, health, and mental health agency staffs and administrators are preparing in many instances for a stormy period. Federal, state, and local funds, regulations, and programs have been drastically reduced under the attack on social programs by President Ronald Reagan and his appointees and legislative supporters. Some agency staff members have already been released in anticipation of slashed budgets. Some vacated positions will not be filled. The use of consultants may be severely curtailed in the immediate future. Travel and professional development funds may be drastically lowered.

As a result, many individuals and families that formerly qualified for services (and still would, by social work standards) may find their basic needs unmet. These new policies will have several social and psychological consequences. It is quite probable that more social workers, especially those primarily clinical in orientation, will try to become engaged in part-time practice. Some may feel forced to turn to it as the quantity and quality of jobs in agency practice diminish and as agency salaries are worth less every year. It is also possible that social agencies, both public and private, will wish to use private clinicians by buying blocks of their time for direct practice, thus saving the costs of full-time salaries and benefits. If agency social workers cannot travel widely for conferences and workshops related to professional development, it may be practical and wise to use local experts through consultation and other arrangements.

As social workers enter private practice (whether regulated or not), they will have to demonstrate their effectiveness in competition with other social workers, psychologists, psychiatrists, and counselors with various backgrounds, training, and experience. The passage of licensing laws in those states that are still unregulated will determine who may enter the marketplace as a social worker. Once in practice, such factors as reputation for effectiveness, location of office, business management capabilities, and resourcefulness and flexibility will determine which professionals survive.

Many potential consumers of private social work services do not understand that social work clinicians in private practice are an option that is available to them. Many clients have great difficulty identifying the social worker as a clinician; this designation does not fit the stereotype of the social worker. If the profession really accepts private practice as an option for its clinicians, it must more clearly state that some social workers practice in this way. The common language needs to include the proper terminology.

Private clinicians in social work, some of whom have doctorates, are often competing with psychologists and psychiatrists, most of whom have doctorates. This can be a disadvantage to master's degree social workers in some situations. An additional disadvantage can be the varied social statuses of the three professions, in which the social worker may be seen at this time by the public and by other professions at the lowest level of the three. The initial assumption by other professions may be that the social worker is the least informed, knowledgeable, and skillful member of the three groups. This assumption can, however, be balanced by demonstrating competence, knowledge, persistence, assertive practice management, and constructive interaction with other professionals.

Within the social work profession, as in other areas of life, there are emotional responses to a largely rational question, namely, shall social workers contribute to the social functioning of *all* people, regardless of their economic or social status, and also participate in social action to alleviate and alter conditions that are destructive or detrimental to effective social functioning? I hope that this question will some day be answered with a resounding "yes!" by all of us. The energy that continues to go into this unnecessary debate can be better used in developing the knowledge, values, and skills of social workers in all settings.

The social worker who is in the best position to have a comprehensive private practice seems obviously to be one who is both a generalist and a specialist. The idea that a social worker must choose between community organization and clinical practice, or between generalist and specialist practice, has had detrimental effects on the development of the profession. An inclusive attitude affirms that social workers can develop a comprehensive practice and continue to grow in knowledge and skills throughout life.

The current status of private clinical social work is an improvement over the past. However, it has not yet arrived at its proper status, where it is accepted that private clinicians have a particular niche to fill in social work's service to society.

Regulatory Promise and Problems. More than half the states now have some form of licensing or registration laws. Other state chapters of NASW are currently attempting to get laws passed.

The legislative attitude across the nation has been one of increasing wariness of the multitude of licensing efforts in recent years by members of many professions and occupations. The social work profession has been slow to realize the need for such legislation. Such professions as marriage and family therapy, rehabilitation counseling, sex therapy, mental health counseling, and drug and alcohol counseling—all formerly considered fields of practice rather than professions—have recently been actively pursuing their own licensing and title-protection laws. In some cases, social workers have been excluded from coverage in these bills; in most instances, they have not, so issues of multiple licensing arise.

A recent development has been the passage by state legislatures of governmental review laws, or "sunset" laws, whereby the reexamination of licensing and program-establishing legislation must be done within a five- to ten-year period after the first passage of such legislation. The idea of reviewing the need and justification for continuing state regulation of a profession has merit, and yet, such requirements do consume much of the time, energy, and money of professional organizations as they defend laws that are considered to be desirable and necessary for both the public and the profession.

Another consideration affecting the passage of social work regulatory legislation has been dissension within the profession itself. So large a constituency inevitably will include radically opposed views on many matters, and this particular matter of licensing has been a difficult issue for many social workers. Although NASW has taken a favorable position on social work regulation, some leaders and rank-and-file members are opposed to it. Subgroups opposed have been represented by state departments of social services and by the Black Social Workers Association (BSWA), for example.

The BSWA has taken the position that licensing laws would provide the social establishment a further opportunity to discriminate against blacks by creating licensing boards with authority to regulate the practice of professional social workers. It is believed that these licensing boards would not represent the views of many blacks and that, in fact, the entire effort to license social workers is elitist and runs counter to the egalitarian values of social work. Other black social workers endorse the NASW position that regulatory board members, usually appointed by governors from lists prepared by the state chapters of NASW, are bound by professional ethics not to discriminate against any groups of people. There is no way to guarantee the placing of particular representatives of different groups on the boards, but individual chapters can influence this issue as they compose the lists of names for gubernatorial consideration.

One feature of the licensing acts that does delineate particular representation on the boards is the requirement that the levels of practice and education specified in the bill be represented (such as social work clinicians, bachelors of social work, social service technicians, or aides).

In North Carolina, one of the states currently attempting to secure passage of a licensing act, influential groups have testified in hearings against the proposed bill, including members of the BSWA. The organization representing social workers (both trained and untrained) of the 100 departments of social services in the state shifted from early opposition to support of the bill, but other groups, such as the state department of personnel, the state education department, some mental health systems, some health departments, and the state association of county commissioners, have opposed passage of the bill or demanded exemption from its requirements for particular social work positions. The opponents' position is primarily that such a law would increase their costs since they would have to employ professionals for social work-designated positions now occupied by less-trained people.

Currently, state and private agencies can employ almost anyone to be a social worker and can represent this person as such to clients, communities, and other professionals. Recently, one county's department of social services secured permission from the state personnel department to employ a person with only a high school education as a Social Worker I. When psychology secured title-protection legislation, social worker categories became the last positions for which almost anyone with any academic background could be hired by mental health systems, departments of social services, health departments, and hospitals.

Licensing efforts have bogged down in many states. Several states are attempting to pass legislation regulating a cluster of groups under a name such as *mental health professionals.* The groups may include rehabilitation counselors, guidance counselors, drug and alcohol counselors, and social workers. Most social workers are opposing such legislation for several reasons, especially because the title under which they would be covered does not adequately reflect the comprehensive practice of social work, which includes community organization, social planning, and social welfare administration.

What are the reasons for supporting social work licensing legislation? An obvious one is to restrict the use of the title *social worker.* Another is to specify standards for performance that should apply to all social workers at all levels of education and experience. The implication of this point is that social workers who are not NASW members will be accountable for appropriate practice. The public then would have access to a legitimate professional board in every state, whether the worker was a member of NASW or not.

Many social work licensing acts have been opposed, or at least not supported, by members of the profession because of the belief that such legislation is solely an effort to protect the clinicians so that, as recognized providers of services, they can secure third-party payments. It is difficult for many social workers to perceive the benefits that can accrue to all members of the profession and to society when the state protects the title and acknowledges legally the existence, knowledge, and expertise of the profession.

Several states have clinical features in their licensing acts or laws. It is difficult to develop standards and regulations of clinical practice that are acceptable both to clinical and nonclinical social workers, who often have differing ideas of what should be required. For example, a community organizer, administrator, or educator may wish someday to do some part-time clinical private practice, without the benefit of clinical training or recent clinical practice. Without regulation, there would be no legal obstacles to his or her doing so that would protect the public from lack of competence in that area.

The primary point remains the welfare of society and of clients. Clients should be informed about the qualifications of those who are called social workers. Clients should have recourse to a licensing body if they believe they have been recipients of malpractice by social workers in any setting.

Existing licensing laws that regulate private practice in some states primarily require clinical social work education and training in graduate programs accredited by CSWE, postgraduate experience under clinical supervision, and passing a board-developed examination. Regulation by the states is one way to help reduce the widespread public and professional confusion abut who is a social worker and what kinds of work social workers do. Also, the definitional dilemma social workers face can be addressed through social work licensing laws.

Third-Party Payments. The issue of third-party payments, inextricably related to the passage of social work licensing laws, continues to be a problem. The term refers to the payment of illness and disability costs by a third party, usually a private insurance company or a self-insured or government-sponsored plan for reimbursement. Historically, health insurance was developed specifically for physical health problems. Eventually, as a branch of medicine, psychiatry urged inclusion of coverage of treatment for mental and emotional disorders.

This treatment, psychiatrists held, could and should include coverage for the costs of psychotherapy whether or not such treatment included prescription of medications or drugs. The insurance industry accepted the expansion of the original concept, although some plans offer participants very low mental health coverage in contrast to physical health benefits. However, insurance companies have tended to restrict insurance reimbursement to physicians, thus limiting the clinical practice of other professions by making more economic the selection of a psychiatrist as a provider of service.

There are serious problems with state legislation and with health insurance policy that restrict reimbursement for services of nonmedical providers to those "supervised by physicians." In most instances, it is inappropriate to require one profession to supervise another, since this infringes upon the professional autonomy of the second profession and raises questions about the qualifications of the first to do so. In many instances, fraudulent practice has been encouraged by such legal requirements since social workers develop plans and carry them out independently, and physicians often only sign the insurance claims.

It has been clear for some time that qualified professionals from a variety of disciplines may be equally effective clinicians. The trend is toward the licensing of professional groups as independent providers, enabling them to offer services to the public within the scope of their training.

Some states have passed insurance legislation that provides freedom of choice among qualified practitioners of mental health services. These laws make it illegal for third-party payers to discriminate among providers who are licensed and otherwise qualified to provide services that are covered under their contracts. People covered under these contracts therefore are not restricted to selecting a psychiatrist in seeking mental health services. Such states as California, Utah, Wisconsin, and Louisiana had freedom of choice legislation by the end of the 1970s.

Some specific progress has been made. Some of the insurance companies that reimburse for social work services are Bankers Life of Des Moines, Iowa, Union Labor Life of New York, and Loyal Protective Insurance Company of Boston. Some union contracts cover social work services, such as those of longshoremen locals and building employees in Chicago. A few companies have added social workers to their list of qualified providers, for example, Standard Oil of California. If a health maintenance organization is federally supported, social workers are entitled to reimbursement (*Psychotherapy Economics,* 1977). But, even when social workers are recognized as legitimate providers of service, it is frequently more difficult for them to get reimbursement than for clinicians of other professions. Freedom of choice legislation on the state level following licensing laws seems to be the most desirable goal for the social work profession.

Third-party payments for clinical social workers, including private practitioners, represent much more than simply a source of reimbursement. Prepaid group health insurance and other sources of third-party payment make it possible for people across the socioeconomic spectrum to obtain mental health services from qualified providers of their own choosing. The issues of professional competence and autonomy for social workers and public acknowledgment of them through legislative action are at the very heart of the question of social sanction to do our work in this society as an independent profession.

Private Practice Considerations. Beginning and building a private practice requires knowledge of many matters, including the community and its resources, the interprofessional network, and practice management, and it requires of the clinician many choices and decisions. The curriculum of private practice courses is based on these considerations.

NASW's revised *Handbook on the Private Practice of Social Work* (1974) is the most helpful source book currently available for clinicians interested in this option. Its sections examine such matters as the personal and professional aspects of private practice; management of the practice; variations of practice arrangements, including solo and group practice; special concerns for casework issues; maintenance of relationships with social agencies; building interprofessional relationships; and ethical considerations that are particularly relevant. A useful bibliography follows the text, which includes pertinent materials developed through 1973; frequent revision and updating of this bibliography is urgently needed. The *Handbook* also includes appendices that present such basic documents as NASW Statements on Privileged Communication to the House Judiciary Committee and NASW's Model Statute. The *Handbook* is a basic reference in the private clinician's library.

Social workers considering entry into private practice even on a part-time basis should examine not only their practical knowledge and needs but also their own qualities and characteristics, which may be assets or liabilities in independent practice. Participating in professional associations; continuing professional development through reading, peer consultation, and continuing education; and involvement with consultation, research, teaching, training, and social and professional action all help to lessen the problem of isolation for the private clinician and maintain the contribution she or he can make to the profession, community, and society. Important personal characteristics include the ability to take responsibility, flexibility, the ability to learn from experience and change practice patterns when appropriate, self-discipline, a sense of humor, ethical awareness, organizational ability, and the ability to meet many personal needs in other ways than through professional practice.

Private practitioners must also be sensitive to the sexual, cultural, ethnic, and religious characteristics of the client. Sources of stress for the clinician and sources of personal and professional growth should be periodically reevaluated. Consumer rights and consumer education should also be explored: What choices do potential clients really have in terms of providers of services and what do clients need to know about the social work clinician in private practice?

One may need to become skillful at building a referral network. There is a multitude of practical considerations, such as how to advertise, how to set and collect fees, how much insurance (including malpractice insurance) the clinician should carry, what record-keeping systems (financial and clinical) are most useful, and what initial expenses are likely to be for office space, utilities, supplies, telephone answering arrangements, furnishings, and equipment. The design of office space; renting, leasing, or owning space; location of the office to accommodate zoning regulations, parking, and the clients' need for privacy; and the pros and cons of sharing space are basic concerns. There are particular issues related to case management that must be dealt with skillfully in private practice, such as missed appointments, cancellations, tardiness, gifts, telephone calls, emergencies, confidentiality, follow-up, and client responsibility.

Another major area of interest to private clinicians is that of legal issues, such as the practitioner's legal liabilities, confidentiality and privileged communication, involvement with the courts, and such special problems as sexual issues between client and clinician and suicide calls.

The private practitioner is tested in a wide variety of situations that call for mature judgment and practical sense. A support system seems essential, and some members of that support system should be one's colleagues and friends who can understand the problems, excitement, frustrations, demands, and challenges of the private practice of social work.

Trends and Future Directions. The term *microtrends* will be used to refer to developments within the private practice of social work, and the term *macrotrends* will refer to developments in private clinical practice that emanate from the social work profession, other professions, and society. One microtrend is an increase in the number of social work clinicians in private practice (part time or full time), stimulated by this period of economic stress and by heightened professional and bureaucratic frustrations.

Surveys conducted to date have generally indicated that up to 10 percent of practicing social workers have devoted time to private work (Gabriel, 1977). Sondra Match, NASW staff associate, estimated in 1975 that from 10,000 to 20,000 social workers were in private practice, including nonmembers of NASW.

Another microtrend is exemplified in the increasing development of group practice with other social workers and other professionals, in preference to the earlier form of solo practice. This trend may be more characteristic of recent graduates.

One innovative development of recent years has been the establishment of private practice offices contiguous to offices of medical doctors, after developing contacts and referral sources among these professionals. In some cases, physicians have invited social workers to join a group practice. Some departments in hospitals with social workers as staff members allow private practice on the premises and provide full billing and secretarial services. Research is needed to determine the variety and strengths of different practice arrangements now in effect across the country.

Although many social workers in private practice will continue to work with young adults, adolescents, and older adults on a one-to-one basis, an increasing number consider themselves primarily as family therapists working with the family as a system. Others are concentrating on practice with groups or a mixed practice.

It has seemed difficult in many locations to develop a full-time private practice, aside from the financial risks involved. It usually takes at least several years to do this, unless one has constant sources of referrals. Sometimes, the difficulty can be the location of the practice or the space arrangements; sometimes, the private practice field is too crowded; sometimes, it is difficult to advertise widely enough; and sometimes, it may serve as a deterrent when the social worker is female or a member of an ethnic or racial minority not in favor with potential client populations (although this difference can work in the social worker's favor, as well). It takes time, satisfied clients who tell their friends and colleagues, and many professional contacts to develop a sound reputation. Building a reputation cannot be rushed. Therefore, many clinicians continue to practice privately part time in combination with agency work. Some may have other sources of income to enable them to survive as full-time practitioners until the practice is firmly established and well developed.

Another microtrend is the increased interest on the part of women and men in female therapists. In the past, the image of the preferred therapist has usually been a male father figure. There is indication that some males, once they become willing to seek help, consider women therapists as potentially easier to work with in heavily emotional matters than men therapists. Eventually, this factor may become insignificant if therapists become more skilled and less sexist in their practice.

Younger private clinicians may discover their age and the related assumptions of limited experience to be a deterrent, and young single clinicians have often experienced some disadvantage with new clients who have marriage or family-relationship problems. Such difficulties can all be surmounted in time by therapists' building a reputation of competence, effectiveness, and the necessary professional skills in communicating warmth, empathy, and genuineness.

Macrotrends include more and better information about this form of social work practice among social workers, other professionals, and the general public, as more social workers become involved in it. Licensing efforts provide a unique opportunity to the profession to educate legislators, their staffs, state government officials, and the general public about what professional social workers do.

In politically and socially unstable times, however, some social workers may, in effect, flee into private practice as a survival effort. They may not be particularly fit or prepared for the special demands, responsibilities, and freedom of this new role. One sad and destructive result of this trend could be an aggravation of the old schism within social work itself. If negative social and political attitudes toward the profession and its lower-income and socially disabled clients continue to grow, clinical private practice could be viewed by some as an inexcusable escape from the tough realities of agency work.

The challenge to the social worker interested in private practice is to remain connected to and involved with the concerns and work of the profession at large. Private practice can include interaction with all economic, social, and professional strata in the society and can become a microcosm of the social work profession's knowledge, values, and skills in interaction with people in the social environment.

References

Borenzweig, H. "Agency vs. Private Practice: Similarities and Differences." *Social Work,* 1981, *26,* 239–244.

Cohen, J. "Nature of Clnical Social Work." In P. Ewalt (Ed.), *Toward a Definition of Clinical Social Work.* Washington, D.C.: National Association of Social Workers, 1979.

Cohen, M. "Some Characteristics of Social Workers in Private Practice." *Social Work,* 1966, *11,* 69–77.

Gabriel, E. "The Private Practice of Social Work." In *Encyclopedia of Social Work.* Washington, D.C.: National Association of Social Workers, 1977.

Golton, M. A. "Analysis of Private Practice in Casework." *Social Work,* 1963, *8,* 72–78.

Koret, L. "The Social Worker in Private Practice." *Social Work,* 1958, *3,* 11–17.

Kurzman, P. A. "Third-Party Reimbursement." *Social Work,* 1973, *18,* 15.

Levenstein, S. *Private Practice in Social Casework: A Profession's Changing Pattern.* New York: Columbia University Press, 1964.

National Association of Social Workers. *Handbook on the Private Practice of Social Work.* (Rev. ed.) Washington, D.C.: National Association of Social Workers, 1974.

National Association of Social Workers. *NASW Register of Clinical Social Workers.* (3rd ed.) Washington, D.C.: National Association of Social Workers, 1982.

Psychotherapy Economics (now *Psychotherapy Finances: The Newsletter for Independent Practitioners*). 1977, *4* (4), 1.

Section VIII

Current and Future Trends in Clinical Social Work

Scott Briar
Section Editor

As these pages are written, massive fiscal and ideological assaults on social service programs throughout the country are casting long shadows of doubt across the future of social work. A few pessimists in the profession are even forecasting that social work will not survive this current retreat from social concerns and human services. Although many social workers do not reject completely this terminal prognosis, few consider it to be more than a remote possibility. Nevertheless, social workers and social work programs may be in a stage of retrenchment for some years to come.

At such a time, one of the most important objectives of the profession should be to emerge at the end of the current crisis with greater professional strength and competence than at the beginning. In its attempts to achieve this objective, the profession will be assisted substantially by trends described in the four chapters in this section. These trends, already under way, promise to enhance significantly the profession's effectiveness and competence to address the wide array of human needs and problems that fall within its mission.

The mainstay of clinical social work has been direct work with individual clients. For many decades, clinical social work practice with individuals was shaped primarily by the psychodynamic orientation to diagnosis and intervention derived from Freudian psychoanalytic thought. Although the influence of this perspective continues to be strong among clinical social workers, in recent years other perspectives also have become prominent. One of these, for example, is the behavioral approach to assessment and intervention. This approach carries the advantage of much greater amenability to research than did the psychodynamic perspective. Despite some allegations that the behavioral approach is dehumanizing and inconsistent with social work values, this perspective continues to spread widely among clinical practitioners in social work. The behavioral approach has merged with others into what now is called an empirical approach to practice, in which practice is shaped and continually modified by the findings of empirical research. In this approach, practitioners are guided more by research results than by any particular theoretical perspective, with the result that treatment approaches previously considered to be incompatible for theoretical reasons may be combined with positive empirical results. Within a general empirical perspective on practice, Sharon Berlin reviews in Chapter Fifty-one some of the changes occurring in social work clinical practice and considers the directions these changes may take in the future.

The emergence of empirical approaches to social work practice was made possible by the development of research methods that permitted clinicians to conduct rigorous research within the constraints of clinical practice. Further advances in empirical models for practice are likely to be stimulated not only by the findings of clinical research but in the improvement of clinical research tools and the wider use of them by practitioners. These possibilities and related matters are examined by Steven Paul Schinke in Chapter Fifty on "Data-Based Practice." It seems clear that implementation of data-based practice models will bring many changes in clinical practice, and it seems almost as clear that these changes are likely to bring about a pattern of practice that is more accountable and probably more effective. What is different now compared to a decade ago is that new data-based approaches to clinical practice are feasible and not merely hypothetical.

Over the past fifteen to twenty years, family treatment has emerged as a major focus of interest and activity in clinical practice. There is every reason to expect that family-oriented treatment will be even more important in clinical practice in the future. Jon R. Conte and Terese M. Halpin, in Chapter Fifty-two on services to families, review current trends in family treatment and examine the future implications of these trends.

Since the earliest beginnings of the profession, social workers have recognized the need to move beyond the treatment of problems after they have appeared and to intervene earlier to prevent the occurrence of the problem. However, for decades the call for social workers to engage in preventive efforts was an appeal that could not be followed because, with few exceptions, little if anything was known empirically about how to prevent the problems addressed by social workers. That state of affairs now is changing, a development that could have profound significance for the future course of social work practice. In Chapter Forty-nine, H. John Staulcup reviews current trends in prevention and considers the prospects for increased preventive intervention by social workers in the future.

The future trends surveyed in the chapters in this section do not, of course, exhaust all the developments now under way that can be expected to shape social work practice in the future. They do, however, identify some of the more important and prominent themes. Taken together, they point to an exciting, vigorous, and increasingly effective array of practice advances that promise to make the social worker an even more valuable professional in the society of the future.

49

Primary Prevention

H. John Staulcup

With the ever-increasing number of individuals, children, and families who need treatment for child abuse, alcoholism, divorce, delinquency, and other problems, why is so much attention being given to prevention? How can we take precious resources and use them for prevention when our treatment services are themselves overtaxed and underfunded? The answers to these questions are complex.

The economic cost of treatment has outstripped available funds. According to the National Center on Child Abuse and Neglect, approximately one million children are abused and neglected annually in the United States (Besharov, 1977). Other unofficial estimates indicate that abuse cases may total two million. Since the average cost to society to treat an abuse case is approximately $7,000, the total estimated cost amounts to $14 billion.

Yet, the Department of Health and Human Services presently spends less than $30 million on child abuse and neglect per year, and only a few of these dollars go toward prevention (Gelles, 1980). In addition, there are an estimated 500,000 delinquent juveniles and one million prisoners. A state spends about $10,000 per year to retain a juvenile and almost $8,000 to incarcerate an adult felon; however, our treatment measures do little to improve their lives and fail to deter recidivism. Furthermore, although alcoholism and alcohol abuse result in a staggering $43 billion loss to business and society, federal and state agencies spend less than $500 million for alcohol treatment services and treat less than 10 percent of all addicted individuals and families (Noble, 1979; Staulcup, 1980a). Without

Note: I would like to thank Dr. Martin Bloom at Virginia Commonwealth University School of Social Work, Ms. Betty Blythe at the University of Washington School of Social Work, and Ms. Valerie L. Hughes, attorney at the law firm of Perkins, Coie, Stone, Olsen and Williams in Seattle, Washington, for their editing and substantive comments on earlier drafts of this chapter. I also thank Joan Hiltner and Anna Bolstad for their typing and word processing expertise.

question, our efforts to ameliorate these social problems are costly and often inadequate.

There are alternatives. There is widespread agreement among the private and public sectors and in academia that prevention is a key to reducing the extent of future social and human problems. According to Secretary of Health and Human Services Richard Schweiker, prevention is the number one priority for promotion of health and curtailment of social problems (Schweiker, 1981). Most agree that existing programs tend to address the results of the problem, not the causal factors. In the long term, prevention is cost effective for public agencies, communities, and individuals because it anticipates and minimizes the need for future services. Because our financial and professional resources are limited, we cannot treat all individuals and families who need treatment. Our overtaxed social services presently cannot absorb the pain and suffering that exists, and they will certainly be inadequate for the need that is predicted in the forthcoming austere decades.

The purpose of this chapter is to explain in some detail the current trends in preventive social work. First, a historical perspective is presented to provide a background for current practices. Next, some emerging conceptual and theoretical frameworks are identified. The practice methods currently in use are then examined, with emphasis on the dominant intervention strategies. The chapter concludes with an overview of research in primary preventive social work. I have attempted to present the unique aspects of preventive work in social welfare and at the same time to integrate history with current trends, education with practice, and practice with research. For the most part, this chapter reflects the work of social work practitioners, academics, and researchers.

Historical Perspective

Prevention is not a new concept to the field of social work, although only recently has it gained stature as a viable intervention strategy. Collins and Pancoast (1976) note that early prevention programs were directed toward children and youth. According to Williams and Money (1980), the historical roots of child protective services are based on the efforts of the Society for Prevention of Cruelty to Animals (SPCA) and the New York Society for Prevention of Cruelty to Children (NYSPCC). In the landmark abuse case of Mary Ellen Wilson in 1874, SPCA President Henry Bergh took the first steps toward child abuse prevention. After hearing his humanitarian plea, the court ruled that children should be protected from cruel and unusual punishment, removed Mary Ellen from the custody of her step-parents, and sentenced her mother to one year's imprisonment at hard labor. Bergh's work led to the development of approximately 150 private organizations to prevent child abuse. The SPCC groups, directed for the most part by lawyers, succeeded in placing many children in alternate care away from abusive families. By 1900, however, many more children were being institutionalized than were being placed in foster homes. One report indicated that six children were placed in foster care, whereas 2,400 were placed in institutions in 1900 (Williams and Money, 1980). Also concerned with preventing child abuse and neglect but opposed to institutionalization, social workers began to work with abusive families. Secondary prevention, aimed at restoring the family and thereby reducing future abuse, was their objective. The developmen of social casework methods and the influence of psychoanalysis in the 1920s and 1930s contributed to the shift from protection through law enforcement to treatment through social work.

Early interest in prevention also was evident at the National Conference on Social Welfare Proceedings in 1915. Along with the well-known paper by Abraham Flexner, "Is Social Work a Profession?", six papers were presented with prevention as their focus and addressed such topics as immigration, mental illness, and eugenics. Although the means they advocated would be viewed as coercive today, sterilization of "insane" and "feebleminded" individuals to prevent mental illness (eugenics movement) was nonetheless prevention.

In 1930, Mary Richmond defined prevention as "one of the end results of a series of processes which include research, individual treatment, public education, legislation, and then . . . administrative adaptations." Richmond clearly portrays the long-term and integrative complexity of preventive work (Kendall, 1962, p. 587). Even at these early stages, her work shows that preventive social work had micro and macro dimensions, focusing both on children and families and their problem conditions and on the larger social and political forces that affect such conditions (Wittman, 1980).

The work of Christian Carl Carstens is perhaps the strongest historical link to contemporary preventive social work. Carstens, a key promoter of social reform of services to children, was the most articulate and prolific advocate of prevention during the first third of the twentieth century. As director of the Massachusetts Society for Prevention of Cruelty to Children (MSPCC) from 1904 to 1920 and founder and director of the Child Welfare League of America from 1920 to 1939, Carstens's work is unparalleled. As noted by Antler and Antler (1980, p. 202), in 1920, "Carstens explained in his last report as general agent of the MSPCC [that] child protective agencies needed to pledge themselves to the 'prevention of cruelty and neglect, and not merely to the prevention of its recurrence.'" Carstens believed that the "social structure of communities, as well as the internal life of families, [had] to be strengthened if abuse and neglect were to be stopped at their source" (Antler and Antler, 1980, p. 202). Carstens's work to prevent child abuse and community neglect, to establish a standardized child welfare program that stressed temporary rather than permanent institutional care, and to strengthen the natural family was unrelenting. If it were not for the strength of the Freudian psychoanalytic movement, Carstens's notion of community prevention programming might be considerably further developed today.

Through the influence of Freud and psychoanalysis, social work as well as other helping professions turned to extended therapy for treatment of social-psychosocial problems. Not surprisingly, interest in social reform and widespread social change, including preventive methods, was neglected while psychoanalysis developed, flourished, and then waned. Attention shifted from a community unit of analysis to the individual. Not until the 1950s and 1960s were new methods of human services explored, such as behavior modification, encounter groups, transactional analysis, communal living, and self-help networks. Through this human services renaissance, social services, and particularly child welfare services, once again began to use preventive methods (Reinherz, 1980).

Current Trends

The contemporary emphasis on prevention in government, schools, and private institutions is an outcome of several forces. First is the change in government's position on welfare and community services. With the passage of the Community Mental Health Act of 1963, government agencies at all levels made the first significant step to provide community-wide services. Symbolically, focus has shifted from a preoccupation with case-by-case services to comprehensive planning for entire geographical areas. This shift from individual to community has been referred to as the third mental health revolution. The first mental health revolution occurred when Pinel removed the chains from the mentally ill in Paris, France, and the second is marked by the impact of Freud and psychoanalysis. The fourth revolution is considered to be the effect of preventive thinking during the past ten to fifteen years (Bloom, 1975).

Several political events have lent support to prevention. Agencies of the federal government have been allocating larger portions of their budgets to preventive services, education, and research. The Social Work Education Branch of NIMH, the National Institute on Drug Abuse, the National Institute on Alcohol Abuse and Alcoholism, and the Office of Special Education, among others, address the prevention of social problems. Still other agencies, such as the Public Health Service, the Office of the Surgeon General, and the Disease Control Center, are searching for ways of preventing disease and epidemics. The past and current chiefs of the Social Work Education Branch have been a driving force behind the preventive movement in social work.

The federal Office of Prevention, created in 1979, has funded several research projects aimed at preventing problems in children of "high-risk" parents (alcoholics, divorcing couples, and severely disturbed individuals). The National Institute on Drug Abuse has developed a newsletter, *Prevention Resources,* as well as a National Prevention Evaluation Research Network. The Network provides up-to-date information on research, training, and programs as well as network development. Perhaps the most important recent development in Congress was passage of the Mental Health Systems Act, signed into law by President Carter in October, 1980. Although appropriations for prevention were decreased, prevention remains one of the Act's top five priorities. It is estimated that funds from the Mental Health Systems Act for prevention will total $6 million in 1981, $7 million in 1982, and $8 million in 1983 (Mental Health Systems Act, 1980).

Numerous private prevention organizations and associations have emerged and are actively lobbying, raising funds, and developing large citizen and professional memberships. For example, the National Association of Prevention Professionals and the National Committee for Prevention of Child Abuse have made significant strides to promote and deliver prevention services to children and families. In some areas, social work is at the forefront of knowledge and practice development. The following sections explore such development in theory, practice, and research.

Models for Human Service Delivery

A number of methods have evolved for delivering services to individuals and groups with physical, emotional, or social problems. Traditionally, these methods are subsumed under two distinct models of service delivery, the medical or direct-treatment model and the prevention or active-outreach model (Kessler and Albee, 1975). Since the early days of incarceration of the mentally ill, the treatment model has predominated in mental health and health settings. The past few decades have seen a resurgence of the treatment model with the advent of psychotropic drugs, electroshock therapy, and new forms of psychotherapy. The essence of this model is to classify individuals' symptoms into discrete diagnostic categories, which, in turn, prescribe treatment techniques to mitigate the symptoms. Little attention is given to altering interpersonal or environmental factors. Indeed, when the symptoms are gone, the individual usually returns to the same interpersonal and environmental situation in which the illness began. To paraphrase Kessler and Albee (1975), the treatment model acts as a passive or receptive system with a restorative focus. Unlike the prevention model, little effort is expended to seek out individuals in the preclinical stage or even to follow up on individuals who have recovered from their symptoms. In the past decade, increased attention has turned to the prevention model. The theoretical underpinnings of the prevention model embrace an ecological ideal in which planned efforts are aimed at comprehensive change—to alter the course of negative occurrences and to evoke desirable events. From this perspective, the more traditional case-by-case treatment approach is considered ineffective, narrow in scope, and cosmetic in result.

A cogent depiction of the prevention model is given by Porter (1980). In his conceptual analysis, preventive social work consists of the following elements derived from a range of social and scientific technologies: (1) the methodology of epidemiology, which addresses the incidence and duration of illness; (2) human ecology, which examines the interaction between the person and his social and physical environment, especially the adaptive behavior of individuals or groups; (3) social systems theory, which provides a conceptual framework for integrating knowledge about persons, families, and their environments for the purposes of structuring and conducting prevention programs; and (4) the social psychologies, with their emphasis on the interpersonal process, "positive aspects of growth, institutional supports to enhance optimal socialization, the avoidance of labeling, and the social integration of marginal groups" (p. 13). Porter also acknowledges the contribution of the concept of stress, the social engineering aspects of behavioral methods, and the importance of the developmental processes. Taken together, these methods and sciences form the basis of the developing model of prevention related to social services.

Operational Frameworks. Within the preventive model, two operational frameworks have emerged—the control framework and the socialization framework. Focusing on the management of human behavior or of communities, the control framework places little emphasis on individuals' attitudes, knowledge, or beliefs or on major socialization forces (family, peer group, school, community, or work group) (Lauderdale, 1978). Some consensus polling may be taken, but usually a community board, authority, or elected representative advocates legal or policy change in the "best interest of the community." An external change is illustrated by the recent case of *Coulter* v. *Superior Court of San Mateo County.* The California Supreme Court held, under both common law and the California Business and Professional Code, that a social host who furnishes intoxicating liquor to a visibly intoxicated guest may be liable for harm to third parties when the risk of injury to others is reasonably foreseeable (Hughes-Staulcup, 1979). This example depicts the far-reaching nature of external change processes and yet represents only one avenue in which such change is occurring.

The socialization framework assumes that people are capable of preventing problems on an individual basis and suggests that the key factors involve learning and helping processes, such as education, training, consultation, self-help, and networking. Prevention programs that adopt socialization change methods address the knowledge, attitudes, and values of individuals and communities. Individuals are viewed as able to exercise their own choices in a responsible manner; hence, any preventive intervention requires their active participation.

At times, control and socialization methods of change overlap. A comprehensive plan for primary and secondary prevention of child abuse, for example, might include classes in schools and other community settings addressing sexuality, parenthood, and pregnancy; birthing rooms and hospital procedures that are more conducive to attachment and bonding; and community crisis nurseries and childcare centers (Coolsen, 1980). Each of these programs involves both control and socialization change methods—control methods to obtain authorization and financial resources and socialization methods to deliver the research and service programs.

Stages of Intervention. Interventions can be implemented at any stage of a problem or potential problem. These stages are commonly referred to as primary, secondary, and tertiary prevention, which are essentially prevention, treatment, and rehabilitation, respectively. Primary prevention refers to activities that reduce the incidence of new cases of an identified problem within a population or that promote new coping competencies to fend off anticipated life crises or other stressful events. Activities that promote mental health or skill acquisition, such as anticipatory guidance programs (for example, parenting instruction for parents-to-be, perinatal counseling, premarital training, predivorce counseling, and preretirement training), are also considered primary prevention, especially if they are associated with an impending concern. Hence, primary prevention of emotional and physical stress aims to obviate negative processes or to promote desirable events. Secondary prevention is early identification and prompt treatment of a problem, whereas tertiary prevention refers to a rebuilding process that occurs once the problem behavior or condition has run its course (Hollister, 1980). Primary prevention reduces the prevalence of a problem by diminishing the number of new cases. Secondary and tertiary prevention reduce prevalence by decreasing the duration of a condition (Bloom, 1975).

Despite this three-stage division, the terms *primary, secondary,* and *tertiary* often confuse practitioners and provide a literary guise for treatment efforts, such that the term *prevention* becomes a referent for both prevention and treatment. Inasmuch as prevention and treatment are interdependent counterparts to human services delivery, they are not to be equated. Prevention efforts are "before the fact" efforts with the emphasis on before. They may be "shortly" before or "long" before an undesirable state occurs, but, in all cases, they are before and not during or shortly after a problem arises (Bloom, 1980).

The preventer is an orchestrator of preventive activities and serves as an active consultant to assist others to plan, implement, and evaluate programs.

Bloom (1978) conceptualizes preventive action as a process with the following sequence:

1. One must first develop an orientation toward the undesirable conditions or the desired state of affairs. The orientation provides a direction for action and reflects the individual's or group's attitude or purpose for engaging in a preventive action. An orientation may be derived from a personal belief or from organizational bylaws. For example, the National Committee for Prevention of Child Abuse and its members subscribe to primary and secondary prevention directed toward children and families as their orientation guidepost.
2. Once an orientation is developed, the next step is to specifically identify the goal for action. For example, there is increasing concern about teenage parenthood and consequent child abuse and neglect. The Racine, Wisconsin, area has a particularly high incidence of teenage parents. Thus, a problem statement might be succinctly stated as follows: There is a high incidence of teenage births in Racine, Wisconsin: 26 percent of all births compared to 15 percent nationwide. These young mothers and fathers have many special concerns—continued education, vocational development, marriage, self-identity, an understanding of child growth and development, and child care. As a group, teenage parents are "at risk" for child abuse and neglect as well as for stunted social, vocational, and educational development. (Contingent on steps three through five, the last sentence would include a specific statement of the action to be taken, for example, to develop a home-health visitor program.)
3. Next, a list of program alternatives is generated. The purpose of the project might be to address the special needs of teenage mothers through mother-father-infant bonding, education for parenthood, a home-health visitor program, or a drop-off center for mothers in school or at work.
4. Decision making is the next step—to choose the best action using the available knowledge base, funding, and, perhaps most important, personnel resources. More than one program may be initiated, depending on resource availability.
5. Implementation and evaluation of the programs should occur simultaneously. The evaluation plan should be developed in advance, so that it can be set in motion when the program begins.
6. Terminate or continue the program. Simply stated, if the program is successful or potentially successful through modification, then attempts should be made to continue its funding. If unsuccessful, the program should be ended and a new strategy developed.

This outline provides a structure from which the preventer may organize, implement, and evaluate a specific preventive activity.

A Conceptual Framework for Preventive Social Work

The following analysis is a developing conception of primary prevention in social welfare. It attempts to integrate the processes of prevention with the psychological, social, and physical aspects of life.

Primary prevention is an intervention strategy that has acquired many connotations in recent years. From the various definitions and conceptualizations that have been discussed in the literature, two processes may be abstracted. The first process involves promoting a desired state of affairs, such as improving the quality of life or life opportunities of individual members of a community. Here, emphasis is placed on promoting positive, healthy, or desired events. The second process involves obviating predicted untoward future events (Bloom, 1980; Hollister, 1980; Kessler and Albee, 1975). Examples of efforts to eliminate undesirable future events from the person, the collective, or the environment are disease immunization, fluoridation of community water supplies, and air pollution control, respectively. The first three boxes at the top of Figure 1 refer to the generic goals of primary prevention. These goals represent the three types of objectives that a primary prevention effort may have. Research and practice in primary prevention of individual, social, or environmental conditions have focused on either one or both of these processes.

The next item in Figure 1 is the psychological–social–physical system in which preventive actions may be directed. The dotted lines separating these three spheres indicate their interrelatedness, and a preventive action aimed at one sphere may have an overlapping effect on other spheres. Table 1 lists various preventive actions that may be aimed at the spheres within the system. Note that some of the actions could be operating in more than one sphere.

The last box in Figure 1 refers to the outcomes that occur within the system as a result of a preventive action. As indicated, outcomes can be expected or unexpected. A preventive action may be intended to obviate an undesirable event, and yet, at the same time, it may unexpectedly obviate a desired event. Or, a preventive action may be intended to promote a desired event with an unexpected additional consequence of promoting an undesired event.

Complementarity. Complementarity refers to the balance between obviated and promoted events. Perhaps the best illustration of complementarity is found in in the learning theory concepts of extinction and positive reinforcement. Learning theorists refer to methods of decelerating (extinguishing) undesirable behaviors while at the same time accelerating (positively reinforcing) desirable behaviors to take the place of the ones decelerated. Research has shown that simply eliminating undesirable behavior does not ensure that the void created in a person's behavioral repertoire will necessarily be filled with a desirable behavior; rather, it may well be filled by another undesirable behavior (Bandura, 1969, pp. 48–52). To counter this, learning theorists posit that engaging in both decelerating and accelerating processes is necessary when altering a system, be it an individual, family, community, or society. This same balancing approach is also applicable to the concepts of preventive obviation and promotion.

In preventive intervention, there seem to be three separate and distinct types of complementarity. In the first, when one obviates a predicted untoward future event, a void is created in the system that must be filled with a desired event, or the void may be filled by another competing undesirable event. And, even though one has filled the void created by the obviating process, other unexpected consequences, both desirable and undesirable, may also occur. In the second type of preventive action, promotion of a desired event, no void is created in the system, but rather an addition is made to it. This type of preventive action, however, is also

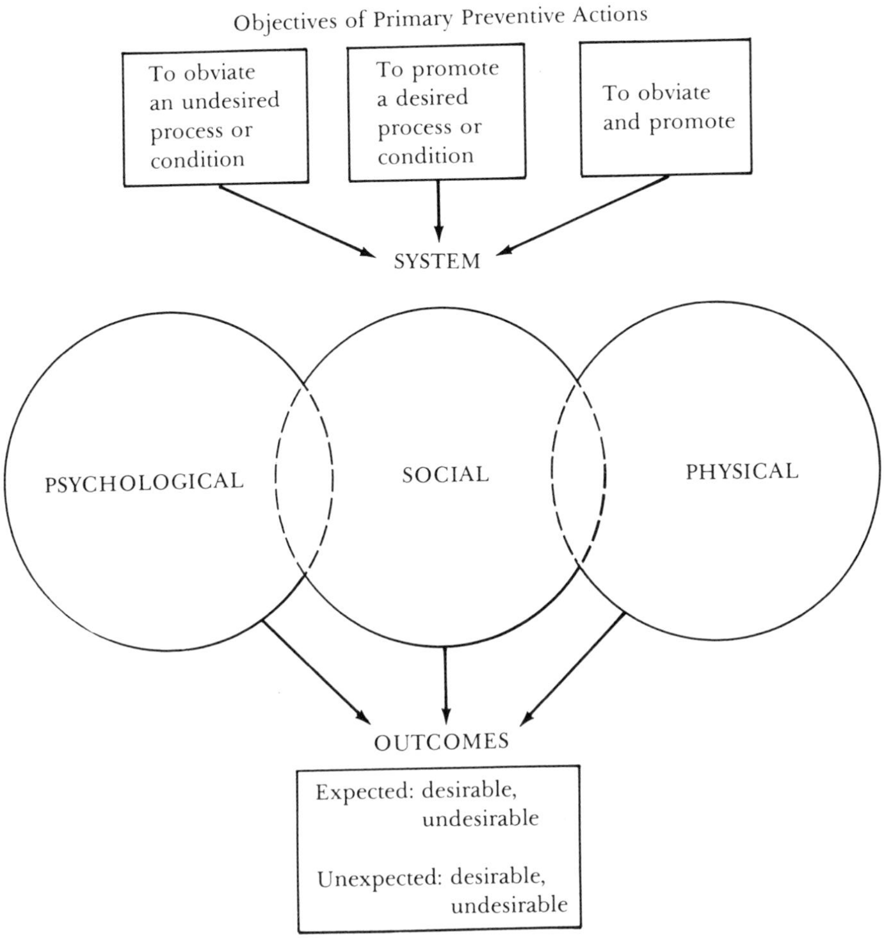

Figure 1. A Conceptual Model for the Process of Primary Preventive Social Work

susceptible to the same unexpected consequences as the first. The third type of preventive action occurs when one obviates an undesirable future event and promotes a desired event to take its place. This outcome represents true complementarity. By filling the void created by the obviation of one event with a designated desirable event, one may reduce the frequency of unexpected undesirable consequences. Three examples of preventive complementarity follow.

Example 1. A social example that illustrates these concepts was the national prohibition of the use of alcohol. In this case, the goal was to eliminate alcohol use from the American culture so as to obviate the problems associated with it, such as alcoholism, alcoholic psychosis, and deaths due to alcohol-related cirrhosis. This goal was partially achieved, in that national consumption of alcohol was reduced by 50 percent (Keller and Gurioli, 1976). The complementarity involved here is that, while national consumption of alcohol was reduced (obviated), such undesirable events as a black market and graft increased. Although the ratifiers of the Eighteenth Amendment must have anticipated some of these undesirable events, they probably did not expect as many as occurred.

Table 1. Some Possible Preventive Actions

Psychological	*Social*	*Physical*
Disease immunization	Community planning	Chlorination
Alcohol education	Social policy	Flouridation
Lead poisoning	Legislation	Air pollution control

Example 2. The Orangeburg Area Project, a federally funded primary alcoholism prevention program, sought both to promote desired events and to obviate predicted untoward events. The specific goals of this project, which was directed toward children of alcoholics, were (1) to improve students' grade-point averages; (2) to improve students' problem-solving and coping skills; and (3) to increase students' knowledge of and foster unfavorable attitudes toward alcohol abuse. This project intended to promote positive events (improved grade-point averages, problem-solving and coping skills) and to induce unfavorable attitudes on the assumption that they would decrease a child's chances of becoming an alcoholic. Here, the complementarity involved obviating future abusive drinking by the children (pending the intermediate step of inducing unfavorable attitudes) and promoting individual skills and achievement. The program was directed specifically toward the individual children (that is, the psychosphere).

The Orangeburg project measured pre–post change in the variables named above. There were no statistically significant differences in these attributes before and after the prevention project, except with regard to knowledge of and attitudes toward alcohol. These differences, however, were significant in the opposite direction expected; that is, knowledge level decreased, and attitudes became more favorable toward alcohol. The evaluator of the project explained these results as follows: "By exposing the experimental children to values different from those being taught by their parents, they may have become confused, thereby performing less well on the posttest measures than did the controls" (Vincent, 1978, p. 14). This situation is a prime example of the unanticipated development of an undesirable consequence in a primary prevention project. The project provided alcohol education to better equip the children to deal with their potential risk for alcoholism, but it in fact may have done more harm than good by creating problems in the family value structure.

Example 3. The third example involves the previously mentioned case of *Coulter* v. *Superior Court of San Mateo County*. In this case, an automobile passenger brought a suit for damages against the host of a party who had furnished intoxicating liquors to the driver of the car in which the passenger was riding. The passenger claimed that the driver's intoxication resulted in the car's collision with a roadway abutment and his subsequent injuries. Furthermore, the passenger alleged that the host knew or should have known that his guest was becoming excessively intoxicated and intended to operate a motor vehicle following her consumption of the liquor. The California Supreme Court held that, under both common law and the California Business and Professional Code, a social host who furnished intoxicating liquor to a visibly intoxicated guest may be liable for harm to third parties when the risk of injury to others was reasonably foreseeable (Hughes-Staulcup, 1979).

The goals of the court decision, as interpreted from the justices' opinions, are (1) to hold social hosts legally responsible for increasing obvious intoxication of a guest under conditions involving a reasonable foreseeable risk of harm to others; (2) more specifically, to obviate the potential danger and risk to persons driving automobiles on the highway; and (3) to allow third parties to sue social hosts for damages resulting from a guest's drinking behavior.

The entire psychological–social–physical system is represented in this case. The decision affects individual drivers, social parties or activities where hosts serve alcoholic beverages, and the physical environment (state highways, roads, and thoroughfares). Due to the recent date of this case, the complementarity can only be hypothesized. It seems that the case may produce some unanticipated consequences. By holding the social host responsible for determining and monitoring the level of intoxication of his guests, the court removes the individual's legal responsibility for his own drinking behavior. Thus, while the decision may serve to improve a third party's ability to collect for damages, it very well may do nothing to reduce alcohol-related traffic accidents.

Preventive Consultation. Preventive consultation and education traditionally have been the essence of prevention efforts in community and school settings—if not in fact, at least in theory. Focusing on public education and addressing such topics as alcohol use, nutrition, immunization, and smoking, public education efforts generally have emanated from community mental health centers. Private preventive consultation has usually been provided to one professional by another following a request. In the past few years, consultants in both the private and public sectors have begun to focus increasingly on prevention because of the increasing need for information on content, programming, and administration.

Caplan (1970) identifies four types of consultation. They are client-centered case consultation, consultee-centered case consultation, program-centered consultation, and administrative-centered consultation. Consultation in the area of prevention programming usually focuses on the last three of Caplan's categories as well as on advocacy consultation, as discussed by Kadushin (1977). Client-centered case consultation involves a direct person-to-person communication with a specific client. Consultee-centered case consultation differs, in that a preventer might train another professional or volunteer, rather than the client, to conduct a specific preventive act, such as a home-health screening session for new mothers and their infants. The primary purpose of consultee-centered case consultation is to transfer the knowledge needed by the consultee to plan the implementation of such a program.

Program-centered consultation, using the same example, might involve working with a hospital pediatric staff to design home-health screening programs and would focus on content, population, and expected program results. Administrative-centered consultation involves information on the day-to-day conduct and logistics of a program (such as screening, training volunteers, and budgeting). Advocacy consultation is generally considered to be outside the boundaries of traditional consultation, in that it involves advocacy of a client's interest through legislation, policy, or lobbying.

Usually consultation is passive in nature. The consultant is generally an objective observer (an outsider) whose function is to identify various options from which the consultee will choose. Advocacy consultation, however, is more directive, in that the consultant promotes a specific program or idea, such as lobbying for legislation. The advocate consultant contracts to work with a particular group for a specific purpose. Illustrative of advocacy consultation is the work of the Kansas Chapter of the National Committee for Prevention of Child Abuse. This volunteer–professional group enlisted the assistance of several consultants to draft legislation to increase the marriage license fee from $3 to $7 to build a funding source for prevention programming for child abuse and family violence. The Kansas legislature enacted the Children and Family Trust Fund on July 1, 1980. It is estimated that this advocacy measure will create a funding base of about $130,000 each year for community prevention efforts (Gelles, 1981).

Anticipatory Guidance Programs. Anticipatory guidance programs are best summed up in the well-known phrase "an ounce of prevention is worth a pound of cure." One can predict that there are milestones at which individuals will encounter difficulties and that these difficulties can be eased or completely avoided with preparation. Examples of anticipatory guidance abound. Among them are preretirement training, premarital training, and predivorce training. One program that is representative of an anticipatory guidance program is a parental training program for expectant teenage parents. A preventer can educate these young parents about the growth and development of their newborn child, help them to continue their own educational and vocational planning to ensure financial support, and secure appropriate childcare support programs that will permit the young parents to pursue their own development. Each of these program elements anticipates specific problems. The beauty of anticipatory programs is the ease with which specific life events can be identified in advance. Interventions can be clearly focused, measured, and evaluated.

Training Efforts. Training can be a tool for disseminating knowledge about prevention. It may take many forms, but ordinarily it is a process of learning special skills, knowledge, behaviors, or attitudes for the conduct of a specific objective (Pittman, 1978).

An ecological model for professional training in preventive methods is presented by Clement-McCulloch (1980). The target groups for ecological training are community mental health prevention workers and supervisors, and the focus of this prevention training program is to "facilitate effective program implementation and evaluation" on the community level (p. 38). The ecological training covers four content areas: (1) understanding patterns of human behavior, (2) community diagnosis and community development, (3) group process and organizational development, and (4) program development and evaluation. Clement-McCulloch's training effort has resulted in over fifty prevention programs. The trained vounteers have reported "positive change" as a result of participating in the training, and ecological training is now being conducted throughout the country.

Another prevention training program recently was developed at the University of Washington School of Social Work. Focusing on several social and health problems among youth, Gilchrist, Schinke, and Blythe (1980) provide a clear example of training in behavioral and cognitive areas. The rationale behind their work is that traditional information and scare-tactic approaches have failed because they do not "transform knowledge or abstract information into personal decisions and personal decisions into overt behavior" (p. 381). Their training programs have demonstrated the process of transforming cognitive material into specific behavior among adolescents in the areas of smoking and sexual behavior.

Training of volunteers is a growing trend. As more and more social services fall victim to inflation and budgetary cutbacks, and as social welfare becomes overshadowed by defense spending, volunteers become extremely important to the provision of necessary services. Although professionals like to view themselves as the providers of most human services, there is no question that the bulk of human services are provided by volunteers. Imagine a town without the Jaycees, Junior League, Lions Club, Moose Club, Young Men's Christian Association, Young Women's Christian Association, Parents Anonymous, Alcoholics Anonymous, and United Way. These groups rely on volunteers and financial support from private citizens, and the community, in turn, is dependent on their services. These groups support prevention activities, and training for prevention is beginning to affect these private groups.

One example of the magnitude of education and training in the private sector is the work of the National Committee for Prevention of Child Abuse (NCPCA). NCPCA conducts a national public awareness and education program that includes a media campaign, publications, audio-visual training materials for professional and volunteer groups, and training conferences and workshops at the national, regional, and state levels. Each year, NCPCA hosts a National Leadership Conference with ten to fifteen training workshops on administration, child and parent programs, motivation of volunteers, board development, fundraising, and legislative advocacy. Each workshop is presented in a training format, and workshop participants are assisted in following through with their newly learned skills.

Education in Preventive Social Work. In the traditional social work curricula, education about prevention, if it exists at all, is ordinarily a component of either community mental health courses (consultation and education) or community organization courses (community development, networking, self-help groups, and collective or consumer-oriented programs). Only within the past five years have schools of social work begun to include courses that treat preventive social work as an autonomous subject—at Adelphi University, University of Minnesota at Minneapolis, Portland State University, San Francisco State University, University of Tennessee at Memphis, University of West Virginia, George Williams College, Washington University, Hunter College, and University of North Carolina. Some schools are also beginning to include preventive content in core courses (policy, human behavior and social environment).

A recent indication of interest in prevention curricula is marked by the Council on Social Work Education's Primary Prevention Project. The Council received a three-year grant to survey social work curricula for preventive content, to hold conferences to identify and develop materials, and to disseminate to social work schools all relevant materials in a sourcebook. Now in its second year, the CSWE Prevention Project has held one conference, identified several curricular aids, and conducted a pretest and posttest survey to assess the impact of prevention education among twelve different graduate schools. (The findings of this study are available by writing Milton Nobel, D.S.W., Council on Social Work Education, 111 Eighth Avenue, New York, NY 10011.)

The longest training effort in preventive social work education is that at the George Warren Brown School of Social Work, Washington University. In the fall of 1977, the Social Work Education Branch of NIMH awarded the Brown School of Social Work in St. Louis a five-year grant to train master's students in preventive service and research in social work. Now beginning its fifth year, the Prevention Speciality Program has developed and implemented a model curriculum in which primary prevention content is integrated into the total social work curriculum, along with courses on direct practice (secondary prevention) and rehabilitation (tertiary prevention). All students at the school are instructed in prevention, and the preventive orientation is taught in core courses, schoolwide lectures, symposia, and special presentations in such courses as community development, family therapy, gerontology, and social policy. Trainees in Primary Prevention (TIPP), and other students who volunteer, receive further specialized training in preventive theory, research, and practice methods. A field practicum experience consisting of ten semester credit hours is constructed to enable each training fellow to develop knowledge and skills in the entire range of preventive approaches. Working individually and in teams over a two-year period, the training fellows may experience the longitudinal nature of preventive service and evaluation as well as the developmental stages inherent in the work (Staulcup, 1980b).

Research in Preventive Social Work. To gain full acceptance, primary prevention programs need to establish that they either reduce the incidence of social problems or promote positive growth and development. Without such documentation, we cannot expect that prevention programs will be taken seriously. This section will discuss selected research studies that address some of the topics raised throughout this chapter.

A recent study of the professional staff at three community mental health centers investigated the role of social work in primary prevention. Social workers were found to do more primary prevention than other professionals and were more experienced in prevention methods. Interestingly enough, however, social workers do not conceptualize these activities as preventive, nor do they embrace a preventive ideology (Matus and Nuehring, 1979).

In a survey of 141 social workers at 33 Chicago area mental health agencies, Walsh (1978) investigated the organizational and educational factors associated with the use of primary prevention by social workers. Prevention programs were associated with education, ideology, and federal funding in the agency's budget. Younger M.S.W. respondents (those under age 40) were more likely to be conducting prevention programs.

These two studies indicate that social workers are taking a leading role in primary prevention programming, and yet, they have not adopted a theoretical framework that distinguishes prevention as a special part of social work. Alternatively, social workers, especially younger professionals, do not perceive prevention as something outside social work and therefore attach no more special significance to it than to other social work methods. These findings suggest that prevention has entered the mainstream of social work.

Perhaps the most extensive research on prevention networks is that presented by Collins and Pancoast (1976). In their book *Natural Helping Networks: A Strategy for Prevention,* the authors describe a demonstration project designed to develop an information and referral exchange for family daycare providers and users. Their goal was to develop and test ways that social workers could support and broaden the scope of these networks. Collins and Pancoast (p. 19) believe that "using the concept of network as an analytical tool focuses attention on real relationships between real people in a way that suggests both useful information and appropriate intervention for social workers."

A professional worker can gain an understanding of the density, range, and pathways of a network by identifying a central figure in the network, sometimes referred to as the indigenous natural leader. In Collins and Pancoast's study of daycare, the stereotyped natural leader was the home-centered woman who played a central role of support and assistance for other families in the neighborhood. The researchers ranked 27 women who were family daycare providers in terms of performance and personality. The highest-ranked individuals were less mobile, had intact families, had children of school age or younger, and had a mature interest in other people. During this initial survey, the researchers were asked for assistance in finding daycare for individuals and discovered that a flourishing hidden network existed. Natural leaders in the network acted voluntarily as advisers and matchmakers for those needing services.

It is obvious from Collins and Pancoast's work that very strong neighborhood networks exist in our country, that these networks are, for the most part, untapped, and that through organized networking efforts an immense amount of primary prevention services may be harnessed. Already, many networks have emerged, including Parents Anonymous, Parents Without Partners, The National Committee for Prevention of Child Abuse, The National Association of Prevention Professionals, and many other local and state groups. These groups are providing training, service, research, and public awareness activities. Networking can become a means for joining volunteer and professional efforts.

Public awareness of health and social problems is increasing steadily. Radio and television announcements addressing problems of heart disease, smoking, alcohol use, or child abuse and carrying a preventive message are quite frequent. The research of Maccoby and Alexander (1979) suggests that these announcements are an important medium for further prevention efforts. In a study that assessed the effectiveness of three separate media approaches (no treatment, treatment by media only, and treatment by media plus intensive interpersonal instruction) in three "roughly comparable" communities, Maccoby and Alexander examined the effectiveness of the media to prevent heart disease by reducing smoking, high serum cholesterol intake, and hypertension among persons aged thirty-five to fifty-nine. The researchers evaluated the success of the interventions through survey data and medical examinations designed to measure knowledge, attitudes, and behavior related to cardiovascular risk. According to the researchers (p. 79), "The main finding is that both the media treatment and media plus face-to-face instruction treatment . . . show evidence of positive risk-reduction effects after two years, as compared to the reference group. At the end of the second year, the level of estimated coronary disease risk decreased by 17 to 18 percent in the treatment community samples, but it increased by more than 6 percent in the no treatment community."

The media hold great promise for future prevention programs. The task before us is to build relations with local media and to design programs in awareness, education, and referral.

Gradually, more methods for evaluating prevention programs are being developed. Two methods that were developed by social workers specifically for prevention are discussed here. First, a short handbook for evaluation entitled *A Handbook for the Practitioner in Primary Prevention: How to Do Program Evaluation* has been written by McCann (1980). This booklet is short on research detail, and yet it provides the essential ingredients of evaluation as well as references to a number of more sophisticated evaluation materials. Research steps covered in this booklet include identification of an "at risk" population and a target population, stating measurable objectives, measuring change, selecting an evaluation design, maximizing validity, collecting and analyzing data, and writing an evaluation report.

A second, more detailed, handbook designed specifically for child abuse prevention programs has been prepared by Gray and DiLeonardi (in press). This handbook discusses various evaluation designs, barriers to evaluation in child abuse prevention, issues of validity and reliability, and a variety of specific program examples. It also includes a section on writing an evaluation report.

Conclusion

Compared to treatment, prevention activities are much more difficult to initiate, maintain, and evaluate. They often involve broadbased political, social, and economic change. Hence, one can readily imagine the many barriers to prevention practice. Nuehring (1978) identifies several types of barriers—lack of resources, limited knowledge or methods, lack of mandate (although this is beginning to change), community resistance, and organizational or structural problems (no place for prevention). Nuehring contends that all these issues are the result of the irrationality or ambiguity of prevention methods. Once the methods are improved to acceptable scientific standards and prevention becomes more than ideological dogma, these barriers will disappear. Without specific objectives, methods, and results, preventive work will continue to waiver. It is encouraging that more and more research and interest is centering on prevention in social work.

References

Antler, J., and Antler S. "From Child Rescue to Family Protection: The Evolution of the Child Protection Movement in the United States." *Children and Youth Services Review,* 1979, *1* (2), 177–204.

Bandura, A. *Principles of Behavior Modification.* New York: Holt, Rinehart and Winston, 1969.

Besharov, D. J. "U.S. National Center on Child Abuse and Neglect: Three Years of Experience." *Child Abuse and Neglect: The International Journal,* 1977, *1,* 173–177.

Bloom, B. L. *Community Mental Health: A General Introduction.* Monterey, Calif.: Brooks/Cole, 1975.

Bloom, M. Notes from a course titled "Prevention: Theory, Research, and Practice." St. Louis: The George Warren Brown School of Social Work, Washington University, 1978. (Mimeographed.)

Bloom, M. "A Working Definition of Primary Prevention Related to Social Concerns." *The Journal of Prevention,* 1980, *1* (1), 15–23.

Caplan, *Theory and Practice of Mental Health Consultation.* Scranton, Pa.: Basic Books, 1970.

Clement-McCulloch, P. "The Ecological Model: A Framework for Operationalizing Prevention." *The Journal of Prevention,* 1980, *1* (1), 35–43.

Collins, A. H., and Pancoast, D. L. *Natural Helping Networks: A Strategy for Prevention.* Washington, D.C.: National Association of Social Workers, 1976.

Coolsen, P. "Community Involvement in the Prevention of Child Abuse and Neglect." *Children Today,* 1980, *9* (5), 5–8.

Gelles, R. Keynote Address, Annual Meeting of Kansas Chapter, National Committee for Prevention of Child Abuse, September 21, 1981.

Gilchrist, L. D., Schinke, S. P., and Blythe, B. J. "Primary Prevention Services for Children and Youth." *Children and Youth Services Review,* 1980, *1* (4), 379–391.

Gray, E., and DiLeonardi, J. *Evaluating Primary Prevention of Child Abuse Programs: A Handbook.* Chicago: The National Committee for Prevention of Child Abuse, in press.

Hollister, W. G. "The Relationship Between Mental Health Prevention and Mental Health Promotion." *The Journal of Prevention,* 1980, *1* (1), 49–51.

Hughes-Staulcup, V. "Recent Developments: Torts–Common Law Liability—Social Host May Be Liable to Third Parties." *Washington University Law Quarterly,* 1979, *1,* 293–297.

Kadushin, A. *Consultation in Social Work.* New York: Columbia University Press, 1977.

Keller, M., and Gurioli, C. "Statistics on Consumption of Alcohol and on Alcoholism." *Journal of Studies on Alcohol,* 1976.

Kendall, K. A. "Discussion." *The Social Forum.* New York: Columbia University Press, 1969.

Kessler, M., and Albee, G. W. "Primary Prevention." *Annual Review of Psychology,* 1975, *26,* 557–591.

Klein, D. C., and Goldston, S. E. (Eds.). *Primary Prevention: An Idea Whose Time Has Come.* (DHEW Publication No. (ADM) 77-447.) Washington, D.C.: U.S. Government Printing Office, 1977.

Lauderdale, M. L. "An Analysis of the Control Theory of Alcoholism." In *Education Commission of the States Task Force on Responsible Decisions About Alcohol: A Technical Document.* Denver: Education Commission of the States, 1978.

McCann, M. *A Handbook for the Practitioner in Primary Prevention: How to Do Program Evaluation,* 1980. 6188 McPherson, St. Louis, Mo. 63112.

Maccoby, N., and Alexander, J. "Reducing Heart Disease Risk Using the Mass Media: Comparing the Effects on Three Communities." In R. F. Muñoz, L. R. Snowden, and J. G. Kelly (Eds.), *Social and Psychological Research in Community Settings.* San Francisco: Jossey-Bass, 1979.

Matus, R., and Nuehring, E. M. "Social Workers in Primary Prevention: Action and Ideology in Mental Health." *Community Mental Health Journal,* 1979, *15* (1), 33–40.

Mental Health Systems Act, 1980. Public Law 96-398, Title 9, 1980, added to by Public Law 97-35.

National Committee for Prevention of Child Abuse. *Prevent Child Abuse.* Chicago: National Committee for Prevention of Child Abuse, 1976. (Mimeographed.)

Noble, E. P. (Ed.). *Alcohol and Health.* (DHEW Publication No. (ADM) 79-832.) Washington, D.C.: U.S. Government Printing Office, 1979.

Nuehring, E. M. "The Technological Character of Barriers to Primary Preventive Activity in Mental Health: A Framework for Analysis." *Administration in Social Work,* 1978, *2* (4), 451–468.

Pittman, D. Notes from a course titled "Seminar in Alcoholism Prevention." 1978. (Mimeographed.)

Porter, R. A. "Conceptual Parameters of Primary Prevention." Paper presented at the CSWE Conference on Primary Prevention in Social Work Education, Louisville, October 22, 1980.

Reinherz, H. "Primary Prevention of Emotional Disorders of Children: Mirage or Reality." *The Journal of Prevention,* 1980, *1* (1), 4–14.

Schinke, S. P., and Gilchrist, L. D. "Adolescent Pregnancy: An Interpersonal Skill Training Approach to Prevention." *Social Work in Health Care,* 1977, *3* (2), 159–167.

Schweiker, R. "News Note." *ADAMA NEWS,* 1981, *7* (14), 1.

Staulcup, H. J. "Knowledge and Attitudes as Determinants of Alcohol Use in Youth: Testing the Alcohol Education Assumption." Unpublished doctoral dissertation, 1980a.

Staulcup, H. J. (Ed.). *Primary Prevention in Social Work: Concepts and Training.* St. Louis: The George Warren Brown School of Social Work, Washington University, 1980b.

Vincent, E. S. *The Development of Services for Children of Problem-Drinker Parents: An Evaluation of the Orangeburg Elementary Children's Program.* Orangeburg, S.C.: Orangeburg Area Committee for Economic Progress, 1978.

Walsh, J. A., Jr. "Organizational and Educational Factors Associated with the Use of Primary Prevention by Social Workers in Primary Prevention by Social Workers in Community Mental Health Practice." Unpublished doctoral dissertation, Department of Social Work, University of Michigan, 1978.

Williams, G. J., and Money, J. *Traumatic Abuse and Neglect of Children at Home.* Baltimore: Johns Hopkins University Press, 1980.

Wittman, M. "The Challenge of Primary Prevention to Social Work: Past, Present, and Future Directions." In H. J. Staulcup (Ed.), *Primary Prevention in Social Work: Concepts and Training.* St. Louis: The George Warren Brown School of Social Work, Washington University, 1980.

50

Data-Based Practice

Steven Paul Schinke

The social work profession's mandate for responsive services to various populations in various settings calls for an approach that is empirically grounded. To be effective, social workers must be guided by prior experiences. Social change efforts can be more successful when they are guided by quantifiable feedback about previous successes and failures. Scarce funds and resources demand cost-effective professional activities, which can best be determined by collecting, interpreting, and disseminating data that accurately portray practice activities.

This chapter summarizes the status of data-based clinical social work. The first section defines the term *data* and indicates how data may serve as a basis for client services. A discussion of the historical background of empirical social work is followed by a case illustration. Data-based practice is then illustrated by a summary of the past two decades of published clinical social work. A discussion of the implications of future clinical practice concludes the chapter.

Data as a Base for Practice

In the context of direct service social work, data is information about professional practice with clients. Information can be qualitative or quantitative.

Note: I warmly thank Edith Watson, Thomas Edward Smith, Joan Hiltner, and Anna Bolstad. Funding was by Maternal and Child Health Training Project 913 from the Bureau of Community Health Services (Health Services Administration) and by Mental Retardation and Developmental Disabilities Branch Grant HD 02274 from the National Institute of Child Health and Human Development (National Institutes of Health), administered through the United States Public Health Service, Department of Health and Human Services, and awarded to the University of Washington Child Development and Mental Retardation Center.

Qualitative information includes subjective impressions ("I've had a super day"), values ("Rob is a bad boy"), and progress descriptions ("Compared to our first meeting, Mr. Barth is a lot less anxious"). Quantitative information is information that can be measured ("Today I was promoted to Social Worker III and got a $115 per month pay raise") ("Rob cut school three times this week and was caught shoplifting") ("When Mr. Barth started therapy, he did not stay seated for more than five minutes and never stopped fidgeting").

This chapter argues that clinical social work is best served by quantitative information. The rationale for the argument is straightforward. Quantitative data can be expressed as numerical measurements that can be compared and interpreted more easily than qualitative data. ("Seventy-six percent of my clients are single parents. Of these, the mothers' average age is 28.5; the mean age of the single fathers is 35.33." "Before treatment, Betty had an average of six temper tantrums a day. For the last two weeks, her daily rate was .5—roughly one temper tantrum every two days.")

Data are essential for social work practice. Data are used at the beginning of treatment to diagnose client problems and indicate treatment methods. During the treatment process, data may be used to answer such questions as: Are clinical goals realistic? Is treatment working? Are clients satisfied?

At the conclusion of clinical practice, quantitative information may be used to evaluate the outcome. Data can also be used to describe the efficiency with which outcomes were achieved. Practice results (whether successful or not) can be succinctly expressed through tables, graphs, and written reports.

Historical Background

Antedating today's interest in data-based social work is a history of integrated practice and research. Half a century ago, Richmond (1917) provided guidelines for gathering data. Richmond's approach was discussed in Milford Conference deliberations from 1923 to 1928. These conferences, held in Milford, Pennsylvania, brought together direct-service staff from the Family Welfare Association of America, American Association of Hospital Social Workers, American Association of Psychiatric Social Workers, Child Welfare League of America, International Migration Service, National Association of Travelers' Aid Societies, National Committee on Visiting Teachers, and National Probation Association. The goals of the Conference were to identify social work missions, define social casework, and discuss issues of agency competence, personnel deployment, and professional education. Regarding data-based practice, the Milford conferees' perspicacity is mirrored in the report of the American Association of Social Workers (1929, p. 12):

> There is no greater responsibility facing social case work at the present time than the responsibility of organizing continuous research into the concepts, problems, and methods of its field. There is need not for one treatise on social case work but for a library of treatises. Social case workers cannot leave the responsibility for research to foundations and universities. They must do it themselves, and participation by social case workers in such research must be widespread. The results of such studies embodied in articles, papers, pamphlets, monographs, and books are needed for the train-

> ing of case workers. They are needed for the development of sounder methods of supervision in social case work agencies, and they are needed for the service of the individual social case worker in his own professional development.

Following the early years, a vanguard of social workers carried on the cause of scientifically grounded practice. Relevant are postulates of Briar and Miller (1971): "The social caseworker, like the scientist, must be skeptical of his knowledge and procedures. Theory, even within the so-called 'hard' sciences, is always partial, tentative, and subject to revision. Social work knowledge is seen by the professional as temporary, and techniques, to the extent that they follow from knowledge, are always being supplanted by new and different ones. Skepticism toward existing procedures and an open-mindedness toward new conceptions, then, become the hallmarks of the social caseworker" (p. 81). These authors claim that scientists and social workers share techniques for constructing their data bases: "Stemming from the tradition of science is the paradigm of observation–hypothesis–experiment. This model is analogous to the traditional social casework formula of study, diagnosis, and treatment" (p. 81).

Six years later, in an issue of *Social Work* on conceptual frameworks, Reid (1977, p. 378) called for data-based practice to test treatment modalities: "Models capable of being tested can be assessed through a variety of techniques, from controlled experimentation to the collection of data secured as part of applying a model in ordinary practice situations. Although testing of the latter sort, which would be more common than planned experimentation, might not yield conclusive data on a model's effectiveness, it would provide a basis for assessment and development of the model."

Fischer's *Effective Casework Practice* (1978b, p. 3) criticized the neglect of data-based clinical work: "Traditionally, critical skills for theory and research analysis have not been a central part of social work students' and practitioners' knowledge base. But no profession can, or should, expect to survive—let alone provide effective services to its clients—without building into its training and practice the capacity for such ongoing evaluation. Without continuing critical analysis, for example, the profession, or individual professionals, would never be in a position of knowing when to update, revise, or radically change its typical methods of operation. Without such critical evaluation, professionals could never make optimal choices as to which approaches to implement in practice, nor as to which approaches are most (or least) effective."

Tripodi and Epstein (1978, p. 77) echoed this theme: "Social work practitioners and researchers should develop, implement, and evaluate strategies for incorporating research methods into social work practice."

Consequently, models for data-based practice are being developed. The University of Washington School of Social Work has implemented a model to teach scientific social work (Briar, 1973a, 1979; Jayaratne and Levy, 1979; Levy and Olson, 1979; Mundt and others, 1977). The practitioner so trained "is a professional who combines clinical methods in direct practice with skills in scientific evaluation. Clinical competence takes in the areas of assessment, case planning, and the delivery of social work services to individuals, families, groups, and the community. Scientific competence means an ability to document effectiveness through rigorous research methods and empirical data. Thus, clinical scientists recognize a logical compatibility between clinical practice and research activities" (Schinke, 1979a, p. 28). Other social work schools adopting the data-based model include those at the University of Hawaii; University of Texas, Arlington; University of Wisconsin, Milwaukee; and State University of New York, Albany (Bloom, 1978; Duehn and Mayadas, 1977; Gingerich, 1977; Hudson, 1978b).

This legacy has fostered diverse applications of empirical social work. A cursory search of the literature manifests such practice in group work with antisocial children, habilitation with underachieving students, social competency skills for children, assertive training with gay teenagers, dating among young adults, group treatment with depressed women, couple counseling, sex therapy, child management for single parents, child abuse, control of obesity, alcoholism, and cigarette smoking, and independent living skills for older people (McKinlay, Kelly, and Patterson, 1977; Mutschler, 1979; Schinke, 1981a). Despite the diversity of problems and approaches, data-based social workers are achieving remarkably positive results.

Case Illustration

A case illustration can show some of the main features of data-based practice relative to a presenting problem of national concern: unanticipated teenage pregnancy. Like many social problems, teenage pregnancy drew large-scale attention only after its consequences began to burden the public and private sectors (Gilchrist, Schinke, and Blythe, 1979; Gilchrist and others, in press). Adolescents' unwanted conceptions are seldom considered until childbearing cannot be avoided through contraception or elective abortion (Schinke, 1978; Schinke, Gilchrist, and Smith, 1980). Policies and programs for teenagers therefore aim to ameliorate the miseries of young parents and their babies rather than to remediate the antecedent conditions through primary prevention (Chilman, 1979; Schinke, 1979c). To contribute to a reversal of this trend, Blythe, Gilchrist, and I began a program to prevent unwanted teenage pregnancy (Blythe, Gilchrist, and Schinke, 1981; Schinke, 1982; Schinke, Gilchrist, and Blythe, 1980).

Methods. In a suburban high school, sophomore women and men were queried about their interest in a clinical program to prevent unplanned pregnancy. Students were informed that the program encompassed pretreatment assessment, treatment, and posttreatment evaluation and that not everyone would participate in each phase. Those wanting involvement gave written consent and obtained parental permission. From this pool, 36 youths were randomly assigned to four groups of nine each. Group I participated in all three phases. Group II participated in treatment and evaluation with no prior assessment. Group III completed assessment and evaluation but was untreated. Involved in evaluation, Group IV was not preassessed or treated. By forewarning students that participation would differ, random assignment posed no ethical dilemma (see Schinke, 1981b). Supplemental designs for data-based social work also run low risks of violating professional ethics as long as clients are told of all exigencies (Grinnell, 1981; Hersen and Barlow, 1976; Jayaratne and Levy, 1979; Kratochwill, 1978; Witkin and Harrison, 1979).

Pretreatment assessment with Groups I and III included several measures. A paper and pencil test measured youths' facts and myths about human reproduction. Another measured students' knowledge of contraceptive methods. Tape recordings were made of the teenagers' verbal statements that showed evidence of their problem solving and decision making. Youths' ability to interpersonally communicate important decisions about dating, sex, and birth control was assessed by a videotaped procedure. This procedure entailed face-to-face interactions with peers who acted like dating partners. The peers followed scripted instructions in eight situations that elicited each student's nonverbal and verbal behavior. For example, one situation required individual youths to refuse to attend an all-night party.

Assessment completed, Groups I and II were treated. The primary prevention program was based on earlier research data proving that adolescents do not use contraceptives because of several factors. Young people sometimes lack accurate facts about human reproduction. Other times, teenagers risk pregnancy because they cannot solve personal and interpersonal problems related to their sexuality. Still other times, teenaged women and men seem unable to make responsible decisions during interactions with their sexual partners concerning birth control. Support for these factors from hundreds of cases of unwanted teenage pregnancy indicated that all three be covered in the present prevention program (Schinke and Gilchrist, 1977; Schinke, Gilchrist, and Small, 1979). Two graduate social workers led the groups of nine teenagers through fourteen 50-minute sessions in which they learned reproductive biology, contraceptive methods, problem solving, decision making, and methods of nonverbal and verbal communication (Schinke, 1981d). The students were assigned homework tasks to apply this information. Typical tasks required students to discuss contraception with the sexual partner, to buy birth-control devices when needed, and to not engage in sex if unwilling or if unprotected.

When Groups I and II finished treatment, all youths took measures identical to those administered at pretreatment. Six months later, they reported their attitudes toward family planning and they also reported their sexual behavior, birth-control practices, and recent history of pregnancy. Groups I and II filled out questionnaires on treatment aspects they liked, did not like, did not understand, and wanted to change. These students noted whether they applied prevention to their lives and whether the experiences were positive or negative.

Results. Pretreatment assessment revealed no differences between Groups I and III. Posttreatment data on the four Groups are shown in Figure 1. As is evident in graph A, young people participating in treatment groups correctly answered more questions about human reproduction and contraception than did youths in the assessment and evaluation group and those in the evaluation-only group. Two-sample independent t tests (Goodman, 1978; Hays, 1973; Jayaratne, 1978; Kazdin, 1976; Parsonson and Baer, 1978) juxtaposing Groups I and II with Groups III and IV verify the statistical differences of these results, $t(34) = 2.37$, $p < .05$, $t(34) = 2.63$, $p < .02$. Audiotaped samples of youths' problem solving and decision making were transcribed and scored according to standard protocols (Platt and others, 1974; Spivack, Platt, and Shure, 1976). Graph B shows that young people in Groups I and II are better able to specify problems, identify obstacles to solving them, and derive solutions to problems than were youths in Groups III and IV, $t(34) = 3.84$, $p < .001$.

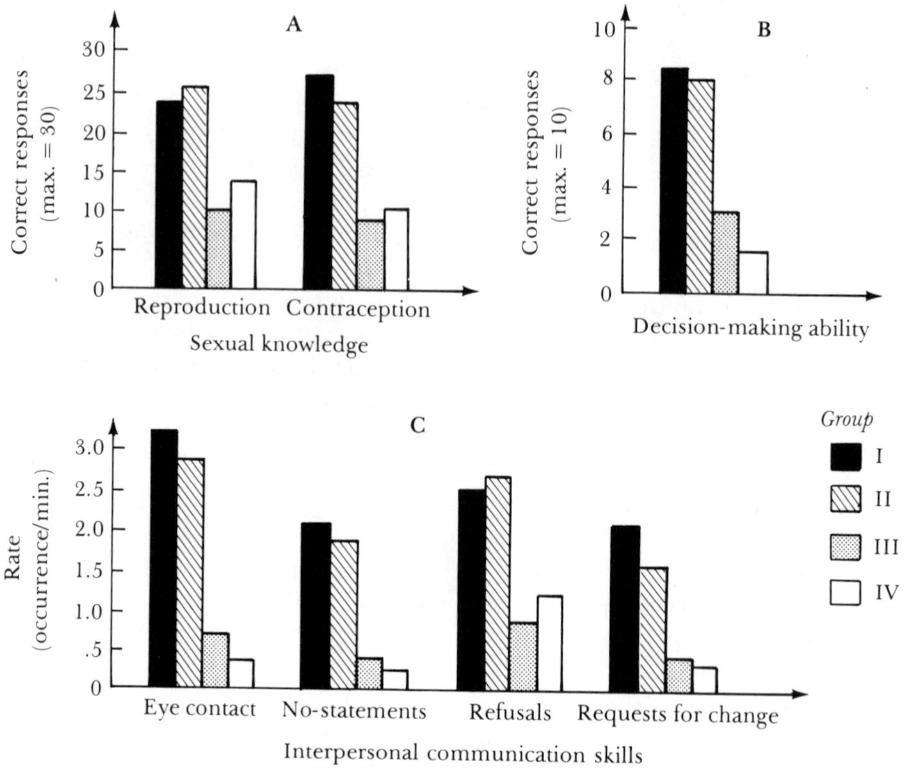

Figure 1. Group mean scores on posttreatment evaluation measures of reproductive and contraceptive knowledge (graph A), decision making (graph B), and interpersonal communication (graph C). Each group of nine adolescent women and men was given different clinical services. Group I received pretreatment assessment, treatment, and posttreatment evaluation. With no previous assessment, Group II was treated and evaluated. Group III completed assessment and evaluation only. Group IV was unassessed, untreated, and evaluated.

Videotaped interactions were viewed and rated by two graduate social workers. These two were kept naive of group affiliations and were trained to use Likert scales on youths' nonverbal and verbal performance (Schinke and others, 1978, 1979). Scoring accuracy was computed by correlating separate ratings of the same tapes. Pearson product-moment correlation coefficients ranged from 0.874 to 1.000. Scores were transformed into rates of occurrence to account for interactions of varying length (Schinke and Smith, 1979). As shown in graph C, videotaped ratings distinguished among youths who were treated and those who were not. Raters saw youths in the former two groups as more persuasive when making eye contact with the antagonist, $t(34) = 4.43$, $p < .0001$, saying "no" in response to pressure, $t(34) = 3.04$, $p < .005$, refusing to comply with unreasonable demands (not use birth control, risk pregnancy, act against their best interests), $t(34) = 2.19$,

$p < .05$, and requesting that interpersonal partners seek out and use birth control or otherwise change their comportment, $t(34) = 2.46$, $p < .02$.

Six-month follow-up with all but two of the 36 youths (one each in Groups II and III) confirm the efficacy of prevention treatment. Young people in treated groups, more than those in untreated ones, were favorably disposed toward family planning, $t(32) = 2.08$, $p < .05$, had fewer instances of unprotected intercourse, $t(32) = 3.83$, $p < .001$, had greater habitual use of contraception, $t(32) = 2.38$, $p < .05$, and better protection at last intercourse, $t(32) = 3.26$, $p < .005$, and were less reliant on inadequate contraceptive methods, $t(32) = 4.35$, $p < .0002$. An aborted pregnancy was related by a young woman in the untreated control condition, Group IV. No other youth related an unplanned pregnancy.

Consumer satisfaction data (Kazdin,1977) from the treated groups lend warmth to the results. With some exceptions, participants liked all treatment sessions, used their learning often and with beneficial results, and suggested modifying primarily logistical arrangements (different room, time of day, physical layout). Young persons' open-ended responses suggested that they enjoyed the groups and that they were personally interested in treatment.

Participant feedback was corroborated by unsolicited comments from parents. The mother of one young woman wrote, "I'm happy about the groups E. attended. She talks with me and her sister about problems we never used to talk about." Teachers had similar sentiments. A collective of advisors to the sophomore class wrote, "Thanks to you, our students are now able to discuss their concerns on a variety of subjects, not only sex, but lots of other important issues as well. Please accept our appreciation."

Conclusions. This case teaches several lessons about data-based social work. Empirical practice that ends well starts ahead of the first treatment session. Before assessment, data-based clinicians plan each treatment phase. An overall plan then dictates client involvement in pretreatment assessment, treatment, and posttreatment evaluation. Anticipating various phases affects negotiations with clients. Treatment modalities for data-based social work appear in the literature and are familiar to clinicians. Giving clients unknown or untried treatment is risky at best, and clinicians should avoid treatment modalities that are not supported by at least some research. Practitioners assisting people with their difficulties ought to collect quantitative information on any therapy provided. Tests of experimental intervention are wisely restricted to research with nonclinical populations and to such analogue problems as anxiety induced in the laboratory with paid volunteers as subjects.

The example illustrates how attitudes toward the problem of teenage pregnancy can be measured using parameters of cognitions and behavior. By focusing on the attitudes that lead to pregnancy, we were able to use several reliable prevention methods. If original methods had been used, our conclusions might be criticized on the basis that measurement, treatment, or a combination of the two were responsible for the outcomes. If outcomes were only evaluated in terms of the incidence of pregnancy, the prevention program could be erroneously judged as ineffective. For example, the reported abortion in one untreated group only suggests that no treatment is less effective than treatment; it does not prove treatment is effective.

The results of data-based practice can raise more questions than answers. Although fourteen treatment sessions were judged to be successful, might briefer intervention be equally effective? The small group context appeared to be appropriate, but would large groups have better cost-benefit ratios? Without doubt the unwanted teenage pregnancy can be avoided by primary prevention (Gilchrist, Schinke, and Blythe, 1979; Gilchrist and others, in press). Are teenage alcohol and drug abuse, delinquency, family conflicts, and career decisions equally amenable to preventive social work? Empirical practice puts our modest achievements in perspective and raises possibilities for future endeavors.

The Present State of Data-Based Social Work

Clinical social work engages clients in a helping relationship. The main feature of data-based social work is that quantitative information is used to guide and evaluate practice.

This feature distinguishes data-based activities from other clinical practice. Is this type of practice increasing? One way of testing this hypothesis is to survey the professional literature. Published articles can be retrieved; they show the range of practice areas and give a contemporary picture of social work for a particular time period of interest. Notwithstanding weaknesses in the journal system (Lindsey, 1978a, 1978b), a recent survey of thirty social work periodicals discovered "a healthy diversity among the journals . . . [that] is an appropriate reflection of the diversity of the profession" (Else, 1978, p. 272). Smith and I collaborated to study the state of data-based clinical practice as presented in the professional social work literature.

Procedure. Using Else's (1978) listing, twenty-two social work journals that appeared from 1960 through 1979 were scanned for three nonexclusive indices—total articles, articles on clinical practice, and clinical articles that supported their findings with numerical, quantitative data. Articles were defined as authored reports. Thus, an anonymous announcement, a piece of poetry, a letter to the editor, and any other paper without an author or one that did not report on professional activity was not evaluated as an article. Articles in each of the three considered categories were grouped in five-year intervals, and mean scores were derived for each five-year period. Means for journals having less than five years' longevity were figured by dividing the total number of articles by the number of years of publication. Percentages of change between periods were computed with the algorithm mean of later period − mean of earlier period ÷ mean of earlier period × 100.

Findings. Table 1 lists annual means of total articles (A_T), clinical articles (A_C), and data-based clinical articles (A_{DB}) published in the twenty-two social work journals from 1960 through 1979, grouped by five-year periods. Overall, the findings reveal the increase of data-based social work practice in the professional literature.

Our survey confirms the relative growth of publications about clinical social work. Of sixteen journals launched since 1970, nine devote at least half their space to clinical practice. Even the seven not aimed at direct service (*Aretê, Journal of Applied Social Sciences, Journal of Social Service Research, Journal of Sociology and Social Welfare, Journal of Social Welfare, Social Perspectives,* and *Social*

Table 1. Annual Mean of Total Articles (A_T), Clinical Articles (A_C), and Data-Based Clinical Articles (A_{DB}) in 22 Social Work Journals from 1960 Through 1979, by Five-Year Period

	1960–1964			*1965–1969*			*1970–1974*			*1975–1979*		
	A_T	A_C	A_{DB}	A_T	A_C	A_{DB}	A_T	A_C	A_{DB}	A_T	A_C	A_{DB}
Aretê							9.8	2.9	0.0	9.2	2.2	0.8
Child Welfare	62.2	43.2	5.2	66.8	49.2	11.6	64.2	48.0	10.2	62.0	51.8	15.0
Clinical Social Work Journal							21.4	16.4	1.0	22.5	17.0	0.5
Health and Social Work										42.3	31.5	10.3
Journal of Applied Social Sciences										19.0	3.0	3.0
Journal of Education for Social Work							15.8	4.8	0.0	45.6	17.0	4.4
Journal of Gerontological Social Work										26.0	16.7	7.3
Journal of Social Service Research										26.0	11.2	10.0
Journal of Sociology and Social Welfare							49.3	5.3	0.0	44.4	18.4	4.6
Journal of Social Welfare										15.6	6.6	2.8
Practice Digest										43.5	38.0	3.5
School Social Work Quarterly										22.0	15.0	4.0
Smith College Studies in Social Work	11.1	6.4	4.3	8.8	4.4	1.8	8.4	3.2	3.8	7.8	3.8	3.2
Social Casework	51.0	41.8	6.8	51.0	38.4	8.2	58.8	43.6	9.6	70.6	52.4	10.2
Social Perspectives										19.4	6.0	1.4
Social Service Review	28.6	12.2	2.8	27.2	13.4	5.0	26.0	14.4	8.2	34.2	15.6	9.0
Social Thought										19.4	4.6	1.4
Social Work	56.6	34.2	5.8	50.8	26.4	6.8	73.6	38.2	11.2	84.0	53.8	19.6
Social Work in Education										22.4	15.0	4.0
Social Work in Health Care										31.8	23.8	8.8
Social Work Research and Abstracts										21.5	10.9	9.8
Social Work with Groups										27.5	20.0	3.5

Thought) published a number of clinical papers. As journals become less academic and more responsive to the majority of social workers, future publications will probably move toward a practice orientation. The fledgling *Practice Digest* is an instance of such movement.

Table 2 shows changing percentages of total articles, clinical articles, and data-based clinical articles between five-year periods for the last twenty years. Data-based clinical reports are generally increasing in the nine journals with two or more comparison intervals. For example, the *Journal of Education for Social Work* and *Smith College Studies in Social Work* increased the number of data-based articles by over 100 percent between 1965–1969 and 1970–1974. The periods 1970–1974 and 1975–1979 show a large increase in the number of data-based reports. The *Journal of Sociology and Social Welfare* increased such coverage by 459 percent, and the *Journal of Education for Social Work* increased its coverage by 214 percent.

Three journals decreased the number of data-based papers, and three published more about data-based practice despite fewer client-related articles. During the twenty-year period, *Smith College Studies in Social Work* decreased their data-based papers by 25 percent, and *Child Welfare, Social Casework, Social Service Review,* and *Social Work* showed increases of 188 percent, 50 percent, 221 percent, and 238 percent, respectively. Taber and Shapiro's (1965) survey of *Social Casework, Social Service Review*, and *Social Work* from 1920 to 1964, with Howe and Shuerman's (1974) coverage of the same three in 1957 and from 1967 through 1972 and Simpson's (1978) review of *Social Work* from 1956 to 1977, corroborates our finding of an increase in the number of data-based articles in our best-known journals.

Our survey verifies the accent on data-based practice in clinical social work journals. As social work journals proliferate, direct service to clients is getting deserved recognition. Our survey supports our hypothesis that most published articles have quantitative indicators.

Future Clinical Practice

Our survey indicates an auspicious future for data-based practice. Many social workers support the continuance of quantitative description of clinical methods and results. The following quotes indicate increasing support for data-based practice: "The goal of developing a scientifically based practice is too important to abandon" (Taubman, 1978, p. 249). "We must endeavor to evaluate continually our effectiveness and how it can be quantified in terms of explicit, concrete, and measurable problem formulation and measurable, focused, problem-solving techniques" (Wertkin, 1978, p. 517). "The tools that previously only researchers possessed should be brought to bear on social work practice" (Levitt and Brown, 1978, p. 251). "Scientific practice—that is, practice which is explicitly guided by the empirical information from the scientific knowledge base, but more particularly, from the ongoing evaluation of that practice—offers a clear response to the challenge of accountability" (Bloom, 1978, p. 584). "If you cannot measure the client's problem, you cannot treat it" (Hudson, 1978a, p. 66). "If you cannot measure your intervention, it cannot be implemented" (Gingerich, 1978, p. 252). "An activity that cannot be defined is not worth measuring, and if it

Table 2. Percentage of Change Between Five-Year Periods for Total Articles (A_T), Clinical Articles (A_C), and Data-Based Clinical Articles (A_{DB}) in Nine Social Work Journals from 1960 Through 1979

	1960–1964 to 1965–1969			*1965–1969 to 1970–1974*			*1970–1974 to 1975–1979*			*1960–1964 to 1975–1979*		
	A_T	A_C	A_{DB}	A_T	A_C	A_{DB}	A_T	A_C	A_{DB}	A_T	A_C	A_{DB}
Aretê							−6	−24	+79			
Child Welfare	+7	+14	+123	−4	−2	−12	−3	+8	+47	0	+20	+188
Clinical Social Work Journal							+5	+4	−50			
Journal of Education for Social Work				+65	+96	+139	+75	+81	+214			
Journal of Sociology and Social Welfare							−10	+245	+459			
Social Casework	0	−8	+21	+15	+14	+17	+20	+20	+6	+38	+25	+50
Smith College Studies in Social Work	−21	−31	−58	−5	−27	+111	−7	+19	−16	−30	−41	−25
Social Service Review	−5	+10	+79	−4	+7	+64	+32	+8	+10	+20	+28	+221
Social Work	−10	−23	+17	+45	+45	+45	+14	+41	+75	+48	+57	+238

Note: Percentage of change = Mean of later period − Mean of earlier period ÷ Mean of earlier period × 100.

cannot be measured it is not worth doing" (Anderson, 1979, p. 3). "It is best if researchers are direct service practitioners" (Seidl, 1980, p. 61).

Assuming data-based practice is here to stay, what is its future? One can hope that its future will include better-prepared practitioners, more relevant research methods and technologies, stepped-up scrutiny from inside and outside the profession, an end to the practitioner–researcher split, and greater rewards for data use and production.

Professional education is charged with identifying the needs of the social work community and tailoring appropriate curricula. Regarding empirical practice, much of this effort is happening through the previously mentioned models of simultaneous clinical and research training. One may expect that all accredited graduate programs will soon adopt some of this joint emphasis (Fanshel, 1980a). A few will resist data-based practice, especially those seeing empiricism as antithetical to social work's humanitarianism (Cooper, 1980; Rabichow, 1980; Watson, 1979). But, educators who are listening to their counterparts, students, and consumer agencies will hear the wisdom of scientific practice. Teaching quantitative social work to B.S.W. and continuing education students will not lag far behind (Schinke and Schilling, 1980; Schinke and others, 1981; Wodarski, 1980).

Emerging methods and techniques for gathering and accessing data will help clinicians study their practice. Individual case research is an easy way to investigate clinical phenomena, determine if social work is effective, and decide when to halt treatment and transfer the locus of change solely to clients. Recent and forthcoming handbooks (Grinnell, 1981; Hersen and Barlow, 1976; Jayaratne and Levy, 1979; Kazdin, 1978, 1979; Kratochwill, 1978; Schinke, 1981a) place this methodology within reach of every social worker. A wealth of assessment procedures assist such clinical evaluations (Beere, 1979; Buros, 1978; Chun, Cobb, and French, 1975). And, the advent of computers and desk-top calculators measurably aid data compilation and analysis.

Social work is undergoing scrutiny from within the field and from the public (Briar, 1975; Meyer, 1979; Schinke, 1979b). Most critics constructively seek greater sensitivity to clients and human services inequities (Alexander, 1977; Crouch, 1979; Dean, 1977; Fischer, 1978a); a minority think social work should be disbanded (Bitensky, 1978; Gannon, 1972). Regardless of motive, all see professional efficacy as our top challenge (Briar, 1973a, 1973b; Fischer, 1976; Haselkorn, 1978; Newman and Turem, 1974). This premium on outcome will not become passé. In the short run, the U.S. economy and conservative politics vitiate returning to large, costly public welfare programs with ill-planned evaluations (Bernstein and Freeman, 1975; Masters, Garfinkel, and Bishop, 1978). Over the long term, increased demands for social services and competition from allied disciplines necessitate efficient, efficacious, and accountable practice (Briar, 1979). These pressures imply expanded emphasis on data-based practice. Social workers who concur with the prognosis will prepare for the future by equipping themselves with necessary skills.

To the advantage of workers and clients, the profession is burying the notion that practice and research are mutually exclusive (Fanshel, 1980b). The ceremony will be accompanied by no weeping. If anything, social workers will rejoice that Briar and Miller's (1971) words of ten years ago have finally come true: "Every clinician . . . is a researcher and any dichotomy between research and clinical practice is thus artificial" (p. 82). The near future will surely witness a profession as affable with data as with clients and social agencies. At the same time will come a demise of such argot as *clinician-researcher, practitioner-scientist,* and *clinical social worker*—labels that alienate rather than integrate the profession. Social workers ought to be social workers.

Data-based practice will be infused into the field at a quicker rate if workers get institutional rewards for empirical undertakings. Agencies could provide release time for individuals to collect data, interpret them, and communicate them in writing and in oral presentations. Staff meetings could give part of the agenda to workers telling about and showing their data. Agencies could monitor the gathering of quantitative information and remunerate data-based assessment, evaluation, and referral. One community mental health center has a method for reminding clinicians to keep data and relate objective results to referral sources (Rinn and Vernon, 1975)—staff doing so derive recompense through promotions and pay increases. Though this arrangement is atypical, a forthright commitment to data collection from those hiring social workers will nurture rigorous practice. It is unfair to hand clinicians the tools to study professional work without backing the use of the implements with organizational perquisites. With Briar (1979), this author agrees that "we will have to find ways to help create in the profession and in social agencies the conditions that are necessary if clinical research is to take root and flourish in social work" (p. 140).

The advent of data-based practice is an unprecedented chance for social work to prove its worth. The multiple settings in which clinicians practice will equally prosper from a quantitative approach. Agencies, institutions, and treatment centers can make inherent promises explicit and supported by quantitative facts. Workers in private practice can shore professional competency with information on successful and predictable results. Should data indicate that individuals or agencies are not fulfilling their missions, persons most able to change will be the first to know (Agras and Berkowitz, 1980). Goals, procedures, and methods can be reexamined, refined, and modified by using such information.

Empirical clinicians shaping the field are ensuring professional survival and therefore benefiting the next generations of social workers and clients. Disciplines vying for the human services dollar—psychology, psychiatry, education, public health, nursing (Bornstein and Wallersheim, 1978; Sykes, 1978)—pose no threat when social workers bear out clinical efforts with numbers. Cuts in social services may be abated by incontrovertible direct-practice results. In short, the future of data-based social work is bright.

References

Agras, W. S., and Berkowitz, R. "Clinical Research in Behavior Therapy: Halfway There?" *Behavior Therapy,* 1980, *11,* 472–487.

Alexander, C. A. "Social Work Practice: A Unitary Conception." *Social Work,* 1977, *22,* 407–414.

American Association of Social Workers. *Social Case Work: Generic and Specific: A Report of the Milford Conference.* New York: American Association of Social Workers, 1929.

Anderson, R. J. "Accountability, Means, and Ends." *Social Work in Education,* 1979, *1,* 2–4.

Beere, C. A. *Women and Women's Issues: A Handbook of Tests and Measures.* San Francisco: Jossey-Bass, 1979.

Bernstein, I. N., and Freeman, H. E. *Academic and Entrepreneurial Research.* New York: Russell Sage Foundation, 1975.

Bitensky, R. "Social Work: A Non-Existent Profession in Search of Itself." *New Universities Quarterly,* 1978, *2,* 65–73.

Bloom, M. "Challenges to the Helping Professions and the Response of Scientific Practice." *Social Service Review,* 1978, *52,* 584–595.

Bloom, M., and Block, S. R. "Evaluating One's Own Effectiveness and Efficiency." *Social Work,* 1977, *22,* 130–136.

Blythe, B. J., Gilchrist, L. D., and Schinke, S. P. "Pregnancy-Prevention Groups for Adolescents." *Social Work,* 1981, *26,* 503–504.

Bornstein, P. H., and Wollersheim, J. P. "Scientist–Practitioner Activities Among Psychologists of Behavioral and Nonbehavioral Orientations." *Professional Psychology,* 1978, *9,* 659–664.

Briar, S. "Effective Social Work Intervention in Direct Practice: Implications for Education." In Council on Social Work Education (Ed.), *Facing the Challenge: Plenary Session Papers from the 19th Annual Program Meeting.* New York: Council on Social Work Education, 1973a.

Briar, S. "The Age of Accountability." *Social Work,* 1973b, *18,* 2, 114.

Briar, S. "Professional Awareness: 1975." *Social Work,* 1975, *20,* 258.

Briar, S. "Incorporating Research into Education for Clinical Practice in Social Work: Toward a Clinical Science in Social Work." In A. Rubin and A. Rosenblatt (Eds.), *Sourcebook on Research Utilization.* New York: Council on Social Work Education, 1979.

Briar, S., and Miller, H. *Problems and Issues in Social Casework.* New York: Columbia University, 1971.

Buros, O. K. (Ed.). *The Eighth Mental Measurements Yearbook.* Vols. 1 and 2. Highland Park, N.J.: Gryphon Press, 1978.

Chilman, C. S. *Adolescent Sexuality in a Changing American Society: Social and Psychological Perspectives.* Washington, D.C.: U.S. Government Printing Office, 1979.

Chun, K., Cobb, S., and French, J.R.P., Jr. *Measures for Psychological Assessment: A Guide to over 3,000 Original Sources and Their Applications.* Ann Arbor: Institute for Social Research, University of Michigan, 1975.

Cooper, S. "The Master's and Beyond." In Judith Mishne (Ed.), *Psychotherapy and Training in Clinical Social Work.* New York: Gardner Press, 1980.

Crouch, R. C. "Social Work Defined." *Social Work,* 1979, *24,* 46–48.

Dean, W. R., Jr. "Back to Activism." *Social Work,* 1977, *22,* 369–373.

Duehn, W. D., and Mayadas, N. S. "Entrance and Exit Requirements of Professional Social Work Education." *Journal of Education for Social Work,* 1977, *13,* 22–29.

Else, J. F. "Social Work Journals: Purposes and Trends." *Social Work,* 1978, *23,* 267–273.

Fanshel, D. (Ed.). *Future of Social Work Research.* Washington, D.C.: National Association of Social Workers, 1980a.

Fanshel, D. "The Future of Social Work Research: Strategies for Coming Years." In D. Fanshel (Ed.), *Future of Social Work Research.* Washington, D.C.: National Association of Social Workers, 1980b.

Fischer, J. *The Effectiveness of Social Casework.* Springfield, Ill.: Thomas, 1976.

Fischer, J. "Does Anything Work?" *Journal of Social Service Research,* 1978a, *1,* 215–243.

Fischer, J. *Effective Casework Practice: An Eclectic Approach.* New York: McGraw-Hill, 1978b.

Gannon, J. P. "Second-Term Script: If President Wins Again, the Nation May Have a Do-Less Government." *The Wall Street Journal,* October 18, 1972, pp. 1, 20.

Gilchrist, L. D., Schinke, S. P., and Blythe, B. J. "Primary Prevention Services for Children and Youth." *Children and Youth Services Review,* 1979, *1,* 379–391.

Gilchrist, L. D., and others. "Prevention and Health Promotion Services for Adolescents: Validation of a Model." In J. R. Anderson (Ed.), *Social Work in Health Care: Fission or Fusion.* Seattle: University of Washington Press, in press.

Gingerich, W. J. "The Evaluation of Clinical Practice: A Graduate Level Course." *Journal of Social Welfare,* 1977, *14,* 109–118.

Gingerich, W. J. "Measuring the Process." *Social Work,* 1978, *23,* 251–252.

Goodman, L. A. *Analyzing Qualitative/Categorical Data.* Cambridge, Mass.: Abt Books, 1978.

Grinnell, R. M., Jr. (Ed.). *Applied Social Work Research and Evaluation.* Itasca, Ill.: Peacock, 1981.

Haselkorn, F. "Accountability in Clinical Practice." *Social Casework,* 1978, *59,* 330–336.

Hays, W. C. *Statistics for the Social Sciences.* (2nd ed.) New York: Holt, Rinehart and Winston, 1973.

Hersen, M., and Barlow, D. (Eds.). *Single-Case Experimental Designs: Strategies for Studying Behavior Change.* Elmsford, N.Y.: Pergamon Press, 1976.

Howe, M. W., and Schuerman, J. R. "Trends in Social Work Literature: 1957–1972." *Social Service Review,* 1974, *48,* 279–285.

Hudson, W. W. "First Axioms of Treatment." *Social Work,* 1978a, *23,* 66.

Hudson, W. W. "Research Training in Professional Social Work Education." *Social Service Review,* 1978b, *52,* 116–121.

Jayaratne, S. "Analytic Procedures for Single-Subject Designs." *Social Work Research and Abstracts,* 1978, *14,* 30–40.

Jayaratne, S., and Levy, R. L. *Empirical Clinical Practice.* New York: Columbia University Press, 1979.

Kazdin, A. E. "Statistical Analyses for Single-Case Experimental Designs." In M. Hersen and D. Barlow (Eds.), *Single-Case Experimental Designs: Strategies for Studying Behavior Change.* New York: Pergamon Press, 1976.

Kazdin, A. E. "Assessing the Clinical or Applied Importance of Behavior Change Through Social Validation." *Behavior Modification,* 1977, *1,* 427–452.

Kazdin, A. E. "Methodological and Interpretive Problems of Single-Case Experimental Designs." *Journal of Consulting and Clinical Psychology,* 1978, *46,* 629–642.

Kazdin, A. E. "Data Evaluation for Intrasubject-Replication Research." *Journal of Social Service Research,* 1979, *3,* 79–97.
Kratochwill, T. E. (Ed.). *Single Subject Research: Strategies for Evaluating Change.* New York: Academic Press, 1978.
Levitt, J. L., and Brown, L. B. "Research and Practice." *Social Work,* 1978, *23,* 251.
Levy, R. L., and Olson, D. G. "The Single-Subject Methodology in Clinical Practice: An Overview." *Journal of Social Service Research,* 1979, *3,* 25–49.
Lindsey, D. "The Operation of Professional Journals in Social Work." *Journal of Sociology and Social Welfare,* 1978a, *5,* 273–298.
Lindsey, D. *The Scientific Publication System in Social Science: A Study in the Operation of Leading Professional Journals in Psychology, Sociology, and Social Work.* San Francisco: Jossey-Bass, 1978b.
McKinley, T., Kelly, J. A., and Patterson, J. "Teaching Assertive Skills to a Passive Homosexual Adolescent: An Illustrative Case Study." *Journal of Homosexuality,* 1977, *3,* 163–170.
Masters, S., Garfinkel, I., and Bishop, J. "Benefit-Cost Analysis in Program Evaluation." *Journal of Social Service Research,* 1978, *2,* 79–93.
Meyer, C. H. "What Direction for Direct Practice?" *Social Work,* 1979, *24,* 267–272.
Mundt, L., and others. "The Clinical-Scientist Model for Graduate Training in the Field." Paper presented at the Annual Program Meeting of the Council on Social Work Education, Phoenix, Arizona, February 1977.
Mutschler, E. "Using Single-Case Evaluation Procedures in a Family and Children's Service Agency." *Journal of Social Service Research,* 1979, *3,* 115–134.
Newman, E., and Turem, J. "The Crisis of Accountability." *Social Work,* 1974, *19,* 5–16.
Parsonson, B. S., and Baer, D. M. "The Analysis and Presentation of Graphic Data." In T. R. Kratochwill (Ed.), *Single Subject Research: Strategies for Evaluating Change.* New York: Academic Press, 1978.
Platt, J. J., and others. "Adolescent Problem-Solving Thinking." *Journal of Consulting and Clinical Psychology,* 1974, *42,* 787–793.
Rabichow, H. G. "Dilemmas in Agency Practice." In J. Mishne (Ed.), *Psychotherapy and Training in Clinical Social Work.* New York: Gardner Press, 1980.
Reid, W. J. "Social Work for Social Problems." *Social Work,* 1977, *22,* 374–381.
Richmond, M. E. *Social Diagnosis.* New York: Russell Sage Foundation, 1917.
Rinn, C., and Vernon, J. C. "Process Evaluation of Outpatient Treatment in a Community Mental Health Center." *Journal of Behavior Therapy and Experimental Psychiatry,* 1975, *6,* 5–11.
Schinke, S. P. "Teenage Pregnancy: The Need for Multiple Casework Services." *Social Casework,* 1978, *59,* 406–410.
Schinke, S. P. "Bridging the Accountability Gap." *Practice Digest,* 1979a, *1,* 28–29.
Schinke, S. P. "Evaluating Social Work Practice: A Conceptual Model and Example." *Social Casework,* 1979b, *60,* 195–200.
Schinke, S. P. "Research in Adolescent Health: Social Work Implications." In W. T. Hall and C. L. Young (Eds.), *Health and Social Needs of the Adolescent:*

Professional Responsibilities. Pittsburgh: University of Pittsburgh Graduate School of Public Health, 1979c.

Schinke, S. P. (Ed.). *Behavioral Methods in Social Welfare.* Hawthorne, N.Y.: Aldine, 1981a.

Schinke, S. P. "Ethics." In R. M. Grinnell, Jr. (Ed.), *Applied Social Work Research and Evaluation.* Itasca, Ill.: Peacock, 1981b.

Schinke, S. P. "Individual Case Evaluation." In S. P. Schinke (Ed.), *Behavioral Methods in Social Welfare.* Hawthorne, N.Y.: Aldine, 1981c.

Schinke, S. P. "Interpersonal-Skills Training with Adolescents." In M. Hersen, R. M. Eisler, and P. M. Miller (Eds.), *Progress in Behavior Modification.* Vol. 2. New York: Academic Press, 1981d.

Schinke, S. P. "A School-Based Model for Teenage Pregnancy Prevention." *Social Work in Education,* 1982, *4,* 34–42.

Schinke, S. P., and Gilchrist, L. D. "Adolescent Pregnancy: An Interpersonal Skill Training Approach to Prevention." *Social Work in Health Care,* 1977, *3,* 159–167.

Schinke, S. P., Gilchrist, L. D., and Blythe, B. J. "Role of Communication in the Prevention of Teenage Pregnancy." *Health and Social Work,* 1980, *5,* 54–59.

Schinke, S. P., Gilchrist, L. D., and Small, R. W. "Preventing Unwanted Adolescent Pregnancy: A Cognitive-Behavioral Approach." *American Journal of Orthopsychiatry,* 1979, *49,* 81–88.

Schinke, S. P., Gilchrist, L. D., and Smith, T. E. "Increasing the Economic Self-Sufficiency of Teenager Mothers." In S. J. Bahr (Ed.), *Economics and The Family.* Lexington, Mass.: Heath, 1980.

Schinke, S. P., and Schilling, R. F., II. "Needs Assessment and Child Care Staff Training." *Child Care Quarterly,* 1980, *9,* 73–81.

Schinke, S. P., and Smith, T. E. "A Videotape Character Generator for Training and Research." *Behavioral Engineering,* 1979, *5,* 101–104.

Schinke, S. P., and others. "Improving Teenage Mothers' Ability to Compete for Jobs." *Social Work Research and Abstracts,* 1978, *14,* 25–29.

Schinke, S. P., and others. "Group Interpersonal Skills Training in a Natural Setting. An Experimental Study." *Behaviour Research and Therapy,* 1979, *17,* 149–154.

Schinke, S. P., and others. "Measuring the Impact of Continuing Education," *Journal of Education for Social Work,* 1981, *17,* 59–64.

Seidl, F. W. "Making Research Relevant for Practitioners." In D. Fanshel (Ed.), *Future of Social Work Research.* Washington, D.C.: National Association of Social Workers, 1980.

Simpson, R. L. "Is Research Utilization for Social Workers?" *Journal of Social Service Research,* 1978, *2,* 143–157.

Spivack, G., Platt, J. J., and Shure, M. B. *The Problem-Solving Approach to Adjustment: A Guide to Research and Intervention.* San Francisco: Jossey-Bass, 1976.

Sykes, D. H. "The Clinical Psychologist as Scientist/Researcher: Implications for Training." *Bulletin of the British Psychological Society,* 1978, *31,* 419.

Taber, M., and Shapiro, I. "Social Work and Its Knowledge Base: A Content Analysis of the Periodical Literature." *Social Work,* 1965, *10,* 100–106.

Taubman, S. B. "Educating the Practitioner-Researcher." *Social Work,* 1978, *23,* 249–250.

Tripodi, T., and Epstein, I. *Journal of Social Service Research,* 1978, *2,* 65–78.

Watson, K. W. "Social Work and Stress and Personal Belief." *Child Welfare,* 1979, *58,* 3–12.

Wertkin, R. A. "Measurable Terms." *Social Work,* 1978, *23,* 517.

Witkin, S. L., and Harrison, D. F. "Single-Case Designs in Marital Research and Therapy." *Journal of Social Service Research,* 1979, *3,* 51–66.

Wodarski, J. S. "Requisites for the Establishment and Implementation of Competency Based Agency Practice." *Aretê,* 1980, *6,* 17–28.

51

Cognitive-Behavioral Approaches

Sharon Berlin

How social work direct practitioners will work with clients in the future will be—at least should be—as much determined by theoretical, philosophical, and task commitments as by available practice methods. Inevitably, methods influence practice perspectives, including goals, problem definitions, and areas of enquiry. But, unless we prefer to play it safe and ignore whole areas of complicated real-life problems, pragmatics should not be the only force shaping social work direct practice. Techniques to alleviate human problems sould be guided by the conceptualization of such problems and refined through empirical tests.

By now, it is well known that empirical tests of direct practice efforts during the past two decades have uncovered minimal positive effects (Mullen and Dumpson, 1972; Wood, 1978). In addition to lack of specificity about the interventions actually used, reviews of this body of research point to rather amazing discrepancies between the scope of the problems and the scope of the interventions used to alleviate them. The existence of such large power differentials between natural influences and practitioner influences on client problems suggests either that the social workers did not clearly understand the problems (did not account for all the environmental and personal factors that served to maintain them) or that they did not know what to do with all of these problem correlates.

Reasonable, simple, and familiar, the practice guidelines that several theoreticians (Meyer, 1972; Reid, 1972, 1978; Wood, 1978) have extracted from these research findings are: (1) to analyze target problems broadly, accounting for multiple social and psychological causal influences; (2) to define client goals narrowly, in specific, feasible terms and according to the client's request; and (3) to devise a problem-reduction strategy that the worker and client can implement to counterinfluence the major dimensions of the problem situation. Several major responses in the form of social work practice models or perspectives have been developed to address these implications. For example, Reid and Epstein's (1972; Epstein, 1980; Reid, 1978) task-centered treatment system directs practitioners to focus on client-identified problems (unsatisfied wants) as they are influenced through the interaction of beliefs, behavior, affect, and social systems factors and directs workers how to go about helping clients to achieve modest and specific problem-reduction goals. Taking an epidemiological rather than a methodological perspective, Meyer (1972, 1976, 1979) reminds us to conceptualize the units of attention broadly in order to incorporate the problem context—that is, the personal, social-environmental, and organizational factors interacting with the problem. Similarly, Germain and Gitterman (1979, 1980; Germain, 1979) find useful metaphors for describing person–situation reciprocity within an ecological perspective. Similarly, Pincus and Minahan (1973) focus on the interaction of people and resource systems.

In spite of, or perhaps because of, the profession's chronic ambivalence about intrapsychic versus social determinism and its chronic failure to change either the structures of personalities or societies, there is finally some consensus that direct practice goals need to correspond closely to client requests and to focus on enhancing client coping and reducing specific conflicts rather than on curing people, changing lifestyles, or altering society. There is also agreement that personal problems exist in a social context; these problems influence and are influenced by social, biological, and psychological factors. This consensus will shape the course of clinical practice during the next decade. At the same time that we are abandoning grandiose goals in favor of sophisticated problem analysis, we are exposing the need for a range of equally sophisticated social and psychological intervention tactics.

There is credibility for the idea that, if one conducts a careful and accurate problem assessment, effective solutions will present themselves. However, it may not be so simple. Many discussions of how to think about problems assume that we already have ample intervention strategies to solve them, but questions about methods and strategies continue to puzzle social work theoreticians as well as individual practitioners. Optimally, "the situation will generate the tasks to be accomplished" (Meyer, 1979, p. 269), but how to carry out those tasks remains a legitimate and often an unanswered question (Briar, 1973).

Given this context—the need for a broad, interactional theoretical perspective and for effective methods to address specific, limited goals—the remainder of the chapter discusses the implications of a cognitive-learning perspective for social work direct practice methods. Even though another theoretical perspective from another discipline is not the whole answer, this relatively new and developing view of human functioning and change provides some answers, and directions to other answers, about how to help people cope with life problems, and it does so from a framework that is very compatible with social work's person-in-situation commitment (Berlin, 1980a; 1982).

Representing a synthesis of views from cognitive psychology, social learning theory, and psychodynamic theory, the cognitive–behavioral model explains human functioning as the product of reciprocal interaction between personal and environmental variables and provides a rationale for differentially altering cognition, behavior, affect, and interpersonal and social situations (Mahoney, 1974, 1980). Variations of cognitive-behavioral therapies have been effectively used to reduce several human problems, including depression (Rush and others, 1977); anxiety (Goldfried, 1979); anger (Novaco, 1976); pain (Turk, 1978); impulsivity (Meichenbaum and Goodman, 1971); interpersonal reticence (Linehan, 1979); alcoholism (Marlatt, 1979); and self-criticism (Berlin, 1980c).

A Cognitive-Behavioral Perspective on Coping

Life circumstances are demanding, difficult, and uncertain. Many people long for the "simple life," some try to create it, and day to day all of us try to cope with life. "Coping refers to behavior that protects people from being psychologically [or materially] harmed by problematic social experience, a behavior that importantly mediates the impact that societies have on their members" (Pearlin and Schooler, 1978, p. 2). Although coping sometimes connotes enduring or making the best of awful circumstances, it also encompasses attempts to alter the stress-inducing situation. Coping is a transactional process, both a reaction to and a shaper of environmental demands (Lazarus and Launier, 1978).

Everybody copes. We all do what we think we can to soften the blows of living in the world. But, people differ in the success of their coping efforts. Some of us get dealt a lot more blows than others, and some of us have more social and personal coping resources and specific coping skills than others. Unfortunately, but not accidentally, persons who are exposed to more hardship (for example, persons who are poor, uneducated, and female) tend to be less likely to have the means to fend off the attendant stresses (Pearlin and Schooler, 1978). Problems are a fact of life, and experiencing pain is a part of being human. But whether or not people are systematically oppressed and whether or not they have a varied repertoire of coping skills, positive self-attitudes and expectancies and access to social resources affects how they avoid, alleviate, or exacerbate the impact of problems. It often happens that people who bear the brunt of hardships and personal devaluation messages learn more about the unjust nature of society and their own impotence than they learn about successful coping. Because they are deficient in skills, social support, and personal confidence, their troubles often become worse.

A cognitive-behavioral analysis of coping suggests that the transactions between people and their environments are primarily in the form of information exchange. As individuals grow up, they incorporate information from the social environment about how things work, what kinds of behavior are valued, what to expect from others, and the effectiveness of their actions. The social environment (parents, friends, school, community, culture) provides the data for ideas and expectations about life. These ideas and expectations in turn influence which stimuli are attended to and how they are interpreted and then what actions are undertaken (Arnkoff, 1980). Frequently, our ideas and expectations and symbolic representations of reality are simplistic and inaccurate and thus lead to dysfunctional responses (Mahoney, 1974). If, for example, people do not pay attention to internal and external signals of trouble, if they only attend to negative information, if they primarily hang on to painful memories and anticipate similarly painful futures, if they interpret every event to mean personal failure, if they lack basic life skills, or if they relentlessly and urgently attempt to control all events, the negative concomitants of cognitive appraisals tend to maintain, if not magnify, their original problems (Berlin, 1980a). As people become aware of the possibility of alternative perspectives about themselves and the world, they are in a position to enlarge both their representational systems and response repertoires, to gradually divest themselves of internalized social imperatives, and to exert more effective influence on their enviornment.

Awareness and appraisal of problem events, personal attributions and expectations, skills, and access to social resources and interpersonal support are key targets for social workers and clients in their attempts to develop effective coping responses. In addition to fostering specific solutions to the problem at hand, the intervention goal is also to teach clients problem-solving strategies that they can use in dealing with ongoing life difficulties. Several sources describe, and in some instances verify, the utility of a problem-solving orientation to clinical practice (D'Zurilla and Goldfried, 1971; Epstein, 1980; Haley, 1976; Mahoney, 1979; Perlman, 1957; Reid, 1978; Spivak, Platt and Shure, 1976). Adapted from the foregoing approaches, problem solving is viewed here both as a model for therapeutic intervention and as a way of managing one's life. It is represented as a basic nine-step overlapping sequence (see Figure 1).

Awareness. People who do not register signals that trouble is coming have missed an early opportunity to influence events when they may be more amenable and less devastating (Kanfer, 1979; Marlatt and Gordon, 1978). If, for example, one is not quite aware that the first letter sent home by the child's teacher commenting on his listlessness is something different than the notice of the P.T.A. meeting; or that stopping by the favorite tavern just to talk to old friends is a warning cue to the recovering alcoholic; or one is not aware that increasing feelings of anxiety mean that one is threatened and needs to find an effective means of protection, the problem may grow. If the person in question waits to pay attention until her child has become seriously depressed, or until she has gone on a five-day binge, or until he has had a full-blown panic attack, it is already late in the game.

Although life is often capricious, there remain certain relatively predictable patterns of cause and effect or antecedent and consequence. If individuals know their internal patterns and have information about their social environment, they can discriminate forewarnings, the early warning cues that come both from internal and external sources. External cues are events that signal potential problematic scenarios. Depending on individual patterns, the baby's diaper rash, a second notice of a utilities bill, not having a phone call from mother in a month, being late for work four days in a row, forgetting a clinic appointment, and slapping one's child can all be the harbingers of more trouble or the early signals to cope. Emotions are additional important sources of information about when and how to cope. For many, strong emotions are seen as personal flaws ("I shouldn't be feeling this way, what's wrong with me?") and may generate fear of losing control. However, negative emotions, such as feeling frustrated, sad, or unconfident, can be cues to begin efforts at self-understanding and coping. Denial of emotions leaves one bereft of important signals about how one is and what one needs. Problem solving requires that internal cues are recognized ("I'm really feeling sad"), accepted ("This is an important feeling, a normal feeling"), experienced, and used as a cue to cope ("I'll feel better if I let someone comfort me").

	Awareness	
Not aware		Aware of early warning cues (internal and external)
	Expectations	
Expect that I can't cope with this Expect that nothing I can do will help		Expect I can solve this problem Expect I can influence a better outcome
	Defining problem	
Stay stuck in a general feeling of unease		Specify exactly *what* is wrong Figure out the conditions (inside of you and outside of you) that influence the problem
	Think of solution alternatives (Discriminate areas of personal control)	
Keep possibilities narrow		Based on probable causes and creative thinking, generate a variety of possibilities, including doing nothing
	Analyze options and decide	
Be led by force of habit		Figure out task requirements Look at costs and benefits of each option
	Take action and persevere	
Don't ever start, get bogged down by anxiety and self-doubt Give up after a few setbacks		Review alternatives, prepare, and take action Give new plan a fair trial, expect setbacks, analyze them, and help yourself through them
	Attributions	
Look primarily at shortcomings, blame them on personal inadequacy, and decide you are helpless Attribute any successes to luck or factors outside self		Take credit for successful efforts and positive abilities Figure out if and how you can cope with remaining problems
	Analyze progress and modify plan	
Stay hazy about the effects of new work Attribute failure to inadequate abilities and success to luck or other external factors		Look at what is working, what is not working, and what needs to be changed; modify plan Attribute success to ability and effort, and attribute failure to modifiable effort on external factors
	Maintenance of change	
Assume success is final or assume failure at first nonmaintenance		Anticipate and prepare for high-risk situations Know that one nonmaintenance does not make a failure

Figure 1. Schematic Outline of a Personal Problem-Solving Process

In enhancing awareness of early warning cues, social workers can use several operations:

1. Provide an explanation (Meichenbaum, 1977) for the importance of attending to problem antecedents, and relate awareness-enhancing activities to the problem at hand as well as to problem solving in general.
2. Help clients reflect about events and feelings leading to their awareness of the current problem, and then help them to identify similar sequences of events that led to other related problems.
3. Give clients information they are lacking about relevant social, familial, or organizational dynamics—for example, about how the school works, or the welfare department, or the gas company; about how babies grow or how women get pregnant; and about how people solve problems.
4. Elicit information about the client's emotions; show clients how emotions can be used as information for coping.

The idea here is not to indulge in emotional dramas (Fadiman, 1980) but to note the emotion and to use its meaning to guide constructive actions. Specific means to advance these purposes may include:

1. Verbal persuasion—questioning, examining, clarifying, and sharing information (Bandura, 1977).
2. Modeling—talking about how you, the worker, might think your way through the beginnings of problem solving by identifying a feeling, accepting its normalcy, and figuring out its implications for coping (Rosenthal and Bandura, 1978).
3. Imagery—directing the client to shut his eyes and reexperience the events, thoughts, and feelings preceding problem occurrence (Meichenbaum, 1977).
4. Client self-monitoring—asking the client to systematically attend to and report on problem antecedents (Mahoney, 1979; Thoresen and Mahoney, 1974).

For some people, however, awareness takes the form of preoccupation with thoughts and emotions and undue concern with danger, possible problems, and encroaching disaster. Here awareness can engender immobilizing caution, alienating self-centeredness, and escalation of arousal. Rather than acting as a signal for coping action, emotions are sometimes used as a substitute for action; people can become obsessed with their present emotions and can imagine potential difficulties that never occur. In such situations, cognitive modification methods (addressed later in the chapter) are used to alter processes of misperception, selective focusing, and self-induced arousal.

Expectations. Expectations about alternative courses of action, of the ability to exert control over one's destiny, and of one's ability to solve problems are an important motivational source (Rotter, 1978). Extensive documentation (Kanfer, 1979) suggests that persons are more likely to show positive change when they perceive that they can choose among alternatives and that they retain some control over the outcome.

Bandura (1977) goes even further in elevating the importance of expectations by suggesting that all psychological change is mediated by expectations of personal efficacy, by assessment of one's coping competency. People who are confident of their ability to perform a task or cope with a problem are likely to persist longer, be more tolerant of obstacles, and experience more favorable outcomes (Bandura and others, 1980; Bandura and Adams, 1977; Bandura, Adams, and Beyer, 1977). Efficacy judgments are arrived at through a process of inferring the relative contributions of personal and situational factors to one's previous successes and failures. For example, a person may try but fail to achieve a positive outcome and thus carry forward a weak sense of personal efficacy. She may also retain a weak efficacy expectation even following success by attributing that outcome to easiness of the task, to having expended a huge amount of effort, to a "one time only" flash of brilliance, or to getting assistance from others. However, negative outcomes can enhance future coping efforts if failure is attributed to lack of effort rather than to deficient ability or fate (Frieze and others, 1978).

Stereotypically expecting that one can exert no influence and has no choice is personally dangerous. Such negative expectations lead to decreased trying, self-denigration, distress, unfavorable outcomes, and ultimately a kind of "learned helplessness" (Bandura and others, 1980; Abramson, Seligman, and Teasdale, 1978). Nor is it healthy or useful to approach each life situation with a sense of urgency to control or to keep knocking one's head against "the brick wall" (Goldfried, 1980). It is probably the case, however, that most situations allow some element of choice or influence. Often, the choice is not between having a problematic event occur or not occur, but of what to make of it, what to do with it, how much involvement to give it, how to learn from it. "In every situation, for every person, there is a realm of freedom and a realm of constraint. One may live in either realm. One must recognize the irresistible forces . . . but, knowing them, one may turn away and live in the realm of one's freedom. A farmer must know the fence which bounds his land but need not spend his life standing there, looking out, beating his fists on the rails; better he till his soil, think of what to grow, where to plant the fruit trees" (Wheelis, 1973, p. 31).

An early step in helping a client out of a problem situation is to get him to differentiate between externally imposed necessities and those that are self-perpetuated and subjective, and then to pinpoint where his choices lie. The goal is recognition that the self-imposed "necessities" are among a number of alternative ways of being, thinking, and doing in response to a given situation and that one has the capability of finding a preferable alternative.

Practitioners work to enhance clients' positive expectations for change throughout the entire intervention process. First, in the problem-definition and assessment stage, workers help clients to reconceptualize their problems in ways that make them understandable and amenable to change. Later, workers help clients take a first step in reducing their problems. The importance of clients making an early competent move is underscored by Bandura (1977). He suggests that, even though information from various sources—performance, vicarious experiences, affective arousal, and verbal persuasion—can all influence efficacy expectations, the most powerful information comes from successful action.

Problem Definition. Drawing further from Bandura's delineation of influence sources, the problem-definition stage relies primarily on verbalization. Verbal strategies have limited effects as the sole means of influence, but they are useful in setting the stage for increased effort. At the outset, clients are often confused, flooded by emotion, feeling overwhelmed and out of control. They are not exactly sure what is the matter. They refer to "these problems," "these decisions," "these situations," but often conclude that all they really know is that "things" are getting away from them and they just cannot cope any more. The worker elicits and listens to the client's story and gives it back to her in a more organized, less punishing, more understandable way. The worker continues to ask questions and to ponder and reflect with the client about the behavioral, cognitive, interpersonal, situational, and emotional causes and components of problems (Epstein, 1980; Peterson, 1968) until she and the client have arrived at a common conceptualization of the problem. This shared perspective normalizes the problem, makes it understandable and reasonable in its context, and transforms its global, amorphous nature into specific components that can be dealt with. Instead of being reprehensible, bizarre, and a sign of deviance to keep hidden, problems are accepted as being reasonable reactions, as understandable events, given the situational factors, available skills, fears or other feelings, competing interests, and basic assumptions of the client. Organizing the facts, pinpointing targets, and positively connoting the problem make it seem more solvable, and generate hope that coping responses can be found. Moreover, clients can be persuaded by the social worker's perception of their desire to "do right." The worker sees and communicates that, despite the struggle and confusion and negative consequences, at least on some level, the client tries hard, wants the best, and cares deeply.

Generalizable problem-definition guidelines include the following:

1. Problems are normal and inevitable.
2. The causes of problems can be located in situations, behaviors, beliefs, and emotions.
3. Pinpointing specific aspects of the problem and the conditions that cause or maintain it provide targets amenable to change.
4. Pinpointing the problem means being able to say: "This is what is wrong, and these factors—these old beliefs and socialized expectations, this fear, this skill deficit, this bureaucratic regulation, this self-devaluing response, this interpersonal agenda—all contribute to the problem state" (Mahoney, 1979).

Formulating and Implementing Solution Alternatives. As already noted, accurate definition of a problem can be an important step toward finding solution strategies. Since problems consist of or are maintained by some interactive combination of personal and situational factors, solution strategies are aimed at changing those conditions. In devising intervention strategies, the social worker acts to supplement the client's own solution resources so that work proceeds from the client's frame of reference and optimally expands that frame. Making the client a problem solver not only gives her practice in problem-solving thinking, it also avoids placing her in a position counseling of feeling imposed upon by and then reacting against worker-devised strategies (Brehm, 1966).

COGNITIVE STRATEGIES. Coping outcomes are a function of situational demands and cognitive appraisals of both the nature of the demands and of one's resources to meet them (Lazarus, Averill, and Opton, 1970; Lazarus and Launier, 1978; Roskies and Lazarus, 1979). When clients misappraise the implications of demanding events, the social worker's central task is to teach them to make more realistic assessments of both the demands they face and the resources they have to draw from. Whether this turns out to be hard, moderately hard, or relatively easy depends on a lot of unpredictable, complex, and interactive factors, central among which is whether the new "realistic" appraisal guidelines fit somewhere in the person's cognitive structures—that is, whether they have referents in the client's mind. Indeed, variations in psychotherapy are sometimes viewed as alternative ways to help clients learn and internalize more functional perspectives. The therapeutic relationship, new enactive experiences, new awareness, feedback imagery, and emotional release are variously emphasized by different theoretical schools as central mind-changing ingredients (Goldfried, 1980). Cognitive therapies have also recently emerged to address this teaching-learning task (Mahoney and Arnkoff, 1978).

Although recent cognitive therapy literature suggests a profusion of explanations for and procedures to accomplish cognitive change, differences among these appear to be in the degree of emphasis given to altering overriding cognitive schema or meaning systems (Mahoney, 1980; Sollod and Wachtel, 1980) versus attending primarily to specific cognitive distortions (Beck and others, 1979; D'Zurilla and Goldfried, 1971; Ellis, 1962; Meichenbaum, 1977). Mahoney (1980) suggests that changes to alter specific and delimited problems are more likely achieved and maintained when they are incorporated into existing cognitive structures. Core cognitive changes occur much less reliably, with great effort, and are appropriately undertaken when clients find that their major assumptions and rules are no longer valid and do not seem to work any more. Drawing from Kuhn's (1962) description of scientific revolutions, Mahoney suggests that, in these latter instances, persons are experiencing "paradigmatic crisis" and, like scientists whose favored hypotheses are not holding up, may either retrench and fight to hang on to their sense of order or set to work on revising previous assumptions. Despite Mahoney's dichotomy of specific versus core cognitive change, we need to remember that cognitive change is not an all-or-nothing proposition. Between these two approaches can be varying degrees of attention to changing core assumptions—the degree depending in part on how much specific attitude changes are compatible with or threaten basic beliefs and how much these old views seem to prescribe maladaptive behaviors, fruitless interactions, and emotional pain. For reasons already mentioned, as social workers, we are rarely involved in total personality restructuring, but neither are we advised to keep our cognitive change efforts at the minimum level. At the least, we need to take care to anchor all our change efforts in the client's existing paradigm or help her to consider alternative conceptualizations that she can consciously apply as part of her coping efforts.

Social workers can facilitate cognitive change by:

1. Gaining understanding of and communicating from the client's system of meanings (Goldfried, 1979).
2. Initially accepting the "internal validity" of the client's personal views (Beck and others, 1979) and understanding the ways in which environmental responses, personal behaviors, and emotional reactions maintain them (Sollod and Wachtel, 1980).
3. Gradually facilitating the client's ability to consider other possible meanings by putting the same facts or situations into other conceptual or emotional

frames (Watzlawick, 1976) or by casually offering various understandable alternative viewpoints, reactions, and feelings (Sollod and Wachtel, 1977).

4. Building client awareness of the relationships among cognitive appraisals, emotions, behaviors, and interpersonal reactions and awareness of the possibility that some cognitive appraisals may be inaccurate. Goldfried (1979) suggests using hypothetical or worker-related examples to first facilitate a somewhat theoretical understanding of this intervention rationale before exploring discrepancies between client views about the problem and the "facts."
5. Focusing the client's attention on her own expectations and interpretations of events and considering with her their "evidential" warrant (Meichenbaum and Butler, 1980). Client self-monitoring is useful in increasing awareness of cognitions so that they can be evaluated and changed (Thoresen and Mahoney, 1974) and in allowing the client to disengage from them by promoting the view that thoughts are data rather than absolute, immutable facts. Likewise, gently questioning, showing a willingness to accept the worst possible constructions if the data support them, and Socratic dialogue have also been found helpful in leading clients to their own conclusions and avoiding resistance likely evoked by a frontal attack on their personal opinions (Beck and others, 1979).
6. Helping the client construct alternative, more adaptive meanings, expectations, and self-instructions (Berlin, 1980c; Mahoney, 1980; Meichenbaum, 1977). This step often involves revising personal standards of conduct. It is important that the new standards are the result of careful consideration and hold some personal appeal (for example, "I'd like to be the kind of person who takes mistakes in her stride and then figures out what to do next").
7. Providing experiences that give new evidence to support changed views and counter old ones. Task assignments and behavioral experiments (Beck and others, 1979) are useful here both in terms of assisting the client to improve his circumstances and to test old absolute assumptions.

It is hard for all of us to give up favored assumptions, even in the face of contrary evidence. When confronted by disconfirming evidence, researchers usually overcome the awful temptation to "fudge" the data but typically go on to make strenuous efforts to discredit their unexpected findings. Numerous replications are sometimes required before they are ready to make adjustments in the original hypothesis. It is often the same with clients. Accepting new beliefs requires a lot of evidence, a lot of self-encouragement, a lot of experience in acting in accord with the assumptions, and a lot of indications that the changes are being tolerated, if not encouraged by important others. Since old beliefs are never completely eradicated from memory, the emphasis on building or strengthening competing parallel beliefs seems warranted (Mahoney, 1980). Although it is not always necessary to emphasize insight into the origins of problematic cognitions or to uncover repressed memories (Bedrosian and Beck, 1980), in some instances understanding the context in which the beliefs were formulated is another means of disengaging from them—of prompting the realization that they are repetitions of "old dramas" (Fadiman, 1980) that are now out of context. In his treatise on change, Wheelis (1973) says something similar: "For what has made my father's voice so irresistible all these years, his judgment of me so implacably my destiny, has been the continuing silent and unnoticed reception of his message. So soon as I translate it into audible sound, it becomes feasible for me to disagree, to become, if need be, vehement and angry in disagreement. I have resources beyond those of that child under the awning, and, if the old drama now takes place visibly and audibly, these resources become for the first time available to me, may achieve a different outcome" (pp. 83–84).

Based on assessment information and client requests, cognitive distortions may be viewed as interventive targets of primary, secondary, or even less importance. Rarely are they totally ignored or isolated as the sole interventive target. Because of the reciprocal influence among behaviors, cognitions, emotions, and situations, change in any one factor affects all the other factors.

BEHAVIORAL STRATEGIES. Even though clients' perceptions of personal incompetence or inability to cope may be exaggerated or overgeneralized, these views are usually not completely erroneous. Individuals may truly not know how to manage particular aspects of their lives effectively. They may in fact be alienating their friends, ignoring their children, losing their tempers on the job, or sitting in their nightgowns all day and never moving from the rocking chair. Social worker practitioners are well advised to look for the grain of truth in every "cognitive distortion" and engage with the client in seeing what else can be done. Alternative behaviors must be specified, modeled, rehearsed, adjusted, and repeatedly enacted. We have all experienced and reexperienced the scenario in which the client reports back, "I tried it, but it didn't work"—"I tried taking a few minutes for myself after work, but my kids wouldn't leave me alone"; "I tried walking down to the corner, but I got too anxious"; "I tried to work on my resume, but then I thought that I'd never get a job anyway"; "I called a friend to go out, but she was busy"—as if "that took care of that." Ourselves benefactors of repetition, we have learned better than anyone else that doing things differently often arouses opposing forces—resistance from significant others, anxiety associated with self-expectations of humiliation and failure, growing attachment to the positive parts of the dysfunctional actions and interactions. We know that performance change must be protected and practiced countless times, and so we can say in response, "Of course it didn't work" or, better yet, warn in advance, "Don't expect to take care of your whole problem in just this one week, the idea is to take this first step and keep track of what happens, of what the positive effects are and what is hard about implementing these actions so we can adjust our plan."

As noted earlier in the chapter, persistence is influenced by the ways in which clients explain their progress or lack thereof. Attribution research supports the notion that positive change is more likely to occur and be maintained if the individual perceives progress as a result of personal, global, and long-lasting factors, such as skill and ability, rather than external, specific, and short-lived factors, such as fortuitous circumstances, extreme effort, or external aids. However, negative outcomes can promote problem-solving efforts if they are attributed to delimited personal causes, such as specific skill deficit, lack of effort, or fatigue (Frieze and others, 1978). Clients may need help to reconsider the facts and to attribute responsibilities for progress and difficulties accurately. The most problematic attributional patterns to be undone are extremist ones in which clients shoulder full responsibility for failures and view them as resulting from negative personality traits or blame them totally on the external world and in either case see no avenues for personal influence.

The strategy is to get a little change going—to give the client the skills, supportive conditions, and incentives to assist him in attributing mastery to his own abilities and efforts—and then to build from there by guiding the client's performance through increasingly difficult and independent tasks. From their review of the interactional skills treatment research, Rosenthal and Bandura (1978) extracted several intervention guidelines. Modified for the purposes of this chapter, they include:

1. Generalizable principles of behavior change are explained.
2. Clients' learning goals are organized into achievable graduated tasks.
3. Specific rules of conduct corresponding to each task are explained and demonstrated.
4. Clients' rehearsal is guided by specific instruction, encouragement, and feedback that credits successes and provides suggestions about correcting errors.
5. Once the client can enact the necessary behaviors in the practice setting with worker assistance, she is given the opportunity for more independent performance to promote a sense of personal efficacy. This transition to independent mastery may include withdrawal of worker assistance and sessions in other environments.
6. Attention is given to performance obstacles both in the environment and in the client's belief system. The client is at least encouraged to suspend judgment and keep trying; more profitably, she is encouraged to guide her performance efforts by self-instructions rather than allowing demoralizing doubts and associated emotional distress to interfere with them (Berlin, 1980c, 1981a). Extra interventive steps may also need to be taken by the worker or client to engage the cooperation of others.
7. Finally, clients test their newly acquired skills in increasingly demanding situations.

When inadequate coping is largely a matter of inhibited performance, the social worker's primary effort is directed to helping clients anticipate and deal with interfering cognitive, emotional, and situational factors. But when people seem to lack basic coping skills (for example, skills related to such tasks as interviewing for a job, playing with one's children, making friends, shopping for groceries, communicating assertively), demonstration is an essential part of the intervention. Here, social workers need to concentrate on developing modeling procedures that help the client "attend to modeled activities, grasp their meaning, code the gist into durable symbols, retain the guidance in accessible form, and [develop] the response competence to execute it" (Rosenthal and Bandura, 1978, p. 629). To help clients learn coping skills, the social worker first labels and later summarizes the main components of the skill. By presenting well-organized, salient, comprehensible information that is not too anxiety arousing, the worker limits distractions and avoids stimulus overload and observer fatigue. Attention can be further facilitated if models are similar to the client in sex, race, age, and background. "Coping" models who face and overcome performance difficulties have also been found to be more compelling than "mastery" models who appear effortlessly perfect (Marlatt and Perry, 1976). Modeled information is more likely to be retained if the client recodes it into personally meaningful forms. Acronym, metaphor, imagery, and analogy can be used to encode central messages and facilitate their retention. Symbolic representation of behaviors guides the client's performance, but response competence also depends on whether the client has previously enacted component behaviors. When clients have little experience with the skill in question, it is crucial to follow modeling with opportunities for practice. Finally, if individuals see no benefits or anticipate negative sanctions for performing modeled behaviors, they are unlikely to perform them. In addition to affecting performance, incentive expectations can also prompt attention, deliberate coding, and active rehearsal. It is useful for clients to review the positive benefits of goal completion, to deliver positive self-evaluations for task achievement, and to receive feedback and support from others.

It also may help the client to look at reasons for her reluctance to adopt new skills. The possibility that she is scared, unconvinced, or overwhelmed needs to be assessed and dealt with, along with her reluctance to give up the positive aspects of the old ways. As problematic as they may have been, the old behaviors must have been functional in some respects. Clients can be helped to identify how these patterns served them and to acknowledge the possible advantages to just leaving things be. As long as resistance remains unacknowledged, it operates as a powerful, shadowy saboteur. But, if you say, "When you think about making some changes, you may also think of reasons why not to," the possibility of no change becomes a conscious alternative choice and its subconscious power becomes disarmed.

AFFECTIVE STRATEGIES. It has been difficult to understand fully the interaction between cognition and emotion because they are not entirely separable response modes (Arnkoff, 1980). Contrary to common understanding, cognitions are not purely rational or intellectual but incorporate emotional associations (Goldfried, 1980; Meichenbaum, 1977). Emotions have been described as physiological sensations and the meanings assigned to them (Schacter, 1964). Evaluation of events has been found to mediate emotional arousal (Beck, 1976). But, the evaluation itself includes emotional meanings, and the arousal experience is not complete until it is labeled and thus experienced as being depressed or anxious or angry, as falling in love or falling apart.

It is often difficult to alter beliefs because they tend to be encumbered by strong affective associations that make the beliefs seem true. By contrast, alternative constructions that might replace old, maladaptive beliefs may seem rather "intellectual" and emotionally barren. A first step in helping the client to cope with emotional associations is to help the client identify, experience, and accept them. It is quite common that people are afraid of their emotions. Uncomfortable feelings are often taken as bad feelings, as signs of personal weakness. Fearful avoidance of affective experiences does not, however, lead to their demise; rather, it seems to endow emotions with even greater perceived potential for creating personal catastrophe. Similarly, guilt or annoyance at emotions do not seem to lessen their intensity. There are many who repeatedly ask with a kind of petulant incredulity, "Why am I feeling this way?" "What's the matter with me?" "Why do these feelings always come to me?" without ever stopping to answer their questions. Struggling to adhere to societal injunctions to stay in control does not necessarily get rid of emotional associations but deprives individuals of information that can be used in planning for an adaptive next step. Practitioners can begin to assist clients in availing themselves of emotional information by asking what they are feeling, using evocative terms to facilitate emotional expression, demonstrating comfort with strong feelings, and explicating the point of view that emotions are natural and informative. Expressing the feeling will not necessarily make it go away, but avoiding such judgments as "This is intolerable," "I'm falling apart," or "I can't stand this," will help to dissipate some of its power.

Many individuals cling to their preferred emotional meanings. Some people seem always to find something in any situation to justify (and hence perpetuate) their anger or self-pity or sadness. No one likes to be wrong about his or her beliefs, and the same is often true of affective components. Referring to the predictable and repetitive nature of personal dramas, Fadiman (1980) suggests that there comes a point after which these familiar scenarios become an indulgence that interferes with adaptive functioning: "A different way of viewing the kind of personal drama performed in therapy groups might be the following: It is my turn to perform a personal drama, as is my right as a member of this group. I wish the rest of the group to stop their concerns with themselves and give me a lot of attention while I run through it. I will now do 'my mother really loved my sister more than me' followed by a chorus of 'my sexual feelings are frozen up inside me' and a final riff of 'sometimes I wish I were a lesbian, but if I were, I'd kill myself'" (p. 43).

Most of us know, or with a little assistance can know, our personal dramas. And, knowing them, we can usefully detach ourselves from them. We explain to our clients that detaching does not mean denying or avoiding, but experiencing, labeling, and letting go. We say, "Just because you hear the music, doesn't mean you have to dance." In Fadiman's terms, it is useful to develop detached awareness, or "witness consciousness," to enable observation of dramas without either praise or blame—"Now I'm feeling anxious," "Now I'm doing the last chorus of 'nobody cares how I feel,'" "Now I'm ready for a good fight"—and that's all. One need not dwell on, invest in, or overvalue the old needs and opinions of the self. They are there, but so what? In meditation, one can observe the occurrence of thoughts and feelings—watch them arise, name them, and let them go: "Feelings arise. Thoughts arise. The 'planning mind,' the 'judging mind.' Awareness experiences the process of their movement. It doesn't get lost in content. Observe thought passing through the vast space of mind" (Levine, 1979, p. 35).

As another way to limit emotional arousal, clients can be instructed in deep breathing (Meichenbaum, 1974, Benson, 1975) and muscle relaxation (Jacobson, 1974). Even though relaxation does not make a significant contribution to desensitization procedures (Kazdin and Wilcoxin, 1976; Kazdin and Wilson, 1978); it can be useful as an active coping strategy for anxiety-related problems (Goldfried, 1980). Typically, clients are taught to become more aware of bodily cues (such as muscular tension) associated with anxiety and then to use relaxation procedures to reduce the muscular tension and thus the anxiety (Goldfried and Davison, 1976).

Even thought guidance about weakening old dysfunctional emotional associations is relatively sparse and in some instances quite speculative, we are probably better informed and more influential here than in facilitating affective enrichment of new constructions. Certainly, we are continually assailed with some variation of the response, "I know it intellectually, but not on an emotional level." The clients are right. Compared to the old, familiar, emotionally loaded assumptions, the new ones seem pretty flat. In this situation, it helps to know that emotional attachment to new beliefs comes slowly. If clients can be persuaded to continue to use alternative interpretations, even though these new thoughts seem somewhat alien, and to notice and disengage from old rival thoughts, comfort with and emotional attachment to the new views gradually increases. And, we might usefully suggest that, since clients are already practicing alternative self-statements, it might help if they used a little affect in their messages to themselves. "As long as the information you want to give yourself seems accurate on the face of it, then why not use the words, intonation, and gestures that indicate strength of opinion and commitment." Since there is some evidence to suggest that people infer their internal states from external behaviors and revise beliefs on the basis of what they observe themselves doing (Bem, 1970; 1972), acting appropriately sincere, intense, fervent, or compassionate in conjunction with modified self-statements may enhance their believability. However, a grim, mechanical repetition of "I'm ok" is not very convincing.

Kelly (1955) has written about facilitating change by having the client play a whole new role with a new and explicit supporting personal history. Similarly, neurolinguistic programming (NLP) addresses the necessity of providing clients with historical foundations for alternative views and behaviors (Bandler and Grinder, 1979). NLP prescribes specific imagery-based experiential procedures to get the client to imagine dealing with earlier significant events in different and more resourceful ways—ways that can give a background for the new behaviors she wants to develop.

When new perspectives begin to pay off in terms of better solutions, then associated reactions of personal pride or group identity or interpersonal closeness may also occur to validate and emotionally enrich these alternative views. For example, Jo Ann, a woman in the self-criticism reduction group (Berlin, 1980b), wanted to be more compassionate with herself as well as with the important people in her life. In pursuing this goal, she instigated what turned out to be a long and mutually disclosive talk with her husband. Among other things, she told him that she thought her attempts to be easier on herself would also allow her to be less demanding of him. Her husband responded positively, wanted her not to be so hard on herself, and then talked about his own "low times" and how he clung to them to avoid making decisions or risking actions. This revival of intimacy was important to Jo Ann and her husband and provided a positive emotional association for Jo Ann's new perspective. Unfortunately, such heartwarming interpersonal responses to one's struggles to change do not always occur, despite our best efforts.

SOCIAL-ENVIRONMENTAL STRATEGIES. All the foregoing change strategies continually highlight reciprocity among personal subsystems of cognition, behavior, and affect. However, the cognitive-behavioral literature contains remarkably little discussion of the influence of social factors (interpersonal relationships, friendship support, access to material resources and opportunity) in enhancing or obstructing coping efforts. Rather, here and in other psychological and coping literature, there is an implication that social circumstances are fixed—too big, too overwhelming—and thus attention is most fruitfully directed toward more modifiable psychological factors (Roskies and Lazarus, 1979; Wilson, 1979). Certainly there is a place for enduring, retreating from, and even denying the impact of social demands. There are all kinds of circumstances in which altering personal appraisals, arousal level, and skills can mute the effects of difficult events and make life better. But, there is also something insidious and shortsighted in the refrain that hard times are inevitable, and the best one can do is to adjust to them or make the best of them. Since hard times are not equally distributed, it is difficult to know which ones are inevitable or under what conditions they are inevitable. Is it inevitable that women are unsafe on the streets at night, that children may be beaten and neglected, that women and minorities are discriminated against in the job market? If we say yes, our focus turns almost exclusively to personal adjustment, and then, when personal adjustment is missing, we are in jeopardy of blaming clients for their problems. It is mistaken to assume that all problems are responsive to individual coping efforts (Pearlin and Schooler, 1978). Care is also needed not to confuse cultural norms or values with necessities. Never before the women's movement have certain "inevitabilities" (for example, women's lesser sense of morality, their inability to think logically, their need to be protected and guided) been so thoroughly exposed as shared and culturally transmitted delusions (Meyer, 1980).

The problems of poverty, unemployment, and sexual and racial oppression are commonly encountered by social workers, but we have pretty much persisted in trying to find ways to deal with them on a case by case basis. Meyer (1980) suggests that "people's responses are shaped by their culture, and inevitably they conspire to maintain that culture" (p. 2). According to Selye (1956), "knowing what hurts you has an inherent curative value" (p. 260). It helps clients to know where the trouble is coming from, to discriminate where choices lie, and then to refuse to be an accomplice in their own devaluation. To find out that my problems are not a result of my personal inadequacy is a relief. To know that the present circumstances are not necessarily one's lot in life gives one freedom and at the same time burdens one with personal responsibility. Understanding society's "shared delusions" allows one, for the first time, to refuse to participate in them.

Having conducted several years of research on "learned helplessness," Seligman (1974) has concluded that early uncontrollable aversive experiences may dramatically impair subsequent learning and lead to learned-helplessness depression. The recent attributional analysis of helplessness suggests that global and stable and internal personal explanations for helplessness are more likely to result in symptoms of depression than external, specific, and short-lived reasons. The implications of this formulation are to work with clients to change unrealistic attributions for failure to external, specific, and unstable explanations and to change erroneous attributions for success to internal, global, and stable explanations (Abramson, Seligman, and Teasdale, 1978).

Perception of social consensus operates powerfully to maintain or change personal beliefs (Bem, 1970). In isolation, people are more likely to conclude that, for everyone else, life goes along smoothly in compliance with traditional views, that these views are right, and that they themselves are out of step and are wrong. "A person in isolation cannot detect common sources of pain" (Wykoff, 1977,

p. 15). As social workers, we are in a unique position to identify such common sources—social barriers, organizational rigidity, and misplaced values and expectations. Social workers are learning that the "American dream" was never meant for everyone and that, at best, it is not all that wonderful. In reality, there are not many of those "ideal" families in which mom stays home, dad goes out to work, and the kids are in school. Indeed, the nuclear family may not be worthy of the extreme measures people take to protect it. Women, we know, don't ask to be battered or raped, and the sex segregation and sexual discrimination found in the structure of the labor market, as well as the profit motive, and not personal laziness, largely account for a significantly lower wage for women than for men and contribute to unemployment. We need to bring our isolated individuals together to discover for themselves their common sources of pain, to receive and extend social support, and to take collective action.

Numerous studies have found a positive relationship between social support (interchange providing affirmation, a sense of belonging, and mutual aid) and personal adjustment (Brown and Harris, 1978; Cobb, 1976; Pearlin and Johnson, 1977; Miller and Ingham, 1976). Further evidence of the influence of social support is provided by experimental research on affiliation—when under stress, people prefer to be with others, and this proximity tends to improve performance and reduce physiological arousal (Heller, 1979). Despite the correlational nature of much of the social support evidence and the current inability to identify ingredients of support and affiliation, we are sufficiently informed to know that helping clients locate, develop, and maintain social ties is a promising strategy. Social workers' activities can focus on strengthening natural support networks (Collins and Pancoast, 1976); mobilizing extended family networks (Rueveni, 1979); acting as a part of a long-term support system (Test and Stein, 1977); and forming new self-help networks based on common issues (Burden, 1980; Crow, 1980).

Besides working with clients in natural or formed groups and thereby providing a means through which they can bolster each others' inner resources, we should not avoid directing clients' attention to social barriers to adjustment and helping them consider avenues for collective action (Chamberlin, 1978). For numerous reasons, including client priorities, values, and levels of stress and trust, it is not always feasible to offer clients social action possibilities, but such possibilities must at least exist in our own minds so that opportunities may be seized when they exist. Collective action is important both because it is necessary to influence the social causes of individual problems and because effective action is the most powerful conveyer of a sense of personal efficacy. Without exhuming the old individual versus social change arguments, perhaps it is enough to reiterate that the issue has never required and "either/or" answer and that our commitment to individual service almost always takes us beyond individuals. Various combinations of personal preferences, training, job mandates, and theoretical and empirical backing may lead us to spend much of our professional time on work with single clients, but, unlike many colleagues in other human service professions (such as psychology and psychiatry), we know that social policies are not fixed, resources are not static, and organizations are not immoveable. This awareness, along with an understanding of the social causes of individual problems, compels us to find the opportunities to involve ourselves in organizational, educational, and political efforts to alter oppressive circumstances.

Analyzing Progress and Modifying the Plan. Recently, there has been a great deal written about the importance of evaluating clinical practice on a case-by-case basis (Fischer, 1978; Jayaratne and Levy, 1979). A rationale for single case evaluation is that keeping careful records of progress and interventive operations provides information about the status of target concerns and directs attention to factors that may be promoting or interfering with change efforts. Evaluation thus provides directions about how intervention and coping efforts need to be modified. An additional benefit from recording progress and teaching clients to record progress is that, when a dramatic improvement is not forthcoming, people often tend to assume there has been no improvement at all. Since change usually occurs a little bit at a time, it is important to acknowledge those little bits and build from them. Also, there is something quite gratifying and motivating about seeing the gradual upward slope of the trend line on one's personal graph.

The sequence of steps in analyzing progress is, first, figure out which indicators of problem change (problem frequency, intensity, duration, patterns) are most meaningful, and, second, decide how that information can best be recorded. The most feasible data collection options are usually client self-observation, using such formats as structured diary, daily rating scale, and behavioral checklists, or interview methods such as paper-and-pencil inventories, uniform interview questions or role-play tests. Third, display changes graphically on a progress chart so that patterns of improvement and setbacks can be noted and used to prompt analysis of causal conditions.

Maintaining Change. "We set out with wild enthusiasm (and often unrealistic goals), and we plunge forward with boldness and determination. When our poorly conceived solution fails, we are crestfallen: we "give up" and crawl back to our old patterns. Gradually, over a period of months, we decide to have another go at it, and we rush forward again. . . . Once again we are met with failure, and slowly, over time, our determination and enthusiasm begin to decline. We begin to believe that we are butting our head against a brick wall, and we begin to expect failure" (Mahoney, 1979, p. 126).

Although our expectations are often otherwise, problem coping is not a one-time-only, all-or-nothing endeavor, and direct practice intervention does not necessarily produce lasting change. Presumably, intervention will have effected specific problem change, but there is no reason to believe that this change will be automatically maintained after formal contact has ceased and the client goes on about her daily life (Kazdin and Wilson, 1978). A coping-skills approach to personal problems provides the client with a set of coping guidelines and practice in understanding and responding to problems, including responding to the reemergence of old problems. A clear advantage of a coping orientation toward clinical work is the dual goal of helping clients to reduce problems and at the same time to learn the therapeutic process well enough to apply it on their own to other life problems. But, unless the client has learned how to cope with setbacks, she has not learned how to cope.

In their analysis of relapse for addictive behaviors, Marlatt and Gordon (1978) suggest that relapse is most likely to occur in high-risk situations (primarily involving negative emotional states, social pressure, and interpersonal conflict) in which the person fails to cope with an emerging problem. Failure to cope is seen as leading to diminished expectations that one can handle the difficulty and then giving up: "Here I am right back where I started, the therapy didn't work, I didn't change, and I may as well forget about things ever being different." Experimental tests of interventions derived from this cognitive-behavioral analysis have found that relapse-prevention coping-skills approaches are significantly more effective than traditional discussion groups (and no treatment) in reducing posttreatment drinking behaviors among chronic male alcoholics (Chaney, O'Leary, and Marlatt, 1978), and they are more effective than behavioral weight-loss procedures in maintaining and increasing weight loss among overweight men and women during a sixty-day posttreatment follow-up period (Rosenthal and Marx, 1979). Preliminary work is under way to determine implications of the Marlatt and Gordon model for maintenance of intervention gains with other clinical problems (Berlin, 1980b). In working to help clients avoid slipping back into old debilitating patterns once treatment is ended, it may be useful for practitioners to (1) share the perspective that slip-ups are inevitable and can be taken as cues for coping rather than as signs of personal failure and helplessness; (2) help clients identify and analyze their high-risk situations—circumstances that are most likely to precipitate problem behavior; (3) identify the early warning cues (internal and external) that signal vulnerability to difficult situations; and (4) plan and practice cognitive and behavioral responses that can be used to cope with high-risk situations and reduce the probability of relapse. Any setbacks that occur during the course of intervention provide a good opportunity to help clients to explore their reactions to slip-ups, to understand how viewing reemergence of problems as signs of total failure stops coping precisely at the time when one needs to cope the most, and in general to gain the experience and tools to handle the setbacks that will occur once they are on their own. It is also worth remembering that being on one's own is not an all-or-nothing event. Coping with high-risk situations often means using supportive resources, including the social work practitioner. It is expected that clients will call back when they find themselves faltering. Experience suggests that it is often useful to arrange in advance for follow-up booster sessions to review progress, fortify coping efforts, and promote a continuing process of learning to manage life difficulties.

Summary and Conclusions

This chapter has presented a coping-skills conceptualization of social work direct practice that emphasizes helping clients to cope with immediate pressing problems as well as making therapeutic procedures explicit so that they can use them to manage future life problems. This perspective emphasizes the transactional influence of person and environment on stress and coping. Individuals are seen as both responding to and acting to change their external circumstances. Cognitive appraisal of the nature of demands and of one's own coping options is central in determining actions undertaken, emotions experienced, and changes engendered in the environment. Attempts to modify cognitive mediating factors and problem states may differentially focus on enhancing awareness of early warning cues, creating positive expectancies for and attributions of change, and altering the cognitive, affective, behavioral, and social causes or effects of problems. These strategies are used to achieve clearly specified outcomes to well-defined problems, and they are remodeled until the outcomes are achieved.

Recent efforts to understand the influences of cognitions in human functioning, primarily in the field of clinical behavioral psychology, have led to a fortification of behavioral strategies with procedures to correct maladaptive appraisal processes and have resulted in cognitive-behavioral therapies that some view as "on the cutting edge of current empirical developments and refinements in psychotherapy" (Mahoney, 1980, p. 158). Equally important, these shifts have fostered a kind of disciplined, methodological eclecticism supported by loosely connected theoretical assumptions about aspects of the transactional nature of human behavior. These assumptions provide guidelines to help us explore, understand, and intervene into the numerous variations of personal-environmental transactions that we encounter. Notwithstanding the fresh possibilities of this current period of theoretical openness, our endorsement of cognitively based explanations of personal behavior needs to be cautious. Understanding of memory processes—of the ways people attend to, construct, integrate, and retrieve information—is by no means complete. Theoreticians have devised competing models that all rely on hypothetical mechanisms (deep structure, sensory register, schemata) to explain cognitive events. In Kanfer's (1979) words, "It is obvious that our framework is tentative and heuristic. It is a patchwork of related empirical facts and logical inferences and speculations held together by practical experiences that give it some credence and utility" (p. 191).

Liberated from theories that are restricted to discrete, observable behaviors, many theorists are exploring the influences of nonconscious cognitions, rediscovering the power of emotions, and focusing on cognitive development and information processing. Caution is also required here. The commitment to empiricism has always been the strength of behavioral practice and is the most important contribution behaviorists can make to cognitive-behavioral endeavors. Without arduous efforts to validate explanations and demonstrate intervention effectiveness, all the creative exploration and moves toward paradigm integration will remain little more than esoteric speculation and will have nothing to do with our main purpose of client problem reduction.

Firmly committed to effective intervention, social work is also called upon to shape the emerging paradigm by focusing attention on the social arrangements and institutions that facilitate or impede change. Working with people upon whom social conditions make the heaviest demands, we have a broad perspective on the scope of personal problems and solutions. We see that change often involves intrapersonal, interpersonal, and personal-societal processes. Very little is known about the content and consequences of various coping strategies as they are used in various environments. Because of our experience, work settings, and clientele, we are in optimal positions to engage in systematic attempts to describe the content of effective coping, including individual and collective efforts to alter environments.

References

Abramson, L. Y., Seligman, M.E.P., and Teasdale, T. D. "Learned Helplessness in Humans: Critique and Reformulation." *Journal of Abnormal Psychology*, 1978, *87*,49-74.

Arnkoff, D. B. "Psychotherapy from the Perspective of Cognitive Theory." In M. J. Mahoney (Ed.), *Psychotherapy Process: Current Issues and Future Directions.* New York: Plenum, 1980.

Bandler, R., and Grinder, J. *Frogs into Princes: Neurolinguistic Programming.* Moab, Utah: Real People Press, 1979.

Bandura, A. "Self-Efficacy: Toward a Unifying Theory of Behavior Change." *Psychological Review,* 1977, *84,* 191–215.

Bandura, A., and Adams, N. E. "Analysis of Self-Efficacy Theory of Behavioral Change." *Cognitive Therapy and Research,* 1977, *1,* 287–310.

Bandura, A., Adams, N. E., and Beyer, J. "Cognitive Processes Mediating Behavioral Change." *Journal of Personality and Social Psychology,* 1977, *35,* 125–139.

Bandura, A., and others. "Tests of the Generality of Self-Efficacy." *Cognitive Therapy and Research,* 1980, *4,* 39–66.

Beck, A. T. *Cognitive Therapy and the Emotional Disorders.* New York: International Universities Press, 1976.

Beck, A. T., and others. *Cognitive Therapy of Depression.* New York: The Guilford Press, 1979.

Bedrosian, R. C., and Beck, A. T. "Principles of Cognitive Therapy." In M. J. Mahoney (Ed.), *Psychotherapy Process: Current Issues and Future Directions.* New York: Plenum, 1980.

Bem, D. J. *Beliefs, Attitudes, and Human Affairs.* Monterey, Calif.: Brooks/Cole, 1970.

Bem, D. J. "Self-Perception Theory." In L. Berkowitz (Ed.), *Advances in Experimental Social Psychology.* Vol. 6. New York: Academic Press, 1972.

Benson, H. *The Relaxation Response.* New York: Morrow, 1975.

Berlin, S. B. "A Cognitive-Learning Perspective for Social Work." *Social Service Review,* 1980a, *4,* 537–555.

Berlin, S. B. "An Investigation of the Effects of Relapse Prevention Interventions on Durability of Self-Criticism Problem Change." Unpublished manuscript, University of Wisconsin, Madison, 1980b.

Berlin, S. B. "Cognitive-Behavioral Intervention for Problems of Self-Criticism Among Women." *Social Work Research and Abstracts,* 1980c, *4,* 19–28.

Berlin, S. B. "Cognitive-Behavioral Interventions for Social Work Practice." *Social Work,* 1982, *3,* 218–228.

Brehm, J. W. *A Theory of Psychological Reactance.* New York: Academic Press, 1966.

Briar, S. "Effective Social Work Intervention in Direct Practice: Implications for Education." In S. Briar and others (Eds.), *Facing the Challenge.* New York: Council of Social Work Education, 1973.

Brown, G. W., and Harris, T. *Social Origins of Depression.* New York: Free Press, 1978.

Burden, D. "Women as Single Parents: Alternative Services for a Neglected Population." In N. Gottlieb (Ed.), *Alternative Social Services for Women.* New York: Columbia University Press, 1980.

Chamberlin, J. *On Our Own.* New York: McGraw-Hill, 1978.

Chaney, E. F., O'Leary, M. R., and Marlatt, G. A. "Skill Training with Alcoholics." *Journal of Consulting and Clinical Psychology,* 1978, *46,* 1092–1104.

Cobb, S. "Social Support as a Moderator of Life Stress." *Psychosomatic Medicine,* 1976, *38,* 300–314.

Collins, A. H., and Pancoast, D. L. *Natural Helping Networks: A Strategy for Prevention.* New York: National Association of Social Workers, 1976.

Crow, G. N. "Abused Women's Network." Paper presented at NASW Conference on Social Work Practice in a Sexist Society, Washington, D.C., September 1980.

D'Zurilla, T. J., and Goldfried, M. R. "Problem Solving and Behavior Modification." *Journal of Abnormal Psychology,* 1971, *78,* 107–126.

Ellis, A. *Reason and Emotion in Psychotherapy.* New York: Stuart, 1962.

Epstein, L. *Helping People: The Task Centered Approach.* St. Louis, Mo.: Mosby, 1980.

Fadiman, J. "The Transpersonal Stance." In M. J. Mahoney (Ed.), *Psychotherapy Process: Current Issues and Future Directions.* New York: Plenum Press, 1980.

Fischer, J. *Effective Casework Practice: An Eclectic Approach.* New York: McGraw-Hill, 1978.

Frieze, I. H., and others. "Attributions of the Causes of Success and Failure as Internal and External Barriers to Achievement in Women." In J. Sherman and F. Denmark (Eds.), *Psychology of Women: Future Direction of Research.* New York: Psychology Dimension, 1978.

Goldfried, M. R. "Anxiety Reduction Through Cognitive–Behavioral Intervention." In P. C. Kendall and S. D. Hollon (Eds.), *Cognitive–Behavioral Interventions: Theory, Research and Practice.* New York: Academic Press, 1979.

Goldfried, M. R. "Psychotherapy as Coping Skill Training." In M. J. Mahoney (Ed.), *Psychotherapy Process: Current Issues and Future Directions.* New York: Plenum, 1980.

Goldfried, M. R., and Davison, G. C. *Clinical Behavior Therapy.* New York: Holt, Rinehart and Winston, 1976.

Germain, C. B. (Ed.). *Social Work Practice: People and Environments.* New York: Columbia University Press, 1979.

Germain, C. B., and Gitterman, A. "The Life Model of Social Work Practice." In F. Turner (Ed.), *Social Work Treatment: Interlocking Theoretical Approaches.* (2nd ed.) New York: Free Press, 1979.

Germain, C. B., and Gitterman, A. *The Life Model of Social Work Practice.* New York: Columbia University Press, 1980.

Haley, J. *Problem-Solving Therapy: New Strategies for Effective Family Therapy.* San Francisco: Jossey-Bass, 1976.

Heller, K. "The Effects of Social Support: Prevention and Treatment Implications." In A. P. Goldstein and F. H. Kanfer (Eds.), *Maximizing Treatment Gains: Transfer Enhancement in Psychotherapy.* New York: Academic Press, 1979.

Jacobson, E. *Progressive Relaxation.* (3rd ed.) Chicago: University of Chicago Press, 1974.

Jayaratne, S., and Levy, R. L. *The Clinical-Research Model of Intervention.* New York: Columbia University Press, 1979.

Kanfer, F. H. "Self-Management: Strategies and Tactics." In A. P. Goldstein and F. H. Kanfer (Eds.), *Maximizing Treatment Gains: Transfer Enhancement in Psychotherapy.* New York: Academic Press, 1979.

Kazdin, A. E., and Wilcoxon, L. "Systematic Desensitization and Nonspecific Treatment Effects: A Methodological Evaluation." *Psychological Bulletin,* 1976, *5,* 719–728.

Kazdin, A. E., and Wilson, G. T. *Evaluation of Behavior Therapy.* Cambridge, Mass.: Ballinger, 1978.

Kelly, G. *The Psychology of Personal Constructs.* Vols. 1 and 2. New York: Norton, 1955.

Kuhn, T. S. *The Structures of Scientific Revolutions.* Chicago: University of Chicago Press, 1962.

Lazarus, R. S., Averill, J. R., and Opton, E. M., Jr. "Toward a Cognitive Theory of Emotion." In M. Arnold (Ed.), *Feeling and Emotions.* New York: Academic Press, 1970.

Lazarus, R. S., and Launier, R. "Stress-Related Transactions Between Person and Environment." In L. A. Pervin and M. Lewis (Eds.), *Perspectives in Interactional Psychology.* New York: Plenum, 1978.

Levine, S. *A Gradual Awakening.* New York: Anchor Books, 1979.

Linehan, M. M. "Structured Cognitive–Behavioral Treatment of Assertion Problems." In P. C. Kendall and S. D. Hollon (Eds.), *Cognitive–Behavioral Interventions: Theory, Research, and Practice.* New York: Academic Press, 1979.

Mahoney, M. J. *Cognition and Behavior Modification.* Cambridge, Mass.: Ballinger, 1974.

Mahoney, M. J. *Self-Change: Strategies for Solving Personal Problems.* New York: Norton, 1979.

Mahoney, M. J. (Ed.). *Psychotherapy Process: Current Issues and Future Directions.* New York: Plenum Press, 1980.

Mahoney, M. J., and Arnkoff, D. "Cognitive and Self-Control Therapies." In S. L. Garfield and A. E. Bergin (Eds.), *Handbook of Psychotherapy and Behavior Change: An Empirical Analysis.* New York: Wiley, 1978.

Marlatt, G. A. "Alcohol Use and Problem Drinking: A Cognitive–Behavioral Analysis." In P. C. Kendall and S. D. Hollon (Eds.), *Cognitive–Behavioral Interventions: Theory, Research, and Practice.* New York: Academic Press, 1979.

Marlatt, G. A., and Gordon, J. R. *Determinants of Relapse: Implications for the Maintenance of Behavior Change.* Technical Report No. 78-07. Seattle: University of Washington, Alcoholism and Drug Abuse Institute, 1978.

Marlatt, G. A., and Perry, M. A. "Modeling Methods." In F. H. Kanfer and A. P. Goldstein (Eds.), *Helping People Change.* New York: Pergamon Press, 1976.

Meichenbaum, D. "Therapist Manual for Cognitive Behavior Modification." Unpublished manuscript, University of Waterloo, 1974.

Meichenbaum, D. *Cognitive–Behavior Modification: An Integrative Approach.* New York: Plenum, 1977.

Meichenbaum, D., and Butler, L. "Egocentrism and Evidence: Making Piaget Kosher." In M. J. Mahoney, *Psychotherapy Process: Current Issues and Future Directions.* New York: Plenum, 1980.

Meichenbaum, D., and Goodman, J. "Training Impulsive Children to Talk to Themselves: A Means of Developing Self-Control." *Journal of Abnormal Psychology,* 1971, *77,* 115–126.

Meyer, C. H. "Practice on Microsystem Level." In E. J. Mullen and J. R. Dumpson (Eds.), *Evaluation of Social Intervention.* San Francisco: Jossey-Bass, 1972.

Meyer, C. H. *Social Work Practice: The Changing Landscape.* (2nd ed.) New York: Free Press, 1976.

Meyer, C. H. "What Directions for Direct Practice." *Social Work,* 1979, *24,* 267–273.

Meyer, C. H. "Issues for Women in a Women's Profession." Paper presented at NASW Conference on Social Work Practice in a Sexist Society, Washington, D.C., September 1980.

Miller, P., and Ingham, J. G. "Friends, Confidants and Symptoms." *Social Psychiatry,* 1976, *11,* 51–58.

Mullen, E. J., and Dumpson, J. R. (Eds.). *Evaluation of Social Intervention.* San Francisco: Jossey-Bass, 1972.

Novaco, R. W. "Treatment of Chronic Anger Through Cognitive and Relaxation Controls." *Journal of Consulting and Clinical Psychology,* 1976, *44,* 681.

Pearlin, L., and Johnson, J. "Marital Status, Life-Strains, and Depression." *American Sociological Review,* 1977, *42,* 704–715.

Pearlin, L. I., and Schooler, C. "The Structure of Coping." *Journal of Health and Social Behavior,* 1978, *19,* 2–21.

Perlman, H. H. *Social Casework: A Problem-Solving Process.* Chicago: University of Chicago Press, 1957.

Peterson, D. *The Clinical Study of Social Behavior.* New York: Appleton-Century-Crofts, 1968.

Pincus, A., and Minahan, A. *Social Work Practice: Model and Method.* Itasca, Ill.: Peacock, 1973.

Reid, W. J. *The Task-Centered System.* New York: Columbia University Press, 1978.

Reid, W. J., and Epstein, L. *Task-Centered Casework.* New York: Columbia University Press, 1972.

Rosenthal, B. S., and Marx, R. D. "A Comparison of Standard Behavioral and Relapse Prevention Weight Reduction." Paper presented at a meeting of the Association for the Advancement of Behavior Therapy, San Francisco, 1979.

Rosenthal, T., and Bandura, A. "Psychological Modeling: Theory and Practice." In S. L. Garfield and A. E. Bergin (Eds.), *Handbook of Psychotherapy and Behavior Change: An Empirical Analysis.* New York: Wiley, 1978.

Roskies, E., and Lazarus, R. S. "Coping Theory and the Teaching of Coping Skills." In P. Davidson (Ed.), *Behavioral Medicine: Changing Lifestyles.* New York: Brunner/Mazel, 1979.

Rotter, J. B. "Generalized Expectancies for Problem Solving and Psychotherapy." *Cognitive Therapy and Research,* 1978, *2,* 1–10.

Rueveni, U. *Networking Families in Crisis.* New York: Human Services Press, 1979.

Rush, A. J., and others. "Comparative Efficacy of Cognitive Therapy and Pharmacotherapy in the Treatment of Depressed Outpatients." *Cognitive Therapy and Research,* 1977, *1,* 17–38.

Schacter, S. "The Interaction of Cognitive and Physiological Determinants of Emotional State." In L. Berkowitz (Ed.), *Advances in Experimental Social Psychology.* Vol. 1. New York: Academic Press, 1964.

Seligman, M.E.P. "Depression and Learned Helplessness." In R. J. Friedman and M. M. Katz (Eds.), *The Psychology of Depression: Contemporary Theory and Research.* Washington, D.C.: Winston, 1974.
Selye, H. *The Stress of Life.* New York: McGraw-Hill, 1956.
Sollod, R. N., and Wachtel, P. L. "A Structural and Transactional Approach to Cognition in Clinical Problems." In M. J. Mahoney (Ed.), *Psychotherapy Process: Current Issues and Future Directions.* New York: Plenum Press, 1980.
Spivack, G., Platt, J. J., and Shure, M. D. *The Problem-Solving Approach to Adjustment.* San Francisco: Jossey-Bass, 1976.
Test, M. A., and Stein, L. I. "A Community Approach to the Chronically Disabled Patient." *Social Policy,* 1977, *8,* 8-16.
Thoresen, C. E., and Mahoney, M. J. *Behavioral Self-Control.* New York: Holt, Rinehart and Winston, 1974.
Turk, D. C. "Cognitive-Behavioral Techniques in the Management of Pain." In J. P. Foreyt and D. P. Rathjen (Eds.), *Cognitive Behavior Therapy: Research and Application.* New York: Plenum, 1978.
Watzlawick, P. "The Psychotherapeutic Technique of 'Reframing.'" In J. Claghorn (Ed.), *Successful Psychotherapy.* New York: Bruner/Mazel, 1976.
Wheelis, A. *How People Change.* New York: Harper & Row, 1973.
Wilson, G. T. "Cognitive Factors in Lifestyle Changes." In P. Davidson (Ed.), *Behavioral Medicine: Changing Health Lifestyles.* New York: Brunner/Mazel, 1979.
Wood, K. M. "Casework Effectiveness: A New Look at Research Evidence." *Social Work,* 1978, *23,* 437-459.
Wyckoff, H. *Solving Women's Problems.* New York: Grove Press, 1977.

52

New Services for Families

Jon R. Conte
Terese M. Halpin

Our objective in this chapter is to discuss demographic trends in American families and social work's response to providing service to troubled families. As the chapter will illustrate, there is a clear trend in the helping literature toward an increase in the range of services offered to families. The following discussion will be restricted to issues concerning clinical work with families. Specifically, we are interested in services to children *and* adults with relational bonds. We specifically exclude from consideration services for individuals and for the adult dyad (for example, marital counseling).

The definition of the term *clinical* is a controversial issue in social work. It is an unfortunate concept. It is derived from Latin and means "bed-ridden person," which carries strong medical or disease connotations. It also is unfortunate that many social workers use the term *clinician* as a means of separating themselves from other social workers, just as others use the labels *therapist, family therapist,* or *university professor* instead of *social worker.*

Our view of practice is broad; we recognize a wide range of direct service models and direct practice roles. Our view is also political, in that we believe the future of social work depends in part on the vitality and knowledge that can develop as practitioners exchange different viewpoints and approaches to practice. We use the term *clinical* to denote a direct service practitioner who may provide a wide range of services in casework with individuals, families, and small client groups.

The purpose of this chapter is to raise a number of issues concerning services to families and to suggest possible future directions for clinical interventions. Specifically, the chapter critically analyzes minisystem (family therapy) and megasystem (ecological) perspectives for practice, identifies innovative services for consideration, and attempts to forecast a number of trends that may influence family services in the future.

Demographic Trends

A number of demographic trends describe potentially significant changes in the American family (U.S. Bureau of the Census, 1978).

1. The average size of the American family is decreasing. The average number of persons living in a family in 1960 was 3.33, as compared with 2.81 in 1978. Although the divorce rate accounts for some of this decrease, the declining birth rate accounts for most of the reduction in family size over the past twenty-five years.
2. An increasing number of women are postponing marriage. The proportion of women 24 years of age who have never married increased by one-third from 1970 to 1978 (36 percent to 48 percent).
3. Divorce and remarriage rates are high. There are approximately 90 divorced persons for every 1,000 married (a 91 percent increase since 1970, and a 157 percent increase since 1960). Estimates indicate that one out of every three marriages will end in divorce.
4. The marriage rate is increasing slightly. The rate of marriage per 1,000 population has increased 3 percent from 1976 to 1978. There are almost twice as many marriages as divorces.
5. The number of women in the labor force is increasing. About 50 percent of all women are in the labor force. The proportion of working mothers with children under 6 years old in the labor force increased from 19 percent in 1969 to 42 percent in 1978.
6. Most households are family households. Three of four households in 1978 were family households, an increase of only 11 percent since 1970 and less than half of the total household growth over the nine years. The one of four nonfamily households increased by 60 percent and accounted for 56 percent of the total increase in households from 1970 to 1978. Persons living alone account for 88 percent of all nonfamily households. This is 22 percent of all households.
7. The number of female-headed households is increasing. Family households maintained by women living without husbands accounted for 11 percent of all households in 1978 (an increase of 46 percent since 1970). Family households headed by divorced women account for 34 percent of all female-headed households.
8. The number of one-parent families is increasing. One-parent families represented 7 percent of all households in 1978 (an increase from 4 percent in 1960). In 1979, 38 percent of one-parent families were headed by a divorced mother (up from 24 percent in 1960). The proportion of one-parent families headed by never-married mothers increased from 7 percent to 15 percent in the same time period. Many of these never-married mothers are teenagers. There has not been a disproportionate increase in one-parent families headed by fathers.

9. Family victimization affects large numbers of people. One million children may be abused or neglected, and 1.6 million wives beaten each year (Delegate Workbook, White House Conference on Families). Although estimates vary, one out of ten boys and one out of five girls may be sexually exploited by the time they reach adulthood (Finkelhor, 1979). An overwhelming proportion of sexually abused children are exploited by members of their own families (Conte and Berliner, 1981).
10. Americans believe that family life is deteriorating. Fifty percent of Americans believe that family life has gotten worse over the past fifteen years (*Listening to America's Families,* 1980, p. 180).

Summarizing specific trends, it appears that families are smaller and have fewer children, although most Americans continue to live in families. There are more single-parent families, and many of these families experience major financial problems associated with the loss in income when moving from a two-parent to a single-parent head. The divorce rate is high, and a large number of children are exposed to divorce and its effects. The remarriage rate is also high, as is the marriage rate generally. Perhaps most significantly, regardless of the meaning of these trends, most Americans believe family life is deteriorating.

There are scholars who see these trends as reflecting a general breakdown in the American family, which in turn threatens "more basic processes" (Zimmerman, 1972). There are also those who conclude that the family is "here to stay" and stronger than anyone expected (Bane, 1976; Featherstone, 1979). There is no agreement whether these trends reflect changes only in the structure of families or in the functions, such as childrearing and support of family members, as well. Featherstone (1979) suggests that it does not matter which is changing. He concludes, "Change in structure and function and individual roles are not to be confused with the collapse of the family" (p. 37).

It would appear that whether one views these trends as negative or positive depends on the values and biases that one brings to such an analysis. Indeed, Demos (1974) notes: "There is no golden age of the family glaring at us from far back in the historical past. And there is no good reason to construe recent trends in terms of decline and decay. To every point alleged as an adverse reflection on traditional family life, one can offer a direct rejoinder" (p. 444).

Implications for Practice. These trends seem to indicate that, while Americans continue to believe in marriage and family, the structure of any given marriage and family may change during the course of the family's life together. Whereas there is nothing pathogenic or necessarily negative about any particular family structure or change in structure, *some* families do experience difficulty in association with these changes. Changes in family structure (especially divorce) are associated with economic, social, and emotional crises; large numbers of family members are victimized by other family members, especially as a consequence of family violence of sexual exploitation; and young parents, especially teenage mothers, may lack the knowledge and skills for effective parenting.

These data suggest the importance of a range of services. The National Commission on Families and Public Policy of the National Conference on Social Work (1978) called attention to the need for a range of services to support families. These support services include income and employment, physical and mental health, childrearing (daycare and parental support services), and personal social services. The personal social services identified by the Commission included information, advice, referral, and case advocacy related to all social problems; protective programs; substitute care arrangements; concrete support services (homemaker, delivered or congregate meals, home health, and escort or chore services); advice services and counseling related to childrearing, budgeting, family planning, abortion, and so on; mutual aid programs for families with common problems; and counseling and concrete help related to environmental, interpersonal, or intrapsychic emergencies.

The clinical social worker may assume a variety of roles in the provision of mental health, health, and personal social services. These roles include, but are not limited to, direct provision of service, advocacy on behalf of specific cases, brokerage or case management, and supervision of paraprofessionals. Whatever role she may play, the clinical social worker should understand the intrafamily and extrafamily variables associated with the family's problems. Some specific clinical roles might include (1) training parents (especially teenagers) to discipline their children without inflicting physical injury; (2) helping divorcing parents to negotiate child custody and living arrangements so that both the parents' desires to maintain contact with the child and the child's emotional and psychological needs are met; (3) working with a community group to obtain state and United Way funds to establish a shelter for battered family members, and developing a treatment program for the violent family member.

The selection of any particular clinical role will depend in part on the practice perspective used by the social worker. Two major perspectives are the minisystems (family therapy) and the megasystems (ecological) perspectives.

Minisystems Perspective

Much clinical work with families consists of providing services to individual family members with attention directed to the mutual influence of the family on the individual and the individual on the family unit. There is an expanding body of literature describing approaches to family therapy (Glick and Kessler, 1980; Goldenberg and Goldenberg, 1980; Janzen and Harris, 1980). The four major family therapy models tend to stress different aspects of human functioning, as will be seen in the following descriptions. The psychodynamic model views family dysfunction in terms of interlocking pathologies, in which symptoms are a function of the pathological relationships between family members. The communications model emphasizes dysfunctional relationships in the patterns of communication between family members. The structural model emphasizes the activities of various subsystems and the family system as a whole. The behavioral model emphasizes the specific behavior patterns resulting from exchanges of reinforcement and punishment among family members.

Glick and Kessler (1980) have suggested that all family therapy may be divided into three basic approaches:

1. The insight–awareness approach, in which observation, clarification, and interpretations are used to foster understanding (and presumably, change).

2. The structural–behavioral approach, in which manipulations are devised to alter family structures and conduct.
3. The experiential approach, in which emotional experience is designed to change the way family members see and react to one another.

In spite of the obvious differences between each of the major family therapy models and approaches to practice, they share some common assumptions and problems.

First, in all models, emphasis is placed on activities that take place within the family. Although external forces are acknowledged as contributing to family stress and dysfunction, the focus of assessment and intervention is on processes that take place among family members. Consequently, therapist attention is directed within the family.

Second, with the exception of occasional use of treatment within the family's own home, family therapy takes place in an environment foreign to the family (for example, the therapist's office). There is no research evidence to support the assumption that patterns of behavior, emotions, cognitions, or motoric behavior exhibited by family members during a therapy session are similar to those patterns exhibited at home or in other environments. Indeed, there is ample evidence in the behavioral literature to suggest that behavior is setting-specific (Conway and Bucher, 1976). As a corollary to this point, there is no evidence to support the assumption that change in the family produced in therapy will generalize to posttherapy settings.

Third, the connection between a model's description of family dysfunction (an assessment statement) and the appropriate intervention strategies are often unclear. Indeed, whereas both family diagnosis or assessment and family therapy are rich in concepts and techniques, theory is particularly weak on connecting the two.

Assessment of families may take place from a number of different perspectives and in terms of a number of characteristics. For example, the therapist may attempt to determine how well families perform life-maintaining tasks (feeding, clothing, nurturing) or how successfully they handle the stress associated with changes through the family life cycle (birth of a new member, children leaving home for first time at school, or death of a spouse). Important concepts of family functioning that may also be assessed include problem solving, communication, roles, affective responsiveness, affective involvement, and behavior control (Epstein, Bishop, and Levin, 1978).

What has not been well developed is the practice implications of any particular combination of assessment facts. Given a particular combination of facts about a family's functioning, theory is not helpful in determining which intervention techniques should be used to help the family relieve the stress. The lack of such theory has resulted in a large number of specific techniques for which the parameters of use have not been delineated. Lantz (1978) identifies a set of presumably effective family therapy techniques, including provocative exaggeration, boundary setting, bringing symptoms alive in the interview, and sculpting. However, the specific family characteristics or interaction patterns for which these techniques are effective is not indicated.

Fourth, systems theory, especially as used in structural and communication models, is a descriptive theory and not a theory of change. A system perspective on the family calls attention to the family as an "interactive milieu," with transactions constantly taking place between components (Glick and Kessler, 1980). Families may be thought of as consisting of numerous subsystems, such as the parental, adult–child, or child–child systems. It may also be helpful to think of ways in which each component and subsystem is affected by and affects each other component and subsystem. The concept of the family system seeking to maintain a state of equilibrium may also be helpful. None of these concepts, however, explains change in families. To make the statement that the family system is changed as the therapist enters the family, thereby disrupting the family equilibrium, is to describe *what* has taken place, *not why* or *how* it happened. For example, a systems view of the environment (ecology) may make the statement that a particular type of hawk is threatened with extinction because its food source of fish in a marsh has been killed by runoff of silt from a nearby new housing development. This statement describes a causal chain of events from the housing development to the threatened extinction of the hawk. Such causal chains are not provided in family systems theory.

Research. An increasing number of reviews of research have been published over the past few years, including reviews of process research (Pinsof, 1980), multiple family group therapy (Strelnick, 1977), family therapy for problem children (Masten, 1979), parent training (Conte, 1979), family therapy outcomes (Gurman and Kniskern, 1978b; Wells and Dezen, 1978), and deterioration in marital and family therapy (Gurman and Kniskern, 1978a). The reviews of family therapy outcome, especially the review by social workers Wells and Dezen (1978), have been the subject of some debate among family therapy researchers (see Gurman and Kniskern, 1978; Stanton and Todd, 1980; and Wells, 1980, for a rejoinder). Although methodologists will never completely agree on their criticisms of various study designs, the reviews of family therapy outcome do seem to agree on at least two points. First, over the past few years, there has been an increase in the number of research studies evaluating family therapy. Second, a large proportion of these studies are either poorly controlled or subject to other major methodological difficulties (such as multiple treatment interference). Hodgson and Lewis (1979) report a trend analysis of research on family therapy published between 1969 and 1976 and note relatively unsophisticated methodologies. Specifically, they found that questionnaires and interviews are the predominant data-collection strategy, although they do note an increase in the number of studies reporting the use of observation. Also, most studies continue to report percentage data and to use nonrandom selection of subjects.

From a clinical social work perspective, these reviews identify a number of problems inherent in much of the family therapy research to date that limit the utility of this research for clinicians. First, many of the family therapy outcome studies treat family therapy as if it were a unitary intervention. The term *family therapy* by itself means little, since it can refer to such a wide variety of procedures. Even a more specific term, such as *systems family therapy*, may imply a wide variety of procedures. Paul (1967) long ago suggested that the accountability question is not "Does therapy work?" but "What treatment, by whom, is most effective for this individual with that specific problem, and under which set of circumstances?" Studies that attempt to answer the global question "Does family therapy work?", even within a tightly controlled research design, provide little information to the clinician who cannot subsequently replicate the treatment procedures used in the research. Research studies demonstrating the utility of imprecise procedures are not very helpful. The development of detailed training materials, along with research evaluating the effectiveness of the particular treatment approach, is far more valuable.

Second, the research typically does not tell the clinician *how* to practice. To be useful to the clinical social worker, research needs to evaluate procedures or variables that can be manipulated by the clinician to provide more effective service to clients. For example, in their excellent and extensive review, Gurman and Kniskern (1978b) identify a few such variables that do inform practice. These include the positive relationship between therapist and client of the same sex and prevention of premature termination, the positive relationship between the activity level of family therapists and maintaining the family in treatment, and the importance of involving the father in therapy if the family is to continue in treatment and show improvement. These are variables that can be manipulated in the delivery of service to clients. More research in this tradition is sorely needed. However, such an approach is often criticized, as Gurman and Kniskern (1978c) suggest, for too great an emphasis on "technolatry." We see nothing in an emphasis on evaluating the techniques of family therapy which negates the importance of a therapist's ability to relate to and have unconditioned positive regard for families. However the development of the plethora of family therapy techniques (such as sculpting, paradoxical instruction, behavioral contracting) is a reflection of the fact that the relationship alone often will not produce a complete improvement. To date what is lacking is evidence as to the effects of family therapy techniques in addition to a positive worker and client relationship.

Third, reviews of research continue to dichotomize behavioral and nonbehavioral family therapy. Gurman and Kniskern (1978b) indicate that this separation was made in spite of the fact that they "do not believe the world of psychotherapy is easily or meaningfully divided into nonbehavioral and behavioral camps" (p. 845). However, their presentation of the behavioral marital and family research begins with an axiological analysis not performed elsewhere in their review. It is not at all clear that clinicians continue to make these discriminations between behavioral and nonbehavioral therapies. The pressure on those involved with families is to find solutions that work. Combinations of techniques and approaches may provide those solutions.

Fourth, in many ways, the approach to family research has been misguided. What Kazdin and Wilson (1978) call the box score approach, in which the results from a number of poorly controlled studies are added together to make some statement about an area of interest, has yielded little clinically useful information. There is an urgent need for social work agencies and social work clinicians to commence ongoing research on service to families. The response to such a suggestion is often one expressing what Bergin (1971) has called "the bugaboo of complexity," namely, that families and family therapy are too complex for research. In fact, complexity is primarily a function of the particular research questions asked and the resulting number of variables. It is not a function of the number of people present in a therapy room.

We now have the research designs, especially the single case experimental variety (see Hersen and Barlow, 1976; Jayaratne and Levy, 1979) and the measurement procedures (see Cromwell, Olson, and Fournier, 1976) needed to begin the necessary research efforts. What seems lacking is a commitment on the part of many social work family therapists and agencies. Mash (1976), in a review of the history of behavioral research and intervention, has pointed out that complexity in intervention and research developed slowly over a number of years. Such a developmental view would require only that social work agencies begin *a process* of research into family service. Indeed, within social work, we have a methodology in the developmental research paradigm that is well suited for such a process (Rothman, 1980). The question remains whether social work will begin such efforts.

Megasystems Perspectives

From its earliest beginnings social work has recognized a duality to its approach to practice. As Mary Richmond described this duality, it involved both *direct* "action of man on man" and "*indirect* action through social environment." Since Richmond's time, social workers have never agreed exactly what this duality implies for practice. The debate continues today and has been extenuated by the conceptualization of social work practice into at least two domains: direct (micro) and indirect (macro).

Within direct practice, there have been a number of formulations regarding the meaning of "action through the social environment" and the place of "indirect" services. Turner (1978) has recently defined psychosocial therapy as "the form of psychotherapeutic practice in which the bio-psycho-social knowledge of human and societal behavior; skills in relating to individuals, families, groups, and communities; and competence in mobilizing available resources are combined in the medium of individual, group, or familial relationships to help persons alter their personality, behavior, or situation" (p. 5). In part, Turner describes a view of clinical practice in which the focus is on individual cases (individuals or families) and the ways social conditions or forces affect the individual case. Clinical intervention seeks change in client cognitions, emotions, behaviors, and environments. He states that "the theoretical basis of milieu change is the belief that alterations of a client's outer world can bring about changes in behavior, emotional responses, and understanding" (p. 49). The change activities may be addressed either by increasing a client's access to material resources or by the provision of services (for example, substitute care).

Turner's definition stresses efforts to help individual cases change aspects of themselves or their situations. Whittaker (1974) offers a somewhat different focus when he defines social treatment as "an approach to interpersonal helping which utilizes direct and indirect strategies of intervention to aid individuals, families, and small groups in improving social functioning and coping with social problems" (p. 49). Whittaker (1974) extends the view of clinical practice as he describes worker roles in the social treatment model; these roles include change agent, teacher-counselor, and advocate-ombudsman. The latter includes such activities as helping the client to obtain legal services, seek or hold employment, or deal with a public welfare department. This view sees the clinical social worker *moving into* the client's social world to act with and on behalf of the client. This view begins to view practice within an ecological perspective.

An Ecological Perspective. The past few years have witnessed a steady increase in the number of articles that propose an ecological view of practice. As will be seen in this section, this view of practice has been conceptualized in a number of different ways. One of the most consistent voices describing an ecological view of practice has been Germain (1973, 1979, 1980), who indicates that she does not see it as a new form of casework as much as a broader definition. Her ecological view directs professional attention to the person-in-environment. It suggests that organisms and environments can be thought of in terms of an adaptive balance (goodness-to-fit) between the two (Germain and Gitterman, 1979). To the extent that these "fits" violate physical, psychological, or social needs, people experience stress or disjunction between the individual's needs and "environmental nutriments."

The ecological perspective defines human problems as the outcomes of transactions between environments and people. One such transaction appears in cases of child abuse (Garbarino, 1976; Garbarino and Crouter, 1978; Garbarino and Sherman, 1980). In a series of studies, Garbarino and his colleagues have found significant relationships between child abuse and specific environmental conditions: social isolation, socioeconomic stress without adequate social support systems, and high-risk neighborhoods characterized by high social impoverishment (low socioeconomic status, families headed by females, high percentages of women in the work force with children under six years of age, and a high percentage of residences less than one year old).

Within an ecological model of practice, three general goals for intervention can be identified: (1) to relieve, develop, and strengthen people's innate capacity for growth and creative adaptation; (2) to remove environmental blocks and obstacles to growth and development; and (3) to increase the nutritive properties of the environment (Germain, 1979).

A number of recent reports in the literature have identified themselves as originating from an ecological perspective. Aponte (1979) discusses the importance of understanding the effects of minority status and cultural values relating to family roles and expectations in the treatment of a Mexican–American family. Aponte (1976) describes a family–school interview with a ten-year-old child, his parents, school counselor, teacher, and principal. An ecological perspective was used to call attention to possible contexts of intervention, including the boy himself (whose bravado indicated a shy and awkward child), his family (especially his father, who was withdrawn), and the school counselor (who was overprotective and served to screen information between the school and family).

Joseph and Conrad (1980) describe the parish neighborhood as a natural ecological system in which both direct services, such as access services, counseling, volunteer activities, and work with the aged, and indirect services, such as planning special community programs, service coordination, and advocating for legislation, were provided.

Hellenbrand and Yesser (1977) describe a social service program sponsored by industry to help people at their place of work. A careful reading shows that these reports reflect only two kinds of application of the ecological perspective. First, they restate the importance of understanding the effects of physical, social, and cultural environments on the lives of individuals and individual families. Second, they suggest service delivery arrangements in environments (systems) where people live and work. In spite of the value of these reports, there is a third aspect of practice to which the ecological perspective calls attention—the importance of working to change conditions that produce stress. Indeed, this aspect may potentially be its most significant contribution.

The ecological view calls attention to those areas in which the person-environment fit does not meet the physical, emotional, or social needs of people. "Disjunction" between environment and person may occur in any environment. Because of their proximity to clients and their environments, clinical social workers are in an excellent position to identify instances of environment-person disjunction and to take action to correct the environmental conditions resulting in client stress. This aspect of the ecological perspective would appear obvious. Consequently, it is surprising that almost no discussions of efforts to change environments have been forthcoming within this perspective.

There are a number of other potential problems with the ecological perspective. In spite of Germain's (1973) early warning that the ecological view is merely a broader definition of casework, many of its adherents offer it as a model of practice. Yet, it has failed to develop many important aspects of a model of practice, such as procedures for conducting assessments, a set of intervention techniques, and strategies and rationales for their use. Aside from reminding us of social work's dual concern with the person and the environment and suggesting service delivery in the client's environment, the ecological perspective has added little to our understanding of or ability to resolve clients' problems. Nevertheless, it is only relatively recently that discussions of this perspective have appeared in the social work literature. Perhaps with time this perspective will be developed into a model of practice with the necessary specificity and comprehensiveness to direct clinical activities on behalf of clients. To date, this is the perspective's promise, not its reality.

Service Trends

As the title of the recently published proceedings of the North American Symposium on Family Practice (1980) suggests, there are many dimensions of family practice. This section briefly summarizes the major dimensions in this expanding area of social work practice and discusses three areas—networking, family life education, and advocacy.

Extensions of Service. A number of articles have described extensions of traditional family therapy either in terms of who is part of the therapy team or where service is provided. For example, Haufrecht and Mitchell (1978) describe the addition of a learning specialist to a family therapy team providing service to families with children who have learning disabilities. Burnett and others (1976) describe police crisis teams consisting of social workers and plainclothes officers who are able to respond quickly to family crises. Cutting and Prosser (1979) describe a family agency's services to families of a military research and development center, where they estimate that ten percent of the employees experienced serious emotional problems. A number of articles describe in-home services for families. For example, Cautley (1980) presents evaluative data on a multimethod in-home program in which parents were trained in behavior-modification skills. In addition, role playing and coaching were used to model positive parent–child interactions, other family therapy methods were used to model positive parent–child interactions, and still other family therapy methods were used as needed. Similarly, Golner (1971) describes Home Family Counseling, which combined in-home family therapy and a dual ecological intervention (coordinating community social services for the family and getting the family involved with a "key helper"). In another ecological intervention, Vassil (1978) describes a family residential camp where disadvantaged families spent time. Parents assumed major responsibilities for such activities as taking care of groups of children and forming a camp council in which parents made most decisions pertaining to the operation of the camp. Anecdotal results suggest that families developed an increased appreciation for other family members, developed or expanded interpersonal skills, and felt less socially isolated as a result of the camping experience.

In addition to these descriptions of services to families, attention in the literature has been directed to several major social concerns that have arisen in part because of demographic changes in the family. These include sexism, family violence, and divorce.

SEXISM. During the past few years, there has been considerable discussion of various issues relating to sexism in practice. Rauch (1978) identifies several areas of sexism in social work that have been neglected—for example, the sex-role stereotypes in social science components of curricula in schools of social work, such as sex-role stereotyping of women in psychopathology or in the relationships depicted between clients and workers. Wesley (1975) has criticized the sexist bias of psychodynamic thought. Brown and Hellinger (1975) have examined therapist attitudes toward women. Hare-Muston (1978) described a feminist approach to family therapy, and Smith (1980) has pointed out the importance for family therapists to understand their own sexual biases in working with egalitarian marriages.

Continued attention to issues concerning sexism seems important for the social worker who works with families. Not only are many of the changes facing families traced to the push for women's liberation (see Lipman-Bluman, 1976), but it is within family life that many issues of sexism, changes in sex roles, and negotiations between individual needs and family group needs take place. Increased awareness of the therapist's own sexual biases, the sexual biases of helping theories, and sexist assumptions of service delivery requirements should receive continuing attention.

FAMILY VIOLENCE. There appears to be a growing awareness that family violence affects many American homes. Such violence includes child, spouse, and sibling abuse, incest, spouse rape, physical abuse of elders by middle-aged children, and parent abuse by adolescent children. In terms of wife beating, Star (1980) points out that low awareness of the problem, general acceptance, and denial have, until recently, accounted for professional silence. Nichols (1976) points out that the "abused wife problem" is a problem for social workers, who have tended to treat it as a symptom of a more serious family problem and consequently minimized its importance. Wife-beating is increasingly recognized as a multifaceted problem (Star 1978; Star and others, 1979). The abused wife potentially faces insensitivity and sexism from law enforcement, legal and judicial agencies, medical facilities, and social services. Both McShane (1979) and Higgins (1978) have pointed out the importance of emergency services, including crisis telephone services, information and referral, and emergency room protocol. They also stress the importance of police officers who will respond to calls reporting wife beating, housing, financial and legal assistance, counseling, and therapy.

Violence directed against women by family members (including boyfriends) poses a major challenge in social work. It is a challenge not only to confront insensitivity and sexism from the society as a whole in working with victimized women but to confront the biases of the profession's intervention theories and techniques. Such violence also suggests the need for both a person-changing and situation-changing perspective by providing a wide range of personal social services to the abused wife, her children, and the abusing partner.

DIVORCE. Also receiving a considerable amount of attention in the literature have been issues concerning divorce and remarriage (for a review, see Walker, Rogers, and Messinger, 1977). Several articles have suggested viewing divorce as a continuum from separation to remarriage (Chiancola, 1978; Goldmeier, 1980). Woody (1978) has called for preventive interventions for children with divorcing parents by increased social work collaboration with divorce lawyers and divorce counseling with a strong emphasis on helping the adults consider the needs of the children. She also calls for education formats for divorcing families and for more aggressive outreach efforts to public welfare agencies, private and public health facilities, work settings, and schools.

Effron (1980) describes a twelve-week program in a school for preadolescent children whose parents are divorcing. The group used role playing, affective education techniques (games and audiovisual materials), and creative writing to explore the children's reactions to the divorce. Several articles have described the problems and characteristics of step-families (Jacobson, 1979; Johnson, 1980). Keshet and Rosenthal (1978) have described the problems in fathering after marital separation, such as establishing a parenting schedule and coordinating two households. These articles suggest that social workers and others are addressing the problems experienced by families who undergo divorce and remarriage. The responses of social workers have included active outreach efforts to provide services in the clients' environment and new forms of interventions.

Networking. Consistent with the ecological perspective for practice are several approaches that attempt to connect or reconnect hurting individuals and families with social networks (Collins, 1980; Collins and Pancoast, 1976; Pancoast, 1980; Speck and Attneave, 1973; Rueveni, 1979). One approach has been to use natural helping networks that already exist in communities or can be formed around a person who has both the personal characteristics to be a helper and is in a position to help (Collins and Pancoast, 1976). The professional social worker consults with the natural helper, provides community resources, and helps solve problems. Another approach has been to create support networks in the form of self-help groups. A third approach is frequently referred to as *networking*. According to Rueveni (1979), "Family network intervention is an attempt to mobilize the social network support system in a collaborative effort to solve an emotional crisis. It is a time-limited, goal-directed approach that will help family members in crisis to assemble and mobilize their own social network of relatives, friends, and neighbors; this network will become collectively involved in developing new options and solutions for dealing with a difficult crisis" (p. 26).

Social networks are links between people and can be described in terms of density, or the ratio of actual links to potential links; range, or the number of individuals involved in the network; and pathways, or the indirect links between two individuals through at least one intermediary (Collins and Pancoast, 1976). Hartman (1978) describes the use of an eco-map, which is a graphical depiction of a family's relationships with systems in their environment, and a genogram, which is a family's place in the generational history of the extended family. Both of these devices may easily be used to depict the family's social network graphically. Especially useful in this regard is Hartman's eco-map, since it includes symbols to represent the nature of the relationships between the family and its social network.

According to Rueveni (1979, p. 72), the goals of networking are:

1. To facilitate rapid connections, familiarity, and readiness to participate, which increases the level of involvement and energy of the network;
2. To develop and encourage sharing of the problems and concerns by members of the immediate family, which allows for increased involvement and exchange of a variety of viewpoints by network members;
3. To facilitate communication between the family and the extended network system, which emphasizes the need for network activities;
4. To provide direct intervention and a deeper exploration of the nature of the difficulty during impasse periods, which leads to crisis resolution; and
5. To assist in the development and formulation of temporary support groups, which serve as resource consultants.

In network intervention, the therapist becomes a convener of the family's social network and acts as a facilitator during the beginning stages as the network forms an interacting support group. During this process, the network progresses through a series of stages referred to as retribalization, polarization, mobilization, depression, breakthrough, and exhaustion–elation (Rueveni, 1979, pp. 33–37). As the network progresses through the phases, the therapist becomes less involved in directing the process. The therapist may, however, continue to act as a consultant to various subnetworks that form as support groups to various members of the family. These support groups essentially help the family to resolve problems by developing alternatives and by supporting individual family members as they undertake new courses of action. Intervention techniques include many that family therapists are familiar with, such as "the empty chair," in which a chair is placed in the middle of the assembled network and anyone wishing to talk must sit in the chair; the "death ceremony," which is described as a powerful technique for dealing with disengagement, in which a family member imagines he or she is dead and the network eulogizes him or her; and "sculpting," in which family members spatially depict their feelings for each other.

Although it is not completely clear from the descriptions of actual networking cases (Speck and Attneave, 1973), this intervention appears to have two major elements. First, using techniques of traditional family therapy (especially humanistic ones), the network convener works with the family to pinpoint the problem and the variables associated with the problem. The presence of the family's social network may serve to intensify the impact of the convener's activities with the family. Second, individuals in the family's social network gradually become more intensely involved or "reconnected" with the family. These individuals frequently form support groups around individual family members and assist the family in moving toward problem resolution. Often, this resolution involves new resources developed or provided by the network. When networking activities include all the social service agencies involved with many social work client families, a renewed commitment and coordination of services may take place.

In the absence of research data describing the effects of networking efforts, it is impossible to regard it as more than a *promising* service strategy. However, on an impressionistic basis, several aspects of networking do seem noteworthy. If anecdotal descriptions are accurate, networking families in crisis can serve to facilitate change in troubled families. These changes can be produced with an intensive but relatively short period of professional involvement. Also, the formulation of an activated network with a history of helping a particular family may serve as a means of ensuring the generalization of treatment effects into the future.

Many people who seek service from clinical social workers are socially isolated. Whether this isolation is a function of a real lack of a social network or a consequence of the problem they experience is an empirical question. However, we suspect that frequently it is the "family problem" and their reaction to or perception of it that serves to isolate the family from their network. For example, Kozloff (1979) has done an excellent job of describing the effects on families of having a "problem behavior" child. These effects include an increased amount of work, a negative perception of self, a real or imagined social stigma, and an increased social vulnerability. Such families would seem good candidates for networking intervention.

On the negative side, several issues require attention. Part of the language of networking interventions (for example, retribalization) seems to serve no useful communicative purpose that more traditional small group concepts could not more easily accomplish. More importantly, such terminology may impede the dissemination of networking ideas. Evaluative research describing the process and especially the effects of networking interventions are nonexistent. Without such studies, networking should be approached cautiously. Some descriptions of networking almost suggest some magical and unspecified event or condition that produces change. In fact, change comes about as the result of specific solutions developed by and often implemented by subgroups within the activated social network.

Family Life Education. Educational approaches to prevention and treatment appear to be an increasingly popular form of service in social work agencies. Since 1976, the national board of the Family Service Association of America (FSAA) has recognized family life education as being of equal importance with family counseling and family advocacy. In their 1970 survey of member agencies, FSAA found that 78 percent of the membership offered some form of family life education (Beck, Tileston, and Keston, 1977).

Several tensions run through discussions about family life education activities. There is a question whether it is a counseling or therapeutic strategy. For example, Cantoni (1975) describes family life education as a treatment modality and then distinguishes it from group counseling because participants come to family life courses without professional diagnosis as a prerequisite. However, the difference between therapy and family life education may not be an important one. What may be a more important issue has to do with the relative emphasis placed on skill-building versus understanding. Ambrosino (1979) has recently expressed a major orientation in family life education, which stresses understanding, sensitivity, or awareness: "Family life education programs provide a unique opportunity for groups to learn, to listen, to express concerns, clarify confusions, give and receive support, and to review options for improving relationships" (p. 582). Fine (1980), in defining parent education, expresses both understanding and skill building: "Parent education . . . refers to systematic and conceptually based programs, intended to impart information, awareness, or skills to the participants. . . . The format usually includes the presentation of specific ideas, some group discussion, sharing or processing of ideas and experiences, and some skill-building activities" (pp. 2–3).

The emphasis on understanding, awareness, or sensitivity seems to be a function both of the humanistic perspective of many family life educators and of the assumption that these qualities will solve the problems experienced by those who take family life education services. Research on family life education is so lacking that it is impossible to support or reject these assumptions about the relative merit of emphasizing understanding or awareness over skill building.

Whether it is viewed as a preventive or therapeutic service, and regardless of the mix of skill building versus understanding experiences, family life education has the following characteristics (Prochaska and Coyle, 1979):

1. It is goal directed and topic specific.
2. It is nonthreatening and encourages participants to examine issues they might normally avoid.
3. The group format allows for both professional and peer feedback.
4. The group format is an economical use of professional time.
5. The format can encourage problem solving, and other group members can help clarify issues.
6. Family life education reduces the stigma associated with asking for and receiving help.
7. The educational format can help set limits to topics and intensity of participation. This creates a sense of psychological safety among group members.

Most groups use a combination of methods, including short lectures and reading assignments, group discussions, film, and role plays, and some kind of homework. Groups or classes are offered on a wide range of topics. For example, Simon (1976) describes a Personal and Family Life Development Program offered by the Family and Child Service of Seattle that included classes on parenting (focusing on improving communication and family relationships); couples and groups (focusing on individual identity, communication skills, and issues concerning intimacy); a support and awareness group for women with mastectomies; a university black students' group dealing with race as a factor in their lives; and a family enrichment series for groups of families focusing on awareness and growth of the family unit. Similarly, Levin (1975) describes course offerings of the Jewish Family and Children's Bureau of Atlanta that included such topics as marriage, single parents, divorce, changing roles and values, problems of being an adolescent, women over forty, and senior citizens. The Family Service Association of America has developed a series of models for family life education that includes parent–child communication (Riley, Apgar, and Eaton, 1977) and separation and divorce (Callahan, 1979). Fine (1980) has just published a *Handbook on Parent Education* that includes descriptions of several different models of parent education.

Advocacy. The advocacy role of the clinical social worker, although long a part of the social work tradition, is a source of some tension among clinical social workers. The Family Service Association of America has defined advocacy as "a professional service designed to improve life conditions for people by harnessing direct and expert knowledge of family needs with the commitment to action and the application of skills to produce the necessary community change. The purpose of family advocacy service is to insure that the system and institutions with direct bearing on families work for those families, rather than against them. Family advocacy goals include not only improvement of existing public and voluntary services and their delivery, but also development of new or changed forms of social services" (Mauser, 1973, p. 1).

Two approaches to advocacy have been identified, the casework advocate and the community advocate (Panitch, 1974), or the client advocate and the political advocate (Hallowitz, 1974). The casework advocate acts on behalf of the individual case and its dealings with agencies or institutions. The community advocate works on behalf of an entire group or class of clients suffering a common problem caused, aggravated, or ignored by institutions or agencies in the community. There is some disagreement about how these different roles can be combined by the clinical social worker who identifies a disjunction between client and environment. In spite of discussions suggesting the importance of advocacy efforts in the context of treatment (Hallowitz, 1974) and as a vital role of the voluntary agency (O'Connell, 1978), the place of advocacy efforts within social work continues to be debated.

There are a number of obstacles to greater use of advocacy efforts within clinical practice. These include a preference for and preoccupation with a narrow definition of clinical practice, a combination of timidity and naiveté in influencing policy, the community effect of the increased use of government funds to purchase service (O'Connell, 1978), professional values in support of consensus over conflict (Panitch, 1974), and lack of technical expertise in advocacy skills (Rice, 1977). Other obstacles have to do with the different processes involved in advocacy versus other kinds of clinical practice, which make it difficult for one clinician to perform both roles. For example, advocacy may require extensive and often spontaneous meetings with people in authority, whereas clinical practice requires that regular time be allocated for appointments with clients. Agencies also may fear adverse publicity that will incur the wrath of the powerful as their caseworkers try to change conditions affecting some groups of clients. Yet, much of what causes family problems are environmental conditions or events. Both the tradition of social work and the emerging ecological perspective for practice call attention to the importance of moving into the client's environment to change those situations that are problematic for clients. For example, the problems faced by abused women, while they may originate in the actions of men, also take place within the social framework, which includes laws and law enforcement responses.

These problems require the full range of direct service arrangements (Higgins, 1978; McShane, 1979). It seems likely that the search for a comfortable mix of advocacy and other direct service skills will continue to face social workers.

Summary

As this chapter has illustrated, clinical social work's responses to family problems are varied. In terms of the locations in which services are provided, the family problems confronted, and the perspectives brought to bear on these problems, the profession has many accomplishments of which it can be proud. In many ways, the profession is moving beyond the notion that clinical social work takes place only within an office during a fifty-minute hour. In spite of these very encouraging and admirable trends, a number of concerns face clinical social work in the foreseeable future. It is not clear what the profession's response will be to these issues.

First, *the Reagan administration has launched a major attack on social services.* As this chapter is written, it is too early in President Reagan's administration to determine the full extent of his proposed budget cuts or the full impact of his policies on social services. Nevertheless, these is every indication that his plans represent a major attempt to dismantle federal support for and influence on the nation's social services. This policy may mean substantial reductions in services for families, including, for example, income and employment supports, child nutrition programs, and daycare. It is likely that these changes will present major hardships for American families and will be associated with increases in mental, social, and physical problems.

Concurrent with the problem of increased numbers of families experiencing difficulties is the likely decrease in the number of social workers available to respond to these families as states eliminate programs or institute hiring freezes. If these decreases do substantially materialize, and if the trend toward deprofessionalization continues in the jobs that remain, the future looks bleak for the profession. Several responses seem important to us in the immediate future in light of this attack on social services.

First, we need to document and publicize the impact of budgetary cuts, changes in eligibility, and the shift in responsibility for social services from the federal government to the states. The specific effects of these policies need to be described to the public. The profession has always had a difficult time communicating the knowledge and experiences of the social worker to those who make decisions in a form that is readily usable. Clinical social workers in a variety of settings should develop case studies and assist in the collection of data on a number of cases that describe the effects of Reagan's changes in social services. These effects should be publicized through every available channel because it is not clear that, if informed, the American people will support such a radical change in approach to social services. In almost every community, there is a radio or television talk show on which local human service personnel discuss how to treat problem children, how to improve marriages, or how to deal with depression. These shows could become a forum for discussing the treatment, causes, and effects of changes of the federal role in social services to families. Such efforts should serve to destroy the myths perpetrated by the Reagan administration that the "truly needy" will not be affected by their attack on social services.

Second, *accountability is here to stay.* Questions about the effectiveness of social casework and the accountability of social work are not likely to go away. The autonomy of the social worker to do basically as she pleases with only minimal reporting responsibilities to her supervisor is a thing of the past. There is every indication that "intrusion" into clinical practice by the social work agency, funding source, and accrediting bodies will continue. Demands for increased reporting, documentation, and proof of effectiveness will continue. Taking Briar's (1973) address to the Council on Social Work Education as a benchmark, there has been a considerable number of discussions among social workers as to the meaning of accountability, the meaning of the findings of outcome studies, and various methodological issues in the design of social work effectiveness research. To date, however, there has been only a handful of actual studies evaluating the effects of social work services. *Almost none* of these studies has been in the area of services to families. Consequently, it is not clear whether clinical social workers, including those working with families, will develop the skills and carry out the procedures to determine and report on the effects of clinical services. The potential tragedy of the refusal to begin this process may not become clear until social workers have been replaced by other professions more willing and apparently more able to conduct such activities.

Third, *the duality within social work is inherent and can be our strength.* The duality noted by Mary Richmond and continually discussed today will not be easily resolved into a single view of practice, nor should it. Perhaps each social work agency and each clinical social worker will have to respond to this duality in their own ways. The creation of separate clinical organizations of social workers is an unfortunate move that threatens the strength and vitality of the profession. Other professions, such as psychology, have found it possible to include a wide variety of roles in subdivisions of one professional organization.

In part, the strength of social work is its dual perspective for practice. Only social work has continually called attention to the needs of individual families *and* the need to change the social conditions and events that create the problems families experience. There may always be tension between the two components of this duality, people-changing and context-changing. This tension can be the source of creative responses in social work research, practice theory, program development, and service delivery. Balancing efforts between the poles of this duality may be the contribution that social work brings to resolving families' problems.

Fourth, *services for families will continue to be varied.* There will not be agreement, nor is it desirable for there to be agreement, on a single set of services for families. Different perspectives applied in different fields of practice will respond with a variety of family treatment approaches. There is some indication within social work in many communities that the period of doctrinaire rigidity is giving way to a more open sharing and acceptance of different approaches to family treatment. Within single settings, a variety of services, even from different theoretical models, are offered to families.

Increasingly, the criterion for selecting an approach or technique may be "what works?" and not "how does it fit into my theoretical model?" Indeed, in a tight social service economy, there will be increasing pressure to justify services and techniques in terms of their power to solve the problems that brought the client to the social worker. It may even be a disguised blessing that one of the positive effects of President Reagan's assault on social services will be to identify services with the greatest potential effectiveness.

Fifth, *family therapy will increase in popularity.* There is every indication that professional interest in family therapy as a potential service approach for dysfunctional families will grow in the foreseeable future. Although developments may continue to originate within major models (systems, communications, or behavioral), there appears to be some suggestion that research efforts within family therapy are increasing and that, within practice, social workers are integrating components from various models toward the end of more effective service. It is too early to determine if these indications will become real trends affecting both family therapy theory and practice. Certainly, the history of family therapy, with its overemphasis on technique and its antiresearch tradition, works against the identification of family therapy approaches and techniques with demonstrated effectiveness. It seems likely that, in the foreseeable future, family therapy, like other family services, either will have to prove that it offers change-producing potential for families or in time lose ground to services that can. It is not clear whether family therapists will respond to this challenge in time to ensure that family therapy will be an available resource for families. An additional danger for social work family therapists is that their adaptation of approaches to family therapy developed outside of social work will restrict them to a narrow definition of clinical social work, a definition that ignores the need for and potential contribution of "context-changing" efforts.

Perhaps at no other time in recent history have the dangers facing American families been greater and their need for services been more acute. Unfortunately, at no other time have the threats to social work's ability to respond to these needs been greater. Although the dangers and challenges are great, there is every indication that the profession is capable of responding on behalf of families. The real question remains, will social workers begin the necessary endeavors in time?

References

Ambrosino, S. "Integrating Counseling, Family Life Education, and Family Advocacy." *Social Casework*, 1979, *60* (10), 579–585.

Aponte, H. J. "The Family–School Interview: An Eco-Structural Approach." *Family Process,* 1976, *15* (3), 303–311.

Aponte, H. J. "Diagnosis in Family Therapy." In C. Germain (Ed.), *Social Work Practice: People and Environments.* New York: Columbia University Press, 1979.

Bane, M. J. *Here to Stay.* New York: Basic Books, 1976.

Beck, D. F., Tileston, C., and Keston, S. *Educational Programs of Family Agencies.* New York: Family Service Association of America, 1977.

Bergin, A. E. "The Evaluation of Therapeutic Outcomes." In A. E. Bergin and S. L. Garfield (Eds.), *Handbook of Psychotherapy and Behavior Change.* New York: Wiley, 1971.

Briar, S., and Conte, J. R. "Families." In H. S. Maas (Ed.), *Social Service Research: Reviews of Studies.* Washington, D.C.: National Association of Social Workers, 1978.

Briar, S., and others. *Facing the Challenge.* New York: Council on Social Work Education, 1973.

Brown, C. R., and Hellinger, M. L. "Therapists' Attitudes Toward Women." *Social Work,* 1975, *20* (4), 266–270.

Burnett, B., and others. "Police and Social Workers in a Community Outreach Program." *Social Casework,* 1976, *57* (1), 41–47.

Callahan, B. N. *Separation and Divorce.* New York: Family Service Association of America, 1979.

Cantoni, L. "Family Life Education: A Treatment Modality." *Child Welfare,* 1975, *54* (9), 658–665.

Cautley, P. W. "Treating Dysfunctional Families at Home." *Social Work,* 1980, *25* (5), 380–386.

Chiancola, S. P. "The Process of Separation and Divorce: A New Approach." *Social Casework,* 1978, *59* (8), 494–499.

Collins, A. H. "Helping Neighbors Intervene in Cases of Maltreatment." In J. Garbarino and S. H. Stocking (Eds.), *Protecting Children from Abuse and Neglect.* San Francisco: Jossey-Bass, 1980.

Collins, A. H., and Pancoast, D. L. *Natural Helping Networks: A Strategy for Prevention.* Washington, D.C.: National Association of Social Workers, 1976.

Conte, J. R. "Helping Groups of Parents Change Their Children's Behavior." *Child and Youth Services,* 1979, *2* (3), 1–13.

Conte, J. R., and Berliner, L. "Sexual Abuse of Children: Implications for Practice." *Social Casework,* 1981, *62* (10), 601–606.

Conway, J., and Bucher, B. "Transfer and Maintenance of Behavior Change in Children." In E. Mash, L. Hamerlynck, and L. Handy (Eds.), *Behavior Modification and Families.* New York: Brunner/Mazel, 1976.

Cromwell, R. E., Olson, D.H.L., and Fournier, D. G. "Diagnosis and Evaluation in Marital and Family Counseling." In D.H.L. Olson (Ed.), *Treating Relationships,* Lake Mills, Iowa: Graphic, 1976.

Cutting, A. R., and Posser, F. J. "Family Oriented Mental Health Consultation to a Naval Research Group." *Social Casework,* 1979, *60* (4), 236–242.

Delegate Workbook. White House Conference on Families.

Demos, J. "The American Family in Past Time." *American Scholar,* 1974, *43* (3), 422–446.

Effron, A. K. "Children and Divorce: Help from an Elementary School." *Social Casework,* 1980, *61* (5), 305–312.

Epstein, N. B., Bishop, D. S., and Levin, S. "The McMaster Model of Family Functioning." *Journal of Marriage and Family Counseling,* 1978, *4,* 19–31.

Family Service Association of America. *The Many Dimensions of Family Practice.* Proceedings of the North American Symposium on Family Practice. New York: Family Service Association of America, 1980.

Featherstone, J. "Family Matters." *Harvard Educational Review,* 1979, *49* (1), 20–52.

Fine, M. J. *Handbook on Parent Education.* New York: Academic Press, 1980.

Finkelhor, D. *Sexually Victimized Children.* New York: Free Press, 1979.

Garbarino, J. "A Preliminary Study of Some Ecological Correlates of Child Abuse." *Child Development,* 1976, *47* (1), 178–185.

Garbarino, J., and Crouter, A. "Defining the Community Context for Parent–Child Relations." *Child Development,* 1978, *49* (3), 604–616.

Garbarino, J., and Sherman, D. "High-Risk Neighborhoods and High-Risk Families." *Child Development,* 1980, *51* (1), 188–198.

Garbarino, J., and Stocking, S. H. *Protecting Children from Abuse and Neglect,* San Francisco: Jossey-Bass, 1980.

Germain, C. B. "An Ecological Perspective in Casework Practice." *Social Casework,* 1973, *54* (6), 323–330.

Germain, C. B. *Social Work Practice: People and Environments.* New York: Columbia University Press, 1979.

Germain, C. B. "Social Context of Clinical Social Work." *Social Work,* 1980, *25* (6), 483–488.

Germain, C. B., and Gitterman, A. "The Life Model of Social Work Practice." In F. J. Turner (Ed.), *Social Work Treatment.* New York: Free Press, 1979.

Glick, I. D., and Kessler, D. R. *Marital and Family Therapy.* New York: Grune & Stratton, 1980.

Goldenberg, I., and Goldenberg, H. *Family Therapy: An Overview.* Monterey, Calif.: Brooks/Cole, 1980.

Goldmeier, J. "Intervention in the Continuum from Divorce to Family Reconstitution." *Social Casework,* 1980, *61* (1), 39–47.

Golner, J. H. "Home Family Counseling." *Social Work,* 1971, *16* (4), 63–70.

Gurman, A. S., and Kniskern, D. P. "Deterioration in Marital and Family Therapy: Empirical, Clinical, and Conceptual Issues." *Family Process,* 1978a, *17* (1), 3–20.

Gurman, A. S., and Kniskern, D. P. "Research on Marital and Family Therapy: Progress, Perspective, and Prospect." In S. L. Garfield and A. E. Bergin (Eds.), *Handbook of Psychotherapy and Behavior Change.* New York: Wiley, 1978b.

Gurman, A. S., and Kniskern, D. P. "Technolatry, Methodolatry, and the Results of Family Therapy." *Family Process,* 1978c, *17* (3), 275–281.

Hallowitz, D. "Advocacy in the Context of Treatment." *Social Casework,* 1974, *55* (7), 416–420.

Hare-Mustin, R. T. "A Feminist Approach to Family Therapy." *Family Process,* 1978, (17), 181–194.

Hartman, A. "Diagrammatic Assessment of Family Relationships." *Social Casework,* 1978, *59* (8), 465–476.

Haufrecht, B., and Mitchell, C. "Family Systems and Learning Problems: A Treatment Model." *Social Casework,* 1978, *59* (10), 579–587.

Hellenbrand, S., and Yasser, R. "Social Work in Industrial Social Welfare." In F. Sobey (Ed.), *Changing Roles in Social Work Practice.* Philadelphia: Temple University Press, 1977.

Hersen, M., and Barlow, D. H. *Single Case Experimental Designs.* Elmsford, N.Y.: Pergamon Press, 1976.

Higgins, J. G. "Social Services for Abused Wives." *Social Casework,* 1978, *59* (5), 266–271.

Hodgson, J. S., and Lewis, R. A. "Pilgrim's Progress III: A Trend Analysis of Family Therapy and Methodology." *Family Process,* 1979, *18* (2), 163–173.

Jacobson, D. S. "Stepfamilies: Myth and Realities." *Social Work,* 1979, *24* (3), 202–207.

Janzen, C., and Harris, O. *Family Treatment in Social Work Practice.* Itasca, Ill.: Peacock, 1980.

Jayaratne, S., and Levy, R. *Empirical Clinical Practice.* New York: Columbia University Press, 1979.

Johnson, H. C. "Working with Stepfamilies: Principles of Practice." *Social Work,* 1980, *25* (4), 304–308.

Joseph, M. V., and Conrad, A. P. "A Parish Neighborhood Model for Social Work Practice." *Social Casework,* 1980, *61* (7), 423–432.

Kazdin, A. E., and Wilson, G. T. *Evaluation of Behavior Therapy.* Cambridge, Mass.: Ballanger, 1978.

Keshet, H. F., and Rosenthal, K. M. "Fathering After Marital Separation." *Social Work,* 1978, *59* (1), 11–18.

Kozloff, M. A. *A Program for Families of Children with Learning and Behavior Problems.* New York: Wiley, 1979.

Lantz, J. E. *Family and Marital Therapy: A Transactional Approach.* New York: Appleton-Century-Crofts, 1978.

Levin, E. "Development of a Family Life Education Program in a Community Social Service Agency." *The Family Coordinator,* 1975, *24* (3), 343–349.

Lipman-Blumen, J. "The Implications for Family Structure of Changing Sex Roles." *Social Casework,* 1976, *57* (2), 67–79.

Listening to America's Families. A Report to the President, Congress, and Families of the Nation, White House Conference on Families, Washington, D.C., October 1980.

McShane, C. "Community Services for Battered Women." *Social Work,* 1979, *24* (1), 34–39.

Mash, E. "Behavior Modification and Methodology: A Developmental Perspective." *The Journal of Educational Thought,* 1976, *10* (1), 5–21.

Masten, A. S. "Family Therapy as a Treatment for Children: A Critical Review of Outcome Research." *Family Process,* 1979, *18* (3), 323–335.

Mauser, E. *Family Advocacy: A Manual for Action.* New York: Family Service Association of America, 1973.

National Commission on Families and Public Policy. *Families and Public Policies in the United States: Final Report of the Commission.* National Conference on Social Welfare, New York, 1978.

Nichols, B. "The Abused Wife Problem." *Social Casework,* 1976, *57* (1), 27–32.

Norton, A. J., and Glick, P. C. "Changes in American Family Life." *Children Today,* 1976, *5* (3), 2–4, 44.

O'Connell, B. "From Service to Advocacy to Empowerment." *Social Casework,* 1978, *59* (4), 195–202.

Pancoast, D. L. "Finding and Enlisting Neighbors to Support Families." In J. Garbarino and S. H. Stocking (Eds.), *Protecting Children from Abuse and Neglect.* San Francisco: Jossey-Bass, 1980.

Panitch, A. "Advocacy Practice." *Social Work,* 1974, *19* (3), 326–332.

Paul, G. "Strategy of Outcome Research in Psychotherapy." *Journal of Consulting Psychology,* 1967, *319* (2), 109–113.

Pinsof, W. M. "Family Therapy Process Research." In A. S. Gurman and D. P. Kniskern (Eds.), *Handbook of Family Therapy.* New York: Brunner/Mazel, 1980.

Prochaska, J., and Coyle, J. P. "Choosing Parenthood: A Needed Family Life Education Group." *Social Casework,* 1979, *60* (5), 323–327.

Rauch, J. B. "Gender as a Factor in Practice." *Social Work,* 1978, *23* (5), 388–393.

Rice, R. M. *A Survey of a Sample of 22 Member Agencies of the Family Service Association of America Concerning Changes in Family Problems.* New York: Family Service Association of America, 1977.

Riley, D. P., Apgar, K., and Eaton, J. *Parent–Child Communication.* New York: Family Service Association of America, 1977.

Rothman, J. *Social R and D: Research and Development in the Human Services.* Englewood Cliffs, N.J.: Prentice-Hall, 1980.

Roundaville, B. J. "Theories in Marital Violence: Evidence from a Study of Battered Women." *Victimology: An International Journal,* 1978, *3* (1–2), 11–31.

Rueveni, U. *Networking Families in Crisis.* New York: Human Sciences Press, 1979.

Simon, D. S. "A Systematic Approach to Family Life Education." *Social Casework,* 1976, *57* (8), 511–516.

Smith, A. O. "Egalitarian Marriage: Implications for Practice and Policy." *Social Casework,* 1980, *61* (5), 288–295.

Speck, R. V., and Attneave, C. L. *Family Networks.* New York: Pantheon Books, 1973.

Stanton, M. D., and Todd, T. C. "A Critique of the Wells and Dezen Review of the Results of Nonbehavioral Family Therapy." *Family Process,* 1980, *19* (2), 169–178.

Star, B. "Comparing Battered and Non-Battered Women." *Victimology: An International Journal,* 1978, *3* (1–2), 32–44.

Star, B. "Patterns in Family Violence." *Social Casework,* 1980, *61* (6), 339–346.

Star, B., and others. "Psychosocial Aspects of Wife Battering." *Social Casework,* 1979, *60* (8), 479–488.

Strelnick, A. H. "Multiple Family Group Therapy: A Review of the Literature." *Family Process,* 1977, *16* (3), 307–325.

Turner, F. J. *Psychosocial Therapy.* New York: Free Press, 1978.

U.S. Bureau of the Census. *Current Population Reports.* Series p-20, No. 336. Washington, D.C.: U.S. Department of Commerce, Bureau of the Census, 1978.

Vassil, T. V. "Residential Family Camping: Altering Family Patterns." *Social Casework,* 1978, *59* (10), 605–613.

Walker, K. N., Rogers, J., and Messinger, L. "Remarriage after Divorce: A Review." *Social Casework,* 1977, *58* (5), 276–285.

Wells, R. A. "Tempests, Teapots and Research Design: A Rejoinder to Stanton and Todd." *Family Process,* 1980, *19* (2), 177–178.

Wells, R. A., and Dezen, A. E. "The Results of Family Therapy Revisited: The Nonbehavioral Methods." *Family Process,* 1978, *17* (3), 251–274.

Name Index

A

Name Index

C

Name Index

H

Name Index

I

J

K

L

N

Name Index

R

S

Name Index

T

U

V

Subject Index

B

D

G

N

T

Subject Index